1004820757

GOVERNMENT
FINANCE
STATISTICS
YEARBOOK

GOVERNMENT FINANCE STATISTICS YEARBOOK

Vol. XXIX, 2005
Prepared by the IMF Statistics Department
Robert W. Edwards, Director
Keith G. Dublin, Division Chief,
    Government Finance Division

For information related to this publication, please:
    fax the Statistics Department at (202) 623-6460,
    or write Statistics Department
        International Monetary Fund
        Washington, D.C. 20431
    or telephone (202) 623-6180.
For copyright inquiries, please fax the Editorial Division at (202) 623-6579.
For purchases only, please contact Publication Services (see information below).

Address orders to:
International Monetary Fund
Attention: Publication Services
Washington, D.C. 20431
U.S.A.
Telephone: (202) 623-7430
Telefax: (202) 623-7201
E-mail: publications@imf.org
Internet: http://www.imf.org

ISSN 0250-7374
ISBN 1-58906-462-3

Recycled paper

INTERNATIONAL MONETARY FUND

Government
Finance Statistics

Yearbook 2005

SELECTION OF STATISTICAL PUBLICATIONS

International Financial Statistics (IFS)

Acknowledged as a standard source of statistics on all aspects of international and domestic finance, *IFS* publishes, for most countries of the world, current data on exchange rates, international liquidity, international banking, money and banking, interest rates, prices, production, international transactions (including balance of payments and international investment position), government finance, and national accounts. Information is presented in tables for specific countries and in tables for area and world aggregates. *IFS* is published monthly and annually. *Price:* Subscription price is US$495 a year (US$247 to university faculty and students) for twelve monthly issues and the yearbook. Single copy price is US$72 for a monthly issue and US$105 for a yearbook issue.

Balance of Payments Statistics Yearbook (BOPSY)

Issued in three parts, this annual publication contains balance of payments and international investment position data. Part 1 provides detailed tables on balance of payments statistics for approximately 170 countries and international investment position data for 104 countries. Part 2 presents tables of regional and world totals of major balance of payments components. Part 3 contains descriptions of methodologies, compilation practices, and data sources used by reporting countries Price: US$108.

Direction of Trade Statistics (DOTS)

Quarterly issues of this publication provide, for about 156 countries, tables with current data (or estimates) on the value of imports from and exports to their most important trading partners. In addition, similar summary tables for the world, industrial countries, and developing countries are included. The yearbook provides, for the most recent seven years, detailed trade data by country for approximately 186 countries, the world, and major areas. *Price:* Subscription price is US$155 a year (US$129 to university faculty and students) for the quarterly issues and the yearbook. Price for a quarterly issue only is US$28, the yearbook only is US$77, and a guide only is US$12.50.

Government Finance Statistics Yearbook (GFSY)

This annual publication provides detailed data on transactions in revenue, expense, net acquisition of assets and liabilities, other economic flows, and balances of assets and liabilities of general government and its subsectors. The data are compiled according to the framework of the 2001 *Government Finance Statistics Manual,* which provides for several summary measures of government fiscal performance. *Price:* US$88.

CD-ROM Subscriptions

International Financial Statistics (IFS), Balance of Payments Statistics (BOPS), Direction of Trade Statistics (DOTS), and *Government Finance Statistics (GFS)* are available on CD-ROM by annual subscription. The CD-ROMs incorporate a Windows-based browser facility, as well as a flat file of the database in scientific notation. *Price of each subscription:* US$450 a year for single-user PC license (US$225 for university faculty and students). Network and redistribution licenses are negotiated on a case-by-case basis. Please contact Publication Services for information.

Subscription Packages

Combined Subscription Package

The combined subscription package includes all issues of *IFS, DOTS, BOPSY, GFSY,* and *Staff Papers,* the Fund's economic journal. *Combined subscription price:* US$749 a year. Airspeed delivery available at additional cost; please inquire.

Combined Statistical Yearbook Subscription

This subscription comprises *BOPSY, GFSY, IFSY,* and *DOTSY* at a combined rate of US$265. Because of different publication dates of the four yearbooks, it may take up to one year to service an order. Airspeed delivery available at additional cost; please inquire.

IFS on the Internet

The Statistics Department of the Fund is pleased to make available to subscribers the *International Financial Statistics (IFS)* database through an easy-to-use online service. The *IFS* database contains time series data beginning in 1948. The browser software provides a familiar and easy-to-use Windows interface for browsing the database, selecting series of interest, displaying the selected series in a spreadsheet format, and saving the selected series for transfer to other software systems, such as Microsoft Excel®. Single user license price for the *IFS Online Service* is $495, and $247 for academic users. Dependent on certain criteria, a range of scaled discounts is available. For full details of qualification for these discounts and online payment, please visit http://www.imfstatistics.org or email us directly at publications@imf.org.

Address orders to

Publication Services, IMF, Washington, DC 20431, USA
Telephone: (202) 623-7430   Telefax: (202) 623-7201   E-mail: publications@imf.org
Internet: http://www.imf.org

Note: Prices include the cost of delivery by surface mail. Enhanced delivery is available for an additional charge.

CONTENTS

"Country" in this publication does not always refer to a territorial entity that is a state as understood by international law and practice; the term also covers the euro area and some nonsovereign territorial entities, for which statistical data are provided internationally on a separate basis.

"Country" in this publication does not always refer to a territorial entity that is a state as understood by international law and practice; the term also covers the euro area and some nonsovereign territorial entities, for which statistical data are provided internationally on a separate basis.

PREFACE

The *2005 Government Finance Statistics Yearbook (GFS Yearbook)*, contains detailed data on revenue, expense, transactions in assets and liabilities, and stocks of assets and liabilities for the general government sector and its subsectors. The data and related information are presented in world, country, and institutional tables for 130 reporting countries presented in the framework of the *Government Finance Statistics Manual 2001 (GFSM 2001)*.[1]

The *GFSM 2001* introduces a comprehensive analytical framework that uses detailed accrual data for recording government resource flows and aggregate cash transactions for measuring government liquidity. It presents balance sheet information, which integrates transactions and other economic flows with stock positions, and defines several balancing items appropriate for contemporary fiscal analysis. Moreover, the concepts and principles set out in the *GFSM 2001* are harmonized with the other macroeconomic statistical standards[2] to facilitate consistency of statistical analysis. **The *GFSM 2001* analytic framework, though conceived from an accrual perspective, can be used to present data generated by a variety of accounting practices, including cash. Annex I to this preface illustrates the salient features of the *GFSM 2001*.**

The *GFSM 2001* reporting format was introduced in 2003, and the *2005 GFS Yearbook* builds on this process. Given that a number of countries still use the *GFSM 1986* framework for their reporting systems, **Annex II describes the reclassification of historical data from the GFSM 1986 to the GFSM 2001 framework.**

The rest of this preface elaborates on the composition of the world, country, and institutional tables, the symbols and conventions, and the GFS CD-ROM.

World, Country, and Institutional Tables

World tables

The *GFS Yearbook* world tables provide cross-country comparisons of data for general and central government, showing the *GFSM 2001* major aggregates and key balances, as well as the components of the major aggregates, as a percent of gross domestic product (GDP).[3]

The world tables are supported by a set of detailed country tables that incorporate an integrated classification coding system of stocks and flows.[4]

Country tables

To facilitate international comparisons, the *GFSM 2001* emphasizes the presentation of fiscal data for the general government sector, which is uniformly defined across countries, consistent with the *1993 SNA*.

The central and general government sectors are shown for each country in the hard copy of the *GFS Yearbook*. In addition, two other subsectors are shown on the basis of the institutional structure of the particular country, that is, based on the subsectors that exist in a country. All subsectors, as relevant, are shown on the GFS CD-ROM.

If no data are available for the published subsectors for a specific detailed classification table or summary statement, only the table or statement headings are presented in the hard copy of the *GFS Yearbook*.

Data reported for the latest three years are presented in the hard copy of the *GFS Yearbook*. The oldest data shown in this edition of the *GFS Yearbook* are for 1996–98. Countries whose most recently reported data are older than 1998 are included only on the GFS CD-ROM.[5]

Table A of the Guide to Country Tables, provided at the front of this volume, indicates the sectors and years for which data are available for each country on the GFS CD-ROM and in the hard copy. Table B of the Guide to Country Tables indicates the current accounting basis of recording the data in the individual country tables for each subsector of general government. The basis of recording is identified as cash or noncash, where the latter includes any recording basis other than cash (including accrual). An ellipsis (....) indicates nonavailability of information, and a dash (—) indicates that a subsector does not exist.

For countries reporting noncash data for all or some subsectors of general government, all data are presented, according to the relevant basis of recording, in the detailed classification tables (Tables 1–8), and all data (including subsectors on a cash basis) are summarized in the Statement of Government Operations. The corresponding cash flow data, where available, are presented in the Statement of Sources and Uses of Cash. For those subsectors reported on a cash basis, data in the Statement of Government Operations and the Statement of Sources and Uses of Cash are identical.

For countries reporting cash data for *all* subsectors of general government, data are presented in the detailed classification tables (Tables 1–3 and 6–8) and are summarized only in the Statement of Sources and Uses of Cash.

Because of the nonavailability of data on the consumption of fixed capital, the *net operating balance* (change in net worth owing to transactions, including consumption of fixed capital) is not published for some countries that report data on a noncash basis.

---

[1]The text of the *GFSM 2001* which replaced *A Manual on Government Finance Statistics, 1986 (GFSM 1986)*, is available on the IMF website: http://www.imf.org/external/np/sta/index.htm.
    [2]*System of National Accounts 1993*; *Balance of Payments Manual*, fifth edition, 1993; and *Monetary and Financial Statistics Manual 2000*.
    [3] Calendar year GDP data are used for all countries, regardless of their fiscal year-end.
    [4] The detailed classification tables are presented in Appendix 4 of the *GFSM 2001*.

[5]In the GFS database, all historic data from 1990 onward were reclassified from the *GFSM 1986* framework to the *GFSM 2001* framework.

Users should exercise caution when making country comparisons using the Classification of the Functions of Government (Table 7), insofar as the definition of outlays may differ among countries or over time. The *GFSM 2001* framework defines outlays by function of government as the sum of expense and the *net* acquisition of nonfinancial assets. This is a change from the definition under the *GFSM 1986*, which defined outlays as the sum of expense and *gross* acquisition of nonfinancial assets, that is, expenditure. Outlays in Table 7 may be defined in either way.

Institutional tables

For each country, a standardized institutional table describes the structure of the general government sector. In addition, the institutional table provides data coverage details, information on accounting practices, and countries' *GFSM 2001* implementation plans, where available. The institutional table explains breaks in the comparability of time series from 1990 onward.

Symbols, Conventions, and Statistical Adjustment

The following symbols and conventions are used for the data presented in the *GFS Yearbook* and GFS CD-ROM:

Captions or subheaders identify the units in which data are expressed.

Billion means one thousand million.

A dash (—) indicates that a figure is zero or less than half of a significant digit.

An ellipsis (....) indicates the nonavailability of data.

The letter f denotes forecasted or projected data.

The letter p denotes data that are preliminary or provisional.

The symbol † (k on the GFS CD-ROM) marks a break in the comparability of data; that is, data appearing after the symbol do not form a consistent time series with those for earlier years. Typically, break symbols will appear in the detailed classification tables (Tables 1–8) or summary statements when, for example, changes have occurred in the coverage and classification of data or when the basis of recording has changed from cash to noncash. **Break symbols in the time series of individual countries are explained in the coverage note included in the institutional table for that country**.

For data relating to a fiscal year, the country and world tables present the data within the calendar year for which the greatest number of monthly observations exist. For fiscal years ending June 30, the tables present the data in the calendar year when the fiscal year ends. For example, the fiscal year July 1, 2000–June 30, 2001 is shown as calendar year 2001. Changes in fiscal years are indicated by the break symbol † (k on the GFS CD-ROM).

The *GFS Yearbook* database contains statistical adjustment lines for most aggregates, all of which are included on the GFS CD-ROM. However, only two of the statistical adjustment lines are presented in the hard copy of the *GFS Yearbook*: (i) the Statement of Government Operations includes a line for the statistical discrepancy between net lending/borrowing and financing; and (ii) the Classification of the Functions of Government (Table 7) includes a line for the statistical discrepancy between the reported components and total outlays.

Minor differences between published totals and the sum of components are attributable to rounding.

GFS CD-ROM

The *Government Finance Statistics Database and Browser on CD-ROM*, referred to here as the GFS CD-ROM, contains time series for all reported subsectors of general government for 140 countries from 1990 onwards, presented in the framework of the *GFSM 2001*. Users should exercise caution when comparing data over time insofar as breaks in the series (e.g., currency units and magnitudes) may exist.

At present, the GFS CD-ROM is issued monthly and updated as countries report new data. For most countries, the data reported in 2002 and/or earlier were converted from the *GFSM 1986* framework to conform as closely as possible to the *GFSM 2001* framework.

The GFS CD-ROM also has a browser that enables users to view and extract data for analytical purposes. The browser software is an easy-to-use Windows interface for accessing the database, selecting specific data series, displaying the selected series in a spreadsheet format, and saving the selected series for transfer to other software systems, such as Microsoft Excel.

There are four complementary views for browsing the database contained within the GFS CD-ROM:

- a "table view" corresponding to the tables contained within the *2005 GFS Yearbook* publication;
- an "economic concept view" that provides access to comparable analytical concepts across countries; and
- a view/search facility based on the structure of the time series codes.
- a multiple year "matrix view" for enhanced data analysis based on *GFSM 2001* statements and tables for any combination of the subsectors of general government.

An extensive on-line help facility is incorporated into the browser, including a list of frequently-asked-questions (FAQs).

For users seeking access to historical GFS data, the *Historical Government Finance Statistics Database and Browser on CD-ROM* is now available. This Historical GFS CD-ROM contains time series for 149 countries from 1972 to 1989, presented in the framework of the *GFSM 1986*.

For those users interested in converting the historical time series into the *GFSM 2001* framework using a bridge table, the document "*Classification of GFSM 1986 Data to the GFSM 2001 Framework*" is available on the IMFS's website: (http://www.imf.org/external/pubs/ft/gfs/manual/comp.htm).

This annex provides a synopsis of the GFS system as it relates to the treatment of stocks and flow data, the four financial statements that comprise the analytical framework of the *GFSM 2001*, and salient features of coverage, classification, basis of recording, and valuation under the *GFSM 2001*.

The Treatment of Balance Sheet and Flow Data

The *GFSM 2001* is a framework that fully integrates flows (used to report the results of events that occur during the accounting period) and stocks (used to compile the Balance Sheet at the beginning and end of the accounting period). The comprehensive treatment of flows in the GFS system enables the opening and closing stocks to be fully reconciled. In other words, the following relationship is valid for each item on the Balance Sheet:

$$S_1 = S_0 + F$$

where $S0$ and $S1$ represent the values of an item on the Balance Sheet at two points in time $(0,1)$ and F represents the cumulative value of all flows between times 0 and 1 that affect that particular item. More generally, any stock, including net worth, is the cumulative value of all flows affecting that stock that have occurred over the lifetime of the item.

The *GFSM 2001* framework provides a range of possibilities for fiscal analysis, especially concerning fiscal liquidity and policy sustainability issues. The liquidity constraint, measured as the *net change in the stock of cash,* should prove useful for fiscal policy decision makers. This measure is shown in the Statement of Sources and Uses of Cash, which also contains information on the types of aggregate receipts and payments that contribute to the change in the stock of cash.

A major innovation of the *GFSM 2001* framework is that the Statement of Government Operations parallels a set of business accounts, allowing a nuanced view of fiscal sustainability through the measurement of *net worth,* as well as an *operating balance* and *net lending/borrowing.* When compiled using comprehensive accrual information, these measures reflect more accurately the impact of resource flows. The analysis of *net worth* (the stock of assets minus liabilities) should focus policy attention on the structure of the government's balance sheet and the portfolio choice among assets (and liabilities). The *net operating balance* is a summary measure of the change in net worth owing to transactions that occurred in the period; revenue and expense are the only transactions that affect *net worth. Net lending/borrowing* shows the extent to which the government absorbs or provides financial resources to the rest of the economy and the rest of the world.

The Four Financial Statements of the *GFSM 2001*

The core of the analytic framework is a set of four financial statements. Three of the statements can be combined to demonstrate that all changes in stocks result from flows (see Figure 1). These are (1) the Statement of Government Operations, (2) the Statement of Other Economic Flows, and (3) the Balance Sheet. The fourth statement—the Statement of Sources and Uses of Cash— provides key information on liquidity.

The **Statement of Government Operations** summarizes all transactions and derives important analytic balances from this information. Revenue minus expense equals the *net operating balance,* which is a summary measure of the effect of the government's transactions on *net worth.* The subsequent deduction of the net acquisition of nonfinancial assets from the net operating balance produces a balance called *net lending/borrowing,* which measures the extent to which government either provides financial resources to the other sectors of the economy and the rest of the world (*net lending*) or uses financial resources generated by the other sectors (*net borrowing*). *Net lending/borrowing,* also, is equal to the government financing requirement derived as the net of transactions in financial assets and liabilities. It is a measure of the financial impact of government activity on the rest of the economy.

STATEMENT OF GOVERNMENT OPERATIONS	
1	Revenue
2	Expense
	Net operating balance (1–2=31+32–33)
31	Net acquisition of nonfinancial assets
	Net lending/borrowing (1–2–31=32–33)
32	Net acquisition of financial assets
33	Net incurrence of liabilities

The Statement of Other Economic Flows presents information on changes in *net worth* that arise from flows other than transactions. These flows are classified as either changes in the value (revaluations, or holding gains or losses) or the volume of assets and liabilities. The balancing item of this statement is the *change in net worth resulting from other economic flows.*

STATEMENT OF OTHER ECONOMIC FLOWS	
4,5	Change in net worth resulting from other economic flows (41+42–43+51+52–53)
41,51	Change in nonfinancial assets
42,52	Change in financial assets
43,53	Change in liabilities

Figure 1: Structure of the GFS Analytical Framework

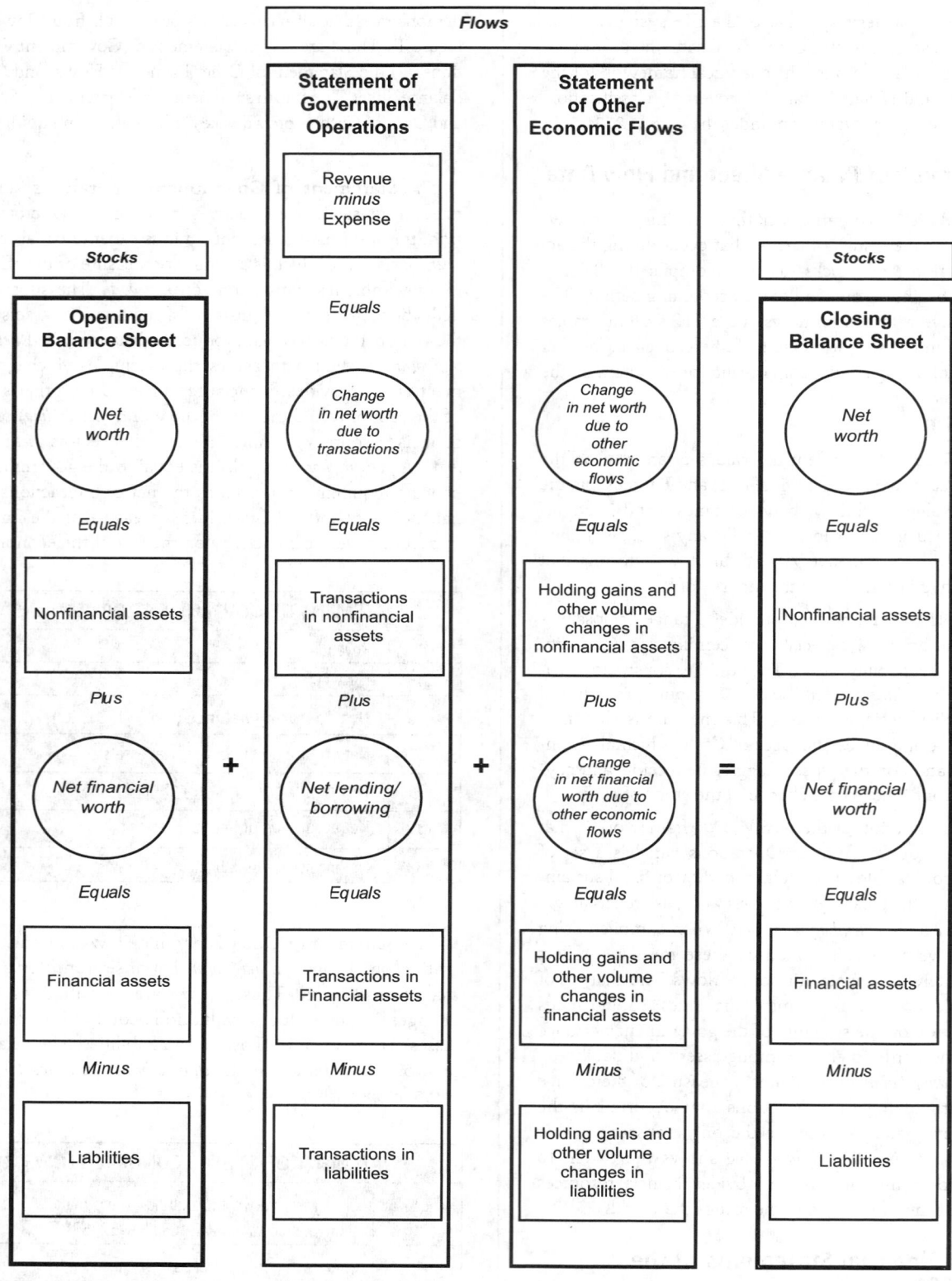

The **Balance Sheet** presents the stocks of assets, liabilities, and *net worth* at the end of the accounting period. The government's *net worth* is defined as the difference between total assets and total liabilities. Another balancing item that can be derived from the Balance Sheet is *net financial worth*, which is defined as total financial assets minus total liabilities.

BALANCE SHEET	
6	Net worth (61+62–63)
61	Nonfinancial assets
62	Financial assets
63	Liabilities

The **Statement of Sources and Uses of Cash** shows the amounts of cash generated and used in operations, transactions in nonfinancial assets, and transactions involving financial assets and liabilities, excluding cash itself. The balancing item, *net change in the stock of cash,* is the sum of the net cash received from these three sources of cash flows.

STATEMENT OF SOURCES AND USES OF CASH	
1	Cash receipts from operating activities
2	Cash payments for operating activities
	Net cash inflow from operating activities (1–2)
31	Net cash outflow from investments in nonfinancial assets
	Cash surplus/deficit (1–2–31)
32x	Net acquisition of financial assets other than cash
33	Net incurrence of liabilities
	Net cash inflow from financing activities (–32x+33)
	Net change in the stock of cash (1–2–31–32x+33=3212+3222)[1]

Coverage of the *GFSM 2001* System

The main focus of the coverage of the *GFSM 2001* system is the general government sector as defined in the *System of National Accounts, 1993 (1993 SNA)*, which is defined on the basis of institutional units. The comprehensive conceptual and accounting framework of the *GFSM 2001* applies to both the general government and the broader public sector; however, the coverage of the *GFS Yearbook* database has not been extended yet to include the public sector.[2]

Government units are institutional units[3] that carry out the functions of government as their primary activity. That is, they:

- have legislative, judicial, or executive authority over other institutional units within a given area;
- assume responsibility for the provision of goods and services to the community as a whole or to individual households on a nonmarket basis;
- make transfer payments to redistribute income and wealth; and
- finance their activities, directly or indirectly, mainly by means of taxes and other compulsory transfers from units in other sectors.

All government units are members of the general government sector, which also consists of all nonmarket nonprofit institutions (NPIs) that are controlled by government units. These are legally nongovernment entities, but they are considered to be carrying out government policies and effectively are part of government. The general government sector does not include public corporations or quasi-corporations.

Frequently, units of the broader public sector (nonfinancial public corporations and financial public corporations) carry out some functions of government. To capture the fiscal transactions and activities taking place outside the general government sector, the *GFSM 2001* encourages the identification of transactions between units of the general government sector and public corporations in the compilation of statistics on the public sector. However, it should be noted that this volume of the *GFS Yearbook* does not yet include these data.

In the GFS system, provision is made for subsectors of general government: central; state, provincial, or regional; and local; plus social security schemes, as relevant.[4] Not all countries will have all three levels; some may have only a central government or a central government and one lower level. Other countries may have more than three levels. In such cases, the various units should all be classified as one of the three levels suggested in the *GFSM 2001*.

The central government subsector is large and complex in most countries. It is generally composed of a central group of departments or ministries that make up a single institutional unit plus, in many countries, other units operating under the authority of the central government with a separate legal identity and enough autonomy to form additional government units (extrabudgetary accounts/funds and social security funds). These units may also exist at the state or local

---

[1] Domestic currency and deposits (3212) and foreign currency and deposits (3222).

[2] The general government sector consists of entities that implement public policy through the provision of primarily nonmarket services and the redistribution of income and wealth, with both activities supported mainly by compulsory levies on other sectors. The public sector consists of the general government sector plus

[2] (cont.) government-controlled entities, known as public corporations, whose primary activity is to engage in commercial activities.

[3] This type of unit can, in its own right, own assets, incur liabilities, and engage in economic activities and transactions with other entities.

[4] The *GFS Yearbook* does not separately disclose data on social security. These data are available on the GFS CD-ROM in the respective tables and statements.

government levels. The *GFSM 2001* encourages the creation of subsectors at each level of government based on whether the units are financed by the legislative budgets of that level of government or by extrabudgetary sources.[5]

The *GFSM 2001* Classifications

Classification codes are used in the GFS system to identify types of transactions, other economic flows, and stocks of assets and liabilities. The overall organization of the codes is outlined in Figure 2.

Codes beginning with 1 refer to revenue; codes beginning with 2 refer to expense; and codes beginning with 3 refer to transactions in nonfinancial assets, financial assets, and liabilities. For financial assets and liabilities, code 3 also signifies that they have been classified by financial instrument.

The first digit of the classification code for an other economic flow is always 4 or 5. Codes beginning with 4 refer to holding gains or losses and codes beginning with 5 refer to other changes in the volume of assets and liabilities. The first digit of the classification code for a stock of a type of asset or liability is always 6.

Transactions in assets and liabilities, other economic flows, and stocks of assets and liabilities all refer to types of assets and liabilities. Hence, the second and subsequent digits of each code are identical for each type of asset or liability. That is, 311 refers to transactions in fixed assets, 411 to holding gains in fixed assets, 511 to other changes in the volume of fixed assets, and 611 to the stock of fixed assets.

Expense transactions and transactions in nonfinancial assets can also be classified using the Classification of Functions of Government (COFOG).[6] All COFOG classification codes begin with 7. Transactions in financial assets and liabilities can be classified according to the sector of the other party to the financial instrument as well as according to the type of financial instrument. When classified by sector, the classification codes for these transactions begin with 8.

The *GFSM 2001* also encourages the recording of memorandum items to provide supplemental information about items related to, but not included on, the Balance Sheet. Where reported, these data have been included in the *GFS Yearbook* and on the GFS CD-ROM.

Basis and Time of Recording

In the *GFSM 2001* system, flows are recorded on an accrual basis, which means that flows are recorded at the time economic value is created, transformed, exchanged, transferred, or extinguished. Using the accrual basis also means that nonmonetary transactions are fully integrated in the revised GFS system. The *GFSM 2001* system also records flows on a cash basis. These data are reported in the Statement of Sources and Uses of Cash in the Country Tables of the *GFS Yearbook* and on the GFS CD-ROM.

Valuation of Flows and Stocks

Flows as well as stocks of assets, liabilities, and net worth (a balancing item) are valued at current market prices in the *GFSM 2001*, but with a provision for recording the nominal value of debt securities as a memorandum item.[7] In particular, flows are to be valued at prices current on the dates for which they are recorded, while stocks are to be valued at current prices on the Balance Sheet date.

---

[5] Separately classifying these units is analytically useful in distinguishing their differing sources of finance and differing types of public oversight of their operations.

[6] Data are collected and published for a selected subset of functions.

[7] The nominal value is the amount that the debtor owes to the creditor at any moment. Conceptually, the nominal value is equal to the required future payments of principal and interest discounted at the existing contractual interest rate. It reflects the value of the instrument at creation and subsequent economic flows, such as transactions, valuation changes (excluding market price changes) , and other changes such as debt forgiveness.

Figure 2: The Classification Coding System for GFS

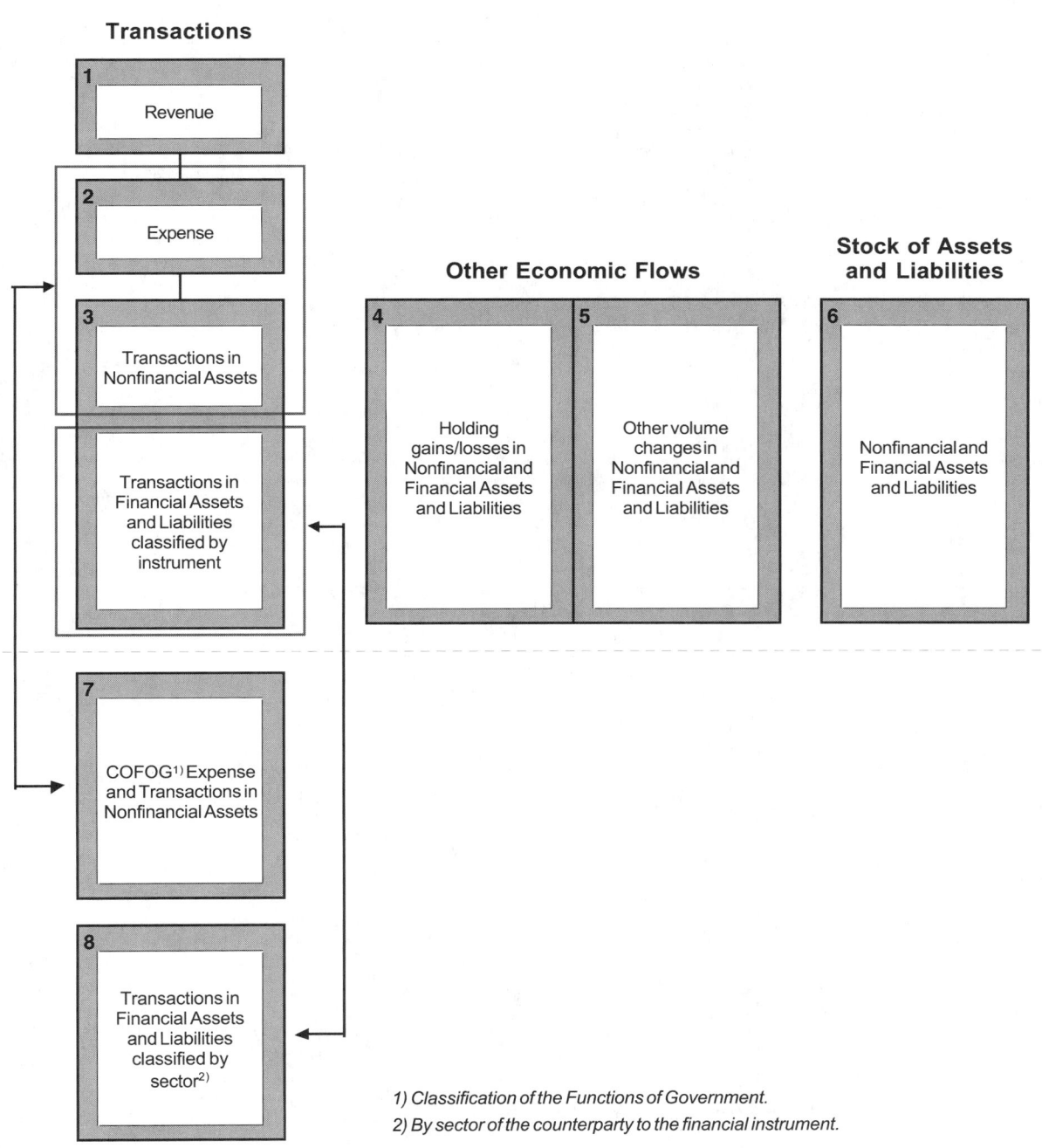

Transactions

1 Revenue

2 Expense

3 Transactions in Nonfinancial Assets

Transactions in Financial Assets and Liabilities classified by instrument

Other Economic Flows

4 Holding gains/losses in Nonfinancial and Financial Assets and Liabilities

5 Other volume changes in Nonfinancial and Financial Assets and Liabilities

Stock of Assets and Liabilities

6 Nonfinancial and Financial Assets and Liabilities

7 COFOG[1] Expense and Transactions in Nonfinancial Assets

8 Transactions in Financial Assets and Liabilities classified by sector[2]

1) Classification of the Functions of Government.
2) By sector of the counterparty to the financial instrument.

All historical data in the GFS database from 1990 onward have been reclassified to conform as closely as possible to the *GFSM 2001*. The main features of the reclassification are described below and illustrated in broad terms in Figure 3.

Revenue

The *GFSM 1986* categories total revenue and grants (A.I), excluding sales of fixed capital assets, stocks, and land and intangible assets (A14–16), were classified to the *GFSM 2001* category revenue (1). In addition, the following explains the classification of the historical *GFSM 1986* revenue items to the *GFSM 2001* categories:

- *Other taxes (116)*: For state and local governments, other taxes (116) also include taxes on payroll and workforce (112), and taxes on international trade (115), because these data were not separately collected in the *GFS Yearbook* Questionnaire (*GFSM 1986* format).

- *Grants from abroad (131)*: For all subsectors of general government, this category includes grants from international organizations (132), except grants from supranational organizations, because these data were not separately collected in the *GFS Yearbook* Questionnaire (*GFSM 1986* format). Grants from supranational organizations, separately available in the *GFSM 1986* historical data (where applicable), are classified in the *GFSM 2001* category grants from international organizations (132).

- *Property income (141)*: For all subsectors of general government, this category includes cash operating surpluses of departmental enterprise sales (*GFSM 1986* category A8.1). See *Operations of market establishments* below.

- *Voluntary transfers other than grants (144)*: For all subsectors of general government, this category excludes current transfers from nongovernment sources because these data were not separately collected in the *GFS Yearbook* Questionnaire (*GFSM 1986* format). These transfers are included in the *GFSM 1986* category other nontax revenue (A12), which has been reclassified to the *GFSM 2001* category miscellaneous and unidentified revenue (145).

- *Other revenue (145)*: For all subsectors of general government, this category includes current voluntary transfers other than grants because these data were not separately collected in the *GFS Yearbook* Questionnaire (*GFSM 1986* format). For state and local governments, miscellaneous and unidentified revenue (145) also includes fines, forfeits, and penalties (144) because these data were not separately collected in the *GFS Yearbook* Questionnaire (*GFSM 1986* format).

Expense

The *GFSM 1986* categories total current expenditure (C.III) and total capital transfers (C7) were classified to the *GFSM 2001* category expense (2). In addition, the following specific comments relate to the classification of the historical *GFSM 1986* expenditure items to the *GFSM 2001* categories.

- *Total expense (2)*: For state and local governments, only three components of expense (wages and salaries, use of goods and services, and interest) can be derived from the *GFSM 1986* data. Subsidies, grants, social benefits and other expense cannot be derived because these data were not separately collected in the *GFS Yearbook* Questionnaire (*GFSM 1986* format).

- *Wages and salaries (211)*: For state and local governments, this category includes social contributions by government as employer (212) because these data were not separately collected in the *GFS Yearbook* Questionnaire (*GFSM 1986* format).

- *Use of goods and services (22)*: For all subsectors of general government, this category includes property expense other than interest (281) because these data were not separately collected in the *GFS Yearbook* Questionnaire (*GFSM 1986* format).

- *Subsidies (25)*: For all subsectors of central government, this category includes the *GFSM 1986* category cash operating deficits of departmental enterprise sales (C3.1.3). See *Operations of market establishments* below. For state and local governments, subsidies (25) cannot be calculated because these data were not separately collected in the *GFS Yearbook* Questionnaire (*GFSM 1986* format).

- *Grants to foreign governments (261)*: For all subsectors of central government, this category includes grants to international organizations (262) because these data were not separately collected in the *GFS Yearbook* Questionnaire (*GFSM 1986* format). For state and local governments, grants (26) cannot be calculated because data other than grants to other general government units were not separately collected in the *GFS Yearbook* Questionnaire (*GFSM 1986* format).

- *Social benefits (27)*: For all subsectors of central government, the *GFSM 1986* category current transfers to nonprofit institutions and households (C3.3–4) was used as a proxy for social benefits owing to lack of details. Therefore, social benefits (27) may be overstated because it includes other (current) transfers to nonprofit institutions and households, which should be classified to miscellaneous other expense (282), if available. For state and local governments, social benefits (27) cannot be calculated because current transfers to nonprofit institutions and households were not separately collected in the *GFS Yearbook* Questionnaire (*GFSM 1986* format).

- *Other expense (28)*: For all subsectors of central government, this category excludes property expense other than interest because these data were not separately collected in the

GFS Yearbook Questionnaire (*GFSM 1986* format). See *Use of goods and services* above.

- *Miscellaneous other expense (282)*: For all subsectors of central government, this category only includes domestic capital transfers to all units except general government units (*GFSM 1986* categories C7.1.2–5). Current transfers to nonprofit institutions and households other than social benefits are excluded because these data were not separately collected in the *GFS Yearbook* Questionnaire (*GFSM 1986* format). See *Social benefits* above.

Net acquisition of nonfinancial assets

The *GFSM 1986* expenditure categories acquisition of fixed capital assets (C4), purchases of stocks (C5), and purchases of land and intangible assets (C6) were classified to the *GFSM 2001* category purchases of nonfinancial assets (31.1). The revenue categories sales of fixed capital assets, stocks, and land and intangible assets (A14–16) were classified to the *GFSM 2001* category sales of nonfinancial assets (31.2). The net acquisition of nonfinancial assets was calculated as category 31.1 minus 31.2.

Figure 3: Broad Overview of Relationships Between GFSM 1986 and GFSM 2001 Classification Systems

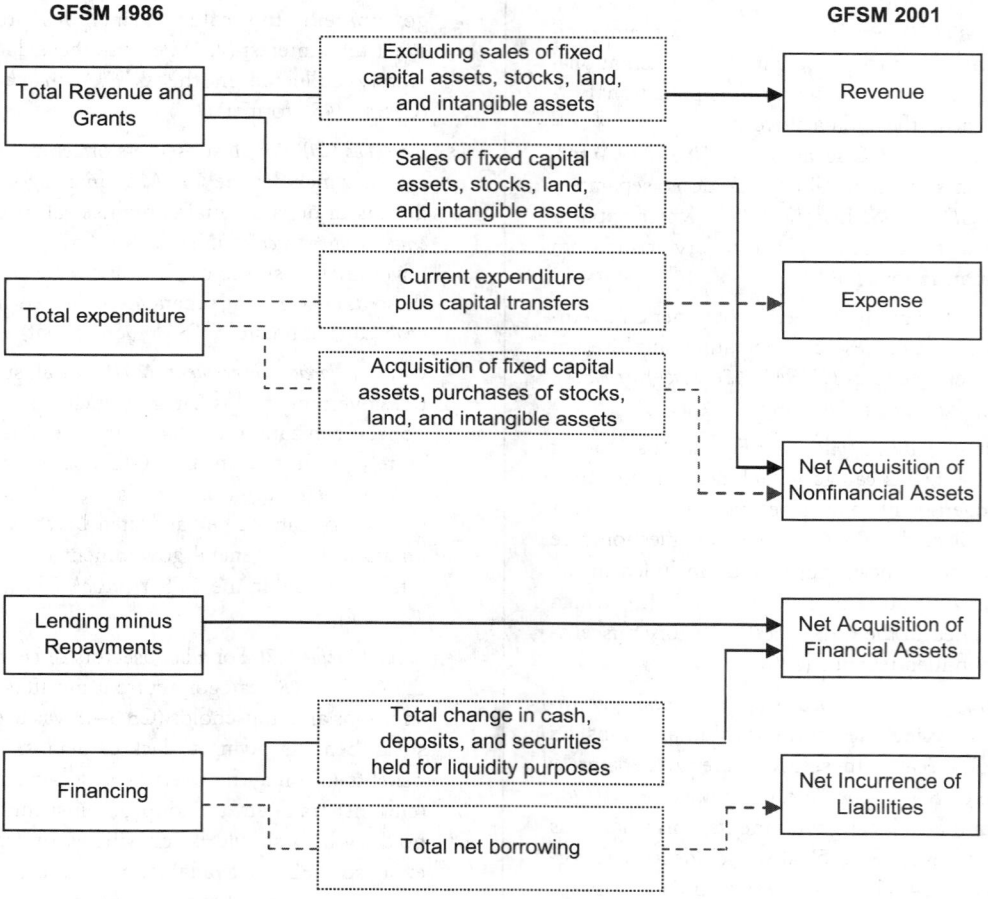

The acquisition and disposal of valuables were not separately collected in the *GFS Yearbook* Questionnaire (*GFSM 1986* format).

For state and local governments, sales of fixed capital assets (311.2) include capital transfers received from nongovernment sources because these data were not separately collected in the *GFS Yearbook* Questionnaire (*GFSM 1986* format).

Net acquisition of financial assets

The *GFSM 1986* categories total lending minus repayments (C.V) and total change in cash, deposits, and securities held for liquidity purposes (E6 and E12) are classified to the *GFSM 2001* categories net acquisition of financial assets (32, 82).

Owing to lack of detail in the *GFSM 1986* classifications, most of the components of the domestic and foreign net acquisition of financial assets are not available.

For state and local governments, net acquisition of financial assets excludes change in cash, deposits, and securities held for liquidity purposes: abroad (E12) because these data were not separately collected in the *GFS Yearbook* Questionnaire (*GFSM 1986* format). (See *Net incurrence of liabilities* below.)

Net incurrence of liabilities

All *GFSM 1986* financing categories (Tables D or E), excluding total change in cash, deposits, and securities held for liquidity purposes (E6 and E12), are classified to the *GFSM 2001* categories net incurrence of liabilities (33, 83).

For state and local governments, net incurrence of liabilities includes change in cash, deposits, and securities held for liquidity purposes: abroad (E12) because these data were not separately collected in the *GFS Yearbook* Questionnaire (*GFSM 1986* format). (See *Net acquisition of financial assets* above.)

Liabilities

For all subsectors of general government, domestic, foreign and total outstanding debt (*GFSM 1986* data) were classified to the *GFSM 2001* categories domestic (631), foreign (632), and total liabilities (63), respectively.

For the historical *GFS Yearbook* data (*GFSM 1986* format), therefore, liabilities are valued in accordance with the *GFSM 1986* methodology and not according to their market values (*GFSM 2001* methodology).

Total outlays

In the historical *GFS Yearbook* data (*GFSM 1986* format), total outlays (7) represents expense plus the (gross) acquisition of nonfinancial assets because the disposals/sales of nonfinancial assets were not classified by function of government. Only total expenditure (expense plus the acquisition of nonfinancial assets) was classified by function of government. In the *GFSM 2001*, total outlays represent expense plus the *net* acquisition of nonfinancial assets (acquisitions minus disposals).

Outlays on the protection of the environment (705) were not separately collected in the *GFS Yearbook* Questionnaire (*GFSM 1986* format).

Adjustments to the *GFSM 1986* data categories

The *GFS Yearbook* Questionnaire (*GFSM 1986* format) included several country-specific adjustment lines to the aggregates and/or subcategories of revenue and grants, expenditure and lending minus repayments, and financing. These adjustments were due to imbalances between the aggregates and the sum of their components. To maintain the balance in the data, these adjustments were included in the reclassification of the historical *GFSM 1986* data to the *GFSM 2001* categories. In the hard copy of the *GFS Yearbook,* published components may not sum to the aggregates as displayed because the adjustments are not published. These adjustment data are available on the GFS CD-ROM in the respective tables and statements.

Adjustment for the *GFSM 1986* consolidation method

For each subsector of central government in the Statement of Sources and Uses of Cash, the balancing item *net cash inflow from operating activities* (CIO) includes an adjustment to compensate for the *GFSM 1986* method of consolidating central government data. This adjustment line is not shown in the hard copy publication of the *GFS Yearbook* but is available on the GFS CD-ROM.

In pre–2003 GFS yearbooks based on the *GFSM 1986*, budgetary central government, extrabudgetary accounts/funds, and social security funds were combined to form the consolidated central government, where data were available. Data for state and/or local governments were also published, as available, but no general government data (consolidating central government, state governments and local governments, as relevant) were compiled and published.

In both the *GFSM 1986* and the *GFSM 2001*, consolidation involves the elimination of all transactions and debtor-creditor relationships that occur among the units that have been consolidated (i.e., presenting the statistics of a set of units as if they constituted a single unit). However, the method for consolidation in the *GFSM 2001* differs from that applied in the *GFSM 1986* and in previous GFS yearbooks. The difference can be explained as follows: The operations of central government's budgetary accounts (BA), extrabudgetary accounts/funds (EA), and social security funds (SS) are combined to form the consolidated central government (CG). Furthermore, also assume all transactions between these units are X (= $X_{ba} + X_{ea} + X_{ss}$). In the *GFSM 2001*, CG = BA + EA + SS − X. The subsectors are presented on a gross basis and the consolidation is done separately. In the *GFSM 1986*, CG = (BA − X_{ba}) + (EA - X_{ea}) + (SS - X_{ss}). The subsectors are presented on a net basis, i.e., after consolidation. This difference means that the *GFSM 2001* data for each subsector of gov-

ernment are presented on a gross basis, while the *GFSM 1986* data for each subsector of government are presented on a net basis. The presentation of the *GFSM 1986* above-the-line data for the subsectors of central government on a net basis resulted in a mismatch between the deficit/surplus and financing data for these subsectors.

The reclassification of the historical GFS yearbook data to the *GFSM 2001* Statement of Sources and Uses of Cash has required an adjustment of budgetary central government accounts, extrabudgetary accounts/funds, and social security funds data from a net basis to a gross basis. This adjustment was needed so that the respective balancing items (net cash inflow from operating activities, cash surplus/deficit, and net change in the stock of cash) in the Statement of Sources and Uses of Cash are correctly shown on a gross basis. If no financing data were reported for the budgetary, extrabudgetary, and social security subsectors, this adjustment for consolidation could not be made. As a result, the Statement of Sources and Uses of Cash shows data for the balancing items "net cash inflow from operating activities" and "cash surplus/deficit" as being not available for these subsectors.

Operations of market establishments

In the *GFSM 2001*, the **operations of market establishments** are recorded on a **gross basis**. That is, their gross rev-
enues are classified to the appropriate revenue categories, and their gross expenses are classified to the appropriate expense categories. In the *GFSM 1986*, operations of market establishments are recorded on a net basis. Only cash operating surpluses or deficits of departmental enterprises were included as revenue (entrepreneurial and property income) or expenditure (current transfers) in the *GFSM 1986* framework. Because of this, the use of unadjusted *GFSM 1986* data—as in the case of reclassifying the historical *GFSM 1986* data to the *GFSM 2001* categories—will understate both revenue and expense.

Social contributions by government as employer

In the *GFSM 2001*, **social contributions by government as employer** are "rerouted" so that the government is seen paying its employees, who then make payments of the same amount to the social insurance scheme. As a result, such contributions are not eliminated in consolidation of the general government subsectors. In the *GFSM 1986*, social contributions by government as employer are eliminated in consolidation of government data, because these transactions were considered to be between the contributing level of government and the social security fund. Because of this, the use of unadjusted *GFSM 1986* data—as in the case of reclassifying the historical *GFSM 1986* data to the *GFSM 2001* categories—will understate both revenue and expense.

GUIDE TO COUNTRY TABLES

Table A: Sector and Data Availability

Government Sector

BA	Budgetary Central Government
EA	Extra-Budgetary Units/Entities
SS	Social Security Funds
CG	Central Government (consolidated)
SG	State Governments
LG	Local Governments
GG	General Government (consolidated)

For each country listed:
- Existing Sectors corresponds to those described in the Institutional Tables published in this edition of the *GFS Yearbook*.
- Reported Sectors GFS CD-ROM refers to those sectors for which the country has actually reported data over the period beginning in 1990 (all reported sectors may not be available for each year of the series included on the GFS CD-ROM).
- Reported Sectors *GFS Yearbook* refers to the most recent three-year period for which data on the indicated sector(s) are published in the *GFS Yearbook*.
- The *GFS Yearbook* only includes countries that have reported data for 1998 or subsequent years.

For EU countries listed:
   In line with the presentation adopted within the European Union, data on BA operations may include the operations of EA.

Country Code	Country	Existing Sectors	Reported Sectors GFS CD-ROM: 140 Countries Sectors	Years	GFS Yearbook: 130 Countries Sectors	Years
512	Afghanistan, I.R. of	BA, EA, SS, CG, SG, GG	BA	2003-2004	BA	2003-2004
914	Albania	BA, EA, SS, CG, LG, GG	BA, EA, SS, CG, LG, GG	1995-2002	GG	2002
612	Algeria	BA, EA, SS, CG, LG, GG	BA	1994-2002	BA	2000-2002
213	Argentina	BA, EA, SS, CG, SG, LG, GG	BA, EA, SS, CG, SG, LG, GG	1990-2004	CG, SG, LG, GG	2002-2004
911	Armenia, Republic of	BA, EA, SS, CG, LG, GG	BA, EA, SS, CG, LG, GG	2003-2004	BA, CG, LG, GG	2003-2004
193	Australia	BA, EA, CG, SG, LG, GG	CG, SG, LG, GG	1990-2004	CG, SG, LG, GG	2002-2004
122	Austria	BA, EA, SS, CG, SG, LG, GG	BA, EA, SS, CG, SG, LG, GG	1990-2003	CG, SG, LG, GG	2001-2003
912	Azerbaijan, Republic of	BA, EA, SS, CG, LG, GG	CG, LG	1994-1999	CG, LG	1997-1999
313	Bahamas, The	BA, SS, CG, GG	BA	1990-2004	BA	2002-2004
419	Bahrain, Kingdom of	BA, EA, SS, CG, LG, GG	BA, EA, SS, CG, LG	1990-2004	BA, CG	2002-2004
513	Bangladesh	BA, CG, LG, GG	BA, CG	2000-2004	BA, CG	2002-2004
316	Barbados	BA, EA, SS, CG, GG	BA, EA, SS, CG, GG	2003-2004	BA, EA, CG, GG	2003-2004
913	Belarus	BA, SS, CG, LG, GG	BA, SS, CG, LG, GG	1992-2004	BA, CG, LG, GG	2002-2004
124	Belgium	BA, EA, SS, CG, SG, LG, GG	BA, EA, SS, CG, SG, LG, GG	1990-2003	CG, SG, LG, GG	2001-2003
339	Belize	BA, SS, CG, LG, GG	BA	1990-1997		
514	Bhutan	BA, CG, GG	BA, CG, GG	1990-2004	BA, CG, GG	2002-2004
218	Bolivia	BA, EA, SS, CG, SG, LG, GG	BA, EA, SS, CG, SG, LG, GG	1990-2004	CG, SG, LG, GG	2002-2004
963	Bosnia & Herzegovina	BA, EA, SS, CG, LG, GG	BA, SS, CG	2003-2004	BA, CG	2003-2004
616	Botswana	BA, EA, CG, LG, GG	BA, LG	1990-1996		
223	Brazil	BA, EA, SS, CG, SG, LG, GG	BA, EA, SS, CG, SG, LG	1990-1998	CG, SG, LG	1997-1998
918	Bulgaria	BA, EA, SS, CG, LG, GG	BA, EA, SS, CG, LG, GG	1990-2004	BA, CG, LG, GG	2002-2004
618	Burundi	BA, EA, SS, CG, LG, GG	BA, EA, SS, CG	1991-1999	BA, CG	1997-1999
522	Cambodia	BA, CG, LG, GG	BA, CG	2002-2004	BA, CG	2002-2004
622	Cameroon	BA, EA, SS, CG, LG, GG	BA, EA, SS, CG	1990-1999	BA	1998-1999
156	Canada	BA, EA, SS, CG, SG, LG, GG	BA, EA, SS, CG, SG, LG, GG	1990-2004	CG, SG, LG, GG	2002-2004
228	Chile	BA, EA, SS, CG, LG, GG	BA, EA, CG, LG, GG	1990-2004	BA, CG, LG, GG	2002-2004
924	China, P.R.: Mainland	BA, EA, SS, CG, LG, GG	BA, EA, SS, LG	1990-2003	BA, LG	2001-2003
532	China, P.R.: Hong Kong	GG	GG	2001-2003	GG	2001-2003
546	China, P.R.: Macao	BA, EA, SS, CG, GG	BA, EA, SS, CG, GG	1996-2004	BA, EA, CG, GG	2002-2004
233	Colombia	BA, EA, SS, CG, SG, LG, GG	BA, EA, SS, CG, SG, LG, GG	1990-2004	BA, EA	2002-2004
636	Congo, Dem. Rep. of	BA, EA, SS, CG, LG, GG	BA, EA, SS, CG	1990-2002	BA, CG	2000-2002

Country Code	Country	Existing Sectors	Reported Sectors			
			GFS CD-ROM: 140 Countries		GFS Yearbook: 130 Countries	
			Sectors	Years	Sectors	Years
634	Congo, Republic of	BA, EA, SS, CG, LG, GG	BA, EA, SS, CG, LG, GG	1990-2003	BA, CG, LG, GG	2001-2003
238	Costa Rica	BA, EA, SS, CG, LG, GG	BA, EA, SS, CG, LG, GG	1990-2004	BA, CG, LG, GG	2002-2004
662	Cote d'Ivoire	BA, EA, SS, CG, LG, GG	BA, EA, SS, CG	1990-2003	BA, CG	2001-2003
960	Croatia	BA, EA, SS, CG, LG, GG	BA, EA, SS, CG, LG, GG	1991-2004	BA, CG, LG, GG	2002-2004
423	Cyprus	BA, EA, SS, CG, LG, GG	BA, EA, SS, CG	1990-1998	BA, EA, CG	1996-1998
935	Czech Republic	BA, EA, SS, CG, LG, GG	BA, EA, SS, CG, LG, GG	1993-2004	BA, CG, LG, GG	2002-2004
128	Denmark	BA, EA, SS, CG, LG, GG	BA, SS, CG, LG, GG	1998-2004	BA, CG, LG, GG	2002-2004
243	Dominican Republic	BA, EA, SS, CG, LG, GG	BA, EA, SS, CG, LG	1990-2003	BA, CG	2001-2003
248	Ecuador	BA, EA, SS, CG, LG, GG	BA	1990-1994		
469	Egypt	BA, EA, SS, CG, GG	BA, EA, SS, CG,	1990-2002	BA	2000-2002
253	El Salvador	BA, EA, SS, CG, LG, GG	BA, EA, SS, CG, LG, GG	1990-2004	BA, CG, LG, GG	2002-2004
939	Estonia	BA, EA, SS, CG, LG, GG	BA, EA, SS, CG, LG	1991-2001	BA, CG, LG	1999-2001
644	Ethiopia	BA, EA, SS, CG, SG, LG, GG	BA, EA, SS, CG, SG	1990-2002	BA, CG	2001-2002
819	Fiji	BA, EA, CG, LG, GG	BA, LG	1990-2004	BA	2004
172	Finland	BA, EA, SS, CG, LG, GG	BA, EA, SS, CG, LG, GG	1990-2004	BA, CG, LG, GG	2002-2004
132	France	BA, EA, SS, CG, LG, GG	BA, EA, SS, CG, LG, GG	1990-2004	BA, CG, LG, GG	2002-2004
648	Gambia, The	BA, EA, CG, LG, GG	BA, EA, CG	1990-1993		
915	Georgia	BA, EA, SS, CG, LG, GG	BA, EA, SS, CG, LG, GG	1995-2004	BA, CG, LG, GG	2002-2004
134	Germany	BA, EA, SS, CG, SG, LG, GG	BA, EA, SS, CG, SG, LG, GG	1990-2004	CG, SG, LG, GG	2002-2004
652	Ghana	BA, EA, CG, LG, GG	BA	1990-2004	BA	2002-2004
174	Greece	BA, EA, SS, CG, LG, GG	BA, EA, SS, CG, LG, GG	1990-2000	BA, CG, LG, GG	1998-2000
328	Grenada	BA, EA, SS, CG, GG	BA	1991-1995		
258	Guatemala	BA, EA, SS, CG, LG, GG	BA, LG	1990-2004	BA	2002-2004
656	Guinea	BA, SS, CG, LG, GG	BA, CG	1990-1999	BA	1998-1999
944	Hungary	BA, EA, SS, CG, LG, GG	BA, EA, SS, CG, LG, GG	1990-2003	BA, CG, LG, GG	2001-2003
176	Iceland	BA, SS, CG, LG, GG	BA, SS, CG, LG, GG	1990-2002	BA, CG, LG, GG	2000-2002
534	India	BA, CG, SG, LG, GG	BA, CG, SG, GG	1990-2004	CG, GG	2002-2004
536	Indonesia	BA, EA, SS, CG, SG, LG, GG	BA, EA, SS, CG, SG, LG	1990-2004	BA, CG	2002-2004
429	Iran, Islamic Republic of	BA, EA, SS, CG, LG, GG	BA, EA, SS, CG, LG, GG	1990-2005	BA, CG, LG, GG	2003-2005
178	Ireland	BA, SS, CG, LG, GG	BA, SS, CG, LG	1990-1997		
436	Israel	BA, EA, SS, CG, LG, GG	BA, EA, SS, CG, LG, GG	1990-2004	BA, CG, LG, GG	2002-2004
136	Italy	BA, EA, SS, CG, LG, GG	BA, EA, SS, CG, LG, GG	1990-2003	BA, CG, LG, GG	2001-2003
343	Jamaica	BA, EA, SS, CG, LG, GG	BA, EA, SS, CG, LG, GG	1992-2003	BA, CG, LG, GG	2001-2003
158	Japan	BA, EA, SS, CG, LG, GG	BA, SS, CG, GG	1990-2003	GG	2001-2003
439	Jordan	BA, EA, SS, CG, LG, GG	BA	1990-2004	BA	2002-2004
916	Kazakhstan	BA, EA, SS, CG, LG, GG	BA, EA, SS, CG, LG, GG	1997-2004	CG, LG, GG	2002-2004
664	Kenya	BA, EA, SS, CG, LG, GG	BA, LG	1990-2002	BA	2000-2002
542	Korea, Republic of	BA, EA, CG, SG, LG, GG	BA, EA, CG	1990-2001	BA, CG	1999-2001
443	Kuwait	BA, EA, SS, CG, GG	BA, EA, SS, CG, GG	1997-2003	BA, EA, CG, GG	2001-2003
917	Kyrgyz Republic	BA, EA, SS, CG, LG, GG	BA, LG	1993-2001	BA, LG	1999-2001
941	Latvia	BA, SS, CG, LG, GG	BA, EA, SS, CG, LG, GG	1994-2004	BA, CG, LG, GG	2002-2004
446	Lebanon	BA, EA, SS, CG, LG, GG	BA, CG	1993-2003	BA	2001-2003

Country Code	Country	Existing Sectors	GFS CD-ROM: 140 Countries		GFS Yearbook: 130 Countries	
			Reported Sectors			
			Sectors	Years	Sectors	Years
666	Lesotho	BA, EA, CG, GG	CG, GG	1990-2004	CG, GG	2002-2004
946	Lithuania	BA, EA, SS, CG, LG, GG	BA, EA, SS, CG, LG, GG	1991-2004	BA, CG, LG, GG	2002-2004
137	Luxembourg	BA, EA, SS, CG, LG, GG	BA, EA, SS, CG, LG, GG	1990-2004	BA, CG, LG, GG	2002-2004
674	Madagascar	BA, EA, SS, CG, LG, GG	BA, EA, CG	1990-2004	CG	2002-2004
548	Malaysia	BA, EA, SS, CG, SG, LG, GG	EA, CG, SG, LG, GG	1990-2003	CG, SG, LG, GG	2001-2003
556	Maldives	BA, CG, GG	BA, CG, GG	1990-2005	BA, CG, GG	2003-2005
181	Malta	BA, EA, CG, GG	BA, EA, CG, GG	1990-2001	BA, CG, GG	1999-2001
684	Mauritius	BA, EA, SS, CG, SG, LG, GG	BA, EA, SS, CG, SG, LG, GG	1990-2004	CG, SG, LG, GG	2002-2004
273	Mexico	BA, SS, CG, SG, LG, GG	BA, SS, CG, SG, LG	1990-2000	CG, SG, LG	1998-2000
921	Moldova	BA, EA, SS, CG, LG, GG	BA, EA, SS, CG, LG, GG	1995-2004	BA, CG, LG, GG	2002-2004
948	Mongolia	BA, EA, SS, CG, LG, GG	BA, EA, SS, CG, LG, GG	1992-2003	BA, CG, LG, GG	2001-2003
686	Morocco	BA, EA, SS, CG, LG, GG	BA, EA, SS, CG	1990-1999	BA, CG	1997-1999
518	Myanmar	BA, SS, CG, LG, GG	BA, SS, CG	1990-2002	CG	2000-2002
728	Namibia	BA, EA, CG, LG, GG	BA	1990-2003	BA	2001-2003
558	Nepal	BA, CG, LG, GG	BA, CG	1990-2004	BA, CG	2002-2004
138	Netherlands	BA, EA, SS, CG, LG, GG	BA, EA, SS, CG, LG, GG	1990-2004	BA, CG, LG, GG	2002-2004
353	Netherlands Antilles	BA, EA, SS, CG, LG, GG	BA, EA, SS, CG, LG	1990-1995		
196	New Zealand	BA, EA, SS, CG, LG, GG	BA, EA, SS, CG, LG, GG	1990-2004	BA, CG, LG, GG	2002-2004
278	Nicaragua	BA, EA, SS, CG, SG, LG, GG	BA, SS, CG, LG	1990-2004	BA, CG	2002-2004
142	Norway	BA, EA, SS, CG, LG, GG	BA, EA, CG, LG, GG	1990-2004	BA, CG, LG, GG	2002-2004
449	Oman	BA, EA, CG, GG	BA	1990-2001	BA	1999-2001
564	Pakistan	BA, CG, SG, LG, GG	BA, CG	1990-2006	CG	2004-2006
283	Panama	BA, EA, SS, CG, LG, GG	BA, EA, SS, CG	1990-2001	BA, CG	1999-2001
853	Papua New Guinea	BA, EA, CG, SG, LG, GG	BA	1990-2002	BA	2000-2002
288	Paraguay	BA, EA, SS, CG, SG, LG, GG	BA, LG	1990-2004	BA	2002-2004
293	Peru	BA, EA, SS, CG, SG, LG, GG	BA, EA, SS, CG, SG, LG, GG	1990-2004	CG, SG, LG, GG	2002-2004
566	Philippines	BA, EA, SS, CG, LG, GG	BA, LG	1990-2004	BA	2002-2004
964	Poland	BA, EA, SS, CG, LG, GG	BA, EA, SS, CG, LG, GG	1994-2003	BA, CG, LG, GG	2001-2003
182	Portugal	BA, EA, SS, CG, LG, GG	BA, EA, SS, CG, LG, GG	1990-2002	BA, CG, LG, GG	2000-2002
968	Romania	BA, EA, SS, CG, LG, GG	BA, EA, SS, CG, LG, GG	1990-2002	BA, CG, LG, GG	2000-2002
922	Russian Federation	BA, EA, SS, CG, LG, GG	BA, EA, SS, CG, LG, GG	1994-2004	BA, CG, LG, GG	2002-2004
714	Rwanda	BA, EA, SS, CG, LG, GG	BA, EA, SS, CG	1990-1993		
361	St. Kitts and Nevis	BA, EA, SS, CG, GG	BA, SS, CG, GG	1990-2003	BA, CG, GG	2003
364	St. Vincent and Grenadines	BA, SS, CG, LG, GG	BA, GG	1990-2004	GG	2002-2004
135	San Marino	BA, EA, SS, CG, GG	BA, EA, SS, CG, GG	1995-2002	BA, EA, CG, GG	2002
722	Senegal	BA, EA, SS, CG, LG, GG	BA, LG	1996-2001	BA, LG	1999-2001
965	Serbia & Montenegro	BA, SS, CG, SG, LG, GG	BA, SS, CG, SG, LG, GG	2002	CG, SG, LG, GG	2002
718	Seychelles	BA, SS, CG, GG	BA, SS, CG, GG	1990-2004	CG, GG	2002-2004
724	Sierra Leone	BA, EA, CG, LG, GG	BA	1990-1999	BA	1997-1999
576	Singapore	BA, EA, CG, GG	BA, EA, CG, GG	1990-2004	BA, EA, CG, GG	2002-2004
936	Slovak Republic	BA, EA, SS, CG, LG, GG	BA, EA, SS, CG, LG, GG	1996-2003	BA, CG, LG, GG	2001-2003
961	Slovenia	BA, EA, SS, CG, LG, GG	BA, EA, SS, CG, LG, GG	1992-2004	BA, CG, LG, GG	2002-2004

Country Code	Country	Existing Sectors	Reported Sectors			
			GFS CD-ROM: 140 Countries		GFS Yearbook: 130 Countries	
			Sectors	Years	Sectors	Years
199	South Africa	BA, EA, SS, CG, SG, LG, GG	BA, EA, SS, CG, SG, LG, GG	1990-2004	CG, SG, LG, GG	2002-2004
184	Spain	BA, EA, SS, CG, SG, LG, GG	BA, SS, CG, SG, LG, GG	1990-2003	CG, SG, LG, GG	2001-2003
524	Sri Lanka	BA, EA, CG, SG, LG, GG	BA, CG, LG	1990-2002	BA, LG	2000-2002
732	Sudan	BA, EA, SS, CG, SG, LG, GG	BA	1998-1999	BA	1998-1999
734	Swaziland	BA, EA, CG, LG, GG	BA, LG	1999-2003	BA, LG	2001-2003
144	Sweden	BA, SS, CG, LG, GG	BA, SS, CG, LG, GG	1990-2003	BA, CG, LG, GG	2001-2003
146	Switzerland	BA, EA, SS, CG, SG, LG, GG	BA, EA, SS, CG, SG, LG, GG	1990-2002	CG, SG, LG, GG	2000-2002
463	Syrian Arab Republic	BA, EA, CG, LG, GG	BA, CG	1990-1999	CG	1997-1999
923	Tajikistan	BA, SS, CG, LG, GG	BA, SS, CG, LG, GG	1998-2004	BA, CG, LG, GG	2003-2004
578	Thailand	BA, EA, SS, CG, LG, GG	BA, EA, SS, CG, LG, GG	1990-2004	BA, CG, LG, GG	2002-2004
369	Trinidad and Tobago	BA, EA, SS, CG, LG, GG	BA, EA, SS, CG, LG	1993-1995		
744	Tunisia	BA, EA, SS, CG, LG, GG	BA, EA, SS, CG	1990-2005	BA, CG	2003-2005
186	Turkey	BA, EA, SS, CG, LG, GG	BA, EA, SS, CG	1990-2001	BA, EA	1999-2001
746	Uganda	BA, EA, SS, CG, LG, GG	BA, LG	1998-2003	BA, LG	2001-2003
926	Ukraine	BA, SS, CG, LG, GG	BA, SS, CG, LG, GG	1992-2004	BA, CG, LG, GG	2002-2004
466	United Arab Emirates	BA, CG, SG, GG	BA, CG	1990-1999	CG	1997-1999
112	United Kingdom	BA, EA, SS, CG, LG, GG	CG, LG, GG	1998-2004	CG, LG, GG	2002-2004
111	United States	BA, SS, CG, SG, LG, GG	BA, SS, CG, SG, LG, GG	1990-2005	CG, GG	2003-2005
298	Uruguay	BA, EA, SS, CG, LG, GG	BA, EA, SS, CG, LG, GG	1990-2004	BA, CG, LG, GG	2002-2004
846	Vanuatu	BA, EA, CG, LG, GG	BA, EA, CG	1990-1999	BA, CG	1997-1999
299	Venezuela, Rep. Bol.	BA, EA, SS, CG, SG, LG, GG	BA, EA, SS, CG	1990-2003	CG	2001-2003
582	Vietnam	BA, EA, SS, CG, LG, GG	GG	1990-2004	GG	2002-2004
474	Yemen, Republic of	BA, EA, SS, CG, GG	BA	1990-1999	BA	1997-1999
754	Zambia	BA, EA, SS, CG, LG, GG	BA	1990-1999	BA	1997-1999
698	Zimbabwe	BA, EA, CG, LG, GG	CG, LG	1990-1997		

GUIDE TO COUNTRY TABLES

Table B: Basis of Recording for Latest Year Reported

Government Sector			C	Cash basis of recording
BA	Budgetary Central Government		N	Noncash basis of recording (including accrual basis)
EA	Extra-Budgetary Units/Entities		–	Sector does not exist
SS	Social Security Funds		….	Information Not Available
CG	Central Government (consolidated)			
SG	State Governments			For EU countries listed:
LG	Local Governments			In line with the presentation adopted within the European
GG	General Government (consolidated)			Union, data on BA operations may include the operations of EA.

Country Code	Country	BA	EA	SS	CG	SG	LG	GG
512	Afghanistan, I.R. of	C	….	….	….	….	–	….
914	Albania	….	….	….	….	–	….	C
612	Algeria	C	….	….	….	–	….	….
213	Argentina	N	N	N	N	N	N	N
911	Armenia, Republic of	C	C	C	C	–	C	C
193	Australia	….	….	–	N	N	N	N
122	Austria	N	N	N	N	N	N	N
912	Azerbaijan, Republic of	….	….	….	C	–	C	….
313	Bahamas, The	C	–	….	….	–	….	….
419	Bahrain, Kingdom of	C	C	C	C	–	….	….
513	Bangladesh	C	–	–	C	–	….	….
316	Barbados	C	C	C	C	–	–	C
913	Belarus	C	–	C	C	–	C	C
124	Belgium	N	N	N	N	N	N	N
339	Belize	C	–	….	….	–	….	….
514	Bhutan	C	–	–	C	–	–	C
218	Bolivia	N	N	N	N	N	N	N
963	Bosnia & Herzegovina	N	….	N	N	–	….	….
616	Botswana	C	….	–	….	–	….	….
223	Brazil	C	C	C	C	C	C	….
918	Bulgaria	C	C	C	C	–	C	C
618	Burundi	C	….	C	C	–	….	….
522	Cambodia	N	–	–	N	….	….	….
622	Cameroon	C	….	….	….	–	….	….
156	Canada	C	C	C	C	C	C	C
228	Chile	N	N	….	N	–	N	N
924	China, P.R.: Mainland	C	C	….	….	–	C	….
532	China, P.R.: Hong Kong	–	–	–	–	–	–	N
546	China, P.R.: Macao	C	C	C	C	–	–	C
233	Colombia	N	N	N	….	….	….	….
636	Congo, Dem. Rep. of	C	C	C	C	–	….	….

Country Code	Country	BA	EA	SS	CG	SG	LG	GG
634	Congo, Republic of	N	N	N	N	-	N	N
238	Costa Rica	C	C	C	C	-	C	C
662	Cote d'Ivoire	C	C	C	C	-	....	....
960	Croatia	C	C	C	C	-	C	C
423	Cyprus	C	C	C	C	-	....	....
935	Czech Republic	N	N	N	N	-	N	N
128	Denmark	N	....	N	N	-	N	N
243	Dominican Republic	C	C	C	C	-	....	....
248	Ecuador	C	....	....	....	-	....	....
469	Egypt	C	....	....	....	-	-	....
253	El Salvador	N	N	N	N	-	N	N
939	Estonia	C	C	C	C	-	C	....
644	Ethiopia	C	C	C	C	C	....	....
819	Fiji	C	....	....	....	-	....	....
172	Finland	N	....	N	N	-	N	N
132	France	N	....	N	N	-	N	N
648	Gambia, The	C	C	-	C	....	....	....
915	Georgia	C	C	C	C	-	C	C
134	Germany	N	....	N	N	N	N	N
652	Ghana	C	....	-	....	-	....	....
174	Greece	N	N	N	N	-	N	N
328	Grenada	C	C	C	C	-	C	C
258	Guatemala	C	....	....	....	-	....	....
656	Guinea	C	-	....	....	-	....	....
944	Hungary	N	N	N	N	-	N	N
176	Iceland	N	-	N	N	-	N	N
534	India	C	-	-	C	....	....	....
536	Indonesia	C	C	C	C	....	....	....
429	Iran, Islamic Republic of	C	C	C	C	-	C	C
178	Ireland	C	-	C	C	-	C	....
436	Israel	N	N	N	N	-	N	N
136	Italy	N	N	N	N	-	N	N
343	Jamaica	C	C	C	C	-	C	C
158	Japan	....	....	....	....	-	....	N
439	Jordan	C	....	....	....	-	....	....
916	Kazakhstan	....	....	....	C	-	C	C
664	Kenya	C	....	....	....	-	....	....
542	Korea, Republic of	C	C	-	C	....	....	....
443	Kuwait	C	C	C	C	-	-	C
917	Kyrgyz Republic	C	....	....	....	-	C	....
941	Latvia	C	-	C	C	-	C	C
446	Lebanon	N	....	....	....	-	....	....

Country Code	Country	BA	EA	SS	CG	SG	LG	GG
666	Lesotho	....	....	-	C	-	-	C
946	Lithuania	N	N	N	N	-	N	N
137	Luxembourg	N	....	N	N	-	N	N
674	Madagascar	....	....	....	N	-	....	....
548	Malaysia	....	....	....	C	C	C	C
556	Maldives	C	-	-	C	-	-	C
181	Malta	C	....	-	C	-	-	C
684	Mauritius	C	C	C	C	C	C	C
273	Mexico	C	-	C	C	C	C	....
921	Moldova	C	C	C	C	-	C	C
948	Mongolia	C	N	C	N	-	C	N
686	Morocco	C	C	C	C	-	....	....
518	Myanmar	....	-	....	C	-	....	....
728	Namibia	C	....	-	....	-	....	....
558	Nepal	C	-	-	C	-	....	....
138	Netherlands	N	....	N	N	-	N	N
353	Netherlands Antilles	C	C	C	C	-	C	....
196	New Zealand	N	N	N	N	-	N	N
278	Nicaragua	C	....	C	C	....	....	....
142	Norway	N	N	....	N	-	N	N
449	Oman	C	....	-	....	-	-	....
564	Pakistan	C	-	-	C	....	....	....
283	Panama	C	C	C	C	-	....	....
853	Papua New Guinea	C	....	....	....	....	....	....
288	Paraguay	C	....	....	....	....	....	....
293	Peru	C	C	C	C	C	C	C
566	Philippines	C	....	....	....	-	....	....
964	Poland	N	N	N	N	-	N	N
182	Portugal	N	....	N	N	-	N	N
968	Romania	N	N	N	N	-	N	N
922	Russian Federation	N	N	N	N	-	N	N
714	Rwanda	C	C	C	C	-	....	....
361	St. Kitts and Nevis	C	....	C	C	-	-	C
364	St. Vincent and Grenadines	....	-	....	....	-	....	C
135	San Marino	N	N	N	N	-	-	N
722	Senegal	C	....	....	....	-	C	....
965	Serbia & Montenegro	C	-	C	C	C	C	C
718	Seychelles	....	-	....	C	-	-	C
724	Sierra Leone	C	....	-	....	-	....	....
576	Singapore	C	C	-	C	-	-	C
936	Slovak Republic	N	N	N	N	-	N	N
961	Slovenia	C	C	C	C	-	C	C

Country Code	Country	BA	EA	SS	CG	SG	LG	GG
199	South Africa	C	N	N	N	C	C	N
184	Spain	N	....	N	N	N	N	N
524	Sri Lanka	C	....	-	....	....	C	....
732	Sudan	C	....	....	....	....	....	....
734	Swaziland	C	....	-	....	-	C	....
144	Sweden	N	-	N	N	-	N	N
146	Switzerland	C	C	C	C	C	C	C
463	Syrian Arab Republic	....	....	-	C	-	....	....
923	Tajikistan	C	-	C	C	-	C	C
578	Thailand	C	N	N	N	-	C	N
369	Trinidad and Tobago	C	C	C	C	-	C	....
744	Tunisia	C	....	C	C	-	....	....
186	Turkey	C	C	....	....	-	....	....
746	Uganda	C	....	....	....	-	C	....
926	Ukraine	C	-	C	C	-	C	C
466	United Arab Emirates	C	-	-	C	-	....	....
112	United Kingdom	....	....	....	N	-	N	N
111	United States	....	-	....	N	....	....	....
298	Uruguay	C	C	C	C	-	C	C
846	Vanuatu	C	C	-	C	-	....	....
299	Venezuela, Rep. Bol.	C	....	C	C	....	....	....
582	Vietnam	....	....	....	....	-	....	C
474	Yemen, Republic of	C	....	....	....	-	-	....
754	Zambia	C	....	....	....	-	....	....
698	Zimbabwe	....	....	-	C	-	....	....

WORLD
and
AREA TABLES

Table W1. Main Balances: General and Central Government

(Percent of GDP)

		Cash Surplus/Deficit						Net Lending/Borrowing					
		1999	2000	2001	2002	2003	2004	1999	2000	2001	2002	2003	2004
General Government													
	Industrial Countries												
111	United States	....	4.18	....	....	....	....	....	....	−.27	−3.68	−4.85	−4.60
156	Canada	....	2.66	.62	−.05	.20	.94p	....	....	....	....	....	....
193	Australia	.82	2.60	1.16	.52	1.44	1.76	.80	2.46	.71	−.50	1.01	1.22
158	Japan	....	....	1.80	.45	1.37p	....	....	....	−6.59	−8.23	−7.54p	....
196	New Zealand	....	....	....	....	2.70p	3.27p	....	....	....	....	2.87p	3.55p
	Euro Area												
122	Austria	....	....	....	....	....	....	−2.34	−1.60	.11	−.41	−1.25	....
124	Belgium	....	....	....	....	....	....	−2.08	.12	−.92	−1.49	−1.26	....
172	Finland	....	....	....	....	....	....	2.19	7.18	7.15	5.91	2.31p	1.90p
132	France	....	....	....	....	....	....	−1.59	−1.38	−1.51	−3.17	−4.20p	−3.65p
134	Germany	....	....	....	....	....	....	−1.46	1.31	−2.82	−3.71	−4.00	−3.66
174	Greece	....	....	....	....	....	....	....	....	....	....	....	....
136	Italy	....	....	....	....	....	....	−1.76	−.67	−2.67	−2.41	−2.50	....
137	Luxembourg	....	....	....	....	....	....	3.53	6.27	6.07	2.11	.20p	−.62p
138	Netherlands	....	....	....	....	....	....	†.66	2.20	−.25	−1.99	−3.16p	−2.08p
182	Portugal	....	....	....	....	....	....	−2.87	−2.97	−4.42	−2.72	....	....
184	Spain	....	....	....	....	....	....	−1.18	−.87	−.37	−.06p	.32p	....
128	Denmark	....	....	....	....	....	....	3.15	2.27	1.19	.26	−.23p	1.11p
176	Iceland	....	....	....	....	....	....	2.42	2.46	.17	−.99	....	....
142	Norway	....	11.79	13.94	8.95	7.66p	9.24p	....	15.61	13.67	9.27	7.61p	11.45p
135	San Marino	....	....	....	....	....	....	....	....	....	1.29	....	....
144	Sweden	....	....	....	....	....	....	1.30	3.66	4.56	−.26	.05	....
146	Switzerland	.22	3.06	.58	†.65	....	....	....	....	....	....	....	....
112	United Kingdom	....	....	....	....	....	....	1.14	1.64	.79	−1.58	−3.24	−3.08
	Developing Countries												
	Africa												
612	Algeria	....	....	....	....	....	....	....	....	....	....	....	....
618	Burundi	....	....	....	....	....	....	....	....	....	....	....	....
622	Cameroon	....	....	....	....	....	....	....	....	....	....	....	....
636	Congo, Dem. Rep. of	....	....	....	....	....	....	....	....	....	....	....	....
634	Congo, Rep. of	....	....	....	....	....	....	....	....	....	....	6.51	....
662	Côte d'Ivoire	....	....	....	....	....	....	....	....	....	....	....	....
644	Ethiopia	....	....	....	....	....	....	....	....	....	....	....	....
652	Ghana	....	....	....	....	....	....	....	....	....	....	....	....
656	Guinea	....	....	....	....	....	....	....	....	....	....	....	....
664	Kenya	....	....	....	....	....	....	....	....	....	....	....	....
666	Lesotho	−6.42	−3.68	−2.53	−3.63	.61p	....	....	....	....	....	....	....
674	Madagascar	....	....	....	....	....	....	....	....	....	....	....	....
684	Mauritius	....	....	....	†−3.55	−3.16	−3.00	....	....	....	....	....	....
686	Morocco	....	....	....	....	....	....	....	....	....	....	....	....
728	Namibia	....	....	....	....	....	....	....	....	....	....	....	....
722	Senegal	....	....	....	....	....	....	....	....	....	....	....	....
718	Seychelles	....	....	....	−14.35	....	....	....	....	....	....	....	....
724	Sierra Leone	....	....	....	....	....	....	....	....	....	....	....	....
199	South Africa	−1.76	−1.96	−.93	−1.83	−2.89p	−2.39p	....	−2.23	−1.17	−2.37	−2.89p	−2.39p
732	Sudan	....	....	....	....	....	....	....	....	....	....	....	....
734	Swaziland	....	....	....	....	....	....	....	....	....	....	....	....
744	Tunisia	....	....	....	....	....	....	....	....	....	....	....	....
746	Uganda	....	....	....	....	....	....	....	....	....	....	....	....
754	Zambia	....	....	....	....	....	....	....	....	....	....	....	....

Table W1. Main Balances: General and Central Government

(Percent of GDP)

		Cash Surplus/Deficit						Net Lending/Borrowing					
		1999	2000	2001	2002	2003	2004	1999	2000	2001	2002	2003	2004
	Asia												
512	Afghanistan, I.R. of........	....	....	....	....	....	....	....	....	....	....	....	....
513	Bangladesh...........	....	....	....	....	....	....	....	....	....	....	....	....
514	Bhutan..............	−1.91	−2.19	....	....	....	....	....	....	....	....	....	....
522	Cambodia.............	....	....	....	....	....	....	....	....	....	....	....	....
924	China, P.R.: Mainland............	....	....	....	....	....	....	....	....	....	....	....	....
532	China, P.R.: Hong Kong........	....	....	....	−5.09	−4.77	....	....	....	....	−6.95	−6.00	....
546	China, P.R.: Macao.........	−.60	1.64	3.62	2.88	4.99	8.05	....	....	....	....	....	....
819	Fiji........	....	....	....	....	....	....	....	....	....	....	....	....
534	India.............	−7.02	−7.67	−7.98	−7.80	....	....	....	....	....	....	....	....
536	Indonesia............	....	....	....	....	....	....	....	....	....	....	....	....
542	Korea, Rep. of.........	....	....	....	....	....	....	....	....	....	....	....	....
548	Malaysia...........	−3.17	−3.36	−3.80	−6.56	−4.82p	....	....	....	....	....	....	....
556	Maldives...........	−3.89	−5.00	−6.02	−6.01	−6.11	−4.40p	....	....	....	....	....	....
948	Mongolia...........	....	....	....	−1.05	....	....	....	....	....	....	−.36p	....
518	Myanmar..........	....	....	....	....	....	....	....	....	....	....	....	....
558	Nepal.............	....	....	....	....	....	....	....	....	....	....	....	....
564	Pakistan............	....	....	....	....	....	....	....	....	....	....	....	....
853	Papua New Guinea.........	....	....	....	....	....	....	....	....	....	....	....	....
566	Philippines...........	....	....	....	....	....	....	....	....	....	....	....	....
576	Singapore...........	....	....	5.74	4.77	3.09	4.16	....	....	....	....	....	....
524	Sri Lanka...........	....	....	....	....	....	....	....	....	....	....	....	....
578	Thailand............	−8.96	−1.77	†−1.76	−6.60	....	....	....	....	....	....	2.06	1.14p
846	Vanuatu............	....	....	....	....	....	....	....	....	....	....	....	....
582	Vietnam............	−1.58	−2.81	−3.23	−2.57	−3.50p	−3.98f	....	....	....	....	....	....
	Europe (excluding industrial countries)												
914	Albania............	....	....	....	−6.18	....	....	....	....	....	....	....	....
911	Armenia............	....	....	....	....	−.65p	−.80p	....	....	....	....	....	....
912	Azerbaijan...........	....	....	....	....	....	....	....	....	....	....	....	....
913	Belarus............	....	....	....	....	−.60p	.59p	....	....	....	....	....	....
963	Bosnia and Herzegovina............	....	....	....	....	....	....	....	....	....	....	....	....
918	Bulgaria............	.17	−.63	.20	−.64	—	1.73	....	....	....	....	....	....
960	Croatia............	....	....	....	−3.17	−3.96	−4.03	....	....	....	....	....	....
423	Cyprus............	....	....	....	....	....	....	....	....	....	....	....	....
935	Czech Republic...........	....	....	....	....	....	....	....	−4.05p	−4.65p	−6.34p	−5.04p	−3.53p
939	Estonia............	....	....	....	....	....	....	....	....	....	....	....	....
915	Georgia............	....	....	....	....	....	....	....	....	....	....	....	....
944	Hungary............	....	−4.09	−3.75	−9.49	−6.09p	....	....	−3.00	−4.70	−9.36	−6.29p	....
916	Kazakhstan...........	....	.54	.24	.18	−.50	−.02	....	....	....	....	....	....
917	Kyrgyz Republic...........	....	....	....	....	....	....	....	....	....	....	....	....
941	Latvia............	....	....	....	−2.60	−1.66	−1.05	....	....	....	....	....	....
946	Lithuania...........	....	−2.91	−1.75	−1.43	−1.36	−1.50p	....	−2.80	−2.07	−1.30	−1.21	−1.44p
181	Malta............	−6.13	−5.39	−5.83	....	....	....	....	....	....	....	....	....
921	Moldova............	....	....	....	†.53	2.42	.52	....	....	....	....	....	....
964	Poland............	....	....	....	....	....	....	....	−3.15	−3.94	−3.59	....	....
968	Romania............	....	....	....	−2.33p	....	....	....	....	−2.00p	....	....	....
922	Russia Federation...........	....	3.48	†2.74	1.24	1.72	5.31	....	....	†6.90	1.89	5.89	....
965	Serbia and Montenegro..........	....	....	....	....	....	....	....	....	....	....	....	....
936	Slovak Republic...........	....	−9.74	−5.48p	−6.23p	−3.91p	....	....	....	....	−3.46p	....	....
961	Slovenia............	....	−1.02	−1.15	−2.82	−1.37	−1.25	....	....	....	....	....	....
923	Tajikistan...........	....	....	....	....	....	....	....	....	....	....	....	....
186	Turkey............	....	....	....	....	....	....	....	....	....	....	....	....
926	Ukraine............	....	....	−.94	.54	.01p	−3.42p	....	....	....	....	....	....
	Middle East												
419	Bahrain, Kingdom of..........	....	....	....	....	....	....	....	....	....	....	....	....
469	Egypt............	....	....	....	....	....	....	....	....	....	....	....	....
429	Iran, I.R. of............	....	....	1.06	.82	2.08	4.12p	....	....	....	....	....	....
436	Israel............	....	−.58	−3.67	−4.47	−5.60	−4.44p	....	−2.03	−3.91	−4.24	−6.69	−5.08p
439	Jordan............	....	....	....	....	....	....	....	....	....	....	....	....
443	Kuwait............	....	....	....	7.55	6.46	....	....	....	....	....	....	....
446	Lebanon............	....	....	....	....	....	....	....	....	....	....	....	....
449	Oman............	....	....	....	....	....	....	....	....	....	....	....	....
463	Syrian Arab Republic..........	....	....	....	....	....	....	....	....	....	....	....	....
466	United Arab Emirates..........	....	....	....	....	....	....	....	....	....	....	....	....
474	Yemen, Republic of..........	....	....	....	....	....	....	....	....	....	....	....	....

Table W1. Main Balances: General and Central Government

(Percent of GDP)

		Cash Surplus/Deficit						Net Lending/Borrowing					
		1999	2000	2001	2002	2003	2004	1999	2000	2001	2002	2003	2004
	Western Hemisphere												
213	Argentina	....	....	....	....	....	....	....	....	....	−6.41p	−2.37p	.67p
313	Bahamas, The	....	....	....	....	....	....	....	....	....	....	....	....
316	Barbados	....	....	....	....	....	....	....	....	....	....	....	....
218	Bolivia	−3.25	−3.90	−6.61	−6.60	−4.43	−4.03	....	....	....	−7.62	−6.01	−4.42
223	Brazil	....	....	....	....	....	....	....	....	....	....	....	....
228	Chile	....	....	.36	−.36	.20	2.67	....	....	−.48	−1.22	−.41	2.14
233	Colombia	−7.13	−3.85	....	....	....	....	....	....	....	....	....	....
238	Costa Rica	....	....	....	−3.26	−1.55	....	....	....	....	....	....	....
243	Dominican Republic	....	....	....	....	....	....	....	....	....	....	....	....
253	El Salvador	....	....	....	−4.69	−3.59	−3.64	....	....	....	−4.76	−2.57	−3.19
258	Guatemala	....	....	....	....	....	....	....	....	....	....	....	....
343	Jamaica	....	....	....	....	....	....	....	....	....	....	....	....
273	Mexico	....	....	....	....	....	....	....	....	....	....	....	....
278	Nicaragua	....	....	....	....	....	....	....	....	....	....	....	....
283	Panama	....	....	....	....	....	....	....	....	....	....	....	....
288	Paraguay	....	....	....	....	....	....	....	....	....	....	....	....
293	Peru	−2.46	−2.01	−2.05	−1.34p	−1.56p	−.99p	....	....	....	....	....	....
361	St. Kitts and Nevis	....	....	....	....	−4.48		....	....	....	....	....	....
364	St. Vincent and the Grenadines	−2.96	−2.25	1.99	3.58	2.85	....	....	....	....	....	....	....
298	Uruguay	....	....	−4.59	−4.82	−4.64	−2.49p	....	....	....	....	....	....
299	Venezuela, Rep. Bol.	....	....	....	....	....	....	....	....	....	....	....	....

Central Government

		Cash Surplus/Deficit						Net Lending/Borrowing					
		1999	2000	2001	2002	2003	2004	1999	2000	2001	2002	2003	2004
	Industrial Countries												
111	United States	1.34	2.33	....	....	....	....	....	....	.49	−2.54	−3.87	−3.83
156	Canada	.87	1.44	1.31	.87	.97	1.35p	....	....	....	....	....	....
193	Australia	.73	1.87	.79	−.12	.99	.99	.57	2.05	.85	−.44	.84	.80
158	Japan	....	....	....	....	....	....	....	....	....	....	....	....
196	New Zealand	....	....	.99	1.88	2.77	3.39p	....	....	....	1.71	2.95	3.72p
	Euro Area												
122	Austria	....	....	....	....	....	....	−2.60	−1.87	−.66	−1.08	−1.88	....
124	Belgium	....	....	....	....	....	....	−1.17	.12	−.10	−.02	−.29	....
172	Finland	....	....	....	....	....	....	2.36	6.88	6.00	4.62	2.78p	2.53p
132	France	....	....	....	....	....	....	−1.94	−1.58	−1.65	−3.31	−4.23p	−3.53p
134	Germany	....	....	....	....	....	....	−1.26	1.39	−1.48	−2.01	−2.20	−2.36
174	Greece	....	....	....	....	....	....	....	....	....	....	....	....
136	Italy	....	....	....	....	....	....	−1.32	−.62	−2.41	−1.76	−2.25	....
137	Luxembourg	....	....	....	....	....	....	3.31	5.70	5.92	1.98	.23p	−.49p
138	Netherlands	....	....	....	....	....	....	†.52	2.13	−.17	−1.51	−2.85p	−1.65p
182	Portugal	....	....	....	....	....	....	−3.13	−2.57	−4.01	−2.25	....	....
184	Spain	....	....	....	....	....	....	−1.01	−.52	.15	.26p	.56p	....
128	Denmark	1.99	....	....	....	....	....	3.05	1.66	.82	.29	.33p	1.82p
176	Iceland	....	....	....	....	....	....	2.87	2.80	.89	−.42	....	....
142	Norway	4.80	12.16	14.50	8.56	8.73p	9.82p	....	15.86	14.22	9.22	8.52p	11.84p
135	San Marino	....	....	....	....	....	....	....	....	....	1.29	....	....
144	Sweden	.56	....	....	....	....	....	1.64	3.27	4.79	.31	.31	....
146	Switzerland	−.17	2.22	.32	†.56	....	....	....	....	....	....	....	....
112	United Kingdom	.43	....	....	....	....	....	1.15	1.71	.81	−1.71	−3.48	−3.21

Table W1. Main Balances: General and Central Government

(Percent of GDP)

		Cash Surplus/Deficit						Net Lending/Borrowing					
		1999	2000	2001	2002	2003	2004	1999	2000	2001	2002	2003	2004
	Developing Countries												
	Africa												
612	Algeria	....	....	....	....	....	....	....	....	....	....	....	....
618	Burundi	−4.52	....	....	....	....	....	....	....	....	....	....	....
622	Cameroon	....	....	....	....	....	....	....	....	....	....	....	....
636	Congo, Dem. Rep. of	−5.58	−4.03	−.06	−.05	....	....	....	....	....	....	....	....
634	Congo, Rep. of	−5.62	1.86	....	....	....	....	....	....	−1.27	−5.25	6.43	....
662	Côte d'Ivoire	−2.24	−1.05	.87	−1.59	−2.60	....	....	....	....	....	....	....
644	Ethiopia	....	....	....	....	....	....	....	....	....	....	....	....
652	Ghana	....	....	....	....	....	....	....	....	....	....	....	....
656	Guinea	....	....	....	....	....	....	....	....	....	....	....	....
664	Kenya	....	....	....	....	....	....	....	....	....	....	....	....
666	Lesotho	−6.42	−3.68	−2.53	−3.63	.61p	....	....	....	....	....	....	....
674	Madagascar	....	−2.28	−3.94	−3.64	−2.92	−3.97	....	−2.04	−3.85	−4.45	−3.69	−4.50
684	Mauritius	†−2.09	−1.07	†−3.80	†−3.58	−3.22	−2.99	....	....	....	....	....	....
686	Morocco	−2.68	....	....	....	....	....	....	....	....	....	....	....
728	Namibia	....	....	....	....	....	....	....	....	....	....	....	....
722	Senegal	....	....	....	....	....	....	....	....	....	....	....	....
718	Seychelles	−11.18	−13.82	−8.86	−14.35	....	....	....	....	....	....	....	....
724	Sierra Leone	....	....	....	....	....	....	....	....	....	....	....	....
199	South Africa	−1.81	−1.69	−.67	−1.08	−2.30p	−1.95p	....	−1.96	−.92	−1.63	−2.30p	−1.95p
732	Sudan	....	....	....	....	....	....	....	....	....	....	....	....
734	Swaziland	....	....	....	....	....	....	....	....	....	....	....	....
744	Tunisia	−2.44	−2.65	−2.34	−2.35	−2.37	−2.35p	....	....	....	....	....	....
746	Uganda	....	....	....	....	....	....	....	....	....	....	....	....
754	Zambia	....	....	....	....	....	....	....	....	....	....	....	....
	Asia												
512	Afghanistan, I.R. of	....	....	....	....	....	....	....	....	....	....	....	....
513	Bangladesh	....	....	−.66	−.17	−.12	....	....	....	....	....	....	....
514	Bhutan	−1.91	−2.19	....	....	....	....	....	....	....	....	....	....
522	Cambodia	....	....	....	....	....	....	....	....	....	−3.55	−4.68	−2.24
924	China, P.R.: Mainland	....	....	....	....	....	....	....	....	....	....	....	....
546	China, P.R.: Macao	−.60	1.64	3.62	2.88	4.99	8.05	....	....	....	....	....	....
819	Fiji	....	....	....	....	....	....	....	....	....	....	....	....
534	India	−3.37	−3.90	−4.43	−4.72	−3.68p	−3.59f	....	....	....	....	....	....
536	Indonesia	−2.47	....	−3.03	−.29	−2.28	−1.10p	....	....	....	....	....	....
542	Korea, Republic of	1.33	4.56	2.85	....	....	....	....	....	....	....	....	....
548	Malaysia	−3.23	−3.15	−3.02	−6.28	−4.30p	....	....	....	....	....	....	....
556	Maldives	−3.89	−5.00	−6.02	−6.01	−6.11	−4.40p	....	....	....	....	....	....
948	Mongolia	−3.17	.22	1.24	−1.58	....	....	....	....	....	....	−.51p	....
518	Myanmar	−1.39	−3.40	−3.00	−1.30	....	....	....	....	....	....	....	....
558	Nepal	−4.55	−3.85	−5.00	−4.35	−1.85	−2.13p	....	....	....	....	....	....
564	Pakistan	−5.54	−4.12	−3.79	−2.89p	−2.92p	−2.02	....	....	....	....	....	....
853	Papua New Guinea	....	....	....	....	....	....	....	....	....	....	....	....
566	Philippines	....	....	....	....	....	....	....	....	....	....	....	....
576	Singapore	12.69	11.45	5.74	4.77	3.09	4.16	....	....	....	....	....	....
524	Sri Lanka	....	....	....	....	....	....	....	....	....	....	....	....
578	Thailand	−8.99	−1.86	†−2.19	−7.19	....	....	....	....	....	....	1.48	.55p
846	Vanuatu	−.78	....	....	....	....	....	....	....	....	....	....	....
582	Vietnam	....	....	....	....	....	....	....	....	....	....	....	....

Table W1. Main Balances: General and Central Government

(Percent of GDP)

		Cash Surplus/Deficit						Net Lending/Borrowing					
		1999	2000	2001	2002	2003	2004	1999	2000	2001	2002	2003	2004
	Europe (excluding industrial countries)												
914	Albania	....	....	....	....	....	....	....	....	....	....	....	....
911	Armenia	....	....	....	....	−.74p	−.85p	....	....	....	....	....	....
912	Azerbaijan	....	....	....	....	....	....	....	....	....	....	....	....
913	Belarus	−1.90	.07	−.83	1.13	−1.06p	−.16p	....	....	....	....	....	....
963	Bonsia and Herzegovina	....	....	....	....	....	....	....	....	....	....	.78	
918	Bulgaria	.41	−.39	.20	−.55	.20	1.65	....	....	....	....	....	....
960	Croatia	−5.32	−6.20	−4.80	−3.63	−4.10	−4.01	....	....	....	....	....	....
423	Cyprus	....	....	....	....	....	....	....	....	....	....	....	....
935	Czech Republic	−2.21	....	....	....	....	....	....	−3.65p	−4.13p	−6.12p	−4.90p	−3.25p
939	Estonia	−3.81	−.69	.95	....	....	....	....	....	....	....	....	....
915	Georgia	−2.21	−1.62	.21	−1.84	....	....	....	....	....	....	....	....
944	Hungary	−5.84	−4.00	−3.77	−8.83	−5.90p	....	....	−2.83	−4.49	−8.62	−6.26p	....
916	Kazakhstan	−2.70	.09	.07	.35	−.63	.23	....	....	....	....	....	....
917	Kyrgyz Republic	....	....	....	....	....	....	....	....	....	....	....	....
941	Latvia	−3.09	−2.27	−1.14	−1.84	−1.28	−.96	....	....	....	....	....	....
946	Lithuania	−5.10	−2.86	−1.37	−1.48	−1.37	−1.51p	....	−2.75	−1.69	−1.34	−1.22	−1.58p
181	Malta	−6.13	−5.39	−5.83	....	....	....	....	....	....	....	....	....
921	Moldova	−2.92	−1.49	.96	†.18	1.99	.44	....	....	....	....	....	....
964	Poland	−2.40	−3.11	....	....	....	....	....	....	−2.86	−3.29	−3.43	....
968	Romania	−2.93	−4.47	−3.61	−2.33p	....	....	....	....	....	−1.98p	....	....
922	Russia Federation	†−.12p	2.47	†2.63	1.53	1.85	4.88	....	....	....	†7.02	2.20	5.37
965	Serbia and Montenegro	....	....	....	....	....	....	....	....	....	....	....	....
936	Slovak Republic	−.21	−9.58	−5.45p	−6.14p	−3.98p	....	....	....	....	....	−3.28p	....
961	Slovenia	−.66	−1.14	−1.13	−2.69	−1.36	−1.27	....	....	....	....	....	....
923	Tajikistan	....	....	....	....	....	....	....	....	....	....	....	....
186	Turkey	....	....	....	....	....	....	....	....	....	....	....	....
926	Ukraine	−2.09	−.60	−.79	.33	−.19p	−3.20p	....	....	....	....	....	....
	Middle East												
419	Bahrain, Kingdom of	−.33	10.27	6.05	−.32	2.47	5.70p	....	....	....	....	....	....
469	Egypt	....	....	....	....	....	....	....	....	....	....	....	....
429	Iran, I.R. of	.12	1.79	.98	.71	1.63	3.64p	....	....	....	....	....	....
436	Israel	−2.89	−.38	−3.31	−4.07	−5.36	−4.15p	....	−1.82	−3.56	−3.84	−6.45	−4.79p
439	Jordan	....	....	....	....	....	....	....	....	....	....	....	....
443	Kuwait	−9.44	....	....	7.55	6.46	....	....	....	....	....	....	....
446	Lebanon	....	....	....	....	....	....	....	....	....	....	....	....
449	Oman	....	....	....	....	....	....	....	....	....	....	....	....
463	Syrian Arab Rep	.71	....	....	....	....	....	....	....	....	....	....	....
466	United Arab Emirates	....	....	....	....	....	....	....	....	....	....	....	....
474	Yemen, Republic of	....	....	....	....	....	....	....	....	....	....	....	....
	Western Hemisphere												
213	Argentina	−2.92	−2.77	−3.32	−.91	.80	2.94	....	....	....	−5.71	−2.83	−.46
313	Bahamas, The	....	....	....	....	....	....	....	....	....	....	....	....
316	Barbados	....	....	....	....	....	....	....	....	....	....	....	....
218	Bolivia	−3.21	−4.00	−6.61	−7.51	−6.06	−4.48	....	....	....	−8.69	−7.56	−5.39
223	Brazil	....	....	....	....	....	....	....	....	....	....	....	....
228	Chile	−1.34	.27	.35	−.38	.18	2.68	....	....	−.50	−1.24	−.43	2.15
233	Colombia	−6.11	−3.72	....	....	....	....	....	....	....	....	....	....
238	Costa Rica	−1.41	−1.31	−1.21	−3.41	−1.60	....	....	....	....	....	....	....
243	Dominican Republic	−.46	1.00	.31	−.18	1.42	....	....	....	....	....	....	....
253	El Salvador	−1.31	2.26	†−3.33	−4.64	−3.53	−3.64	....	....	....	−4.73	−2.52	−3.28
258	Guatemala	....	....	....	....	....	....	....	....	....	....	....	....
343	Jamaica	−4.54	−2.65	−3.72	−7.43	−9.84	....	....	....	....	....	....	....
273	Mexico	−1.52	−1.21	....	....	....	....	....	....	....	....	....	....
278	Nicaragua	−2.18	−3.10	−5.92	−1.66	−1.86p	−1.04p	....	....	....	....	....	....
283	Panama	.18	−.84	.91	....	....	....	....	....	....	....	....	....
293	Peru	−2.35	−2.06	−2.06	−1.40p	−1.69p	−1.16p	....	....	....	....	....	....
361	St. Kitts and Nevis	....	....	....	....	....	−4.49	....	....	....	....	....	....
364	St. Vincent and the Grenadines	....	....	....	....	....	....	....	....	....	....	....	....
298	Uruguay	†−3.75	−3.42	−4.50	−4.87	−4.57	−2.51p	....	....	....	....	....	....
299	Venezuela, Rep. Bol	−1.55	−1.24	−4.00	−3.23	−4.12p	....	....	....	....	....	....	....

Table W2. Other Balances: General and Central Government

(Percent of GDP)

		Gross Operating Balance						Net Financial Worth					
		1999	2000	2001	2002	2003	2004	1999	2000	2001	2002	2003	2004
General Government													
Industrial Countries													
111	United States	....	....	2.40	−.93	−2.20	−2.04	....	....	....	....	....	....
156	Canada	....	....	....	....	....	....	....	....	....	....	....	....
193	Australia	2.98	4.29	2.64	1.61	3.00	3.32	−6.34	−5.14	−4.14	−2.33	−.24	3.43
158	Japan	....	....	−1.06	−2.99	−2.74p	....	....	....	−64.52	−71.53	−76.04p	....
196	New Zealand	....	....	....	....	5.67p	6.66p	....	....	....	....	−15.64p	−10.08p
	Euro Area												
122	Austria	−.64	−.53	1.20	.82	−.10	....	−44.51	−42.92	−43.83	−45.11	−43.08	....
124	Belgium	1.32	1.93	2.05	1.62	1.88	....	−103.45	−102.43	−42.50	−44.15	−43.84	....
172	Finland	4.99	9.79	8.23	7.20	5.23p	4.88p	50.72	31.40	32.12	31.82	40.29p	....
132	France	1.50	1.90	1.67	−.11	−.95p	−.32p	....	....	....	−41.51	−43.96p	−45.11p
134	Germany	.31	.54	−1.14	−2.12	−2.55	−2.34	−44.69	−41.86	−43.50	−47.54	−50.48	−54.30
174	Greece	....	....	....	....	....	....	....	....	....	....	....	....
136	Italy	.74	.53	−.19	−.52	.15	....	−102.07	....	....	....	....	....
137	Luxembourg	7.93	10.02	8.62	7.20	5.20p	4.02p	....	51.66	56.50	56.04	56.68p	53.39p
138	Netherlands	†3.21	4.41	2.90	1.48	.32p	.99p	†−36.56	−35.11	−33.03	−34.89	−36.13p	−37.79p
182	Portugal	1.32	.67	−.44	.35	....	....	−27.20	−27.14	−26.54	−30.17	....	....
184	Spain	2.30	2.18	2.83	3.26p	3.66p	....	−46.19	−41.93	....	....	....	....
128	Denmark	4.82	3.92	2.93	2.02	1.39p	2.99p	....	−24.48	−18.94	−18.10	−17.13p	−14.54p
176	Iceland	6.57	6.21	4.49	3.09	....	....	−35.69	−38.04	−37.76	−24.00	....	....
142	Norway	....	18.21	16.26	12.03	10.57p	14.18p	....	60.61	71.92	71.28	83.40p	....
135	San Marino	....	....	....	1.61	....	....	....	....	....	−5.45	....	....
144	Sweden	3.62	5.57	7.37	2.88	2.96	....	−9.90	−1.68	3.12	−3.68	....	....
146	Switzerland	....	....	....	....	....	....	....	....	....	....	....	....
112	United Kingdom	2.13	2.66	2.09	−.20	−1.68	−1.39	−36.45	−33.49	−33.31	−34.09	−34.56	−36.79
Developing Countries													
Africa													
612	Algeria	....	....	....	....	....	....	....	....	....	....	....	....
618	Burundi	....	....	....	....	....	....	....	....	....	....	....	....
622	Cameroon	....	....	....	....	....	....	....	....	....	....	....	....
636	Congo, Dem. Rep. of	....	....	....	....	....	....	....	....	....	....	....	....
634	Congo, Rep. of	....	....	....	....	11.81		....	....	....	....	....	....
662	Côte d'Ivoire	....	....	....	....	....	....	....	....	....	....	....	....
644	Ethiopia	....	....	....	....	....	....	....	....	....	....	....	....
652	Ghana	....	....	....	....	....	....	....	....	....	....	....	....
656	Guinea	....	....	....	....	....	....	....	....	....	....	....	....
664	Kenya	....	....	....	....	....	....	....	....	....	....	....	....
666	Lesotho	....	....	....	....	....	....	....	....	....	....	....	....
674	Madagascar	....	....	....	....	....	....	....	....	....	....	....	....
684	Mauritius	....	....	....	....	....	....	....	....	....	....	....	....
686	Morocco	....	....	....	....	....	....	....	....	....	....	....	....
728	Namibia	....	....	....	....	....	....	....	....	....	....	....	....
722	Senegal	....	....	....	....	....	....	....	....	....	....	....	....
718	Seychelles	....	....	....	....	....	....	....	....	....	....	....	....
724	Sierra Leone	....	....	....	....	....	....	....	....	....	....	....	....
199	South Africa	....	−.05	1.24	.12	−.34p	.06p	....	....	....	....	....	....
732	Sudan	....	....	....	....	....	....	....	....	....	....	....	....
734	Swaziland	....	....	....	....	....	....	....	....	....	....	....	....
744	Tunisia	....	....	....	....	....	....	....	....	....	....	....	....
746	Uganda	....	....	....	....	....	....	....	....	....	....	....	....
754	Zambia	....	....	....	....	....	....	....	....	....	....	....	....

Table W2. Other Balances: General and Central Government

(Percent of GDP)

		Gross Operating Balance						Net Financial Worth					
		1999	2000	2001	2002	2003	2004	1999	2000	2001	2002	2003	2004
Asia													
512	Afghanistan, I.R. of	....	....	....	....	....	....	....	....	....	....	....	....
513	Bangladesh	....	....	....	....	....	....	....	....	....	....	....	....
514	Bhutan	....	....	....	....	....	....	....	....	....	....	....	....
522	Cambodia	....	....	....	....	....	....	....	....	....	....	....	....
924	China, P.R.: Mainland	....	....	....	....	....	....	....	....	....	....	....	....
532	China, P.R.: Hong Kong	....	....	....	−6.25	−4.87	....	....	....	19.07	12.63	7.24	....
546	China, P.R.: Macao	....	....	....	....	....	....	....	....	....	....	....	....
819	Fiji	....	....	....	....	....	....	....	....	....	....	....	....
534	India	....	....	....	....	....	....	....	....	....	....	....	....
536	Indonesia	....	....	....	....	....	....	....	....	....	....	....	....
542	Korea, Rep. of	....	....	....	....	....	....	....	....	....	....	....	....
548	Malaysia	....	....	....	....	....	....	....	....	....	....	....	....
556	Maldives	....	....	....	....	....	....	....	....	....	....	....	....
948	Mongolia	....	....	....	....	9.84p	....	....	....	....	....	−20.43p	....
518	Myanmar	....	....	....	....	....	....	....	....	....	....	....	....
558	Nepal	....	....	....	....	....	....	....	....	....	....	....	....
564	Pakistan	....	....	....	....	....	....	....	....	....	....	....	....
853	Papua New Guinea	....	....	....	....	....	....	....	....	....	....	....	....
566	Philippines	....	....	....	....	....	....	....	....	....	....	....	....
576	Singapore	....	....	....	....	....	....	....	....	....	....	....	....
524	Sri Lanka	....	....	....	....	....	....	....	....	....	....	....	....
578	Thailand	....	....	....	....	5.64	4.21p	....	....	....	....	....	....
846	Vanuatu	....	....	....	....	....	....	....	....	....	....	....	....
582	Vietnam	....	....	....	....	....	....	....	....	....	....	....	....
Europe (excluding industrial countries)													
914	Albania	....	....	....	....	....	....	....	....	....	....	....	....
911	Armenia	....	....	....	....	....	....	....	....	....	....	....	....
912	Azerbaijan	....	....	....	....	....	....	....	....	....	....	....	....
913	Belarus	....	....	....	....	....	....	....	....	....	....	....	....
963	Bosnia and Herzegovina	....	....	....	....	....	....	....	....	....	....	....	....
918	Bulgaria	....	....	....	....	....	....	....	....	....	....	....	....
960	Croatia	....	....	....	....	....	....	....	....	....	....	....	....
423	Cyprus	....	....	....	....	....	....	....	....	....	....	....	....
935	Czech Republic	....	−1.26p	−1.96p	−3.78p	−2.47p	−.87p	....	....	....	....	....	....
939	Estonia	....	....	....	....	....	....	....	....	....	....	....	....
915	Georgia	....	....	....	....	....	....	....	....	....	....	....	....
944	Hungary	....	.69	−.22	−3.65	−2.86p	....	....	....	....	....	....	....
916	Kazakhstan	....	....	....	....	....	....	....	....	....	....	....	....
917	Kyrgyz Republic	....	....	....	....	....	....	....	....	....	....	....	....
941	Latvia	....	....	....	....	....	....	....	....	....	....	....	....
946	Lithuania	....	....	.31	1.59	1.93	1.82p	....	....	....	....	−18.83	−17.15p
181	Malta	....	....	....	....	....	....	....	....	....	....	....	....
921	Moldova	....	....	....	....	....	....	....	....	....	....	....	−47.71
964	Poland	....	....	−.92	−1.50	−1.29	....	....	....	....	....	....	....
968	Romania	....	....	....	.79p	....	....	....	....	....	....	....	....
922	Russia Federation	....	....	....	†12.70	7.27	10.76	....	....	−5.37	†−2.52	....	....
965	Serbia and Montenegro	....	....	....	....	....	....	....	....	....	....	....	....
936	Slovak Republic	....	....	....	....	−.99p	....	....	.14	14.65p	20.09p	2.71p	....
961	Slovenia	....	....	....	....	....	....	....	....	....	....	....	....
923	Tajikistan	....	....	....	....	....	....	....	....	....	....	....	....
186	Turkey	....	....	....	....	....	....	....	....	....	....	....	....
926	Ukraine	....	....	....	....	....	....	....	....	....	....	....	....
Middle East													
419	Bahrain, Kingdom of	....	....	....	....	....	....	....	....	....	....	....	....
469	Egypt	....	....	....	....	....	....	....	....	....	....	....	....
429	Iran, I.R. of	....	....	....	....	....	....	....	....	....	....	....	....
436	Israel	....	.44	−1.32	−1.52	−4.01	−2.59p	....	....	....	....	....	....
439	Jordan	....	....	....	....	....	....	....	....	....	....	....	....
443	Kuwait	....	....	....	....	....	....	....	....	....	....	....	....
446	Lebanon	....	....	....	....	....	....	....	....	....	....	....	....
449	Oman	....	....	....	....	....	....	....	....	....	....	....	....
463	Syrian Arab Republic	....	....	....	....	....	....	....	....	....	....	....	....
466	United Arab Emirates	....	....	....	....	....	....	....	....	....	....	....	....
474	Yemen, Republic of	....	....	....	....	....	....	....	....	....	....	....	....

Table W2. Other Balances: General and Central Government

(Percent of GDP)

		Gross Operating Balance						Net Financial Worth					
		1999	2000	2001	2002	2003	2004	1999	2000	2001	2002	2003	2004
	Western Hemisphere												
213	Argentina	....	....	....	−5.53p	−1.05p	2.48p	....	....	....	....	....	....
313	Bahamas, The	....	....	....	....	....	....	....	....	....	....	....	....
316	Barbados	....	....	....	....	....	....	....	....	....	....	....	....
218	Bolivia	....	....	....	−1.05	−.04	2.13	....	....	....	....	....	....
223	Brazil	....	....	....	....	....	....	....	....	....	....	....	....
228	Chile	....	....	2.15	1.38	1.93	4.29	....	....	....	....	....	....
233	Colombia	....	....	....	....	....	....	−16.85	−17.71	....	....	....	....
238	Costa Rica	....	....	....	....	....	....	....	....	....	....	....	....
243	Dominican Republic	....	....	....	....	....	....	....	....	....	....	....	....
253	El Salvador	....	....	....	−1.57	.40	−.47	....	....	....	....	−34.90	−34.23
258	Guatemala	....	....	....	....	....	....	....	....	....	....	....	....
343	Jamaica	....	....	....	....	....	....	....	....	....	....	....	....
273	Mexico	....	....	....	....	....	....	....	....	....	....	....	....
278	Nicaragua	....	....	....	....	....	....	....	....	....	....	....	....
283	Panama	....	....	....	....	....	....	....	....	....	....	....	....
288	Paraguay	....	....	....	....	....	....	....	....	....	....	....	....
293	Peru	....	....	....	....	....	....	....	....	....	....	....	....
361	St. Kitts and Nevis	....	....	....	....	....	....	....	....	....	....	....	....
364	St. Vincent and the Grenadines	....	....	....	....	....	....	....	....	....	....	....	....
298	Uruguay	....	....	....	....	....	....	....	....	−39.83	−82.19	−94.52	−74.93p
299	Venezuela, Rep. Bol.	....	....	....	....	....	....	....	....	....	....	....	....

Central Government

		Gross Operating Balance						Net Financial Worth					
		1999	2000	2001	2002	2003	2004	1999	2000	2001	2002	2003	2004
	Industrial Countries												
111	United States	....	....	.84	−2.16	−3.52	−3.49	....	....	....	....	....	....
156	Canada	....	....	....	....	....	....	....	....	....	....	....	....
193	Australia	.94	2.24	1.04	−.11	1.16	1.21	−10.93	−11.16	−11.08	−10.55	−10.31	−8.11
158	Japan	....	....	....	....	....	....	....	....	....	....	....	....
196	New Zealand	....	....	2.87	4.00	4.66	5.60p	....	....	−6.98	−5.10	−18.17	−12.33p
	Euro Area												
122	Austria	−2.13	−1.83	−.32	−.78	−1.64	....	....	....	−48.94	−50.15	−48.40	....
124	Belgium	−.65	.37	−.09	.30	.08	....	....	....	−36.56	−37.61	−37.37	....
172	Finland	3.53	7.93	6.82	5.58	3.90p	3.76p	46.97	27.24	28.81	28.42	37.17p	....
132	France	−.91	−.66	−.75	−2.37	−3.22p	−2.52p	....	....	....	−37.34	−39.94p	−41.14p
134	Germany	−.84	−.74	−1.11	−1.65	−1.85	−2.02	....	....	....	....	....	....
174	Greece	....	....	....	....	....	....	....	....	....	....	....	....
136	Italy	−.64	−1.19	−1.83	−1.83	−1.63	....	....	....	....	....	....	....
137	Luxembourg	5.68	7.81	6.61	4.99	3.08p	2.27p	....	48.79	53.38	53.13	54.08p	50.91p
138	Netherlands	†1.53	2.51	1.10	−.09	−1.48p	−.44p	....	−34.49	−31.90	−33.27	−34.51p	−35.77p
182	Portugal	−1.08	−1.14	−2.48	−1.53	....	....	....	....	....	....	....	....
184	Spain	.04	.43	1.23	1.37p	1.69p	....	....	....	....	....	....	....
128	Denmark	3.74	2.28	1.43	.88	.81p	2.49p	....	−22.24	−17.35	−16.11	−14.70p	−12.99p
176	Iceland	4.77	4.45	2.80	1.40	....	....	−28.07	−29.90	−29.96	−29.11	....	....
142	Norway	....	16.84	15.12	10.45	9.78p	13.10p	....	62.41	74.24	72.81	85.93p	....
135	San Marino	....	....	....	1.61	....	....	....	....	....	−5.45	....	....
144	Sweden	2.73	4.30	6.11	1.79	1.81	....	....	....	....	−3.04	....	....
146	Switzerland	....	....	....	....	....	....	....	....	....	....	....	....
112	United Kingdom	1.57	2.18	1.41	−1.03	−2.71	−2.41	−31.81	−29.10	....	....	....	....

Table W2. Other Balances: General and Central Government

(Percent of GDP)

		Gross Operating Balance						Net Financial Worth					
		1999	2000	2001	2002	2003	2004	1999	2000	2001	2002	2003	2004
	Developing Countries												
	Africa												
612	Algeria	....	....	....	....	....	....	....	....	....	....	....	....
618	Burundi	....	....	....	....	....	....	....	....	....	....	....	....
622	Cameroon	....	....	....	....	....	....	....	....	....	....	....	....
636	Congo, Dem. Rep. of	....	....	....	....	....	....	....	....	....	....	....	....
634	Congo, Rep. of	....	....	9.09	4.05	11.59	....	....	....	....	....	....	....
662	Côte d'Ivoire	....	....	....	....	....	....	....	....	....	....	....	....
644	Ethiopia	....	....	....	....	....	....	....	....	....	....	....	....
652	Ghana	....	....	....	....	....	....	....	....	....	....	....	....
656	Guinea	....	....	....	....	....	....	....	....	....	....	....	....
664	Kenya	....	....	....	....	....	....	....	....	....	....	....	....
666	Lesotho	....	....	....	....	....	....	....	....	....	....	....	....
674	Madagascar	....	4.68	3.22	.19	4.01	7.71	....	....	....	....	....	....
684	Mauritius	....	....	....	....	....	....	....	....	....	....	....	....
686	Morocco	....	....	....	....	....	....	....	....	....	....	....	....
728	Namibia	....	....	....	....	....	....	....	....	....	....	....	....
722	Senegal	....	....	....	....	....	....	....	....	....	....	....	....
718	Seychelles	....	....	....	....	....	....	....	....	....	....	....	....
724	Sierra Leone	....	....	....	....	....	....	....	....	....	....	....	....
199	South Africa	....	−1.45	−.27	−1.03	−1.70p	−1.34p	....	....	....	....	....	....
732	Sudan	....	....	....	....	....	....	....	....	....	....	....	....
734	Swaziland	....	....	....	....	....	....	....	....	....	....	....	....
744	Tunisia	....	....	....	....	....	....	....	....	....	....	....	....
746	Uganda	....	....	....	....	....	....	....	....	....	....	....	....
754	Zambia	....	....	....	....	....	....	....	....	....	....	....	....
	Asia												
512	Afghanistan, I.R. of	....	....	....	....	....	....	....	....	....	....	....	....
513	Bangladesh	....	....	....	....	....	....	....	....	....	....	....	....
514	Bhutan	....	....	....	....	....	....	....	....	....	....	....	....
522	Cambodia	....	....	....	4.97	2.06	3.67	....	....	....	....	....	....
924	China, P.R.: Mainland	....	....	....	....	....	....	....	....	....	....	....	....
546	China, P.R.: Macao	....	....	....	....	....	....	....	....	....	....	....	....
819	Fiji	....	....	....	....	....	....	....	....	....	....	....	....
534	India	....	....	....	....	....	....	....	....	....	....	....	....
536	Indonesia	....	....	....	....	....	....	....	....	....	....	....	....
542	Korea, Republic of	....	....	....	....	....	....	....	....	....	....	....	....
548	Malaysia	....	....	....	....	....	....	....	....	....	....	....	....
556	Maldives	....	....	....	....	....	....	....	....	....	....	....	....
948	Mongolia	....	....	....	....	9.30p	....	....	....	−4.80	−10.64	−24.03p	....
518	Myanmar	....	....	....	....	....	....	....	....	....	....	....	....
558	Nepal	....	....	....	....	....	....	....	....	....	....	....	....
564	Pakistan	....	....	....	....	....	....	....	....	....	....	....	....
853	Papua New Guinea	....	....	....	....	....	....	....	....	....	....	....	....
566	Philippines	....	....	....	....	....	....	....	....	....	....	....	....
576	Singapore	....	....	....	....	....	....	....	....	....	....	....	....
524	Sri Lanka	....	....	....	....	....	....	....	....	....	....	....	....
578	Thailand	....	....	....	....	3.73	2.45p	....	....	....	....	....	....
846	Vanuatu	....	....	....	....	....	....	....	....	....	....	....	....
582	Vietnam	....	....	....	....	....	....	....	....	....	....	....	....

Table W2. Other Balances: General and Central Government
(Percent of GDP)

		Gross Operating Balance						Net Financial Worth					
		1999	2000	2001	2002	2003	2004	1999	2000	2001	2002	2003	2004
	Europe (excluding industrial countries)												
914	Albania....................	....	....	....	....	....	....	....	....	....	....	....	....
911	Armenia....................	....	....	....	....	....	....	....	....	....	....	....	....
912	Azerbaijan....................	....	....	....	....	....	....	....	....	....	....	....	....
913	Belarus....................	....	....	....	....	....	....	....	....	....	....	....	....
963	Bonsia and Herzegovina..........	....	....	....	....	2.21		....	....	....	....	....	....
918	Bulgaria....................	....	....	....	....	....	....	....	....	....	....	....	....
960	Croatia....................	....	....	....	....	....	....	....	....	....	....	....	....
423	Cyprus....................	....	....	....	....	....	....	....	....	....	....	....	....
935	Czech Republic....................	....	−2.89p	−3.50p	−5.67p	−4.38p	−2.75p	....	....	....	....	....	....
939	Estonia....................	....	....	....	....	....	....	....	....	....	....	....	....
915	Georgia....................	....	....	....	....	....	....	....	....	....	....	....	....
944	Hungary....................	....	−.69	−1.76	−4.92	−4.36p	....	−39.77	−37.08	−39.23	−44.81	−44.33p	....
916	Kazakhstan....................	....	....	....	....	....	....	....	....	....	....	....	....
917	Kyrgyz Republic....................	....	....	....	....	....	....	....	....	....	....	....	....
941	Latvia....................	....	....	....	....	....	....	....	....	....	....	....	....
946	Lithuania....................	....	....	.42	.91	1.42	.93p	....	....	....	....	−17.97	−16.74p
181	Malta....................	....	....	....	....	....	....	....	....	....	....	....	....
921	Moldova....................	....	....	....	....	....	....	....	....	....	....	....	−48.47
964	Poland....................	....	....	−2.22	−2.37	−2.45	....	....	....	....	....	....	....
968	Romania....................	....	....	....	.20p	....	....	....	....	....	....	....	....
922	Russia Federation....................	....	....	....	†9.20	4.53	7.16	....	....	−5.66	†−2.61	....	....
965	Serbia and Montenegro..........	....	....	....	....	....	....	....	....	....	....	....	....
936	Slovak Republic....................	....	....	....	....	−1.63p	....	....	−1.66	12.93p	17.89p	.63p	....
961	Slovenia....................	....	....	....	....	....	....	....	....	....	....	....	....
923	Tajikistan....................	....	....	....	....	....	....	....	....	....	....	....	....
186	Turkey....................	....	....	....	....	....	....	....	....	....	....	....	....
926	Ukraine....................	....	....	....	....	....	....	....	....	....	....	....	....
	Middle East												
419	Bahrain, Kingdom of....................	....	....	....	....	....	....	....	....	....	....	....	....
469	Egypt....................	....	....	....	....	....	....	....	....	....	....	....	....
429	Iran, I.R. of....................	....	....	....	....	....	....	....	....	....	....	....	....
436	Israel....................	....	−.73	−2.38	−2.58	−5.18	−3.69p	....	....	....	....	....	....
439	Jordan....................	....	....	....	....	....	....	....	....	....	....	....	....
443	Kuwait....................	....	....	....	....	....	....	....	....	....	....	....	....
446	Lebanon....................	....	....	....	....	....	....	....	....	....	....	....	....
449	Oman....................	....	....	....	....	....	....	....	....	....	....	....	....
463	Syrian Arab Rep....................	....	....	....	....	....	....	....	....	....	....	....	....
466	United Arab Emirates....................	....	....	....	....	....	....	....	....	....	....	....	....
474	Yemen, Republic of....................	....	....	....	....	....	....	....	....	....	....	....	....
	Western Hemisphere												
213	Argentina....................	....	....	....	−5.60	−2.62	−.09	....	....	....	....	....	....
313	Bahamas, The....................	....	....	....	....	....	....	....	....	....	....	....	....
316	Barbados....................	....	....	....	....	....	....	....	....	....	....	....	....
218	Bolivia....................	....	....	....	−6.69	−5.08	−2.61	....	....	....	....	....	....
223	Brazil....................	....	....	....	....	....	....	....	....	....	....	....	....
228	Chile....................	....	....	1.72	.95	1.54	3.95	....	....	....	....	....	....
233	Colombia....................	....	....	....	....	....	....	−15.79	−16.66	....	....	....	....
238	Costa Rica....................	....	....	....	....	....	....	....	....	....	....	....	....
243	Dominican Republic....................	....	....	....	....	....	....	....	....	....	....	....	....
253	El Salvador....................	....	....	....	−1.79	.11	−.98	....	....	....	−31.77	−35.33	−34.82
258	Guatemala....................	....	....	....	....	....	....	....	....	....	....	....	....
343	Jamaica....................	....	....	....	....	....	....	....	....	....	....	....	....
273	Mexico....................	....	....	....	....	....	....	....	....	....	....	....	....
278	Nicaragua....................	....	....	....	....	....	....	....	....	....	....	....	....
283	Panama....................	....	....	....	....	....	....	....	....	....	....	....	....
288	Paraguay....................	....	....	....	....	....	....	....	....	....	....	....	....
293	Peru....................	....	....	....	....	....	....	....	....	....	....	....	....
361	St. Kitts and Nevis....................	....	....	....	....	....	....	....	....	....	....	....	....
364	St. Vincent and the Grenadines.......	....	....	....	....	....	....	....	....	....	....	....	....
298	Uruguay....................	....	....	....	....	....	....	....	....	−38.39	−80.15	−92.53	−73.38p
299	Venezuela, Rep. Bol....................	....	....	....	....	....	....	....	....	....	....	....	....

Table W3. Major Categories: General and Central Government

(Percent of GDP)

| | | | Revenue | Expense plus Net Acquisition of Nonfinancial Assets | | | Net Acquisition of Financial Assets | Net Incurrence of Liabilities |
				Expense	Net Acquisition of Nonfinancial Assets	Total Outlays		
General Government								
Industrial Countries								
111	United States.............................	2004	31.59	34.92	1.27	36.19	....	....
156	Canada.....................................	2004	41.02p	37.55p	2.53p	40.15p	1.19p	0.25p
193	Australia...................................	2004	37.07	35.20	0.65	35.85	−0.09	−1.31
158	Japan.......................................	2003	30.02p	35.52p	2.05p	37.56p	6.49p	13.51p
196	New Zealand.............................	2004	39.21p	34.43p	1.23p	35.67p	....	....
	Euro Area							
122	Austria..................................	2003	49.08	50.47	−0.14	50.33	0.29	1.58
124	Belgium................................	2003	51.30	50.99	1.57	52.57	−2.01	−2.10
172	Finland.................................	2004	52.96p	50.46p	0.60p	51.06p	....	....
132	France..................................	2004	50.12p	52.90p	0.87p	53.77p	0.45p	4.11p
134	Germany...............................	2004	43.19	47.12	−0.27	46.85	−0.32	3.29
174	Greece.................................	2000	....	....	....	....	....	....
136	Italy.....................................	2003	46.66	47.83	1.32	49.15	−4.30	−1.69
137	Luxembourg..........................	2004	44.65p	42.58p	2.69p	45.26p	−0.43p	0.33p
138	Netherlands..........................	2004	44.32p	45.81p	0.58p	46.40p	−1.19p	0.90p
182	Portugal...............................	2002	42.98	44.75	0.94	45.70	2.00	4.72
184	Spain...................................	2003	38.00p	34.34p	3.34p	37.68p	0.71p	0.39p
128	Denmark...................................	2004	56.59p	55.52p	−0.04p	55.48p	−1.42p	−2.53p
176	Iceland.....................................	2002	45.54	44.53	2.00	46.53	−0.47	0.52
142	Norway.....................................	2004	57.96p	45.74p	0.77p	46.51p	....	....
135	San Marino...............................	2002	46.95	46.73	−1.07	45.66	−0.77	−2.06
144	Sweden....................................	2003	58.75	58.13	0.58	58.70	3.06	1.92
146	Switzerland..............................	2002	†38.35	†35.17	†2.53	†37.69	†−0.09	†−0.75
112	United Kingdom........................	2004	40.63	42.95	0.76	43.71	0.64	3.86
Developing Countries								
Africa								
612	Algeria.....................................	2002	....	....	....	....	....	....
618	Burundi....................................	1999	....	....	....	....	....	....
622	Cameroon.................................	1999	....	....	....	....	....	....
636	Congo, Dem. Rep. of.................	2002	....	....	....	....	....	....
634	Congo, Rep. of..........................	2003	31.83	20.02	5.30	....	....	....
662	Côte d'Ivoire.............................	2003	....	....	....	....	....	....
644	Ethiopia...................................	2001	....	....	....	....	....	....
652	Ghana......................................	2004	....	....	....	....	....	....
656	Guinea.....................................	1999	....	....	....	....	....	....
664	Kenya......................................	2002	....	....	....	....	....	....
666	Lesotho....................................	2003	41.97p	35.11p	6.25p	41.36p	....	....
674	Madagascar...............................	2004	....	....	....	....	....	....
684	Mauritius..................................	2004	21.36	20.56	3.80	24.36	−4.80	−1.80
686	Morocco...................................	1999	....	....	....	....	....	....
728	Namibia....................................	2001	....	....	....	....	....	....
722	Senegal....................................	2001	....	....	....	....	....	....
718	Seychelles................................	2002	41.96	47.27	9.03	56.30	−5.64	8.71
724	Sierra Leone.............................	1999	....	....	....	....	....	....
199	South Africa..............................	2004	33.57p	33.51p	2.45p	35.96p	1.51p	3.90p
732	Sudan......................................	1999	....	....	....	....	....	....
734	Swaziland.................................	2003	....	....	....	....	....	....
744	Tunisia.....................................	2004	....	....	....	....	....	....
746	Uganda....................................	2003	....	....	....	....	....	....
754	Zambia.....................................	1999	....	....	....	....	....	....
Asia								
512	Afghanistan, I.R. of...................	2004	....	....	....	....	....	....
513	Bangladesh...............................	2003	....	....	....	....	....	....
514	Bhutan.....................................	2004	....	....	....	....	....	....
522	Cambodia.................................	2004	....	....	....	....	....	....
924	China, P.R.: Mainland.................	2003	....	....	....	....	....	....

Table W3. Major Categories: General and Central Government

(Percent of GDP)

			Revenue	Expense plus Net Acquisition of Nonfinancial Assets			Net Acquisition of Financial Assets	Net Incurrence of Liabilities
				Expense	Net Acquisition of Nonfinancial Assets	Total Outlays		
532	China, P.R.: Hong Kong	2003	16.92	22.10	0.82	22.92	−4.82	1.19
546	China, P.R.: Macao	2004	24.49	12.24	4.20	16.44	8.05	—
819	Fiji	2004	....	....	....	....	....	....
534	India	2003	....	....	....	....	....	....
536	Indonesia	2004	....	....	....	....	....	....
542	Korea, Rep. of	2001	....	....	....	....	....	....
548	Malaysia	2003	26.12p	21.30p	9.64p	30.94p		
556	Maldives	2004	40.90p	32.19p	13.10p	45.52p	−1.77p	2.62p
948	Mongolia	2003	†44.04p	†34.20p	†10.21p	†44.40p	†4.03p	†4.64p
518	Myanmar	2002	....	....	....	....	....	....
558	Nepal	2004	....	....	....	....	....	....
564	Pakistan	2004	....	....	....	....	....	....
853	Papua New Guinea	2002	....	....	....	....	....	....
566	Philippines	2004	....	....	....	....	....	....
576	Singapore	2004	20.23	15.50	0.57	17.23	13.46	9.29
524	Sri Lanka	2002	....	....	....	....	....	....
578	Thailand	2004	21.00p	16.80p	3.06p	19.87p	4.85p	3.71p
846	Vanuatu	1999	....	....	....	....	....	....
582	Vietnam	2003	24.09p	....	....	29.10p	−1.56p	1.94p
	Europe (excluding industrial countries)							
914	Albania	2002	24.32	24.06	6.43	29.70	−0.52	5.65
911	Armenia	2004	19.69p	17.61p	2.88p	20.52p	1.33p	2.13p
912	Azerbaijan	1999	....	....	....	....	....	....
913	Belarus	2004	46.36p	39.86p	5.91p	46.03p	1.56p	0.97p
963	Bosnia and Herzegovina	2003	....	....	....	....	....	....
918	Bulgaria	2004	41.21	36.60	2.88	39.48	−0.26	−1.98
960	Croatia	2004	46.15	45.12	5.07	50.19	0.05	4.08
423	Cyprus	1998	....	....	....	....	....	....
935	Czech Republic	2004	38.86p	39.73p	2.67p	42.78p	0.32p	3.85p
939	Estonia	2001	....	....	....	....	....	....
915	Georgia	2002	....	....	....	....	....	....
944	Hungary	2003	44.06p	46.92p	3.43p	50.36p	−0.35p	5.93p
916	Kazakhstan	2004	22.71	18.33	4.40	23.07	0.20	0.22
917	Kyrgyz Republic	2001	....	....	....	....	....	....
941	Latvia	2004	34.39	33.57	1.88	35.45	0.88	1.93
946	Lithuania	2004	31.93p	31.21p	2.16p	33.37p	−1.03p	0.40p
181	Malta	2001	34.00	36.57	3.25	39.95	−0.68	5.15
921	Moldova	2004	35.58	31.83	3.23	35.06	1.26	0.74
964	Poland	2003	40.47	43.45	0.61	44.06	0.92	4.51
968	Romania	2002	†32.30p	†31.51p	†2.80p	†34.31p	†0.61p	†2.12p
922	Russia Federation	2004	40.43	32.03	2.51	34.54	4.94	−0.94
965	Serbia and Montenegro	2002	....	....	....	....	....	....
936	Slovak Republic	2003	†38.34p	†39.34p	†2.46p	†41.80p	†−0.59p	†2.65p
961	Slovenia	2004	45.97	44.61	2.61	47.59	0.33	1.58
923	Tajikistan	2004	....	....	....	....	....	....
186	Turkey	2001	....	....	....	....	....	....
926	Ukraine	2004	37.03p	38.03p	2.42p	41.18p	0.07p	3.49p
	Middle East							
419	Bahrain, Kingdom of	2004	....	....	....	....	....	....
469	Egypt	2002	....	....	....	....	....	....
429	Iran, I.R. of	2004	30.87p	20.85p	5.90p	26.75p	3.51p	−0.61p
436	Israel	2004	47.60p	51.69p	1.00p	52.68p	....	....
439	Jordan	2003	....	....	....	....	....	....
443	Kuwait	2003	54.40	43.33	4.60	47.94	....	....
446	Lebanon	2003	....	....	....	....	....	....
449	Oman	2001	....	....	....	....	....	....
463	Syrian Arab Republic	1999	....	....	....	....	....	....
466	United Arab Emirates	1999	....	....	....	....	....	....

Table W3. Major Categories: General and Central Government
(Percent of GDP)

| | | | Revenue | Expense plus Net Acquisition of Nonfinancial Assets | | | Net Acquisition of Financial Assets | Net Incurrence of Liabilities |
				Expense	Net Acquisition of Nonfinancial Assets	Total Outlays		
474	Yemen, Republic of..........................	1999	....	....	....	....	....	....
	Western Hemisphere							
213	Argentina......................................	2004	29.43p	26.95p	1.80p	28.76p	3.62p	2.94p
313	Bahamas, The...............................	2004	....	....	....	....	....	....
316	Barbados......................................	2002	....	....	....	....	....	....
218	Bolivia..	2004	30.36	28.41	6.37	34.78	2.84	7.26
223	Brazil...	1998	....	....	....	....	....	....
228	Chile..	2004	24.20	19.91	2.15	....	1.37	−0.77
233	Colombia......................................	2004	....	....	....	....	....	....
238	Costa Rica....................................	2003	23.37	23.84	1.09	24.93	....	....
243	Dominican Republic........................	2003	....	....	....	....	....	....
253	El Salvador...................................	2004	16.53	17.28	2.44	19.72	−2.74	2.58
258	Guatemala....................................	2004	....	....	....	....	....	....
343	Jamaica.......................................	2003	33.05	42.37	....	....	....	....
273	Mexico...	2000	....	....	....	....	....	....
278	Nicaragua.....................................	2004	....	....	....	....	....	....
283	Panama..	2001	....	....	....	....	....	....
288	Paraguay......................................	2003	....	....	....	....	....	....
293	Peru..	2004	17.85p	16.52p	2.33p	18.84p	3.64p	4.63p
361	St. Kitts and Nevis.........................	2003	37.88	36.63	....	....	....	....
364	St. Vincent and the Grenadines.........	2003	34.70	....	....	31.85	....	....
298	Uruguay.......................................	2004	....	....	....	....	−1.05p	1.33p
299	Venezuela, Rep. Bol.......................	2003	....	....	....	....	....	....

Central Government
Industrial Countries
111	United States................................	2004	17.14	20.88	0.09	20.97	−0.30	3.15
156	Canada..	2004	19.72p	18.08p	0.29p	18.38p	0.71p	−0.64p
193	Australia.......................................	2004	27.36	26.44	0.12	26.56	0.39	−0.41
158	Japan...	2003	....	....	....	....	....	....
196	New Zealand.................................	2004	36.21p	31.88p	0.61p	32.49p	3.08p	−0.64p
	Euro Area							
122	Austria...	2003	37.84	40.00	−0.28	39.72	0.34	2.22
124	Belgium..	2003	43.81	43.91	0.19	44.10	−2.84	−2.76
172	Finland...	2004	39.56p	36.87p	0.16p	37.03p	....	....
132	France..	2004	43.64p	47.05p	0.12p	47.17p	0.09p	3.64p
134	Germany.......................................	2004	28.85	31.21	—	31.21	....	....
174	Greece...	2000	....	....	....	....	....	....
136	Italy..	2003	37.86	39.99	0.12	40.11	−4.56	−2.19
137	Luxembourg..................................	2004	41.80p	40.63p	1.67p	42.30p	−0.09p	0.71p
138	Netherlands..................................	2004	39.34p	40.66p	0.33p	40.99p	−0.81p	0.84p
182	Portugal.......................................	2002	39.33	41.59	—	41.58	2.16	4.40
184	Spain...	2003	31.40p	29.71p	1.13p	30.84p	0.62p	0.06p
128	Denmark.......................................	2004	36.58p	34.86p	−0.10p	34.76p	−0.69p	−2.51p
176	Iceland...	2002	33.80	33.86	0.36	34.22	−0.51	−0.09
142	Norway...	2004	49.35p	37.22p	0.29p	37.51p	....	....
135	San Marino...................................	2002	46.95	46.73	−1.07	45.66	−0.77	−2.06
144	Sweden..	2003	38.27	37.47	0.49	37.95	2.65	1.62
146	Switzerland...................................	2002	†19.93	†19.16	†0.21	†19.37	†−0.01	†−0.56
112	United Kingdom.............................	2004	36.84	39.74	0.31	40.05	0.37	3.59
	Developing Countries							
	Africa							
612	Algeria...	2002	....	....	....	....	....	....
618	Burundi..	1999	18.29	20.65	....	23.09	1.63	6.15
622	Cameroon.....................................	1999	....	....	....	....	....	....
636	Congo, Dem. Rep. of......................	2002	8.24	....	....	8.29	....	....
634	Congo, Rep. of..............................	2003	31.46	19.88	5.16	25.03	....	....
662	Côte d'Ivoire.................................	2003	17.17	17.12	....	....	6.35	8.96
644	Ethiopia..	2001	....	....	....	....	....	....

Table W3. Major Categories: General and Central Government

(Percent of GDP)

| | | | Revenue | Expense plus Net Acquisition of Nonfinancial Assets | | | Net Acquisition of Financial Assets | Net Incurrence of Liabilities |
				Expense	Net Acquisition of Nonfinancial Assets	Total Outlays		
652	Ghana	2004	....	....	....	....	....	....
656	Guinea	1999	....	....	....	....	....	....
664	Kenya	2002	....	....	....	....	....	....
666	Lesotho	2003	41.97p	35.11p	6.25p	41.36p	....	....
674	Madagascar	2004	20.31	12.60	12.22	24.82	1.13	5.64
684	Mauritius	2004	20.99	20.61	3.36	23.98	−4.80	−1.82
686	Morocco	1999	29.64	28.52	3.80	32.55	−1.80	0.89
728	Namibia	2001	....	....	....	....	....	....
722	Senegal	2001	....	....	....	....	....	....
718	Seychelles	2002	41.96	47.27	9.03	56.30	−5.64	8.71
724	Sierra Leone	1999	....	....	....	....	....	....
199	South Africa	2004	28.03p	29.36p	0.61p	29.97p	1.34p	3.28p
732	Sudan	1999	....	....	....	....	....	....
734	Swaziland	2003	....	....	....	....	....	....
744	Tunisia	2004	29.85p	28.35p	3.86p	32.23p	−0.80p	1.55p
746	Uganda	2003	....	....	....	....	....	....
754	Zambia	1999	....	....	....	....	....	....
	Asia							
512	Afghanistan, I.R. of	2004	....	....	....	....	....	....
513	Bangladesh	2003	11.20	9.08	2.24	11.33	2.52	2.64
514	Bhutan	2004	....	....	....	....	....	....
522	Cambodia	2004	12.79	9.12	5.90	15.03	−0.18	1.89
924	China, P.R.: Mainland	2003	....	....	....	....	....	....
532	China, P.R.: Hong Kong	2003	....	....	....	....	....	....
546	China, P.R.: Macao	2004	24.49	12.24	4.20	16.44	8.05	—
819	Fiji	2004	....	....	....	....	....	....
534	India	2003	12.04p	15.82p	−0.10p	16.27p	−0.21p	3.47p
536	Indonesia	2004	18.32p	16.80p	2.62p	19.42p	−1.54p	−0.44p
542	Korea, Republic of	2001	22.80	18.56	1.39	20.16	0.48	−2.37
548	Malaysia	2003	23.75p	20.13p	7.92p	28.05p	....	....
556	Maldives	2004	40.90p	32.19p	13.10p	45.52p	−1.77p	2.62p
948	Mongolia	2003	†42.34p	†33.03p	†9.82p	†42.85p	†3.93p	†4.78p
518	Myanmar	2002	4.97	....	....	6.28	−0.01	....
558	Nepal	2004	14.41p	....	....	16.65p	−0.66p	1.47p
564	Pakistan	2004	14.57	14.92	1.67	16.59	....	....
853	Papua New Guinea	2002	....	....	....	....	....	....
566	Philippines	2004	....	....	....	....	....	....
576	Singapore	2004	20.23	15.50	0.57	17.23	13.46	9.29
524	Sri Lanka	2002	....	....	....	....	....	....
578	Thailand	2004	19.39p	16.95p	1.89p	18.84p	4.25p	3.70p
846	Vanuatu	1999	22.36	21.25	1.90	23.24	1.00	1.78
582	Vietnam	2003	....	....	....	....	....	....
	Europe (excluding industrial countries)							
914	Albania	2002	....	....	....	....	....	....
911	Armenia	2004	19.03p	17.06p	2.83p	19.92p	1.28p	2.13p
912	Azerbaijan	1999	....	....	....	....	....	....
913	Belarus	2004	30.66p	28.49p	2.34p	31.02p	0.97p	1.13p
963	Bonsia and Herzegovina	2003	43.65	41.44	1.42	42.87	2.63	1.85
918	Bulgaria	2004	39.33	35.32	2.36	37.69	−0.41	−2.05
960	Croatia	2004	42.02	41.98	4.04	46.03	0.01	4.02
423	Cyprus	1998	30.29	32.77	2.82	35.61	0.70	6.00
935	Czech Republic	2004	33.14p	35.89p	0.50p	36.42p	0.32p	3.57p
939	Estonia	2001	28.62	26.67	1.00	27.99	0.78	−0.17
915	Georgia	2002	10.76	11.26	1.34	12.60	0.05	1.88
944	Hungary	2003	37.82p	42.18p	1.90p	44.08p	−0.43p	5.72p
916	Kazakhstan	2004	17.12	14.80	2.09	17.00	0.50	0.27
917	Kyrgyz Republic	2001	....	....	....	....	....	....
941	Latvia	2004	28.04	28.15	0.85	29.00	1.14	2.09

Table W3. Major Categories: General and Central Government

(Percent of GDP)

| | | | Revenue | Expense plus Net Acquisition of Nonfinancial Assets | | | Net Acquisition of Financial Assets | Net Incurrence of Liabilities |
				Expense	Net Acquisition of Nonfinancial Assets	Total Outlays		
946	Lithuania	2004	28.76p	28.54p	1.81p	30.35p	−1.30p	0.28p
181	Malta	2001	34.00	36.57	3.25	39.95	−0.68	5.15
921	Moldova	2004	29.29	27.12	1.73	28.85	1.00	0.55
964	Poland	2003	35.21	39.31	−0.67	38.64	0.63	4.05
968	Romania	2002	†26.11p	†25.91p	†2.17p	†28.08p	†0.61p	†2.10p
922	Russia Federation	2004	27.51	21.93	0.21	22.14	4.01	−1.36
965	Serbia and Montenegro	2002	....	....	....	....	....	....
936	Slovak Republic	2003	†35.18p	†36.80p	†1.66p	†38.46p	†−0.56p	†2.63p
961	Slovenia	2004	41.06	40.80	1.53	42.41	0.22	1.50
923	Tajikistan	2004	....	....	....	....	....	....
186	Turkey	2001	....	....	....	....	....	....
926	Ukraine	2004	31.37p	33.06p	1.51p	34.81p	−0.11p	3.09p
	Middle East							
419	Bahrain, Kingdom of	2004	32.29p	24.09p	2.49p	26.59p	3.31p	−2.40p
469	Egypt	2002	....	....	....	....	....	....
429	Iran, I.R. of	2004	28.90p	20.20p	5.07p	25.26p	3.03p	−0.61p
436	Israel	2004	44.29p	48.76p	0.32p	49.08	....	....
439	Jordan	2003	....	....	....	....	....	....
443	Kuwait	2003	54.40	43.33	4.60	47.94	....	....
446	Lebanon	2003	....	....	....	....	....	....
449	Oman	2001	....	....	....	....	....	....
463	Syrian Arab Rep	1999	23.94	....	....	23.23	....	....
466	United Arab Emirates	1999	....	....	....	....	....	....
474	Yemen, Republic of	1999	....	....	....	....	....	....
	Western Hemisphere							
213	Argentina	2004	18.20	18.30	0.36	18.67	2.43	2.89
313	Bahamas, The	2004	....	....	....	....	....	....
316	Barbados	2002	....	....	....	....	....	....
218	Bolivia	2004	24.43	27.21	2.61	29.82	1.78	7.17
223	Brazil	1998	24.24	26.21	−1.11	26.80	....	....
228	Chile	2004	22.31	18.37	1.80	20.20	1.38	−0.77
233	Colombia	2004	....	....	....	....	....	....
238	Costa Rica	2003	22.66	23.33	0.93	24.26	....	....
243	Dominican Republic	2003	16.73	13.38	1.93	15.31	4.71	3.30
253	El Salvador	2004	15.76	17.02	2.02	19.04	−2.88	2.51
258	Guatemala	2004	....	....	....	....	....	....
343	Jamaica	2003	32.56	41.77	0.64	42.40	....	....
273	Mexico	2000	14.76	15.46	0.48	15.95	....	....
278	Nicaragua	2004	24.57p	19.74p	5.87p	25.61p	....	....
283	Panama	2001	25.75	23.17	1.67	24.85	....	....
288	Paraguay	2003	....	....	....	....	....	....
293	Peru	2004	16.85p	16.86p	1.15p	18.01p	3.46p	4.62p
361	St. Kitts and Nevis	2003	37.88	36.63	....	....	....	....
364	St. Vincent and the Grenadines	2003	....	....	....	....	....	....
298	Uruguay	2004	26.52p	27.54p	1.49p	29.03p	−1.12p	1.28p
299	Venezuela, Rep. Bol.	2003	24.03p	25.16p	3.00p	28.15p	2.30p	6.42p

Table W4. Revenue Categories: General and Central Government

(Percent of GDP)

			Taxes								
			Taxes on Income, Profits, & Capital Gains	Taxes on Payroll and Work Force	Taxes on Property	Taxes on Goods and Services	Taxes on Inter-national Trade	Other Taxes	Total	Social Contri-butions	Grants	Other Revenue
General Government												
	Industrial Countries											
111	United States...........................	2004	11.03	—	3.06	4.47	0.20	—	18.75	7.01	—	5.83
156	Canada...................................	2004	15.86p	0.69p	3.55p	8.54p	0.24p	0.11p	28.98p	5.48p	—p	6.56p
193	Australia.................................	2004	16.97	1.68	2.91	8.45	0.67	—	30.68	—	—	6.39
158	Japan.....................................	2003	6.89p	....	....	....	....	....	15.87p	10.41p	—p	3.74p
196	New Zealand............................	2004	19.09p	—p	1.89p	10.55p	1.03p	—p	32.55p	0.08p	—p	6.59p
	Euro Area											
122	Austria...................................	2003	12.71	2.14	0.54	12.29	—	0.02	27.71	16.26	0.24	4.88
124	Belgium..................................	2003	16.35	0.01	2.98	10.91	—	0.12	30.38	16.48	0.05	4.40
172	Finland...................................	2004	17.09p	—p	1.14p	13.91p	—p	0.03p	32.17p	12.07p	0.20p	8.51p
132	France....................................	2004	10.20p	1.15p	4.43p	11.14p	0.02p	0.01p	26.95p	18.09p	0.09p	4.99p
134	Germany.................................	2004	10.96	—	0.81	10.15	—	—	21.91	17.84	0.18	3.25
174	Greece...................................	2000	....	....	....	....	....	....	....	....	....	....
136	Italy......................................	2003	13.32	—	1.51	12.97	—	1.87	29.68	13.15	0.35	3.48
137	Luxembourg............................	2004	13.23p	—p	1.50p	13.64p	—p	0.05p	28.43p	12.34p	0.02p	3.86p
138	Netherlands............................	2004	9.11p	0.08p	1.78p	12.06p	0.25p	—p	23.29p	15.02p	0.09p	5.91p
182	Portugal.................................	2002	9.35	—	0.55	13.98	—	0.79	24.67	12.18	2.26	3.87
184	Spain.....................................	2003	9.54p	—p	2.67p	9.24p	—p	—p	21.44p	12.78p	0.99p	2.78p
128	Denmark.................................	2004	29.59p	0.20p	1.85p	16.10p	—p	0.01p	47.75p	2.10p	0.15p	6.59p
176	Iceland...................................	2002	16.83	—	3.36	14.79	0.32	0.24	35.54	3.12	—	6.87
142	Norway...................................	2004	20.82p	—p	1.15p	13.07p	0.11p	—p	35.16p	9.70p	—p	13.10p
135	San Marino.............................	2002	10.94	—	1.18	10.87	0.47	0.05	23.52	10.09	0.50	12.84
144	Sweden..................................	2003	18.49	3.01	1.54	13.09	—	0.12	36.25	15.10	0.05	7.35
146	Switzerland.............................	2002	†12.99	†—	†2.59	†6.56	†0.24	†—	†22.39	†7.71	†—	†8.25
112	United Kingdom.......................	2004	13.44	—	1.76	13.39	—	0.42	29.02	8.24	0.36	3.02
	Developing Countries											
	Africa											
612	Algeria...................................	2002	....	....	....	....	....	....	....	....		....
618	Burundi..................................	1999	....	....	....	....	....	....	....	....		....
622	Cameroon...............................	1999	....	....	....	....	....	....	....	....		....
636	Congo, Dem. Rep. of................	2002	....	....	....	....	....	....	....	....		....
634	Congo, Rep. of........................	2003	1.27	—	0.05	5.20	2.09	0.22	8.84	1.33	0.50	21.16
662	Côte d'Ivoire...........................	2003	....	....	....	....	....	....	....	....		....
644	Ethiopia..................................	2001	....	....	....	....	....	....	....	....		....
652	Ghana....................................	2004	....	....	....	....	....	....	....	....		....
656	Guinea...................................	1999	....	....	....	....	....	....	....	....		....
664	Kenya....................................	2002	....	....	....	....	....	....	....	....		....
666	Lesotho..................................	2003	9.89p	—p	—p	7.00p	16.50p	0.12p	33.50p	—p	2.06p	6.40p
674	Madagascar.............................	2004	....	....	....	....	....	....	....	....		....
684	Mauritius................................	2004	2.68	0.11	0.98	9.10	4.23	0.01	17.11	0.80	0.35	3.10
686	Morocco.................................	1999	....	....	....	....	....	....	....	....		....
728	Namibia..................................	2001	....	....	....	....	....	....	....	....		....
722	Senegal..................................	2001	....	....	....	....	....	....	....	....		....
718	Seychelles...............................	2002	6.61	—	0.51	8.39	10.18	0.40	26.09	6.62	0.66	8.59
724	Sierra Leone............................	1999	....	....	....	....	....	....	....	....		....
199	South Africa............................	2004	14.23p	0.32p	1.80p	10.17p	0.87p	0.41p	27.81p	0.68p	0.02p	5.06p
732	Sudan....................................	1999	....	....	....	....	....	....	....	....		....
734	Swaziland...............................	2003	....	....	....	....	....	....	....	....		....
744	Tunisia...................................	2004	....	....	....	....	....	....	....	....		....
746	Uganda..................................	2003	....	....	....	....	....	....	....	....		....
754	Zambia...................................	1999	....	....	....	....	....	....	....	....		....
	Asia											
512	Afghanistan, I.R. of.................	2004	....	....	....	....	....	....	....	....		....
513	Bangladesh..............................	2003	....	....	....	....	....	....	....	....		....
514	Bhutan...................................	2004	....	....	....	....	....	....	....	....		....
522	Cambodia................................	2004	....	....	....	....	....	....	....	....		....
924	China, P.R.: Mainland................	2003	....	....	....	....	....	....	....	....		....

Table W4. Revenue Categories: General and Central Government

(Percent of GDP)

			Taxes							Social Contri-butions	Grants	Other Revenue
			Taxes on Income, Profits, & Capital Gains	Taxes on Payroll and Work Force	Taxes on Property	Taxes on Goods and Services	Taxes on Inter-national Trade	Other Taxes	Total			
532	China, P.R.: Hong Kong	2003	6.58	—	1.97	2.14	0.07	0.08	10.84	—	—	6.07
546	China, P.R.: Macao	2004	1.17	—	0.89	19.58	—	0.32	21.96	0.13	—	2.40
819	Fiji	2004	....	....	....	....	....	....	....	....	....	....
534	India	2003	....	....	....	....	....	....	....	....	....	....
536	Indonesia	2004	....	....	....	....	....	....	....	....	....	....
542	Korea, Rep. of	2001	....	....	....	....	....	....	....	....	....	....
548	Malaysia	2003	....	....	....	....	....	....	18.57p	—p	—p	7.55p
556	Maldives	2004	0.59p	—p	0.01p	5.47p	13.65p	0.13p	19.84p	—p	0.90p	20.16p
948	Mongolia	2003	†7.16p	†—p	†0.93p	†15.41p	†2.40p	†0.06p	†25.97p	†6.67p	†0.64p	†10.77p
518	Myanmar	2002	....	....	....	....	....	....	....	....	....	....
558	Nepal	2004	....	....	....	....	....	....	....	....	....	....
564	Pakistan	2004	....	....	....	....	....	....	....	....	....	....
853	Papua New Guinea	2002	....	....	....	....	....	....	....	....	....	....
566	Philippines	2004	....	....	....	....	....	....	....	....	....	....
576	Singapore	2004	5.57	—	1.14	4.78	0.01	0.99	12.50	—	—	7.73
524	Sri Lanka	2002	....	....	....	....	....	....	....	....	....	....
578	Thailand	2004	6.20p	—p	0.44p	8.82p	1.63p	0.10p	17.19p	0.94p	0.03p	2.83p
846	Vanuatu	1999	....	....	....	....	....	....	....	....	....	....
582	Vietnam	2003	8.21p	—p	0.42p	8.58p	3.51p	—p	20.72p	—p	0.48p	2.89p
	Europe (excluding industrial countries)											
914	Albania	2002	3.32	—	—	10.68	2.13	0.26	16.37	3.96	0.65	3.33
911	Armenia	2004	2.76p	—p	0.38p	5.96p	0.60p	4.83p	14.54p	2.68p	0.72p	1.74p
912	Azerbaijan	1999	....	....	....	....	....	....	....	....	....	....
913	Belarus	2004	7.10p	0.99p	1.94p	19.30p	2.21p	2.38p	33.92p	10.87p	—p	1.57p
963	Bosnia and Herzegovina	2003	....	....	....	....	....	....	....	....	....	....
918	Bulgaria	2004	5.75	—	1.13	15.76	0.77	0.02	23.42	10.73	1.16	5.89
960	Croatia	2004	5.87	—	0.35	20.08	0.77	0.17	27.25	14.23	0.01	4.67
423	Cyprus	1998	....	....	....	....	....	....	....	....	....	....
935	Czech Republic	2004	9.15p	—p	0.55p	10.76p	0.15p	0.01p	20.61p	15.05p	0.90p	2.30p
939	Estonia	2001	....	....	....	....	....	....	....	....	....	....
915	Georgia	2002	....	....	....	....	....	....	....	....	....	....
944	Hungary	2003	9.42p	0.13p	0.83p	15.19p	0.72p	0.49p	26.79p	12.55p	0.14p	4.59p
916	Kazakhstan	2004	8.62	3.01	0.68	7.89	0.90	0.14	21.25	—	—	1.46
917	Kyrgyz Republic	2001	....	....	....	....	....	....	....	....	....	....
941	Latvia	2004	7.68	—	0.77	10.09	0.23	0.11	18.89	8.74	2.11	4.65
946	Lithuania	2004	8.69p	0.04p	0.40p	10.57p	0.13p	—p	19.83p	9.20p	0.90p	2.01p
181	Malta	2001	9.64	—	0.92	12.33	1.27	—	24.16	6.15	0.08	3.61
921	Moldova	2004	4.93	—	0.70	14.39	1.55	—	21.58	7.79	0.39	5.82
964	Poland	2003	6.19	—	1.38	12.03	0.46	—	20.06	14.14	0.15	6.12
968	Romania	2002	†5.19p	†—p	†0.69p	†10.72p	†0.66p	†0.01p	†17.27p	†10.85p	†0.33p	†3.86p
922	Russia Federation	2004	9.05	—	1.27	8.16	5.13	0.06	23.68	7.55	—	9.21
965	Serbia and Montenegro	2002	....	....	....	....	....	....	....	....	....	....
936	Slovak Republic	2003	†6.72p	†—p	†0.44p	†10.70p	†0.34p	†—p	†18.20p	†14.04p	†0.02p	†6.09p
961	Slovenia	2004	8.11	1.37	0.63	13.70	0.31	0.12	24.24	15.75	0.72	5.25
923	Tajikistan	2004	....	....	....	....	....	....	....	....	....	....
186	Turkey	2001	....	....	....	....	....	....	....	....	....	....
926	Ukraine	2004	8.87p	0.05p	0.45p	7.39p	1.71p	0.01p	18.47p	11.88p	0.12p	6.55p
	Middle East											
419	Bahrain, Kingdom of	2004	....	....	....	....	....	....	....	....	....	....
469	Egypt	2002	....	....	....	....	....	....	....	....	....	....
429	Iran, I.R. of	2004	2.69p	—p	0.29p	1.02p	2.35p	1.13p	7.49p	3.77p	—p	19.61p
436	Israel	2004	12.87p	1.85p	3.09p	13.18p	0.30p	0.17p	31.47p	7.51p	2.10p	6.52p
439	Jordan	2003	....	....	....	....	....	....	....	....	....	....
443	Kuwait	2003	0.24	—	0.08	—	1.18	—	1.50	—	—	52.90
446	Lebanon	2003	....	....	....	....	....	....	....	....	....	....
449	Oman	2001	....	....	....	....	....	....	....	....	....	....
463	Syrian Arab Republic	1999	....	....	....	....	....	....	....	....	....	....
466	United Arab Emirates	1999	....	....	....	....	....	....	....	....	....	....

Table W4. Revenue Categories: General and Central Government

(Percent of GDP)

			Taxes							Social Contributions	Grants	Other Revenue
			Taxes on Income, Profits, & Capital Gains	Taxes on Payroll and Work Force	Taxes on Property	Taxes on Goods and Services	Taxes on International Trade	Other Taxes	Total			
474	Yemen, Republic of.................................	1999	....	....	....	....	....	....	....	....	....	....
	Western Hemisphere											
213	Argentina...	2004	5.18p	0.08p	2.64p	10.97p	2.88p	1.17p	22.91p	3.01p	0.01p	3.49p
313	Bahamas, The.....................................	2004	....	....	....	....	....	....	....	....	....	....
316	Barbados..	2002	....	....	....	....	....	....	....	....	....	....
218	Bolivia...	2004	2.12	—	3.33	10.99	0.96	1.48	18.89	1.92	4.12	5.43
223	Brazil..	1998	....	....	....	....	....	....	....	....	....	....
228	Chile..	2004	4.09	—	0.63	10.94	0.45	1.17	17.27	1.44	—	5.48
233	Colombia..	2004	....	....	....	....	....	....	....	....	....	....
238	Costa Rica..	2003	3.34	—	0.62	8.84	1.03	0.03	13.86	7.33	—	2.19
243	Dominican Republic...............................	2003	....	....	....	....	....	....	....	....	....	....
253	El Salvador.......................................	2004	3.32	—	0.10	6.46	1.10	0.25	11.23	2.26	0.22	2.82
258	Guatemala..	2004	....	....	....	....	....	....	....	....	....	....
343	Jamaica...	2003	....	....	0.30	....	2.99	....	....	2.18	0.05	....
273	Mexico..	2000	....	....	....	....	....	....	....	....	....	....
278	Nicaragua...	2004	....	....	....	....	....	....	....	....	....	....
283	Panama...	2001	....	....	....	....	....	....	....	....	....	....
288	Paraguay..	2003	....	....	....	....	....	....	....	....	....	....
293	Peru..	2004	4.03p	—p	0.22p	8.90p	1.17p	0.75p	13.59p	1.60p	0.11p	2.56p
361	St. Kitts and Nevis...............................	2003	4.34	2.16	0.53	3.20	11.85	1.70	23.78	4.88	0.04	9.19
364	St. Vincent and the Grenadines................	2003	7.58	—	0.27	5.24	13.10	—	26.18	1.99	1.55	4.99
298	Uruguay...	2004	....	....	....	....	....	....	....	....	....	....
299	Venezuela, Rep. Bol.............................	2003	....	....	....	....	....	....	....	....	....	....

Central Government

			Taxes							Social Contributions	Grants	Other Revenue
			Taxes on Income, Profits, & Capital Gains	Taxes on Payroll and Work Force	Taxes on Property	Taxes on Goods and Services	Taxes on International Trade	Other Taxes	Total			
	Industrial Countries											
111	United States......................................	2004	8.76	—	0.21	0.60	0.20	—	9.77	6.84	—	0.53
156	Canada..	2004	10.28p	—p	—p	3.47p	0.24p	—p	13.98p	4.50p	0.05p	1.18p
193	Australia..	2004	16.97	0.43	—	6.91	0.67	—	24.99	—	0.03	2.34
158	Japan...	2003	....	....	....	....	....	....	....	....	....	....
196	New Zealand......................................	2004	19.09p	—p	—p	10.53p	1.03p	—p	30.65p	0.08p	—p	5.48p
	Euro Area											
122	Austria..	2003	9.35	1.30	0.11	9.61	—	0.02	20.39	15.25	−0.20	2.41
124	Belgium...	2003	15.55	0.01	0.31	9.89	—	0.06	25.82	15.09	0.13	2.77
172	Finland...	2004	8.36	—p	0.68p	13.90p	—p	0.03p	22.98p	12.06p	0.46p	4.06p
132	France..	2004	10.20p	0.85p	0.91p	10.41p	—p	0.01p	22.38p	18.06p	0.34p	2.86p
134	Germany..	2004	4.53	—	—	6.31	—	—	10.84	17.05	0.34	0.62
174	Greece..	2000	....	....	....	....	....	....	....	....	....	....
136	Italy..	2003	11.70	—	0.53	8.97	—	1.65	22.85	13.06	0.12	1.83
137	Luxembourg.......................................	2004	11.45p	—p	1.37p	13.60p	—p	0.05p	26.47p	12.32p	0.36p	2.65p
138	Netherlands.......................................	2004	9.11p	0.08p	1.09p	11.21p	0.25p	—p	21.75p	14.53p	0.11p	2.95p
182	Portugal..	2002	8.86	—	0.08	12.78	—	0.77	22.49	12.11	1.77	2.96
184	Spain...	2003	7.15p	—p	0.02p	4.58p	—p	—p	11.75p	12.73p	5.38p	1.54p
128	Denmark..	2004	13.78p	0.20p	0.68p	16.09p	—p	0.01p	30.76p	1.58p	0.40p	3.84p
176	Iceland...	2002	9.06	—	1.43	14.79	0.32	0.10	25.71	3.12	—	4.97
142	Norway...	2004	15.31p	—p	0.60p	12.94p	0.11p	—p	28.97p	9.70p	0.05p	10.64p
135	San Marino.......................................	2002	10.94	—	1.18	10.87	0.47	0.05	23.52	10.09	0.50	12.84
144	Sweden...	2003	1.97	3.01	1.54	13.09	—	0.12	19.73	14.67	0.26	3.61
146	Switzerland.......................................	2002	†3.24	†—	†0.51	†6.05	†0.24	†—	†10.04	†7.71	†0.55	†1.63
112	United Kingdom..................................	2004	13.44	—	1.75	11.75	—	0.42	27.36	7.99	0.31	1.19
	Developing Countries											
	Africa											
612	Algeria..	2002	....	....	....	....	....	....	....	....	....	....
618	Burundi...	1999	3.32	0.14	—	6.95	3.19	0.01	13.60	1.18	2.49	1.02
622	Cameroon...	1999	....	....	....	....	....	....	....	....	....	....
636	Congo, Dem. Rep. of............................	2002	2.02	0.04	0.04	1.95	2.26	—	6.32	—	0.31	1.61
634	Congo, Rep. of...................................	2003	1.27	—	—	4.96	2.09	0.22	8.54	1.33	0.49	21.10
662	Côte d'Ivoire.....................................	2003	1.33	1.70	0.50	3.16	7.89	—	14.58	1.34	0.48	0.77
644	Ethiopia...	2001	....	....	....	....	....	....	....	....	....	....

Table W4. Revenue Categories: General and Central Government

(Percent of GDP)

			Taxes							Social Contri-butions	Grants	Other Revenue
			Taxes on Income, Profits, & Capital Gains	Taxes on Payroll and Work Force	Taxes on Property	Taxes on Goods and Services	Taxes on Inter-national Trade	Other Taxes	Total			
652	Ghana	2004	....	....	....	....	....	....	....	....	....	....
656	Guinea	1999	....	....	....	....	....	....	....	....	....	....
664	Kenya	2002	....	....	....	....	....	....	....	....	....	....
666	Lesotho	2003	9.89p	—p	—p	7.00p	16.50p	0.12p	33.50p	—p	2.06p	6.40p
674	Madagascar	2004	1.26	0.60	0.23	3.25	5.46	0.08	10.88	—	8.23	1.21
684	Mauritius	2004	2.68	0.11	0.84	8.98	4.23	0.01	16.84	0.80	0.35	3.00
686	Morocco	1999	7.13	—	0.57	10.76	4.71	0.31	23.47	2.59	—	3.58
728	Namibia	2001	....	....	....	....	....	....	....	....	....	....
722	Senegal	2001	....	....	....	....	....	....	....	....	....	....
718	Seychelles	2002	6.61	—	0.51	8.39	10.18	0.40	26.09	6.62	0.66	8.59
724	Sierra Leone	1999	....	....	....	....	....	....	....	....	....	....
199	South Africa	2004	14.23p	0.32p	0.66p	9.87p	0.87p	0.05p	26.00p	0.68p	0.25p	1.10p
732	Sudan	1999	....	....	....	....	....	....	....	....	....	....
734	Swaziland	2003	....	....	....	....	....	....	....	....	....	....
744	Tunisia	2004	6.79p	0.34p	0.42p	10.50p	2.14p	0.44p	20.64p	5.52p	0.21p	3.49p
746	Uganda	2003	....	....	....	....	....	....	....	....	....	....
754	Zambia	1999	....	....	....	....	....	....	....	....	....	....
	Asia											
512	Afghanistan, I.R. of	2004										
513	Bangladesh	2003	1.27	0.02	—	3.63	2.82	0.35	8.07	—	1.10	2.03
514	Bhutan	2004	....	....	....	....	....	....	....	....	....	....
522	Cambodia	2004	0.80	—	—	4.80	3.01	0.02	8.63	—	2.05	2.11
924	China, P.R.: Mainland	2003	....	....	....	....	....	....	....	....	....	....
532	China, P.R.: Hong Kong	2003	....	....	....	....	....	....	....	....	....	....
546	China, P.R.: Macao	2004	1.17	—	0.89	19.58	—	0.32	21.96	0.13	—	2.40
819	Fiji	2004	....	....	....	....	....	....	....	....	....	....
534	India	2003	3.74p	—p	0.01p	3.70p	1.79p	—p	9.24p	0.04p	0.10p	2.66p
536	Indonesia	2004	5.16p	—p	0.64p	5.87p	0.55p	0.07p	12.29p	0.50p	0.01p	5.51p
542	Korea, Republic of	2001	5.73	—	0.47	7.04	0.95	1.20	15.40	3.39	—	4.01
548	Malaysia	2003	11.26p	—p	0.05p	5.09p	1.33p	−0.11p	17.62p	—p	—p	6.12p
556	Maldives	2004	0.59p	—p	0.01p	5.47p	13.65p	0.13p	19.84p	—p	0.90p	20.16p
948	Mongolia	2003	†6.83p	†—p	†—p	†14.99p	†2.40p	†—p	†24.22p	†6.67p	†1.73p	†9.71p
518	Myanmar	2002	0.81	—	—	1.10	0.09	—	2.00	—	0.01	2.96
558	Nepal	2004	1.64p	0.28p	0.38p	4.27p	3.12p	—p	9.70p	—p	2.32p	2.40p
564	Pakistan	2004	2.95	—	0.01	4.80	1.59	1.28	10.63	—	0.63	3.31
853	Papua New Guinea	2002	....	....	....	....	....	....	....	....	....	....
566	Philippines	2004	....	....	....	....	....	....	....	....	....	....
576	Singapore	2004	5.57	—	1.14	4.78	0.01	0.99	12.50	—	—	7.73
524	Sri Lanka	2002	....	....	....	....	....	....	....	....	....	....
578	Thailand	2004	6.20p	—p	0.01p	7.77p	1.63p	0.10p	15.71p	0.94p	0.03p	2.71p
846	Vanuatu	1999	—	—	0.37	10.40	7.52	—	18.28	—	1.62	2.46
582	Vietnam	2003	....	....	....	....	....	....	....	....	....	....
	Europe (excluding industrial countries)											
914	Albania	2002	....	....	....	....	....	....	....	....	....	....
911	Armenia	2004	2.76p	—p	—p	5.96p	0.60p	4.76p	14.08p	2.68p	0.72p	1.55p
912	Azerbaijan	1999	....	....	....	....	....	....	....	....	....	....
913	Belarus	2004	2.33p	0.99p	—p	11.00p	2.21p	2.04p	18.57p	10.87p	0.05p	1.17p
963	Bonsia and Herzegovina	2003	0.78	1.76	0.05	12.47	7.89	0.61	23.55	14.37	0.41	5.30
918	Bulgaria	2004	5.75	—	—	15.76	0.77	0.02	22.30	10.73	1.15	5.15
960	Croatia	2004	3.02	—	0.17	19.94	0.77	0.16	24.06	14.23	0.13	3.59
423	Cyprus	1998	6.17	0.55	0.54	8.31	1.15	2.94	19.66	4.59	0.02	6.03
935	Czech Republic	2004	6.53p	—p	0.38p	8.90p	0.15p	0.01p	15.96p	15.05p	0.94p	1.18p
939	Estonia	2001	3.74	—	—	11.66	0.04	—	15.44	10.02	0.60	2.56
915	Georgia	2002	0.37	—	—	6.56	0.68	—	7.62	2.08	0.30	0.77
944	Hungary	2003	7.22p	0.12p	0.29p	13.53p	0.72p	0.49p	22.37p	12.55p	0.20p	2.70p
916	Kazakhstan	2004	6.86	—	—	6.84	0.90	0.03	14.63	—	1.19	1.30
917	Kyrgyz Republic	2001	....	....	....	....	....	....	....	....	....	....
941	Latvia	2004	3.43	—	—	10.05	0.23	0.08	13.80	8.74	2.11	3.39

Table W4. Revenue Categories: General and Central Government

(Percent of GDP)

			Taxes							Social Contri-butions	Grants	Other Revenue
			Taxes on Income, Profits, & Capital Gains	Taxes on Payroll and Work Force	Taxes on Property	Taxes on Goods and Services	Taxes on Inter-national Trade	Other Taxes	Total			
946	Lithuania	2004	6.39p	0.04p	—p	10.48p	0.13p	—p	17.03p	9.20p	0.90p	1.63p
181	Malta	2001	9.64	—	0.92	12.33	1.27	—	24.16	6.15	0.08	3.61
921	Moldova	2004	0.88	—	—	13.95	1.55	—	16.38	7.79	0.48	4.65
964	Poland	2003	4.92	—	0.03	11.92	0.46	—	17.34	14.14	0.15	3.58
968	Romania	2002	†2.42p	†—p	†0.13p	†8.52p	†0.66p	†0.01p	†11.74p	†10.85p	†0.33p	†3.19p
922	Russia Federation	2004	1.22	—	—	7.09	5.13	—	13.45	7.55	0.21	6.29
965	Serbia and Montenegro	2002	....	....	....	....	....	....	....	....	....	....
936	Slovak Republic	2003	†5.94p	†—p	†0.12p	†10.31p	†0.34p	†—p	†16.72p	†14.04p	†0.02p	†4.41p
961	Slovenia	2004	5.97	1.52	0.05	13.37	0.31	0.12	21.34	15.75	0.78	3.20
923	Tajikistan	2004	....	....	....	....	....	....	....	....	....	....
186	Turkey	2001	....	....	....	....	....	....	....	....	....	....
926	Ukraine	2004	4.84p	—p	—p	6.74p	1.71p	0.01p	13.30p	11.88p	0.59p	5.59p
	Middle East											
419	Bahrain, Kingdom of	2004	1.32p	0.41p	0.29p	0.50p	1.38p	1.13p	5.04p	1.27p	0.53p	25.45p
469	Egypt	2002	....	....	....	....	....	....	....	....	....	....
429	Iran, I.R. of	2004	2.69p	—p	0.29p	0.68p	2.35p	—p	6.01p	3.77p	—p	19.11p
436	Israel	2004	12.87p	1.85p	0.57p	13.04p	0.30p	0.17p	28.80p	7.51p	2.71p	5.27p
439	Jordan	2003	....	....	....	....	....	....	....	....	....	....
443	Kuwait	2003	0.24	—	0.08	—	1.18	—	1.50	—	—	52.90
446	Lebanon	2003	....	....	....	....	....	....	....	....	....	....
449	Oman	2001	....	....	....	....	....	....	....	....	....	....
463	Syrian Arab Rep	1999	8.98	0.74	0.25	4.57	2.36	0.54	17.43	0.06	—	6.45
466	United Arab Emirates	1999	....	....	....	....	....	....	....	....	....	....
474	Yemen, Republic of	1999	....	....	....	....	....	....	....	....	....	....
	Western Hemisphere											
213	Argentina	2004	3.44	0.08	1.63	5.31	2.88	0.87	14.21	3.01	0.05	0.93
313	Bahamas, The	2004										
316	Barbados	2002	....	....	....	....	....	....	....	....	....	....
218	Bolivia	2004	1.71	—	1.82	9.25	0.76	1.47	15.02	1.92	4.18	3.30
223	Brazil	1998	5.04	1.08	0.02	5.28	0.72	—	12.15	8.48	0.01	4.22
228	Chile	2004	4.09	—	—	10.12	0.45	1.23	15.89	1.44	0.01	4.98
233	Colombia	2004	....	....	....	....	....	....	....	....	....	....
238	Costa Rica	2003	3.34	—	0.49	8.56	1.03	—	13.42	7.33	0.05	1.86
243	Dominican Republic	2003	4.05	—	0.25	6.85	3.49	0.03	14.67	0.50	0.19	1.37
253	El Salvador	2004	3.32	—	0.10	6.46	1.10	—	10.98	2.26	0.23	2.29
258	Guatemala	2004	....	....	....	....	....	....	....	....	....	....
343	Jamaica	2003	....	....	—	....	2.99	....	....	2.18	0.05	....
273	Mexico	2000	5.04	—	—	9.17	0.60	0.11	11.67	1.55	—	1.55
278	Nicaragua	2004	4.37p	—p	—p	10.16p	0.94p	0.02p	15.50p	3.96p	3.27p	1.84p
283	Panama	2001	3.85	—	0.36	2.29	2.21	0.56	9.26	5.04	0.20	11.26
288	Paraguay	2003	....	....	....	....	....	....	....	....	....	....
293	Peru	2004	4.03p	—p	—p	8.87p	1.17p	0.70p	13.29p	1.60p	0.11p	1.85p
361	St. Kitts and Nevis	2003	4.34	2.16	0.53	3.20	11.85	1.70	23.78	4.88	0.04	9.19
364	St. Vincent and the Grenadines	2003	....	....	....	....	....	....	....	....	....	....
298	Uruguay	2004	2.54p	1.30p	1.78p	12.91p	1.43p	−1.48p	18.48p	4.97p	—p	3.07p
299	Venezuela, Rep. Bol	2003	3.22p	—p	1.73p	5.64p	0.85p	0.09p	11.54p	0.59p	—p	11.90p

Table W5. Expense Categories: General and Central Government
(Percent of GDP)

			Compen-sation of Employees	Use of Goods and Services	Consump-tion of Fixed Capital	Interest	Subsidies	Grants	Social Benefits	Other Expense
General Government										
	Industrial Countries									
111	United States	2004	10.06	8.10	1.29	2.63	0.37	0.22	11.91	0.34
156	Canada	2004	12.74p	7.85p	....	3.60p	1.14p	0.30p	9.09p	2.83p
193	Australia	2004	9.59	6.71	1.45	1.78	1.36	0.17	11.25	2.88
158	Japan	2003	6.35p	3.51p	2.76p	2.79p	0.79p	0.07p	17.17p	2.09p
196	New Zealand	2004	8.79p	9.81p	1.88p	1.80p	0.26p	0.18p	11.01p	0.70p
	Euro Area									
122	Austria	2003	9.51	4.59	1.29	3.10	3.18	1.01	23.48	4.31
124	Belgium	2003	12.12	3.42	1.57	5.43	1.61	0.30	23.28	3.26
172	Finland	2004	13.80p	9.16p	2.38p	1.80p	1.28p	1.05p	19.08p	1.90p
132	France	2004	13.46p	5.77p	2.45p	2.75p	1.50p	0.36p	23.30p	3.31p
134	Germany	2004	7.61	4.04	1.59	2.84	1.31	0.83	26.47	2.42
174	Greece	2000	....	....	....	....	....	....	....	....
136	Italy	2003	11.04	5.31	1.33	5.38	1.12	0.89	19.79	2.98
137	Luxembourg	2004	8.73p	3.51p	1.95p	0.23p	1.69p	1.12p	20.84p	4.52p
138	Netherlands	2004	10.04p	7.07p	2.49p	2.59p	1.41p	1.40p	19.74p	1.08p
182	Portugal	2002	15.29	4.26	2.13	3.05	1.45	0.31	14.96	3.30
184	Spain	2003	9.84p	4.16p	....	2.46p	1.06p	0.08p	13.70p	3.03p
128	Denmark	2004	17.87p	8.68p	1.92p	3.18p	2.35p	2.07p	18.40p	1.05p
176	Iceland	2002	16.21	11.60	2.08	3.38	1.79	0.09	6.67	2.71
142	Norway	2004	13.67p	6.92p	1.96p	1.48p	2.10p	0.85p	17.37p	1.38p
135	San Marino	2002	15.88	8.48	1.39	1.06	0.93	—	12.65	6.33
144	Sweden	2003	16.63	11.34	2.34	2.39	1.54	0.48	21.45	1.97
146	Switzerland	2002	†11.03	†5.65	....	†1.82	†3.50	†0.55	†9.15	†3.47
112	United Kingdom	2004	10.41	11.83	0.93	2.04	0.58	0.27	13.44	3.46
	Developing Countries									
	Africa									
612	Algeria	2002	....	....	....	....	....	....	....	....
618	Burundi	1999	....	....	....	....	....	....	....	....
622	Cameroon	1999	....	....	....	....	....	....	....	....
636	Congo, Dem. Rep. of	2002	....	....	....	....	....	....	....	....
634	Congo, Rep. of	2003	7.66	5.90	....	5.69	—	—	0.65	0.11
662	Côte d'Ivoire	2003	....	....	....	....	....	....	....	....
644	Ethiopia	2001	....	....	....	....	....	....	....	....
652	Ghana	2004	....	....	....	....	....	....	....	....
656	Guinea	1999	....	....	....	....	....	....	....	....
664	Kenya	2002	....	....	....	....	....	....	....	....
666	Lesotho	2003	13.03p	10.86p	....	2.51p	7.32p	—p	1.38p	—p
674	Madagascar	2004	....	....	....	....	....	....	....	....
684	Mauritius	2004	8.71	2.85	....	2.91	0.55	0.08	4.76	0.70
686	Morocco	1999	....	....	....	....	....	....	....	....
728	Namibia	2001	....	....	....	....	....	....	....	....
722	Senegal	2001	....	....	....	....	....	....	....	....
718	Seychelles	2002	13.27	11.67	....	8.02	2.75	—	11.55	0.01
724	Sierra Leone	1999	....	....	....	....	....	....	....	....
199	South Africa	2004	12.38p	9.50p	....	3.68p	0.49p	0.81p	3.89p	2.76p
732	Sudan	1999	....	....	....	....	....	....	....	....
734	Swaziland	2003	....	....	....	....	....	....	....	....
744	Tunisia	2004	....	....	....	....	....	....	....	....
746	Uganda	2003	....	....	....	....	....	....	....	....
754	Zambia	1999	....	....	....	....	....	....	....	....
	Asia									
512	Afghanistan, I.R. of	2004	....	....	....	....	....	....		....
513	Bangladesh	2003	....	....	....	....	....	....		....
514	Bhutan	2004	....	....	....	....	....	....		....
522	Cambodia	2004	....	....	....	....	....	....		....
924	China, P.R.: Mainland	2003	....	....	....	....	....	....		....

Table W5. Expense Categories: General and Central Government

(Percent of GDP)

			Compensation of Employees	Use of Goods and Services	Consumption of Fixed Capital	Interest	Subsidies	Grants	Social Benefits	Other Expense
532	China, P.R.: Hong Kong	2003	5.69	5.00	0.31	—	0.02	—	5.20	5.86
546	China, P.R.: Macao	2004	6.08	2.50	....	—	0.53	0.01	1.27	1.85
819	Fiji	2004	....	....	....	....	....	....	....	....
534	India	2003	....	....	....	....	....	....	....	....
536	Indonesia	2004	....	....	....	....	....	....	....	....
542	Korea, Rep. of	2001	....	....	....	....	....	....	....	....
548	Malaysia	2003	....	....	....	....	....	—p	....	....
556	Maldives	2004	8.42p	21.54p	....	1.63p	0.60p	—p	—p	—p
948	Mongolia	2003	†10.49p	†13.08p	....	†1.30p	†0.69p	†0.05p	†8.57p	†0.01p
518	Myanmar	2002	....	....	....	....	....	....	....	....
558	Nepal	2004	....	....	....	....	....	....	....	....
564	Pakistan	2004	....	....	....	....	....	....	....	....
853	Papua New Guinea	2002	....	....	....	....	....	....	....	....
566	Philippines	2004	....	....	....	....	....	....	....	....
576	Singapore	2004	4.82	5.36	....	0.16	—	2.35	2.81	—
524	Sri Lanka	2002	....	....	....	....	....	....	....	....
578	Thailand	2004	5.97p	4.45p	....	1.29p	1.03p	0.02p	2.73p	1.29p
846	Vanuatu	1999	....	....	....	....	....	....	....	....
582	Vietnam	2003	....	....	....	1.04p	....	....	....	....
	Europe (excluding industrial countries)									
914	Albania	2002	7.36	3.55	....	3.93	1.01	—	1.38	6.83
911	Armenia	2004	3.34p	7.58p	....	0.52p	0.73p	—p	4.17p	1.26p
912	Azerbaijan	1999	....	....	....	....	....	....	....	....
913	Belarus	2004	10.00p	10.02p	....	0.49p	5.04p	0.25p	13.01p	1.04p
963	Bosnia and Herzegovina	2003	....	....	....	....	....	....	....	....
918	Bulgaria	2004	6.77	10.08	....	1.83	2.28	—	14.58	1.05
960	Croatia	2004	12.32	4.67	....	2.14	2.75	0.08	19.81	3.36
423	Cyprus	1998	....	....	....	....	....	....	....	....
935	Czech Republic	2004	4.05p	4.27p	....	1.10p	8.60p	0.50p	17.30p	3.91p
939	Estonia	2001	....	....	....	....	....	....	....	....
915	Georgia	2002	....	....	....	....	....	....	....	....
944	Hungary	2003	12.80p	6.74p	....	4.20p	2.94p	—p	16.46p	3.77p
916	Kazakhstan	2004	4.25	6.87	....	0.63	0.54	0.03	4.57	1.43
917	Kyrgyz Republic	2001	....	....	....	....	....	....	....	....
941	Latvia	2004	8.92	5.91	....	0.74	0.53	—	9.29	8.18
946	Lithuania	2004	8.88p	4.73p	1.09p	1.00p	0.70p	0.53p	12.44p	1.83p
181	Malta	2001	11.95	3.43	....	3.58	2.68	0.74	13.92	0.27
921	Moldova	2004	7.72	5.80	....	2.43	2.22	0.13	9.66	3.86
964	Poland	2003	9.71	8.18	1.69	2.80	0.70	0.05	18.29	2.03
968	Romania	2002	†6.92p	†7.42p	....	†2.19p	†1.97p	†0.04p	†9.62p	†3.34p
922	Russia Federation	2004	7.84	7.88	....	1.26	3.35	—	9.14	0.20
965	Serbia and Montenegro	2002	....	....	....	....	....	....	....	....
936	Slovak Republic	2003	†8.61p	†6.38p	....	†2.53p	†1.75p	†0.07p	†17.40p	†2.59p
961	Slovenia	2004	11.75	8.75	....	1.49	1.32	0.66	19.03	1.61
923	Tajikistan	2004	....	....	....	....	....	....	....	....
186	Turkey	2001	....	....	....	....	....	....	....	....
926	Ukraine	2004	9.73p	5.99p	....	0.91p	2.39p	0.06p	15.56p	3.38p
	Middle East									
419	Bahrain, Kingdom of	2004	....	....	....	....	....	....	....	....
469	Egypt	2002	....	....	....	....	....	....	....	....
429	Iran, I.R. of	2004	....	....	....	0.23p	....	....	....	....
436	Israel	2004	14.13p	14.58p	1.49p	6.14p	0.90p	0.06p	10.70p	3.68p
439	Jordan	2003	....	....	....	....	....	....	....	....
443	Kuwait	2003	14.67	11.54	....	0.14	6.51	0.51	4.49	5.47
446	Lebanon	2003	....	....	....	....	....	....	....	....
449	Oman	2001	....	....	....	....	....	....	....	....
463	Syrian Arab Republic	1999	....	....	....	....	....	....	....	....
466	United Arab Emirates	1999	....	....	....	....	....	....	....	....

Table W5. Expense Categories: General and Central Government

(Percent of GDP)

		Compensation of Employees	Use of Goods and Services	Consumption of Fixed Capital	Interest	Subsidies	Grants	Social Benefits	Other Expense
474	Yemen, Republic of............ 1999	....	....	....	....	....	....	....	....
	Western Hemisphere								
213	Argentina........................ 2004	8.50p	3.03p	....	5.19p	0.60p	0.08p	6.14p	3.40p
313	Bahamas, The.................. 2004	....	....	....	....	....	....	....	....
316	Barbados......................... 2002	....	....	....	....	....	....	....	....
218	Bolivia............................ 2004	12.45	6.26	....	2.70	0.46	0.05	4.92	1.39
223	Brazil.............................. 1998	....	....	....	....	....	....	....	....
228	Chile.............................. 2004	5.40	2.47	....	0.98	4.62	—	4.93	1.52
233	Colombia......................... 2004	....	....	....	....	....	....	....	....
238	Costa Rica....................... 2003	10.35	3.17	....	4.30	—	—	4.88	1.14
243	Dominican Republic............ 2003	....	....	....	....	....	....	....	....
253	El Salvador...................... 2004	7.52	2.55	0.29	2.30	—	0.04	0.25	4.34
258	Guatemala....................... 2004	....	....	....	....	....	....	....	....
343	Jamaica........................... 2003	13.27	5.92	....	19.29	—	—	0.64	3.25
273	Mexico............................ 2000	....	....	....	....	....	....	....	....
278	Nicaragua........................ 2004	....	....	....	....	....	....	....	....
283	Panama........................... 2001	....	....	....	....	....	....	....	....
288	Paraguay......................... 2003	....	....	....	....	....	....	....	....
293	Peru............................... 2004	6.06p	4.55p	....	2.05p	—p	—p	3.27p	0.59p
361	St. Kitts and Nevis............. 2003	15.03	7.47	....	7.56	—	1.42	3.90	1.24
364	St. Vincent and the Grenadines.. 2003	....	....	....	....	....	....	....	....
298	Uruguay.......................... 2004	....	....	....	....	....	....	....	....
299	Venezuela, Rep. Bol........... 2003	....	....	....	....	....	....	....	....

Central Government

		Compensation of Employees	Use of Goods and Services	Consumption of Fixed Capital	Interest	Subsidies	Grants	Social Benefits	Other Expense
	Industrial Countries								
111	United States................... 2004	2.71	3.24	0.25	1.88	0.37	3.59	8.67	0.19
156	Canada........................... 2004	2.04p	1.37p	....	1.56p	0.28p	4.08p	7.64p	1.10p
193	Australia......................... 2004	2.72	2.67	0.29	1.09	0.75	6.96	10.92	1.05
158	Japan............................. 2003	....	....	....	....	....	....	....	....
196	New Zealand.................... 2004	8.09p	8.44p	1.27p	1.71p	0.07p	0.53p	11.01p	0.76p
	Euro Area								
122	Austria........................... 2003	5.12	2.09	0.52	3.00	2.04	5.62	20.21	1.41
124	Belgium........................... 2003	3.09	1.16	0.19	4.98	0.88	11.18	20.66	1.77
172	Finland........................... 2004	3.75p	3.59p	1.07p	1.70	1.20p	6.33p	17.65p	1.59
132	France............................ 2004	10.34p	3.34p	0.90p	2.58p	0.80p	4.32p	22.41p	2.38p
134	Germany......................... 2004	1.71	1.35	0.34	1.77	0.39	2.47	22.28	0.90
174	Greece............................ 2000	....	....	....	....	....	....	....	....
136	Italy............................... 2003	6.57	1.66	0.50	5.21	0.46	6.98	17.11	1.50
137	Luxembourg..................... 2004	6.68p	2.31p	1.09p	0.17p	1.56p	3.71p	20.77p	4.34p
138	Netherlands..................... 2004	3.42p	2.81p	0.88p	2.17p	0.86p	12.15p	17.85p	0.53p
182	Portugal.......................... 2002	13.28	3.03	0.73	2.95	1.33	2.65	14.79	2.83
184	Spain............................. 2003	4.95p	1.86p	....	2.09p	0.57p	5.45p	13.49p	1.30p
128	Denmark.......................... 2004	4.69p	3.32p	0.77p	3.06p	1.53p	14.60p	6.13p	0.78p
176	Iceland........................... 2002	10.03	8.38	1.45	2.86	1.47	1.36	6.15	2.16
142	Norway........................... 2004	5.96p	4.28p	0.97p	1.05p	1.78p	5.89p	16.28p	1.02p
135	San Marino...................... 2002	15.88	8.48	1.39	1.06	0.93	—	12.65	6.33
144	Sweden........................... 2003	3.99	4.42	1.00	2.05	1.05	5.51	17.77	1.68
146	Switzerland...................... 2002	†1.41	†1.71	....	†0.91	†0.98	†4.05	†9.15	†0.96
112	United Kingdom................ 2004	5.28	7.48	0.49	2.00	0.39	8.81	11.96	3.33
	Developing Countries								
	Africa								
612	Algeria........................... 2002	....	....	....	....	....	....	....	....
618	Burundi........................... 1999	....	....	....	....	....	....	....	2.87
622	Cameroon........................ 1999	....	....	....	....	....	....	....	....
636	Congo, Dem. Rep. of.......... 2002	....	....	....	....	....	....	....	....
634	Congo, Rep. of................. 2003	7.35	5.77	....	5.69	—	0.34	0.65	0.07
662	Côte d'Ivoire.................... 2003	6.61	5.05	....	2.66	1.25	—	1.41	0.14
644	Ethiopia.......................... 2001	....	....	....	....	....	....	....	....

Table W5. Expense Categories: General and Central Government

(Percent of GDP)

			Compensation of Employees	Use of Goods and Services	Consumption of Fixed Capital	Interest	Subsidies	Grants	Social Benefits	Other Expense
652	Ghana	2004	....	....	....	....	....	....	....	....
656	Guinea	1999	....	....	....	....	....	....	....	....
664	Kenya	2002	....	....	....	....	....	....	....	....
666	Lesotho	2003	13.03p	10.86p	....	2.51p	7.32p	—p	1.38p	—p
674	Madagascar	2004	4.91	1.80	....	2.94	1.35	—	—	1.60
684	Mauritius	2004	7.96	2.50	....	2.91	0.55	1.38	4.64	0.68
686	Morocco	1999	11.72	3.37	....	4.89	1.04	1.94	4.27	1.29
728	Namibia	2001	....	....	....	....	....	....	....	....
722	Senegal	2001	....	....	....	....	....	....	....	....
718	Seychelles	2002	13.27	11.67	....	8.02	2.75	—	11.55	0.01
724	Sierra Leone	1999	....	....	....	....	....	....	....	....
199	South Africa	2004	4.16p	3.40p	....	3.57p	0.37p	15.27p	0.78p	1.82p
732	Sudan	1999	....	....	....	....	....	....	....	....
734	Swaziland	2003	....	....	....	....	....	....	....	....
744	Tunisia	2004	11.38p	2.09p	....	2.81p	....	....	....	....
746	Uganda	2003	....	....	....	....	....	....	....	....
754	Zambia	1999	....	....	....	....	....	....	....	....
	Asia									
512	Afghanistan, I.R. of	2004	....	....	....	....	....	....	....	....
513	Bangladesh	2003	2.30	1.46	....	1.87	0.31	1.43	0.85	0.86
514	Bhutan	2004	....	....	....	....	....	....	....	....
522	Cambodia	2004	3.26	2.87	....	0.25	0.33	0.58	0.72	1.12
924	China, P.R.: Mainland	2003	....	....	....	....	....	....	....	....
532	China, P.R.: Hong Kong	2003	....	....	....	....	....	....	....	....
546	China, P.R.: Macao	2004	6.08	2.50	....	—	0.53	0.01	1.27	1.85
819	Fiji	2004	....	....	....	....	....	....	....	....
534	India	2003	1.55p	1.92p	....	4.39p	....	....	....	....
536	Indonesia	2004	2.14p	1.28p	....	2.71p	3.98p	5.65p	1.01p	0.03p
542	Korea, Republic of	2001	1.99	2.22	....	1.16	0.09	7.54	2.74	2.83
548	Malaysia	2003	5.96p	5.23p	....	2.50p	3.98p	1.18p	1.17p	0.11p
556	Maldives	2004	8.42p	21.54p	....	1.63p	0.60p	—p	—p	—p
948	Mongolia	2003	†9.76p	†11.85p	....	†1.30p	†0.62p	†0.95p	†8.54p	†0.01p
518	Myanmar	2002	....	....	....	....	....	....	....	....
558	Nepal	2004	....	....	....	1.69p	....	....	....	....
564	Pakistan	2004	0.68	4.61	....	5.82	0.80	3.00	—	—
853	Papua New Guinea	2002	....	....	....	....	....	....	....	....
566	Philippines	2004	....	....	....	....	....	....	....	....
576	Singapore	2004	4.82	5.36	....	0.16	—	2.35	2.81	—
524	Sri Lanka	2002	....	....	....	....	....	....	....	....
578	Thailand	2004	5.44p	3.48p	....	1.29p	1.03p	1.84p	2.71p	1.14p
846	Vanuatu	1999	11.75	6.85	....	0.76	....	....	....	—
582	Vietnam	2003	....	....	....	....	....	....	....	....
	Europe (excluding industrial countries)									
914	Albania	2002	....	....	....	....	....	....	....	....
911	Armenia	2004	2.91p	7.09p	....	0.52p	0.69p	0.62p	4.17p	1.06p
912	Azerbaijan	1999	....	....	....	....	....	....	....	....
913	Belarus	2004	3.65p	5.28p	....	0.47p	2.12p	3.41p	12.57p	0.99p
963	Bonsia and Herzegovina	2003	12.01	11.08	....	0.89	1.11	1.25	13.85	1.26
918	Bulgaria	2004	4.02	7.67	....	1.82	2.05	4.18	14.57	1.01
960	Croatia	2004	11.24	3.06	....	2.10	2.40	1.04	19.63	2.52
423	Cyprus	1998	9.44	2.90	....	5.54	0.70	1.26	10.55	—
935	Czech Republic	2004	3.04p	2.13p	....	1.02p	4.23p	5.46p	16.79p	3.21p
939	Estonia	2001	2.65	8.45	....	0.16	0.77	3.31	11.28	0.05
915	Georgia	2002	1.50	2.44	....	1.97	....	....	....	—
944	Hungary	2003	6.11p	3.36p	....	4.14p	2.77p	6.69p	15.84p	3.28p
916	Kazakhstan	2004	1.34	3.64	....	0.61	0.17	3.78	4.10	1.16
917	Kyrgyz Republic	2001	....	....	....	....	....	....	....	....
941	Latvia	2004	4.57	3.51	....	0.68	0.51	2.87	9.00	7.00

Table W5. Expense Categories: General and Central Government

(Percent of GDP)

			Compensation of Employees	Use of Goods and Services	Consumption of Fixed Capital	Interest	Subsidies	Grants	Social Benefits	Other Expense
946	Lithuania	2004	5.23p	3.47p	0.70p	0.97p	0.64p	4.30p	11.53p	1.69p
181	Malta	2001	11.95	3.43	....	3.58	2.68	0.74	13.92	0.27
921	Moldova	2004	4.09	4.80	....	2.42	1.05	2.84	9.43	2.50
964	Poland	2003	4.81	5.26	1.64	2.70	0.58	5.48	17.68	1.17
968	Romania	2002	†4.08p	†5.59p	....	†2.18p	†1.46p	†0.31p	†9.27p	†3.01p
922	Russia Federation	2004	3.89	5.06	....	1.11	0.30	2.43	7.37	0.19
965	Serbia and Montenegro	2002	....	....	....	....	....	....	....	....
936	Slovak Republic	2003	†4.91p	†4.30p	....	†2.47p	†1.53p	†4.18p	†17.40p	†2.00p
961	Slovenia	2004	7.73	6.43	....	1.47	1.24	4.69	18.26	0.98
923	Tajikistan	2004	....	....	....	....	....	....	....	....
186	Turkey	2001	....	....	....	....	....	....	....	....
926	Ukraine	2004	5.19p	3.76p	....	0.89p	1.67p	4.95p	14.03p	2.57p
	Middle East									
419	Bahrain, Kingdom of	2004	13.95p	3.52p	....	1.11p	0.41p	1.79p	—p	3.31p
469	Egypt	2002	....	....	....	....	....	....	....	....
429	Iran, I.R. of	2004	9.15p	2.46p	....	0.23p	3.05p	0.39p	3.47p	1.44p
436	Israel	2004	11.86p	12.91p	0.78p	5.90p	0.90p	2.65p	10.70p	3.06p
439	Jordan	2003	....	....	....	....	....	....	....	....
443	Kuwait	2003	14.67	11.54	....	0.14	6.51	0.51	4.49	5.47
446	Lebanon	2003	....	....	....	....	....	....	....	....
449	Oman	2001	....	....	....	....	....	....	....	....
463	Syrian Arab Rep.	1999	....	....	....	....	....	....	....	....
466	United Arab Emirates	1999	....	....	....	....	....	....	....	....
474	Yemen, Republic of	1999	....	....	....	....	....	....	....	....
	Western Hemisphere									
213	Argentina	2004	2.11	0.84	....	4.82	0.60	2.43	6.14	1.37
313	Bahamas, The	2004	....	....	....	....	....	....	....	....
316	Barbados	2002	....	....	....	....	....	....	....	....
218	Bolivia	2004	6.62	4.58	....	2.55	0.45	6.76	4.83	1.23
223	Brazil	1998	3.44	2.49	....	3.83	1.59	4.78	10.15	—
228	Chile	2004	4.01	1.74	....	0.98	4.36	0.87	4.93	1.47
233	Colombia	2004	....	....	....	....	....	....	....	....
238	Costa Rica	2003	10.00	3.00	....	4.28	—	0.07	4.88	1.11
243	Dominican Republic	2003	6.04	2.16	....	1.56	1.95	—	0.12	1.55
253	El Salvador	2004	7.07	2.29	0.28	2.28	—	0.55	0.25	4.31
258	Guatemala	2004	....	....	....	....	....	....	....	....
343	Jamaica	2003	13.25	5.38	....	19.29	—	—	0.64	3.21
273	Mexico	2000	2.64	1.22	....	2.06	....	....	....	....
278	Nicaragua	2004	5.96p	3.06p	....	2.04p	—p	5.84p	2.38p	0.47p
283	Panama	2001	8.59	3.82	....	4.97	0.37	0.07	5.35	—
288	Paraguay	2003	....	....	....	....	....	....	....	....
293	Peru	2004	3.57p	3.57p	....	2.01p	—p	4.64p	2.74p	0.33p
361	St. Kitts and Nevis	2003	15.03	7.47	....	7.56	—	1.42	3.90	1.24
364	St. Vincent and the Grenadines	2003	....	....	....	....	....	....	....	....
298	Uruguay	2004	6.00p	3.90p	....	4.92p	2.52p	—p	10.20p	—p
299	Venezuela, Rep. Bol.	2003	4.86p	1.90p	....	4.69p	—p	11.55p	1.76p	0.39p

Table W6. Outlays by Function: General and Central Government

(Percent of Total Outlays)

			General Public Services	Defense	Public Order and Safety	Economic Affairs	Environ- mental Protection	Housing & Com- munity Amenities	Health	Recrea- tion, Culture, & Religion	Education	Social Protection
General Government												
	Industrial Countries											
111	United States...........................	2004	12.91	11.60	5.81	10.05	....	1.95	20.51	0.89	16.76	19.50
156	Canada...................................	2004	13.83p	2.71p	5.11p	8.81p	1.72p	2.08p	18.56p	2.60p	14.77p	29.81p
193	Australia.................................	2004	12.07	4.37	4.69	11.87	1.25	2.30	17.24	2.58	14.68	28.96
158	Japan.....................................	2003	14.46p	2.59p	3.75p	11.33p	3.76p	1.90p	18.15p	0.44p	10.78p	31.32p
196	New Zealand............................	2004	8.66p	2.50p	3.93p	8.26p	1.73p	2.13p	15.84p	5.00p	18.74p	33.20p
	Euro Area											
122	Austria...................................	2003	14.78	1.76	2.81	10.27	0.74	1.57	13.01	2.04	11.26	41.75
124	Belgium..................................	2003	38.04	2.28	3.80	9.98	1.38	0.71	13.49	2.38	15.73	43.31
172	Finland...................................	2004	....	....	....	....	....	....	....	....	....	....
132	France....................................	2004	....	....	....	....	....	....	....	....	....	....
134	Germany.................................	2004	....	....	....	....	....	....	....	....	....	....
174	Greece....................................	2000	....	....	....	....	....	....	....	....	....	....
136	Italy.......................................	2003	18.43	2.75	4.26	7.72	1.72	1.66	13.20	2.40	10.60	37.26
137	Luxembourg............................	2004	16.54p	0.66p	2.54p	11.12p	2.71p	2.25p	12.11p	4.85p	13.00p	61.04p
138	Netherlands............................	2004	16.14p	3.17p	3.83p	10.65p	1.78p	2.84p	9.73p	3.08p	11.40p	37.37p
182	Portugal.................................	2002	13.65	2.95	4.32	10.83	1.40	1.90	15.28	2.62	15.48	31.59
184	Spain.....................................	2003	....	....	....	....	....	....	....	....	....	....
128	Denmark.................................	2004	13.47p	2.88p	1.85p	6.53p	0.96p	1.27p	13.40p	3.09p	14.82p	41.74p
176	Iceland...................................	2002	16.06	—	4.20	14.85	....	2.46	19.86	6.51	15.75	20.32
142	Norway...................................	2004	9.35p	3.91p	2.38p	9.01p	1.33p	1.02p	17.19p	2.52p	13.59p	39.69p
135	San Marino..............................	2002	14.52	—	2.94	14.32	3.23	2.34	18.14	2.30	9.40	32.80
144	Sweden...................................	2003	14.04	3.53	2.45	8.50	0.57	1.54	12.40	1.85	12.65	42.45
146	Switzerland.............................	2002	†13.86	†3.17	†4.63	†11.38	†1.74	†1.17	†11.07	†2.46	†15.38	†35.13
112	United Kingdom.......................	2004	10.49	6.37	5.86	6.54	1.43	1.60	16.55	1.01	12.85	37.31
	Developing Countries											
	Africa											
612	Algeria....................................	2002	....	....	....	....	....	....	....	....	....	....
618	Burundi..................................	1999	....	....	....	....	....	....	....	....	....	....
622	Cameroon...............................	1999	....	....	....	....	....	....	....	....	....	....
636	Congo, Dem. Rep. of................	2002	....	....	....	....	....	....	....	....	....	....
634	Congo, Rep. of........................	2003	....	....	....	....	....	....	....	....	....	....
662	Côte d'Ivoire...........................	2003	....	....	....	....	....	....	....	....	....	....
644	Ethiopia.................................	2001	....	....	....	....	....	....	....	....	....	....
652	Ghana....................................	2004	....	....	....	....	....	....	....	....	....	....
656	Guinea...................................	1999	....	....	....	....	....	....	....	....	....	....
664	Kenya.....................................	2002	....	....	....	....	....	....	....	....	....	....
666	Lesotho..................................	2003	14.09p	5.79p	8.80p	8.25p	....	1.72p	6.32p	1.36p	24.10p	3.91p
674	Madagascar.............................	2004	....	....	....	....	....	....	....	....	....	....
684	Mauritius................................	2004	21.11	0.73	8.40	12.08	4.46	4.86	9.18	2.36	15.98	20.83
686	Morocco.................................	1999	....	....	....	....	....	....	....	....	....	....
728	Namibia..................................	2001	....	....	....	....	....	....	....	....	....	....
722	Senegal..................................	2001	....	....	....	....	....	....	....	....	....	....
718	Seychelles...............................	2002	35.74	3.65	3.76	7.67	....	2.53	6.33	1.10	9.82	14.00
724	Sierra Leone............................	1999	....	....	....	....	....	....	....	....	....	....
199	South Africa............................	2004	....	....	....	....	....	....	....	....	....	....
732	Sudan.....................................	1999	....	....	....	....	....	....	....	....	....	....
734	Swaziland...............................	2003	....	....	....	....	....	....	....	....	....	....
744	Tunisia...................................	2004	....	....	....	....	....	....	....	....	....	....
746	Uganda...................................	2003	....	....	....	....	....	....	....	....	....	....
754	Zambia...................................	1999	....	....	....	....	....	....	....	....	....	....
	Asia											
512	Afghanistan, I.R. of..................	2004	....	....	....	....	....	....	....	....	....	....
513	Bangladesh.............................	2003	....	....	....	....	....	....	....	....	....	....
514	Bhutan...................................	2004	36.44	—	5.64	29.84	—	5.12	8.49	1.59	13.30	—
522	Cambodia...............................	2004	....	....	....	....	....	....	....	....	....	....
924	China, P.R.: Mainland...............	2003	....	....	....	....	....	....	....	....	....	....

Table W6. Outlays by Function: General and Central Government

(Percent of Total Outlays)

			General Public Services	Defense	Public Order and Safety	Economic Affairs	Environ-mental Protection	Housing & Com-munity Amenities	Health	Recrea-tion, Culture, & Religion	Education	Social Protection
532	China, P.R.: Hong Kong	2003	17.30	—	10.07	10.14	3.64	11.24	12.55	3.11	19.78	12.16
546	China, P.R.: Macao	2004	16.51	—	17.25	13.55	2.38	0.89	10.46	14.84	14.03	10.10
819	Fiji	2004	....	....	....	....	....	....	....	....	....	
534	India	2003	....	....	....	....	....	....	....	....		
536	Indonesia	2004	....	....	....	....	....	....	....	....		
542	Korea, Rep. of	2001	....	....	....	....	....	....	....	....		
548	Malaysia	2003	....	....	....	....	....	....	....	....		
556	Maldives	2004	24.48p	9.95p	3.21p	15.88p	—p	11.29p	11.28p	—p	19.60p	4.31p
948	Mongolia	2003	....	....	....	....	....	....	....	....		
518	Myanmar	2002	....	....	....	....	....	....	....	....		
558	Nepal	2004	....	....	....	....	....	....	....	....		
564	Pakistan	2004	....	....	....	....	....	....	....	....		
853	Papua New Guinea	2002	....	....	....	....	....	....	....	....		
566	Philippines	2004	....	....	....	....	....	....	....	....		
576	Singapore	2004	9.03	28.83	6.15	12.10	....	13.23	5.75	0.06	21.60	3.24
524	Sri Lanka	2002	....	....	....	....	....	....	....	....		
578	Thailand	2004	....	....	....	....	....	....	....	....		
846	Vanuatu	1999	....	....	....	....	....	....	....	....		
582	Vietnam	2003	....	....	....	....	....	....	....	....		9.21p
	Europe (excluding industrial countries)											
914	Albania	2002	26.18	4.03	6.38	15.01	—	4.82	7.33	1.39	10.17	24.68
911	Armenia	2004	....	....	....	....	....	....	....	....		
912	Azerbaijan	1999	....	....	....	....	....	....	....	....		
913	Belarus	2004	9.55p	2.13p	4.51p	20.05p	1.38p	6.72p	10.29p	3.26p	13.36p	28.75p
963	Bosnia and Herzegovina	2003	....	....	....	....	....	....	....	....		
918	Bulgaria	2004	10.81	5.83	7.14	12.59	—	3.91	11.79	2.02	11.01	34.89
960	Croatia	2004	....	....	....	....	....	....	....	....		
423	Cyprus	1998	....	....	....	....	....	....	....	....		
935	Czech Republic	2004	11.29p	4.51p	3.87p	15.44p	2.85p	4.67p	14.82p	2.54p	9.86p	30.15p
939	Estonia	2001	....	....	....	....	....	....	....	....		
915	Georgia	2002	....	....	....	....	....	....	....	....		
944	Hungary	2003	....	....	....	....	....	....	....	....		
916	Kazakhstan	2004	15.51	4.50	9.21	15.23	0.63	5.36	10.19	3.41	14.81	21.15
917	Kyrgyz Republic	2001	....	....	....	....	....	....	....	....		
941	Latvia	2004	15.64	3.47	6.30	11.66	....	5.19	9.45	3.66	16.54	28.10
946	Lithuania	2004	11.75p	4.33p	5.57p	11.47p	1.34p	1.33p	13.82p	2.95p	17.73p	29.71p
181	Malta	2001	16.23	1.64	3.96	13.51	1.27	2.37	12.09	1.48	12.78	34.67
921	Moldova	2004	16.07	1.22	5.70	4.08	0.44	3.19	17.66	1.52	17.07	33.06
964	Poland	2003	12.10	2.92	4.31	7.35	1.85	2.87	9.58	1.64	13.08	44.29
968	Romania	2002	†11.86p	†4.13p	†6.87p	†15.42p	†0.36p	†5.77p	†11.50p	†2.35p	†12.10p	†29.81p
922	Russia Federation	2004	19.34	7.72	7.81	12.97	0.33	5.04	4.98	2.84	10.16	28.79
965	Serbia and Montenegro	2002	....	....	....	....	....	....	....	....		
936	Slovak Republic	2003	†11.89p	†4.33p	†4.77p	†11.13p	†1.82p	†2.71p	†20.03p	†2.10p	†10.41p	†31.60p
961	Slovenia	2004	11.14	2.80	4.00	9.78	1.62	1.38	13.62	2.71	15.61	37.35
923	Tajikistan	2004	....	....	....	....	....	....	....	....		
186	Turkey	2001	....	....	....	....	....	....	....	....		
926	Ukraine	2004	8.54p	3.60p	5.54p	15.17p	0.63p	2.12p	9.39p	1.98p	12.69p	40.34p
	Middle East											
419	Bahrain, Kingdom of	2004	....	....	....	....	....	....	....	....		
469	Egypt	2002	....	....	....	....	....	....	....	....		
429	Iran, I.R. of	2004	9.71p	12.81p	5.03p	21.89p	0.69p	5.49p	6.70p	3.20p	6.52p	27.95p
436	Israel	2004	15.95p	16.66p	3.77p	6.07p	1.77p	1.48p	12.15p	2.78p	15.86p	23.52p
439	Jordan	2003	....	....	....	....	....	....	....	....		
443	Kuwait	2003	9.24	15.93	8.65	12.91	0.10	7.08	6.22	3.17	12.46	14.64
446	Lebanon	2003	....	....	....	....	....	....	....	....		
449	Oman	2001	....	....	....	....	....	....	....	....		
463	Syrian Arab Republic	1999	....	....	....	....	....	....	....	....		
466	United Arab Emirates	1999	....	....	....	....	....	....	....	....		

Table W6. Outlays by Function: General and Central Government

(Percent of Total Outlays)

		General Public Services	Defense	Public Order and Safety	Economic Affairs	Environ-mental Protection	Housing & Community Amenities	Health	Recrea-tion, Culture, & Religion	Education	Social Protection
474	Yemen, Republic of....................	1999	....	....	....	....	....	....	....	....	....	....
	Western Hemisphere											
213	Argentina....................	2004	31.66p	1.97p	6.03p	7.34p	0.19p	1.96p	7.74p	0.39p	13.40p	25.81p
313	Bahamas, The....................	2004										
316	Barbados....................	2002	....	....	....	....	....	....	....	....	....	....
218	Bolivia....................	2004	18.50	4.83	5.99	19.67	1.52	3.83	9.37	1.69	19.69	14.90
223	Brazil....................	1998	....	....	....	....	....	....	....	....	....	....
228	Chile....................	2004	....	....	....	....	....	....	....	....	....	....
233	Colombia....................	2004	....	....	....	....	....	....	....	....	....	....
238	Costa Rica....................	2003	21.62	—	7.34	9.47	—	2.05	20.29	0.76	21.04	16.83
243	Dominican Republic....................	2003										
253	El Salvador....................	2004										
258	Guatemala....................	2004										
343	Jamaica....................	2003										
273	Mexico....................	2000										
278	Nicaragua....................	2004										
283	Panama....................	2001										
288	Paraguay....................	2003	....	....	....	....	....	....	....	....	....	....
293	Peru....................	2004	....	....	....	....	....	....	....	....	....	....
361	St. Kitts and Nevis....................	2003	....	....	....	....	....	....	....	....	....	....
364	St. Vincent and the Grenadines................	2003	43.26	—	8.00	9.43	1.42	1.55	10.72	0.25	13.94	11.43
298	Uruguay....................	2004	....	....	....	....	....	....	....	....	....	....
299	Venezuela, Rep. Bol....................	2003	....	....	....	....	....	....	....	....	....	....

Central Government

		General Public Services	Defense	Public Order and Safety	Economic Affairs	Environ-mental Protection	Housing & Community Amenities	Health	Recrea-tion, Culture, & Religion	Education	Social Protection
	Industrial Countries											
111	United States....................	2004	11.81	20.18	1.50	6.53	....	1.91	24.15	0.18	2.75	30.99
156	Canada....................	2004	24.27p	5.93p	3.70p	5.94p	0.68p	1.22p	9.43p	1.72p	2.08p	45.03p
193	Australia....................	2004	25.40	5.89	1.04	6.37	0.20	0.64	14.30	0.87	9.27	36.02
158	Japan....................	2003	....	....	....	....	....	....	....	....	....	....
196	New Zealand....................	2004	7.45p	2.68p	4.33p	6.91p	−0.42p	1.60p	17.39p	3.48p	20.58p	36.01p
	Euro Area											
122	Austria....................	2003	15.16	2.24	3.09	6.27	0.30	1.12	14.19	0.71	9.77	47.16
124	Belgium....................	2003	36.38	2.72	2.66	5.19	0.04	0.04	15.54	0.22	2.65	43.96
172	Finland....................	2004	....	....	....	....	....	....	....	....	....	....
132	France....................	2004	....	....	....	....	....	....	....	....	....	....
134	Germany....................	2004	....	....	....	....	....	....	....	....	....	....
174	Greece....................	2000	....	....	....	....	....	....	....	....	....	....
136	Italy....................	2003	28.61	3.36	4.63	3.92	0.39	0.08	3.05	1.68	10.16	44.12
137	Luxembourg....................	2004	14.86p	0.70p	2.47p	9.52p	1.36p	1.40p	12.93p	3.42p	10.41p	64.67p
138	Netherlands....................	2004	20.45p	3.59p	4.03p	6.59p	0.38p	0.66p	10.37p	0.83p	11.14p	41.95p
182	Portugal....................	2002	16.61	3.24	4.52	8.15	0.33	0.16	15.95	1.05	15.66	34.34
184	Spain....................	2003	....	....	....	....	....	....	....	....	....	....
128	Denmark....................	2004	28.14p	4.55p	2.69p	6.30p	0.62p	1.32p	0.93p	2.51p	12.21p	40.73p
176	Iceland....................	2002	18.47	—	4.91	15.71	....	0.91	26.24	3.14	9.96	20.67
142	Norway....................	2004	16.74p	4.85p	2.55p	9.91p	0.33p	0.17p	16.25p	1.24p	6.25p	41.71p
135	San Marino....................	2002	14.52	—	2.94	14.32	3.23	2.34	18.14	2.30	9.40	32.80
144	Sweden....................	2003	21.30	5.48	3.09	9.90	0.43	0.55	3.31	0.88	6.11	48.95
146	Switzerland....................	2002	†17.91	†5.73	†0.85	†13.49	†0.26	†0.58	†0.28	†0.61	†3.92	†56.38
112	United Kingdom....................	2004	....	....	....	....	....	....	....	....	....	....
	Developing Countries											
	Africa											
612	Algeria....................	2002	....	....	....	....	....	....	....	....	....	....
618	Burundi....................	1999	....	....	....	....	....	....	....	....	....	....
622	Cameroon....................	1999	....	....	....	....	....	....	....	....	....	....
636	Congo, Dem. Rep. of....................	2002	....	....	....	....	....	....	....	....	....	....
634	Congo, Rep. of....................	2003	69.21	9.52	4.09	10.38	0.30	4.36	3.81	3.43	3.53	0.81
662	Côte d'Ivoire....................	2003	....	....	....	....	....	....	....	....	....	....
644	Ethiopia....................	2001	....	....	....	....	....	....	....	....	....	....

Table W6. Outlays by Function: General and Central Government

(Percent of Total Outlays)

			General Public Services	Defense	Public Order and Safety	Economic Affairs	Environmental Protection	Housing & Community Amenities	Health	Recreation, Culture, & Religion	Education	Social Protection
652	Ghana......................	2004	....	....	....	....	....	....	....	....	....	....
656	Guinea......................	1999	....	....	....	....	....	....	....	....	....	....
664	Kenya......................	2002	....	....	....	....	....	....	....	....	....	....
666	Lesotho......................	2003	14.09p	5.79p	8.80p	8.25p	....	1.72p	6.32p	1.36p	24.10p	3.91p
674	Madagascar..............	2004	40.02	5.03	1.83	30.96	—	—	7.52	0.11	13.29	1.25
684	Mauritius..................	2004	25.56	0.74	8.49	10.64	3.86	3.29	9.02	1.90	15.82	20.68
686	Morocco....................	1999	40.50	12.92	6.95	8.06	—	0.45	3.22	0.81	17.78	9.30
728	Namibia....................	2001	....	....	....	....	....	....	....	....	....	....
722	Senegal....................	2001	....	....	....	....	....	....	....	....	....	....
718	Seychelles................	2002	35.74	3.65	3.76	7.67	....	2.53	6.33	1.10	9.82	14.00
724	Sierra Leone.............	1999	....	....	....	....	....	....	....	....	....	....
199	South Africa..............	2004	....	....	....	....	....	....	....	....	....	....
732	Sudan......................	1999	....	....	....	....	....	....	....	....	....	....
734	Swaziland.................	2003	....	....	....	....	....	....	....	....	....	....
744	Tunisia.....................	2004	15.94p	4.89p	7.71p	16.62p	....	5.32p	5.33p	2.96p	19.96p	21.26p
746	Uganda.....................	2003	....	....	....	....	....	....	....	....	....	....
754	Zambia.....................	1999	....	....	....	....	....	....	....	....	....	....
	Asia											
512	Afghanistan, I.R. of......	2004	....	....	....	....	....	....	....	....	....	....
513	Bangladesh................	2003	28.29	10.09	5.73	18.47	0.12	7.73	6.75	1.38	17.94	3.49
514	Bhutan.....................	2004	36.44	—	5.64	29.84	—	5.12	8.49	1.59	13.30	—
522	Cambodia..................	2004	....	....	....	....	....	....	....	....	....	....
924	China, P.R.: Mainland.....	2003	....	....	....	....	....	....	....	....	....	....
532	China, P.R.: Hong Kong...	2003	....	....	....	....	....	....	....	....	....	....
546	China, P.R.: Macao........	2004	16.51	—	17.25	13.55	2.38	0.89	10.46	14.84	14.03	10.10
819	Fiji.........................	2004	....	....	....	....	....	....	....	....	....	....
534	India.......................	2003	60.63p	13.41p	....	16.82p	....	5.28p	1.50p	....	2.36p	....
536	Indonesia..................	2004	74.06p	6.59p	0.70p	6.23p	....	0.85p	1.38p	0.59p	3.97p	5.64p
542	Korea, Republic of........	2001	25.23	12.52	5.05	21.52	....	2.19	0.44	1.01	17.72	14.33
548	Malaysia...................	2003	....	....	....	....	....	....	....	....	....	....
556	Maldives...................	2004	24.48p	9.95p	3.21p	15.88p	—p	11.29p	11.28p	—p	19.60p	4.31p
948	Mongolia...................	2003	....	....	....	....	....	....	....	....	....	....
518	Myanmar...................	2002	23.37	21.53	—	31.43	—	1.00	5.33	0.67	14.63	2.03
558	Nepal.......................	2004	24.56p	10.17p	8.36p	24.68p	—p	4.39p	5.34p	—p	17.47p	5.03p
564	Pakistan...................	2004	66.46	19.94	1.70	8.47	0.02	0.33	0.79	0.25	1.88	0.17
853	Papua New Guinea........	2002	....	....	....	....	....	....	....	....	....	....
566	Philippines................	2004	....	....	....	....	....	....	....	....	....	....
576	Singapore..................	2004	9.03	28.83	6.15	12.10	....	13.23	5.75	0.06	21.60	3.24
524	Sri Lanka...................	2002	....	....	....	....	....	....	....	....	....	....
578	Thailand...................	2004	15.64p	6.55p	5.47p	24.30p	0.91p	0.88p	9.52p	0.60p	21.38p	14.74p
846	Vanuatu....................	1999	....	....	....	....	....	....	....	....	....	....
582	Vietnam....................	2003	....	....	....	....	....	....	....	....	....	....
	Europe (excluding industrial countries)											
914	Albania....................	2002	....	....	....	....	....	....	....	....	....	....
911	Armenia....................	2004	....	....	....	....	....	....	....	....	....	....
912	Azerbaijan.................	1999	32.32f	11.08f	11.33f	8.50f	....	0.04f	0.81f	1.28f	3.20f	33.14f
913	Belarus....................	2004	19.04p	3.12p	5.61p	21.23p	0.51p	0.30p	3.29p	2.12p	3.78p	41.00p
963	Bonsia and Herzegovina...	2003	....	....	....	....	....	....	....	....	....	....
918	Bulgaria...................	2004	21.06	6.02	7.37	11.75	—	0.71	11.57	1.38	4.95	35.19
960	Croatia....................	2004	9.40	3.88	5.76	8.25	0.25	2.65	13.35	1.30	7.60	36.52
423	Cyprus.....................	1998	22.37	3.94	5.30	13.43	....	3.94	6.32	1.64	11.84	24.52
935	Czech Republic...........	2004	13.26p	5.26p	4.07p	13.60p	1.47p	2.49p	16.69p	1.03p	9.55p	32.58p
939	Estonia....................	2001	19.43	4.96	7.17	9.46	....	—	16.29	3.96	7.31	31.43
915	Georgia....................	2002	36.37	5.11	8.56	7.82	....	0.46	5.41	2.79	4.69	28.80
944	Hungary...................	2003	....	....	....	....	....	....	....	....	....	....
916	Kazakhstan................	2004	30.62	5.08	9.99	17.69	0.57	2.77	3.08	2.00	3.64	24.55
917	Kyrgyz Republic...........	2001	....	....	....	....	....	....	....	....	....	....
941	Latvia......................	2004	22.25	4.29	7.28	13.66	....	1.45	11.01	2.15	6.10	31.81

Table W6. Outlays by Function: General and Central Government

(Percent of Total Outlays)

			General Public Services	Defense	Public Order and Safety	Economic Affairs	Environ-mental Protection	Housing & Com-munity Amenities	Health	Recrea-tion, Culture, & Religion	Education	Social Protection
946	Lithuania	2004	23.91p	4.72p	5.95p	11.45p	0.80p	−0.03p	14.82p	1.82p	7.32p	29.25p
181	Malta	2001	16.23	1.64	3.96	13.51	1.27	2.37	12.09	1.48	12.78	34.67
921	Moldova	2004	19.13	1.44	5.88	3.98	0.53	0.03	20.89	0.78	7.98	39.35
964	Poland	2003	12.47	3.36	4.70	5.95	0.35	0.80	10.63	0.60	11.69	49.43
968	Romania	2002	†12.99p	†5.04p	†8.12p	†15.99p	†0.45p	†1.97p	†13.95p	†1.50p	†6.56p	†33.46p
922	Russia Federation	2004	29.15	12.04	9.59	5.08	0.33	—	1.24	2.06	3.27	37.23
965	Serbia and Montenegro	2002	....	....	....	....	....	....	....	....	....	....
936	Slovak Republic	2003	†20.64p	†4.70p	†5.00p	†10.17p	†0.75p	†0.84p	†20.29p	†1.19p	†3.40p	†33.17p
961	Slovenia	2004	12.27	3.11	4.27	8.94	0.82	0.31	14.71	1.72	12.57	41.28
923	Tajikistan	2004	....	....	....	....	....	....	....	....	....	....
186	Turkey	2001	....	....	....	....	....	....	....	....	....	....
926	Ukraine	2004	21.92p	4.26p	6.43p	13.58p	0.45p	0.53p	3.93p	0.91p	6.25p	41.74p
	Middle East											
419	Bahrain, Kingdom of	2004	37.80p	16.35p	10.24p	1.81p	—p	3.03p	8.03p	0.20p	15.40p	7.15p
469	Egypt	2002	....	....	....	....	....	....	....	....	....	....
429	Iran, I.R. of	2004	10.29p	13.57p	5.33p	20.17p	0.63p	5.39p	7.09p	2.94p	6.91p	27.68p
436	Israel	2004	16.24p	17.83p	3.76p	5.56p	0.25p	1.25p	12.97p	1.82p	15.34p	24.97p
439	Jordan	2003	....	....	....	....	....	....	....	....	....	....
443	Kuwait	2003	9.24	15.93	8.65	12.91	0.10	7.08	6.22	3.17	12.46	14.64
446	Lebanon	2003	....	....	....	....	....	....	....	....	....	....
449	Oman	2001	....	....	....	....	....	....	....	....	....	....
463	Syrian Arab Rep.	1999	12.91	23.64	—	44.04	....	1.00	2.34	1.54	9.21	5.31
466	United Arab Emirates	1999	20.78p	30.06p	13.78p	4.54p	—p	1.64p	7.22p	1.45p	17.33p	3.20p
474	Yemen, Republic of	1999	....	....	....	....	....	....	....	....	....	....
	Western Hemisphere											
213	Argentina	2004	32.65	3.04	4.40	7.17	0.29	1.83	5.30	0.18	5.19	39.94
313	Bahamas, The	2004	....	....	....	....	....	....	....	....	....	....
316	Barbados	2002	....	....	....	....	....	....	....	....	....	....
218	Bolivia	2004	20.34	5.64	6.84	17.37	0.70	0.81	9.88	0.46	21.71	16.25
223	Brazil	1998	28.44	3.49	3.19	4.84	....	0.64	6.21	0.07	6.14	47.26
228	Chile	2004	9.53	7.05	6.28	12.13	0.33	1.12	13.99	0.63	18.12	30.83
233	Colombia	2004	....	....	....	....	....	....	....	....	....	....
238	Costa Rica	2003	22.21	—	7.55	9.73	—	0.03	20.85	0.78	21.61	17.29
243	Dominican Republic	2003	24.88	4.49	4.83	16.31	0.74	6.30	9.52	0.84	12.59	19.51
253	El Salvador	2004	....	....	....	....	....	....	....	....	....	....
258	Guatemala	2004	....	....	....	....	....	....	....	....	....	....
343	Jamaica	2003	....	....	....	....	....	....	....	....	....	....
273	Mexico	2000	38.36	3.04	2.72	8.11	....	6.92	4.95	0.56	24.73	20.12
278	Nicaragua	2004	....	....	....	....	....	....	....	....	....	....
283	Panama	2001	27.55	—	6.67	5.99	—	3.66	17.98	1.33	16.25	20.57
288	Paraguay	2003	....	....	....	....	....	....	....	....	....	....
293	Peru	2004	....	....	....	....	....	....	....	....	....	....
361	St. Kitts and Nevis	2003	....	....	....	....	....	....	....	....	....	....
364	St. Vincent and the Grenadines	2003	....	....	....	....	....	....	....	....	....	....
298	Uruguay	2004	....	....	....	....	....	....	....	....	....	....
299	Venezuela, Rep. Bol.	2003	47.66p	4.41p	2.97p	5.01p	—p	3.46p	7.55p	1.54p	18.51p	8.90p

COUNTRY TABLES

Afghanistan, Islamic Republic of   512

In Millions of Afghanis / Year Ending March 20 / Cash Reporter

	Budgetary Central Government			Extrabudgetary Accounts			Central Government			General Government		
	2002	2003	2004	2002	2003	2004	2002	2003	2004	2002	2003	2004
Statement of government operations												
Statement of other economic flows												
Balance sheet												
6 *Net worth*............	....	....	....	....	....	....	....	....	....	....	....	....
61 Nonfinancial assets.................	....	....	....	....	....	....	....	....	....	....	....	....
62 Financial assets.....................	....	....	....	....	....	....	....	....	....	....	....	....
63 Liabilities.........................	....	20,020	29,209	....	....	....	....	....	....	....	....	....
Statement of sources and uses of cash												
1 Cash receipts from operating activities...........	....	26,612	39,787	....	....	....	....	....	....	....	....	....
11 Taxes..........................	....	5,456	9,722	....	....	....	....	....	....	....	....	....
12 Social contributions................	....	72	314	....	....	....	....	....	....	....	....	....
13 Grants............................	....	16,343	27,007	....	....	....	....	....	....	....	....	....
14 Other receipts......................	....	4,740	2,743	....	....	....	....	....	....	....	....	....
2 Cash payments for operating activities...........	....	24,367	36,281	....	....	....	....	....	....	....	....	....
21 Compensation of employees............	....	11,729	15,262	....	....	....	....	....	....	....	....	....
22 Purchases of goods and services..................	....	10,922	18,649	....	....	....	....	....	....	....	....	....
24 Interest...........................	....	42	98	....	....	....	....	....	....	....	....	....
25 Subsidies.........................	....	181	48	....	....	....	....	....	....	....	....	....
26 Grants...........................	....	768	284	....	....	....	....	....	....	....	....	....
27 Social benefits......................	....	686	1,366	....	....	....	....	....	....	....	....	....
28 Other payments.....................	....	39	574	....	....	....	....	....	....	....	....	....
CIO *Net cash inflow from oper. activities.....*	....	*2,244*	*3,506*	....	....	....	....	....	....	....	....	....
31.1 Purchases of nonfinancial assets.................	....	6,205	5,389	....	....	....	....	....	....	....	....	....
31.2 Sales of nonfinancial assets.....................	....	25	32	....	....	....	....	....	....	....	....	....
31 Net cash outflow from investments in nonfinancial assets................	....	6,180	5,357	....	....	....	....	....	....	....	....	....
CSD *Cash surplus/deficit.................*	....	*−3,936*	*−1,851*	....	....	....	....	....	....	....	....	....
32x Net acquisition of fin assets, excl. cash...........	....	—	268	....	....	....	....	....	....	....	....	....
321x Domestic........................	....	—	268	....	....	....	....	....	....	....	....	....
322x Foreign.........................	....	—	—	....	....	....	....	....	....	....	....	....
323 Monetary gold and SDRs................	....	—	—	....	....	....	....	....	....	....	....	....
33 Net incurrence of liabilities.............	....	4,587	9,969	....	....	....	....	....	....	....	....	....
331 Domestic........................	....	—	724	....	....	....	....	....	....	....	....	....
332 Foreign.........................	....	4,587	9,245	....	....	....	....	....	....	....	....	....
NFB Net cash inflow from fin. activities.........	....	4,587	9,701	....	....	....	....	....	....	....	....	....
NCB *Net change in the stock of cash.............*	....	*651*	*7,850*	....	....	....	....	....	....	....	....	....
Table 1 Revenue												
1 **Revenue**...................	....	26,612	39,787	....	....	....	....	....	....	....	....	....
11 **Taxes**.....................	....	5,456	9,722	....	....	....	....	....	....	....	....	....
111 Taxes on income, profits, & capital gains......	....	365	1,014	....	....	....	....	....	....	....	....	....
1111 Individuals........................	....	212	370	....	....	....	....	....	....	....	....	....
1112 Corporations and other enterprises.............	....	154	643	....	....	....	....	....	....	....	....	....
112 Taxes on payroll and workforce..................	....	—	—	....	....	....	....	....	....	....	....	....
113 Taxes on property.....................	....	36	54	....	....	....	....	....	....	....	....	....
114 Taxes on goods and services........................	....	282	1,185	....	....	....	....	....	....	....	....	....
1141 General taxes on goods and services..........	....	266	1,170	....	....	....	....	....	....	....	....	....
1142 Excises.........................	....	—	—	....	....	....	....	....	....	....	....	....
115 Taxes on int'l. trade and transactions...........	....	4,565	7,021	....	....	....	....	....	....	....	....	....
116 Other taxes.......................	....	208	449	....	....	....	....	....	....	....	....	....
12 **Social contributions**................	....	72	314	....	....	....	....	....	....	....	....	....
121 Social security contributions..............	....	72	314	....	....	....	....	....	....	....	....	....
122 Other social contributions..............	....	—	—	....	....	....	....	....	....	....	....	....
13 **Grants**..................	....	16,343	27,007	....	....	....	....	....	....	....	....	....
131 From foreign governments................	....	....	4,373	....	....	....	....	....	....	....	....	....
132 From international organizations................	....	....	22,634	....	....	....	....	....	....	....	....	....
133 From other general government units...........	....	....	—	....	....	....	....	....	....	....	....	....
14 **Other revenue**..................	....	4,740	2,743	....	....	....	....	....	....	....	....	....
Table 2 Expense by economic type												
2 **Expense**.....................	....	24,367	36,281	....	....	....	....	....	....	....	....	....
21 **Compensation of employees**....................	....	11,729	15,262	....	....	....	....	....	....	....	....	....
211 Wages and salaries................	....	11,729	15,262	....	....	....	....	....	....	....	....	....
212 Social contributions.................	....	—	—	....	....	....	....	....	....	....	....	....
22 **Use of goods and services**..................	....	10,922	18,649	....	....	....	....	....	....	....	....	....
23 **Consumption of fixed capital**...............	....	....	....	....	....	....	....	....	....	....	....	....
24 **Interest**.....................	....	42	98	....	....	....	....	....	....	....	....	....
25 **Subsidies**.....................	....	181	48	....	....	....	....	....	....	....	....	....

	Budgetary Central Government			Extrabudgetary Accounts			Central Government			General Government		
	2002	2003	2004	2002	2003	2004	2002	2003	2004	2002	2003	2004
26 **Grants**.........................	....	768	284	....	....	....	....	....	....	....	....	....
261 To foreign govenments...................	....	—	—	....	....	....	....	....	....	....	....	....
262 To international organizations.............	....	—	—	....	....	....	....	....	....	....	....	....
263 To other general government units..............	....	768	284	....	....	....	....	....	....	....	....	....
2631 Current.................	....	768	215	....	....	....	....	....	....	....	....	....
2632 Capital.................	....	—	70	....	....	....	....	....	....	....	....	....
27 **Social benefits**..................	....	686	1,366	....	....	....	....	....	....	....	....	....
28 **Other expense**......................	....	39	574	....	....	....	....	....	....	....	....	....
281 Property expense other than interest............	....	—	—	....	....	....	....	....	....	....	....	....
282 Miscellaneous other expense..................	....	39	574	....	....	....	....	....	....	....	....	....
2821 Current..................	....	39	561	....	....	....	....	....	....	....	....	....
2822 Capital..................	....	—	13	....	....	....	....	....	....	....	....	....
Table 3 Transactions in assets and liabilities												
3 **Change in net worth from transactns**....	....	....	....	....	....	....	....	....	....	....	....	....
31 **Net acquisition of nonfinancial assets**...	....	6,180	5,357	....	....	....	....	....	....	....	....	....
311 Fixed assets......................	....	6,203	5,386	....	....	....	....	....	....	....	....	....
3111 Buildings and structures....................	....	1,552	3,425	....	....	....	....	....	....	....	....	....
3112 Machinery and equipment..................	....	4,651	1,962	....	....	....	....	....	....	....	....	....
3113 Other fixed assets.....................	....	—	—	....	....	....	....	....	....	....	....	....
312 Inventories.....................	....	—	—	....	....	....	....	....	....	....	....	....
313 Valuables.....................	....	2	—	....	....	....	....	....	....	....	....	....
314 Nonproduced assets.....................	....	−25	−29	....	....	....	....	....	....	....	....	....
3141 Land.....................	....	−7	−29	....	....	....	....	....	....	....	....	....
3142 Subsoil assets.....................	....	−18	—	....	....	....	....	....	....	....	....	....
3143 Other naturally occurring assets.................	....	—	—	....	....	....	....	....	....	....	....	....
3144 Intangible nonproduced assets...........	....	—	—	....	....	....	....	....	....	....	....	....
32 **Net acquisition of financial assets**........	....	651	8,118	....	....	....	....	....	....	....	....	....
321 Domestic....................	....	8	2,373	....	....	....	....	....	....	....	....	....
3212 Currency and deposits..................	....	8	2,105	....	....	....	....	....	....	....	....	....
3213 Securities other than shares....................	....	—	—	....	....	....	....	....	....	....	....	....
3214 Loans.....................	....	—	268	....	....	....	....	....	....	....	....	....
3215 Shares and other equity.....................	....	—	—	....	....	....	....	....	....	....	....	....
3216 Insurance technical reserves.....................	....	—	—	....	....	....	....	....	....	....	....	....
3217 Financial derivatives.....................	....	—	—	....	....	....	....	....	....	....	....	....
3218 Other accounts receivable.....................	....	....	....	....	....	....	....	....	....	....	....	....
322 Foreign....................	....	643	5,745	....	....	....	....	....	....	....	....	....
3222 Currency and deposits....................	....	643	5,745	....	....	....	....	....	....	....	....	....
3223 Securities other than shares....................	....	—	—	....	....	....	....	....	....	....	....	....
3224 Loans.....................	....	—	—	....	....	....	....	....	....	....	....	....
3225 Shares and other equity.....................	....	—	—	....	....	....	....	....	....	....	....	....
3226 Insurance technical reserves....................	....	—	—	....	....	....	....	....	....	....	....	....
3227 Financial derivatives.....................	....	—	—	....	....	....	....	....	....	....	....	....
3228 Other accounts receivable................	....	....	....	....	....	....	....	....	....	....	....	....
323 Monetary gold and SDRs.................	....	....	....	....	....	....	....	....	....	....	....	....
33 **Net incurrence of liabilities**...................	....	4,587	9,969	....	....	....	....	....	....	....	....	....
331 Domestic.....................	....	—	724	....	....	....	....	....	....	....	....	....
3312 Currency and deposits.....................	....	—	724	....	....	....	....	....	....	....	....	....
3313 Securities other than shares....................	....	—	—	....	....	....	....	....	....	....	....	....
3314 Loans.....................	....	—	—	....	....	....	....	....	....	....	....	....
3316 Insurance technical reserves....................	....	—	—	....	....	....	....	....	....	....	....	....
3317 Financial derivatives.....................	....	—	—	....	....	....	....	....	....	....	....	....
3318 Other accounts payable....................	....	....	....	....	....	....	....	....	....	....	....	....
332 Foreign....................	....	4,587	9,245	....	....	....	....	....	....	....	....	....
3322 Currency and deposits....................	....	—	—	....	....	....	....	....	....	....	....	....
3323 Securities other than shares....................	....	—	—	....	....	....	....	....	....	....	....	....
3324 Loans.....................	....	4,587	9,245	....	....	....	....	....	....	....	....	....
3326 Insurance technical reserves....................	....	—	—	....	....	....	....	....	....	....	....	....
3327 Financial derivatives....................	....	—	—	....	....	....	....	....	....	....	....	....
3328 Other accounts payable...........................	....	....	....	....	....	....	....	....	....	....	....	....

Afghanistan, Islamic Republic of   512

In Millions of Afghanis / Year Ending March 20 / Cash Reporter

	Budgetary Central Government			Extrabudgetary Accounts			Central Government			General Government		
	2002	2003	2004	2002	2003	2004	2002	2003	2004	2002	2003	2004
Table 4 Holding gains in assets and liabilities												
Table 5 Other changes in the volume of assets and liabilities												
Table 6 Balance sheet												
6 Net worth....................	....	....	....	....	....	....	....	....	....	....	....	....
61 Nonfinancial assets....................	....	....	....	....	....	....	....	....	....	....	....	....
611 Fixed assets....................	....	....	....	....	....	....	....	....	....	....	....	....
6111 Buildings and structures....................	....	....	....	....	....	....	....	....	....	....	....	....
6112 Machinery and equipment....................	....	....	....	....	....	....	....	....	....	....	....	....
6113 Other fixed assets....................	....	....	....	....	....	....	....	....	....	....	....	....
612 Inventories....................	....	....	....	....	....	....	....	....	....	....	....	....
613 Valuables....................	....	....	....	....	....	....	....	....	....	....	....	....
614 Nonproduced assets....................	....	....	....	....	....	....	....	....	....	....	....	....
6141 Land....................	....	....	....	....	....	....	....	....	....	....	....	....
6142 Subsoil assets....................	....	....	....	....	....	....	....	....	....	....	....	....
6143 Other naturally occurring assets....................	....	....	....	....	....	....	....	....	....	....	....	....
6144 Intangible nonproduced assets....................	....	....	....	....	....	....	....	....	....	....	....	....
62 Financial assets....................	....	....	....	....	....	....	....	....	....	....	....	....
621 Domestic....................	....	....	....	....	....	....	....	....	....	....	....	....
6212 Currency and deposits....................	....	....	....	....	....	....	....	....	....	....	....	....
6213 Securities other than shares....................	....	....	....	....	....	....	....	....	....	....	....	....
6214 Loans....................	....	....	....	....	....	....	....	....	....	....	....	....
6215 Shares and other equity....................	....	....	....	....	....	....	....	....	....	....	....	....
6216 Insurance technical reserves....................	....	....	....	....	....	....	....	....	....	....	....	....
6217 Financial derivatives....................	....	....	....	....	....	....	....	....	....	....	....	....
6218 Other accounts receivable....................	....	....	....	....	....	....	....	....	....	....	....	....
622 Foreign....................	....	....	....	....	....	....	....	....	....	....	....	....
6222 Currency and deposits....................	....	....	....	....	....	....	....	....	....	....	....	....
6223 Securities other than shares....................	....	....	....	....	....	....	....	....	....	....	....	....
6224 Loans....................	....	....	....	....	....	....	....	....	....	....	....	....
6225 Shares and other equity....................	....	....	....	....	....	....	....	....	....	....	....	....
6226 Insurance technical reserves....................	....	....	....	....	....	....	....	....	....	....	....	....
6227 Financial derivatives....................	....	....	....	....	....	....	....	....	....	....	....	....
6228 Other accounts receivable....................	....	....	....	....	....	....	....	....	....	....	....	....
623 Monetary gold and SDRs....................	....	....	....	....	....	....	....	....	....	....	....	....
63 Liabilities....................	....	**20,020**	**29,209**	....	....	....	....	....	....	....	....	....
631 Domestic....................	....	—	—	....	....	....	....	....	....	....	....	....
6312 Currency and deposits....................	....	....	....	....	....	....	....	....	....	....	....	....
6313 Securities other than shares....................	....	....	....	....	....	....	....	....	....	....	....	....
6314 Loans....................	....	....	....	....	....	....	....	....	....	....	....	....
6316 Insurance technical reserves....................	....	....	....	....	....	....	....	....	....	....	....	....
6317 Financial derivatives....................	....	....	....	....	....	....	....	....	....	....	....	....
6318 Other accounts payable....................	....	....	....	....	....	....	....	....	....	....	....	....
632 Foreign....................	....	20,020	29,209	....	....	....	....	....	....	....	....	....
6322 Currency and deposits....................	....	....	....	....	....	....	....	....	....	....	....	....
6323 Securities other than shares....................	....	....	....	....	....	....	....	....	....	....	....	....
6324 Loans....................	....	....	....	....	....	....	....	....	....	....	....	....
6326 Insurance technical reserves....................	....	....	....	....	....	....	....	....	....	....	....	....
6327 Financial derivatives....................	....	....	....	....	....	....	....	....	....	....	....	....
6328 Other accounts payable....................	....	....	....	....	....	....	....	....	....	....	....	....
Memorandum items:												
6M2 Net financial worth....................	....	....	....	....	....	....	....	....	....	....	....	....
6M3 Debt at market value....................	....	....	....	....	....	....	....	....	....	....	....	....
6M4 Debt at nominal value....................	....	....	....	....	....	....	....	....	....	....	....	....
6M5 Arrears....................	....	....	....	....	....	....	....	....	....	....	....	....
6M6 Obligations for social security benefits....................	....	....	....	....	....	....	....	....	....	....	....	....
6M7 Contingent liabilities....................	....	....	....	....	....	....	....	....	....	....	....	....
6M8 Uncapitalized military weapons, systems....................	....	....	....	....	....	....	....	....	....	....	....	....
Table 7 Outlays by functions of govt.												
7 Total outlays....................	....	**30,548**	**41,638**	....	....	....	....	....	....	....	....	....
701 General public services....................	....	**4,797**	**3,251**	....	....	....	....	....	....	....	....	....
7017 Public debt transactions....................	....	42	98	....	....	....	....	....	....	....	....	....
7018 General transfers between levels of govt.....	....	....	....	....	....	....	....	....	....	....	....	....
702 Defense....................	....	**5,991**	**5,759**	....	....	....	....	....	....	....	....	....
703 Public order and safety....................	....	**5,397**	**8,141**	....	....	....	....	....	....	....	....	....

In Millions of Afghanis / Year Ending March 20 / Cash Reporter

		Budgetary Central Government			Extrabudgetary Accounts			Central Government			General Government		
		2002	2003	2004	2002	2003	2004	2002	2003	2004	2002	2003	2004
704	**Economic affairs**..................	....	**7,247**	**13,067**	....	....	....	....	....	....	....	....	....
7042	Agriculture, forestry, fishing, and hunting.....	....	1,627	6,501	....	....	....	....	....	....	....	....	....
7043	Fuel and energy....................	....	1,053	376	....	....	....	....	....	....	....	....	....
7044	Mining, manufacturing, and construction.....	....	1,390	180	....	....	....	....	....	....	....	....	....
7045	Transport............................	....	1,995	5,190	....	....	....	....	....	....	....	....	....
7046	Communication....................	....	....	....	....	....	....	....	....	....	....	....	....
705	**Environmental protection**....................	....	—	—	....	....	....	....	....	....	....	....	....
706	**Housing and community amenities**........	....	**205**	**552**	....	....	....	....	....	....	....	....	....
707	**Health**....................	....	**1,211**	**3,017**	....	....	....	....	....	....	....	....	....
7072	Outpatient services....................	....	58	....	....	....	....	....	....	....	....	....	....
7073	Hospital services....................	....	312	....	....	....	....	....	....	....	....	....	....
7074	Public health services....................	....	....	....	....	....	....	....	....	....	....	....	....
708	**Recreation, culture, and religion**..........	....	**509**	**642**	....	....	....	....	....	....	....	....	....
709	**Education**....................	....	**3,912**	**5,793**	....	....	....	....	....	....	....	....	....
7091	Pre-primary and primary education..............	....	....	....	....	....	....	....	....	....	....	....	....
7092	Secondary education....................	....	3,806	5,550	....	....	....	....	....	....	....	....	....
7094	Tertiary education....................	....	99	227	....	....	....	....	....	....	....	....	....
710	**Social protection**....................	....	**560**	**1,447**	....	....	....	....	....	....	....	....	....
7	Statistical discrepancy: Total outlays..............	....	718	−32	....	....	....	....	....	....	....	....	....
Table 8	**Transactions in financial assets and liabilities by sector**												
82	**Net acquisition of financial assets**........	....	**651**	**8,118**	....	....	....	....	....	....	....	....	....
821	Domestic....................	....	8	2,373	....	....	....	....	....	....	....	....	....
8211	General government....................	....	—	96	....	....	....	....	....	....	....	....	....
8212	Central bank....................	....	8	....	....	....	....	....	....	....	....	....	....
8213	Other depository corporations....................	....	—	....	....	....	....	....	....	....	....	....	....
8214	Financial corporations n.e.c....................	....	—	....	....	....	....	....	....	....	....	....	....
8215	Nonfinancial corporations....................	....	—	173	....	....	....	....	....	....	....	....	....
8216	Households & NPIs serving households......	....	—	....	....	....	....	....	....	....	....	....	....
822	Foreign....................	....	643	5,745	....	....	....	....	....	....	....	....	....
8221	General government....................	....	....	....	....	....	....	....	....	....	....	....	....
8227	International organizations....................	....	....	....	....	....	....	....	....	....	....	....	....
8228	Financial corporations other than international organizations..............	....	....	....	....	....	....	....	....	....	....	....	....
8229	Other nonresidents....................	....	....	....	....	....	....	....	....	....	....	....	....
823	Monetary gold and SDRs....................	....	—	—	....	....	....	....	....	....	....	....	....
83	**Net incurrence of liabilities**....................	....	**4,587**	**9,969**	....	....	....	....	....	....	....	....	....
831	Domestic....................	....	—	724	....	....	....	....	....	....	....	....	....
8311	General government....................	....	—	....	....	....	....	....	....	....	....	....	....
8312	Central bank....................	....	—	....	....	....	....	....	....	....	....	....	....
8313	Other depository corporations....................	....	—	....	....	....	....	....	....	....	....	....	....
8314	Financial corporations n.e.c....................	....	—	....	....	....	....	....	....	....	....	....	....
8315	Nonfinancial corporations....................	....	—	....	....	....	....	....	....	....	....	....	....
8316	Households & NPIs serving households......	....	—	....	....	....	....	....	....	....	....	....	....
832	Foreign....................	....	4,587	9,245	....	....	....	....	....	....	....	....	....
8321	General government....................	....	—	—	....	....	....	....	....	....	....	....	....
8327	International organizations....................	....	4,587	9,245	....	....	....	....	....	....	....	....	....
8328	Financial corporations other than international organizations..............	....	—	—	....	....	....	....	....	....	....	....	....
8329	Other nonresidents....................	....	—	—	....	....	....	....	....	....	....	....	....

Albania 914

In Millions of Leks / Year Ending December 31 / Cash Reporter

	Budgetary Central Government			Central Government			Local Government			General Government		
	2000	2001	2002	2000	2001	2002	2000	2001	2002	2000	2001	2002
Statement of government operations												
Statement of other economic flows												
Balance sheet												
Statement of sources and uses of cash												
1 Cash receipts from operating activities...........	....	....	....	....	....	....	....	....	....	....	....	153,197
11 Taxes.......	....	....	....	....	....	....	....	....	....	....	....	103,162
12 Social contributions...................	....	....	....	....	....	....	....	....	....	....	....	24,920
13 Grants...................	....	....	....	....	....	....	....	....	....	....	....	4,119
14 Other receipts..................	....	....	....	....	....	....	....	....	....	....	....	20,996
2 Cash payments for operating activities...........	....	....	....	....	....	....	....	....	....	....	....	151,598
21 Compensation of employees..................	....	....	....	....	....	....	....	....	....	....	....	46,346
22 Purchases of goods and services..............	....	....	....	....	....	....	....	....	....	....	....	22,367
24 Interest..................	....	....	....	....	....	....	....	....	....	....	....	24,762
25 Subsidies..................	....	....	....	....	....	....	....	....	....	....	....	6,354
26 Grants..................	....	....	....	....	....	....	....	....	....	....	....	—
27 Social benefits..................	....	....	....	....	....	....	....	....	....	....	....	8,713
28 Other payments..................	....	....	....	....	....	....	....	....	....	....	....	43,056
CIO *Net cash inflow from oper. activities.....*	....	....	....	....	....	....	....	....	....	....	....	*1,599*
31.1 Purchases of nonfinancial assets................	....	....	....	....	....	....	....	....	....	....	....	40,917
31.2 Sales of nonfinancial assets....................	....	....	....	....	....	....	....	....	....	....	....	407
31 Net cash outflow from investments in nonfinancial assets....................	....	....	....	....	....	....	....	....	....	....	....	40,510
CSD *Cash surplus/deficit....................*	....	....	....	....	....	....	....	....	....	....	....	*−38,911*
32x Net acquisition of fin assets, excl. cash...........	....	....	....	....	....	....	....	....	....	....	....	−2,030
321x Domestic................	....	....	....	....	....	....	....	....	....	....	....	−2,030
322x Foreign................	....	....	....	....	....	....	....	....	....	....	....	
323 Monetary gold and SDRs..............	....	....	....	....	....	....	....	....	....	....	....	—
33 Net incurrence of liabilities..............	....	....	....	....	....	....	....	....	....	....	....	35,613
331 Domestic..............	....	....	....	....	....	....	....	....	....	....	....	19,521
332 Foreign..............	....	....	....	....	....	....	....	....	....	....	....	16,092
NFB Net cash inflow from fin. activities................	....	....	....	....	....	....	....	....	....	....	....	37,643
NCB *Net change in the stock of cash............*	....	....	....	....	....	....	....	....	....	....	....	*−1,268*
Table 1 Revenue												
1 **Revenue.....................**	....	....	....	....	....	....	....	....	....	....	....	**153,197**
11 **Taxes.......................**	....	....	....	....	....	....	....	....	....	....	....	**103,162**
111 Taxes on income, profits, & capital gains......	....	....	....	....	....	....	....	....	....	....	....	20,894
1111 Individuals...................	....	....	....	....	....	....	....	....	....	....	....	6,149
1112 Corporations and other enterprises............	....	....	....	....	....	....	....	....	....	....	....	14,745
112 Taxes on payroll and workforce..................	....	....	....	....	....	....	....	....	....	....	....	—
113 Taxes on property..................	....	....	....	....	....	....	....	....	....	....	....	—
114 Taxes on goods and services.................	....	....	....	....	....	....	....	....	....	....	....	67,255
1141 General taxes on goods and services..........	....	....	....	....	....	....	....	....	....	....	....	46,113
1142 Excises.................	....	....	....	....	....	....	....	....	....	....	....	9,324
115 Taxes on int'l. trade and transactions...........	....	....	....	....	....	....	....	....	....	....	....	13,401
116 Other taxes.................	....	....	....	....	....	....	....	....	....	....	....	1,611
12 **Social contributions.........................**	....	....	....	....	....	....	....	....	....	....	....	**24,920**
121 Social security contributions................	....	....	....	....	....	....	....	....	....	....	....	24,920
122 Other social contributions................	....	....	....	....	....	....	....	....	....	....	....	—
13 **Grants.........................**	....	....	....	....	....	....	....	....	....	....	....	**4,119**
131 From foreign governments................	....	....	....	....	....	....	....	....	....	....	....	4,119
132 From international organizations............	....	....	....	....	....	....	....	....	....	....	....	—
133 From other general government units...........	....	....	....	....	....	....	....	....	....	....	....	—
14 **Other revenue....................**	....	....	....	....	....	....	....	....	....	....	....	**20,996**
Table 2 Expense by economic type												
2 **Expense....................**	....	....	....	....	....	....	....	....	....	....	....	**151,598**
21 **Compensation of employees...................**	....	....	....	....	....	....	....	....	....	....	....	**46,346**
211 Wages and salaries...................	....	....	....	....	....	....	....	....	....	....	....	36,882
212 Social contributions...................	....	....	....	....	....	....	....	....	....	....	....	9,464
22 **Use of goods and services...................**	....	....	....	....	....	....	....	....	....	....	....	**22,367**
23 **Consumption of fixed capital.................**	....	....	....	....	....	....	....	....	....	....	....	....
24 **Interest......................**	....	....	....	....	....	....	....	....	....	....	....	**24,762**
25 **Subsidies......................**	....	....	....	....	....	....	....	....	....	....	....	**6,354**

2005, International Monetary Fund: *Government Finance Statistics Yearbook*

Albania 914

In Millions of Leks / Year Ending December 31 / Cash Reporter

		Budgetary Central Government			Central Government			Local Government			General Government		
		2000	2001	2002	2000	2001	2002	2000	2001	2002	2000	2001	2002
26	Grants............	....	....	....	....	....	....	....	....	....	....	....	—
261	To foreign govenments............	....	....	....	....	....	....	....	....	....	....	....	—
262	To international organizations............	....	....	....	....	....	....	....	....	....	....	....	—
263	To other general government units............	....	....	....	....	....	....	....	....	....	....	....	—
2631	Current............	....	....	....	....	....	....	....	....	....	....	....	—
2632	Capital............	....	....	....	....	....	....	....	....	....	....	....	—
27	Social benefits............	....	....	....	....	....	....	....	....	....	....	....	8,713
28	Other expense............	....	....	....	....	....	....	....	....	....	....	....	43,056
281	Property expense other than interest............	....	....	....	....	....	....	....	....	....	....	....	....
282	Miscellaneous other expense............	....	....	....	....	....	....	....	....	....	....	....	....
2821	Current............	....	....	....	....	....	....	....	....	....	....	....	....
2822	Capital............	....	....	....	....	....	....	....	....	....	....	....	....

Table 3 Transactions in assets and liabilities

		Budgetary Central Government			Central Government			Local Government			General Government		
		2000	2001	2002	2000	2001	2002	2000	2001	2002	2000	2001	2002
3	Change in net worth from transactns....	....	....	....	....	....	....	....	....	....	....	....	....
31	Net acquisition of nonfinancial assets...	....	....	....	....	....	....	....	....	....	....	....	40,510
311	Fixed assets............	....	....	....	....	....	....	....	....	....	....	....	....
3111	Buildings and structures............	....	....	....	....	....	....	....	....	....	....	....	....
3112	Machinery and equipment............	....	....	....	....	....	....	....	....	....	....	....	....
3113	Other fixed assets............	....	....	....	....	....	....	....	....	....	....	....	....
312	Inventories............	....	....	....	....	....	....	....	....	....	....	....	....
313	Valuables............	....	....	....	....	....	....	....	....	....	....	....	....
314	Nonproduced assets............	....	....	....	....	....	....	....	....	....	....	....	....
3141	Land............	....	....	....	....	....	....	....	....	....	....	....	....
3142	Subsoil assets............	....	....	....	....	....	....	....	....	....	....	....	....
3143	Other naturally occurring assets............	....	....	....	....	....	....	....	....	....	....	....	....
3144	Intangible nonproduced assets............	....	....	....	....	....	....	....	....	....	....	....	....
32	Net acquisition of financial assets............	....	....	....	....	....	....	....	....	....	....	....	−3,298
321	Domestic............	....	....	....	....	....	....	....	....	....	....	....	−2,862
3212	Currency and deposits............	....	....	....	....	....	....	....	....	....	....	....	−832
3213	Securities other than shares............	....	....	....	....	....	....	....	....	....	....	....	—
3214	Loans............	....	....	....	....	....	....	....	....	....	....	....	−1,545
3215	Shares and other equity............	....	....	....	....	....	....	....	....	....	....	....	−485
3216	Insurance technical reserves............	....	....	....	....	....	....	....	....	....	....	....	—
3217	Financial derivatives............	....	....	....	....	....	....	....	....	....	....	....	—
3218	Other accounts receivable............	....	....	....	....	....	....	....	....	....	....	....	—
322	Foreign............	....	....	....	....	....	....	....	....	....	....	....	−436
3222	Currency and deposits............	....	....	....	....	....	....	....	....	....	....	....	−436
3223	Securities other than shares............	....	....	....	....	....	....	....	....	....	....	....	—
3224	Loans............	....	....	....	....	....	....	....	....	....	....	....	—
3225	Shares and other equity............	....	....	....	....	....	....	....	....	....	....	....	—
3226	Insurance technical reserves............	....	....	....	....	....	....	....	....	....	....	....	—
3227	Financial derivatives............	....	....	....	....	....	....	....	....	....	....	....	—
3228	Other accounts receivable............	....	....	....	....	....	....	....	....	....	....	....	....
323	Monetary gold and SDRs............	....	....	....	....	....	....	....	....	....	....	....	—
33	Net incurrence of liabilities............	....	....	....	....	....	....	....	....	....	....	....	35,613
331	Domestic............	....	....	....	....	....	....	....	....	....	....	....	19,521
3312	Currency and deposits............	....	....	....	....	....	....	....	....	....	....	....	−87
3313	Securities other than shares............	....	....	....	....	....	....	....	....	....	....	....	19,593
3314	Loans............	....	....	....	....	....	....	....	....	....	....	....	15
3316	Insurance technical reserves............	....	....	....	....	....	....	....	....	....	....	....	—
3317	Financial derivatives............	....	....	....	....	....	....	....	....	....	....	....	—
3318	Other accounts payable............	....	....	....	....	....	....	....	....	....	....	....	....
332	Foreign............	....	....	....	....	....	....	....	....	....	....	....	16,092
3322	Currency and deposits............	....	....	....	....	....	....	....	....	....	....	....	—
3323	Securities other than shares............	....	....	....	....	....	....	....	....	....	....	....	—
3324	Loans............	....	....	....	....	....	....	....	....	....	....	....	16,092
3326	Insurance technical reserves............	....	....	....	....	....	....	....	....	....	....	....	—
3327	Financial derivatives............	....	....	....	....	....	....	....	....	....	....	....	—
3328	Other accounts payable............	....	....	....	....	....	....	....	....	....	....	....	....

In Millions of Leks / Year Ending December 31 / Cash Reporter

	Budgetary Central Government			Central Government			Local Government			General Government		
	2000	2001	2002	2000	2001	2002	2000	2001	2002	2000	2001	2002
Table 4 Holding gains in assets and liabilities												
Table 5 Other changes in the volume of assets and liabilities												
Table 6 Balance sheet												
Table 7 Outlays by functions of govt.												
7 **Total outlays**....................	....	....	....	....	....	....	....	....	....	....	....	**187,109**
701 **General public services**........................	....	....	....	....	....	....	....	....	....	....	....	**48,983**
7017 Public debt transactions............................	....	....	....	....	....	....	....	....	....	....	....	24,762
7018 General transfers between levels of govt......	....	....	....	....	....	....	....	....	....	....	....	24,220
702 **Defense**........................	....	....	....	....	....	....	....	....	....	....	....	**7,537**
703 **Public order and safety**........................	....	....	....	....	....	....	....	....	....	....	....	**11,944**
704 **Economic affairs**........................	....	....	....	....	....	....	....	....	....	....	....	**28,080**
7042 Agriculture, forestry, fishing, and hunting.....	....	....	....	....	....	....	....	....	....	....	....	7,158
7043 Fuel and energy............................	....	....	....	....	....	....	....	....	....	....	....	4,949
7044 Mining, manufacturing, and construction.....	....	....	....	....	....	....	....	....	....	....	....	1,112
7045 Transport............................	....	....	....	....	....	....	....	....	....	....	....	14,861
7046 Communication............................	....	....	....	....	....	....	....	....	....	....	....	—
705 **Environmental protection**......................	....	....	....	....	....	....	....	....	....	....	....	—
706 **Housing and community amenities**........	....	....	....	....	....	....	....	....	....	....	....	**9,021**
707 **Health**........................	....	....	....	....	....	....	....	....	....	....	....	**13,719**
7072 Outpatient services............................	....	....	....	....	....	....	....	....	....	....	....	....
7073 Hospital services............................	....	....	....	....	....	....	....	....	....	....	....	....
7074 Public health services............................	....	....	....	....	....	....	....	....	....	....	....	....
708 **Recreation, culture, and religion**............	....	....	....	....	....	....	....	....	....	....	....	**2,609**
709 **Education**........................	....	....	....	....	....	....	....	....	....	....	....	**19,034**
7091 Pre-primary and primary education............	....	....	....	....	....	....	....	....	....	....	....	....
7092 Secondary education............................	....	....	....	....	....	....	....	....	....	....	....	....
7094 Tertiary education............................	....	....	....	....	....	....	....	....	....	....	....	....
710 **Social protection**........................	....	....	....	....	....	....	....	....	....	....	....	**46,183**
7 Statistical discrepancy: Total outlays............	....	....	....	....	....	....	....	....	....	....	....	—
Table 8 Transactions in financial assets and liabilities by sector												
82 **Net acquisition of financial assets**.........	....	....	....	....	....	....	....	....	....	....	....	**−3,298**
821 Domestic............................	....	....	....	....	....	....	....	....	....	....	....	−2,862
8211 General government............................	....	....	....	....	....	....	....	....	....	....	....	....
8212 Central bank............................	....	....	....	....	....	....	....	....	....	....	....	....
8213 Other depository corporations............	....	....	....	....	....	....	....	....	....	....	....	....
8214 Financial corporations n.e.c................	....	....	....	....	....	....	....	....	....	....	....	....
8215 Nonfinancial corporations............	....	....	....	....	....	....	....	....	....	....	....	....
8216 Households & NPIs serving households......	....	....	....	....	....	....	....	....	....	....	....	....
822 Foreign............................	....	....	....	....	....	....	....	....	....	....	....	−436
8221 General government............................	....	....	....	....	....	....	....	....	....	....	....	....
8227 International organizations..................	....	....	....	....	....	....	....	....	....	....	....	....
8228 Financial corporations other than international organizations..............	....	....	....	....	....	....	....	....	....	....	....	....
8229 Other nonresidents............................	....	....	....	....	....	....	....	....	....	....	....	....
823 Monetary gold and SDRs............	....	....	....	....	....	....	....	....	....	....	....	—
83 **Net incurrence of liabilities**..................	....	....	....	....	....	....	....	....	....	....	....	**35,613**
831 Domestic............................	....	....	....	....	....	....	....	....	....	....	....	19,521
8311 General government............................	....	....	....	....	....	....	....	....	....	....	....	....
8312 Central bank............................	....	....	....	....	....	....	....	....	....	....	....	....
8313 Other depository corporations............	....	....	....	....	....	....	....	....	....	....	....	....
8314 Financial corporations n.e.c................	....	....	....	....	....	....	....	....	....	....	....	....
8315 Nonfinancial corporations............	....	....	....	....	....	....	....	....	....	....	....	....
8316 Households & NPIs serving households......	....	....	....	....	....	....	....	....	....	....	....	....
832 Foreign............................	....	....	....	....	....	....	....	....	....	....	....	16,092
8321 General government............................	....	....	....	....	....	....	....	....	....	....	....	....
8327 International organizations..................	....	....	....	....	....	....	....	....	....	....	....	....
8328 Financial corporations other than international organizations..............	....	....	....	....	....	....	....	....	....	....	....	....
8329 Other nonresidents............................	....	....	....	....	....	....	....	....	....	....	....	....

In Billions of Dinars / Year Ending December 31 / Cash Reporter

	Budgetary Central Government			Central Government			Local Government			General Government		
	2000	2001	2002	2000	2001	2002	2000	2001	2002	2000	2001	2002
Statement of government operations												
Statement of other economic flows												
Balance sheet												
6 *Net worth*	....	....	....	....	....	....	....	....	....	....	....	....
61 Nonfinancial assets	....	....	....	....	....	....	....	....	....	....	....	....
62 Financial assets	....	....	....	....	....	....	....	....	....	....	....	....
63 Liabilities	2,559.4	2,407.9	2,140.8	....	....	....	....	....	....	....	....	....
Statement of sources and uses of cash												
1 Cash receipts from operating activities	1,578.2	1,505.5	1,603.2	....	....	....	....	....	....	....	....	....
11 Taxes	1,522.7	1,354.6	1,425.8	....	....	....	....	....	....	....	....	....
12 Social contributions	—	—	—	....	....	....	....	....	....	....	....	....
13 Grants	—	—	—	....	....	....	....	....	....	....	....	....
14 Other receipts	55.4	150.9	177.4	....	....	....	....	....	....	....	....	....
2 Cash payments for operating activities	856.2	963.6	1,097.7	....	....	....	....	....	....	....	....	....
21 Compensation of employees	289.6	324.0	346.2	....	....	....	....	....	....	....	....	....
22 Purchases of goods and services	54.6	46.3	68.5	....	....	....	....	....	....	....	....	....
24 Interest	162.3	147.5	137.2	....	....	....	....	....	....	....	....	....
25 Subsidies	—	—	—	....	....	....	....	....	....	....	....	....
26 Grants	92.0	114.6	137.6	....	....	....	....	....	....	....	....	....
27 Social benefits	257.7	331.2	408.1	....	....	....	....	....	....	....	....	....
28 Other payments	—	—	—	....	....	....	....	....	....	....	....	....
CIO *Net cash inflow from oper. activities*	*722.0*	*541.9*	*505.5*	....	....	....	....	....	....	....	....	....
31.1 Purchases of nonfinancial assets	321.9	357.4	452.9	....	....	....	....	....	....	....	....	....
31.2 Sales of nonfinancial assets	—	—	—	....	....	....	....	....	....	....	....	....
31 Net cash outflow from investments in nonfinancial assets	321.9	357.4	452.9	....	....	....	....	....	....	....	....	....
CSD *Cash surplus/deficit*	*400.0*	*184.5*	*52.5*	....	....	....	....	....	....	....	....	....
32x Net acquisition of fin assets, excl. cash	1.2	13.5	42.1	....	....	....	....	....	....	....	....	....
321x Domestic	1.2	13.5	42.1	....	....	....	....	....	....	....	....	....
322x Foreign	—	—	—	....	....	....	....	....	....	....	....	....
323 Monetary gold and SDRs	—	—	—	....	....	....	....	....	....	....	....	....
33 Net incurrence of liabilities	−78.7	−74.7	7.2	....	....	....	....	....	....	....	....	....
331 Domestic	18.3	35.9	82.0	....	....	....	....	....	....	....	....	....
332 Foreign	−97.1	−110.6	−74.9	....	....	....	....	....	....	....	....	....
NFB Net cash inflow from fin. activities	−79.9	−88.1	−35.0	....	....	....	....	....	....	....	....	....
NCB *Net change in the stock of cash*	*320.2*	*96.4*	*17.6*	....	....	....	....	....	....	....	....	....
Table 1 Revenue												
1 **Revenue**	**1,578.2**	**1,505.5**	**1,603.2**	....	....	....	....	....	....	....	....	....
11 **Taxes**	**1,522.7**	**1,354.6**	**1,425.8**	....	....	....	....	....	....	....	....	....
111 Taxes on income, profits, & capital gains	1,255.3	1,054.9	1,055.1	....	....	....	....	....	....	....	....	....
1111 Individuals	34.9	45.5	52.7	....	....	....	....	....	....	....	....	....
1112 Corporations and other enterprises	47.1	53.0	59.6	....	....	....	....	....	....	....	....	....
112 Taxes on payroll and workforce	—	—	—	....	....	....	....	....	....	....	....	....
113 Taxes on property	—	—	—	....	....	....	....	....	....	....	....	....
114 Taxes on goods and services	110.5	118.4	144.3	....	....	....	....	....	....	....	....	....
1141 General taxes on goods and services	47.8	55.0	70.9	....	....	....	....	....	....	....	....	....
1142 Excises	62.6	63.4	73.4	....	....	....	....	....	....	....	....	....
115 Taxes on int'l. trade and transactions	140.8	164.5	207.5	....	....	....	....	....	....	....	....	....
116 Other taxes	16.2	16.8	18.9	....	....	....	....	....	....	....	....	....
12 **Social contributions**	**—**	**—**	**—**	....	....	....	....	....	....	....	....	....
121 Social security contributions	—	—	—	....	....	....	....	....	....	....	....	....
122 Other social contributions	—	—	—	....	....	....	....	....	....	....	....	....
13 **Grants**	**—**	**—**	**—**	....	....	....	....	....	....	....	....	....
131 From foreign governments	—	—	—	....	....	....	....	....	....	....	....	....
132 From international organizations	—	—	—	....	....	....	....	....	....	....	....	....
133 From other general government units	—	—	—	....	....	....	....	....	....	....	....	....
14 **Other revenue**	**55.4**	**150.9**	**177.4**	....	....	....	....	....	....	....	....	....
Table 2 Expense by economic type												
2 **Expense**	**856.2**	**963.6**	**1,097.7**	....	....	....	....	....	....	....	....	....
21 **Compensation of employees**	**289.6**	**324.0**	**346.2**	....	....	....	....	....	....	....	....	....
211 Wages and salaries	231.7	259.2	277.0	....	....	....	....	....	....	....	....	....
212 Social contributions	57.9	64.8	69.2	....	....	....	....	....	....	....	....	....
22 **Use of goods and services**	**54.6**	**46.3**	**68.5**	....	....	....	....	....	....	....	....	....
23 **Consumption of fixed capital**	....	....	....	....	....	....	....	....	....	....	....	....
24 **Interest**	**162.3**	**147.5**	**137.2**	....	....	....	....	....	....	....	....	....
25 **Subsidies**	**—**	**—**	**—**	....	....	....	....	....	....	....	....	....

In Billions of Dinars / Year Ending December 31 / Cash Reporter

		Budgetary Central Government			Central Government			Local Government			General Government		
		2000	2001	2002	2000	2001	2002	2000	2001	2002	2000	2001	2002
26	**Grants**............................	**92.0**	**114.6**	**137.6**	....	....	....	....	....	....	....	....	....
261	To foreign govenments...............	—	—	—	....	....	....	....	....	....	....	....	....
262	To international organizations.......	—	—	—	....	....	....	....	....	....	....	....	....
263	To other general government units..............	92.0	114.6	137.6	....	....	....	....	....	....	....	....	....
2631	Current............................	92.0	114.6	137.6	....	....	....	....	....	....	....	....	....
2632	Capital............................	—	—	—	....	....	....	....	....	....	....	....	....
27	**Social benefits**...................	**257.7**	**331.2**	**408.1**	....	....	....	....	....	....	....	....	....
28	**Other expense**....................	—	—	—	....	....	....	....	....	....	....	....	....
281	Property expense other than interest............	—	—	—	....	....	....	....	....	....	....	....	....
282	Miscellaneous other expense.......................	—	—	—	....	....	....	....	....	....	....	....	....
2821	Current............................	—	—	—	....	....	....	....	....	....	....	....	....
2822	Capital............................	—	—	—	....	....	....	....	....	....	....	....	....
Table 3 Transactions in assets and liabilities													
3	**Change in net worth from transactns....**	....	....	....	....	....	....	....	....	....	....	....	....
31	**Net acquisition of nonfinancial assets...**	**321.9**	**357.4**	**452.9**	....	....	....	....	....	....	....	....	....
311	Fixed assets............................	321.9	357.4	452.9	....	....	....	....	....	....	....	....	....
3111	Buildings and structures...............	....	....	....	....	....	....	....	....	....	....	....	....
3112	Machinery and equipment.......................	....	....	....	....	....	....	....	....	....	....	....	....
3113	Other fixed assets...............	....	....	....	....	....	....	....	....	....	....	....	....
312	Inventories............................	—	—	—	....	....	....	....	....	....	....	....	....
313	Valuables............................	—	—	—	....	....	....	....	....	....	....	....	....
314	Nonproduced assets..................	—	—	—	....	....	....	....	....	....	....	....	....
3141	Land............................	—	—	—	....	....	....	....	....	....	....	....	....
3142	Subsoil assets............................	—	—	—	....	....	....	....	....	....	....	....	....
3143	Other naturally occurring assets................	—	—	—	....	....	....	....	....	....	....	....	....
3144	Intangible nonproduced assets............	—	—	—	....	....	....	....	....	....	....	....	....
32	**Net acquisition of financial assets........**	**321.3**	**109.8**	**59.7**	....	....	....	....	....	....	....	....	....
321	Domestic............................	321.3	109.8	59.7	....	....	....	....	....	....	....	....	....
3212	Currency and deposits.......................	320.2	96.4	17.6	....	....	....	....	....	....	....	....	....
3213	Securities other than shares...............	—	—	—	....	....	....	....	....	....	....	....	....
3214	Loans............................	1.2	13.5	42.1	....	....	....	....	....	....	....	....	....
3215	Shares and other equity..................	—	—	—	....	....	....	....	....	....	....	....	....
3216	Insurance technical reserves.......................	—	—	—	....	....	....	....	....	....	....	....	....
3217	Financial derivatives...............	—	—	—	....	....	....	....	....	....	....	....	....
3218	Other accounts receivable...............	....	....	....	....	....	....	....	....	....	....	....	....
322	Foreign............................	—	—	—	....	....	....	....	....	....	....	....	....
3222	Currency and deposits...............	—	—	—	....	....	....	....	....	....	....	....	....
3223	Securities other than shares...............	—	—	—	....	....	....	....	....	....	....	....	....
3224	Loans............................	—	—	—	....	....	....	....	....	....	....	....	....
3225	Shares and other equity...............	—	—	—	....	....	....	....	....	....	....	....	....
3226	Insurance technical reserves...............	—	—	—	....	....	....	....	....	....	....	....	....
3227	Financial derivatives...............	—	—	—	....	....	....	....	....	....	....	....	....
3228	Other accounts receivable...............	....	....	....	....	....	....	....	....	....	....	....	....
323	Monetary gold and SDRs...............	—	—	—	....	....	....	....	....	....	....	....	....
33	**Net incurrence of liabilities...................**	**−78.7**	**−74.7**	**7.2**	....	....	....	....	....	....	....	....	....
331	Domestic............................	18.3	35.9	82.0	....	....	....	....	....	....	....	....	....
3312	Currency and deposits.......................	63.2	−4.8	−31.0	....	....	....	....	....	....	....	....	....
3313	Securities other than shares.......................	−81.7	−56.0	−16.3	....	....	....	....	....	....	....	....	....
3314	Loans............................	....	....	....	....	....	....	....	....	....	....	....	....
3316	Insurance technical reserves...............	....	....	....	....	....	....	....	....	....	....	....	....
3317	Financial derivatives...............	....	....	....	....	....	....	....	....	....	....	....	....
3318	Other accounts payable...............	....	....	....	....	....	....	....	....	....	....	....	....
332	Foreign............................	−97.1	−110.6	−74.9	....	....	....	....	....	....	....	....	....
3322	Currency and deposits...............	—	—	—	....	....	....	....	....	....	....	....	....
3323	Securities other than shares...............	—	—	—	....	....	....	....	....	....	....	....	....
3324	Loans............................	−97.1	−110.6	−74.9	....	....	....	....	....	....	....	....	....
3326	Insurance technical reserves...............	—	—	—	....	....	....	....	....	....	....	....	....
3327	Financial derivatives...............	—	—	—	....	....	....	....	....	....	....	....	....
3328	Other accounts payable...............	....	....	....	....	....	....	....	....	....	....	....	....

In Billions of Dinars / Year Ending December 31 / Cash Reporter

	Budgetary Central Government			Central Government			Local Government			General Government		
	2000	2001	2002	2000	2001	2002	2000	2001	2002	2000	2001	2002
Table 4 Holding gains in assets and liabilities												
Table 5 Other changes in the volume of assets and liabilities												
Table 6 Balance sheet												
6 **Net worth**..............	....	....	....	....	....	....	....	....	....	....	....	....
61 **Nonfinancial assets**..............	....	....	....	....	....	....	....	....	....	....	....	....
611 Fixed assets..............	....	....	....	....	....	....	....	....	....	....	....	....
6111 Buildings and structures..............	....	....	....	....	....	....	....	....	....	....	....	....
6112 Machinery and equipment..............	....	....	....	....	....	....	....	....	....	....	....	....
6113 Other fixed assets..............	....	....	....	....	....	....	....	....	....	....	....	....
612 Inventories..............	....	....	....	....	....	....	....	....	....	....	....	....
613 Valuables..............	....	....	....	....	....	....	....	....	....	....	....	....
614 Nonproduced assets..............	....	....	....	....	....	....	....	....	....	....	....	....
6141 Land..............	....	....	....	....	....	....	....	....	....	....	....	....
6142 Subsoil assets..............	....	....	....	....	....	....	....	....	....	....	....	....
6143 Other naturally occurring assets..............	....	....	....	....	....	....	....	....	....	....	....	....
6144 Intangible nonproduced assets..............	....	....	....	....	....	....	....	....	....	....	....	....
62 **Financial assets**..............	....	....	....	....	....	....	....	....	....	....	....	....
621 Domestic..............	....	....	....	....	....	....	....	....	....	....	....	....
6212 Currency and deposits..............	....	....	....	....	....	....	....	....	....	....	....	....
6213 Securities other than shares..............	....	....	....	....	....	....	....	....	....	....	....	....
6214 Loans..............	....	....	....	....	....	....	....	....	....	....	....	....
6215 Shares and other equity..............	....	....	....	....	....	....	....	....	....	....	....	....
6216 Insurance technical reserves..............	....	....	....	....	....	....	....	....	....	....	....	....
6217 Financial derivatives..............	....	....	....	....	....	....	....	....	....	....	....	....
6218 Other accounts receivable..............	....	....	....	....	....	....	....	....	....	....	....	....
622 Foreign..............	....	....	....	....	....	....	....	....	....	....	....	....
6222 Currency and deposits..............	....	....	....	....	....	....	....	....	....	....	....	....
6223 Securities other than shares..............	....	....	....	....	....	....	....	....	....	....	....	....
6224 Loans..............	....	....	....	....	....	....	....	....	....	....	....	....
6225 Shares and other equity..............	....	....	....	....	....	....	....	....	....	....	....	....
6226 Insurance technical reserves..............	....	....	....	....	....	....	....	....	....	....	....	....
6227 Financial derivatives..............	....	....	....	....	....	....	....	....	....	....	....	....
6228 Other accounts receivable..............	....	....	....	....	....	....	....	....	....	....	....	....
623 Monetary gold and SDRs..............	....	....	....	....	....	....	....	....	....	....	....	....
63 **Liabilities**..............	**2,559.4**	**2,407.9**	**2,140.8**	....	....	....	....	....	....	....	....	....
631 Domestic..............	1,022.9	999.4	976.1	....	....	....	....	....	....	....	....	....
6312 Currency and deposits..............	....	....	....	....	....	....	....	....	....	....	....	....
6313 Securities other than shares..............	....	....	....	....	....	....	....	....	....	....	....	....
6314 Loans..............	....	....	....	....	....	....	....	....	....	....	....	....
6316 Insurance technical reserves..............	....	....	....	....	....	....	....	....	....	....	....	....
6317 Financial derivatives..............	....	....	....	....	....	....	....	....	....	....	....	....
6318 Other accounts payable..............	....	....	....	....	....	....	....	....	....	....	....	....
632 Foreign..............	1,536.5	1,408.5	1,164.7	....	....	....	....	....	....	....	....	....
6322 Currency and deposits..............	....	....	....	....	....	....	....	....	....	....	....	....
6323 Securities other than shares..............	....	....	....	....	....	....	....	....	....	....	....	....
6324 Loans..............	....	....	....	....	....	....	....	....	....	....	....	....
6326 Insurance technical reserves..............	....	....	....	....	....	....	....	....	....	....	....	....
6327 Financial derivatives..............	....	....	....	....	....	....	....	....	....	....	....	....
6328 Other accounts payable..............	....	....	....	....	....	....	....	....	....	....	....	....
Memorandum items:												
6M2 Net financial worth..............	....	....	....	....	....	....	....	....	....	....	....	....
6M3 Debt at market value..............	....	....	....	....	....	....	....	....	....	....	....	....
6M4 Debt at nominal value..............	....	....	....	....	....	....	....	....	....	....	....	....
6M5 Arrears..............	....	....	....	....	....	....	....	....	....	....	....	....
6M6 Obligations for social security benefits..............	....	....	....	....	....	....	....	....	....	....	....	....
6M7 Contingent liabilities..............	....	....	....	....	....	....	....	....	....	....	....	....
6M8 Uncapitalized military weapons, systems..............	....	....	....	....	....	....	....	....	....	....	....	....
Table 7 Outlays by functions of govt.												
7 **Total outlays**..............	**1,178.1**	**1,321.0**	**1,550.6**	....	....	....	....	....	....	....	....	....
701 **General public services**..............	....	....	....	....	....	....	....	....	....	....	....	....
7017 Public debt transactions..............	162.3	147.5	137.2	....	....	....	....	....	....	....	....	....
7018 General transfers between levels of govt..............	....	....	....	....	....	....	....	....	....	....	....	....
702 **Defense**..............	....	....	....	....	....	....	....	....	....	....	....	....
703 **Public order and safety**..............	....	....	....	....	....	....	....	....	....	....	....	....

Algeria   612

In Billions of Dinars / Year Ending December 31 / Cash Reporter

	Budgetary Central Government			Central Government			Local Government			General Government		
	2000	2001	2002	2000	2001	2002	2000	2001	2002	2000	2001	2002
704 **Economic affairs**.............................	....	....	....	....	....	....	....	....	....	....	....	....
7042 Agriculture, forestry, fishing, and hunting.....	....	....	....	....	....	....	....	....	....	....	....	....
7043 Fuel and energy...........................	....	....	....	....	....	....	....	....	....	....	....	....
7044 Mining, manufacturing, and construction......	....	....	....	....	....	....	....	....	....	....	....	....
7045 Transport...................................	....	....	....	....	....	....	....	....	....	....	....	....
7046 Communication.............................	....	....	....	....	....	....	....	....	....	....	....	....
705 **Environmental protection**.....................	....	....	....	....	....	....	....	....	....	....	....	....
706 **Housing and community amenities**........	....	....	....	....	....	....	....	....	....	....	....	....
707 **Health**..	....	....	....	....	....	....	....	....	....	....	....	....
7072 Outpatient services........................	....	....	....	....	....	....	....	....	....	....	....	....
7073 Hospital services...........................	....	....	....	....	....	....	....	....	....	....	....	....
7074 Public health services.....................	....	....	....	....	....	....	....	....	....	....	....	....
708 **Recreation, culture, and religion**...........	....	....	....	....	....	....	....	....	....	....	....	....
709 **Education**....................................	....	....	....	....	....	....	....	....	....	....	....	....
7091 Pre-primary and primary education..............	....	....	....	....	....	....	....	....	....	....	....	....
7092 Secondary education......................	....	....	....	....	....	....	....	....	....	....	....	....
7094 Tertiary education.........................	....	....	....	....	....	....	....	....	....	....	....	....
710 **Social protection**............................	....	....	....	....	....	....	....	....	....	....	....	....
7 Statistical discrepancy: Total outlays.............	....	....	....	....	....	....	....	....	....	....	....	....
Table 8 Transactions in financial assets and liabilities by sector												
82 **Net acquisition of financial assets**........	**321.3**	**109.8**	**59.7**	....	....	....	....	....	....	....	....	....
821 Domestic..	321.3	109.8	59.7	....	....	....	....	....	....	....	....	....
8211 General government........................	1.2	13.5	42.1	....	....	....	....	....	....	....	....	....
8212 Central bank.................................	323.4	104.0	16.5	....	....	....	....	....	....	....	....	....
8213 Other depository corporations................	....	....	....	....	....	....	....	....	....	....	....	....
8214 Financial corporations n.e.c...................	....	....	....	....	....	....	....	....	....	....	....	....
8215 Nonfinancial corporations..................	—	—	—	....	....	....	....	....	....	....	....	....
8216 Households & NPIs serving households......	....	....	....	....	....	....	....	....	....	....	....	....
822 Foreign..	—	—	—	....	....	....	....	....	....	....	....	....
8221 General government........................	—	—	—	....	....	....	....	....	....	....	....	....
8227 International organizations..................	—	—	—	....	....	....	....	....	....	....	....	....
8228 Financial corporations other than international organizations..............	—	—	—	....	....	....	....	....	....	....	....	....
8229 Other nonresidents.........................	—	—	—	....	....	....	....	....	....	....	....	....
823 Monetary gold and SDRs.....................	—	—	—	....	....	....	....	....	....	....	....	....
83 **Net incurrence of liabilities**...................	**−78.7**	**−74.7**	**7.2**	....	....	....	....	....	....	....	....	....
831 Domestic..	18.3	35.9	82.0	....	....	....	....	....	....	....	....	....
8311 General government........................	36.5	86.0	38.9	....	....	....	....	....	....	....	....	....
8312 Central bank.................................	....	....	....	....	....	....	....	....	....	....	....	....
8313 Other depository corporations................	....	....	....	....	....	....	....	....	....	....	....	....
8314 Financial corporations n.e.c...................	....	....	....	....	....	....	....	....	....	....	....	....
8315 Nonfinancial corporations..................	....	....	....	....	....	....	....	....	....	....	....	....
8316 Households & NPIs serving households......	....	....	....	....	....	....	....	....	....	....	....	....
832 Foreign..	−97.1	−110.6	−74.9	....	....	....	....	....	....	....	....	....
8321 General government........................	—	—	—	....	....	....	....	....	....	....	....	....
8327 International organizations..................	—	—	—	....	....	....	....	....	....	....	....	....
8328 Financial corporations other than international organizations..............	—	—	—	....	....	....	....	....	....	....	....	....
8329 Other nonresidents.........................	−97.1	−110.6	−74.9	....	....	....	....	....	....	....	....	....

2005, International Monetary Fund: *Government Finance Statistics Yearbook*

Argentina 213

In Millions of Pesos / Year Ending December 31 / Noncash Reporter

		Central Government			State Government			Local Government			General Government		
		2002	2003	2004	2002p	2003p	2004p	2002f	2003f	2004p	2002p	2003p	2004p
Statement of government operations													
1	Revenue	44,015	64,711	81,428	31,823	41,962	56,207	7,376	8,526	11,050	74,265	103,839	131,639
2	Expense	61,507	74,569	81,870	31,878	37,194	46,293	7,111	7,390	9,448	91,546	107,795	120,565
GOB	*Gross operating balance*	*−17,492*	*−9,858*	*−414*	*−55*	*4,767*	*9,915*	*265*	*1,136*	*1,602*	*−17,281*	*−3,955*	*11,102*
NOB	*Net operating balance*	....	....	....	....	....	....	....	....	....	....	....	....
31	Net acquisition of nonfinancial assets	345	778	1,621	1,711	3,140	5,043	708	1,033	1,408	2,764	4,951	8,072
NLB	*Net lending/borrowing*	*−17,837*	*−10,636*	*−2,063*	*−1,766*	*1,628*	*4,872*	*−443*	*102*	*193*	*−20,046*	*−8,906*	*3,002*
32	Net acquisition of financial assets	−1,360	17,590	10,852	−624	2,080	5,089	−30	3	230	−2,013	19,673	16,170
33	Net incurrence of liabilities	16,477	28,226	12,915	1,142	452	217	413	−99	37	18,032	28,579	13,168
NLB	Statistical discrepancy	—	—	—	—	—	—	—	—	—	—	—	—
Statement of other economic flows													
Balance sheet													
Statement of sources and uses of cash													
1	Cash receipts from operating activities	44,124	64,276	81,906	....	....	....	....	....	....	....	....	....
11	Taxes	30,717	47,057	63,554	....	....	....	....	....	....	....	....	....
12	Social contributions	8,661	10,488	13,363	....	....	....	....	....	....	....	....	....
13	Grants	124	56	1,016	....	....	....	....	....	....	....	....	....
14	Other receipts	4,622	6,676	3,974	....	....	....	....	....	....	....	....	....
2	Cash payments for operating activities	46,723	60,489	67,279	....	....	....	....	....	....	....	....	....
21	Compensation of employees	7,013	8,659	9,339	....	....	....	....	....	....	....	....	....
22	Purchases of goods and services	2,304	2,908	3,491	....	....	....	....	....	....	....	....	....
24	Interest	6,726	7,706	6,334	....	....	....	....	....	....	....	....	....
25	Subsidies	460	1,306	2,277	....	....	....	....	....	....	....	....	....
26	Grants	5,322	6,926	11,905	....	....	....	....	....	....	....	....	....
27	Social benefits	20,741	25,405	28,009	....	....	....	....	....	....	....	....	....
28	Other payments	4,156	7,578	5,923	....	....	....	....	....	....	....	....	....
CIO	*Net cash inflow from oper. activities*	*−2,599*	*3,788*	*14,628*	....	....	....	....	....	....	....	....	....
31.1	Purchases of nonfinancial assets	256	787	1,484	....	....	....	....	....	....	....	....	....
31.2	Sales of nonfinancial assets	16	16	17	....	....	....	....	....	....	....	....	....
31	Net cash outflow from investments in nonfinancial assets	240	771	1,467	....	....	....	....	....	....	....	....	....
CSD	*Cash surplus/deficit*	*−2,839*	*3,016*	*13,161*	....	....	....	....	....	....	....	....	....
32x	Net acquisition of fin assets, excl. cash	3,341	8,864	5,295	....	....	....	....	....	....	....	....	....
321x	Domestic	3,411	8,525	5,037	....	....	....	....	....	....	....	....	....
322x	Foreign	−71	339	257	....	....	....	....	....	....	....	....	....
323	Monetary gold and SDRs	—	—	—	....	....	....	....	....	....	....	....	....
33	Net incurrence of liabilities	−1,429	8,548	−8,221	....	....	....	....	....	....	....	....	....
331	Domestic	6,235	10,125	24	....	....	....	....	....	....	....	....	....
332	Foreign	−7,664	−1,577	−8,245	....	....	....	....	....	....	....	....	....
NFB	Net cash inflow from fin. activities	−4,770	−316	−13,515	....	....	....	....	....	....	....	....	....
NCB	*Net change in the stock of cash*	*−4,709*	*8,779*	*4,529*	....	....	....	....	....	....	....	....	....
Table 1 Revenue													
1	**Revenue**	**†44,015**	**64,711**	**81,428**	**†31,823**	**41,962**	**56,207**	**†7,376**	**8,526**	**11,050**	**†74,265**	**103,839**	**131,639**
11	**Taxes**	**†30,692**	**47,059**	**63,554**	**†22,016**	**29,273**	**38,722**	**†167**	**165**	**221**	**†52,875**	**76,497**	**102,497**
111	Taxes on income, profits, & capital gains	†5,740	10,374	15,382	†3,227	5,452	7,771	†—	—	—	†8,967	15,826	23,152
1111	Individuals	†1,741	3,130	4,626	†1,014	1,696	2,436	†—	—	—	†2,754	4,826	7,062
1112	Corporations and other enterprises	†4,000	7,244	10,755	†2,213	3,756	5,335	†—	—	—	†6,213	11,000	16,090
112	Taxes on payroll and workforce	†165	198	349	†—	—	—	†—	—	—	†165	198	349
113	Taxes on property	†4,518	5,667	7,306	†2,488	3,882	4,503	†—	—	—	†7,006	9,549	11,810
114	Taxes on goods and services	†12,201	17,230	23,766	†12,872	18,183	25,313	†—	—	—	†25,072	35,413	49,079
1141	General taxes on goods and services	†6,460	9,844	14,878	†11,417	16,260	22,884	†—	—	—	†17,877	26,104	37,762
1142	Excises	†4,291	4,760	5,544	†799	1,048	1,437	†—	—	—	†5,091	5,808	6,981
115	Taxes on int'l. trade and transactions	†6,003	10,659	12,865	†—	—	—	†—	—	—	†6,003	10,659	12,865
116	Other taxes	†2,065	2,930	3,886	†3,430	1,756	1,135	†167	165	221	†5,662	4,852	5,242
12	**Social contributions**	**†8,661**	**10,501**	**13,481**	**†—**	**—**	**—**	**†—**	**—**	**—**	**†8,661**	**10,501**	**13,481**
121	Social security contributions	†8,506	10,196	13,097	†—	—	—	†—	—	—	†8,506	10,196	13,097
122	Other social contributions	†155	305	384	†—	—	—	†—	—	—	†155	305	384
13	**Grants**	**†78**	**56**	**245**	**†5,179**	**6,757**	**10,551**	**†3,711**	**4,566**	**6,280**	**†19**	**19**	**30**
131	From foreign governments	†1	2	7	†—	—	—	†—	—	—	†1	2	7
132	From international organizations	†18	17	23	†—	—	—	†—	—	—	†18	17	23
133	From other general government units	†60	37	215	†5,179	6,757	10,551	†3,711	4,566	6,280	†—	—	—
14	**Other revenue**	**†4,583**	**7,095**	**4,148**	**†4,628**	**5,932**	**6,935**	**†3,499**	**3,794**	**4,548**	**†12,710**	**16,821**	**15,631**

In Millions of Pesos / Year Ending December 31 / Noncash Reporter

	Central Government			State Government			Local Government			General Government		
	2002	2003	2004	2002p	2003p	2004p	2002f	2003f	2004p	2002p	2003p	2004p
Table 2 Expense by economic type												
2 **Expense**.....................	†61,507	74,569	81,870	†31,878	37,194	46,293	†7,111	7,390	9,448	†91,546	107,795	120,565
21 **Compensation of employees**..................	†6,978	8,703	9,420	†18,118	19,123	23,058	†4,542	4,525	5,555	†29,638	32,351	38,033
211 Wages and salaries..........	....	....	8,156	....	....	....	....	....	....	....	....	....
212 Social contributions...........	....	....	1,264	....	....	....	....	....	....	....	....	....
22 **Use of goods and services**.....................	†2,467	2,739	3,750	†3,735	5,228	6,662	†2,092	2,415	3,141	†8,293	10,382	13,553
23 **Consumption of fixed capital**................	....	....	....	....	....	....	....	....	....	....	....	....
24 **Interest**........................	†21,088	22,377	21,543	†1,478	1,808	1,636	†68	45	58	†22,633	24,231	23,236
25 **Subsidies**......................	†435	1,317	2,666	†—	—	—	†—	—	—	†435	1,317	2,666
26 **Grants**........................	†5,292	7,164	10,872	†3,776	4,618	6,528	†—	—	—	†120	423	355
261 To foreign governents..........	†—	—	—	†—	—	—	†—	—	—	†—	—	—
262 To international organizations....................	†114	407	322	†6	16	33	†—	—	—	†120	423	355
263 To other general government units..............	†5,179	6,757	10,551	†3,770	4,603	6,495	†—	—	—	†—	—	—
2631 Current.......................	†3,418	4,661	7,764	†3,679	4,493	6,310	†—	—	—	†—	—	—
2632 Capital.......................	†1,761	2,096	2,787	†92	109	185	†—	—	—	†—	—	—
27 **Social benefits**.............	†20,987	24,744	27,476	†—	—	—	†—	—	—	†20,987	24,744	27,476
28 **Other expense**.............	†4,260	7,526	6,114	†4,772	6,417	8,409	†409	405	695	†9,441	14,348	15,218
281 Property expense other than interest...........	†149	4	—	†—	—	—	†—	—	—	†149	4	—
282 Miscellaneous other expense......................	†4,111	7,522	6,114	†4,772	6,417	8,409	†409	405	695	†9,292	14,344	15,218
2821 Current.......................	†4,104	7,377	5,844	†4,593	5,982	7,423	†399	395	685	†9,097	13,755	13,952
2822 Capital.......................	†7	144	269	†178	435	986	†10	10	10	†195	589	1,266
Table 3 Transactions in assets and liabilities												
3 **Change in net worth from transactns....**	....	....	....	....	....	....	....	....	....	....	....	....
31 **Net acquisition of nonfinancial assets...**	†345	778	1,621	†1,711	3,140	5,043	†708	1,033	1,408	†2,764	4,951	8,072
311 Fixed assets..............	†344	779	1,615	†1,692	3,102	4,968	†707	1,023	1,398	†2,743	4,904	7,982
3111 Buildings and structures....................	†234	574	1,210	†1,572	2,858	4,526	†627	953	1,281	†2,433	4,384	7,017
3112 Machinery and equipment...............	†103	196	396	†114	241	381	†80	71	117	†297	508	894
3113 Other fixed assets..........	†7	8	10	†7	4	61	†—	—	—	†13	13	71
312 Inventories..................	†—	—	—	†19	37	75	†1	10	10	†20	47	85
313 Valuables....................	†3	4	6	†—	—	—	†—	—	—	†3	4	6
314 Nonproduced assets..........	†−1	−4	—	†—	—	—	†—	—	—	†−1	−4	—
3141 Land.........................	†−1	−4	—	†—	—	—	†—	—	—	†−1	−4	—
3142 Subsoil assets...............	†—	—	—	†—	—	—	†—	—	—	†—	—	—
3143 Other naturally occurring assets...............	†—	—	—	†—	—	—	†—	—	—	†—	—	—
3144 Intangible nonproduced assets....................	†—	—	—	†—	—	—	†—	—	—	†—	—	—
32 **Net acquisition of financial assets.........**	†−1,360	17,590	10,852	†−624	2,080	5,089	†−30	3	230	†−2,013	19,673	16,170
321 Domestic....................	†−1,217	17,250	10,596	†−624	2,080	5,089	†−30	3	230	†−1,871	19,333	15,915
3212 Currency and deposits........	†−4,709	8,779	4,529	....	....	—	....	....	....	....	....	....
3213 Securities other than shares..........	†273	46	39	....	....	2,820	....	....	....	....	....	....
3214 Loans.......................	†2,996	8	2,355	....	....	229	....	....	....	....	....	....
3215 Shares and other equity.........	†20	−15	648	....	....	435	....	....	....	....	....	....
3216 Insurance technical reserves..........	†—	—	—	....	....	—	....	....	....	....	....	....
3217 Financial derivatives.........	†—	—	—	....	....	—	....	....	....	....	....	....
3218 Other accounts receivable........	†203	8,431	3,025	....	....	1,604	....	....	....	....	....	....
322 Foreign....................	†−142	340	256	†—	—	—	†—	—	—	†−142	340	256
3222 Currency and deposits........	†—	—	—	†—	—	—	†—	—	—	†—	—	—
3223 Securities other than shares..........	†−338	—	—	†—	—	—	†—	—	—	†−338	—	—
3224 Loans.......................	†—	—	—	†—	—	—	†—	—	—	†—	—	—
3225 Shares and other equity.........	†—	—	1	†—	—	—	†—	—	—	†—	—	1
3226 Insurance technical reserves..........	....	—	—	†—	—	—	†—	—	—	†—	—	—
3227 Financial derivatives.........	....	—	—	†—	—	—	†—	—	—	†—	—	—
3228 Other accounts receivable........	†195	340	255	†—	—	—	†—	—	—	†195	340	255
323 Monetary gold and SDRs..........	†—	—	—	†—	—	—	†—	—	—	†—	—	—
33 **Net incurrence of liabilities...................**	†16,477	28,226	12,915	†1,142	452	217	†413	−99	37	†18,032	28,579	13,168
331 Domestic....................	†10,263	15,191	6,048	†1,487	822	307	....	....	37	....	....	6,391
3312 Currency and deposits........	†—	—	—	†—	—	—	....	....	....	....	....	....
3313 Securities other than shares..........	†−11,686	625	−10,214	†3,170	−4,915	−263	....	....	....	....	....	....
3314 Loans.......................	†6,154	4,054	346	†−1,253	—	−107	....	....	....	....	....	....
3316 Insurance technical reserves..........	†—	161	—	†—	—	—	....	....	....	....	....	....
3317 Financial derivatives.........	†—	—	—	†—	—	—	....	....	....	....	....	....
3318 Other accounts payable........	†15,794	10,351	15,916	†−430	5,737	677	....	....	....	....	....	....

In Millions of Pesos / Year Ending December 31 / Noncash Reporter

		Central Government			State Government			Local Government			General Government		
		2002	2003	2004	2002p	2003p	2004p	2002f	2003f	2004p	2002p	2003p	2004p
332	Foreign....................................	†6,215	13,035	6,867	†–345	–370	–90	....	....	—	....	....	6,777
3322	Currency and deposits.....................	†—	—	—	†—	—	—	....	....	—	....	....	....
3323	Securities other than shares...............	†–11,613	–18,303	–27,389	†–175	—	—	....	....	—	....	....	....
3324	Loans..	†–8,207	–2,831	–10,385	†–170	–370	–90	....	....	—	....	....	....
3326	Insurance technical reserves...............	†—	—	—	†—	—	—	....	....	—	....	....	....
3327	Financial derivatives......................	†—	—	—	†—	—	—	....	....	—	....	....	....
3328	Other accounts payable.....................	†26,035	34,168	44,641	†—	—	—	....	....	—	....	....	....

Table 4   Holding gains in assets and liabilities

Table 5   Other changes in the volume of assets and liabilities

Table 6   Balance sheet

Table 7   Outlays by functions of govt.

		Central Government			State Government			Local Government			General Government		
7	**Total outlays........................**	**†61,852**	**75,347**	**83,491**	**†33,589**	**40,334**	**51,336**	**†7,819**	**8,423**	**10,856**	**†94,311**	**112,746**	**128,637**
701	**General public services............**	**†23,819**	**26,789**	**27,259**	**†9,843**	**12,081**	**15,508**	....	....	....	....	....	**40,732**
7017	Public debt transactions.................	†21,088	22,377	21,543	†1,478	1,808	1,636	†68	45	58	†22,633	24,231	23,236
7018	General transfers between levels of govt.....	†1,058	1,887	1,993	....	....	—	....	....	....	....	....	—
702	**Defense................................**	**†1,979**	**2,265**	**2,537**	**†—**	**—**	**—**	....	....	....	....	....	**2,537**
703	**Public order and safety............**	**†2,499**	**3,129**	**3,677**	**†3,102**	**3,500**	**4,170**	....	....	....	....	....	**7,757**
704	**Economic affairs....................**	**†3,256**	**6,407**	**5,987**	**†2,338**	**3,209**	**4,270**	....	....	....	....	....	**9,438**
7042	Agriculture, forestry, fishing, and hunting.....	†215	233	316	†422	627	897	....	....	....	....	....	1,208
7043	Fuel and energy...........................	†363	553	1,554	†701	1,020	1,374	....	....	....	....	....	2,598
7044	Mining, manufacturing, and construction.....	†67	119	128	†46	55	79	....	....	....	....	....	206
7045	Transport.................................	†1,104	2,150	3,145	†520	722	899	....	....	....	....	....	3,663
7046	Communication............................	†76	112	143	†—	....	—	....	....	....	....	....	143
705	**Environmental protection............**	**†63**	**61**	**242**	**†—**	**—**	**—**	....	....	....	....	....	**241**
706	**Housing and community amenities......**	**†819**	**1,094**	**1,531**	**†1,253**	**1,672**	**2,315**	....	....	....	....	....	**2,519**
707	**Health................................**	**†3,360**	**4,377**	**4,424**	**†3,960**	**4,707**	**5,754**	....	....	....	....	....	**9,957**
7072	Outpatient services.......................	†—	—	—	....	....	....	....	....	....	....	....	....
7073	Hospital services.........................	†—	—	—	....	....	....	....	....	....	....	....	....
7074	Public health services....................	†—	—	—	....	....	....	....	....	....	....	....	....
708	**Recreation, culture, and religion............**	**†111**	**147**	**154**	**†179**	**280**	**352**	....	....	....	....	....	**505**
709	**Education.............................**	**†2,481**	**3,426**	**4,337**	**†10,425**	**11,342**	**14,252**	....	....	....	....	....	**17,244**
7091	Pre-primary and primary education...............	†—	....	—	....	....	....	....	....	....	....	....	....
7092	Secondary education........................	†—	....	—	....	....	....	....	....	....	....	....	....
7094	Tertiary education.........................	†—	....	—	....	....	....	....	....	....	....	....	....
710	**Social protection....................**	**†23,467**	**27,652**	**33,343**	**†2,490**	**3,541**	**4,714**	....	....	....	....	....	**33,197**
7	Statistical discrepancy: Total outlays...............	†—	—	—	†—	—	—	....	....	....	....	....	4,511

Table 8   Transactions in financial assets and liabilities by sector

		Central Government			State Government			Local Government			General Government		
82	**Net acquisition of financial assets........**	**†–1,360**	**17,590**	**10,852**	**†–624**	**2,080**	**5,089**	**†–30**	**3**	**230**	**†–2,013**	**19,673**	**16,170**
821	Domestic.................................	†–1,217	17,250	10,596	†–624	2,080	5,089	†–30	3	230	†–1,871	19,333	15,915
8211	General government........................	....	....	....	....	....	....	....	....	....	....	....	....
8212	Central bank..............................	....	....	....	....	....	....	....	....	....	....	....	....
8213	Other depository corporations..............	....	....	....	....	....	....	....	....	....	....	....	....
8214	Financial corporations n.e.c...............	....	....	....	....	....	....	....	....	....	....	....	....
8215	Nonfinancial corporations..................	....	....	....	....	....	....	....	....	....	....	....	....
8216	Households & NPIs serving households.......	....	....	....	....	....	....	....	....	....	....	....	....
822	Foreign..................................	†–142	340	256	†—	—	—	†—	—	—	†–142	340	256
8221	General government........................	....	....	....	†—	—	—	†—	—	—	....	....	....
8227	International organizations................	....	....	....	†—	—	—	†—	—	—	....	....	....
8228	Financial corporations other than international organizations...............	....	....	....	†—	—	—	†—	—	—	....	....	....
8229	Other nonresidents........................	....	....	....	†—	—	—	†—	—	—	....	....	....
823	Monetary gold and SDRs....................	†—	—	—	†—	—	—	†—	—	—	†—	—	—
83	**Net incurrence of liabilities............**	**†16,477**	**28,226**	**12,915**	**†1,142**	**452**	**217**	**†413**	**–99**	**37**	**†18,032**	**28,579**	**13,168**
831	Domestic.................................	†10,263	15,191	6,048	†1,487	822	307	....	....	37	....	....	6,391
8311	General government........................	....	....	....	....	....	....	....	....	....	....	....	....
8312	Central bank..............................	....	....	....	....	....	....	....	....	....	....	....	....
8313	Other depository corporations..............	....	....	....	....	....	....	....	....	....	....	....	....
8314	Financial corporations n.e.c...............	....	....	....	....	....	....	....	....	....	....	....	....
8315	Nonfinancial corporations..................	....	....	....	....	....	....	....	....	....	....	....	....
8316	Households & NPIs serving households.......	....	....	....	....	....	....	....	....	....	....	....	....

In Millions of Pesos / Year Ending December 31 / Noncash Reporter

		Central Government			State Government			Local Government			General Government		
		2002	2003	2004	2002p	2003p	2004p	2002f	2003f	2004p	2002p	2003p	2004p
832	Foreign...............................	†6,215	13,035	6,867	†–345	–370	–90	....	....	—	....	....	6,777
8321	General government....................	....	....	....	....	....	....	....	....	—	....	....	....
8327	International organizations........................	....	....	....	....	....	....	....	....	—	....	....	....
8328	Financial corporations other than international organizations..............	....	....	....	....	....	....	....	....	—	....	....	....
8329	Other nonresidents.................................	....	....	....	....	....	....	....	....	—	....	....	....

Armenia, Republic of   911

In Millions of Dram / Year ending December 31 / Cash Reporter

	Budgetary Central Government			Central Government			Local Government			General Government		
	2002	2003p	2004p	2002	2003p	2004p	2002	2003p	2004p	2002	2003p	2004p
Statement of government operations												
Statement of other economic flows												
Balance sheet												
Statement of sources and uses of cash												
1 Cash receipts from operating activities.........	....	292,035	293,155	....	338,463	360,933	....	22,796	24,410	....	351,883	373,364
11 Taxes......................................	....	227,447	267,044	....	227,447	267,044	....	6,794	8,704	....	234,241	275,748
12 Social contributions..............................	....	—	—	....	44,711	50,828	....			....	44,711	50,828
13 Grants..	....	50,480	13,717	....	50,480	13,717	....	10,127	11,811	....	51,231	13,734
14 Other receipts.................................	....	14,109	12,394	....	15,826	29,343	....	5,875	3,895	....	21,701	33,054
2 Cash payments for operating activities..........	....	222,296	262,812	....	266,680	323,511	....	18,795	22,392	....	276,098	333,924
21 Compensation of employees......................	....	13,736	24,241	....	13,736	55,188	....	6,779	8,178	....	20,515	63,365
22 Purchases of goods and services.................	....	140,887	160,517	....	141,400	134,427	....	8,547	9,584	....	149,947	143,827
24 Interest..	....	11,398	9,835	....	11,398	9,835	....	3	—	....	11,401	9,835
25 Subsidies......................................	....	14,523	12,724	....	14,523	13,116	....	244	753	....	14,768	13,869
26 Grants...	....	21,089	32,303	....	9,750	11,795	....	—	—	....		374
27 Social benefits.................................	....	14,252	15,779	....	65,682	79,108	....	39	52	....	65,721	79,160
28 Other payments...............................	....	6,411	7,413	....	10,191	20,043	....	3,182	3,826	....	13,374	23,868
CIO *Net cash inflow from oper. activities.....*	....	*69,739*	*30,343*	....	*71,783*	*37,422*	....	*4,002*	*2,018*	....	*75,785*	*39,439*
31.1 Purchases of nonfinancial assets..............	....	83,803	60,618	....	83,803	62,833	....	2,589	4,583	....	86,392	67,417
31.2 Sales of nonfinancial assets...................	....	—	9,094	....	—	9,224	....	—	3,616	....	—	12,840
31 Net cash outflow from investments in nonfinancial assets..............	....	83,803	51,525	....	83,803	53,609	....	2,589	967	....	86,392	54,577
CSD *Cash surplus/deficit............................*	....	*−14,064*	*−21,182*	....	*−12,020*	*−16,188*	....	*1,412*	*1,051*	....	*−10,608*	*−15,137*
32x Net acquisition of fin assets, excl. cash.........	....	6,598	10,539	....	6,598	10,539	....	—	—	....	6,598	10,539
321x Domestic...................................	....	−2,827	−585	....	−2,827	−585	....	—	—	....	−2,827	−585
322x Foreign....................................	....	9,426	11,124	....	9,426	11,124	....	—	—	....	9,426	11,124
323 Monetary gold and SDRs....................	....			....			....			....		
33 Net incurrence of liabilities..................	....	40,342	40,451	....	40,342	40,451	....	−2	—	....	40,340	40,451
331 Domestic....................................	....	1,903	5,591	....	1,903	5,591	....	−2	—	....	1,901	5,591
332 Foreign....................................	....	38,439	34,860	....	38,439	34,860	....	—	—	....	38,439	34,860
NFB Net cash inflow from fin. activities.................	....	33,743	29,912	....	33,743	29,912	....	−2	—	....	33,742	29,912
NCB *Net change in the stock of cash............*	....	*19,679*	*8,730*	....	*21,723*	*13,725*	....	*1,411*	*1,051*	....	*23,134*	*14,775*
Table 1 Revenue												
1 **Revenue..**	....	**292,035**	**293,155**	....	**338,463**	**360,933**	....	**22,796**	**24,410**	....	**351,883**	**373,364**
11 **Taxes..**	....	**227,447**	**267,044**	....	**227,447**	**267,044**	....	**6,794**	**8,704**	....	**234,241**	**275,748**
111 Taxes on income, profits, & capital gains......	....	34,408	52,424	....	34,408	52,424	....	—	—	....	34,408	52,424
1111 Individuals................................	....	16,780	20,413	....	16,780	20,413	....	—	—	....	16,781	20,413
1112 Corporations and other enterprises...........	....	17,627	32,011	....	17,627	32,011	....	—	—	....	17,627	32,011
112 Taxes on payroll and workforce.................	....	—	—	....	—	—	....	—	—	....	—	—
113 Taxes on property..........................	....	93	−67	....	93	−67	....	5,977	7,358	....	6,069	7,291
114 Taxes on goods and services................	....	146,873	113,048	....	146,873	113,048	....	—	—	....	146,873	113,048
1141 General taxes on goods and services..........	....	107,769	102,584	....	107,769	102,584	....	—	—	....	107,769	102,584
1142 Excises....................................	....	39,104	10,464	....	39,104	10,464	....	—	—	....	39,104	10,464
115 Taxes on int'l. trade and transactions........	....	10,724	11,390	....	10,724	11,390	....	—	—	....	10,724	11,390
116 Other taxes.................................	....	35,349	90,249	....	35,349	90,249	....	818	1,346	....	36,166	91,595
12 **Social contributions...............................**	....	—	—	....	**44,711**	**50,828**	....	—	—	....	**44,711**	**50,828**
121 Social security contributions..................	....	—	—	....	44,711	50,828	....	—	—	....	44,711	50,828
122 Other social contributions.....................	....	—	—	....	—	—	....			....	—	—
13 **Grants...**	....	**50,480**	**13,717**	....	**50,480**	**13,717**	....	**10,127**	**11,811**	....	**51,231**	**13,734**
131 From foreign governments....................	....	3,840	742	....	3,840	742	....	—	—	....	3,840	742
132 From international organizations.................	....	46,639	12,976	....	46,639	12,976	....	751	16	....	47,390	12,992
133 From other general government units............	....			....			....	9,376	11,795	....	—	—
14 **Other revenue.................................**	....	**14,109**	**12,394**	....	**15,826**	**29,343**	....	**5,875**	**3,895**	....	**21,701**	**33,054**
Table 2 Expense by economic type												
2 **Expense..**	....	**222,296**	**262,812**	....	**266,680**	**323,511**	....	**18,795**	**22,392**	....	**276,098**	**333,924**
21 **Compensation of employees...................**	....	**13,736**	**24,241**	....	**13,736**	**55,188**	....	**6,779**	**8,178**	....	**20,515**	**63,365**
211 **Wages and salaries............................**	....	....	24,241	....	....	55,188	....	....	8,178	....	....	63,365
212 **Social contributions..........................**	....	....	....	....	....	....	....	....	....	....	....	....
22 **Use of goods and services.....................**	....	**140,887**	**160,517**	....	**141,400**	**134,427**	....	**8,547**	**9,584**	....	**149,947**	**143,827**
23 **Consumption of fixed capital................**	....	....	....	....	....	....	....	....	....	....	....	....
24 **Interest..**	....	**11,398**	**9,835**	....	**11,398**	**9,835**	....	**3**	**—**	....	**11,401**	**9,835**
25 **Subsidies...**	....	**14,523**	**12,724**	....	**14,523**	**13,116**	....	**244**	**753**	....	**14,768**	**13,869**

In Millions of Dram / Year ending December 31 / Cash Reporter

		Budgetary Central Government			Central Government			Local Government			General Government		
		2002	2003p	2004p	2002	2003p	2004p	2002	2003p	2004p	2002	2003p	2004p
26	**Grants**...........................	....	**21,089**	**32,303**	....	**9,750**	**11,795**	....	**—**	**—**	....	**374**	**—**
261	To foreign govenments..................	....	—	—	....	—	—	....	—	—	....	—	—
262	To international organizations..........	....	—	—	....	—	—	....	—	—	....	—	—
263	To other general government units...............	....	21,089	32,303	....	9,750	11,795	....	—	—	....	374	—
2631	Current....................	....	20,873	32,303	....	9,533	11,795	....	—	—	....	374	—
2632	Capital.....................	....	216	—	....	216	—	....	—	—	....	—	—
27	**Social benefits**.........................	....	**14,252**	**15,779**	....	**65,682**	**79,108**	....	**39**	**52**	....	**65,721**	**79,160**
28	**Other expense**..........................	....	**6,411**	**7,413**	....	**10,191**	**20,043**	....	**3,182**	**3,826**	....	**13,374**	**23,868**
281	Property expense other than interest............	....	—	—	....	—	—	....	—	—	....	—	—
282	Miscellaneous other expense......................	....	6,411	7,413	....	10,191	20,043	....	3,182	3,826	....	13,374	23,868
2821	Current............................	....	6,411	7,413	....	10,191	20,043	....	3,182	3,826	....	13,374	23,868
2822	Capital............................	....	—	—	....	—	—	....	—	—	....	—	—
Table 3	**Transactions in assets and liabilities**												
3	**Change in net worth from transactns....**	....	....	....	....	....	....	....	....	....	....	....	....
31	**Net acquisition of nonfinancial assets...**	....	**83,803**	**51,525**	....	**83,803**	**53,609**	....	**2,589**	**967**	....	**86,392**	**54,577**
311	Fixed assets............................	....	82,488	49,455	....	82,488	51,539	....	2,589	964	....	85,077	52,503
3111	Buildings and structures...................	....	....	....	....	....	....	....	....	....	....	....	....
3112	Machinery and equipment..................	....	....	....	....	....	....	....	....	....	....	....	....
3113	Other fixed assets........................	....	....	....	....	....	....	....	....	....	....	....	....
312	Inventories............................	....	1,315	2,070	....	1,315	2,070	....	—	4	....	1,315	2,073
313	Valuables............................	....	—	—	....	—	—	....	—	—	....	—	—
314	Nonproduced assets......................	....	—	—	....	—	—	....	—	—	....	—	—
3141	Land....................	....	—	—	....	—	—	....	—	—	....	—	—
3142	Subsoil assets.......................	....	—	—	....	—	—	....	—	—	....	—	—
3143	Other naturally occurring assets...........	....	—	—	....	—	—	....	—	—	....	—	—
3144	Intangible nonproduced assets................	....	—	—	....	—	—	....	—	—	....	—	—
32	**Net acquisition of financial assets........**	....	**26,277**	**19,269**	....	**28,321**	**24,263**	....	**1,411**	**1,051**	....	**29,732**	**25,314**
321	Domestic...........................	....	16,852	8,145	....	18,896	13,139	....	1,411	1,051	....	20,306	14,190
3212	Currency and deposits....................	....	19,679	8,730	....	21,723	13,725	....	1,411	1,051	....	23,134	14,775
3213	Securities other than shares...............	....	—	—	....	—	—	....	—	—	....	—	—
3214	Loans....................	....	−2,827	−585	....	−2,827	−585	....	—	—	....	−2,827	−585
3215	Shares and other equity..................	....	—	—	....	—	—	....	—	—	....	—	—
3216	Insurance technical reserves..................	....	—	—	....	—	—	....	—	—	....	—	—
3217	Financial derivatives..................	....	—	—	....	—	—	....	—	—	....	—	—
3218	Other accounts receivable................	....	....	....	....	....	....	....	....	....	....	....	....
322	Foreign............................	....	9,426	11,124	....	9,426	11,124	....	—	—	....	9,426	11,124
3222	Currency and deposits....................	....	—	—	....	—	—	....	—	—	....	—	—
3223	Securities other than shares................	....	—	—	....	—	—	....	—	—	....	—	—
3224	Loans....................	....	9,426	11,124	....	9,426	11,124	....	—	—	....	9,426	11,124
3225	Shares and other equity..................	....	—	—	....	—	—	....	—	—	....	—	—
3226	Insurance technical reserves..................	....	—	—	....	—	—	....	—	—	....	—	—
3227	Financial derivatives..................	....	—	—	....	—	—	....	—	—	....	—	—
3228	Other accounts receivable................	....	—	—	....	—	—	....	—	—	....	—	—
323	Monetary gold and SDRs..................	....	—	—	....	—	—	....	—	—	....	—	—
33	**Net incurrence of liabilities...................**	....	**40,342**	**40,451**	....	**40,342**	**40,451**	....	**−2**	**—**	....	**40,340**	**40,451**
331	Domestic...........................	....	1,903	5,591	....	1,903	5,591	....	−2	—	....	1,901	5,591
3312	Currency and deposits....................	....	....	—	....	....	—	....	—	—	....	....	—
3313	Securities other than shares.................	....	1,740	5,591	....	1,740	5,591	....	—	—	....	1,740	5,591
3314	Loans....................	....	....	—	....	....	—	....	−2	—	....	....	—
3316	Insurance technical reserves..................	....	—	—	....	—	—	....	—	—	....	—	—
3317	Financial derivatives..................	....	—	—	....	—	—	....	—	—	....	—	—
3318	Other accounts payable..................	....	....	....	....	....	....	....	....	....	....	....	....
332	Foreign............................	....	38,439	34,860	....	38,439	34,860	....	—	—	....	38,439	34,860
3322	Currency and deposits....................	....	....	—	....	....	—	....	—	—	....	....	—
3323	Securities other than shares................	....	....	—	....	....	—	....	—	—	....	....	—
3324	Loans....................	....	36,098	34,860	....	36,098	34,860	....	—	—	....	36,098	34,860
3326	Insurance technical reserves..................	....	....	—	....	....	—	....	—	—	....	....	—
3327	Financial derivatives..................	....	....	—	....	....	—	....	—	—	....	....	—
3328	Other accounts payable..................	....	....	....	....	....	....	....	....	....	....	....	....

In Millions of Dram / Year ending December 31 / Cash Reporter

	Budgetary Central Government			Central Government			Local Government			General Government		
	2002	2003p	2004p	2002	2003p	2004p	2002	2003p	2004p	2002	2003p	2004p
Table 4 Holding gains in assets and liabilities												
Table 5 Other changes in the volume of assets and liabilities												
Table 6 Balance sheet												
6 Net worth....................	....	....	....	....	....	....	....	....	....	....	....	....
61 **Nonfinancial assets**...............	....	....	....	....	....	....	....	....	....	....	....	....
611 Fixed assets................	....	....	....	....	....	....	....	....	....	....	....	....
6111 Buildings and structures........	....	....	....	....	....	....	....	....	....	....	....	....
6112 Machinery and equipment.......	....	....	....	....	....	....	....	....	....	....	....	....
6113 Other fixed assets..........	....	....	....	....	....	....	....	....	....	....	....	....
612 Inventories................	....	....	....	....	....	....	....	....	....	....	....	....
613 Valuables..................	....	....	....	....	....	....	....	....	....	....	....	....
614 Nonproduced assets..........	....	....	....	....	....	....	....	....	....	....	....	....
6141 Land.....................	....	....	....	....	....	....	....	....	....	....	....	....
6142 Subsoil assets.............	....	....	....	....	....	....	....	....	....	....	....	....
6143 Other naturally occurring assets....	....	....	....	....	....	....	....	....	....	....	....	....
6144 Intangible nonproduced assets......	....	....	....	....	....	....	....	....	....	....	....	....
62 **Financial assets**..................	....	....	....	....	....	....	....	....	....	....	....	....
621 Domestic..................	....	....	....	....	....	....	....	....	....	....	....	....
6212 Currency and deposits.........	....	....	....	....	....	....	....	....	....	....	....	....
6213 Securities other than shares......	....	....	....	....	....	....	....	....	....	....	....	....
6214 Loans....................	....	....	....	....	....	....	....	....	....	....	....	....
6215 Shares and other equity........	....	....	....	....	....	....	....	....	....	....	....	....
6216 Insurance technical reserves......	....	....	....	....	....	....	....	....	....	....	....	....
6217 Financial derivatives..........	....	....	....	....	....	....	....	....	....	....	....	....
6218 Other accounts receivable.......	....	....	....	....	....	....	....	....	....	....	....	....
622 Foreign...................	....	....	....	....	....	....	....	....	....	....	....	....
6222 Currency and deposits.........	....	....	....	....	....	....	....	....	....	....	....	....
6223 Securities other than shares......	....	....	....	....	....	....	....	....	....	....	....	....
6224 Loans....................	....	....	....	....	....	....	....	....	....	....	....	....
6225 Shares and other equity........	....	....	....	....	....	....	....	....	....	....	....	....
6226 Insurance technical reserves......	....	....	....	....	....	....	....	....	....	....	....	....
6227 Financial derivatives..........	....	....	....	....	....	....	....	....	....	....	....	....
6228 Other accounts receivable.......	....	....	....	....	....	....	....	....	....	....	....	....
623 Monetary gold and SDRs........	....	....	....	....	....	....	....	....	....	....	....	....
63 **Liabilities**....................	....	658,097	618,575	....	....	....	....	....	....	....	....	....
631 Domestic..................	....	40,965	46,406	....	....	....	....	....	....	....	....	....
6312 Currency and deposits.........	....	—	—	....	....	....	....	....	....	....	....	....
6313 Securities other than shares......	....	40,965	46,406	....	....	....	....	....	....	....	....	....
6314 Loans....................	....	—	—	....	....	....	....	....	....	....	....	....
6316 Insurance technical reserves......	....	—	—	....	....	....	....	....	....	....	....	....
6317 Financial derivatives..........	....	—	—	....	....	....	....	....	....	....	....	....
6318 Other accounts payable.........	....	....	....	....	....	....	....	....	....	....	....	....
632 Foreign...................	....	617,132	572,169	....	....	....	....	....	....	....	....	....
6322 Currency and deposits.........	....	—	—	....	....	....	....	....	....	....	....	....
6323 Securities other than shares......	....	—	—	....	....	....	....	....	....	....	....	....
6324 Loans....................	....	617,132	572,169	....	....	....	....	....	....	....	....	....
6326 Insurance technical reserves......	....	....	....	....	....	....	....	....	....	....	....	....
6327 Financial derivatives..........	....	—	—	....	....	....	....	....	....	....	....	....
6328 Other accounts payable.........	....	....	....	....	....	....	....	....	....	....	....	....
Memorandum items:												
6M2 Net financial worth............	....	....	....	....	....	....	....	....	....	....	....	....
6M3 Debt at market value..........	....	....	....	....	....	....	....	....	....	....	....	....
6M4 Debt at nominal value.........	....	....	....	....	....	....	....	....	....	....	....	....
6M5 Arrears...................	....	....	....	....	....	....	....	....	....	....	....	....
6M6 Obligations for social security benefits....	....	....	....	....	....	....	....	....	....	....	....	....
6M7 Contingent liabilities..........	....	....	....	....	....	....	....	....	....	....	....	....
6M8 Uncapitalized military weapons, systems....	....	....	....	....	....	....	....	....	....	....	....	....
Table 7 Outlays by functions of govt.												
7 **Total outlays**..................	....	306,100	314,337	....	350,483	377,781	....	21,384	23,359	....	362,491	389,162
701 **General public services**..........	....	....	....	....	....	....	....	....	....	....	....	....
7017 Public debt transactions........	....	11,398	9,835	....	11,398	9,835	....	3	—	....	11,401	9,835
7018 General transfers between levels of govt....	....	....	....	....	....	....	....	....	....	....	....	....
702 **Defense**....................	....	....	....	....	....	....	....	....	....	....	....	....
703 **Public order and safety**..........	....	....	....	....	....	....	....	....	....	....	....	....

		Budgetary Central Government			Central Government			Local Government			General Government		
		2002	2003p	2004p	2002	2003p	2004p	2002	2003p	2004p	2002	2003p	2004p
704	**Economic affairs**..............................	....	....	....	....	....	....	....	....	....	....	....	....
7042	Agriculture, forestry, fishing, and hunting.....	....	....	....	....	....	....	....	....	....	....	....	....
7043	Fuel and energy....................................	....	....	....	....	....	....	....	....	....	....	....	....
7044	Mining, manufacturing, and construction.....	....	....	....	....	....	....	....	....	....	....	....	....
7045	Transport...	....	....	....	....	....	....	....	....	....	....	....	....
7046	Communication......................................	....	....	....	....	....	....	....	....	....	....	....	....
705	**Environmental protection**......................	....	....	....	....	....	....	....	....	....	....	....	....
706	**Housing and community amenities**........	....	....	....	....	....	....	....	....	....	....	....	....
707	**Health**..	....	....	....	....	....	....	....	....	....	....	....	....
7072	Outpatient services................................	....	....	....	....	....	....	....	....	....	....	....	....
7073	Hospital services...................................	....	....	....	....	....	....	....	....	....	....	....	....
7074	Public health services............................	....	....	....	....	....	....	....	....	....	....	....	....
708	**Recreation, culture, and religion**...........	....	....	....	....	....	....	....	....	....	....	....	....
709	**Education**..	....	....	....	....	....	....	....	....	....	....	....	....
7091	Pre-primary and primary education............	....	....	....	....	....	....	....	....	....	....	....	....
7092	Secondary education..............................	....	....	....	....	....	....	....	....	....	....	....	....
7094	Tertiary education..................................	....	....	....	....	....	....	....	....	....	....	....	....
710	**Social protection**................................	....	....	....	....	....	....	....	....	....	....	....	....
7	Statistical discrepancy: Total outlays.............	....	....	....	....	....	....	....	....	....	....	....	....

Table 8   Transactions in financial assets and liabilities by sector

		Budgetary Central Government			Central Government			Local Government			General Government		
		2002	2003p	2004p	2002	2003p	2004p	2002	2003p	2004p	2002	2003p	2004p
82	**Net acquisition of financial assets**........	....	26,277	19,269	....	28,321	24,263	....	1,411	1,051	....	29,732	25,314
821	Domestic...	....	16,852	8,145	....	18,896	13,139	....	1,411	1,051	....	20,306	14,190
8211	General government...............................	....	—	—	....	—	—	....	—	—	....	—	—
8212	Central bank..	....	19,679	8,730	....	21,723	9,045	....	1,411	1,051	....	23,134	10,096
8213	Other depository corporations...................	....	−7,948	−585	....	−7,948	4,094	....	—	—	....	−7,948	4,094
8214	Financial corporations n.e.c....................	....	—	—	....	—	—	....	—	—	....	—	—
8215	Nonfinancial corporations........................	....	5,121	—	....	5,121	—	....	—	—	....	5,121	—
8216	Households & NPIs serving households......	....	—	—	....	—	—	....	—	—	....	—	—
822	Foreign...	....	9,426	11,124	....	9,426	11,124	....	—	—	....	9,426	11,124
8221	General government...............................	....	9,426	11,124	....	9,426	11,124	....	—	—	....	9,426	11,124
8227	International organizations.......................	....	—	—	....	—	—	....	—	—	....	—	—
8228	Financial corporations other than international organizations..............	....	—	—	....	—	—	....	—	—	....	—	—
8229	Other nonresidents................................	....	—	—	....	—	—	....	—	—	....	—	—
823	Monetary gold and SDRs.........................	....	—	—	....	—	—	....	—	—	....	—	—
83	**Net incurrence of liabilities**....................	....	40,342	40,451	....	40,342	40,451	....	−2	—	....	40,340	40,451
831	Domestic...	....	1,903	5,591	....	1,903	5,591	....	−2	—	....	1,901	5,591
8311	General government...............................	....	—	—	....	—	—	....	—	—	....	—	—
8312	Central bank..	....	−589	4,840	....	−589	4,840	....	—	—	....	−589	4,840
8313	Other depository corporations...................	....	−484	3,474	....	−484	3,474	....	−2	—	....	−486	3,474
8314	Financial corporations n.e.c....................	....	—	—	....	—	—	....	—	—	....	—	—
8315	Nonfinancial corporations........................	....	2,977	−2,723	....	2,977	−2,723	....	—	—	....	2,977	−2,723
8316	Households & NPIs serving households......	....	—	—	....	—	—	....	—	—	....	—	—
832	Foreign...	....	38,439	34,860	....	38,439	34,860	....	—	—	....	38,439	34,860
8321	General government...............................	....	188	—	....	188	—	....	—	—	....	188	—
8327	International organizations.......................	....	44,529	33,246	....	44,529	33,246	....	—	—	....	44,529	33,246
8328	Financial corporations other than international organizations..............	....	—	1,614	....	—	1,614	....	—	—	....	—	1,614
8329	Other nonresidents................................	....	−6,279	—	....	−6,279	—	....	—	—	....	−6,279	—

In Millions of Dollars / Year Ending June 30 / Noncash Reporter

		Central Government			State Government			Local Government			General Government		
		2002	2003	2004	2002	2003	2004	2002	2003	2004	2002	2003	2004
Statement of government operations													
1	Revenue	196,294	213,538	229,012	106,183	113,210	123,352	18,114	19,018	20,312	262,613	286,526	310,265
2	Expense	199,464	207,007	221,329	104,177	109,615	117,305	16,507	17,555	18,272	262,158	275,023	294,618
GOB	*Gross operating balance*	*−811*	*9,088*	*10,148*	*7,377*	*9,275*	*11,911*	*5,260*	*5,220*	*5,887*	*11,837*	*23,497*	*27,823*
NOB	*Net operating balance*	*−3,170*	*6,531*	*7,683*	*2,006*	*3,595*	*6,047*	*1,607*	*1,463*	*2,040*	*455*	*11,503*	*15,647*
31	Net acquisition of nonfinancial assets	77	−56	965	3,094	2,317	2,593	973	1,311	1,858	4,144	3,572	5,416
NLB	*Net lending/borrowing*	*−3,247*	*6,587*	*6,718*	*−1,088*	*1,278*	*3,454*	*634*	*152*	*182*	*−3,689*	*7,931*	*10,231*
32	Net acquisition of financial assets	−6,022	2,572	3,291	2,953	2,996	5,260	657	876	651	−1,269	6,529	−726
33	Net incurrence of liabilities	−2,775	−4,017	−3,426	4,041	1,717	1,808	23	724	477	2,419	−1,404	−10,958
NLB	Statistical discrepancy	—	2	−1	—	1	−2	—	—	−8	1	2	1
Statement of other economic flows													
Balance sheet													
6	*Net worth*	*−23,210*	*−24,771*	*−6,831*	*271,861*	*307,964*	*341,239*	*153,912*	*162,200*	*173,227*	*402,564*	*445,396*	*507,636*
61	Nonfinancial assets	54,452	55,987	61,085	211,978	230,479	246,698	153,277	160,811	171,152	419,704	447,280	478,936
62	Financial assets	112,972	116,615	126,282	173,336	197,965	217,277	9,555	10,468	11,455	291,125	320,371	350,728
63	Liabilities	190,634	197,373	194,198	113,453	120,480	122,736	8,920	9,079	9,380	308,265	322,255	322,028
Statement of sources and uses of cash													
1	Cash receipts from operating activities	192,614	210,007	223,884	107,585	114,670	125,336	17,595	18,075	19,179	259,628	283,798	306,664
11	Taxes	174,323	191,388	205,328	33,436	35,909	40,078	6,700	7,166	7,722	214,128	234,074	252,768
12	Social contributions	—	—	—	—	—	—	—	—	—	—	—	—
13	Grants	425	555	264	53,199	54,961	57,416	3,196	2,647	2,650	946	1,580	1,059
14	Other receipts	17,866	18,064	18,292	20,950	23,800	27,842	7,699	8,262	8,807	44,554	48,144	52,837
2	Cash payments for operating activities	191,183	199,290	212,701	95,700	103,367	110,341	13,206	14,332	14,981	241,926	258,035	276,288
21	Compensation of employees	....	....	....	....	....	....	....	....	....	....	....	....
22	Purchases of goods and services	....	....	....	....	....	....	....	....	....	....	....	....
24	Interest	....	....	....	....	....	....	....	....	....	....	....	....
25	Subsidies	....	....	....	....	....	....	....	....	....	....	....	....
26	Grants	....	....	....	....	....	....	....	....	....	....	....	....
27	Social benefits	....	....	....	....	....	....	....	....	....	....	....	....
28	Other payments	....	....	....	....	....	....	....	....	....	....	....	....
CIO	*Net cash inflow from oper. activities*	*1,431*	*10,717*	*11,183*	*11,885*	*11,303*	*14,995*	*4,389*	*3,743*	*4,198*	*17,702*	*25,763*	*30,376*
31.1	Purchases of nonfinancial assets	3,321	4,538	3,940	9,216	9,038	9,770	4,365	4,755	5,233	16,902	18,332	18,942
31.2	Sales of nonfinancial assets	990	1,559	1,028	1,410	1,530	1,526	606	738	734	3,006	3,827	3,288
31	Net cash outflow from investments in nonfinancial assets	2,331	2,979	2,912	7,806	7,508	8,244	3,759	4,017	4,499	13,896	14,505	15,654
CSD	*Cash surplus/deficit*	*−900*	*7,738*	*8,271*	*4,079*	*3,795*	*6,751*	*630*	*−274*	*−301*	*3,806*	*11,258*	*14,722*
32x	Net acquisition of fin assets, excl. cash	−6,424	2,114	3,775	−284	1,943	3,634	193	75	119	−5,378	4,222	7,781
321x	Domestic	....	....	....	....	....	....	....	....	....	....	....	....
322x	Foreign	....	....	....	....	....	....	....	....	....	....	....	....
323	Monetary gold and SDRs	—	—	—	—	—	—	—	—	—	—	—	—
33	Net incurrence of liabilities	−4,345	−5,319	−5,032	−1,898	−770	−1,598	−38	1,098	925	−5,137	−4,892	−15,516
331	Domestic	....	....	....	....	....	....	....	....	....	....	....	....
332	Foreign	....	....	....	....	....	....	....	....	....	....	....	....
NFB	Net cash inflow from fin. activities	2,079	−7,433	−8,807	−1,614	−2,713	−5,232	−231	1,023	806	241	−9,114	−23,297
NCB	*Net change in the stock of cash*	*1,179*	*305*	*−536*	*2,465*	*1,082*	*1,519*	*399*	*749*	*505*	*4,047*	*2,144*	*−8,575*
Table 1 Revenue													
1	**Revenue**	**196,294**	**213,538**	**229,012**	**106,183**	**113,210**	**123,352**	**18,114**	**19,018**	**20,312**	**262,613**	**286,526**	**310,265**
11	**Taxes**	**177,463**	**194,479**	**209,170**	**33,339**	**36,401**	**40,389**	**6,757**	**7,216**	**7,662**	**217,160**	**237,664**	**256,766**
111	Taxes on income, profits, & capital gains	119,032	131,278	142,066	—	—	—	—	—	—	119,032	131,278	142,066
1111	Individuals	86,112	91,484	98,979	—	—	—	—	—	—	86,112	91,484	98,979
1112	Corporations and other enterprises	31,782	38,696	41,990	—	—	—	—	—	—	31,782	38,696	41,990
112	Taxes on payroll and workforce	3,814	3,060	3,632	9,675	10,158	10,839	—	—	—	13,097	12,796	14,027
113	Taxes on property	12	13	13	12,431	14,164	16,679	6,757	7,216	7,662	19,193	21,383	24,346
114	Taxes on goods and services	49,391	54,555	57,837	11,233	12,079	12,871	—	—	—	60,624	66,634	70,705
1141	General taxes on goods and services	28,180	32,153	35,123	—	—	—	—	—	—	28,180	32,153	35,123
1142	Excises	20,489	21,645	21,903	5	—	4	—	—	—	20,494	21,648	21,907
115	Taxes on int'l. trade and transactions	5,214	5,573	5,622	—	—	—	—	—	—	5,214	5,573	5,622
116	Other taxes	—	—	—	—	—	—	—	—	—	—	—	—
12	**Social contributions**	—	—	—	—	—	—	—	—	—	—	—	—
121	Social security contributions	—	—	—	—	—	—	—	—	—	—	—	—
122	Other social contributions	—	—	—	—	—	—	—	—	—	—	—	—
13	**Grants**	**233**	**225**	**255**	**52,415**	**53,709**	**56,435**	**3,160**	**2,746**	**3,017**	**1**	**11**	**6**
131	From foreign governments	—	—	—	1	11	6	—	—	—	1	11	6
132	From international organizations	—	—	—	—	—	—	—	—	—	—	—	—
133	From other general government units	233	225	255	52,414	53,698	56,429	3,160	2,746	3,017	—	—	—
14	**Other revenue**	**18,598**	**18,834**	**19,587**	**20,429**	**23,100**	**26,528**	**8,197**	**9,056**	**9,633**	**45,452**	**48,851**	**53,493**

In Millions of Dollars / Year Ending June 30 / Noncash Reporter

	Central Government			State Government			Local Government			General Government		
	2002	2003	2004	2002	2003	2004	2002	2003	2004	2002	2003	2004
Table 2 Expense by economic type												
2 **Expense**.........	**199,464**	**207,007**	**221,329**	**104,177**	**109,615**	**117,305**	**16,507**	**17,555**	**18,272**	**262,158**	**275,023**	**294,618**
21 **Compensation of employees**..........	**19,281**	**21,234**	**22,741**	**43,961**	**47,509**	**50,901**	**5,713**	**6,250**	**6,604**	**68,948**	**74,983**	**80,238**
211 Wages and salaries.............	17,063	18,265	19,773	40,120	43,017	46,011	5,336	5,747	6,104	62,511	67,020	71,881
212 Social contributions.............	2,218	2,969	2,968	3,841	4,492	4,890	377	503	500	6,437	7,963	8,357
22 **Use of goods and services**.............	**19,143**	**20,832**	**22,341**	**25,789**	**27,049**	**28,472**	**6,582**	**6,936**	**7,250**	**50,088**	**53,029**	**56,180**
23 **Consumption of fixed capital**.............	**2,359**	**2,557**	**2,465**	**5,371**	**5,680**	**5,864**	**3,653**	**3,757**	**3,847**	**11,382**	**11,994**	**12,176**
24 **Interest**.............	**10,522**	**10,338**	**9,139**	**5,112**	**5,419**	**5,602**	**363**	**386**	**373**	**15,776**	**15,926**	**14,906**
25 **Subsidies**.............	**5,007**	**5,470**	**6,253**	**4,592**	**4,794**	**5,181**	—	**7**	—	**9,575**	**10,257**	**11,410**
26 **Grants**.............	**52,909**	**55,857**	**58,236**	**2,873**	**2,680**	**2,876**	—	—	—	—	**1,884**	**1,445**
261 To foreign govenments.............	—	....	....	—	—	—	—	—	—	—	....	....
262 To international organizations.............	—	....	....	—	—	—	—	—	—	—	....	....
263 To other general government units.............	52,909	53,973	56,791	2,873	2,680	2,876	—	—	—	—	—	—
2631 Current.............	49,780	51,448	54,463	2,200	2,025	2,237	—	—	—	—	—	—
2632 Capital.............	3,129	2,525	2,328	673	655	639	—	—	—	—	—	—
27 **Social benefits**.............	**78,996**	**81,590**	**91,354**	**2,611**	**2,651**	**2,836**	—	—	—	**81,607**	**84,241**	**94,191**
28 **Other expense**.............	**11,247**	**9,129**	**8,800**	**13,868**	**13,833**	**15,573**	**196**	**219**	**198**	**24,782**	**22,709**	**24,072**
281 Property expense other than interest.............	—	—	—	—	—	1	—	—	—	—	—	1
282 Miscellaneous other expense.............	11,247	9,129	8,800	13,868	13,833	15,572	196	219	198	24,782	22,709	24,071
2821 Current.............	10,128	8,523	8,146	10,331	11,338	12,514	176	199	178	20,121	19,605	20,363
2822 Capital.............	1,119	606	654	3,537	2,495	3,058	20	20	20	4,661	3,104	3,708
Table 3 Transactions in assets and liabilities												
3 **Change in net worth from transactns**....	**−3,170**	**6,533**	**7,682**	**2,006**	**3,596**	**6,045**	**1,607**	**1,463**	**2,032**	**456**	**11,505**	**15,648**
31 **Net acquisition of nonfinancial assets**...	**77**	**−56**	**965**	**3,094**	**2,317**	**2,593**	**973**	**1,311**	**1,858**	**4,144**	**3,572**	**5,416**
311 Fixed assets.............	−151	840	613	3,334	2,470	2,694	843	1,194	1,667	4,026	4,504	4,974
3111 Buildings and structures.............	....	....	....	....	....	....	....	....	....	....	....	....
3112 Machinery and equipment.............	....	....	....	....	....	....	....	....	....	....	....	....
3113 Other fixed assets.............	....	....	....	....	....	....	....	....	....	....	....	....
312 Inventories.............	182	−452	780	−15	24	−1	−10	−17	4	157	−445	783
313 Valuables.............	57	83	109	−2	5	−71	20	—	—	75	88	38
314 Nonproduced assets.............	−11	−527	−537	−223	−182	−29	120	134	187	−114	−575	−379
3141 Land.............	....	....	....	−235	−229	−78	120	134	187	....	....	....
3142 Subsoil assets.............	....	....	....	—	—	—	—	—	—	....	....	....
3143 Other naturally occurring assets.............	....	....	....	—	—	—	—	—	—	....	....	....
3144 Intangible nonproduced assets.............	....	....	....	12	45	49	—	—	—	....	....	....
32 **Net acquisition of financial assets**.........	**−6,022**	**2,572**	**3,291**	**2,953**	**2,996**	**5,260**	**657**	**876**	**651**	**−1,269**	**6,529**	**−726**
321 Domestic.............	....	....	....	....	....	....	....	....	....	....	....	....
3212 Currency and deposits.............	....	....	....	....	....	....	....	....	....	....	....	....
3213 Securities other than shares.............	....	....	....	....	....	....	....	....	....	....	....	....
3214 Loans.............	....	....	....	....	....	....	....	....	....	....	....	....
3215 Shares and other equity.............	....	....	....	....	....	....	....	....	....	....	....	....
3216 Insurance technical reserves.............	....	....	....	....	....	....	....	....	....	....	....	....
3217 Financial derivatives.............	....	....	....	....	....	....	....	....	....	....	....	....
3218 Other accounts receivable.............	....	....	....	....	....	....	....	....	....	....	....	....
322 Foreign.............	....	....	....	....	....	....	....	....	....	....	....	....
3222 Currency and deposits.............	....	....	....	....	....	....	....	....	....	....	....	....
3223 Securities other than shares.............	....	....	....	....	....	....	....	....	....	....	....	....
3224 Loans.............	....	....	....	....	....	....	....	....	....	....	....	....
3225 Shares and other equity.............	....	....	....	....	....	....	....	....	....	....	....	....
3226 Insurance technical reserves.............	....	....	....	....	....	....	....	....	....	....	....	....
3227 Financial derivatives.............	....	....	....	....	....	....	....	....	....	....	....	....
3228 Other accounts receivable.............	....	....	....	....	....	....	....	....	....	....	....	....
323 Monetary gold and SDRs.............	—	—	—	—	—	—	—	—	—	—	—	—
33 **Net incurrence of liabilities**.............	**−2,775**	**−4,017**	**−3,426**	**4,041**	**1,717**	**1,808**	**23**	**724**	**477**	**2,419**	**−1,404**	**−10,958**
331 Domestic.............	....	....	....	....	....	....	....	....	....	....	....	....
3312 Currency and deposits.............	....	....	....	....	....	....	....	....	....	....	....	....
3313 Securities other than shares.............	....	....	....	....	....	....	....	....	....	....	....	....
3314 Loans.............	....	....	....	....	....	....	....	....	....	....	....	....
3316 Insurance technical reserves.............	....	....	....	....	....	....	....	....	....	....	....	....
3317 Financial derivatives.............	....	....	....	....	....	....	....	....	....	....	....	....
3318 Other accounts payable.............	....	....	....	....	....	....	....	....	....	....	....	....

In Millions of Dollars / Year Ending June 30 / Noncash Reporter

		Central Government			State Government			Local Government			General Government		
		2002	2003	2004	2002	2003	2004	2002	2003	2004	2002	2003	2004
332	Foreign............................	....	....	....	....	....	....	....	....	....	....	....	....
3322	Currency and deposits................	....	....	....	....	....	....	....	....	....	....	....	....
3323	Securities other than shares............	....	....	....	....	....	....	....	....	....	....	....	....
3324	Loans.................................	....	....	....	....	....	....	....	....	....	....	....	....
3326	Insurance technical reserves............	....	....	....	....	....	....	....	....	....	....	....	....
3327	Financial derivatives...................	....	....	....	....	....	....	....	....	....	....	....	....
3328	Other accounts payable.................	....	....	....	....	....	....	....	....	....	....	....	....

Table 4   Holding gains in assets and liabilities

Table 5   Other changes in the volume of assets and liabilities

Table 6   Balance sheet

		Central Government			State Government			Local Government			General Government		
		2002	2003	2004	2002	2003	2004	2002	2003	2004	2002	2003	2004
6	**Net worth................**	**−23,210**	**−24,771**	**−6,831**	**271,861**	**307,964**	**341,239**	**153,912**	**162,200**	**173,227**	**402,564**	**445,396**	**507,636**
61	**Nonfinancial assets.........**	**54,452**	**55,987**	**61,085**	**211,978**	**230,479**	**246,698**	**153,277**	**160,811**	**171,152**	**419,704**	**447,280**	**478,936**
611	Fixed assets.................	39,081	36,958	38,964	155,435	165,348	169,237	108,889	112,967	118,640	303,405	315,275	326,841
6111	Buildings and structures......	23,575	25,340	26,484	146,669	156,235	159,820	105,550	108,647	114,238	275,794	290,223	300,542
6112	Machinery and equipment.....	14,106	10,010	10,666	8,365	8,640	8,875	3,263	4,305	4,386	25,734	22,956	23,927
6113	Other fixed assets............	1,400	1,608	1,814	401	473	542	76	15	16	1,877	2,096	2,372
612	Inventories...................	3,953	4,124	4,919	683	713	728	1,034	1,036	1,163	5,671	5,873	6,811
613	Valuables....................	2,106	6,907	8,361	6,416	7,430	7,556	2	2	2	8,524	14,339	15,919
614	Nonproduced assets...........	9,312	7,998	8,841	49,444	56,988	69,177	43,352	46,806	51,347	102,104	111,793	129,365
6141	Land........................	7,304	7,653	8,528	47,900	55,221	67,180	42,296	45,125	49,545	97,500	107,999	125,253
6142	Subsoil assets................	—	—	—	—	—	—	—	—	—	—	—	—
6143	Other naturally occurring assets....	1,992	308	273	1,473	1,669	1,863	1,056	1,681	1,802	4,517	3,659	3,938
6144	Intangible nonproduced assets.......	16	37	40	71	98	134	—	—	—	87	135	174
62	**Financial assets................**	**112,972**	**116,615**	**126,282**	**173,336**	**197,965**	**217,277**	**9,555**	**10,468**	**11,455**	**291,125**	**320,371**	**350,728**
621	Domestic....................	112,972	116,615	126,282	173,336	197,965	217,277	9,555	10,468	11,455	291,125	320,371	350,728
6212	Currency and deposits.........	2,989	3,245	2,579	7,843	7,474	8,253	3,382	4,001	4,508	14,203	14,716	15,341
6213	Securities other than shares.....	46,041	48,541	52,196	30,221	33,404	37,529	3,869	4,202	4,586	75,711	81,815	90,297
6214	Loans........................	—	—	—	—	—	—	—	—	—	—	—	—
6215	Shares and other equity........	47,735	44,811	49,651	123,446	144,559	157,409	425	566	598	171,605	189,935	207,657
6216	Insurance technical reserves......	—	—	—	—	—	—	—	—	—	—	—	—
6217	Financial derivatives...........	—	—	—	—	—	—	—	—	—	—	—	—
6218	Other accounts receivable........	16,207	20,018	21,856	11,826	12,528	14,086	1,879	1,699	1,763	29,606	33,905	37,433
622	Foreign.....................	....	....	....	....	....	....	....	....	....	....	....	....
6222	Currency and deposits.........	....	....	....	....	....	....	....	....	....	....	....	....
6223	Securities other than shares.....	....	....	....	....	....	....	....	....	....	....	....	....
6224	Loans........................	....	....	....	....	....	....	....	....	....	....	....	....
6225	Shares and other equity........	....	....	....	....	....	....	....	....	....	....	....	....
6226	Insurance technical reserves......	....	....	....	....	....	....	....	....	....	....	....	....
6227	Financial derivatives...........	....	....	....	....	....	....	....	....	....	....	....	....
6228	Other accounts receivable........	....	....	....	....	....	....	....	....	....	....	....	....
623	Monetary gold and SDRs.........												
63	**Liabilities..................**	**190,634**	**197,373**	**194,198**	**113,453**	**120,480**	**122,736**	**8,920**	**9,079**	**9,380**	**308,265**	**322,255**	**322,028**
631	Domestic....................	190,634	197,373	194,198	113,453	120,480	122,736	8,920	9,079	9,380	308,265	322,255	322,028
6312	Currency and deposits.........	2,380	2,496	2,608	1,374	1,370	1,379	143	293	342	3,886	4,155	4,329
6313	Securities other than shares.....	78,435	72,093	66,553	33,714	31,847	30,202	5,272	5,118	5,142	113,002	104,726	97,883
6314	Loans........................	—	—	—	—	—	—	—	—	—	—	—	—
6316	Insurance technical reserves......	84,018	92,124	90,919	48,847	55,043	56,047	—	—	—	132,865	147,167	146,966
6317	Financial derivatives...........	—	—	—	—	—	—	—	—	—	—	—	—
6318	Other accounts payable.........	25,801	30,660	34,118	29,518	32,220	35,108	3,505	3,668	3,896	58,512	66,207	72,850
632	Foreign.....................	....	....	....	....	....	....	....	....	....	....	....	....
6322	Currency and deposits.........	....	....	....	....	....	....	....	....	....	....	....	....
6323	Securities other than shares.....	....	....	....	....	....	....	....	....	....	....	....	....
6324	Loans........................	....	....	....	....	....	....	....	....	....	....	....	....
6326	Insurance technical reserves......	....	....	....	....	....	....	....	....	....	....	....	....
6327	Financial derivatives...........	....	....	....	....	....	....	....	....	....	....	....	....
6328	Other accounts payable.........	....	....	....	....	....	....	....	....	....	....	....	....

In Millions of Dollars / Year Ending June 30 / Noncash Reporter

	Central Government			State Government			Local Government			General Government		
	2002	2003	2004	2002	2003	2004	2002	2003	2004	2002	2003	2004
Memorandum items:												
6M2 Net financial worth..............	−77,662	−80,758	−67,916	59,883	77,485	94,541	635	1,389	2,075	−17,140	−1,884	28,700
6M3 Debt at market value................	....	....	....	....	....	....	....	....	....	....	....	....
6M4 Debt at nominal value...............	....	....	....	....	....	....	....	....	....	....	....	....
6M5 Arrears............................	....	....	....	....	....	....	....	....	....	....	....	....
6M6 Obligations for social security benefits...........	....	....	....	....	....	....	....	....	....	....	....	....
6M7 Contingent liabilities................	....	....	....	....	....	....	....	....	....	....	....	....
6M8 Uncapitalized military weapons, systems.......	....	....	....	....	....	....	....	....	....	....	....	....
Table 7 Outlays by functions of govt.												
7 **Total outlays......................**	**199,541**	**206,951**	**222,294**	**107,271**	**111,932**	**119,898**	**17,480**	**18,866**	**20,130**	**266,302**	**278,595**	**300,034**
701 **General public services.....................**	**53,032**	**54,855**	**56,456**	**12,194**	**11,838**	**13,647**	**3,753**	**4,000**	**4,262**	**33,777**	**34,209**	**36,216**
7017 Public debt transactions......................	10,522	10,338	9,139	5,112	5,419	5,602	363	386	373	15,776	15,926	14,906
7018 General transfers between levels of govt......	33,476	34,324	36,030	1,237	1,048	1,138	—	2	6	573	101	267
702 **Defense..........................**	**11,697**	**13,483**	**13,098**	—	—	—	—	—	—	**11,697**	**13,483**	**13,098**
703 **Public order and safety......................**	**1,880**	**1,939**	**2,319**	**10,195**	**10,684**	**11,563**	**385**	**456**	**453**	**12,226**	**12,903**	**14,069**
704 **Economic affairs.....................**	**14,143**	**13,317**	**14,155**	**17,341**	**17,302**	**18,448**	**5,257**	**5,685**	**5,884**	**33,691**	**33,801**	**35,602**
7042 Agriculture, forestry, fishing, and hunting.....	1,726	1,979	2,017	2,443	2,219	2,218	45	50	52	3,972	4,040	3,833
7043 Fuel and energy........................	3,194	3,589	3,688	1,039	1,037	1,201	21	47	42	3,210	3,587	3,688
7044 Mining, manufacturing, and construction.....	2,210	1,490	1,579	520	392	448	183	266	292	2,210	1,490	1,579
7045 Transport............................	2,445	1,757	2,301	10,755	10,650	11,754	4,470	4,692	4,830	15,014	14,912	16,605
7046 Communication........................	497	634	340	58	130	132	1	1	2	536	765	463
705 **Environmental protection.....................**	**621**	**499**	**446**	**1,370**	**−326**	**1,575**	**1,943**	**1,588**	**1,802**	**3,665**	**1,595**	**3,748**
706 **Housing and community amenities........**	**1,600**	**1,391**	**1,414**	**4,895**	**4,303**	**4,033**	**2,274**	**2,809**	**3,071**	**6,859**	**6,833**	**6,904**
707 **Health..........................**	**27,622**	**29,148**	**31,777**	**24,710**	**26,880**	**28,685**	**267**	**298**	**318**	**44,578**	**47,520**	**51,730**
7072 Outpatient services.....................	....	....	....	....	....	....	....	....	....	....	....	....
7073 Hospital services......................	....	....	....	....	....	....	....	....	....	....	....	....
7074 Public health services..................	....	....	....	....	....	....	....	....	....	....	....	....
708 **Recreation, culture, and religion...........**	**1,843**	**1,916**	**1,941**	**2,254**	**4,480**	**2,844**	**2,653**	**2,877**	**3,127**	**6,378**	**9,131**	**7,736**
709 **Education............................**	**17,994**	**19,104**	**20,611**	**27,782**	**29,776**	**31,563**	**47**	**76**	**69**	**38,647**	**41,652**	**44,038**
7091 Pre-primary and primary education..............	....	....	....	....	....	....	....	....	....	....	....	....
7092 Secondary education....................	....	....	....	....	....	....	....	....	....	....	....	....
7094 Tertiary education......................	....	....	....	....	....	....	....	....	....	....	....	....
710 **Social protection.....................**	**69,107**	**71,297**	**80,076**	**6,533**	**6,996**	**7,540**	**902**	**1,076**	**1,151**	**74,781**	**77,467**	**86,892**
7 Statistical discrepancy: Total outlays..............	2	2	1	−3	−1	—	−1	1	−7	3	1	1
Table 8 Transactions in financial assets and liabilities by sector												

Austria   122

In Millions of Euros / Year Ending December 31 / Noncash Reporter

		Central Government			State Government			Local Government			General Government		
		2001	2002	2003	2001	2002	2003	2001	2002	2003	2001	2002	2003
Statement of government operations													
1	Revenue................................	84,519	85,200	85,890	21,145	21,580	21,444	17,905	18,285	18,437	109,381	110,330	111,395
2	Expense................................	86,423	88,106	90,783	20,017	20,306	20,086	17,469	17,750	18,057	109,720	111,428	114,550
GOB	*Gross operating balance........*	*−688*	*−1,713*	*−3,717*	*1,502*	*1,653*	*1,747*	*1,772*	*1,877*	*1,736*	*2,586*	*1,817*	*−234*
NOB	*Net operating balance........*	*−1,903*	*−2,906*	*−4,892*	*1,128*	*1,273*	*1,358*	*436*	*535*	*380*	*−339*	*−1,098*	*−3,155*
31	Net acquisition of nonfinancial assets...........	−481	−526	−635	23	355	337	−120	−22	−23	−577	−193	−321
NLB	*Net lending/borrowing........*	*−1,423*	*−2,379*	*−4,257*	*1,105*	*918*	*1,021*	*556*	*557*	*403*	*238*	*−905*	*−2,833*
32	Net acquisition of financial assets..............	2,879	3,277	767	2,327	510	921	100	−62	−621	4,778	3,491	665
33	Net incurrence of liabilities..................	3,728	5,884	5,049	1,834	−377	−23	−491	−672	−1,036	4,543	4,601	3,588
NLB	Statistical discrepancy............	574	−228	−25	−612	−31	−76	35	54	12	−3	−205	−89
Statement of other economic flows													
Balance sheet													
6	*Net worth................*	....	....	....	....	....	....	....	....	....	....	....	....
61	Nonfinancial assets...............	....	....	....	....	....	....	....	....	....	....	....	....
62	Financial assets..................	33,574	36,627	37,774	19,544	18,578	19,125	6,198	6,141	5,520	56,753	58,548	59,220
63	Liabilities..................	139,215	147,304	147,628	7,064	6,556	6,655	7,667	7,045	5,911	151,383	158,109	156,995
Statement of sources and uses of cash													
Table 1 Revenue													
1	**Revenue.................**	**84,519**	**85,200**	**85,890**	**21,145**	**21,580**	**21,444**	**17,905**	**18,285**	**18,437**	**109,381**	**110,330**	**111,395**
11	**Taxes.................**	**45,363**	**45,810**	**46,276**	**6,742**	**6,619**	**6,438**	**10,651**	**10,353**	**10,171**	**62,757**	**62,781**	**62,885**
111	Taxes on income, profits, & capital gains......	22,601	21,551	21,232	3,850	3,662	3,612	4,416	4,071	4,009	30,867	29,284	28,853
1111	Individuals..................	16,885	16,991	17,286	2,910	2,905	2,893	3,319	3,244	3,234	23,115	23,140	23,414
1112	Corporations and other enterprises............	4,997	3,728	3,602	939	757	718	1,097	827	775	7,034	5,311	5,096
112	Taxes on payroll and workforce............	2,821	2,892	2,941	—	—	—	1,820	1,869	1,912	4,641	4,761	4,854
113	Taxes on property...........	244	229	248	57	50	52	929	901	934	1,230	1,179	1,234
114	Taxes on goods and services............	19,641	21,093	21,809	2,836	2,908	2,774	3,485	3,512	3,316	25,963	27,513	27,899
1141	General taxes on goods and services..........	11,395	12,502	12,873	2,142	2,175	1,997	2,705	2,728	2,510	16,243	17,405	17,379
1142	Excises..................	5,245	5,475	5,750	203	221	232	174	173	175	5,623	5,869	6,157
115	Taxes on int'l. trade and transactions...........	−6	−1	−1	—	—	—	—	—	—	−6	−1	−1
116	Other taxes..................	62	46	46	—	—	—	—	—	—	62	46	46
12	**Social contributions.................**	**33,237**	**33,775**	**34,610**	**1,411**	**1,384**	**1,384**	**870**	**847**	**900**	**35,518**	**36,006**	**36,894**
121	Social security contributions............	30,983	31,523	32,286	377	391	396	395	365	372	31,754	32,279	33,054
122	Other social contributions...........	2,254	2,252	2,324	1,034	993	988	475	482	528	3,764	3,727	3,840
13	**Grants.................**	**521**	**41**	**−464**	**10,881**	**11,527**	**11,586**	**3,181**	**3,730**	**3,790**	**395**	**564**	**536**
131	From foreign governments............	—	—	—	—	—	—	—	—	—	—	—	—
132	From international organizations............	335	534	454	54	27	73	6	3	9	395	564	536
133	From other general government units...........	186	−493	−918	10,827	11,500	11,513	3,176	3,728	3,781	—	—	—
14	**Other revenue.................**	**5,398**	**5,575**	**5,469**	**2,111**	**2,049**	**2,036**	**3,202**	**3,354**	**3,575**	**10,712**	**10,978**	**11,080**
Table 2 Expense by economic type													
2	**Expense.................**	**86,423**	**88,106**	**90,783**	**20,017**	**20,306**	**20,086**	**17,469**	**17,750**	**18,057**	**109,720**	**111,428**	**114,550**
21	**Compensation of employees.................**	**11,199**	**11,283**	**11,614**	**5,543**	**5,633**	**5,631**	**4,201**	**4,199**	**4,344**	**20,943**	**21,115**	**21,589**
211	Wages and salaries..................	8,162	8,221	8,441	4,137	4,200	4,207	3,291	3,274	3,357	15,590	15,696	16,005
212	Social contributions..................	3,036	3,062	3,173	1,407	1,433	1,424	910	925	987	5,353	5,420	5,584
22	**Use of goods and services.................**	**4,392**	**4,568**	**4,736**	**1,878**	**1,986**	**2,042**	**3,285**	**3,578**	**3,643**	**9,555**	**10,133**	**10,421**
23	**Consumption of fixed capital.................**	**1,215**	**1,193**	**1,176**	**374**	**379**	**390**	**1,336**	**1,343**	**1,356**	**2,925**	**2,915**	**2,921**
24	**Interest.................**	**7,280**	**7,132**	**6,809**	**249**	**154**	**100**	**216**	**143**	**119**	**7,745**	**7,429**	**7,027**
25	**Subsidies.................**	**3,935**	**4,381**	**4,626**	**1,221**	**1,364**	**1,259**	**1,368**	**1,337**	**1,333**	**6,524**	**7,082**	**7,218**
26	**Grants.................**	**11,488**	**12,310**	**12,751**	**2,382**	**2,320**	**1,639**	**2,195**	**2,186**	**2,274**	**1,876**	**2,081**	**2,288**
261	To foreign governments............	—	—	—	—	—	—	—	—	—	—	—	—
262	To international organizations..................	1,870	2,076	2,283	6	3	4	—	1	1	1,876	2,081	2,288
263	To other general government units............	9,618	10,233	10,468	2,376	2,316	1,635	2,195	2,185	2,273	—	—	—
2631	Current..................	8,725	9,282	9,485	1,482	1,554	966	2,039	2,068	2,147	—	—	—
2632	Capital..................	893	951	983	894	762	669	156	116	126	—	—	—
27	**Social benefits.................**	**42,927**	**44,022**	**45,868**	**4,553**	**4,683**	**4,789**	**2,529**	**2,568**	**2,643**	**50,009**	**51,273**	**53,300**
28	**Other expense.................**	**3,986**	**3,217**	**3,205**	**3,818**	**3,787**	**4,237**	**2,339**	**2,396**	**2,345**	**10,143**	**9,401**	**9,787**
281	Property expense other than interest...........	—	—	—	—	—	—	—	—	—	—	—	—
282	Miscellaneous other expense..................	3,986	3,217	3,205	3,818	3,787	4,237	2,339	2,396	2,345	10,143	9,401	9,787
2821	Current..................	843	1,069	833	2,850	2,669	3,263	944	992	1,033	4,637	4,730	5,129
2822	Capital..................	3,143	2,148	2,372	968	1,118	974	1,395	1,404	1,312	5,506	4,670	4,658

In Millions of Euros / Year Ending December 31 / Noncash Reporter

	Central Government			State Government			Local Government			General Government		
	2001	2002	2003	2001	2002	2003	2001	2002	2003	2001	2002	2003
Table 3 Transactions in assets and liabilities												
3 Change in net worth from transactns....	−1,329	−3,133	−4,917	516	1,242	1,281	472	589	392	−342	−1,303	−3,244
31 Net acquisition of nonfinancial assets...	−481	−526	−635	23	355	337	−120	−22	−23	−577	−193	−321
311 Fixed assets..............................	−431	−475	−579	16	310	376	−61	40	51	−477	−126	−153
3111 Buildings and structures...................	−432	−514	−565	8	298	363	−76	—	19	−500	−216	−183
3112 Machinery and equipment............	18	47	−6	13	15	12	21	43	36	51	105	42
3113 Other fixed assets....................	−18	−8	−8	−5	−4	—	−6	−4	−4	−28	−15	−12
312 Inventories.................................	—	—	—	—	—	—	—	—	—	—	—	—
313 Valuables.................................	3	1	1	—	—	—	—	—	—	3	1	1
314 Nonproduced assets....................	−52	−52	−56	7	46	−39	−59	−62	−74	−104	−68	−169
3141 Land....................................	....	....	....	....	....	....	....	....	....	....	....	....
3142 Subsoil assets.........................	....	....	....	....	....	....	....	....	....	....	....	....
3143 Other naturally occurring assets....	....	....	....	....	....	....	....	....	....	....	....	....
3144 Intangible nonproduced assets.........	....	....	....									
32 Net acquisition of financial assets........	2,879	3,277	767	2,327	510	921	100	−62	−621	4,778	3,491	665
321 Domestic................................	2,879	3,277	767	2,327	510	921	100	−62	−621	4,778	3,491	665
3212 Currency and deposits................	−60	−568	572	2,642	15	−499	100	−188	−621	2,683	−741	−548
3213 Securities other than shares.........	26	1,627	−1,535	—	2,442	—	—	—	—	26	4,069	−1,535
3214 Loans...................................	2,512	1,370	−150	−316	−2,073	1,203	—	126	—	1,669	−812	651
3215 Shares and other equity.............	177	299	164	—	126	217	—	—	—	177	425	381
3216 Insurance technical reserves........	—	—	—	—	—	—	—	—	—	—	—	—
3217 Financial derivatives.................	—	—	—	—	—	—	—	—	—	—	—	—
3218 Other accounts receivable...........	223	550	1,716	—	—	—	—	—	—	223	550	1,716
322 Foreign................................	....	....	....	....	....	....						
3222 Currency and deposits...............	....	....	....	....	....	....						
3223 Securities other than shares........	....	....	....	....	....	....						
3224 Loans..................................	....	....	....	....	....	....						
3225 Shares and other equity.............	....	....	....	....	....	....						
3226 Insurance technical reserves........	....	....	....	....	....	....						
3227 Financial derivatives.................	....	....	....	....	....	....						
3228 Other accounts receivable...........	....	....	....	....	....	....						
323 Monetary gold and SDRs.............	—	—	—	—	—	—	—	—	—	—	—	—
33 Net incurrence of liabilities...................	3,728	5,884	5,049	1,834	−377	−23	−491	−672	−1,036	4,543	4,601	3,588
331 Domestic................................	3,728	5,884	5,049	1,834	−377	−23	−491	−672	−1,036	4,543	4,601	3,588
3312 Currency and deposits................	—	—	—	—	—	—	—	—	—	—	—	—
3313 Securities other than shares.........	4,426	7,042	6,325	−102	−177	−70	−136	−182	−492	4,189	6,682	5,764
3314 Loans..................................	−1,009	−1,513	−1,473	1,935	−200	47	−355	−490	−688	43	−2,437	−2,517
3316 Insurance technical reserves........	—	—	—	—	—	—	—	—	—			
3317 Financial derivatives.................	307	440	334	—	—	—	—	—	—	307	440	334
3318 Other accounts payable.............	3	−84	−137	—	—	—	—	—	144	3	−84	7
332 Foreign................................	....	....	....	....	....	....	....	....	....	....	....	....
3322 Currency and deposits...............	....	....	....	....	....	....	....	....	....	....	....	....
3323 Securities other than shares........	....	....	....	....	....	....	....	....	....	....	....	....
3324 Loans..................................	....	....	....	....	....	....	....	....	....	....	....	....
3326 Insurance technical reserves........	....	....	....	....	....	....	....	....	....	....	....	....
3327 Financial derivatives.................	....	....	....	....	....	....	....	....	....	....	....	....
3328 Other accounts payable.............	....	....	....	....	....	....	....	....	....	....	....	....
Table 4 Holding gains in assets and liabilities												
Table 5 Other changes in the volume of assets and liabilities												
Table 6 Balance sheet												
6 Net worth..............................	....	....	....	....	....	....	....	....	....	....	....	....
61 Nonfinancial assets......................	....	....	....	....	....	....	....	....	....	....	....	....
611 Fixed assets..............................	....	....	....	....	....	....	....	....	....	....	....	....
6111 Buildings and structures...............	....	....	....	....	....	....	....	....	....	....	....	....
6112 Machinery and equipment............	....	....	....	....	....	....	....	....	....	....	....	....
6113 Other fixed assets....................	....	....	....	....	....	....	....	....	....	....	....	....
612 Inventories.................................	....	....	....	....	....	....	....	....	....	....	....	....
613 Valuables.................................	....	....	....	....	....	....	....	....	....	....	....	....
614 Nonproduced assets....................	....	....	....	....	....	....	....	....	....	....	....	....
6141 Land....................................	....	....	....	....	....	....	....	....	....	....	....	....
6142 Subsoil assets.........................	....	....	....	....	....	....	....	....	....	....	....	....
6143 Other naturally occurring assets....	....	....	....	....	....	....	....	....	....	....	....	....
6144 Intangible nonproduced assets..........	....	....	....	....	....	....	....	....	....	....	....	....

Austria 122

In Millions of Euros / Year Ending December 31 / Noncash Reporter

		Central Government			State Government			Local Government			General Government		
		2001	2002	2003	2001	2002	2003	2001	2002	2003	2001	2002	2003
62	**Financial assets**	**33,574**	**36,627**	**37,774**	**19,544**	**18,578**	**19,125**	**6,198**	**6,141**	**5,520**	**56,753**	**58,548**	**59,220**
621	Domestic	33,574	36,627	37,774	19,544	18,578	19,125	6,198	6,141	5,520	56,753	58,548	59,220
6212	Currency and deposits	5,148	4,470	5,056	3,208	3,222	2,728	3,446	3,258	2,636	11,802	10,950	10,420
6213	Securities other than shares	2,259	3,826	2,254	—	2,442	2,442	—	—	—	2,259	6,268	4,696
6214	Loans	15,729	17,131	16,980	16,291	12,744	13,568	2,753	2,883	2,884	32,210	29,960	30,232
6215	Shares and other equity	9,993	10,205	10,773	44	170	387	—	—	—	10,037	10,375	11,160
6216	Insurance technical reserves	—	—	—	—	—	—	—	—	—	—	—	—
6217	Financial derivatives	—	—	—	—	—	—	—	—	—	—	—	—
6218	Other accounts receivable	445	995	2,710	—	—	—	—	—	—	445	995	2,710
622	Foreign	....	....	....	....	....	....	....	....	....	....	....	....
6222	Currency and deposits	....	....	....	....	....	....	....	....	....	....	....	....
6223	Securities other than shares	....	....	....	....	....	....	....	....	....	....	....	....
6224	Loans	....	....	....	....	....	....	....	....	....	....	....	....
6225	Shares and other equity	....	....	....	....	....	....	....	....	....	....	....	....
6226	Insurance technical reserves	....	....	....	....	....	....	....	....	....	....	....	....
6227	Financial derivatives	....	....	....	....	....	....	....	....	....	....	....	....
6228	Other accounts receivable	....	....	....	....	....	....	....	....	....	....	....	....
623	Monetary gold and SDRs	—	—	—	—	—	—	—	—	—	—	—	—
63	**Liabilities**	**139,215**	**147,304**	**147,628**	**7,064**	**6,556**	**6,655**	**7,667**	**7,045**	**5,911**	**151,383**	**158,109**	**156,995**
631	Domestic	139,215	147,304	147,628	7,064	6,556	6,655	7,667	7,045	5,911	151,383	158,109	156,995
6312	Currency and deposits	—	—	—	—	—	—	—	—	—	—	—	—
6313	Securities other than shares	118,603	128,372	130,380	495	186	238	1,668	1,538	1,005	120,766	130,095	131,623
6314	Loans	19,761	18,166	16,619	6,568	6,370	6,417	5,562	5,019	4,273	29,328	26,758	24,109
6316	Insurance technical reserves	—	—	—	—	—	—	—	—	—	—	—	—
6317	Financial derivatives	—	—	—	—	—	—	—	—	—	—	—	—
6318	Other accounts payable	851	767	630	—	—	—	437	489	633	1,288	1,256	1,263
632	Foreign	....	....	....	....	....	....	....	....	....	....	....	....
6322	Currency and deposits	....	....	....	....	....	....	....	....	....	....	....	....
6323	Securities other than shares	....	....	....	....	....	....	....	....	....	....	....	....
6324	Loans	....	....	....	....	....	....	....	....	....	....	....	....
6326	Insurance technical reserves	....	....	....	....	....	....	....	....	....	....	....	....
6327	Financial derivatives	....	....	....	....	....	....	....	....	....	....	....	....
6328	Other accounts payable	....	....	....	....	....	....	....	....	....	....	....	....
	Memorandum items:												
6M2	Net financial worth	−105,641	−110,677	−109,854	12,480	12,022	12,470	−1,468	−905	−391	−94,629	−99,561	−97,775
6M3	Debt at market value	....	....	....	....	....	....	....	....	....	....	....	....
6M4	Debt at nominal value	....	....	....	....	....	....	....	....	....	....	....	....
6M5	Arrears	....	....	....	....	....	....	....	....	....	....	....	....
6M6	Obligations for social security benefits	....	....	....	....	....	....	....	....	....	....	....	....
6M7	Contingent liabilities	....	....	....	....	....	....	....	....	....	....	....	....
6M8	Uncapitalized military weapons, systems	....	....	....	....	....	....	....	....	....	....	....	....

Table 7   Outlays by functions of govt.

		Central Government			State Government			Local Government			General Government		
		2001	2002	2003	2001	2002	2003	2001	2002	2003	2001	2002	2003
7	**Total outlays**	**85,942**	**87,579**	**90,147**	**20,041**	**20,662**	**20,423**	**17,349**	**17,728**	**18,034**	**109,143**	**111,235**	**114,228**
701	**General public services**	**14,146**	**13,606**	**13,668**	**2,516**	**2,490**	**2,147**	**3,266**	**3,124**	**3,093**	**18,113**	**16,964**	**16,881**
7017	Public debt transactions	7,280	7,132	6,809	249	154	100	216	143	119	7,745	7,429	7,027
7018	General transfers between levels of govt.	....	....	....	....	....	....	....	....	....	....	....	....
702	**Defense**	**1,911**	**1,910**	**2,015**	—	—	—	—	—	—	**1,911**	**1,910**	**2,015**
703	**Public order and safety**	**2,645**	**2,680**	**2,784**	**99**	**121**	**110**	**336**	**392**	**409**	**2,987**	**3,090**	**3,206**
704	**Economic affairs**	**5,276**	**5,646**	**5,650**	**3,705**	**3,911**	**4,285**	**2,920**	**2,462**	**2,623**	**10,997**	**11,154**	**11,731**
7042	Agriculture, forestry, fishing, and hunting	....	....	....	....	....	....	....	....	....	....	....	....
7043	Fuel and energy	....	....	....	....	....	....	....	....	....	....	....	....
7044	Mining, manufacturing, and construction	....	....	....	....	....	....	....	....	....	....	....	....
7045	Transport	....	....	....	....	....	....	....	....	....	....	....	....
7046	Communication	....	....	....	....	....	....	....	....	....	....	....	....
705	**Environmental protection**	**425**	**230**	**271**	**185**	**174**	**173**	**449**	**438**	**486**	**841**	**734**	**841**
706	**Housing and community amenities**	**1,129**	**990**	**1,012**	**1,055**	**980**	**1,048**	**736**	**701**	**622**	**2,195**	**1,807**	**1,798**
707	**Health**	**11,984**	**12,453**	**12,795**	**4,125**	**4,316**	**4,031**	**2,232**	**3,086**	**3,080**	**12,939**	**14,693**	**14,866**
7072	Outpatient services	....	....	....	....	....	....	....	....	....	....	....	....
7073	Hospital services	....	....	....	....	....	....	....	....	....	....	....	....
7074	Public health services	....	....	....	....	....	....	....	....	....	....	....	....
708	**Recreation, culture, and religion**	**668**	**700**	**638**	**433**	**404**	**436**	**1,291**	**1,348**	**1,337**	**2,315**	**2,349**	**2,331**

In Millions of Euros / Year Ending December 31 / Noncash Reporter

		Central Government			State Government			Local Government			General Government		
		2001	2002	2003	2001	2002	2003	2001	2002	2003	2001	2002	2003
709	**Education**................	**8,468**	**8,778**	**8,804**	**3,766**	**3,927**	**3,917**	**2,912**	**3,002**	**3,098**	**12,108**	**12,552**	**12,865**
7091	Pre-primary and primary education.............	....	....	....	....	....	....	....	....	....	....	....	....
7092	Secondary education................	....	....	....	....	....	....	....	....	....	....	....	....
7094	Tertiary education................	....	....	....	....	....	....	....	....	....	....	....	....
710	**Social protection**................	**39,290**	**40,586**	**42,512**	**4,157**	**4,339**	**4,277**	**3,207**	**3,175**	**3,287**	**44,738**	**45,982**	**47,696**
7	Statistical discrepancy: Total outlays.............	—	—	—	—	—	—	—	—	—	—	—	—
Table 8 Transactions in financial assets and liabilities by sector													
82	**Net acquisition of financial assets**........	**2,879**	**3,277**	**767**	**2,327**	**510**	**921**	**100**	**−62**	**−621**	**4,778**	**3,491**	**665**
821	Domestic................	2,879	3,277	767	2,327	510	921	100	−62	−621	4,778	3,491	665
8211	General government................	....	....	....	....	....	....	....	....	....	....	....	....
8212	Central bank................	....	....	....	....	....	....	....	....	....	....	....	....
8213	Other depository corporations................	....	....	....	....	....	....	....	....	....	....	....	....
8214	Financial corporations n.e.c................	....	....	....	....	....	....	....	....	....	....	....	....
8215	Nonfinancial corporations................	....	....	....	....	....	....	....	....	....	....	....	....
8216	Households & NPIs serving households......	....	....	....	....	....	....	....	....	....	....	....	....
822	Foreign................	....	....	....	....	....	....	....	....	....	....	....	....
8221	General government................	....	....	....	....	....	....	....	....	....	....	....	....
8227	International organizations................	....	....	....	....	....	....	....	....	....	....	....	....
8228	Financial corporations other than international organizations.............	....	....	....	....	....	....	....	....	....	....	....	....
8229	Other nonresidents................	....	....	....	....	....	....	....	....	....	....	....	....
823	Monetary gold and SDRs................	—	—	—	—	—	—	—	—	—	—	—	—
83	**Net incurrence of liabilities**................	**3,728**	**5,884**	**5,049**	**1,834**	**−377**	**−23**	**−491**	**−672**	**−1,036**	**4,543**	**4,601**	**3,588**
831	Domestic................	3,728	5,884	5,049	1,834	−377	−23	−491	−672	−1,036	4,543	4,601	3,588
8311	General government................	....	....	....	....	....	....	....	....	....	....	....	....
8312	Central bank................	....	....	....	....	....	....	....	....	....	....	....	....
8313	Other depository corporations................	....	....	....	....	....	....	....	....	....	....	....	....
8314	Financial corporations n.e.c................	....	....	....	....	....	....	....	....	....	....	....	....
8315	Nonfinancial corporations................	....	....	....	....	....	....	....	....	....	....	....	....
8316	Households & NPIs serving households......	....	....	....	....	....	....	....	....	....	....	....	....
832	Foreign................	....	....	....	....	....	....	....	....	....	....	....	....
8321	General government................	....	....	....	....	....	....	....	....	....	....	....	....
8327	International organizations................	....	....	....	....	....	....	....	....	....	....	....	....
8328	Financial corporations other than international organizations.............	....	....	....	....	....	....	....	....	....	....	....	....
8329	Other nonresidents................	....	....	....	....	....	....	....	....	....	....	....	....

Azerbaijan, Republic of   912

In Billions of Manat / Year Ending December 31 / Cash Reporter

	Budgetary Central Government			Central Government			Local Government			General Government		
	1997	1998	1999	1997	1998	1999f	1997	1998	1999f	1997	1998	1999
Statement of government operations												
Statement of other economic flows												
Balance sheet												
Statement of sources and uses of cash												
1 Cash receipts from operating activities............	....	....	....	2,402.0	3,143.0	3,380.2	997.6	1,137.1	1,192.8	....	....	....
11 Taxes...	....	....	....	1,688.7	2,181.2	2,403.5	640.9	630.0	496.1	....	....	....
12 Social contributions.........................	....	....	....	548.8	723.9	733.0	—	—	—	....	....	....
13 Grants..	....	....	....	52.0	67.0	63.2	331.4	474.2	600.7	....	....	....
14 Other receipts.................................	....	....	....	112.5	170.9	180.5	25.3	32.9	96.0	....	....	....
2 Cash payments for operating activities..........	....	....	....	2,561.6	3,228.6	3,588.1	956.1	1,084.6	1,161.5	....	....	....
21 Compensation of employees................	....	....	....	316.5	383.1	....	560.7	735.2	747.7	....	....	....
22 Purchases of goods and services..........	....	....	....	784.2	918.5	....	307.5	328.5	329.3	....	....	....
24 Interest...	....	....	....	71.2	61.4	81.8	—	—	—	....	....	....
25 Subsidies.......................................	....	....	....	.8	1.0	.8	....	....	....	....	....	....
26 Grants..	....	....	....	364.2	524.5	648.7	....	....	....	....	....	....
27 Social benefits................................	....	....	....	981.1	1,260.0	1,463.1	....	....	....	....	....	....
28 Other payments..............................	....	....	....	43.5	80.2	61.4	....	....	....	....	....	....
CIO *Net cash inflow from oper. activities.....*	....	....	....	*−159.6*	*−85.6*	*−208.0*	*41.5*	*52.5*	*31.3*	....	....	....
31.1 Purchases of nonfinancial assets..................	....	....	....	467.0	764.5	672.8	41.5	52.5	31.3			
31.2 Sales of nonfinancial assets..........................	....	....	....	—	—	—						
31 Net cash outflow from investments in nonfinancial assets................	....	....	....	467.0	764.5	672.8	41.5	52.5	31.3	....	....	....
CSD *Cash surplus/deficit..............................*	....	....	....	*−626.5*	*−850.1*	*−880.8*	—	—	—			
32x Net acquisition of fin assets, excl. cash..........	....	....	....	−284.7	−227.1	−401.3	....	....	....			
321x Domestic..	....	....	....	−284.7	−227.1	−401.3	....	....	....			
322x Foreign..	....	....	....	—	—	—	....	....	....			
323 Monetary gold and SDRs..................	....	....	....	—	—	—	....	....	....			
33 Net incurrence of liabilities..............	....	....	....	....	....	....	....	....	....			
331 Domestic..	....	....	....	....	....	....	....	....	....			
332 Foreign..	....	....	....	....	....	....	....	....	....			
NFB Net cash inflow from fin. activities................	....	....	....	....	....	....	....	....	....			
NCB *Net change in the stock of cash.............*	....	....	....	....	....	....	....	....	....	....	....	....
Table 1 Revenue												
1 **Revenue...**	....	....	....	**2,402.0**	**3,143.0**	**3,380.2**	**997.6**	**1,137.1**	**1,192.8**	....	....	....
11 **Taxes...**	....	....	....	**1,688.7**	**2,181.2**	**2,403.5**	**640.9**	**630.0**	**496.1**	....	....	....
111 Taxes on income, profits, & capital gains......	....	....	....	479.9	645.5	725.4	253.9	268.5	209.6	....	....	....
1111 Individuals...	....	....	....	180.1	265.3	344.9	107.3	115.7	120.1	....	....	....
1112 Corporations and other enterprises..........	....	....	....	266.9	360.1	380.5	....	....	....	....	....	....
112 Taxes on payroll and workforce..........	....	....	....	8.9	10.3	11.6						
113 Taxes on property...........................	....	....	....	35.6	72.9	59.7	15.0	39.2	33.3			
114 Taxes on goods and services..............	....	....	....	967.6	1,172.7	1,323.8	325.7	252.7	221.2			
1141 General taxes on goods and services..........	....	....	....	479.1	603.2	692.6	....	....	....			
1142 Excises...	....	....	....	177.0	238.0	377.2						
115 Taxes on int'l. trade and transactions...........	....	....	....	196.7	280.0	283.0	—	—	—			
116 Other taxes.....................................	....	....	....	—	—	—	46.3	69.6	32.0			
12 **Social contributions.........................**	....	....	....	**548.8**	**723.9**	**733.0**	—	—	—	....	....	....
121 Social security contributions..........................	....	....	....	548.8	723.9	733.0	—	—	—	....	....	
122 Other social contributions..........................	....	....	....	—	—	—	....	....	....	....	....	
13 **Grants...**	....	....	....	**52.0**	**67.0**	**63.2**	**331.4**	**474.2**	**600.7**	....	....	....
131 From foreign governments...........................	....	....	....	52.0	67.0	63.2	—	—	—			
132 From international organizations.................	....	....	....	—	—	—	—	—	—			
133 From other general government units...........	....	....	....	—	—	—	331.4	474.2	600.7			
14 **Other revenue..................................**	....	....	....	**112.5**	**170.9**	**180.5**	**25.3**	**32.9**	**96.0**	....	....	....
Table 2 Expense by economic type												
2 **Expense..**	....	....	....	**2,561.6**	**3,228.6**	**3,588.1**	**956.1**	**1,084.6**	**1,161.5**	....	....	....
21 **Compensation of employees................**	....	....	....	**316.5**	**383.1**	....	**560.7**	**735.2**	**747.7**	....	....	....
211 Wages and salaries...........................	....	....	....	316.5	383.1	....	560.7	735.2	747.7			
212 Social contributions.........................	....	....	....	—	—	....	....	....	....			
22 **Use of goods and services.....................**	....	....	....	**784.2**	**918.5**	....	**307.5**	**328.5**	**329.3**			
23 **Consumption of fixed capital.................**	....	....	....	....	....	....	....	....	....			
24 **Interest..**	....	....	....	**71.2**	**61.4**	**81.8**	—	—	—	....	....	....
25 **Subsidies..**	....	....	....	**.8**	**1.0**	**.8**	....	....	....	....	....	....

In Billions of Manat / Year Ending December 31 / Cash Reporter

		Budgetary Central Government			Central Government			Local Government			General Government		
		1997	1998	1999	1997	1998	1999f	1997	1998	1999f	1997	1998	1999
26	**Grants**....................	....	....	....	**364.2**	**524.5**	**648.7**	....	....	....	....	....	....
261	To foreign govenments....................	....	....	....	32.8	50.2	48.0	....	....	....	....	....	....
262	To international organizations....................	....	....	....	—	—	—	....	....	....	....	....	....
263	To other general government units..............	....	....	....	331.4	474.2	600.7	—	—	—	....	....	....
2631	Current....................	....	....	....	331.4	474.2	600.7	—	—	—	....	....	....
2632	Capital....................	....	....	....	—	—	—	—	—	—	....	....	....
27	**Social benefits**....................	....	....	....	**981.1**	**1,260.0**	**1,463.1**	....	....	....	....	....	....
28	**Other expense**....................	....	....	....	**43.5**	**80.2**	**61.4**	....	....	....	....	....	....
281	Property expense other than interest............	....	....	....	—	—	—	....	....	....	....	....	....
282	Miscellaneous other expense....................	....	....	....	43.5	80.2	61.4	....	....	....	....	....	....
2821	Current....................	....	....	....	—	—	—	....	....	....	....	....	....
2822	Capital....................	....	....	....	43.5	80.2	61.4	....	....	....	....	....	....

Table 3   Transactions in assets and liabilities

		Budgetary Central Government			Central Government			Local Government			General Government		
		1997	1998	1999	1997	1998	1999f	1997	1998	1999f	1997	1998	1999
3	**Change in net worth from transactns**....	....	....	....	....	....	....	....	....	....	....	....	....
31	**Net acquisition of nonfinancial assets**...	....	....	....	**467.0**	**764.5**	**672.8**	**41.5**	**52.5**	**31.3**	....	....	....
311	Fixed assets....................	....	....	....	186.8	277.0	218.4	....	....	....	....	....	....
3111	Buildings and structures....................	....	....	....	....	....	....	....	....	....	....	....	....
3112	Machinery and equipment....................	....	....	....	....	....	....	....	....	....	....	....	....
3113	Other fixed assets....................	....	....	....	....	....	....	....	....	....	....	....	....
312	Inventories....................	....	....	....	280.1	487.5	454.4	....	....	....	....	....	....
313	Valuables....................	....	....	....	—	—	—	....	....	....	....	....	....
314	Nonproduced assets....................	....	....	....	—	—	—	....	....	....	....	....	....
3141	Land....................	....	....	....	—	—	—	....	....	....	....	....	....
3142	Subsoil assets....................	....	....	....	—	—	—	....	....	....	....	....	....
3143	Other naturally occurring assets....................	....	....	....	—	—	—	....	....	....	....	....	....
3144	Intangible nonproduced assets....................	....	....	....	—	—	—	....	....	....	....	....	....
32	**Net acquisition of financial assets**....................	....	....	....	....	....	....	....	....	....	....	....	....
321	Domestic....................	....	....	....	....	....	....	....	....	....	....	....	....
3212	Currency and deposits....................	....	....	....	....	....	....	....	....	....	....	....	....
3213	Securities other than shares....................	....	....	....	....	....	....	....	....	....	....	....	....
3214	Loans....................	....	....	....	....	....	....	....	....	....	....	....	....
3215	Shares and other equity....................	....	....	....	....	....	....	....	....	....	....	....	....
3216	Insurance technical reserves....................	....	....	....	....	....	....	....	....	....	....	....	....
3217	Financial derivatives....................	....	....	....	....	....	....	....	....	....	....	....	....
3218	Other accounts receivable....................	....	....	....	....	....	....	....	....	....	....	....	....
322	Foreign....................	....	....	....	....	....	....	....	....	....	....	....	....
3222	Currency and deposits....................	....	....	....	....	....	....	....	....	....	....	....	....
3223	Securities other than shares....................	....	....	....	....	....	....	....	....	....	....	....	....
3224	Loans....................	....	....	....	....	....	....	....	....	....	....	....	....
3225	Shares and other equity....................	....	....	....	....	....	....	....	....	....	....	....	....
3226	Insurance technical reserves....................	....	....	....	....	....	....	....	....	....	....	....	....
3227	Financial derivatives....................	....	....	....	....	....	....	....	....	....	....	....	....
3228	Other accounts receivable....................	....	....	....	....	....	....	....	....	....	....	....	....
323	Monetary gold and SDRs....................	....	....	....	....	....	....	....	....	....	....	....	....
33	**Net incurrence of liabilities**....................	....	....	....	....	....	....	....	....	....	....	....	....
331	Domestic....................	....	....	....	....	....	....	....	....	....	....	....	....
3312	Currency and deposits....................	....	....	....	....	....	....	....	....	....	....	....	....
3313	Securities other than shares....................	....	....	....	....	....	....	....	....	....	....	....	....
3314	Loans....................	....	....	....	....	....	....	....	....	....	....	....	....
3316	Insurance technical reserves....................	....	....	....	....	....	....	....	....	....	....	....	....
3317	Financial derivatives....................	....	....	....	....	....	....	....	....	....	....	....	....
3318	Other accounts payable....................	....	....	....	....	....	....	....	....	....	....	....	....
332	Foreign....................	....	....	....	....	....	....	....	....	....	....	....	....
3322	Currency and deposits....................	....	....	....	....	....	....	....	....	....	....	....	....
3323	Securities other than shares....................	....	....	....	....	....	....	....	....	....	....	....	....
3324	Loans....................	....	....	....	....	....	....	....	....	....	....	....	....
3326	Insurance technical reserves....................	....	....	....	....	....	....	....	....	....	....	....	....
3327	Financial derivatives....................	....	....	....	....	....	....	....	....	....	....	....	....
3328	Other accounts payable....................	....	....	....	....	....	....	....	....	....	....	....	....

Azerbaijan, Republic of   912

In Billions of Manat / Year Ending December 31 / Cash Reporter

	Budgetary Central Government			Central Government			Local Government			General Government		
	1997	1998	1999	1997	1998	1999f	1997	1998	1999f	1997	1998	1999
Table 4 Holding gains in assets and liabilities												
Table 5 Other changes in the volume of assets and liabilities												
Table 6 Balance sheet												
Table 7 Outlays by functions of govt.												
7 **Total outlays**	....	....	....	3,028.6	3,993.1	4,260.9	997.6	1,137.1	1,192.8	....	....	....
701 **General public services**	....	....	....	823.2	1,333.4	1,377.3	41.3	48.6	120.0	....	....	....
7017 Public debt transactions	....	....	....	71.2	61.4	81.8	—	—	—	....	....	....
7018 General transfers between levels of govt.	....	....	....	....	....	....	....	....	....	....	....	....
702 **Defense**	....	....	....	357.8	463.1	472.1	—	—	—	....	....	....
703 **Public order and safety**	....	....	....	256.4	380.2	482.9	—	—	—	....	....	....
704 **Economic affairs**	....	....	....	358.4	418.4	362.4	76.6	10.2	9.4	....	....	....
7042 Agriculture, forestry, fishing, and hunting	....	....	....	151.7	160.5	169.7	2.7	3.4	4.0	....	....	....
7043 Fuel and energy	....	....	....	—						....	....	....
7044 Mining, manufacturing, and construction	....	....	....	121.9	177.5	125.5	—	—	—	....	....	....
7045 Transport	....	....	....	45.6	56.0	56.0	73.9	6.8	5.4	....	....	....
7046 Communication	....	....	....	....	....	....	....	....	....	....	....	....
705 **Environmental protection**	....	....	....	....	....	....	....	....	....	....	....	....
706 **Housing and community amenities**	....	....	....	1.5	1.7	1.5	82.8	84.9	94.2	....	....	....
707 **Health**	....	....	....	149.4	45.1	34.7	208.5	245.1	185.7	....	....	....
7072 Outpatient services	....	....	....	....	....	....	....	....	....	....	....	....
7073 Hospital services	....	....	....	....	....	....	....	....	....	....	....	....
7074 Public health services	....	....	....	....	....	....	....	....	....	....	....	....
708 **Recreation, culture, and religion**	....	....	....	52.4	61.4	54.7	42.9	50.1	45.8	....	....	....
709 **Education**	....	....	....	117.0	140.8	136.3	534.9	685.1	723.9	....	....	....
7091 Pre-primary and primary education	....	....	....	....	....	....	....	....	....	....	....	....
7092 Secondary education	....	....	....	....	....	....	....	....	....	....	....	....
7094 Tertiary education	....	....	....	....	....	....	....	....	....	....	....	....
710 **Social protection**	....	....	....	964.9	1,227.3	1,412.1	10.8	13.3	13.9	....	....	....
7 Statistical discrepancy: Total outlays	....	....	....	−52.4	−78.1	−73.0	—	—	—	....	....	....
Table 8 Transactions in financial assets and liabilities by sector												
82 **Net acquisition of financial assets**	....	....	....	....	....	....	....	....	....	....	....	....
821 Domestic	....	....	....	....	....	....	....	....	....	....	....	....
8211 General government	....	....	....	....	223.3	.2	....	....	....	....	....	....
8212 Central bank	....	....	....	....	....	....	....	....	....	....	....	....
8213 Other depository corporations	....	....	....	....	....	....	....	....	....	....	....	....
8214 Financial corporations n.e.c.	....	....	....	....	....	....	....	....	....	....	....	....
8215 Nonfinancial corporations	....	....	....	....	−450.4	−401.5	....	....	....	....	....	....
8216 Households & NPIs serving households	....	....	....	....	....	....	....	....	....	....	....	....
822 Foreign	....	....	....	....	....	....	....	....	....	....	....	....
8221 General government	....	....	....	....	....	....	....	....	....	....	....	....
8227 International organizations	....	....	....	....	....	....	....	....	....	....	....	....
8228 Financial corporations other than international organizations	....	....	....	....	....	....	....	....	....	....	....	....
8229 Other nonresidents	....	....	....	....	....	....	....	....	....	....	....	....
823 Monetary gold and SDRs	....	....	....	....	....	—	....	....	....	....	....	....
83 **Net incurrence of liabilities**	....	....	....	....	....	....	....	....	....	....	....	....
831 Domestic	....	....	....	....	....	....	....	....	....	....	....	....
8311 General government	....	....	....	....	....	....	....	....	....	....	....	....
8312 Central bank	....	....	....	....	....	....	....	....	....	....	....	....
8313 Other depository corporations	....	....	....	....	....	....	....	....	....	....	....	....
8314 Financial corporations n.e.c.	....	....	....	....	....	....	....	....	....	....	....	....
8315 Nonfinancial corporations	....	....	....	....	....	....	....	....	....	....	....	....
8316 Households & NPIs serving households	....	....	....	....	....	....	....	....	....	....	....	....
832 Foreign	....	....	....	....	....	....	....	....	....	....	....	....
8321 General government	....	....	....	....	....	....	....	....	....	....	....	....
8327 International organizations	....	....	....	....	....	....	....	....	....	....	....	....
8328 Financial corporations other than international organizations	....	....	....	....	....	....	....	....	....	....	....	....
8329 Other nonresidents	....	....	....	....	....	....	....	....	....	....	....	....

	Budgetary Central Government			Extrabudgetary Accounts			Central Government			General Government		
	2002	2003	2004	2002	2003	2004	2002	2003	2004	2002	2003	2004
Statement of government operations												
Statement of other economic flows												
Balance sheet												
Statement of sources and uses of cash												
1 Cash receipts from operating activities...........	887.6	901.1	944.5	....	....	....	....	....	....	....	....	....
11 Taxes..	799.2	823.9	853.8	....	....	....	....	....	....	....	....	....
12 Social contributions.................................	—	—	—	....	....	....	....	....	....	....	....	....
13 Grants...	—	—	—	....	....	....	....	....	....	....	....	....
14 Other receipts...	88.4	77.2	90.7	....	....	....	....	....	....	....	....	....
2 Cash payments for operating activities...........	922.7	999.0	1,021.3	....	....	....	....	....	....	....	....	....
21 Compensation of employees.......................	400.5	421.3	450.1	....	....	....	....	....	....	....	....	....
22 Purchases of goods and services.................	201.5	233.2	199.1	....	....	....	....	....	....	....	....	....
24 Interest...	98.3	107.0	113.9	....	....	....	....	....	....	....	....	....
25 Subsidies..	114.4	138.0	138.7	....	....	....	....	....	....	....	....	....
26 Grants...	15.6	16.8	20.3	....	....	....	....	....	....	....	....	....
27 Social benefits.......................................	87.2	78.1	93.6	....	....	....	....	....	....	....	....	....
28 Other payments......................................	5.2	4.6	5.5	....	....	....	....	....	....	....	....	....
CIO *Net cash inflow from oper. activities.....*	*−35.1*	*−97.9*	*−76.8*	....	....	....	....	....	....	....	....	....
31.1 Purchases of nonfinancial assets...................	95.5	68.5	98.4	....	....	....	....	....	....	....	....	....
31.2 Sales of nonfinancial assets........................	1.3	.7	.7	....	....	....	....	....	....	....	....	....
31 Net cash outflow from investments in nonfinancial assets..................................	94.2	67.8	97.7	....	....	....	....	....	....	....	....	....
CSD *Cash surplus/deficit....................*	*−129.3*	*−165.7*	*−174.5*	....	....	....	....	....	....	....	....	....
32x Net acquisition of fin assets, excl. cash.........	5.0	42.0	22.5	....	....	....	....	....	....	....	....	....
321x Domestic..	5.0	42.0	22.5	....	....	....	....	....	....	....	....	....
322x Foreign..	—	—	—	....	....	....	....	....	....	....	....	....
323 Monetary gold and SDRs..........................	—	—	—	....	....	....	....	....	....	....	....	....
33 Net incurrence of liabilities......................	145.6	226.5	206.4	....	....	....	....	....	....	....	....	....
331 Domestic..	167.2	29.4	210.8	....	....	....	....	....	....	....	....	....
332 Foreign..	−21.6	197.1	−4.4	....	....	....	....	....	....	....	....	....
NFB Net cash inflow from fin. activities.................	140.6	184.5	183.9	....	....	....	....	....	....	....	....	....
NCB *Net change in the stock of cash...........*	*11.3*	*18.8*	*9.3*	....	....	....	....	....	....	....	....	....
Table 1 Revenue												
1 **Revenue.............................**	**887.6**	**901.1**	**944.5**	....	....	....	....	....	....	....	....	....
11 **Taxes.................................**	**799.2**	**823.9**	**853.8**	....	....	....	....	....	....	....	....	....
111 Taxes on income, profits, & capital gains......	—	—	—	....	....	....	....	....	....	....	....	....
1111 Individuals..	—	—	—	....	....	....	....	....	....	....	....	....
1112 Corporations and other enterprises............	—	—	—	....	....	....	....	....	....	....	....	....
112 Taxes on payroll and workforce..................	—	—	—	....	....	....	....	....	....	....	....	....
113 Taxes on property...................................	83.1	77.9	116.6	....	....	....	....	....	....	....	....	....
114 Taxes on goods and services.....................	54.7	47.9	50.4	....	....	....	....	....	....	....	....	....
1141 General taxes on goods and services..........	—	—	—	....	....	....	....	....	....	....	....	....
1142 Excises..	—	—	—	....	....	....	....	....	....	....	....	....
115 Taxes on int'l. trade and transactions...........	506.7	529.0	483.6	....	....	....	....	....	....	....	....	....
116 Other taxes..	154.7	169.1	203.1	....	....	....	....	....	....	....	....	....
12 **Social contributions............................**	**—**	**—**	**—**	....	....	....	....	....	....	....	....	....
121 Social security contributions.....................	—	—	—	....	....	....	....	....	....	....	....	....
122 Other social contributions........................	—	—	—	....	....	....	....	....	....	....	....	....
13 **Grants.................................**	**—**	**—**	**—**	....	....	....	....	....	....	....	....	....
131 From foreign governments........................	—	—	—	....	....	....	....	....	....	....	....	....
132 From international organizations................	—	—	—	....	....	....	....	....	....	....	....	....
133 From other general government units..........	—	—	—	....	....	....	....	....	....	....	....	....
14 **Other revenue....................**	**88.4**	**77.2**	**90.7**	....	....	....	....	....	....	....	....	....
Table 2 Expense by economic type												
2 **Expense................................**	**922.7**	**999.0**	**1,021.3**	....	....	....	....	....	....	....	....	....
21 **Compensation of employees..................**	**400.5**	**421.3**	**450.1**	....	....	....	....	....	....	....	....	....
211 Wages and salaries.................................	389.9	410.9	439.4	....	....	....	....	....	....	....	....	....
212 Social contributions.................................	10.6	10.4	10.7	....	....	....	....	....	....	....	....	....
22 **Use of goods and services......................**	**201.5**	**233.2**	**199.1**	....	....	....	....	....	....	....	....	....
23 **Consumption of fixed capital...............**	....	....	....	....	....	....	....	....	....	....	....	....
24 **Interest................................**	**98.3**	**107.0**	**113.9**	....	....	....	....	....	....	....	....	....
25 **Subsidies...............................**	**114.4**	**138.0**	**138.7**	....	....	....	....	....	....	....	....	....

In Millions of Dollars / Year Ending December 31 / Cash Reporter

		Budgetary Central Government			Extrabudgetary Accounts			Central Government			General Government		
		2002	2003	2004	2002	2003	2004	2002	2003	2004	2002	2003	2004
26	**Grants**....................................	**15.6**	**16.8**	**20.3**	....	....	....	....	....	....	....	....	....
261	To foreign govenments......................	—	—	—	....	....	....	....	....	....	....	....	....
262	To international organizations..............	—	—	—	....	....	....	....	....	....	....	....	....
263	To other general government units........	15.6	16.8	20.3	....	....	....	....	....	....	....	....	....
2631	Current...	11.6	12.6	15.7	....	....	....	....	....	....	....	....	....
2632	Capital...	4.0	4.2	4.6	....	....	....	....	....	....	....	....	....
27	**Social benefits**.............................	**87.2**	**78.1**	**93.6**	....	....	....	....	....	....	....	....	....
28	**Other expense**.............................	**5.2**	**4.6**	**5.5**	....	....	....	....	....	....	....	....	....
281	Property expense other than interest......	—	—	—	....	....	....	....	....	....	....	....	....
282	Miscellaneous other expense...............	5.2	4.6	5.5	....	....	....	....	....	....	....	....	....
2821	Current...	5.2	4.6	5.5	....	....	....	....	....	....	....	....	....
2822	Capital...	—	—	—	....	....	....	....	....	....	....	....	....

Table 3   Transactions in assets and liabilities

		2002	2003	2004	2002	2003	2004	2002	2003	2004	2002	2003	2004
3	**Change in net worth from transactns....**	....	....	....	....	....	....	....	....	....	....	....	....
31	**Net acquisition of nonfinancial assets...**	**94.2**	**67.8**	**97.7**	....	....	....	....	....	....	....	....	....
311	Fixed assets...................................	89.5	65.8	73.2	....	....	....	....	....	....	....	....	....
3111	Buildings and structures....................	....	....	73.4	....	....	....	....	....	....	....	....	....
3112	Machinery and equipment..................	....	....	−.2	....	....	....	....	....	....	....	....	....
3113	Other fixed assets...........................	....	....	—	....	....	....	....	....	....	....	....	....
312	Inventories....................................	−.2	−.4	−.2	....	....	....	....	....	....	....	....	....
313	Valuables......................................	—	—	—	....	....	....	....	....	....	....	....	....
314	Nonproduced assets.........................	4.9	2.4	24.7	....	....	....	....	....	....	....	....	....
3141	Land..	4.9	2.4	24.7	....	....	....	....	....	....	....	....	....
3142	Subsoil assets................................	—	—	—	....	....	....	....	....	....	....	....	....
3143	Other naturally occurring assets...........	—	—	—	....	....	....	....	....	....	....	....	....
3144	Intangible nonproduced assets.............	—	—	—	....	....	....	....	....	....	....	....	....
32	**Net acquisition of financial assets........**	**16.3**	**60.8**	**31.8**	....	....	....	....	....	....	....	....	....
321	Domestic.......................................	16.3	60.8	31.8	....	....	....	....	....	....	....	....	....
3212	Currency and deposits.......................	11.3	18.8	9.3	....	....	....	....	....	....	....	....	....
3213	Securities other than shares................	—	—	—	....	....	....	....	....	....	....	....	....
3214	Loans...	5.0	42.0	37.5	....	....	....	....	....	....	....	....	....
3215	Shares and other equity.....................	—	—	−15.0	....	....	....	....	....	....	....	....	....
3216	Insurance technical reserves................	—	—	—	....	....	....	....	....	....	....	....	....
3217	Financial derivatives.........................	—	—	—	....	....	....	....	....	....	....	....	....
3218	Other accounts receivable...................	....	....	....	....	....	....	....	....	....	....	....	....
322	Foreign...	—	—	—	....	....	....	....	....	....	....	....	....
3222	Currency and deposits.......................	—	—	—	....	....	....	....	....	....	....	....	....
3223	Securities other than shares................	—	—	—	....	....	....	....	....	....	....	....	....
3224	Loans...	—	—	—	....	....	....	....	....	....	....	....	....
3225	Shares and other equity.....................	—	—	—	....	....	....	....	....	....	....	....	....
3226	Insurance technical reserves................	—	—	—	....	....	....	....	....	....	....	....	....
3227	Financial derivatives.........................	—	—	—	....	....	....	....	....	....	....	....	....
3228	Other accounts receivable...................	....	....	....	....	....	....	....	....	....	....	....	....
323	Monetary gold and SDRs....................	—	—	—	....	....	....	....	....	....	....	....	....
33	**Net incurrence of liabilities..................**	**145.6**	**226.5**	**206.4**	....	....	....	....	....	....	....	....	....
331	Domestic.......................................	167.2	29.4	210.8	....	....	....	....	....	....	....	....	....
3312	Currency and deposits.......................	−5.9	45.9	62.5	....	....	....	....	....	....	....	....	....
3313	Securities other than shares................	95.3	77.8	165.7	....	....	....	....	....	....	....	....	....
3314	Loans...	77.8	−94.3	−17.5	....	....	....	....	....	....	....	....	....
3316	Insurance technical reserves................	—	—	—	....	....	....	....	....	....	....	....	....
3317	Financial derivatives.........................	—	—	—	....	....	....	....	....	....	....	....	....
3318	Other accounts payable......................	....	....	....	....	....	....	....	....	....	....	....	....
332	Foreign...	−21.6	197.1	−4.4	....	....	....	....	....	....	....	....	....
3322	Currency and deposits.......................	—	—	—	....	....	....	....	....	....	....	....	....
3323	Securities other than shares................	−25.6	200.0	—	....	....	....	....	....	....	....	....	....
3324	Loans...	4.0	−2.9	−4.4	....	....	....	....	....	....	....	....	....
3326	Insurance technical reserves................	—	—	—	....	....	....	....	....	....	....	....	....
3327	Financial derivatives.........................	—	—	—	....	....	....	....	....	....	....	....	....
3328	Other accounts payable......................	....	....	....	....	....	....	....	....	....	....	....	....

In Millions of Dollars / Year Ending December 31 / Cash Reporter

	Budgetary Central Government			Extrabudgetary Accounts			Central Government			General Government		
	2002	2003	2004	2002	2003	2004	2002	2003	2004	2002	2003	2004
Table 4 Holding gains in assets and liabilities												
Table 5 Other changes in the volume of assets and liabilities												
Table 6 Balance sheet												
6 **Net worth**............	....	....	....	....	....	....	....	....	....	....	....	....
61 **Nonfinancial assets**............	....	....	....	....	....	....	....	....	....	....	....	....
611 Fixed assets............	....	....	....	....	....	....	....	....	....	....	....	....
6111 Buildings and structures............	....	....	....	....	....	....	....	....	....	....	....	....
6112 Machinery and equipment............	....	....	....	....	....	....	....	....	....	....	....	....
6113 Other fixed assets............	....	....	....	....	....	....	....	....	....	....	....	....
612 Inventories............	....	....	....	....	....	....	....	....	....	....	....	....
613 Valuables............	....	....	....	....	....	....	....	....	....	....	....	....
614 Nonproduced assets............	....	....	....	....	....	....	....	....	....	....	....	....
6141 Land............	....	....	....	....	....	....	....	....	....	....	....	....
6142 Subsoil assets............	....	....	....	....	....	....	....	....	....	....	....	....
6143 Other naturally occurring assets............	....	....	....	....	....	....	....	....	....	....	....	....
6144 Intangible nonproduced assets............	....	....	....	....	....	....	....	....	....	....	....	....
62 **Financial assets**............	....	....	....	....	....	....	....	....	....	....	....	....
621 Domestic............	....	....	....	....	....	....	....	....	....	....	....	....
6212 Currency and deposits............	....	....	....	....	....	....	....	....	....	....	....	....
6213 Securities other than shares............	....	....	....	....	....	....	....	....	....	....	....	....
6214 Loans............	....	....	....	....	....	....	....	....	....	....	....	....
6215 Shares and other equity............	....	....	....	....	....	....	....	....	....	....	....	....
6216 Insurance technical reserves............	....	....	....	....	....	....	....	....	....	....	....	....
6217 Financial derivatives............	....	....	....	....	....	....	....	....	....	....	....	....
6218 Other accounts receivable............	....	....	....	....	....	....	....	....	....	....	....	....
622 Foreign............	....	....	....	....	....	....	....	....	....	....	....	....
6222 Currency and deposits............	....	....	....	....	....	....	....	....	....	....	....	....
6223 Securities other than shares............	....	....	....	....	....	....	....	....	....	....	....	....
6224 Loans............	....	....	....	....	....	....	....	....	....	....	....	....
6225 Shares and other equity............	....	....	....	....	....	....	....	....	....	....	....	....
6226 Insurance technical reserves............	....	....	....	....	....	....	....	....	....	....	....	....
6227 Financial derivatives............	....	....	....	....	....	....	....	....	....	....	....	....
6228 Other accounts receivable............	....	....	....	....	....	....	....	....	....	....	....	....
623 Monetary gold and SDRs............	....	....	....	....	....	....	....	....	....	....	....	....
63 **Liabilities**............	....	....	....	....	....	....	....	....	....	....	....	....
631 Domestic............	....	....	....	....	....	....	....	....	....	....	....	....
6312 Currency and deposits............	....	....	....	....	....	....	....	....	....	....	....	....
6313 Securities other than shares............	1,488.5	1,566.3	1,732.0	....	....	....	....	....	....	....	....	....
6314 Loans............	....	....	81.3	....	....	....	....	....	....	....	....	....
6316 Insurance technical reserves............	....	....	....	....	....	....	....	....	....	....	....	....
6317 Financial derivatives............	....	....	....	....	....	....	....	....	....	....	....	....
6318 Other accounts payable............	....	....	....	....	....	....	....	....	....	....	....	....
632 Foreign............	96.1	292.1	287.7	....	....	....	....	....	....	....	....	....
6322 Currency and deposits............	—	—	—	....	....	....	....	....	....	....	....	....
6323 Securities other than shares............	25.0	225.0	225.0	....	....	....	....	....	....	....	....	....
6324 Loans............	71.1	67.1	62.7	....	....	....	....	....	....	....	....	....
6326 Insurance technical reserves............	—	—	—	....	....	....	....	....	....	....	....	....
6327 Financial derivatives............	—	—	—	....	....	....	....	....	....	....	....	....
6328 Other accounts payable............	....	....	....	....	....	....	....	....	....	....	....	....
Memorandum items:												
6M2 Net financial worth............	....	....	....	....	....	....	....	....	....	....	....	....
6M3 Debt at market value............	....	....	....	....	....	....	....	....	....	....	....	....
6M4 Debt at nominal value............	....	....	....	....	....	....	....	....	....	....	....	....
6M5 Arrears............	....	....	....	....	....	....	....	....	....	....	....	....
6M6 Obligations for social security benefits............	....	....	....	....	....	....	....	....	....	....	....	....
6M7 Contingent liabilities............	417.7	462.9	432.3	....	....	....	....	....	....	....	....	....
6M8 Uncapitalized military weapons, systems........	....	....	....	....	....	....	....	....	....	....	....	....
Table 7 Outlays by functions of govt.												
7 **Total outlays**............	1,018.2	1,067.5	1,119.7	....	....	....	....	....	....	....	....	....
701 **General public services**............	246.1	295.7	307.1	....	....	....	....	....	....	....	....	....
7017 Public debt transactions............	98.3	107.0	113.9	....	....	....	....	....	....	....	....	....
7018 General transfers between levels of govt......	....	....	....	....	....	....	....	....	....	....	....	....
702 **Defense**............	28.5	30.9	34.3	....	....	....	....	....	....	....	....	....
703 **Public order and safety**............	119.9	129.3	135.8	....	....	....	....	....	....	....	....	....

		Budgetary Central Government			Extrabudgetary Accounts			Central Government			General Government		
		2002	2003	2004	2002	2003	2004	2002	2003	2004	2002	2003	2004
704	**Economic affairs**............................	**200.0**	**166.1**	**172.9**	....	....	....	....	....	....	....	....	....
7042	Agriculture, forestry, fishing, and hunting.....	12.1	12.9	13.5	....	....	....	....	....	....	....	....	....
7043	Fuel and energy..................................	....	....	....	....	....	....	....	....	....	....	....	....
7044	Mining, manufacturing, and construction.....	....	....	....	....	....	....	....	....	....	....	....	....
7045	Transport..	19.4	20.7	22.6	....	....	....	....	....	....	....	....	....
7046	Communication..................................	1.4	3.0	3.8	....	....	....	....	....	....	....	....	....
705	**Environmental protection**....................	....	....	....	....	....	....	....	....	....	....	....	....
706	**Housing and community amenities**........	**8.7**	**12.3**	**14.7**	....	....	....	....	....	....	....	....	....
707	**Health**..	**158.6**	**173.3**	**184.8**	....	....	....	....	....	....	....	....	....
7072	Outpatient services.............................	....	....	....	....	....	....	....	....	....	....	....	....
7073	Hospital services................................	105.9	117.2	....	....	....	....	....	....	....	....	....	....
7074	Public health services..........................	....	....	....	....	....	....	....	....	....	....	....	....
708	**Recreation, culture, and religion**..........	—	—	—	....	....	....	....	....	....	....	....	....
709	**Education**..	**193.9**	**199.5**	**208.9**	....	....	....	....	....	....	....	....	....
7091	Pre-primary and primary education..............	....	....	....	....	....	....	....	....	....	....	....	....
7092	Secondary education............................	....	....	....	....	....	....	....	....	....	....	....	....
7094	Tertiary education...............................	....	....	....	....	....	....	....	....	....	....	....	....
710	**Social protection**...............................	**62.5**	**60.4**	**61.1**	....	....	....	....	....	....	....	....	....
7	Statistical discrepancy: Total outlays..............	—	—	—	....	....	....	....	....	....	....	....	....

Table 8 Transactions in financial assets and liabilities by sector

		Budgetary Central Government			Extrabudgetary Accounts			Central Government			General Government		
82	**Net acquisition of financial assets**........	**16.3**	**60.8**	**31.8**	....	....	....	....	....	....	....	....	....
821	Domestic...	16.3	60.8	31.8	....	....	....	....	....	....	....	....	....
8211	General government.............................	....	....	....	....	....	....	....	....	....	....	....	....
8212	Central bank.....................................	....	....	....	....	....	....	....	....	....	....	....	....
8213	Other depository corporations..................	11.3	....	....	....	....	....	....	....	....	....	....	....
8214	Financial corporations n.e.c....................	....	....	....	....	....	....	....	....	....	....	....	....
8215	Nonfinancial corporations.......................	....	....	....	....	....	....	....	....	....	....	....	....
8216	Households & NPIs serving households......	....	....	....	....	....	....	....	....	....	....	....	....
822	Foreign..	—	—	—	....	....	....	....	....	....	....	....	....
8221	General government.............................	—	—	—	....	....	....	....	....	....	....	....	....
8227	International organizations......................	—	—	—	....	....	....	....	....	....	....	....	....
8228	Financial corporations other than international organizations..............	—	—	—	....	....	....	....	....	....	....	....	....
8229	Other nonresidents.............................	—	—	—	....	....	....	....	....	....	....	....	....
823	Monetary gold and SDRs.......................	—	—	—	....	....	....	....	....	....	....	....	....
83	**Net incurrence of liabilities**...................	**145.6**	**226.5**	**206.4**	....	....	....	....	....	....	....	....	....
831	Domestic...	167.2	29.4	210.8	....	....	....	....	....	....	....	....	....
8311	General government.............................	....	....	....	....	....	....	....	....	....	....	....	....
8312	Central bank.....................................	−7.7	....	34.7	....	....	....	....	....	....	....	....	....
8313	Other depository corporations..................	43.5	....	....	....	....	....	....	....	....	....	....	....
8314	Financial corporations n.e.c....................	....	....	....	....	....	....	....	....	....	....	....	....
8315	Nonfinancial corporations.......................	....	....	....	....	....	....	....	....	....	....	....	....
8316	Households & NPIs serving households......	....	....	83.4	....	....	....	....	....	....	....	....	....
832	Foreign..	−21.6	197.1	−4.4	....	....	....	....	....	....	....	....	....
8321	General government.............................	—	—	—	....	....	....	....	....	....	....	....	....
8327	International organizations......................	9.1	2.3	.7	....	....	....	....	....	....	....	....	....
8328	Financial corporations other than international organizations..............	—	—	—	....	....	....	....	....	....	....	....	....
8329	Other nonresidents.............................	−30.7	194.8	−5.2	....	....	....	....	....	....	....	....	....

In Millions of Dinars / Year Ending December 31 / Cash Reporter

	Budgetary Central Government			Central Government			Local Government			General Government		
	2002	2003	2004p	2002	2003	2004p	2002	2003	2004	2002	2003	2004
Statement of government operations												
Statement of other economic flows												
Balance sheet												
6 *Net worth*...................	....	....	....	....	....	....	....	....	....	....	....	....
61 Nonfinancial assets...................	....	....	....	....	....	....	....	....	....	....	....	....
62 Financial assets...................	....	....	....	....	....	....	....	....	....	....	....	....
63 Liabilities...................	1,023.7	1,351.4	1,453.6	1,023.7	1,351.4	1,453.6	....	....	....	....	....	....
Statement of sources and uses of cash												
1 Cash receipts from operating activities...	972.9	1,089.8	1,284.1	1,025.7	1,144.8	1,336.8	....	....	....	....	....	....
11 Taxes...................	129.1	137.7	208.5	129.1	137.7	208.5	....	....	....	....	....	....
12 Social contributions...................	—	—	—	52.8	55.0	52.7	....	....	....	....	....	....
13 Grants...................	38.2	18.8	22.0	38.2	18.8	22.0	....	....	....	....	....	....
14 Other receipts...................	805.6	933.3	1,053.6	805.6	933.3	1,053.6	....	....	....	....	....	....
2 Cash payments for operating activities...	836.2	868.9	957.7	870.5	907.8	997.6	....	....	....	....	....	....
21 Compensation of employees...................	449.0	519.4	537.8	453.6	558.3	577.7	....	....	....	....	....	....
22 Purchases of goods and services...................	141.6	134.4	145.7	141.6	134.4	145.7	....	....	....	....	....	....
24 Interest...................	35.9	49.4	45.9	35.9	49.4	45.9	....	....	....	....	....	....
25 Subsidies...................	38.0	54.3	17.1	38.0	54.3	17.1	....	....	....	....	....	....
26 Grants...................	....	111.4	74.1	....	111.4	74.1	....	....	....	....	....	....
27 Social benefits...................	—	—	—	29.7	—	—	....	....	....	....	....	....
28 Other payments...................	....	—	137.1	....	—	137.1	....	....	....	....	....	....
CIO *Net cash inflow from oper. activities...*	*212.6*	*−62.2*	*202.2*	*155.2*	*237.0*	*339.2*	....	....	....	....	....	....
31.1 Purchases of nonfinancial assets...................	166.0	147.7	103.5	166.0	147.7	103.5	....	....	....	....	....	....
31.2 Sales of nonfinancial assets...................	.6	.7	.5	.6	.7	.5	....	....	....	....	....	....
31 Net cash outflow from investments in nonfinancial assets...................	165.4	147.0	103.0	165.4	147.0	103.0	....	....	....	....	....	....
CSD *Cash surplus/deficit...*	*47.2*	*−209.2*	*99.2*	*−10.2*	*90.0*	*236.2*	....	....	....	....	....	....
32x Net acquisition of fin assets, excl. cash...	—	—	—	−83.2	299.3	219.7	....	....	....	....	....	....
321x Domestic...................	—	—	—	−83.2	299.3	219.7	....	....	....	....	....	....
322x Foreign...................	—	—	—	—	—	—	....	....	....	....	....	....
323 Monetary gold and SDRs...................	—	—	—	—	—	—	....	....	....	....	....	....
33 Net incurrence of liabilities...................	−54.6	133.9	−191.9	−62.0	209.2	−99.2	....	....	....	....	....	....
331 Domestic...................	−95.6	−123.8	−203.3	−103.0	−48.5	−110.6	....	....	....	....	....	....
332 Foreign...................	41.0	257.7	11.4	41.0	257.7	11.4	....	....	....	....	....	....
NFB Net cash inflow from fin. activities...	−54.6	133.9	−191.9	21.2	−90.1	−318.9	....	....	....	....	....	....
NCB *Net change in the stock of cash...*	*−7.4*	*−75.3*	*−92.7*	*11.0*	*−.1*	*−82.7*	....	....	....	....	....	....
Table 1 Revenue												
1 **Revenue**...................	972.9	1,089.8	1,284.1	1,025.7	1,144.8	1,336.8	....	....	....	....	....	....
11 **Taxes**...................	129.1	137.7	208.5	129.1	137.7	208.5	....	....	....	....	....	....
111 Taxes on income, profits, & capital gains...	40.8	40.9	54.7	40.8	40.9	54.7	....	....	....	....	....	....
1111 Individuals...................	—	—	—	—	—	—	....	....	....	....	....	....
1112 Corporations and other enterprises...	40.8	40.9	54.7	40.8	40.9	54.7	....	....	....	....	....	....
112 Taxes on payroll and workforce...................	15.1	16.3	17.1	15.1	16.3	17.1	....	....	....	....	....	....
113 Taxes on property...................	6.6	9.6	12.0	6.6	9.6	12.0	....	....	....	....	....	....
114 Taxes on goods and services...................	19.6	21.1	20.8	19.6	21.1	20.8	....	....	....	....	....	....
1141 General taxes on goods and services...	—	—	—	—	—	—	....	....	....	....	....	....
1142 Excises...................	2.4	2.5	—	2.4	2.5	—	....	....	....	....	....	....
115 Taxes on int'l. trade and transactions...	47.0	49.8	57.1	47.0	49.8	57.1	....	....	....	....	....	....
116 Other taxes...................	—	—	46.8	—	—	46.8	....	....	....	....	....	....
12 **Social contributions**...................	—	—	—	52.8	55.0	52.7	....	....	....	....	....	....
121 Social security contributions...................	—	—	—	52.8	55.0	52.7	....	....	....	....	....	....
122 Other social contributions...................	—	—	—	—	—	—	....	....	....	....	....	....
13 **Grants**...................	38.2	18.8	22.0	38.2	18.8	22.0	....	....	....	....	....	....
131 From foreign governments...................	38.2	18.8	22.0	38.2	18.8	22.0	....	....	....	....	....	....
132 From international organizations...................	—	—	—	—	—	—	....	....	....	....	....	....
133 From other general government units...	—	—	—	—	—	—	....	....	....	....	....	....
14 **Other revenue**...................	805.6	933.3	1,053.6	805.6	933.3	1,053.6	....	....	....	....	....	....
Table 2 Expense by economic type												
2 **Expense**...................	836.2	868.9	957.7	870.5	907.8	997.6	....	....	....	....	....	....
21 **Compensation of employees**...................	449.0	519.4	537.8	453.6	558.3	577.7	....	....	....	....	....	....
211 Wages and salaries...................	449.0	515.0	537.8	453.6	....	577.7	....	....	....	....	....	....
212 Social contributions...................	—	4.4	—	—	....	—	....	....	....	....	....	....
22 **Use of goods and services**...................	141.6	134.4	145.7	141.6	134.4	145.7	....	....	....	....	....	....
23 **Consumption of fixed capital**...................	....	....	....	....	....	....	....	....	....	....	....	....
24 **Interest**...................	35.9	49.4	45.9	35.9	49.4	45.9	....	....	....	....	....	....
25 **Subsidies**...................	38.0	54.3	17.1	38.0	54.3	17.1	....	....	....	....	....	....

		Budgetary Central Government			Central Government			Local Government			General Government		
		2002	2003	2004p	2002	2003	2004p	2002	2003	2004	2002	2003	2004
26	Grants....................	....	111.4	74.1	....	111.4	74.1	....	....	....	....	....	....
261	To foreign govenments...........	....	....	—	....	....	—	....	....	....	....	....	....
262	To international organizations...........	....	....	—	....	....	—	....	....	....	....	....	....
263	To other general government units...........	....	....	74.1	....	....	74.1	....	....	....	....	....	....
2631	Current...........	46.6	....	74.1	46.6	....	74.1	....	....	....	....	....	....
2632	Capital...........	....	....	—	....	....	—	....	....	....	....	....	....
27	Social benefits....................	—	—	—	29.7	—	—	....	....	....	....	....	....
28	Other expense....................	....	—	137.1	....	—	137.1	....	....	....	....	....	....
281	Property expense other than interest...........	....	—	—	....	—	—	....	....	....	....	....	....
282	Miscellaneous other expense...........	....	—	137.1	....	—	137.1	....	....	....	....	....	....
2821	Current...........	....	—	—	....	—	—	....	....	....	....	....	....
2822	Capital...........	....	—	137.1	....	—	137.1	....	....	....	....	....	....

Table 3 Transactions in assets and liabilities

		Budgetary Central Government			Central Government			Local Government			General Government		
3	Change in net worth from transactns....	....	....	....	....	....	....	....	....	....	....	....	....
31	Net acquisition of nonfinancial assets...	165.4	147.0	103.0	165.4	147.0	103.0	....	....	....	....	....	....
311	Fixed assets...........	165.7	147.2	103.5	165.7	147.2	103.5	....	....	....	....	....	....
3111	Buildings and structures...........	....	....	....	....	....	....	....	....	....	....	....	....
3112	Machinery and equipment...........	....	....	....	....	....	....	....	....	....	....	....	....
3113	Other fixed assets...........	....	....	....	....	....	....	....	....	....	....	....	....
312	Inventories...........	−.2	−.2	−.1	−.2	−.2	−.1	....	....	....	....	....	....
313	Valuables...........	—	—	—	—	—	—	....	....	....	....	....	....
314	Nonproduced assets...........	−.1	—	−.4	−.1	—	−.4	....	....	....	....	....	....
3141	Land...........	....	—	....	....	—	....	....	....	....	....	....	....
3142	Subsoil assets...........	....	—	....	....	—	....	....	....	....	....	....	....
3143	Other naturally occurring assets...........	....	—	....	....	—	....	....	....	....	....	....	....
3144	Intangible nonproduced assets...........	....	—	....	....	—	....	....	....	....	....	....	....
32	Net acquisition of financial assets........	−7.4	−75.3	−92.7	−72.2	299.2	137.0	....	....	....	....	....	....
321	Domestic...........	−7.4	−75.3	−92.7	−72.2	299.2	137.0	....	....	....	....	....	....
3212	Currency and deposits...........	−7.4	−75.3	−92.7	11.0	−.1	−82.7	....	....	....	....	....	....
3213	Securities other than shares...........	—	—	—	....	....	—	....	....	....	....	....	....
3214	Loans...........	—	—	—	....	....	219.7	....	....	....	....	....	....
3215	Shares and other equity...........	—	—	—	....	....	—	....	....	....	....	....	....
3216	Insurance technical reserves...........	—	—	—	....	....	—	....	....	....	....	....	....
3217	Financial derivatives...........	—	—	—	....	....	—	....	....	....	....	....	....
3218	Other accounts receivable...........	....	....	....	....	....	—	....	....	....	....	....	....
322	Foreign...........	—	—	—	—	—	—	....	....	....	....	....	....
3222	Currency and deposits...........	—	—	—	—	—	—	....	....	....	....	....	....
3223	Securities other than shares...........	—	—	—	—	—	—	....	....	....	....	....	....
3224	Loans...........	—	—	—	—	—	—	....	....	....	....	....	....
3225	Shares and other equity...........	—	—	—	—	—	—	....	....	....	....	....	....
3226	Insurance technical reserves...........	—	—	—	—	—	—	....	....	....	....	....	....
3227	Financial derivatives...........	—	—	—	—	—	—	....	....	....	....	....	....
3228	Other accounts receivable...........	....	....	....	....	....	....	....	....	....	....	....	....
323	Monetary gold and SDRs...........							....	....	....	....	....	....
33	Net incurrence of liabilities....................	−54.6	133.9	−191.9	−62.0	209.2	−99.2	....	....	....	....	....	....
331	Domestic...........	−95.6	−123.8	−203.3	−103.0	−48.5	−110.6	....	....	....	....	....	....
3312	Currency and deposits...........	−179.7	−193.8	−300.0	−179.7	−193.8	−300.0	....	....	....	....	....	....
3313	Securities other than shares...........	26.4	−5.5	—	19.0	69.8	92.7	....	....	....	....	....	....
3314	Loans...........	57.7	75.5	96.7	57.7	75.5	96.7	....	....	....	....	....	....
3316	Insurance technical reserves...........	—	—	—	—	—	—	....	....	....	....	....	....
3317	Financial derivatives...........	—	—	—	—	—	—	....	....	....	....	....	....
3318	Other accounts payable...........	....	....	....	....	....	....	....	....	....	....	....	....
332	Foreign...........	41.0	257.7	11.4	41.0	257.7	11.4	....	....	....	....	....	....
3322	Currency and deposits...........	—	—	—	—	—	—	....	....	....	....	....	....
3323	Securities other than shares...........	—	—	—	—	—	—	....	....	....	....	....	....
3324	Loans...........	41.0	257.7	11.4	41.0	257.7	11.4	....	....	....	....	....	....
3326	Insurance technical reserves...........	—	—	—	—	—	—	....	....	....	....	....	....
3327	Financial derivatives...........	—	—	—	—	—	—	....	....	....	....	....	....
3328	Other accounts payable...........	....	....	....	....	....	....	....	....	....	....	....	....

	Budgetary Central Government 2002	2003	2004p	Central Government 2002	2003	2004p	Local Government 2002	2003	2004	General Government 2002	2003	2004
Table 4 Holding gains in assets and liabilities												
Table 5 Other changes in the volume of assets and liabilities												
Table 6 Balance sheet												
6 **Net worth**	....	....	....	....	....	....	....	....	....	....	....	....
61 **Nonfinancial assets**	....	....	....	....	....	....	....	....	....	....	....	....
611 Fixed assets	....	....	....	....	....	....	....	....	....	....	....	....
6111 Buildings and structures	....	....	....	....	....	....	....	....	....	....	....	....
6112 Machinery and equipment	....	....	....	....	....	....	....	....	....	....	....	....
6113 Other fixed assets	....	....	....	....	....	....	....	....	....	....	....	....
612 Inventories	....	....	....	....	....	....	....	....	....	....	....	....
613 Valuables	....	....	....	....	....	....	....	....	....	....	....	....
614 Nonproduced assets	....	....	....	....	....	....	....	....	....	....	....	....
6141 Land	....	....	....	....	....	....	....	....	....	....	....	....
6142 Subsoil assets	....	....	....	....	....	....	....	....	....	....	....	....
6143 Other naturally occurring assets	....	....	....	....	....	....	....	....	....	....	....	....
6144 Intangible nonproduced assets	....	....	....	....	....	....	....	....	....	....	....	....
62 **Financial assets**	....	....	....	....	....	....	....	....	....	....	....	....
621 Domestic	....	....	....	....	....	....	....	....	....	....	....	....
6212 Currency and deposits	....	....	....	....	....	....	....	....	....	....	....	....
6213 Securities other than shares	....	....	....	....	....	....	....	....	....	....	....	....
6214 Loans	....	....	....	....	....	....	....	....	....	....	....	....
6215 Shares and other equity	....	....	....	....	....	....	....	....	....	....	....	....
6216 Insurance technical reserves	....	....	....	....	....	....	....	....	....	....	....	....
6217 Financial derivatives	....	....	....	....	....	....	....	....	....	....	....	....
6218 Other accounts receivable	....	....	....	....	....	....	....	....	....	....	....	....
622 Foreign	....	....	....	....	....	....	....	....	....	....	....	....
6222 Currency and deposits	....	....	....	....	....	....	....	....	....	....	....	....
6223 Securities other than shares	....	....	....	....	....	....	....	....	....	....	....	....
6224 Loans	....	....	....	....	....	....	....	....	....	....	....	....
6225 Shares and other equity	....	....	....	....	....	....	....	....	....	....	....	....
6226 Insurance technical reserves	....	....	....	....	....	....	....	....	....	....	....	....
6227 Financial derivatives	....	....	....	....	....	....	....	....	....	....	....	....
6228 Other accounts receivable	....	....	....	....	....	....	....	....	....	....	....	....
623 Monetary gold and SDRs	....	....	....	....	....	....	....	....	....	....	....	....
63 **Liabilities**	**1,023.7**	**1,351.4**	**1,453.6**	**1,023.7**	**1,351.4**	**1,453.6**	....	....	....	....	....	....
631 Domestic	841.5	911.5	1,002.3	841.5	911.5	1,002.3	....	....	....	....	....	....
6312 Currency and deposits	....	....	....	....	....	....	....	....	....	....	....	....
6313 Securities other than shares	....	....	....	....	....	....	....	....	....	....	....	....
6314 Loans	....	....	....	....	....	....	....	....	....	....	....	....
6316 Insurance technical reserves	....	....	....	....	....	....	....	....	....	....	....	....
6317 Financial derivatives	....	....	....	....	....	....	....	....	....	....	....	....
6318 Other accounts payable	....	....	....	....	....	....	....	....	....	....	....	....
632 Foreign	182.2	439.9	451.3	182.2	439.9	451.3	....	....	....	....	....	....
6322 Currency and deposits	....	....	....	....	....	....	....	....	....	....	....	....
6323 Securities other than shares	....	....	....	....	....	....	....	....	....	....	....	....
6324 Loans	....	....	....	....	....	....	....	....	....	....	....	....
6326 Insurance technical reserves	....	....	....	....	....	....	....	....	....	....	....	....
6327 Financial derivatives	....	....	....	....	....	....	....	....	....	....	....	....
6328 Other accounts payable	....	....	....	....	....	....	....	....	....	....	....	....
Memorandum items:												
6M2 Net financial worth	....	....	....	....	....	....	....	....	....	....	....	....
6M3 Debt at market value	....	....	....	....	....	....	....	....	....	....	....	....
6M4 Debt at nominal value	....	....	....	....	....	....	....	....	....	....	....	....
6M5 Arrears	....	....	....	....	....	....	....	....	....	....	....	....
6M6 Obligations for social security benefits	....	....	....	....	....	....	....	....	....	....	....	....
6M7 Contingent liabilities	....	....	....	....	....	....	....	....	....	....	....	....
6M8 Uncapitalized military weapons, systems	....	....	....	....	....	....	....	....	....	....	....	....
Table 7 Outlays by functions of govt.												
7 **Total outlays**	**1,002.2**	**1,016.6**	**1,061.2**	**1,036.5**	**1,055.5**	**1,101.1**	....	....	....	....	....	....
701 **General public services**	**444.1**	**349.5**	**416.2**	**444.1**	**349.5**	**416.2**	....	....	....	....	....	....
7017 Public debt transactions	35.9	49.4	45.9	35.9	49.4	45.9	....	....	....	....	....	....
7018 General transfers between levels of govt	....	....	....	....	....	....	....	....	....	....	....	....
702 **Defense**	**149.5**	**174.5**	**180.0**	**149.5**	**174.5**	**180.0**	....	....	....	....	....	....
703 **Public order and safety**	**106.5**	**111.4**	**112.7**	**106.5**	**111.4**	**112.7**	....	....	....	....	....	....

In Millions of Dinars / Year Ending December 31 / Cash Reporter

		Budgetary Central Government			Central Government			Local Government			General Government		
		2002	2003	2004p	2002	2003	2004p	2002	2003	2004	2002	2003	2004
704	**Economic affairs**................................	**16.6**	**19.9**	**19.9**	**16.6**	**19.9**	**19.9**	....	....	....	....	....	....
7042	Agriculture, forestry, fishing, and hunting.....	3.7	5.3	5.6	3.7	5.3	5.6	....	....	....	....	....	....
7043	Fuel and energy............................	1.5	1.6	1.6	1.5	1.6	1.6	....	....	....	....	....	....
7044	Mining, manufacturing, and construction.....	2.8	5.3	5.3	2.8	5.3	5.3	....	....	....	....	....	....
7045	Transport....................................	8.4	7.4	2.4	8.4	7.4	2.4	....	....	....	....	....	....
7046	Communication.............................	....	....	....	....	....	....	....	....	....	....	....	....
705	**Environmental protection**....................	—	—	—	—	—	—	....	....	....	....	....	....
706	**Housing and community amenities**........	**41.2**	**105.0**	**33.4**	**41.2**	**105.0**	**33.4**	....	....	....	....	....	....
707	**Health**.......................................	**71.1**	**80.6**	**88.4**	**71.1**	**80.6**	**88.4**	....	....	....	....	....	....
7072	Outpatient services...........................	—	—	—	—	—	—	....	....	....	....	....	....
7073	Hospital services.............................	71.1	80.6	88.4	71.1	80.6	88.4	....	....	....	....	....	....
7074	Public health services.........................	—	—	—	—	—	—	....	....	....	....	....	....
708	**Recreation, culture, and religion**...........	**5.4**	**5.6**	**2.2**	**5.4**	**5.6**	**2.2**	....	....	....	....	....	....
709	**Education**....................................	**131.1**	**162.8**	**169.6**	**131.1**	**162.8**	**169.6**	....	....	....	....	....	....
7091	Pre-primary and primary education.............			....			....	....	....	....	....	....	....
7092	Secondary education..........................	110.6	129.6	141.7	110.6	129.6	141.7	....	....	....	....	....	....
7094	Tertiary education............................	20.5	33.2	27.9	20.5	33.2	27.9	....	....	....	....	....	....
710	**Social protection**.............................	**36.7**	**7.3**	**38.8**	**71.0**	**46.2**	**78.7**	....	....	....	....	....	....
7	Statistical discrepancy: Total outlays.............	—	—	—	—	—	—	....	....	....	....	....	....

Table 8   Transactions in financial assets and liabilities by sector

		Budgetary Central Government			Central Government			Local Government			General Government		
82	**Net acquisition of financial assets**........	**−7.4**	**−75.3**	**−92.7**	**−72.2**	**299.2**	**137.0**	....	....	....	....	....	....
821	Domestic....................................	−7.4	−75.3	−92.7	−72.2	299.2	137.0	....	....	....	....	....	....
8211	General government.............................	....	—	—	....	299.3	219.7	....	....	....	....	....	....
8212	Central bank.................................	....	....	....	....	....	....	....	....	....	....	....	....
8213	Other depository corporations..................	....	....	....	....	....	....	....	....	....	....	....	....
8214	Financial corporations n.e.c...................	....	....	....	....	....	....	....	....	....	....	....	....
8215	Nonfinancial corporations.....................	....	....	....	....	....	....	....	....	....	....	....	....
8216	Households & NPIs serving households......	....	....	....	....	....	....	....	....	....	....	....	....
822	Foreign.....................................	—	—	—	—	—	—	....	....	....	....	....	....
8221	General government.............................	—	—	—	—	—	—	....	....	....	....	....	....
8227	International organizations.....................	—	—	—	—	—	—	....	....	....	....	....	....
8228	Financial corporations other than international organizations..............	—	—	—	—	—	—	....	....	....	....	....	....
8229	Other nonresidents...........................	—	—	—	—	—	—	....	....	....	....	....	....
823	Monetary gold and SDRs.......................	—	—	—	—	—	—	....	....	....	....	....	....
83	**Net incurrence of liabilities**.................	**−54.6**	**133.9**	**−191.9**	**−62.0**	**209.2**	**−99.2**	....	....	....	....	....	....
831	Domestic....................................	−95.6	−123.8	−203.3	−103.0	−48.5	−110.6	....	....	....	....	....	....
8311	General government.............................	....	....	....	....	....	....	....	....	....	....	....	....
8312	Central bank.................................	....	....	....	....	....	....	....	....	....	....	....	....
8313	Other depository corporations..................	....	....	....	....	....	....	....	....	....	....	....	....
8314	Financial corporations n.e.c...................	....	....	....	....	....	....	....	....	....	....	....	....
8315	Nonfinancial corporations.....................	....	....	....	....	....	....	....	....	....	....	....	....
8316	Households & NPIs serving households......	....	....	....	....	....	....	....	....	....	....	....	....
832	Foreign.....................................	41.0	257.7	11.4	41.0	257.7	11.4	....	....	....	....	....	....
8321	General government.............................	—	—	—	—	—	—	....	....	....	....	....	....
8327	International organizations.....................	41.0	257.7	11.4	41.0	257.7	11.4	....	....	....	....	....	....
8328	Financial corporations other than international organizations..............	—	—	—	—	—	—	....	....	....	....	....	....
8329	Other nonresidents...........................	—	—	—	—	—	—	....	....	....	....	....	....

		Budgetary Central Government			Central Government			Local Government			General Government		
		2002	2003	2004	2002	2003	2004	2002	2003	2004	2002	2003	2004
	Statement of government operations												
	Statement of other economic flows												
	Balance sheet												
	Statement of sources and uses of cash												
1	Cash receipts from operating activities..........	298,672	336,680	347,303	298,672	336,680	347,303	....	....	....	....	....	....
11	Taxes.....................................	210,297	242,612	270,086	210,297	242,612	270,086	....	....	....	....	....	....
12	Social contributions.....................	—	—	—	—	—	—	....	....	....	....	....	....
13	Grants...................................	19,759	33,092	15,495	19,759	33,092	15,495	....	....	....	....	....	....
14	Other receipts...........................	68,616	60,976	61,722	68,616	60,976	61,722	....	....	....	....	....	....
2	Cash payments for operating activities..........	247,877	272,945	291,494	247,877	272,945	291,494	....	....	....	....	....	....
21	Compensation of employees.................	65,394	69,137	74,314	65,394	69,137	74,314	....	....	....	....	....	....
22	Purchases of goods and services..................	35,371	43,907	49,298	35,371	43,907	49,298	....	....	....	....	....	....
24	Interest..................................	49,217	56,160	56,864	49,217	56,160	56,864	....	....	....	....	....	....
25	Subsidies................................	3,419	9,384	8,883	3,419	9,384	8,883	....	....	....	....	....	....
26	Grants...................................	37,851	42,898	48,828	37,851	42,898	48,828	....	....	....	....	....	....
27	Social benefits...........................	21,425	25,597	28,145	21,425	25,597	28,145	....	....	....	....	....	....
28	Other payments..........................	35,200	25,862	25,163	35,200	25,862	25,163	....	....	....	....	....	....
CIO	*Net cash inflow from oper. activities.....*	*50,795*	*63,735*	*55,808*	*50,795*	*63,735*	*55,808*	....	....	....	....	....	....
31.1	Purchases of nonfinancial assets..................	56,208	68,021	80,328	56,208	68,021	80,328	....	....	....	....	....	....
31.2	Sales of nonfinancial assets.........................	640	637	329	640	637	329	....	....	....	....	....	....
31	Net cash outflow from investments in nonfinancial assets...................	55,568	67,384	79,999	55,568	67,384	79,999	....	....	....	....	....	....
CSD	*Cash surplus/deficit....................*	*–4,773*	*–3,649*	*–24,191*	*–4,773*	*–3,649*	*–24,191*	....	....	....	....	....	....
32x	Net acquisition of fin assets, excl. cash..........	79,750	78,732	31,976	79,750	78,732	31,976	....	....	....	....	....	....
321x	Domestic.................................	79,750	78,732	31,976	79,750	78,732	31,976	....	....	....	....	....	....
322x	Foreign..................................	—	—	—	—	—	—	....	....	....	....	....	....
323	Monetary gold and SDRs....................	—	—	—	—	—	—	....	....	....	....	....	....
33	Net incurrence of liabilities.................	84,223	79,362	105,976	84,223	79,362	105,976	....	....	....	....	....	....
331	Domestic.................................	56,656	49,052	76,916	56,656	49,052	76,916	....	....	....	....	....	....
332	Foreign..................................	27,567	30,311	29,060	27,567	30,311	29,060	....	....	....	....	....	....
NFB	Net cash inflow from fin. activities.........	4,473	630	74,000	4,473	630	74,000	....	....	....	....	....	....
NCB	*Net change in the stock of cash.............*	*–300*	*–3,019*	*49,809*	*–300*	*–3,019*	*49,809*	....	....	....	....	....	....
	Table 1 Revenue												
1	**Revenue........................**	**298,672**	**336,680**	**347,303**	**298,672**	**336,680**	**347,303**	....	....	....	....	....	....
11	**Taxes.............................**	**210,297**	**242,612**	**270,086**	**210,297**	**242,612**	**270,086**	....	....	....	....	....	....
111	Taxes on income, profits, & capital gains......	35,152	38,064	42,809	35,152	38,064	42,809	....	....	....	....	....	....
1111	Individuals...........................	16,621	22,154	24,013	16,621	22,154	24,013	....	....	....	....	....	....
1112	Corporations and other enterprises............	18,531	15,910	18,796	18,531	15,910	18,796	....	....	....	....	....	....
112	Taxes on payroll and workforce..................	—	500	985	—	500	985	....	....	....	....	....	....
113	Taxes on property........................	9	75	10	9	75	10	....	....	....	....	....	....
114	Taxes on goods and services...................	75,228	108,949	100,540	75,228	108,949	100,540	....	....	....	....	....	....
1141	General taxes on goods and services..........	70,477	103,609	95,025	70,477	103,609	95,025	....	....	....	....	....	....
1142	Excises.................................	2,962	3,064	2,987	2,962	3,064	2,987	....	....	....	....	....	....
115	Taxes on int'l. trade and transactions..........	89,395	84,610	113,076	89,395	84,610	113,076	....	....	....	....	....	....
116	Other taxes..............................	10,513	10,414	12,666	10,513	10,414	12,666	....	....	....	....	....	....
12	**Social contributions...................**	**—**	**—**	**—**	**—**	**—**	**—**	....	....	....	....	....	....
121	Social security contributions.............	—	—	—	—	—	—	....	....	....	....	....	....
122	Other social contributions...............	—	—	—	—	—	—	....	....	....	....	....	....
13	**Grants.............................**	**19,759**	**33,092**	**15,495**	**19,759**	**33,092**	**15,495**	....	....	....	....	....	....
131	From foreign governments.................	19,759	33,092	15,495	19,759	33,092	15,495	....	....	....	....	....	....
132	From international organizations.................	—	—	—	—	—	—	....	....	....	....	....	....
133	From other general government units..........	—	—	—	—	—	—	....	....	....	....	....	....
14	**Other revenue.....................**	**68,616**	**60,976**	**61,722**	**68,616**	**60,976**	**61,722**	....	....	....	....	....	....
	Table 2 Expense by economic type												
2	**Expense............................**	**247,877**	**272,945**	**291,494**	**247,877**	**272,945**	**291,494**	....	....	....	....	....	....
21	**Compensation of employees............**	**65,394**	**69,137**	**74,314**	**65,394**	**69,137**	**74,314**	....	....	....	....	....	....
211	Wages and salaries.......................	65,394	69,137	74,314	65,394	69,137	74,314	....	....	....	....	....	....
212	Social contributions.....................	—	—	—	—	—	—	....	....	....	....	....	....
22	**Use of goods and services.................**	**35,371**	**43,907**	**49,298**	**35,371**	**43,907**	**49,298**	....	....	....	....	....	....
23	**Consumption of fixed capital...............**	....	....	....	....	....	....	....	....	....	....	....	....
24	**Interest............................**	**49,217**	**56,160**	**56,864**	**49,217**	**56,160**	**56,864**	....	....	....	....	....	....
25	**Subsidies..........................**	**3,419**	**9,384**	**8,883**	**3,419**	**9,384**	**8,883**	....	....	....	....	....	....

		Budgetary Central Government			Central Government			Local Government			General Government		
		2002	2003	2004	2002	2003	2004	2002	2003	2004	2002	2003	2004
26	Grants....................................	37,851	42,898	48,828	37,851	42,898	48,828	....	....	....	....	....	....
261	To foreign govenments................	—	—	—	—	—	—	....	....	....	....	....	....
262	To international organizations.......	—	—	—	—	—	—	....	....	....	....	....	....
263	To other general government units......	37,851	42,898	48,828	37,851	42,898	48,828	....	....	....	....	....	....
2631	Current................................	37,851	42,898	48,828	37,851	42,898	48,828	....	....	....	....	....	....
2632	Capital.................................	—	—	—	—	—	—	....	....	....	....	....	....
27	Social benefits........................	21,425	25,597	28,145	21,425	25,597	28,145	....	....	....	....	....	....
28	Other expense........................	35,200	25,862	25,163	35,200	25,862	25,163	....	....	....	....	....	....
281	Property expense other than interest..........	—	—	—	—	—	—	....	....	....	....	....	....
282	Miscellaneous other expense......................	35,200	25,862	25,163	35,200	25,862	25,163	....	....	....	....	....	....
2821	Current..............................	35,200	25,862	25,163	35,200	25,862	25,163	....	....	....	....	....	....
2822	Capital..............................	—	—	—	—	—	—	....	....	....	....	....	....
Table 3 Transactions in assets and liabilities													
3	Change in net worth from transactns....	....	....	....	....	....	....	....	....	....	....	....	....
31	Net acquisition of nonfinancial assets...	55,568	67,384	79,999	55,568	67,384	79,999	....	....	....	....	....	....
311	Fixed assets............................	54,887	66,888	79,198	54,887	66,888	79,198	....	....	....	....	....	....
3111	Buildings and structures..........................	1,685	1,374	3,295	1,685	1,374	3,295	....	....	....	....	....	....
3112	Machinery and equipment......................	7,739	7,317	8,490	7,739	7,317	8,490	....	....	....	....	....	....
3113	Other fixed assets........................	45,464	58,197	67,413	45,464	58,197	67,413	....	....	....	....	....	....
312	Inventories................................	—	—	—	—	—	—	....	....	....	....	....	....
313	Valuables................................	—	—	—	—	—	—	....	....	....	....	....	....
314	Nonproduced assets....................	680	496	801	680	496	801	....	....	....	....	....	....
3141	Land..................................	680	496	801	680	496	801	....	....	....	....	....	....
3142	Subsoil assets.........................	—	—	—	—	—	—	....	....	....	....	....	....
3143	Other naturally occurring assets................	—	—	—	—	—	—	....	....	....	....	....	....
3144	Intangible nonproduced assets.................	—	—	—	—	—	—	....	....	....	....	....	....
32	Net acquisition of financial assets........	79,450	75,713	81,785	79,450	75,713	81,785	....	....	....	....	....	....
321	Domestic................................	79,450	75,713	81,785	79,450	75,713	81,785	....	....	....	....	....	....
3212	Currency and deposits.............................	−300	−3,019	49,809	−300	−3,019	49,809	....	....	....	....	....	....
3213	Securities other than shares...................	—	—	—	—	—	—	....	....	....	....	....	....
3214	Loans.................................	8,962	13,752	13,053	8,962	13,752	13,053	....	....	....	....	....	....
3215	Shares and other equity....................	70,788	64,980	18,923	70,788	64,980	18,923	....	....	....	....	....	....
3216	Insurance technical reserves.................	—	—	—	—	—	—	....	....	....	....	....	....
3217	Financial derivatives.......................	—	—	—	—	—	—	....	....	....	....	....	....
3218	Other accounts receivable.......................	....	....	....	....	....	....	....	....	....	....	....	....
322	Foreign.................................	—	—	—	—	—	—	....	....	....	....	....	....
3222	Currency and deposits........................	—	—	—	—	—	—	....	....	....	....	....	....
3223	Securities other than shares...............	—	—	—	—	—	—	....	....	....	....	....	....
3224	Loans.................................	—	—	—	—	—	—	....	....	....	....	....	....
3225	Shares and other equity..................	—	—	—	—	—	—	....	....	....	....	....	....
3226	Insurance technical reserves.................	—	—	—	—	—	—	....	....	....	....	....	....
3227	Financial derivatives.......................	—	—	—	—	—	—	....	....	....	....	....	....
3228	Other accounts receivable....................	....	....	....	....	....	....	....	....	....	....	....	....
323	Monetary gold and SDRs.................	—	—	—	—	—	—	....	....	....	....	....	....
33	Net incurrence of liabilities.................	84,223	79,362	105,976	84,223	79,362	105,976	....	....	....	....	....	....
331	Domestic................................	56,656	49,052	76,916	56,656	49,052	76,916	....	....	....	....	....	....
3312	Currency and deposits..........................	—	—	—	—	—	—	....	....	....	....	....	....
3313	Securities other than shares....................	44,760	43,640	40,945	44,760	43,640	40,945	....	....	....	....	....	....
3314	Loans.................................	11,896	5,411	35,971	11,896	5,411	35,971	....	....	....	....	....	....
3316	Insurance technical reserves.................	—	—	—	—	—	—	....	....	....	....	....	....
3317	Financial derivatives.......................	—	—	—	—	—	—	....	....	....	....	....	....
3318	Other accounts payable......................	....	....	....	....	....	....	....	....	....	....	....	....
332	Foreign.................................	27,567	30,311	29,060	27,567	30,311	29,060	....	....	....	....	....	....
3322	Currency and deposits........................	—	—	—	—	—	—	....	....	....	....	....	....
3323	Securities other than shares................	—	—	—	—	—	—	....	....	....	....	....	....
3324	Loans.................................	27,567	30,311	29,060	27,567	30,311	29,060	....	....	....	....	....	....
3326	Insurance technical reserves.................	—	—	—	—	—	—	....	....	....	....	....	....
3327	Financial derivatives.......................	—	—	—	—	—	—	....	....	....	....	....	....
3328	Other accounts payable......................	....	....	....	....	....	....	....	....	....	....	....	....

In Millions of Taka / Year Ending June 30 / Cash Reporter

	Budgetary Central Government			Central Government			Local Government			General Government		
	2002	2003	2004	2002	2003	2004	2002	2003	2004	2002	2003	2004
Table 4 Holding gains in assets and liabilities												
Table 5 Other changes in the volume of assets and liabilities												
Table 6 Balance sheet												
Table 7 Outlays by functions of govt.												
7 Total outlays..........	**303,445**	**340,329**	**371,493**	**303,445**	**340,329**	**371,493**	....	....	....	....	....	....
701 General public services..........	**83,425**	**96,293**	**136,523**	**83,425**	**96,293**	**136,523**	....	....	....	....	....	....
7017 Public debt transactions..........	49,217	56,160	56,864	49,217	56,160	56,864	....	....	....	....	....	....
7018 General transfers between levels of govt......	....	....	....	....	....	....	....	....	....	....	....	....
702 Defense..........	**34,401**	**34,354**	**36,852**	**34,401**	**34,354**	**36,852**	....	....	....	....	....	....
703 Public order and safety..........	**17,078**	**19,511**	**22,257**	**17,078**	**19,511**	**22,257**	....	....	....	....	....	....
704 Economic affairs..........	**56,584**	**62,874**	**31,071**	**56,584**	**62,874**	**31,071**	....	....	....	....	....	....
7042 Agriculture, forestry, fishing, and hunting.....	9,571	9,785	11,378	9,571	9,785	11,378	....	....	....	....	....	....
7043 Fuel and energy..........	2,467	5,642	6,059	2,467	5,642	6,059	....	....	....	....	....	....
7044 Mining, manufacturing, and construction.....	55	49	44	55	49	44	....	....	....	....	....	....
7045 Transport..........	18,868	19,666	22,697	18,868	19,666	22,697	....	....	....	....	....	....
7046 Communication..........	10	14	11	10	14	11	....	....	....	....	....	....
705 Environmental protection..........	**400**	**413**	**430**	**400**	**413**	**430**	....	....	....	....	....	....
706 Housing and community amenities.......	**21,854**	**26,307**	**34,620**	**21,854**	**26,307**	**34,620**	....	....	....	....	....	....
707 Health..........	**19,371**	**22,959**	**25,988**	**19,371**	**22,959**	**25,988**	....	....	....	....	....	....
7072 Outpatient services..........	13,196	16,110	17,034	13,196	16,110	17,034	....	....	....	....	....	....
7073 Hospital services..........	2,266	2,537	4,432	2,266	2,537	4,432	....	....	....	....	....	....
7074 Public health services..........	3,908	4,313	4,522	3,908	4,313	4,522	....	....	....	....	....	....
708 Recreation, culture, and religion..........	**3,694**	**4,685**	**5,890**	**3,694**	**4,685**	**5,890**	....	....	....	....	....	....
709 Education..........	**56,000**	**61,059**	**63,333**	**56,000**	**61,059**	**63,333**	....	....	....	....	....	....
7091 Pre-primary and primary education..........	23,376	25,302	24,193	23,376	25,302	24,193	....	....	....	....	....	....
7092 Secondary education..........	10,121	11,844	12,036	10,121	11,844	12,036	....	....	....	....	....	....
7094 Tertiary education..........	22,502	23,913	27,104	22,502	23,913	27,104	....	....	....	....	....	....
710 Social protection..........	**10,639**	**11,874**	**14,529**	**10,639**	**11,874**	**14,529**	....	....	....	....	....	....
7 Statistical discrepancy: Total outlays..........	—	—	—	—	—	—	....	....	....	....	....	....
Table 8 Transactions in financial assets and liabilities by sector												
82 Net acquisition of financial assets.........	**79,450**	**75,713**	**81,785**	**79,450**	**75,713**	**81,785**	....	....	....	....	....	....
821 Domestic..........	79,450	75,713	81,785	79,450	75,713	81,785	....	....	....	....	....	....
8211 General government..........	11,551	9,819	6,067	11,551	9,819	6,067	....	....	....	....	....	....
8212 Central bank..........	−355	−3,453	−133	−355	−3,453	−133	....	....	....	....	....	....
8213 Other depository corporations..........	71,455	76,911	87,009	71,455	76,911	87,009	....	....	....	....	....	....
8214 Financial corporations n.e.c..........	−638	−586	−489	−638	−586	−489	....	....	....	....	....	....
8215 Nonfinancial corporations..........	−2,472	−6,594	−10,445	−2,472	−6,594	−10,445	....	....	....	....	....	....
8216 Households & NPIs serving households......	−91	−384	−224	−91	−384	−224	....	....	....	....	....	....
822 Foreign..........	—	—	—	—	—	—	....	....	....	....	....	....
8221 General government..........	—	—	—	—	—	—	....	....	....	....	....	....
8227 International organizations..........	—	—	—	—	—	—	....	....	....	....	....	....
8228 Financial corporations other than international organizations..........	—	—	—	—	—	—	....	....	....	....	....	....
8229 Other nonresidents..........	—	—	—	—	—	—	....	....	....	....	....	....
823 Monetary gold and SDRs..........	—	—	—	—	—	—	....	....	....	....	....	....
83 Net incurrence of liabilities..........	**84,223**	**79,362**	**105,976**	**84,223**	**79,362**	**105,976**	....	....	....	....	....	....
831 Domestic..........	56,656	49,052	76,916	56,656	49,052	76,916	....	....	....	....	....	....
8311 General government..........	—	—	—	—	—	—	....	....	....	....	....	....
8312 Central bank..........	21,452	−6,419	21,451	21,452	−6,419	21,451	....	....	....	....	....	....
8313 Other depository corporations..........	4,599	1,964	6,081	4,599	1,964	6,081	....	....	....	....	....	....
8314 Financial corporations n.e.c..........	—	—	—	—	—	—	....	....	....	....	....	....
8315 Nonfinancial corporations..........	—	—	—	—	—	—	....	....	....	....	....	....
8316 Households & NPIs serving households......	30,605	53,507	49,384	30,605	53,507	49,384	....	....	....	....	....	....
832 Foreign..........	27,567	30,311	29,060	27,567	30,311	29,060	....	....	....	....	....	....
8321 General government..........	10,091	4,617	12,559	10,091	4,617	12,559	....	....	....	....	....	....
8327 International organizations..........	17,476	25,694	16,501	17,476	25,694	16,501	....	....	....	....	....	....
8328 Financial corporations other than international organizations..........	—	—	—	—	—	—	....	....	....	....	....	....
8329 Other nonresidents..........	—	—	—	—	—	—	....	....	....	....	....	....

Barbados   316

In Millions of Barbados Dollars / Year Ending December 31 / Cash Reporter

		Budgetary Central Government			Extrabudgetary Accounts			Central Government			General Government		
		2002	2003	2004f	2002	2003	2004f	2002	2003	2004f	2002	2003	2004f
	Statement of government operations												
	Statement of other economic flows												
	Balance sheet												
	Statement of sources and uses of cash												
1	Cash receipts from operating activities	....	1,827.5	1,980.7	....	394.1	502.9	....	2,276.1	2,467.0	....	2,276.1	2,467.0
11	Taxes	....	1,620.4	1,775.5	....	6.9	—	....	1,627.3	1,775.5	....	1,627.3	1,775.5
12	Social contributions	....	100.4	118.8	....	—	—	....	428.7	483.9	....	428.7	483.9
13	Grants	....	9.1	9.3	....	369.9	486.7	....	—	—	....	—	—
14	Other receipts	....	97.6	77.1	....	17.3	16.2	....	220.1	207.6	....	220.1	207.6
2	Cash payments for operating activities	....	1,732.1	1,776.8	....	358.9	361.7	....	2,034.6	1,932.7	....	2,034.6	1,932.7
21	Compensation of employees	....	783.0	738.3	....	94.3	90.2	....	877.2	828.5	....	877.2	828.5
22	Purchases of goods and services	....	208.2	185.4	....	117.8	119.1	....	339.3	304.5	....	339.3	304.5
24	Interest	....	274.2	271.7	....	1.6	1.3	....	275.9	273.0	....	275.9	273.0
25	Subsidies	....	27.6	23.1	....	6.2	2.2	....	33.8	25.3	....	33.8	25.3
26	Grants	....	369.8	498.5	....	12.8	1.3	....	12.7	13.1	....	12.7	13.1
27	Social benefits	....	42.0	33.5	....	.4	.4	....	340.4	314.8	....	340.4	314.8
28	Other payments	....	27.3	26.3	....	125.9	147.2	....	155.3	173.5	....	155.3	173.5
CIO	*Net cash inflow from oper. activities*	....	*95.4*	*203.9*	....	*35.2*	*141.2*	....	*241.5*	*534.3*	....	*241.5*	*534.3*
31.1	Purchases of nonfinancial assets	....	249.5	325.6	....	16.3	—	....	272.9	325.6	....	272.9	325.6
31.2	Sales of nonfinancial assets	....	—	—	....			....	—	—	....	—	—
31	Net cash outflow from investments in nonfinancial assets	....	249.5	325.6	....	16.3	—	....	272.9	325.6	....	272.9	325.6
CSD	*Cash surplus/deficit*	....	*−154.1*	*−121.7*	....	*18.8*	*141.2*	....	*−31.3*	*208.7*	....	*−31.3*	*208.7*
32x	Net acquisition of fin assets, excl. cash	....	220.2	....	....	18.1	....	....	347.0	....	....	347.0	....
321x	Domestic	....	220.2	....	....	18.1	....	....	341.8	....	....	341.8	....
322x	Foreign	....	—	....	....	—	....	....	5.2	....	....	5.2	....
323	Monetary gold and SDRs	....	—	....	....	—	....	....	—	....	....	—	....
33	Net incurrence of liabilities	....	66.8	....	....	−5.0	....	....	63.1	....	....	63.1	....
331	Domestic	....	112.1	....	....	−5.0	....	....	108.4	....	....	108.4	....
332	Foreign	....	−45.3	....	....			....	−45.3	....	....	−45.3	....
NFB	Net cash inflow from fin. activities	....	−153.3	....	....	−23.1	....	....	−283.9	....	....	−283.9	....
NCB	*Net change in the stock of cash*	....	*−307.4*	....	....	*−4.2*	....	....	*−315.2*	....	....	*−315.2*	....

Table 1   Revenue

		2002	2003	2004f	2002	2003	2004f	2002	2003	2004f	2002	2003	2004f
1	**Revenue**	....	**1,827.5**	**1,980.8**	....	**394.1**	**502.9**	....	**2,276.1**	**2,467.1**	....	**2,276.1**	**2,467.1**
11	**Taxes**	....	**1,620.4**	**1,775.6**	....	**6.9**	**—**	....	**1,627.3**	**1,775.6**	....	**1,627.3**	**1,775.6**
111	Taxes on income, profits, & capital gains	....	604.7	596.5	....	—	—	....	604.7	596.5	....	604.7	596.5
1111	Individuals	....	358.4	331.1	....	—	—	....	358.4	331.1	....	358.4	331.1
1112	Corporations and other enterprises	....	220.3	232.4	....	—	—	....	220.3	232.4	....	220.3	232.4
112	Taxes on payroll and workforce	....	—	—	....	—	—	....	—	—	....	—	—
113	Taxes on property	....	116.8	133.2	....	—	—	....	116.8	133.2	....	116.8	133.2
114	Taxes on goods and services	....	703.1	821.5	....	—	—	....	703.1	821.5	....	703.1	821.5
1141	General taxes on goods and services	....	494.6	572.2	....	—	—	....	494.6	572.2	....	494.6	572.2
1142	Excises	....	114.2	153.0	....	—	—	....	114.2	153.0	....	114.2	153.0
115	Taxes on int'l. trade and transactions	....	166.6	196.3	....	6.9	—	....	173.6	196.3	....	173.6	196.3
116	Other taxes	....	29.1	28.1	....	—	—	....	29.1	28.1	....	29.1	28.1
12	**Social contributions**	....	**100.4**	**118.8**	....	**—**	**—**	....	**428.7**	**483.9**	....	**428.7**	**483.9**
121	Social security contributions	....	1.2	.9	....	—	—	....	329.5	366.0	....	329.5	366.0
122	Other social contributions	....	99.2	117.9	....	—	—	....	99.2	117.9	....	99.2	117.9
13	**Grants**	....	**9.1**	**9.3**	....	**369.9**	**486.7**	....	**—**	**—**	....	**—**	**—**
131	From foreign governments	....	—	—	....	—	—	....	—	—	....	—	—
132	From international organizations	....	—	—	....	—	—	....	—	—	....	—	—
133	From other general government units	....	9.1	9.3	....	369.9	486.7	....	—	—	....	—	—
14	**Other revenue**	....	**97.6**	**77.1**	....	**17.3**	**16.2**	....	**220.1**	**207.6**	....	**220.1**	**207.6**

Table 2   Expense by economic type

		2002	2003	2004f	2002	2003	2004f	2002	2003	2004f	2002	2003	2004f
2	**Expense**	....	**1,732.1**	**1,777.0**	....	**358.9**	**361.7**	....	**2,034.6**	**1,932.9**	....	**2,034.6**	**1,932.9**
21	**Compensation of employees**	....	**783.0**	**738.4**	....	**94.3**	**90.2**	....	**877.2**	**828.6**	....	**877.2**	**828.6**
211	Wages and salaries	....	642.1	580.1	....	68.2	85.2	....	710.3	665.3	....	710.3	665.3
212	Social contributions	....	140.9	158.3	....	26.1	5.0	....	167.0	163.3	....	167.0	163.3
22	**Use of goods and services**	....	**208.2**	**185.4**	....	**117.8**	**119.1**	....	**339.3**	**304.5**	....	**339.3**	**304.5**
23	**Consumption of fixed capital**	....	....	....	....	....	....	....	....	....	....	....	....
24	**Interest**	....	**274.3**	**271.7**	....	**1.6**	**1.3**	....	**275.9**	**273.0**	....	**275.9**	**273.0**
25	**Subsidies**	....	**27.6**	**23.1**	....	**6.2**	**2.2**	....	**33.8**	**25.3**	....	**33.8**	**25.3**

In Millions of Barbados Dollars / Year Ending December 31 / Cash Reporter

		Budgetary Central Government			Extrabudgetary Accounts			Central Government			General Government		
		2002	2003	2004f	2002	2003	2004f	2002	2003	2004f	2002	2003	2004f
26	**Grants**....................	....	**369.8**	**498.6**	....	**12.8**	**1.3**	....	**12.7**	**13.2**	....	**12.7**	**13.2**
261	To foreign govenments.................	....	—	—	....	—		....	—	—	....	—	—
262	To international organizations....................	....	11.3	11.9	....	1.2	1.3	....	12.5	13.2	....	12.5	13.2
263	To other general government units..............	....	358.5	486.7	....	11.5	—	....	.2	—	....	.2	—
2631	Current.................	....	297.7	430.4	....	—	—	....	.1	—	....	.1	—
2632	Capital.................	....	60.8	56.3	....	11.5	—	....	.1	—	....	.1	—
27	**Social benefits**..................	....	**42.0**	**33.5**	....	**.4**	**.4**	....	**340.4**	**314.8**	....	**340.4**	**314.8**
28	**Other expense**..................	....	**27.3**	**26.3**	....	**125.9**	**147.2**	....	**155.3**	**173.5**	....	**155.3**	**173.5**
281	Property expense other than interest............	....	—		....	—		....	—		....	—	
282	Miscellaneous other expense....................	....	27.3	26.3	....	125.9	147.2	....	155.3	173.5	....	155.3	173.5
2821	Current.................	....	23.7	22.3	....	85.3	101.8	....	111.0	124.1	....	111.0	124.1
2822	Capital.................	....	3.6	4.0	....	40.6	45.4	....	44.2	49.4	....	44.2	49.4
Table 3	**Transactions in assets and liabilities**												
3	**Change in net worth from transactns....**	....	....	....	....	....	....	....	....	....	....	....	....
31	**Net acquisition of nonfinancial assets...**	....	**249.5**	**325.6**	....	**16.3**	**—**	....	**272.9**	**325.6**	....	**272.9**	**325.6**
311	Fixed assets.................	....	249.5	325.6	....	16.3	—	....	272.9	325.6	....	272.9	325.6
3111	Buildings and structures.................	....	211.4	....	....	10.8		....	223.7	....	....	223.7	....
3112	Machinery and equipment.................	....	38.1	....	....	5.6		....	44.9	....	....	44.9	....
3113	Other fixed assets.................	....	—	....	....	—		....	4.3	....	....	4.3	....
312	Inventories.................	....	—		....	—		....	—	—	....	—	—
313	Valuables.................	....	—		....	—		....	—	—	....	—	—
314	Nonproduced assets.................	....	—		....	—		....	—	—	....	—	—
3141	Land.................	....	—		....	—		....	—	—	....	—	—
3142	Subsoil assets.................	....	—	—	....	—		....	—	—	....	—	—
3143	Other naturally occurring assets.................	....	—	—	....	—		....	—	—	....	—	—
3144	Intangible nonproduced assets.................	....	—	—	....	—		....	—	—	....	—	—
32	**Net acquisition of financial assets.........**	....	**−87.3**	**....**	....	**13.9**	**....**	....	**31.8**	**....**	....	**31.8**	**....**
321	Domestic.................	....	−87.3	....	....	13.9	....	....	26.6	....	....	26.6	....
3212	Currency and deposits.................	....	−307.4	....	....	−4.2	....	....	−315.2	....	....	−315.2	....
3213	Securities other than shares.................	....	6.0	....	....	8.7	....	....	114.7	....	....	114.7	....
3214	Loans.................	....	214.2	....	....	.6	....	....	207.9	....	....	207.9	....
3215	Shares and other equity.................	....	—	....	....	8.7	....	....	19.2	....	....	19.2	....
3216	Insurance technical reserves.................	....	—	....	....	—	....	....	—	....	....	—	....
3217	Financial derivatives.................	....	—	....	....	—	....	....	—	....	....	—	....
3218	Other accounts receivable.................	....	....	....	....	....	....	....	....	....	....	....	....
322	Foreign.................	....	—	....	....	—	....	....	5.2	....	....	5.2	....
3222	Currency and deposits.................	....	—	....	....	—	....	....	—	....	....	—	....
3223	Securities other than shares.................	....	—	....	....	—	....	....	5.2	....	....	5.2	....
3224	Loans.................	....	—	....	....	—	....	....	—	....	....	—	....
3225	Shares and other equity.................	....	—	....	....	—	....	....	—	....	....	—	....
3226	Insurance technical reserves.................	....	—	....	....	—	....	....	—	....	....	—	....
3227	Financial derivatives.................	....	—	....	....	—	....	....	—	....	....	—	....
3228	Other accounts receivable.................	....	....	....	....	....	....	....	....	....	....	....	....
323	Monetary gold and SDRs.................	....	—	....	....	—	....	....	—	....	....	—	....
33	**Net incurrence of liabilities...................**	....	**66.8**	**....**	....	**−5.0**	**....**	....	**63.1**	**....**	....	**63.1**	**....**
331	Domestic.................	....	112.1	....	....	−5.0	....	....	108.4	....	....	108.4	....
3312	Currency and deposits.................	....	−28.5	....	....	—	....	....	−28.5	....	....	−28.5	....
3313	Securities other than shares.................	....	.1	....	....	−.8	....	....	−.7	....	....	−.7	....
3314	Loans.................	....	259.2	....	....	−1.0	....	....	259.4	....	....	259.4	....
3316	Insurance technical reserves.................	....	−118.7	....	....	−3.1	....	....	−121.8	....	....	−121.8	....
3317	Financial derivatives.................	....	—	....	....	—	....	....	—	....	....	—	....
3318	Other accounts payable.................	....	....	....	....	....	....	....	....	....	....	....	....
332	Foreign.................	....	−45.3	....	....	—	....	....	−45.3	....	....	−45.3	....
3322	Currency and deposits.................	....	—	....	....	—	....	....	—	....	....	—	....
3323	Securities other than shares.................	....	—	....	....	—	....	....	—	....	....	—	....
3324	Loans.................	....	−45.3	....	....	—	....	....	−45.3	....	....	−45.3	....
3326	Insurance technical reserves.................	....	—	....	....	—	....	....	—	....	....	—	....
3327	Financial derivatives.................	....	—	....	....	—	....	....	....	....	....	—	....
3328	Other accounts payable.................	....	....	....	....	....	....	....	....	....	....	....	....

Barbados   316

In Millions of Barbados Dollars / Year Ending December 31 / Cash Reporter

	Budgetary Central Government			Extrabudgetary Accounts			Central Government			General Government		
	2002	2003	2004f	2002	2003	2004f	2002	2003	2004f	2002	2003	2004f
Table 4 Holding gains in assets and liabilities												
Table 5 Other changes in the volume of assets and liabilities												
Table 6 Balance sheet												
Table 7 Outlays by functions of govt.												
7 Total outlays..........................	....	1,981.6	2,102.6	....	375.3	361.7	....	2,307.4	2,258.5	....	2,307.4	2,258.5
701 **General public services**..........................	....	570.7	....	....	....	....	....	....	....	....	....	....
7017 Public debt transactions..........................	....	274.2	271.7	....	1.6	1.3	....	275.9	273.0	....	275.9	273.0
7018 General transfers between levels of govt......	....	....	....	....	....	....	....	....	....	....	....	....
702 **Defense**..........................	....	39.9	....	....	....	....	....	....	....	....	....	....
703 **Public order and safety**..........................	....	127.8	....	....	....	....	....	....	....	....	....	....
704 **Economic affairs**..........................	....	321.2	....	....	....	....	....	....	....	....	....	....
7042 Agriculture, forestry, fishing, and hunting.....	....	55.6	....	....								
7043 Fuel and energy..........................	....	1.1	....									
7044 Mining, manufacturing, and construction.....	....	—	....									
7045 Transport..........................	....	129.5	....									
7046 Communication..........................	....	24.4	....									
705 **Environmental protection**..........................	....	131.2	....	....	....	....	....	....	....	....	....	....
706 **Housing and community amenities**........	....	28.8	....	....	....	....	....	....	....	....	....	....
707 **Health**..........................	....	231.5	....	....	....	....	....	....	....	....	....	....
7072 Outpatient services..........................	....	22.0	....									
7073 Hospital services..........................	....	135.7	....									
7074 Public health services..........................	....	17.9	....									
708 **Recreation, culture, and religion**...........	....	42.7	....	....								
709 **Education**..........................	....	381.8	....	....								
7091 Pre-primary and primary education..........	....	91.9	....									
7092 Secondary education..........................	....	123.0	....									
7094 Tertiary education..........................	....	104.6	....									
710 **Social protection**..........................	....	106.0	....	....	....	....	....	....	....	....	....	....
7 Statistical discrepancy: Total outlays..............	....	—	....	....	....	....	....	....	....	....	....	....
Table 8 Transactions in financial assets and liabilities by sector												
82 **Net acquisition of financial assets**.........	....	−87.3	....	....	13.9	....	....	31.8	....		31.8	....
821 Domestic..........................	....	−87.3	....	....	13.9	....	....	26.6	....	....	26.6	....
8211 General government..........................	....	....	....	....	....	....	....	....	....	....	....	....
8212 Central bank..........................	....	....	....	....	....	....	....	....	....	....	....	....
8213 Other depository corporations..........................	....	....	....	....	....	....	....	....	....	....	....	....
8214 Financial corporations n.e.c..........................	....	....	....	....	....	....	....	....	....	....	....	....
8215 Nonfinancial corporations..........................	....	....	....	....	....	....	....	....	....	....	....	....
8216 Households & NPIs serving households......	....	....	....	....	....	....	....	....	....	....	....	....
822 Foreign..........................	....	—	....	....	—	....	....	5.2	....	....	5.2	....
8221 General government..........................	....	—	....	....	....	....	....	....	....	....	....	....
8227 International organizations..........................	....	—	....	....	....	....	....	....	....	....	....	....
8228 Financial corporations other than international organizations..............	....	—	....	....	—	....	....	....	....	....	....	....
8229 Other nonresidents..........................	....	—	....	....	—	....	....	....	....	....	....	....
823 Monetary gold and SDRs..........................	....	—	....	....	—	....	....	—	....	....	—	....
83 **Net incurrence of liabilities**..................	....	66.8	....	....	−5.0	....	....	63.1	....	....	63.1	....
831 Domestic..........................	....	112.1	....	....	−5.0	....	....	108.4	....	....	108.4	....
8311 General government..........................	....	....	....	....	....	....	....	....	....	....	....	....
8312 Central bank..........................	....	....	....	....	....	....	....	....	....	....	....	....
8313 Other depository corporations..........................	....	....	....	....	....	....	....	....	....	....	....	....
8314 Financial corporations n.e.c..........................	....	....	....	....	....	....	....	....	....	....	....	....
8315 Nonfinancial corporations..........................	....	....	....	....	....	....	....	....	....	....	....	....
8316 Households & NPIs serving households......	....	....	....	....	....	....	....	....	....	....	....	....
832 Foreign..........................	....	−45.3	....	....	—	....	....	−45.3	....	....	−45.3	....
8321 General government..........................	....	....	....	....	—	....	....	....	....	....	....	....
8327 International organizations..........................	....	....	....	....	—	....	....	....	....	....	....	....
8328 Financial corporations other than international organizations..............	....	....	....	....	—	....	....	....	....	....	....	....
8329 Other nonresidents..........................	....	....	....	....	—	....	....	....	....	....	....	....

In Billions of Rubels / Year Ending December 31 / Cash Reporter

	Budgetary Central Government			Central Government			Local Government			General Government		
	2002	2003p	2004p	2002	2003p	2004p	2002	2003p	2004p	2002	2003p	2004p
Statement of government operations												
Statement of other economic flows												
Balance sheet												
6 *Net worth*......	....	....	....	....	....	....	....	....	....	....	....	....
61 Nonfinancial assets......	....	....	....	....	....	....	....	....	....		....	....
62 Financial assets......	....	....	....	....	....	....	....	....	....	....	....	....
63 Liabilities......	3,224.6	....	....	3,224.6	....	....	....	....	....	....	....	....
Statement of sources and uses of cash												
1 Cash receipts from operating activities......	4,062.6	†6,775.8	9,745.4	6,960.4	10,749.6	15,162.1	4,741.6	7,226.9	9,343.8	....	16,747.3	22,921.5
11 Taxes......	3,711.9	†6,467.6	9,184.2	3,711.9	6,467.6	9,184.2	3,670.4	5,892.4	7,588.4	....	12,360.0	16,772.6
12 Social contributions......	73.9	†—	—	2,845.6	3,882.8	5,374.2	330.4	—	—	....	3,882.8	5,374.2
13 Grants......	3.5	†27.7	23.0	16.1	27.7	23.0	654.7	1,201.5	1,561.4	....	—	—
14 Other receipts......	273.4	†280.4	538.2	386.8	371.5	580.7	86.0	133.1	193.9	....	504.5	774.7
2 Cash payments for operating activities......	3,397.0	†6,390.3	8,871.8	6,450.5	10,316.0	14,085.8	4,015.8	5,760.4	7,205.2	....	14,847.2	19,706.6
21 Compensation of employees......	886.0	†1,255.7	1,790.1	886.0	1,255.7	1,804.5	1,756.2	2,390.3	3,139.2	....	3,646.0	4,943.7
22 Purchases of goods and services......	767.5	†1,708.0	2,589.3	803.9	1,738.8	2,609.5	1,196.1	1,577.0	2,344.8	....	3,315.8	4,954.4
24 Interest......	142.3	†184.0	233.9	142.3	184.0	233.9	1.1	2.2	9.4	....	186.2	243.3
25 Subsidies......	197.9	†516.8	1,046.9	197.9	516.8	1,046.9	....	1,294.9	1,446.5	....	1,811.7	2,493.4
26 Grants......	613.3	†1,367.0	1,685.8	613.3	1,304.8	1,685.8	....	27.7	23.0	....	103.3	124.4
27 Social benefits......	596.9	†711.5	1,036.9	3,614.0	4,668.6	6,216.2	....	222.7	214.9	....	4,891.3	6,431.2
28 Other payments......	193.2	†647.3	488.8	193.2	647.3	488.8	....	245.6	27.5	....	893.0	516.3
CIO *Net cash inflow from oper. activities*......	*451.7*	*†385.4*	*873.6*	*509.9*	*433.6*	*1,076.3*	*725.8*	*1,466.5*	*2,138.6*	....	*1,900.1*	*3,214.9*
31.1 Purchases of nonfinancial assets......	638.4	†898.5	1,240.1	638.4	898.5	1,252.1	670.8	1,328.5	1,803.2	....	2,227.1	3,055.4
31.2 Sales of nonfinancial assets......	424.3	†78.7	94.4	424.3	78.7	94.4	24.9	27.6	37.6	....	106.4	132.0
31 Net cash outflow from investments in nonfinancial assets......	214.2	†819.8	1,145.7	214.2	819.8	1,157.7	645.9	1,300.9	1,765.6	....	2,120.7	2,923.3
CSD *Cash surplus/deficit*......	*237.5*	*†−434.4*	*−272.1*	*295.8*	*−386.2*	*−81.4*	*79.9*	*165.6*	*373.0*	....	*−220.6*	*291.6*
32x Net acquisition of fin assets, excl. cash......	215.9	†125.0	−41.2	215.9	125.0	−41.2	249.5	204.6	127.7	....	295.6	214.4
321x Domestic......	195.0	†125.0	−41.2	195.0	125.0	−41.2	249.5	204.6	127.7	....	295.6	214.4
322x Foreign......	20.9	†—	—	20.9	—	—	—	—	—	....	—	—
323 Monetary gold and SDRs......	—	†—	—	—	—	—	—	—	—	....	—	—
33 Net incurrence of liabilities......	124.0	†458.5	559.1	124.0	458.5	559.1	—	118.2	−207.5	....	542.7	479.5
331 Domestic......	146.9	†573.5	323.0	146.9	573.5	323.0	—	118.2	−207.5	....	657.7	243.4
332 Foreign......	−23.0	†−115.0	236.1	−23.0	−115.0	236.1	—	—	—	....	−115.0	236.1
NFB Net cash inflow from fin. activities......	−91.9	†333.5	600.3	−91.9	333.5	600.3	−249.5	−86.4	−335.1	....	247.1	265.1
NCB *Net change in the stock of cash*......	*145.6*	*†−100.9*	*328.1*	*203.8*	*−52.7*	*518.8*	*−169.6*	*79.3*	*37.8*	....	*26.6*	*556.7*
Table 1 Revenue												
1 **Revenue**......	**4,062.6**	**†6,775.8**	**9,745.4**	**6,960.4**	**10,749.6**	**15,162.1**	**4,741.6**	**7,226.9**	**9,343.8**	....	**16,747.3**	**22,921.5**
11 **Taxes**......	**3,711.9**	**†6,467.6**	**9,184.2**	**3,711.9**	**6,467.6**	**9,184.2**	**3,670.4**	**5,892.4**	**7,588.4**	....	**12,360.0**	**16,772.6**
111 Taxes on income, profits, & capital gains......	457.2	†687.8	1,153.3	457.2	687.8	1,153.3	1,227.3	1,616.3	2,358.0	....	2,304.1	3,511.3
1111 Individuals......	—	†—	—	—	—	—	773.1	1,024.5	1,403.8	....	1,024.5	1,403.8
1112 Corporations and other enterprises......	457.2	†687.8	1,153.3	457.2	687.8	1,153.3	....	422.9	716.0	....	1,110.8	1,869.3
112 Taxes on payroll and workforce......	220.4	†358.8	489.7	220.4	358.8	489.7	—	—	—	....	358.8	489.7
113 Taxes on property......	—	†—	—	—	—	—	390.0	730.6	957.0	....	730.6	957.0
114 Taxes on goods and services......	2,510.8	†3,701.9	5,439.9	2,510.8	3,701.9	5,439.9	1,919.9	3,440.7	4,103.8	....	7,142.6	9,543.7
1141 General taxes on goods and services......	1,364.2	†2,821.3	4,389.6	1,364.2	2,821.3	4,389.6	....	2,813.4	3,140.1	....	5,634.7	7,529.7
1142 Excises......	445.1	†694.1	953.3	445.1	694.1	953.3	....	315.4	438.1	....	1,009.5	1,391.4
115 Taxes on int'l. trade and transactions......	523.6	†957.2	1,094.8	523.6	957.2	1,094.8	—	—	—	....	957.2	1,094.8
116 Other taxes......	—	†761.9	1,006.5	—	761.9	1,006.5	133.2	104.8	169.6	....	866.7	1,176.1
12 **Social contributions**......	**73.9**	**†—**	**—**	**2,845.6**	**3,882.8**	**5,374.2**	**330.4**	**—**	**—**	....	**3,882.8**	**5,374.2**
121 Social security contributions......	73.9	†—	—	2,845.6	3,882.8	5,374.2	—	—	—	....	3,882.8	5,374.2
122 Other social contributions......	—	†—	—	—	—	—	330.4	—	—	....	—	—
13 **Grants**......	**3.5**	**†27.7**	**23.0**	**16.1**	**27.7**	**23.0**	**654.7**	**1,201.5**	**1,561.4**	....	**—**	**—**
131 From foreign governments......	—	†—	—	—	—	—	—	—	—	....	—	—
132 From international organizations......	—	†—	—	—	—	—	—	—	—	....	—	—
133 From other general government units......	3.5	†27.7	23.0	16.1	27.7	23.0	654.7	1,201.5	1,561.4	....	—	—
14 **Other revenue**......	**273.4**	**†280.4**	**538.2**	**386.8**	**371.5**	**580.7**	**86.0**	**133.1**	**193.9**	....	**504.5**	**774.7**
Table 2 Expense by economic type												
2 **Expense**......	**3,397.0**	**†6,390.3**	**8,871.8**	**6,450.5**	**10,316.0**	**14,085.8**	**4,015.8**	**5,760.4**	**7,205.2**	....	**14,847.2**	**19,706.6**
21 **Compensation of employees**......	**886.0**	**†1,255.7**	**1,790.1**	**886.0**	**1,255.7**	**1,804.5**	**1,756.2**	**2,390.3**	**3,139.2**	....	**3,646.0**	**4,943.7**
211 Wages and salaries......	741.8	†1,058.9	1,500.0	741.8	1,058.9	1,510.7	1,319.6	1,806.6	2,369.0	....	2,865.5	3,879.6
212 Social contributions......	144.1	†196.8	290.0	144.1	196.8	293.8	436.6	583.7	770.2	....	780.5	1,064.0
22 **Use of goods and services**......	**767.5**	**†1,708.0**	**2,589.3**	**803.9**	**1,738.8**	**2,609.5**	**1,196.1**	**1,577.0**	**2,344.8**	....	**3,315.8**	**4,954.4**
23 **Consumption of fixed capital**......	....	....	....	....	....	....	....	....	....	....	....	....
24 **Interest**......	**142.3**	**†184.0**	**233.9**	**142.3**	**184.0**	**233.9**	**1.1**	**2.2**	**9.4**	....	**186.2**	**243.3**
25 **Subsidies**......	**197.9**	**†516.8**	**1,046.9**	**197.9**	**516.8**	**1,046.9**	....	**1,294.9**	**1,446.5**	....	**1,811.7**	**2,493.4**

Belarus   913

In Billions of Rubels / Year Ending December 31 / Cash Reporter

		Budgetary Central Government			Central Government			Local Government			General Government		
		2002	2003p	2004p	2002	2003p	2004p	2002	2003p	2004p	2002	2003p	2004p
26	Grants..........................	613.3	†1,367.0	1,685.8	613.3	1,304.8	1,685.8	....	27.7	23.0	....	103.3	124.4
261	To foreign govenments....................	1.6	†56.0	55.6	1.6	56.0	55.6	....	—	—	....	56.0	55.6
262	To international organizations..............	....	†47.3	68.9	....	47.3	68.9	....	—	—	....	47.3	68.9
263	To other general government units...........	611.7	†1,263.7	1,561.4	611.7	1,201.5	1,561.4	26.1	27.7	23.0	....	—	—
2631	Current....................	560.6	†1,206.8	1,521.9	560.6	1,144.6	1,521.9	—	—	23.0	....	—	—
2632	Capital....................	51.1	†56.9	39.5	51.1	56.9	39.5	26.1	27.7	—	....	—	—
27	Social benefits........................	596.9	†711.5	1,036.9	3,614.0	4,668.6	6,216.2	....	222.7	214.9	....	4,891.3	6,431.2
28	Other expense........................	193.2	†647.3	488.8	193.2	647.3	488.8	....	245.6	27.5	....	893.0	516.3
281	Property expense other than interest...........	—	†—		....			....			....		
282	Miscellaneous other expense..................	193.2	†647.3	488.8	193.2	647.3	488.8	....	245.6	27.5	....	893.0	516.3
2821	Current....................	—	†225.7	—	—	225.7	—	....	238.8	—	....	464.5	—
2822	Capital....................	193.2	†421.7	488.8	193.2	421.7	488.8	....	6.8	27.5	....	428.5	516.3
Table 3 Transactions in assets and liabilities													
3	Change in net worth from transactns....	....	....	....	....	....	....	....	....	....		....	....
31	Net acquisition of nonfinancial assets...	214.2	†819.8	1,145.7	214.2	819.8	1,157.7	645.9	1,300.9	1,765.6	....	2,120.7	2,923.3
311	Fixed assets........................	181.3	†766.5	1,165.2	181.3	766.5	1,177.3	....	1,302.1	1,769.3	....	2,068.5	2,946.6
3111	Buildings and structures..............	....	†—	784.4	....	—	795.3	....	—	1,393.6	....	—	2,188.9
3112	Machinery and equipment......................	....	†—	377.6	....	—	378.7	....	—	375.2	....	—	753.9
3113	Other fixed assets....................	....	†766.5	3.3	....	766.5	3.3	....	1,302.1	.5	....	2,068.5	3.8
312	Inventories....................	30.6	†48.1	−17.0	30.6	48.1	−17.0	....	—	−1.2	....	48.1	−18.2
313	Valuables....................	—	†3.3	−2.5	—	3.3	−2.5	....	—	—	....	3.3	−2.5
314	Nonproduced assets....................	2.3	†2.0	—	2.3	2.0	—	....	−1.2	−2.5	....	.8	−2.5
3141	Land....................	....	†—	—	....	—	—	....	−1.6	−2.5	....	−1.6	−2.5
3142	Subsoil assets....................	....	†—	—	....	—	—	....	—	—	....	—	—
3143	Other naturally occurring assets..................	....	†—	—	....	—	—	....	—	—	....	—	—
3144	Intangible nonproduced assets..................	....	†2.0	—	....	2.0	—	....	.4	—	....	2.4	—
32	Net acquisition of financial assets........	361.5	†24.1	286.9	419.7	72.3	477.7	79.9	283.9	165.5	....	322.2	771.1
321	Domestic....................	340.6	†24.1	286.9	398.8	72.3	477.7	79.9	283.9	165.5	....	322.2	771.1
3212	Currency and deposits....................	145.6	†−100.9	328.1	203.8	−52.7	518.8	−169.6	79.3	37.8	....	26.6	556.7
3213	Securities other than shares....................	....	†—		....			....					
3214	Loans....................	....	†128.3	−38.1	....	128.3	−38.1	....	237.1	164.3	....	331.4	254.2
3215	Shares and other equity....................	....	†−3.3	−3.1	....	−3.3	−3.1	....	−32.5	−36.6	....	−35.8	−39.7
3216	Insurance technical reserves....................	....	†—	—	....	—	—	....	—	—	....	—	—
3217	Financial derivatives....................	....	†—	—	....	—	—	....	—	—	....	—	—
3218	Other accounts receivable....................	....	....	....	....	....	....	....	....	....		....	....
322	Foreign....................	20.9	†—	—	20.9	—	—	—	—	—	....	—	—
3222	Currency and deposits....................	—	†—	—	—	—	—	—	—	—	....	—	—
3223	Securities other than shares....................	—	†—	—	—	—	—	—	—	—	....	—	—
3224	Loans....................	—	†—	—	....	—	—	—	—	—			
3225	Shares and other equity....................	—	†—	—	....	—	—	—	—	—			
3226	Insurance technical reserves....................	—	†—	—	....	—	—	—	—	—			
3227	Financial derivatives....................	—	†—	—	....	—	—	—	—	—			
3228	Other accounts receivable....................	....	....	....	....	....	....	....	....	....			
323	Monetary gold and SDRs....................	—	†—	—	—	—	—	....	—	—	....	—	—
33	Net incurrence of liabilities..................	124.0	†458.5	559.1	124.0	458.5	559.1	—	118.2	−207.5	....	542.7	479.5
331	Domestic....................	146.9	†573.5	323.0	146.9	573.5	323.0	—	118.2	−207.5	....	657.7	243.4
3312	Currency and deposits....................	—	†—	−15.0	—	—	−15.0	—	—	—	....	—	−15.0
3313	Securities other than shares....................	146.9	†282.2	343.8	146.9	282.2	343.8	—	—	—	....	282.2	343.8
3314	Loans....................	—	†291.3	−5.8	—	291.3	−5.8	—	118.2	−207.5	....	375.5	−85.4
3316	Insurance technical reserves....................	—	†—	—	—	—	—	—	—	—			
3317	Financial derivatives....................	—	†—	—	—	—	—	—	—	—			
3318	Other accounts payable....................	....	....	....	....	....	....	....	....	....			
332	Foreign....................	−23.0	†−115.0	236.1	−23.0	−115.0	236.1	—	—	—	....	−115.0	236.1
3322	Currency and deposits....................	9.2	†—	—	9.2	—	—	—	—	—			
3323	Securities other than shares....................	−32.2	†—	55.7	−32.2	—	55.7	—	—	—	....	—	55.7
3324	Loans....................	—	†−2.6	180.4	—	−2.6	180.4	—	—	—	....	−2.6	180.4
3326	Insurance technical reserves....................	—	†−112.5	—	—	−112.5	—	—	—	—	....	−112.5	—
3327	Financial derivatives....................	—	†—	—	—	—	—	—	—	—			
3328	Other accounts payable....................	....	....	....	....	....	....	....	....	....		....	....

In Billions of Rubels / Year Ending December 31 / Cash Reporter

	Budgetary Central Government			Central Government			Local Government			General Government		
	2002	2003p	2004p	2002	2003p	2004p	2002	2003p	2004p	2002	2003p	2004p
Table 4 Holding gains in assets and liabilities												
Table 5 Other changes in the volume of assets and liabilities												
Table 6 Balance sheet												
6 Net worth....................	....	....	....	....	....	....	....	....	....	....	....	....
61 Nonfinancial assets....................	....	....	....	....	....	....	....	....	....	....	....	....
611 Fixed assets....................	....	....	....	....	....	....	....	....	....	....	....	....
6111 Buildings and structures....................	....	....	....	....	....	....	....	....	....	....	....	....
6112 Machinery and equipment....................	....	....	....	....	....	....	....	....	....	....	....	....
6113 Other fixed assets....................	....	....	....	....	....	....	....	....	....	....	....	....
612 Inventories....................	....	....	....	....	....	....	....	....	....	....	....	....
613 Valuables....................	....	....	....	....	....	....	....	....	....	....	....	....
614 Nonproduced assets....................	....	....	....	....	....	....	....	....	....	....	....	....
6141 Land....................	....	....	....	....	....	....	....	....	....	....	....	....
6142 Subsoil assets....................	....	....	....	....	....	....	....	....	....	....	....	....
6143 Other naturally occurring assets....................	....	....	....	....	....	....	....	....	....	....	....	....
6144 Intangible nonproduced assets....................	....	....	....	....	....	....	....	....	....	....	....	....
62 Financial assets....................	....	....	....	....	....	....	....	....	....	....	....	....
621 Domestic....................	....	....	....	....	....	....	....	....	....	....	....	....
6212 Currency and deposits....................	....	....	....	....	....	....	....	....	....	....	....	....
6213 Securities other than shares....................	....	....	....	....	....	....	....	....	....	....	....	....
6214 Loans....................	....	....	....	....	....	....	....	....	....	....	....	....
6215 Shares and other equity....................	....	....	....	....	....	....	....	....	....	....	....	....
6216 Insurance technical reserves....................	....	....	....	....	....	....	....	....	....	....	....	....
6217 Financial derivatives....................	....	....	....	....	....	....	....	....	....	....	....	....
6218 Other accounts receivable....................	....	....	....	....	....	....	....	....	....	....	....	....
622 Foreign....................	....	....	....	....	....	....	....	....	....	....	....	....
6222 Currency and deposits....................	....	....	....	....	....	....	....	....	....	....	....	....
6223 Securities other than shares....................	....	....	....	....	....	....	....	....	....	....	....	....
6224 Loans....................	....	....	....	....	....	....	....	....	....	....	....	....
6225 Shares and other equity....................	....	....	....	....	....	....	....	....	....	....	....	....
6226 Insurance technical reserves....................	....	....	....	....	....	....	....	....	....	....	....	....
6227 Financial derivatives....................	....	....	....	....	....	....	....	....	....	....	....	....
6228 Other accounts receivable....................	....	....	....	....	....	....	....	....	....	....	....	....
623 Monetary gold and SDRs....................	....	....	....	....	....	....	....	....	....	....	....	....
63 **Liabilities**....................	**3,224.6**	....	....	**3,224.6**	....	....	....	....	....	....	....	....
631 Domestic....................	1,663.6	....	....	1,663.6	....	....	....	....	....	....	....	....
6312 Currency and deposits....................	....	....	....	....	....	....	....	....	....	....	....	....
6313 Securities other than shares....................	....	....	....	....	....	....	....	....	....	....	....	....
6314 Loans....................	....	....	....	....	....	....	....	....	....	....	....	....
6316 Insurance technical reserves....................	....	....	....	....	....	....	....	....	....	....	....	....
6317 Financial derivatives....................	....	....	....	....	....	....	....	....	....	....	....	....
6318 Other accounts payable....................	....	....	....	....	....	....	....	....	....	....	....	....
632 Foreign....................	1,561.0	....	....	1,561.0	....	....	....	....	....	....	....	....
6322 Currency and deposits....................	....	....	....	....	....	....	....	....	....	....	....	....
6323 Securities other than shares....................	....	....	....	....	....	....	....	....	....	....	....	....
6324 Loans....................	....	....	....	....	....	....	....	....	....	....	....	....
6326 Insurance technical reserves....................	....	....	....	....	....	....	....	....	....	....	....	....
6327 Financial derivatives....................	....	....	....	....	....	....	....	....	....	....	....	....
6328 Other accounts payable....................	....	....	....	....	....	....	....	....	....	....	....	....
Memorandum items:												
6M2 Net financial worth....................	....	....	....	....	....	....	....	....	....	....	....	....
6M3 Debt at market value....................	....	....	....	....	....	....	....	....	....	....	....	....
6M4 Debt at nominal value....................	....	....	....	....	....	....	....	....	....	....	....	....
6M5 Arrears....................	....	....	....	....	....	....	....	....	....	....	....	....
6M6 Obligations for social security benefits....................	....	....	....	....	....	....	....	....	....	....	....	....
6M7 Contingent liabilities....................	....	....	....	....	....	....	....	....	....	....	....	....
6M8 Uncapitalized military weapons, systems....................	....	....	....	....	....	....	....	....	....	....	....	....
Table 7 Outlays by functions of govt.												
7 **Total outlays**....................	**4,035.5**	**†7,288.9**	**10,111.9**	**7,089.0**	**11,214.5**	**15,337.9**	**4,686.6**	**7,089.0**	**9,008.4**	**....**	**17,074.3**	**22,762.0**
701 **General public services**....................	**1,484.8**	**†2,346.0**	**2,920.5**	**1,484.8**	**2,346.0**	**2,920.5**	**716.3**	**523.1**	**684.6**	**....**	**1,798.7**	**2,173.5**
7017 Public debt transactions....................	142.3	†184.0	233.9	142.3	184.0	233.9	1.1	2.2	9.4	....	186.2	243.3
7018 General transfers between levels of govt......	....	†1,070.4	1,408.6	....	1,070.4	1,408.6	....	—	23.0	....	—	—
702 **Defense**....................	**323.6**	**†380.6**	**478.2**	**323.6**	**380.6**	**478.2**	**2.9**	**4.0**	**5.8**	**....**	**384.6**	**484.0**
703 **Public order and safety**....................	**311.8**	**†605.0**	**860.5**	**311.8**	**605.0**	**860.5**	**57.2**	**116.0**	**166.4**	**....**	**721.0**	**1,026.8**

In Billions of Rubels / Year Ending December 31 / Cash Reporter

		Budgetary Central Government			Central Government			Local Government			General Government	
		2002	2003p	2004p	2002	2003p	2004p	2002	2003p	2004p	2002	2003p	2004p
704	**Economic affairs**........................	**924.8**	**†2,115.8**	**3,255.8**	**924.8**	**2,115.8**	**3,255.8**	**848.4**	**1,235.7**	**1,381.0**	....	**3,265.3**	**4,564.1**
7042	Agriculture, forestry, fishing, and hunting.....	411.2	†745.1	1,491.0	411.2	745.1	1,491.0	403.1	768.6	605.0	....	1,456.6	2,056.0
7043	Fuel and energy.........................	21.2	†42.8	7.2	21.2	42.8	7.2	20.7	25.2	34.2	....	68.0	41.3
7044	Mining, manufacturing, and construction.....	3.4	†—	9.5	3.4	—	9.5	15.2	5.6	7.2	....	5.6	16.7
7045	Transport...............................	357.5	†453.9	713.3	357.5	453.9	713.3	346.2	510.6	715.4	....	935.3	1,396.0
7046	Communication...........................	....	†1.9	2.7	....	1.9	2.7	....	—	.6	....	1.9	3.3
705	**Environmental protection**...............	....	**†42.0**	**79.0**	....	**42.0**	**79.0**	....	**138.2**	**235.6**	....	**180.2**	**314.6**
706	**Housing and community amenities**........	**1.3**	**†9.4**	**45.6**	**1.3**	**9.4**	**45.6**	**611.1**	**1,193.1**	**1,484.8**	....	**1,202.5**	**1,530.4**
707	**Health**...................................	**253.4**	**†385.5**	**504.0**	**253.4**	**385.5**	**504.0**	**938.6**	**1,393.7**	**1,839.2**	....	**1,779.2**	**2,343.2**
7072	Outpatient services.......................	—	....	....	—	....	....	....	....	....	....	....	....
7073	Hospital services.........................	—	....	....	—	....	....	....	....	....	....	....	....
7074	Public health services....................	....	....	....	....	....	....	....	....	....	....	....	....
708	**Recreation, culture, and religion**...........	**101.4**	**†218.5**	**325.8**	**101.4**	**218.5**	**325.8**	**149.8**	**307.9**	**415.1**	....	**526.4**	**740.9**
709	**Education**...............................	**293.5**	**†426.5**	**580.2**	**293.5**	**426.5**	**580.2**	**1,444.6**	**1,959.5**	**2,461.2**	....	**2,386.0**	**3,041.4**
7091	Pre-primary and primary education.............	....	....	....	....	....	....	....	....	....	....	....	....
7092	Secondary education......................	94.8	....	....	94.8	....	....	....	....	....	....	....	....
7094	Tertiary education........................	184.2	†257.2	....	184.2	257.2	....	....	....	....	....	....	....
710	**Social protection**........................	**340.8**	**†759.6**	**1,062.3**	**3,394.3**	**4,685.3**	**6,288.4**	**79.5**	**223.5**	**334.6**	....	**4,858.3**	**6,543.0**
7	Statistical discrepancy: Total outlays.............	—	†—	—	—	.1	—	—	−5.7	—	....	−27.9	—
Table 8	**Transactions in financial assets and liabilities by sector**												
82	**Net acquisition of financial assets**........	**361.5**	**†24.1**	**286.9**	**419.7**	**72.3**	**477.6**	**79.9**	**283.9**	**165.5**	....	**322.2**	**771.1**
821	Domestic..............................	340.6	†24.1	286.9	398.8	72.3	477.6	79.9	283.9	165.5	....	322.2	771.1
8211	General government...................	78.6	†−68.9	330.6	78.6	−20.7	521.3	....	76.4	32.0	....	21.7	681.2
8212	Central bank.........................	....	†—	—	....	—	—	....	—	—	....	—	—
8213	Other depository corporations..................	....	†—	—	....	—	—	....	—	—	....	—	—
8214	Financial corporations n.e.c................	....	†—	—	....	—	—	....	—	—	....	—	—
8215	Nonfinancial corporations..................	91.4	†93.0	−43.7	91.4	93.0	−43.7	....	207.5	133.5	....	300.5	89.8
8216	Households & NPIs serving households......	....	†—	—	....	—	—	....	—	—	....	—	—
822	Foreign................................	20.9	†—	—	20.9	—	—	—	—	—	....	—	—
8221	General government...................	....	†—	—	....	—	—	—	—	—	....	—	—
8227	International organizations..................	....	†—	—	....	—	—	—	—	—	....	—	—
8228	Financial corporations other than international organizations...............	....	†—	—	....	—	—	—	—	—	....	—	—
8229	Other nonresidents.......................	....	†—	—	....	—	—	—	—	—	....	—	—
823	Monetary gold and SDRs....................	—	†—	—	—	—	—	—	—	—	....	—	—
83	**Net incurrence of liabilities**..................	**124.0**	**†458.5**	**559.1**	**124.0**	**458.5**	**559.1**	**—**	**118.2**	**−207.5**	....	**542.7**	**479.5**
831	Domestic..............................	146.9	†573.5	323.0	146.9	573.5	323.0	—	118.2	−207.5	....	657.7	243.4
8311	General government...................	....	†—	—	....	—	—	—	118.2	−127.9	....	84.2	—
8312	Central bank.........................	....	†283.7	−3.4	....	283.7	−3.4	—	—	—	....	283.7	−3.4
8313	Other depository corporations..................	....	†289.8	251.4	....	289.8	251.4	—	—	−79.5	....	289.8	171.8
8314	Financial corporations n.e.c...............	....	†—	—	....	—	—	—	—	—	....	—	—
8315	Nonfinancial corporations..................	....	†—	75.3	....	—	75.3	—	—	—	....	—	75.3
8316	Households & NPIs serving households......	....	†—	−.3	....	—	−.3	—	—	—	....	—	−.3
832	Foreign................................	−23.0	†−115.0	236.1	−23.0	−115.0	236.1	—	—	—	....	−115.0	236.1
8321	General government...................	....	†−25.5	240.0	....	−25.5	240.0	—	—	—	....	−25.5	240.0
8327	International organizations..................	....	†−86.9	−59.6	....	−86.9	−59.6	—	—	—	....	−86.9	−59.6
8328	Financial corporations other than international organizations...............	....	†—	—	....	—	—	—	—	—	....	—	—
8329	Other nonresidents.......................	—	†−2.6	55.7	—	−2.6	55.7	—	—	—	....	−2.6	55.7

Belgium   124

In Millions of Euros / Year Ending December 31 / Noncash Reporter

	Central Government			State Government			Local Government			General Government		
	2001	2002	2003	2001	2002	2003	2001	2002	2003	2001	2002	2003
Statement of government operations												
1 Revenue......	111,565	112,436	118,083	35,496	35,861	38,102	16,072	17,357	18,719	126,876	131,364	138,285
2 Expense......	111,805	112,067	118,359	33,449	36,232	37,695	16,433	17,174	18,017	125,429	131,183	137,451
GOB *Gross operating balance......*	*−223*	*789*	*229*	*3,823*	*1,513*	*2,113*	*1,621*	*1,939*	*2,730*	*5,221*	*4,240*	*5,072*
NOB *Net operating balance......*	*−240*	*369*	*−275*	*2,047*	*−371*	*407*	*−360*	*183*	*702*	*1,447*	*181*	*834*
31 Net acquisition of nonfinancial assets......	17	420	504	1,775	1,884	1,706	1,981	1,756	2,028	3,774	4,059	4,238
NLB *Net lending/borrowing......*	*−257*	*−51*	*−779*	*272*	*−2,255*	*−1,299*	*−2,342*	*−1,573*	*−1,326*	*−2,327*	*−3,878*	*−3,403*
32 Net acquisition of financial assets......	−252	−1,419	−7,667	1,518	−975	−826	−108	173	631	244	−1,586	−5,414
33 Net incurrence of liabilities......	868	−1,035	−7,445	−295	−110	−1,153	467	323	475	126	−188	−5,673
NLB Statistical discrepancy......	−863	−333	556	1,541	1,390	1,625	1,767	1,423	1,482	2,445	2,480	3,663
Statement of other economic flows												
Balance sheet												
6 *Net worth......*	....	....	....	....	....	....	....	....	....	....	....	....
61 Nonfinancial assets......	....	....	....	....	....	....	....	....	....	....	....	....
62 Financial assets......	279,632	281,887	276,421	6,774	6,153	4,379	9,149	8,384	9,130	286,606	288,109	285,663
63 Liabilities......	372,550	380,102	377,162	17,043	17,321	16,168	13,977	14,300	14,775	394,622	403,408	403,839
Statement of sources and uses of cash												
Table 1 Revenue												
1 **Revenue......**	**111,565**	**112,436**	**118,083**	**35,496**	**35,861**	**38,102**	**16,072**	**17,357**	**18,719**	**126,876**	**131,364**	**138,285**
11 **Taxes......**	**69,837**	**69,568**	**69,591**	**3,057**	**5,446**	**5,943**	**5,363**	**5,889**	**6,348**	**78,257**	**80,903**	**81,882**
111 Taxes on income, profits, & capital gains......	41,543	42,328	41,909	—	−223	−1	1,881	2,028	2,173	43,424	44,133	44,081
1111 Individuals......	33,255	34,001	33,693	—	−223	−1	1,881	2,028	2,173	35,136	35,806	35,865
1112 Corporations and other enterprises......	8,092	8,087	7,906	—	—	—	—	—	—	8,092	8,087	7,906
112 Taxes on payroll and workforce......	24	22	22	—	—	—	—	—	—	24	22	22
113 Taxes on property......	2,108	856	833	2,025	3,339	3,627	2,915	3,267	3,569	7,047	7,461	8,028
114 Taxes on goods and services......	26,005	26,203	26,671	895	2,148	2,141	567	594	606	27,468	28,946	29,417
1141 General taxes on goods and services......	16,728	17,825	17,958	—	—	—	—	—	—	16,728	17,825	17,958
1142 Excises......	5,645	5,956	6,186	327	336	361	—	—	—	5,972	6,292	6,548
115 Taxes on int'l. trade and transactions......	—	—	—	—	—	—	—	—	—	—	—	—
116 Other taxes......	158	160	157	137	181	176	—	—	—	295	341	333
12 **Social contributions......**	**38,427**	**40,000**	**40,685**	**2,399**	**2,612**	**2,795**	**867**	**908**	**950**	**41,693**	**43,521**	**44,429**
121 Social security contributions......	36,610	38,148	38,909	—	—	—	16	16	16	36,626	38,164	38,925
122 Other social contributions......	1,817	1,852	1,776	2,399	2,612	2,795	851	892	934	5,067	5,357	5,505
13 **Grants......**	**414**	**413**	**344**	**28,518**	**25,926**	**27,428**	**7,486**	**8,105**	**8,840**	**266**	**267**	**124**
131 From foreign governments......	—	—	—	—	—	—	—	—	—	—	—	—
132 From international organizations......	192	211	36	75	56	88	—	—	—	266	267	124
133 From other general government units......	222	202	308	28,443	25,870	27,340	7,486	8,105	8,840	—	—	—
14 **Other revenue......**	**2,886**	**2,455**	**7,464**	**1,523**	**1,877**	**1,937**	**2,356**	**2,455**	**2,581**	**6,660**	**6,673**	**11,851**
Table 2 Expense by economic type												
2 **Expense......**	**111,805**	**112,067**	**118,359**	**33,449**	**36,232**	**37,695**	**16,433**	**17,174**	**18,017**	**125,429**	**131,183**	**137,451**
21 **Compensation of employees......**	**7,916**	**8,076**	**8,323**	**13,014**	**14,021**	**14,657**	**8,659**	**9,297**	**9,691**	**29,590**	**31,394**	**32,671**
211 Wages and salaries......	5,593	5,697	5,896	9,618	10,344	10,729	6,381	6,845	6,933	21,592	22,885	23,558
212 Social contributions......	2,323	2,379	2,427	3,396	3,678	3,928	2,279	2,452	2,758	7,998	8,509	9,113
22 **Use of goods and services......**	**2,924**	**2,985**	**3,116**	**3,010**	**3,637**	**3,757**	**2,127**	**2,239**	**2,333**	**8,062**	**8,861**	**9,206**
23 **Consumption of fixed capital......**	**17**	**420**	**504**	**1,775**	**1,884**	**1,706**	**1,981**	**1,756**	**2,028**	**3,774**	**4,059**	**4,238**
24 **Interest......**	**15,381**	**14,386**	**13,414**	**764**	**742**	**702**	**709**	**675**	**653**	**16,749**	**15,689**	**14,639**
25 **Subsidies......**	**2,046**	**1,990**	**2,381**	**1,532**	**1,624**	**1,572**	**375**	**384**	**395**	**3,953**	**3,998**	**4,349**
26 **Grants......**	**30,349**	**28,267**	**30,147**	**6,286**	**6,408**	**6,940**	**193**	**222**	**199**	**676**	**721**	**797**
261 To foreign govenments......	—	—	—	—	—	—	—	—	—	—	—	—
262 To international organizations......	543	563	634	83	99	104	50	58	59	676	721	797
263 To other general government units......	29,805	27,704	29,513	6,203	6,308	6,836	143	164	140	—	—	—
2631 Current......	29,719	27,657	29,392	5,566	5,815	6,366	140	162	137	—	—	—
2632 Capital......	87	47	121	638	493	470	3	3	2	—	—	—
27 **Social benefits......**	**49,961**	**52,409**	**55,694**	**4,161**	**4,704**	**4,948**	**1,825**	**2,015**	**2,115**	**55,948**	**59,129**	**62,757**
28 **Other expense......**	**3,210**	**3,535**	**4,779**	**2,906**	**3,212**	**3,413**	**562**	**586**	**603**	**6,678**	**7,333**	**8,794**
281 Property expense other than interest......	—	—	—	—	—	—	—	—	—	—	—	—
282 Miscellaneous other expense......	3,210	3,535	4,779	2,906	3,212	3,413	562	586	603	6,678	7,333	8,794
2821 Current......	2,330	2,568	2,880	1,505	1,619	1,778	501	502	512	4,336	4,690	5,170
2822 Capital......	879	967	1,900	1,401	1,593	1,634	61	83	90	2,342	2,643	3,624

In Millions of Euros / Year Ending December 31 / Noncash Reporter

		Central Government			State Government			Local Government			General Government		
		2001	2002	2003	2001	2002	2003	2001	2002	2003	2001	2002	2003
Table 3	**Transactions in assets and liabilities**												
3	**Change in net worth from transactns....**	−1,103	36	281	3,588	1,019	2,032	1,407	1,606	2,184	3,892	2,661	4,497
31	**Net acquisition of nonfinancial assets...**	17	420	504	1,775	1,884	1,706	1,981	1,756	2,028	3,774	4,059	4,238
311	Fixed assets..........	428	577	488	1,775	1,882	1,703	2,004	1,784	2,070	4,207	4,243	4,261
3111	Buildings and structures..........	....	....	....	....	....	....	....	....	....	....	....	....
3112	Machinery and equipment..........	....	....	....	....	....	....	....	....	....	....	....	....
3113	Other fixed assets..........	....	....	....	....	....	....	....	....	....	....	....	....
312	Inventories..........	−11	26	15	—	2	3	—	—	—	−11	28	18
313	Valuables..........	—	—	—				—	—	—	—	—	—
314	Nonproduced assets..........	−400	−183	1	—	—	—	−23	−29	−42	−422	−211	−41
3141	Land..........	....	....	....				....	....	....	....	....	....
3142	Subsoil assets..........	....	....	....				....	....	....	....	....	....
3143	Other naturally occurring assets..........	....	....	....	—	—	—	....	....	....	....	....	....
3144	Intangible nonproduced assets..........	....	....	....	—	—	—	....	....	....	....	....	....
32	**Net acquisition of financial assets.........**	−252	−1,419	−7,667	1,518	−975	−826	−108	173	631	244	−1,586	−5,414
321	Domestic..........	340	−1,615	−7,977	1,518	−905	−851	−240	254	716	704	−1,632	−5,663
3212	Currency and deposits..........	159	−867	152	325	−243	69	−288	346	346	196	−763	567
3213	Securities other than shares..........	107	151	−151	938	−784	307	−262	74	746	−4	114	126
3214	Loans..........	−527	−223	−7,677	−69	−92	−1,325	—	3	7	−380	−69	−6,309
3215	Shares and other equity..........	−94	−371	−185	−6	107	68	154	165	245	54	−100	128
3216	Insurance technical reserves..........	—	—	—	—	—	—	—	—	—	—	—	—
3217	Financial derivatives..........	−139	−133	−128	—	—	—	—	—	—	−139	−133	−128
3218	Other accounts receivable..........	835	−172	12	329	108	29	157	−334	−628	978	−681	−48
322	Foreign..........	−592	197	310	—	−70	24	132	−81	−85	−461	46	249
3222	Currency and deposits..........	−898	—	—	—	—	—	—	—	—	−898	—	—
3223	Securities other than shares..........	—	—	—	—	−62	18	−7	−12	−7	−7	−74	12
3224	Loans..........	2	261	112	—	—	—	—	—	—	2	261	112
3225	Shares and other equity..........	128	112	53	—	−8	6	138	−69	−78	266	36	−19
3226	Insurance technical reserves..........	—	—	—	—	—	—	—	—	—	—	—	—
3227	Financial derivatives..........	—	—	—	—	—	—	—	—	—	—	—	—
3228	Other accounts receivable..........	176	−176	145	—	—	—	—	—	—	176	−176	145
323	Monetary gold and SDRs..........	—	—	—	—	—	—	—	—	—	—	—	—
33	**Net incurrence of liabilities...................**	868	−1,035	−7,445	−295	−110	−1,153	467	323	475	126	−188	−5,673
331	Domestic..........	−10,879	−11,163	−12,393	−361	−663	−1,197	467	323	475	−11,687	−10,869	−10,666
3312	Currency and deposits..........	−118	70	138	—	—	—	—	—	—	−118	70	138
3313	Securities other than shares..........	−7,907	−10,526	−10,856	−325	500	−539	39	7	24	−8,980	−9,346	−12,148
3314	Loans..........	−1,877	−431	−1,789	−87	−1,212	−746	434	318	447	−1,314	−1,081	599
3316	Insurance technical reserves..........	—	—	—	—	−19	29	−17	−6	−2	−17	−25	27
3317	Financial derivatives..........	—	—	—	—	—	—	—	—	—	—	—	—
3318	Other accounts payable..........	−977	−275	114	51	67	59	11	4	6	−1,258	−487	718
332	Foreign..........	11,747	10,128	4,948	66	553	44	—	—	—	11,813	10,681	4,992
3322	Currency and deposits..........	—	—	—	—	—	—	—	—	—	—	—	—
3323	Securities other than shares..........	11,473	10,603	5,492	21	488	41	—	—	—	11,494	11,091	5,533
3324	Loans..........	−212	−29	−234	44	65	3	—	—	—	−167	36	−231
3326	Insurance technical reserves..........	—	—	—	—	—	—	—	—	—	—	—	—
3327	Financial derivatives..........	—	—	—	—	—	—	—	—	—	—	—	—
3328	Other accounts payable..........	485	−446	−310	—	—	—	—	—	—	485	−446	−310
Table 4	**Holding gains in assets and liabilities**												
Table 5	**Other changes in the volume of assets and liabilities**												
Table 6	**Balance sheet**												
6	**Net worth..........**	....	....	....	....	....	....	....	....	....	....	....	....
61	**Nonfinancial assets..........**	....	....	....	....	....	....	....	....	....	....	....	....
611	Fixed assets..........	....	....	....	....	....	....	....	....	....	....	....	....
6111	Buildings and structures..........	....	....	....	....	....	....	....	....	....	....	....	....
6112	Machinery and equipment..........	....	....	....	....	....	....	....	....	....	....	....	....
6113	Other fixed assets..........	....	....	....	....	....	....	....	....	....	....	....	....
612	Inventories..........	....	....	....	....	....	....	....	....	....	....	....	....
613	Valuables..........	....	....	....	....	....	....	....	....	....	....	....	....
614	Nonproduced assets..........	....	....	....	....	....	....	....	....	....	....	....	....
6141	Land..........	....	....	....	....	....	....	....	....	....	....	....	....
6142	Subsoil assets..........	....	....	....	....	....	....	....	....	....	....	....	....
6143	Other naturally occurring assets..........	....	....	....	....	....	....	....	....	....	....	....	....
6144	Intangible nonproduced assets..........	....	....	....	....	....	....	....	....	....	....	....	....

In Millions of Euros / Year Ending December 31 / Noncash Reporter

		Central Government			State Government			Local Government			General Government		
		2001	2002	2003	2001	2002	2003	2001	2002	2003	2001	2002	2003
62	**Financial assets**.................	**279,632**	**281,887**	**276,421**	**6,774**	**6,153**	**4,379**	**9,149**	**8,384**	**9,130**	**286,606**	**288,109**	**285,663**
621	Domestic...........................	28,347	27,786	20,578	6,774	6,082	4,283	8,358	7,674	8,504	34,530	33,226	29,099
6212	Currency and deposits..........	2,063	1,255	1,355	737	509	578	2,294	2,640	2,986	5,094	4,404	4,918
6213	Securities other than shares....	2,116	2,747	858	1,068	284	591	1,135	1,210	1,956	1,590	2,184	571
6214	Loans................................	9,080	8,305	788	3,070	2,949	—	—	3	9	6,828	6,179	6
6215	Shares and other equity.........	1,547	1,773	3,731	1,209	1,543	2,287	3,744	2,971	3,331	6,500	6,286	9,349
6216	Insurance technical reserves.....	—	—	—	—	—	—	—	—	—	—	—	—
6217	Financial derivatives.............	—	—	—	—	—	—	—	—	—	—	—	—
6218	Other accounts receivable.......	13,540	13,705	13,847	690	798	828	1,185	851	223	14,518	14,174	14,255
622	Foreign.............................	226	337	611	—	72	96	791	710	625	1,017	1,118	1,332
6222	Currency and deposits..........	—	—	—	—	—	—	—	—	—	—	—	—
6223	Securities other than shares....	—	337	466	—	39	57	56	44	37	56	419	560
6224	Loans................................	50	—	—	—	—	—	—	—	—	50	—	—
6225	Shares and other equity.........	—	—	—	—	33	39	735	666	588	735	699	627
6226	Insurance technical reserves.....	—	—	—	—	—	—	—	—	—	—	—	—
6227	Financial derivatives.............	—	—	—	—	—	—	—	—	—	—	—	—
6228	Other accounts receivable.......	176	—	145	—	—	—	—	—	—	176	—	145
623	Monetary gold and SDRs........	251,060	253,765	255,232	—	—	—	—	—	—	251,060	253,765	255,232
63	**Liabilities**........................	**372,550**	**380,102**	**377,162**	**17,043**	**17,321**	**16,168**	**13,977**	**14,300**	**14,775**	**394,622**	**403,408**	**403,839**
631	Domestic...........................	259,358	258,511	250,477	16,036	15,760	14,564	13,977	14,300	14,775	280,422	280,256	275,549
6312	Currency and deposits..........	144,216	134,548	128,077	—	—	—	—	—	—	144,216	134,548	128,077
6313	Securities other than shares....	−1,300	−114	−1,356	2,683	3,183	2,644	103	109	133	−1,244	1,122	−1,413
6314	Loans................................	2,899	467	−5,470	12,359	11,247	10,501	13,583	13,901	14,348	23,520	20,537	18,589
6316	Insurance technical reserves.....	—	—	—	—	270	299	102	96	94	102	365	393
6317	Financial derivatives.............	181	237	268	—	—	—	—	—	—	181	237	268
6318	Other accounts payable..........	113,362	123,373	128,957	994	1,061	1,120	190	194	200	113,648	123,447	129,636
632	Foreign.............................	113,193	121,591	126,685	1,007	1,560	1,605	—	—	—	114,200	123,151	128,290
6322	Currency and deposits..........	104,402	114,797	120,298	—	—	—	—	—	—	104,402	114,797	120,298
6323	Securities other than shares....	2,281	2,264	2,236	592	1,080	1,121	—	—	—	2,873	3,344	3,357
6324	Loans................................	267	290	56	415	480	483	—	—	—	682	770	539
6326	Insurance technical reserves.....	—	—	—	—	—	—	—	—	—	—	—	—
6327	Financial derivatives.............	—	—	—	—	—	—	—	—	—	—	—	—
6328	Other accounts payable..........	6,243	4,241	4,096	—	—	—	—	—	—	6,243	4,241	4,096
	Memorandum items:												
6M2	Net financial worth...............	−92,918	−98,215	−100,741	−10,269	−11,167	−11,789	−4,829	−5,916	−5,646	−108,016	−115,298	−118,176
6M3	Debt at market value.............	....	....	....	....	....	....	....	....	....	....	....	....
6M4	Debt at nominal value...........	....	....	....	....	....	....	....	....	....	....	....	....
6M5	Arrears..............................	....	....	....	....	....	....	....	....	....	....	....	....
6M6	Obligations for social security benefits...........	....	....	....	....	....	....	....	....	....	....	....	....
6M7	Contingent liabilities.............	....	....	....	....	....	....	....	....	....	....	....	....
6M8	Uncapitalized military weapons, systems........	....	....	....	....	....	....	....	....	....	....	....	....
	Table 7 Outlays by functions of govt.												
7	**Total outlays**....................	**111,822**	**112,487**	**118,862**	**35,224**	**38,116**	**39,400**	**18,414**	**18,930**	**20,045**	**129,202**	**135,242**	**141,689**
701	**General public services**...........	**45,694**	**42,603**	**43,247**	**5,383**	**5,688**	**6,411**	**3,982**	**4,137**	**4,240**	**55,059**	**52,428**	**53,897**
7017	Public debt transactions............	15,381	14,386	13,414	764	742	702	709	675	653	16,749	15,689	14,639
7018	General transfers between levels of govt......	....	....	....									
702	**Defense**...........................	**3,199**	**3,224**	**3,228**	—	—	—	—	—	—	**3,199**	**3,224**	**3,228**
703	**Public order and safety**..........	**2,553**	**2,883**	**3,157**	**63**	**80**	**78**	**1,584**	**1,994**	**2,143**	**4,200**	**4,956**	**5,378**
704	**Economic affairs**.................	**4,394**	**4,607**	**6,170**	**5,608**	**6,031**	**5,943**	**1,926**	**1,817**	**2,021**	**11,929**	**12,455**	**14,135**
7042	Agriculture, forestry, fishing, and hunting.....	....	....	....	....	....	....	....	....	....	....	....	....
7043	Fuel and energy......................	....	....	....	....	....	....	....	....	....	....	....	....
7044	Mining, manufacturing, and construction.....	....	....	....	....	....	....	....	....	....	....	....	....
7045	Transport.............................	....	....	....	....	....	....	....	....	....	....	....	....
7046	Communication......................	....	....	....	....	....	....	....	....	....	....	....	....
705	**Environmental protection**......................	**44**	**46**	**43**	**1,180**	**1,115**	**1,009**	**881**	**872**	**898**	**2,104**	**2,032**	**1,950**
706	**Housing and community amenities**........	—	—	**49**	**561**	**688**	**641**	**303**	**289**	**318**	**863**	**977**	**1,009**
707	**Health**.............................	**16,256**	**16,854**	**18,471**	**266**	**283**	**282**	**325**	**337**	**365**	**16,846**	**17,474**	**19,118**
7072	Outpatient services..................	....	....	....	....	....	....	....	....	....	....	....	....
7073	Hospital services.....................	....	....	....	....	....	....	....	....	....	....	....	....
7074	Public health services................	....	....	....	....	....	....	....	....	....	....	....	....
708	**Recreation, culture, and religion**............	**269**	**255**	**267**	**769**	**1,498**	**1,549**	**1,474**	**1,457**	**1,553**	**2,512**	**3,210**	**3,368**

		Central Government			State Government			Local Government			General Government		
		2001	2002	2003	2001	2002	2003	2001	2002	2003	2001	2002	2003
709	**Education**................................	**2,763**	**2,956**	**3,153**	**14,316**	**15,021**	**15,557**	**3,369**	**3,474**	**3,578**	**20,448**	**21,450**	**22,288**
7091	Pre-primary and primary education..............	....	....	....	....	....	....	....	....	....	....	....	....
7092	Secondary education............................	....	....	....	....	....	....	....	....	....	....	....	....
7094	Tertiary education..............................	....	....	....	....	....	....	....	....	....	....	....	....
710	**Social protection**.............................	**50,346**	**49,892**	**52,246**	**5,303**	**5,829**	**6,226**	**2,590**	**2,799**	**2,900**	**58,239**	**58,520**	**61,372**
7	Statistical discrepancy: Total outlays..............	−13,696	−10,832	−11,168	1,775	1,884	1,706	1,981	1,756	2,028	−46,196	−41,484	−44,053

Table 8   Transactions in financial assets and liabilities by sector

		Central Government			State Government			Local Government			General Government		
82	**Net acquisition of financial assets**.........	**−252**	**−1,418**	**−7,667**	**1,518**	**−975**	**−826**	**−108**	**173**	**631**	**244**	**−1,586**	**−5,414**
821	Domestic...	340	−1,615	−7,977	1,518	−905	−851	−240	254	716	705	−1,632	−5,663
8211	General government...........................	3	26	−1,496	1,078	−773	−1,026	−167	113	73	—	—	—
8212	Central bank....................................	162	−571	−358	—	—	—	—	—	—	162	−571	−358
8213	Other depository corporations..................	−41	−1,001	−12	325	−250	69	−292	345	344	−8	−905	401
8214	Financial corporations n.e.c...................	−133	−55	−3,543	−102	60	1	−4	47	7	−239	52	−3,535
8215	Nonfinancial corporations......................	301	166	148	168	63	93	172	68	331	641	296	572
8216	Households & NPIs serving households......	48	−181	−2,716	50	−5	12	50	−318	−39	148	−504	−2,743
822	Foreign..	−592	197	310	—	−70	24	132	−81	−85	−461	46	249
8221	General government...........................	....	....	....	....	....	....	....	....	....	....	....	....
8227	International organizations....................	....	....	....	....	....	....	....	....	....	....	....	....
8228	Financial corporations other than international organizations..............	....	....	....	....	....	....	....	....	....	....	....	....
8229	Other nonresidents............................	....	....	....	....	....	....	....	....	....	....	....	....
823	Monetary gold and SDRs.......................	—	—	—	—	—	—	—	—	—	—	—	—
83	**Net incurrence of liabilities**..................	**869**	**−1,035**	**−7,445**	**−295**	**−110**	**−1,152**	**467**	**323**	**475**	**126**	**−188**	**−5,673**
831	Domestic...	−10,879	−11,162	−12,393	−361	−663	−1,197	467	323	475	−11,687	−10,869	−10,665
8311	General government...........................	1,044	−911	−1,510	−111	252	−959	−19	25	20	—	—	—
8312	Central bank....................................	76	−285	−154	—	—	—	—	—	—	76	−285	−154
8313	Other depository corporations..................	−11,936	−8,453	−8,043	−251	−873	−342	428	330	440	−11,759	−8,996	−7,945
8314	Financial corporations n.e.c...................	−140	−470	−1,664	−36	17	−14	—	—	—	−176	−453	−1,677
8315	Nonfinancial corporations......................	−252	−920	1,093	−13	−108	29	64	−30	11	−202	−1,058	1,133
8316	Households & NPIs serving households......	329	−123	−2,116	51	48	88	−6	−2	5	374	−77	−2,023
832	Foreign..	11,747	10,128	4,948	66	553	44	—	—	—	11,813	10,681	4,992
8321	General government...........................	....	....	....	....	....	....	—	—	—	....	....	....
8327	International organizations....................	....	....	....	....	....	....	—	—	—	....	....	....
8328	Financial corporations other than international organizations..............	....	....	....	....	....	....	—	—	—	....	....	....
8329	Other nonresidents............................	....	....	....	....	....	....	—	—	—	....	....	....

Bhutan   514

In Millions of Ngultrum / Year Ending June 30 / Cash Reporter

	Budgetary Central Government			Extrabudgetary Accounts			Central Government			General Government		
	2002	2003	2004	2002	2003	2004	2002	2003	2004	2002	2003	2004
Statement of government operations												
Statement of other economic flows												
Balance sheet												
6 *Net worth*	....	....	....	....	....	....	....	....	....	....	....	....
61 Nonfinancial assets	....	....	....	....	....	....	....	....	....	....	....	....
62 Financial assets	....	....	....	....	....	....	....	....	....	....	....	....
63 Liabilities	14,715.7	19,931.0	23,959.3	....	....	....	14,715.7	19,931.0	23,959.3	14,715.7	19,931.0	23,959.3
Statement of sources and uses of cash												
1 Cash receipts from operating activities	8,792.0	7,015.3	10,371.5	....	....	....	8,792.0	7,015.3	10,371.5	8,792.0	7,015.3	10,371.5
11 Taxes	2,414.6	2,713.6	2,446.6	....	....	....	2,414.6	2,713.6	2,446.6	2,414.6	2,713.6	2,446.6
12 Social contributions	—	—	—	....	....	....	—	—	—	—	—	—
13 Grants	3,748.5	2,269.1	5,367.4	....	....	....	3,748.5	2,269.1	5,367.4	3,748.5	2,269.1	5,367.4
14 Other receipts	2,628.9	2,032.7	2,557.5	....	....	....	2,628.9	2,032.7	2,557.5	2,628.9	2,032.7	2,557.5
2 Cash payments for operating activities	4,827.1	5,373.2	5,409.2	....	....	....	4,827.1	5,373.2	5,409.2	4,827.1	5,373.2	5,409.2
21 Compensation of employees	1,897.1	1,947.0	2,086.8	....	....	....	1,897.1	1,947.0	2,086.8	1,897.1	1,947.0	2,086.8
22 Purchases of goods and services	2,161.2	2,093.2	2,386.6	....	....	....	2,161.2	2,093.2	2,386.6	2,161.2	2,093.2	2,386.6
24 Interest	115.8	168.9	220.3	....	....	....	115.8	168.9	220.3	115.8	168.9	220.3
25 Subsidies	65.1	143.9	114.3	....	....	....	65.1	143.9	114.3	65.1	143.9	114.3
26 Grants	—	24.0	61.7	....	....	....	—	24.0	61.7	—	24.0	61.7
27 Social benefits	228.7	203.9	279.6	....	....	....	228.7	203.9	279.6	228.7	203.9	279.6
28 Other payments	359.2	792.3	260.0	....	....	....	359.2	792.3	260.0	359.2	792.3	260.0
CIO *Net cash inflow from oper. activities*	*3,965.0*	*1,642.1*	*4,962.2*	....	....	....	*3,965.0*	*1,642.1*	*4,962.2*	*3,965.0*	*1,642.1*	*4,962.2*
31.1 Purchases of nonfinancial assets	4,953.4	4,517.2	4,393.0	....	....	....	4,953.4	4,517.2	4,393.0	4,953.4	4,517.2	4,393.0
31.2 Sales of nonfinancial assets	34.7	25.0	73.5	....	....	....	34.7	25.0	73.5	34.7	25.0	73.5
31 Net cash outflow from investments in nonfinancial assets	4,918.7	4,492.2	4,319.5	....	....	....	4,918.7	4,492.2	4,319.5	4,918.7	4,492.2	4,319.5
CSD *Cash surplus/deficit*	*–953.7*	*–2,850.1*	*642.7*	....	....	....	*–953.7*	*–2,850.1*	*642.7*	*–953.7*	*–2,850.1*	*642.7*
32x Net acquisition of fin assets, excl. cash	271.6	40.8	62.9	....	....	....	271.6	40.8	62.9	271.6	40.8	62.9
321x Domestic	271.6	40.8	62.9	....	....	....	271.6	40.8	62.9	271.6	40.8	62.9
322x Foreign	—	—	—	....	....	....	—	—	—	—	—	—
323 Monetary gold and SDRs	—	—	—	....	....	....	—	—	—	—	—	—
33 Net incurrence of liabilities	1,181.4	2,895.7	–556.3	....	....	....	1,181.4	2,895.7	–556.3	1,181.4	2,895.7	–556.3
331 Domestic	–215.3	1,358.4	–1,488.4	....	....	....	–215.3	1,358.4	–1,488.4	–215.3	1,358.4	–1,488.4
332 Foreign	1,396.7	1,537.3	932.1	....	....	....	1,396.7	1,537.3	932.1	1,396.7	1,537.3	932.1
NFB Net cash inflow from fin. activities	909.8	2,854.9	–619.2	....	....	....	909.8	2,854.9	–619.2	909.8	2,854.9	–619.2
NCB *Net change in the stock of cash*	*–44.0*	*4.7*	*23.5*	....	....	....	*–44.0*	*4.7*	*23.5*	*–44.0*	*4.7*	*23.5*
Table 1 Revenue												
1 **Revenue**	**8,792.0**	**7,015.3**	**10,371.5**	....	....	....	**8,792.0**	**7,015.3**	**10,371.5**	**8,792.0**	**7,015.3**	**10,371.5**
11 **Taxes**	**2,414.6**	**2,713.6**	**2,446.6**	....	....	....	**2,414.6**	**2,713.6**	**2,446.6**	**2,414.6**	**2,713.6**	**2,446.6**
111 Taxes on income, profits, & capital gains	1,305.0	1,272.7	1,419.4	....	....	....	1,305.0	1,272.7	1,419.4	1,305.0	1,272.7	1,419.4
1111 Individuals	317.2	350.2	404.0	....	....	....	317.2	350.2	404.0	317.2	350.2	404.0
1112 Corporations and other enterprises	987.8	922.5	1,015.4	....	....	....	987.8	922.5	1,015.4	987.8	922.5	1,015.4
112 Taxes on payroll and workforce	73.6	100.5	113.5	....	....	....	73.6	100.5	113.5	73.6	100.5	113.5
113 Taxes on property	9.6	1.5	1.4	....	....	....	9.6	1.5	1.4	9.6	1.5	1.4
114 Taxes on goods and services	915.0	1,219.5	750.1	....	....	....	915.0	1,219.5	750.1	915.0	1,219.5	750.1
1141 General taxes on goods and services	360.0	435.0	495.5	....	....	....	360.0	435.0	495.5	360.0	435.0	495.5
1142 Excises	444.9	657.8	129.3	....	....	....	444.9	657.8	129.3	444.9	657.8	129.3
115 Taxes on int'l. trade and transactions	106.8	115.9	153.8	....	....	....	106.8	115.9	153.8	106.8	115.9	153.8
116 Other taxes	4.5	3.5	3.3	....	....	....	4.5	3.5	3.3	4.5	3.5	3.3
12 **Social contributions**	**—**	**—**	**—**	....	....	....	**—**	**—**	**—**	**—**	**—**	**—**
121 Social security contributions	—	—	—	....	....	....	—	—	—	—	—	—
122 Other social contributions	—	—	—	....	....	....	—	—	—	—	—	—
13 **Grants**	**3,748.5**	**2,269.1**	**5,367.4**	....	....	....	**3,748.5**	**2,269.1**	**5,367.4**	**3,748.5**	**2,269.1**	**5,367.4**
131 From foreign governments	3,748.5	2,269.1	5,367.4	....	....	....	3,748.5	2,269.1	5,367.4	3,748.5	2,269.1	5,367.4
132 From international organizations	—	—	—	....	....	....	—	—	—	—	—	—
133 From other general government units	—	—	—	....	....	....	—	—	—	—	—	—
14 **Other revenue**	**2,628.9**	**2,032.7**	**2,557.5**	....	....	....	**2,628.9**	**2,032.7**	**2,557.5**	**2,628.9**	**2,032.7**	**2,557.5**
Table 2 Expense by economic type												
2 **Expense**	**4,827.1**	**5,373.2**	**5,409.2**	....	....	....	**4,827.1**	**5,373.2**	**5,409.2**	**4,827.1**	**5,373.2**	**5,409.2**
21 **Compensation of employees**	**1,897.1**	**1,947.0**	**2,086.8**	....	....	....	**1,897.1**	**1,947.0**	**2,086.8**	**1,897.1**	**1,947.0**	**2,086.8**
211 Wages and salaries	1,745.8	1,844.8	1,979.7	....	....	....	1,745.8	1,844.8	1,979.7	1,745.8	1,844.8	1,979.7
212 Social contributions	151.4	102.2	107.1	....	....	....	151.4	102.2	107.1	151.4	102.2	107.1
22 **Use of goods and services**	**2,161.2**	**2,093.2**	**2,386.6**	....	....	....	**2,161.2**	**2,093.2**	**2,386.6**	**2,161.2**	**2,093.2**	**2,386.6**
23 **Consumption of fixed capital**	....	....	....	....	....	....	....	....	....	....	....	....
24 **Interest**	**115.8**	**168.9**	**220.3**	....	....	....	**115.8**	**168.9**	**220.3**	**115.8**	**168.9**	**220.3**
25 **Subsidies**	**65.1**	**143.9**	**114.3**	....	....	....	**65.1**	**143.9**	**114.3**	**65.1**	**143.9**	**114.3**

In Millions of Ngultrum / Year Ending June 30 / Cash Reporter

	Budgetary Central Government			Extrabudgetary Accounts			Central Government			General Government		
	2002	2003	2004	2002	2003	2004	2002	2003	2004	2002	2003	2004
26 Grants..................................	—	24.0	61.7	....	....	....	—	24.0	61.7	—	24.0	61.7
261 To foreign govenments................	—	24.0	61.7	....	....	....	—	24.0	61.7	—	24.0	61.7
262 To international organizations.........	—	—	—	....	....	....	—	—	—	—	—	—
263 To other general government units....	—	—	—	....	....	....	—	—	—	—	—	—
2631 Current................................	—	—	—	....	....	....	—	—	—	—	—	—
2632 Capital.................................	—	—	—	....	....	....	—	—	—	—	—	—
27 Social benefits..........................	228.7	203.9	279.6	....	....	....	228.7	203.9	279.6	228.7	203.9	279.6
28 Other expense..........................	359.2	792.3	260.0	....	....	....	359.2	792.3	260.0	359.2	792.3	260.0
281 Property expense other than interest....	—	—	—	....	....	....	—	—	—	—	—	—
282 Miscellaneous other expense..........	359.2	792.3	260.0	....	....	....	359.2	792.3	260.0	359.2	792.3	260.0
2821 Current................................	—	—	—	....	....	....	—	—	—	—	—	—
2822 Capital.................................	359.2	792.3	260.0	....	....	....	359.2	792.3	260.0	359.2	792.3	260.0

Table 3 Transactions in assets and liabilities

	Budgetary Central Government			Extrabudgetary Accounts			Central Government			General Government		
	2002	2003	2004	2002	2003	2004	2002	2003	2004	2002	2003	2004
3 Change in net worth from transactns....	....	....	....	....	....	....	....	....	....	....	....	....
31 Net acquisition of nonfinancial assets...	4,918.7	4,492.2	4,319.5	....	....	....	4,918.7	4,492.2	4,319.5	4,918.7	4,492.2	4,319.5
311 Fixed assets............................	4,293.6	3,654.6	3,650.3	....	....	....	4,293.6	3,654.6	3,650.3	4,293.6	3,654.6	3,650.3
3111 Buildings and structures............	....	....	....	....	....	....	....	....	....	....	....	....
3112 Machinery and equipment.........	....	....	....	....	....	....	....	....	....	....	....	....
3113 Other fixed assets..................	....	....	....	....	....	....	....	....	....	....	....	....
312 Inventories.............................	—	—	—	....	....	....	—	—	—	—	—	—
313 Valuables..............................	—	—	—	....	....	....	—	—	—	—	—	—
314 Nonproduced assets..................	625.0	837.6	669.2	....	....	....	625.0	837.6	669.2	625.0	837.6	669.2
3141 Land.................................	....	....	....	....	....	....	....	....	....	....	....	....
3142 Subsoil assets......................	....	....	....	....	....	....	....	....	....	....	....	....
3143 Other naturally occurring assets....	....	....	....	....	....	....	....	....	....	....	....	....
3144 Intangible nonproduced assets.....	....	....	....	....	....	....	....	....	....	....	....	....
32 Net acquisition of financial assets........	227.7	45.6	86.4	....	....	....	227.7	45.6	86.4	227.7	45.6	86.4
321 Domestic..............................	227.7	45.6	86.4	....	....	....	227.7	45.6	86.4	227.7	45.6	86.4
3212 Currency and deposits.............	−44.0	4.7	23.5	....	....	....	−44.0	4.7	23.5	−44.0	4.7	23.5
3213 Securities other than shares.......	....	....	....	....	....	....	....	....	....	....	....	....
3214 Loans...............................	....	....	....	....	....	....	....	....	....	....	....	....
3215 Shares and other equity...........	....	....	....	....	....	....	....	....	....	....	....	....
3216 Insurance technical reserves......	....	....	....	....	....	....	....	....	....	....	....	....
3217 Financial derivatives...............	....	....	....	....	....	....	....	....	....	....	....	....
3218 Other accounts receivable.........	....	....	....	....	....	....	....	....	....	....	....	....
322 Foreign...............................	—	—	—	....	....	....	—	—	—	—	—	—
3222 Currency and deposits.............	—	—	—	....	....	....	—	—	—	—	—	—
3223 Securities other than shares.......	—	—	—	....	....	....	—	—	—	—	—	—
3224 Loans...............................	—	—	—	....	....	....	—	—	—	—	—	—
3225 Shares and other equity...........	—	—	—	....	....	....	—	—	—	—	—	—
3226 Insurance technical reserves......	—	—	—	....	....	....	—	—	—	—	—	—
3227 Financial derivatives...............	—	—	—	....	....	....	—	—	—	—	—	—
3228 Other accounts receivable.........	....	....	....	....	....	....	....	....	....	....	....	....
323 Monetary gold and SDRs..........	—	—	—	....	....	....	—	—	—	—	—	—
33 Net incurrence of liabilities..................	1,181.4	2,895.7	−556.3	....	....	....	1,181.4	2,895.7	−556.3	1,181.4	2,895.7	−556.3
331 Domestic..............................	−215.3	1,358.4	−1,488.4	....	....	....	−215.3	1,358.4	−1,488.4	−215.3	1,358.4	−1,488.4
3312 Currency and deposits.............	—	—	—	....	....	....	—	—	—	—	—	—
3313 Securities other than shares.......	500.0	250.0	—	....	....	....	500.0	250.0	—	500.0	250.0	—
3314 Loans...............................	−715.3	1,108.4	−1,488.4	....	....	....	−715.3	1,108.4	−1,488.4	−715.3	1,108.4	−1,488.4
3316 Insurance technical reserves......	—	—	—	....	....	....	—	—	—	—	—	—
3317 Financial derivatives...............	—	—	—	....	....	....	—	—	—	—	—	—
3318 Other accounts payable...........	....	....	....	....	....	....	....	....	....	....	....	....
332 Foreign...............................	1,396.7	1,537.3	932.1	....	....	....	1,396.7	1,537.3	932.1	1,396.7	1,537.3	932.1
3322 Currency and deposits.............	—	—	—	....	....	....	—	—	—	—	—	—
3323 Securities other than shares.......	—	—	—	....	....	....	—	—	—	—	—	—
3324 Loans...............................	1,396.7	1,537.3	932.1	....	....	....	1,396.7	1,537.3	932.1	1,396.7	1,537.3	932.1
3326 Insurance technical reserves......	—	—	—	....	....	....	—	—	—	—	—	—
3327 Financial derivatives...............	—	—	—	....	....	....	—	—	—	—	—	—
3328 Other accounts payable...........	....	....	....	....	....	....	....	....	....	....	....	....

	Budgetary Central Government			Extrabudgetary Accounts			Central Government			General Government		
	2002	2003	2004	2002	2003	2004	2002	2003	2004	2002	2003	2004
Table 4 Holding gains in assets and liabilities												
Table 5 Other changes in the volume of assets and liabilities												
Table 6 Balance sheet												
6 Net worth..................	....	....	....	....	....	....	....	....	....	....	....	....
61 **Nonfinancial assets**...................	....	....	....	....	....	....	....	....	....	....	....	....
611 Fixed assets........................	....	....	....	....	....	....	....	....	....	....	....	....
6111 Buildings and structures.............	....	....	....	....	....	....	....	....	....	....	....	....
6112 Machinery and equipment............	....	....	....	....	....	....	....	....	....	....	....	....
6113 Other fixed assets................	....	....	....	....	....	....	....	....	....	....	....	....
612 Inventories......................	....	....	....	....	....	....	....	....	....	....	....	....
613 Valuables......................	....	....	....	....	....	....	....	....	....	....	....	....
614 Nonproduced assets.................	....	....	....	....	....	....	....	....	....	....	....	....
6141 Land..........................	....	....	....	....	....	....	....	....	....	....	....	....
6142 Subsoil assets.....................	....	....	....	....	....	....	....	....	....	....	....	....
6143 Other naturally occurring assets..........	....	....	....	....	....	....	....	....	....	....	....	....
6144 Intangible nonproduced assets...........	....	....	....	....	....	....	....	....	....	....	....	....
62 **Financial assets**........................	....	....	....	....	....	....	....	....	....	....	....	....
621 Domestic.........................	....	....	....	....	....	....	....	....	....	....	....	....
6212 Currency and deposits................	....	....	....	....	....	....	....	....	....	....	....	....
6213 Securities other than shares.............	....	....	....	....	....	....	....	....	....	....	....	....
6214 Loans...........................	....	....	....	....	....	....	....	....	....	....	....	....
6215 Shares and other equity..............	....	....	....	....	....	....	....	....	....	....	....	....
6216 Insurance technical reserves.............	....	....	....	....	....	....	....	....	....	....	....	....
6217 Financial derivatives.................	....	....	....	....	....	....	....	....	....	....	....	....
6218 Other accounts receivable..............	....	....	....	....	....	....	....	....	....	....	....	....
622 Foreign..........................	....	....	....	....	....	....	....	....	....	....	....	....
6222 Currency and deposits................	....	....	....	....	....	....	....	....	....	....	....	....
6223 Securities other than shares.............	....	....	....	....	....	....	....	....	....	....	....	....
6224 Loans...........................	....	....	....	....	....	....	....	....	....	....	....	....
6225 Shares and other equity..............	....	....	....	....	....	....	....	....	....	....	....	....
6226 Insurance technical reserves.............	....	....	....	....	....	....	....	....	....	....	....	....
6227 Financial derivatives.................	....	....	....	....	....	....	....	....	....	....	....	....
6228 Other accounts receivable..............	....	....	....	....	....	....	....	....	....	....	....	....
623 Monetary gold and SDRs...............	....	....	....	....	....	....	....	....	....	....	....	....
63 **Liabilities**........................	**14,715.7**	**19,931.0**	**23,959.3**	....	....	....	**14,715.7**	**19,931.0**	**23,959.3**	**14,715.7**	**19,931.0**	**23,959.3**
631 Domestic.........................	500.0	750.0	500.0	....	....	....	500.0	750.0	500.0	500.0	750.0	500.0
6312 Currency and deposits................	....	....	....	....	....	....	....	....	....	....	....	....
6313 Securities other than shares.............	....	....	....	....	....	....	....	....	....	....	....	....
6314 Loans...........................	....	....	....	....	....	....	....	....	....	....	....	....
6316 Insurance technical reserves.............	....	....	....	....	....	....	....	....	....	....	....	....
6317 Financial derivatives.................	....	....	....	....	....	....	....	....	....	....	....	....
6318 Other accounts payable..............	....	....	....	....	....	....	....	....	....	....	....	....
632 Foreign..........................	14,215.7	19,181.0	23,459.3	....	....	....	14,215.7	19,181.0	23,459.3	14,215.7	19,181.0	23,459.3
6322 Currency and deposits................	....	....	....	....	....	....	....	....	....	....	....	....
6323 Securities other than shares.............	....	....	....	....	....	....	....	....	....	....	....	....
6324 Loans...........................	....	....	....	....	....	....	....	....	....	....	....	....
6326 Insurance technical reserves.............	....	....	....	....	....	....	....	....	....	....	....	....
6327 Financial derivatives.................	....	....	....	....	....	....	....	....	....	....	....	....
6328 Other accounts payable..............	....	....	....	....	....	....	....	....	....	....	....	....
Memorandum items:												
6M2 Net financial worth..................	....	....	....	....	....	....	....	....	....	....	....	....
6M3 Debt at market value.................	....	....	....	....	....	....	....	....	....	....	....	....
6M4 Debt at nominal value.................	....	....	....	....	....	....	....	....	....	....	....	....
6M5 Arrears...........................	....	....	....	....	....	....	....	....	....	....	....	....
6M6 Obligations for social security benefits...........	....	....	....	....	....	....	....	....	....	....	....	....
6M7 Contingent liabilities.................	....	....	....	....	....	....	....	....	....	....	....	....
6M8 Uncapitalized military weapons, systems........	....	....	....	....	....	....	....	....	....	....	....	....
Table 7 Outlays by functions of govt.												
7 **Total outlays**..................	**9,780.4**	**9,890.5**	**9,802.3**	....	....	....	**9,780.4**	**9,890.5**	**9,802.3**	**9,780.4**	**9,890.5**	**9,802.3**
701 **General public services**..................	**2,320.3**	**3,202.8**	**3,571.6**	....	....	....	**2,320.3**	**3,202.8**	**3,571.6**	**2,320.3**	**3,202.8**	**3,571.6**
7017 Public debt transactions.................	115.8	168.9	220.3	....	....	....	115.8	168.9	220.3	115.8	168.9	220.3
7018 General transfers between levels of govt......	....	....	....	....	....	....	....	....	....	....	....	....
702 **Defense**...........................	—	—	—	....	....	....	—	—	—	—	—	—
703 **Public order and safety**..................	**482.4**	**519.8**	**552.7**	....	....	....	**482.4**	**519.8**	**552.7**	**482.4**	**519.8**	**552.7**

	Budgetary Central Government			Extrabudgetary Accounts			Central Government			General Government		
	2002	2003	2004	2002	2003	2004	2002	2003	2004	2002	2003	2004
704 **Economic affairs**.................................	**3,876.6**	**3,291.9**	**2,925.4**	....	....	....	**3,876.6**	**3,291.9**	**2,925.4**	**3,876.6**	**3,291.9**	**2,925.4**
7042 Agriculture, forestry, fishing, and hunting.....	883.2	1,115.3	989.1	....	....	....	883.2	1,115.3	989.1	883.2	1,115.3	989.1
7043 Fuel and energy................................	1,835.1	1,015.6	789.5	....	....	....	1,835.1	1,015.6	789.5	1,835.1	1,015.6	789.5
7044 Mining, manufacturing, and construction.....	106.4	156.3	75.5	....	....	....	106.4	156.3	75.5	106.4	156.3	75.5
7045 Transport...	979.5	946.8	1,042.7	....	....	....	979.5	946.8	1,042.7	979.5	946.8	1,042.7
7046 Communication..................................	....	....	....	....	....	....	....	....	....	....	....	....
705 **Environmental protection**......................	—	—	—	....	....	....	—	—	—	—	—	—
706 **Housing and community amenities**........	**340.8**	**411.1**	**501.7**	....	....	....	**340.8**	**411.1**	**501.7**	**340.8**	**411.1**	**501.7**
707 **Health**...	**1,142.8**	**848.7**	**831.8**	....	....	....	**1,142.8**	**848.7**	**831.8**	**1,142.8**	**848.7**	**831.8**
7072 Outpatient services.............................	....	....	....	....	....	....	....	....	....	....	....	....
7073 Hospital services................................	....	....	....	....	....	....	....	....	....	....	....	....
7074 Public health services..........................	....	....	....	....	....	....	....	....	....	....	....	....
708 **Recreation, culture, and religion**...........	**183.6**	**139.6**	**155.7**	....	....	....	**183.6**	**139.6**	**155.7**	**183.6**	**139.6**	**155.7**
709 **Education**...	**1,434.0**	**1,476.5**	**1,303.3**	....	....	....	**1,434.0**	**1,476.5**	**1,303.3**	**1,434.0**	**1,476.5**	**1,303.3**
7091 Pre-primary and primary education.............	....	....	....	....	....	....	....	....	....	....	....	....
7092 Secondary education............................	....	....	....	....	....	....	....	....	....	....	....	....
7094 Tertiary education...............................	....	....	....	....	....	....	....	....	....	....	....	....
710 **Social protection**................................	—	—	—	....	....	....	—	—	—	—	—	—
7 Statistical discrepancy: Total outlays..............	—	—	−40.0	....	....	....	—	—	−40.0	—	—	−40.0

Table 8   Transactions in financial assets and liabilities by sector

	Budgetary Central Government			Extrabudgetary Accounts			Central Government			General Government		
82 **Net acquisition of financial assets**........	**227.7**	**45.6**	**86.4**	....	....	....	**227.7**	**45.6**	**86.4**	**227.7**	**45.6**	**86.4**
821 Domestic..	227.7	45.6	86.4	....	....	....	227.7	45.6	86.4	227.7	45.6	86.4
8211 General government.............................	—	....	....	....	....	....	....	....	....	....	....	....
8212 Central bank....................................	....	....	....	....	....	....	....	....	....	....	....	....
8213 Other depository corporations..................	....	....	....	....	....	....	....	....	....	....	....	....
8214 Financial corporations n.e.c....................	....	....	....	....	....	....	....	....	....	....	....	....
8215 Nonfinancial corporations......................	56.2	....	....	....	....	....	56.2	....	....	56.2	....	....
8216 Households & NPIs serving households......	....	....	....	....	....	....	....	....	....	....	....	....
822 Foreign..	—	—	—	....	....	....	—	—	—	—	—	—
8221 General government.............................	—	—	—	....	....	....	—	—	—	—	—	—
8227 International organizations......................	—	—	—	....	....	....	—	—	—	—	—	—
8228 Financial corporations other than international organizations..............	—	—	—	....	....	....	—	—	—	—	—	—
8229 Other nonresidents.............................	—	—	—	....	....	....	—	—	—	—	—	—
823 Monetary gold and SDRs........................	—	—	—	....	....	....	—	—	—	—	—	—
83 **Net incurrence of liabilities**..................	**1,181.4**	**2,895.7**	**−556.3**	....	....	....	**1,181.4**	**2,895.7**	**−556.3**	**1,181.4**	**2,895.7**	**−556.3**
831 Domestic..	−215.3	1,358.4	−1,488.4	....	....	....	−215.3	1,358.4	−1,488.4	−215.3	1,358.4	−1,488.4
8311 General government.............................	....	....	....	....	....	....	....	....	....	....	....	....
8312 Central bank....................................	....	....	....	....	....	....	....	....	....	....	....	....
8313 Other depository corporations..................	....	....	....	....	....	....	....	....	....	....	....	....
8314 Financial corporations n.e.c....................	....	....	....	....	....	....	....	....	....	....	....	....
8315 Nonfinancial corporations......................	....	....	....	....	....	....	....	....	....	....	....	....
8316 Households & NPIs serving households......	....	....	....	....	....	....	....	....	....	....	....	....
832 Foreign..	1,396.7	1,537.3	932.1	....	....	....	1,396.7	1,537.3	932.1	1,396.7	1,537.3	932.1
8321 General government.............................	450.0	562.2	462.0	....	....	....	450.0	562.2	462.0	450.0	562.2	462.0
8327 International organizations......................	946.7	975.2	470.2	....	....	....	946.7	975.2	470.2	946.7	975.2	470.2
8328 Financial corporations other than international organizations..............	—	—	—	....	....	....	—	—	—	—	—	—
8329 Other nonresidents.............................	—	—	—	....	....	....	—	—	—	—	—	—

In Millions of Bolivianos / Year Ending December 31 / Noncash Reporter

	Central Government			State Government			Local Government			General Government		
	2002	2003	2004	2002	2003	2004	2002	2003	2004	2002	2003	2004
Statement of government operations												
1 Revenue..........	12,516	14,123	17,008	4,117	4,697	5,172	3,237	3,309	4,007	15,480	17,568	21,140
2 Expense..........	16,316	17,462	18,946	3,085	3,553	4,251	1,067	1,332	1,629	16,077	17,785	19,780
GOB *Gross operating balance..........*	*−3,799*	*−3,148*	*−1,815*	*1,033*	*1,145*	*921*	*2,170*	*1,977*	*2,378*	*−597*	*−26*	*1,483*
NOB *Net operating balance..........*	....	....	....	....	....	....	....	....	....	....	....	....
31 Net acquisition of nonfinancial assets..........	1,138	1,344	1,814	807	525	699	1,786	1,634	1,922	3,731	3,503	4,434
NLB *Net lending/borrowing..........*	*−4,938*	*−4,683*	*−3,752*	*226*	*620*	*222*	*383*	*343*	*456*	*−4,328*	*−3,721*	*−3,074*
32 Net acquisition of financial assets..........	−1,221	681	1,241	179	583	260	231	280	273	−845	1,461	1,980
33 Net incurrence of liabilities..........	3,717	5,365	4,993	−47	−37	38	−153	−63	−183	3,483	5,182	5,054
NLB Statistical discrepancy..........	—	—	—	—	—	—	—	—	—	—	—	—
Statement of other economic flows												
Balance sheet												
Statement of sources and uses of cash												
1 Cash receipts from operating activities..........	10,741	12,949	15,467	3,688	4,498	4,604	2,812	2,976	3,628	12,859	16,188	19,521
11 Taxes..........	6,635	7,183	9,308	323	258	255	1,761	1,935	2,448	8,717	9,374	11,997
12 Social contributions..........	1,049	1,232	1,280	—	—	—	—	—	—	1,049	1,232	1,280
13 Grants..........	1,289	2,498	2,747	2,771	3,385	3,368	765	624	753	472	2,304	2,704
14 Other receipts..........	1,768	2,036	2,133	594	855	981	287	417	426	2,620	3,278	3,541
2 Cash payments for operating activities..........	14,642	15,372	16,699	2,890	3,436	3,883	977	1,188	1,533	14,125	15,761	17,937
21 Compensation of employees..........	3,790	3,853	4,266	2,421	2,854	3,202	430	478	536	6,641	7,185	8,004
22 Purchases of goods and services..........	2,418	2,712	2,980	235	234	249	341	540	851	2,994	3,486	4,080
24 Interest..........	1,334	1,537	1,774	29	30	45	79	71	67	1,414	1,608	1,886
25 Subsidies..........	117	75	121	—	—	—	19	30	7	136	105	128
26 Grants..........	3,702	3,965	4,140	142	254	278	13	7	8	−495	23	263
27 Social benefits..........	2,817	2,914	3,123	44	44	45	8	11	9	2,869	2,969	3,177
28 Other payments..........	464	316	295	19	20	65	86	51	55	566	385	399
CIO *Net cash inflow from oper. activities.....*	*−3,901*	*−2,423*	*−1,232*	*798*	*1,062*	*721*	*1,836*	*1,787*	*2,095*	*−1,267*	*427*	*1,584*
31.1 Purchases of nonfinancial assets..........	550	1,355	1,954	706	485	658	1,412	1,359	1,849	2,669	3,199	4,460
31.2 Sales of nonfinancial assets..........	183	26	63	—	1	—	2	2	5	185	29	68
31 Net cash outflow from investments in nonfinancial assets..........	367	1,330	1,891	706	484	658	1,411	1,356	1,843	2,483	3,170	4,392
CSD *Cash surplus/deficit..........*	*−4,268*	*−3,753*	*−3,122*	*92*	*578*	*63*	*425*	*431*	*252*	*−3,750*	*−2,743*	*−2,808*
32x Net acquisition of fin assets, excl. cash..........	−1,251	−35	616	−144	13	15	212	−31	21	−1,190	−121	652
321x Domestic..........	−1,305	−114	530	−144	13	15	212	−30	21	−1,245	−198	566
322x Foreign..........	55	78	86	—	—	—	—	−1	—	55	77	86
323 Monetary gold and SDRs..........	—	—	—	—	—	—	—	—	—	—	—	—
33 Net incurrence of liabilities..........	2,838	4,446	4,343	−21	11	155	−43	−93	−61	2,767	4,295	4,437
331 Domestic..........	484	1,588	1,833	−37	−68	−75	−70	−72	−97	369	1,380	1,660
332 Foreign..........	2,355	2,858	2,511	16	79	230	27	−22	36	2,397	2,915	2,777
NFB Net cash inflow from fin. activities..........	4,089	4,481	3,727	123	−2	140	−255	−62	−82	3,957	4,416	3,785
NCB *Net change in the stock of cash..........*	*−179*	*728*	*605*	*215*	*576*	*203*	*171*	*369*	*169*	*207*	*1,673*	*978*
Table 1 Revenue												
1 **Revenue..........**	†12,516	14,123	17,008	†4,117	4,697	5,172	†3,237	3,309	4,007	†15,480	17,568	21,140
11 **Taxes..........**	†7,473	8,031	10,455	†323	258	255	†1,761	1,935	2,455	†9,553	10,222	13,151
111 Taxes on income, profits, & capital gains......	†841	893	1,193	†—	—	—	†172	195	287	†1,013	1,088	1,479
1111 Individuals..........	†—	—	—	†—	—	—	†—	—	—	†—	—	—
1112 Corporations and other enterprises..........	†841	893	1,193	†—	—	—	†172	195	287	†1,013	1,088	1,479
112 Taxes on payroll and workforce..........	†—	—	—	†—	—	—	†—	—	—	†—	—	—
113 Taxes on property..........	†874	992	1,271	†—	—	—	†756	835	1,049	†1,630	1,826	2,319
114 Taxes on goods and services..........	†5,109	5,447	6,440	†323	258	255	†711	789	971	†6,140	6,492	7,653
1141 General taxes on goods and services..........	†2,993	3,230	3,522	†—	—	—	†650	729	875	†3,640	3,957	4,384
1142 Excises..........	†2,103	2,201	2,581	†323	258	255	†58	56	91	†2,484	2,515	2,927
115 Taxes on int'l. trade and transactions..........	†488	455	528	†—	—	—	†118	112	145	†605	567	672
116 Other taxes..........	†160	244	1,024	†—	—	—	†4	4	3	†164	248	1,027
12 **Social contributions..........**	†1,085	1,431	1,339	†—	—	—	†—	—	—	†1,085	1,431	1,339
121 Social security contributions..........	†1,085	1,431	1,339	†—	—	—	†—	—	—	†1,085	1,431	1,339
122 Other social contributions..........	†—	—	—	†—	—	—	†—	—	—	†—	—	—
13 **Grants..........**	†2,100	2,487	2,914	†3,194	3,581	3,907	†1,171	886	1,056	†2,105	2,427	2,871
131 From foreign governments..........	†385	864	977	†49	2	7	†127	39	37	†562	905	1,020
132 From international organizations..........	†1,505	1,357	1,671	†12	62	33	†27	103	146	†1,544	1,522	1,851
133 From other general government units..........	†210	267	266	†3,132	3,517	3,868	†1,017	744	873	†—	—	—
14 **Other revenue..........**	†1,859	2,174	2,300	†601	858	1,009	†305	487	496	†2,737	3,489	3,780

In Millions of Bolivianos / Year Ending December 31 / Noncash Reporter

	Central Government			State Government			Local Government			General Government		
	2002	2003	2004	2002	2003	2004	2002	2003	2004	2002	2003	2004
Table 2 Expense by economic type												
2 Expense..............................	†16,316	17,462	18,946	†3,085	3,553	4,251	†1,067	1,332	1,629	†16,077	17,785	19,780
21 **Compensation of employees**..................	†4,122	4,238	4,612	†2,486	2,898	3,476	†456	513	582	†7,064	7,650	8,669
211 Wages and salaries.............................	†3,754	3,875	4,209	†2,062	2,396	2,850	†409	460	522	†6,225	6,731	7,581
212 Social contributions.........................	†368	363	403	†424	503	626	†47	53	60	†838	919	1,088
22 **Use of goods and services**.....................	†2,648	2,930	3,190	†284	262	292	†394	632	876	†3,326	3,824	4,358
23 **Consumption of fixed capital**..............	....	....	....	....	....	....	....	....	....	....	....	....
24 **Interest**...............................	†1,334	1,566	1,774	†30	42	49	†81	81	82	†1,418	1,659	1,879
25 **Subsidies**................................	†211	365	311	†—	—	—	†24	31	9	†235	396	320
26 **Grants**..................................	†4,152	4,278	4,710	†220	285	321	†15	7	9	†28	41	34
261 To foreign govenments......................	†1	—	—	†—	—	—	†—	—	—	†1	—	—
262 To international organizations..................	†27	41	34	†—	—	—	†—	—	—	†27	41	34
263 To other general government units............	†4,124	4,237	4,676	†220	285	321	†15	7	9	†—	—	—
2631 Current..................................	†3,002	3,437	3,752	†74	56	64	†—	2	—	†—	—	—
2632 Capital...................................	†1,122	800	924	†146	228	257	†15	5	9	†—	—	—
27 **Social benefits**............................	†2,902	3,139	3,366	†45	44	48	†11	14	10	†2,959	3,197	3,425
28 **Other expense**............................	†946	755	859	†19	21	65	†87	53	61	†1,047	826	971
281 Property expense other than interest..........	†—	1	1	†—	—	—	†—	—	—	†—	1	1
282 Miscellaneous other expense....................	†946	754	859	†19	21	65	†87	53	61	†1,047	825	970
2821 Current..................................	†700	445	657	†3	5	5	†49	31	38	†748	479	684
2822 Capital...................................	†246	309	202	†15	17	61	†38	22	23	†299	347	286
Table 3 Transactions in assets and liabilities												
3 **Change in net worth from transactns....**	....	....	....	....	....	....	....	....	....	....	....	....
31 **Net acquisition of nonfinancial assets...**	†1,138	1,344	1,814	†807	525	699	†1,786	1,634	1,922	†3,731	3,503	4,434
311 Fixed assets................................	†1,141	1,331	1,817	†808	524	695	†1,769	1,619	1,886	†3,718	3,474	4,399
3111 Buildings and structures...................	†1,035	1,268	1,675	†786	503	663	†1,649	1,471	1,683	†3,470	3,243	4,021
3112 Machinery and equipment................	†256	79	159	†22	21	32	†119	144	202	†398	245	393
3113 Other fixed assets.....................	†−150	−17	−17	†—	—	1	†1	3	1	†−150	−13	−15
312 Inventories................................	†—	—	—	†—	—	—	†—	—	—	†—	—	—
313 Valuables.................................	†—	—	—	†—	—	—	†—	—	—	†—	—	—
314 Nonproduced assets.........................	†−2	14	−3	†−1	—	3	†17	15	36	†13	29	36
3141 Land....................................	†−9	14	−3	†−1	—	3	†16	15	36	†6	29	36
3142 Subsoil assets...........................	†—	—	—	†—	—	—	†—	—	—	†—	—	—
3143 Other naturally occurring assets..............	†—	—	—	†—	—	—	†—	—	—	†—	—	—
3144 Intangible nonproduced assets............	†6	—	—	†—	—	—	†1	—	—	†8	—	—
32 **Net acquisition of financial assets**........	†−1,221	681	1,241	†179	583	260	†231	280	273	†−845	1,461	1,980
321 Domestic.................................	†−1,275	603	1,155	†179	583	260	†231	281	273	†−900	1,384	1,894
3212 Currency and deposits....................	†−179	728	605	†215	576	204	†171	369	169	†207	1,673	978
3213 Securities other than shares...............	†−118	−15	80	†−20	—	−32	†−2	—	22	†−140	−140	101
3214 Loans..................................	†−1,012	−47	516	†—	−2	−1	†3	−2	—	†−1,043	−8	691
3215 Shares and other equity....................	†2	—	−33	†—	14	47	†4	—	—	†6	15	14
3216 Insurance technical reserves..................	†—	—	—	†—	—	—	†—	—	—	†—	—	—
3217 Financial derivatives.....................	†—	—	—	†—	—	—	†—	—	—	†—	—	—
3218 Other accounts receivable..................	†32	−64	−13	†−16	−6	42	†55	−86	83	†70	−156	111
322 Foreign..................................	†55	78	86	†—	—	—	†—	−1	—	†55	77	86
3222 Currency and deposits....................	†—	—	—	†—	—	—	†—	—	—	†—	—	—
3223 Securities other than shares...............	†—	—	—	†—	—	—	†—	—	—	†—	—	—
3224 Loans..................................	†−8	−1	−1	†—	—	—	†—	−1	—	†−8	−2	−1
3225 Shares and other equity....................	†63	79	87	†—	—	—	†—	—	—	†63	79	87
3226 Insurance technical reserves..................	†—	—	—	†—	—	—	†—	—	—	†—	—	—
3227 Financial derivatives.....................	†—	—	—	†—	—	—	†—	—	—	†—	—	—
3228 Other accounts receivable..................	†—	—	—	†—	—	—	†—	—	—	†—	—	—
323 Monetary gold and SDRs....................	†—	—	—	†—	—	—	†—	—	—	†—	—	—
33 **Net incurrence of liabilities**..................	†3,717	5,365	4,993	†−47	−37	38	†−153	−63	−183	†3,483	5,182	5,054
331 Domestic.................................	†1,360	2,507	2,483	†−74	−120	−195	†−180	−44	−220	†1,073	2,258	2,274
3312 Currency and deposits....................	†—	—	—	†—	—	—	†—	—	—	†—	—	—
3313 Securities other than shares...............	†3,463	3,741	4,543	†—	—	—	†—	21	8	†3,463	3,637	4,582
3314 Loans..................................	†−2,889	−1,371	−2,022	†−37	−68	−75	†−47	−53	−66	†−3,006	−1,450	−1,987
3316 Insurance technical reserves..................	†—	—	—	†—	—	—	†—	—	—	†—	—	—
3317 Financial derivatives.....................	†—	—	—	†—	—	—	†—	—	—	†—	—	—
3318 Other accounts payable....................	†786	136	−38	†−37	−53	−120	†−133	−12	−162	†616	72	−320

Bolivia   218

In Millions of Bolivianos / Year Ending December 31 / Noncash Reporter

		Central Government			State Government			Local Government			General Government		
		2002	2003	2004	2002	2003	2004	2002	2003	2004	2002	2003	2004
332	Foreign..............................	†2,357	2,858	2,510	†27	84	232	†27	−19	38	†2,410	2,923	2,779
3322	Currency and deposits................	†—	—	—	†—	—	—	†—	—	—	†—	—	—
3323	Securities other than shares............	†—	806	392	†—	—	—	†—	—	—	†—	806	392
3324	Loans....................................	†2,357	2,052	2,117	†27	84	232	†27	−19	38	†2,410	2,118	2,387
3326	Insurance technical reserves............	†—	—	—	†—	—	—	†—	—	—	†—	—	—
3327	Financial derivatives....................	†—	—	—	†—	—	—	†—	—	—	†—	—	—
3328	Other accounts payable.................	†—	—	—	†—	—	—	†—	—	—	†—	—	—

Table 4   Holding gains in assets and liabilities

Table 5   Other changes in the volume of assets and liabilities

Table 6   Balance sheet

Table 7   Outlays by functions of govt.

7	Total outlays.............................	†17,454	18,806	20,760	†3,891	4,077	4,950	†2,854	2,966	3,551	†19,808	21,289	24,214
701	**General public services.....................**	†2,869	3,716	4,223	†200	242	290	†498	478	530	†3,143	4,087	4,480
7017	Public debt transactions................	†1,334	1,566	1,774	†30	42	49	†81	81	82	†1,418	1,659	1,879
7018	General transfers between levels of govt.....	†330	896	1,094	†11	46	95	†—	1	29	†14	658	678
702	**Defense.............................**	†1,041	1,157	1,171	†—	—	—	†—	2	—	†1,041	1,159	1,171
703	**Public order and safety.....................**	†1,248	1,368	1,420	†3	8	8	†14	23	22	†1,264	1,399	1,449
704	**Economic affairs.........................**	†2,941	2,955	3,606	†957	760	905	†624	608	829	†3,720	3,720	4,764
7042	Agriculture, forestry, fishing, and hunting.....	†324	352	371	†223	74	157	†83	78	106	†530	451	617
7043	Fuel and energy........................	†255	443	299	†37	38	98	†27	36	28	†311	503	410
7044	Mining, manufacturing, and construction.....	†61	54	58	†13	6	5	†7	7	11	†81	67	74
7045	Transport..............................	†1,186	1,543	2,003	†476	413	517	†453	430	624	†2,037	2,229	2,890
7046	Communication........................	†28	27	35	†—	—	—	†—	—	—	†28	28	35
705	**Environmental protection.....................**	†149	169	145	†79	65	71	†215	236	193	†440	450	368
706	**Housing and community amenities........**	†233	159	169	†46	79	88	†598	581	727	†829	797	927
707	**Health.....................**	†1,580	1,798	2,051	†428	472	538	†181	336	376	†1,646	1,992	2,270
7072	Outpatient services....................	†447	704	778	†—	—	2	†88	152	99	†524	850	865
7073	Hospital services......................	†347	175	208	†16	3	2	†30	102	198	†388	275	386
7074	Public health services..................	†186	137	130	†13	6	147	†5	10	12	†204	153	289
708	**Recreation, culture, and religion...........**	†109	36	95	†32	20	17	†175	178	299	†315	233	410
709	**Education.....................**	†4,156	4,249	4,508	†1,965	2,305	2,855	†495	489	506	†4,078	4,104	4,768
7091	Pre-primary and primary education.....	†101	87	83	†2	—	4	†295	193	172	†360	228	220
7092	Secondary education....................	†148	62	18	†—	—	3	†69	153	110	†75	154	96
7094	Tertiary education......................	†1,262	1,119	1,162	†—	3	32	†—	1	2	†1,262	1,122	1,170
710	**Social protection.....................**	†3,130	3,200	3,373	†181	126	179	†55	36	70	†3,330	3,349	3,608
7	Statistical discrepancy: Total outlays..............	†—	—	—	†—	—	—	†—	—	—	†—	—	—

Table 8   Transactions in financial assets and liabilities by sector

82	**Net acquisition of financial assets.........**	†−1,221	681	1,241	†179	583	260	†231	280	273	†−845	1,461	1,980
821	Domestic................................	†−1,275	603	1,155	†179	583	260	†231	281	273	†−900	1,384	1,894
8211	General government.....................	†−637	−104	−92	†−21	—	−32	†—	−2	—	†−692	−189	82
8212	Central bank...........................	†−179	616	624	†215	576	204	†171	369	191	†207	1,561	1,019
8213	Other depository corporations..................	†−438	−31	−9	†2	—	—	†—	—	—	†−436	−31	−9
8214	Financial corporations n.e.c.............	†−34	−34	7	†—	—	47	†−2	−91	—	†−36	−124	55
8215	Nonfinancial corporations..............	†12	155	625	†−16	7	41	†62	5	83	†58	167	748
8216	Households & NPIs serving households......	†—	—	—	†—	—	—	†—	—	—	†—	—	—
822	Foreign.................................	†55	78	86	†—	—	—	†—	−1	—	†55	77	86
8221	General government.....................	†—	−1	−1	†—	—	—	†—	—	—	†—	−1	−1
8227	International organizations.............	†55	79	87	†—	—	—	†—	—	—	†55	79	87
8228	Financial corporations other than international organizations.............	†—	—	—	†—	—	—	†—	—	—	†—	—	—
8229	Other nonresidents....................	†—	—	—	†—	—	—	†—	−1	—	†—	−1	—
823	Monetary gold and SDRs.................	†—	—	—	†—	—	—	†—	—	—	†—	—	—
83	**Net incurrence of liabilities...................**	†3,717	5,365	4,993	†−47	−37	38	†−153	−63	−183	†3,483	5,182	5,054
831	Domestic................................	†1,360	2,507	2,484	†−74	−120	−195	†−180	−44	−220	†1,073	2,258	2,274
8311	General government.....................	†−17	327	−215	†—	5	−4	†64	−30	49	†13	218	36
8312	Central bank...........................	†332	579	455	†—	—	—	†—	—	—	†332	579	455
8313	Other depository corporations..................	†−478	1,495	−244	†−40	−59	−47	†−116	−4	−103	†−634	1,432	−394
8314	Financial corporations n.e.c.............	†−80	−13	−5	†—	−16	−28	†—	−3	—	†−80	−32	−33
8315	Nonfinancial corporations..............	†1,445	204	2,220	†−33	−51	−113	†−116	50	−185	†1,296	203	1,923
8316	Households & NPIs serving households......	†158	−86	272	†—	1	−4	†−12	−57	18	†146	−141	287

In Millions of Bolivianos / Year Ending December 31 / Noncash Reporter

		Central Government			State Government			Local Government			General Government		
		2002	2003	2004	2002	2003	2004	2002	2003	2004	2002	2003	2004
832	Foreign..	†2,357	2,858	2,510	†27	84	232	†27	−19	38	†2,410	2,923	2,780
8321	General government................................	†−71	−219	20	†17	—	40	†—	—	16	†−54	−218	77
8327	International organizations......................	†2,429	3,077	2,489	†8	83	192	†20	24	21	†2,457	3,184	2,702
8328	Financial corporations other than international organizations.............	†—	—	—	†—	—	—	†—	—	—	†—	—	—
8329	Other nonresidents.................................	†−1	—	—	†2	—	—	†7	−43	1	†7	−43	1

Bosnia and Herzegovina   963

In Millions of Convertible Marka / Year Ending December 31 / Noncash Reporter

	Budgetary Central Government			Central Government			Local Government			General Government		
	2002	2003	2004p	2002	2003	2004p	2002	2003	2004	2002	2003	2004
Statement of government operations												
1 Revenue.................................	....	3,519.1	3,654.7	....	5,311.9	5,573.6	....	....	....	....	....	....
2 Expense.................................	....	3,267.0	3,349.6	....	5,043.3	5,191.4	....	....	....	....	....	....
GOB *Gross operating balance.....................*	....	*252.1*	*305.1*	....	*268.5*	*382.2*	....	....	....	....	....	....
NOB *Net operating balance...................*	....	....	....	....	....	....	....	....	....	....	....	....
31 Net acquisition of nonfinancial assets...........	....	167.3	133.7	....	173.4	138.0	....	....	....	....	....	....
NLB *Net lending/borrowing..................*	....	*84.8*	*171.5*	....	*95.1*	*244.2*	....	....	....	....	....	....
32 Net acquisition of financial assets.................	....	237.9	293.9	....	319.9	395.5	....	....	....	....	....	....
33 Net incurrence of liabilities.....................	....	153.1	122.4	....	224.7	151.3	....	....	....	....	....	....
NLB Statistical discrepancy..........................	....	—	—	....			....	....	....	....	....	....
Statement of other economic flows												
Balance sheet												
Statement of sources and uses of cash												
Table 1 Revenue												
1 **Revenue**	....	**3,519.1**	**3,654.7**	....	**5,311.9**	**5,573.6**	....	....	....	....	....	....
11 **Taxes**	....	**2,866.6**	**3,004.2**	....	**2,866.6**	**3,004.2**	....	....	....	....	....	....
111 Taxes on income, profits, & capital gains......	....	94.7	128.9	....	94.7	128.9	....	....	....	....	....	....
1111 Individuals...........................	....	94.7	128.9	....	94.7	128.9	....	....	....	....	....	....
1112 Corporations and other enterprises............	....	—	—	....	—	—	....	....	....	....	....	....
112 Taxes on payroll and workforce..................	....	213.6	231.2	....	213.6	231.2	....	....	....	....	....	....
113 Taxes on property.........................	....	6.6	6.6	....	6.6	6.6	....	....	....	....	....	....
114 Taxes on goods and services..................	....	1,517.3	2,010.0	....	1,517.3	2,010.0	....	....	....	....	....	....
1141 General taxes on goods and services..........	....	1,157.8	1,312.9	....	1,157.8	1,312.9	....	....	....	....	....	....
1142 Excises.................................	....	359.4	697.2	....	359.4	697.2	....	....	....	....	....	....
115 Taxes on int'l. trade and transactions...........	....	960.2	546.5	....	960.2	546.5	....	....	....	....	....	....
116 Other taxes.................................	....	74.3	80.9	....	74.3	80.9	....	....	....	....	....	....
12 **Social contributions**	....	**11.3**	**17.5**	....	**1,749.3**	**1,908.0**	....	....	....	....	....	....
121 Social security contributions.....................	....	11.3	17.5	....	1,749.3	1,908.0	....	....	....	....	....	....
122 Other social contributions...........................	....	—	—	....	—	—	....	....	....	....	....	....
13 **Grants**	....	**50.5**	**39.3**	....	**50.5**	**39.3**	....	....	....	....	....	....
131 From foreign governments.....................	....	—	—	....	—	—	....	....	....	....	....	....
132 From international organizations.................	....	—	—	....	—	—	....	....	....	....	....	....
133 From other general government units...........	....	50.5	39.3	....	50.5	39.3	....	....	....	....	....	....
14 **Other revenue**	....	**590.7**	**593.7**	....	**645.5**	**622.0**	....	....	....	....	....	....
Table 2 Expense by economic type												
2 **Expense**	....	**3,267.0**	**3,349.6**	....	**5,043.3**	**5,191.4**	....	....	....	....	....	....
21 **Compensation of employees**	....	**1,532.4**	**1,518.3**	....	**1,461.2**	**1,478.3**	....	....	....	....	....	....
211 Wages and salaries..........................	....	1,409.9	1,424.0	....	1,461.2	1,478.3	....	....	....	....	....	....
212 Social contributions........................	....	122.5	94.3	....	—	—	....	....	....	....	....	....
22 **Use of goods and services**	....	**568.9**	**444.7**	....	**1,348.0**	**1,223.5**	....	....	....	....	....	....
23 **Consumption of fixed capital**	....	....	....	....	....	....	....	....	....	....	....	....
24 **Interest**	....	**105.5**	**81.3**	....	**107.9**	**82.8**	....	....	....	....	....	....
25 **Subsidies**	....	**124.1**	**147.4**	....	**134.7**	**168.3**	....	....	....	....	....	....
26 **Grants**	....	**157.5**	**261.7**	....	**152.3**	**100.9**	....	....	....	....	....	....
261 To foreign govenments......................	....	—	—	....	—	—	....	....	....	....	....	....
262 To international organizations......................	....	—	—	....	—	—	....	....	....	....	....	....
263 To other general government units.............	....	157.5	261.7	....	152.3	100.9	....	....	....	....	....	....
2631 Current.................................	....	157.5	261.7	....	152.3	100.9	....	....	....	....	....	....
2632 Capital.................................	....	—	—	....	—	—	....	....	....	....	....	....
27 **Social benefits**	....	**632.0**	**687.6**	....	**1,686.0**	**1,888.5**	....	....	....	....	....	....
28 **Other expense**	....	**146.6**	**208.6**	....	**153.2**	**249.1**	....	....	....	....	....	....
281 Property expense other than interest............	....	—	—	....	—	—	....	....	....	....	....	....
282 Miscellaneous other expense..................	....	146.6	208.6	....	153.2	249.1	....	....	....	....	....	....
2821 Current.................................	....	146.6	208.6	....	153.2	249.1	....	....	....	....	....	....
2822 Capital.................................	....	—	—	....	—	—	....	....	....	....	....	....

In Millions of Convertible Marka / Year Ending December 31 / Noncash Reporter

	Budgetary Central Government			Central Government			Local Government			General Government		
	2002	2003	2004p	2002	2003	2004p	2002	2003	2004	2002	2003	2004
Table 3 Transactions in assets and liabilities												
3 **Change in net worth from transactns....**	....	....	....	....	....	....	....	....	....	....	....	....
31 **Net acquisition of nonfinancial assets...**	....	167.3	133.7	....	173.4	138.0	....	....	....	....	....	....
311 Fixed assets...	....	165.2	111.0	....	168.7	115.0	....	....	....	....	....	....
3111 Buildings and structures...........................	....	165.2	111.0	....	168.7	115.0	....	....	....	....	....	....
3112 Machinery and equipment..........................	....	—	—	....	—	—	....	....	....	....	....	....
3113 Other fixed assets...................................	....	—	—	....	—	—	....	....	....	....	....	....
312 Inventories...	....	—	—	....	—	—	....	....	....	....	....	....
313 Valuables...	....	—	—	....	—	—	....	....	....	....	....	....
314 Nonproduced assets..................................	....	2.1	22.7	....	4.7	23.0	....	....	....	....	....	....
3141 Land...	....	—	—	....	—	—	....	....	....	....	....	....
3142 Subsoil assets...	....	—	—	....	—	—	....	....	....	....	....	....
3143 Other naturally occurring assets.................	....	—	—	....	—	—	....	....	....	....	....	....
3144 Intangible nonproduced assets...................	....	2.1	22.7	....	4.7	23.0	....	....	....	....	....	....
32 **Net acquisition of financial assets.........**	....	237.9	293.9	....	319.9	395.5	....	....	....	....	....	....
321 Domestic..	....	237.9	293.9	....	319.9	395.5	....	....	....	....	....	....
3212 Currency and deposits..............................	....	—	—	....	—	—	....	....	....	....	....	....
3213 Securities other than shares......................	....	—	—	....	—	—	....	....	....	....	....	....
3214 Loans...	....	237.9	293.9	....	319.9	395.5	....	....	....	....	....	....
3215 Shares and other equity............................	....	—	—	....	—	—	....	....	....	....	....	....
3216 Insurance technical reserves......................	....	—	—	....	—	—	....	....	....	....	....	....
3217 Financial derivatives................................	....	—	—	....	—	—	....	....	....	....	....	....
3218 Other accounts receivable.........................	....	—	—	....	—	—	....	....	....	....	....	....
322 Foreign..	....	—	—	....	—	—	....	....	....	....	....	....
3222 Currency and deposits..............................	....	—	—	....	—	—	....	....	....	....	....	....
3223 Securities other than shares......................	....	—	—	....	—	—	....	....	....	....	....	....
3224 Loans...	....	—	—	....	—	—	....	....	....	....	....	....
3225 Shares and other equity............................	....	—	—	....	—	—	....	....	....	....	....	....
3226 Insurance technical reserves......................	....	—	—	....	—	—	....	....	....	....	....	....
3227 Financial derivatives................................	....	—	—	....	—	—	....	....	....	....	....	....
3228 Other accounts receivable.........................	....	—	—	....	—	—	....	....	....	....	....	....
323 Monetary gold and SDRs............................	....	—	—	....	—	—	....	....	....	....	....	....
33 **Net incurrence of liabilities...................**	....	153.1	122.4	....	224.7	151.3	....	....	....	....	....	....
331 Domestic..	....	73.7	−13.9	....	145.3	15.0	....	....	....	....	....	....
3312 Currency and deposits..............................	....	—	—	....	—	—	....	....	....	....	....	....
3313 Securities other than shares......................	....	—	—	....	—	—	....	....	....	....	....	....
3314 Loans...	....	73.7	−13.9	....	145.3	15.0	....	....	....	....	....	....
3316 Insurance technical reserves......................	....	—	—	....	—	—	....	....	....	....	....	....
3317 Financial derivatives................................	....	—	—	....	—	—	....	....	....	....	....	....
3318 Other accounts payable............................	....	—	—	....	—	—	....	....	....	....	....	....
332 Foreign..	....	79.4	136.3	....	79.4	136.3	....	....	....	....	....	....
3322 Currency and deposits..............................	....	—	—	....	—	—	....	....	....	....	....	....
3323 Securities other than shares......................	....	—	—	....	—	—	....	....	....	....	....	....
3324 Loans...	....	79.4	136.3	....	79.4	136.3	....	....	....	....	....	....
3326 Insurance technical reserves......................	....	—	—	....	—	—	....	....	....	....	....	....
3327 Financial derivatives................................	....	—	—	....	—	—	....	....	....	....	....	....
3328 Other accounts payable............................	....	—	—	....	—	—	....	....	....	....	....	....
Table 4 Holding gains in assets and liabilities												
Table 5 Other changes in the volume of assets and liabilities												
Table 6 Balance sheet												
Table 7 Outlays by functions of govt.												
Table 8 Transactions in financial assets and liabilities by sector												

In Millions of Reais / Year Ending December 31 / Cash Reporter

	Central Government 1996	1997	1998	State Government 1996	1997	1998	Local Government 1996	1997	1998	General Government 1996	1997	1998
Statement of government operations												
Statement of other economic flows												
Balance sheet												
Statement of sources and uses of cash												
1 Cash receipts from operating activities...........	....	204,768	221,604	....	102,003	108,098	....	49,291	53,730	....	....	....
11 Taxes........	....	97,070	111,086	....	66,147	67,367	....	9,280	10,672	....	....	....
12 Social contributions........	....	75,408	77,492	....	4,941	4,185	....	201	621	....	....	....
13 Grants........	....	9	71	....	22,305	26,520	....	32,627	34,945	....	....	....
14 Other receipts........	....	34,959	38,614	....	8,610	10,026	....	7,184	7,491	....	....	....
2 Cash payments for operating activities........	....	207,704	239,585	....	97,765	113,168	....	43,348	46,806	....	....	....
21 Compensation of employees........	....	24,096	31,405	....	38,443	41,599	....	21,759	22,965	....	....	....
22 Purchases of goods and services........	....	18,790	22,784	....	14,015	17,935	....	16,251	18,151	....	....	....
24 Interest........	....	29,789	35,013	....	6,177	6,029	....	943	995	....	....	....
25 Subsidies........	....	8,830	14,534	....	....	....	....	....	....	....	....	....
26 Grants........	....	37,953	43,743	....	....	....	....	....	....	....	....	....
27 Social benefits........	....	90,404	92,762	....	....	....	....	....	....	....	....	....
28 Other payments........	....	—	—	....	....	....	....	....	....	....	....	....
CIO *Net cash inflow from oper. activities.....*	....	*−2,936*	*−17,981*	....	*4,238*	*−5,069*	....	*5,943*	*6,924*	....	....	....
31.1 Purchases of nonfinancial assets........	....	5,780	5,447	....	8,050	10,858	....	10,555	11,040	....	....	....
31.2 Sales of nonfinancial assets........	....	8,650	15,583	....	12,088	10,909	....	454	122	....	....	....
31 Net cash outflow from investments in nonfinancial assets........	....	−2,870	−10,136	....	−4,039	−51	....	10,101	10,917	....	....	....
CSD *Cash surplus/deficit........*	....	*−67*	*−7,845*	....	*8,277*	*−5,018*	....	*−4,157*	*−3,993*	....	....	....
32x Net acquisition of fin assets, excl. cash........	....	63,597	63,034	....	15,207	14,521	....	384	419	....	....	....
321x Domestic........	....	....	....	....	....	....	....	....	....	....	....	....
322x Foreign........	....	....	....	....	....	....	....	....	....	....	....	....
323 Monetary gold and SDRs........	....	....	....	....	....	....	....	....	....	....	....	....
33 Net incurrence of liabilities........	....	....	....	....	....	....	....	....	....	....	....	....
331 Domestic........	....	....	....	....	....	....	....	....	....	....	....	....
332 Foreign........	....	....	....	....	....	....	....	....	....	....	....	....
NFB Net cash inflow from fin. activities........	....	....	....	....	....	....	....	....	....	....	....	....
NCB *Net change in the stock of cash........*	....	....	....	....	....	....	....	....	....	....	....	....
Table 1 Revenue												
1 **Revenue........**	....	**204,768**	**221,604**	....	**102,003**	**108,098**	....	**49,291**	**53,730**	....	....	....
11 **Taxes........**	....	**97,070**	**111,086**	....	**66,147**	**67,367**	....	**9,280**	**10,672**	....	....	....
111 Taxes on income, profits, & capital gains......	....	34,358	46,096	....	—	—	....	—	—	....	....	....
1111 Individuals........	....	2,793	2,978	....	—	—	....	—	—	....	....	....
1112 Corporations and other enterprises........	....	13,158	11,834	....	—	—	....	—	—	....	....	....
112 Taxes on payroll and workforce........	....	10,428	9,913	....	—	—	....	—	—	....	....	....
113 Taxes on property........	....	260	224	....	4,039	4,631	....	4,468	5,297	....	....	....
114 Taxes on goods and services........	....	46,882	48,255	....	59,263	59,939	....	4,812	5,375	....	....	....
1141 General taxes on goods and services........	....	18,198	18,719	....	....	....	....	....	....	....	....	....
1142 Excises........	....	16,727	16,392	....	....	....	....	....	....	....	....	....
115 Taxes on int'l. trade and transactions........	....	5,143	6,597	....	—	—	....	—	—	....	....	....
116 Other taxes........	....	—	—	....	2,845	2,797	....	—	—	....	....	....
12 **Social contributions........**	....	**75,408**	**77,492**	....	**4,941**	**4,185**	....	**201**	**621**	....	....	....
121 Social security contributions........	....	75,261	77,491	....	4,941	4,185	....	201	621	....	....	....
122 Other social contributions........	....	147	1	....	—	—	....	—	—	....	....	....
13 **Grants........**	....	**9**	**71**	....	**22,305**	**26,520**	....	**32,627**	**34,945**	....	....	....
131 From foreign governments........	....	6	45	....	....	....	....	....	....	....	....	....
132 From international organizations........	....	—	—	....	....	....	....	....	....	....	....	....
133 From other general government units........	....	2	27	....	22,305	26,520	....	32,627	34,945	....	....	....
14 **Other revenue........**	....	**34,959**	**38,614**	....	**8,610**	**10,026**	....	**7,184**	**7,491**	....	....	....
Table 2 Expense by economic type												
2 **Expense........**	....	**207,704**	**239,585**	....	**97,765**	**113,168**	....	**43,348**	**46,806**	....	....	....
21 **Compensation of employees........**	....	**24,096**	**31,405**	....	**38,443**	**41,599**	....	**21,759**	**22,965**	....	....	....
211 Wages and salaries........	....	22,070	29,600	....	38,443	41,599	....	21,759	22,965	....	....	....
212 Social contributions........	....	2,026	1,805	....	....	....	....	....	....	....	....	....
22 **Use of goods and services........**	....	**18,790**	**22,784**	....	**14,015**	**17,935**	....	**16,251**	**18,151**	....	....	....
23 **Consumption of fixed capital........**	....	....	....	....	....	....	....	....	....	....	....	....
24 **Interest........**	....	**29,789**	**35,013**	....	**6,177**	**6,029**	....	**943**	**995**	....	....	....
25 **Subsidies........**	....	**8,830**	**14,534**	....	....	....	....	....	....	....	....	....

		Central Government			State Government			Local Government			General Government		
		1996	1997	1998	1996	1997	1998	1996	1997	1998	1996	1997	1998
26	**Grants**..	....	**37,953**	**43,743**	....	....	....	....	....	....	....	....	....
261	To foreign govenments......................	....	189	345	....	....	....	....	....	....	....	....	....
262	To international organizations..............	....	—	—	....	....	....	....	....	....	....	....	....
263	To other general government units...........	....	37,764	43,398	....	18,010	19,864	....	107	57	....	....	....
2631	Current..	....	37,764	43,398	....	18,010	19,864	....	54	57	....	....	....
2632	Capital...	....	—	—	....	—	—	....	54	—	....	....	....
27	**Social benefits**...............................	....	**90,404**	**92,762**	....	....	....	....	....	....	....	....	....
28	**Other expense**................................	....	**—**		....	....	....	....	....	....	....	....	....
281	Property expense other than interest.........	....	—	—	....	....	....	....	....	....	....	....	....
282	Miscellaneous other expense................	....	—	—	....	....	....	....	....	....	....	....	....
2821	Current..	....	—	—	....	....	....	....	....	....	....	....	....
2822	Capital...	....	—	—	....	....	....	....	....	....	....	....	....
Table 3 Transactions in assets and liabilities													
3	**Change in net worth from transactns....**	....	....	....	....	....	....	....	....	....	....	....	....
31	**Net acquisition of nonfinancial assets...**	....	**−2,870**	**−10,136**	....	**−4,039**	**−51**	....	**10,101**	**10,917**	....	....	....
311	Fixed assets...................................	....	775	−267	....	....	....	....	....	....	....	....	....
3111	Buildings and structures..................	....	....	....	....	....	....	....	....	....	....	....	....
3112	Machinery and equipment.................	....	....	....	....	....	....	....	....	....	....	....	....
3113	Other fixed assets.........................	....	....	....	....	....	....	....	....	....	....	....	....
312	Inventories....................................	....	−660	−496	....	....	....	....	....	....	....	....	....
313	Valuables......................................	....	—	—	....	....	....	....	....	....	....	....	....
314	Nonproduced assets.........................	....	−2,985	−9,373	....	....	....	....	....	....	....	....	....
3141	Land...	....	....	....	....	....	....	....	....	....	....	....	....
3142	Subsoil assets...............................	....	....	....	....	....	....	....	....	....	....	....	....
3143	Other naturally occurring assets..........	....	....	....	....	....	....	....	....	....	....	....	....
3144	Intangible nonproduced assets............	....	....	....	....	....	....	....	....	....	....	....	....
32	**Net acquisition of financial assets.........**	....	....	....	....	....	....	....	....	....	....	....	....
321	Domestic......................................	....	....	....	....	....	....	....	....	....	....	....	....
3212	Currency and deposits.....................	....	....	....	....	....	....	....	....	....	....	....	....
3213	Securities other than shares..............	....	....	....	....	....	....	....	....	....	....	....	....
3214	Loans..	....	....	....	....	....	....	....	....	....	....	....	....
3215	Shares and other equity...................	....	....	....	....	....	....	....	....	....	....	....	....
3216	Insurance technical reserves..............	....	....	....	....	....	....	....	....	....	....	....	....
3217	Financial derivatives.......................	....	....	....	....	....	....	....	....	....	....	....	....
3218	Other accounts receivable.................	....	....	....	....	....	....	....	....	....	....	....	....
322	Foreign..	....	....	....	....	....	....	....	....	....	....	....	....
3222	Currency and deposits.....................	....	....	....	....	....	....	....	....	....	....	....	....
3223	Securities other than shares..............	....	....	....	....	....	....	....	....	....	....	....	....
3224	Loans..	....	....	....	....	....	....	....	....	....	....	....	....
3225	Shares and other equity...................	....	....	....	....	....	....	....	....	....	....	....	....
3226	Insurance technical reserves..............	....	....	....	....	....	....	....	....	....	....	....	....
3227	Financial derivatives.......................	....	....	....	....	....	....	....	....	....	....	....	....
3228	Other accounts receivable.................	....	....	....	....	....	....	....	....	....	....	....	....
323	Monetary gold and SDRs....................	....	....	....	....	....	....	....	....	....	....	....	....
33	**Net incurrence of liabilities...................**	....	....	....	....	....	....	....	....	....	....	....	....
331	Domestic......................................	....	....	....	....	....	....	....	....	....	....	....	....
3312	Currency and deposits.....................	....	....	....	....	....	....	....	....	....	....	....	....
3313	Securities other than shares..............	....	....	....	....	....	....	....	....	....	....	....	....
3314	Loans..	....	....	....	....	....	....	....	....	....	....	....	....
3316	Insurance technical reserves..............	....	....	....	....	....	....	....	....	....	....	....	....
3317	Financial derivatives.......................	....	....	....	....	....	....	....	....	....	....	....	....
3318	Other accounts payable....................	....	....	....	....	....	....	....	....	....	....	....	....
332	Foreign..	....	....	....	....	....	....	....	....	....	....	....	....
3322	Currency and deposits.....................	....	....	....	....	....	....	....	....	....	....	....	....
3323	Securities other than shares..............	....	....	....	....	....	....	....	....	....	....	....	....
3324	Loans..	....	....	....	....	....	....	....	....	....	....	....	....
3326	Insurance technical reserves..............	....	....	....	....	....	....	....	....	....	....	....	....
3327	Financial derivatives.......................	....	....	....	....	....	....	....	....	....	....	....	....
3328	Other accounts payable....................	....	....	....	....	....	....	....	....	....	....	....	....

In Millions of Reais / Year Ending December 31 / Cash Reporter

	Central Government			State Government			Local Government			General Government		
	1996	1997	1998	1996	1997	1998	1996	1997	1998	1996	1997	1998
Table 4 Holding gains in assets and liabilities												
Table 5 Other changes in the volume of assets and liabilities												
Table 6 Balance sheet												
Table 7 Outlays by functions of govt.												
7 **Total outlays**....................	....	213,484	245,032	....	105,815	124,025	....	53,903	57,845	....	....	....
701 **General public services**..........................	....	65,995	69,692	....	....	....	....	....	....	....	....	....
7017 Public debt transactions............................	....	29,789	35,013	....	6,177	6,029	....	943	995	....	....	....
7018 General transfers between levels of govt......	....	....	....	....	....	....	....	....	....	....	....	....
702 **Defense**...	....	8,519	8,542	....	....	....	....	....	....	....	....	....
703 **Public order and safety**........................	....	5,717	7,822	....	....	....	....	....	....	....	....	....
704 **Economic affairs**...............................	....	12,497	11,857	....	....	....	....	....	....	....	....	....
7042 Agriculture, forestry, fishing, and hunting.....	....	5,511	6,131	....	....	....	....	....	....	....	....	....
7043 Fuel and energy.............................	....	350	803	....	....	....	....	....	....	....	....	....
7044 Mining, manufacturing, and construction.....	....	295	320	....	....	....	....	....	....	....	....	....
7045 Transport....................................	....	3,267	3,042	....	....	....	....	....	....	....	....	....
7046 Communication...............................	....	....	....	....	....	....	....	....	....	....	....	....
705 **Environmental protection**........................	....	....	....	....	....	....	....	....	....	....	....	....
706 **Housing and community amenities**........	....	1,543	1,561	....	....	....	....	....	....	....	....	....
707 **Health**..	....	15,912	15,226	....	....	....	....	....	....	....	....	....
7072 Outpatient services...........................	....	14,638	13,604	....	....	....	....	....	....	....	....	....
7073 Hospital services.............................	....	....	—	....	....	....	....	....	....	....	....	....
7074 Public health services.........................	....	....	....	....	....	....	....	....	....	....	....	....
708 **Recreation, culture, and religion**............	....	178	166	....	....	....	....	....	....	....	....	....
709 **Education**....................................	....	9,520	15,033	....	....	....	....	....	....	....	....	....
7091 Pre-primary and primary education..............	....	....	....	....	....	....	....	....	....	....	....	....
7092 Secondary education............................	....	4,546	9,261	....	....	....	....	....	....	....	....	....
7094 Tertiary education.............................	....	4,724	4,985	....	....	....	....	....	....	....	....	....
710 **Social protection**...........................	....	95,760	115,791	....	....	....	....	....	....	....	....	....
7 Statistical discrepancy: Total outlays..............	....	−2,157	−656	....	....	....	....	....	....	....	....	....
Table 8 Transactions in financial assets and liabilities by sector												

2005, International Monetary Fund: *Government Finance Statistics Yearbook*

In Millions of Leva / Year Ending December 31 / Cash Reporter

	Budgetary Central Government			Central Government			Local Government			General Government		
	2002	2003	2004	2002	2003	2004	2002	2003	2004	2002	2003	2004
Statement of government operations												
Statement of other economic flows												
Balance sheet												
Statement of sources and uses of cash												
1 Cash receipts from operating activities..........	7,922	8,505	10,352	11,116	12,484	14,950	2,451	2,093	2,303	12,415	13,817	15,662
11 Taxes..	5,437	6,527	8,474	5,438	6,527	8,474	1,227	1,107	429	6,666	7,634	8,903
12 Social contributions.............................	—	—	—	3,075	3,654	4,080	—	—	—	3,075	3,654	4,080
13 Grants...	496	61	30	432	306	439	1,022	766	1,591	302	311	440
14 Other receipts.................................	1,989	1,916	1,848	2,171	1,997	1,957	202	220	282	2,372	2,218	2,239
2 Cash payments for operating activities..........	7,294	8,029	9,194	10,533	11,711	13,426	2,281	1,955	2,076	11,662	12,906	13,911
21 Compensation of employees.....................	1,082	1,308	1,469	1,123	1,356	1,528	823	957	1,046	1,946	2,313	2,575
22 Purchases of goods and services.................	2,425	2,640	2,779	2,535	2,740	2,915	758	769	915	3,292	3,509	3,830
24 Interest..	700	720	692	701	721	693	11	2	4	712	723	697
25 Subsidies......................................	552	684	689	587	738	778	185	202	90	772	940	868
26 Grants...	2,136	1,958	2,782	1,011	758	1,590	141	2	—	—	—	—
27 Social benefits.................................	238	554	576	4,349	5,122	5,537	347	6	5	4,696	5,128	5,542
28 Other payments................................	161	166	206	227	276	384	17	17	15	244	293	399
CIO *Net cash inflow from oper. activities.....*	*628*	*476*	*1,158*	*583*	*773*	*1,524*	*170*	*138*	*227*	*753*	*911*	*1,751*
31.1 Purchases of nonfinancial assets.................	651	724	787	813	871	977	251	291	307	1,064	1,162	1,284
31.2 Sales of nonfinancial assets....................	53	162	79	54	165	79	50	87	111	104	253	190
31 Net cash outflow from investments in nonfinancial assets.........................	598	562	708	759	706	898	201	204	196	961	909	1,094
CSD *Cash surplus/deficit...............................*	*30*	*–86*	*449*	*–177*	*67*	*625*	*–31*	*–66*	*31*	*–208*	*1*	*657*
32x Net acquisition of fin assets, excl. cash..........	–1,140	–317	–1,172	–1,167	–257	–1,183	–53	–55	–46	–1,223	–312	–1,230
321x Domestic....................................	–128	–255	–684	–156	–195	–696	–53	–55	–46	–211	–250	–742
322x Foreign.....................................	–1,012	–62	–487	–1,012	–62	–487	—	—	—	–1,012	–62	–487
323 Monetary gold and SDRs......................	—	—	—	—	—	—	—	—	—	—	—	—
33 Net incurrence of liabilities.....................	–402	214	–766	–366	204	–780	–14	33	26	–383	237	–754
331 Domestic....................................	127	304	374	125	306	358	10	17	3	132	324	360
332 Foreign.....................................	–529	–90	–1,140	–491	–102	–1,138	–24	15	24	–514	–87	–1,114
NFB Net cash inflow from fin. activities..............	738	531	406	801	461	403	39	87	73	840	549	476
NCB *Net change in the stock of cash...........*	*768*	*445*	*855*	*624*	*529*	*1,029*	*8*	*21*	*104*	*632*	*550*	*1,132*

Table 1   Revenue

	Budgetary Central Government			Central Government			Local Government			General Government		
	2002	2003	2004	2002	2003	2004	2002	2003	2004	2002	2003	2004
1 **Revenue**..................................	**7,922**	**8,505**	**10,352**	**11,116**	**12,484**	**14,950**	**2,451**	**2,093**	**2,303**	**12,415**	**13,817**	**15,662**
11 **Taxes**.....................................	**5,437**	**6,527**	**8,474**	**5,438**	**6,527**	**8,474**	**1,227**	**1,107**	**429**	**6,666**	**7,634**	**8,903**
111 Taxes on income, profits, & capital gains......	1,088	1,477	2,186	1,088	1,477	2,186	915	724	—	2,004	2,201	2,186
1111 Individuals..................................	532	416	1,248	532	416	1,248	520	724	—	1,052	1,140	1,248
1112 Corporations and other enterprises.............	512	969	858	512	969	858	394	—	—	905	969	858
112 Taxes on payroll and workforce................	—	—	—	—	—	—	—	—	—	—	—	—
113 Taxes on property............................	—	—	1	—	—	1	305	383	429	305	383	430
114 Taxes on goods and services...................	4,157	4,813	5,988	4,159	4,813	5,988	7	—	—	4,166	4,813	5,988
1141 General taxes on goods and services..........	2,688	3,101	3,891	2,688	3,101	3,891	—	—	—	2,688	3,101	3,891
1142 Excises....................................	1,312	1,544	1,885	1,314	1,544	1,885	—	—	—	1,314	1,544	1,885
115 Taxes on int'l. trade and transactions...........	188	231	292	188	231	292	—	—	—	188	231	292
116 Other taxes.................................	3	6	7	3	6	7	—	—	—	3	6	7
12 **Social contributions**........................	**—**	**—**	**—**	**3,075**	**3,654**	**4,080**	**—**	**—**	**—**	**3,075**	**3,654**	**4,080**
121 Social security contributions..................	—	—	—	3,075	3,654	4,080	—	—	—	3,075	3,654	4,080
122 Other social contributions....................	—	—	—	—	—	—	—	—	—	—	—	—
13 **Grants**...................................	**496**	**61**	**30**	**432**	**306**	**439**	**1,022**	**766**	**1,591**	**302**	**311**	**440**
131 From foreign governments....................	—	—	—	—	—	—	—	—	—	—	—	—
132 From international organizations...............	26	46	26	291	303	439	10	8	1	302	311	440
133 From other general government units..........	470	15	3	140	2	—	1,011	758	1,590	—	—	—
14 **Other revenue**.............................	**1,989**	**1,916**	**1,848**	**2,171**	**1,997**	**1,957**	**202**	**220**	**282**	**2,372**	**2,218**	**2,239**

Table 2   Expense by economic type

	Budgetary Central Government			Central Government			Local Government			General Government		
	2002	2003	2004	2002	2003	2004	2002	2003	2004	2002	2003	2004
2 **Expense**.................................	**7,294**	**8,029**	**9,194**	**10,533**	**11,711**	**13,426**	**2,281**	**1,955**	**2,076**	**11,662**	**12,906**	**13,911**
21 **Compensation of employees**.................	**1,082**	**1,308**	**1,469**	**1,123**	**1,356**	**1,528**	**823**	**957**	**1,046**	**1,946**	**2,313**	**2,575**
211 Wages and salaries..........................	825	990	1,108	856	1,027	1,154	612	716	779	1,468	1,743	1,933
212 Social contributions.........................	257	317	360	267	328	374	212	241	267	478	570	642
22 **Use of goods and services**....................	**2,425**	**2,640**	**2,779**	**2,535**	**2,740**	**2,915**	**758**	**769**	**915**	**3,292**	**3,509**	**3,830**
23 **Consumption of fixed capital**................	....	....	....	....	....	....	....	....	....	....	....	....
24 **Interest**..................................	**700**	**720**	**692**	**701**	**721**	**693**	**11**	**2**	**4**	**712**	**723**	**697**
25 **Subsidies**.................................	**552**	**684**	**689**	**587**	**738**	**778**	**185**	**202**	**90**	**772**	**940**	**868**

In Millions of Leva / Year Ending December 31 / Cash Reporter

		Budgetary Central Government			Central Government			Local Government			General Government		
		2002	2003	2004	2002	2003	2004	2002	2003	2004	2002	2003	2004
26	Grants..................................	2,136	1,958	2,782	1,011	758	1,590	141	2	—	—	—	—
261	To foreign govenments...........	—	—	—	—	—	—	—	—	—	—	—	—
262	To international organizations......	—	—	—	—	—	—	—	—	—	—	—	—
263	To other general government units..........	2,136	1,958	2,782	1,011	758	1,590	141	2	—	—	—	—
2631	Current...............	2,136	1,958	2,782	1,011	758	1,590	141	2	—	—	—	—
2632	Capital.............	238	554	576	4,349	5,122	5,537	347	6	5	4,696	5,128	5,542
27	Social benefits............................	238	554	576	4,349	5,122	5,537	347	6	5	4,696	5,128	5,542
28	Other expense............................	161	166	206	227	276	384	17	17	15	244	293	399
281	Property expense other than interest..........	—	—	—	—	—	—	—	—	—	—	—	—
282	Miscellaneous other expense...............	161	166	206	227	276	384	17	17	15	244	293	399
2821	Current..............	44	47	49	74	82	89	10	11	11	84	93	100
2822	Capital...............	117	118	157	153	194	296	7	6	4	160	200	300

Table 3 Transactions in assets and liabilities

		Budgetary Central Government			Central Government			Local Government			General Government		
3	Change in net worth from transactns....	....	....	....	....	....	....	....	....	....	....	....	....
31	Net acquisition of nonfinancial assets...	598	562	708	759	706	898	201	204	196	961	909	1,094
311	Fixed assets........................	587	577	677	748	721	864	230	264	274	978	985	1,138
3111	Buildings and structures.............	....	....	—	....	....	—	....	....	—	....	....	—
3112	Machinery and equipment.............	....	....	—	....	....	—	....	....	—	....	....	—
3113	Other fixed assets..................	....	....	677	....	....	864	....	....	274	....	....	1,138
312	Inventories.........................	13	–13	–8	13	–13	–8	—	—	—	13	–13	–8
313	Valuables..........................	—	—	—	—	—	—	—	—	—	—	—	—
314	Nonproduced assets.................	–1	–3	39	–1	–3	42	–29	–60	–78	–30	–63	–36
3141	Land..............................	–1	–2	–3	–1	–2	–3	–28	–55	–73	–30	–57	–76
3142	Subsoil assets......................	—	—	—	—	—	—	—	—	—	—	—	—
3143	Other naturally occurring assets...............	—	—	—	—	—	—	—	—	—	—	—	—
3144	Intangible nonproduced assets.................	—	—	42	—	—	45	–1	–5	–6	–1	–5	40
32	Net acquisition of financial assets........	–372	128	–317	–543	272	–155	–45	–33	58	–591	238	–97
321	Domestic...........................	640	190	171	469	333	333	–45	–33	58	421	300	390
3212	Currency and deposits...............	768	445	855	624	529	1,029	8	21	104	632	550	1,132
3213	Securities other than shares..........	—	—	—	—	—	—	—	—	—	–2	—	—
3214	Loans.............................	14	–4	19	9	63	63	1	1	—	10	63	63
3215	Shares and other equity.............	–142	–251	–703	–164	–258	–759	–55	–55	–47	–219	–313	–805
3216	Insurance technical reserves..........	—	—	—	—	—	—	—	—	—	—	—	—
3217	Financial derivatives................	—	—	—	—	—	—	—	—	—	—	—	—
3218	Other accounts receivable............	....	....	....	....	....	....	....	....	....	....	....	....
322	Foreign...........................	–1,012	–62	–487	–1,012	–62	–487	—	—	—	–1,012	–62	–487
3222	Currency and deposits...............	—	—	—	—	—	—	—	—	—	—	—	—
3223	Securities other than shares..........	–993	–44	–469	–993	–44	–469	—	—	—	–993	–44	–469
3224	Loans.............................	–18	–17	–19	–18	–17	–19	—	—	—	–18	–17	–19
3225	Shares and other equity..............	—	—	—	—	—	—	—	—	—	—	—	—
3226	Insurance technical reserves..........	—	—	—	—	—	—	—	—	—	—	—	—
3227	Financial derivatives................	—	—	—	—	—	—	—	—	—	—	—	—
3228	Other accounts receivable...........	....	....	....	....	....	....	....	....	....	....	....	....
323	Monetary gold and SDRs............	—	—	—	—	—	—	—	—	—	—	—	—
33	Net incurrence of liabilities..................	–402	214	–766	–366	204	–780	–14	33	26	–383	237	–754
331	Domestic...........................	127	304	374	125	306	358	10	17	3	132	324	360
3312	Currency and deposits...............	—	—	—	—	—	—	—	—	—	—	—	—
3313	Securities other than shares..........	332	194	448	329	195	437	6	2	2	333	198	439
3314	Loans.............................	–205	110	–74	–205	111	–79	4	15	1	–201	126	–78
3316	Insurance technical reserves..........	—	—	—	—	—	—	—	—	—	—	—	—
3317	Financial derivatives................	—	—	—	—	—	—	—	—	—	—	—	—
3318	Other accounts payable.............	....	....	....	....	....	....	....	....	....	....	....	....
332	Foreign...........................	–529	–90	–1,140	–491	–102	–1,138	–24	15	24	–514	–87	–1,114
3322	Currency and deposits...............	—	—	—	—	—	—	—	—	—	—	—	—
3323	Securities other than shares.........	–92	–179	–1,286	–92	–179	–1,286	–28	—	—	–120	–179	–1,286
3324	Loans.............................	–436	88	147	–398	77	148	4	15	24	–394	92	172
3326	Insurance technical reserves.........	—	—	—	—	—	—	—	—	—	—	—	—
3327	Financial derivatives...............	—	—	—	—	—	—	—	—	—	—	—	—
3328	Other accounts payable.............	....	....	....	....	....	....	....	....	....	....	....	....

In Millions of Leva / Year Ending December 31 / Cash Reporter

	Budgetary Central Government			Central Government			Local Government			General Government		
	2002	2003	2004	2002	2003	2004	2002	2003	2004	2002	2003	2004
Table 4 Holding gains in assets and liabilities												
Table 5 Other changes in the volume of assets and liabilities												
Table 6 Balance sheet												
Table 7 Outlays by functions of govt.												
7 **Total outlays**................................	7,892	8,591	9,902	11,293	12,417	14,324	2,482	2,159	2,271	12,623	13,816	15,005
701 **General public services**......................	3,446	3,324	4,208	2,339	2,127	3,017	366	202	196	1,554	1,569	1,622
7017 Public debt transactions.............................	701	720	692	702	721	693	11	2	4	713	724	697
7018 General transfers between levels of govt......	2,136	1,958	2,782	1,011	758	1,590	141	2	—	—	—	—
702 **Defense**..	821	815	862	821	815	862	7	11	13	828	826	875
703 **Public order and safety**......................	863	949	1,056	865	949	1,056	15	13	16	879	962	1,071
704 **Economic affairs**.............................	1,031	1,097	1,149	1,318	1,477	1,683	187	191	207	1,505	1,668	1,890
7042 Agriculture, forestry, fishing, and hunting.....	279	312	305	322	368	378	11	3	4	334	371	382
7043 Fuel and energy.....................................	54	57	41	55	57	41	—	—	—	55	57	41
7044 Mining, manufacturing, and construction.....	—	—	2	—	—	2	—	—	—	—	—	2
7045 Transport...	505	551	626	515	551	626	131	141	149	646	692	775
7046 Communication.....................................	....	....	....	....	....	....	....	....	....	....	....	....
705 **Environmental protection**......................	—	—	—	—	—	—	—	—	—	—	—	—
706 **Housing and community amenities**........	99	85	101	105	87	101	398	410	485	503	497	586
707 **Health**...	610	703	776	1,228	1,479	1,658	210	219	111	1,437	1,698	1,769
7072 Outpatient services..................................	....	....	....	....	....	....	....	....	....	....	....	....
7073 Hospital services....................................	....	335	....	....	549	....	....	166	....	....	715	....
7074 Public health services..............................	....	....	....	....	....	....	....	....	....	....	....	....
708 **Recreation, culture, and religion**...........	150	193	198	151	195	198	72	92	106	223	286	304
709 **Education**..	566	651	707	568	651	709	786	854	944	1,353	1,505	1,652
7091 Pre-primary and primary education..............	115	129	147	116	129	147	....	....	....	....	....	....
7092 Secondary education...............................	140	165	170	141	165	172	....	....	....	....	....	....
7094 Tertiary education..................................	311	356	390	311	356	390	....	....	....	....	....	....
710 **Social protection**................................	307	775	846	3,898	4,637	5,041	442	168	195	4,340	4,805	5,235
7 Statistical discrepancy: Total outlays............	—	—	—	—	—	—	—	—	—	—	—	—
Table 8 Transactions in financial assets and liabilities by sector												
82 **Net acquisition of financial assets**........	−372	128	−317	−543	272	−155	−45	−33	58	−591	238	−97
821 Domestic..	640	190	171	469	333	333	−45	−33	58	421	300	390
8211 General government...............................	—	—	—	—	—	—	—	—	—	−2	—	—
8212 Central bank..	817	105	1,769	640	133	1,875	—	—	—	640	133	1,875
8213 Other depository corporations....................	−66	340	−914	−33	396	−846	8	21	104	−25	417	−743
8214 Financial corporations n.e.c......................	—	—	—	—	—	—	—	—	—	—	—	—
8215 Nonfinancial corporations........................	−111	−255	−684	−139	−195	−696	−53	−55	−46	−192	−250	−742
8216 Households & NPIs serving households......	—	—	—	—	—	—	—	—	—	—	—	—
822 Foreign...	−1,012	−62	−487	−1,012	−62	−487	—	—	—	−1,012	−62	−487
8221 General government...............................	−1,012	−62	−487	−1,012	−62	−487	—	—	—	−1,012	−62	−487
8227 International organizations.......................	—	—	—	—	—	—	—	—	—	—	—	—
8228 Financial corporations other than international organizations.............	—	—	—	—	—	—	—	—	—	—	—	—
8229 Other nonresidents................................	—	—	—	—	—	—	—	—	—	—	—	—
823 Monetary gold and SDRs.........................	—	—	—	—	—	—	—	—	—	—	—	—
83 **Net incurrence of liabilities**..................	−402	214	−766	−366	204	−780	−14	33	26	−383	237	−754
831 Domestic...	127	304	374	125	306	358	10	17	3	132	324	360
8311 General government...............................	−1	1	7	−1	2	−9	—	1	1	−1	3	−8
8312 Central bank..	−202	109	−87	−202	109	−87	—	—	—	−202	109	−87
8313 Other depository corporations....................	330	194	448	328	195	448	9	17	2	335	212	450
8314 Financial corporations n.e.c......................	—	—	5	—	—	5	—	—	—	—	—	5
8315 Nonfinancial corporations........................	—	—	—	—	—	—	—	—	—	—	—	—
8316 Households & NPIs serving households......	—	—	—	—	—	—	—	—	—	—	—	—
832 Foreign...	−529	−90	−1,140	−491	−102	−1,138	−24	15	24	−514	−87	−1,114
8321 General government...............................	—	—	—	—	—	—	—	—	—	—	—	—
8327 International organizations.......................	−63	−171	−112	−65	−172	−114	—	—	—	−65	−172	−114
8328 Financial corporations other than international organizations.............	−189	217	−933	−149	217	−933	−25	15	19	−174	232	−914
8329 Other nonresidents................................	−277	−137	−95	−277	−146	−92	2	—	5	−275	−146	−87

In Millions of Francs / Year Ending December 31 / Cash Reporter

	Budgetary Central Government			Central Government			Local Government			General Government		
	1997	1998	1999	1997	1998	1999	1997	1998	1999	1997	1998	1999
Statement of government operations												
Statement of other economic flows												
Balance sheet												
6 *Net worth*....................	....	....	....	....	....	....	....	....	....	....	....	....
61 Nonfinancial assets..............	....	....	....	....	....	....	....	....	....	....	....	....
62 Financial assets..................	....	....	....	....	....	....	....	....	....	....	....	....
63 Liabilities.........................	....	....	....	460,199	605,411	740,305	....	....	....	....	....	....
Statement of sources and uses of cash												
1 Cash receipts from operating activities..........	41,498	59,087	63,536	56,416	76,744	83,291	....	....	....	....	....	....
11 Taxes......	39,149	55,445	59,956	39,149	57,419	61,923	....	....	....	....	....	....
12 Social contributions..............	—	—	—	3,731	4,281	5,357	....	....	....	....	....	....
13 Grants...............................	—	—	—	10,271	10,474	11,355	....	....	....	....	....	....
14 Other receipts......................	2,349	3,642	3,580	3,265	4,569	4,656	....	....	....	....	....	....
2 Cash payments for operating activities..........	62,609	75,989	82,246	....	88,357	94,029	....	....	....	....	....	....
21 Compensation of employees.......................	24,063	27,231	30,344	....	....	....	....	....	....	....	....	....
22 Purchases of goods and services.................	18,275	20,477	21,245	....	....	....	....	....	....	....	....	....
24 Interest.............................	6,069	6,840	9,507	....	....	....	....	....	....	....	....	....
25 Subsidies...........................	4,503	5,724	6,199	....	....	....	....	....	....	....	....	....
26 Grants..............................	230	250	234	....	....	....	....	....	....	....	....	....
27 Social benefits.....................	886	1,192	1,654	....	....	....	....	....	....	....	....	....
28 Other payments.....................	8,583	14,275	13,063	8,583	14,275	13,063	....	....	....	....	....	....
CIO *Net cash inflow from oper. activities*.....	....	....	....	....	*−11,613*	*−10,738*	....	....	....	....	....	....
31.1 Purchases of nonfinancial assets...................	3,476	5,443	6,347	....	....	....	....	....	....	....	....	....
31.2 Sales of nonfinancial assets..........................	108	60	111	108	64	111	....	....	....	....	....	....
31 Net cash outflow from investments in nonfinancial assets.................................	3,368	5,383	6,237	....	....	....	....	....	....	....	....	....
CSD *Cash surplus/deficit*....................	....	....	....	*−21,138*	*−17,773*	*−20,589*	....	....	....	....	....	....
32x Net acquisition of fin assets, excl. cash..........	−2,803	319	−1,654	....	319	−1,584	....	....	....	....	....	....
321x Domestic............................	....	....	....	....	....	....	....	....	....	....	....	....
322x Foreign.............................	....	....	....	....	....	....	....	....	....	....	....	....
323 Monetary gold and SDRs...........	—	—	—	—	—	—	....	....	....	....	....	....
33 Net incurrence of liabilities........	....	....	....	18,555	25,600	27,991	....	....	....	....	....	....
331 Domestic............................	....	....	....	8,135	9,670	14,869	....	....	....	....	....	....
332 Foreign.............................	....	....	....	10,420	15,930	13,121	....	....	....	....	....	....
NFB Net cash inflow from fin. activities.................	....	....	....	21,138	25,281	29,575	....	....	....	....	....	....
NCB *Net change in the stock of cash*...........	....	....	....	....	*7,508*	*8,986*	....	....	....	....	....	....
Table 1 Revenue												
1 **Revenue**........	**41,498**	**59,087**	**63,536**	**56,416**	**76,744**	**83,291**	....	....	....	....	....	....
11 **Taxes**......	**39,149**	**55,445**	**59,956**	**39,149**	**57,419**	**61,923**	....	....	....	....	....	....
111 Taxes on income, profits, & capital gains......	10,322	13,139	15,122	10,322	13,139	15,122	....	....	....	....	....	....
1111 Individuals..............	4,471	5,753	6,604	4,471	5,753	6,604	....	....	....	....	....	....
1112 Corporations and other enterprises............	5,148	6,402	7,664	5,148	6,402	7,664	....	....	....	....	....	....
112 Taxes on payroll and workforce......	130	106	618	130	106	618	....	....	....	....	....	....
113 Taxes on property..................	—	—	—	—	—	—	....	....	....	....	....	....
114 Taxes on goods and services......	20,744	25,305	31,640	20,744	25,305	31,640	....	....	....	....	....	....
1141 General taxes on goods and services..........	7,281	11,435	12,643	7,281	11,435	12,643	....	....	....	....	....	....
1142 Excises..............................	13,155	13,567	18,601	13,155	13,567	18,601	....	....	....	....	....	....
115 Taxes on int'l. trade and transactions..........	7,229	16,855	12,542	7,229	18,829	14,508	....	....	....	....	....	....
116 Other taxes........................	724	41	35	724	41	35	....	....	....	....	....	....
12 **Social contributions**..............	—	—	—	**3,731**	**4,281**	**5,357**	....	....	....	....	....	....
121 Social security contributions........	—	—	—	3,731	4,281	5,357	....	....	....	....	....	....
122 Other social contributions..........	—	—	—	—	—	—	....	....	....	....	....	....
13 **Grants**..............................	—	—	—	**10,271**	**10,474**	**11,355**	....	....	....	....	....	....
131 From foreign governments.........	—	—	—	1,972	1,113	854	....	....	....	....	....	....
132 From international organizations.....	—	—	—	8,299	9,361	10,501	....	....	....	....	....	....
133 From other general government units..........	—	—	—	—	—	—	....	....	....	....	....	....
14 **Other revenue**......................	**2,349**	**3,642**	**3,580**	**3,265**	**4,569**	**4,656**	....	....	....	....	....	....
Table 2 Expense by economic type												
2 **Expense**........	**62,609**	**75,989**	**82,246**	....	**88,357**	**94,029**	....	....	....	....	....	....
21 **Compensation of employees**..........	**24,063**	**27,231**	**30,344**	....	....	....	....	....	....	....	....	....
211 Wages and salaries..................	24,063	27,231	30,344	....	....	....	....	....	....	....	....	....
212 Social contributions.................	—	—	—	....	....	....	....	....	....	....	....	....
22 **Use of goods and services**........	**18,275**	**20,477**	**21,245**	....	....	....	....	....	....	....	....	....
23 **Consumption of fixed capital**.............	....	....	....	....	....	....	....	....	....	....	....	....
24 **Interest**........	**6,069**	**6,840**	**9,507**	....	....	....	....	....	....	....	....	....
25 **Subsidies**........	**4,503**	**5,724**	**6,199**	....	....	....	....	....	....	....	....	....

Burundi 618

In Millions of Francs / Year Ending December 31 / Cash Reporter

		Budgetary Central Government			Central Government			Local Government			General Government		
		1997	1998	1999	1997	1998	1999	1997	1998	1999	1997	1998	1999
26	**Grants**..............	**230**	**250**	**234**	....	....	....	....	....	....	....	....	....
261	To foreign govements............	230	250	234	....	....	....	....	....	....	....	....	....
262	To international organizations...........	—	—	—	....	....	....	....	....	....	....	....	....
263	To other general government units..........	—	—	—	....	....	....	....	....	....	....	....	....
2631	Current..............	—	—	—	....	....	....	....	....	....	....	....	....
2632	Capital..............	—	—	—	....	....	....	....	....	....	....	....	....
27	**Social benefits**..............	**886**	**1,192**	**1,654**	....	....	....	....	....	....	....	....	....
28	**Other expense**..............	**8,583**	**14,275**	**13,063**	**8,583**	**14,275**	**13,063**	....	....	....	....	....	....
281	Property expense other than interest...........	—	—	—	—	—	—	....	....	....	....	....	....
282	Miscellaneous other expense..................	8,583	14,275	13,063	8,583	14,275	13,063	....	....	....	....	....	....
2821	Current..............	—	—	—	—	—	—	....	....	....	....	....	....
2822	Capital..............	8,583	14,275	13,063	8,583	14,275	13,063	....	....	....	....	....	....

Table 3 Transactions in assets and liabilities

		1997	1998	1999	1997	1998	1999	1997	1998	1999	1997	1998	1999
3	**Change in net worth from transactns**....	....	....	....	....	....	....	....	....	....	....	....	....
31	**Net acquisition of nonfinancial assets**...	**3,368**	**5,383**	**6,237**	....	....	....	....	....	....	....	....	....
311	Fixed assets..............	3,407	5,391	6,281	....	....	....	....	....	....	....	....	....
3111	Buildings and structures..............	....	....	....	....	....	....	....	....	....	....	....	....
3112	Machinery and equipment..............	....	....	....	....	....	....	....	....	....	....	....	....
3113	Other fixed assets..............	....	....	....	....	....	....	....	....	....	....	....	....
312	Inventories..............	—	—	—	....	....	....	....	....	....	....	....	....
313	Valuables..............	—	—	—	....	....	....	....	....	....	....	....	....
314	Nonproduced assets..............	−39	−8	−44	....	....	....	....	....	....	....	....	....
3141	Land..............	....	....	....	....	....	....	....	....	....	....	....	....
3142	Subsoil assets..............	....	....	....	....	....	....	....	....	....	....	....	....
3143	Other naturally occurring assets..............	....	....	....	....	....	....	....	....	....	....	....	....
3144	Intangible nonproduced assets..............	....	....	....	....	....	....	....	....	....	....	....	....
32	**Net acquisition of financial assets**........	....	....	....	**−2,583**	**7,827**	**7,402**	....	....	....	....	....	....
321	Domestic..............	....	....	....	....	....	....	....	....	....	....	....	....
3212	Currency and deposits..............	....	....	....	....	7,508	8,986	....	....	....	....	....	....
3213	Securities other than shares..............	....	....	....	....	....	....	....	....	....	....	....	....
3214	Loans..............	....	....	....	....	....	....	....	....	....	....	....	....
3215	Shares and other equity..............	....	....	....	....	....	....	....	....	....	....	....	....
3216	Insurance technical reserves..............	....	....	....	....	....	....	....	....	....	....	....	....
3217	Financial derivatives..............	....	....	....	....	....	....	....	....	....	....	....	....
3218	Other accounts receivable..............	....	....	....	....	....	....	....	....	....	....	....	....
322	Foreign..............	....	....	....	....	....	....	....	....	....	....	....	....
3222	Currency and deposits..............	....	....	....	....	—	—	....	....	....	....	....	....
3223	Securities other than shares..............	....	....	....	....	....	....	....	....	....	....	....	....
3224	Loans..............	....	....	....	....	....	....	....	....	....	....	....	....
3225	Shares and other equity..............	....	....	....	....	....	....	....	....	....	....	....	....
3226	Insurance technical reserves..............	....	....	....	....	....	....	....	....	....	....	....	....
3227	Financial derivatives..............	....	....	....	....	....	....	....	....	....	....	....	....
3228	Other accounts receivable..............	....	....	....	....	....	....	....	....	....	....	....	....
323	Monetary gold and SDRs..............	....	....	....	....	....	....	....	....	....	....	....	....
33	**Net incurrence of liabilities**..................	....	....	....	**18,555**	**25,600**	**27,991**	....	....	....	....	....	....
331	Domestic..............	....	....	....	8,135	9,670	14,869	....	....	....	....	....	....
3312	Currency and deposits..............	....	....	....	—	—	—	....	....	....	....	....	....
3313	Securities other than shares..............	....	....	....	8,135	9,670	14,869	....	....	....	....	....	....
3314	Loans..............	....	....	....	—	—	—	....	....	....	....	....	....
3316	Insurance technical reserves..............	....	....	....	—	—	—	....	....	....	....	....	....
3317	Financial derivatives..............	....	....	....	—	—	—	....	....	....	....	....	....
3318	Other accounts payable..............	....	....	....	....	....	....	....	....	....	....	....	....
332	Foreign..............	....	....	....	10,420	15,930	13,121	....	....	....	....	....	....
3322	Currency and deposits..............	....	....	....	....	....	....	....	....	....	....	....	....
3323	Securities other than shares..............	....	....	....	....	....	....	....	....	....	....	....	....
3324	Loans..............	....	....	....	....	....	....	....	....	....	....	....	....
3326	Insurance technical reserves..............	....	....	....	....	....	....	....	....	....	....	....	....
3327	Financial derivatives..............	....	....	....	....	....	....	....	....	....	....	....	....
3328	Other accounts payable..............	....	....	....	....	....	....	....	....	....	....	....	....

	Budgetary Central Government			Central Government			Local Government			General Government		
	1997	1998	1999	1997	1998	1999	1997	1998	1999	1997	1998	1999
Table 4 Holding gains in assets and liabilities												
Table 5 Other changes in the volume of assets and liabilities												
Table 6 Balance sheet												
6 **Net worth**.................	....	....	....	....	....	....	....	....	....	....	....	....
61 **Nonfinancial assets**.................	....	....	....	....	....	....	....	....	....	....	....	....
611 Fixed assets.................	....	....	....	....	....	....	....	....	....	....	....	....
6111 Buildings and structures.................	....	....	....	....	....	....	....	....	....	....	....	....
6112 Machinery and equipment.................	....	....	....	....	....	....	....	....	....	....	....	....
6113 Other fixed assets.................	....	....	....	....	....	....	....	....	....	....	....	....
612 Inventories.................	....	....	....	....	....	....	....	....	....	....	....	....
613 Valuables.................	....	....	....	....	....	....	....	....	....	....	....	....
614 Nonproduced assets.................	....	....	....	....	....	....	....	....	....	....	....	....
6141 Land.................	....	....	....	....	....	....	....	....	....	....	....	....
6142 Subsoil assets.................	....	....	....	....	....	....	....	....	....	....	....	....
6143 Other naturally occurring assets.................	....	....	....	....	....	....	....	....	....	....	....	....
6144 Intangible nonproduced assets.................	....	....	....	....	....	....	....	....	....	....	....	....
62 **Financial assets**.................	....	....	....	....	....	....	....	....	....	....	....	....
621 Domestic.................	....	....	....	....	....	....	....	....	....	....	....	....
6212 Currency and deposits.................	....	....	....	....	....	....	....	....	....	....	....	....
6213 Securities other than shares.................	....	....	....	....	....	....	....	....	....	....	....	....
6214 Loans.................	....	....	....	....	....	....	....	....	....	....	....	....
6215 Shares and other equity.................	....	....	....	....	....	....	....	....	....	....	....	....
6216 Insurance technical reserves.................	....	....	....	....	....	....	....	....	....	....	....	....
6217 Financial derivatives.................	....	....	....	....	....	....	....	....	....	....	....	....
6218 Other accounts receivable.................	....	....	....	....	....	....	....	....	....	....	....	....
622 Foreign.................	....	....	....	....	....	....	....	....	....	....	....	....
6222 Currency and deposits.................	....	....	....	....	....	....	....	....	....	....	....	....
6223 Securities other than shares.................	....	....	....	....	....	....	....	....	....	....	....	....
6224 Loans.................	....	....	....	....	....	....	....	....	....	....	....	....
6225 Shares and other equity.................	....	....	....	....	....	....	....	....	....	....	....	....
6226 Insurance technical reserves.................	....	....	....	....	....	....	....	....	....	....	....	....
6227 Financial derivatives.................	....	....	....	....	....	....	....	....	....	....	....	....
6228 Other accounts receivable.................	....	....	....	....	....	....	....	....	....	....	....	....
623 Monetary gold and SDRs.................	....	....	....	....	....	....	....	....	....	....	....	....
63 **Liabilities**.................	....	....	....	460,199	605,411	740,305	....	....	....	....	....	....
631 Domestic.................	....	....	....	35,457	49,659	64,528	....	....	....	....	....	....
6312 Currency and deposits.................	....	....	....	....	....	....	....	....	....	....	....	....
6313 Securities other than shares.................	....	....	....	....	....	....	....	....	....	....	....	....
6314 Loans.................	....	....	....	....	....	....	....	....	....	....	....	....
6316 Insurance technical reserves.................	....	....	....	....	....	....	....	....	....	....	....	....
6317 Financial derivatives.................	....	....	....	....	....	....	....	....	....	....	....	....
6318 Other accounts payable.................	....	....	....	....	....	....	....	....	....	....	....	....
632 Foreign.................	....	....	....	424,742	555,752	675,777	....	....	....	....	....	....
6322 Currency and deposits.................	....	....	....	....	....	....	....	....	....	....	....	....
6323 Securities other than shares.................	....	....	....	....	....	....	....	....	....	....	....	....
6324 Loans.................	....	....	....	....	....	....	....	....	....	....	....	....
6326 Insurance technical reserves.................	....	....	....	....	....	....	....	....	....	....	....	....
6327 Financial derivatives.................	....	....	....	....	....	....	....	....	....	....	....	....
6328 Other accounts payable.................	....	....	....	....	....	....	....	....	....	....	....	....
Memorandum items:												
6M2 Net financial worth.................	....	....		....	....		....	....		....	....	
6M3 Debt at market value.................	....	....		....	....		....	....		....	....	
6M4 Debt at nominal value.................	....	....		....	....		....	....		....	....	
6M5 Arrears.................	....	....		....	....		....	....		....	....	
6M6 Obligations for social security benefits.................	....	....		....	....		....	....		....	....	
6M7 Contingent liabilities.................	....	....		....	....		....	....		....	....	
6M8 Uncapitalized military weapons, systems.................	....	....		....	....		....	....		....	....	
Table 7 Outlays by functions of govt.												
7 **Total outlays**.................	66,085	81,432	88,593	80,800	98,061	105,181	....	....	....	....	....	....
701 **General public services**.................	....	34,787	38,185	....	....	....	....	....	....	....	....	....
7017 Public debt transactions.................	6,069	6,840	9,507	....	....	....	....	....	....	....	....	....
7018 General transfers between levels of govt.................	....	....	....	....	....	....	....	....	....	....	....	....
702 **Defense**.................	21,100	23,325	24,564	....	....	....	....	....	....	....	....	....
703 **Public order and safety**.................	1,334	2,153	2,502	....	....	....	....	....	....	....	....	....

2005, International Monetary Fund: *Government Finance Statistics Yearbook*

In Millions of Francs / Year Ending December 31 / Cash Reporter

		Budgetary Central Government			Central Government			Local Government			General Government		
		1997	1998	1999	1997	1998	1999	1997	1998	1999	1997	1998	1999
704	**Economic affairs**....................	....	**4,024**	**4,568**	....	....	....	....	....	....	....	....	....
7042	Agriculture, forestry, fishing, and hunting.....	....	1,499	1,941	....	....	....	....	....	....	....	....	....
7043	Fuel and energy....................	....	232	543	....	....	....	....	....	....	....	....	....
7044	Mining, manufacturing, and construction.....	....	995	1,068	....	....	....	....	....	....	....	....	....
7045	Transport....................	....	336	169	....	....	....	....	....	....	....	....	....
7046	Communication....................	....	....	....	....	....	....	....	....	....	....	....	....
705	**Environmental protection**....................	....	....	....	....	....	....	....	....	....	....	....	....
706	**Housing and community amenities**........	—	—	—	....	....	....	....	....	....	....	....	....
707	**Health**....................	**2,085**	**2,421**	**2,271**	....	....	....	....	....	....	....	....	....
7072	Outpatient services....................	....	....	....	....	....	....	....	....	....	....	....	....
7073	Hospital services....................	....	....	....	....	....	....	....	....	....	....	....	....
7074	Public health services....................	....	....	....	....	....	....	....	....	....	....	....	....
708	**Recreation, culture, and religion**..........	**334**	**286**	**345**	....	....	....	....	....	....	....	....	....
709	**Education**....................	**11,204**	**14,080**	**15,991**	....	....	....	....	....	....	....	....	....
7091	Pre-primary and primary education...............	....	....	....	....	....	....	....	....	....	....	....	....
7092	Secondary education....................	....	....	....	....	....	....	....	....	....	....	....	....
7094	Tertiary education....................	....	....	....	....	....	....	....	....	....	....	....	....
710	**Social protection**....................	**276**	**356**	**168**	....	....	....	....	....	....	....	....	....
7	Statistical discrepancy: Total outlays............	—	—	—	....	....	....	....	....	....	....	....	....

Table 8 Transactions in financial assets and liabilities by sector

		Budgetary Central Government			Central Government			Local Government			General Government		
82	**Net acquisition of financial assets**........	....	....	....	**−2,583**	**7,827**	**7,402**	....	....	....	....	....	....
821	Domestic....................	....	....	....	....	....	....	....	....	....	....	....	....
8211	General government....................	....	....	....	....	....	....	....	....	....	....	....	....
8212	Central bank....................	....	....	....	....	....	....	....	....	....	....	....	....
8213	Other depository corporations....................	....	....	....	....	....	....	....	....	....	....	....	....
8214	Financial corporations n.e.c....................	....	....	....	....	....	....	....	....	....	....	....	....
8215	Nonfinancial corporations....................	....	....	....	....	....	....	....	....	....	....	....	....
8216	Households & NPIs serving households......	....	....	....	....	....	....	....	....	....	....	....	....
822	Foreign....................	....	....	....	....	....	....	....	....	....	....	....	....
8221	General government....................	....	....	....	....	....	....	....	....	....	....	....	....
8227	International organizations....................	....	....	....	....	....	....	....	....	....	....	....	....
8228	Financial corporations other than international organizations..............	....	....	....	....	....	....	....	....	....	....	....	....
8229	Other nonresidents....................	....	....	....	....	....	....	....	....	....	....	....	....
823	Monetary gold and SDRs....................	....	....	....	—	—	—	....	....	....	....	....	....
83	**Net incurrence of liabilities**....................	....	....	....	**18,555**	**25,600**	**27,991**	....	....	....	....	....	....
831	Domestic....................	....	....	....	8,135	9,670	14,869	....	....	....	....	....	....
8311	General government....................	....	....	....	....	....	....	....	....	....	....	....	....
8312	Central bank....................	....	....	....	....	....	....	....	....	....	....	....	....
8313	Other depository corporations....................	....	....	....	....	....	....	....	....	....	....	....	....
8314	Financial corporations n.e.c....................	....	....	....	....	....	....	....	....	....	....	....	....
8315	Nonfinancial corporations....................	....	....	....	....	....	....	....	....	....	....	....	....
8316	Households & NPIs serving households......	....	....	....	....	....	....	....	....	....	....	....	....
832	Foreign....................	....	....	....	10,420	15,930	13,121	....	....	....	....	....	....
8321	General government....................	....	....	....	—	—	—	....	....	....	....	....	....
8327	International organizations....................	....	....	....	10,420	15,930	13,121	....	....	....	....	....	....
8328	Financial corporations other than international organizations..............	....	....	....	—		—	....	....	....	....	....	....
8329	Other nonresidents....................	....	....	....	—	—	—	....	....	....	....	....	....

In Billions of Riels / Year Ending December 31 / Noncash Reporter

	Budgetary Central Government			Central Government			Local Government			General Government		
	2002	2003	2004	2002	2003	2004	2002	2003	2004	2002	2003	2004
Statement of government operations												
1 Revenue..	1,820.6	1,785.4	2,119.1	2,369.5	2,114.9	2,510.3	....	....	....	....	....	....
2 Expense...	1,574.1	1,758.1	1,790.6	1,574.1	1,758.1	1,790.6	....	....	....	....	....	....
GOB *Gross operating balance*................	*246.5*	*27.3*	*328.5*	*795.4*	*356.8*	*719.7*	....	....	....	....	....	....
NOB *Net operating balance*....................	....	....	....	....	....	....	....	....	....	....	....	....
31 Net acquisition of nonfinancial assets...........	322.1	301.8	231.4	1,363.4	1,167.3	1,158.8	....	....	....	....	....	....
NLB *Net lending/borrowing*....................	*−75.6*	*−274.5*	*97.2*	*−568.0*	*−810.5*	*−439.1*	....	....	....	....	....	....
32 Net acquisition of financial assets.................	80.2	30.7	−13.8	109.4	56.5	−35.9	....	....	....	....	....	....
33 Net incurrence of liabilities........................	44.2	299.5	−143.0	565.8	861.3	371.2	....	....	....	....	....	....
NLB Statistical discrepancy.................................	111.5	5.6	32.0	111.5	5.6	32.0	....	....	....	....	....	....
Statement of other economic flows												
Balance sheet												
Statement of sources and uses of cash												
Table 1 Revenue												
1 **Revenue**..	**1,820.6**	**1,785.4**	**2,119.1**	**2,369.5**	**2,114.9**	**2,510.3**	....	....	....	....	....	....
11 **Taxes**...	**1,371.5**	**1,397.2**	**1,693.7**	**1,371.5**	**1,397.2**	**1,693.7**	....	....	....	....	....	....
111 Taxes on income, profits, & capital gains......	134.2	150.4	157.9	134.2	150.4	157.9	....	....	....	....	....	....
1111 Individuals...................................	27.2	40.5	40.6	27.2	40.5	40.6	....	....	....	....	....	....
1112 Corporations and other enterprises............	107.0	109.9	117.3	107.0	109.9	117.3	....	....	....	....	....	....
112 Taxes on payroll and workforce...................	—	—	—	—	—	—	....	....	....	....	....	....
113 Taxes on property....................................	—	—	—	—	—	—	....	....	....	....	....	....
114 Taxes on goods and services.......................	703.5	689.5	941.8	703.5	689.5	941.8	....	....	....	....	....	....
1141 General taxes on goods and services..........	457.2	460.4	598.0	457.2	460.4	598.0	....	....	....	....	....	....
1142 Excises....................................	210.4	197.6	304.4	210.4	197.6	304.4	....	....	....	....	....	....
115 Taxes on int'l. trade and transactions...........	529.9	541.0	590.2	529.9	541.0	590.2	....	....	....	....	....	....
116 Other taxes..	3.9	16.3	3.8	3.9	16.3	3.8	....	....	....	....	....	....
12 **Social contributions**.............................	—	—	—	—	—	—	....	....	....	....	....	....
121 Social security contributions........................	—	—	—	—	—	—	....	....	....	....	....	....
122 Other social contributions..........................	—	—	—	—	—	—	....	....	....	....	....	....
13 **Grants**...	**93.0**	**52.2**	**11.8**	**641.9**	**381.7**	**403.0**	....	....	....	....	....	....
131 From foreign governments...........................	93.0	52.2	11.8	641.9	381.7	403.0	....	....	....	....	....	....
132 From international organizations....................	—	—	—	—	—	—	....	....	....	....	....	....
133 From other general government units...........	—	—	—	—	—	—	....	....	....	....	....	....
14 **Other revenue**....................................	**356.2**	**336.0**	**413.6**	**356.2**	**336.0**	**413.6**	....	....	....	....	....	....
Table 2 Expense by economic type												
2 **Expense**...	**1,574.1**	**1,758.1**	**1,790.6**	**1,574.1**	**1,758.1**	**1,790.6**	....	....	....	....	....	....
21 **Compensation of employees**....................	**586.7**	**614.7**	**639.6**	**586.7**	**614.7**	**639.6**	....	....	....	....	....	....
211 Wages and salaries..............................	586.7	614.7	639.6	586.7	614.7	639.6	....	....	....	....	....	....
212 Social contributions...................................	—	—	—	—	—	—	....	....	....	....	....	....
22 **Use of goods and services**.....................	**551.3**	**596.0**	**564.1**	**551.3**	**596.0**	**564.1**	....	....	....	....	....	....
23 **Consumption of fixed capital**.................	....	....	....	....	....	....	....	....	....	....	....	....
24 **Interest**...	**27.6**	**34.1**	**48.6**	**27.6**	**34.1**	**48.6**	....	....	....	....	....	....
25 **Subsidies**...	**50.2**	**60.1**	**63.8**	**50.2**	**60.1**	**63.8**	....	....	....	....	....	....
26 **Grants**...	**56.4**	**106.1**	**114.0**	**56.4**	**106.1**	**114.0**	....	....	....	....	....	....
261 To foreign governments..............................	—	—	—	—	—	—	....	....	....	....	....	....
262 To international organizations.......................	—	—	—	—	—	—	....	....	....	....	....	....
263 To other general government units..............	56.4	106.1	114.0	56.4	106.1	114.0	....	....	....	....	....	....
2631 Current....................................	....	....	....	....	....	....	....	....	....	....	....	....
2632 Capital.....................................	....	....	....	....	....	....	....	....	....	....	....	....
27 **Social benefits**...................................	**136.4**	**164.7**	**141.2**	**136.4**	**164.7**	**141.2**	....	....	....	....	....	....
28 **Other expense**...................................	**165.5**	**182.5**	**219.3**	**165.5**	**182.5**	**219.3**	....	....	....	....	....	....
281 Property expense other than interest...........	—	—	—	—	—	—	....	....	....	....	....	....
282 Miscellaneous other expense......................	165.5	182.5	219.3	165.5	182.5	219.3	....	....	....	....	....	....
2821 Current....................................	....	....	....	....	....	....	....	....	....	....	....	....
2822 Capital.....................................	....	....	....	....	....	....	....	....	....	....	....	....

In Billions of Riels / Year Ending December 31 / Noncash Reporter

	Budgetary Central Government			Central Government			Local Government			General Government		
	2002	2003	2004	2002	2003	2004	2002	2003	2004	2002	2003	2004
Table 3 Transactions in assets and liabilities												
3 Change in net worth from transactns....	....	....	....	....	....	....	....	....	....	....	....	....
31 **Net acquisition of nonfinancial assets...**	**322.1**	**301.8**	**231.4**	**1,363.4**	**1,167.3**	**1,158.8**	....	....	....	....	....	....
311 Fixed assets....................	322.1	301.8	231.4	1,363.4	1,167.3	1,158.8	....	....	....	....	....	....
3111 Buildings and structures..........	....	....	....	....	....	....	....	....	....	....	....	....
3112 Machinery and equipment............	....	....	....	....	....	....	....	....	....	....	....	....
3113 Other fixed assets.................	....	....	....	....	....	....	....	....	....	....	....	....
312 Inventories......................	—	—	—	—	—	—	....	....	....	....	....	....
313 Valuables.......................	—	—	—	—	—	—	....	....	....	....	....	....
314 Nonproduced assets..............	—	—	—	—	—	—	....	....	....	....	....	....
3141 Land.........................	—	—	—	—	—	—	....	....	....	....	....	....
3142 Subsoil assets...............	—	—	—	—	—	—	....	....	....	....	....	....
3143 Other naturally occurring assets....	—	—	—	—	—	—	....	....	....	....	....	....
3144 Intangible nonproduced assets.......	—	—	—	—	—	—	....	....	....	....	....	....
32 **Net acquisition of financial assets........**	**80.2**	**30.7**	**−13.8**	**109.4**	**56.5**	**−35.9**	....	....	....	....	....	....
321 Domestic.........................	80.2	30.7	−13.8	109.4	56.5	−35.9	....	....	....	....	....	....
3212 Currency and deposits..........	80.2	30.7	−13.8	109.4	56.5	−35.9	....	....	....	....	....	....
3213 Securities other than shares.......	—	—	—	—	—	—	....	....	....	....	....	....
3214 Loans..........................	—	—	—	—	—	—	....	....	....	....	....	....
3215 Shares and other equity...........	—	—	—	—	—	—	....	....	....	....	....	....
3216 Insurance technical reserves.......	—	—	—	—	—	—	....	....	....	....	....	....
3217 Financial derivatives..............	—	—	—	—	—	—	....	....	....	....	....	....
3218 Other accounts receivable.........	—	—	—	—	—	—	....	....	....	....	....	....
322 Foreign..........................	—	—	—	—	—	—	....	....	....	....	....	....
3222 Currency and deposits............	—	—	—	—	—	—	....	....	....	....	....	....
3223 Securities other than shares.......	—	—	—	—	—	—	....	....	....	....	....	....
3224 Loans..........................	—	—	—	—	—	—	....	....	....	....	....	....
3225 Shares and other equity...........	—	—	—	—	—	—	....	....	....	....	....	....
3226 Insurance technical reserves.......	—	—	—	—	—	—	....	....	....	....	....	....
3227 Financial derivatives..............	—	—	—	—	—	—	....	....	....	....	....	....
3228 Other accounts receivable.........	—	—	—	—	—	—	....	....	....	....	....	....
323 Monetary gold and SDRs..............	—	—	—	—	—	—	....	....	....	....	....	....
33 **Net incurrence of liabilities...................**	**44.2**	**299.5**	**−143.0**	**565.8**	**861.3**	**371.2**	....	....	....	....	....	....
331 Domestic.........................	−32.5	328.6	−139.6	−32.5	328.6	−139.6	....	....	....	....	....	....
3312 Currency and deposits.............	−46.0	106.5	−118.0	−46.0	106.5	−118.0	....	....	....	....	....	....
3313 Securities other than shares.......	—	49.9	—	—	49.9	—	....	....	....	....	....	....
3314 Loans..........................	—	—	—	—	—	—	....	....	....	....	....	....
3316 Insurance technical reserves.......	—	—	—	—	—	—	....	....	....	....	....	....
3317 Financial derivatives..............	—	—	—	—	—	—	....	....	....	....	....	....
3318 Other accounts payable............	13.4	172.2	−21.6	13.4	172.2	−21.6	....	....	....	....	....	....
332 Foreign..........................	76.8	−29.1	−3.4	598.4	532.7	510.8	....	....	....	....	....	....
3322 Currency and deposits.............	—	—	—	—	—	—	....	....	....	....	....	....
3323 Securities other than shares.......	—	—	—	—	—	—	....	....	....	....	....	....
3324 Loans..........................	76.8	−29.1	−3.4	598.4	532.7	510.8	....	....	....	....	....	....
3326 Insurance technical reserves.......	—	—	—	—	—	—	....	....	....	....	....	....
3327 Financial derivatives..............	—	—	—	—	—	—	....	....	....	....	....	....
3328 Other accounts payable............	—	—	—	—	—	—	....	....	....	....	....	....
Table 4 Holding gains in assets and liabilities												
Table 5 Other changes in the volume of assets and liabilities												
Table 6 Balance sheet												
Table 7 Outlays by functions of govt.												
7 **Total outlays........................**	**1,896.2**	**2,060.0**	**2,022.0**	**2,937.5**	**2,925.4**	**2,949.4**	....	....	....	....	....	....
701 **General public services....................**	....	....	....	....	....	....	....	....	....	....	....	....
7017 Public debt transactions............	27.6	34.1	48.6	27.6	34.1	48.6	....	....	....	....	....	....
7018 General transfers between levels of govt......	....	....	....	....	....	....	....	....	....	....	....	....
702 **Defense........................**	....	....	....	....	....	....	....	....	....	....	....	....
703 **Public order and safety........................**	....	....	....	....	....	....	....	....	....	....	....	....
704 **Economic affairs...................................**	....	....	....	....	....	....	....	....	....	....	....	....
7042 Agriculture, forestry, fishing, and hunting.....	....	....	....	....	....	....	....	....	....	....	....	....
7043 Fuel and energy.........................	....	....	....	....	....	....	....	....	....	....	....	....
7044 Mining, manufacturing, and construction.....	....	....	....	....	....	....	....	....	....	....	....	....
7045 Transport.............................	....	....	....	....	....	....	....	....	....	....	....	....
7046 Communication........................	....	....	....	....	....	....	....	....	....	....	....	....

		Budgetary Central Government			Central Government			Local Government			General Government		
		2002	2003	2004	2002	2003	2004	2002	2003	2004	2002	2003	2004
705	**Environmental protection**.....................	....	....	....	....	....	....	....	....	....	....	....	....
706	**Housing and community amenities**........	....	....	....	....	....	....	....	....	....	....	....	....
707	**Health**...	....	....	....	....	....	....	....	....	....	....	....	....
7072	Outpatient services..............................	....	....	....	....	....	....	....	....	....	....	....	....
7073	Hospital services.................................	....	....	....	....	....	....	....	....	....	....	....	....
7074	Public health services...........................	....	....	....	....	....	....	....	....	....	....	....	....
708	**Recreation, culture, and religion**..........	....	....	....	....	....	....	....	....	....	....	....	....
709	**Education**..	....	....	....	....	....	....	....	....	....	....	....	....
7091	Pre-primary and primary education............	....	....	....	....	....	....	....	....	....	....	....	....
7092	Secondary education.............................	....	....	....	....	....	....	....	....	....	....	....	....
7094	Tertiary education................................	....	....	....	....	....	....	....	....	....	....	....	....
710	**Social protection**................................	....	....	....	....	....	....	....	....	....	....	....	....
7	Statistical discrepancy: Total outlays..........	....	....	....	....	....	....	....	....	....	....	....	....

Table 8 Transactions in financial assets and liabilities by sector

		Budgetary Central Government			Central Government			Local Government			General Government		
82	**Net acquisition of financial assets**........	**80.2**	**30.7**	**−13.8**	**109.4**	**56.5**	**−35.9**	....	....	....	....	....	....
821	Domestic..	80.2	30.7	−13.8	109.4	56.5	−35.9	....	....	....	....	....	....
8211	General government.............................	....	....	....	....	....	....	....	....	....	....	....	....
8212	Central bank......................................	....	....	....	....	....	....	....	....	....	....	....	....
8213	Other depository corporations..................	....	....	....	....	....	....	....	....	....	....	....	....
8214	Financial corporations n.e.c....................	....	....	....	....	....	....	....	....	....	....	....	....
8215	Nonfinancial corporations.......................	....	....	....	....	....	....	....	....	....	....	....	....
8216	Households & NPIs serving households......	....	....	....	....	....	....	....	....	....	....	....	....
822	Foreign...	—	—	—	—	—	—	....	....	....	....	....	....
8221	General government.............................	—	—	—	—	—	—	....	....	....	....	....	....
8227	International organizations......................	—	—	—	—	—	—	....	....	....	....	....	....
8228	Financial corporations other than international organizations............	—	—	—	—	—	—	....	....	....	....	....	....
8229	Other nonresidents..............................	—	—	—	—	—	—	....	....	....	....	....	....
823	Monetary gold and SDRs.......................	—	—	—	—	—	—	....	....	....	....	....	....
83	**Net incurrence of liabilities**.................	**44.2**	**299.5**	**−143.0**	**565.8**	**861.3**	**371.2**	....	....	....	....	....	....
831	Domestic..	−32.5	328.6	−139.6	−32.5	328.6	−139.6	....	....	....	....	....	....
8311	General government.............................	....	....	....	....	....	....	....	....	....	....	....	....
8312	Central bank......................................	....	....	....	....	....	....	....	....	....	....	....	....
8313	Other depository corporations..................	....	....	....	....	....	....	....	....	....	....	....	....
8314	Financial corporations n.e.c....................	....	....	....	....	....	....	....	....	....	....	....	....
8315	Nonfinancial corporations.......................	....	....	....	....	....	....	....	....	....	....	....	....
8316	Households & NPIs serving households......	....	....	....	....	....	....	....	....	....	....	....	....
832	Foreign...	76.8	−29.1	−3.4	598.4	532.7	510.8	....	....	....	....	....	....
8321	General government.............................	....	....	....	....	....	....	....	....	....	....	....	....
8327	International organizations......................	....	....	....	....	....	....	....	....	....	....	....	....
8328	Financial corporations other than international organizations............	....	....	....	....	....	....	....	....	....	....	....	....
8329	Other nonresidents..............................	....	....	....	....	....	....	....	....	....	....	....	....

In Billions of Francs / Year Ending June 30 / Cash Reporter

	Budgetary Central Government			Central Government			Local Government			General Government		
	1997	1998	1999	1997	1998	1999	1997	1998	1999	1997	1998	1999
Statement of government operations												
Statement of other economic flows												
Balance sheet												
6 *Net worth*...................	....	....	....	....	....	....	....	....	....	....	....	....
61 Nonfinancial assets...................	....	....	....	....	....	....	....	....	....	....	....	....
62 Financial assets...................	....	....	....	....	....	....	....	....	....	....	....	....
63 Liabilities...................	....	5,652.91	5,656.16	....	....	....	....	....	....	....	....	....
Statement of sources and uses of cash												
1 Cash receipts from operating activities..........	....	862.31	867.46	....	....	....	....	....	....	....	....	....
11 Taxes...................	....	646.18	690.99	....	....	....	....	....	....	....	....	....
12 Social contributions...................	....	17.75	18.71	....	....	....	....	....	....	....	....	....
13 Grants...................	....	—	—	....	....	....	....	....	....	....	....	....
14 Other receipts...................	....	198.38	157.76	....	....	....	....	....	....	....	....	....
2 Cash payments for operating activities..........	....	674.60	740.60	....	....	....	....	....	....	....	....	....
21 Compensation of employees...................	....	259.20	274.70	....	....	....	....	....	....	....	....	....
22 Purchases of goods and services...................	....	143.00	169.20	....	....	....	....	....	....	....	....	....
24 Interest...................	....	168.20	166.20	....	....	....	....	....	....	....	....	....
25 Subsidies...................	....	97.20	125.50	....	....	....	....	....	....	....	....	....
26 Grants...................	....	—	—	....	....	....	....	....	....	....	....	....
27 Social benefits...................	....	—	—	....	....	....	....	....	....	....	....	....
28 Other payments...................	....	—	—	....	....	....	....	....	....	....	....	....
CIO *Net cash inflow from oper. activities*.....	....	187.71	126.86	....	....	....	....	....	....	....	....	....
31.1 Purchases of nonfinancial assets...................	....	103.00	119.20	....	....	....	....	....	....	....	....	....
31.2 Sales of nonfinancial assets...................	....			....	....	....	....	....	....	....	....	....
31 Net cash outflow from investments in nonfinancial assets...................	....	103.00	119.20	....	....	....	....	....	....	....	....	....
CSD *Cash surplus/deficit*...................	....	84.71	7.66	....	....	....	....	....	....	....	....	....
32x Net acquisition of fin assets, excl. cash...................	....	1.00	.50	....	....	....	....	....	....	....	....	....
321x Domestic...................	....	1.00	.50	....	....	....	....	....	....	....	....	....
322x Foreign...................	....	—	—	....	....	....	....	....	....	....	....	....
323 Monetary gold and SDRs...................	....	—	—	....	....	....	....	....	....	....	....	....
33 Net incurrence of liabilities...................	....	....	....	....	....	....	....	....	....	....	....	....
331 Domestic...................	....	....	....	....	....	....	....	....	....	....	....	....
332 Foreign...................	....	....	....	....	....	....	....	....	....	....	....	....
NFB Net cash inflow from fin. activities...................	....	....	....	....	....	....	....	....	....	....	....	....
NCB *Net change in the stock of cash*..........	....	....	....	....	....	....	....	....	....	....	....	....
Table 1 Revenue												
1 **Revenue**...................	....	862.31	867.46	....	....	....	....	....	....	....	....	....
11 **Taxes**...................	....	646.18	690.99	....	....	....	....	....	....	....	....	....
111 Taxes on income, profits, & capital gains......	....	163.69	179.98	....	....	....	....	....	....	....	....	....
1111 Individuals...................	....	80.49	75.38	....	....	....	....	....	....	....	....	....
1112 Corporations and other enterprises...........	....	83.20	104.60	....	....	....	....	....	....	....	....	....
112 Taxes on payroll and workforce...................	....	—	—	....	....	....	....	....	....	....	....	....
113 Taxes on property...................	....	5.49	9.17	....	....	....	....	....	....	....	....	....
114 Taxes on goods and services...................	....	183.82	223.75	....	....	....	....	....	....	....	....	....
1141 General taxes on goods and services...........	....	154.90	192.90	....	....	....	....	....	....	....	....	....
1142 Excises...................	....	23.10	24.80	....	....	....	....	....	....	....	....	....
115 Taxes on int'l. trade and transactions...........	....	260.02	245.12	....	....	....	....	....	....	....	....	....
116 Other taxes...................	....	28.16	28.97	....	....	....	....	....	....	....	....	....
12 **Social contributions**...................	....	17.75	18.71	....	....	....	....	....	....	....	....	....
121 Social security contributions...................	....	—	—	....	....	....	....	....	....	....	....	....
122 Other social contributions...................	....	17.75	18.71	....	....	....	....	....	....	....	....	....
13 **Grants**...................	....	—	—	....	....	....	....	....	....	....	....	....
131 From foreign governments...................	....	—	—	....	....	....	....	....	....	....	....	....
132 From international organizations...................	....	—	—	....	....	....	....	....	....	....	....	....
133 From other general government units...........	....	—	—	....	....	....	....	....	....	....	....	....
14 **Other revenue**...................	....	198.38	157.76	....	....	....	....	....	....	....	....	....
Table 2 Expense by economic type												
2 **Expense**...................	....	674.60	740.60	....	....	....	....	....	....	....	....	....
21 **Compensation of employees**...................	....	259.20	274.70	....	....	....	....	....	....	....	....	....
211 Wages and salaries...................	....	259.20	274.70	....	....	....	....	....	....	....	....	....
212 Social contributions...................	....			....	....	....	....	....	....	....	....	....
22 **Use of goods and services**...................	....	143.00	169.20	....	....	....	....	....	....	....	....	....
23 **Consumption of fixed capital**...................	....	....	....	....	....	....	....	....	....	....	....	....
24 **Interest**...................	....	168.20	166.20	....	....	....	....	....	....	....	....	....
25 **Subsidies**...................	....	97.20	125.50	....	....	....	....	....	....	....	....	....

	Budgetary Central Government			Central Government			Local Government			General Government		
	1997	1998	1999	1997	1998	1999	1997	1998	1999	1997	1998	1999
26 **Grants**.....	....	—	—	....	....	....	....	....	....	....	....	....
261 To foreign govenments.....	....	—	—	....	....	....	....	....	....	....	....	....
262 To international organizations.....	....	—	—	....	....	....	....	....	....	....	....	....
263 To other general government units.....	....	—	—	....	....	....	....	....	....	....	....	....
2631 Current.....	....	—	—	....	....	....	....	....	....	....	....	....
2632 Capital.....	....	—	—	....	....	....	....	....	....	....	....	....
27 **Social benefits**.....	....	—	—	....	....	....	....	....	....	....	....	....
28 **Other expense**.....	....	—	—	....	....	....	....	....	....	....	....	....
281 Property expense other than interest.....	....	—	—	....	....	....	....	....	....	....	....	....
282 Miscellaneous other expense.....	....	—	—	....	....	....	....	....	....	....	....	....
2821 Current.....	....	—	—	....	....	....	....	....	....	....	....	....
2822 Capital.....	....	—	—	....	....	....	....	....	....	....	....	....
Table 3 Transactions in assets and liabilities												
3 **Change in net worth from transactns**.....	....	....	....	....	....	....	....	....	....	....	....	....
31 **Net acquisition of nonfinancial assets**.....	....	103.00	119.20	....	....	....	....	....	....	....	....	....
311 Fixed assets.....	....	103.00	119.20	....	....	....	....	....	....	....	....	....
3111 Buildings and structures.....	....	....	....	....	....	....	....	....	....	....	....	....
3112 Machinery and equipment.....	....	....	....	....	....	....	....	....	....	....	....	....
3113 Other fixed assets.....	....	....	....	....	....	....	....	....	....	....	....	....
312 Inventories.....	....	—	—	....	....	....	....	....	....	....	....	....
313 Valuables.....	....	—	—	....	....	....	....	....	....	....	....	....
314 Nonproduced assets.....	....	—	—	....	....	....	....	....	....	....	....	....
3141 Land.....	....	—	—	....	....	....	....	....	....	....	....	....
3142 Subsoil assets.....	....	—	—	....	....	....	....	....	....	....	....	....
3143 Other naturally occurring assets.....	....	—	—	....	....	....	....	....	....	....	....	....
3144 Intangible nonproduced assets.....	....	—	—	....	....	....	....	....	....	....	....	....
32 **Net acquisition of financial assets**.....	....	....	....	....	....	....	....	....	....	....	....	....
321 Domestic.....	....	....	....	....	....	....	....	....	....	....	....	....
3212 Currency and deposits.....	....	....	....	....	....	....	....	....	....	....	....	....
3213 Securities other than shares.....	....	....	....	....	....	....	....	....	....	....	....	....
3214 Loans.....	....	....	....	....	....	....	....	....	....	....	....	....
3215 Shares and other equity.....	....	....	....	....	....	....	....	....	....	....	....	....
3216 Insurance technical reserves.....	....	....	....	....	....	....	....	....	....	....	....	....
3217 Financial derivatives.....	....	....	....	....	....	....	....	....	....	....	....	....
3218 Other accounts receivable.....	....	....	....	....	....	....	....	....	....	....	....	....
322 Foreign.....	....	....	....	....	....	....	....	....	....	....	....	....
3222 Currency and deposits.....	....	....	....	....	....	....	....	....	....	....	....	....
3223 Securities other than shares.....	....	....	....	....	....	....	....	....	....	....	....	....
3224 Loans.....	....	....	....	....	....	....	....	....	....	....	....	....
3225 Shares and other equity.....	....	....	....	....	....	....	....	....	....	....	....	....
3226 Insurance technical reserves.....	....	....	....	....	....	....	....	....	....	....	....	....
3227 Financial derivatives.....	....	....	....	....	....	....	....	....	....	....	....	....
3228 Other accounts receivable.....	....	....	....	....	....	....	....	....	....	....	....	....
323 Monetary gold and SDRs.....	....	....	....	....	....	....	....	....	....	....	....	....
33 **Net incurrence of liabilities**.....	....	....	....	....	....	....	....	....	....	....	....	....
331 Domestic.....	....	....	....	....	....	....	....	....	....	....	....	....
3312 Currency and deposits.....	....	....	....	....	....	....	....	....	....	....	....	....
3313 Securities other than shares.....	....	....	....	....	....	....	....	....	....	....	....	....
3314 Loans.....	....	....	....	....	....	....	....	....	....	....	....	....
3316 Insurance technical reserves.....	....	....	....	....	....	....	....	....	....	....	....	....
3317 Financial derivatives.....	....	....	....	....	....	....	....	....	....	....	....	....
3318 Other accounts payable.....	....	....	....	....	....	....	....	....	....	....	....	....
332 Foreign.....	....	....	....	....	....	....	....	....	....	....	....	....
3322 Currency and deposits.....	....	....	....	....	....	....	....	....	....	....	....	....
3323 Securities other than shares.....	....	....	....	....	....	....	....	....	....	....	....	....
3324 Loans.....	....	....	....	....	....	....	....	....	....	....	....	....
3326 Insurance technical reserves.....	....	....	....	....	....	....	....	....	....	....	....	....
3327 Financial derivatives.....	....	....	....	....	....	....	....	....	....	....	....	....
3328 Other accounts payable.....	....	....	....	....	....	....	....	....	....	....	....	....

	Budgetary Central Government			Central Government			Local Government			General Government		
	1997	1998	1999	1997	1998	1999	1997	1998	1999	1997	1998	1999
Table 4 Holding gains in assets and liabilities												
Table 5 Other changes in the volume of assets and liabilities												
Table 6 Balance sheet												
6 Net worth..	....	....	....	....	....	....	....	....	....	....	....	....
61 **Nonfinancial assets............................**	....	....	....	....	....	....	....	....	....	....	....	....
611 Fixed assets...................................	....	....	....	....	....	....	....	....	....	....	....	....
6111 Buildings and structures...................	....	....	....	....	....	....	....	....	....	....	....	....
6112 Machinery and equipment....................	....	....	....	....	....	....	....	....	....	....	....	....
6113 Other fixed assets.........................	....	....	....	....	....	....	....	....	....	....	....	....
612 Inventories................................	....	....	....	....	....	....	....	....	....	....	....	....
613 Valuables..................................	....	....	....	....	....	....	....	....	....	....	....	....
614 Nonproduced assets.........................	....	....	....	....	....	....	....	....	....	....	....	....
6141 Land.....................................	....	....	....	....	....	....	....	....	....	....	....	....
6142 Subsoil assets.............................	....	....	....	....	....	....	....	....	....	....	....	....
6143 Other naturally occurring assets..............	....	....	....	....	....	....	....	....	....	....	....	....
6144 Intangible nonproduced assets................	....	....	....	....	....	....	....	....	....	....	....	....
62 **Financial assets..............................**	....	....	....	....	....	....	....	....	....	....	....	....
621 Domestic...................................	....	....	....	....	....	....	....	....	....	....	....	....
6212 Currency and deposits......................	....	....	....	....	....	....	....	....	....	....	....	....
6213 Securities other than shares...............	....	....	....	....	....	....	....	....	....	....	....	....
6214 Loans.....................................	....	....	....	....	....	....	....	....	....	....	....	....
6215 Shares and other equity...................	....	....	....	....	....	....	....	....	....	....	....	....
6216 Insurance technical reserves..............	....	....	....	....	....	....	....	....	....	....	....	....
6217 Financial derivatives.....................	....	....	....	....	....	....	....	....	....	....	....	....
6218 Other accounts receivable.................	....	....	....	....	....	....	....	....	....	....	....	....
622 Foreign...................................	....	....	....	....	....	....	....	....	....	....	....	....
6222 Currency and deposits.....................	....	....	....	....	....	....	....	....	....	....	....	....
6223 Securities other than shares..............	....	....	....	....	....	....	....	....	....	....	....	....
6224 Loans.....................................	....	....	....	....	....	....	....	....	....	....	....	....
6225 Shares and other equity...................	....	....	....	....	....	....	....	....	....	....	....	....
6226 Insurance technical reserves..............	....	....	....	....	....	....	....	....	....	....	....	....
6227 Financial derivatives.....................	....	....	....	....	....	....	....	....	....	....	....	....
6228 Other accounts receivable.................	....	....	....	....	....	....	....	....	....	....	....	....
623 Monetary gold and SDRs....................	....	....	....	....	....	....	....	....	....	....	....	....
63 **Liabilities...................................**	....	**5,652.91**	**5,656.16**	....	....	....	....	....	....	....	....	....
631 Domestic..................................	....	1,391.38	1,224.04	....	....	....	....	....	....	....	....	....
6312 Currency and deposits.....................	....	....	....	....	....	....	....	....	....	....	....	....
6313 Securities other than shares..............	....	....	....	....	....	....	....	....	....	....	....	....
6314 Loans.....................................	....	....	....	....	....	....	....	....	....	....	....	....
6316 Insurance technical reserves..............	....	....	....	....	....	....	....	....	....	....	....	....
6317 Financial derivatives.....................	....	....	....	....	....	....	....	....	....	....	....	....
6318 Other accounts payable....................	....	....	....	....	....	....	....	....	....	....	....	....
632 Foreign...................................	....	4,261.53	4,432.12	....	....	....	....	....	....	....	....	....
6322 Currency and deposits.....................	....	....	....	....	....	....	....	....	....	....	....	....
6323 Securities other than shares..............	....	....	....	....	....	....	....	....	....	....	....	....
6324 Loans.....................................	....	....	....	....	....	....	....	....	....	....	....	....
6326 Insurance technical reserves..............	....	....	....	....	....	....	....	....	....	....	....	....
6327 Financial derivatives.....................	....	....	....	....	....	....	....	....	....	....	....	....
6328 Other accounts payable....................	....	....	....	....	....	....	....	....	....	....	....	....
Memorandum items:												
6M2 Net financial worth............................	....	....	....	....	....	....	....	....	....	....	....	....
6M3 Debt at market value...........................	....	....	....	....	....	....	....	....	....	....	....	....
6M4 Debt at nominal value..........................	....	....	....	....	....	....	....	....	....	....	....	....
6M5 Arrears..	....	....	....	....	....	....	....	....	....	....	....	....
6M6 Obligations for social security benefits...........	....	....	....	....	....	....	....	....	....	....	....	....
6M7 Contingent liabilities..........................	....	....	....	....	....	....	....	....	....	....	....	....
6M8 Uncapitalized military weapons, systems........	....	....	....	....	....	....	....	....	....	....	....	....
Table 7 Outlays by functions of govt.												
7 **Total outlays..................................**	....	**777.60**	**859.80**	....	....	....	....	....	....	....	....	....
701 **General public services.........................**	....	**360.45**	**375.22**	....	....	....	....	....	....	....	....	....
7017 Public debt transactions....................	....	168.20	166.20	....	....	....	....	....	....	....	....	....
7018 General transfers between levels of govt.......	....	....	....	....	....	....	....	....	....	....	....	....
702 **Defense..**	....	**72.54**	**81.83**	....	....	....	....	....	....	....	....	....
703 **Public order and safety.........................**	....	**28.12**	**34.02**	....	....	....	....	....	....	....	....	....

In Billions of Francs / Year Ending June 30 / Cash Reporter

		Budgetary Central Government			Central Government			Local Government			General Government		
		1997	1998	1999	1997	1998	1999	1997	1998	1999	1997	1998	1999
704	**Economic affairs**.....................	....	**49.08**	**58.74**	....	....	....	....	....	....	....	....	....
7042	Agriculture, forestry, fishing, and hunting.....	....	22.31	23.83	....	....	....	....	....	....	....	....	....
7043	Fuel and energy....................	....	—	—	....	....	....	....	....	....	....	....	....
7044	Mining, manufacturing, and construction.....	....	1.01	1.22	....	....	....	....	....	....	....	....	....
7045	Transport....................	....	23.50	29.89	....	....	....	....	....	....	....	....	....
7046	Communication....................	....	....	....	....	....	....	....	....	....	....	....	....
705	**Environmental protection**......................	....	—	—	....	....	....	....	....	....	....	....	....
706	**Housing and community amenities**........	....	**7.07**	**8.23**	....	....	....	....	....	....	....	....	....
707	**Health**....................	....	**25.45**	**29.63**	....	....	....	....	....	....	....	....	....
7072	Outpatient services....................	....	....	....	....	....	....	....	....	....	....	....	....
7073	Hospital services....................	....	....	....	....	....	....	....	....	....	....	....	....
7074	Public health services....................	....	....	....	....	....	....	....	....	....	....	....	....
708	**Recreation, culture, and religion**............	....	**5.17**	**6.30**	....	....	....	....	....	....	....	....	....
709	**Education**....................	....	**94.99**	**103.15**	....	....	....	....	....	....	....	....	....
7091	Pre-primary and primary education..............	....	....	....	....	....	....	....	....	....	....	....	....
7092	Secondary education....................	....	81.51	88.57	....	....	....	....	....	....	....	....	....
7094	Tertiary education....................	....	10.25	10.46	....	....	....	....	....	....	....	....	....
710	**Social protection**....................	....	**2.92**	**3.92**	....	....	....	....	....	....	....	....	....
7	Statistical discrepancy: Total outlays..............	....	131.81	158.76	....	....	....	....	....	....	....	....	....

Table 8 Transactions in financial assets and liabilities by sector

In Billions of Dollars / Year Beginning April 1 (except Local Government) / Cash Reporter

	Central Government			State Government			Local Government			General Government		
	2002	2003	2004p	2002	2003	2004p	2002	2003	2004p	2002	2003	2004p
Statement of government operations												
Statement of other economic flows												
Balance sheet												
6 *Net worth*.....	....	....	....	....	....	....	....	....	....	....	....	....
61 Nonfinancial assets.....	....	....	....	....	....	....	....	....	....	....	....	....
62 Financial assets.....	....	....	....	....	....	....	....	....	....	....	....	....
63 Liabilities.....	630.30	629.30	619.09	513.97	531.15	553.91	64.20	66.03	65.50	1,208.47	1,226.49	1,238.50
Statement of sources and uses of cash												
1 Cash receipts from operating activities.....	228.29	240.20	254.45	236.90	249.48	271.59	85.94	89.36	92.09	477.66	500.08	529.27
11 Taxes.....	158.78	168.37	180.43	139.39	143.25	155.11	35.36	37.20	38.37	333.53	348.82	373.91
12 Social contributions.....	55.12	58.07	58.12	11.29	12.21	12.58	—	—	—	66.41	70.28	70.70
13 Grants.....	.55	.68	.67	36.27	40.67	49.33	34.31	35.28	36.55	—	—	—
14 Other receipts.....	13.84	13.07	15.23	49.96	53.34	54.58	16.26	16.88	17.17	77.71	80.99	84.65
2 Cash payments for operating activities.....	214.17	224.15	233.25	235.16	244.14	259.98	72.93	77.21	80.11	448.79	466.55	484.47
21 Compensation of employees.....	24.17	25.30	26.36	80.95	87.14	88.70	44.39	46.85	49.26	149.51	159.29	164.32
22 Purchases of goods and services.....	18.08	18.02	17.73	50.53	52.30	62.99	20.64	22.35	22.80	87.13	90.41	101.26
24 Interest.....	22.72	21.19	20.14	23.26	23.18	23.40	3.01	2.98	2.97	48.76	47.30	46.45
25 Subsidies.....	3.56	3.99	3.61	9.85	10.74	9.38	1.56	1.70	1.76	14.97	16.43	14.74
26 Grants.....	39.34	44.92	52.58	34.44	34.39	37.80	.07	.05	.05	2.72	2.72	3.88
27 Social benefits.....	93.82	96.06	98.63	17.83	18.26	18.65	—	—	—	111.64	114.32	117.28
28 Other payments.....	12.48	14.67	14.20	18.32	18.12	19.07	3.26	3.29	3.28	34.06	36.08	36.55
CIO *Net cash inflow from oper. activities*.....	*14.12*	*16.04*	*21.21*	*1.74*	*5.34*	*11.61*	*13.01*	*12.15*	*11.98*	*28.87*	*33.53*	*44.79*
31.1 Purchases of nonfinancial assets.....	4.20	4.41	3.93	13.10	14.23	14.43	12.92	13.24	15.16	30.22	31.88	33.52
31.2 Sales of nonfinancial assets.....	.09	.18	.18	.52	.46	.54	.15	.16	.15	.76	.81	.86
31 Net cash outflow from investments in nonfinancial assets.....	4.11	4.23	3.75	12.58	13.76	13.89	12.77	13.08	15.01	29.46	31.07	32.65
CSD *Cash surplus/deficit*.....	*10.01*	*11.82*	*17.46*	*−10.84*	*−8.42*	*−2.28*	*.24*	*−.93*	*−3.03*	*−.59*	*2.46*	*12.14*
32x Net acquisition of fin assets, excl. cash.....	1.26	3.94	3.78	1.43	3.81	2.59	.04	.23	.04	2.73	7.98	6.41
321x Domestic.....	2.01	4.44	3.99	1.43	3.81	2.59	.04	.23	.04	3.47	8.48	6.62
322x Foreign.....	−.75	−.50	−.21	—	—	—	—	—	—	−.75	−.50	−.21
323 Monetary gold and SDRs.....	—	—	—	—	—	—	—	—	—	—	—	—
33 Net incurrence of liabilities.....	−10.02	−.12	−8.27	7.70	20.03	9.00	4.48	2.73	2.54	2.16	22.64	3.27
331 Domestic.....	−15.97	−.90	−12.53	17.37	26.30	17.15	4.49	2.55	1.92	5.90	27.95	6.53
332 Foreign.....	5.94	.78	4.26	−9.67	−6.27	−8.15	−.01	.18	.62	−3.74	−5.32	−3.26
NFB Net cash inflow from fin. activities.....	−11.28	−4.06	−12.05	6.27	16.22	6.41	4.44	2.50	2.50	−.57	14.66	−3.14
NCB *Net change in the stock of cash*.....	*−1.27*	*7.76*	*5.41*	*−4.57*	*7.79*	*4.12*	*4.68*	*1.57*	*−.53*	*−1.17*	*17.12*	*9.00*
Table 1 Revenue												
1 **Revenue**.....	**228.29**	**240.20**	**254.45**	**236.90**	**249.48**	**271.59**	**85.94**	**89.36**	**92.09**	**477.66**	**500.08**	**529.27**
11 **Taxes**.....	**158.78**	**168.37**	**180.43**	**139.39**	**143.25**	**155.11**	**35.36**	**37.20**	**38.37**	**333.53**	**348.82**	**373.91**
111 Taxes on income, profits, & capital gains.....	114.67	123.77	132.62	62.83	63.99	72.04	—	—	—	177.51	187.76	204.66
1111 Individuals.....	88.32	92.65	97.44	51.38	52.31	56.54	—	—	—	139.70	144.96	153.98
1112 Corporations and other enterprises.....	21.97	26.95	30.36	11.45	11.68	15.50	—	—	—	33.42	38.63	45.86
112 Taxes on payroll and workforce.....	—	—	—	8.29	8.62	8.91	—	—	—	8.29	8.62	8.91
113 Taxes on property.....	—	—	—	8.40	8.63	9.49	32.57	34.88	36.26	40.97	43.51	45.75
114 Taxes on goods and services.....	40.90	41.78	44.77	59.87	62.01	64.67	.70	.74	.75	101.48	104.53	110.19
1141 General taxes on goods and services.....	30.74	31.31	34.22	29.66	30.88	32.13	.08	.08	.08	60.48	62.27	66.43
1142 Excises.....	9.32	9.61	9.68	12.45	13.10	13.54	—	—	—	21.77	22.71	23.22
115 Taxes on int'l. trade and transactions.....	3.20	2.82	3.05	—	—	—	—	—	—	3.20	2.82	3.05
116 Other taxes.....	—	—	—	—	—	—	2.09	1.58	1.36	2.09	1.58	1.36
12 **Social contributions**.....	**55.12**	**58.07**	**58.12**	**11.29**	**12.21**	**12.58**	—	—	—	**66.41**	**70.28**	**70.70**
121 Social security contributions.....	51.06	53.83	53.87	11.29	12.21	12.58	—	—	—	62.35	66.04	66.45
122 Other social contributions.....	4.06	4.24	4.25	—	—	—	—	—	—	4.06	4.24	4.25
13 **Grants**.....	**.55**	**.68**	**.67**	**36.27**	**40.67**	**49.33**	**34.31**	**35.28**	**36.55**	—	—	—
131 From foreign governments.....	—	—	—	—	—	—	—	—	—	—	—	—
132 From international organizations.....	—	—	—	—	—	—	—	—	—	—	—	—
133 From other general government units.....	.55	.68	.67	36.27	40.67	49.33	34.31	35.28	36.55	—	—	—
14 **Other revenue**.....	**13.84**	**13.07**	**15.23**	**49.96**	**53.34**	**54.58**	**16.26**	**16.88**	**17.17**	**77.71**	**80.99**	**84.65**
Table 2 Expense by economic type												
2 **Expense**.....	**214.17**	**224.15**	**233.25**	**235.16**	**244.14**	**259.98**	**72.93**	**77.21**	**80.11**	**448.79**	**466.55**	**484.47**
21 **Compensation of employees**.....	**24.17**	**25.30**	**26.36**	**80.95**	**87.14**	**88.70**	**44.39**	**46.85**	**49.26**	**149.51**	**159.29**	**164.32**
211 Wages and salaries.....	19.03	20.04	21.23	73.84	79.61	81.16	37.56	39.62	41.60	130.44	139.26	144.00
212 Social contributions.....	5.14	5.27	5.13	7.11	7.54	7.54	6.83	7.23	7.66	19.08	20.03	20.32
22 **Use of goods and services**.....	**18.08**	**18.02**	**17.73**	**50.53**	**52.30**	**62.99**	**20.64**	**22.35**	**22.80**	**87.13**	**90.41**	**101.26**
23 **Consumption of fixed capital**.....	....	....	....	....	....	....	....	....	....	....	....	....
24 Interest.....	22.72	21.19	20.14	23.26	23.18	23.40	3.01	2.98	2.97	48.76	47.30	46.45
25 **Subsidies**.....	**3.56**	**3.99**	**3.61**	**9.85**	**10.74**	**9.38**	**1.56**	**1.70**	**1.76**	**14.97**	**16.43**	**14.74**

In Billions of Dollars / Year Beginning April 1 (except Local Government) / Cash Reporter

		Central Government 2002	2003	2004p	State Government 2002	2003	2004p	Local Government 2002	2003	2004p	General Government 2002	2003	2004p
26	Grants....................................	39.34	44.92	52.58	34.44	34.39	37.80	.07	.05	.05	2.72	2.72	3.88
261	To foreign govenments................	1.74	1.98	2.98	—	—	—	—	—	—	1.74	1.98	2.98
262	To international organizations..........	.99	.73	.89	—	—	—	—	—	—	.99	.73	.89
263	To other general government units...........	36.61	42.21	48.71	34.44	34.39	37.80	.07	.05	.05	—	—	—
2631	Current...............................	36.31	42.04	48.51	32.82	33.32	36.95	.07	.05	.05	—	—	—
2632	Capital...............................	.30	.17	.20	1.62	1.07	.85	—	—	—	—	—	—
27	Social benefits..........................	93.82	96.06	98.63	17.83	18.26	18.65	—	—	—	111.64	114.32	117.28
28	Other expense.........................	12.48	14.67	14.20	18.32	18.12	19.07	3.26	3.29	3.28	34.06	36.08	36.55
281	Property expense other than interest..........	6.78	8.79	8.77	2.04	2.25	2.13	—	—	—	8.81	11.04	10.90
282	Miscellaneous other expense................	5.70	5.89	5.43	16.28	15.87	16.94	3.26	3.29	3.28	25.25	25.04	25.64
2821	Current...............................	3.51	4.20	3.82	15.67	15.50	16.06	3.26	3.29	3.28	22.43	22.99	23.16
2822	Capital...............................	2.20	1.69	1.61	.61	.37	.88	—	—	—	2.81	2.05	2.49

Table 3   Transactions in assets and liabilities

		Central Government 2002	2003	2004p	State Government 2002	2003	2004p	Local Government 2002	2003	2004p	General Government 2002	2003	2004p
3	Change in net worth from transactns....	....	....	....	....	....	....	....	....	....	....	....	....
31	Net acquisition of nonfinancial assets...	4.11	4.23	3.75	12.58	13.76	13.89	12.77	13.08	15.01	29.46	31.07	32.65
311	Fixed assets..........................	4.11	4.23	3.75	12.58	13.76	13.89	12.77	13.08	15.01	29.46	31.07	32.65
3111	Buildings and structures...............	....	....	....	....	....	....	....	....	....	....	....	....
3112	Machinery and equipment..........	....	....	....	....	....	....	....	....	....	....	....	....
3113	Other fixed assets.................	....	....	....	....	....	....	....	....	....	....	....	....
312	Inventories............................	—	—	—	—	—	—	—	—	—	—	—	—
313	Valuables.............................	—	—	—	—	—	—	—	—	—	—	—	—
314	Nonproduced assets....................	—	—	—	—	—	—	—	—	—	—	—	—
3141	Land.................................	—	—	—	—	—	—	—	—	—	—	—	—
3142	Subsoil assets........................	—	—	—	—	—	—	—	—	—	—	—	—
3143	Other naturally occurring assets........	—	—	—	—	—	—	—	—	—	—	—	—
3144	Intangible nonproduced assets.........	—	—	—	—	—	—	—	—	—	—	—	—
32	Net acquisition of financial assets........	−.01	11.70	9.18	−3.14	11.60	6.72	4.71	1.80	−.49	1.56	25.10	15.41
321	Domestic.............................	1.08	12.41	9.40	−3.14	11.60	6.72	4.71	1.80	−.49	2.65	25.81	15.63
3212	Currency and deposits................	−.93	7.97	5.42	−4.57	7.79	4.12	4.68	1.57	−.53	−.82	17.33	9.01
3213	Securities other than shares..........	....	....	....	....	....	....	....	....	....	....	....	....
3214	Loans...............................	....	....	....	....	....	....	....	....	....	....	....	....
3215	Shares and other equity..............	....	....	....	....	....	....	....	....	....	....	....	....
3216	Insurance technical reserves..........	....	....	....	....	....	....	....	....	....	....	....	....
3217	Financial derivatives.................	....	....	....	....	....	....	....	....	....	....	....	....
3218	Other accounts receivable............	....	....	....	....	....	....	....	....	....	....	....	....
322	Foreign..............................	−1.09	−.71	−.22	—	—	—	—	—	—	−1.09	−.71	−.22
3222	Currency and deposits................	−.34	−.21	−.01	—	—	—	—	—	—	−.34	−.21	−.01
3223	Securities other than shares..........	....	....	....	—	—	—	—	—	—	....	....	....
3224	Loans...............................	....	....	....	—	—	—	—	—	—	....	....	....
3225	Shares and other equity..............	....	....	....	—	—	—	—	—	—	....	....	....
3226	Insurance technical reserves..........	....	....	....	—	—	—	—	—	—	....	....	....
3227	Financial derivatives.................	....	....	....	—	—	—	—	—	—	....	....	....
3228	Other accounts receivable............	....	....	....	....	....	....	....	....	....	....	....	....
323	Monetary gold and SDRs..............	....	....	....	....	....	....	....	....	....	....	....	....
33	Net incurrence of liabilities.................	−10.02	−.12	−8.27	7.70	20.03	9.00	4.48	2.73	2.54	2.16	22.64	3.27
331	Domestic.............................	−15.97	−.90	−12.53	17.37	26.30	17.15	4.49	2.55	1.92	5.90	27.95	6.53
3312	Currency and deposits................	—	—	—	—	—	—	—	—	—	—	—	—
3313	Securities other than shares...........	−3.25	2.72	.75	−18.68	−16.35	−44.82	−3.73	2.45	−.41	−25.66	−11.18	−44.48
3314	Loans...............................	−3.90	−4.58	−15.57	36.05	42.65	61.97	8.22	.10	2.32	40.37	38.17	48.72
3316	Insurance technical reserves..........	....	....	....	—	—	—	—	—	—	....	....	....
3317	Financial derivatives.................	....	....	....	—	—	—	—	—	—	....	....	....
3318	Other accounts payable..............	....	....	....	....	....	....	....	....	....	....	....	....
332	Foreign..............................	5.94	.78	4.26	−9.67	−6.27	−8.15	−.01	.18	.62	−3.74	−5.32	−3.26
3322	Currency and deposits................	—	—	—	....	....	....	....	....	....	....	....	....
3323	Securities other than shares..........	5.99	.79	4.13	....	....	....	....	....	....	....	....	....
3324	Loans...............................	−.04	−.01	.13	....	....	....	....	....	....	....	....	....
3326	Insurance technical reserves..........	—	—	—	....	....	....	....	....	....	....	....	....
3327	Financial derivatives.................	—	—	—	....	....	....	....	....	....	....	....	....
3328	Other accounts payable..............	....	....	....	....	....	....	....	....	....	....	....	....

In Billions of Dollars / Year Beginning April 1 (except Local Government) / Cash Reporter

	Central Government			State Government			Local Government			General Government		
	2002	2003	2004p	2002	2003	2004p	2002	2003	2004p	2002	2003	2004p
Table 4 Holding gains in assets and liabilities												
Table 5 Other changes in the volume of assets and liabilities												
Table 6 Balance sheet												
6 **Net worth**............................	....	....	....	....	....	....	....	....	....	....	....	....
61 **Nonfinancial assets**..............................	....	....	....	....	....	....	....	....	....	....	....	....
611 Fixed assets............................	....	....	....	....	....	....	....	....	....	....	....	....
6111 Buildings and structures....................	....	....	....	....	....	....	....	....	....	....	....	....
6112 Machinery and equipment.....................	....	....	....	....	....	....	....	....	....	....	....	....
6113 Other fixed assets........................	....	....	....	....	....	....	....	....	....	....	....	....
612 Inventories...............................	....	....	....	....	....	....	....	....	....	....	....	....
613 Valuables................................	....	....	....	....	....	....	....	....	....	....	....	....
614 Nonproduced assets......................	....	....	....	....	....	....	....	....	....	....	....	....
6141 Land..................................	....	....	....	....	....	....	....	....	....	....	....	....
6142 Subsoil assets..........................	....	....	....	....	....	....	....	....	....	....	....	....
6143 Other naturally occurring assets...........	....	....	....	....	....	....	....	....	....	....	....	....
6144 Intangible nonproduced assets..............	....	....	....	....	....	....	....	....	....	....	....	....
62 **Financial assets**............................	....	....	....	....	....	....	....	....	....	....	....	....
621 Domestic...............................	....	....	....	....	....	....	....	....	....	....	....	....
6212 Currency and deposits....................	....	....	....	....	....	....	....	....	....	....	....	....
6213 Securities other than shares..............	....	....	....	....	....	....	....	....	....	....	....	....
6214 Loans.................................	....	....	....	....	....	....	....	....	....	....	....	....
6215 Shares and other equity..................	....	....	....	....	....	....	....	....	....	....	....	....
6216 Insurance technical reserves..............	....	....	....	....	....	....	....	....	....	....	....	....
6217 Financial derivatives.....................	....	....	....	....	....	....	....	....	....	....	....	....
6218 Other accounts receivable................	....	....	....	....	....	....	....	....	....	....	....	....
622 Foreign................................	....	....	....	....	....	....	....	....	....	....	....	....
6222 Currency and deposits....................	....	....	....	....	....	....	....	....	....	....	....	....
6223 Securities other than shares..............	....	....	....	....	....	....	....	....	....	....	....	....
6224 Loans.................................	....	....	....	....	....	....	....	....	....	....	....	....
6225 Shares and other equity..................	....	....	....	....	....	....	....	....	....	....	....	....
6226 Insurance technical reserves..............	....	....	....	....	....	....	....	....	....	....	....	....
6227 Financial derivatives.....................	....	....	....	....	....	....	....	....	....	....	....	....
6228 Other accounts receivable................	....	....	....	....	....	....	....	....	....	....	....	....
623 Monetary gold and SDRs...................	....	....	....	....	....	....	....	....	....	....	....	....
63 **Liabilities**................................	630.30	629.30	619.09	513.97	531.15	553.91	64.20	66.03	65.50	1,208.47	1,226.49	1,238.50
631 Domestic...............................	608.01	607.86	608.52	471.54	492.81	523.54	63.59	65.24	64.10	1,143.14	1,165.90	1,196.16
6312 Currency and deposits....................	....	....	....	....	....	....	....	....	....	....	....	....
6313 Securities other than shares..............	....	....	....	....	....	....	....	....	....	....	....	....
6314 Loans.................................	....	....	....	....	....	....	....	....	....	....	....	....
6316 Insurance technical reserves..............	....	....	....	....	....	....	....	....	....	....	....	....
6317 Financial derivatives.....................	....	....	....	....	....	....	....	....	....	....	....	....
6318 Other accounts payable..................	....	....	....	....	....	....	....	....	....	....	....	....
632 Foreign................................	22.28	21.45	10.57	42.43	38.34	30.37	.61	.79	1.41	65.32	60.58	42.34
6322 Currency and deposits....................	....	....	....	....	....	....	....	....	....	....	....	....
6323 Securities other than shares..............	....	....	....	....	....	....	....	....	....	....	....	....
6324 Loans.................................	....	....	....	....	....	....	....	....	....	....	....	....
6326 Insurance technical reserves..............	....	....	....	....	....	....	....	....	....	....	....	....
6327 Financial derivatives.....................	....	....	....	....	....	....	....	....	....	....	....	....
6328 Other accounts payable..................	....	....	....	....	....	....	....	....	....	....	....	....
Memorandum items:												
6M2 Net financial worth......................	....	....	....	....	....	....	....	....	....	....	....	....
6M3 Debt at market value....................	....	....	....	....	....	....	....	....	....	....	....	....
6M4 Debt at nominal value....................	....	....	....	....	....	....	....	....	....	....	....	....
6M5 Arrears................................	....	....	....	....	....	....	....	....	....	....	....	....
6M6 Obligations for social security benefits...........	....	....	....	....	....	....	....	....	....	....	....	....
6M7 Contingent liabilities.....................	....	....	....	....	....	....	....	....	....	....	....	....
6M8 Uncapitalized military weapons, systems........	....	....	....	....	....	....	....	....	....	....	....	....
Table 7 Outlays by functions of govt.												
7 **Total outlays**..........................	218.37	228.56	237.18	248.26	258.37	274.41	85.86	90.45	95.27	479.01	498.43	517.99
701 **General public services**......................	67.33	66.36	57.56	30.78	31.37	31.75	7.55	7.85	7.91	73.73	72.69	71.65
7017 Public debt transactions....................	22.72	21.19	20.14	23.26	23.18	23.40	3.01	2.98	2.97	48.76	47.30	46.45
7018 General transfers between levels of govt.......	28.94	29.63	21.99	1.28	1.35	1.75	—	—	—	—	—	—
702 **Defense**................................	12.99	13.47	14.06	—	—	—	—	—	—	12.98	13.45	14.04
703 **Public order and safety**........................	6.86	7.62	8.77	7.41	9.55	9.94	7.89	8.36	8.88	21.04	24.26	26.49

In Billions of Dollars / Year Beginning April 1 (except Local Government) / Cash Reporter

		Central Government			State Government			Local Government			General Government		
		2002	2003	2004p	2002	2003	2004p	2002	2003	2004p	2002	2003	2004p
704	**Economic affairs**................................	**14.07**	**15.80**	**14.08**	**23.71**	**21.03**	**22.81**	**10.91**	**11.71**	**12.23**	**45.04**	**44.87**	**45.61**
7042	Agriculture, forestry, fishing, and hunting.....	4.10	5.67	4.23	7.00	.18	.60	.18	.18	.16	9.84	5.06	4.36
7043	Fuel and energy...............................	.18	.26	.43	.19	—	—	—	—	—	.29	.08	.28
7044	Mining, manufacturing, and construction.....	—	—	—	.21	—	—	—	—	—	.21	—	—
7045	Transport....................................	2.01	1.99	2.05	9.04	9.21	10.37	9.52	10.22	10.80	18.97	19.54	21.18
7046	Communication...............................	.22	.18	.26	.26	—	—	—	—	—	.48	.18	.25
705	**Environmental protection**....................	**1.39**	**1.48**	**1.61**	**1.18**	**1.80**	**1.87**	**4.62**	**4.99**	**5.92**	**6.93**	**7.82**	**8.90**
706	**Housing and community amenities**........	**2.78**	**2.93**	**2.88**	**3.38**	**3.19**	**3.32**	**5.89**	**6.38**	**7.23**	**9.37**	**9.83**	**10.75**
707	**Health**......................................	**3.51**	**6.81**	**22.38**	**79.02**	**85.50**	**92.80**	**1.30**	**1.41**	**1.38**	**82.53**	**89.29**	**96.16**
7072	Outpatient services...........................	.51	.69	.74	34.34	36.80	39.46	—	—	—	34.75	37.22	39.52
7073	Hospital services.............................	.07	1.58	4.36	27.74	30.47	33.41	.09	.08	.06	27.88	30.59	33.55
7074	Public health services.........................	.81	.83	1.20	2.40	2.64	2.78	.61	.64	.65	3.54	3.83	4.36
708	**Recreation, culture, and religion**..........	**3.64**	**4.05**	**4.09**	**2.43**	**2.60**	**2.75**	**6.07**	**6.68**	**6.83**	**11.96**	**13.11**	**13.45**
709	**Education**...................................	**4.99**	**5.18**	**4.94**	**58.29**	**60.31**	**64.02**	**36.26**	**37.44**	**39.24**	**70.16**	**72.68**	**76.50**
7091	Pre-primary and primary education..............	....	....	....	....	....	....	....	....	....	....	....	....
7092	Secondary education..........................	....	....	....	....	....	....	....	....	....	....	....	....
7094	Tertiary education............................	1.43	1.52	1.43	26.14	26.94	28.64	.05	.03	.03	27.09	28.01	29.61
710	**Social protection**............................	**100.82**	**104.87**	**106.80**	**42.05**	**43.03**	**45.15**	**5.38**	**5.62**	**5.66**	**145.27**	**150.42**	**154.43**
7	Statistical discrepancy: Total outlays..............	—	—	—	—	—	—	—	—	—	—	—	—

Table 8   Transactions in financial assets and liabilities by sector

		Central Government			State Government			Local Government			General Government		
82	**Net acquisition of financial assets**........	**−.01**	**11.70**	**9.18**	**−3.14**	**11.60**	**6.72**	**4.71**	**1.80**	**−.49**	**1.56**	**25.10**	**15.41**
821	Domestic....................................	1.08	12.41	9.40	−3.14	11.60	6.72	4.71	1.80	−.49	2.65	25.81	15.63
8211	General government...........................	....	....	....	....	....	....	....	....	....	....	....	....
8212	Central bank.................................	....	....	....	....	....	....	....	....	....	....	....	....
8213	Other depository corporations.................	....	....	....	....	....	....	....	....	....	....	....	....
8214	Financial corporations n.e.c...................	....	....	....	....	....	....	....	....	....	....	....	....
8215	Nonfinancial corporations.....................	....	....	....	....	....	....	....	....	....	....	....	....
8216	Households & NPIs serving households......	....	....	....	....	....	....	....	....	....	....	....	....
822	Foreign.....................................	−1.09	−.71	−.22	—	—	—	—	—	—	−1.09	−.71	−.22
8221	General government...........................	....	....	....	—	—	—	—	—	—	....	....	....
8227	International organizations.....................	....	....	....	—	—	—	—	—	—	....	....	....
8228	Financial corporations other than international organizations...........	....	....	....	—	—	—	—	—	—	....	....	....
8229	Other nonresidents...........................	....	....	....	—	—	—	—	—	—	....	....	....
823	Monetary gold and SDRs......................	—	—	—	—	—	—	—	—	—	—	—	—
83	**Net incurrence of liabilities**..................	**−10.02**	**−.12**	**−8.27**	**7.70**	**20.03**	**9.00**	**4.48**	**2.73**	**2.54**	**2.16**	**22.64**	**3.27**
831	Domestic....................................	−15.97	−.90	−12.53	17.37	26.30	17.15	4.49	2.55	1.92	5.90	27.95	6.53
8311	General government...........................	....	....	....	....	....	....	....	....	....	....	....	....
8312	Central bank.................................	....	....	....	....	....	....	....	....	....	....	....	....
8313	Other depository corporations.................	....	....	....	....	....	....	....	....	....	....	....	....
8314	Financial corporations n.e.c...................	....	....	....	....	....	....	....	....	....	....	....	....
8315	Nonfinancial corporations.....................	....	....	....	....	....	....	....	....	....	....	....	....
8316	Households & NPIs serving households......	....	....	....	....	....	....	....	....	....	....	....	....
832	Foreign.....................................	5.94	.78	4.26	−9.67	−6.27	−8.15	−.01	.18	.62	−3.74	−5.32	−3.26
8321	General government...........................	....	....	....	....	....	....	....	....	....	....	....	....
8327	International organizations.....................	....	....	....	....	....	....	....	....	....	....	....	....
8328	Financial corporations other than international organizations.............	....	....	....	....	....	....	....	....	....	....	....	....
8329	Other nonresidents...........................	....	....	....	....	....	....	....	....	....	....	....	....

Chile 228

In Billions of Pesos / Year Ending December 31 / Noncash Reporter

	Budgetary Central Government			Central Government			Local Government			General Government		
	2002	2003	2004	2002	2003	2004	2002	2003	2004	2002	2003	2004
Statement of government operations												
1 Revenue..........	9,592.3	10,418.8	12,455.7	9,770.8	10,604.4	12,798.4	1,513.5	1,584.6	1,585.1	10,765.6	11,667.6	13,879.9
2 Expense..........	8,879.4	9,408.3	10,029.1	9,331.7	9,820.7	10,534.2	1,315.4	1,388.8	1,388.1	10,128.4	10,688.1	11,418.6
GOB *Gross operating balance......*	*712.9*	*1,010.5*	*2,426.6*	*439.1*	*783.7*	*2,264.2*	*198.1*	*195.8*	*197.1*	*637.2*	*979.5*	*2,461.2*
NOB *Net operating balance......*	....	....	....	....	....	....	....	....	....	....	....	....
31 Net acquisition of nonfinancial assets.......	1,013.3	1,001.8	1,030.8	1,013.3	1,001.8	1,030.8	190.2	185.2	203.1	1,203.5	1,187.0	1,233.9
NLB *Net lending/borrowing......*	*−300.4*	*8.7*	*1,395.8*	*−574.2*	*−218.1*	*1,233.3*	*7.9*	*10.7*	*−6.0*	*−566.3*	*−207.5*	*1,227.3*
32 Net acquisition of financial assets.......	−730.2	−184.1	621.5	−747.9	−200.4	789.6	7.8	10.6	−5.0	−740.1	−189.8	784.6
33 Net incurrence of liabilities.......	−429.9	−192.8	−774.3	−173.7	17.7	−443.8	—	—	1.0	−173.8	17.7	−442.8
NLB Statistical discrepancy.......	—	—	—	—	—	—	—	—	—	—	—	—
Statement of other economic flows												
Balance sheet												
Statement of sources and uses of cash												
1 Cash receipts from operating activities.......	9,592.3	10,403.5	12,455.7	9,770.8	10,589.1	12,798.4	1,513.5	1,584.6	1,585.1	10,765.6	11,652.3	13,879.9
11 Taxes.......	7,709.0	8,117.3	9,111.8	7,727.9	8,121.7	9,112.3	723.1	788.2	795.0	8,450.9	8,910.0	9,907.4
12 Social contributions.......	678.9	728.0	827.6	678.9	728.0	827.6	—	—	—	678.9	728.0	827.6
13 Grants.......	3.6	3.5	3.2	3.6	3.5	3.2	515.1	517.8	500.5	—	—	—
14 Other receipts.......	1,200.8	1,554.7	2,513.1	1,360.4	1,735.8	2,855.2	275.4	278.6	289.6	1,635.8	2,014.4	3,144.9
2 Cash payments for operating activities.......	8,795.2	9,393.1	10,029.1	8,933.9	9,494.4	10,231.9	1,315.4	1,388.8	1,388.1	9,730.6	10,361.8	11,116.3
21 Compensation of employees.......	2,011.1	2,131.3	2,301.6	2,011.1	2,131.3	2,301.6	773.5	806.2	796.3	2,784.6	2,937.5	3,098.0
22 Purchases of goods and services.......	713.4	764.9	803.2	831.5	834.9	999.0	387.4	419.9	416.4	1,219.0	1,254.8	1,415.4
24 Interest.......	135.1	270.0	254.8	142.0	277.8	258.3				142.0	277.8	258.3
25 Subsidies.......	2,189.5	2,283.1	2,499.0	2,203.1	2,306.7	2,502.6	126.3	135.1	144.8	2,329.4	2,441.7	2,647.4
26 Grants.......	515.1	517.8	500.5	515.1	517.8	500.5	3.6	3.5	3.2	—	—	—
27 Social benefits.......	2,570.6	2,690.3	2,824.9	2,570.6	2,690.3	2,824.9	4.5	1.2	.6	2,575.1	2,691.5	2,825.5
28 Other payments.......	660.5	735.7	845.1	660.5	735.7	845.1	20.0	22.9	26.8	680.6	758.6	871.9
CIO *Net cash inflow from oper. activities....*	*797.1*	*1,010.5*	*2,426.6*	*836.9*	*1,094.7*	*2,566.4*	*198.1*	*195.8*	*197.1*	*1,035.0*	*1,290.5*	*2,763.5*
31.1 Purchases of nonfinancial assets.......	1,032.5	1,013.1	1,051.7	1,032.5	1,013.1	1,051.7	199.0	195.6	216.4	1,231.5	1,208.7	1,268.1
31.2 Sales of nonfinancial assets.......	19.2	11.3	20.9	19.2	11.3	20.9	8.7	10.4	13.3	28.0	21.7	34.2
31 Net cash outflow from investments in nonfinancial assets.......	1,013.3	1,001.8	1,030.8	1,013.3	1,001.8	1,030.8	190.2	185.2	203.1	1,203.5	1,187.0	1,233.9
CSD *Cash surplus/deficit.......*	*−216.2*	*8.7*	*1,395.8*	*−176.4*	*92.9*	*1,535.6*	*7.9*	*10.7*	*−6.0*	*−168.5*	*103.6*	*1,529.6*
32x Net acquisition of fin assets, excl. cash.......	−128.2	90.2	570.0	−130.3	88.2	568.4	2.9	2.9	6.4	−127.4	91.1	574.8
321x Domestic.......	−128.2	90.2	570.0	−130.3	88.2	568.4	2.9	2.9	6.4	−127.4	91.1	574.8
322x Foreign.......	—	—	—	—	—	—	—	—	—	—	—	—
323 Monetary gold and SDRs.......	—	—	—	—	—	—	—	—	—	—	—	—
33 Net incurrence of liabilities.......	−429.9	−192.8	−774.3	−487.3	−293.3	−746.1	—	—	1.0	−487.3	−293.3	−745.0
331 Domestic.......	−880.2	−782.6	−867.5	−880.2	−782.6	−867.5	—	—	1.0	−880.3	−782.7	−866.5
332 Foreign.......	450.4	589.9	93.3	393.0	489.3	121.5	—	—	—	393.0	489.3	121.5
NFB Net cash inflow from fin. activities.......	−301.7	−283.0	−1,344.3	−357.0	−381.5	−1,314.4	−2.9	−2.9	−5.4	−359.9	−384.5	−1,319.8
NCB *Net change in the stock of cash.......*	*−517.8*	*−274.3*	*51.5*	*−533.4*	*−288.6*	*221.2*	*4.9*	*7.7*	*−11.4*	*−528.5*	*−280.9*	*209.8*
Table 1 Revenue												
1 **Revenue.......**	**9,592.3**	**10,418.8**	**12,455.7**	**9,770.8**	**10,604.4**	**12,798.4**	**1,513.5**	**1,584.6**	**1,585.1**	**10,765.6**	**11,667.6**	**13,879.9**
11 **Taxes.......**	**7,709.0**	**8,117.3**	**9,111.8**	**7,727.9**	**8,121.7**	**9,112.3**	**723.1**	**788.2**	**795.0**	**8,450.9**	**8,910.0**	**9,907.4**
111 Taxes on income, profits, & capital gains......	2,138.5	2,197.1	2,343.7	2,138.5	2,197.1	2,343.7	—	—	—	2,138.5	2,197.1	2,343.7
1111 Individuals.......	....	....	....	....	....	....	—	—	—	....	....	....
1112 Corporations and other enterprises.......	....	....	....	....	....	....	—	—	—	....	....	....
112 Taxes on payroll and workforce.......	—	—	—	—	—	—	—	—	—	—	—	—
113 Taxes on property.......	—	—	—	—	—	—	326.9	365.0	358.9	326.9	365.0	358.9
114 Taxes on goods and services.......	4,782.6	5,185.4	5,801.9	4,801.5	5,189.8	5,802.4	424.3	456.5	470.8	5,225.8	5,646.3	6,273.2
1141 General taxes on goods and services.......	3,728.5	4,096.8	4,693.2	3,728.5	4,096.8	4,693.2	—	—	—	3,728.5	4,096.8	4,693.2
1142 Excises.......	1,054.2	1,088.6	1,108.7	1,073.0	1,093.0	1,109.2	—	—	—	1,073.0	1,093.0	1,109.2
115 Taxes on int'l. trade and transactions.......	436.6	317.4	259.9	436.6	317.4	259.9	—	—	—	436.6	317.4	259.9
116 Other taxes.......	351.3	417.5	706.2	351.3	417.5	706.2	−28.1	−33.3	−34.7	323.2	384.2	671.6
12 **Social contributions.......**	**678.9**	**728.0**	**827.6**	**678.9**	**728.0**	**827.6**	**—**	**—**	**—**	**678.9**	**728.0**	**827.6**
121 Social security contributions.......	678.9	728.0	827.6	678.9	728.0	827.6	—	—	—	678.9	728.0	827.6
122 Other social contributions.......	—	—	—	—	—	—	—	—	—	—	—	—
13 **Grants.......**	**3.6**	**3.5**	**3.2**	**3.6**	**3.5**	**3.2**	**515.1**	**517.8**	**500.5**	**—**	**—**	**—**
131 From foreign governments.......	—	—	—	—	—	—	—	—	—	—	—	—
132 From international organizations.......	—	—	—	—	—	—	—	—	—	—	—	—
133 From other general government units.......	3.6	3.5	3.2	3.6	3.5	3.2	515.1	517.8	500.5	—	—	—
14 **Other revenue.......**	**1,200.8**	**1,570.0**	**2,513.1**	**1,360.4**	**1,751.1**	**2,855.2**	**275.4**	**278.6**	**289.6**	**1,635.8**	**2,029.7**	**3,144.9**

Chile   228

In Billions of Pesos / Year Ending December 31 / Noncash Reporter

	Budgetary Central Government			Central Government			Local Government			General Government		
	2002	2003	2004	2002	2003	2004	2002	2003	2004	2002	2003	2004
Table 2 Expense by economic type												
2 Expense..............................	8,879.4	9,408.3	10,029.1	9,331.7	9,820.7	10,534.2	1,315.4	1,388.8	1,388.1	10,128.4	10,688.1	11,418.6
21 Compensation of employees..................	2,011.1	2,131.3	2,301.6	2,011.1	2,131.3	2,301.6	773.5	806.2	796.3	2,784.6	2,937.5	3,098.0
211 Wages and salaries..................	2,011.1	2,131.3	2,301.6	2,011.1	2,131.3	2,301.6	773.5	806.2	796.3	2,784.6	2,937.5	3,098.0
212 Social contributions..................	—	—	—	—	—	—	—	—	—	—	—	—
22 Use of goods and services..................	713.4	764.9	803.2	831.5	834.9	999.0	387.4	419.9	416.4	1,219.0	1,254.8	1,415.4
23 Consumption of fixed capital..................	....	....	....	....	....	....	....	....	....			
24 Interest..................	219.3	270.0	254.8	539.8	588.8	560.6	—	—	—	539.8	588.8	560.6
25 Subsidies..................	2,189.5	2,283.1	2,499.0	2,203.1	2,306.7	2,502.6	126.3	135.1	144.8	2,329.4	2,441.7	2,647.4
26 Grants..................	515.1	517.8	500.5	515.1	517.8	500.5	3.6	3.5	3.2	—	—	—
261 To foreign govenments..................	—	—	—	—	—	—	—	—	—	—	—	—
262 To international organizations..................	—	—	—	—	—	—	—	—	—	—	—	—
263 To other general government units..................	515.1	517.8	500.5	515.1	517.8	500.5	3.6	3.5	3.2			
2631 Current..................	454.1	467.1	453.6	454.1	467.1	453.6	3.6	3.5	3.2			
2632 Capital..................	61.0	50.7	46.9	61.0	50.7	46.9	—	—	—			
27 Social benefits..................	2,570.6	2,705.6	2,824.9	2,570.6	2,705.6	2,824.9	4.5	1.2	.6	2,575.1	2,706.8	2,825.5
28 Other expense..................	660.5	735.7	845.1	660.5	735.7	845.1	20.0	22.9	26.8	680.6	758.6	871.9
281 Property expense other than interest..................	—	—	—	—	—	—	—	—	—	—	—	—
282 Miscellaneous other expense..................	660.5	735.7	845.1	660.5	735.7	845.1	20.0	22.9	26.8	680.6	758.6	871.9
2821 Current..................	91.4	82.5	77.9	91.4	82.5	77.9	15.6	17.3	20.7	107.0	99.9	98.6
2822 Capital..................	569.1	653.2	767.2	569.1	653.2	767.2	4.5	5.6	6.1	573.6	658.7	773.3
Table 3 Transactions in assets and liabilities												
3 Change in net worth from transactns....	....	....	....	....	....	....	....	....	....	....	....	....
31 Net acquisition of nonfinancial assets...	1,013.3	1,001.8	1,030.8	1,013.3	1,001.8	1,030.8	190.2	185.2	203.1	1,203.5	1,187.0	1,233.9
311 Fixed assets..................	1,013.3	1,001.8	1,030.8	1,013.3	1,001.8	1,030.8	190.2	185.2	203.1	1,203.5	1,187.0	1,233.9
3111 Buildings and structures..................	....	....	....	....	....	....	....	....	....	....	....	....
3112 Machinery and equipment..................	....	....	....	....	....	....	....	....	....	....	....	....
3113 Other fixed assets..................	....	....	....	....	....	....	....	....	....	....	....	....
312 Inventories..................	—	—	—	—	—	—	—	—	—	—	—	—
313 Valuables..................	—	—	—	—	—	—	—	—	—	—	—	—
314 Nonproduced assets..................	—	—	—	—	—	—	—	—	—	—	—	—
3141 Land..................	—	—	—	—	—	—	—	—	—	—	—	—
3142 Subsoil assets..................	—	—	—	—	—	—	—	—	—	—	—	—
3143 Other naturally occurring assets..................	—	—	—	—	—	—	—	—	—	—	—	—
3144 Intangible nonproduced assets..................	—	—	—	—	—	—	—	—	—	—	—	—
32 Net acquisition of financial assets..................	−730.2	−184.1	621.5	−747.9	−200.4	789.6	7.8	10.6	−5.0	−740.1	−189.8	784.6
321 Domestic..................	−730.2	−184.1	621.5	−747.9	−200.4	789.6	7.8	10.6	−5.0	−740.1	−189.8	784.6
3212 Currency and deposits..................	−517.8	−274.3	51.5	−533.4	−288.6	221.2	4.9	7.7	−11.4	−528.5	−280.9	209.8
3213 Securities other than shares..................	−112.2	124.7	555.3	−112.2	124.7	555.3	1.8	3.7	8.4	−110.4	128.4	563.8
3214 Loans..................	−16.0	−34.5	14.7	−18.1	−36.5	13.0	1.1	−.8	−2.0	−17.0	−37.3	11.0
3215 Shares and other equity..................	—	—	—	—	—	—	—	—	—	—	—	—
3216 Insurance technical reserves..................	—	—	—	—	—	—	—	—	—	—	—	—
3217 Financial derivatives..................	—	—	—	—	—	—	—	—	—	—	—	—
3218 Other accounts receivable..................	−84.2	—	—	−84.2	—	—	—	—	—	−84.2	—	—
322 Foreign..................	—	—	—	—	—	—	—	—	—	—	—	—
3222 Currency and deposits..................	—	—	—	—	—	—	—	—	—	—	—	—
3223 Securities other than shares..................	—	—	—	—	—	—	—	—	—	—	—	—
3224 Loans..................	—	—	—	—	—	—	—	—	—	—	—	—
3225 Shares and other equity..................	—	—	—	—	—	—	—	—	—	—	—	—
3226 Insurance technical reserves..................	—	—	—	—	—	—	—	—	—	—	—	—
3227 Financial derivatives..................	—	—	—	—	—	—	—	—	—	—	—	—
3228 Other accounts receivable..................	—	—	—	—	—	—	—	—	—	—	—	—
323 Monetary gold and SDRs..................	—	—	—	—	—	—	—	—	—	—	—	—
33 Net incurrence of liabilities..................	−429.9	−192.8	−774.3	−173.7	17.7	−443.8	—	—	1.0	−173.8	17.7	−442.8
331 Domestic..................	−880.2	−782.6	−867.5	−566.7	−471.6	−565.3	—	—	1.0	−566.7	−471.6	−564.2
3312 Currency and deposits..................	—	—	—	—	—	—	—	—	—	—	—	—
3313 Securities other than shares..................	−487.4	−573.2	−649.0	−173.8	−262.2	−346.7	—	—	—	−173.8	−262.2	−346.7
3314 Loans..................	−392.9	−209.4	−218.6	−392.9	−209.4	−218.6	—	—	1.0	−392.9	−209.5	−217.5
3316 Insurance technical reserves..................	—	—	—	—	—	—	—	—	—	—	—	—
3317 Financial derivatives..................	—	—	—	—	—	—	—	—	—	—	—	—
3318 Other accounts payable..................	—	—	—	—	—	—	—	—	—	—	—	—

2005, International Monetary Fund: *Government Finance Statistics Yearbook*

In Billions of Pesos / Year Ending December 31 / Noncash Reporter

		Budgetary Central Government			Central Government			Local Government			General Government		
		2002	2003	2004	2002	2003	2004	2002	2003	2004	2002	2003	2004
332	Foreign..................................	450.4	589.9	93.3	393.0	489.3	121.5	—	—	—	393.0	489.3	121.5
3322	Currency and deposits..........................	—	—	—	—	—	—	—	—	—	—	—	—
3323	Securities other than shares..................	—	—	—	—	—	—	—	—	—	—	—	—
3324	Loans..	450.4	589.9	93.3	393.0	489.3	121.5	—	—	—	393.0	489.3	121.5
3326	Insurance technical reserves.................	—	—	—	—	—	—	—	—	—	—	—	—
3327	Financial derivatives.........................	—	—	—	—	—	—	—	—	—	—	—	—
3328	Other accounts payable........................	—	—	—	—	—	—	—	—	—	—	—	—

Table 4 Holding gains in assets and liabilities

Table 5 Other changes in the volume of assets and liabilities

Table 6 Balance sheet

Table 7 Outlays by functions of govt.

		Budgetary Central Government			Central Government			Local Government			General Government		
		2002	2003	2004	2002	2003	2004	2002	2003	2004	2002	2003	2004
7	**Total outlays..........................**	**9,911.9**	**10,421.5**	**11,080.8**	**10,364.2**	**10,833.8**	**11,585.9**	....	....	....	....	....	....
701	**General public services.....................**	**707.7**	**746.4**	**798.6**	**1,028.1**	**1,065.2**	**1,104.4**	....	....	....	....	....	....
7017	Public debt transactions.......................	219.3	270.0	254.8	539.8	588.8	560.6	....	....	....	....	....	....
7018	General transfers between levels of govt......	....	....	....	....	....	....	....	....	....	....	....	....
702	**Defense.................................**	**613.4**	**612.3**	**620.7**	**731.5**	**682.3**	**816.4**	....	....	....	....	....	....
703	**Public order and safety.................**	**611.2**	**670.2**	**727.2**	**611.2**	**670.2**	**727.2**	....	....	....	....	....	....
704	**Economic affairs.......................**	**1,263.7**	**1,326.4**	**1,401.4**	**1,277.3**	**1,349.9**	**1,405.0**	....	....	....	....	....	....
7042	Agriculture, forestry, fishing, and hunting.....	147.5	149.2	149.6	147.5	149.2	149.6	....	....	....	....	....	....
7043	Fuel and energy...............................	18.8	23.7	22.4	32.5	47.3	26.0	....	....	....	....	....	....
7044	Mining, manufacturing, and construction.....	18.1	17.2	15.3	18.1	17.2	15.3	....	....	....	....	....	....
7045	Transport.....................................	760.9	850.5	910.9	760.9	850.5	910.9	....	....	....	....	....	....
7046	Communication................................	5.0	5.5	5.5	5.0	5.5	5.5	....	....	....	....	....	....
705	**Environmental protection.................**	**39.4**	**35.9**	**38.0**	**39.4**	**35.9**	**38.0**	....	....	....	....	....	....
706	**Housing and community amenities........**	**90.9**	**93.8**	**130.2**	**90.9**	**93.8**	**130.2**	....	....	....	....	....	....
707	**Health.................................**	**1,390.4**	**1,515.3**	**1,620.9**	**1,390.4**	**1,515.3**	**1,620.9**	....	....	....	....	....	....
7072	Outpatient services...........................	—	—	—	—	—	—	....	....	....	....	....	....
7073	Hospital services.............................	1,047.3	1,135.3	1,218.8	1,047.3	1,135.3	1,218.8	....	....	....	....	....	....
7074	Public health services........................	54.9	57.6	59.8	54.9	57.6	59.8	....	....	....	....	....	....
708	**Recreation, culture, and religion...........**	**66.8**	**69.9**	**73.2**	**66.8**	**69.9**	**73.2**	....	....	....	....	....	....
709	**Education...............................**	**1,849.3**	**1,928.5**	**2,099.2**	**1,849.3**	**1,928.5**	**2,099.2**	....	....	....	....	....	....
7091	Pre-primary and primary education...............	1,406.0	1,472.9	1,650.2	1,406.0	1,472.9	1,650.2	....	....	....	....	....	....
7092	Secondary education...........................	....	....	....	....	....	....	....	....	....	....	....	....
7094	Tertiary education............................	213.9	215.4	231.0	213.9	215.4	231.0	....	....	....	....	....	....
710	**Social protection.......................**	**3,279.2**	**3,422.9**	**3,571.4**	**3,279.2**	**3,422.9**	**3,571.4**	....	....	....	....	....	....
7	Statistical discrepancy: Total outlays..............	—	—	—	—	—	—	....	....	....	....	....	....

Table 8 Transactions in financial assets and liabilities by sector

		Budgetary Central Government			Central Government			Local Government			General Government		
		2002	2003	2004	2002	2003	2004	2002	2003	2004	2002	2003	2004
82	**Net acquisition of financial assets.........**	**−730.2**	**−184.1**	**621.5**	**−747.9**	**−200.4**	**789.6**	**7.8**	**10.6**	**−5.0**	**−740.1**	**−189.8**	**784.6**
821	Domestic...................................	−730.2	−184.1	621.5	−747.9	−200.4	789.6	7.8	10.6	−5.0	−740.1	−189.8	784.6
8211	General government...........................	....	....	....	....	....	....	....	....	....	....	....	....
8212	Central bank.................................	....	....	....	....	....	....	....	....	....	....	....	....
8213	Other depository corporations................	....	....	....	....	....	....	....	....	....	....	....	....
8214	Financial corporations n.e.c.................	....	....	....	....	....	....	....	....	....	....	....	....
8215	Nonfinancial corporations....................	....	....	....	....	....	....	....	....	....	....	....	....
8216	Households & NPIs serving households......	....	....	....	....	....	....	....	....	....	....	....	....
822	Foreign....................................	—	—	—	—	—	—	—	—	—	—	—	—
8221	General government...........................	—	—	—	—	—	—	—	—	—	—	—	—
8227	International organizations..................	—	—	—	—	—	—	—	—	—	—	—	—
8228	Financial corporations other than international organizations.............	—	—	—	—	—	—	—	—	—	—	—	—
8229	Other nonresidents...........................	—	—	—	—	—	—	—	—	—	—	—	—
823	Monetary gold and SDRs..........................	—	—	—	—	—	—	—	—	—	—	—	—
83	**Net incurrence of liabilities...................**	**−429.9**	**−192.8**	**−774.3**	**−173.7**	**17.7**	**−443.8**	**—**	**—**	**1.0**	**−173.8**	**17.7**	**−442.8**
831	Domestic...................................	−880.2	−782.6	−867.5	−566.7	−471.6	−565.3	—	—	1.0	−566.7	−471.6	−564.2
8311	General government...........................	....	....	....	....	....	....	—	—	....	....	....	....
8312	Central bank.................................	....	....	....	....	....	....	—	—	....	....	....	....
8313	Other depository corporations................	....	....	....	....	....	....	—	—	....	....	....	....
8314	Financial corporations n.e.c.................	....	....	....	....	....	....	—	—	....	....	....	....
8315	Nonfinancial corporations....................	....	....	....	....	....	....	—	—	....	....	....	....
8316	Households & NPIs serving households......	....	....	....	....	....	....	—	—	....	....	....	....

		Budgetary Central Government			Central Government			Local Government			General Government		
		2002	2003	2004	2002	2003	2004	2002	2003	2004	2002	2003	2004
832	Foreign............................	450.4	589.9	93.3	393.0	489.3	121.5	—	—	—	393.0	489.3	121.5
8321	General government................	....	....	....	....	....	....	—	—	—	....	....	....
8327	International organizations............	....	....	....	....	....	....	—	—	—	....	....	....
8328	Financial corporations other than international organizations...........	....	....	....	....	....	....	—	—	—	....	....	....
8329	Other nonresidents....................	....	....	....	....	....	....	—	—	—	....	....	....

China, P.R.: Mainland   924

In Billions of Yuan / Year Ending December 31 / Cash Reporter

		Budgetary Central Government			Central Government			Local Government			General Government		
		2001	2002	2003	2001	2002	2003	2001	2002	2003	2001	2002	2003
	Statement of government operations												
	Statement of other economic flows												
	Balance sheet												
	Statement of sources and uses of cash												
1	Cash receipts from operating activities...........	921.2	1,107.2	1,251.6	....	....	....	1,620.2	2,391.3	2,692.4	....	....	....
11	Taxes..	811.7	1,023.2	1,159.8	....	....	....	691.0	761.2	827.8	....	....	....
12	Social contributions.................................	—	—	—	....	....	....	213.5	323.9	388.8	....	....	....
13	Grants...	59.1	63.8	61.9	....	....	....	600.2	790.5	880.5	....	....	....
14	Other receipts...	50.4	20.2	30.0	....	....	....	115.6	515.7	595.3	....	....	....
2	Cash payments for operating activities...........	....	1,291.6	1,419.1	....	....	....	....	2,076.3	2,334.7	....	....	....
21	Compensation of employees......................	....	....	....	....	....	....	....	....	....	....	....	....
22	Purchases of goods and services.................	....	....	....	....	....	....	....	....	....	....	....	....
24	Interest..	....	67.9	95.5	....	....	....	....	—	.9	....	....	....
25	Subsidies..	....	34.8	31.0	....	....	....	....	72.5	75.6	....	....	....
26	Grants...	....	788.4	834.0	....	....	....	....	133.2	158.3	....	....	....
27	Social benefits..	....	11.1	19.2	....	....	....	....	455.3	526.3	....	....	....
28	Other payments.......................................	....	.1	—	....	....	....	....	98.5	88.8	....	....	....
CIO	*Net cash inflow from oper. activities.....*	....	*−184.4*	*−167.5*	....	....	....	....	*314.9*	*357.7*	....	....	....
31.1	Purchases of nonfinancial assets..................	....	125.3	152.3	....	....	....	....	214.6	215.4	....	....	....
31.2	Sales of nonfinancial assets........................	....	—	—	....	....	....	....	—	—	....	....	....
31	Net cash outflow from investments in nonfinancial assets................................	....	125.3	152.3				....	214.6	215.4			
CSD	*Cash surplus/deficit...............................*	*−460.4*	*−309.7*	*−319.8*	....	....	....	*−14.5*	*100.3*	*142.3*	....	....	....
32x	Net acquisition of fin assets, excl. cash.........	....	....	....	....	....	....	....	....	....	....	....	....
321x	Domestic...	....	....	....	....	....	....	....	....	....	....	....	....
322x	Foreign..	....	....	....	....	....	....	....	....	....	....	....	....
323	Monetary gold and SDRs...........................	....	....	....	....	....	....	....	....	....	....	....	....
33	Net incurrence of liabilities........................	....	....	....	....	....	....	....	....	....	....	....	....
331	Domestic...	....	....	....	....	....	....	....	....	....	....	....	....
332	Foreign..	....	....	....	....	....	....	....	....	....	....	....	....
NFB	Net cash inflow from fin. activities...............	....	....	....	....	....	....	....	....	....	....	....	....
NCB	*Net change in the stock of cash............*	....	....	....	....	....	....	....	....	....	....	....	....
	Table 1 Revenue												
1	**Revenue....................................**	**921.2**	**1,107.2**	**1,251.6**	....	....	....	**1,620.2**	**2,391.3**	**2,692.4**	....	....	....
11	**Taxes......................................**	**811.7**	**1,023.2**	**1,159.8**	....	....	....	**691.0**	**761.2**	**827.8**	....	....	....
111	Taxes on income, profits, & capital gains......	101.9	248.8	258.5	....	....	....	234.4	180.6	161.1	....	....	....
1111	Individuals...	27.9	60.6	85.1	....	....	....	71.6	60.6	56.7	....	....	....
1112	Corporations and other enterprises.............	73.9	188.2	173.5	....	....	....	162.8	120.1	104.3	....	....	....
112	Taxes on payroll and workforce...................	—	—	—	....	....	....	—	—	—	....	....	....
113	Taxes on property....................................	26.6	10.9	12.4	....	....	....	32.3	38.5	95.9	....	....	....
114	Taxes on goods and services......................	599.2	807.3	994.5	....	....	....	393.1	542.1	570.8	....	....	....
1141	General taxes on goods and services..........	479.8	665.2	872.4	....	....	....	357.1	492.7	555.3	....	....	....
1142	Excises...	93.8	142.1	122.1	....	....	....	—	—	—	....	....	....
115	Taxes on int'l. trade and transactions...........	84.1	−43.7	−105.6	....	....	....	—	—	—	....	....	....
116	Other taxes..	—	—	—	....	....	....	31.1	—	—	....	....	....
12	**Social contributions............................**	**—**	**—**	**—**	....	....	....	**213.5**	**323.9**	**388.8**	....	....	....
121	Social security contributions......................	—	—	—	....	....	....	213.5	323.9	388.8	....	....	....
122	Other social contributions.........................	—	—	—	....	....	....	—	—	—	....	....	....
13	**Grants..**	**59.1**	**63.8**	**61.9**	....	....	....	**600.2**	**790.5**	**880.5**	....	....	....
131	From foreign governments.........................	—	—	—	....	....	....	—	—	—	....	....	....
132	From international organizations..................	—	—	—	....	....	....	—	—	—	....	....	....
133	From other general government units...........	59.1	63.8	61.9	....	....	....	600.2	790.5	880.5	....	....	....
14	**Other revenue...............................**	**50.4**	**20.2**	**30.0**	....	....	....	**115.6**	**515.7**	**595.3**	....	....	....
	Table 2 Expense by economic type												
2	**Expense......................................**	....	**1,291.6**	**1,419.1**	....	....	....	....	**2,076.3**	**2,334.7**	....	....	....
21	**Compensation of employees..................**	....	....	....	....	....	....	....	....	....	....	....	....
211	Wages and salaries...................................	....	....	....	....	....	....	....	....	....	....	....	....
212	Social contributions.................................	....	....	....	....	....	....	....	....	....	....	....	....
22	**Use of goods and services.....................**	....	....	....	....	....	....	....	....	....	....	....	....
23	**Consumption of fixed capital.................**	....	....	....	....	....	....	....	....	....	....	....	....
24	Interest..	....	67.9	95.5	....	....	....	....	—	.9	....	....	....
25	**Subsidies..**	....	34.8	31.0	....	....	....	....	72.5	75.6	....	....	....

In Billions of Yuan / Year Ending December 31 / Cash Reporter

		Budgetary Central Government			Central Government			Local Government			General Government		
		2001	2002	2003	2001	2002	2003	2001	2002	2003	2001	2002	2003
26	**Grants**	....	**788.4**	**834.0**	....	....	....	....	**133.2**	**158.3**	....	....	....
261	To foreign govenments	....	—	5.2	....	....	....	....	....	—	....	....	....
262	To international organizations	....	—	—	....	....	....	....	....	—	....	....	....
263	To other general government units	....	788.4	828.7	....	....	....	....	....	158.3	....	....	....
2631	Current	....	....	....	....	....	....	....	....	....	....	....	....
2632	Capital	....	....	....	....	....	....	....	....	....	....	....	....
27	**Social benefits**	....	**11.1**	**19.2**	....	....	....	....	**455.3**	**526.3**	....	....	....
28	**Other expense**	....	**.1**	**—**	....	....	....	....	**98.5**	**88.8**	....	....	....
281	Property expense other than interest	....	—	—	....	....	....	....	—	—	....	....	....
282	Miscellaneous other expense	....	.1	—	....	....	....	....	98.5	88.8	....	....	....
2821	Current	....	....	—	....	....	....	....	....	....	....	....	....
2822	Capital	....	....	—	....	....	....	....	....	....	....	....	....

Table 3   Transactions in assets and liabilities

Table 4   Holding gains in assets and liabilities

Table 5   Other changes in the volume of assets and liabilities

Table 6   Balance sheet

Table 7   Outlays by functions of govt.

		Budgetary Central Government			Central Government			Local Government			General Government		
7	**Total outlays**	1,381.6	1,416.9	1,571.4	....	....	....	1,634.6	2,291.0	2,530.6	....	....	....
701	**General public services**	945.4	874.8	997.5	....	....	....	262.5	725.5	999.5	....	....	....
7017	Public debt transactions	....	67.9	95.5	....	....	....	....	—	.9	....	....	....
7018	General transfers between levels of govt	....	736.0	....	....	....	....	....	77.9	115.4	....	....	....
702	**Defense**	143.0	169.5	188.9	....	....	....	1.7	2.2	3.3	....	....	....
703	**Public order and safety**	28.4	29.9	32.6	....	....	....	97.0	111.3	131.5	....	....	....
704	**Economic affairs**	189.6	246.3	289.4	....	....	....	467.3	483.8	302.1	....	....	....
7042	Agriculture, forestry, fishing, and hunting	....	19.3	19.7	....	....	....	....	131.0	124.1	....	....	....
7043	Fuel and energy	....	6.8	6.3	....	....	....	....	1.2	1.8	....	....	....
7044	Mining, manufacturing, and construction	....	11.0	8.6	....	....	....	....	....	37.7	....	....	....
7045	Transport	....	23.3	17.8	....	....	....	....	26.8	21.1	....	....	....
7046	Communication	....	2.2	1.4	....	....	....	....	—	—	....	....	....
705	**Environmental protection**	.2	.2	.4	....	....	....	13.9	89.3	105.6	....	....	....
706	**Housing and community amenities**	6.1	6.8	5.2	....	....	....	85.2	4.1	6.4	....	....	....
707	**Health**	2.1	2.4	2.7	....	....	....	70.0	66.2	83.1	....	....	....
7072	Outpatient services	....	.2	.2	....	....	....	....	2.6	2.8	....	....	....
7073	Hospital services	....	....	....	....	....	....	....	....	....	....	....	....
7074	Public health services	....	1.7	2.0	....	....	....	....	36.3	42.4	....	....	....
708	**Recreation, culture, and religion**	5.0	5.4	6.2	....	....	....	29.7	32.1	33.9	....	....	....
709	**Education**	20.9	23.8	28.1	....	....	....	231.6	300.8	334.2	....	....	....
7091	Pre-primary and primary education	....	.1	....	....	....	....	....	95.7	....	....	....	....
7092	Secondary education	....	.2	.3	....	....	....	....	78.1	....	....	....	....
7094	Tertiary education	....	19.3	21.1	....	....	....	....	34.2	....	....	....	....
710	**Social protection**	40.8	51.6	15.0	....	....	....	375.7	454.2	531.0	....	....	....
7	Statistical discrepancy: Total outlays	—	6.2	5.4	....	....	....	—	21.4	—	....	....	....

Table 8   Transactions in financial assets and liabilities by sector

China, P.R.: Hong Kong   532

In Millions of Hong Kong Dollars / Year Ending March 31 / Noncash Reporter

		Budgetary Central Government			Extrabudgetary Accounts			Central Government			General Government		
		2001	2002	2003	2001	2002	2003	2001	2002	2003	2001	2002	2003
Statement of government operations													
1	Revenue	....	....	....	....	....	....	....	....	....	....	190,532	204,324
2	Expense	....	....	....	....	....	....	....	....	....	....	272,083	266,967
GOB	*Gross operating balance*	....	....	....	....	....	....	....	....	....	....	*−77,988*	*−58,861*
NOB	*Net operating balance*	....	....	....	....	....	....	....	....	....	....	*−81,551*	*−62,643*
31	Net acquisition of nonfinancial assets	....	....	....	....	....	....	....	....	....	....	5,191	9,868
NLB	*Net lending/borrowing*	....	....	....	....	....	....	....	....	....	....	*−86,742*	*−72,511*
32	Net acquisition of financial assets	....	....	....	....	....	....	....	....	....	....	−66,481	−58,183
33	Net incurrence of liabilities	....	....	....	....	....	....	....	....	....	....	20,261	14,328
NLB	Statistical discrepancy	....	....	....	....	....	....	....	....	....	....	—	—
Statement of other economic flows													
4	*Change in net worth from holding gains*	....	....	....	....	....	....	....	....	....	....	*1,530*	*2,461*
41	Nonfinancial assets	....	....	....	....	....	....	....	....	....	....	−566	68
42	Financial assets	....	....	....	....	....	....	....	....	....	....	2,096	2,393
43	Liabilities	....	....	....	....	....	....	....	....	....	....	—	—
5	*Change in net worth from other volume changes*	....	....	....	....	....	....	....	....	....	....	—	—
51	Nonfinancial assets	....	....	....	....	....	....	....	....	....	....	—	—
52	Financial assets	....	....	....	....	....	....	....	....	....	....	—	—
53	Liabilities	....	....	....	....	....	....	....	....	....	....	—	—
Balance sheet													
6	*Net worth*	....	....	....	....	....	....	....	....	....	*364,300*	*284,279*	*224,097*
61	Nonfinancial assets	....	....	....	....	....	....	....	....	....	122,071	126,696	136,632
62	Financial assets	....	....	....	....	....	....	....	....	....	575,305	510,920	455,130
63	Liabilities	....	....	....	....	....	....	....	....	....	333,076	353,337	367,665
Statement of sources and uses of cash													
1	Cash receipts from operating activities	....	....	....	....	....	....	....	....	....	....	184,726	196,894
11	Taxes	....	....	....	....	....	....	....	....	....	....	116,167	130,933
12	Social contributions	....	....	....	....	....	....	....	....	....	....	26	23
13	Grants	....	....	....	....	....	....	....	....	....	....	—	—
14	Other receipts	....	....	....	....	....	....	....	....	....	....	68,533	65,938
2	Cash payments for operating activities	....	....	....	....	....	....	....	....	....	....	240,887	244,132
21	Compensation of employees	....	....	....	....	....	....	....	....	....	....	70,614	68,772
22	Purchases of goods and services	....	....	....	....	....	....	....	....	....	....	57,568	60,561
24	Interest	....	....	....	....	....	....	....	....	....	....	50	35
25	Subsidies	....	....	....	....	....	....	....	....	....	....	72	247
26	Grants	....	....	....	....	....	....	....	....	....	....	55	52
27	Social benefits	....	....	....	....	....	....	....	....	....	....	61,857	60,412
28	Other payments	....	....	....	....	....	....	....	....	....	....	50,671	54,053
CIO	*Net cash inflow from oper. activities*	....	....	....	....	....	....	....	....	....	....	*−56,161*	*−47,238*
31.1	Purchases of nonfinancial assets	....	....	....	....	....	....	....	....	....	....	7,431	10,425
31.2	Sales of nonfinancial assets	....	....	....	....	....	....	....	....	....	....	14	—
31	Net cash outflow from investments in nonfinancial assets	....	....	....	....	....	....	....	....	....	....	7,417	10,425
CSD	*Cash surplus/deficit*	....	....	....	....	....	....	....	....	....	....	*−63,578*	*−57,663*
32x	Net acquisition of fin assets, excl. cash	....	....	....	....	....	....	....	....	....	....	−60,771	−60,765
321x	Domestic	....	....	....	....	....	....	....	....	....	....	−60,771	−60,765
322x	Foreign	....	....	....	....	....	....	....	....	....	....	—	—
323	Monetary gold and SDRs	....	....	....	....	....	....	....	....	....	....	—	—
33	Net incurrence of liabilities	....	....	....	....	....	....	....	....	....	....	−3,084	−2,932
331	Domestic	....	....	....	....	....	....	....	....	....	....	−3,084	−2,932
332	Foreign	....	....	....	....	....	....	....	....	....	....	—	—
NFB	Net cash inflow from fin. activities	....	....	....	....	....	....	....	....	....	....	57,687	57,833
NCB	*Net change in the stock of cash*	....	....	....	....	....	....	....	....	....	....	*−5,891*	*170*
Table 1 Revenue													
1	**Revenue**	....	....	....	....	....	....	....	....	....	....	**190,532**	**204,324**
11	**Taxes**	....	....	....	....	....	....	....	....	....	....	**116,167**	**130,933**
111	Taxes on income, profits, & capital gains	....	....	....	....	....	....	....	....	....	....	71,848	79,491
1111	Individuals	....	....	....	....	....	....	....	....	....	....	33,049	30,721
1112	Corporations and other enterprises	....	....	....	....	....	....	....	....	....	....	38,799	48,770
112	Taxes on payroll and workforce	....	....	....	....	....	....	....	....	....	....	—	—
113	Taxes on property	....	....	....	....	....	....	....	....	....	....	18,452	23,851
114	Taxes on goods and services	....	....	....	....	....	....	....	....	....	....	24,082	25,877
1141	General taxes on goods and services	....	....	....	....	....	....	....	....	....	....	—	—
1142	Excises	....	....	....	....	....	....	....	....	....	....	6,620	6,422

China, P.R.: Hong Kong   532

In Millions of Hong Kong Dollars / Year Ending March 31 / Noncash Reporter

		Budgetary Central Government			Extrabudgetary Accounts			Central Government			General Government		
		2001	2002	2003	2001	2002	2003	2001	2002	2003	2001	2002	2003
115	Taxes on int'l. trade and transactions...........	....	....	....	....	....	....	....	....	....	....	700	805
116	Other taxes...	....	....	....	....	....	....	....	....	....	....	1,085	909
12	**Social contributions.........................**	....	....	....	....	....	....	....	....	....	....	**26**	**23**
121	Social security contributions.....................	....	....	....	....	....	....	....	....	....	....	26	23
122	Other social contributions........................	....	....	....	....	....	....	....	....	....	....	—	—
13	**Grants...**	....	....	....	....	....	....	....	....	....	....	—	—
131	From foreign governments.........................	....	....	....	....	....	....	....	....	....	....	—	—
132	From international organizations.................	....	....	....	....	....	....	....	....	....	....	—	—
133	From other general government units..........	....	....	....	....	....	....	....	....	....	....	—	—
14	**Other revenue................................**	....	....	....	....	....	....	....	....	....	....	**74,339**	**73,368**

Table 2   Expense by economic type

		Budgetary Central Government			Extrabudgetary Accounts			Central Government			General Government		
		2001	2002	2003	2001	2002	2003	2001	2002	2003	2001	2002	2003
2	**Expense...**	....	....	....	....	....	....	....	....	....	....	**272,083**	**266,967**
21	**Compensation of employees...................**	....	....	....	....	....	....	....	....	....	....	**70,614**	**68,772**
211	Wages and salaries..................................	....	....	....	....	....	....	....	....	....	....	60,672	58,647
212	Social contributions................................	....	....	....	....	....	....	....	....	....	....	9,942	10,125
22	**Use of goods and services......................**	....	....	....	....	....	....	....	....	....	....	**61,675**	**60,421**
23	**Consumption of fixed capital................**	....	....	....	....	....	....	....	....	....	....	**3,563**	**3,782**
24	**Interest..**	....	....	....	....	....	....	....	....	....	....	**50**	**35**
25	**Subsidies...**	....	....	....	....	....	....	....	....	....	....	**72**	**247**
26	**Grants...**	....	....	....	....	....	....	....	....	....	....	**55**	**52**
261	To foreign govenments............................	....	....	....	....	....	....	....	....	....	....	18	15
262	To international organizations.....................	....	....	....	....	....	....	....	....	....	....	37	37
263	To other general government units.............	....	....	....	....	....	....	....	....	....	....	—	—
2631	Current...	....	....	....	....	....	....	....	....	....	....	—	—
2632	Capital..	....	....	....	....	....	....	....	....	....	....	—	—
27	**Social benefits.................................**	....	....	....	....	....	....	....	....	....	....	**69,861**	**62,870**
28	**Other expense.................................**	....	....	....	....	....	....	....	....	....	....	**66,193**	**70,788**
281	Property expense other than interest...........	....	....	....	....	....	....	....	....	....	....	15,495	16,637
282	Miscellaneous other expense.....................	....	....	....	....	....	....	....	....	....	....	50,698	54,151
2821	Current...	....	....	....	....	....	....	....	....	....	....	45,874	47,641
2822	Capital..	....	....	....	....	....	....	....	....	....	....	4,824	6,510

Table 3   Transactions in assets and liabilities

		Budgetary Central Government			Extrabudgetary Accounts			Central Government			General Government		
		2001	2002	2003	2001	2002	2003	2001	2002	2003	2001	2002	2003
3	**Change in net worth from transactns....**	....	....	....	....	....	....	....	....	....	....	**−81,551**	**−62,643**
31	**Net acquisition of nonfinancial assets...**	....	....	....	....	....	....	....	....	....	....	**5,191**	**9,868**
311	Fixed assets...	....	....	....	....	....	....	....	....	....	....	2,578	7,538
3111	Buildings and structures.........................	....	....	....	....	....	....	....	....	....	....	3,641	6,211
3112	Machinery and equipment........................	....	....	....	....	....	....	....	....	....	....	−49	−89
3113	Other fixed assets.................................	....	....	....	....	....	....	....	....	....	....	−1,014	1,416
312	Inventories...	....	....	....	....	....	....	....	....	....	....	2,613	2,330
313	Valuables...	....	....	....	....	....	....	....	....	....	....	—	—
314	Nonproduced assets................................	....	....	....	....	....	....	....	....	....	....	—	—
3141	Land...	....	....	....	....	....	....	....	....	....	....	—	—
3142	Subsoil assets..................................	....	....	....	....	....	....	....	....	....	....	—	—
3143	Other naturally occurring assets.............	....	....	....	....	....	....	....	....	....	....	—	—
3144	Intangible nonproduced assets..............	....	....	....	....	....	....	....	....	....	....	—	—
32	**Net acquisition of financial assets.........**	....	....	....	....	....	....	....	....	....	....	**−66,481**	**−58,183**
321	Domestic..	....	....	....	....	....	....	....	....	....	....	−66,481	−58,183
3212	Currency and deposits.............................	....	....	....	....	....	....	....	....	....	....	−5,891	170
3213	Securities other than shares......................	....	....	....	....	....	....	....	....	....	....	—	—
3214	Loans...	....	....	....	....	....	....	....	....	....	....	−3,673	−19,487
3215	Shares and other equity...........................	....	....	....	....	....	....	....	....	....	....	−56,674	−42,999
3216	Insurance technical reserves......................	....	....	....	....	....	....	....	....	....	....	—	—
3217	Financial derivatives...............................	....	....	....	....	....	....	....	....	....	....	—	—
3218	Other accounts receivable........................	....	....	....	....	....	....	....	....	....	....	−243	4,133
322	Foreign...	....	....	....	....	....	....	....	....	....	....	—	—
3222	Currency and deposits.............................	....	....	....	....	....	....	....	....	....	....	—	—
3223	Securities other than shares......................	....	....	....	....	....	....	....	....	....	....	—	—
3224	Loans...	....	....	....	....	....	....	....	....	....	....	—	—
3225	Shares and other equity...........................	....	....	....	....	....	....	....	....	....	....	—	—
3226	Insurance technical reserves......................	....	....	....	....	....	....	....	....	....	....	—	—
3227	Financial derivatives...............................	....	....	....	....	....	....	....	....	....	....	—	—
3228	Other accounts receivable........................	....	....	....	....	....	....	....	....	....	....	—	—
323	Monetary gold and SDRs..........................	....	....	....	....	....	....	....	....	....	....	—	—

		Budgetary Central Government			Extrabudgetary Accounts			Central Government			General Government		
		2001	2002	2003	2001	2002	2003	2001	2002	2003	2001	2002	2003
33	Net incurrence of liabilities......	....	....	....	....	....	....	....	....	....	....	20,261	14,328
331	Domestic......	....	....	....	....	....	....	....	....	....	....	20,261	14,328
3312	Currency and deposits......	....	....	....	....	....	....	....	....	....	....	—	—
3313	Securities other than shares......	....	....	....	....	....	....	....	....	....	....	—	—
3314	Loans......	....	....	....	....	....	....	....	....	....	....	—	—
3316	Insurance technical reserves......	....	....	....	....	....	....	....	....	....	....	—	—
3317	Financial derivatives......	....	....	....	....	....	....	....	....	....	....	—	—
3318	Other accounts payable......	....	....	....	....	....	....	....	....	....	....	20,261	14,328
332	Foreign......	....	....	....	....	....	....	....	....	....	....	—	—
3322	Currency and deposits......	....	....	....	....	....	....	....	....	....	....	—	—
3323	Securities other than shares......	....	....	....	....	....	....	....	....	....	....	—	—
3324	Loans......	....	....	....	....	....	....	....	....	....	....	—	—
3326	Insurance technical reserves......	....	....	....	....	....	....	....	....	....	....	—	—
3327	Financial derivatives......	....	....	....	....	....	....	....	....	....	....	—	—
3328	Other accounts payable......	....	....	....	....	....	....	....	....	....	....	—	—
Table 4	**Holding gains in assets and liabilities**												
4	Change in net worth from hold. gains...	....	....	....	....	....	....	....	....	....	....	1,530	2,461
41	Nonfinancial assets......	....	....	....	....	....	....	....	....	....	....	−566	68
411	Fixed assets......	....	....	....	....	....	....	....	....	....	....	—	—
412	Inventories......	....	....	....	....	....	....	....	....	....	....	−566	68
413	Valuables......	....	....	....	....	....	....	....	....	....	....	—	—
414	Nonproduced assets......	....	....	....	....	....	....	....	....	....	....	—	—
42	Financial assets......	....	....	....	....	....	....	....	....	....	....	2,096	2,393
421	Domestic......	....	....	....	....	....	....	....	....	....	....	2,096	2,393
422	Foreign......	....	....	....	....	....	....	....	....	....	....	—	—
423	Monetary gold and SDRs......	....	....	....	....	....	....	....	....	....	....	—	—
43	Liabilities......	....	....	....	....	....	....	....	....	....	....	—	—
431	Domestic......	....	....	....	....	....	....	....	....	....	....	—	—
432	Foreign......	....	....	....	....	....	....	....	....	....	....	—	—
Table 5	**Other changes in the volume of assets and liabilities**												
5	Change in net worth from vol. chngs.....	....	....	....	....	....	....	....	....	....	....	—	—
51	Nonfinancial assets......	....	....	....	....	....	....	....	....	....	....	—	—
511	Fixed assets......	....	....	....	....	....	....	....	....	....	....	—	—
512	Inventories......	....	....	....	....	....	....	....	....	....	....	—	—
513	Valuables......	....	....	....	....	....	....	....	....	....	....	—	—
514	Nonproduced assets......	....	....	....	....	....	....	....	....	....	....	—	—
52	Financial assets......	....	....	....	....	....	....	....	....	....	....	—	—
521	Domestic......	....	....	....	....	....	....	....	....	....	....	—	—
522	Foreign......	....	....	....	....	....	....	....	....	....	....	—	—
523	Monetary gold and SDRs......	....	....	....	....	....	....	....	....	....	....	—	—
53	Liabilities......	....	....	....	....	....	....	....	....	....	....	—	—
531	Domestic......	....	....	....	....	....	....	....	....	....	....	—	—
532	Foreign......	....	....	....	....	....	....	....	....	....	....	—	—
Table 6	**Balance sheet**												
6	Net worth......	....	....	....	....	....	....	....	....	....	364,300	284,279	224,097
61	Nonfinancial assets......	....	....	....	....	....	....	....	....	....	122,071	126,696	136,632
611	Fixed assets......	....	....	....	....	....	....	....	....	....	....	112,614	120,153
6111	Buildings and structures......	....	....	....	....	....	....	....	....	....	....	98,881	105,093
6112	Machinery and equipment......	....	....	....	....	....	....	....	....	....	....	442	353
6113	Other fixed assets......	....	....	....	....	....	....	....	....	....	....	13,291	14,707
612	Inventories......	....	....	....	....	....	....	....	....	....	....	14,082	16,479
613	Valuables......	....	....	....	....	....	....	....	....	....	....	—	—
614	Nonproduced assets......	....	....	....	....	....	....	....	....	....	....	—	—
6141	Land......	....	....	....	....	....	....	....	....	....	....	—	—
6142	Subsoil assets......	....	....	....	....	....	....	....	....	....	....	—	—
6143	Other naturally occurring assets......	....	....	....	....	....	....	....	....	....	....	—	—
6144	Intangible nonproduced assets......	....	....	....	....	....	....	....	....	....	....	—	—

In Millions of Hong Kong Dollars / Year Ending March 31 / Noncash Reporter

		Budgetary Central Government			Extrabudgetary Accounts			Central Government			General Government		
		2001	2002	2003	2001	2002	2003	2001	2002	2003	2001	2002	2003
62	**Financial assets**	....	....	....	....	....	....	....	....	....	**575,305**	**510,920**	**455,130**
621	Domestic	....	....	....	....	....	....	....	....	....	....	510,920	455,130
6212	Currency and deposits	....	....	....	....	....	....	....	....	....	....	10,233	10,403
6213	Securities other than shares	....	....	....	....	....	....	....	....	....	....	—	—
6214	Loans	....	....	....	....	....	....	....	....	....	....	37,358	17,871
6215	Shares and other equity	....	....	....	....	....	....	....	....	....	....	462,174	421,568
6216	Insurance technical reserves	....	....	....	....	....	....	....	....	....	....	—	—
6217	Financial derivatives	....	....	....	....	....	....	....	....	....	....	—	—
6218	Other accounts receivable	....	....	....	....	....	....	....	....	....	....	1,155	5,288
622	Foreign	....	....	....	....	....	....	....	....	....	....	—	—
6222	Currency and deposits	....	....	....	....	....	....	....	....	....	....	—	—
6223	Securities other than shares	....	....	....	....	....	....	....	....	....	....	—	—
6224	Loans	....	....	....	....	....	....	....	....	....	....	—	—
6225	Shares and other equity	....	....	....	....	....	....	....	....	....	....	—	—
6226	Insurance technical reserves	....	....	....	....	....	....	....	....	....	....	—	—
6227	Financial derivatives	....	....	....	....	....	....	....	....	....	....	—	—
6228	Other accounts receivable	....	....	....	....	....	....	....	....	....	....	—	—
623	Monetary gold and SDRs	....	....	....	....	....	....	....	....	....	—	—	—
63	**Liabilities**	....	....	....	....	....	....	....	....	....	**333,076**	**353,337**	**367,665**
631	Domestic	....	....	....	....	....	....	....	....	....	333,076	353,337	367,665
6312	Currency and deposits	....	....	....	....	....	....	....	....	....	....	....	....
6313	Securities other than shares	....	....	....	....	....	....	....	....	....	....	....	....
6314	Loans	....	....	....	....	....	....	....	....	....	....	....	....
6316	Insurance technical reserves	....	....	....	....	....	....	....	....	....	....	....	....
6317	Financial derivatives	....	....	....	....	....	....	....	....	....	....	....	....
6318	Other accounts payable	....	....	....	....	....	....	....	....	....	....	....	....
632	Foreign	....	....	....	....	....	....	....	....	....	—	—	—
6322	Currency and deposits	....	....	....	....	....	....	....	....	....	—	—	—
6323	Securities other than shares	....	....	....	....	....	....	....	....	....	—	—	—
6324	Loans	....	....	....	....	....	....	....	....	....	—	—	—
6326	Insurance technical reserves	....	....	....	....	....	....	....	....	....	—	—	—
6327	Financial derivatives	....	....	....	....	....	....	....	....	....	—	—	—
6328	Other accounts payable	....	....	....	....	....	....	....	....	....	—	—	—
Memorandum items:													
6M2	Net financial worth	....	....	....	....	....	....	....	....	....	242,229	157,583	87,465
6M3	Debt at market value	....	....	....	....	....	....	....	....	....	....	....	....
6M4	Debt at nominal value	....	....	....	....	....	....	....	....	....	....	....	....
6M5	Arrears	....	....	....	....	....	....	....	....	....	....	....	....
6M6	Obligations for social security benefits	....			....			....			....		
6M7	Contingent liabilities	....	....	....	....	....	....	....	....	....	....	46,295	39,107
6M8	Uncapitalized military weapons, systems	....	....	....	....	....	....	....	....	....	....	....	....
Table 7 Outlays by functions of govt.													
7	**Total outlays**	....	....	....	....	....	....	....	....	....	....	**277,274**	**276,834**
701	**General public services**	....	....	....	....	....	....	....	....	....	....	**55,453**	**47,901**
7017	Public debt transactions	....	....	....	....	....	....	....	....	....	....	50	35
7018	General transfers between levels of govt	....	....	....	....	....	....	....	....	....	....	—	—
702	**Defense**	....	....	....	....	....	....	....	....	....	....	—	—
703	**Public order and safety**	....	....	....	....	....	....	....	....	....	....	**28,418**	**27,885**
704	**Economic affairs**	....	....	....	....	....	....	....	....	....	....	**25,995**	**28,073**
7042	Agriculture, forestry, fishing, and hunting	....	....	....	....	....	....	....	....	....	....	330	311
7043	Fuel and energy	....	....	....	....	....	....	....	....	....	....	25	24
7044	Mining, manufacturing, and construction	....	....	....	....	....	....	....	....	....	....	9,292	8,640
7045	Transport	....	....	....	....	....	....	....	....	....	....	9,007	10,617
7046	Communication	....	....	....	....	....	....	....	....	....	....	1,012	937
705	**Environmental protection**	....	....	....	....	....	....	....	....	....	....	**10,624**	**10,070**
706	**Housing and community amenities**	....	....	....	....	....	....	....	....	....	....	**29,256**	**31,126**
707	**Health**	....	....	....	....	....	....	....	....	....	....	**33,602**	**34,736**
7072	Outpatient services	....	....	....	....	....	....	....	....	....	....	....	....
7073	Hospital services	....	....	....	....	....	....	....	....	....	....	....	....
7074	Public health services	....	....	....	....	....	....	....	....	....	....	....	....
708	**Recreation, culture, and religion**	....	....	....	....	....	....	....	....	....	....	**8,634**	**8,618**

2005, International Monetary Fund: *Government Finance Statistics Yearbook*

In Millions of Hong Kong Dollars / Year Ending March 31 / Noncash Reporter

		Budgetary Central Government			Extrabudgetary Accounts			Central Government			General Government		
		2001	2002	2003	2001	2002	2003	2001	2002	2003	2001	2002	2003
709	**Education**.................	....	....	....	....	....	....	....	....	....	....	**53,023**	**54,764**
7091	Pre-primary and primary education..............	....	....	....	....	....	....	....	....	....	....	12,878	13,719
7092	Secondary education.................	....	....	....	....	....	....	....	....	....	....	17,170	17,915
7094	Tertiary education.................	....	....	....	....	....	....	....	....	....	....	14,335	14,821
710	**Social protection**.................	....	....	....	....	....	....	....	....	....	....	**32,269**	**33,661**
7	Statistical discrepancy: Total outlays.............	....	....	....	....	....	....	....	....	....	....	—	—

Table 8 Transactions in financial assets and liabilities by sector

		Budgetary Central Government			Extrabudgetary Accounts			Central Government			General Government		
		2001	2002	2003	2001	2002	2003	2001	2002	2003	2001	2002	2003
82	**Net acquisition of financial assets**.........	....	....	....	....	....	....	....	....	....	....	**−66,481**	**−58,183**
821	Domestic.................	....	....	....	....	....	....	....	....	....	....	−66,481	−58,183
8211	General government.................	....	....	....	....	....	....	....	....	....	....	....	....
8212	Central bank.................	....	....	....	....	....	....	....	....	....	....	....	....
8213	Other depository corporations.................	....	....	....	....	....	....	....	....	....	....	....	....
8214	Financial corporations n.e.c.	....	....	....	....	....	....	....	....	....	....	....	....
8215	Nonfinancial corporations.................	....	....	....	....	....	....	....	....	....	....	....	....
8216	Households & NPIs serving households......	....	....	....	....	....	....	....	....	....	....	....	....
822	Foreign.................	....	....	....	....	....	....	....	....	....	....	—	—
8221	General government.................	....	....	....	....	....	....	....	....	....	....	—	—
8227	International organizations.................	....	....	....	....	....	....	....	....	....	....	—	—
8228	Financial corporations other than international organizations.............	....	....	....	....	....	....	....	....	....	....	—	—
8229	Other nonresidents.................	....	....	....	....	....	....	....	....	....	....	—	—
823	Monetary gold and SDRs.................	....	....	....	....	....	....	....	....	....	....	—	—
83	**Net incurrence of liabilities**.................	....	....	....	....	....	....	....	....	....	....	**20,261**	**14,328**
831	Domestic.................	....	....	....	....	....	....	....	....	....	....	20,261	14,328
8311	General government.................	....	....	....	....	....	....	....	....	....	....	....	....
8312	Central bank.................	....	....	....	....	....	....	....	....	....	....	....	....
8313	Other depository corporations.................	....	....	....	....	....	....	....	....	....	....	....	....
8314	Financial corporations n.e.c.	....	....	....	....	....	....	....	....	....	....	....	....
8315	Nonfinancial corporations.................	....	....	....	....	....	....	....	....	....	....	....	....
8316	Households & NPIs serving households......	....	....	....	....	....	....	....	....	....	....	....	....
832	Foreign.................	....	....	....	....	....	....	....	....	....	....	—	—
8321	General government.................	....	....	....	....	....	....	....	....	....	....	—	—
8327	International organizations.................	....	....	....	....	....	....	....	....	....	....	—	—
8328	Financial corporations other than international organizations.............	....	....	....	....	....	....	....	....	....	....	—	—
8329	Other nonresidents.................	....	....	....	....	....	....	....	....	....	....	—	—

China,P.R.:Macao 546

In Millions of Patakas / Year Ending December 31 / Cash Reporter

	Budgetary Central Government			Extrabudgetary Accounts			Central Government			General Government		
	2002	2003	2004	2002	2003	2004	2002	2003	2004	2002	2003	2004
Statement of government operations												
Statement of other economic flows												
Balance sheet												
Statement of sources and uses of cash												
1 Cash receipts from operating activities..........	11,049.0	14,062.9	19,303.2	3,729.2	5,065.9	4,848.6	11,895.2	15,289.1	20,248.6	11,895.2	15,289.1	20,248.6
11 Taxes.....	10,108.0	12,739.3	18,044.3	98.5	521.6	115.3	10,206.5	13,260.9	18,159.5	10,206.5	13,260.9	18,159,5
12 Social contributions.....	—	—	—	16.9	16.1	16.8	95.8	98.0	105.5	95.8	98.0	105.5
13 Grants.....	42.2	43.0	—	2,929.1	3,885.0	3,995.1	—	—	—	—	—	—
14 Other receipts.....	898.8	1,280.5	1,258.9	684.7	643.1	721.5	1,592.9	1,930.2	1,983.5	1,592.9	1,930.2	1,983.5
2 Cash payments for operating activities..........	7,919.6	8,981.8	9,644.6	3,828.5	4,257.2	4,456.1	8,841.6	9,643.8	10,120.2	8,841.6	9,643.8	10,120.2
21 Compensation of employees.....	2,761.1	2,840.2	2,941.1	1,871.0	1,963.1	2,069.9	4,647.9	4,821.8	5,030.2	4,647.9	4,821.8	5,030.2
22 Purchases of goods and services.....	490.1	539.3	662.8	1,197.8	1,488.4	1,403.3	1,688.2	2,031.9	2,070.6	1,688.2	2,031.9	2,070.6
24 Interest.....												
25 Subsidies.....	233.2	295.4	305.9	143.1	134.2	128.3	376.3	429.6	434.2	376.3	429.6	434.2
26 Grants.....	3,232.6	4,108.6	4,461.5	43.1	44.0	4.4	1.9	2.2	5.6	1.9	2.2	5.6
27 Social benefits.....	285.6	238.6	247.6	281.7	181.7	349.7	915.6	950.6	1,050.5	915.6	950.6	1,050.5
28 Other payments.....	917.0	959.6	1,025.7	291.8	445.7	500.4	1,211.6	1,407.7	1,529.0	1,211.6	1,407.7	1,529.0
CIO *Net cash inflow from oper. activities.....*	*3,129.5*	*5,081.1*	*9,658.6*	*−99.4*	*808.7*	*392.5*	*3,053.5*	*5,645.4*	*10,128.4*	*3,053.5*	*5,645.4*	*10,128.4*
31.1 Purchases of nonfinancial assets.....	1,288.1	2,192.5	3,182.5	213.9	321.7	321.2	1,503.3	2,516.9	3,504.2	1,503.3	2,516.9	3,504.2
31.2 Sales of nonfinancial assets.....	.2	—	—	26.2	46.1	33.7	26.5	46.1	33.7	26.5	46.1	33.7
31 Net cash outflow from investments in nonfinancial assets.....	1,287.9	2,192.5	3,182.5	187.7	275.6	287.5	1,476.9	2,470.8	3,470.5	1,476.9	2,470.8	3,470.5
CSD *Cash surplus/deficit.....*	*1,841.6*	*2,888.6*	*6,476.0*	*−287.0*	*533.1*	*105.1*	*1,576.7*	*3,174.6*	*6,657.9*	*1,576.7*	*3,174.6*	*6,657.9*
32x Net acquisition of fin assets, excl. cash..........	45.0	252.0	309.0	27.5	125.4	35.7	43.2	377.4	344.7	43.2	377.4	344.7
321x Domestic.....	45.0	252.0	309.0	27.5	125.4	35.7	72.5	377.4	344.7	72.5	377.4	344.7
322x Foreign.....	—	—	—	—	—	—	−29.4	—	—	−29.4	—	—
323 Monetary gold and SDRs.....	—	—	—	—	—	—	—	—	—	—	—	—
33 Net incurrence of liabilities.....	—	—	—	—	—	—	—	—	—	—	—	—
331 Domestic.....	—	—	—	—	—	—	—	—	—	—	—	—
332 Foreign.....	—	—	—	—	—	—	—	—	—	—	—	—
NFB Net cash inflow from fin. activities.....	−45.0	−252.0	−309.0	−27.5	−125.4	−35.7	−43.2	−377.4	−344.7	−43.2	−377.4	−344.7
NCB *Net change in the stock of cash.....*	*1,796.6*	*2,636.6*	*6,167.0*	*−314.5*	*407.7*	*69.4*	*1,533.5*	*2,797.2*	*6,313.2*	*1,533.5*	*2,797.2*	*6,313.2*
Table 1 Revenue												
1 **Revenue.....**	**11,049.0**	**14,062.9**	**19,303.2**	**3,729.2**	**5,065.9**	**4,848.6**	**11,895.2**	**15,289.1**	**20,248.6**	**11,895.2**	**15,289.1**	**20,248.6**
11 **Taxes.....**	**10,108.0**	**12,739.3**	**18,044.3**	**98.5**	**521.6**	**115.3**	**10,206.5**	**13,260.9**	**18,159.5**	**10,206.5**	**13,260.9**	**18,159.5**
111 Taxes on income, profits, & capital gains......	873.4	780.8	967.6	—	—	—	873.4	780.8	967.6	873.4	780.8	967.6
1111 Individuals.....	259.5	212.4	248.1	—	—	—	259.5	212.4	248.1	259.5	212.4	248.1
1112 Corporations and other enterprises.....	613.9	568.4	719.5	—	—	—	613.9	568.4	719.5	613.9	568.4	719.5
112 Taxes on payroll and workforce.....	—	—	—	—	—	—	—	—	—	—	—	—
113 Taxes on property.....	470.5	520.5	736.5	—	—	—	470.5	520.5	736.5	470.5	520.5	736.5
114 Taxes on goods and services.....	8,528.2	11,211.3	16,072.1	98.5	521.6	115.3	8,626.7	11,732.9	16,187.4	8,626.7	11,732.9	16,187.4
1141 General taxes on goods and services..........	—		—	—	—	—	—	—	—	—	—	—
1142 Excises.....	447.3	516.9	582.4	—	—	—	447.3	516.9	582.4	447.3	516.9	582.4
115 Taxes on int'l. trade and transactions..........	—	—	—	—	—	—	—	—	—	—	—	—
116 Other taxes.....	235.9	226.7	268.0	—	—	—	235.9	226.7	268.0	235.9	226.7	268.0
12 **Social contributions.....**	—	—	—	**16.9**	**16.1**	**16.8**	**95.8**	**98.0**	**105.5**	**95.8**	**98.0**	**105.5**
121 Social security contributions.....	—	—	—	16.9	16.1	16.8	95.8	98.0	105.5	95.8	98.0	105.5
122 Other social contributions.....	—	—	—	—	—	—	—	—	—	—	—	—
13 **Grants.....**	**42.2**	**43.0**	—	**2,929.1**	**3,885.0**	**3,995.1**	—	—	—	—	—	—
131 From foreign governments.....	—	—	—	—	—	—	—	—	—	—	—	—
132 From international organizations.....	—	—	—	—	—	—	—	—	—	—	—	—
133 From other general government units..........	42.2	43.0	—	2,929.1	3,885.0	3,995.1	—	—	—	—	—	—
14 **Other revenue.....**	**898.8**	**1,280.5**	**1,258.9**	**684.7**	**643.1**	**721.5**	**1,592.9**	**1,930.2**	**1,983.5**	**1,592.9**	**1,930.2**	**1,983.5**
Table 2 Expense by economic type												
2 **Expense.....**	**7,919.6**	**8,981.8**	**9,644.6**	**3,828.5**	**4,257.2**	**4,456.1**	**8,841.6**	**9,643.8**	**10,120.2**	**8,841.6**	**9,643.8**	**10,120.2**
21 **Compensation of employees.....**	**2,761.1**	**2,840.2**	**2,941.1**	**1,871.0**	**1,963.1**	**2,069.9**	**4,647.9**	**4,821.8**	**5,030.2**	**4,647.9**	**4,821.8**	**5,030.2**
211 Wages and salaries.....	2,761.1	2,840.2	2,941.1	1,871.0	1,963.1	2,069.9	4,647.9	4,803.3	5,030.2	4,647.9	4,803.3	5,030.2
212 Social contributions.....	—	—	—	—	—	—	—	18.5	—	—	18.5	—
22 **Use of goods and services.....**	**490.1**	**539.3**	**662.8**	**1,197.8**	**1,488.4**	**1,403.3**	**1,688.2**	**2,031.9**	**2,070.6**	**1,688.2**	**2,031.9**	**2,070.6**
23 **Consumption of fixed capital.....**	....	....	....	....	....	....	....	....	....	....	....	....
24 **Interest.....**	—	—	—	—	—	—	—	—	—	—	—	—
25 **Subsidies.....**	**233.2**	**295.4**	**305.9**	**143.1**	**134.2**	**128.3**	**376.3**	**429.6**	**434.2**	**376.3**	**429.6**	**434.2**

In Millions of Patakas / Year Ending December 31 / Cash Reporter

		Budgetary Central Government			Extrabudgetary Accounts			Central Government			General Government		
		2002	2003	2004	2002	2003	2004	2002	2003	2004	2002	2003	2004
26	Grants...................................	3,232.6	4,108.6	4,461.5	43.1	44.0	4.4	1.9	2.2	5.6	1.9	2.2	5.6
261	To foreign govenments................	—	—	—									
262	To international organizations........	1.0	1.2	1.2	.9	1.0	4.4	1.9	2.2	5.6	1.9	2.2	5.6
263	To other general government units...	3,231.5	4,107.5	4,460.3	42.2	43.0	—						
2631	Current...............................	3,177.3	3,992.3	4,214.8	42.2	43.0	—						
2632	Capital...............................	54.2	115.1	245.5			—						
27	Social benefits............................	285.6	238.6	247.6	281.7	181.7	349.7	915.6	950.6	1,050.5	915.6	950.6	1,050.5
28	Other expense............................	917.0	959.6	1,025.7	291.8	445.7	500.4	1,211.6	1,407.7	1,529.0	1,211.6	1,407.7	1,529.0
281	Property expense other than interest....	....	340.0	357.6	....	122.3	136.0	....	464.6	495.9	....	464.6	495.9
282	Miscellaneous other expense............	....	619.6	668.2	....	323.4	364.4	....	943.0	1,033.1	....	943.0	1,033.1
2821	Current...............................	....	593.4	646.9	....	323.4	364.4	....	916.9	1,011.8	....	916.9	1,011.8
2822	Capital...............................	....	26.1	21.2	....	—	—	....	26.1	21.2	....	26.1	21.2

Table 3　Transactions in assets and liabilities

		Budgetary Central Government			Extrabudgetary Accounts			Central Government			General Government		
		2002	2003	2004	2002	2003	2004	2002	2003	2004	2002	2003	2004
3	Change in net worth from transactns....	....	....	....	....	....	....	....	....	....	....	....	....
31	Net acquisition of nonfinancial assets...	1,287.9	2,192.5	3,182.5	187.7	275.6	287.5	1,476.9	2,470.8	3,470.5	1,476.9	2,470.8	3,470.5
311	Fixed assets...........................	1,287.9	2,192.7	3,182.5	187.7	275.6	287.5	1,476.9	2,471.0	3,470.5	1,476.9	2,471.0	3,470.5
3111	Buildings and structures.............	386.9	1,763.6	2,594.9	37.6	96.3	131.6	425.3	1,859.9	2,726.7	425.3	1,859.9	2,726.7
3112	Machinery and equipment.............	889.8	414.4	586.1	150.1	179.3	155.9	1,040.4	596.4	742.4	1,040.4	596.4	742.4
3113	Other fixed assets...................	11.2	14.7	1.5	—	—	—	11.2	14.7	1.5	11.2	14.7	1.5
312	Inventories.............................	—	—	—	—	—	—	—	—	—	—	—	—
313	Valuables..............................	—	—	—	—	—	—	—	—	—	—	—	—
314	Nonproduced assets...................	—	–.2	—	—	—	—	—	–.2	—	—	–.2	—
3141	Land.................................	—	–.2	—	—	—	—	—	–.2	—	—	–.2	—
3142	Subsoil assets.......................	—	—	—	—	—	—	—	—	—	—	—	—
3143	Other naturally occurring assets.....	—	—	—	—	—	—	—	—	—	—	—	—
3144	Intangible nonproduced assets........	—	—	—	—	—	—	—	—	—	—	—	—
32	Net acquisition of financial assets........	1,841.6	2,888.6	6,476.0	−287.0	533.1	105.1	1,576.7	3,174.6	6,657.9	1,576.7	3,174.6	6,657.9
321	Domestic...............................	1,841.6	2,888.6	6,476.0	−287.0	533.1	105.1	1,606.0	3,174.6	6,657.9	1,606.0	3,174.6	6,657.9
3212	Currency and deposits.................	1,796.6	2,636.6	6,167.0	−314.5	407.7	69.4	1,533.5	2,797.2	6,313.2	1,533.5	2,797.2	6,313.2
3213	Securities other than shares..........	—	—	—				—	—	—			
3214	Loans.................................				22.5	97.4	25.9	22.5	97.4	25.9	22.5	97.4	25.9
3215	Shares and other equity..............	45.0	252.0	309.0	5.0	28.0	9.8	50.0	280.0	318.8	50.0	280.0	318.8
3216	Insurance technical reserves..........	—	—	—	—	—	—	—	—	—	—	—	—
3217	Financial derivatives.................	—	—	—	—	—	—	—	—	—	—	—	—
3218	Other accounts receivable.............	....	....	....	....	....	....	....	....	....	....	....	....
322	Foreign................................	—	—	—	—	—	—	−29.4	—	—	−29.4	—	—
3222	Currency and deposits.................	—	—	—	—	—	—	—	—	—	—	—	—
3223	Securities other than shares..........	—	—	—	—	—	—	−29.4	—	—	−29.4	—	—
3224	Loans.................................	—	—	—	—	—	—	—	—	—	—	—	—
3225	Shares and other equity..............	—	—	—	—	—	—	—	—	—	—	—	—
3226	Insurance technical reserves..........	—	—	—	—	—	—	—	—	—	—	—	—
3227	Financial derivatives.................	—	—	—	—	—	—	—	—	—	—	—	—
3228	Other accounts receivable.............	....	....	....	....	....	....	....	....	....	....	....	....
323	Monetary gold and SDRs...............	—	—	—	—	—	—	—	—	—	....	....	....
33	Net incurrence of liabilities..................	—	—	—	—	—	—	—	—	—	—	—	—
331	Domestic...............................	—	—	—	—	—	—	—	—	—	—	—	—
3312	Currency and deposits.................	—	—	—	—	—	—	—	—	—	—	—	—
3313	Securities other than shares..........	—	—	—	—	—	—	—	—	—	—	—	—
3314	Loans.................................	—	—	—	—	—	—	—	—	—	—	—	—
3316	Insurance technical reserves..........	—	—	—	—	—	—	—	—	—	—	—	—
3317	Financial derivatives.................	—	—	—	—	—	—	—	—	—	—	—	—
3318	Other accounts payable................	....	....	....	....	....	....	....	....	....	....	....	....
332	Foreign................................	—	—	—	—	—	—	—	—	—	—	—	—
3322	Currency and deposits.................	—	—	—	—	—	—	—	—	—	—	—	—
3323	Securities other than shares..........	—	—	—	—	—	—	—	—	—	—	—	—
3324	Loans.................................	—	—	—	—	—	—	—	—	—	—	—	—
3326	Insurance technical reserves..........	—	—	—	—	—	—	—	—	—	—	—	—
3327	Financial derivatives.................	—	—	—	—	—	—	—	—	—	—	—	—
3328	Other accounts payable................	....	....	....	....	....	....	....	....	....	....	....	....

In Millions of Patakas / Year Ending December 31 / Cash Reporter

	Budgetary Central Government			Extrabudgetary Accounts			Central Government			General Government		
	2002	2003	2004	2002	2003	2004	2002	2003	2004	2002	2003	2004
Table 4 Holding gains in assets and liabilities												
Table 5 Other changes in the volume of assets and liabilities												
Table 6 Balance sheet												
Table 7 Outlays by functions of govt.												
7 Total outlays............	9,207.5	11,174.3	12,827.2	4,016.2	4,532.8	4,743.6	10,318.5	12,114.6	13,590.7	10,318.5	12,114.6	13,590.7
701 **General public services**...........	4,311.4	5,205.5	5,655.7	911.0	1,033.2	1,047.8	1,948.7	2,088.3	2,243.2	1,948.7	2,088.3	2,243.2
7017 Public debt transactions...........	—	—	—	—	—	—	—	—	—	—	—	—
7018 General transfers between levels of govt......	3,231.5	4,107.5	....	42.2	43.0	....	—	—	....	—	—	....
702 **Defense**...........	—	—	—	—	—	—	—	—	—	—	—	—
703 **Public order and safety**...........	1,662.8	1,926.5	2,019.7	281.6	288.5	324.3	1,944.4	2,214.9	2,344.0	1,944.4	2,214.9	2,344.0
704 **Economic affairs**...........	1,138.7	1,096.5	1,682.2	109.5	197.0	159.2	1,248.2	1,293.5	1,841.4	1,248.2	1,293.5	1,841.4
7042 Agriculture, forestry, fishing, and hunting.....	....	....	....	....	....	....	....	....	....	....	....	....
7043 Fuel and energy...........	....	....	....	....	....	....	....	....	....	....	....	....
7044 Mining, manufacturing, and construction.....	....	....	....	....	....	....	....	....	....	....	....	....
7045 Transport...........	....	....	....	....	....	....	....	....	....	....	....	....
7046 Communication...........	....	....	....	....	....	....	....	....	....	....	....	....
705 **Environmental protection**...........	210.8	328.3	302.4	13.3	23.5	21.7	224.1	351.8	324.1	224.1	351.8	324.1
706 **Housing and community amenities**........	—	33.3	13.2	70.2	57.3	107.4	70.2	90.6	120.6	70.2	90.6	120.6
707 **Health**...........	13.1	19.3	68.0	1,225.9	1,364.7	1,352.9	1,239.0	1,384.1	1,421.0	1,239.0	1,384.1	1,421.0
7072 Outpatient services...........	....	....	....	....	....	....	....	....	....	....	....	....
7073 Hospital services...........	....	....	....	....	....	....	....	....	....	....	....	....
7074 Public health services...........	....	....	....	....	....	....	....	....	....	....	....	....
708 **Recreation, culture, and religion**............	443.7	1,105.4	1,577.3	345.1	397.5	439.5	788.8	1,502.9	2,016.9	788.8	1,502.9	2,016.9
709 **Education**............	953.1	1,030.5	1,056.2	730.5	808.0	851.1	1,683.6	1,838.5	1,907.3	1,683.6	1,838.5	1,907.3
7091 Pre-primary and primary education...........	....	....	....	....	....	....	....	....	....	....	....	....
7092 Secondary education...........	....	....	....	....	....	....	....	....	....	....	....	....
7094 Tertiary education...........	....	....	....	....	....	....	....	....	....	....	....	....
710 **Social protection**...........	473.9	428.9	452.4	329.1	363.0	439.7	1,171.5	1,349.9	1,372.4	1,171.5	1,349.9	1,372.4
7 Statistical discrepancy: Total outlays...........	—	—	—	—	—	—	—	—	—	—	—	—
Table 8 Transactions in financial assets and liabilities by sector												
82 **Net acquisition of financial assets**........	1,841.6	2,888.6	6,476.0	−287.0	533.1	105.1	1,576.7	3,174.6	6,657.9	1,576.7	3,174.6	6,657.9
821 Domestic...........	1,841.6	2,888.6	6,476.0	−287.0	533.1	105.1	1,606.0	3,174.6	6,657.9	1,606.0	3,174.6	6,657.9
8211 General government...........	....	2,888.6	6,476.0	....	533.1	105.1	....	3,174.6	6,657.9	....	3,174.6	6,657.9
8212 Central bank...........	....	—	—	....	—	—	....	—	—	....	—	—
8213 Other depository corporations...........	....	—	—	....	—	—	....	—	—	....	—	—
8214 Financial corporations n.e.c...........	....	—	—	....	—	—	....	—	—	....	—	—
8215 Nonfinancial corporations...........	45.0	—	—	5.0	—	—	50.0	—	—	50.0	—	—
8216 Households & NPIs serving households......	....	—	—	22.5	—	—	22.5	—	—	22.5	—	—
822 Foreign...........	—	—	—	—	—	—	−29.4	—	—	−29.4	—	—
8221 General government...........	—	—	—	—	—	—	—	—	—	—	—	—
8227 International organizations...........	—	—	—	—	—	—	—	—	—	—	—	—
8228 Financial corporations other than international organizations............	—	—	—	—	—	—	−29.4	—	—	−29.4	—	—
8229 Other nonresidents...........	—	—	—	—	—	—	—	—	—	—	—	—
823 Monetary gold and SDRs...........	—	—	—	—	—	—	—	—	—	—	—	—
83 **Net incurrence of liabilities**...........	—	—	—	—	—	—	—	—	—	—	—	—
831 Domestic...........	—	—	—	—	—	—	—	—	—	—	—	—
8311 General government...........	—	—	—	—	—	—	—	—	—	—	—	—
8312 Central bank...........	—	—	—	—	—	—	—	—	—	—	—	—
8313 Other depository corporations...........	—	—	—	—	—	—	—	—	—	—	—	—
8314 Financial corporations n.e.c...........	—	—	—	—	—	—	—	—	—	—	—	—
8315 Nonfinancial corporations...........	—	—	—	—	—	—	—	—	—	—	—	—
8316 Households & NPIs serving households......	—	—	—	—	—	—	—	—	—	—	—	—
832 Foreign...........	—	—	—	—	—	—	—	—	—	—	—	—
8321 General government...........	—	—	—	—	—	—	—	—	—	—	—	—
8327 International organizations...........	—	—	—	—	—	—	—	—	—	—	—	—
8328 Financial corporations other than international organizations...........	—	—	—	—	—	—	—	—	—	—	—	—
8329 Other nonresidents...........	—	—	—	—	—	—	—	—	—	—	—	—

In Billions of Pesos / Year Ending December 31 / Noncash Reporter

		Budgetary Central Government			Extrabudgetary Accounts			Central Government			General Government		
		2002	2003	2004	2002	2003	2004	2002	2003	2004	2002	2003	2004
Statement of government operations													
1	Revenue	34,476	42,446	44,077	4,512	4,562	6,415	....	....	....	....	....	....
2	Expense	43,315	51,849	58,945	4,031	4,656	5,352	....	....	....	....	....	....
GOB	*Gross operating balance*	*−8,236*	*−8,783*	*−14,868*	*594*	*—*	*1,172*	....	....	....	....	....	....
NOB	*Net operating balance*	*−8,839*	*−9,403*	*−14,868*	*481*	*−94*	*1,063*	....	....	....	....	....	....
31	Net acquisition of nonfinancial assets	10,732	1,000	5,799	199	−732	258	....	....	....	....	....	....
NLB	*Net lending/borrowing*	*−19,570*	*−10,402*	*−20,667*	*282*	*638*	*805*	....	....	....	....	....	....
32	Net acquisition of financial assets	4,809	7,572	−6,001	648	409	902	....	....	....	....	....	....
33	Net incurrence of liabilities	24,380	17,974	14,666	366	−229	97	....	....	....	....	....	....
NLB	Statistical discrepancy	—	—	—	—	—	—	....	....	....	....	....	....
Statement of other economic flows													
4	*Change in net worth from holding gains*	....	....	*571*	....	....	*306*	....	....	....	....	....	....
41	Nonfinancial assets	....	....	−490	....	....	232	....	....	....	....	....	....
42	Financial assets	....	....	1,061	....	....	74	....	....	....	....	....	....
43	Liabilities	....	....	—	....	....	—	....	....	....	....	....	....
5	*Change in net worth from other volume changes*	....	....	*−5,260*	....	....	*−76*	....	....	....	....	....	....
51	Nonfinancial assets	....	....	−5,260	....	....	−79	....	....	....	....	....	....
52	Financial assets	....	....	—	....	....	3	....	....	....	....	....	....
53	Liabilities	....	....	—	....	....	—	....	....	....	....	....	....
Balance sheet													
6	*Net worth*	....	....	*−75,068*	....	....	*6,901*	....	....	....	....	....	....
61	Nonfinancial assets	....	....	20,962	....	....	2,886	....	....	....	....	....	....
62	Financial assets	....	....	52,094	....	....	5,623	....	....	....	....	....	....
63	Liabilities	....	....	148,124	....	....	1,608	....	....	....	....	....	....
Statement of sources and uses of cash													
1	Cash receipts from operating activities	34,503	52,182	62,179	4,667	4,633	5,029	....	....	....	....	....	....
11	Taxes	28,102	35,693	34,121	1,879	2,222	630	....	....	....	....	....	....
12	Social contributions	19	....	1,221	99	104	1,987	....	....	....	....	....	....
13	Grants	....	....	408	....	....	957	....	....	....	....	....	....
14	Other receipts	....	....	26,429	....	....	1,455	....	....	....	....	....	....
2	Cash payments for operating activities	44,899	49,588	69,500	3,872	4,126	5,441	....	....	....	....	....	....
21	Compensation of employees	6,491	10,572	7,458	723	919	697	....	....	....	....	....	....
22	Purchases of goods and services	3,942	5,292	4,025	2,464	2,897	2,454	....	....	....	....	....	....
24	Interest	9,651	11,171	12,080	21	26	25	....	....	....	....	....	....
25	Subsidies	....	....	635	....	....	16	....	....	....	....	....	....
26	Grants	....	....	27,688	....	....	1,210	....	....	....	....	....	....
27	Social benefits	788	2,335	4,452	195	63	485	....	....	....	....	....	....
28	Other payments	....	....	13,162	....	....	554	....	....	....	....	....	....
CIO	*Net cash inflow from oper. activities*	*−10,396*	*2,594*	*−7,321*	*795*	*507*	*−412*	....	....	....	....	....	....
31.1	Purchases of nonfinancial assets	996	285	6,216	....	74	1,296	....	....	....	....	....	....
31.2	Sales of nonfinancial assets	820	680	92	....	103	107	....	....	....	....	....	....
31	Net cash outflow from investments in nonfinancial assets	176	−395	6,123	−55	−28	1,189	....	....	....	....	....	....
CSD	*Cash surplus/deficit*	*−10,572*	*2,988*	*−13,445*	*850*	*535*	*−1,601*	....	....	....	....	....	....
32x	Net acquisition of fin assets, excl. cash	−2,531	1,671	−1,537	−51	678	471	....	....	....	....	....	....
321x	Domestic	445	868	−2,417	−57	633	471	....	....	....	....	....	....
322x	Foreign	−2,976	804	880	7	45	—	....	....	....	....	....	....
323	Monetary gold and SDRs	—	—	—	—	—	—	....	....	....	....	....	....
33	Net incurrence of liabilities	21,264	12,391	8,247	115	75	26	....	....	....	....	....	....
331	Domestic	11,855	6,853	12,730	130	69	−177	....	....	....	....	....	....
332	Foreign	9,409	5,537	−4,483	−14	6	203	....	....	....	....	....	....
NFB	Net cash inflow from fin. activities	23,794	10,719	9,784	166	−603	−445	....	....	....	....	....	....
NCB	*Net change in the stock of cash*	*1,345*	*1,768*	*808*	*33*	*−2*	*65*	....	....	....	....	....	....
Table 1 Revenue													
1	**Revenue**	**34,476**	**42,446**	**44,077**	**4,512**	**4,562**	**6,415**	....	....	....	....	....
11	**Taxes**	**24,277**	**31,472**	**35,468**	**1,879**	**2,222**	**—**	....	....	....	....	....
111	Taxes on income, profits, & capital gains	10,842	15,281	15,570	201	351	—	....	....	....	....	....	....
1111	Individuals	121	19	2,510	—	—	—	....	....	....	....	....	....
1112	Corporations and other enterprises	10,537	12,231	13,060	201	328	—	....	....	....	....	....	....
112	Taxes on payroll and workforce	—	—	—	1,580	1,683	—	....	....	....	....	....	....
113	Taxes on property	1,445	1,686	2,293	—	—	—	....	....	....	....	....	....
114	Taxes on goods and services	10,423	12,211	15,234	—	—	—	....	....	....	....	....	....
1141	General taxes on goods and services	8,912	10,234	12,738	—	—	—	....	....	....	....	....	....
1142	Excises	980	1,026	1,264	—	—	—	....	....	....	....	....	....

		Budgetary Central Government			Extrabudgetary Accounts			Central Government			General Government		
		2002	2003	2004	2002	2003	2004	2002	2003	2004	2002	2003	2004
115	Taxes on int'l. trade and transactions...........	2,172	2,238	2,310	—	—	—	....	....	....	....	....	....
116	Other taxes.....	−605	55	60	98	187	—	....	....	....	....	....	....
12	**Social contributions.....**	**25**	**124**	**3**	**99**	**104**	**99**	....	....	....	....	....	....
121	Social security contributions.....	25	124	3	99	104	99	....	....	....	....	....	....
122	Other social contributions.....	—	—	—	—	—	—	....	....	....	....	....	....
13	**Grants.....**	....	....	**163**	....	....	**802**	....	....	....	....	....	....
131	From foreign governments.....	....	....	163	....	....	5	....	....	....	....	....	....
132	From international organizations.....	....	....	—	....	....	—	....	....	....	....	....	....
133	From other general government units.....	....	....	—	....	....	798	....	....	....	....	....	....
14	**Other revenue.....**	....	....	**8,442**	....	....	**5,513**	....	....	....	....	....	....

Table 2   Expense by economic type

		Budgetary Central Government			Extrabudgetary Accounts			Central Government			General Government		
2	**Expense.....**	**43,315**	**51,849**	**58,945**	**4,031**	**4,656**	**5,352**	....	....	....	....	....	....
21	**Compensation of employees.....**	**10,462**	**10,673**	**8,294**	**935**	**924**	**999**	....	....	....	....	....	....
211	Wages and salaries.....	5,782	5,573	6,666	607	557	580	....	....	....	....	....	....
212	Social contributions.....	4,680	5,101	1,628	328	367	419	....	....	....	....	....	....
22	**Use of goods and services.....**	**3,685**	**5,327**	**4,676**	**2,492**	**3,041**	**3,620**	....	....	....	....	....	....
23	**Consumption of fixed capital.....**	**603**	**620**	**—**	**113**	**94**	**109**	....	....	....	....	....	....
24	**Interest.....**	**10,373**	**11,941**	**12,080**	**22**	**37**	**24**	....	....	....	....	....	....
25	**Subsidies.....**	....	....	**290**	....	....	—	....	....	....	....	....	....
26	**Grants.....**	....	....	**13,868**	....	....	**158**	....	....	....	....	....	....
261	To foreign governments.....	....	....	—	....	....	—	....	....	....	....	....	....
262	To international organizations.....	....	....	—	....	....	—	....	....	....	....	....	....
263	To other general government units.....	....	....	13,868	....	....	158	....	....	....	....	....	....
2631	Current.....	....	....	13,622	....	....	158	....	....	....	....	....	....
2632	Capital.....	....	....	247	....	....	—	....	....	....	....	....	....
27	**Social benefits.....**	**238**	**747**	**771**	**1**	**64**	**68**	....	....	....	....	....	....
28	**Other expense.....**	....	....	**18,965**	....	....	**372**	....	....	....	....	....	....
281	Property expense other than interest.....	108	125	111	11	12	13	....	....	....	....	....	....
282	Miscellaneous other expense.....	....	....	18,854	....	....	359	....	....	....	....	....	....
2821	Current.....	....	....	18,851	....	....	359	....	....	....	....	....	....
2822	Capital.....	....	....	3	....	....	—	....	....	....	....	....	....

Table 3   Transactions in assets and liabilities

		Budgetary Central Government			Extrabudgetary Accounts			Central Government			General Government		
3	**Change in net worth from transactns....**	**−8,839**	**−9,403**	**−14,868**	**481**	**−94**	**1,063**	....	....	....	....	....	....
31	**Net acquisition of nonfinancial assets...**	**10,732**	**1,000**	**5,799**	**199**	**−732**	**258**	....	....	....	....	....	....
311	Fixed assets.....	1,362	763	1,084	135	126	224	....	....	....	....	....	....
3111	Buildings and structures.....	896	45	525	59	42	219	....	....	....	....	....	....
3112	Machinery and equipment.....	436	682	447	76	78	517	....	....	....	....	....	....
3113	Other fixed assets.....	30	36	111	—	5	−511	....	....	....	....	....	....
312	Inventories.....	387	−24	−139	−50	10	99	....	....	....	....	....	....
313	Valuables.....	2	1	−124	3	3	14	....	....	....	....	....	....
314	Nonproduced assets.....	8,981	259	4,978	111	−870	−79	....	....	....	....	....	....
3141	Land.....	67	38	237	2	17	51	....	....	....	....	....	....
3142	Subsoil assets.....	8,733	176	4,640	109	−983	−34	....	....	....	....	....	....
3143	Other naturally occurring assets.....	182	38	43	—	—	—	....	....	....	....	....	....
3144	Intangible nonproduced assets.....	—	8	58	—	95	−96	....	....	....	....	....	....
32	**Net acquisition of financial assets.....**	**4,809**	**7,572**	**−6,001**	**648**	**409**	**902**	....	....	....	....	....	....
321	Domestic.....	7,785	6,688	−6,946	641	391	877	....	....	....	....	....	....
3212	Currency and deposits.....	1,345	1,768	776	33	−19	42	....	....	....	....	....	....
3213	Securities other than shares.....	−570	29	−1,002	213	653	433	....	....	....	....	....	....
3214	Loans.....	2,372	44	−1,233	139	102	88	....	....	....	....	....	....
3215	Shares and other equity.....	−335	4,139	−1,660	17	30	−67	....	....	....	....	....	....
3216	Insurance technical reserves.....	—	—	17	—	—	1	....	....	....	....	....	....
3217	Financial derivatives.....	—	—	—	—	—	—	....	....	....	....	....	....
3218	Other accounts receivable.....	4,975	708	−3,843	241	−376	378	....	....	....	....	....	....
322	Foreign.....	−2,976	884	945	7	17	26	....	....	....	....	....	....
3222	Currency and deposits.....	—	—	33	—	17	22	....	....	....	....	....	....
3223	Securities other than shares.....	−2,976	804	887	7	—	3	....	....	....	....	....	....
3224	Loans.....	—	—	—	—	—	—	....	....	....	....	....	....
3225	Shares and other equity.....	—	81	25	—	—	—	....	....	....	....	....	....
3226	Insurance technical reserves.....	—	—	—	—	—	—	....	....	....	....	....	....
3227	Financial derivatives.....	—	—	—	—	—	—	....	....	....	....	....	....
3228	Other accounts receivable.....	—	—	—	—	—	—	....	....	....	....	....	....
323	Monetary gold and SDRs.....	—	—	—	—	—	—	....	....	....	....	....	....

In Billions of Pesos / Year Ending December 31 / Noncash Reporter

		Budgetary Central Government			Extrabudgetary Accounts			Central Government			General Government		
		2002	2003	2004	2002	2003	2004	2002	2003	2004	2002	2003	2004
33	Net incurrence of liabilities..................	24,380	17,974	14,666	366	−229	97	....	....	....	....	....	....
331	Domestic....................................	13,960	12,142	19,148	380	−223	−106	....	....	....	....	....	....
3312	Currency and deposits....................	—	—	—	—	13	−13	....	....	....	....	....	....
3313	Securities other than shares............	12,970	9,423	12,949	135	−6	7	....	....	....	....	....	....
3314	Loans......................................	−74	−166	−72	−1	−44	−199	....	....	....	....	....	....
3316	Insurance technical reserves.............	—	—	—	—	—	—	....	....	....	....	....	....
3317	Financial derivatives.....................	—	—	—	—	—	—	....	....	....	....	....	....
3318	Other accounts payable..................	1,064	2,884	6,271	246	−186	99	....	....	....	....	....	....
332	Foreign......................................	10,420	5,832	−4,482	−14	−6	202	....	....	....	....	....	....
3322	Currency and deposits....................	—	—	—	—	—	—	....	....	....	....	....	....
3323	Securities other than shares............	6,364	−332	−2,208	—	—	—	....	....	....	....	....	....
3324	Loans......................................	3,967	6,226	−2,172	−2	−7	203	....	....	....	....	....	....
3326	Insurance technical reserves.............	—	—	—	—	—	—	....	....	....	....	....	....
3327	Financial derivatives.....................	—	—	—	—	—	—	....	....	....	....	....	....
3328	Other accounts payable..................	89	−62	−102	−12	—	—	....	....	....	....	....	....
Table 4	**Holding gains in assets and liabilities**												
4	**Change in net worth from hold. gains...**	....	....	**571**	....	....	**306**	....	....	....	....	....	....
41	**Nonfinancial assets............................**	....	....	**−490**	....	....	**232**	....	....	....	....	....	....
411	Fixed assets..............................	....	....	−95	....	....	139	....	....	....	....	....	....
412	Inventories...............................	....	....	—	....	....	—	....	....	....	....	....	....
413	Valuables.................................	....	....	—	....	....	—	....	....	....	....	....	....
414	Nonproduced assets.....................	....	....	−395	....	....	94	....	....	....	....	....	....
42	**Financial assets..............................**	....	....	**1,061**	....	....	**74**	....	....	....	....	....	....
421	Domestic.................................	....	....	−97	....	....	74	....	....	....	....	....	....
422	Foreign...................................	....	....	1,158	....	....	—	....	....	....	....	....	....
423	Monetary gold and SDRs.................	....	....	—	....	....		....	....	....	....	....	....
43	**Liabilities.................................**	....	....	**—**	....	....	**—**	....	....	....	....	....	....
431	Domestic.................................	....	....	—	....	....	—	....	....	....	....	....	....
432	Foreign...................................	....	....	—	....	....	—	....	....	....	....	....	....
Table 5	**Other changes in the volume of assets and liabilities**												
5	**Change in net worth from vol. chngs.....**	....	....	**−5,260**	....	....	**−76**	....	....	....	....	....	....
51	**Nonfinancial assets............................**	....	....	**−5,260**	....	....	**−79**	....	....	....	....	....	....
511	Fixed assets..............................	....	....	−1,060	....	....	−60	....	....	....	....	....	....
512	Inventories...............................	....	....	4	....	....	−19	....	....	....	....	....	....
513	Valuables.................................	....	....	—	....	....	—	....	....	....	....	....	....
514	Nonproduced assets.....................	....	....	−4,204	....	....	—	....	....	....	....	....	....
52	**Financial assets..............................**	....	....	**—**	....	....	**3**	....	....	....	....	....	....
521	Domestic.................................	....	....	—	....	....	3	....	....	....	....	....	....
522	Foreign...................................	....	....	—	....	....	—	....	....	....	....	....	....
523	Monetary gold and SDRs.................	....	....	—	....	....	—	....	....	....	....	....	....
53	**Liabilities.................................**	....	....	**—**	....	....	**—**	....	....	....	....	....	....
531	Domestic.................................	....	....	—	....	....	—	....	....	....	....	....	....
532	Foreign...................................	....	....	—	....	....		....	....	....	....	....	....
Table 6	**Balance sheet**												
6	**Net worth..**	....	....	**−75,068**	....	....	**6,901**	....	....	....	....	....	....
61	**Nonfinancial assets............................**	....	....	**20,962**	....	....	**2,886**	....	....	....	....	....	....
611	Fixed assets..............................	....	....	19,072	....	....	2,130	....	....	....	....	....	....
6111	Buildings and structures................	....	....	11,441	....	....	674	....	....	....	....	....	....
6112	Machinery and equipment..............	....	....	7,432	....	....	1,392	....	....	....	....	....	....
6113	Other fixed assets......................	....	....	199	....	....	64	....	....	....	....	....	....
612	Inventories...............................	....	....	203	....	....	516	....	....	....	....	....	....
613	Valuables.................................	....	....	205	....	....	38	....	....	....	....	....	....
614	Nonproduced assets.....................	....	....	1,481	....	....	202	....	....	....	....	....	....
6141	Land.....................................	....	....	783	....	....	177	....	....	....	....	....	....
6142	Subsoil assets...........................	....	....	—	....	....	—	....	....	....	....	....	....
6143	Other naturally occurring assets........	....	....	593	....	....	—	....	....	....	....	....	....
6144	Intangible nonproduced assets..........	....	....	105	....	....	25	....	....	....	....	....	....

In Billions of Pesos / Year Ending December 31 / Noncash Reporter

	Budgetary Central Government			Extrabudgetary Accounts			Central Government			General Government		
	2002	2003	2004	2002	2003	2004	2002	2003	2004	2002	2003	2004
62 **Financial assets**............................	....	....	**52,094**	....	....	**5,623**	....	....	....	....	....	....
621 Domestic................................	....	....	48,414	....	....	5,474	....	....	....	....	....	....
6212 Currency and deposits................	....	....	7,861	....	....	396	....	....	....	....	....	....
6213 Securities other than shares.......	....	....	463	....	....	2,460	....	....	....	....	....	....
6214 Loans......................................	....	....	12,057	....	....	901	....	....	....	....	....	....
6215 Shares and other equity............	....	....	22,168	....	....	—	....	....	....	....	....	....
6216 Insurance technical reserves.......	....	....	—	....	....	—	....	....	....	....	....	....
6217 Financial derivatives..................	....	....	—	....	....	—	....	....	....	....	....	....
6218 Other accounts receivable..........	....	....	5,865	....	....	1,717	....	....	....	....	....	....
622 Foreign.................................	....	....	3,680	....	....	148	....	....	....	....	....	....
6222 Currency and deposits................	....	....	33	....	....	110	....	....	....	....	....	....
6223 Securities other than shares.......	....	....	2,768	....	....	38	....	....	....	....	....	....
6224 Loans......................................	....	....	—	....	....	—	....	....	....	....	....	....
6225 Shares and other equity............	....	....	879	....	....	—	....	....	....	....	....	....
6226 Insurance technical reserves.......	....	....	—	....	....	—	....	....	....	....	....	....
6227 Financial derivatives..................	....	....	—	....	....	—	....	....	....	....	....	....
6228 Other accounts receivable..........	....	....	—	....	....	—	....	....	....	....	....	....
623 Monetary gold and SDRs..........	....	....	—	....	....	—	....	....	....	....	....	....
63 **Liabilities**................................	....	....	**148,124**	....	....	**1,608**	....	....	....	....	....	....
631 Domestic................................	....	....	93,116	....	....	1,386	....	....	....	....	....	....
6312 Currency and deposits................	....	....	—	....	....	2	....	....	....	....	....	....
6313 Securities other than shares.......	....	....	74,076	....	....	154	....	....	....	....	....	....
6314 Loans......................................	....	....	1,875	....	....	41	....	....	....	....	....	....
6316 Insurance technical reserves.......	....	....	—	....	....	—	....	....	....	....	....	....
6317 Financial derivatives..................	....	....	—	....	....	—	....	....	....	....	....	....
6318 Other accounts payable.............	....	....	17,165	....	....	1,188	....	....	....	....	....	....
632 Foreign.................................	....	....	55,008	....	....	222	....	....	....	....	....	....
6322 Currency and deposits................	....	....	—	....	....	—	....	....	....	....	....	....
6323 Securities other than shares.......	....	....	30,335	....	....	—	....	....	....	....	....	....
6324 Loans......................................	....	....	24,598	....	....	221	....	....	....	....	....	....
6326 Insurance technical reserves.......	....	....	—	....	....	—	....	....	....	....	....	....
6327 Financial derivatives..................	....	....	—	....	....	—	....	....	....	....	....	....
6328 Other accounts payable.............	....	....	75	....	....	1	....	....	....	....	....	....
Memorandum items:												
6M2 Net financial worth..................	....	....	−96,030	....	....	4,015	....	....	....	....	....	....
6M3 Debt at market value...............	....	....	....	....	....	....	....	....	....	....	....	....
6M4 Debt at nominal value..............	....	....	....	....	....	....	....	....	....	....	....	....
6M5 Arrears...................................	....	....	....	....	....	....	....	....	....	....	....	....
6M6 Obligations for social security benefits...........	....	....	....	....	....	....	....	....	....	....	....	....
6M7 Contingent liabilities.................	....	....	....	....	....	....	....	....	....	....	....	....
6M8 Uncapitalized military weapons, systems........	....	....	....	....	....	....	....	....	....	....	....	....
Table 7 Outlays by functions of govt.												
7 **Total outlays**............................	54,046	52,849	64,744	4,231	3,925	5,610	....	....	....	....	....	....
701 **General public services**....................	....	....	....	....	....	....	....	....	....	....	....	....
7017 Public debt transactions.............	10,373	11,941	12,080	22	37	24	....	....	....	....	....	....
7018 General transfers between levels of govt......	....	....	....	....	....	....	....	....	....	....	....	....
702 **Defense**......................................	....	....	....	....	....	....	....	....	....	....	....	....
703 **Public order and safety**....................	....	....	....	....	....	....	....	....	....	....	....	....
704 **Economic affairs**............................	....	....	....	....	....	....	....	....	....	....	....	....
7042 Agriculture, forestry, fishing, and hunting......	....	....	....	....	....	....	....	....	....	....	....	....
7043 Fuel and energy.........................	....	....	....	....	....	....	....	....	....	....	....	....
7044 Mining, manufacturing, and construction.....	....	....	....	....	....	....	....	....	....	....	....	....
7045 Transport..................................	....	....	....	....	....	....	....	....	....	....	....	....
7046 Communication...........................	....	....	....	....	....	....	....	....	....	....	....	....
705 **Environmental protection**....................	....	....	....	....	....	....	....	....	....	....	....	....
706 **Housing and community amenities**........	....	....	....	....	....	....	....	....	....	....	....	....
707 **Health**.......................................	....	....	....	....	....	....	....	....	....	....	....	....
7072 Outpatient services.....................	....	....	....	....	....	....	....	....	....	....	....	....
7073 Hospital services........................	....	....	....	....	....	....	....	....	....	....	....	....
7074 Public health services..................	....	....	....	....	....	....	....	....	....	....	....	....
708 **Recreation, culture, and religion**............	....	....	....	....	....	....	....	....	....	....	....	....

In Billions of Pesos / Year Ending December 31 / Noncash Reporter

		Budgetary Central Government			Extrabudgetary Accounts			Central Government			General Government		
		2002	2003	2004	2002	2003	2004	2002	2003	2004	2002	2003	2004
709	**Education**....................	....	....	....	....	....	....	....	....	....	....	....	....
7091	Pre-primary and primary education..............	....	....	....	....	....	....	....	....	....	....	....	....
7092	Secondary education................	....	....	....	....	....	....	....	....	....	....	....	....
7094	Tertiary education................	....	....	....	....	....	....	....	....	....	....	....	....
710	**Social protection**................	....	....	....	....	....	....	....	....	....	....	....	....
7	Statistical discrepancy: Total outlays..............	....	....	....	....	....	....	....	....	....	....	....	....
Table 8 Transactions in financial assets and liabilities by sector													
82	**Net acquisition of financial assets.........**	**4,809**	**7,572**	**−6,001**	**648**	**409**	**902**	....	....	....	....	....	....
821	Domestic....................	7,785	6,688	−6,946	641	391	877	....	....	....	....	....	....
8211	General government....................	−3,155	9,494	−3,806	347	564	418	....	....	....	....	....	....
8212	Central bank....................	−84	142	−157	—	—	6	....	....	....	....	....	....
8213	Other depository corporations....................	−3,817	1,906	221	−13	−3	120	....	....	....	....	....	....
8214	Financial corporations n.e.c.	5	193	−66	—	−85	−53	....	....	....	....	....	....
8215	Nonfinancial corporations....................	15,266	−5,677	−645	133	−218	46	....	....	....	....	....	....
8216	Households & NPIs serving households......	−429	630	−2,492	174	133	339	....	....	....	....	....	....
822	Foreign....................	−2,976	884	945	7	17	26	....	....	....	....	....	....
8221	General government....................	—	—	—	—	....	—	....	....	....	....	....	....
8227	International organizations....................	−2,983	81	25	—	....	—	....	....	....	....	....	....
8228	Financial corporations other than international organizations..............	7	804	920	7	....	6	....	....	....	....	....	....
8229	Other nonresidents....................	—	—	—	—	....	20	....	....	....	....	....	....
823	Monetary gold and SDRs....................	—	—	—	—	....	—	....	....	....	....	....	....
83	**Net incurrence of liabilities...................**	**24,380**	**17,974**	**14,666**	**366**	**−229**	**97**	....	....	....	....	....	....
831	Domestic....................	13,960	12,142	19,148	380	−223	−106	....	....	....	....	....	....
8311	General government....................	....	2,426	−823	10	70	95	....	....	....	....	....	....
8312	Central bank....................	....	−1,715	—	—	—	—	....	....	....	....	....	....
8313	Other depository corporations....................	....	885	−355	114	−43	−199	....	....	....	....	....	....
8314	Financial corporations n.e.c.	....	24	−53	−117	6	5	....	....	....	....	....	....
8315	Nonfinancial corporations....................	....	9,806	12,326	190	−223	125	....	....	....	....	....	....
8316	Households & NPIs serving households......	....	717	8,054	183	−33	−132	....	....	....	....	....	....
832	Foreign....................	10,420	5,832	−4,482	−14	−6	202	....	....	....	....	....	....
8321	General government....................	−13	−58	−74	—	—	—	....	....	....	....	....	....
8327	International organizations....................	—	—	—	—	—	—	....	....	....	....	....	....
8328	Financial corporations other than international organizations..............	3,978	6,284	−2,098	−2	−7	203	....	....	....	....	....	....
8329	Other nonresidents....................	6,455	−394	−2,310	−12	—	—	....	....	....	....	....	....

Congo, Democratic Republic of   636

In Millions of Francs / Year Ending December 31 / Cash Reporter

		Budgetary Central Government			Central Government			Local Government			General Government		
		2000	2001	2002	2000	2001	2002	2000	2001	2002	2000	2001	2002
Statement of government operations													
Statement of other economic flows													
Balance sheet													
Statement of sources and uses of cash													
1	Cash receipts from operating activities...........	11,093	66,644	138,988	15,490	138,403	158,395	....	....	....	....	....	....
11	Taxes..	10,270	61,420	108,945	10,270	61,420	121,448	....	....	....	....	....	....
12	Social contributions.............................	—	—	—	—	—	—	....	....	....	....	....	....
13	Grants...	—	—	—	4,397	71,759	6,047	....	....	....	....	....	....
14	Other receipts...................................	823	5,224	30,044	823	5,224	30,901	....	....	....	....	....	....
2	Cash payments for operating activities...........	22,348	65,747	....	25,440	114,130	....	....	....	....	....	....	....
21	Compensation of employees.......................	6,964	24,030	....	6,964	24,030	....	....	....	....	....	....	....
22	Purchases of goods and services.................	15,114	41,500	....	15,114	41,500	....	....	....	....	....	....	....
24	Interest...	—	—	....	—	—	....	....	....	....	....	....	....
25	Subsidies..	—	—	....	—	—	....	....	....	....	....	....	....
26	Grants...	4	80	....	3,096	48,463	....	....	....	....	....	....	....
27	Social benefits..................................	266	137	....	266	137	....	....	....	....	....	....	....
28	Other payments...................................	—	—	....	—	—	....	....	....	....	....	....	....
CIO	*Net cash inflow from oper. activities.....*	*−11,255*	*897*	....	*−9,950*	*24,273*	....	....	....	....	....	....	....
31.1	Purchases of nonfinancial assets................	731	1,694	....	2,036	25,070	....	....	....	....	....	....	....
31.2	Sales of nonfinancial assets....................	—	—	....	—	—	....	....	....	....	....	....	....
31	Net cash outflow from investments in nonfinancial assets..............	731	1,694	....	2,036	25,070	....	....	....	....	....	....	....
CSD	*Cash surplus/deficit.....................*	*−11,986*	*−797*	*−8,638*	*−11,986*	*−797*	*−1,002*	....	....	....	....	....	....
32x	Net acquisition of fin assets, excl. cash........	....	....	....	....	....	....	....	....	....	....	....	....
321x	Domestic..	....	....	....	....	....	....	....	....	....	....	....	....
322x	Foreign...	....	....	....	....	....	....	....	....	....	....	....	....
323	Monetary gold and SDRs..........................	....	....	....	....	....	....	....	....	....	....	....	....
33	Net incurrence of liabilities....................	....	....	....	....	....	....	....	....	....	....	....	....
331	Domestic..	....	....	....	....	....	....	....	....	....	....	....	....
332	Foreign...	....	....	....	....	....	....	....	....	....	....	....	....
NFB	Net cash inflow from fin. activities.............	....	....	....	....	....	....	....	....	....	....	....	....
NCB	*Net change in the stock of cash...........*	....	....	....	....	....	....	....	....	....	....	....	....
Table 1 Revenue													
1	**Revenue**......................................	**11,093**	**66,644**	**138,988**	**15,490**	**138,403**	**158,395**	....	....	....	....	....	....
11	**Taxes**..	**10,270**	**61,420**	**108,945**	**10,270**	**61,420**	**121,448**	....	....	....	....	....	....
111	Taxes on income, profits, & capital gains......	1,299	10,239	36,703	1,299	10,239	38,870	....	....	....	....	....	....
1111	Individuals....................................	846	5,611	10,847	846	5,611	10,847	....	....	....	....	....	....
1112	Corporations and other enterprises............	453	4,516	25,857	453	4,516	28,023	....	....	....	....	....	....
112	Taxes on payroll and workforce.................	—	—	863	—	—	863	....	....	....	....	....	....
113	Taxes on property..............................	—	—	790	—	—	790	....	....	....	....	....	....
114	Taxes on goods and services....................	2,446	14,451	28,503	2,446	14,451	37,471	....	....	....	....	....	....
1141	General taxes on goods and services...........	562	4,199	1,751	562	4,199	1,751	....	....	....	....	....	....
1142	Excises..	1,418	9,085	19,009	1,418	9,085	27,977	....	....	....	....	....	....
115	Taxes on int'l. trade and transactions.........	2,540	21,292	42,028	2,540	21,292	43,397	....	....	....	....	....	....
116	Other taxes....................................	3,985	15,438	58	3,985	15,438	58	....	....	....	....	....	....
12	**Social contributions**........................	—	—	—	—	—	—	....	....	....	....	....	....
121	Social security contributions.................	—	—	—	—	—	—	....	....	....	....	....	....
122	Other social contributions....................	—	—	—	—	—	—	....	....	....	....	....	....
13	**Grants**......................................	—	—	—	**4,397**	**71,759**	**6,047**	....	....	....	....	....	....
131	From foreign governments......................	—	—	—	4,397	71,759	6,047	....	....	....	....	....	....
132	From international organizations..............	—	—	—	—	—	—	....	....	....	....	....	....
133	From other general government units...........	—	—	—	—	—	—	....	....	....	....	....	....
14	**Other revenue**...............................	**823**	**5,224**	**30,044**	**823**	**5,224**	**30,901**	....	....	....	....	....	....
Table 2 Expense by economic type													
2	**Expense**.....................................	**22,348**	**65,747**	....	**25,440**	**114,130**	....	....	....	....	....	....	....
21	**Compensation of employees**...................	**6,964**	**24,030**	....	**6,964**	**24,030**	....	....	....	....	....	....	....
211	Wages and salaries.............................	6,964	24,030	....	6,964	24,030	....	....	....	....	....	....	....
212	Social contributions..........................	—	—	....	—	—	....	....	....	....	....	....	....
22	**Use of goods and services**...................	**15,114**	**41,500**	....	**15,114**	**41,500**	....	....	....	....	....	....	....
23	**Consumption of fixed capital**................	....	....	....	....	....	....	....	....	....	....	....	....
24	**Interest**....................................	—	—	....	—	—	....	....	....	....	....	....	....
25	**Subsidies**...................................	—	—	....	—	—	....	....	....	....	....	....	....

		Budgetary Central Government			Central Government			Local Government			General Government		
		2000	2001	2002	2000	2001	2002	2000	2001	2002	2000	2001	2002
26	**Grants**.....................................	4	80	....	3,096	48,463	....	....	....	....	....	....	....
261	To foreign govenments.................	4	80	....	4	80	....	....	....	....	....	....	....
262	To international organizations.........	—	—	....	—	—	....	....	....	....	....	....	....
263	To other general government units........	—	—	....	3,092	48,383	....	....	....	....	....	....	....
2631	Current......................................	—	—	....	3,092	48,383	....	....	....	....	....	....	....
2632	Capital......................................	—	—	....	—	—	....	....	....	....	....	....	....
27	**Social benefits**...........................	266	137	....	266	137	....	....	....	....	....	....	....
28	**Other expense**...........................	—	—	....	—	—	....	....	....	....	....	....	....
281	Property expense other than interest...........	—	—	....	—	—	....	....	....	....	....	....	....
282	Miscellaneous other expense....................	—	—	....	—	—	....	....	....	....	....	....	....
2821	Current......................................	—	—	....	—	—	....	....	....	....	....	....	....
2822	Capital......................................	—	—	....	—	—	....	....	....	....	....	....	....

Table 3   Transactions in assets and liabilities

		Budgetary Central Government			Central Government			Local Government			General Government		
		2000	2001	2002	2000	2001	2002	2000	2001	2002	2000	2001	2002
3	**Change in net worth from transactns....**	....	....	....	....	....	....	....	....	....	....	....	....
31	**Net acquisition of nonfinancial assets...**	731	1,694	....	2,036	25,070	....	....	....	....	....	....	....
311	Fixed assets................................	731	1,694	....	2,036	25,070	....	....	....	....	....	....	....
3111	Buildings and structures..................	....	....	....	....	....	....	....	....	....	....	....	....
3112	Machinery and equipment..................	....	....	....	....	....	....	....	....	....	....	....	....
3113	Other fixed assets........................	....	....	....	....	....	....	....	....	....	....	....	....
312	Inventories.................................	—	—	....	—	—	....	....	....	....	....	....	....
313	Valuables...................................	—	—	....	—	—	....	....	....	....	....	....	....
314	Nonproduced assets........................	—	—	....	—	—	....	....	....	....	....	....	....
3141	Land.......................................	—	—	....	—	—	....	....	....	....	....	....	....
3142	Subsoil assets.............................	....	....	....	....	....	....	....	....	....	....	....	....
3143	Other naturally occurring assets................	....	....	....	....	....	....	....	....	....	....	....	....
3144	Intangible nonproduced assets................	—	—	....	—	—	....	....	....	....	....	....	....
32	**Net acquisition of financial assets........**	....	....	....	....	....	....	....	....	....	....	....	....
321	Domestic....................................	....	....	....	....	....	....	....	....	....	....	....	....
3212	Currency and deposits.....................	....	....	....	....	....	....	....	....	....	....	....	....
3213	Securities other than shares..............	....	....	....	....	....	....	....	....	....	....	....	....
3214	Loans......................................	....	....	....	....	....	....	....	....	....	....	....	....
3215	Shares and other equity...................	....	....	....	....	....	....	....	....	....	....	....	....
3216	Insurance technical reserves..............	....	....	....	....	....	....	....	....	....	....	....	....
3217	Financial derivatives......................	....	....	....	....	....	....	....	....	....	....	....	....
3218	Other accounts receivable.................	....	....	....	....	....	....	....	....	....	....	....	....
322	Foreign.....................................	....	....	....	....	....	....	....	....	....	....	....	....
3222	Currency and deposits.....................	....	....	....	....	....	....	....	....	....	....	....	....
3223	Securities other than shares..............	....	....	....	....	....	....	....	....	....	....	....	....
3224	Loans......................................	....	....	....	....	....	....	....	....	....	....	....	....
3225	Shares and other equity...................	....	....	....	....	....	....	....	....	....	....	....	....
3226	Insurance technical reserves..............	....	....	....	....	....	....	....	....	....	....	....	....
3227	Financial derivatives......................	....	....	....	....	....	....	....	....	....	....	....	....
3228	Other accounts receivable.................	....	....	....	....	....	....	....	....	....	....	....	....
323	Monetary gold and SDRs....................	....	....	....	....	....	....	....	....	....	....	....	....
33	**Net incurrence of liabilities.............**	....	....	....	....	....	....	....	....	....	....	....	....
331	Domestic....................................	....	....	....	....	....	....	....	....	....	....	....	....
3312	Currency and deposits.....................	....	....	....	....	....	....	....	....	....	....	....	....
3313	Securities other than shares..............	....	....	....	....	....	....	....	....	....	....	....	....
3314	Loans......................................	....	....	....	....	....	....	....	....	....	....	....	....
3316	Insurance technical reserves..............	....	....	....	....	....	....	....	....	....	....	....	....
3317	Financial derivatives......................	....	....	....	....	....	....	....	....	....	....	....	....
3318	Other accounts payable....................	....	....	....	....	....	....	....	....	....	....	....	....
332	Foreign.....................................	....	....	....	....	....	....	....	....	....	....	....	....
3322	Currency and deposits.....................	....	....	....	....	....	....	....	....	....	....	....	....
3323	Securities other than shares..............	....	....	....	....	....	....	....	....	....	....	....	....
3324	Loans......................................	....	....	....	....	....	....	....	....	....	....	....	....
3326	Insurance technical reserves..............	....	....	....	....	....	....	....	....	....	....	....	....
3327	Financial derivatives......................	....	....	....	....	....	....	....	....	....	....	....	....
3328	Other accounts payable....................	....	....	....	....	....	....	....	....	....	....	....	....

	Budgetary Central Government			Central Government			Local Government			General Government		
	2000	2001	2002	2000	2001	2002	2000	2001	2002	2000	2001	2002
Table 4 Holding gains in assets and liabilities												
Table 5 Other changes in the volume of assets and liabilities												
Table 6 Balance sheet												
Table 7 Outlays by functions of govt.												
7 Total outlays..............................	23,079	67,441	147,626	27,476	139,200	159,397	....	....	....	....	....	....
701 **General public services.....................**	....	....	....	....	....	....	....	....	....	....	....	....
7017 Public debt transactions........................	—	—	14,685	—	—	14,777	....	....	....	....	....	....
7018 General transfers between levels of govt......	....	....	....	....	....	....	....	....	....	....	....	....
702 **Defense..**	....	....	....	....	....	....	....	....	....	....	....	....
703 **Public order and safety.........................**	....	....	....	....	....	....	....	....	....	....	....	....
704 **Economic affairs..................................**	....	....	....	....	....	....	....	....	....	....	....	....
7042 Agriculture, forestry, fishing, and hunting.....	....	....	....	....	....	....	....	....	....	....	....	....
7043 Fuel and energy.....................................	....	....	....	....	....	....	....	....	....	....	....	....
7044 Mining, manufacturing, and construction.....	....	....	....	....	....	....	....	....	....	....	....	....
7045 Transport..	....	....	....	....	....	....	....	....	....	....	....	....
7046 Communication.......................................	....	....	....	....	....	....	....	....	....	....	....	....
705 **Environmental protection......................**	....	....	....	....	....	....	....	....	....	....	....	....
706 **Housing and community amenities........**	....	....	....	....	....	....	....	....	....	....	....	....
707 **Health...**	....	....	....	....	....	....	....	....	....	....	....	....
7072 Outpatient services.................................	....	....	....	....	....	....	....	....	....	....	....	....
7073 Hospital services....................................	....	....	....	....	....	....	....	....	....	....	....	....
7074 Public health services.............................	....	....	....	....	....	....	....	....	....	....	....	....
708 **Recreation, culture, and religion............**	....	....	....	....	....	....	....	....	....	....	....	....
709 **Education...**	....	....	....	....	....	....	....	....	....	....	....	....
7091 Pre-primary and primary education..............	....	....	....	....	....	....	....	....	....	....	....	....
7092 Secondary education................................	....	....	....	....	....	....	....	....	....	....	....	....
7094 Tertiary education...................................	....	....	....	....	....	....	....	....	....	....	....	....
710 **Social protection...................................**	....	....	....	....	....	....	....	....	....	....	....	....
7 Statistical discrepancy: Total outlays..............	....	....	....	....	....	....	....	....	....	....	....	....
Table 8 Transactions in financial assets and liabilities by sector												

	Budgetary Central Government			Central Government			Local Government			General Government		
	2001	2002	2003	2001	2002	2003	2001	2002	2003	2001	2002	2003
Statement of government operations												
1 Revenue	630.30	642.50	613.50	670.51	675.48	651.27	13.07	12.58	14.60	....	....	658.80
2 Expense	440.60	564.10	397.12	484.42	590.24	411.41	12.64	12.88	10.04	....	....	414.39
GOB *Gross operating balance*	*189.70*	*78.40*	*216.38*	*186.09*	*85.23*	*239.86*	*.43*	*−.30*	*4.55*	....	....	*244.41*
NOB *Net operating balance*	....	....	....	....	....	....	....	....	....	....	....	....
31 Net acquisition of nonfinancial assets	205.40	191.40	105.60	212.07	195.59	106.74	2.97	1.60	2.94	....	....	109.68
NLB *Net lending/borrowing*	*−15.70*	*−113.00*	*110.79*	*−25.98*	*−110.36*	*133.12*	*−2.54*	*−1.90*	*1.61*	....	....	*134.73*
32 Net acquisition of financial assets	....	....	....	....	....	....	....	....	....	....	....	....
33 Net incurrence of liabilities	....	....	....	....	....	....	....	....	....	....	....	....
NLB Statistical discrepancy	....	....	....	....	....	....	....	....	....	....	....	....
Statement of other economic flows												
Balance sheet												
6 *Net worth*	....	....	....	....	....	....	....	....	....	....	....	....
61 Nonfinancial assets	....	....	....	....	....	....	....	....	....	....	....	....
62 Financial assets	....	....	....	....	....	....	....	....	....	....	....	....
63 Liabilities	....	....	4.35	....	....	4.35	....	....	—	....	....	4.35
Statement of sources and uses of cash												
Table 1 Revenue												
1 **Revenue**	**630.30**	**642.50**	**613.50**	**670.51**	**675.48**	**651.27**	**13.07**	**12.58**	**14.60**	....	....	**658.80**
11 **Taxes**	**185.80**	**171.40**	**175.70**	**188.76**	**176.00**	**176.82**	**5.06**	**5.68**	**6.19**	....	....	**183.01**
111 Taxes on income, profits, & capital gains	—	—	25.30	—	—	26.31	—	—	—	....	....	26.31
1111 Individuals	—	—	25.30	—	—	26.31	—	—	—	....	....	26.31
1112 Corporations and other enterprises	—	—	—	—	—	—	—	—	—	....	....	—
112 Taxes on payroll and workforce	—	—	—	—	—	—	—	—	—	....	....	—
113 Taxes on property	—	—	—	—	—	—	2.12	2.28	1.14	....	....	1.14
114 Taxes on goods and services	142.50	135.30	102.40	142.50	135.26	102.59	2.93	3.40	5.06	....	....	107.65
1141 General taxes on goods and services	126.90	125.30	65.40	126.90	125.26	65.40	—	—	—	....	....	65.40
1142 Excises	15.60	10.00	7.10	15.60	10.00	7.10	—	.34	—	....	....	7.10
115 Taxes on int'l. trade and transactions	43.30	36.10	43.30	45.90	40.43	43.30	—	—	—	....	....	43.30
116 Other taxes	—	—	4.70	.36	.31	4.61	.01	—	—	....	....	4.61
12 **Social contributions**	**—**	**—**	**—**	**25.32**	**23.21**	**27.46**	**—**	**—**	**—**	....	....	**27.46**
121 Social security contributions	—	—	—	24.41	22.23	27.46	—	—	—	....	....	27.46
122 Other social contributions	—	—	—	.91	.97	—	—	—	—	....	....	—
13 **Grants**	**3.70**	**3.70**	**9.90**	**9.53**	**3.79**	**10.22**	**7.40**	**6.31**	**7.21**	....	....	**10.38**
131 From foreign governments	—	—	9.90	—	—	9.90	....	....	—	....	....	9.90
132 From international organizations	3.70	3.70	—	3.70	3.70	.32	.64	.17	.16	....	....	.48
133 From other general government units	—	—	—	5.83	.09	—	....	....	7.05	....	....	—
14 **Other revenue**	**440.80**	**467.40**	**427.90**	**446.90**	**472.48**	**436.76**	**.60**	**.59**	**1.19**	....	....	**437.95**
Table 2 Expense by economic type												
2 **Expense**	**440.60**	**564.10**	**397.12**	**484.42**	**590.25**	**411.41**	**12.64**	**12.88**	**10.04**	....	....	**414.39**
21 **Compensation of employees**	**118.10**	**120.40**	**120.20**	**137.57**	**131.80**	**152.09**	**7.35**	**7.23**	**6.42**	....	....	**158.51**
211 Wages and salaries	118.10	120.40	120.20	137.36	131.62	139.66	6.65	6.48	5.96	....	....	145.62
212 Social contributions	—	—	—	.21	.18	12.43	.70	.76	.46	....	....	12.89
22 **Use of goods and services**	**87.10**	**151.70**	**113.13**	**94.35**	**159.30**	**119.44**	**2.64**	**3.42**	**2.78**	....	....	**122.22**
23 **Consumption of fixed capital**	....	....	....	....	....	....	....	....	....	....	....	....
24 **Interest**	**152.00**	**177.80**	**117.80**	**152.01**	**177.80**	**117.80**	**—**	**—**	**—**	....	....	**117.80**
25 **Subsidies**	**—**	**—**	**—**	**.46**	**.43**	**—**	**1.48**	**.53**	**—**	....	....	**—**
26 **Grants**	**83.40**	**114.20**	**45.99**	**59.56**	**101.84**	**7.05**	**1.11**	**.27**	**—**	....	....	**—**
261 To foreign govenments	....	....	—	....	....	—	....	....	—	....	....	—
262 To international organizations	....	....	—	....	....	—	....	....	—	....	....	—
263 To other general government units	....	....	45.99	....	....	7.05	....	....	—	....	....	—
2631 Current	....	....	45.36	....	....	6.97	....	....	—	....	....	—
2632 Capital	....	....	.63	....	....	.08	....	....	—	....	....	—
27 **Social benefits**	**—**	**—**	**—**	**20.86**	**16.33**	**13.47**	**.06**	**.25**	**.05**	....	....	**13.52**
28 **Other expense**	**—**	**—**	**—**	**19.61**	**2.75**	**1.55**	**—**	**1.18**	**.79**	....	....	**2.33**
281 Property expense other than interest	—	—	—	17.48	.95	.02	—	—	.01	....	....	.02
282 Miscellaneous other expense	—	—	—	2.14	1.80	1.53	—	1.18	.78	....	....	2.30
2821 Current	—	—	—	2.14	1.80	.98	—	1.18	.58	....	....	1.55
2822 Capital	—	—	—	—	—	.55	—	—	.20	....	....	.75

Congo, Republic of   634

In Billions of Francs / Year Ending December 31 / Noncash Reporter

	Budgetary Central Government			Central Government			Local Government			General Government		
	2001	2002	2003	2001	2002	2003	2001	2002	2003	2001	2002	2003
Table 3 Transactions in assets and liabilities												
3 Change in net worth from transactns....	....	....	....	....	....	....	....	....	....	....	....	....
31 **Net acquisition of nonfinancial assets...**	**205.40**	**191.40**	**105.60**	**212.07**	**195.59**	**106.74**	**2.99**	**1.60**	**2.94**	....	....	**109.68**
311 Fixed assets..	205.40	191.40	104.97	212.07	195.57	106.12	2.97	1.48	2.94	....	....	109.06
3111 Buildings and structures...................	....	—	62.29	....	.10	62.60	1.37	.77	1.24	....	....	63.84
3112 Machinery and equipment.................	....	—	28.76	....	.30	29.48	.37	.22	.06	....	....	29.54
3113 Other fixed assets...........................	....	191.40	13.92	....	195.20	14.03	1.23	.49	1.64	....	....	15.68
312 Inventories...	—	—	.25	—	—	.25	—	—	—	....	....	.25
313 Valuables...	—	—	—	—	—	—	—	—	—	....	....	—
314 Nonproduced assets................................	—	—	.38	.01	.02	.38	.02	.11	—	....	....	.38
3141 Land...	—	—	—	—	—	—	—	.09	—	....	....	—
3142 Subsoil assets....................................	—	—	—	—	—	—	—	—	—	....	....	—
3143 Other naturally occurring assets.........	—	—	—	—	—	—	—	—	—	....	....	—
3144 Intangible nonproduced assets..........	—	—	.38	—	—	.38	—	.02	—	....	....	.38
32 **Net acquisition of financial assets.........**	....	....	....	....	....	....	....	....	....	....	....	....
321 Domestic...	....	....	....	....	....	....	....	....	....	....	....	....
3212 Currency and deposits......................	....	....	....	....	....	....	....	....	....	....	....	....
3213 Securities other than shares..............	....	....	....	....	....	....	....	....	....	....	....	....
3214 Loans..	....	....	....	....	....	....	....	....	....	....	....	....
3215 Shares and other equity....................	....	....	....	....	....	....	....	....	....	....	....	....
3216 Insurance technical reserves..............	....	....	....	....	....	....	....	....	....	....	....	....
3217 Financial derivatives.........................	....	....	....	....	....	....	....	....	....	....	....	....
3218 Other accounts receivable.................	....	....	....	....	....	....	....	....	....	....	....	....
322 Foreign...	....	....	....	....	....	....	....	....	....	....	....	....
3222 Currency and deposits......................	....	....	....	....	....	....	....	....	....	....	....	....
3223 Securities other than shares..............	....	....	....	....	....	....	....	....	....	....	....	....
3224 Loans..	....	....	....	....	....	....	....	....	....	....	....	....
3225 Shares and other equity....................	....	....	....	....	....	....	....	....	....	....	....	....
3226 Insurance technical reserves..............	....	....	....	....	....	....	....	....	....	....	....	....
3227 Financial derivatives.........................	....	....	....	....	....	....	....	....	....	....	....	....
3228 Other accounts receivable.................	....	....	....	....	....	....	....	....	....	....	....	....
323 Monetary gold and SDRs..........................	....	....	....	....	....	....	....	....	....	....	....	....
33 **Net incurrence of liabilities....................**	....	....	....	....	....	....	....	....	....	....	....	....
331 Domestic...	....	....	....	....	....	....	....	....	....	....	....	....
3312 Currency and deposits......................	....	....	....	....	....	....	....	....	....	....	....	....
3313 Securities other than shares..............	....	....	....	....	....	....	....	....	....	....	....	....
3314 Loans..	....	....	....	....	....	....	....	....	....	....	....	....
3316 Insurance technical reserves..............	....	....	....	....	....	....	....	....	....	....	....	....
3317 Financial derivatives.........................	....	....	....	....	....	....	....	....	....	....	....	....
3318 Other accounts payable.....................	....	....	....	....	....	....	....	....	....	....	....	....
332 Foreign...	....	....	....	....	....	....	....	....	....	....	....	....
3322 Currency and deposits......................	....	....	....	....	....	....	....	....	....	....	....	....
3323 Securities other than shares..............	....	....	....	....	....	....	....	....	....	....	....	....
3324 Loans..	....	....	....	....	....	....	....	....	....	....	....	....
3326 Insurance technical reserves..............	....	....	....	....	....	....	....	....	....	....	....	....
3327 Financial derivatives.........................	....	....	....	....	....	....	....	....	....	....	....	....
3328 Other accounts payable.....................	....	....	....	....	....	....	....	....	....	....	....	....
Table 4 Holding gains in assets and liabilities												
Table 5 Other changes in the volume of assets and liabilities												
Table 6 Balance sheet												
6 **Net worth...**	....	....	....	....	....	....	....	....	....	....	....	....
61 **Nonfinancial assets.............................**	....	....	....	....	....	....	....	....	....	....	....	....
611 Fixed assets...	....	....	....	....	....	....	....	....	....	....	....	....
6111 Buildings and structures...................	....	....	....	....	....	....	....	....	....	....	....	....
6112 Machinery and equipment.................	....	....	....	....	....	....	....	....	....	....	....	....
6113 Other fixed assets...........................	....	....	....	....	....	....	....	....	....	....	....	....
612 Inventories...	....	....	....	....	....	....	....	....	....	....	....	....
613 Valuables...	....	....	....	....	....	....	....	....	....	....	....	....
614 Nonproduced assets................................	....	....	....	....	....	....	....	....	....	....	....	....
6141 Land...	....	....	....	....	....	....	....	....	....	....	....	....
6142 Subsoil assets....................................	....	....	....	....	....	....	....	....	....	....	....	....
6143 Other naturally occurring assets.........	....	....	....	....	....	....	....	....	....	....	....	....
6144 Intangible nonproduced assets..........	....	....	....	....	....	....	....	....	....	....	....	....

2005, International Monetary Fund: *Government Finance Statistics Yearbook*

In Billions of Francs / Year Ending December 31 / Noncash Reporter

		Budgetary Central Government			Central Government			Local Government			General Government		
		2001	2002	2003	2001	2002	2003	2001	2002	2003	2001	2002	2003
62	**Financial assets**...............	....	....	....	....	....	....	....	....	....	....	....	....
621	Domestic...............	....	....	....	....	....	....	....	....	....	....	....	....
6212	Currency and deposits...............	....	....	....	....	....	....	....	....	....	....	....	....
6213	Securities other than shares...............	....	....	....	....	....	....	....	....	....	....	....	....
6214	Loans...............	....	....	....	....	....	....	....	....	....	....	....	....
6215	Shares and other equity...............	....	....	....	....	....	....	....	....	....	....	....	....
6216	Insurance technical reserves...............	....	....	....	....	....	....	....	....	....	....	....	....
6217	Financial derivatives...............	....	....	....	....	....	....	....	....	....	....	....	....
6218	Other accounts receivable...............	....	....	....	....	....	....	....	....	....	....	....	....
622	Foreign...............	....	....	....	....	....	....	....	....	....	....	....	....
6222	Currency and deposits...............	....	....	....	....	....	....	....	....	....	....	....	....
6223	Securities other than shares...............	....	....	....	....	....	....	....	....	....	....	....	....
6224	Loans...............	....	....	....	....	....	....	....	....	....	....	....	....
6225	Shares and other equity...............	....	....	....	....	....	....	....	....	....	....	....	....
6226	Insurance technical reserves...............	....	....	....	....	....	....	....	....	....	....	....	....
6227	Financial derivatives...............	....	....	....	....	....	....	....	....	....	....	....	....
6228	Other accounts receivable...............	....	....	....	....	....	....	....	....	....	....	....	....
623	Monetary gold and SDRs...............	....	....	....	....	....	....	....	....	....	....	....	....
63	**Liabilities**...............	....	....	**4.35**	....	....	**4.35**	....	....	—	....	....	**4.35**
631	Domestic...............	....	....	.56	....	....	.56	....	....	—	....	....	.56
6312	Currency and deposits...............	....	....	—	....	....	—	....	....	—	....	....	—
6313	Securities other than shares...............	....	....	—	....	....	—	....	....	—	....	....	—
6314	Loans...............	....	....	.56	....	....	.56	....	....	—	....	....	.56
6316	Insurance technical reserves...............	....	....	—	....	....	—	....	....	—	....	....	—
6317	Financial derivatives...............	....	....	—	....	....	—	....	....	—	....	....	—
6318	Other accounts payable...............	....	....	....	....	....	....	....	....	....	....	....	....
632	Foreign...............	....	....	3.79	....	....	3.79	....	....	—	....	....	3.79
6322	Currency and deposits...............	....	....	—	....	....	—	....	....	—	....	....	—
6323	Securities other than shares...............	....	....	—	....	....	—	....	....	—	....	....	—
6324	Loans...............	....	....	3.79	....	....	3.79	....	....	—	....	....	3.79
6326	Insurance technical reserves...............	....	....	—	....	....	—	....	....	—	....	....	—
6327	Financial derivatives...............	....	....	—	....	....	—	....	....	—	....	....	—
6328	Other accounts payable...............	....	....	....	....	....	....	....	....	....	....	....	....
Memorandum items:													
6M2	Net financial worth...............	....	....	....	....	....	....	....	....	....	....	....	....
6M3	Debt at market value...............	....	....	4.35	....	....	4.35	....	....	....	....	....	4.35
6M4	Debt at nominal value...............	....	....	....	....	....	....	....	....	....	....	....	....
6M5	Arrears...............	....	....	2.84	....	....	2.84	....	....	....	....	....	2.84
6M6	Obligations for social security benefits...............	....	....	....	....	....	....	....	....	....	....	....	....
6M7	Contingent liabilities...............	....	....	....	....	....	....	....	....	....	....	....	....
6M8	Uncapitalized military weapons, systems...............	....	....	....	....	....	....	....	....	....	....	....	....

Table 7   Outlays by functions of govt.

		Budgetary Central Government			Central Government			Local Government			General Government		
		2001	2002	2003	2001	2002	2003	2001	2002	2003	2001	2002	2003
7	**Total outlays**...............	....	....	**502.71**	....	....	**518.15**	....	....	....	....	....	....
701	**General public services**...............	....	....	....	....	....	**358.60**	....	....	....	....	....	....
7017	Public debt transactions...............	....	....	117.80	....	....	117.80	....	....	....	....	....	....
7018	General transfers between levels of govt...............	....	....	....	....	....	....	....	....	....	....	....	....
702	**Defense**...............	....	....	....	....	....	**49.33**	....	....	....	....	....	....
703	**Public order and safety**...............	....	....	....	....	....	**21.17**	....	....	....	....	....	....
704	**Economic affairs**...............	....	....	....	....	....	**53.80**	....	....	....	....	....	....
7042	Agriculture, forestry, fishing, and hunting...............	....	....	....	....	....	5.66	....	....	....	....	....	....
7043	Fuel and energy...............	....	....	....	....	....	30.12	....	....	....	....	....	....
7044	Mining, manufacturing, and construction...............	....	....	....	....	....	2.09	....	....	....	....	....	....
7045	Transport...............	....	....	....	....	....	12.03	....	....	....	....	....	....
7046	Communication...............	....	....	....	....	....	1.52	....	....	....	....	....	....
705	**Environmental protection**...............	....	....	....	....	....	**1.56**	....	....	....	....	....	....
706	**Housing and community amenities**...............	....	....	....	....	....	**22.58**	....	....	....	....	....	....
707	**Health**...............	....	....	....	....	....	**19.77**	....	....	....	....	....	....
7072	Outpatient services...............	....	....	....	....	....	—	....	....	....	....	....	....
7073	Hospital services...............	....	....	....	....	....	....	....	....	....	....	....	....
7074	Public health services...............	....	....	....	....	....	12.46	....	....	....	....	....	....
708	**Recreation, culture, and religion**...............	....	....	....	....	....	**17.77**	....	....	....	....	....	....

In Billions of Francs / Year Ending December 31 / Noncash Reporter

		Budgetary Central Government			Central Government			Local Government			General Government		
		2001	2002	2003	2001	2002	2003	2001	2002	2003	2001	2002	2003
709	**Education**..............................	....	....	....	....	....	**18.27**	....	....	....	....	....	....
7091	Pre-primary and primary education..............	....	....	....	....	....	.12	....	....	....	....	....	....
7092	Secondary education............................	....	....	....	....	....	1.20	....	....	....	....	....	....
7094	Tertiary education...............................	....	....	....	....	....	15.53	....	....	....	....	....	....
710	**Social protection**..............................	....	....	....	....	....	**4.22**	....	....	....	....	....	....
7	Statistical discrepancy: Total outlays..............	....	....	....	....	....	−48.92	....	....	....	....	....	....

Table 8   Transactions in financial assets and liabilities by sector

In Billions of Colones / Year Ending December 31 / Cash Reporter

		Budgetary Central Government			Central Government			Local Government			General Government		
		2002	2003	2004	2002	2003	2004	2002	2003	2004	2002	2003	2004
	Statement of government operations												
	Statement of other economic flows												
	Balance sheet												
	Statement of sources and uses of cash												
1	Cash receipts from operating activities..........	809.0	981.6	1,111.9	1,370.5	1,579.4	1,819.8	58.6	58.4	77.0	1,420.2	1,629.2	1,883.7
11	Taxes.....................................	778.4	906.7	1,057.9	797.5	935.4	1,088.8	25.3	30.7	37.0	822.7	966.1	1,125.7
12	Social contributions.............................	23.1	25.1	28.0	456.1	510.7	580.4	—	—	—	456.1	510.7	580.4
13	Grants...	2.3	42.1	17.6	3.2	3.8	1.6	5.7	4.8	13.0	—	—	1.5
14	Other receipts..	5.2	7.7	8.4	113.7	129.5	148.9	27.7	22.9	27.1	141.4	152.4	176.0
2	Cash payments for operating activities..........	1,029.0	1,149.5	1,312.0	1,467.2	1,626.5	1,835.9	45.3	43.7	62.4	1,503.6	1,661.6	1,885.1
21	Compensation of employees.....................	361.0	414.9	468.7	599.9	697.1	781.9	23.1	24.2	32.1	623.0	721.3	813.9
22	Purchases of goods and services..................	36.2	31.3	40.9	176.6	209.0	213.0	15.5	12.1	21.1	192.2	221.1	234.0
24	Interest..	259.4	297.3	333.0	260.6	298.5	333.8	1.3	1.1	1.0	261.9	299.6	334.8
25	Subsidies...	—	—	—	—	—	—	—	—	—	—	—	—
26	Grants..	152.9	194.3	221.7	5.7	4.8	14.9	3.2	3.8	.1	—	—	1.8
27	Social benefits......................................	209.8	208.9	244.8	384.2	339.9	453.4	1.6	—	—	385.8	339.9	453.4
28	Other payments....................................	9.7	2.8	2.9	40.3	77.2	39.0	.5	2.5	8.1	40.8	79.7	47.1
CIO	*Net cash inflow from oper. activities.....*	−220.0	−167.9	−200.1	−96.7	−47.1	−16.1	13.4	14.7	14.6	−83.4	−32.4	−1.4
31.1	Purchases of nonfinancial assets................	21.8	17.7	17.8	109.7	64.5	92.0	4.6	11.4	6.2	114.4	75.9	98.1
31.2	Sales of nonfinancial assets......................	—	—	—	—	—	—	—	—	—	—	—	—
31	Net cash outflow from investments in nonfinancial assets..................................	21.8	17.7	17.8	109.7	64.5	92.0	4.6	11.4	6.2	114.4	75.9	98.1
CSD	*Cash surplus/deficit.............................*	−241.8	−185.6	−217.9	−206.4	−111.6	−108.0	8.7	3.3	8.5	−197.8	−108.3	−99.6
32x	Net acquisition of fin assets, excl. cash....	....	....	....	....	....	....	....	....	....	....	....	....
321x	Domestic..	....	....	....	....	....	....	....	....	....	....	....	....
322x	Foreign..	....	....	....	....	....	....	....	....	....	....	....	....
323	Monetary gold and SDRs.........................	....	....	....	....	....	....	....	....	....	....	....	....
33	Net incurrence of liabilities.....................	....	....	....	....	....	....	....	....	....	....	....	....
331	Domestic..	....	....	....	....	....	....	....	....	....	....	....	....
332	Foreign..	....	....	....	....	....	....	....	....	....	....	....	....
NFB	Net cash inflow from fin. activities..........	....	....	....	....	....	....	....	....	....	....	....	....
NCB	*Net change in the stock of cash.............*	....	....	....	....	....	....	....	....	....	....	....	....

Table 1　Revenue

		2002	2003	2004	2002	2003	2004	2002	2003	2004	2002	2003	2004
1	**Revenue........................**	809.0	981.6	1,111.9	1,370.5	1,579.4	1,819.8	58.6	58.4	77.0	1,420.2	1,629.2	1,883.7
11	**Taxes..........................**	778.4	906.7	1,057.9	797.5	935.4	1,088.8	25.3	30.7	37.0	822.7	966.1	1,125.7
111	Taxes on income, profits, & capital gains......	185.7	233.1	267.4	185.7	233.1	268.0	—	—	—	185.7	233.1	268.0
1111	Individuals..	....	....	....	....	....	....	—	—	—	....	....	....
1112	Corporations and other enterprises............	....	....	....	....	....	....	—	—	—	....	....	....
112	Taxes on payroll and workforce.................	—	—	—	—	—	—	—	—	—	—	—	—
113	Taxes on property.................................	22.1	34.0	36.0	22.1	34.0	36.0	7.5	8.9	12.1	29.6	42.9	48.1
114	Taxes on goods and services.....................	513.8	571.2	665.2	522.2	596.6	692.3	14.6	19.7	24.9	536.7	616.3	717.2
1141	General taxes on goods and services..........	297.6	331.5	397.4	297.6	331.5	397.4	—	—	—	297.6	331.5	397.4
1142	Excises...	65.4	66.1	73.1	65.4	66.1	73.1	—	—	—	65.4	66.1	73.1
115	Taxes on int'l. trade and transactions..........	56.9	68.4	89.1	60.2	71.7	92.3	—	—	—	60.2	71.7	92.3
116	Other taxes...	—	—	—	7.3			3.2	2.1	—	10.6	2.1	—
12	**Social contributions.............................**	23.1	25.1	28.0	456.1	510.7	580.4	—	—	—	456.1	510.7	580.4
121	Social security contributions.....................	—	—	—	363.4	401.1	455.4	—	—	—	363.4	401.1	455.4
122	Other social contributions.......................	23.1	25.1	28.0	92.7	109.6	125.0	—	—	—	—	109.6	125.0
13	**Grants...**	2.3	42.1	17.6	3.2	3.8	1.6	5.7	4.8	13.0	—	—	1.5
131	From foreign governments.......................	—	—	—	—	—	—	—	—	—	—	—	—
132	From international organizations................	—	—	—	—	—	1.5	—	—	—	—	—	1.5
133	From other general government units..........	2.3	42.1	17.6	3.2	3.8	.1	5.7	4.8	13.0	—	—	—
14	**Other revenue.....................................**	5.2	7.7	8.4	113.7	129.5	148.9	27.7	22.9	27.1	141.4	152.4	176.0

Table 2　Expense by economic type

		2002	2003	2004	2002	2003	2004	2002	2003	2004	2002	2003	2004
2	**Expense...........................**	1,029.0	1,149.5	1,312.0	1,467.2	1,626.5	1,835.9	45.3	43.7	62.4	1,503.6	1,661.6	1,885.1
21	**Compensation of employees.................**	361.0	414.9	468.7	599.9	697.1	781.9	23.1	24.2	32.1	623.0	721.3	813.9
211	Wages and salaries.................................	314.7	362.4	409.2	542.3	628.6	707.2	23.1	21.2	28.4	565.5	649.8	735.6
212	Social contributions...............................	46.3	52.5	59.6	57.6	68.5	74.7	—	3.0	3.7	57.6	71.5	78.4
22	**Use of goods and services.....................**	36.2	31.3	40.9	176.6	209.0	213.0	15.5	12.1	21.1	192.2	221.1	234.0
23	**Consumption of fixed capital.................**	....	....	....	....	....	....	....	....	....	....	....	....
24	**Interest...**	259.4	297.3	333.0	260.6	298.5	333.8	1.3	1.1	1.0	261.9	299.6	334.8
25	**Subsidies..**	—	—	—	—	—	—	—	—	—	—	—	—

In Billions of Colones / Year Ending December 31 / Cash Reporter

		Budgetary Central Government			Central Government			Local Government			General Government		
		2002	2003	2004	2002	2003	2004	2002	2003	2004	2002	2003	2004
26	Grants..................................	152.9	194.3	221.7	5.7	4.8	14.9	3.2	3.8	.1	—	—	1.8
261	To foreign govenments.................	—	—	—	—	—	—	—	—	—	—	—	—
262	To international organizations.........	—	—	1.2	—	—	1.8	—	—	—	—	—	1.8
263	To other general government units......	152.9	194.3	220.5	5.7	4.8	13.0	3.2	3.8	.1	—	—	—
2631	Current................................	97.2	139.6	149.7	4.0	3.5	1.6	....	....	.1			
2632	Capital................................	55.7	54.7	70.9	1.7	1.3	11.4	....	....	—			
27	Social benefits.......................	209.8	208.9	244.8	384.2	339.9	453.4	1.6	—	—	385.8	339.9	453.4
28	Other expense.........................	9.7	2.8	2.9	40.3	77.2	39.0	.5	2.5	8.1	40.8	79.7	47.1
281	Property expense other than interest....	—	—	—	—	—	—	—	—	—	—	—	—
282	Miscellaneous other expense...........	9.7	2.8	2.9	40.3	77.2	39.0	.5	2.5	8.1	40.8	79.7	47.1
2821	Current................................	3.4	1.4	2.9	5.8	47.6	39.0	—	2.5	8.1	5.8	50.1	47.1
2822	Capital................................	6.4	1.4	—	34.5	29.6	—	.5	—	—	35.0	29.6	—

Table 3   Transactions in assets and liabilities

3	Change in net worth from transactns....	....	....	....	....	....	....	....	....	....	....	....	....
31	Net acquisition of nonfinancial assets...	21.8	17.7	17.8	109.7	64.5	92.0	4.6	11.4	6.2	114.4	75.9	98.1
311	Fixed assets..........................	21.7	16.1	15.9	104.4	56.7	86.9	4.4	10.7	5.9	108.8	67.4	92.8
3111	Buildings and structures..............	....	10.6	10.3	....	36.8	63.8	....	8.3	2.6	....	45.1	66.4
3112	Machinery and equipment...............	....	5.5	5.6	....	19.9	23.1	....	2.4	3.3	....	22.3	26.4
3113	Other fixed assets....................	....	—	—	....	—	—	....	—	—	....	—	—
312	Inventories...........................	—	—	—	—	—	—	—	—	—	—	—	—
313	Valuables.............................	—	—	—	—	—	—	—	—	—	—	—	—
314	Nonproduced assets....................	.1	1.6	1.9	5.4	7.8	5.1	.3	.7	.3	5.6	8.5	5.4
3141	Land..................................	....	1.6	1.9	....	7.8	5.1	....	.7	.3	....	8.5	5.4
3142	Subsoil assets........................	....	—	—	....	—	—	....	—	—	....	—	—
3143	Other naturally occurring assets......	....	—	—	....	—	—	....	—	—	....	—	—
3144	Intangible nonproduced assets.........	....	—	—	....	—	—	....	—	—	....	—	—
32	Net acquisition of financial assets........	....	....	....	....	....	....	....	....	....	....	....	....
321	Domestic..............................	....	....	....	....	....	....	....	....	....	....	....	....
3212	Currency and deposits.................	....	....	....	....	....	....	....	....	....	....	....	....
3213	Securities other than shares..........	....	....	....	....	....	....	....	....	....	....	....	....
3214	Loans.................................	....	....	....	....	....	....	....	....	....	....	....	....
3215	Shares and other equity...............	....	....	....	....	....	....	....	....	....	....	....	....
3216	Insurance technical reserves..........	....	....	....	....	....	....	....	....	....	....	....	....
3217	Financial derivatives.................	....	....	....	....	....	....	....	....	....	....	....	....
3218	Other accounts receivable.............	....	....	....	....	....	....	....	....	....	....	....	....
322	Foreign...............................	....	....	....	....	....	....	....	....	....	....	....	....
3222	Currency and deposits.................	....	....	....	....	....	....	....	....	....	....	....	....
3223	Securities other than shares..........	....	....	....	....	....	....	....	....	....	....	....	....
3224	Loans.................................	....	....	....	....	....	....	....	....	....	....	....	....
3225	Shares and other equity...............	....	....	....	....	....	....	....	....	....	....	....	....
3226	Insurance technical reserves..........	....	....	....	....	....	....	....	....	....	....	....	....
3227	Financial derivatives.................	....	....	....	....	....	....	....	....	....	....	....	....
3228	Other accounts receivable.............	....	....	....	....	....	....	....	....	....	....	....	....
323	Monetary gold and SDRs................	....	....	....	....	....	....	....	....	....	....	....	....
33	Net incurrence of liabilities...................	....	....	....	....	....	....	....	....	....	....	....	....
331	Domestic..............................	....	....	....	....	....	....	....	....	....	....	....	....
3312	Currency and deposits.................	....	....	....	....	....	....	....	....	....	....	....	....
3313	Securities other than shares..........	....	....	....	....	....	....	....	....	....	....	....	....
3314	Loans.................................	....	....	....	....	....	....	....	....	....	....	....	....
3316	Insurance technical reserves..........	....	....	....	....	....	....	....	....	....	....	....	....
3317	Financial derivatives.................	....	....	....	....	....	....	....	....	....	....	....	....
3318	Other accounts payable................	....	....	....	....	....	....	....	....	....	....	....	....
332	Foreign...............................	....	....	....	....	....	....	....	....	....	....	....	....
3322	Currency and deposits.................	....	....	....	....	....	....	....	....	....	....	....	....
3323	Securities other than shares..........	....	....	....	....	....	....	....	....	....	....	....	....
3324	Loans.................................	....	....	....	....	....	....	....	....	....	....	....	....
3326	Insurance technical reserves..........	....	....	....	....	....	....	....	....	....	....	....	....
3327	Financial derivatives.................	....	....	....	....	....	....	....	....	....	....	....	....
3328	Other accounts payable................	....	....	....	....	....	....	....	....	....	....	....	....

In Billions of Colones / Year Ending December 31 / Cash Reporter

	Budgetary Central Government			Central Government			Local Government			General Government		
	2002	2003	2004	2002	2003	2004	2002	2003	2004	2002	2003	2004
Table 4 Holding gains in assets and liabilities												
Table 5 Other changes in the volume of assets and liabilities												
Table 6 Balance sheet												
Table 7 Outlays by functions of govt.												
7 **Total outlays**...........................	1,050.8	1,167.2	1,329.9	1,576.9	1,691.0	1,927.8	49.9	55.1	68.6	1,618.0	1,737.5	1,983.2
701 **General public services**..........................	334.2	360.2	406.9	....	375.6	....	1.3	—	—	....	375.6	....
7017 Public debt transactions.................................	259.4	297.3	333.0	....	298.5	333.8	1.3	1.1	1.0	....	299.6	334.8
7018 General transfers between levels of govt......	....	....	....	....	....	....	....	....	....	....	....	....
702 **Defense**..	—	—	—	....	—	....	—	—	—	....	—	....
703 **Public order and safety**..........................	118.1	127.0	144.1	....	127.6	....	—	—	—	....	127.6	....
704 **Economic affairs**....................................	108.3	86.3	104.4	....	164.6	....	—	—	—	....	164.6	....
7042 Agriculture, forestry, fishing, and hunting....	10.2	21.9	34.1	....	42.0	....	—	—	—	....	42.0	....
7043 Fuel and energy...	—	—	—	....	1.6	....	—	—	—	....	1.6	....
7044 Mining, manufacturing, and construction.....	36.6	4.6	—	....	16.2	....	—	—	—	....	16.2	....
7045 Transport..	61.5	59.8	70.3	....	104.8	....	—	—	—	....	104.8	....
7046 Communication..	—	—	—	....	—	....	—	—	—	....	—	....
705 **Environmental protection**......................	9.9	—	12.5	....	—	....	—	—	—	....	....	....
706 **Housing and community amenities**........	.6	.5	.7	....	.5	....	49.9	39.9	68.6	....	35.6	....
707 **Health**..	29.6	37.4	34.5	....	352.6	....	—	—	—	....	352.6	....
7072 Outpatient services......................................	....	....	....	....	....	....	—	—	—	....	....	....
7073 Hospital services..	....	....	....	....	....	....	—	—	—	....	....	....
7074 Public health services..................................	....	....	....	....	....	....	—	—	—	....	....	....
708 **Recreation, culture, and religion**............	8.4	7.3	8.6	....	13.2	....	—	—	—	....	13.2	....
709 **Education**..	296.3	343.1	398.1	....	365.5	....	—	—	—	....	365.5	....
7091 Pre-primary and primary education...............	....	....	....	....	....	....	—	—	—	....	....	....
7092 Secondary education....................................	....	....	....	....	....	....	—	—	—	....	....	....
7094 Tertiary education.......................................	....	....	....	....	....	....	—	—	—	....	....	....
710 **Social protection**....................................	162.8	211.3	220.0	....	292.4	....	—	—	—	....	292.4	....
7 Statistical discrepancy: Total outlays..............	−17.3	−5.9	—	....	−1.0	....	−1.3	15.2	—	....	10.4	....
Table 8 Transactions in financial assets and liabilities by sector												

In Billions of Francs / Year Ending December 31 / Cash Reporter

	Budgetary Central Government			Central Government			Local Government			General Government		
	2001	2002	2003	2001	2002	2003	2001	2002	2003	2001	2002	2003
Statement of government operations												
Statement of other economic flows												
Balance sheet												
Statement of sources and uses of cash												
1 Cash receipts from operating activities..........	1,262.4	1,343.7	1,281.9	1,376.6	1,469.6	1,401.4	....	....	....	....	....	....
11 Taxes..................................	1,174.1	1,259.3	1,190.1	1,174.1	1,259.3	1,190.1	....	....	....	....	....	....
12 Social contributions....................	—	—	—	114.2	113.1	109.1	....	....	....	....	....	....
13 Grants................................	40.3	28.4	39.1	40.3	28.4	39.1	....	....	....	....	....	....
14 Other receipts........................	48.0	56.0	52.7	48.0	68.7	63.0	....	....	....	....	....	....
2 Cash payments for operating activities..........	1,021.2	1,137.6	1,253.5	1,163.5	1,335.3	1,397.3	....	....	....	....	....	....
21 Compensation of employees................	484.1	523.5	539.4	484.1	523.5	539.4	....	....	....	....	....	....
22 Purchases of goods and services.............	208.3	263.2	389.3	244.4	347.2	412.4	....	....	....	....	....	....
24 Interest...............................	259.7	265.6	217.4	259.7	265.6	217.4	....	....	....	....	....	....
25 Subsidies.............................	61.0	74.9	101.9	61.0	74.9	101.9	....	....	....	....	....	....
26 Grants................................	—	—	—	—	—	—	....	....	....	....	....	....
27 Social benefits........................	4.4	3.1	3.1	101.0	104.0	114.7	....	....	....	....	....	....
28 Other payments........................	3.8	7.2	2.4	13.3	20.1	11.5	....	....	....	....	....	....
CIO *Net cash inflow from oper. activities.....*	*241.3*	*206.2*	*28.4*	*213.2*	*134.2*	*4.0*	....	....	....	....	....	....
31.1 Purchases of nonfinancial assets...............	....	....	....	....	....	....						
31.2 Sales of nonfinancial assets................	....	....	....	....	....	....						
31 Net cash outflow from investments in nonfinancial assets..................	....	....	....	....	....	....						
CSD *Cash surplus/deficit..................*	*68.1*	*−129.4*	*−212.6*	*68.1*	*−129.4*	*−212.6*	....	....	....	....	....	....
32x Net acquisition of fin assets, excl. cash.......	....	....	....	....	....	....	....	....	....	....	....	....
321x Domestic.............................	....	....	....	....	....	....						
322x Foreign..............................	....	....	....	....	....	....						
323 Monetary gold and SDRs.................	—	—	—	—	—	—						
33 Net incurrence of liabilities...............	416.5	1,079.2	731.1	416.5	1,079.2	731.1	....	....	....	....	....	....
331 Domestic.............................	21.3	35.7	190.7	21.3	35.7	190.7	....	....	....	....	....	....
332 Foreign..............................	395.2	1,043.5	540.4	395.2	1,043.5	540.4	....	....	....	....	....	....
NFB Net cash inflow from fin. activities.........	....	....	....	....	....	....						
NCB *Net change in the stock of cash...........*	....	....	....	....	....	....						
Table 1 Revenue												
1 **Revenue**........................	**1,262.4**	**1,343.7**	**1,281.9**	**1,376.6**	**1,469.6**	**1,401.4**	....	....	....	....	....	....
11 **Taxes**...........................	**1,174.1**	**1,259.3**	**1,190.1**	**1,174.1**	**1,259.3**	**1,190.1**	....	....	....	....	....	....
111 Taxes on income, profits, & capital gains......	140.6	136.2	108.7	140.6	136.2	108.7	....	....	....	....	....	....
1111 Individuals..........................	—											
1112 Corporations and other enterprises...........	115.8	111.5	86.9	115.8	111.5	86.9						
112 Taxes on payroll and workforce............	133.5	143.3	138.4	133.5	143.3	138.4						
113 Taxes on property......................	52.5	51.1	40.6	52.5	51.1	40.6						
114 Taxes on goods and services...............	295.5	296.4	258.2	295.5	296.4	258.2						
1141 General taxes on goods and services..........	191.6	199.0	137.2	191.6	199.0	137.2						
1142 Excises.............................	8.1	8.2	8.5	8.1	8.2	8.5						
115 Taxes on int'l. trade and transactions..........	552.0	632.3	644.2	552.0	632.3	644.2						
116 Other taxes...........................	—	—	—									
12 **Social contributions....................**	**—**	**—**	**—**	**114.2**	**113.1**	**109.1**	....	....	....	....	....	....
121 Social security contributions..............	—	—	—	114.2	113.1	109.1						
122 Other social contributions...............	—	—	—									
13 **Grants......................**	**40.3**	**28.4**	**39.1**	**40.3**	**28.4**	**39.1**	....	....	....	....	....	....
131 From foreign governments...............	40.3	28.4	39.1	40.3	28.4	39.1						
132 From international organizations............	—	—	—	—	—	—						
133 From other general government units..........	—	—	—	—	—	—						
14 **Other revenue........................**	**48.0**	**56.0**	**52.7**	**48.0**	**68.7**	**63.0**	....	....	....	....	....	....
Table 2 Expense by economic type												
2 **Expense.........................**	**1,021.2**	**1,137.6**	**1,253.5**	**1,163.5**	**1,335.3**	**1,397.3**	....	....	....	....	....	....
21 **Compensation of employees................**	**484.1**	**523.5**	**539.4**	**484.1**	**523.5**	**539.4**	....	....	....	....	....	....
211 Wages and salaries......................	458.8	496.0	511.1	458.8	496.0	511.1	....	....	....	....	....	....
212 Social contributions....................	25.3	27.5	28.3	25.3	27.5	28.3	....	....	....	....	....	....
22 **Use of goods and services....................**	**208.3**	**263.2**	**389.3**	**244.4**	**347.2**	**412.4**	....	....	....	....	....	....
23 **Consumption of fixed capital...............**	....	....	....	....	....	....	....	....	....	....	....	....
24 **Interest........................**	**259.7**	**265.6**	**217.4**	**259.7**	**265.6**	**217.4**	....	....	....	....	....	....
25 **Subsidies........................**	**61.0**	**74.9**	**101.9**	**61.0**	**74.9**	**101.9**	....	....	....	....	....	....

In Billions of Francs / Year Ending December 31 / Cash Reporter

	Budgetary Central Government			Central Government			Local Government			General Government		
	2001	2002	2003	2001	2002	2003	2001	2002	2003	2001	2002	2003
26 Grants.................................	—	—	—	—	—	—	....	....	....	....	....	....
261 To foreign govenments....................	—	—	—	—	—	—	....	....	....	....	....	....
262 To international organizations..................	—	—	—	—	—	—	....	....	....	....	....	....
263 To other general government units..............	—	—	—	—	—	—	....	....	....	....	....	....
2631 Current...................................	—	—	—	—	—	—	....	....	....	....	....	....
2632 Capital....................................	—	—	—	—	—	—	....	....	....	....	....	....
27 Social benefits............................	4.4	3.1	3.1	101.0	104.0	114.7	....	....	....	....	....	....
28 Other expense...........................	3.8	7.2	2.4	13.3	20.1	11.5	....	....	....	....	....	....
281 Property expense other than interest............	—	—	—	—	—	—	....	....	....	....	....	....
282 Miscellaneous other expense....................	3.8	7.2	2.4	13.3	20.1	11.5	....	....	....	....	....	....
2821 Current..................................	—	—	—	9.6	12.9	9.1	....	....	....	....	....	....
2822 Capital...................................	3.8	7.2	2.4	3.8	7.2	2.4	....	....	....	....	....	....
Table 3 Transactions in assets and liabilities												
3 Change in net worth from transactns....	....	....	....	....	....	....	....	....	....	....	....	....
31 Net acquisition of nonfinancial assets...	....	....	....	....	....	....	....	....	....	....	....	....
311 Fixed assets................................	....	....	....	....	....	....	....	....	....	....	....	....
3111 Buildings and structures....................	....	....	....	....	....	....	....	....	....	....	....	....
3112 Machinery and equipment...................	....	....	....	....	....	....	....	....	....	....	....	....
3113 Other fixed assets........................	....	....	....	....	....	....	....	....	....	....	....	....
312 Inventories.................................	....	....	....	....	....	....	....	....	....	....	....	....
313 Valuables..................................	....	....	....	....	....	....	....	....	....	....	....	....
314 Nonproduced assets..........................	....	....	....	....	....	....	....	....	....	....	....	....
3141 Land.....................................	....	....	....	....	....	....	....	....	....	....	....	....
3142 Subsoil assets...........................	....	....	....	....	....	....	....	....	....	....	....	....
3143 Other naturally occurring assets..................	....	....	....	....	....	....	....	....	....	....	....	....
3144 Intangible nonproduced assets................	....	....	....	....	....	....	....	....	....	....	....	....
32 Net acquisition of financial assets........	484.6	949.8	518.5	484.6	949.8	518.5	....	....	....	....	....	....
321 Domestic..................................	127.4	2.0	117.3	127.4	2.0	117.3	....	....	....	....	....	....
3212 Currency and deposits....................	....	....	....	....	....	....	....	....	....	....	....	....
3213 Securities other than shares......................	....	....	....	....	....	....	....	....	....	....	....	....
3214 Loans....................................	....	....	....	....	....	....	....	....	....	....	....	....
3215 Shares and other equity....................	....	....	....	....	....	....	....	....	....	....	....	....
3216 Insurance technical reserves..................	....	....	....	....	....	....	....	....	....	....	....	....
3217 Financial derivatives.........................	....	....	....	....	....	....	....	....	....	....	....	....
3218 Other accounts receivable.....................	....	....	....	....	....	....	....	....	....	....	....	....
322 Foreign..................................	357.2	947.8	401.2	357.2	947.8	401.2	....	....	....	....	....	....
3222 Currency and deposits....................	....	....	....	....	....	....	....	....	....	....	....	....
3223 Securities other than shares...................	....	....	....	....	....	....	....	....	....	....	....	....
3224 Loans....................................	....	....	....	....	....	....	....	....	....	....	....	....
3225 Shares and other equity....................	....	....	....	....	....	....	....	....	....	....	....	....
3226 Insurance technical reserves..................	....	....	....	....	....	....	....	....	....	....	....	....
3227 Financial derivatives.........................	....	....	....	....	....	....	....	....	....	....	....	....
3228 Other accounts receivable.....................	....	....	....	....	....	....	....	....	....	....	....	....
323 Monetary gold and SDRs..........................	—	—	—	—	—	—	....	....	....	....	....	....
33 Net incurrence of liabilities..................	416.5	1,079.2	731.1	416.5	1,079.2	731.1	....	....	....	....	....	....
331 Domestic..................................	21.3	35.7	190.7	21.3	35.7	190.7	....	....	....	....	....	....
3312 Currency and deposits....................	....	....	....	....	....	....	....	....	....	....	....	....
3313 Securities other than shares...................	....	....	....	....	....	....	....	....	....	....	....	....
3314 Loans....................................	....	....	....	....	....	....	....	....	....	....	....	....
3316 Insurance technical reserves..................	....	....	....	....	....	....	....	....	....	....	....	....
3317 Financial derivatives.........................	....	....	....	....	....	....	....	....	....	....	....	....
3318 Other accounts payable.....................	....	....	....	....	....	....	....	....	....	....	....	....
332 Foreign..................................	395.2	1,043.5	540.4	395.2	1,043.5	540.4	....	....	....	....	....	....
3322 Currency and deposits....................	....	....	....	....	....	....	....	....	....	....	....	....
3323 Securities other than shares...................	....	....	....	....	....	....	....	....	....	....	....	....
3324 Loans....................................	....	....	....	....	....	....	....	....	....	....	....	....
3326 Insurance technical reserves..................	....	....	....	....	....	....	....	....	....	....	....	....
3327 Financial derivatives.........................	....	....	....	....	....	....	....	....	....	....	....	....
3328 Other accounts payable.....................	....	....	....	....	....	....	....	....	....	....	....	....

	Budgetary Central Government			Central Government			Local Government			General Government		
	2001	2002	2003	2001	2002	2003	2001	2002	2003	2001	2002	2003
Table 4 Holding gains in assets and liabilities												
Table 5 Other changes in the volume of assets and liabilities												
Table 6 Balance sheet												
Table 7 Outlays by functions of govt.												
Table 8 Transactions in financial assets and liabilities by sector												
82 **Net acquisition of financial assets**.........	**484.6**	**949.8**	**518.5**	**484.6**	**949.8**	**518.5**	....	....	....	....	....	....
821 Domestic...................................	127.4	2.0	117.3	127.4	2.0	117.3	....	....	....	....	....	....
8211 General government..............................	.3	—	—	.3	—	—	....	....	....	....	....	....
8212 Central bank......................................	48.7	—	117.3	48.7	—	117.3	....	....	....	....	....	....
8213 Other depository corporations..................	23.2	—	—	23.2	—	—	....	....	....	....	....	....
8214 Financial corporations n.e.c......................	52.9	—	—	52.9	—	—	....	....	....	....	....	....
8215 Nonfinancial corporations.........................	2.3	2.0	—	2.3	2.0	—	....	....	....	....	....	....
8216 Households & NPIs serving households......	—	—	—	—	—	—	....	....	....	....	....	....
822 Foreign..	357.2	947.8	401.2	357.2	947.8	401.2	....	....	....	....	....	....
8221 General government..............................	—	5.2	6.7	—	5.2	6.7	....	....	....	....	....	....
8227 International organizations.......................	357.2	914.4	394.5	357.2	914.4	394.5	....	....	....	....	....	....
8228 Financial corporations other than international organizations.............	—	—	—	—	—	—	....	....	....	....	....	....
8229 Other nonresidents...............................	—	28.2	—	—	28.2	—	....	....	....	....	....	....
823 Monetary gold and SDRs......................	—	—	—	—	—	—	....	....	....	....	....	....
83 **Net incurrence of liabilities**...................	**416.5**	**1,079.2**	**731.1**	**416.5**	**1,079.2**	**731.1**	....	....	....	....	....	....
831 Domestic..	21.3	35.7	190.7	21.3	35.7	190.7	....	....	....	....	....	....
8311 General government..............................	15.2	6.7	1.9	15.2	6.7	1.9	....	....	....	....	....	....
8312 Central bank......................................	—	4.1	—	—	4.1	—	....	....	....	....	....	....
8313 Other depository corporations..................	—	—	—	—	—	—	....	....	....	....	....	....
8314 Financial corporations n.e.c......................	—	19.6	56.4	—	19.6	56.4	....	....	....	....	....	....
8315 Nonfinancial corporations.........................	6.1	5.3	132.3	6.1	5.3	132.3	....	....	....	....	....	....
8316 Households & NPIs serving households......	—	—	—	—	—	—	....	....	....	....	....	....
832 Foreign..	395.2	1,043.5	540.4	395.2	1,043.5	540.4	....	....	....	....	....	....
8321 General government..............................	—	—	—	—	—	—	....	....	....	....	....	....
8327 International organizations.......................	395.2	1,011.2	540.4	395.2	1,011.2	540.4	....	....	....	....	....	....
8328 Financial corporations other than international organizations.............	—	32.2	—	—	32.2	—	....	....	....	....	....	....
8329 Other nonresidents...............................	—	—	—	—	—	—	....	....	....	....	....	....

Croatia 960

In Millions of Kunas / Year Ending December 31 / Cash Reporter

	Budgetary Central Government			Central Government			Local Government			General Government		
	2002	2003	2004	2002	2003	2004	2002	2003	2004	2002	2003	2004
Statement of government operations												
Statement of other economic flows												
Balance sheet												
Statement of sources and uses of cash												
1 Cash receipts from operating activities..........	†69,651	74,677	80,464	75,064	80,787	87,019	†9,098	10,075	10,829	82,465	88,842	95,578
11 Taxes.......	†42,810	45,281	47,150	45,171	47,912	49,834	†5,494	5,923	6,592	50,666	53,835	56,426
12 Social contributions................	†25,190	27,417	29,478	25,200	27,425	29,478	†—	—	—	25,200	27,425	29,478
13 Grants........	†—	10	10	143	379	277	1,556	1,652	2,007	1	12	14
14 Other receipts........	†1,651	1,969	3,826	4,550	5,071	7,431	2,048	2,500	2,230	6,598	7,571	9,661
2 Cash payments for operating activities..........	†70,397	77,075	83,131	75,448	80,715	86,941	†7,136	8,127	8,766	80,888	86,824	93,438
21 Compensation of employees................	†19,534	21,226	22,268	20,288	22,068	23,266	†1,894	1,997	2,240	22,182	24,065	25,505
22 Purchases of goods and services..........	†4,392	4,171	4,359	6,870	6,292	6,328	†2,902	3,203	3,352	9,773	9,494	9,679
24 Interest........	†3,264	3,587	3,973	3,646	3,956	4,344	†115	83	80	3,761	4,039	4,423
25 Subsidies........	†2,105	4,293	4,968	3,564	4,293	4,968	†583	623	726	4,146	4,916	5,695
26 Grants........	†4,162	3,747	3,420	1,659	1,737	2,163	†142	367	267	105	85	160
27 Social benefits........	†34,257	36,204	39,731	35,839	37,940	40,646	†290	315	376	36,129	38,255	41,022
28 Other payments........	†2,684	3,848	4,412	3,582	4,430	5,227	†1,211	1,540	1,726	4,792	5,970	6,954
CIO *Net cash inflow from oper. activities.....*	*†–746*	*–2,398*	*–2,668*	*–384*	*71*	*78*	*†1,961*	*1,947*	*2,063*	*1,577*	*2,019*	*2,141*
31.1 Purchases of nonfinancial assets........	†1,595	2,055	1,664	6,376	8,272	8,648	†1,541	2,127	2,711	7,917	10,398	11,360
31.2 Sales of nonfinancial assets........	†218	243	244	247	276	275	†406	458	590	652	734	865
31 Net cash outflow from investments in nonfinancial assets........	†1,377	1,812	1,419	6,129	7,996	8,374	†1,136	1,668	2,121	7,265	9,664	10,495
CSD *Cash surplus/deficit................*	*†–2,123*	*–4,210*	*–4,087*	*–6,514*	*–7,925*	*–8,296*	*†825*	*279*	*–59*	*–5,688*	*–7,646*	*–8,354*
32x Net acquisition of fin assets, excl. cash........	†1,290	–2,467	1,336	–1,041	–2,600	920	†1	182	64	–1,040	–2,419	983
321x Domestic........	†1,276	–2,477	1,327	–1,054	–2,609	910	†2	189	66	–1,052	–2,422	975
322x Foreign........	†14	10	10	14	10	10	†–2	–7	–2	12	3	8
323 Monetary gold and SDRs........	†—	—	—	—	—	—	†—	—	—	—	—	—
33 Net incurrence of liabilities........	†3,773	2,890	4,309	7,030	6,962	8,324	†–40	–82	135	6,990	6,878	8,459
331 Domestic........	†1,425	–160	4,039	2,079	949	4,108	†–27	7	232	2,052	954	4,339
332 Foreign........	†2,348	3,050	270	4,951	6,013	4,216	†–13	–89	–97	4,938	5,924	4,119
NFB Net cash inflow from fin. activities........	†2,483	5,357	2,973	8,070	9,561	7,405	†–41	–264	71	8,030	9,297	7,476
NCB *Net change in the stock of cash........*	*†360*	*1,147*	*–1,114*	*1,557*	*1,636*	*–891*	*†785*	*15*	*12*	*2,342*	*1,651*	*–879*
Table 1 Revenue												
1 **Revenue........**	†69,651	74,677	80,464	75,064	80,787	87,019	†9,098	10,075	10,829	82,465	88,842	95,578
11 **Taxes........**	†42,810	45,281	47,150	45,171	47,912	49,834	†5,494	5,923	6,592	50,666	53,835	56,426
111 Taxes on income, profits, & capital gains......	†6,022	6,189	6,260	6,022	6,189	6,260	†4,918	5,327	5,901	10,941	11,517	12,161
1111 Individuals........	†3,363	3,115	3,128	3,363	3,115	3,128	†3,863	4,083	4,636	7,227	7,198	7,765
1112 Corporations and other enterprises........	†2,659	3,075	3,131	2,659	3,075	3,131	†1,055	1,244	1,265	3,714	4,319	4,396
112 Taxes on payroll and workforce........	†—	—	—	—	—	—	†—	—	—	—	—	—
113 Taxes on property........	†295	290	356	295	290	356	†329	316	375	624	606	731
114 Taxes on goods and services........	†33,974	36,651	38,602	36,335	39,282	41,286	†228	265	302	36,564	39,547	41,588
1141 General taxes on goods and services........	†26,089	28,260	30,014	26,089	28,260	30,014	†39	43	44	26,128	28,303	30,057
1142 Excises........	†7,474	7,851	7,942	9,835	10,482	10,625	†—	—	—	9,835	10,482	10,625
115 Taxes on int'l. trade and transactions........	†2,051	1,811	1,591	2,051	1,811	1,591	†—	—	—	2,051	1,811	1,591
116 Other taxes........	†469	340	341	469	340	341	†18	14	14	487	354	355
12 **Social contributions........**	†25,190	27,417	29,478	25,200	27,425	29,478	†—	—	—	25,200	27,425	29,478
121 Social security contributions........	†25,190	27,417	29,478	25,200	27,425	29,478	†—	—	—	25,200	27,425	29,478
122 Other social contributions........	†—	—	—	—	—	—	†—	—	—	—	—	—
13 **Grants........**	†—	10	10	143	379	277	1,556	1,652	2,007	1	12	14
131 From foreign governments........	†—	—	1	—	1	1	†—	—	4	—	2	5
132 From international organizations........	†—	10	9	—	10	9	†1	—	—	1	10	9
133 From other general government units........	†—	—	—	142	367	267	1,555	1,652	2,003	—	—	—
14 **Other revenue........**	†1,651	1,969	3,826	4,550	5,071	7,431	2,048	2,500	2,230	6,598	7,571	9,661
Table 2 Expense by economic type												
2 **Expense........**	†70,397	77,075	83,131	75,448	80,715	86,941	†7,136	8,127	8,766	80,888	86,824	93,438
21 **Compensation of employees........**	†19,534	21,226	22,268	20,288	22,068	23,266	†1,894	1,997	2,240	22,182	24,065	25,505
211 Wages and salaries........	†16,677	18,037	18,889	17,327	18,763	19,751	†1,640	1,733	1,973	18,966	20,496	21,724
212 Social contributions........	†2,857	3,189	3,380	2,962	3,306	3,515	†254	264	267	3,216	3,570	3,782
22 **Use of goods and services........**	†4,392	4,171	4,359	6,870	6,292	6,328	†2,902	3,203	3,352	9,773	9,494	9,679
23 **Consumption of fixed capital........**	....	....	....	....	....	....	....	....	....	....	....	....
24 **Interest........**	†3,264	3,587	3,973	3,646	3,956	4,344	†115	83	80	3,761	4,039	4,423
25 **Subsidies........**	†2,105	4,293	4,968	3,564	4,293	4,968	†583	623	726	4,146	4,916	5,695

In Millions of Kunas / Year Ending December 31 / Cash Reporter

		Budgetary Central Government			Central Government			Local Government			General Government		
		2002	2003	2004	2002	2003	2004	2002	2003	2004	2002	2003	2004
26	Grants..................................	†4,162	3,747	3,420	1,659	1,737	2,163	†142	367	267	105	85	160
261	To foreign govenments...............	†66	44	77	66	44	77	†—	—	—	66	44	77
262	To international organizations..................	†39	41	83	39	41	83	†—	—	—	39	41	83
263	To other general government units...............	†4,057	3,662	3,260	1,555	1,652	2,003	†142	367	267	—	—	—
2631	Current...............	†3,957	3,199	2,499	1,288	1,231	1,572	†142	136	91	—	—	—
2632	Capital...............	†100	463	762	267	421	431	†—	231	176	—	—	—
27	Social benefits........................	†34,257	36,204	39,731	35,839	37,940	40,646	†290	315	376	36,129	38,255	41,022
28	Other expense.......................	†2,684	3,848	4,412	3,582	4,430	5,227	†1,211	1,540	1,726	4,792	5,970	6,954
281	Property expense other than interest............	†1	7	4	1	7	4	†—	—	—	1	7	4
282	Miscellaneous other expense..................	†2,684	3,841	4,408	3,581	4,423	5,224	†1,211	1,540	1,726	4,792	5,963	6,950
2821	Current...............	†1,331	2,326	1,843	1,626	2,310	1,870	†938	1,261	1,274	2,564	3,571	3,145
2822	Capital...............	†1,353	1,515	2,566	1,955	2,113	3,353	†273	279	452	2,227	2,392	3,805

Table 3   Transactions in assets and liabilities

		Budgetary Central Government			Central Government			Local Government			General Government		
		2002	2003	2004	2002	2003	2004	2002	2003	2004	2002	2003	2004
3	Change in net worth from transactns....	....	....	....	....	....	....	....	....	....	....	....	....
31	Net acquisition of nonfinancial assets...	†1,377	1,812	1,419	6,129	7,996	8,374	†1,136	1,668	2,121	7,265	9,664	10,495
311	Fixed assets.............................	†1,284	1,795	1,385	5,898	7,867	8,158	†1,173	1,676	2,213	7,071	9,543	10,371
3111	Buildings and structures...................	†716	1,200	812	5,200	7,197	7,400	†1,000	1,418	1,927	6,200	8,615	9,326
3112	Machinery and equipment...............	†388	517	519	502	584	698	†151	214	223	653	797	921
3113	Other fixed assets...................	†180	79	54	196	86	60	†22	45	64	218	131	124
312	Inventories...................	†—	—	—	—	—	—	†—	—	—	—	—	—
313	Valuables...................	†69	5	8	70	5	8	†2	2	—	72	7	8
314	Nonproduced assets...................	†24	12	27	161	124	208	†–39	–9	–92	122	115	116
3141	Land...................	†–2	–18	7	117	89	182	†–56	–47	–120	60	42	61
3142	Subsoil assets...................	†—	—	—	—	—	—	†—	2	—	—	2	—
3143	Other naturally occurring assets...........	†—	—	—	—	—	—	†—	—	—	—	—	—
3144	Intangible nonproduced assets..................	†26	30	20	44	35	26	†18	36	28	62	71	55
32	Net acquisition of financial assets.........	†1,649	–1,320	222	516	–963	28	†785	197	76	1,302	–768	104
321	Domestic...................	†1,636	–1,330	212	503	–973	19	†787	204	78	1,290	–771	96
3212	Currency and deposits...................	†360	1,147	–1,114	1,557	1,636	–891	†785	15	12	2,342	1,651	–879
3213	Securities other than shares...................	†—	—	—	—	—	—	†—	—	—	—	—	—
3214	Loans...................	†690	393	1,003	355	242	736	†62	174	58	416	414	794
3215	Shares and other equity...............	†587	–2,870	324	–1,409	–2,851	174	†–62	15	–4	–1,471	–2,836	170
3216	Insurance technical reserves.............	†—	—	—	—	—	—	†—	—	—	—	—	—
3217	Financial derivatives...................	†—	—	—	—	—	—	†—	—	—	—	—	—
3218	Other accounts receivable.............	....	....	....	....	....	....	....	....	....	....	....	....
322	Foreign...................	†14	10	10	14	10	10	†–2	–7	–2	12	3	8
3222	Currency and deposits...................	†—	—	—	—	—	—	†—	—	—	—	—	—
3223	Securities other than shares...................	†—	—	—	—	—	—	†—	—	—	—	—	—
3224	Loans...................	†—	—	—	—	—	—	†–2	–7	–2	–2	–7	–2
3225	Shares and other equity...............	†14	10	10	14	10	10	†—	—	—	14	10	10
3226	Insurance technical reserves.............	†—	—	—	—	—	—	†—	—	—	—	—	—
3227	Financial derivatives...................	†—	—	—	—	—	—	†—	—	—	—	—	—
3228	Other accounts receivable.............	....	....	....	....	....	....	....	....	....	....	....	....
323	Monetary gold and SDRs...................	†—	—	—	—	—	—	†—	—	—	—	—	—
33	Net incurrence of liabilities..................	†3,773	2,890	4,309	7,030	6,962	8,324	†–40	–82	135	6,990	6,878	8,459
331	Domestic...................	†1,425	–160	4,039	2,079	949	4,108	†–27	7	232	2,052	954	4,339
3312	Currency and deposits...................	†—	—	—	—	—	—	†—	—	—	—	—	—
3313	Securities other than shares...................	†1,297	636	6,358	1,297	1,166	6,351	†21	3	208	1,318	1,169	6,559
3314	Loans...................	†128	–796	–2,319	781	–217	–2,243	†–48	4	24	734	–215	–2,219
3316	Insurance technical reserves.............	†—	—	—	—	—	—	†—	—	—	—	—	—
3317	Financial derivatives...................	†—	—	—	—	—	—	†—	—	—	—	—	—
3318	Other accounts payable...................	....	....	....	....	....	....	....	....	....	....	....	....
332	Foreign...................	†2,348	3,050	270	4,951	6,013	4,216	†–13	–89	–97	4,938	5,924	4,119
3322	Currency and deposits...................	†—	—	—	—	—	—	†—	—	—	—	—	—
3323	Securities other than shares...................	†3,024	4,051	1,215	3,024	5,176	1,215	†—	—	—	3,024	5,176	1,215
3324	Loans...................	†–677	–1,001	–945	1,927	837	3,001	†–13	–89	–97	1,914	748	2,904
3326	Insurance technical reserves.............	†—	—	—	—	—	—	†—	—	—	—	—	—
3327	Financial derivatives...................	†—	—	—	—	—	—	†—	—	—	—	—	—
3328	Other accounts payable...................	....	....	....	....	....	....	....	....	....	....	....	....

In Millions of Kunas / Year Ending December 31 / Cash Reporter

	Budgetary Central Government			Central Government			Local Government			General Government		
	2002	2003	2004	2002	2003	2004	2002	2003	2004	2002	2003	2004
Table 4 Holding gains in assets and liabilities												
Table 5 Other changes in the volume of assets and liabilities												
Table 6 Balance sheet												
Table 7 Outlays by functions of govt.												
7 **Total outlays**........................	71,774	78,888	84,551	81,578	88,711	95,315	8,272	9,796	10,888	88,153	96,488	103,932
701 **General public services**.................	†7,374	8,202	8,958	7,374	8,202	8,958	†1,404	1,545	....	8,778	9,747	....
7017 Public debt transactions.................	†3,264	3,587	3,973	3,646	3,956	4,344	†115	83	80	3,761	4,039	4,423
7018 General transfers between levels of govt......	†1,049	1,104	1,194	1,049	1,104	1,194	†41	42	....	1,090	1,145	....
702 **Defense**....................................	†4,352	4,088	3,701	4,352	4,088	3,701	†—	—	....	4,352	4,088	....
703 **Public order and safety**................	†4,791	5,176	5,488	4,791	5,176	5,488	†244	261	....	5,034	5,437	....
704 **Economic affairs**......................	†5,747	6,632	7,866	5,747	6,632	7,866	†1,416	1,473	....	7,163	8,105	....
7042 Agriculture, forestry, fishing, and hunting.....	†1,890	2,311	2,088	1,890	2,311	2,088	†54	67	....	1,944	2,379	....
7043 Fuel and energy........................	†2	1	1	2	1	1	†115	7	....	116	9	....
7044 Mining, manufacturing, and construction.....	†535	649	560	535	649	560	†53	22	....	589	671	....
7045 Transport..............................	†1,910	1,606	3,290	1,910	1,606	3,290	†944	1,146	....	2,854	2,751	....
7046 Communication.........................	†108	74	23	108	74	23	†1	2	....	109	76	....
705 **Environmental protection**............	†264	311	234	264	311	234	†282	319	....	546	629	....
706 **Housing and community amenities**.......	†1,411	1,830	2,529	1,411	1,830	2,529	†1,607	2,210	....	3,019	4,040	....
707 **Health**.................................	†10,704	11,609	12,720	10,704	11,609	12,720	†477	541	....	11,181	12,150	....
7072 Outpatient services....................	†4,080	2,357	539	4,080	2,357	539	†54	71	....	4,134	2,428	....
7073 Hospital services......................	†3,881	6,452	6,983	3,881	6,452	6,983	†39	51	....	3,920	6,503	....
7074 Public health services.................	†15	25	15	15	25	15	†53	28	....	68	53	....
708 **Recreation, culture, and religion**...........	†994	1,085	1,242	994	1,085	1,242	†1,035	1,229	....	2,029	2,314	....
709 **Education**..............................	†6,315	6,807	7,245	6,315	6,807	7,245	†1,729	2,181	....	8,044	8,988	....
7091 Pre-primary and primary education..............	†3,173	3,296	3,533	3,173	3,296	3,533	†1,324	1,659	....	4,496	4,954	....
7092 Secondary education...................	†1,504	1,651	1,751	1,504	1,651	1,751	†315	428	....	1,819	2,079	....
7094 Tertiary education.....................	†1,564	1,627	1,708	1,564	1,627	1,708	†20	15	....	1,584	1,641	....
710 **Social protection**.....................	†32,219	33,391	34,812	32,219	33,391	34,812	†487	538	....	32,706	33,929	....
7 Statistical discrepancy: Total outlays..............	−2,396	−243	−245	7,407	9,581	10,520	−409	−501	....	5,301	7,062	....
Table 8 Transactions in financial assets and liabilities by sector												
82 **Net acquisition of financial assets**........	†1,649	−1,320	222	516	−963	28	785	197	76	1,301	−768	104
821 Domestic.................................	†1,636	−1,330	212	503	−973	19	787	204	78	1,290	−771	96
8211 General government....................	†69	58	84	—	6	10	†—	—	—	—	4	10
8212 Central bank..........................	†−242	1,184	−1,070	−242	1,184	−1,070	†—	—	—	−242	1,184	−1,070
8213 Other depository corporations.........	†1,043	368	290	2,241	857	514	†722	82	23	2,963	939	537
8214 Financial corporations n.e.c..........	†—	—	—	—	—	—	†—	—	—	—	—	—
8215 Nonfinancial corporations............	†684	−3,213	677	−1,578	−3,294	334	†50	103	46	−1,528	−3,190	380
8216 Households & NPIs serving households......	†82	273	231	82	273	231	15	19	8	97	292	239
822 Foreign.................................	†14	10	10	14	10	10	−2	−7	−2	12	3	8
8221 General government....................	†—	—	—	—	—	—	†—	—	—			
8227 International organizations...........	†14	10	10	14	10	10	†—	—	—	14	10	10
8228 Financial corporations other than international organizations...............	†—	—	—	—	—	—	†—	—	—			
8229 Other nonresidents....................	†—	—	—	—	—	—	−2	−7	−2	−2	−7	−2
823 Monetary gold and SDRs..................	†—	—	—	—	—	—	†—	—	—			
83 **Net incurrence of liabilities**..................	†3,773	2,890	4,309	7,030	6,962	8,324	†−40	−82	135	6,990	6,878	8,459
831 Domestic.................................	†1,425	−160	4,039	2,079	949	4,108	†−27	7	232	2,052	954	4,339
8311 General government....................	†—	—	—	—	—	—	†—	2	1	—	—	—
8312 Central bank..........................	†—	—	—	—	—	—	†—	—	—			
8313 Other depository corporations.........	†1,335	246	4,025	1,988	1,355	4,094	†−18	62	285	1,971	1,416	4,379
8314 Financial corporations n.e.c..........	†90	−406	14	90	−406	14	†—	—	—	90	−406	14
8315 Nonfinancial corporations............	†—	—	—	—	—	—	†−9	−56	−54	−9	−56	−54
8316 Households & NPIs serving households......	†—	—	—	—	—	—	†—	—	—	—	—	—
832 Foreign.................................	†2,348	3,050	270	4,951	6,013	4,216	†−13	−89	−97	4,938	5,924	4,119
8321 General government....................	†−302	−330	−347	−302	−330	−347	†—	—	—	−302	−330	−347
8327 International organizations...........	†729	774	90	729	774	90	†—	—	—	729	774	90
8328 Financial corporations other than international organizations.............	†1,921	2,606	540	4,524	5,569	4,486	†−13	−89	−97	4,511	5,480	4,389
8329 Other nonresidents....................	†—	—	−12	—	—	−12	†—	—	—	—	—	−12

In Millions of Pounds / Year Ending December 31 / Cash Reporter

		Budgetary Central Government			Extrabudgetary Accounts			Central Government			General Government		
		1996	1997	1998	1996	1997	1998	1996	1997	1998	1996	1997	1998
Statement of government operations													
Statement of other economic flows													
Balance sheet													
6	*Net worth......*	....	....	....	....	....	....	....	....	....	....	....	....
61	Nonfinancial assets......	....	....	....	....	....	....	....	....	....	....	....	....
62	Financial assets......	....	....	....	....	....	....	....	....	....	....	....	....
63	Liabilities......	2,095.5	2,399.9	2,712.6	145.1	102.7	82.9	2,240.5	2,502.7	2,795.5	....	....	....
Statement of sources and uses of cash													
1	Cash receipts from operating activities......	887.8	914.1	955.5	153.2	158.1	188.2	1,322.9	1,374.4	1,473.0	....		....
11	Taxes......	737.6	739.7	795.1	123.2	126.3	160.7	860.8	866.0	955.8			
12	Social contributions......	2.6	2.8	3.3	—	—	—	200.1	209.2	223.1			
13	Grants......	.8	.5	.6	1.7	1.2	.1	2.4	1.6	.7			
14	Other receipts......	146.9	171.2	156.5	28.3	30.7	27.4	259.7	297.7	293.3			
2	Cash payments for operating activities......	915.1	1,019.2	1,125.3	209.2	219.7	203.9	1,351.2	1,485.1	1,593.5			
21	Compensation of employees......	392.0	424.7	453.5	1.5	1.7	1.7	396.8	429.9	458.9			
22	Purchases of goods and services......	105.6	121.0	130.7	5.2	9.1	9.5	111.5	131.8	141.1			
24	Interest......	205.7	212.8	253.9	16.1	17.2	15.3	221.7	230.0	269.2			
25	Subsidies......	18.8	19.6	21.0	27.7	16.7	12.9	46.5	36.3	33.9			
26	Grants......	29.3	40.7	45.7	19.1	20.0	15.7	48.4	60.6	61.4			
27	Social benefits......	163.8	200.5	220.6	26.4	28.3	33.1	413.0	469.7	513.3			
28	Other payments......	—	—	—	—	—	—	—	—	—			
CIO	*Net cash inflow from oper. activities.....*	−193.5	−295.5	−317.7	164.4	184.8	189.0	−28.2	−110.7	−120.5			
31.1	Purchases of nonfinancial assets......	96.9	105.6	125.9	14.7	12.8	12.3	111.6	118.4	138.3			
31.2	Sales of nonfinancial assets......	.7	.5	.8	.1	—	.1	.8	.6	.9			
31	Net cash outflow from investments in nonfinancial assets......	96.2	105.1	125.1	14.6	12.8	12.3	110.8	117.9	137.4	....		....
CSD	*Cash surplus/deficit......*	−289.7	−400.6	−442.8	149.8	172.1	176.7	−139.1	−228.5	−257.8			
32x	Net acquisition of fin assets, excl. cash......	1.5	2.3	−.6	.4	.6	1.7	3.0	2.7	−.2			
321x	Domestic......	1.5	2.3	−.6	.4	.6	1.7	3.0	2.7	−.2			
322x	Foreign......	—	—	—	—	—	—	—	—	—			
323	Monetary gold and SDRs......	—	—	—	—	—	—	—	—	—	....		
33	Net incurrence of liabilities......	294.3	413.1	470.6	−144.0	−178.2	−179.0	150.3	234.9	291.6			
331	Domestic......	310.7	275.7	307.2	−98.5	−128.9	−163.8	212.2	146.8	143.4			
332	Foreign......	−16.4	137.3	163.5	−45.5	−49.3	−15.2	−61.8	88.1	148.3			
NFB	Net cash inflow from fin. activities......	292.9	410.8	471.2	−144.4	−178.8	−180.7	147.3	232.1	291.9			
NCB	*Net change in the stock of cash......*	3.2	10.2	28.4	5.5	−6.7	−4.0	8.3	3.6	34.1	....		....
Table 1 Revenue													
1	**Revenue......**	**887.8**	**914.1**	**955.5**	**153.2**	**158.1**	**188.2**	**1,322.9**	**1,374.4**	**1,473.0**	....		....
11	**Taxes......**	**737.6**	**739.7**	**795.1**	**123.2**	**126.3**	**160.7**	**860.8**	**866.0**	**955.8**	....		....
111	Taxes on income, profits, & capital gains......	250.7	266.3	297.5	4.2	2.4	2.6	254.9	268.7	300.1	....		
1111	Individuals......	147.1	158.2	166.3	—	—	—	147.1	158.2	166.3			
1112	Corporations and other enterprises......	96.7	102.0	124.4	—	—	—	96.7	102.0	124.4			
112	Taxes on payroll and workforce......	—	—	—	21.4	22.1	26.7	21.4	22.1	26.7			
113	Taxes on property......	24.3	24.3	26.1	—	—	—	24.3	24.3	26.1			
114	Taxes on goods and services......	365.7	366.8	404.3	—	—	—	365.7	366.8	404.3			
1141	General taxes on goods and services......	198.0	206.4	225.8	—	—	—	198.0	206.4	225.8			
1142	Excises......	117.5	107.7	120.0	—	—	—	117.5	107.7	120.0			
115	Taxes on int'l. trade and transactions......	84.4	69.4	53.4	11.1	7.1	2.3	95.5	76.5	55.7			
116	Other taxes......	12.4	12.9	13.8	86.5	94.6	129.2	98.9	107.5	143.0			
12	**Social contributions......**	**2.6**	**2.8**	**3.3**	—	—	—	**200.1**	**209.2**	**223.1**	....		....
121	Social security contributions......	—	—	—	—	—	—	197.5	206.4	219.9			
122	Other social contributions......	2.6	2.8	3.3	—	—	—	2.6	2.8	3.3			
13	**Grants......**	**.8**	**.5**	**.6**	**1.7**	**1.2**	**.1**	**2.4**	**1.6**	**.7**	....		....
131	From foreign governments......	.8	.5	.6	1.7	1.2	.1	2.4	1.6	.7			
132	From international organizations......	—	—	—	—	—	—	—	—	—			
133	From other general government units......	—	—	—	—	—	—	—	—	—	....		
14	**Other revenue......**	**146.9**	**171.2**	**156.5**	**28.3**	**30.7**	**27.4**	**259.7**	**297.7**	**293.3**	....		....
Table 2 Expense by economic type													
2	**Expense......**	**915.1**	**1,019.2**	**1,125.3**	**209.2**	**219.7**	**203.9**	**1,351.2**	**1,485.1**	**1,593.5**	....		....
21	**Compensation of employees......**	**392.0**	**424.7**	**453.5**	**1.5**	**1.7**	**1.7**	**396.8**	**429.9**	**458.9**	....		....
211	Wages and salaries......	392.0	424.7	453.5	1.5	1.7	1.7	396.8	429.9	458.9			
212	Social contributions......	—	—	—	—	—	—	—	—	—			
22	**Use of goods and services......**	**105.6**	**121.0**	**130.7**	**5.2**	**9.1**	**9.5**	**111.5**	**131.8**	**141.1**	....		....
23	**Consumption of fixed capital......**	....	....	....	....	....	....	....	....	....	....		....
24	**Interest......**	**205.7**	**212.8**	**253.9**	**16.1**	**17.2**	**15.3**	**221.7**	**230.0**	**269.2**	....		....
25	**Subsidies......**	**18.8**	**19.6**	**21.0**	**27.7**	**16.7**	**12.9**	**46.5**	**36.3**	**33.9**	....		....

	Budgetary Central Government			Extrabudgetary Accounts			Central Government			General Government		
	1996	1997	1998	1996	1997	1998	1996	1997	1998	1996	1997	1998
26 Grants.............................	29.3	40.7	45.7	19.1	20.0	15.7	48.4	60.6	61.4	....	....	....
261 To foreign governments...........	9.7	12.2	13.8	—	—	—	9.7	12.2	13.8	....	....	....
262 To international organizations........	—	—	—	—	—	—	—	—	—	....	....	....
263 To other general government units........	19.6	28.5	31.9	19.1	20.0	15.7	38.7	48.4	47.6	....	....	....
2631 Current...........	5.8	5.9	7.7	—	—	—	5.8	5.9	7.7	....	....	....
2632 Capital...........	13.9	22.5	24.2	19.1	20.0	15.7	33.0	42.5	39.9	....	....	....
27 Social benefits..................	163.8	200.5	220.6	26.4	28.3	33.1	413.0	469.7	513.3	....	....	....
28 Other expense..................	—	—	—	—	—	—	—	—	—	....	....	....
281 Property expense other than interest...........	—	—	—	—	—	—	—	—	—	....	....	....
282 Miscellaneous other expense..............	—	—	—	—	—	—	—	—	—	....	....	....
2821 Current..............	—	—	—	—	—	—	—	—	—	....	....	....
2822 Capital..............	—	—	—	—	—	—	—	—	—	....	....	....

Table 3   Transactions in assets and liabilities

	Budgetary Central Government			Extrabudgetary Accounts			Central Government			General Government		
3 Change in net worth from transactns....	....	....	....	....	....	....	....	....	....	....	....	....
31 Net acquisition of nonfinancial assets...	96.2	105.1	125.1	14.6	12.8	12.3	110.8	117.9	137.4	....	....	....
311 Fixed assets............	82.2	94.5	112.6	14.6	12.8	12.3	96.8	107.2	124.9	....	....	....
3111 Buildings and structures............	....	....	....	....	....	....	....	....	....	....	....	....
3112 Machinery and equipment............	....	....	....	....	....	....	....	....	....	....	....	....
3113 Other fixed assets............	....	....	....	....	....	....	....	....	....	....	....	....
312 Inventories...............	—	—	—	—	—	—	—	—	—	....	....	....
313 Valuables...............	—	—	—	—	—	—	—	—	—	....	....	....
314 Nonproduced assets...............	14.0	10.6	12.5	—	—	—	14.0	10.6	12.5	....	....	....
3141 Land...............	....	....	....	—	—	—	....	....	....	....	....	....
3142 Subsoil assets...............	....	....	....	—	—	—	....	....	....	....	....	....
3143 Other naturally occurring assets........	....	....	....	—	—	—	....	....	....	....	....	....
3144 Intangible nonproduced assets........	....	....	....	—	—	—	....	....	....	....	....	....
32 Net acquisition of financial assets........	4.6	12.5	27.8	5.8	−6.1	−2.3	11.3	6.4	33.8	....	....	....
321 Domestic...........	4.6	12.5	27.8	5.8	−6.1	−2.3	11.3	6.4	33.8	....	....	....
3212 Currency and deposits............	3.2	10.2	28.4	5.5	−6.7	−4.0	8.3	3.6	34.1	....	....	....
3213 Securities other than shares............	....	....	....	....	....	....	....	....	....	....	....	....
3214 Loans............	....	....	....	....	....	....	....	....	....	....	....	....
3215 Shares and other equity............	....	....	....	....	....	....	....	....	....	....	....	....
3216 Insurance technical reserves............	....	....	....	....	....	....	....	....	....	....	....	....
3217 Financial derivatives............	....	....	....	....	....	....	....	....	....	....	....	....
3218 Other accounts receivable............	....	....	....	....	....	....	....	....	....	....	....	....
322 Foreign............	—	—	—	—	—	—	—	—	—	....	....	....
3222 Currency and deposits............	—	—	—	—	—	—	—	—	—	....	....	....
3223 Securities other than shares............	—	—	—	—	—	—	—	—	—	....	....	....
3224 Loans............	—	—	—	—	—	—	—	—	—	....	....	....
3225 Shares and other equity............	—	—	—	—	—	—	—	—	—	....	....	....
3226 Insurance technical reserves............	—	—	—	—	—	—	—	—	—	....	....	....
3227 Financial derivatives............	—	—	—	—	—	—	—	—	—	....	....	....
3228 Other accounts receivable............	....	....	....	....	....	....	....	....	....	....	....	....
323 Monetary gold and SDRs............	—	—	—	—	—	—	—	—	—	....	....	....
33 Net incurrence of liabilities..................	294.3	413.1	470.6	−144.0	−178.2	−179.0	150.3	234.9	291.6	....	....	....
331 Domestic...........	310.7	275.7	307.2	−98.5	−128.9	−163.8	212.2	146.8	143.4	....	....	....
3312 Currency and deposits............	—	—	—	—	—	—	—	—	—	....	....	....
3313 Securities other than shares............	338.4	280.9	270.4	−94.2	−124.5	−163.0	244.2	156.4	107.4	....	....	....
3314 Loans............	−27.7	−5.2	36.8	−4.4	−4.4	−.8	−32.1	−9.6	36.0	....	....	....
3316 Insurance technical reserves............	—	—	—	—	—	—	—	—	—	....	....	....
3317 Financial derivatives............	—	—	—	—	—	—	—	—	—	....	....	....
3318 Other accounts payable............	....	....	....	....	....	....	....	....	....	....	....	....
332 Foreign............	−16.4	137.3	163.5	−45.5	−49.3	−15.2	−61.8	88.1	148.3	....	....	....
3322 Currency and deposits............	—	—	—	−3.3	−.5	−.1	−3.3	−.5	−.1	....	....	....
3323 Securities other than shares............	−17.2	146.4	163.1	—	—	—	−17.2	146.4	163.1	....	....	....
3324 Loans............	.8	−9.1	.4	−42.2	−48.8	−15.1	−41.4	−57.8	−14.7	....	....	....
3326 Insurance technical reserves............	—	—	—	—	—	—	—	—	—	....	....	....
3327 Financial derivatives............	—	—	—	—	—	—	—	—	—	....	....	....
3328 Other accounts payable............	....	....	....	....	....	....	....	....	....	....	....	....

In Millions of Pounds / Year Ending December 31 / Cash Reporter

	Budgetary Central Government			Extrabudgetary Accounts			Central Government			General Government		
	1996	1997	1998	1996	1997	1998	1996	1997	1998	1996	1997	1998
Table 4 Holding gains in assets and liabilities												
Table 5 Other changes in the volume of assets and liabilities												
Table 6 Balance sheet												
6　　Net worth	....	....	....	....	....	....	.....	....	....	....	....	....
61　　Nonfinancial assets	....	....	....	....	....	....	....	....	....	....	....	....
611　　Fixed assets	....	....	....	....	....	....	....	....	....			
6111　　Buildings and structures	....	....	....	....	....	....	....	....	....			
6112　　Machinery and equipment	....	....	....	....	....	....	....	....	....			
6113　　Other fixed assets	....	....	....	....	....	....	....	....	....			
612　　Inventories	....	....	....	....	....	....	....	....	....			
613　　Valuables	....	....	....	....	....	....	....	....	....			
614　　Nonproduced assets	....	....	....	....	....	....	....	....	....			
6141　　Land	....	....	....	....	....	....	....	....	....			
6142　　Subsoil assets	....	....	....	....	....	....	....	....	....			
6143　　Other naturally occurring assets	....	....	....	....	....	....	....	....	....			
6144　　Intangible nonproduced assets	....	....	....	....	....	....	....	....	....			
62　　Financial assets	....	....	....	....	....	....	....	....	....	....	....	....
621　　Domestic	....	....	....	....	....	....	....	....	....			
6212　　Currency and deposits	....	....	....	....	....	....	....	....	....			
6213　　Securities other than shares	....	....	....	....	....	....	....	....	....			
6214　　Loans	....	....	....	....	....	....	....	....	....			
6215　　Shares and other equity	....	....	....	....	....	....	....	....	....			
6216　　Insurance technical reserves	....	....	....	....	....	....	....	....	....			
6217　　Financial derivatives	....	....	....	....	....	....	....	....	....			
6218　　Other accounts receivable	....	....	....	....	....	....	....	....	....			
622　　Foreign	....	....	....	....	....	....	....	....	....			
6222　　Currency and deposits	....	....	....	....	....	....	....	....	....			
6223　　Securities other than shares	....	....	....	....	....	....	....	....	....			
6224　　Loans	....	....	....	....	....	....	....	....	....			
6225　　Shares and other equity	....	....	....	....	....	....	....	....	....			
6226　　Insurance technical reserves	....	....	....	....	....	....	....	....	....			
6227　　Financial derivatives	....	....	....	....	....	....	....	....	....			
6228　　Other accounts receivable	....	....	....	....	....	....	....	....	....			
623　　Monetary gold and SDRs	....	....	....	....	....	....	....	....	....			
63　　Liabilities	**2,095.5**	**2,399.9**	**2,712.6**	**145.1**	**102.7**	**82.9**	**2,240.5**	**2,502.7**	**2,795.5**	....	....	....
631　　Domestic	1,831.0	1,982.3	2,126.4	6.5	5.1	4.3	1,837.6	1,987.4	2,130.7			
6312　　Currency and deposits	....	....	....	....	....	....	....	....	....			
6313　　Securities other than shares	....	....	....	....	....	....	....	....	....			
6314　　Loans	....	....	....	....	....	....	....	....	....			
6316　　Insurance technical reserves	....	....	....	....	....	....	....	....	....			
6317　　Financial derivatives	....	....	....	....	....	....	....	....	....			
6318　　Other accounts payable	....	....	....	....	....	....	....	....	....			
632　　Foreign	264.4	417.7	586.2	138.5	97.6	78.6	403.0	515.3	664.8	....	....	....
6322　　Currency and deposits	....	....	....	....	....	....	....	....	....			
6323　　Securities other than shares	....	....	....	....	....	....	....	....	....			
6324　　Loans	....	....	....	....	....	....	....	....	....			
6326　　Insurance technical reserves	....	....	....	....	....	....	....	....	....			
6327　　Financial derivatives	....	....	....	....	....	....	....	....	....			
6328　　Other accounts payable	....	....	....	....	....	....	....	....	....			
Memorandum items:												
6M2　Net financial worth												
6M3　Debt at market value												
6M4　Debt at nominal value												
6M5　Arrears												
6M6　Obligations for social security benefits												
6M7　Contingent liabilities												
6M8　Uncapitalized military weapons, systems	....	....	....									
Table 7 Outlays by functions of govt.												
7　　Total outlays	1,012.0	1,124.9	1,251.2	223.9	232.5	216.2	1,462.8	1,603.5	1,731.7	....	....	....
701　　**General public services**	**308.1**	**323.4**	**370.9**	**17.3**	**18.4**	**16.5**	**325.5**	**341.8**	**387.5**	....	....	....
7017　　Public debt transactions	205.7	212.8	253.9	16.1	17.2	15.3	221.7	230.0	269.2			
7018　　General transfers between levels of govt.	....	....	....				....	....	....			
702　　**Defense**	**53.5**	**61.5**	**68.3**	—	—	—	**53.5**	**61.5**	**68.3**	....	....	....
703　　**Public order and safety**	**80.6**	**89.6**	**91.8**	—	—	—	**80.6**	**89.6**	**91.8**	....	....	....

In Millions of Pounds / Year Ending December 31 / Cash Reporter

		Budgetary Central Government			Extrabudgetary Accounts			Central Government			General Government		
		1996	1997	1998	1996	1997	1998	1996	1997	1998	1996	1997	1998
704	**Economic affairs**....................	**169.3**	**188.1**	**217.1**	**30.3**	**19.1**	**15.5**	**199.6**	**207.2**	**232.6**	....	....	....
7042	Agriculture, forestry, fishing, and hunting.....	67.9	72.6	79.9	28.5	17.5	13.7	96.4	90.0	93.6	....	....	....
7043	Fuel and energy..........................	—	—	—				—	—	—	....	....	....
7044	Mining, manufacturing, and construction.....	.1	.2	.2	—	—	—	.1	.2	.2	....	....	....
7045	Transport................................	68.2	70.6	92.4	1.3	1.4	1.4	69.5	71.9	93.9	....	....	....
7046	Communication.........................	....	....	....	....	....	....	....	....	....	....	....	....
705	**Environmental protection**................	....	....	....	....	....	....	....	....	....	....	....	....
706	**Housing and community amenities**........	**27.8**	**33.9**	**39.7**	**30.6**	**31.1**	**28.5**	**58.4**	**64.9**	**68.2**	....	....	....
707	**Health**.................................	**88.4**	**101.3**	**109.2**	**.1**	**.1**	**.2**	**88.5**	**101.3**	**109.4**	....	....	....
7072	Outpatient services.......................	....	....	....	....	....	....	....	....	....			
7073	Hospital services.........................	....	....	....	....	....	....	....	....	....			
7074	Public health services.....................	....	....	....	....	....	....	....	....	....			
708	**Recreation, culture, and religion**...........	**22.9**	**27.1**	**28.4**	**.1**	**.3**	**.1**	**23.1**	**27.5**	**28.5**	....	....	....
709	**Education**...............................	**159.8**	**189.1**	**203.7**	**1.6**	**1.3**	**1.3**	**161.4**	**190.3**	**205.0**	....	....	....
7091	Pre-primary and primary education..............	....	....	....	....	....	....	....	....	....			
7092	Secondary education.......................	....	....	....	....	....	....	....	....	....			
7094	Tertiary education........................	....	....	....	....	....	....	....	....	....			
710	**Social protection**........................	**101.5**	**111.1**	**122.1**	**30.5**	**35.4**	**38.3**	**358.8**	**392.7**	**424.7**	....	....	....
7	Statistical discrepancy: Total outlays..............	—	—	—	113.3	126.8	115.8	113.3	126.8	115.8	....	....	....
Table 8 Transactions in financial assets and liabilities by sector													
82	**Net acquisition of financial assets**.........	**4.6**	**12.5**	**27.8**	**5.8**	**−6.1**	**−2.3**	**11.3**	**6.4**	**33.8**	....	....	....
821	Domestic................................	4.6	12.5	27.8	5.8	−6.1	−2.3	11.3	6.4	33.8	....	....	....
8211	General government.......................	....	....	....	....	....	....	....	....	....			
8212	Central bank.............................	....	....	....	....	....	....	....	....	....			
8213	Other depository corporations.................	....	....	....	....	....	....	....	....	....			
8214	Financial corporations n.e.c.................	....	....	....	....	....	....	....	....	....			
8215	Nonfinancial corporations..................	....	....	....	....	....	....	....	....	....			
8216	Households & NPIs serving households......	....	....	....	....	....	....	....	....	....			
822	Foreign.................................	—	—	—	—	—	—	—	—	—	....	....	....
8221	General government.......................	—	—	—	—	—	—	—	—	—			
8227	International organizations..................	—	—	—	—	—	—	—	—	—	....	....	....
8228	Financial corporations other than international organizations..............	—	—	—	—	—	—	—	—	—			
8229	Other nonresidents.......................	—	—	—	—	—	—	—	—	—			
823	Monetary gold and SDRs...................	—	—	—	—	—	—	—	—	—			
83	**Net incurrence of liabilities**..................	**294.3**	**413.1**	**470.6**	**−144.0**	**−178.2**	**−179.0**	**150.3**	**234.9**	**291.6**	....	....	....
831	Domestic................................	310.7	275.7	307.2	−98.5	−128.9	−163.8	212.2	146.8	143.4	....	....	....
8311	General government.......................	....	....	....	....	....	....	....	....	....			
8312	Central bank.............................	....	....	....	....	....	....	....	....	....			
8313	Other depository corporations.................	....	....	....	....	....	....	....	....	....			
8314	Financial corporations n.e.c.................	....	....	....	....	....	....	....	....	....			
8315	Nonfinancial corporations..................	....	....	....	....	....	....	....	....	....			
8316	Households & NPIs serving households......	....	....	....	....	....	....	....	....	....			
832	Foreign.................................	−16.4	137.3	163.5	−45.5	−49.3	−15.2	−61.8	88.1	148.3	....	....	....
8321	General government.......................	−.7	−.6	−.5	—	—	—	−.7	−.6	−.5			
8327	International organizations..................	.8	−12.9	−12.7	−38.7	−48.0	−14.8	−37.9	−60.8	−27.5	....	....	....
8328	Financial corporations other than international organizations..............	—	—	—	—	—	—	—	—	—	....	....	....
8329	Other nonresidents.......................	−16.5	150.8	176.7	−6.8	−1.3	−.4	−23.3	149.5	176.3	....	....	....

In Billions of Koruny / Year Ending December 31 / Noncash Reporter

	Budgetary Central Government			Central Government			Local Government			General Government		
	2002p	2003p	2004p	2002p	2003p	2004p	2002p	2003p	2004p	2002p	2003p	2004p
Statement of government operations												
1 Revenue...............................	671.28	699.54	762.12	781.59	849.32	917.13	228.08	289.59	297.00	921.80	999.80	1,075.57
2 Expense................................	724.48	778.66	806.62	918.46	961.27	993.27	182.46	240.78	244.82	1,013.04	1,062.93	1,099.53
GOB *Gross operating balance......................*	*−53.20*	*−79.12*	*−44.50*	*−136.86*	*−111.94*	*−76.14*	*45.62*	*48.81*	*52.19*	*−91.24*	*−63.13*	*−23.96*
NOB *Net operating balance...................*	....	....	....	....	....	....	....	....	....	....	....	....
31 Net acquisition of nonfinancial assets.............	10.10	12.29	12.54	10.96	13.29	13.84	50.88	52.31	59.95	61.83	65.59	73.78
NLB *Net lending/borrowing....................*	*−63.30*	*−91.41*	*−57.04*	*−147.82*	*−125.23*	*−89.98*	*−5.25*	*−3.49*	*−7.76*	*−153.07*	*−128.72*	*−97.74*
32 Net acquisition of financial assets.................	−12.26	4.57	42.54	−115.33	−30.21	8.74	1.78	10.44	−1.23	−113.15	−20.97	8.84
33 Net incurrence of liabilities....................	51.03	95.97	99.58	32.50	95.02	98.72	7.03	13.93	6.53	39.93	107.75	106.58
NLB Statistical discrepancy........................	—	—	—	—	—	—	—	—	—	—	—	—
Statement of other economic flows												
Balance sheet												
6 *Net worth...................*	....	....	....	....	....	....	....	....	....	....	....	....
61 Nonfinancial assets........................	....	....	....	....	....	....	....	....	....	....	....	....
62 Financial assets............................	....	....	....	....	....	....	....	....	....	....	....	....
63 Liabilities...............................	....	....	....	396.06	491.06	589.01	....	....	....	....	....	....
Statement of sources and uses of cash												
Table 1 Revenue												
1 **Revenue..............................**	**671.28**	**699.54**	**762.12**	**781.59**	**849.32**	**917.13**	**228.08**	**289.59**	**297.00**	**921.80**	**999.80**	**1,075.57**
11 **Taxes.....................................**	**368.52**	**395.37**	**419.25**	**388.36**	**416.10**	**441.84**	**109.72**	**118.89**	**128.71**	**498.08**	**534.99**	**570.54**
111 Taxes on income, profits, & capital gains......	159.03	172.91	180.74	159.03	172.91	180.74	61.09	66.02	72.40	220.12	238.93	253.14
1111 Individuals............................	82.14	88.63	95.22	82.14	88.63	95.22	32.26	34.39	38.11	114.40	123.02	133.33
1112 Corporations and other enterprises............	76.89	84.27	85.52	76.89	84.27	85.52	28.82	31.64	34.29	105.72	115.91	119.81
112 Taxes on payroll and workforce..................	—	—	—	—	—	—	—	—	—	—	—	—
113 Taxes on property.............................	7.86	8.77	10.38	7.86	8.77	10.38	4.57	4.83	4.92	12.43	13.60	15.30
114 Taxes on goods and services.................	191.74	203.10	223.76	211.58	223.82	246.35	44.05	48.03	51.38	255.62	271.86	297.72
1141 General taxes on goods and services.........	118.39	125.66	136.20	118.39	125.66	136.20	36.05	38.73	41.39	154.44	164.39	177.59
1142 Excises.....................................	68.61	72.76	82.80	79.49	84.17	95.85	—	—	—	79.49	84.17	95.85
115 Taxes on int'l. trade and transactions.........	9.78	10.25	4.09	9.78	10.25	4.09	—	—	—	9.78	10.25	4.09
116 Other taxes................................	.11	.35	.29	.11	.35	.29	.01	.01	.01	.13	.35	.30
12 **Social contributions.............................**	**258.51**	**273.11**	**294.14**	**363.00**	**387.25**	**416.65**	—	—	—	**363.00**	**387.25**	**416.65**
121 Social security contributions........................	258.51	273.11	294.14	363.00	387.25	416.65	—	—	—	363.00	387.25	416.65
122 Other social contributions............................	—	—	—	—	—	—	—	—	—	—	—	—
13 **Grants.................................**	**27.32**	**16.14**	**26.49**	**3.30**	**12.90**	**25.90**	**87.07**	**138.51**	**137.46**	**2.49**	**12.31**	**24.81**
131 From foreign governments.........................	—	—	—	—	—	—	—	.02	.02	—	.02	.02
132 From international organizations..................	2.43	12.23	24.78	2.43	12.23	24.78	.06	.06	.02	2.49	12.29	24.79
133 From other general government units...........	24.89	3.91	1.72	.87	.67	1.12	87.00	138.43	137.43	—	—	—
14 **Other revenue................................**	**16.92**	**14.92**	**22.24**	**26.93**	**33.08**	**32.74**	**31.30**	**32.19**	**30.83**	**58.23**	**65.25**	**63.57**
Table 2 Expense by economic type												
2 **Expense................................**	**724.48**	**778.66**	**806.62**	**918.46**	**961.27**	**993.27**	**182.46**	**240.78**	**244.82**	**1,013.04**	**1,062.93**	**1,099.53**
21 **Compensation of employees...................**	**87.12**	**79.26**	**80.95**	**89.95**	**82.26**	**84.19**	**21.16**	**27.20**	**28.01**	**111.12**	**109.46**	**112.20**
211 Wages and salaries...........................	64.90	59.23	60.43	67.00	61.28	62.64	16.02	20.51	21.13	83.02	81.79	83.77
212 Social contributions............................	22.22	20.02	20.52	22.95	20.99	21.55	5.15	6.68	6.88	28.10	27.67	28.42
22 **Use of goods and services......................**	**63.86**	**60.90**	**55.07**	**71.66**	**65.10**	**59.05**	**53.62**	**57.63**	**59.00**	**125.28**	**122.73**	**118.05**
23 **Consumption of fixed capital................**	....	....	....	....	....	....	....	....	....	....	....	....
24 **Interest.............................**	**12.79**	**17.91**	**28.32**	**13.66**	**17.97**	**28.34**	**2.05**	**1.90**	**2.15**	**15.71**	**19.86**	**30.49**
25 **Subsidies.............................**	**108.97**	**89.07**	**89.87**	**156.91**	**124.80**	**117.00**	**79.81**	**119.38**	**120.91**	**236.72**	**244.18**	**237.90**
26 **Grants.............................**	**115.31**	**170.74**	**190.45**	**88.73**	**140.73**	**151.19**	**.87**	**.67**	**1.12**	**1.73**	**2.30**	**13.76**
261 To foreign governments........................	—	—	—	—	—	—	—	—	—	—	—	—
262 To international organizations...................	1.72	2.29	13.76	1.72	2.29	13.76	—	—	—	1.73	2.30	13.76
263 To other general government units.............	113.58	168.45	176.70	87.00	138.43	137.43	.87	.67	1.12	—	—	—
2631 Current.............................	102.01	152.71	155.03	68.73	114.14	111.63	.87	.67	1.12	—	—	—
2632 Capital.............................	11.58	15.74	21.66	18.28	24.30	25.81	—	—	—	—	—	—
27 **Social benefits.............................**	**293.34**	**305.03**	**313.26**	**425.88**	**447.23**	**464.58**	**11.57**	**14.15**	**14.32**	**437.45**	**461.38**	**478.89**
28 **Other expense.............................**	**43.10**	**55.76**	**48.70**	**71.67**	**83.18**	**88.93**	**13.37**	**19.86**	**19.31**	**85.03**	**103.03**	**108.23**
281 Property expense other than interest............	—	—	—	—	—	—	—	—	—	—	—	—
282 Miscellaneous other expense...................	43.10	55.76	48.70	71.67	83.18	88.93	13.37	19.86	19.31	85.03	103.03	108.23
2821 Current.................................	23.01	35.69	26.85	24.88	36.96	28.12	3.31	4.37	4.74	28.19	41.32	32.85
2822 Capital.................................	20.09	20.07	21.85	46.78	46.22	60.81	10.06	15.49	14.57	56.84	61.71	75.38

In Millions of Pounds / Year Ending December 31 / Cash Reporter

		Budgetary Central Government			Extrabudgetary Accounts			Central Government			General Government		
		1996	1997	1998	1996	1997	1998	1996	1997	1998	1996	1997	1998
704	**Economic affairs**.............................	**169.3**	**188.1**	**217.1**	**30.3**	**19.1**	**15.5**	**199.6**	**207.2**	**232.6**	....	....	....
7042	Agriculture, forestry, fishing, and hunting.....	67.9	72.6	79.9	28.5	17.5	13.7	96.4	90.0	93.6	....	....	....
7043	Fuel and energy....................................	—	—	—	—	—	—	—	—	—	....	....	....
7044	Mining, manufacturing, and construction.....	.1	.2	.2	—	—	—	.1	.2	.2	....	....	....
7045	Transport..	68.2	70.6	92.4	1.3	1.4	1.4	69.5	71.9	93.9	....	....	....
7046	Communication....................................	....	....	....	....	....	....	....	....	....	....	....	....
705	**Environmental protection**..................	....	....	....	....	....	....	....	....	....	....	....	....
706	**Housing and community amenities**........	**27.8**	**33.9**	**39.7**	**30.6**	**31.1**	**28.5**	**58.4**	**64.9**	**68.2**	....	....	....
707	**Health**..	**88.4**	**101.3**	**109.2**	**.1**	**.1**	**.2**	**88.5**	**101.3**	**109.4**	....	....	....
7072	Outpatient services...............................	....	....	....	....	....	....	....	....	....			
7073	Hospital services..................................	....	....	....	....	....	....	....	....	....			
7074	Public health services............................	....	....	....	....	....	....	....	....	....			
708	**Recreation, culture, and religion**...........	**22.9**	**27.1**	**28.4**	**.1**	**.3**	**.1**	**23.1**	**27.5**	**28.5**	....	....	....
709	**Education**..	**159.8**	**189.1**	**203.7**	**1.6**	**1.3**	**1.3**	**161.4**	**190.3**	**205.0**	....	....	....
7091	Pre-primary and primary education............	....	....	....	....	....	....	....	....	....			
7092	Secondary education..............................	....	....	....	....	....	....	....	....	....			
7094	Tertiary education..................................	....	....	....	....	....	....	....	....	....			
710	**Social protection**...............................	**101.5**	**111.1**	**122.1**	**30.5**	**35.4**	**38.3**	**358.8**	**392.7**	**424.7**	....	....	....
7	Statistical discrepancy: Total outlays.............	—	—	—	113.3	126.8	115.8	113.3	126.8	115.8	....	....	....

Table 8   Transactions in financial assets and liabilities by sector

82	**Net acquisition of financial assets**.........	**4.6**	**12.5**	**27.8**	**5.8**	**−6.1**	**−2.3**	**11.3**	**6.4**	**33.8**	....	....	....
821	Domestic...	4.6	12.5	27.8	5.8	−6.1	−2.3	11.3	6.4	33.8	....	....	....
8211	General government...............................	....	....	....	....	....	....	....	....	....	....	....	....
8212	Central bank..	....	....	....	....	....	....	....	....	....	....	....	....
8213	Other depository corporations..................	....	....	....	....	....	....	....	....	....	....	....	....
8214	Financial corporations n.e.c.....................	....	....	....	....	....	....	....	....	....	....	....	....
8215	Nonfinancial corporations........................	....	....	....	....	....	....	....	....	....	....	....	....
8216	Households & NPIs serving households......	....	....	....	....	....	....	....	....	....	....	....	....
822	Foreign...	—	—	—	—	—	—	—	—	—			
8221	General government...............................	—	—	—	—	—	—	—	—	—			
8227	International organizations.......................	—	—	—	—	—	—	—	—	—			
8228	Financial corporations other than international organizations..........	—	—	—	—	—	—	—	—	—	....	....	....
8229	Other nonresidents................................	—	—	—	—	—	—	—	—	—	....	....	....
823	Monetary gold and SDRs.........................	—	—	—	—	—	—	—	—	—			
83	**Net incurrence of liabilities**..................	**294.3**	**413.1**	**470.6**	**−144.0**	**−178.2**	**−179.0**	**150.3**	**234.9**	**291.6**	....	....	....
831	Domestic...	310.7	275.7	307.2	−98.5	−128.9	−163.8	212.2	146.8	143.4	....	....	....
8311	General government...............................	....	....	....	....	....	....	....	....	....	....	....	....
8312	Central bank..	....	....	....	....	....	....	....	....	....	....	....	....
8313	Other depository corporations..................	....	....	....	....	....	....	....	....	....	....	....	....
8314	Financial corporations n.e.c.....................	....	....	....	....	....	....	....	....	....	....	....	....
8315	Nonfinancial corporations........................	....	....	....	....	....	....	....	....	....	....	....	....
8316	Households & NPIs serving households......	....	....	....	....	....	....	....	....	....	....	....	....
832	Foreign...	−16.4	137.3	163.5	−45.5	−49.3	−15.2	−61.8	88.1	148.3	....	....	....
8321	General government...............................	−.7	−.6	−.5	—	—	—	−.7	−.6	−.5	....	....	....
8327	International organizations.......................	.8	−12.9	−12.7	−38.7	−48.0	−14.8	−37.9	−60.8	−27.5	....	....	....
8328	Financial corporations other than international organizations..............	—	—	—	—	—	—	—	—	—	....	....	....
8329	Other nonresidents................................	−16.5	150.8	176.7	−6.8	−1.3	−.4	−23.3	149.5	176.3	....	....	....

In Billions of Koruny / Year Ending December 31 / Noncash Reporter

	Budgetary Central Government			Central Government			Local Government			General Government		
	2002p	2003p	2004p	2002p	2003p	2004p	2002p	2003p	2004p	2002p	2003p	2004p
Statement of government operations												
1 Revenue..................	671.28	699.54	762.12	781.59	849.32	917.13	228.08	289.59	297.00	921.80	999.80	1,075.57
2 Expense..................	724.48	778.66	806.62	918.46	961.27	993.27	182.46	240.78	244.82	1,013.04	1,062.93	1,099.53
GOB *Gross operating balance*........	*−53.20*	*−79.12*	*−44.50*	*−136.86*	*−111.94*	*−76.14*	*45.62*	*48.81*	*52.19*	*−91.24*	*−63.13*	*−23.96*
NOB *Net operating balance*........	....	....	....	....	....	....	....	....	....	....	....	....
31 Net acquisition of nonfinancial assets........	10.10	12.29	12.54	10.96	13.29	13.84	50.88	52.31	59.95	61.83	65.59	73.78
NLB *Net lending/borrowing*........	*−63.30*	*−91.41*	*−57.04*	*−147.82*	*−125.23*	*−89.98*	*−5.25*	*−3.49*	*−7.76*	*−153.07*	*−128.72*	*−97.74*
32 Net acquisition of financial assets........	−12.26	4.57	42.54	−115.33	−30.21	8.74	1.78	10.44	−1.23	−113.15	−20.97	8.84
33 Net incurrence of liabilities........	51.03	95.97	99.58	32.50	95.02	98.72	7.03	13.93	6.53	39.93	107.75	106.58
NLB Statistical discrepancy........	—	—	—	—	—	—	—	—	—	—	—	—
Statement of other economic flows												
Balance sheet												
6 *Net worth*........	....	....	....	....	....	....	....	....	....	....	....	....
61 Nonfinancial assets........	....	....	....	....	....	....	....	....	....	....	....	....
62 Financial assets........	....	....	....	....	....	....	....	....	....	....	....	....
63 Liabilities........	....	....	....	396.06	491.06	589.01	....	....	....	....	....	....
Statement of sources and uses of cash												
Table 1 Revenue												
1 **Revenue**........	**671.28**	**699.54**	**762.12**	**781.59**	**849.32**	**917.13**	**228.08**	**289.59**	**297.00**	**921.80**	**999.80**	**1,075.57**
11 **Taxes**........	**368.52**	**395.37**	**419.25**	**388.36**	**416.10**	**441.84**	**109.72**	**118.89**	**128.71**	**498.08**	**534.99**	**570.54**
111 Taxes on income, profits, & capital gains........	159.03	172.91	180.74	159.03	172.91	180.74	61.09	66.02	72.40	220.12	238.93	253.14
1111 Individuals........	82.14	88.63	95.22	82.14	88.63	95.22	32.26	34.39	38.11	114.40	123.02	133.33
1112 Corporations and other enterprises........	76.89	84.27	85.52	76.89	84.27	85.52	28.82	31.64	34.29	105.72	115.91	119.81
112 Taxes on payroll and workforce........	—	—	—	—	—	—	—	—	—	—	—	—
113 Taxes on property........	7.86	8.77	10.38	7.86	8.77	10.38	4.57	4.83	4.92	12.43	13.60	15.30
114 Taxes on goods and services........	191.74	203.10	223.76	211.58	223.82	246.35	44.05	48.03	51.38	255.62	271.86	297.72
1141 General taxes on goods and services........	118.39	125.66	136.20	118.39	125.66	136.20	36.05	38.73	41.39	154.44	164.39	177.59
1142 Excises........	68.61	72.76	82.80	79.49	84.17	95.85	—	—	—	79.49	84.17	95.85
115 Taxes on int'l. trade and transactions........	9.78	10.25	4.09	9.78	10.25	4.09	—	—	—	9.78	10.25	4.09
116 Other taxes........	.11	.35	.29	.11	.35	.29	.01	.01	.01	.13	.35	.30
12 **Social contributions**........	**258.51**	**273.11**	**294.14**	**363.00**	**387.25**	**416.65**	—	—	—	**363.00**	**387.25**	**416.65**
121 Social security contributions........	258.51	273.11	294.14	363.00	387.25	416.65	—	—	—	363.00	387.25	416.65
122 Other social contributions........	—	—	—	—	—	—	—	—	—	—	—	—
13 **Grants**........	**27.32**	**16.14**	**26.49**	**3.30**	**12.90**	**25.90**	**87.07**	**138.51**	**137.46**	**2.49**	**12.31**	**24.81**
131 From foreign governments........	—	—	—	—	—	—	—	.02	.02	—	.02	.02
132 From international organizations........	2.43	12.23	24.78	2.43	12.23	24.78	.06	.06	.02	2.49	12.29	24.79
133 From other general government units........	24.89	3.91	1.72	.87	.67	1.12	87.00	138.43	137.43	—	—	—
14 **Other revenue**........	**16.92**	**14.92**	**22.24**	**26.93**	**33.08**	**32.74**	**31.30**	**32.19**	**30.83**	**58.23**	**65.25**	**63.57**
Table 2 Expense by economic type												
2 **Expense**........	**724.48**	**778.66**	**806.62**	**918.46**	**961.27**	**993.27**	**182.46**	**240.78**	**244.82**	**1,013.04**	**1,062.93**	**1,099.53**
21 **Compensation of employees**........	**87.12**	**79.26**	**80.95**	**89.95**	**82.26**	**84.19**	**21.16**	**27.20**	**28.01**	**111.12**	**109.46**	**112.20**
211 Wages and salaries........	64.90	59.23	60.43	67.00	61.28	62.64	16.02	20.51	21.13	83.02	81.79	83.77
212 Social contributions........	22.22	20.02	20.52	22.95	20.99	21.55	5.15	6.68	6.88	28.10	27.67	28.42
22 **Use of goods and services**........	**63.86**	**60.90**	**55.07**	**71.66**	**65.10**	**59.05**	**53.62**	**57.63**	**59.00**	**125.28**	**122.73**	**118.05**
23 **Consumption of fixed capital**........	....	....	....	....	....	....	....	....	....	....	....	....
24 **Interest**........	**12.79**	**17.91**	**28.32**	**13.66**	**17.97**	**28.34**	**2.05**	**1.90**	**2.15**	**15.71**	**19.86**	**30.49**
25 **Subsidies**........	**108.97**	**89.07**	**89.87**	**156.91**	**124.80**	**117.00**	**79.81**	**119.38**	**120.91**	**236.72**	**244.18**	**237.90**
26 **Grants**........	**115.31**	**170.74**	**190.45**	**88.73**	**140.73**	**151.19**	**.87**	**.67**	**1.12**	**1.73**	**2.30**	**13.76**
261 To foreign governments........	—	—	—	—	—	—	—	—	—	—	—	—
262 To international organizations........	1.72	2.29	13.76	1.72	2.29	13.76	—	—	—	1.73	2.30	13.76
263 To other general government units........	113.58	168.45	176.70	87.00	138.43	137.43	.87	.67	1.12	—	—	—
2631 Current........	102.01	152.71	155.03	68.73	114.14	111.63	.87	.67	1.12	—	—	—
2632 Capital........	11.58	15.74	21.66	18.28	24.30	25.81	—	—	—	—	—	—
27 **Social benefits**........	**293.34**	**305.03**	**313.26**	**425.88**	**447.23**	**464.58**	**11.57**	**14.15**	**14.32**	**437.45**	**461.38**	**478.89**
28 **Other expense**........	**43.10**	**55.76**	**48.70**	**71.67**	**83.18**	**88.93**	**13.37**	**19.86**	**19.31**	**85.03**	**103.03**	**108.23**
281 Property expense other than interest........	—	—	—	—	—	—	—	—	—	—	—	—
282 Miscellaneous other expense........	43.10	55.76	48.70	71.67	83.18	88.93	13.37	19.86	19.31	85.03	103.03	108.23
2821 Current........	23.01	35.69	26.85	24.88	36.96	28.12	3.31	4.37	4.74	28.19	41.32	32.85
2822 Capital........	20.09	20.07	21.85	46.78	46.22	60.81	10.06	15.49	14.57	56.84	61.71	75.38

In Billions of Koruny / Year Ending December 31 / Noncash Reporter

	Budgetary Central Government			Central Government			Local Government			General Government		
	2002p	2003p	2004p	2002p	2003p	2004p	2002p	2003p	2004p	2002p	2003p	2004p
Table 3 Transactions in assets and liabilities												
3 Change in net worth from transactns....	....	....	....	....	....	....	....	....	....	....	....	....
31 Net acquisition of nonfinancial assets...	**10.10**	**12.29**	**12.54**	**10.96**	**13.29**	**13.84**	**50.88**	**52.31**	**59.95**	**61.83**	**65.59**	**73.78**
311 Fixed assets............................	9.17	10.58	11.38	10.01	11.55	12.31	51.11	53.02	60.52	61.12	64.57	72.83
3111 Buildings and structures.............	....	....	....	....	....	....	....	....	....	....	....	....
3112 Machinery and equipment.............	....	....	....	....	....	....	....	....	....	....	....	....
3113 Other fixed assets...................	....	....	....	....	....	....	....	....	....	....	....	....
312 Inventories...........................	—	—	—	—	—	—						
313 Valuables.............................	—	—	—	—	—	—	—	—	—	—	—	—
314 Nonproduced assets....................	.93	1.71	1.17	.95	1.74	1.53	−.24	−.71	−.57	.71	1.03	.96
3141 Land................................	....	....	....	....	....	....	....	....	....	....	....	....
3142 Subsoil assets......................	....	....	....	....	....	....	....	....	....	....	....	....
3143 Other naturally occurring assets....	....	....	....	....	....	....	....	....	....	....	....	....
3144 Intangible nonproduced assets.......	....	....	....	....	....	....	....	....	....	....	....	....
32 Net acquisition of financial assets.........	**−12.26**	**4.57**	**42.54**	**−115.33**	**−30.21**	**8.74**	**1.78**	**10.44**	**−1.23**	**−113.15**	**−20.97**	**8.84**
321 Domestic..............................	9.13	6.81	44.25	−93.94	−27.97	10.44	3.10	7.69	5.31	−90.43	−21.47	17.08
3212 Currency and deposits...............	−.69	−3.13	29.66	19.75	−24.59	12.43	3.46	6.33	5.31	23.20	−18.26	17.74
3213 Securities other than shares........	6.67	−5.80	6.26	6.67	−5.80	6.26	.61	1.91	−1.18	7.24	−4.44	5.47
3214 Loans...............................	3.67	15.63	9.13	3.27	15.68	9.09	.11	−1.48	.28	3.83	13.55	10.30
3215 Shares and other equity.............	.13	.07	.04	−122.98	−13.28	−16.49	−1.08	.93	.90	−124.05	−12.35	−15.59
3216 Insurance technical reserves........	—	—	—	—	—	—	—	—	—	—	—	—
3217 Financial derivatives...............	—	—	—	—	—	—	—	—	—	—	—	—
3218 Other accounts receivable...........	−.66	.03	−.84	−.65	.03	−.84	—	—	—	−.65	.03	−.84
322 Foreign...............................	−21.39	−2.24	−1.70	−21.39	−2.24	−1.70	−1.33	2.74	−6.53	−22.72	.50	−8.24
3222 Currency and deposits...............	—	—	—	—	—	—	.17	—	—	.17	—	—
3223 Securities other than shares........	—	—	—	—	—	—	−1.49	2.74	−6.54	−1.49	2.74	−6.54
3224 Loans...............................	−21.51	−2.35	−2.05	−21.51	−2.35	−2.05	—	—	—	−21.51	−2.35	−2.05
3225 Shares and other equity.............	.12	.11	.35	.12	.11	.35	—	—	—	.12	.11	.35
3226 Insurance technical reserves........	—	—	—	—	—	—	—	—	—	—	—	—
3227 Financial derivatives...............	—	—	—	—	—	—	—	—	—	—	—	—
3228 Other accounts receivable...........	—	—	—	—	—	—	—	—	—	—	—	—
323 Monetary gold and SDRs................	—	—	—	—	—	—	—	—	—	—	—	—
33 Net incurrence of liabilities.................	**51.03**	**95.97**	**99.58**	**32.50**	**95.02**	**98.72**	**7.03**	**13.93**	**6.53**	**39.93**	**107.75**	**106.58**
331 Domestic..............................	47.35	81.02	16.25	28.81	80.07	15.39	2.19	2.42	2.35	31.41	81.29	19.07
3312 Currency and deposits...............	—	—	—	—	—	—	—	—	—	—	—	—
3313 Securities other than shares........	47.35	81.02	16.25	48.10	80.98	16.24	—	—	—	48.05	80.44	16.64
3314 Loans...............................	—	—	—	−19.29	−.94	−.85	2.19	2.42	2.35	−16.65	.82	2.43
3316 Insurance technical reserves........	—	—	—	—	—	—	—	—	—	—	—	—
3317 Financial derivatives...............	—	—	—	—	—	—	—	—	—	—	—	—
3318 Other accounts payable..............	—	—	—	—	.03	—	—	—	—	—	.03	—
332 Foreign...............................	3.68	14.96	83.33	3.68	14.96	83.33	4.84	11.51	4.19	8.52	26.47	87.51
3322 Currency and deposits...............	—	—	—	—	—	—	—	—	—	—	—	—
3323 Securities other than shares........	2.61	10.84	74.40	2.61	10.84	74.40	2.59	5.32	3.16	5.19	16.17	77.56
3324 Loans...............................	1.08	4.11	8.93	1.08	4.11	8.93	2.25	6.19	1.42	3.33	10.30	10.34
3326 Insurance technical reserves........	—	—	—	—	—	—	—	—	—	—	—	—
3327 Financial derivatives...............	—	—	—	—	—	—	—	—	—	—	—	—
3328 Other accounts payable..............	—	—	—	—	—	—	—	—	−.39	—	—	−.39
Table 4 Holding gains in assets and liabilities												
Table 5 Other changes in the volume of assets and liabilities												
Table 6 Balance sheet												
6 Net worth.............................	....	....	....	....	....	....	....	....	....	....	....	....
61 Nonfinancial assets...................	....	....	....	....	....	....	....	....	....	....	....	....
611 Fixed assets..........................	....	....	....	....	....	....	....	....	....	....	....	....
6111 Buildings and structures............	....	....	....	....	....	....	....	....	....	....	....	....
6112 Machinery and equipment.............	....	....	....	....	....	....	....	....	....	....	....	....
6113 Other fixed assets..................	....	....	....	....	....	....	....	....	....	....	....	....
612 Inventories...........................	....	....	....	....	....	....	....	....	....	....	....	....
613 Valuables.............................	....	....	....	....	....	....	....	....	....	....	....	....
614 Nonproduced assets....................	....	....	....	....	....	....	....	....	....	....	....	....
6141 Land................................	....	....	....	....	....	....	....	....	....	....	....	....
6142 Subsoil assets......................	....	....	....	....	....	....	....	....	....	....	....	....
6143 Other naturally occurring assets....	....	....	....	....	....	....	....	....	....	....	....	....
6144 Intangible nonproduced assets.......	....	....	....	....	....	....	....	....	....	....	....	....

		Budgetary Central Government			Central Government			Local Government			General Government		
		2002p	2003p	2004p	2002p	2003p	2004p	2002p	2003p	2004p	2002p	2003p	2004p
62	Financial assets.........................	....	....	....	....	....	....	....	....	....	....	....	....
621	Domestic...........................	....	....	....	....	....	....	....	....	....	....	....	....
6212	Currency and deposits...............	....	....	....	....	....	....	....	....	....	....	....	....
6213	Securities other than shares..........	....	....	....	....	....	....	....	....	....	....	....	....
6214	Loans..............................	....	....	....	....	....	....	....	....	....	....	....	....
6215	Shares and other equity.............	....	....	....	....	....	....	....	....	....	....	....	....
6216	Insurance technical reserves.........	....	....	....	....	....	....	....	....	....	....	....	....
6217	Financial derivatives................	....	....	....	....	....	....	....	....	....	....	....	....
6218	Other accounts receivable...........	....	....	....	....	....	....	....	....	....	....	....	....
622	Foreign............................	....	....	....	....	....	....	....	....	....	....	....	....
6222	Currency and deposits...............	....	....	....	....	....	....	....	....	....	....	....	....
6223	Securities other than shares..........	....	....	....	....	....	....	....	....	....	....	....	....
6224	Loans..............................	....	....	....	....	....	....	....	....	....	....	....	....
6225	Shares and other equity.............	....	....	....	....	....	....	....	....	....	....	....	....
6226	Insurance technical reserves.........	....	....	....	....	....	....	....	....	....	....	....	....
6227	Financial derivatives................	....	....	....	....	....	....	....	....	....	....	....	....
6228	Other accounts receivable...........	....	....	....	....	....	....	....	....	....	....	....	....
623	Monetary gold and SDRs.............	....	....	....	....	....	....	....	....	....	....	....	....
63	**Liabilities........................**	....	....	....	396.06	491.06	589.01	....	....	....	....	....	....
631	Domestic...........................	....	....	....	371.67	451.74	467.10	....	....	....	....	....	....
6312	Currency and deposits...............	....	....	....	—	—	—	....	....	....	....	....	....
6313	Securities other than shares..........	....	....	....	368.55	449.53	465.78	....	....	....	....	....	....
6314	Loans..............................	....	....	....	3.12	2.18	1.33	....	....	....	....	....	....
6316	Insurance technical reserves.........	....	....	....	—	—	—	....	....	....	....	....	....
6317	Financial derivatives................	....	....	....	—	—	—	....	....	....	....	....	....
6318	Other accounts payable.............	....	....	....	—	.03	—	....	....	....	....	....	....
632	Foreign............................	....	....	....	24.38	39.32	121.91	....	....	....	....	....	....
6322	Currency and deposits...............	....	....	....	—	—	—	....	....	....	....	....	....
6323	Securities other than shares..........	....	....	....	15.15	25.99	100.39	....	....	....	....	....	....
6324	Loans..............................	....	....	....	7.62	11.73	20.66	....	....	....	....	....	....
6326	Insurance technical reserves.........	....	....	....	—	—	—	....	....	....	....	....	....
6327	Financial derivatives................	....	....	....	—	—	—	....	....	....	....	....	....
6328	Other accounts payable.............	....	....	....	1.62	1.60	.86	....	....	....	....	....	....
Memorandum items:													
6M2	Net financial worth..................	....	....	....	....	....	....	....	....	....	....	....	....
6M3	Debt at market value................	....	....	....	....	....	....	....	....	....	....	....	....
6M4	Debt at nominal value...............	....	....	....	....	....	....	....	....	....	....	....	....
6M5	Arrears.............................	....	....	....	....	....	....	....	....	....	....	....	....
6M6	Obligations for social security benefits.........	....	....	....	....	....	....	....	....	....	....	....	....
6M7	Contingent liabilities................	....	....	....	....	....	....	....	....	....	....	....	....
6M8	Uncapitalized military weapons, systems........	....	....	....	....	....	....	....	....	....	....	....	....

Table 7   Outlays by functions of govt.

		Budgetary Central Government			Central Government			Local Government			General Government		
		2002p	2003p	2004p	2002p	2003p	2004p	2002p	2003p	2004p	2002p	2003p	2004p
7	**Total outlays....................**	736.02	791.45	819.98	930.86	975.19	1,007.97	241.82	302.43	314.50	1,084.81	1,138.50	1,183.92
701	**General public services..........**	110.59	121.69	133.64	111.47	121.75	133.66	38.92	45.46	48.53	130.16	120.99	133.66
7017	Public debt transactions............	12.79	17.91	28.32	13.66	17.97	28.34	2.05	1.90	2.15	15.71	19.86	30.49
7018	General transfers between levels of govt......	18.69	44.84	47.45	18.69	44.84	47.45	.82	.59	1.08	—	—	—
702	**Defense............................**	42.39	45.07	53.00	42.39	45.07	52.99	1.05	2.94	.45	42.52	47.96	53.40
703	**Public order and safety............**	49.86	55.27	41.03	49.86	55.27	41.03	4.07	4.36	4.90	53.85	59.51	45.81
704	**Economic affairs..................**	55.29	75.70	84.58	132.72	134.05	137.12	37.52	49.60	50.69	166.88	178.40	182.76
7042	Agriculture, forestry, fishing, and hunting.....	16.61	23.13	27.86	23.97	25.87	28.54	1.17	1.50	1.66	24.96	26.98	29.60
7043	Fuel and energy....................	2.03	2.18	2.74	2.03	2.18	2.74	.03	.04	.04	2.04	2.20	2.75
7044	Mining, manufacturing, and construction.....	4.61	2.92	3.04	4.61	2.92	3.04	.27	.20	.27	3.62	2.24	2.85
7045	Transport..........................	13.86	20.12	22.04	54.04	61.41	71.31	34.67	46.03	47.22	87.67	104.84	115.61
7046	Communication.....................	....	....	....	....	....	....	....	....	....	....	....	....
705	**Environmental protection............**	4.42	6.01	6.31	10.96	12.53	14.77	16.92	20.47	22.50	24.64	28.68	33.76
706	**Housing and community amenities........**	18.05	20.70	21.53	21.31	24.46	25.08	35.90	36.30	37.90	49.85	52.17	55.31
707	**Health..............................**	46.66	47.21	44.83	153.29	162.20	168.18	2.62	12.03	10.04	155.34	167.84	175.50
7072	Outpatient services.................	.14	.03	.03	.14	.03	.03	.38	.52	.60	.51	.52	.60
7073	Hospital services...................	9.17	9.47	5.95	9.17	9.47	5.95	1.47	9.03	6.54	10.11	12.21	9.86
7074	Public health services...............	....	....	....	....	....	....	....	....	....	....	....	....
708	**Recreation, culture, and religion...........**	9.43	9.35	10.36	9.52	9.40	10.42	16.92	18.60	21.78	24.95	26.42	30.09

2005, International Monetary Fund: *Government Finance Statistics Yearbook*

In Billions of Koruny / Year Ending December 31 / Noncash Reporter

	Budgetary Central Government			Central Government			Local Government			General Government		
	2002p	2003p	2004p	2002p	2003p	2004p	2002p	2003p	2004p	2002p	2003p	2004p
709 **Education**........................	85.94	91.78	96.29	85.94	91.78	96.31	67.92	84.30	88.59	104.49	110.66	116.74
7091 Pre-primary and primary education..........	....	....	....	....	....	....	....	....	....	....	....	....
7092 Secondary education...............	28.79	4.43	....	28.79	4.43	....	59.04	76.76	....	70.46	78.64	....
7094 Tertiary education.................	14.36	19.55	21.41	14.36	19.55	21.41	.57	.63	.72	14.88	20.13	22.12
710 **Social protection**..................	313.39	318.66	328.41	313.39	318.66	328.41	20.00	28.38	29.11	332.14	345.89	356.91
7 Statistical discrepancy: Total outlays..........	—	—	—	—	—	—	—	—	—	—	—	—
Table 8 Transactions in financial assets and liabilities by sector												
82 **Net acquisition of financial assets**........	−12.26	4.57	42.54	−115.33	−30.21	8.74	1.78	10.44	−1.23	−113.15	−20.97	8.84
821 Domestic........................	9.13	6.81	44.25	−93.94	−27.97	10.44	3.10	7.69	5.31	−90.43	−21.47	17.08
8211 General government.............	−.25	.55	−.76	−.45	.66	−.94	.05	.54	−.39	—	—	—
8212 Central bank...................	6.21	−10.58	31.45	6.21	−10.58	31.45	—	—	—	6.21	−10.58	31.45
8213 Other depository corporations......	−.75	1.76	3.68	19.68	−19.71	−13.55	3.46	6.33	5.31	23.14	−13.38	−8.24
8214 Financial corporations n.e.c.......	.96	2.75	.39	.96	2.75	.39	—	.01	—	.96	2.76	.39
8215 Nonfinancial corporations........	2.93	12.31	9.45	−120.43	−1.12	−7.01	−.46	1.18	.51	−120.89	.06	−6.50
8216 Households & NPIs serving households......	.03	.03	.04	.09	.03	.11	.06	−.36	−.12	.15	−.33	−.02
822 Foreign.......................	−21.39	−2.24	−1.70	−21.39	−2.24	−1.70	−1.33	2.74	−6.53	−22.72	.50	−8.24
8221 General government.............	....	....	....	....	....	....	....	....	....	....	....	....
8227 International organizations........	....	....	....	....	....	....	....	....	....	....	....	....
8228 Financial corporations other than international organizations..........	....	....	....	....	....	....	....	....	....	....	....	....
8229 Other nonresidents.............	....	....	....	....	....	....	....	....	....	....	....	....
823 Monetary gold and SDRs...........	—	—	—	—	—	—	—	—	—	—	—	—
83 **Net incurrence of liabilities**..........	51.03	95.97	99.58	32.50	95.02	98.72	7.03	13.93	6.53	39.93	107.75	106.58
831 Domestic.......................	47.35	81.02	16.25	28.81	80.07	15.39	2.19	2.42	2.35	31.41	81.29	19.07
8311 General government.............	−.71	.55	−.46	.05	.54	−1.24	−.45	.66	−.94	—	—	−.85
8312 Central bank...................	−.51	—	—	−.51	—	—	....	....	....	....	....	....
8313 Other depository corporations......	−13.86	161.69	−24.30	−33.15	160.25	−24.30	....	1.76	....	....	162.02	....
8314 Financial corporations n.e.c.......	55.29	−71.89	42.29	55.29	−71.89	42.29	....	—	....	....	−71.89	....
8315 Nonfinancial corporations........	8.88	−9.43	−1.52	8.88	−8.90	−1.52	....	—	....	....	−8.90	....
8316 Households & NPIs serving households......	−1.73	.09	.25	−1.75	.06	.17	....	—	....	....	.06	....
832 Foreign.......................	3.68	14.96	83.33	3.68	14.96	83.33	4.84	11.51	4.19	8.52	26.47	87.51
8321 General government.............	−.46	−1.75	—	−.46	−1.75	—	....	....	....	....	....	....
8327 International organizations........	1.54	5.86	8.93	1.54	5.86	8.93	....	....	....	....	....	....
8328 Financial corporations other than international organizations..........	—	—	—	—	—	—	....	....	....	....	....	....
8329 Other nonresidents.............	2.61	10.84	74.40	2.61	10.84	74.40	....	....	....	....	....	....

Denmark   128

In Millions of Kroner / Year Ending December 31 / Noncash Reporter

	Budgetary Central Government 2002	2003p	2004p	Central Government 2002	2003p	2004p	Local Government 2002	2003p	2004p	General Government 2002	2003p	2004p
Statement of government operations												
1 Revenue	477,511	487,074	529,841	481,407	491,263	534,298	443,312	458,157	478,889	755,827	771,540	826,466
2 Expense	476,326	486,820	505,193	480,277	490,773	509,140	443,332	466,346	488,442	754,716	779,239	810,861
GOB *Gross operating balance*	*12,018*	*11,102*	*35,837*	*11,963*	*11,338*	*36,347*	*15,543*	*8,143*	*7,258*	*27,506*	*19,481*	*43,605*
NOB *Net operating balance*	*1,185*	*254*	*24,648*	*1,130*	*490*	*25,158*	*−20*	*−8,189*	*−9,553*	*1,110*	*−7,699*	*15,605*
31 Net acquisition of nonfinancial assets	−2,764	−4,071	−1,426	−2,760	−4,068	−1,423	288	−454	857	−2,472	−4,522	−566
NLB *Net lending/borrowing*	*3,949*	*4,325*	*26,075*	*3,890*	*4,558*	*26,581*	*−308*	*−7,735*	*−10,410*	*3,583*	*−3,177*	*16,171*
32 Net acquisition of financial assets	13,012	−7,054	−14,500	14,012	−6,477	−10,074	8,221	−325	−13,891	21,725	−7,480	−20,766
33 Net incurrence of liabilities	9,066	−11,380	−40,575	10,123	−11,037	−36,657	8,528	7,410	−3,480	18,144	−4,305	−36,937
NLB Statistical discrepancy	−3	1	—	−1	2	1	1	—	−2	−2	2	—
Statement of other economic flows												
4 *Change in net worth from holding gains*	....	....	....	....	....	....	....	....	....	....	....	....
41 Nonfinancial assets	....	....	....	....	....	....	....	....	....	....	....	....
42 Financial assets	8,803	5,412	873	8,791	5,466	882	1,281	4,775	164	10,091	10,243	1,046
43 Liabilities	7,795	−1,048	3,066	7,795	−1,048	3,066	1,046	114	286	8,860	−932	3,352
5 *Change in net worth from other volume changes*	....	....	....	....	....	....	....	....	....	....	....	....
51 Nonfinancial assets	....	....	....	....	....	....	....	....	....	....	....	....
52 Financial assets	27,645	2,633	−5,453	9,807	2,337	−6,204	−5,876	−3,864	20,037	3,931	−1,527	13,833
53 Liabilities	—	—	—	2,363	—	—	—	—	—	2,363	—	—
Balance sheet												
6 *Net worth*	....	....	....	....	....	....	....	....	....	....	....	....
61 Nonfinancial assets	....	....	....	....	....	....	....	....	....	....	....	....
62 Financial assets	440,669	441,663	422,581	443,336	444,662	429,264	83,941	84,529	90,838	501,986	503,224	497,333
63 Liabilities	660,999	648,572	612,864	662,788	650,704	618,914	111,080	118,604	113,609	748,577	743,341	709,754
Statement of sources and uses of cash												
Table 1 Revenue												
1 Revenue	477,511	487,074	529,841	481,407	491,263	534,298	443,312	458,157	478,889	755,827	771,540	826,466
11 Taxes	405,433	413,347	449,193	405,433	413,347	449,193	234,530	239,649	248,108	639,963	652,996	697,301
111 Taxes on income, profits, & capital gains	174,136	179,640	201,316	174,136	179,640	201,316	218,732	222,948	230,785	392,868	402,589	432,100
1111 Individuals	138,213	138,271	139,128	138,213	138,271	139,128	214,300	218,379	225,845	352,513	356,649	364,973
1112 Corporations and other enterprises	34,855	35,363	41,090	34,855	35,363	41,090	4,432	4,570	4,940	39,287	39,933	46,030
112 Taxes on payroll and workforce	3,342	2,898	2,895	3,342	2,898	2,895	—	—	—	3,342	2,898	2,895
113 Taxes on property	8,063	8,974	9,861	8,063	8,974	9,861	15,641	16,553	17,172	23,704	25,526	27,033
114 Taxes on goods and services	219,820	221,757	235,043	219,820	221,757	235,043	158	148	151	219,978	221,904	235,194
1141 General taxes on goods and services	132,394	135,092	143,503	132,394	135,092	143,503	—	—	—	132,394	135,092	143,503
1142 Excises	70,246	69,135	72,742	70,246	69,135	72,742	158	148	151	70,404	69,283	72,893
115 Taxes on int'l. trade and transactions	—	—	—	—	—	—	—	—	—	—	—	—
116 Other taxes	72	79	78	72	79	78	—	—	—	72	79	78
12 Social contributions	5,883	5,961	6,150	22,140	22,692	23,134	6,685	7,139	7,558	28,825	29,831	30,691
121 Social security contributions	837	779	748	17,094	17,510	17,732	—	—	—	17,094	17,510	17,732
122 Other social contributions	5,046	5,182	5,402	5,046	5,182	5,402	6,685	7,139	7,558	11,731	12,321	12,959
13 Grants	18,443	19,822	18,651	5,875	7,012	5,903	165,170	172,591	183,010	2,152	1,723	2,191
131 From foreign governments	193	174	164	193	174	164	16	17	19	209	191	183
132 From international organizations	1,944	1,533	2,008	1,944	1,533	2,008	—	—	—	1,944	1,533	2,008
133 From other general government units	16,306	18,116	16,480	3,738	5,305	3,731	165,154	172,574	182,990	—	—	—
14 Other revenue	47,752	47,944	55,847	47,959	48,212	56,069	36,926	38,779	40,214	84,886	86,991	96,283
Table 2 Expense by economic type												
2 Expense	476,326	486,820	505,193	480,277	490,773	509,140	443,332	466,346	488,442	754,716	779,239	810,861
21 Compensation of employees	64,048	64,919	65,984	66,451	67,391	68,463	176,328	184,567	192,477	242,779	251,958	260,940
211 Wages and salaries	55,937	54,554	56,968	58,337	57,023	59,444	169,823	177,606	185,104	228,160	234,629	244,548
212 Social contributions	8,111	10,365	9,016	8,114	10,368	9,019	6,505	6,962	7,373	14,619	17,330	16,392
22 Use of goods and services	42,206	43,095	47,629	43,025	43,942	48,476	68,931	71,111	78,288	111,956	115,053	126,764
23 Consumption of fixed capital	10,833	10,848	11,189	10,833	10,848	11,189	15,563	16,332	16,811	26,396	27,180	28,000
24 Interest	49,841	46,319	44,643	49,846	46,324	44,643	1,858	1,706	1,867	51,704	48,030	46,510
25 Subsidies	23,289	22,079	22,337	23,289	22,079	22,337	10,732	10,996	12,045	34,021	33,075	34,382
26 Grants	235,429	249,297	262,024	194,696	202,338	213,199	3,743	5,311	3,737	29,547	29,770	30,215
261 To foreign governments	18,100	17,789	17,388	18,100	17,879	17,388	5	6	7	18,105	17,885	17,395
262 To international organizations	11,442	11,885	12,821	11,442	11,885	12,821	—	—	—	11,442	11,885	12,821
263 To other general government units	205,886	219,622	231,816	165,154	172,574	182,990	3,738	5,305	3,731	—	—	—
2631 Current	205,815	219,549	231,775	165,083	172,501	182,949	3,734	5,305	3,731	—	—	—
2632 Capital	72	73	41	72	73	41	4	—	—	—	—	—

2005, International Monetary Fund: Government Finance Statistics Yearbook

In Millions of Kroner / Year Ending December 31 / Noncash Reporter

		Budgetary Central Government			Central Government			Local Government			General Government		
		2002	2003p	2004p	2002	2003p	2004p	2002	2003p	2004p	2002	2003p	2004p
27	Social benefits.........................	40,631	40,178	40,915	81,889	87,385	89,453	162,920	172,325	179,275	244,809	259,710	268,729
28	Other expense........................	10,050	10,086	10,471	10,247	10,465	11,380	3,258	3,997	3,941	13,505	14,462	15,321
281	Property expense other than interest............	—	—	—									
282	Miscellaneous other expense.....................	10,050	10,086	10,471	10,247	10,465	11,380	3,258	3,997	3,941	13,505	14,462	15,321
2821	Current....................	5,338	5,810	6,650	5,338	5,810	6,650	2,570	3,256	3,352	7,908	9,066	10,002
2822	Capital.....................	4,712	4,277	3,821	4,909	4,656	4,729	687	741	590	5,597	5,396	5,319

Table 3   Transactions in assets and liabilities

		2002	2003p	2004p	2002	2003p	2004p	2002	2003p	2004p	2002	2003p	2004p
3	Change in net worth from transactns....	1,182	255	24,648	1,129	492	25,160	−19	−8,189	−9,555	1,109	−7,697	15,605
31	Net acquisition of nonfinancial assets...	−2,764	−4,071	−1,426	−2,760	−4,068	−1,423	288	−454	857	−2,472	−4,522	−566
311	Fixed assets..............	−2,710	−4,036	−3,396	−2,707	−4,033	−3,393	648	−261	1,173	−2,058	−4,293	−2,220
3111	Buildings and structures..............	....	....	....	....	....	....	....	....	....	....	....	....
3112	Machinery and equipment....................	....	....	....	....	....	....	....	....	....	....	....	....
3113	Other fixed assets..................	....	....	....	....	....	....	....	....	....	....	....	....
312	Inventories........................	33	49	−77	33	49	−77	—	—	—	33	49	−77
313	Valuables....................	−122	−356	1,804	−122	−356	1,804	−143	−130	−183	−266	−486	1,621
314	Nonproduced assets..............	36	271	242	36	271	242	−217	−64	−133	−182	208	109
3141	Land..................	....	....	....	....	....	....	....	....	....	....	....	....
3142	Subsoil assets.............	....	....	....	....	....	....	....	....	....	....	....	....
3143	Other naturally occurring assets...............	....	....	....	....	....	....	....	....	....	....	....	....
3144	Intangible nonproduced assets.................	....	....	....	....	....	....	....	....	....	....	....	....
32	Net acquisition of financial assets........	13,012	−7,054	−14,500	14,012	−6,477	−10,074	8,221	−325	−13,891	21,725	−7,480	−20,766
321	Domestic.................	13,012	−7,054	−14,500	14,012	−6,477	−10,074	8,221	−325	−13,891	21,725	−7,480	−20,766
3212	Currency and deposits.........................	3,151	−11,640	22,823	3,613	−11,279	27,232	1,961	1,454	−61	5,574	−9,825	27,171
3213	Securities other than shares....................	−3,105	−7,502	−4,280	−2,090	−7,667	−4,934	568	2,186	3,726	−640	−6,593	−2,022
3214	Loans....................	8,179	2,279	−7,189	8,179	2,279	−7,189	795	232	7,611	8,974	2,511	422
3215	Shares and other equity....................	4,923	−1,223	77	4,900	−1,254	−10	3,736	5,359	−126	8,636	4,105	−136
3216	Insurance technical reserves.................	13	5	4	13	5	4	45	29	19	58	34	23
3217	Financial derivatives.................	—	—	—	—	—	—	—	—	—	—	—	—
3218	Other accounts receivable.....................	−149	11,027	−25,935	−603	11,439	−25,177	1,116	−9,585	−25,060	−877	2,288	−46,224
322	Foreign.................	....	....	....	....	....	....	....	....	....	....	....	....
3222	Currency and deposits.........	....	....	....	....	....	....	....	....	....	....	....	....
3223	Securities other than shares.........	....	....	....	....	....	....	....	....	....	....	....	....
3224	Loans.........	....	....	....	....	....	....	....	....	....	....	....	....
3225	Shares and other equity.........	....	....	....	....	....	....	....	....	....	....	....	....
3226	Insurance technical reserves.........	....	....	....	....	....	....	....	....	....	....	....	....
3227	Financial derivatives.........	....	....	....	....	....	....	....	....	....	....	....	....
3228	Other accounts receivable.........	....	....	....	....	....	....	....	....	....	....	....	....
323	Monetary gold and SDRs.........	—	—	—	—	—	—	—	—	—	—	—	—
33	Net incurrence of liabilities...................	9,066	−11,380	−40,575	10,123	−11,037	−36,657	8,528	7,410	−3,480	18,144	−4,305	−36,937
331	Domestic.............	9,066	−11,380	−40,575	10,123	−11,037	−36,657	8,528	7,410	−3,480	18,144	−4,305	−36,937
3312	Currency and deposits.........	—	—	—	—	—	—	1,076	186	500	1,076	186	500
3313	Securities other than shares....................	10,493	−15,531	−1,673	10,493	−15,531	−1,673	−126	−233	−102	11,249	−16,876	−2,589
3314	Loans....................	−684	−42	−7,137	−815	254	−7,046	5,420	3,705	4,010	4,605	3,959	−3,036
3316	Insurance technical reserves.................	—	—	—	—	—	—	—	—	—	—	—	—
3317	Financial derivatives.................	—	—	—	—	—	—	—	—	—	—	—	—
3318	Other accounts payable..................	−743	4,193	−31,765	445	4,240	−27,938	2,158	3,752	−7,888	1,214	8,426	−31,812
332	Foreign.................	....	....	....	....	....	....	....	....	....	....	....	....
3322	Currency and deposits.........	....	....	....	....	....	....	....	....	....	....	....	....
3323	Securities other than shares.........	....	....	....	....	....	....	....	....	....	....	....	....
3324	Loans.........	....	....	....	....	....	....	....	....	....	....	....	....
3326	Insurance technical reserves.........	....	....	....	....	....	....	....	....	....	....	....	....
3327	Financial derivatives.........	....	....	....	....	....	....	....	....	....	....	....	....
3328	Other accounts payable.........	....	....	....	....	....	....	....	....	....	....	....	....

Table 4   Holding gains in assets and liabilities

		2002	2003p	2004p	2002	2003p	2004p	2002	2003p	2004p	2002	2003p	2004p
4	Change in net worth from hold. gains...	....	....	....	....	....	....	....	....	....	....	....	....
41	Nonfinancial assets........................	....	....	....	....	....	....	....	....	....	....	....	....
411	Fixed assets.................	....	....	....	....	....	....	....	....	....	....	....	....
412	Inventories................	....	....	....	....	....	....	....	....	....	....	....	....
413	Valuables................	....	....	....	....	....	....	....	....	....	....	....	....
414	Nonproduced assets................	....	....	....	....	....	....	....	....	....	....	....	....
42	Financial assets..............	8,803	5,412	873	8,791	5,466	882	1,281	4,775	164	10,091	10,243	1,046
421	Domestic..............	8,803	5,412	873	8,791	5,466	882	1,281	4,775	164	10,091	10,243	1,046
422	Foreign.................	....	....	....	....	....	....	....	....	....	....	....	....
423	Monetary gold and SDRs......................	—	—	—	....	....	....	—	—	—	—	....	....

Denmark 128

In Millions of Kroner / Year Ending December 31 / Noncash Reporter

		Budgetary Central Government			Central Government			Local Government			General Government		
		2002	2003p	2004p	2002	2003p	2004p	2002	2003p	2004p	2002	2003p	2004p
43	Liabilities..............	7,795	−1,048	3,066	7,795	−1,048	3,066	1,046	114	286	8,860	−932	3,352
431	Domestic...............	7,795	−1,048	3,066	7,795	−1,048	3,066	1,046	114	286	8,860	−932	3,352
432	Foreign................	....	....	....	....	....	....	....	....	....	....	....	....

Table 5 Other changes in the volume of assets and liabilities

		Budgetary Central Government			Central Government			Local Government			General Government		
5	Change in net worth from vol. chngs.....	....	....	....	....	....	....	....	....	....	....	....	....
51	Nonfinancial assets..............	....	....	....	....	....	....	....	....	....	....	....	....
511	Fixed assets...........	....	....	....	....	....	....	....	....	....	....	....	....
512	Inventories...........	....	....	....	....	....	....	....	....	....	....	....	....
513	Valuables.............	....	....	....	....	....	....	....	....	....	....	....	....
514	Nonproduced assets......	....	....	....	....	....	....	....	....	....	....	....	....
52	Financial assets..............	27,645	2,633	−5,453	9,807	2,337	−6,204	−5,876	−3,864	20,037	3,931	−1,527	13,833
521	Domestic...............	27,645	2,633	−5,453	9,807	2,337	−6,204	−5,876	−3,864	20,037	3,931	−1,527	13,833
522	Foreign................	....	....	....	....	....	....	....	....	....	....	....	....
523	Monetary gold and SDRs...........	—	—	—	—	—	—	—	—	—	—	—	—
53	Liabilities..............	—	—	—	2,363	—	—	—	—	—	2,363	—	—
531	Domestic...............	—	—	—	2,363	—	—	—	—	—	2,363	—	—
532	Foreign................	....	....	....	....	....	....	....	....	....	....	....	....

Table 6 Balance sheet

		Budgetary Central Government			Central Government			Local Government			General Government		
6	Net worth...............	....	....	....	....	....	....	....	....	....	....	....	....
61	Nonfinancial assets.............	....	....	....	....	....	....	....	....	....	....	....	....
611	Fixed assets...........	....	....	....	....	....	....	....	....	....	....	....	....
6111	Buildings and structures......	....	....	....	....	....	....	....	....	....	....	....	....
6112	Machinery and equipment........	....	....	....	....	....	....	....	....	....	....	....	....
6113	Other fixed assets......	....	....	....	....	....	....	....	....	....	....	....	....
612	Inventories...........	....	....	....	....	....	....	....	....	....	....	....	....
613	Valuables.............	....	....	....	....	....	....	....	....	....	....	....	....
614	Nonproduced assets......	....	....	....	....	....	....	....	....	....	....	....	....
6141	Land.................	....	....	....	....	....	....	....	....	....	....	....	....
6142	Subsoil assets.........	....	....	....	....	....	....	....	....	....	....	....	....
6143	Other naturally occurring assets...	....	....	....	....	....	....	....	....	....	....	....	....
6144	Intangible nonproduced assets.........	....	....	....	....	....	....	....	....	....	....	....	....
62	Financial assets..............	440,669	441,663	422,581	443,336	444,662	429,264	83,941	84,529	90,838	501,986	503,224	497,333
621	Domestic...............	440,669	441,663	422,581	443,336	444,662	429,264	83,941	84,529	90,838	501,986	503,224	497,333
6212	Currency and deposits......	48,094	36,455	59,278	48,749	37,470	64,702	11,803	13,257	13,196	60,552	50,727	77,898
6213	Securities other than shares.......	29,778	21,803	17,319	31,461	23,334	18,173	14,187	16,209	19,760	41,422	34,207	31,783
6214	Loans.................	62,028	64,308	57,119	62,028	64,308	57,119	21,743	21,976	29,587	83,771	86,284	86,706
6215	Shares and other equity...........	175,400	180,063	181,215	175,585	180,256	181,353	24,499	34,797	35,009	200,084	215,053	216,362
6216	Insurance technical reserves........	97	103	108	97	103	108	385	418	441	482	521	549
6217	Financial derivatives.........	—	—	—	—	—	—						
6218	Other accounts receivable...........	125,272	138,931	107,542	125,416	139,191	107,809	11,324	−2,128	−7,155	115,675	116,432	84,035
622	Foreign................	....	....	....	....	....	....	....	....	....	....	....	....
6222	Currency and deposits......	....	....	....	....	....	....	....	....	....	....	....	....
6223	Securities other than shares.......	....	....	....	....	....	....	....	....	....	....	....	....
6224	Loans.................	....	....	....	....	....	....	....	....	....	....	....	....
6225	Shares and other equity...........	....	....	....	....	....	....	....	....	....	....	....	....
6226	Insurance technical reserves........	....	....	....	....	....	....	....	....	....	....	....	....
6227	Financial derivatives.........	....	....	....	....	....	....	....	....	....	....	....	....
6228	Other accounts receivable...........	....	....	....	....	....	....	....	....	....	....	....	....
623	Monetary gold and SDRs...........	....	....	....	....	....	....	....	....	....	....	....	....
63	Liabilities..............	660,999	648,572	612,864	662,788	650,704	618,914	111,080	118,604	113,609	748,577	743,341	709,754
631	Domestic...............	660,999	648,572	612,864	662,788	650,704	618,914	111,080	118,604	113,609	748,577	743,341	709,754
6312	Currency and deposits......	—	—	—	—	—	—	11,067	11,253	11,753	11,067	11,253	11,753
6313	Securities other than shares.......	623,839	594,582	595,845	623,839	594,582	595,845	2,210	1,961	1,864	621,823	591,207	591,559
6314	Loans.................	7,641	11,019	4,012	7,718	11,392	4,476	51,506	55,341	59,632	59,224	66,733	64,108
6316	Insurance technical reserves........	—	—	—	—	—	—	—	—	—	—	—	—
6317	Financial derivatives.........	—	—	—	—	—	—	—	—	—	—	—	—
6318	Other accounts payable...........	29,519	42,971	13,007	31,231	44,730	18,593	46,297	50,049	40,360	56,463	74,148	42,334
632	Foreign................	....	....	....	....	....	....	....	....	....	....	....	....
6322	Currency and deposits......	....	....	....	....	....	....	....	....	....	....	....	....
6323	Securities other than shares.......	....	....	....	....	....	....	....	....	....	....	....	....
6324	Loans.................	....	....	....	....	....	....	....	....	....	....	....	....
6326	Insurance technical reserves........	....	....	....	....	....	....	....	....	....	....	....	....
6327	Financial derivatives.........	....	....	....	....	....	....	....	....	....	....	....	....
6328	Other accounts payable...........	....	....	....	....	....	....	....	....	....	....	....	....

Denmark 128

In Millions of Kroner / Year Ending December 31 / Noncash Reporter

	Budgetary Central Government			Central Government			Local Government			General Government		
	2002	2003p	2004p	2002	2003p	2004p	2002	2003p	2004p	2002	2003p	2004p
Memorandum items:												
6M2 Net financial worth	−220,330	−206,909	−190,283	−219,452	−206,042	−189,650	−27,139	−34,075	−22,771	−246,591	−240,117	−212,421
6M3 Debt at market value	....	....	....	....	....	....	....	....	....	....	....	....
6M4 Debt at nominal value	....	....	....	....	....	....	....	....	....	....	....	....
6M5 Arrears	....	....	....	....	....	....	....	....	....	....	....	....
6M6 Obligations for social security benefits	....	....	....	....	....	....	....	....	....	....	....	....
6M7 Contingent liabilities	....	....	....	....	....	....	....	....	....	....	....	....
6M8 Uncapitalized military weapons, systems	....	....	....	....	....	....	....	....	....	....	....	....
Table 7 Outlays by functions of govt.												
7 **Total outlays**	473,562	482,749	503,767	477,516	486,704	507,717	443,620	465,892	489,299	752,244	774,717	810,294
701 **General public services**	138,511	135,523	142,847	138,518	135,622	142,852	16,664	19,670	18,797	112,950	109,482	109,126
7017 Public debt transactions	49,841	46,319	44,643	49,846	46,324	44,643	1,858	1,706	1,867	51,704	48,030	46,510
7018 General transfers between levels of govt.	....	....	51,942	....	....	51,942	....	....	491	....	....	—
702 **Defense**	22,080	22,301	23,114	22,080	22,301	23,114	1	242	243	22,080	22,544	23,357
703 **Public order and safety**	12,151	12,836	13,645	12,151	12,836	13,645	1,544	1,361	1,320	13,694	14,195	14,964
704 **Economic affairs**	30,430	29,547	32,009	30,430	29,547	32,009	21,966	22,165	23,751	49,999	49,491	52,952
7042 Agriculture, forestry, fishing, and hunting	2,207	1,642	1,177	2,207	1,642	1,177	—	—	—	2,207	1,642	1,177
7043 Fuel and energy	60	48	294	60	48	294	—	—	—	17	20	268
7044 Mining, manufacturing, and construction	610	440	578	610	440	578	15	6	8	623	435	584
7045 Transport	10,065	10,570	10,703	10,065	10,570	10,703	12,143	12,384	12,924	22,156	22,909	23,592
7046 Communication	450	518	411	450	518	411	—	—	—	450	518	411
705 **Environmental protection**	4,564	3,944	3,144	4,564	3,944	3,144	4,136	4,238	4,689	8,595	8,074	7,768
706 **Housing and community amenities**	6,602	6,691	6,698	6,602	6,691	6,698	3,083	3,186	3,580	9,639	9,859	10,261
707 **Health**	4,663	4,455	4,714	4,663	4,455	4,714	94,127	97,014	106,224	96,226	99,184	108,548
7072 Outpatient services	51	50	51	51	50	51	12,887	13,526	13,831	12,931	13,568	13,876
7073 Hospital services	2,469	2,178	1,519	2,469	2,178	1,519	72,835	74,804	83,087	72,875	74,835	83,112
7074 Public health services	11	19	794	11	19	794	1,167	1,234	1,443	1,177	1,253	1,487
708 **Recreation, culture, and religion**	10,060	10,248	12,752	10,060	10,248	12,752	12,325	13,017	12,558	21,838	22,734	25,005
709 **Education**	57,636	57,907	61,992	57,636	57,907	61,992	61,077	63,741	64,486	112,139	115,358	120,067
7091 Pre-primary and primary education	7,308	8,017	8,034	7,308	8,017	8,034	42,890	44,935	45,794	47,518	50,322	51,111
7092 Secondary education	12,689	14,498	13,986	12,689	14,498	13,986	7,211	7,624	7,611	19,720	21,974	21,477
7094 Tertiary education	22,473	23,138	25,523	22,473	23,138	25,523	519	527	531	22,781	23,658	26,054
710 **Social protection**	186,866	199,299	202,851	190,813	203,154	206,797	228,698	241,258	253,651	305,084	323,796	338,246
7 Statistical discrepancy: Total outlays	—	—	—	—	—	—	—	—	—	—	—	—
Table 8 Transactions in financial assets and liabilities by sector												
82 **Net acquisition of financial assets**	13,012	−7,054	−14,500	14,012	−6,477	−10,074	8,221	−325	−13,891	21,725	−7,480	−20,766
821 Domestic	13,012	−7,054	−14,500	14,012	−6,477	−10,074	8,221	−325	−13,891	21,725	−7,480	−20,766
8211 General government	....	....	....	....	....	....	....	....	....	....	....	....
8212 Central bank	....	....	....	....	....	....	....	....	....	....	....	....
8213 Other depository corporations	....	....	....	....	....	....	....	....	....	....	....	....
8214 Financial corporations n.e.c.	....	....	....	....	....	....	....	....	....	....	....	....
8215 Nonfinancial corporations	....	....	....	....	....	....	....	....	....	....	....	....
8216 Households & NPIs serving households	....	....	....	....	....	....	....	....	....	....	....	....
822 Foreign	....	....	....	....	....	....	....	....	....	....	....	....
8221 General government	....	....	....	....	....	....	....	....	....	....	....	....
8227 International organizations	....	....	....	....	....	....	....	....	....	....	....	....
8228 Financial corporations other than international organizations	....	....	....	....	....	....	....	....	....	....	....	....
8229 Other nonresidents	....	....	....	....	....	....	....	....	....	....	....	....
823 Monetary gold and SDRs	—	—	—	—	—	—	—	—	—	—	—	—
83 **Net incurrence of liabilities**	9,066	−11,380	−40,575	10,123	−11,037	−36,657	8,528	7,410	−3,480	18,144	−4,305	−36,937
831 Domestic	9,066	−11,380	−40,575	10,123	−11,037	−36,657	8,528	7,410	−3,480	18,144	−4,305	−36,937
8311 General government	....	....	....	....	....	....	....	....	....	....	....	....
8312 Central bank	....	....	....	....	....	....	....	....	....	....	....	....
8313 Other depository corporations	....	....	....	....	....	....	....	....	....	....	....	....
8314 Financial corporations n.e.c.	....	....	....	....	....	....	....	....	....	....	....	....
8315 Nonfinancial corporations	....	....	....	....	....	....	....	....	....	....	....	....
8316 Households & NPIs serving households	....	....	....	....	....	....	....	....	....	....	....	....
832 Foreign	....	....	....	....	....	....	....	....	....	....	....	....
8321 General government	....	....	....	....	....	....	....	....	....	....	....	....
8327 International organizations	....	....	....	....	....	....	....	....	....	....	....	....
8328 Financial corporations other than international organizations	....	....	....	....	....	....	....	....	....	....	....	....
8329 Other nonresidents	....	....	....	....	....	....	....	....	....	....	....	....

Dominican Republic   243

In Millions of Pesos / Year Ending December 31 / Cash Reporter

	Budgetary Central Government			Central Government			Local Government			General Government		
	2001	2002	2003	2001	2002	2003	2001	2002	2003	2001	2002	2003
Statement of government operations												
Statement of other economic flows												
Balance sheet												
Statement of sources and uses of cash												
1 Cash receipts from operating activities...........	60,416	66,779	†80,572	63,514	70,158	84,221	....	....	....	....	....	....
11 Taxes..	57,177	63,101	†73,831	57,177	63,101	73,831	....	....	....	....	....	....
12 Social contributions..............................	577	643	†417	2,793	2,974	2,529	....	....	....	....	....	....
13 Grants...	416	516	†926	416	540	981	....	....	....	....	....	....
14 Other receipts....................................	2,245	2,520	†5,398	3,127	3,544	6,879	....	....	....	....	....	....
2 Cash payments for operating activities...........	46,095	53,208	†65,425	52,003	59,249	67,337	....	....	....	....	....	....
21 Compensation of employees.......................	21,496	24,925	†26,108	25,116	28,754	30,409	....	....	....	....	....	....
22 Purchases of goods and services.................	6,716	8,361	†9,615	7,607	9,139	10,850	....	....	....	....	....	....
24 Interest..	3,018	4,432	†7,872	3,071	4,608	7,874	....	....	....	....	....	....
25 Subsidies...	3,826	2,665	†9,540	4,088	2,959	9,811	....	....	....	....	....	....
26 Grants..	1,076	908	†4,533	1,078	910	5	....	....	....	....	....	....
27 Social benefits...................................	4,655	4,367	†—	5,573	5,306	590	....	....	....	....	....	....
28 Other payments...................................	5,308	7,549	†7,758	5,471	7,574	7,798	....	....	....	....	....	....
CIO *Net cash inflow from oper. activities.....*	....	....	*†15,147*	11,510	10,909	16,883	....	....	....	....	....	....
31.1 Purchases of nonfinancial assets..................	9,245	10,257	†8,567	10,426	11,675	9,765	....	....	....	....	....	....
31.2 Sales of nonfinancial assets.....................	19	26	†38	45	50	51	....	....	....	....	....	....
31 Net cash outflow from investments in nonfinancial assets.....................	9,226	10,232	†8,529	10,382	11,625	9,715	....	....	....	....	....	....
CSD *Cash surplus/deficit....................*	....	....	*†6,618*	*1,129*	*−716*	*7,169*	....	....	....	....	....	....
32x Net acquisition of fin assets, excl. cash.........	74	49	†16,470	150	97	17,416	....	....	....	....	....	....
321x Domestic...	74	49	†24	150	97	970	....	....	....	....	....	....
322x Foreign..	—	—	†16,446	—	—	16,446	....	....	....	....	....	....
323 Monetary gold and SDRs...........................	—	—	†—	—	—	—	....	....	....	....	....	....
33 Net incurrence of liabilities.....................	....	....	†17,127	....	....	16,626	....	....	....	....	....	....
331 Domestic..	....	....	†5,556	....	....	5,055	....	....	....	....	....	....
332 Foreign...	....	....	†11,571	....	....	11,571	....	....	....	....	....	....
NFB Net cash inflow from fin. activities..............	....	....	†657	....	....	−791	....	....	....	....	....	....
NCB *Net change in the stock of cash...........*	....	....	*†6,957*	....	....	*6,294*	....	....	....	....	....	....
Table 1 Revenue												
1 **Revenue**............................	**60,416**	**66,779**	**†80,572**	**63,514**	**70,158**	**84,221**	....	....	....	....	....	....
11 **Taxes**..............................	**57,177**	**63,101**	**†73,831**	**57,177**	**63,101**	**73,831**	....	....	....	....	....	....
111 Taxes on income, profits, & capital gains.....	14,303	14,904	†20,385	14,303	14,904	20,385	....	....	....	....	....	....
1111 Individuals......................................	7,014	8,664	†5,668	7,014	8,664	5,668	....	....	....	....	....	....
1112 Corporations and other enterprises............	7,184	6,092	†9,384	7,184	6,092	9,384	....	....	....	....	....	....
112 Taxes on payroll and workforce...................	—	—	†—	—	—	—	....	....	....	....	....	....
113 Taxes on property................................	560	676	†1,246	560	676	1,246	....	....	....	....	....	....
114 Taxes on goods and services......................	22,017	24,419	†34,498	22,017	24,419	34,498	....	....	....	....	....	....
1141 General taxes on goods and services..........	—	—	†19,179	—	—	19,179	....	....	....	....	....	....
1142 Excises..	20,090	22,170	†15,302	20,090	22,170	15,302	....	....	....	....	....	....
115 Taxes on int'l. trade and transactions..........	19,553	22,194	†17,573	19,553	22,194	17,573	....	....	....	....	....	....
116 Other taxes......................................	745	907	†129	745	907	129	....	....	....	....	....	....
12 **Social contributions**...........................	**577**	**643**	**†417**	**2,793**	**2,974**	**2,529**	....	....	....	....	....	....
121 Social security contributions....................	—	—	†—	2,216	2,331	2,113	....	....	....	....	....	....
122 Other social contributions......................	577	643	†417	577	643	417	....	....	....	....	....	....
13 **Grants**..	**416**	**516**	**†926**	**416**	**540**	**981**	....	....	....	....	....	....
131 From foreign governments.........................	416	516	†878	416	516	878	....	....	....	....	....	....
132 From international organizations.................	—	—	†48	—	—	103	....	....	....	....	....	....
133 From other general government units...........	—	—	†—	—	24	—	....	....	....	....	....	....
14 **Other revenue**.................................	**2,245**	**2,520**	**†5,398**	**3,127**	**3,544**	**6,879**	....	....	....	....	....	....
Table 2 Expense by economic type												
2 **Expense**...........................	**46,095**	**53,208**	**†65,425**	**52,003**	**59,249**	**67,337**	....	....	....	....	....	....
21 **Compensation of employees**...................	**21,496**	**24,925**	**†26,108**	**25,116**	**28,754**	**30,409**	....	....	....	....	....	....
211 Wages and salaries...............................	21,496	24,925	†26,075	25,116	28,754	....	....	....	....	....	....	....
212 Social contributions.............................	—	—	†33	—	—	....	....	....	....	....	....	....
22 **Use of goods and services**......................	**6,716**	**8,361**	**†9,615**	**7,607**	**9,139**	**10,850**	....	....	....	....	....	....
23 **Consumption of fixed capital**.................	....	....	....	....	....	....	....	....	....	....	....	....
24 **Interest**..	**3,018**	**4,432**	**†7,872**	**3,071**	**4,608**	**7,874**	....	....	....	....	....	....
25 **Subsidies**..	**3,826**	**2,665**	**†9,540**	**4,088**	**2,959**	**9,811**	....	....	....	....	....	....

In Millions of Pesos / Year Ending December 31 / Cash Reporter

	Budgetary Central Government			Central Government			Local Government			General Government		
	2001	2002	2003	2001	2002	2003	2001	2002	2003	2001	2002	2003
26 **Grants**...........................	**1,076**	**908**	**†4,533**	**1,078**	**910**	**5**	....	....	....	....	....	....
261 To foreign govenments................	46	63	†—	47	64	5	....	....	....	....	....	....
262 To international organizations............	—	—	†—				....	....	....	....	....	....
263 To other general government units.........	1,031	846	†4,533	1,031	846	—	....	....	....	....	....	....
2631 Current.................................	1,031	846	†3,123	1,031	846	—	....	....	....	....	....	....
2632 Capital.................................	—	—	†1,410	—	—	—	....	....	....	....	....	....
27 **Social benefits**.................	**4,655**	**4,367**	**†—**	**5,573**	**5,306**	**590**	....	....	....	....	....	....
28 **Other expense**..................	**5,308**	**7,549**	**†7,758**	**5,471**	**7,574**	**7,798**	....	....	....	....	....	....
281 Property expense other than interest...........	—	—	†—	—	—	—	....	....	....	....	....	....
282 Miscellaneous other expense..................	5,308	7,549	†7,758	5,471	7,574	7,798	....	....	....	....	....	....
2821 Current.................................	28	....	†—	28	....		....	....	....	....	....	....
2822 Capital.................................	5,280	7,549	†7,758	5,443	....	7,798	....	....	....	....	....	....

Table 3 Transactions in assets and liabilities

	Budgetary Central Government			Central Government			Local Government			General Government		
3 **Change in net worth from transactns....**	....	....	....	....	....	....	....	....	....	....	....	....
31 **Net acquisition of nonfinancial assets...**	**9,226**	**10,232**	**†8,529**	**10,382**	**11,625**	**9,715**	....	....	....	....	....	....
311 Fixed assets...........................	9,200	10,185	†8,567	10,260	11,509	9,725	....	....	....	....	....	....
3111 Buildings and structures..................	....	8,773	†7,286	....	9,897	8,281	....	....	....	....	....	....
3112 Machinery and equipment..................	....	1,242	†855	....	1,402	1,004	....	....	....	....	....	....
3113 Other fixed assets......................	....	170	†426	....	210	440	....	....	....	....	....	....
312 Inventories.................................	—	—	†—	—	—	—	....	....	....	....	....	....
313 Valuables.................................	—	—	†—	—	—	—	....	....	....	....	....	....
314 Nonproduced assets........................	26	46	†−38	121	116	−10	....	....	....	....	....	....
3141 Land......................................	....	46	†−38	....	116	−10	....	....	....	....	....	....
3142 Subsoil assets...........................	....	—	†—	....			....	....	....	....	....	....
3143 Other naturally occurring assets...........	....	—	†—	....			....	....	....	....	....	....
3144 Intangible nonproduced assets..............	....	—	†—	....			....	....	....	....	....	....
32 **Net acquisition of financial assets........**	....	....	**†23,428**	....	....	**23,711**	....	....	....	....	....	....
321 Domestic...................................	....	....	†6,981	....	....	7,264	....	....	....	....	....	....
3212 Currency and deposits.....................	....	....	†6,957	....	....	6,294	....	....	....	....	....	....
3213 Securities other than shares...............	....	3	†—	....	22	65	....	....	....	....	....	....
3214 Loans....................................	....	....	†24	....	....	904	....	....	....	....	....	....
3215 Shares and other equity..................	....	....	†—	....	....	—	....	....	....	....	....	....
3216 Insurance technical reserves...............	....	....	†—	....	....	—	....	....	....	....	....	....
3217 Financial derivatives......................	....	....	†—	....	....	—	....	....	....	....	....	....
3218 Other accounts receivable.................	....	....	....	....			....	....	....	....	....	....
322 Foreign....................................	....	—	†16,446	....	—	16,446	....	....	....	....	....	....
3222 Currency and deposits.....................	....	—	†—	....	—	—	....	....	....	....	....	....
3223 Securities other than shares...............	....	—	†—	....	—	—	....	....	....	....	....	....
3224 Loans....................................	....	—	†16,446	....	—	16,446	....	....	....	....	....	....
3225 Shares and other equity..................	....	—	†—	....	—	—	....	....	....	....	....	....
3226 Insurance technical reserves...............	....	—	†—	....	—	—	....	....	....	....	....	....
3227 Financial derivatives......................	....	—	†—	....	—	—	....	....	....	....	....	....
3228 Other accounts receivable.................	....	....	†—	....	....	....	....	....	....	....	....	....
323 Monetary gold and SDRs................	—	—	†—	—	—		....	....	....	....	....	....
33 **Net incurrence of liabilities...................**	....	....	**†17,127**	....	....	**16,626**	....	....	....	....	....	....
331 Domestic...................................	....	....	†5,556	....	....	5,055	....	....	....	....	....	....
3312 Currency and deposits.....................	....	....	....	....	....	....	....	....	....	....	....	....
3313 Securities other than shares...............	....	....	....	....	....	....	....	....	....	....	....	....
3314 Loans....................................	....	....	....	....	....	....	....	....	....	....	....	....
3316 Insurance technical reserves...............	....	....	....	....	....	....	....	....	....	....	....	....
3317 Financial derivatives......................	....	....	....	....	....	....	....	....	....	....	....	....
3318 Other accounts payable..................	....	....	....	....	....	....	....	....	....	....	....	....
332 Foreign....................................	....	....	†11,571	....	....	11,571	....	....	....	....	....	....
3322 Currency and deposits.....................	....	....	†—	....	....	—	....	....	....	....	....	....
3323 Securities other than shares...............	....	....	†—	....	....	—	....	....	....	....	....	....
3324 Loans....................................	....	....	†11,571	....	....	11,571	....	....	....	....	....	....
3326 Insurance technical reserves...............	....	....	†—	....	....	—	....	....	....	....	....	....
3327 Financial derivatives......................	....	....	†—	....	....	—	....	....	....	....	....	....
3328 Other accounts payable..................	....	....	....	....	....	—	....	....	....	....	....	....

In Millions of Pesos / Year Ending December 31 / Cash Reporter

	Budgetary Central Government			Central Government			Local Government			General Government		
	2001	2002	2003	2001	2002	2003	2001	2002	2003	2001	2002	2003
Table 4 Holding gains in assets and liabilities												
Table 5 Other changes in the volume of assets and liabilities												
Table 6 Balance sheet												
Table 7 Outlays by functions of govt.												
7 **Total outlays**............	....	63,440	†73,954	....	70,874	77,052	....	....	....	....	....	....
701 **General public services**..............	....	9,231	†18,487	....	9,911	19,173	....	....	....	....	....	....
7017 Public debt transactions.............	....	4,432	†7,872	....	4,608	7,874	....	....	....	....	....	....
7018 General transfers between levels of govt.....	....	....	....	....	....	....	....	....	....	....	....	....
702 **Defense**...............	....	4,264	†3,463	....	4,264	3,463	....	....	....	....	....	....
703 **Public order and safety**............	....	3,167	†3,718	....	3,167	3,718	....	....	....	....	....	....
704 **Economic affairs**............	....	14,216	†12,466	....	16,676	12,564	....	....	....	....	....	....
7042 Agriculture, forestry, fishing, and hunting.....	....	2,928	†4,230	....	5,057	4,164	....	....	....	....	....	....
7043 Fuel and energy.............	....	2,899	†3,211	....	....	3,240	....	....	....	....	....	....
7044 Mining, manufacturing, and construction.....	....	1,122	†24	....	....	89	....	....	....	....	....	....
7045 Transport.............	....	4,514	†3,152	....	....	3,152	....	....	....	....	....	....
7046 Communication.............	....	822	†205	....	....	205	....	....	....	....	....	....
705 **Environmental protection**............	....	471	†571	....	471	571	....	....	....	....	....	....
706 **Housing and community amenities**.......	....	5,744	†4,834	....	5,928	4,851	....	....	....	....	....	....
707 **Health**............	....	7,372	†6,134	....	9,161	7,333	....	....	....	....	....	....
7072 Outpatient services.............	....	....	....	....	....	....	....	....	....	....	....	....
7073 Hospital services.............	....	....	....	....	....	....	....	....	....	....	....	....
7074 Public health services.............	....	....	....	....	....	....	....	....	....	....	....	....
708 **Recreation, culture, and religion**............	....	—	†645	....	—	645	....	....	....	....	....	....
709 **Education**............	....	10,644	†9,590	....	11,889	9,700	....	....	....	....	....	....
7091 Pre-primary and primary education.............	....	....	....	....	....	....	....	....	....	....	....	....
7092 Secondary education.............	....	....	....	....	....	....	....	....	....	....	....	....
7094 Tertiary education.............	....	....	....	....	....	....	....	....	....	....	....	....
710 **Social protection**.............	....	5,547	†14,046	....	6,690	15,034	....	....	....	....	....	....
7 Statistical discrepancy: Total outlays.............	....	2,784	†—	....	2,718	—	....	....	....	....	....	....
Table 8 Transactions in financial assets and liabilities by sector												
82 **Net acquisition of financial assets**.........	....	....	†23,428	....	....	23,711	....	....	....	....	....	....
821 Domestic.............	....	....	†6,981	....	....	7,264	....	....	....	....	....	....
8211 General government.............	....	....	†—	....	....	—	....	....	....	....	....	....
8212 Central bank.............	....	....	†—	....	....	—	....	....	....	....	....	....
8213 Other depository corporations.............	....	....	†6,957	....	....	6,294	....	....	....	....	....	....
8214 Financial corporations n.e.c.............	....	....	†—	....	....	65	....	....	....	....	....	....
8215 Nonfinancial corporations.............	74	49	†24	150	97	904	....	....	....	....	....	....
8216 Households & NPIs serving households......	....	....	†—	....	....	—	....	....	....	....	....	....
822 Foreign.............	....	—	†16,446	....	—	16,446	....	....	....	....	....	....
8221 General government.............	....	....	†—	....	....	—	....	....	....	....	....	....
8227 International organizations.............	....	—	†16,446	....	—	16,446	....	....	....	....	....	....
8228 Financial corporations other than international organizations.............	....	—	†—	....	—	—	....	....	....	....	....	....
8229 Other nonresidents.............	....	—	†—	....	—	—	....	....	....	....	....	....
823 Monetary gold and SDRs.............	—	—	†—	....	—	—	....	....	....	....	....	....
83 **Net incurrence of liabilities**.............	....	....	†17,127	....	....	16,626	....	....	....	....	....	....
831 Domestic.............	....	....	†5,556	....	....	5,055	....	....	....	....	....	....
8311 General government.............	....	....	....	....	....	....	....	....	....	....	....	....
8312 Central bank.............	....	....	....	....	....	....	....	....	....	....	....	....
8313 Other depository corporations.............	....	....	....	....	....	....	....	....	....	....	....	....
8314 Financial corporations n.e.c.............	....	....	....	....	....	....	....	....	....	....	....	....
8315 Nonfinancial corporations.............	....	....	....	....	....	....	....	....	....	....	....	....
8316 Households & NPIs serving households......	....	....	....	....	....	....	....	....	....	....	....	....
832 Foreign.............	....	....	†11,571	....	....	11,571	....	....	....	....	....	....
8321 General government.............	....	....	†—	....	....	—	....	....	....	....	....	....
8327 International organizations.............	....	....	†11,571	....	....	11,571	....	....	....	....	....	....
8328 Financial corporations other than international organizations.............	....	....	†—	....	....	—	....	....	....	....	....	....
8329 Other nonresidents.............	....	....	†—	....	....	—	....	....	....	....	....	....

In Millions of Pesos / Year Ending December 31 / Cash Reporter

		Budgetary Central Government			Central Government			Local Government			General Government		
		2001	2002	2003	2001	2002	2003	2001	2002	2003	2001	2002	2003
26	**Grants**...............	**1,076**	**908**	**†4,533**	**1,078**	**910**	**5**	....	....	....	....	....	....
261	To foreign govenments...............	46	63	†—	47	64	5	....	....	....	....	....	....
262	To international organizations...............	—	—	†—	—	—	—	....	....	....	....	....	....
263	To other general government units............	1,031	846	†4,533	1,031	846	—	....	....	....	....	....	....
2631	Current...............	1,031	846	†3,123	1,031	846	—	....	....	....	....	....	....
2632	Capital...............	—	—	†1,410	—	—	—	....	....	....	....	....	....
27	**Social benefits**...............	**4,655**	**4,367**	**†—**	**5,573**	**5,306**	**590**	....	....	....	....	....	....
28	**Other expense**...............	**5,308**	**7,549**	**†7,758**	**5,471**	**7,574**	**7,798**	....	....	....	....	....	....
281	Property expense other than interest............	—	—	†—	—	—	—	....	....	....	....	....	....
282	Miscellaneous other expense...............	5,308	7,549	†7,758	5,471	7,574	7,798	....	....	....	....	....	....
2821	Current...............	28	....	†—	28	....		....	....	....	....	....	....
2822	Capital...............	5,280	....	†7,758	5,443		7,798	....	....	....	....	....	....

Table 3   Transactions in assets and liabilities

		Budgetary Central Government			Central Government			Local Government			General Government		
3	**Change in net worth from transactns....**	....	....	....	....	....	....	....	....	....	....	....	....
31	**Net acquisition of nonfinancial assets...**	**9,226**	**10,232**	**†8,529**	**10,382**	**11,625**	**9,715**	....	....	....	....	....	....
311	Fixed assets...............	9,200	10,185	†8,567	10,260	11,509	9,725	....	....	....	....	....	....
3111	Buildings and structures...............	....	8,773	†7,286	....	9,897	8,281	....	....	....	....	....	....
3112	Machinery and equipment...............	....	1,242	†855	....	1,402	1,004	....	....	....	....	....	....
3113	Other fixed assets...............	....	170	†426	....	210	440	....	....	....	....	....	....
312	Inventories...............	—	—	†—	—	—	—	....	....	....	....	....	....
313	Valuables...............	—	—	†—	—	—	—	....	....	....	....	....	....
314	Nonproduced assets...............	26	46	†−38	121	116	−10	....	....	....	....	....	....
3141	Land...............	....	46	†−38	....	116	−10	....	....	....	....	....	....
3142	Subsoil assets...............	....	—	†—	....			....	....	....	....	....	....
3143	Other naturally occurring assets...............	....	—	†—	....		—	....	....	....	....	....	....
3144	Intangible nonproduced assets...............	....	—	†—	....		—	....	....	....	....	....	....
32	**Net acquisition of financial assets**............	....	....	**†23,428**	....	....	**23,711**	....	....	....	....	....	....
321	Domestic...............	....	....	†6,981	....	....	7,264	....	....	....	....	....	....
3212	Currency and deposits...............	....	....	†6,957	....	....	6,294	....	....	....	....	....	....
3213	Securities other than shares...............	....	3	†—	....	22	65	....	....	....	....	....	....
3214	Loans...............	....	....	†24	....	....	904	....	....	....	....	....	....
3215	Shares and other equity...............	....	....	†—	....	....	—	....	....	....	....	....	....
3216	Insurance technical reserves...............	....	....	†—	....	....	—	....	....	....	....	....	....
3217	Financial derivatives...............	....	....	†—	....	....	—	....	....	....	....	....	....
3218	Other accounts receivable...............	....	....	....	....	....	—	....	....	....	....	....	....
322	Foreign...............	....	—	†16,446	....	—	16,446	....	....	....	....	....	....
3222	Currency and deposits...............	....	—	†—	....	—	—	....	....	....	....	....	....
3223	Securities other than shares...............	....	—	†—	....	—	—	....	....	....	....	....	....
3224	Loans...............	....	—	†16,446	....	—	16,446	....	....	....	....	....	....
3225	Shares and other equity...............	....	—	†—	....	—	—	....	....	....	....	....	....
3226	Insurance technical reserves...............	....	—	†—	....	—	—	....	....	....	....	....	....
3227	Financial derivatives...............	....	—	†—	....	—	—	....	....	....	....	....	....
3228	Other accounts receivable...............	....	....	....	....	....	....	....	....	....	....	....	....
323	Monetary gold and SDRs...............	—	—	†—	—	—	....	....	....	....	....	....	....
33	**Net incurrence of liabilities**...............	....	....	**†17,127**	....	....	**16,626**	....	....	....	....	....	....
331	Domestic...............	....	....	†5,556	....	....	5,055	....	....	....	....	....	....
3312	Currency and deposits...............	....	....	....	....	....	....	....	....	....	....	....	....
3313	Securities other than shares...............	....	....	....	....	....	....	....	....	....	....	....	....
3314	Loans...............	....	....	....	....	....	....	....	....	....	....	....	....
3316	Insurance technical reserves...............	....	....	....	....	....	....	....	....	....	....	....	....
3317	Financial derivatives...............	....	....	....	....	....	....	....	....	....	....	....	....
3318	Other accounts payable...............	....	....	....	....	....	....	....	....	....	....	....	....
332	Foreign...............	....	....	†11,571	....	....	11,571	....	....	....	....	....	....
3322	Currency and deposits...............	....	....	†—	....	....	—	....	....	....	....	....	....
3323	Securities other than shares...............	....	....	†—	....	....	—	....	....	....	....	....	....
3324	Loans...............	....	....	†11,571	....	....	11,571	....	....	....	....	....	....
3326	Insurance technical reserves...............	....	....	†—	....	....	—	....	....	....	....	....	....
3327	Financial derivatives...............	....	....	†—	....	....	—	....	....	....	....	....	....
3328	Other accounts payable...............	....	....	....	....	....	....	....	....	....	....	....	....

Dominican Republic   243

In Millions of Pesos / Year Ending December 31 / Cash Reporter

	Budgetary Central Government			Central Government			Local Government			General Government		
	2001	2002	2003	2001	2002	2003	2001	2002	2003	2001	2002	2003
Table 4 Holding gains in assets and liabilities												
Table 5 Other changes in the volume of assets and liabilities												
Table 6 Balance sheet												
Table 7 Outlays by functions of govt.												
7 Total outlays	....	63,440	†73,954	....	70,874	77,052	....	....	....	....	....	....
701 General public services	....	9,231	†18,487	....	9,911	19,173	....	....	....	....	....	....
7017 Public debt transactions	....	4,432	†7,872	....	4,608	7,874	....	....	....	....	....	....
7018 General transfers between levels of govt.	....	....	....	....	....	....	....	....	....	....	....	....
702 Defense	....	4,264	†3,463	....	4,264	3,463	....	....	....	....	....	....
703 Public order and safety	....	3,167	†3,718	....	3,167	3,718	....	....	....	....	....	....
704 Economic affairs	....	14,216	†12,466	....	16,676	12,564	....	....	....	....	....	....
7042 Agriculture, forestry, fishing, and hunting	....	2,928	†4,230	....	5,057	4,164						
7043 Fuel and energy	....	2,899	†3,211	....	....	3,240						
7044 Mining, manufacturing, and construction	....	1,122	†24	....	....	89						
7045 Transport	....	4,514	†3,152	....	....	3,152						
7046 Communication	....	822	†205	....	....	205						
705 Environmental protection	....	471	†571	....	471	571	....	....	....	....	....	....
706 Housing and community amenities	....	5,744	†4,834	....	5,928	4,851	....	....	....	....	....	....
707 Health	....	7,372	†6,134	....	9,161	7,333	....	....	....	....	....	....
7072 Outpatient services	....	....	....	....	....	....						
7073 Hospital services	....	....	....	....	....	....						
7074 Public health services	....	....	....	....	....	....						
708 Recreation, culture, and religion	....	—	†645	....	—	645	....	....	....	....	....	....
709 Education	....	10,644	†9,590	....	11,889	9,700	....	....	....	....	....	....
7091 Pre-primary and primary education	....	....	....	....	....	....						
7092 Secondary education	....	....	....	....	....	....						
7094 Tertiary education	....	....	....	....	....	....						
710 Social protection	....	5,547	†14,046	....	6,690	15,034	....	....	....	....	....	....
7 Statistical discrepancy: Total outlays	....	2,784	†—	....	2,718	—						
Table 8 Transactions in financial assets and liabilities by sector												
82 Net acquisition of financial assets	....	....	†23,428	....	....	23,711	....	....	....	....	....	....
821 Domestic	....	....	†6,981	....	....	7,264	....	....	....	....	....	....
8211 General government	....	....	†—	....	....	—	....	....	....	....	....	....
8212 Central bank	....	....	†—	....	....	—	....	....	....	....	....	....
8213 Other depository corporations	....	....	†6,957	....	....	6,294	....	....	....	....	....	....
8214 Financial corporations n.e.c.	....	....	†—	....	....	65	....	....	....	....	....	....
8215 Nonfinancial corporations	74	49	†24	150	97	904	....	....	....	....	....	....
8216 Households & NPIs serving households	....	....	†—	....	....	—	....	....	....	....	....	....
822 Foreign	....	—	†16,446	....	—	16,446	....	....	....	....	....	....
8221 General government	....	—	†—	....	....	—						
8227 International organizations	....	—	†16,446	....	—	16,446	....	....	....	....	....	....
8228 Financial corporations other than international organizations	....	—	†—	....	—	—	....	....	....	....	....	....
8229 Other nonresidents	....	—	†—	....	—	—	....	....	....	....	....	....
823 Monetary gold and SDRs	—	—	†—	—	—	—						
83 Net incurrence of liabilities	....	....	†17,127	....	....	16,626	....	....	....	....	....	....
831 Domestic	....	....	†5,556	....	....	5,055	....	....	....	....	....	....
8311 General government	....	....	....	....	....	....	....	....	....	....	....	....
8312 Central bank	....	....	....	....	....	....	....	....	....	....	....	....
8313 Other depository corporations	....	....	....	....	....	....	....	....	....	....	....	....
8314 Financial corporations n.e.c.	....	....	....	....	....	....	....	....	....	....	....	....
8315 Nonfinancial corporations	....	....	....	....	....	....	....	....	....	....	....	....
8316 Households & NPIs serving households	....	....	....	....	....	....	....	....	....	....	....	....
832 Foreign	....	....	†11,571	....	....	11,571	....	....	....	....	....	....
8321 General government	....	....	†—	....	....	—	....	....	....	....	....	....
8327 International organizations	....	....	†11,571	....	....	11,571	....	....	....	....	....	....
8328 Financial corporations other than international organizations	....	....	†—	....	....	—	....	....	....	....	....	....
8329 Other nonresidents	....	....	†—	....	....	—	....	....	....	....	....	....

In Millions of Pounds / Year Ending June 30 / Cash Reporter

		Budgetary Central Government			Extrabudgetary Accounts			Central Government			General Government		
		2000	2001	2002	2000	2001	2002	2000	2001	2002	2000	2001	2002
Statement of government operations													
Statement of other economic flows													
Balance sheet													
Statement of sources and uses of cash													
1	Cash receipts from operating activities	74,277	74,347	77,773	....	....	....	....	....	....	....	....	....
11	Taxes	49,621	51,358	51,726	....	....	....	....	....	....	....	....	....
12	Social contributions	—	—	—	....	....	....	....	....	....	....	....	....
13	Grants	1,773	1,571	3,713	....	....	....	....	....	....	....	....	....
14	Other receipts	22,883	21,418	22,334	....	....	....	....	....	....	....	....	....
2	Cash payments for operating activities	69,758	80,843	85,472	....	....	....	....	....	....	....	....	....
21	Compensation of employees	22,180	25,217	28,238	....	....	....	....	....	....	....	....	....
22	Purchases of goods and services	8,974	11,367	8,623	....	....	....	....	....	....	....	....	....
24	Interest	18,597	20,907	22,903	....	....	....	....	....	....	....	....	....
25	Subsidies	5,024	5,330	5,949	....	....	....	....	....	....	....	....	....
26	Grants	—	—	—	....	....	....	....	....	....	....	....	....
27	Social benefits	6,467	8,291	9,541	....	....	....	....	....	....	....	....	....
28	Other payments	8,516	9,731	10,218	....	....	....	....	....	....	....	....	....
CIO	*Net cash inflow from oper. activities*	*4,519*	*–6,496*	*–7,699*	....	....	....	....	....	....	....	....	....
31.1	Purchases of nonfinancial assets	16,706	15,076	15,247	....	....	....	....	....	....	....	....	....
31.2	Sales of nonfinancial assets	1,122	1,769	1,175	....	....	....	....	....	....	....	....	....
31	Net cash outflow from investments in nonfinancial assets	15,584	13,307	14,072	....	....	....	....	....	....	....	....	....
CSD	*Cash surplus/deficit*	*–11,065*	*–19,803*	*–21,771*	....	....	....	....	....	....	....	....	....
32x	Net acquisition of fin assets, excl. cash	2,136	179	414	....	....	....	....	....	....	....	....	....
321x	Domestic	2,136	179	414	....	....	....	....	....	....	....	....	....
322x	Foreign	—	—	—	....	....	....	....	....	....	....	....	....
323	Monetary gold and SDRs	—	—	—	....	....	....	....	....	....	....	....	....
33	Net incurrence of liabilities	....	....	....	....	....	....	....	....	....	....	....	....
331	Domestic	....	....	....	....	....	....	....	....	....	....	....	....
332	Foreign	....	....	....	....	....	....	....	....	....	....	....	....
NFB	Net cash inflow from fin. activities	....	....	....	....	....	....	....	....	....	....	....	....
NCB	*Net change in the stock of cash*	....	....	....	....	....	....	....	....	....	....	....	....
Table 1 Revenue													
1	**Revenue**	**74,277**	**74,347**	**77,773**	....	....	....	....	....	....	....	....	....
11	**Taxes**	**49,621**	**51,358**	**51,726**	....	....	....	....	....	....	....	....	....
111	Taxes on income, profits, & capital gains	18,323	19,120	19,320	....	....	....	....	....	....	....	....	....
1111	Individuals	4,285	4,181	4,700	....	....	....	....	....	....	....	....	....
1112	Corporations and other enterprises	14,038	14,939	14,620	....	....	....	....	....	....	....	....	....
112	Taxes on payroll and workforce	1,780	2,113	2,304	....	....	....	....	....	....	....	....	....
113	Taxes on property	1	2	1	....	....	....	....	....	....	....	....	....
114	Taxes on goods and services	20,085	20,793	20,580	....	....	....	....	....	....	....	....	....
1141	General taxes on goods and services	20,085	20,793	20,580	....	....	....	....	....	....	....	....	....
1142	Excises	—	—	—	....	....	....	....	....	....	....	....	....
115	Taxes on int'l. trade and transactions	9,295	9,184	9,323	....	....	....	....	....	....	....	....	....
116	Other taxes	137	146	198	....	....	....	....	....	....	....	....	....
12	**Social contributions**	**—**	**—**	**—**	....	....	....	....	....	....	....	....	....
121	Social security contributions	—	—	—	....	....	....	....	....	....	....	....	....
122	Other social contributions	—	—	—	....	....	....	....	....	....	....	....	....
13	**Grants**	**1,773**	**1,571**	**3,713**	....	....	....	....	....	....	....	....	....
131	From foreign governments	1,773	1,546	3,687	....	....	....	....	....	....	....	....	....
132	From international organizations	—	—	26	....	....	....	....	....	....	....	....	....
133	From other general government units	—	25	—	....	....	....	....	....	....	....	....	....
14	**Other revenue**	**22,883**	**21,418**	**22,334**	....	....	....	....	....	....	....	....	....
Table 2 Expense by economic type													
2	**Expense**	**69,758**	**80,843**	**85,472**	....	....	....	....	....	....	....	....	....
21	**Compensation of employees**	**22,180**	**25,217**	**28,238**	....	....	....	....	....	....	....	....	....
211	Wages and salaries	19,060	21,902	24,398	....	....	....	....	....	....	....	....	....
212	Social contributions	3,120	3,315	3,840	....	....	....	....	....	....	....	....	....
22	**Use of goods and services**	**8,974**	**11,367**	**8,623**	....	....	....	....	....	....	....	....	....
23	**Consumption of fixed capital**	....	....	....	....	....	....	....	....	....	....	....	....
24	**Interest**	**18,597**	**20,907**	**22,903**	....	....	....	....	....	....	....	....	....
25	**Subsidies**	**5,024**	**5,330**	**5,949**	....	....	....	....	....	....	....	....	....

		Budgetary Central Government			Extrabudgetary Accounts			Central Government			General Government		
		2000	2001	2002	2000	2001	2002	2000	2001	2002	2000	2001	2002
26	Grants	—	—	—	....	....	....	....	....	....	....	....	....
261	To foreign govenments	—	—	—	....	....	....	....	....	....	....	....	....
262	To international organizations	—	—	—	....	....	....	....	....	....	....	....	....
263	To other general government units	—	—	—	....	....	....	....	....	....	....	....	....
2631	Current	—	—	—	....	....	....	....	....	....	....	....	....
2632	Capital	—	—	—	....	....	....	....	....	....	....	....	....
27	**Social benefits**	**6,467**	**8,291**	**9,541**	....	....	....	....	....	....	....	....	....
28	**Other expense**	**8,516**	**9,731**	**10,218**	....	....	....	....	....	....	....	....	....
281	Property expense other than interest	—	—	—	....	....	....	....	....	....	....	....	....
282	Miscellaneous other expense	8,516	9,731	10,218	....	....	....	....	....	....	....	....	....
2821	Current	8,516	9,731	10,218	....	....	....	....	....	....	....	....	....
2822	Capital	—	—	—	....	....	....	....	....	....	....	....	....

Table 3 Transactions in assets and liabilities

		Budgetary Central Government			Extrabudgetary Accounts			Central Government			General Government		
3	**Change in net worth from transactns**	....	....	....	....	....	....	....	....	....	....	....	....
31	**Net acquisition of nonfinancial assets**	**15,584**	**13,307**	**14,072**	....	....	....	....	....	....	...	....	....
311	Fixed assets	14,952	9,895	15,267	....	....	....	....	....	....	....	....	....
3111	Buildings and structures	12,717	10,860	8,601	....	....	....	....	....	....	....	....	....
3112	Machinery and equipment	2,235	801	6,666	....	....	....	....	....	....	....	....	....
3113	Other fixed assets	—	−1,766	—	....	....	....	....	....	....	....	....	....
312	Inventories	—	−23	−20	....	....	....	....	....	....	....	....	....
313	Valuables	—	—	—	....	....	....	....	....	....	....	....	....
314	Nonproduced assets	632	3,435	−1,175	....	....	....	....	....	....	....	....	....
3141	Land	1,730	3,435	−10	....	....	....	....	....	....	....	....	....
3142	Subsoil assets	—	—	—	....	....	....	....	....	....	....	....	....
3143	Other naturally occurring assets	—	—	—	....	....	....	....	....	....	....	....	....
3144	Intangible nonproduced assets	−1,098	—	−1,165	....	....	....	....	....	....	....	....	....
32	**Net acquisition of financial assets**	....	....	....	....	....	....	....	....	....	....	....	....
321	Domestic	....	....	....	....	....	....	....	....	....	....	....	....
3212	Currency and deposits	....	....	....	....	....	....	....	....	....	....	....	....
3213	Securities other than shares	....	....	....	....	....	....	....	....	....	....	....	....
3214	Loans	....	....	....	....	....	....	....	....	....	....	....	....
3215	Shares and other equity	....	....	....	....	....	....	....	....	....	....	....	....
3216	Insurance technical reserves	....	....	....	....	....	....	....	....	....	....	....	....
3217	Financial derivatives	....	....	....	....	....	....	....	....	....	....	....	....
3218	Other accounts receivable	....	....	....	....	....	....	....	....	....	....	....	....
322	Foreign	....	....	....	....	....	....	....	....	....	....	....	....
3222	Currency and deposits	....	....	....	....	....	....	....	....	....	....	....	....
3223	Securities other than shares	....	....	....	....	....	....	....	....	....	....	....	....
3224	Loans	....	....	....	....	....	....	....	....	....	....	....	....
3225	Shares and other equity	....	....	....	....	....	....	....	....	....	....	....	....
3226	Insurance technical reserves	....	....	....	....	....	....	....	....	....	....	....	....
3227	Financial derivatives	....	....	....	....	....	....	....	....	....	....	....	....
3228	Other accounts receivable	....	....	....	....	....	....	....	....	....	....	....	....
323	Monetary gold and SDRs	....	....	....	....	....	....	....	....	....	....	....	....
33	**Net incurrence of liabilities**	....	....	....	....	....	....	....	....	....	....	....	....
331	Domestic	....	....	....	....	....	....	....	....	....	....	....	....
3312	Currency and deposits	....	....	....	....	....	....	....	....	....	....	....	....
3313	Securities other than shares	....	....	....	....	....	....	....	....	....	....	....	....
3314	Loans	....	....	....	....	....	....	....	....	....	....	....	....
3316	Insurance technical reserves	....	....	....	....	....	....	....	....	....	....	....	....
3317	Financial derivatives	....	....	....	....	....	....	....	....	....	....	....	....
3318	Other accounts payable	....	....	....	....	....	....	....	....	....	....	....	....
332	Foreign	....	....	....	....	....	....	....	....	....	....	....	....
3322	Currency and deposits	....	....	....	....	....	....	....	....	....	....	....	....
3323	Securities other than shares	....	....	....	....	....	....	....	....	....	....	....	....
3324	Loans	....	....	....	....	....	....	....	....	....	....	....	....
3326	Insurance technical reserves	....	....	....	....	....	....	....	....	....	....	....	....
3327	Financial derivatives	....	....	....	....	....	....	....	....	....	....	....	....
3328	Other accounts payable	....	....	....	....	....	....	....	....	....	....	....	....

In Millions of Pounds / Year Ending June 30 / Cash Reporter

	Budgetary Central Government			Extrabudgetary Accounts			Central Government			General Government		
	2000	2001	2002	2000	2001	2002	2000	2001	2002	2000	2001	2002
Table 4 Holding gains in assets and liabilities												
Table 5 Other changes in the volume of assets and liabilities												
Table 6 Balance sheet												
Table 7 Outlays by functions of govt.												
7 Total outlays................................	86,464	95,919	100,719	....	....	....	....	....	....	....	....	....
701 **General public services...........................**	28,546	32,622	36,014	....	....	....	....	....	....	....	....	....
7017 Public debt transactions....................	18,597	20,907	22,903	....	....	....	....	....	....	....	....	....
7018 General transfers between levels of govt......	9,949	11,715	13,111	....	....	....	....	....	....	....	....	....
702 **Defense................................**	8,516	9,731	10,218	....	....	....	....	....	....	....	....	....
703 **Public order and safety........................**	5,192	5,522	5,759	....	....	....	....	....	....	....	....	....
704 **Economic affairs................................**	9,021	9,626	9,862	....	....	....	....	....	....	....	....	....
7042 Agriculture, forestry, fishing, and hunting.....	5,922	6,486	6,542	....	....	....	....	....	....	....	....	....
7043 Fuel and energy................................	263	233	280	....	....	....	....	....	....	....	....	....
7044 Mining, manufacturing, and construction.....	110	117	155	....	....	....	....	....	....	....	....	....
7045 Transport..	2,726	2,790	2,885	....	....	....	....	....	....	....	....	....
7046 Communication..................................	—	—	—	....	....	....	....	....	....	....	....	....
705 **Environmental protection......................**	—	—	—	....	....	....	....	....	....	....	....	....
706 **Housing and community amenities........**	4,774	4,931	4,068	....	....	....	....	....	....	....	....	....
707 **Health................................**	3,961	4,435	4,915	....	....	....	....	....	....	....	....	....
7072 Outpatient services...........................	3,597	4,069	4,475	....	....	....	....	....	....	....	....	....
7073 Hospital services..............................	327	329	393	....	....	....	....	....	....	....	....	....
7074 Public health services.........................	37	37	47	....	....	....	....	....	....	....	....	....
708 **Recreation, culture, and religion............**	8,638	9,692	9,709	....	....	....	....	....	....	....	....	....
709 **Education................................**	17,180	18,588	19,305	....	....	....	....	....	....	....	....	....
7091 Pre-primary and primary education............	....	....	....	....	....	....	....	....	....	....	....	....
7092 Secondary education.........................	....	....	....	....	....	....	....	....	....	....	....	....
7094 Tertiary education............................	95	115	120	....	....	....	....	....	....	....	....	....
710 **Social protection..............................**	636	772	869	....	....	....	....	....	....	....	....	....
7 Statistical discrepancy: Total outlays..............	—	—	—	....	....	....	....	....	....	....	....	....
Table 8 Transactions in financial assets and liabilities by sector												

El Salvador   253

In Millions of Dollars / Year Ending December 31 / Noncash Reporter

	Budgetary Central Government			Central Government			Local Government			General Government		
	2002	2003	2004	2002	2003	2004	2002	2003	2004	2002	2003	2004
Statement of government operations												
1 Revenue........	1,727.9	1,922.6	1,948.5	2,304.7	2,312.8	2,493.5	116.6	142.4	204.5	2,380.8	2,400.2	2,615.5
2 Expense........	2,194.8	2,148.4	2,379.2	2,561.0	2,297.1	2,692.5	85.6	98.1	124.8	2,606.1	2,340.2	2,734.8
GOB *Gross operating balance......*	−466.9	−225.8	−408.7	−256.3	15.7	−155.4	31.0	44.3	81.3	−225.3	60.0	−74.1
NOB *Net operating balance......*	....	....	−430.7	....	....	−199.0	....	....	79.7	....	....	−119.3
31 Net acquisition of nonfinancial assets..........	226.1	182.0	121.5	420.9	391.6	320.1	34.8	52.5	65.7	455.7	444.1	385.8
NLB *Net lending/borrowing......*	−693.0	−407.8	−552.2	−677.2	−375.9	−519.1	−3.8	−8.2	14.0	−681.0	−384.1	−505.1
32 Net acquisition of financial assets........	220.5	10.1	−433.5	−78.5	−230.6	−455.0	−1.5	−.6	20.8	−80.0	−231.2	−434.2
33 Net incurrence of liabilities..........	1,065.2	232.6	415.1	1,040.3	238.8	397.7	7.0	9.0	10.2	1,047.3	247.8	407.9
NLB Statistical discrepancy.........	−151.7	185.3	−296.4	−441.6	−93.5	−333.6	−4.7	−1.4	−3.4	−446.3	−94.9	−337.0
Statement of other economic flows												
4 *Change in net worth from holding gains......*	....	−283.2	....	....	−175.4	....	....	−30.1	....	....	−205.5	....
41 Nonfinancial assets........	....	−102.4	....	....	−227.8	....	....	−33.5	....	....	−261.3	....
42 Financial assets........	....	−98.2	....	....	85.9	....	....	6.6	....	....	92.5	....
43 Liabilities........	....	82.6	....	....	33.5	....	....	3.2	....	....	36.7	....
5 *Change in net worth from other volume changes......*	....	....	....	−913.8	−360.1	....	....	....	....	....	....	....
51 Nonfinancial assets........	....	....	....	−180.2	−45.8	....	....	....	....	....	....	....
52 Financial assets........	....	....	....	−590.1	−825.3	....	....	....	....	....	....	....
53 Liabilities........	....	....	....	143.5	−511.0	....	....	....	....	....	....	....
Balance sheet												
6 *Net worth........*	....	−4,649.8	−5,119.5	−2,849.5	−3,462.8	−3,735.7	....	328.0	456.9	....	−3,134.8	−3,278.8
61 Nonfinancial assets........	....	1,135.6	1,120.0	1,697.4	1,815.4	1,773.6	....	264.6	364.3	....	2,080.0	2,137.9
62 Financial assets........	....	1,396.5	1,131.4	3,361.5	2,391.5	2,245.3	....	130.9	175.3	....	2,522.4	2,420.6
63 Liabilities........	....	7,181.9	7,370.9	7,908.4	7,669.7	7,754.6	....	67.5	82.7	....	7,737.2	7,837.3
Statement of sources and uses of cash												
1 Cash receipts from operating activities..........	1,942.8	2,255.4	2,133.3	2,559.8	2,819.1	....	120.1	149.2	203.8	2,646.6	2,913.3	....
11 Taxes........	1,619.9	1,744.5	1,857.5	1,619.9	1,744.5	1,857.5	20.3	25.6	31.9	1,640.2	1,770.1	1,889.4
12 Social contributions........	—	—	—	337.2	343.0	356.2	—	—	—	337.2	343.0	356.2
13 Grants........	6.5	66.9	44.8	34.7	136.2	....	40.0	56.7	83.7	41.4	137.9	....
14 Other receipts........	316.4	444.0	231.0	568.0	595.4	689.0	59.8	66.9	88.2	627.8	662.3	777.2
2 Cash payments for operating activities..........	2,384.1	2,680.1	2,657.3	3,001.7	3,145.3	....	94.5	112.8	148.8	3,062.9	3,203.1	....
21 Compensation of employees........	781.7	734.2	744.1	1,100.4	1,097.8	1,116.2	49.2	57.3	73.6	1,149.6	1,155.1	1,189.8
22 Purchases of goods and services........	269.1	241.3	270.4	471.5	447.6	485.7	28.4	31.7	45.7	499.9	479.3	531.4
24 Interest........	219.4	250.5	412.9	240.0	259.9	432.1	2.1	4.6	6.4	242.1	264.5	438.5
25 Subsidies........	—	—	—	—	—	—	—	—	—	—	—	—
26 Grants........	745.8	855.8	934.5	357.4	310.5	....	2.4	3.4	4.0	326.5	258.9	....
27 Social benefits........	—	—	—	322.7	352.8	374.4	—	—	—	322.7	352.8	374.4
28 Other payments........	368.1	598.3	295.4	509.7	676.7	380.4	12.4	15.8	19.1	522.1	692.5	399.5
CIO *Net cash inflow from oper. activities......*	−441.3	−424.7	−524.0	−441.9	−326.2	....	25.6	36.4	55.0	−416.3	−289.8	....
31.1 Purchases of nonfinancial assets........	135.7	103.9	52.3	228.2	201.5	155.6	32.6	45.5	54.9	260.8	247.0	210.5
31.2 Sales of nonfinancial assets........	1.1	.3	—	5.6	.4	3.0	.1	.2	.4	5.7	.6	3.4
31 Net cash outflow from investments in nonfinancial assets........	134.6	103.6	52.3	222.6	201.1	152.6	32.5	45.3	54.5	255.1	246.4	207.1
CSD *Cash surplus/deficit........*	−575.9	−528.3	−576.3	−664.5	−527.3	−576.0	−6.9	−8.9	.5	−671.4	−536.2	−575.5
32x Net acquisition of fin assets, excl. cash........	19.7	−124.6	−438.6	−55.4	−114.3	−445.6	—	−.3	−.1	−55.4	−114.6	−445.7
321x Domestic........	19.7	−124.6	−438.6	−57.1	−113.1	−444.5	—	−.3	−.1	−57.1	−113.4	−444.6
322x Foreign........	—	—	—	1.7	−1.2	−1.1	—	—	—	1.7	−1.2	−1.1
323 Monetary gold and SDRs........	—	—	—	—	—	—	—	—	—	—	—	—
33 Net incurrence of liabilities........	570.9	276.6	149.6	613.4	264.9	146.1	5.5	6.0	7.4	618.9	270.9	153.5
331 Domestic........	−765.5	−8.1	−10.0	−729.3	−12.5	−13.4	5.5	6.0	7.6	−723.8	−6.5	−5.8
332 Foreign........	1,336.4	284.7	159.6	1,342.7	277.4	159.5	—	—	−.2	1,342.7	277.4	159.3
NFB Net cash inflow from fin. activities........	551.2	401.2	588.2	668.8	379.2	591.7	5.5	6.3	7.5	674.3	385.5	599.2
NCB *Net change in the stock of cash........*	−24.7	−190.9	9.1	4.2	−220.5	9.2	−1.5	−2.4	7.9	2.7	−222.9	17.1
Table 1 Revenue												
1 **Revenue........**	**1,727.9**	**1,922.6**	**1,948.5**	**2,304.7**	**2,312.8**	**2,493.5**	**116.6**	**142.4**	**204.5**	**2,380.8**	**2,400.2**	**2,615.5**
11 **Taxes........**	**1,532.3**	**1,679.1**	**1,736.8**	**1,532.3**	**1,679.1**	**1,736.8**	**24.8**	**26.6**	**40.1**	**1,557.1**	**1,705.7**	**1,776.9**
111 Taxes on income, profits, & capital gains......	471.4	498.1	524.9	471.4	498.1	524.9	—	—	—	471.4	498.1	524.9
1111 Individuals........	271.2	236.1	246.8	271.2	236.1	246.8	—	—	—	271.2	236.1	246.8
1112 Corporations and other enterprises........	200.2	262.0	278.1	200.2	262.0	278.1	—	—	—	200.2	262.0	278.1
112 Taxes on payroll and workforce........	—	—	—	—	—	—	—	—	—	—	—	—
113 Taxes on property........	13.0	14.5	15.3	13.0	14.5	15.3	—	26.6	—	13.0	41.1	15.3
114 Taxes on goods and services........	891.3	986.0	1,022.2	891.3	986.0	1,022.2	—	—	—	891.3	986.0	1,022.2
1141 General taxes on goods and services........	824.8	924.7	945.2	824.8	924.7	945.2	—	—	—	824.8	924.7	945.2
1142 Excises........	66.5	61.3	76.8	66.5	61.3	76.8	—	—	—	66.5	61.3	76.8

In Millions of Dollars / Year Ending December 31 / Noncash Reporter

		Budgetary Central Government			Central Government			Local Government			General Government		
		2002	2003	2004	2002	2003	2004	2002	2003	2004	2002	2003	2004
115	Taxes on int'l. trade and transactions..........	154.8	180.1	174.4	154.8	180.1	174.4	—	—	—	154.8	180.1	174.4
116	Other taxes..	1.8	.4	—	1.8	.4	—	24.8	—	40.1	26.6	.4	40.1
12	**Social contributions...............................**	**—**	**—**	**—**	**340.6**	**344.6**	**358.2**	**—**	**—**	**—**	**340.6**	**344.6**	**358.2**
121	Social security contributions......................	—	—	—	340.6	344.6	358.2	—	—	—	340.6	344.6	358.2
122	Other social contributions..........................	—	—	—	—	—	—	—	—	—	—	—	—
13	**Grants...**	**12.7**	**103.0**	**24.4**	**15.5**	**17.9**	**36.0**	**39.7**	**55.4**	**80.9**	**14.7**	**18.3**	**34.4**
131	From foreign governments...........................	4.7	3.1	16.8	9.1	6.0	29.6	.2	.4	.2	9.3	6.4	29.8
132	From international organizations.................	5.0	11.7	4.0	5.3	11.9	4.3	.1	—	.3	5.4	11.9	4.6
133	From other general government units.........	3.0	88.2	3.6	1.1	—	2.1	39.4	55.0	80.4	—	—	—
14	**Other revenue......................................**	**182.9**	**140.5**	**187.3**	**416.3**	**271.2**	**362.5**	**52.1**	**60.4**	**83.5**	**468.4**	**331.6**	**446.0**

Table 2 Expense by economic type

		2002	2003	2004	2002	2003	2004	2002	2003	2004	2002	2003	2004
2	**Expense..**	**2,194.8**	**2,148.4**	**2,379.2**	**2,561.0**	**2,297.1**	**2,692.5**	**85.6**	**98.1**	**124.8**	**2,606.1**	**2,340.2**	**2,734.8**
21	**Compensation of employees.................**	**783.6**	**733.5**	**738.8**	**1,106.6**	**1,102.1**	**1,118.4**	**50.6**	**59.2**	**72.0**	**1,157.2**	**1,161.3**	**1,190.4**
211	Wages and salaries.....................................	700.3	653.1	657.3	989.0	981.4	994.9	45.6	53.3	64.7	1,034.6	1,034.7	1,059.6
212	Social contributions....................................	83.3	80.4	81.5	117.6	120.7	123.5	5.0	5.9	7.3	122.6	126.6	130.8
22	**Use of goods and services....................**	**253.3**	**209.9**	**239.8**	**384.5**	**335.0**	**361.9**	**28.8**	**30.9**	**41.0**	**413.3**	**365.9**	**402.9**
23	**Consumption of fixed capital...............**	....	....	**22.0**	....	....	**43.6**	....	....	**1.6**	....	....	**45.2**
24	**Interest...**	**266.7**	**250.0**	**346.2**	**288.9**	**260.0**	**360.0**	**2.1**	**2.6**	**3.9**	**291.0**	**262.6**	**363.9**
25	**Subsidies..**	**—**	**—**	**—**	**—**	**—**	**—**	**—**	**1.5**	**—**	**—**	**1.5**	**—**
26	**Grants..**	**539.3**	**843.9**	**810.6**	**46.0**	**61.0**	**87.2**	**1.1**	**—**	**2.1**	**6.6**	**6.0**	**6.8**
261	To foreign govenments..............................	—	—	—	—	—	—	—	—	—	—	—	—
262	To international organizations.....................	6.5	5.8	6.4	6.6	6.0	6.8	—	—	—	6.6	6.0	6.8
263	To other general government units.............	532.8	838.1	804.2	39.4	55.0	80.4	1.1	—	2.1	—	—	—
2631	Current..	426.0	630.0	639.1	6.6	10.1	14.8	1.0	—	1.8	—	—	—
2632	Capital...	106.8	208.1	165.1	32.8	44.9	65.6	.1	—	.3	—	—	—
27	**Social benefits......................................**	**—**	**—**	**—**	**34.6**	**34.8**	**39.3**	**—**	**—**	**—**	**34.6**	**34.8**	**39.3**
28	**Other expense......................................**	**351.9**	**111.1**	**221.8**	**700.4**	**504.2**	**682.1**	**3.0**	**3.9**	**4.2**	**703.4**	**508.1**	**686.3**
281	Property expense other than interest...........	—	—	—	—	—	—	—	—	—	—	—	—
282	Miscellaneous other expense......................	351.9	111.1	221.8	700.4	504.2	682.1	3.0	3.9	4.2	703.4	508.1	686.3
2821	Current..	157.8	82.1	....	501.8	470.6	....	1.6	3.7	4.1	503.4	474.3	....
2822	Capital...	194.1	29.0	....	198.6	33.6	....	1.4	.2	.1	200.0	33.8	....

Table 3 Transactions in assets and liabilities

		2002	2003	2004	2002	2003	2004	2002	2003	2004	2002	2003	2004
3	**Change in net worth from transactns....**	....	....	**−727.1**	....	....	**−532.6**	....	....	**76.3**	....	....	**−456.3**
31	**Net acquisition of nonfinancial assets...**	**226.1**	**182.0**	**121.5**	**420.9**	**391.6**	**320.1**	**34.8**	**52.5**	**65.7**	**455.7**	**444.1**	**385.8**
311	Fixed assets...	199.4	164.2	99.1	298.8	276.1	194.5	33.0	50.9	63.1	331.8	327.0	257.6
3111	Buildings and structures............................	147.1	98.4	89.8	230.5	187.9	178.6	29.0	42.3	59.2	259.5	230.2	237.8
3112	Machinery and equipment..........................	48.5	24.1	8.3	60.2	36.0	14.0	3.6	3.4	3.8	63.8	39.4	17.8
3113	Other fixed assets......................................	3.8	41.7	1.0	8.1	52.2	1.9	.4	5.2	.1	8.5	57.4	2.0
312	Inventories...	14.2	12.9	18.9	107.4	106.3	123.1	1.4	1.1	1.3	108.8	107.4	124.4
313	Valuables..	.3	—	—	.5	—	.1	—	—	—	.5	—	.1
314	Nonproduced assets....................................	12.2	4.9	3.5	14.2	9.2	2.4	.4	.5	1.3	14.6	9.7	3.7
3141	Land...	11.0	2.7	3.5	11.6	3.6	2.4	.4	.4	1.3	12.0	4.0	3.7
3142	Subsoil assets..	—	—	—	—	—	—	—	—	—	—	—	—
3143	Other naturally occurring assets.................	—	—	—	—	—	—	—	—	—	—	—	—
3144	Intangible nonproduced assets...................	1.2	2.2	—	2.6	5.6	—	—	.1	—	2.6	5.7	—
32	**Net acquisition of financial assets........**	**220.5**	**10.1**	**−433.5**	**−78.5**	**−230.6**	**−455.0**	**−1.5**	**−.6**	**20.8**	**−80.0**	**−231.2**	**−434.2**
321	Domestic...	220.5	10.1	−433.5	−80.2	−229.4	−453.9	−1.5	−.6	20.8	−81.7	−230.0	−433.1
3212	Currency and deposits................................	−24.7	−190.9	9.1	4.2	−220.5	9.2	−1.5	−2.4	7.9	2.7	−222.9	17.1
3213	Securities other than shares.......................	−2.5	—	—	−157.6	−2.3	2.9	—	−.3	−.1	−157.6	−2.6	2.8
3214	Loans...	4.2	−36.5	−31.1	26.6	−43.9	−47.2	—	—	—	26.6	−43.9	−47.2
3215	Shares and other equity..............................	—	—	−296.1	−.1	—	−296.1	—	—	—	−.1	—	−296.1
3216	Insurance technical reserves.......................	—	—	—	—	—	—	—	—	—	—	—	—
3217	Financial derivatives..................................	—	—	—	—	—	—	—	—	—	—	—	—
3218	Other accounts receivable...........................	243.5	237.5	−115.4	46.7	37.3	−122.7	—	2.1	13.0	46.7	39.4	−109.7
322	Foreign...	—	—	—	1.7	−1.2	−1.1	—	—	—	1.7	−1.2	−1.1
3222	Currency and deposits................................	—	—	—	—	—	—	—	—	—	—	—	—
3223	Securities other than shares.......................	—	—	—	1.7	−1.2	−1.1	—	—	—	1.7	−1.2	−1.1
3224	Loans...	—	—	—	—	—	—	—	—	—	—	—	—
3225	Shares and other equity..............................	—	—	—	—	—	—	—	—	—	—	—	—
3226	Insurance technical reserves.......................	—	—	—	—	—	—	—	—	—	—	—	—
3227	Financial derivatives..................................	—	—	—	—	—	—	—	—	—	—	—	—
3228	Other accounts receivable...........................	—	—	—	—	—	—	—	—	—	—	—	—
323	Monetary gold and SDRs............................	—	—	—	—	—	—	—	—	—	—	—	—

In Millions of Dollars / Year Ending December 31 / Noncash Reporter

		Budgetary Central Government			Central Government			Local Government			General Government		
		2002	2003	2004	2002	2003	2004	2002	2003	2004	2002	2003	2004
33	Net incurrence of liabilities	1,065.2	232.6	415.1	1,040.3	238.8	397.7	7.0	9.0	10.2	1,047.3	247.8	407.9
331	Domestic	−271.3	−114.8	326.0	−302.5	−101.3	308.7	7.0	9.0	10.4	−295.5	−92.3	319.1
3312	Currency and deposits	13.0	−17.1	−56.7	−19.5	−9.0	−58.1	2.3	.4	2.2	−17.2	−8.6	−55.9
3313	Securities other than shares	−683.8	−2.2	82.3	−642.5	−9.7	78.2	—	—	—	−642.5	−9.7	78.2
3314	Loans	−5.1	−5.9	−7.1	−9.5	−1.5	−10.7	5.8	7.5	7.6	−3.7	6.0	−3.1
3316	Insurance technical reserves	—	—	—	—	—	—	—	—	—	—	—	—
3317	Financial derivatives	—	—	—	—	—	—	—	—	—	—	—	—
3318	Other accounts payable	404.6	−89.6	307.5	369.0	−81.1	299.3	−1.1	1.1	.6	367.9	−80.0	299.9
332	Foreign	1,336.5	347.4	89.1	1,342.8	340.1	89.0	—	—	−.2	1,342.8	340.1	88.8
3322	Currency and deposits	—	—	—	—	—	—	—	—	—	—	—	—
3323	Securities other than shares	1,251.5	348.5	196.8	1,251.5	348.5	196.8	—	—	—	1,251.5	348.5	196.8
3324	Loans	85.0	−1.1	−107.7	91.3	−8.4	−107.8	—	—	−.2	91.3	−8.4	−108.0
3326	Insurance technical reserves	—	—	—	—	—	—	—	—	—	—	—	—
3327	Financial derivatives	—	—	—	—	—	—	—	—	—	—	—	—
3328	Other accounts payable	—	—	—	—	—	—	—	—	—	—	—	—

Table 4 Holding gains in assets and liabilities

Table 5 Other changes in the volume of assets and liabilities

Table 6 Balance sheet

		Budgetary Central Government			Central Government			Local Government			General Government		
6	Net worth	....	−4,649.8	−5,119.5	−2,849.5	−3,462.8	−3,735.7	....	328.0	456.9	....	−3,134.8	−3,278.8
61	Nonfinancial assets	....	1,135.6	1,120.0	1,697.4	1,815.4	1,773.6	....	264.6	364.3	....	2,080.0	2,137.9
611	Fixed assets	....	850.1	886.9	1,162.0	1,207.2	1,250.2	....	101.7	124.7	....	1,308.9	1,374.9
6111	Buildings and structures	....	185.5	690.6	583.2	376.0	934.2	....	72.8	96.7	....	448.8	1,030.9
6112	Machinery and equipment	....	274.7	192.8	330.3	384.5	309.7	....	31.9	27.8	....	416.4	337.5
6113	Other fixed assets	....	389.9	3.5	248.5	446.7	6.3	....	−3.0	.2	....	443.7	6.5
612	Inventories	....	16.4	16.2	207.6	159.5	104.4	....	1.6	1.6	....	161.1	106.0
613	Valuables	....	4.5	.5	4.6	4.7	.6	....	.1	.1	....	4.8	.7
614	Nonproduced assets	....	264.6	216.4	323.2	444.0	418.4	....	161.2	237.9	....	605.2	656.3
6141	Land	....	239.8	216.4	319.1	412.3	418.4	....	161.0	237.9	....	573.3	656.3
6142	Subsoil assets	....	—	—	—	—	—	....	—	—	....	—	—
6143	Other naturally occurring assets	....	—	—	—	—	—	....	—	—	....	—	—
6144	Intangible nonproduced assets	....	24.8	—	4.1	31.7	—	....	.2	—	....	31.9	—
62	Financial assets	....	1,396.5	1,131.4	3,361.5	2,391.5	2,245.3	....	130.9	175.3	....	2,522.4	2,420.6
621	Domestic	....	1,392.9	1,127.6	3,324.3	2,359.0	2,212.6	....	130.9	175.3	....	2,489.9	2,387.9
6212	Currency and deposits	....	584.7	593.8	1,199.7	955.9	963.5	....	24.8	36.2	....	980.7	999.7
6213	Securities other than shares	....	33.7	47.4	365.0	349.5	369.8	....	1.1	2.0	....	350.6	371.8
6214	Loans	....	364.2	337.5	1,258.1	373.7	130.1	....	.6	.1	....	374.3	130.2
6215	Shares and other equity	....	192.1	5.0	17.8	192.1	5.0	....	—	—	....	192.1	5.0
6216	Insurance technical reserves	....	.1	.2	—	5.6	2.4	....	.2	.1	....	5.8	2.5
6217	Financial derivatives	....	—	—	—	—	—	....	—	—	....	—	—
6218	Other accounts receivable	....	218.1	143.7	483.7	482.2	741.8	....	104.2	136.9	....	586.4	878.7
622	Foreign	....	3.6	3.8	37.2	32.5	32.7	....	—	—	....	32.5	32.7
6222	Currency and deposits	....	—	—	—	—	—	....	—	—	....	—	—
6223	Securities other than shares	....	—	—	37.2	28.9	28.9	....	—	—	....	28.9	28.9
6224	Loans	....	—	—	—	—	—	....	—	—	....	—	—
6225	Shares and other equity	....	3.6	3.8	—	3.6	3.8	....	—	—	....	3.6	3.8
6226	Insurance technical reserves	....	—	—	—	—	—	....	—	—	....	—	—
6227	Financial derivatives	....	—	—	—	—	—	....	—	—	....	—	—
6228	Other accounts receivable	....	—	—	—	—	—	....	—	—	....	—	—
623	Monetary gold and SDRs	....	—	—	—	—	—	....	—	—	....	—	—
63	Liabilities	....	7,181.9	7,370.9	7,908.4	7,669.7	7,754.6	....	67.5	82.7	....	7,737.2	7,837.3
631	Domestic	....	2,173.3	2,122.9	3,379.0	2,656.1	2,635.9	....	60.1	75.4	....	2,716.2	2,711.3
6312	Currency and deposits	....	636.5	586.0	730.8	702.9	626.4	....	5.8	6.9	....	708.7	633.3
6313	Securities other than shares	....	—	932.7	1,125.9	—	990.8	....	—	—	....	—	990.8
6314	Loans	....	846.6	33.1	40.1	959.4	−163.9	....	37.7	51.8	....	997.1	−112.1
6316	Insurance technical reserves	....	—	—	—	4.5	—	....	—	—	....	4.5	—
6317	Financial derivatives	....	—	—	—	—	—	....	—	—	....	—	—
6318	Other accounts payable	....	690.2	571.1	1,482.2	989.3	1,182.6	....	16.6	16.7	....	1,005.9	1,199.3
632	Foreign	....	5,008.6	5,248.0	4,529.4	5,013.6	5,118.7	....	7.4	7.3	....	5,021.0	5,126.0
6322	Currency and deposits	....	—	—	—	—	—	....	—	—	....	—	—
6323	Securities other than shares	....	—	2,440.0	1,805.0	—	2,440.0	....	—	—	....	—	2,440.0
6324	Loans	....	5,008.6	2,808.0	2,724.4	5,013.6	2,678.7	....	7.4	7.3	....	5,021.0	2,686.0
6326	Insurance technical reserves	....	—	—	—	—	—	....	—	—	....	—	—
6327	Financial derivatives	....	—	—	—	—	—	....	—	—	....	—	—
6328	Other accounts payable	....	—	—	—	—	—	....	—	—	....	—	—

In Millions of Dollars / Year Ending December 31 / Noncash Reporter

	Budgetary Central Government			Central Government			Local Government			General Government		
	2002	2003	2004	2002	2003	2004	2002	2003	2004	2002	2003	2004
Memorandum items:												
6M2 Net financial worth..............................	....	−5,785.4	−6,239.5	−4,546.9	−5,278.2	−5,509.3	....	63.4	92.6	....	−5,214.8	−5,416.7
6M3 Debt at market value.............................	....	....	....	....	....	....	....	....	....	....	....	....
6M4 Debt at nominal value...........................	....	....	....	....	....	....	....	....	....	....	....	....
6M5 Arrears..	....	....	....	....	....	....	....	....	....	....	....	....
6M6 Obligations for social security benefits...........	....	....	....	....	....	....	....	....	....	....	....	....
6M7 Contingent liabilities.............................	....	....	....	....	....	....	....	....	....	....	....	....
6M8 Uncapitalized military weapons, systems........	....	....	....	....	....	....	....	....	....	....	....	....
Table 7 Outlays by functions of govt.												
7 **Total outlays**..................................	**2,420.9**	**2,330.4**	**2,500.7**	**2,981.9**	**2,688.7**	**3,012.6**	**120.4**	**150.6**	**190.5**	**3,061.8**	**2,784.3**	**3,120.6**
701 **General public services**..........................	**760.6**	**538.6**	**673.2**	**877.8**	**471.9**	....	**73.0**	**58.0**	**71.0**	**930.6**	**529.9**	....
7017 Public debt transactions...........................	266.7	250.0	346.2	288.9	260.0	360.0	2.1	2.6	3.9	291.0	262.6	363.9
7018 General transfers between levels of govt......	33.7	159.9	123.8	21.2	55.0	....	—	—	....	21.2	—	....
702 **Defense**..	**140.5**	**106.6**	**106.6**	**124.9**	**91.1**	....	—	—	—	**124.9**	**91.1**	....
703 **Public order and safety**..........................	**484.1**	**325.7**	**349.5**	**325.8**	**306.6**	....	—	**1.4**	**1.3**	**325.8**	**308.0**	....
704 **Economic affairs**.................................	**180.9**	**242.9**	**281.5**	**229.3**	**273.7**	....	—	—	—	**229.3**	**273.7**	....
7042 Agriculture, forestry, fishing, and hunting.....	46.3	24.4	40.6	45.8	23.5	....	—	—	—	45.8	23.5	....
7043 Fuel and energy...................................	.6	.9	26.7	.5	4.7	....	—	—	—	.5	4.7	....
7044 Mining, manufacturing, and construction.....	....	....	....	19.7	....	....	—	—	—	19.7	—	....
7045 Transport...	4.0	161.2	135.0	55.9	156.7	....	—	—	—	55.9	156.7	....
7046 Communication....................................	10.2	....	....	34.9	....	....	—	—	—	34.9	....	....
705 **Environmental protection**......................	**5.5**	**5.7**	**5.5**	**5.2**	**5.4**	....	—	—	—	**5.2**	**5.4**	....
706 **Housing and community amenities**........	—	**118.9**	**42.0**	**55.3**	**213.2**	....	—	**84.7**	**118.1**	**55.3**	**297.9**	....
707 **Health**...	**218.5**	**224.4**	**233.5**	**402.6**	**358.1**	....	—	—	—	**402.6**	**358.1**	....
7072 Outpatient services................................	....	....	....	174.9	7.8	....	—	—	—	174.9	7.8	....
7073 Hospital services..................................	133.6	202.3	208.3	125.5	267.2	....	—	—	—	125.5	267.2	....
7074 Public health services............................	65.3	....	....	61.2	....	....	—	—	—	61.2	....	....
708 **Recreation, culture, and religion**..........	**55.4**	**31.6**	**22.8**	**67.6**	**31.7**	....	**47.4**	—	—	**101.9**	**31.7**	....
709 **Education**...	**459.2**	**424.1**	**449.7**	**449.8**	**404.5**	....	—	—	—	**449.8**	**404.5**	....
7091 Pre-primary and primary education.............	286.5	32.6	35.7	267.8	31.2	....	—	—	—	267.8	31.2	....
7092 Secondary education.............................	26.5	254.6	285.9	24.2	239.2	....	—	—	—	24.2	239.2	....
7094 Tertiary education.................................	—	28.4	29.4	20.9	26.2	....	—	—	—	20.9	26.2	....
710 **Social protection**................................	**116.2**	**259.8**	**336.4**	**341.6**	**381.0**	....	—	—	—	**341.6**	**381.0**	....
7 Statistical discrepancy: Total outlays............	—	52.1	—	102.0	151.5	....	—	6.5	—	94.8	103.0	....
Table 8 Transactions in financial assets and liabilities by sector												
82 **Net acquisition of financial assets**........	**220.5**	**10.1**	**−433.5**	**−78.5**	**−230.6**	**−455.0**	**−1.5**	**−.6**	**20.8**	**−80.0**	**−231.2**	**−434.2**
821 Domestic...	220.5	10.1	−433.5	−80.2	−229.4	−453.9	−1.5	−.6	20.8	−81.7	−230.0	−433.1
8211 General government.............................	−41.5	16.8	−.5	−102.3	3.5	−19.7	−1.5	.6	.4	−103.8	4.1	−19.3
8212 Central bank......................................	30.2	−188.0	64.1	29.3	−192.1	64.5	—	—	—	29.3	−192.1	64.5
8213 Other depository corporations..................	48.9	43.8	−83.7	−180.1	28.6	−75.2	—	−1.9	7.6	−180.1	26.7	−67.6
8214 Financial corporations n.e.c....................	−82.9	−37.7	—	−82.9	−247.1	.1	—	—	—	−82.9	−247.1	.1
8215 Nonfinancial corporations......................	32.1	−27.3	−295.1	29.2	−9.2	−294.2	—	1.0	2.0	29.2	−8.2	−292.2
8216 Households & NPIs serving households......	233.7	202.5	−118.3	226.6	186.9	−129.4	—	−.3	10.8	226.6	186.6	−118.6
822 Foreign..	—	—	—	1.7	−1.2	−1.1	—	—	—	1.7	−1.2	−1.1
8221 General government.............................	—	—	—	1.7	—	—	—	—	—	1.7	—	—
8227 International organizations.....................	—	—	—	—	—	—	—	—	—	—	—	—
8228 Financial corporations other than international organizations..................	—	—	—	—	−1.2	—	—	—	—	—	−1.2	—
8229 Other nonresidents..............................	—	—	—	—	—	−1.1	—	—	—	—	—	−1.1
823 Monetary gold and SDRs........................	—	—	—	—	—	—	—	—	—	—	—	—
83 **Net incurrence of liabilities**.................	**1,065.2**	**232.6**	**415.1**	**1,040.3**	**238.8**	**397.7**	**7.0**	**9.0**	**10.2**	**1,047.3**	**247.8**	**407.9**
831 Domestic...	−271.3	−114.8	326.0	−302.5	−101.3	308.7	7.0	9.0	10.4	−295.5	−92.3	319.1
8311 General government.............................	−11.9	4.2	−10.6	−28.0	12.3	−20.5	7.0	.4	−1.6	−21.0	12.7	−22.1
8312 Central bank......................................	—	—	—	—	—	—	—	—	—	—	—	—
8313 Other depository corporations..................	−629.2	−5.2	—	−589.3	−12.7	−8.5	—	—	.1	−589.3	−12.7	−8.4
8314 Financial corporations n.e.c....................	—	.6	65.1	—	1.9	64.9	—	7.1	9.2	—	9.0	74.1
8315 Nonfinancial corporations......................	6.9	−496.5	106.0	5.8	−505.4	138.6	—	−.6	8.7	5.8	−506.0	147.3
8316 Households & NPIs serving households......	362.9	382.1	165.5	309.0	402.6	134.2	—	2.1	−6.0	309.0	404.7	128.2
832 Foreign..	1,336.5	347.4	89.1	1,342.8	340.1	89.0	—	—	−.2	1,342.8	340.1	88.8
8321 General government.............................	—	—	−27.2	—	—	−27.2	—	—	—	—	—	−27.2
8327 International organizations.....................	60.0	7.3	−71.8	62.5	7.3	−71.8	—	—	—	62.5	7.3	−71.8
8328 Financial corporations other than international organizations.............	1,276.5	340.1	−12.9	1,280.3	332.8	−13.0	—	—	−.2	1,280.3	332.8	−13.2
8329 Other nonresidents..............................	—	—	201.0	—	—	201.0	—	—	—	—	—	201.0

In Millions of Krooni / Year Ending December 31 / Cash Reporter

	Budgetary Central Government			Central Government			Local Government			General Government		
	1999	2000	2001	1999	2000	2001	1999	2000	2001	1999	2000	2001
Statement of government operations												
Statement of other economic flows												
Balance sheet												
6 *Net worth*............	....	....	....	....	....	....	....	....	....	....	....	....
61 Nonfinancial assets............	....	....	....	....	....	....	....	....	....	....	....	....
62 Financial assets............	....	....	....	....	....	....				....	....	....
63 Liabilities............	3,514	2,716	2,591	3,514	2,716	2,591	1,709	1,579	2,015	....	....	....
Statement of sources and uses of cash												
1 Cash receipts from operating activities...........	15,557	17,481	19,357	23,494	26,531	29,896	6,446	6,400	8,560	....	....	....
11 Taxes............	13,706	14,886	16,128	13,706	14,886	16,128	4,037	4,116	4,415	....	....	....
12 Social contributions............	—	—	—	7,784	8,983	10,471	—	—	—	....	....	....
13 Grants............	303	259	624	303	259	624	1,846	1,713	3,368	....	....	....
14 Other receipts............	1,548	2,336	2,605	1,702	2,404	2,673	563	572	777	....	....	....
2 Cash payments for operating activities............	14,464	15,043	16,363	25,232	25,978	27,857	5,435	5,697	7,847	....	....	....
21 Compensation of employees............	3,392	3,571	2,720	3,428	3,605	2,766	2,190	2,290	3,772			
22 Purchases of goods and services............	4,848	5,315	5,509	8,497	8,613	8,829	2,051	2,149	2,538			
24 Interest............	189	166	164	189	167	167	149	170	138			
25 Subsidies............	690	682	805	690	682	805	....	....	....			
26 Grants............	1,882	1,743	3,402	1,932	1,743	3,453	....	....	....			
27 Social benefits............	3,301	3,555	3,707	10,333	11,156	11,782	....	....	....			
28 Other payments............	163	13	55	163	13	55	1,011	704	714	....	....	....
CIO *Net cash inflow from oper. activities*.....	−715	696	1,167	−1,738	554	2,039	1,544	1,236	1,810			
31.1 Purchases of nonfinancial assets............	1,563	1,395	1,380	1,584	1,395	1,380	151	267	503			
31.2 Sales of nonfinancial assets............	206	202	331	206	202	331						
31 Net cash outflow from investments in nonfinancial assets............	1,358	1,194	1,049	1,378	1,194	1,049	1,392	969	1,306	....	....	....
CSD *Cash surplus/deficit*............	−2,073	−498	118	−3,116	−640	990	−381	−265	−593	....	....	....
32x Net acquisition of fin assets, excl. cash............	−2,986	−847	−1,502	−2,995	−778	−1,502	−37	−266	−728	....	....	....
321x Domestic............	−2,986	−847	−1,502	−2,995	−778	−1,502	−37	−266	−728	....	....	....
322x Foreign............	—	—	—	—	—	—	—	—	—	....	....	....
323 Monetary gold and SDRs............	—	—	—	—	—	—	—	—	—	....	....	....
33 Net incurrence of liabilities............	−40	−648	−180	−40	−648	−180	325	−360	213	....	....	....
331 Domestic............	−122	−129	−30	−122	−129	−30	325	−559	214	....	....	....
332 Foreign............	82	−520	−150	82	−520	−150	—	199	−1	....	....	....
NFB Net cash inflow from fin. activities............	2,946	199	1,322	2,955	129	1,322	361	−94	941	....	....	....
NCB *Net change in the stock of cash*............	873	−299	1,441	−161	−511	2,312	−20	−359	349	....	....	....
Table 1 Revenue												
1 **Revenue**............	15,557	17,481	19,357	23,494	26,531	29,896	6,446	6,400	8,560	....	....	....
11 **Taxes**............	13,706	14,886	16,128	13,706	14,886	16,128	4,037	4,116	4,415	....	....	....
111 Taxes on income, profits, & capital gains......	4,506	3,778	3,905	4,506	3,778	3,905	3,661	3,671	3,942	....	....	....
1111 Individuals............	2,871	2,923	3,157	2,871	2,923	3,157	3,661	3,671	3,942	....	....	....
1112 Corporations and other enterprises............	1,635	855	748	1,635	855	748	—	—	—	....	....	....
112 Taxes on payroll and workforce............	—	—	—	—	—	—	—	—	—	....	....	....
113 Taxes on property............	—	—	—	—	—	—	347	411	435	....	....	....
114 Taxes on goods and services............	9,200	11,073	12,183	9,200	11,073	12,183	29	33	38	....	....	....
1141 General taxes on goods and services............	6,417	8,153	8,639	6,417	8,153	8,639	....	....	....	....	....	....
1142 Excises............	2,687	2,819	3,434	2,687	2,819	3,434	....	....	....	....	....	....
115 Taxes on int'l. trade and transactions............	—	35	40	—	35	40	—	—	—	....	....	....
116 Other taxes............	—	—	—	—	—	—	—	—	—	....	....	....
12 **Social contributions**............	—	—	—	7,784	8,983	10,471	—	—	—	....	....	....
121 Social security contributions............	—	—	—	7,784	8,983	10,471	—	—	—	....	....	....
122 Other social contributions............	—	—	—	—	—	—	—	—	—	....	....	....
13 **Grants**............	303	259	624	303	259	624	1,846	1,713	3,368	....	....	....
131 From foreign governments............	303	259	624	303	259	624	1	9	6	....	....	....
132 From international organizations............	—	—	—	—	—	—	—	—	—	....	....	....
133 From other general government units............	—	—	—	—	—	—	1,844	1,704	3,363	....	....	....
14 **Other revenue**............	1,548	2,336	2,605	1,702	2,404	2,673	563	572	777	....	....	....
Table 2 Expense by economic type												
2 **Expense**............	14,464	15,043	16,363	25,232	25,978	27,857	5,435	5,697	7,847	....	....	....
21 **Compensation of employees**............	3,392	3,571	2,720	3,428	3,605	2,766	2,190	2,290	3,772	....	....	....
211 Wages and salaries............	3,392	3,571	2,720	3,428	3,605	2,766	2,190	2,290	3,772	....	....	....
212 Social contributions............	—	—	—	—	—	—	—	—	—	....	....	....
22 **Use of goods and services**............	4,848	5,315	5,509	8,497	8,613	8,829	2,051	2,149	2,538	....	....	....
23 **Consumption of fixed capital**............	....	....	....	....	....	....	....	....	....	....	....	....
24 Interest............	189	166	164	189	167	167	149	170	138	....	....	....
25 Subsidies............	690	682	805	690	682	805	....	....	....	....	....	....

In Millions of Krooni / Year Ending December 31 / Cash Reporter

		Budgetary Central Government			Central Government			Local Government			General Government		
		1999	2000	2001	1999	2000	2001	1999	2000	2001	1999	2000	2001
26	**Grants**.....................	**1,882**	**1,743**	**3,402**	**1,932**	**1,743**	**3,453**	....	....	....	....	....	....
261	To foreign governments.................	32	39	40	32	39	40	....	....	....	....	....	....
262	To international organizations..............	—	—	—	—	—	—	....	....	....	....	....	....
263	To other general government units..........	1,850	1,704	3,362	1,901	1,704	3,413	....	....	....	....	....	....
2631	Current.........................	1,380	1,470	3,171	1,431	1,470	3,222	....	....	....	....	....	....
2632	Capital........................	470	234	191	470	234	191	....	....	....	....	....	....
27	**Social benefits**...............	**3,301**	**3,555**	**3,707**	**10,333**	**11,156**	**11,782**	....	....	....	....	....	....
28	**Other expense**................	**163**	**13**	**55**	**163**	**13**	**55**	....	....	....	....	....	....
281	Property expense other than interest.........	—	—	—	—	—	—	....	....	....	....	....	....
282	Miscellaneous other expense.............	163	13	55	163	13	55	....	....	....	....	....	....
2821	Current.........................	—	—	—	—	—	—	....	....	....	....	....	....
2822	Capital........................	163	13	55	163	13	55	....	....	....	....	....	....

Table 3 Transactions in assets and liabilities

		Budgetary Central Government			Central Government			Local Government			General Government		
		1999	2000	2001	1999	2000	2001	1999	2000	2001	1999	2000	2001
3	**Change in net worth from transactns....**	....	....	....	....	....	....	....	....	....	....	....	....
31	**Net acquisition of nonfinancial assets...**	**1,358**	**1,194**	**1,049**	**1,378**	**1,194**	**1,049**	**1,392**	**969**	**1,306**	....	....	....
311	Fixed assets......................	1,500	1,343	1,218	1,520	1,343	1,218	....	....	....	....	....	....
3111	Buildings and structures.............	....	....	....	....	....	....	....	....	....	....	....	....
3112	Machinery and equipment...........	....	....	....	....	....	....	....	....	....	....	....	....
3113	Other fixed assets.................	....	....	....	....	....	....	....	....	....	....	....	....
312	Inventories......................	−1	—	—	−1	—	—	....	....	....	....	....	....
313	Valuables.......................	—	—	—	—	—	—	....	....	....	....	....	....
314	Nonproduced assets................	−141	−149	−169	−141	−149	−169	....	....	....	....	....	....
3141	Land..........................	....	....	....	....	....	....	....	....	....	....	....	....
3142	Subsoil assets...................	....	....	....	....	....	....	....	....	....	....	....	....
3143	Other naturally occurring assets.......	....	....	....	....	....	....	....	....	....	....	....	....
3144	Intangible nonproduced assets.........	....	....	....	....	....	....	....	....	....	....	....	....
32	**Net acquisition of financial assets........**	**−2,113**	**−1,146**	**−62**	**−3,156**	**−1,289**	**810**	**−57**	**−625**	**−379**	....	....	....
321	Domestic.......................	−2,544	−677	−226	−3,586	−819	646	−57	−625	−379	....	....	....
3212	Currency and deposits..............	442	171	1,276	−592	−41	2,148	−20	−359	349	....	....	....
3213	Securities other than shares..........	....	....	....	....	....	....	....	....	....	....	....	....
3214	Loans.........................	....	....	....	....	....	....	....	....	....	....	....	....
3215	Shares and other equity.............	....	....	....	....	....	....	....	....	....	....	....	....
3216	Insurance technical reserves..........	....	....	....	....	....	....	....	....	....	....	....	....
3217	Financial derivatives...............	....	....	....	....	....	....	....	....	....	....	....	....
3218	Other accounts receivable............	....	....	....	....	....	....	....	....	....	....	....	....
322	Foreign........................	431	−470	164	431	−470	164	—	—	—	....	....	....
3222	Currency and deposits..............	431	−470	164	431	−470	164	—	—	—	....	....	....
3223	Securities other than shares..........	—	—	—	—	—	—	—	—	—	....	....	....
3224	Loans.........................	—	—	—	—	—	—	—	—	—	....	....	....
3225	Shares and other equity.............	—	—	—	—	—	—	—	—	—	....	....	....
3226	Insurance technical reserves..........	—	—	—	—	—	—	—	—	—	....	....	....
3227	Financial derivatives...............	—	—	—	—	—	—	—	—	—	....	....	....
3228	Other accounts receivable............	....	....	....	....	....	....	—	—	—	....	....	....
323	Monetary gold and SDRs.............	—	—	—	—	—	—	—	—	—	....	....	....
33	**Net incurrence of liabilities...................**	**−40**	**−648**	**−180**	**−40**	**−648**	**−180**	**325**	**−360**	**213**	....	....	....
331	Domestic.......................	−122	−129	−30	−122	−129	−30	325	−559	214	....	....	....
3312	Currency and deposits..............	—	—	—	—	—	—	—	—	—	....	....	....
3313	Securities other than shares..........	−122	−129	−30	−122	−129	−30	75	−300	−121	....	....	....
3314	Loans.........................	—	—	—	—	—	—	250	−259	336	....	....	....
3316	Insurance technical reserves..........	—	—	—	—	—	—	—	—	—	....	....	....
3317	Financial derivatives...............	—	—	—	—	—	—	—	—	—	....	....	....
3318	Other accounts payable.............	....	....	....	....	....	....	—	—	—	....	....	....
332	Foreign........................	82	−520	−150	82	−520	−150	—	199	−1	....	....	....
3322	Currency and deposits..............	—	—	—	—	—	—	....	....	....	....	....	....
3323	Securities other than shares..........	—	—	—	—	—	—	....	....	....	....	....	....
3324	Loans.........................	82	−520	−150	82	−520	−150	—	....	....	....	....	....
3326	Insurance technical reserves..........	—	—	—	—	—	—	—	....	....	....	....	....
3327	Financial derivatives...............	—	—	—	—	—	—	....	....	....	....	....	....
3328	Other accounts payable.............	....	....	....	....	....	....	....	....	....	....	....	....

In Millions of Krooni / Year Ending December 31 / Cash Reporter

	Budgetary Central Government			Central Government			Local Government			General Government		
	1999	2000	2001	1999	2000	2001	1999	2000	2001	1999	2000	2001
Table 4 Holding gains in assets and liabilities												
Table 5 Other changes in the volume of assets and liabilities												
Table 6 Balance sheet												
6 Net worth....................	....	....	....	....	....	....	....	....	....	....	....	....
61 Nonfinancial assets.............	....	....	....	....	....	....	....	....	....	....	....	....
611 Fixed assets...................	....	....	....	....	....	....	....	....	....	....	....	....
6111 Buildings and structures.........	....	....	....	....	....	....	....	....	....	....	....	....
6112 Machinery and equipment.........	....	....	....	....	....	....	....	....	....	....	....	....
6113 Other fixed assets.............	....	....	....	....	....	....	....	....	....	....	....	....
612 Inventories...................	....	....	....	....	....	....	....	....	....	....	....	....
613 Valuables....................	....	....	....	....	....	....	....	....	....	....	....	....
614 Nonproduced assets.............	....	....	....	....	....	....	....	....	....	....	....	....
6141 Land......................	....	....	....	....	....	....	....	....	....	....	....	....
6142 Subsoil assets................	....	....	....	....	....	....	....	....	....	....	....	....
6143 Other naturally occurring assets...	....	....	....	....	....	....	....	....	....	....	....	....
6144 Intangible nonproduced assets...	....	....	....	....	....	....	....	....	....	....	....	....
62 Financial assets...............	....	....	....	....	....	....	....	....	....	....	....	....
621 Domestic....................	....	....	....	....	....	....	....	....	....	....	....	....
6212 Currency and deposits...........	....	....	....	....	....	....	....	....	....	....	....	....
6213 Securities other than shares.......	....	....	....	....	....	....	....	....	....	....	....	....
6214 Loans.....................	....	....	....	....	....	....	....	....	....	....	....	....
6215 Shares and other equity..........	....	....	....	....	....	....	....	....	....	....	....	....
6216 Insurance technical reserves.......	....	....	....	....	....	....	....	....	....	....	....	....
6217 Financial derivatives...........	....	....	....	....	....	....	....	....	....	....	....	....
6218 Other accounts receivable.........	....	....	....	....	....	....	....	....	....	....	....	....
622 Foreign....................	....	....	....	....	....	....	....	....	....	....	....	....
6222 Currency and deposits...........	....	....	....	....	....	....	....	....	....	....	....	....
6223 Securities other than shares.......	....	....	....	....	....	....	....	....	....	....	....	....
6224 Loans.....................	....	....	....	....	....	....	....	....	....	....	....	....
6225 Shares and other equity..........	....	....	....	....	....	....	....	....	....	....	....	....
6226 Insurance technical reserves.......	....	....	....	....	....	....	....	....	....	....	....	....
6227 Financial derivatives...........	....	....	....	....	....	....	....	....	....	....	....	....
6228 Other accounts receivable.........	....	....	....	....	....	....	....	....	....	....	....	....
623 Monetary gold and SDRs...........	....	....	....	....	....	....	....	....	....	....	....	....
63 **Liabilities**....................	**3,514**	**2,716**	**2,591**	**3,514**	**2,716**	**2,591**	**1,709**	**1,579**	**2,015**	....	....	....
631 Domestic....................	339	210	180	339	210	180	1,709	1,380	1,817			
6312 Currency and deposits...........	....	....	....	....	....	....	....	....	....			
6313 Securities other than shares.......	....	....	....	....	....	....	....	....	....			
6314 Loans.....................	....	....	....	....	....	....	....	....	....			
6316 Insurance technical reserves.......	....	....	....	....	....	....	....	....	....			
6317 Financial derivatives...........	....	....	....	....	....	....	....	....	....			
6318 Other accounts payable.........	....	....	....	....	....	....	....	....	....			
632 Foreign....................	3,175	2,506	2,411	3,175	2,506	2,411	—	199	198			
6322 Currency and deposits...........	....	....	....	....	....	....	—	....	....			
6323 Securities other than shares.......	....	....	....	....	....	....	—	....	....			
6324 Loans.....................	....	....	....	....	....	....	—	....	....			
6326 Insurance technical reserves.......	....	....	....	....	....	....	—	....	....			
6327 Financial derivatives...........	....	....	....	....	....	....	—	....	....			
6328 Other accounts payable...........	....	....	....	....	....	....	....	....	....			
Memorandum items:												
6M2 Net financial worth.............				....	....	....						
6M3 Debt at market value...........												
6M4 Debt at nominal value...........												
6M5 Arrears....................												
6M6 Obligations for social security benefits...........	....	....										
6M7 Contingent liabilities............	....	....	....	....	....	....	....	....	....			
6M8 Uncapitalized military weapons, systems........	....	....	....	....	....	....	....	....	....			
Table 7 Outlays by functions of govt.												
7 **Total outlays**...................	**16,028**	**16,439**	**17,743**	**26,816**	**27,373**	**29,237**	**6,978**	**6,932**	**9,656**	....	....	....
701 **General public services**...........	**3,991**	**4,050**	**5,367**	**4,131**	**4,123**	**5,681**	**928**	**997**	**1,101**	....	....	....
7017 Public debt transactions...........	189	166	164	189	167	167	149	170	138	....	....	....
7018 General transfers between levels of govt......	....	....	....	....	....	....	....	....	....	....	....	....
702 **Defense**....................	**1,084**	**1,389**	**1,450**	**1,084**	**1,389**	**1,450**	**1**	**1**	**1**	....	....	....
703 **Public order and safety**.............	**1,978**	**1,955**	**2,092**	**1,986**	**1,955**	**2,095**	**22**	**21**	**94**	....	....	....

		Budgetary Central Government			Central Government			Local Government			General Government		
		1999	2000	2001	1999	2000	2001	1999	2000	2001	1999	2000	2001
704	**Economic affairs**................................	**2,750**	**2,589**	**2,529**	**2,939**	**2,825**	**2,766**	**588**	**527**	**615**	....	....	....
7042	Agriculture, forestry, fishing, and hunting.....	855	697	744	855	724	744	4	3	2	....	....	....
7043	Fuel and energy..................................	11	10	11	11	10	11	112	115	129	....	....	....
7044	Mining, manufacturing, and construction.....	—	—	—	—	—	—	—	—	—	....	....	....
7045	Transport..	1,775	1,762	1,640	1,775	1,762	1,640	325	312	338	....	....	....
7046	Communication..................................	....	....	....	....	....	....	....	....	....	....	....	....
705	**Environmental protection**......................	....	....	....	....	....	....	....	....	....	....	....	....
706	**Housing and community amenities**........	**13**	**66**	**—**	**13**	**66**	**—**	**1,094**	**1,058**	**1,444**	....	....	....
707	**Health**..	**561**	**421**	**495**	**4,474**	**4,505**	**4,763**	**105**	**101**	**134**	....	....	....
7072	Outpatient services..............................	—	—	—	—	—	—	....	....	....	....	....	....
7073	Hospital services.................................	108	102	111	108	102	111	....	....	....	....	....	....
7074	Public health services...........................	....	....	....	....	....	....	....	....	....	....	....	....
708	**Recreation, culture, and religion**...........	**940**	**1,086**	**1,134**	**965**	**1,107**	**1,157**	**752**	**793**	**1,002**	....	....	....
709	**Education**...	**2,476**	**2,769**	**2,109**	**2,521**	**2,804**	**2,137**	**2,749**	**2,699**	**4,383**	....	....	....
7091	Pre-primary and primary education..............	....	....	....	....	....	....	....	....	....	....	....	....
7092	Secondary education.............................	17	17	21	17	17	21	....	....	....	....	....	....
7094	Tertiary education................................	727	719	743	727	719	743	....	....	....	....	....	....
710	**Social protection**................................	**2,234**	**2,114**	**2,567**	**8,702**	**8,600**	**9,188**	**740**	**735**	**883**	....	....	....
7	Statistical discrepancy: Total outlays..............	—	—	—	—	—	—	—	—	—	....	....	....

Table 8 Transactions in financial assets and liabilities by sector

		Budgetary Central Government			Central Government			Local Government			General Government		
82	**Net acquisition of financial assets**........	**−2,113**	**−1,146**	**−62**	**−3,156**	**−1,289**	**810**	**−57**	**−625**	**−379**	....	....	....
821	Domestic...	−2,544	−677	−226	−3,586	−819	646	−57	−625	−379	....	....	....
8211	General government.............................	43	−258	−53	43	−258	−53	−37	−266	−728	....	....	....
8212	Central bank.....................................	....	....	....	....	....	....	....	....	....	....	....	....
8213	Other depository corporations.................	....	....	....	....	....	....	....	....	....	....	....	....
8214	Financial corporations n.e.c....................	....	....	....	....	....	....	....	....	....	....	....	....
8215	Nonfinancial corporations.......................	75	−22	−174	75	−22	−174	....	....	....	....	....	....
8216	Households & NPIs serving households.......	....	....	....	....	....	....	....	....	....	....	....	....
822	Foreign...	431	−470	164	431	−470	164	—	—	—	....	....	....
8221	General government.............................	....	....	....	....	....	....	—	—	—	....	....	....
8227	International organizations......................	....	....	....	....	....	....	—	—	—	....	....	....
8228	Financial corporations other than international organizations..............	....	....	....	....	....	....	—	—	—	....	....	....
8229	Other nonresidents..............................	....	....	....	....	....	....	—	—	—	....	....	....
823	Monetary gold and SDRs.........................	—	—	—	—	—	—	....	....	....	....	....	....
83	**Net incurrence of liabilities**...................	**−40**	**−648**	**−180**	**−40**	**−648**	**−180**	**325**	**−360**	**213**	....	....	....
831	Domestic...	−122	−129	−30	−122	−129	−30	325	−559	214	....	....	....
8311	General government.............................	....	....	....	....	....	....	....	....	....	....	....	....
8312	Central bank.....................................	....	....	....	....	....	....	....	....	....	....	....	....
8313	Other depository corporations.................	....	....	....	....	....	....	....	....	....	....	....	....
8314	Financial corporations n.e.c....................	....	....	....	....	....	....	....	....	....	....	....	....
8315	Nonfinancial corporations.......................	....	....	....	....	....	....	....	....	....	....	....	....
8316	Households & NPIs serving households.......	....	....	....	....	....	....	....	....	....	....	....	....
832	Foreign...	82	−520	−150	82	−520	−150	—	199	−1	....	....	....
8321	General government.............................	—	—	—	—	—	—	—	....	....	....	....	....
8327	International organizations......................	82	−520	−150	82	−520	−150	—	....	....	....	....	....
8328	Financial corporations other than international organizations..............	—	—	—	—	—	—	—	....	....	....	....	....
8329	Other nonresidents..............................	—	—	—	—	—	—	—	—	—	....	....	....

Ethiopia   644

In Millions of Birr / Year Beginning July 7 / Cash Reporter

		Budgetary Central Government			Central Government			Local Government			General Government		
		2000	2001	2002	2000	2001	2002p	2000	2001	2002	2000	2001	2002
	Statement of government operations												
	Statement of other economic flows												
	Balance sheet												
	Statement of sources and uses of cash												
1	Cash receipts from operating activities..........	....	10,951.7	9,874.1	....	....	12,407.6	....	....	....	....	....	....
11	Taxes..	....	5,541.4	6,512.1	....	....	6,773.3	....	....	....	....	....	....
12	Social contributions..........................	....	—	—	....	....	597.0						
13	Grants...	....	2,876.7	1,319.8	....	....	2,899.1						
14	Other receipts.................................	....	2,533.6	2,042.2	....	....	2,138.2						
2	Cash payments for operating activities..........	....	9,948.3	11,566.1	....	....	13,756.9						
21	Compensation of employees...................	....	2,315.9	1,859.9	....	....	1,859.9						
22	Purchases of goods and services...............	....	2,196.5	3,277.6		....	3,322.6						
24	Interest..	....	1,069.9	996.4	....	....	946.4						
25	Subsidies..	....	—	—	....	....	16.8						
26	Grants...	....	4,366.0	4,289.6	....	....	4,289.6						
27	Social benefits.................................	....	—	999.6	....	....	1,463.6						
28	Other payments...............................	....	—	143.0	....	....	1,858.0						
CIO	*Net cash inflow from oper. activities.....*	....	*1,003.4*	*−1,692.0*	....	....	*−1,349.3*	....	....	....			
31.1	Purchases of nonfinancial assets...............	....	3,883.9	3,310.7	....	....	3,682.2						
31.2	Sales of nonfinancial assets...................	....	—	—	....	....	—						
31	Net cash outflow from investments in nonfinancial assets.................	....	3,883.9	3,310.7	....	....	3,682.2						
CSD	*Cash surplus/deficit.............................*	....	*−2,880.5*	*−5,002.7*	....	....	*−5,031.5*						
32x	Net acquisition of fin assets, excl. cash....	....	....	....	....	....	....						
321x	Domestic...	....	....	....	....	....	....						
322x	Foreign..	....	....	....	....	....	....						
323	Monetary gold and SDRs.....................	....	....	....	....	....	....						
33	Net incurrence of liabilities..................	....	2,880.5	5,002.7	....	....	5,387.2						
331	Domestic...	....	559.2	626.4	....	....	626.4						
332	Foreign..	....	2,321.3	4,376.3	....	....	4,760.8						
NFB	Net cash inflow from fin. activities...............	....	....	....	....	....	....						
NCB	*Net change in the stock of cash.............*	....	....	....	....	....	....						
	Table 1 Revenue												
1	**Revenue**..	....	**10,951.7**	**9,874.1**	....	....	**12,407.6**	....	....	....	....	....	....
11	**Taxes**...	....	**5,541.4**	**6,512.1**	....	....	**6,773.3**						
111	Taxes on income, profits, & capital gains......	....	1,574.4	1,914.6	....	....	1,914.6						
1111	Individuals....................................	....	331.3	653.9			653.9						
1112	Corporations and other enterprises...........	....	1,207.9	1,196.9			1,196.9						
112	Taxes on payroll and workforce..............	....	—	—	....	....	—						
113	Taxes on property.............................	....	—	—	....	....	—						
114	Taxes on goods and services..................	....	1,077.5	1,247.5	....	....	1,508.7						
1141	General taxes on goods and services.........	....	509.7	567.8			567.8						
1142	Excises..	....	312.6	350.1			611.3						
115	Taxes on int'l. trade and transactions..........	....	2,831.6	3,304.9	....	....	3,304.9						
116	Other taxes....................................	....	57.9	45.1	....	....	45.1						
12	**Social contributions**.............................	....	—	—	....	....	**597.0**	....	....	....			
121	Social security contributions..................	....	—	—	....	....	597.0						
122	Other social contributions....................	....	—	—	....	....	—						
13	**Grants**..	....	**2,876.7**	**1,319.8**	....	....	**2,899.1**						
131	From foreign governments....................	....	232.7	290.5	....	....	290.5						
132	From international organizations...............	....	2,644.0	1,029.3	....	....	2,608.6						
133	From other general government units..........	....	—	—	....	....	—						
14	**Other revenue**..................................	....	**2,533.6**	**2,042.2**	....	....	**2,138.2**	....	....	....	....	....	....
	Table 2 Expense by economic type												
2	**Expense**..	....	**9,948.3**	**11,566.1**	....	....	**13,756.9**	....	....	....	....	....	....
21	**Compensation of employees**..................	....	**2,315.9**	**1,859.9**	....	....	**1,859.9**	....	....	....	....	....	....
211	Wages and salaries...........................	....	2,144.7	1,730.8	....	....	1,730.8						
212	Social contributions..........................	....	171.2	129.1	....	....	129.1						
22	**Use of goods and services**......................	....	**2,196.5**	**3,277.6**	....	....	**3,322.6**	....	....	....	....	....	....
23	**Consumption of fixed capital**...............	....	....	....	....	....	....	....	....	....	....	....	....
24	**Interest**..	....	**1,069.9**	**996.4**	....	....	**946.4**	....	....	....	....	....	....
25	**Subsidies**......................................	....	—	—	....	....	**16.8**	....	....	....	....	....	....

2005, International Monetary Fund: *Government Finance Statistics Yearbook*

In Millions of Krooni / Year Ending December 31 / Cash Reporter

		Budgetary Central Government			Central Government			Local Government			General Government		
		1999	2000	2001	1999	2000	2001	1999	2000	2001	1999	2000	2001
704	**Economic affairs**............................	**2,750**	**2,589**	**2,529**	**2,939**	**2,825**	**2,766**	**588**	**527**	**615**	....	....	....
7042	Agriculture, forestry, fishing, and hunting.....	855	697	744	855	724	744	4	3	2	....	....	....
7043	Fuel and energy............................	11	10	11	11	10	11	112	115	129	....	....	....
7044	Mining, manufacturing, and construction.....	—	—	—	—	—	—	—	—	—	....	....	....
7045	Transport..................................	1,775	1,762	1,640	1,775	1,762	1,640	325	312	338	....	....	....
7046	Communication............................	....	....	....	....	....	....	....	....	....	....	....	....
705	**Environmental protection**...................	....	....	....	....	....	....	....	....	....	....	....	....
706	**Housing and community amenities**........	**13**	**66**	**—**	**13**	**66**	**—**	**1,094**	**1,058**	**1,444**	....	....	....
707	**Health**...................................	**561**	**421**	**495**	**4,474**	**4,505**	**4,763**	**105**	**101**	**134**	....	....	....
7072	Outpatient services.........................	—	—	—	—	—	—	....	....	....	....	....	....
7073	Hospital services...........................	108	102	111	108	102	111	....	....	....	....	....	....
7074	Public health services.......................	....	....	....	....	....	....	....	....	....	....	....	....
708	**Recreation, culture, and religion**...........	**940**	**1,086**	**1,134**	**965**	**1,107**	**1,157**	**752**	**793**	**1,002**	....	....	....
709	**Education**................................	**2,476**	**2,769**	**2,109**	**2,521**	**2,804**	**2,137**	**2,749**	**2,699**	**4,383**	....	....	....
7091	Pre-primary and primary education............	....	....	....	....	....	....	....	....	....	....	....	....
7092	Secondary education........................	17	17	21	17	17	21	....	....	....	....	....	....
7094	Tertiary education..........................	727	719	743	727	719	743	....	....	....	....	....	....
710	**Social protection**.........................	**2,234**	**2,114**	**2,567**	**8,702**	**8,600**	**9,188**	**740**	**735**	**883**	....	....	....
7	Statistical discrepancy: Total outlays..............	—	—	—	—	—	—	—	—	—	....	....	....

Table 8 Transactions in financial assets and liabilities by sector

		Budgetary Central Government			Central Government			Local Government			General Government		
		1999	2000	2001	1999	2000	2001	1999	2000	2001	1999	2000	2001
82	**Net acquisition of financial assets**.........	**–2,113**	**–1,146**	**–62**	**–3,156**	**–1,289**	**810**	**–57**	**–625**	**–379**	....	....	....
821	Domestic..................................	–2,544	–677	–226	–3,586	–819	646	–57	–625	–379	....	....	....
8211	General government........................	43	–258	–53	43	–258	–53	–37	–266	–728	....	....	....
8212	Central bank..............................	....	....	....	....	....	....	....	....	....	....	....	....
8213	Other depository corporations...............	....	....	....	....	....	....	....	....	....	....	....	....
8214	Financial corporations n.e.c.................	....	....	....	....	....	....	....	....	....	....	....	....
8215	Nonfinancial corporations...................	75	–22	–174	75	–22	–174	....	....	....	....	....	....
8216	Households & NPIs serving households......	....	....	....	....	....	....	....	....	....	....	....	....
822	Foreign...................................	431	–470	164	431	–470	164	—	—	—	....	....	....
8221	General government........................	....	....	....	....	....	....	—	—	—	....	....	....
8227	International organizations...................	....	....	....	....	....	....	—	—	—	....	....	....
8228	Financial corporations other than international organizations..............	....	....	....	....	....	....	—	—	—	....	....	....
8229	Other nonresidents.........................	....	....	....	....	....	....	—	—	—	....	....	....
823	Monetary gold and SDRs....................	—	—	—	—	—	—	—	—	—	....	....	....
83	**Net incurrence of liabilities**.................	**–40**	**–648**	**–180**	**–40**	**–648**	**–180**	**325**	**–360**	**213**	....	....	....
831	Domestic..................................	–122	–129	–30	–122	–129	–30	325	–559	214	....	....	....
8311	General government........................	....	....	....	....	....	....	....	....	....	....	....	....
8312	Central bank..............................	....	....	....	....	....	....	....	....	....	....	....	....
8313	Other depository corporations...............	....	....	....	....	....	....	....	....	....	....	....	....
8314	Financial corporations n.e.c.................	....	....	....	....	....	....	....	....	....	....	....	....
8315	Nonfinancial corporations...................	....	....	....	....	....	....	....	....	....	....	....	....
8316	Households & NPIs serving households......	....	....	....	....	....	....	....	....	....	....	....	....
832	Foreign...................................	82	–520	–150	82	–520	–150	—	199	–1	....	....	....
8321	General government........................	—	—	—	—	—	—	—	....	....	....	....	....
8327	International organizations...................	82	–520	–150	82	–520	–150	—	....	....	....	....	....
8328	Financial corporations other than international organizations..............	—	—	—	—	—	—	—	....	....	....	....	....
8329	Other nonresidents.........................	—	—	—	—	—	—	—	—	—	....	....	....

	Budgetary Central Government			Central Government			Local Government			General Government		
	2000	2001	2002	2000	2001	2002p	2000	2001	2002	2000	2001	2002
Statement of government operations												
Statement of other economic flows												
Balance sheet												
Statement of sources and uses of cash												
1 Cash receipts from operating activities..........	....	10,951.7	9,874.1	....	....	12,407.6	....	....	....	....	....	....
11 Taxes...	....	5,541.4	6,512.1	....	....	6,773.3	....	....	....	....	....	....
12 Social contributions........................	....	—	—	....	....	597.0	....	....	....	....	....	....
13 Grants..	....	2,876.7	1,319.8	....	....	2,899.1	....	....	....	....	....	....
14 Other receipts.................................	....	2,533.6	2,042.2	....	....	2,138.2	....	....	....	....	....	....
2 Cash payments for operating activities..........	....	9,948.3	11,566.1	....	....	13,756.9	....	....	....	....	....	....
21 Compensation of employees....................	....	2,315.9	1,859.9	....	....	1,859.9	....	....	....	....	....	....
22 Purchases of goods and services..............	....	2,196.5	3,277.6	....	....	3,322.6	....	....	....	....	....	....
24 Interest...	....	1,069.9	996.4	....	....	946.4	....	....	....	....	....	....
25 Subsidies..	....	—	—	....	....	16.8	....	....	....	....	....	....
26 Grants..	....	4,366.0	4,289.6	....	....	4,289.6	....	....	....	....	....	....
27 Social benefits..................................	....	—	999.6	....	....	1,463.6	....	....	....	....	....	....
28 Other payments................................	....	—	143.0	....	....	1,858.0	....	....	....	....	....	....
CIO *Net cash inflow from oper. activities.....*	....	*1,003.4*	*−1,692.0*	....	....	*−1,349.3*	....	....	....	....	....	....
31.1 Purchases of nonfinancial assets..................	....	3,883.9	3,310.7	....	....	3,682.2	....	....	....	....	....	....
31.2 Sales of nonfinancial assets.........................	....	—	—	....	....	—	....	....	....	....	....	....
31 Net cash outflow from investments in nonfinancial assets..........................	....	3,883.9	3,310.7	....	....	3,682.2	....	....	....	....	....	....
CSD *Cash surplus/deficit.........................*	....	*−2,880.5*	*−5,002.7*	....	....	*−5,031.5*	....	....	....	....	....	....
32x Net acquisition of fin assets, excl. cash...	....	....	....	....	....	....	....	....	....	....	....	....
321x Domestic..	....	....	....	....	....	....	....	....	....	....	....	....
322x Foreign...	....	....	....	....	....	....	....	....	....	....	....	....
323 Monetary gold and SDRs...................	....	....	....	....	....	....	....	....	....	....	....	....
33 Net incurrence of liabilities..................	....	2,880.5	5,002.7	....	....	5,387.2	....	....	....	....	....	....
331 Domestic..	....	559.2	626.4	....	....	626.4	....	....	....	....	....	....
332 Foreign...	....	2,321.3	4,376.3	....	....	4,760.8	....	....	....	....	....	....
NFB Net cash inflow from fin. activities............	....	....	....	....	....	....	....	....	....	....	....	....
NCB *Net change in the stock of cash............*	....	....	....	....	....	....	....	....	....	....	....	....
Table 1 Revenue												
1 **Revenue**....................................	....	**10,951.7**	**9,874.1**	....	....	**12,407.6**	....	....	....	....	....	....
11 **Taxes**..	....	**5,541.4**	**6,512.1**	....	....	**6,773.3**	....	....	....	....	....	....
111 Taxes on income, profits, & capital gains......	....	1,574.4	1,914.6	....	....	1,914.6	....	....	....	....	....	....
1111 Individuals..................................	....	331.3	653.9	....	....	653.9	....	....	....	....	....	....
1112 Corporations and other enterprises............	....	1,207.9	1,196.9	....	....	1,196.9	....	....	....	....	....	....
112 Taxes on payroll and workforce.........	....	....	....	....	....	....	....	....	....	....	....	....
113 Taxes on property...........................	....	—	—	....	....	—	....	....	....	....	....	....
114 Taxes on goods and services..............	....	1,077.5	1,247.5	....	....	1,508.7	....	....	....	....	....	....
1141 General taxes on goods and services..........	....	509.7	567.8	....	....	567.8	....	....	....	....	....	....
1142 Excises......................................	....	312.6	350.1	....	....	611.3	....	....	....	....	....	....
115 Taxes on int'l. trade and transactions..........	....	2,831.6	3,304.9	....	....	3,304.9	....	....	....	....	....	....
116 Other taxes...................................	....	57.9	45.1	....	....	45.1	....	....	....	....	....	....
12 **Social contributions**..............................	....	—	—	....	....	**597.0**	....	....	....	....	....	....
121 Social security contributions...........	....	—	—	....	....	597.0	....	....	....	....	....	....
122 Other social contributions...............	....	....	....	....	....	....	....	....	....	....	....	....
13 **Grants**......................................	....	**2,876.7**	**1,319.8**	....	....	**2,899.1**	....	....	....	....	....	....
131 From foreign governments.................	....	232.7	290.5	....	....	290.5	....	....	....	....	....	....
132 From international organizations........	....	2,644.0	1,029.3	....	....	2,608.6	....	....	....	....	....	....
133 From other general government units...........	....	—	—	....	....	—	....	....	....	....	....	....
14 **Other revenue**......................................	....	**2,533.6**	**2,042.2**	....	....	**2,138.2**	....	....	....	....	....	....
Table 2 Expense by economic type												
2 **Expense**..	....	**9,948.3**	**11,566.1**	....	....	**13,756.9**	....	....	....	....	....	....
21 **Compensation of employees**..................	....	**2,315.9**	**1,859.9**	....	....	**1,859.9**	....	....	....	....	....	....
211 Wages and salaries..........................	....	2,144.7	1,730.8	....	....	1,730.8	....	....	....	....	....	....
212 Social contributions........................	....	171.2	129.1	....	....	129.1	....	....	....	....	....	....
22 **Use of goods and services**......................	....	**2,196.5**	**3,277.6**	....	....	**3,322.6**	....	....	....	....	....	....
23 **Consumption of fixed capital**..............	....	....	....	....	....	....	....	....	....	....	....	....
24 **Interest**....................................	....	**1,069.9**	**996.4**	....	....	**946.4**	....	....	....	....	....	....
25 **Subsidies**....................................	....	—	—	....	....	**16.8**	....	....	....	....	....	....

In Millions of Birr / Year Beginning July 7 / Cash Reporter

		Budgetary Central Government			Central Government			Local Government			General Government		
		2000	2001	2002	2000	2001	2002p	2000	2001	2002	2000	2001	2002
26	**Grants**.................................	....	**4,366.0**	**4,289.6**	....	....	**4,289.6**	....	....	....	....	....	....
261	To foreign govenments.....................	....	—	—	....	....	—	....	....	....	....	....	....
262	To international organizations..................	....	29.3	34.3	....	....	34.3	....	....	....	....	....	....
263	To other general government units.............	....	4,336.7	4,255.3	....	....	4,255.3	....	....	....	....	....	....
2631	Current................................	....	4,336.7	4,255.3	....	....	4,255.3	....	....	....	....	....	....
2632	Capital................................	....	—	—	....	....	—	....	....	....	....	....	....
27	**Social benefits**...........................	....	—	999.6	....	....	1,463.6	....	....	....	....	....	....
28	**Other expense**...........................	....	—	143.0	....	....	1,858.0	....	....	....	....	....	....
281	Property expense other than interest...........	....	—	—	....	....	—	....	....	....	....	....	....
282	Miscellaneous other expense................	....	—	143.0	....	....	1,858.0	....	....	....	....	....	....
2821	Current................................	....	—	48.0	....	....	1,763.0	....	....	....	....	....	....
2822	Capital................................	....	—	95.0	....	....	95.0	....	....	....	....	....	....

Table 3   Transactions in assets and liabilities

		Budgetary Central Government			Central Government			Local Government			General Government		
		2000	2001	2002	2000	2001	2002p	2000	2001	2002	2000	2001	2002
3	**Change in net worth from transactns....**	....	....	....	....	....	....	....	....	....	....	....	....
31	**Net acquisition of nonfinancial assets...**	....	**3,883.9**	**3,310.7**	....	....	**3,682.2**	....	....	....	....	....	....
311	Fixed assets...........................	....	2,262.6	3,310.7	....	....	3,682.2	....	....	....	....	....	....
3111	Buildings and structures.................	....	504.6	2,356.2	....	....	....	....	....	....	....	....	....
3112	Machinery and equipment...............	....	1,757.9	953.8	....	....	....	....	....	....	....	....	....
3113	Other fixed assets.....................	....	.1	.7	....	....	....	....	....	....	....	....	....
312	Inventories.............................	....	—	—	....	....	—	....	....	....	....	....	....
313	Valuables..............................	....	—	—	....	....	—	....	....	....	....	....	....
314	Nonproduced assets....................	....	1,621.3	—	....	....	—	....	....	....	....	....	....
3141	Land..................................	....	—	—	....	....	—	....	....	....	....	....	....
3142	Subsoil assets.........................	....	—	—	....	....	—	....	....	....	....	....	....
3143	Other naturally occurring assets...........	....	—	—	....	....	—	....	....	....	....	....	....
3144	Intangible nonproduced assets..................	....	1,621.3	—	....	....	—	....	....	....	....	....	....
32	**Net acquisition of financial assets........**	....	....	....	....	....	....	....	....	....	....	....	....
321	Domestic..............................	....	....	....	....	....	....	....	....	....	....	....	....
3212	Currency and deposits....................	....	....	....	....	....	....	....	....	....	....	....	....
3213	Securities other than shares..............	....	....	....	....	....	....	....	....	....	....	....	....
3214	Loans.................................	....	....	....	....	....	....	....	....	....	....	....	....
3215	Shares and other equity.................	....	....	....	....	....	....	....	....	....	....	....	....
3216	Insurance technical reserves..............	....	....	....	....	....	....	....	....	....	....	....	....
3217	Financial derivatives....................	....	....	....	....	....	....	....	....	....	....	....	....
3218	Other accounts receivable................	....	....	....	....	....	....	....	....	....	....	....	....
322	Foreign...............................	....	....	....	....	....	....	....	....	....	....	....	....
3222	Currency and deposits....................	....	....	....	....	....	....	....	....	....	....	....	....
3223	Securities other than shares..............	....	....	....	....	....	....	....	....	....	....	....	....
3224	Loans.................................	....	....	....	....	....	....	....	....	....	....	....	....
3225	Shares and other equity.................	....	....	....	....	....	....	....	....	....	....	....	....
3226	Insurance technical reserves..............	....	....	....	....	....	....	....	....	....	....	....	....
3227	Financial derivatives....................	....	....	....	....	....	....	....	....	....	....	....	....
3228	Other accounts receivable................	....	....	....	....	....	....	....	....	....	....	....	....
323	Monetary gold and SDRs.................	....	....	....	....	....	....	....	....	....	....	....	....
33	**Net incurrence of liabilities...................**	....	**2,880.5**	**5,002.7**	....	....	**5,387.2**	....	....	....	....	....	....
331	Domestic..............................	....	559.2	626.4	....	....	626.4	....	....	....	....	....	....
3312	Currency and deposits...................	....	—	....	....	....	....	....	....	....	....	....	....
3313	Securities other than shares..............	....	—	....	....	....	....	....	....	....	....	....	....
3314	Loans.................................	....	559.2	....	....	....	....	....	....	....	....	....	....
3316	Insurance technical reserves..............	....	—	....	....	....	....	....	....	....	....	....	....
3317	Financial derivatives....................	....	—	....	....	....	....	....	....	....	....	....	....
3318	Other accounts payable..................	....	....	....	....	....	....	....	....	....	....	....	....
332	Foreign...............................	....	2,321.3	4,376.3	....	....	4,760.8	....	....	....	....	....	....
3322	Currency and deposits...................	....	—	—	....	....	—	....	....	....	....	....	....
3323	Securities other than shares..............	....	—	—	....	....	—	....	....	....	....	....	....
3324	Loans.................................	....	2,321.3	4,376.3	....	....	4,760.8	....	....	....	....	....	....
3326	Insurance technical reserves..............	....	—	—	....	....	—	....	....	....	....	....	....
3327	Financial derivatives....................	....	—	—	....	....	—	....	....	....	....	....	....
3328	Other accounts payable..................	....	....	....	....	....	....	....	....	....	....	....	....

In Millions of Birr / Year Beginning July 7 / Cash Reporter

	Budgetary Central Government			Central Government			Local Government			General Government		
	2000	2001	2002	2000	2001	2002p	2000	2001	2002	2000	2001	2002
Table 4 Holding gains in assets and liabilities												
Table 5 Other changes in the volume of assets and liabilities												
Table 6 Balance sheet												
Table 7 Outlays by functions of govt.												
7 **Total outlays**..............................	....	**13,832.2**	**14,876.8**	....	....	**17,439.1**	....	....	....	....	....	....
701 **General public services**......................	....	**5,605.8**	**6,128.2**	....	....	**6,078.2**	....	....	....	....	....	....
7017 Public debt transactions.....................	....	1,069.9	996.4	....	....	946.4	....	....	....	....	....	....
7018 General transfers between levels of govt......	....	4,336.7	4,255.3	....	....	4,255.3	....	....	....	....	....	....
702 **Defense**.....................................	....	**3,642.3**	**2,891.7**	....	....	**2,891.7**	....	....	....	....	....	....
703 **Public order and safety**....................	....	**191.0**	**290.0**	....	....	**290.0**	....	....	....	....	....	....
704 **Economic affairs**...........................	....	**2,340.8**	**2,952.3**	....	....	**3,269.1**	....	....	....	....	....	....
7042 Agriculture, forestry, fishing, and hunting.....	....	549.6	1,094.0	....	....	1,094.0	....	....	....	....	....	....
7043 Fuel and energy............................	....	428.6	29.6	....	....	46.4	....	....	....	....	....	....
7044 Mining, manufacturing, and construction.....	....	913.0	141.2	....	....	141.2	....	....	....	....	....	....
7045 Transport...................................	....	407.8	1,683.1	....	....	1,983.1	....	....	....	....	....	....
7046 Communication..............................	....	41.8	4.4	....	....	4.4	....	....	....	....	....	....
705 **Environmental protection**....................	....	**10.5**	**3.5**	....	....	**3.5**	....	....	....	....	....	....
706 **Housing and community amenities**........	....	**89.7**	**5.9**	....	....	**5.9**	....	....	....	....	....	....
707 **Health**....................................	....	**113.7**	**141.5**	....	....	**141.5**	....	....	....	....	....	....
7072 Outpatient services.........................	....	—	34.4	....	....	34.4	....	....	....	....	....	....
7073 Hospital services...........................	....	20.9	32.4	....	....	32.4	....	....	....	....	....	....
7074 Public health services......................	....	92.8	74.7	....	....	74.7	....	....	....	....	....	....
708 **Recreation, culture, and religion**...........	....	**90.2**	**40.8**	....	....	**40.8**	....	....	....	....	....	....
709 **Education**.................................	....	**344.0**	**844.8**	....	....	**844.8**	....	....	....	....	....	....
7091 Pre-primary and primary education...............	....	233.0	95.2	....	....	95.2	....	....	....	....	....	....
7092 Secondary education.........................	....	108.9	38.5	....	....	38.5	....	....	....	....	....	....
7094 Tertiary education..........................	....	2.1	711.1	....	....	711.1	....	....	....	....	....	....
710 **Social protection**..........................	....	**1,374.9**	**1,578.1**	....	....	**4,167.0**	....	....	....	....	....	....
7 Statistical discrepancy: Total outlays..............	....	29.3	—	....	....	−293.4	....	....	....	....	....	....
Table 8 Transactions in financial assets and liabilities by sector												
82 **Net acquisition of financial assets**........	....	....	....	....	....	....	....	....	....	....	....	....
821 Domestic...................................	....	....	....	....	....	....	....	....	....	....	....	....
8211 General government.........................	....	....	....	....	....	....	....	....	....	....	....	....
8212 Central bank...............................	....	....	....	....	....	....	....	....	....	....	....	....
8213 Other depository corporations................	....	....	....	....	....	....	....	....	....	....	....	....
8214 Financial corporations n.e.c.................	....	....	....	....	....	....	....	....	....	....	....	....
8215 Nonfinancial corporations...................	....	....	....	....	....	....	....	....	....	....	....	....
8216 Households & NPIs serving households......	....	....	....	....	....	....	....	....	....	....	....	....
822 Foreign....................................	....	....	....	....	....	....	....	....	....	....	....	....
8221 General government.........................	....	....	....	....	....	....	....	....	....	....	....	....
8227 International organizations...................	....	....	....	....	....	....	....	....	....	....	....	....
8228 Financial corporations other than international organizations............	....	....	....	....	....	....	....	....	....	....	....	....
8229 Other nonresidents.........................	....	....	....	....	....	....	....	....	....	....	....	....
823 Monetary gold and SDRs...................	....	....	....	....	....	....	....	....	....	....	....	....
83 **Net incurrence of liabilities**.................	....	**2,880.5**	**5,002.7**	....	....	**5,387.2**	....	....	....	....	....	....
831 Domestic...................................	....	559.2	626.4	....	....	626.4	....	....	....	....	....	....
8311 General government.........................	....	....	....	....	....	....	....	....	....	....	....	....
8312 Central bank...............................	....	....	....	....	....	....	....	....	....	....	....	....
8313 Other depository corporations................	....	....	....	....	....	....	....	....	....	....	....	....
8314 Financial corporations n.e.c.................	....	....	....	....	....	....	....	....	....	....	....	....
8315 Nonfinancial corporations...................	....	....	....	....	....	....	....	....	....	....	....	....
8316 Households & NPIs serving households......	....	....	....	....	....	....	....	....	....	....	....	....
832 Foreign....................................	....	2,321.3	4,376.3	....	....	4,760.8	....	....	....	....	....	....
8321 General government.........................	....	....	....	....	....	....	....	....	....	....	....	....
8327 International organizations...................	....	....	....	....	....	....	....	....	....	....	....	....
8328 Financial corporations other than international organizations............	....	....	....	....	....	....	....	....	....	....	....	....
8329 Other nonresidents.........................	....	....	....	....	....	....	....	....	....	....	....	....

2005, International Monetary Fund: *Government Finance Statistics Yearbook*

In Millions of Dollars / Year Ending December 31 / Cash Reporter

		Budgetary Central Government			Central Government			Local Government			General Government		
		2002	2003	2004	2002	2003	2004	2002	2003	2004	2002	2003	2004
Statement of government operations													
Statement of other economic flows													
Balance sheet													
Statement of sources and uses of cash													
1	Cash receipts from operating activities	....	....	1,176.02	....	....	....	....	....	....	....	....	....
11	Taxes	....	....	1,048.87	....	....	....	....	....	....	....	....	....
12	Social contributions	....	....	—	....	....	....	....	....	....	....	....	....
13	Grants	....	....	22.70	....	....	....	....	....	....	....	....	....
14	Other receipts	....	....	104.45	....	....	....	....	....	....	....	....	....
2	Cash payments for operating activities	....	....	1,177.97	....	....	....	....	....	....	....	....	....
21	Compensation of employees	....	....	519.26	....	....	....	....	....	....	....	....	....
22	Purchases of goods and services	....	....	182.70	....	....	....	....	....	....	....	....	....
24	Interest	....	....	119.02	....	....	....	....	....	....	....	....	....
25	Subsidies	....	....	8.21	....	....	....	....	....	....	....	....	....
26	Grants	....	....	194.24	....	....	....	....	....	....	....	....	....
27	Social benefits	....	....	59.41	....	....	....	....	....	....	....	....	....
28	Other payments	....	....	95.13	....	....	....	....	....	....	....	....	....
CIO	*Net cash inflow from oper. activities*	....	....	*−1.95*	....	....	....	....	....	....	....	....	....
31.1	Purchases of nonfinancial assets	....	....	144.55	....	....	....	....	....	....	....	....	....
31.2	Sales of nonfinancial assets	....	....	—	....	....	....	....	....	....	....	....	....
31	Net cash outflow from investments in nonfinancial assets	....	....	144.55	....	....	....	....	....	....	....	....	....
CSD	*Cash surplus/deficit*	....	....	*−146.50*	....	....	....	....	....	....	....	....	....
32x	Net acquisition of fin assets, excl. cash	....	....		....	....	....	....	....	....	....	....	....
321x	Domestic	....	....		....	....	....	....	....	....	....	....	....
322x	Foreign	....	....		....	....	....	....	....	....	....	....	....
323	Monetary gold and SDRs	....	....		....	....	....	....	....	....	....	....	....
33	Net incurrence of liabilities	....	....		....	....	....	....	....	....	....	....	....
331	Domestic	....	....		....	....	....	....	....	....	....	....	....
332	Foreign	....	....		....	....	....	....	....	....	....	....	....
NFB	Net cash inflow from fin. activities	....	....		....	....	....	....	....	....	....	....	....
NCB	*Net change in the stock of cash*	....	....		....	....	....	....	....	....	....	....	....

Table 1   Revenue

1	**Revenue**	....	....	**1,176.02**	....	....	....	....	....	....	....	....	....
11	**Taxes**	....	....	**1,048.87**	....	....	....	....	....	....	....	....	....
111	Taxes on income, profits, & capital gains	....	....	334.61	....	....	....	....	....	....	....	....	....
1111	Individuals	....	....	175.70	....	....	....	....	....	....	....	....	....
1112	Corporations and other enterprises	....	....	127.23	....	....	....	....	....	....	....	....	....
112	Taxes on payroll and workforce	....	....	—	....	....	....	....	....	....	....	....	....
113	Taxes on property	....	....	15.55	....	....	....	....	....	....	....	....	....
114	Taxes on goods and services	....	....	482.62	....	....	....	....	....	....	....	....	....
1141	General taxes on goods and services	....	....	404.36	....	....	....	....	....	....	....	....	....
1142	Excises	....	....	78.26	....	....	....	....	....	....	....	....	....
115	Taxes on int'l. trade and transactions	....	....	215.58	....	....	....	....	....	....	....	....	....
116	Other taxes	....	....	.51	....	....	....	....	....	....	....	....	....
12	**Social contributions**	....	....	**—**	....	....	....	....	....	....	....	....	....
121	Social security contributions	....	....	—	....	....	....	....	....	....	....	....	....
122	Other social contributions	....	....	—	....	....	....	....	....	....	....	....	....
13	**Grants**	....	....	**22.70**	....	....	....	....	....	....	....	....	....
131	From foreign governments	....	....	3.40	....	....	....	....	....	....	....	....	....
132	From international organizations	....	....	19.30	....	....	....	....	....	....	....	....	....
133	From other general government units	....	....	—	....	....	....	....	....	....	....	....	....
14	**Other revenue**	....	....	**104.45**	....	....	....	....	....	....	....	....	....

Table 2   Expense by economic type

2	**Expense**	....	....	**1,177.97**	....	....	....	....	....	....	....	....	....
21	**Compensation of employees**	....	....	**519.26**	....	....	....	....	....	....	....	....	....
211	Wages and salaries	....	....	463.50	....	....	....	....	....	....	....	....	....
212	Social contributions	....	....	55.76	....	....	....	....	....	....	....	....	....
22	**Use of goods and services**	....	....	**182.70**	....	....	....	....	....	....	....	....	....
23	**Consumption of fixed capital**	....	....	....	....	....	....	....	....	....	....	....	....
24	**Interest**	....	....	**119.02**	....	....	....	....	....	....	....	....	....
25	**Subsidies**	....	....	**8.21**	....	....	....	....	....	....	....	....	....

In Millions of Dollars / Year Ending December 31 / Cash Reporter

		Budgetary Central Government			Central Government			Local Government			General Government		
		2002	2003	2004	2002	2003	2004	2002	2003	2004	2002	2003	2004
26	**Grants**.....................	....	....	**194.24**	....	....	....	....	....	....	....	....	....
261	To foreign govenments..............	....	....	—	....	....	....	....	....	....	....	....	....
262	To international organizations.................	....	....	1.42	....	....	....	....	....	....	....	....	....
263	To other general government units.............	....	....	192.82	....	....	....	....	....	....	....	....	....
2631	Current...............	....	....	....	....	....	....	....	....	....	....	....	....
2632	Capital...............	....	....	....	....	....	....	....	....	....	....	....	....
27	**Social benefits**.........................	....	....	**59.41**	....	....	....	....	....	....	....	....	....
28	**Other expense**......................	....	....	**95.13**	....	....	....	....	....	....	....	....	....
281	Property expense other than interest...........	....	....	....	....	....	....	....	....	....	....	....	....
282	Miscellaneous other expense.................	....	....	....	....	....	....	....	....	....	....	....	....
2821	Current...............	....	....	....	....	....	....	....	....	....	....	....	....
2822	Capital...............	....	....	....	....	....	....	....	....	....	....	....	....

Table 3   Transactions in assets and liabilities

Table 4   Holding gains in assets and liabilities

Table 5   Other changes in the volume of assets and liabilities

Table 6   Balance sheet

Table 7   Outlays by functions of govt.

7	**Total outlays**...............	....	....	**1,322.51**	....	....	....	....	....	....	....	....	....
701	**General public services**.......................	....	....	**329.40**	....	....	....	....	....	....	....	....	....
7017	Public debt transactions.......................	....	....	119.02	....	....	....	....	....	....	....	....	....
7018	General transfers between levels of govt......	....	....	—	....	....	....	....	....	....	....	....	....
702	**Defense**........................	....	....	**97.27**	....	....	....	....	....	....	....	....	....
703	**Public order and safety**.........................	....	....	**84.78**	....	....	....	....	....	....	....	....	....
704	**Economic affairs**............................	....	....	**174.80**	....	....	....	....	....	....	....	....	....
7042	Agriculture, forestry, fishing, and hunting.....	....	....	50.82	....	....	....	....	....	....	....	....	....
7043	Fuel and energy.......................	....	....	6.67	....	....	....	....	....	....	....	....	....
7044	Mining, manufacturing, and construction.....	....	....	32.52	....	....	....	....	....	....	....	....	....
7045	Transport.......................	....	....	75.95	....	....	....	....	....	....	....	....	....
7046	Communication.......................	....	....	1.53	....	....	....	....	....	....	....	....	....
705	**Environmental protection**......................	....	....	**13.18**	....	....	....	....	....	....	....	....	....
706	**Housing and community amenities**........	....	....	**134.05**	....	....	....	....	....	....	....	....	....
707	**Health**...........................	....	....	**128.10**	....	....	....	....	....	....	....	....	....
7072	Outpatient services.......................	....	....	—	....	....	....	....	....	....	....	....	....
7073	Hospital services.......................	....	....	100.60	....	....	....	....	....	....	....	....	....
7074	Public health services.......................	....	....	4.07	....	....	....	....	....	....	....	....	....
708	**Recreation, culture, and religion**...........	....	....	**11.75**	....	....	....	....	....	....	....	....	....
709	**Education**...............	....	....	**293.63**	....	....	....	....	....	....	....	....	....
7091	Pre-primary and primary education..............	....	....	121.93	....	....	....	....	....	....	....	....	....
7092	Secondary education.......................	....	....	106.87	....	....	....	....	....	....	....	....	....
7094	Tertiary education.......................	....	....	42.73	....	....	....	....	....	....	....	....	....
710	**Social protection**...........................	....	....	**55.54**	....	....	....	....	....	....	....	....	....
7	Statistical discrepancy: Total outlays...............	....	....	—	....	....	....	....	....	....	....	....	....

Table 8   Transactions in financial assets and liabilities by sector

In Millions of Euros / Year Ending December 31 / Noncash Reporter

	Budgetary Central Government			Central Government			Local Government			General Government		
	2002	2003p	2004p	2002	2003p	2004p	2002	2003p	2004p	2002	2003p	2004p
Statement of government operations												
1 Revenue............................	38,101	38,058	39,651	56,864	56,854	59,227	26,490	27,295	28,479	76,025	76,332	79,289
2 Expense............................	36,104	37,697	39,213	50,522	52,830	55,207	26,016	27,255	28,762	69,209	72,268	75,552
GOB *Gross operating balance*............	*3,367*	*1,788*	*1,891*	*7,854*	*5,603*	*5,625*	*2,289*	*1,914*	*1,676*	*10,143*	*7,517*	*7,301*
NOB *Net operating balance*............	*1,997*	*361*	*438*	*6,342*	*4,024*	*4,020*	*474*	*40*	*−283*	*6,816*	*4,064*	*3,737*
31 Net acquisition of nonfinancial assets.....	−196	−57	77	−166	25	235	−1,346	714	659	−1,512	739	894
NLB *Net lending/borrowing*............	*2,193*	*418*	*361*	*6,508*	*3,999*	*3,785*	*1,820*	*−674*	*−942*	*8,328*	*3,325*	*2,843*
32 Net acquisition of financial assets........	170	4,290	....	6,251	8,148	....	356	−189	....	6,776	8,232	....
33 Net incurrence of liabilities............	−1,910	3,995	....	281	4,518	....	481	688	....	931	5,479	....
NLB Statistical discrepancy............	−113	−123	....	−538	−369	....	−1,945	−203	....	−2,483	−572	....
Statement of other economic flows												
Balance sheet												
6 *Net worth*............	....	....	....	....	....	....	....	....	....	....	....	....
61 Nonfinancial assets............	....	....	....	....	....	....	....	....	....	....	....	....
62 Financial assets............	42,910	53,389	....	103,047	119,290	....	17,328	17,706	....	115,798	132,693	....
63 Liabilities............	67,578	70,300	....	63,015	65,842	....	12,534	13,218	....	70,972	74,757	....
Statement of sources and uses of cash												
Table 1 Revenue												
1 **Revenue............**	**38,101**	**38,058**	**39,651**	**56,864**	**56,854**	**59,227**	**26,490**	**27,295**	**28,479**	**76,025**	**76,332**	**79,289**
11 **Taxes............**	**32,996**	**33,081**	**34,407**	**32,996**	**33,081**	**34,407**	**13,754**	**13,516**	**13,756**	**46,750**	**46,597**	**48,163**
111 Taxes on income, profits, & capital gains......	12,992	12,068	12,524	12,992	12,068	12,524	13,113	12,848	13,065	26,105	24,916	25,589
1111 Individuals............	8,315	8,054	8,196	8,315	8,054	8,196	11,743	11,851	11,981	20,058	19,905	20,177
1112 Corporations and other enterprises............	4,618	3,955	4,273	4,618	3,955	4,273	1,370	997	1,084	5,988	4,952	5,357
112 Taxes on payroll and workforce............	1	1	1	1	1	1	—	—	—	1	1	1
113 Taxes on property............	905	847	1,018	905	847	1,018	634	661	684	1,539	1,508	1,702
114 Taxes on goods and services............	19,065	20,124	20,818	19,065	20,124	20,818	7	7	7	19,072	20,131	20,825
1141 General taxes on goods and services............	11,391	12,124	12,818	11,391	12,124	12,818	—	—	—	11,391	12,124	12,818
1142 Excises............	5,978	6,196	5,967	5,978	6,196	5,967	1	—	—	5,979	6,196	5,967
115 Taxes on int'l. trade and transactions............	—	—	—	—	—	—	—	—	—	—	—	—
116 Other taxes............	33	41	46	33	41	46	—	—	—	33	41	46
12 **Social contributions............**	**1,382**	**1,412**	**1,427**	**17,252**	**17,354**	**18,051**	**20**	**22**	**22**	**17,272**	**17,376**	**18,073**
121 Social security contributions............	1,382	1,412	1,427	17,252	17,354	18,051	20	22	22	17,272	17,376	18,073
122 Other social contributions............	—	—	—	—	—	—	—	—	—	—	—	—
13 **Grants............**	**382**	**336**	**341**	**750**	**700**	**692**	**6,825**	**7,381**	**8,021**	**321**	**316**	**306**
131 From foreign governments............	—	—	—	—	—	—	—	—	—	—	—	—
132 From international organizations............	172	168	155	209	203	186	112	113	120	321	316	306
133 From other general government units............	210	168	186	541	497	506	6,713	7,268	7,901	—	—	—
14 **Other revenue............**	**3,341**	**3,229**	**3,476**	**5,866**	**5,719**	**6,077**	**5,891**	**6,376**	**6,680**	**11,682**	**12,043**	**12,747**
Table 2 Expense by economic type												
2 **Expense............**	**36,104**	**37,697**	**39,213**	**50,522**	**52,830**	**55,207**	**26,016**	**27,255**	**28,762**	**69,209**	**72,268**	**75,552**
21 **Compensation of employees............**	**4,801**	**5,040**	**5,186**	**5,188**	**5,441**	**5,608**	**13,735**	**14,333**	**15,059**	**18,923**	**19,774**	**20,667**
211 Wages and salaries............	3,853	4,053	4,158	4,152	4,368	4,492	10,571	11,032	11,551	14,723	15,400	16,043
212 Social contributions............	948	987	1,028	1,036	1,073	1,116	3,164	3,301	3,508	4,200	4,374	4,624
22 **Use of goods and services............**	**4,388**	**4,616**	**4,892**	**4,816**	**5,062**	**5,370**	**7,202**	**7,745**	**8,350**	**12,018**	**12,807**	**13,720**
23 **Consumption of fixed capital............**	**1,370**	**1,427**	**1,453**	**1,512**	**1,579**	**1,605**	**1,815**	**1,874**	**1,959**	**3,327**	**3,453**	**3,564**
24 **Interest............**	**3,219**	**2,932**	**2,735**	**2,948**	**2,710**	**2,547**	**214**	**197**	**162**	**3,087**	**2,855**	**2,699**
25 **Subsidies............**	**1,828**	**1,811**	**1,801**	**1,828**	**1,811**	**1,801**	**122**	**117**	**114**	**1,950**	**1,928**	**1,915**
26 **Grants............**	**15,374**	**16,542**	**17,580**	**8,016**	**8,747**	**9,478**	**541**	**497**	**506**	**1,303**	**1,479**	**1,577**
261 To foreign govenments............	—	—	—	—	—	—	—	—	—	—	—	—
262 To international organizations............	1,297	1,475	1,568	1,303	1,479	1,577	—	—	—	1,303	1,479	1,577
263 To other general government units............	14,077	15,067	16,012	6,713	7,268	7,901	541	497	506	—	—	—
2631 Current............	13,259	14,203	15,111	6,574	7,132	7,771	541	497	504	—	—	—
2632 Capital............	818	864	901	139	136	130	—	—	2	—	—	—
27 **Social benefits............**	**3,222**	**3,363**	**3,486**	**24,146**	**25,230**	**26,423**	**1,984**	**1,997**	**2,149**	**26,130**	**27,227**	**28,572**
28 **Other expense............**	**1,902**	**1,966**	**2,080**	**2,068**	**2,250**	**2,375**	**403**	**495**	**463**	**2,471**	**2,745**	**2,838**
281 Property expense other than interest............	4	5	5	4	5	5	3	6	6	7	11	11
282 Miscellaneous other expense............	1,898	1,961	2,075	2,064	2,245	2,370	400	489	457	2,464	2,734	2,827
2821 Current............	1,537	1,606	1,705	1,703	1,890	2,000	395	487	455	2,098	2,377	2,455
2822 Capital............	361	355	370	361	355	370	5	2	2	366	357	372

Finland 172

In Millions of Euros / Year Ending December 31 / Noncash Reporter

	Budgetary Central Government			Central Government			Local Government			General Government		
	2002	2003p	2004p	2002	2003p	2004p	2002	2003p	2004p	2002	2003p	2004p
Table 3 Transactions in assets and liabilities												
3 Change in net worth from transactns....	1,884	238	....	5,804	3,655	....	−1,471	−163	....	4,333	3,492	....
31 Net acquisition of nonfinancial assets...	−196	−57	77	−166	25	235	−1,346	714	659	−1,512	739	894
311 Fixed assets.................................	−242	−108	−44	−212	−26	114	−1,281	864	819	−1,493	838	933
3111 Buildings and structures..................	....	....	....	....	....	....	....	....	....	....	....	....
3112 Machinery and equipment...............	....	....	....	....	....	....	....	....	....	....	....	....
3113 Other fixed assets........................	....	....	....	....	....	....	....	....	....	....	....	....
312 Inventories.................................	2	17	80	2	17	80	—	—	—	2	17	80
313 Valuables...................................	—	—	—	—	—	—	—	—	—	—	—	—
314 Nonproduced assets.......................	44	34	41	44	34	41	−65	−150	−160	−21	−116	−119
3141 Land.......................................	16	9	17	16	9	17	−65	−150	−166	−49	−141	−149
3142 Subsoil assets.............................	—	—	—	—	—	—	—	—	—	—	—	—
3143 Other naturally occurring assets........	—	—	—	—	—	—	—	—	—	—	—	—
3144 Intangible nonproduced assets.........	28	25	24	28	25	24	—	—	—	28	25	24
32 Net acquisition of financial assets........	170	4,290	....	6,251	8,148	....	356	−189	....	6,776	8,232	....
321 Domestic...................................	−3,445	−124	....	−3,865	−747	....	250	−230	....	−3,446	−704	....
3212 Currency and deposits...................	456	653	....	609	655	....	355	−204	....	964	451	....
3213 Securities other than shares............	−119	−629	....	−552	−617	....	−302	251	....	−765	−246	....
3214 Loans.....................................	−13	−25	....	−106	−308	....	50	−196	....	−68	−357	....
3215 Shares and other equity.................	−4,110	11	....	−4,091	−584	....	223	78	....	−3,742	−506	....
3216 Insurance technical reserves............	—	—	....	—	—	....	—	1	....	—	1	....
3217 Financial derivatives....................	—	—	....	—	—	....	11	—	....	11	—	....
3218 Other accounts receivable..............	341	−134	....	275	107	....	−87	−160	....	154	−47	....
322 Foreign....................................	3,615	4,414	....	10,116	8,895	....	106	41	....	10,222	8,936	....
3222 Currency and deposits...................	−524	3,776	....	33	3,342	....	—	4	....	33	3,346	....
3223 Securities other than shares............	472	361	....	3,806	1,371	....	90	28	....	3,896	1,399	....
3224 Loans.....................................	−20	—	....	37	−64	....	—	—	....	37	−64	....
3225 Shares and other equity.................	3,494	343	....	5,815	4,528	....	16	9	....	5,831	4,537	....
3226 Insurance technical reserves............	—	—	....	—	—	....	—	—	....	—	—	....
3227 Financial derivatives....................	—	—	....	—	—	....	—	—	....	—	—	....
3228 Other accounts receivable..............	193	−66	....	425	−282	....	—	—	....	425	−282	....
323 Monetary gold and SDRs..................	—	—	....	—	—	....	—	—	....	—	—	....
33 Net incurrence of liabilities..................	−1,910	3,995	....	281	4,518	....	481	688	....	931	5,479	....
331 Domestic...................................	−6,300	−1,192	....	−4,255	−889	....	−36	268	....	−4,122	−348	....
3312 Currency and deposits...................	26	28	....	26	28	....	—	—	....	26	28	....
3313 Securities other than shares............	−6,673	−2,120	....	−4,627	−1,874	....	−170	64	....	−4,723	−1,690	....
3314 Loans.....................................	29	1,160	....	67	1,159	....	−19	272	....	177	1,578	....
3316 Insurance technical reserves............	—	—	....	1	—	....	15	—	....	16	—	....
3317 Financial derivatives....................	—	—	....	—	—	....	—	—	....	—	—	....
3318 Other accounts payable.................	318	−260	....	278	−202	....	138	−68	....	382	−264	....
332 Foreign....................................	4,390	5,187	....	4,536	5,407	....	517	420	....	5,053	5,827	....
3322 Currency and deposits...................	—	—	....	—	—	....	—	—	....	—	—	....
3323 Securities other than shares............	4,444	3,601	....	4,511	3,878	....	−80	46	....	4,431	3,924	....
3324 Loans.....................................	−38	1,593	....	−38	1,593	....	543	432	....	505	2,025	....
3326 Insurance technical reserves............	—	—	....	—	—	....	—	—	....	—	—	....
3327 Financial derivatives....................	—	—	....	—	—	....	—	—	....	—	—	....
3328 Other accounts payable.................	−16	−7	....	63	−64	....	54	−58	....	117	−122	....
Table 4 Holding gains in assets and liabilities												
Table 5 Other changes in the volume of assets and liabilities												
Table 6 Balance sheet												
6 Net worth.................................	....	....	....	....	....	....	....	....	....	....	....	....
61 Nonfinancial assets........................	....	....	....	....	....	....	....	....	....	....	....	....
611 Fixed assets................................	....	....	....	....	....	....	....	....	....	....	....	....
6111 Buildings and structures..................	....	....	....	....	....	....	....	....	....	....	....	....
6112 Machinery and equipment...............	....	....	....	....	....	....	....	....	....	....	....	....
6113 Other fixed assets........................	....	....	....	....	....	....	....	....	....	....	....	....
612 Inventories.................................	....	....	....	....	....	....	....	....	....	....	....	....
613 Valuables...................................	....	....	....	....	....	....	....	....	....	....	....	....
614 Nonproduced assets.......................	....	....	....	....	....	....	....	....	....	....	....	....
6141 Land.......................................	....	....	....	....	....	....	....	....	....	....	....	....
6142 Subsoil assets.............................	....	....	....	....	....	....	....	....	....	....	....	....
6143 Other naturally occurring assets........	....	....	....	....	....	....	....	....	....	....	....	....
6144 Intangible nonproduced assets.........	....	....	....	....	....	....	....	....	....	....	....	....

2005, International Monetary Fund: *Government Finance Statistics Yearbook*

In Millions of Euros / Year Ending December 31 / Noncash Reporter

		Budgetary Central Government			Central Government			Local Government			General Government		
		2002	2003p	2004p	2002	2003p	2004p	2002	2003p	2004p	2002	2003p	2004p
62	**Financial assets.....................**	**42,910**	**53,389**	....	**103,047**	**119,290**	....	**17,328**	**17,706**	....	**115,798**	**132,693**	....
621	Domestic.....................................	33,342	38,981	....	56,464	62,402	....	17,105	17,452	....	68,992	75,551	....
6212	Currency and deposits..................	1,361	2,014	....	2,237	2,892	....	1,200	996	....	3,437	3,888	....
6213	Securities other than shares..........	1,269	620	....	5,117	4,413	....	1,478	1,731	....	6,288	5,955	....
6214	Loans...	11,667	12,643	....	18,247	18,939	....	4,173	3,977	....	20,790	21,433	....
6215	Shares and other equity................	17,676	22,156	....	28,445	33,320	....	7,511	8,164	....	33,568	39,099	....
6216	Insurance technical reserves.........	—	—	....	—	—	....	78	79	....	78	79	....
6217	Financial derivatives....................	—	—	....	—	—	....			....			....
6218	Other accounts receivable.............	1,369	1,548	....	2,418	2,838	....	2,665	2,505	....	4,831	5,097	....
622	Foreign.......................................	9,568	14,408	....	46,583	56,888	....	223	254	....	46,806	57,142	....
6222	Currency and deposits..................	583	4,337	....	1,249	4,569	....	—	4	....	1,249	4,573	....
6223	Securities other than shares..........	1,890	2,212	....	28,242	29,446	....	186	200	....	28,428	29,646	....
6224	Loans...	60	60	....	125	61	....	—	—	....	125	61	....
6225	Shares and other equity................	5,093	5,958	....	14,202	20,364	....	37	50	....	14,239	20,414	....
6226	Insurance technical reserves.........	—	—	....	—	—	....	—	—	....	—	—	....
6227	Financial derivatives....................	—	—	....	—	—	....			....	—	—	....
6228	Other accounts receivable.............	1,942	1,841	....	2,765	2,448	....			....	2,765	2,448	....
623	Monetary gold and SDRs..............	—	—	....			....			....			....
63	**Liabilities...............................**	**67,578**	**70,300**	....	**63,015**	**65,842**	....	**12,534**	**13,218**	....	**70,972**	**74,757**	....
631	Domestic.....................................	18,024	16,903	....	13,330	12,361	....	11,194	11,457	....	19,947	19,515	....
6312	Currency and deposits..................	236	264	....	236	264	....	—	—	....	236	75	....
6313	Securities other than shares..........	13,786	11,529	....	8,891	6,718	....	375	437	....	8,959	5,672	....
6314	Loans...	1,575	2,735	....	1,623	2,780	....	4,556	4,828	....	4,549	7,608	....
6316	Insurance technical reserves.........	—	—	....	—	—	....	—	—	....	—	—	....
6317	Financial derivatives....................	—	—	....	25	38	....	2,388	2,385	....	25	38	....
6318	Other accounts payable................	2,427	2,375	....	2,555	2,561	....	3,875	3,807	....	6,178	6,122	....
632	Foreign.......................................	49,554	53,397	....	49,685	53,481	....	1,340	1,761	....	51,025	55,242	....
6322	Currency and deposits..................			....			....			....			....
6323	Securities other than shares..........	47,100	49,380	....	47,113	49,403	....	69	116	....	47,182	49,519	....
6324	Loans...	2,422	3,992	....	2,422	3,992	....	919	1,351	....	3,341	5,343	....
6326	Insurance technical reserves.........	—	—	....	—	—	....			....	—	—	....
6327	Financial derivatives....................	—	—	....	—	—	....			....	—	—	....
6328	Other accounts payable................	32	25	....	150	86	....	352	294	....	502	380	....
	Memorandum items:												
6M2	Net financial worth......................	−24,668	−16,911	....	40,032	53,448	....	4,794	4,488	....	44,826	57,936	....
6M3	Debt at market value....................	64,453	65,441	....	55,335	59,702	....	5,919	6,732	....	59,562	64,930	....
6M4	Debt at nominal value...................	....	....	....	....	....		....	....	....	....	....	....
6M5	Arrears.......................................	....	....	....	....	....		....	....	....	....	....	....
6M6	Obligations for social security benefits...........	....	....	....	....	....		....	....	....	....	....	....
6M7	Contingent liabilities....................	....	....	....	....	....		....	....	....	....	....	....
6M8	Uncapitalized military weapons, systems........	....	....	....	....	....		....	....	....	....	....	....
	Table 7 Outlays by functions of govt.												
7	**Total outlays........................**	**35,942**	**37,640**	**39,290**	**50,390**	**52,855**	**55,442**	**25,080**	**27,969**	**29,421**	**68,141**	**73,007**	**76,446**
701	**General public services......................**	**7,314**	**7,387**	....	**6,384**	**7,174**	....	**3,193**	**3,421**	....	**8,522**	**8,789**	....
7017	Public debt transactions.............................	3,219	2,932	2,735	2,948	2,710	2,547	214	197	162	3,087	2,855	2,699
7018	General transfers between levels of govt......	....	....		....	....		....	....		....	....	
702	**Defense................................**	**2,024**	**2,239**	....	**2,024**	**2,239**	....	**—**	**—**	....	**2,024**	**2,239**	....
703	**Public order and safety.................**	**1,578**	**1,646**	....	**1,578**	**1,646**	....	**397**	**446**	....	**1,968**	**2,082**	....
704	**Economic affairs......................**	**5,220**	**5,355**	....	**5,220**	**5,282**	....	**1,977**	**2,068**	....	**6,968**	**7,215**	....
7042	Agriculture, forestry, fishing, and hunting......	....	....	....	....	....		....	....		....	....	
7043	Fuel and energy.........................	....	....	....	....	....	....	....	....	....	....	....	....
7044	Mining, manufacturing, and construction......	....	....		....	....		....	....		....	....	
7045	Transport...................................	....	....	....	....	....		....	....		....	....	
7046	Communication...........................	....	....		....	....		....	....		....	....	
705	**Environmental protection.................**	**267**	**280**	....	**267**	**273**	....	**217**	**221**	....	**456**	**484**	....
706	**Housing and community amenities........**	**359**	**316**	....	**359**	**319**	....	**311**	**243**	....	**670**	**559**	....
707	**Health...................................**	**2,755**	**3,074**	....	**4,147**	**4,579**	....	**7,330**	**7,706**	....	**8,846**	**9,335**	....
7072	Outpatient services......................	....	....		....	....		....	....		....	....	
7073	Hospital services.........................	....	....		....	....		....	....		....	....	
7074	Public health services...................	....	....		....	....		....	....		....	....	
708	**Recreation, culture, and religion...........**	**579**	**566**	....	**579**	**566**	....	**1,292**	**1,381**	....	**1,703**	**1,776**	....

		Budgetary Central Government			Central Government			Local Government			General Government		
		2002	2003p	2004p	2002	2003p	2004p	2002	2003p	2004p	2002	2003p	2004p
709	**Education**..............................	**5,539**	**5,724**	....	**6,292**	**5,786**	....	**5,719**	**5,975**	....	**9,172**	**9,504**	....
7091	Pre-primary and primary education.............	....	....	....	....	....	....	....	....	....	....	....	....
7092	Secondary education...................	....	....	....	....	....	....	....	....	....	....	....	....
7094	Tertiary education........................	....	....	....	....	....	....	....	....	....	....	....	....
710	**Social protection**......................	**10,444**	**11,054**	....	**23,800**	**24,992**	....	**6,323**	**6,529**	....	**29,751**	**31,037**	....
7	Statistical discrepancy: Total outlays.............	−137	−1	....	−260	−1	....	−1,679	−21	....	−1,939	−13	....
Table 8 Transactions in financial assets and liabilities by sector													
82	**Net acquisition of financial assets**........	**170**	**4,290**	....	**6,251**	**8,148**	....	**356**	**−189**	....	**6,776**	**8,232**	....
821	Domestic...............................	−3,445	−124	....	−3,865	−747	....	250	−230	....	−3,446	−704	....
8211	General government......................	−117	2	....	−143	11	....	−26	−80	....	—	—	....
8212	Central bank...........................	−1	1	....	1	−1	....	—	—	....	1	−1	....
8213	Other depository corporations..................	325	37	....	322	−225	....	256	194	....	578	173	....
8214	Financial corporations n.e.c...................	−64	294	....	−262	161	....	281	3	....	19	164	....
8215	Nonfinancial corporations...................	−3,530	−359	....	−3,738	−575	....	58	−86	....	−3,680	−661	....
8216	Households & NPIs serving households......	−58	−99	....	−45	−118	....	−319	−261	....	−364	−379	....
822	Foreign................................	3,615	4,414	....	10,116	8,895	....	106	41	....	10,222	8,936	....
8221	General government......................	....	....	....	....	....	....	....	....	....	....	....	....
8227	International organizations..................	....	....	....	....	....	....	....	....	....	....	....	....
8228	Financial corporations other than international organizations.............	....	....	....	....	....	....	....	....	....	....	....	....
8229	Other nonresidents.......................	....	....	....	....	....	....	....	....	....	....	....	....
823	Monetary gold and SDRs................	—	—	....	—	—	....	—	—	....	—	—	....
83	**Net incurrence of liabilities**...................	**−1,910**	**3,995**	....	**281**	**4,518**	....	**481**	**688**	....	**931**	**5,479**	....
831	Domestic...............................	−6,300	−1,192	....	−4,255	−889	....	−36	268	....	−4,122	−348	....
8311	General government......................	−2,018	−335	....	−33	−82	....	−136	−191	....	—	—	....
8312	Central bank...........................	−187	−2	....	−187	−2	....	—	—	....	−187	−2	....
8313	Other depository corporations..................	−3,199	604	....	−3,193	597	....	−31	377	....	−3,224	974	....
8314	Financial corporations n.e.c...................	−1,730	−433	....	−1,705	−423	....	−29	6	....	−1,734	−417	....
8315	Nonfinancial corporations...................	632	−863	....	634	−810	....	84	126	....	718	−684	....
8316	Households & NPIs serving households......	202	−163	....	229	−169	....	76	−50	....	305	−219	....
832	Foreign................................	4,390	5,187	....	4,536	5,407	....	517	420	....	5,053	5,827	....
8321	General government......................	....	....	....	....	....	....	....	....	....	....	....	....
8327	International organizations..................	....	....	....	....	....	....	....	....	....	....	....	....
8328	Financial corporations other than international organizations.............	....	....	....	....	....	....	....	....	....	....	....	....
8329	Other nonresidents.......................	....	....	....	....	....	....	....	....	....	....	....	....

France 132

In Billions of Euros / Year Ending December 31 / Noncash Reporter

	Budgetary Central Government			Central Government			Local Government			General Government		
	2002	2003p	2004p	2002	2003p	2004p	2002	2003p	2004p	2002	2003p	2004p
Statement of government operations												
1 Revenue................................	340.14	338.63	371.26	680.46	690.66	719.30	156.95	165.21	176.78	772.34	787.63	826.17
2 Expense................................	387.88	395.10	413.41	731.64	755.89	775.61	146.69	153.71	166.24	813.26	841.36	871.94
GOB *Gross operating balance................*	*−37.43*	*−46.58*	*−31.91*	*−36.73*	*−50.98*	*−41.54*	*34.99*	*35.88*	*36.23*	*−1.75*	*−15.10*	*−5.31*
NOB *Net operating balance................*	*−47.74*	*−56.48*	*−42.15*	*−51.18*	*−65.23*	*−56.31*	*10.27*	*11.50*	*10.54*	*−40.91*	*−53.73*	*−45.77*
31 Net acquisition of nonfinancial assets.........	−.20	.90	.20	.10	1.90	1.90	8.10	11.00	12.50	8.20	12.90	14.40
NLB *Net lending/borrowing................*	*−47.54*	*−57.38*	*−42.35*	*−51.28*	*−67.13*	*−58.21*	*2.17*	*.50*	*−1.96*	*−49.11*	*−66.63*	*−60.17*
32 Net acquisition of financial assets..........	4.62	25.29	−4.71	15.49	49.02	1.53	2.84	3.53	1.26	15.18	40.46	7.47
33 Net incurrence of liabilities..........	52.11	82.30	38.06	67.35	116.14	59.96	.59	3.03	3.20	64.78	107.08	67.83
NLB Statistical discrepancy..........	.10	.40	−.40	−.60	—	−.20	.10	—	—	−.50	—	−.20
Statement of other economic flows												
4 *Change in net worth from holding gains................*	*−28.76*	*21.37*	....	*−34.82*	*28.51*	....	*54.70*	*69.42*	....	*19.89*	*97.93*	....
41 Nonfinancial assets................	9.56	10.40	....	11.53	12.90	....	54.38	68.90	....	65.91	81.80	....
42 Financial assets................	−21.87	6.21	14.50	−29.95	10.77	17.91	.10	.19	.21	−29.85	10.96	18.11
43 Liabilities................	16.45	−4.76	18.91	16.40	−4.84	19.06	−.23	−.33	−.02	16.17	−5.17	19.04
5 *Change in net worth from other volume changes................*	*−1.55*	*−9.68*	....	*−3.41*	*−3.32*	....	*−1.47*	*−3.30*	....	*−4.88*	*−6.63*	....
51 Nonfinancial assets................	.20	−3.20	....	.20	—	....	−4.20	−3.00	....	−4.00	−3.00	....
52 Financial assets................	−3.35	6.19	18.44	−2.29	−1.01	19.54	−.30	−.22	—	−3.34	−.42	18.44
53 Liabilities................	−1.60	12.67	36.86	1.32	2.31	4.95	−3.03	.08	—	−2.46	3.20	3.85
Balance sheet												
6 *Net worth................*	*−495.52*	*−540.05*	....	*−354.30*	*−397.60*	....	*636.56*	*714.13*	....	*282.26*	*316.54*	....
61 Nonfinancial assets................	175.21	183.20	....	223.96	235.50	....	701.04	777.90	....	925.01	1,013.40	....
62 Financial assets................	223.63	261.32	289.54	389.04	447.81	486.79	54.79	58.29	59.76	387.02	438.02	482.04
63 Liabilities................	894.36	984.57	1,078.39	967.30	1,080.91	1,164.87	119.28	122.06	125.24	1,029.77	1,134.88	1,225.60
Statement of sources and uses of cash												
Table 1 Revenue												
1 **Revenue................**	**340.14**	**338.63**	**371.26**	**680.46**	**690.66**	**719.30**	**156.95**	**165.21**	**176.78**	**772.34**	**787.63**	**826.17**
11 **Taxes................**	**265.50**	**265.73**	**295.49**	**349.68**	**351.73**	**368.88**	**63.75**	**66.75**	**75.39**	**413.43**	**418.48**	**444.27**
111 Taxes on income, profits, & capital gains......	97.51	94.69	100.94	161.74	160.35	168.18	—	—	—	161.74	160.35	168.18
1111 Individuals................	59.29	61.56	62.05	122.28	126.30	128.86	—	—	—	122.28	126.30	128.86
1112 Corporations and other enterprises..........	38.20	33.13	38.89	39.45	34.04	39.32	—	—	—	39.45	34.04	39.32
112 Taxes on payroll and workforce................	11.86	12.22	13.95	12.44	12.74	13.95	4.35	4.73	5.00	16.79	17.47	18.95
113 Taxes on property................	12.67	12.84	15.02	12.89	12.84	15.02	51.88	54.25	58.02	64.77	67.09	73.04
114 Taxes on goods and services................	143.46	145.99	165.48	162.47	165.70	171.62	7.15	7.40	11.97	169.62	173.10	183.60
1141 General taxes on goods and services..........	103.82	107.11	115.53	103.85	107.45	115.55	—	—	—	103.85	107.45	115.55
1142 Excises................	26.30	26.00	29.49	38.80	38.07	32.22	1.08	1.48	5.97	39.88	39.54	38.19
115 Taxes on int'l. trade and transactions..........	—	−.01	.01	—	−.01	.01	.25	.26	.28	.25	.26	.29
116 Other taxes................	—	—	.10	.14	.11	.10	.12	.11	.12	.26	.22	.22
12 **Social contributions................**	**32.33**	**33.64**	**34.47**	**277.83**	**288.80**	**297.65**	**.43**	**.46**	**.49**	**278.26**	**289.27**	**298.14**
121 Social security contributions................	5.63	5.66	5.73	250.32	259.93	267.98	—	—	—	250.32	259.93	267.98
122 Other social contributions................	26.70	27.98	28.74	27.51	28.87	29.67	.43	.46	.49	27.94	29.33	30.16
13 **Grants................**	**11.73**	**12.37**	**12.31**	**5.47**	**5.52**	**5.68**	**60.91**	**63.98**	**65.71**	**1.31**	**1.27**	**1.47**
131 From foreign governments................	—	—	—	—	—	—	—	—	—	—	—	—
132 From international organizations................	.80	.77	.93	.91	.86	1.02	.40	.42	.45	1.31	1.27	1.47
133 From other general government units................	10.93	11.60	11.38	4.56	4.67	4.66	60.51	63.57	65.26	—	—	—
14 **Other revenue................**	**30.58**	**26.90**	**28.99**	**47.49**	**44.60**	**47.10**	**31.86**	**34.01**	**35.19**	**79.35**	**78.62**	**82.29**
Table 2 Expense by economic type												
2 **Expense................**	**387.88**	**395.10**	**413.41**	**731.64**	**755.89**	**775.61**	**146.69**	**153.71**	**166.24**	**813.26**	**841.36**	**871.94**
21 **Compensation of employees................**	**116.48**	**119.25**	**120.95**	**161.99**	**166.68**	**170.45**	**46.49**	**48.96**	**51.36**	**208.48**	**215.65**	**221.82**
211 Wages and salaries................	77.70	78.87	79.93	111.09	113.59	116.09	34.28	36.01	37.72	145.36	149.60	153.81
212 Social contributions................	38.78	40.38	41.03	50.91	53.10	54.36	12.22	12.95	13.65	63.12	66.05	68.01
22 **Use of goods and services................**	**31.06**	**30.44**	**32.48**	**51.34**	**52.02**	**55.02**	**34.33**	**37.30**	**40.05**	**85.68**	**89.32**	**95.07**
23 **Consumption of fixed capital................**	**10.31**	**9.89**	**10.24**	**14.45**	**14.25**	**14.77**	**24.72**	**24.38**	**25.69**	**39.17**	**38.63**	**40.46**
24 **Interest................**	**41.53**	**41.49**	**41.41**	**42.40**	**42.29**	**42.49**	**4.44**	**3.31**	**2.80**	**46.85**	**45.60**	**45.29**
25 **Subsidies................**	**15.96**	**15.45**	**13.12**	**16.10**	**15.45**	**13.12**	**9.80**	**10.50**	**11.63**	**25.90**	**25.95**	**24.76**
26 **Grants................**	**82.51**	**86.10**	**104.21**	**65.67**	**68.51**	**71.18**	**4.56**	**4.67**	**4.66**	**5.16**	**4.94**	**5.92**
261 To foreign governments................	—	—	—	—	—	—	—	—	—	—	—	—
262 To international organizations................	5.16	4.93	5.91	5.16	4.94	5.92	—	—	—	5.16	4.94	5.92
263 To other general government units................	77.35	81.18	98.29	60.51	63.57	65.26	4.56	4.67	4.66	—	—	—
2631 Current................	70.41	72.81	91.06	53.60	56.46	57.98	3.29	3.38	3.44	—	—	—
2632 Capital................	6.94	8.37	7.23	6.91	7.11	7.28	1.27	1.29	1.22	—	—	—

France 132

In Billions of Euros / Year Ending December 31 / Noncash Reporter

		Budgetary Central Government			Central Government			Local Government			General Government		
		2002	2003p	2004p	2002	2003p	2004p	2002	2003p	2004p	2002	2003p	2004p
27	Social benefits	63.70	64.66	62.35	343.29	359.17	369.35	7.41	9.22	14.67	350.70	368.39	384.02
28	Other expense	26.32	27.82	28.65	36.39	37.52	39.22	14.93	15.37	15.38	51.32	52.89	54.60
281	Property expense other than interest	—	—	—	—	—	—	.03	.03	.03	.03	.03	.03
282	Miscellaneous other expense	26.32	27.82	28.65	36.39	37.52	39.22	14.91	15.34	15.35	51.30	52.86	54.57
2821	Current	14.40	17.27	17.38	22.41	24.73	25.39	11.96	12.24	12.31	34.37	36.98	37.70
2822	Capital	11.92	10.55	11.27	13.98	12.78	13.84	2.95	3.10	3.03	16.93	15.88	16.87

Table 3 Transactions in assets and liabilities

		2002	2003p	2004p	2002	2003p	2004p	2002	2003p	2004p	2002	2003p	2004p
3	Change in net worth from transactns	−47.74	−56.11	−42.57	−51.18	−65.22	−56.52	10.27	11.50	10.56	−40.91	−53.72	−45.96
31	Net acquisition of nonfinancial assets	−.20	.90	.20	.10	1.90	1.90	8.10	11.00	12.50	8.20	12.90	14.40
311	Fixed assets	−.60	.70	—	−.30	1.70	1.70	6.50	9.30	10.30	6.20	11.00	12.00
3111	Buildings and structures	−.70	.30	....	−.60	1.00	....	5.40	8.10	....	4.80	9.10	....
3112	Machinery and equipment	−.10	.20	....	—	.40	....	.70	1.00	....	.70	1.40	....
3113	Other fixed assets	.20	.20	....	.30	.30	....	.40	.20	....	.70	.50	....
312	Inventories	.80	.10	.10	.80	.10	.10	.20	.20	.20	1.00	.30	.30
313	Valuables	—	—	—	—	—	—	—	—	—	—	—	—
314	Nonproduced assets	−.40	.10	.10	−.40	.10	.10	1.40	1.50	2.00	1.00	1.60	2.10
3141	Land	.20	.10	....	.20	.10	....	1.40	1.50	....	1.60	1.60	....
3142	Subsoil assets	—	—	....	—	—	....	—	—	....	—	—	....
3143	Other naturally occurring assets	—	—	....	—	—	....	—	—	....	—	—	....
3144	Intangible nonproduced assets	−.60	—	....	−.60	—	....	—	—	....	−.60	—	....
32	Net acquisition of financial assets	4.62	25.29	−4.71	15.49	49.02	1.53	2.84	3.53	1.26	15.18	40.46	7.47
321	Domestic	4.37	22.40	−4.71	15.31	46.02	1.54	2.84	3.53	1.26	15.00	37.47	7.47
3212	Currency and deposits	14.66	12.90	3.75	14.85	11.58	4.54	1.74	2.11	.14	14.46	12.13	4.67
3213	Securities other than shares	−.16	−1.81	.53	−5.21	−3.74	3.10	.29	.15	−.45	−4.88	−3.26	.78
3214	Loans	.25	−.24	.48	.32	−.21	.48	.04	.37	.05	−.07	.07	.47
3215	Shares and other equity	−6.37	10.83	−4.26	1.46	18.37	1.96	.47	.07	−.01	1.94	18.44	1.95
3216	Insurance technical reserves	—	—	—	—	—	—	—	—	—	—	—	—
3217	Financial derivatives	—	—	—	—	—	—	—	—	—	—	—	—
3218	Other accounts receivable	−4.00	.72	−5.21	3.88	20.03	−8.54	.29	.83	1.54	3.55	10.09	−.40
322	Foreign	.24	2.90	−.01	.18	3.00	−.01	—	—	—	.18	3.00	−.01
3222	Currency and deposits	−.02	−.01	.02	−.02	−.01	.02	—	—	—	−.02	−.01	.02
3223	Securities other than shares	—	.08	—	—	.08	—	—	—	—	—	.08	—
3224	Loans	−.67	1.94	−.49	−.67	1.94	−.49	—	—	—	−.67	1.94	−.49
3225	Shares and other equity	—	—	—	—	—	—	—	—	—	—	—	—
3226	Insurance technical reserves	—	—	—	—	—	—	—	—	—	—	—	—
3227	Financial derivatives	—	—	—	—	—	—	—	—	—	—	—	—
3228	Other accounts receivable	.93	.89	.47	.87	.99	.47	—	—	—	.87	.99	.47
323	Monetary gold and SDRs	—	—	—	—	—	—	—	—	—	—	—	—
33	Net incurrence of liabilities	52.11	82.30	38.06	67.35	116.14	59.96	.59	3.03	3.19	64.78	107.08	67.83
331	Domestic	32.86	63.72	11.14	48.10	97.56	33.04	.68	3.25	3.19	45.63	88.72	40.91
3312	Currency and deposits	−4.86	−5.09	.30	−4.86	−5.09	.30	—	—	—	−6.99	−6.65	.30
3313	Securities other than shares	46.99	64.37	44.96	45.48	68.25	44.28	−.59	−.39	−.18	44.93	68.19	42.23
3314	Loans	−1.87	−.21	−24.15	3.89	11.14	−1.70	.61	4.42	2.45	4.06	15.46	.69
3316	Insurance technical reserves	—	—	—	—	—	—	—	—	—	—	—	—
3317	Financial derivatives	—	—	—	—	—	—	—	—	—	—	—	—
3318	Other accounts payable	−7.40	4.65	−9.97	3.59	23.26	−9.84	.66	−.77	.93	3.63	11.72	−2.31
332	Foreign	19.25	18.59	26.92	19.25	18.58	26.92	−.09	−.22	—	19.15	18.36	26.92
3322	Currency and deposits	.20	.42	−1.26	.20	.42	−1.26	—	—	—	.20	.42	−1.26
3323	Securities other than shares	19.67	17.86	27.78	19.67	17.86	27.78	—	—	—	19.67	17.86	27.78
3324	Loans	−.25	−.42	—	−.25	−.42	—	−.09	−.22	—	−.34	−.63	—
3326	Insurance technical reserves	—	—	—	—	—	—	—	—	—	—	—	—
3327	Financial derivatives	—	—	—	—	—	—	—	—	—	—	—	—
3328	Other accounts payable	−.37	.72	.39	−.37	.72	.39	—	—	—	−.37	.72	.39

Table 4 Holding gains in assets and liabilities

		2002	2003p	2004p	2002	2003p	2004p	2002	2003p	2004p	2002	2003p	2004p
4	Change in net worth from hold. gains	−28.76	21.37	....	−34.82	28.51	....	54.70	69.42	....	19.89	97.93	....
41	Nonfinancial assets	9.56	10.40	....	11.53	12.90	....	54.38	68.90	....	65.91	81.80	....
411	Fixed assets	1.99	2.10	....	1.89	1.80	....	12.55	13.70	....	14.44	15.50	....
412	Inventories	−.14	−.10	....	−.14	−.10	....	−.61	−.50	....	−.75	−.60	....
413	Valuables	—	—	....	—	—	....	—	—	....	—	—	....
414	Nonproduced assets	7.71	8.40	....	9.78	11.20	....	42.44	55.70	....	52.22	66.90	....
42	Financial assets	−21.87	6.21	14.50	−29.95	10.77	17.91	.10	.19	.21	−29.85	10.96	18.11
421	Domestic	−21.88	6.22	14.50	−29.95	10.78	17.91	.10	.19	.21	−29.85	10.96	18.11
422	Foreign	.01	−.01	—	.01	−.01	—	—	—	—	.01	−.01	—
423	Monetary gold and SDRs	—	—	—	—	—	—	—	—	—	—	—	—

In Billions of Euros / Year Ending December 31 / Noncash Reporter

		Budgetary Central Government			Central Government			Local Government			General Government		
		2002	2003p	2004p	2002	2003p	2004p	2002	2003p	2004p	2002	2003p	2004p
43	**Liabilities**	**16.45**	**−4.76**	**18.91**	**16.40**	**−4.84**	**19.06**	**−.23**	**−.33**	**−.02**	**16.17**	**−5.17**	**19.04**
431	Domestic	18.03	−4.25	18.91	17.98	−4.33	19.06	−.23	−.33	−.02	17.76	−4.66	19.04
432	Foreign	−1.58	−.51	—	−1.58	−.51	—	—	—	—	−1.58	−.51	—

Table 5 Other changes in the volume of assets and liabilities

		Budgetary Central Government			Central Government			Local Government			General Government		
		2002	2003p	2004p	2002	2003p	2004p	2002	2003p	2004p	2002	2003p	2004p
5	**Change in net worth from vol. chngs**	**−1.55**	**−9.68**	....	**−3.41**	**−3.32**	....	**−1.47**	**−3.30**	....	**−4.88**	**−6.63**	....
51	**Nonfinancial assets**	**.20**	**−3.20**	....	**.20**	**—**	....	**−4.20**	**−3.00**	....	**−4.00**	**−3.00**	....
511	Fixed assets	—	—	....	—	—	....	—	—	....	—	—	....
512	Inventories	—	−3.10	....	—	—	....	—	—	....	—	—	....
513	Valuables	—	—	....	—	—	....	—	—	....	—	—	....
514	Nonproduced assets	.20	−.10	....	.20	—	....	−4.20	−3.00	....	−4.00	−3.00	....
52	**Financial assets**	**−3.35**	**6.19**	**18.44**	**−2.29**	**−1.01**	**19.54**	**−.30**	**−.22**	**—**	**−3.34**	**−.42**	**18.44**
521	Domestic	−2.53	9.37	18.44	−1.54	2.27	19.54	−.30	−.22	—	−2.58	2.86	18.44
522	Foreign	−.82	−3.19	—	−.76	−3.28	—	—	—	—	−.76	−3.28	—
523	Monetary gold and SDRs	—	—	—	—	—	—	—	—	—	—	—	—
53	**Liabilities**	**−1.60**	**12.67**	**36.86**	**1.32**	**2.31**	**4.95**	**−3.03**	**.08**	**—**	**−2.46**	**3.20**	**3.85**
531	Domestic	−8.09	−5.35	36.86	−5.17	−15.71	4.95	−3.03	.08	—	−8.95	−14.82	3.85
532	Foreign	6.49	18.02	—	6.49	18.02	—	—	—	—	6.49	18.02	—

Table 6 Balance sheet

		Budgetary Central Government			Central Government			Local Government			General Government		
		2002	2003p	2004p	2002	2003p	2004p	2002	2003p	2004p	2002	2003p	2004p
6	**Net worth**	**−495.52**	**−540.05**	....	**−354.30**	**−397.60**	....	**636.56**	**714.13**	....	**282.26**	**316.54**	....
61	**Nonfinancial assets**	**175.21**	**183.20**	....	**223.96**	**235.50**	....	**701.04**	**777.90**	....	**925.01**	**1,013.40**	....
611	Fixed assets	122.62	125.40	....	161.15	164.60	....	489.41	512.40	....	650.57	677.00	....
6111	Buildings and structures	106.04	109.20	....	137.42	141.30	....	470.98	493.40	....	608.40	634.70	....
6112	Machinery and equipment	13.66	13.20	....	19.38	18.90	....	15.45	15.90	....	34.82	34.80	....
6113	Other fixed assets	2.93	3.00	....	4.35	4.40	....	2.99	3.10	....	7.34	7.50	....
612	Inventories	13.06	10.00	....	13.06	10.00	....	3.90	3.60	....	16.96	13.60	....
613	Valuables	—	—	....	—	—	....	—	—	....	—	—	....
614	Nonproduced assets	39.53	47.80	....	49.75	60.90	....	207.73	261.90	....	257.48	322.80	....
6141	Land	36.91	46.50	....	47.13	59.60	....	207.73	261.90	....	254.85	321.50	....
6142	Subsoil assets	2.63	1.30	....	2.63	1.30	....	—	—	....	2.63	1.30	....
6143	Other naturally occurring assets	—	—	....	—	—	....	—	—	....	—	—	....
6144	Intangible nonproduced assets	—	—	....	—	—	....	—	—	....	—	—	....
62	**Financial assets**	**223.63**	**261.32**	**289.54**	**389.04**	**447.81**	**486.79**	**54.79**	**58.29**	**59.76**	**387.02**	**438.02**	**482.04**
621	Domestic	211.16	249.14	277.37	375.29	434.35	473.34	54.79	58.29	59.76	373.27	424.56	468.59
6212	Currency and deposits	34.51	48.19	51.95	40.14	53.28	57.82	25.09	27.19	27.33	37.57	50.17	54.85
6213	Securities other than shares	4.56	5.07	6.19	22.44	21.34	25.29	2.66	2.75	2.30	20.95	19.96	21.58
6214	Loans	8.09	7.45	7.94	10.54	9.76	10.25	12.53	12.81	12.86	22.50	21.96	22.43
6215	Shares and other equity	133.70	150.76	178.58	179.16	208.32	245.51	3.81	4.07	4.26	182.97	212.39	249.77
6216	Insurance technical reserves	—	—	—	—	—	—	—	—	—	—	—	—
6217	Financial derivatives	—	—	—	—	—	—	—	—	—	—	—	—
6218	Other accounts receivable	30.30	37.67	32.72	123.02	141.66	134.47	10.71	11.47	13.01	109.28	120.09	119.95
622	Foreign	12.47	12.18	12.17	13.75	13.46	13.45	—	—	—	13.75	13.46	13.45
6222	Currency and deposits	.17	.16	.17	1.46	1.44	1.46	—	—	—	1.46	1.44	1.46
6223	Securities other than shares	.09	.19	.19	.09	.19	.19	—	—	—	.09	.19	.19
6224	Loans	12.04	11.63	11.13	12.04	11.63	11.13	—	—	—	12.04	11.63	11.13
6225	Shares and other equity	—	—	—	—	—	—	—	—	—	—	—	—
6226	Insurance technical reserves	—	—	—	—	—	—	—	—	—	—	—	—
6227	Financial derivatives	—	—	—	—	—	—	—	—	—	—	—	—
6228	Other accounts receivable	.17	.21	.68	.17	.21	.68	—	—	—	.17	.21	.68
623	Monetary gold and SDRs	—	—	—	—	—	—	—	—	—	—	—	—
63	**Liabilities**	**894.36**	**984.57**	**1,078.39**	**967.30**	**1,080.91**	**1,164.87**	**119.28**	**122.06**	**125.24**	**1,029.77**	**1,134.88**	**1,225.60**
631	Domestic	729.25	783.37	850.28	802.19	879.71	936.76	117.00	120.00	123.18	862.38	931.62	995.42
6312	Currency and deposits	38.26	34.23	34.54	38.26	34.23	34.54	—	—	—	10.61	3.94	4.24
6313	Securities other than shares	656.65	700.88	764.75	655.54	703.57	766.92	2.55	2.10	1.90	653.94	701.53	762.82
6314	Loans	7.93	8.08	16.71	25.07	36.21	35.37	101.50	105.91	108.36	126.00	141.50	143.06
6316	Insurance technical reserves	—	—	—	—	—	—	—	—	—	—	—	—
6317	Financial derivatives	—	—	—	—	—	—	—	—	—	—	—	—
6318	Other accounts payable	26.41	40.18	34.28	83.33	105.70	99.93	12.96	12.00	12.92	71.84	84.65	85.31
632	Foreign	165.11	201.20	228.12	165.11	201.20	228.12	2.28	2.06	2.06	167.39	203.26	230.17
6322	Currency and deposits	9.75	10.17	8.91	9.75	10.17	8.91	—	—	—	9.75	10.17	8.91
6323	Securities other than shares	146.50	182.34	210.13	146.50	182.34	210.13	—	—	—	146.50	182.34	210.13
6324	Loans	7.16	6.41	6.41	7.16	6.41	6.41	2.28	2.06	2.06	9.43	8.46	8.46
6326	Insurance technical reserves	—	—	—	—	—	—	—	—	—	—	—	—
6327	Financial derivatives	—	—	—	—	—	—	—	—	—	—	—	—
6328	Other accounts payable	1.71	2.28	2.67	1.71	2.28	2.67	—	—	—	1.71	2.28	2.67

In Billions of Euros / Year Ending December 31 / Noncash Reporter

	Budgetary Central Government			Central Government			Local Government			General Government		
	2002	2003p	2004p	2002	2003p	2004p	2002	2003p	2004p	2002	2003p	2004p
Memorandum items:												
6M2 Net financial worth..............	−670.73	−723.25	−788.85	−578.26	−633.10	−678.08	−64.49	−63.77	−65.48	−642.75	−696.86	−743.56
6M3 Debt at market value.............	....	....	....	....	....	....	....	....	....	....	....	....
6M4 Debt at nominal value............	....	....	....	....	....	....	....	....	....	....	....	....
6M5 Arrears.............................	....	....	....	....	....	....	....	....	....	....	....	....
6M6 Obligations for social security benefits...........	....	....	....	....	....	....	....	....	....	....	....	....
6M7 Contingent liabilities.............	....	....	....	....	....	....	....	....	....	....	....	....
6M8 Uncapitalized military weapons, systems........	....	....	....	....	....	....	....	....	....	....	....	....
Table 7 Outlays by functions of govt.												
7 **Total outlays.................**	387.68	396.00	413.61	731.74	757.79	777.51	154.79	164.71	178.74	821.46	854.26	886.34
701 **General public services..............**	....	....	....	....	....	....	....	....	....	....	....	....
7017 Public debt transactions........	41.53	41.49	41.41	42.40	42.29	42.49	4.44	3.31	2.80	46.85	45.60	45.29
7018 General transfers between levels of govt......	....	....	....	....	....	....	....	....	....	....	....	....
702 **Defense....................**	....	....	....	....	....	....	....	....	....	....	....	....
703 **Public order and safety................**	....	....	....	....	....	....	....	....	....	....	....	....
704 **Economic affairs..............**	....	....	....	....	....	....	....	....	....	....	....	....
7042 Agriculture, forestry, fishing, and hunting.....	....	....	....	....	....	....	....	....	....	....	....	....
7043 Fuel and energy...............	....	....	....	....	....	....	....	....	....	....	....	....
7044 Mining, manufacturing, and construction.....	....	....	....	....	....	....	....	....	....	....	....	....
7045 Transport......................	....	....	....	....	....	....	....	....	....	....	....	....
7046 Communication................	....	....	....	....	....	....	....	....	....	....	....	....
705 **Environmental protection................**	....	....	....	....	....	....	....	....	....	....	....	....
706 **Housing and community amenities.......**	....	....	....	....	....	....	....	....	....	....	....	....
707 **Health.....................**	....	....	....	....	....	....	....	....	....	....	....	....
7072 Outpatient services...............	....	....	....	....	....	....	....	....	....	....	....	....
7073 Hospital services...............	....	....	....	....	....	....	....	....	....	....	....	....
7074 Public health services...........	....	....	....	....	....	....	....	....	....	....	....	....
708 **Recreation, culture, and religion.............**	....	....	....	....	....	....	....	....	....	....	....	....
709 **Education..................**	....	....	....	....	....	....	....	....	....	....	....	....
7091 Pre-primary and primary education............	....	....	....	....	....	....	....	....	....	....	....	....
7092 Secondary education................	....	....	....	....	....	....	....	....	....	....	....	....
7094 Tertiary education.............	....	....	....	....	....	....	....	....	....	....	....	....
710 **Social protection................**	....	....	....	....	....	....	....	....	....	....	....	....
7 Statistical discrepancy: Total outlays............	....	....	....	....	....	....	....	....	....	....	....	....
Table 8 Transactions in financial assets and liabilities by sector												
82 **Net acquisition of financial assets........**	4.62	25.29	−4.71	15.49	49.02	1.53	2.84	3.53	1.26	15.18	40.46	7.47
821 Domestic..................	4.37	22.40	−4.71	15.31	46.02	1.54	2.84	3.53	1.26	15.00	37.47	7.47
8211 General government................	....	....	....	....	....	....	....	....	....	....	....	....
8212 Central bank..................	....	....	....	....	....	....	....	....	....	....	....	....
8213 Other depository corporations........	....	....	....	....	....	....	....	....	....	....	....	....
8214 Financial corporations n.e.c........	....	....	....	....	....	....	....	....	....	....	....	....
8215 Nonfinancial corporations...........	....	....	....	....	....	....	....	....	....	....	....	....
8216 Households & NPIs serving households......	....	....	....	....	....	....	....	....	....	....	....	....
822 Foreign..................	.24	2.90	−.01	.18	3.00	—	—	—	—	.18	3.00	−.01
8221 General government..............	....	....	—	....	....	—	....	....	—	....	....	—
8227 International organizations........	....	....	—	....	....	—	....	....	—	....	....	—
8228 Financial corporations other than international organizations.............	....	....	—	....	....	—	....	....	—	....	....	—
8229 Other nonresidents............	....	....	—	....	....	—	....	....	—	....	....	—
823 Monetary gold and SDRs............	—	—	—	—	—	—	—	—	—	—	—	—
83 **Net incurrence of liabilities...............**	52.11	82.30	38.06	67.35	116.14	59.96	.59	3.03	3.20	64.78	107.08	67.83
831 Domestic..................	32.86	63.72	11.14	48.10	97.56	33.04	.68	3.25	3.19	45.63	88.72	40.91
8311 General government...............	....	....	....	....	....	....	....	....	....	....	....	....
8312 Central bank..................	....	....	....	....	....	....	....	....	....	....	....	....
8313 Other depository corporations........	....	....	....	....	....	....	....	....	....	....	....	....
8314 Financial corporations n.e.c.......	....	....	....	....	....	....	....	....	....	....	....	....
8315 Nonfinancial corporations...........	....	....	....	....	....	....	....	....	....	....	....	....
8316 Households & NPIs serving households......	....	....	....	....	....	....	....	....	....	....	....	....
832 Foreign..................	19.25	18.59	26.92	19.25	18.58	26.92	−.09	−.22	—	19.15	18.36	26.92
8321 General government..............	....	....	....	....	....	....	....	....	—	....	....	....
8327 International organizations........	....	....	....	....	....	....	....	....	—	....	....	....
8328 Financial corporations other than international organizations.............	....	....	....	....	....	....	....	....	—	....	....	....
8329 Other nonresidents.............	....	....	....	....	....	....	....	....	—	....	....	....

In Millions of Lari / Year Ending December 31 / Cash Reporter

	Budgetary Central Government			Central Government			Local Government			General Government		
	2002	2003	2004	2002	2003	2004	2002	2003	2004	2002	2003	2004
Statement of government operations												
Statement of other economic flows												
Balance sheet												
6 *Net worth*	....	....	....	....	....	....	....	....	....		....	....
61 Nonfinancial assets	....	....	....	....	....	....	....	....	....		....	....
62 Financial assets	....	....	....	....	....	....	....	....	....		....	....
63 Liabilities	4,843.3	†4,608.0	4,306.6	4,843.3	†4,608.0	4,306.6	....	....	....		....	....
Statement of sources and uses of cash												
1 Cash receipts from operating activities	617.2	†662.5	1,240.5	802.7	†933.3	1,732.9	....	†481.5	697.6	....	†1,345.0	2,266.9
11 Taxes	531.5	†555.8	901.5	567.9	†602.3	975.3	....	†403.6	554.9	....	†1,005.9	1,530.2
12 Social contributions	6.3	†—	—	154.8	†222.7	402.2	....	†—	—	....	†222.7	402.2
13 Grants	22.6	†48.4	144.7	22.6	†48.4	160.1	....	†69.8	128.2	....	†48.4	124.7
14 Other receipts	56.8	†58.3	194.3	57.4	†59.9	195.3	....	†8.1	14.5	....	†68.0	209.8
2 Cash payments for operating activities	655.8	†653.6	986.9	839.7	†915.6	1,432.2	....	†415.6	567.2	....	†1,261.4	1,835.8
21 Compensation of employees	112.0	†131.5	232.6	112.0	†131.5	233.0	....	†157.1	239.9	....	†288.6	472.9
22 Purchases of goods and services	146.9	†123.6	270.5	182.1	†169.3	319.2	....	†151.0	109.5	....	†320.3	428.7
24 Interest	146.7	†168.5	140.9	146.7	†168.5	142.4	....	†—	10.6	....	†168.5	153.0
25 Subsidies	....	†57.0	112.7	....	†57.0	112.7	....	†48.3	104.7	....	†105.3	217.4
26 Grants	....	†126.7	170.2	....	†69.8	128.2	....	†—	35.4	....	†—	—
27 Social benefits	....	†46.3	43.8	....	†319.5	480.5	....	†59.2	67.1	....	†378.7	547.6
28 Other payments	....	†—	16.2	....	†—	16.2	....	†—	—	....	†—	16.2
CIO *Net cash inflow from oper. activities*	*−38.6*	*†8.9*	*253.6*	*−37.0*	*†17.7*	*300.7*	....	*†65.9*	*130.4*		*†83.6*	*431.1*
31.1 Purchases of nonfinancial assets	100.0	†117.8	295.9	100.0	†117.8	315.1	....	†71.4	110.4	....	†189.2	425.5
31.2 Sales of nonfinancial assets	—	†23.6	67.0	—	†23.6	67.0	....	†6.7	5.7	....	†30.3	72.7
31 Net cash outflow from investments in nonfinancial assets	100.0	†94.2	228.9	100.0	†94.2	248.1	....	†64.7	104.7	....	†158.9	352.8
CSD *Cash surplus/deficit*	*−138.6*	*†−85.3*	*24.7*	*−137.0*	*†−76.5*	*52.6*	....	*†1.2*	*25.7*	....	*†−75.3*	*78.3*
32x Net acquisition of fin assets, excl. cash	47.2	†49.2	51.9	55.2	†53.7	58.8	....	....	—	....	....	58.8
321x Domestic	47.2	†49.2	51.9	55.2	†53.7	58.8	....	....	—	....	....	58.8
322x Foreign	—	†—	—	—	†—	—	....	....	—	....	....	—
323 Monetary gold and SDRs	—	†—	—	—	†—	—	....	....	—	....	....	—
33 Net incurrence of liabilities	140.5	†140.7	41.0	140.5	†140.7	41.0	....	....	−.9	....	....	40.1
331 Domestic	47.6	†50.0	12.5	47.6	†50.0	12.5	....	....	−.9	....	....	11.6
332 Foreign	92.9	†90.7	28.5	92.9	†90.7	28.5	....	....	—	....	....	28.5
NFB Net cash inflow from fin. activities	93.3	†91.5	−10.9	85.3	†87.0	−17.8	....	....	−.9	....	....	−18.7
NCB *Net change in the stock of cash*	*−45.3*	*†6.2*	*13.8*	*−51.7*	*†10.5*	*34.8*	....	....	*24.8*	....	....	*59.6*
Table 1 Revenue												
1 **Revenue**	**617.2**	**†662.5**	**1,240.5**	**802.7**	**†933.3**	**1,732.9**	....	**†481.5**	**697.6**	....	**†1,345.0**	**2,266.9**
11 **Taxes**	**531.5**	**†555.8**	**901.5**	**567.9**	**†602.3**	**975.3**	....	**†403.6**	**554.9**	....	**†1,005.9**	**1,530.2**
111 Taxes on income, profits, & capital gains	27.8	†31.8	27.7	27.8	†31.8	27.7	....	†222.3	402.6	....	†254.1	430.3
1111 Individuals	18.5	†20.0	16.4	18.5	†20.0	16.4	....	†133.0	252.3	....	†153.0	268.7
1112 Corporations and other enterprises	9.3	†11.8	11.3	9.3	†11.8	11.3	....	†89.3	150.3	....	†101.1	161.6
112 Taxes on payroll and workforce	—	†—	—	—	†—	—	....	†—	—	....	†—	—
113 Taxes on property	—	†—	—	—	†—	2.1	....	†70.5	59.9	....	†70.5	62.0
114 Taxes on goods and services	452.8	†457.7	760.6	489.2	†504.2	811.8	....	†96.6	62.3	....	†600.8	874.1
1141 General taxes on goods and services	370.9	†368.5	598.7	370.9	†387.3	631.9	....	†38.4	29.5	....	†425.7	661.4
1142 Excises	81.9	†89.2	161.9	81.9	†105.2	179.9	....	†10.9	1.8	....	†116.1	181.7
115 Taxes on int'l. trade and transactions	50.9	†66.3	111.3	50.9	†66.3	131.8	....	†14.2	12.1	....	†80.5	143.9
116 Other taxes	—	†—	1.9	—	†—	1.9	....	†—	18.0	....	†—	19.9
12 **Social contributions**	**6.3**	**†—**	**—**	**154.8**	**†222.7**	**402.2**	....	**†—**	**—**	....	**†222.7**	**402.2**
121 Social security contributions	6.3	†—	—	154.8	†222.7	402.2	....	†—	—	....	†222.7	402.2
122 Other social contributions	—	†—	—	—	†—	—	....	†—	—	....	†—	—
13 **Grants**	**22.6**	**†48.4**	**144.7**	**22.6**	**†48.4**	**160.1**	....	**†69.8**	**128.2**	....	**†48.4**	**124.7**
131 From foreign governments	22.6	†48.4	48.7	22.6	†48.4	48.7	....	†—	—	....	†48.4	48.7
132 From international organizations	—	†—	76.0	—	†—	76.0	....	†—	—	....	†—	76.0
133 From other general government units	—	†—	20.0	—	†—	35.4	....	†69.8	128.2	....	†—	—
14 **Other revenue**	**56.8**	**†58.3**	**194.3**	**57.4**	**†59.9**	**195.3**	....	**†8.1**	**14.5**	....	**†68.0**	**209.8**
Table 2 Expense by economic type												
2 **Expense**	**655.8**	**†653.6**	**986.9**	**839.7**	**†915.6**	**1,432.2**	....	**†415.6**	**567.2**	....	**†1,261.4**	**1,835.8**
21 **Compensation of employees**	**112.0**	**†131.5**	**232.6**	**112.0**	**†131.5**	**233.0**	....	**†157.1**	**239.9**	....	**†288.6**	**472.9**
211 Wages and salaries	92.0	†113.0	200.3	92.0	†113.0	200.6	....	†133.2	173.8	....	†246.2	374.4
212 Social contributions	20.0	†18.5	32.3	20.0	†18.5	32.4	....	†23.9	66.1	....	†42.4	98.5
22 **Use of goods and services**	**146.9**	**†123.6**	**270.5**	**182.1**	**†169.3**	**319.2**	....	**†151.0**	**109.5**	....	**†320.3**	**428.7**
23 **Consumption of fixed capital**	....	....	....	....	....	....	....	....	....	....	....	....
24 **Interest**	**146.7**	**†168.5**	**140.9**	**146.7**	**†168.5**	**142.4**	....	**†—**	**10.6**	....	**†168.5**	**153.0**
25 **Subsidies**	....	**†57.0**	**112.7**	....	**†57.0**	**112.7**	....	**†48.3**	**104.7**	....	**†105.3**	**217.4**

In Millions of Lari / Year Ending December 31 / Cash Reporter

		Budgetary Central Government			Central Government			Local Government			General Government		
		2002	2003	2004	2002	2003	2004	2002	2003	2004	2002	2003	2004
26	**Grants**..................	....	†126.7	170.2	....	†69.8	128.2	....	†—	35.4	....	†—	—
261	To foreign govenments...........	....	†—	—	....	†—	—	....	†—	—	....	†—	—
262	To international organizations.........	—	†—	—	—	†—	—	....	†—	—	....	†—	—
263	To other general government units........	....	†126.7	170.2	....	†69.8	128.2	....	†—	35.4	....	†—	—
2631	Current..........	....	†126.7	170.2	....	†69.8	128.2	....	†—	35.4	....	†—	—
2632	Capital..........	....	†—	—	....	†—	—	....	†—	—	....	†—	—
27	**Social benefits**................	....	†46.3	43.8	....	†319.5	480.5	....	†59.2	67.1	....	†378.7	547.6
28	**Other expense**................	—	†—	16.2	—	†—	16.2	....	†—	—	....	†—	16.2
281	Property expense other than interest.........	—	†—	—	—	†—	—	....	†—	—	....	†—	—
282	Miscellaneous other expense.........	—	†—	16.2	—	†—	16.2	....	†—	—	....	†—	16.2
2821	Current.........	—	†—	16.2	—	†—	16.2	....	†—	—	....	†—	16.2
2822	Capital.........	—	†—	—	—	†—	—	....	†—	—	....	†—	—

Table 3   Transactions in assets and liabilities

		Budgetary Central Government			Central Government			Local Government			General Government		
		2002	2003	2004	2002	2003	2004	2002	2003	2004	2002	2003	2004
3	**Change in net worth from transactns....**	....	....	....	....	....	....	....	†64.7	104.7	....	†158.9	352.8
31	**Net acquisition of nonfinancial assets...**	100.0	†94.2	228.9	100.0	†94.2	248.1	....	†64.7	104.7	....	†158.9	352.8
311	Fixed assets.......	100.0	†94.2	228.9	100.0	†94.2	248.1	....	†64.7	104.7	....	†158.9	352.8
3111	Buildings and structures.........	....	....	—	....	....	19.2	....	....	—	....	....	19.2
3112	Machinery and equipment..........	....	....	—	....	....	—	....	....	—	....	....	—
3113	Other fixed assets........	....	....	228.9	....	....	228.9	....	....	104.7	....	....	333.6
312	Inventories.........	—	†—	—	—	†—	—	....	†—	—	....	†—	—
313	Valuables.........	—	†—	—	—	†—	—	....	†—	—	....	†—	—
314	Nonproduced assets.........	—	†—	—	—	†—	—	....	†—	—	....	†—	—
3141	Land.........	—	†—	—	—	†—	—	....	†—	—	....	†—	—
3142	Subsoil assets.........	—	†—	—	—	†—	—	....	†—	—	....	†—	—
3143	Other naturally occurring assets.........	—	†—	—	—	†—	—	....	†—	—	....	†—	—
3144	Intangible nonproduced assets.........	—	†—	—	—	†—	—	....	†—	—	....	†—	—
32	**Net acquisition of financial assets........**	1.9	†55.4	65.7	3.5	†64.2	93.6	....	....	24.8	....	....	118.4
321	Domestic.........	1.9	†55.4	65.7	3.5	†64.2	93.6	....	....	24.8	....	....	118.4
3212	Currency and deposits.........	−45.3	†6.2	13.8	−51.7	†10.5	34.8	....	....	24.8	....	....	59.6
3213	Securities other than shares.........	....	†—	—	....	†—	—	....	....	—	....	....	—
3214	Loans.........	....	†49.2	51.9	....	†53.7	58.8	....	....	—	....	....	58.8
3215	Shares and other equity.........	....	†—	—	....	†—	—	....	....	—	....	....	—
3216	Insurance technical reserves.........	....	†—	—	....	†—	—	....	....	—	....	....	—
3217	Financial derivatives.........	....	†—	—	....	†—	—	....	....	—	....	....	—
3218	Other accounts receivable.........	....	....	—	....	†—	—	....	....	—	....	....	—
322	Foreign.........	—	†—	—	—	†—	—	....	....	—	....	....	—
3222	Currency and deposits.........	—	†—	—	—	†—	—	....	....	—	....	....	—
3223	Securities other than shares.........	—	†—	—	—	†—	—	....	....	—	....	....	—
3224	Loans.........	—	†—	—	—	†—	—	....	....	—	....	....	—
3225	Shares and other equity.........	—	†—	—	—	†—	—	....	....	—	....	....	—
3226	Insurance technical reserves.........	—	†—	—	—	†—	—	....	....	—	....	....	—
3227	Financial derivatives.........	—	†—	—	—	†—	—	....	....	—	....	....	—
3228	Other accounts receivable.........	....	....	—	—	†—	—	....	....	—	....	....	—
323	Monetary gold and SDRs.........	—	†—	—	—	†—	—	....	....	—	....	....	—
33	**Net incurrence of liabilities................**	140.5	†140.7	41.0	140.5	†140.7	41.0	....	....	−.9	....	....	40.1
331	Domestic.........	47.6	†50.0	12.5	47.6	†50.0	12.5	....	....	−.9	....	....	11.6
3312	Currency and deposits.........	—	†—	—	—	†—	—	....	....	—	....	....	—
3313	Securities other than shares.........	24.5	†10.8	−9.0	24.5	†10.8	−9.0	....	....	—	....	....	−9.0
3314	Loans.........	23.1	†39.2	21.5	23.1	†39.2	21.5	....	....	−.9	....	....	20.6
3316	Insurance technical reserves.........	—	†—	—	—	†—	—	....	....	—	....	....	—
3317	Financial derivatives.........	—	†—	—	—	†—	—	....	....	—	....	....	—
3318	Other accounts payable.........	....	....	....	....	....	....	....	....	—	....	....	....
332	Foreign.........	92.9	†90.7	28.5	92.9	†90.7	28.5	....	....	—	....	....	28.5
3322	Currency and deposits.........	—	†—	—	—	†—	—	....	....	—	....	....	—
3323	Securities other than shares.........	—	†—	—	—	†—	—	....	....	—	....	....	—
3324	Loans.........	92.9	†90.7	28.5	92.9	†90.7	28.5	....	....	—	....	....	28.5
3326	Insurance technical reserves.........	—	†—	—	—	†—	—	....	....	—	....	....	—
3327	Financial derivatives.........	—	†—	—	—	†—	—	....	....	—	....	....	—
3328	Other accounts payable.........	....	....	....	....	....	....	....	....	....	....	....	....

In Millions of Lari / Year Ending December 31 / Cash Reporter

	Budgetary Central Government			Central Government			Local Government			General Government		
	2002	2003	2004	2002	2003	2004	2002	2003	2004	2002	2003	2004
Table 4 Holding gains in assets and liabilities												
Table 5 Other changes in the volume of assets and liabilities												
Table 6 Balance sheet												
6 Net worth	....	....	....	....	....	....	....	....	....	....	....	....
61 Nonfinancial assets	....	....	....	....	....	....	....	....	....	....	....	....
611 Fixed assets	....	....	....	....	....	....	....	....	....	....	....	....
6111 Buildings and structures	....	....	....	....	....	....	....	....	....	....	....	....
6112 Machinery and equipment	....	....	....	....	....	....	....	....	....	....	....	....
6113 Other fixed assets	....	....	....	....	....	....	....	....	....	....	....	....
612 Inventories	....	....	....	....	....	....	....	....	....	....	....	....
613 Valuables	....	....	....	....	....	....	....	....	....	....	....	....
614 Nonproduced assets	....	....	....	....	....	....	....	....	....	....	....	....
6141 Land	....	....	....	....	....	....	....	....	....	....	....	....
6142 Subsoil assets	....	....	....	....	....	....	....	....	....	....	....	....
6143 Other naturally occurring assets	....	....	....	....	....	....	....	....	....	....	....	....
6144 Intangible nonproduced assets	....	....	....	....	....	....	....	....	....	....	....	....
62 Financial assets	....	....	....	....	....	....	....	....	....	....	....	....
621 Domestic	....	....	....	....	....	....	....	....	....	....	....	....
6212 Currency and deposits	....	....	....	....	....	....	....	....	....	....	....	....
6213 Securities other than shares	....	....	....	....	....	....	....	....	....	....	....	....
6214 Loans	....	....	....	....	....	....	....	....	....	....	....	....
6215 Shares and other equity	....	....	....	....	....	....	....	....	....	....	....	....
6216 Insurance technical reserves	....	....	....	....	....	....	....	....	....	....	....	....
6217 Financial derivatives	....	....	....	....	....	....	....	....	....	....	....	....
6218 Other accounts receivable	....	....	....	....	....	....	....	....	....	....	....	....
622 Foreign	....	....	....	....	....	....	....	....	....	....	....	....
6222 Currency and deposits	....	....	....	....	....	....	....	....	....	....	....	....
6223 Securities other than shares	....	....	....	....	....	....	....	....	....	....	....	....
6224 Loans	....	....	....	....	....	....	....	....	....	....	....	....
6225 Shares and other equity	....	....	....	....	....	....	....	....	....	....	....	....
6226 Insurance technical reserves	....	....	....	....	....	....	....	....	....	....	....	....
6227 Financial derivatives	....	....	....	....	....	....	....	....	....	....	....	....
6228 Other accounts receivable	....	....	....	....	....	....	....	....	....	....	....	....
623 Monetary gold and SDRs	....	....	....	....	....	....	....	....	....	....	....	....
63 Liabilities	4,843.3	†4,608.0	4,306.6	4,843.3	†4,608.0	4,306.6	....	....	....	....	....	....
631 Domestic	1,520.3	†1,567.9	1,575.8	1,520.3	†1,567.9	1,575.8	....	....	....	....	....	....
6312 Currency and deposits	....	†—	—	....	†—	—	....	....	....	....	....	....
6313 Securities other than shares	....	†—	—	....	†—	—	....	....	....	....	....	....
6314 Loans	....	†1,567.9	1,575.8	....	†1,567.9	1,575.8	....	....	....	....	....	....
6316 Insurance technical reserves	....	†—	—	....	†—		....	....	....	....	....	....
6317 Financial derivatives	....	†—	—	....	†—		....	....	....	....	....	....
6318 Other accounts payable	....	....		....	....		....	....	....	....	....	....
632 Foreign	3,323.0	†3,040.1	2,730.8	3,323.0	†3,040.1	2,730.8	....	....	....	....	....	....
6322 Currency and deposits	....	†—	—	....	†—	—	....	....	....	....	....	....
6323 Securities other than shares	....	†—	—	....	†—	—	....	....	....	....	....	....
6324 Loans	....	†3,040.1	2,730.8	....	†3,040.1	2,730.8	....	....	....	....	....	....
6326 Insurance technical reserves	....	†—	—	....	†—		....	....	....	....	....	....
6327 Financial derivatives	....	†—	....	....	†—	—	....	....	....	....	....	....
6328 Other accounts payable	....	....		....	....		....	....	....	....	....	....
Memorandum items:												
6M2 Net financial worth	....	....		....	....		....	....		....	....	
6M3 Debt at market value	....	....		....	....		....	....		....	....	
6M4 Debt at nominal value	....	....		....	....		....	....		....	....	
6M5 Arrears	....	....		....	....		....	....		....	....	
6M6 Obligations for social security benefits	....	....		....	....		....	....		....	....	
6M7 Contingent liabilities	....	....		....	....		....	....		....	....	
6M8 Uncapitalized military weapons, systems	....	....		....	....		....	....		....	....	
Table 7 Outlays by functions of govt.												
7 Total outlays	755.8	†747.8	1,215.8	939.7	†1,009.8	1,680.3	....	†480.3	671.9	....	†1,420.3	2,188.6
701 General public services	341.8	†344.1	501.9	341.8	†344.1	501.9	....	†167.5	95.7	....	†441.8	434.0
7017 Public debt transactions	146.7	†168.5	140.9	146.7	†168.5	142.4	....	†—	10.6	....	†168.5	153.0
7018 General transfers between levels of govt	....	†69.8	....	....	†69.8	....	....	†—		....	†—	
702 Defense	48.0	†60.4	158.7	48.0	†60.4	158.7	....	†.8	1.7	....	†61.2	160.4
703 Public order and safety	80.4	†107.6	237.4	80.4	†107.6	237.4	....	†6.0	34.7	....	†113.6	272.1

Georgia 915

In Millions of Lari / Year Ending December 31 / Cash Reporter

	Budgetary Central Government			Central Government			Local Government			General Government		
	2002	2003	2004	2002	2003	2004	2002	2003	2004	2002	2003	2004
704 Economic affairs	45.9	†53.1	53.7	73.5	†88.5	113.3	....	†3.6	7.0	....	†92.1	120.3
7042 Agriculture, forestry, fishing, and hunting	16.2	†14.7	29.2	16.2	†14.7	29.2	....	†1.3	2.5	....	†16.0	31.7
7043 Fuel and energy	16.9	†36.8	78.4	16.9	†36.8	78.4	....	†—	2.1	....	†36.8	80.5
7044 Mining, manufacturing, and construction	.8	†.8	−55.0	.8	†.8	−55.0	....	†—	.2	....	†.8	−54.8
7045 Transport	1.4	†.8	1.1	29.0	†36.2	60.7	....	†2.3	2.2	....	†38.5	62.9
7046 Communication	....	....	....	....	....	....	....	....	....	....	....	....
705 Environmental protection	....	†—	—	....	†—	—	....	†—	—	....	†—	—
706 Housing and community amenities	4.3	†5.6	2.8	4.3	†5.6	2.8	....	†56.8	137.8	....	†62.4	140.6
707 Health	50.8	†10.3	54.8	50.8	†10.3	54.8	....	†19.2	40.6	....	†29.5	95.4
7072 Outpatient services	....	....	....	....	†—	....	....	†21.7	....	....	†21.7	....
7073 Hospital services	....	....	....	....	†—	....	....	....	....	....	†—	....
7074 Public health services	....	....	....	....	†—	....	....	....	....	....	†—	....
708 Recreation, culture, and religion	26.2	†25.0	33.9	26.2	†25.0	33.9	....	†24.7	46.5	....	†49.7	80.4
709 Education	44.1	†41.0	65.3	44.1	†41.0	65.3	....	†123.1	221.0	....	†164.1	286.3
7091 Pre-primary and primary education	....	....	....	....	†—	....	....	....	....	....	†—	....
7092 Secondary education	....	....	....	....	†—	....	....	....	....	....	†—	....
7094 Tertiary education	....	....	....	....	†—	....	....	....	....	....	†—	....
710 Social protection	114.3	†100.7	107.3	270.6	†327.3	512.2	....	†78.6	86.9	....	†405.9	599.1
7 Statistical discrepancy: Total outlays	—	†—	—	—	†—	—	....	†—	—	....	†—	—

Table 8 Transactions in financial assets and liabilities by sector

	Budgetary Central Government			Central Government			Local Government			General Government		
	2002	2003	2004	2002	2003	2004	2002	2003	2004	2002	2003	2004
82 Net acquisition of financial assets	1.9	†55.4	65.7	3.5	†64.2	93.6	....	....	24.8	....	....	118.4
821 Domestic	1.9	†55.4	65.7	3.5	†64.2	93.6	....	....	24.8	....	....	118.4
8211 General government	—	†−4.5	—	—	†—	—	....	....	24.8	....	....	24.8
8212 Central bank	....	†6.2	13.8	....	†10.5	34.8	....	....	—	....	....	34.8
8213 Other depository corporations	....	†—	—	....	†—	—	....	....	—	....	....	—
8214 Financial corporations n.e.c.	....	†—	—	....	†—	—	....	....	—	....	....	—
8215 Nonfinancial corporations	—	†53.7	51.9	—	†53.7	58.8	....	....	—	....	....	58.8
8216 Households & NPIs serving households	....	†—	—	—	†—	—	....	....	—	....	....	—
822 Foreign	—	†—	—	—	†—	—	....	....	—	....	....	—
8221 General government	—	†—	—	—	†—	—	....	....	—	....	....	—
8227 International organizations	—	†—	—	—	†—	—	....	....	—	....	....	—
8228 Financial corporations other than international organizations	—	†—	—	—	†—	—	....	....	—	....	....	—
8229 Other nonresidents	—	†—	—	—	†—	—	....	....	—	....	....	—
823 Monetary gold and SDRs	—	†—	—	—	†—	—	....	....	—	....	....	—
83 Net incurrence of liabilities	140.5	†140.7	41.0	140.5	†140.7	41.0	....	....	−.9	....	....	40.1
831 Domestic	47.6	†50.0	12.5	47.6	†50.0	12.5	....	....	−.9	....	....	11.6
8311 General government	....	†—	—	....	†—	—	....	....	—	....	....	—
8312 Central bank	....	†39.2	—	....	†39.2	—	....	....	−.9	....	....	−.9
8313 Other depository corporations	....	†10.8	−9.0	....	†10.8	−9.0	....	....	—	....	....	−9.0
8314 Financial corporations n.e.c.	....	†—	—	....	†—	—	....	....	—	....	....	—
8315 Nonfinancial corporations	....	†—	21.5	....	†—	21.5	....	....	—	....	....	21.5
8316 Households & NPIs serving households	....	†—	—	....	†—	—	....	....	—	....	....	—
832 Foreign	92.9	†90.7	28.5	92.9	†90.7	28.5	....	....	—	....	....	28.5
8321 General government	—	†—	—	—	†—	—	....	....	—	....	....	—
8327 International organizations	92.9	†90.7	28.5	92.9	†90.7	28.5	....	....	—	....	....	28.5
8328 Financial corporations other than international organizations	—	†—	—	—	†—	—	....	....	—	....	....	—
8329 Other nonresidents	—	†—	—	—	†—	—	....	....	—	....	....	—

In Billions of Euros / Year Ending December 31 / Noncash Reporter

	Central Government 2002	2003	2004	State Government 2002	2003	2004	Local Government 2002	2003	2004	General Government 2002	2003	2004
Statement of government operations												
1 Revenue	641.77	652.84	639.22	258.47	260.15	262.61	151.68	150.59	155.96	951.19	960.26	956.84
2 Expense	684.60	700.39	691.48	290.67	291.17	288.95	157.31	162.16	164.52	1,031.85	1,050.40	1,044.00
GOB *Gross operating balance*	−35.38	−40.13	−44.81	−24.98	−23.87	−19.11	14.93	8.92	12.05	−45.43	−55.08	−51.87
NOB *Net operating balance*	−42.83	−47.55	−52.26	−32.20	−31.02	−26.34	−5.63	−11.57	−8.56	−80.66	−90.14	−87.16
31 Net acquisition of nonfinancial assets	.21	.05	−.02	−.03	−.32	−1.26	−1.27	−3.32	−4.68	−1.09	−3.59	−5.96
NLB *Net lending/borrowing*	−43.04	−47.60	−52.24	−32.17	−30.70	−25.08	−4.36	−8.25	−3.88	−79.57	−86.55	−81.20
32 Net acquisition of financial assets	....	....	....	....	....	....	....	....	....	−20.76	4.74	−7.12
33 Net incurrence of liabilities	....	....	....	....	....	....	....	....	....	56.69	86.17	72.95
NLB Statistical discrepancy	....	....	....	....	....	....	....	....	....	2.10	5.10	1.13
Statement of other economic flows												
Balance sheet												
Statement of sources and uses of cash												
Table 1 Revenue												
1 **Revenue**	641.77	652.84	639.22	258.47	260.15	262.61	151.68	150.59	155.96	951.19	960.26	956.84
11 **Taxes**	241.16	245.79	240.15	182.64	183.00	184.24	56.66	56.27	61.13	480.46	485.06	485.52
111 Taxes on income, profits, & capital gains	102.99	103.27	100.38	96.31	96.39	94.07	44.65	43.90	48.35	243.95	243.56	242.80
1111 Individuals	94.63	92.38	87.85	86.88	84.61	80.53	26.62	26.36	25.26	208.13	203.35	193.64
1112 Corporations and other enterprises	6.42	8.38	10.86	5.56	7.39	9.65	.35	.30	.28	12.33	16.07	20.79
112 Taxes on payroll and workforce	—	—	—	—	—	—	—	—	—	—	—	—
113 Taxes on property	—	—	—	8.06	8.42	9.03	8.30	8.61	8.84	16.36	17.04	17.87
114 Taxes on goods and services	138.17	142.52	139.77	78.26	78.19	81.14	3.71	3.75	3.94	220.15	224.46	224.85
1141 General taxes on goods and services	65.57	65.69	65.36	63.61	63.79	66.51	2.86	2.89	2.90	132.04	132.37	134.77
1142 Excises	63.84	68.00	65.50	.81	.79	.78	—	—	—	64.65	68.79	66.28
115 Taxes on int'l. trade and transactions	—	—	—	—	—	—	—	—	—	—	—	—
116 Other taxes	—	—	—	—	—	—	—	—	—	—	—	—
12 **Social contributions**	372.15	377.03	377.75	15.04	15.26	15.43	2.05	2.07	2.08	389.24	394.36	395.26
121 Social security contributions	367.38	372.19	372.88	—	—	—	—	—	—	367.38	372.19	372.88
122 Other social contributions	4.77	4.84	4.87	15.04	15.26	15.43	2.05	2.07	2.08	21.86	22.17	22.38
13 **Grants**	7.55	10.62	7.57	44.07	45.20	44.64	52.87	51.59	52.52	4.03	4.40	4.08
131 From foreign governments	—	—	—	—	—	—	—	—	—	—	—	—
132 From international organizations	.95	1.72	1.31	3.08	2.68	2.77	—	—	—	4.03	4.40	4.08
133 From other general government units	6.60	8.90	6.26	40.99	42.52	41.87	52.87	51.59	52.52	—	—	—
14 **Other revenue**	20.91	19.40	13.75	16.72	16.69	18.30	40.10	40.66	40.23	77.46	76.44	71.98
Table 2 Expense by economic type												
2 **Expense**	684.60	700.39	691.48	290.67	291.17	288.95	157.31	162.16	164.52	1,031.85	1,050.40	1,044.00
21 **Compensation of employees**	37.76	38.14	37.99	92.27	91.33	91.11	39.04	39.48	39.58	169.07	168.95	168.68
211 Wages and salaries	....	....	....	....	....	....	....	....	....	....	....	....
212 Social contributions	....	....	....	....	....	....	....	....	....	....	....	....
22 **Use of goods and services**	28.50	29.61	29.92	26.69	25.87	25.63	33.59	33.74	33.95	88.78	89.22	89.50
23 **Consumption of fixed capital**	7.45	7.42	7.45	7.22	7.15	7.23	20.56	20.49	20.61	35.23	35.06	35.29
24 **Interest**	40.10	40.40	39.18	18.55	19.46	19.46	4.50	5.02	4.57	62.88	64.57	62.91
25 **Subsidies**	11.75	10.04	8.55	13.88	13.44	13.56	6.04	6.42	6.84	31.67	29.90	28.95
26 **Grants**	50.84	54.70	54.72	58.34	59.31	57.60	6.84	6.80	6.80	15.56	17.80	18.47
261 To foreign govenments	2.81	2.73	2.84	—	—	—	—	—	—	2.81	2.73	2.84
262 To international organizations	12.75	15.07	15.63	—	—	—	—	—	—	12.75	15.07	15.63
263 To other general government units	35.28	36.90	36.25	58.34	59.31	57.60	6.84	6.80	6.80	—	—	—
2631 Current	28.50	29.41	29.20	47.28	46.47	46.70	6.14	5.95	5.99	—	—	—
2632 Capital	6.78	7.49	7.05	11.06	12.84	10.90	.70	.85	.81	—	—	—
27 **Social benefits**	487.06	498.26	493.75	50.04	50.32	51.27	37.04	39.50	41.56	574.14	588.08	586.58
28 **Other expense**	21.14	21.82	19.92	23.68	24.29	23.09	9.70	10.71	10.61	54.52	56.82	53.62
281 Property expense other than interest	—	—	—	—	—	—	—	—	—	—	—	—
282 Miscellaneous other expense	21.14	21.82	19.92	23.68	24.29	23.09	9.70	10.71	10.61	54.52	56.82	53.62
2821 Current	8.54	8.53	7.89	7.24	7.25	6.98	5.75	6.28	6.45	21.53	22.06	21.32
2822 Capital	12.60	13.29	12.03	16.44	17.04	16.11	3.95	4.43	4.16	32.99	34.76	32.30

In Billions of Euros / Year Ending December 31 / Noncash Reporter

	Central Government			State Government			Local Government			General Government		
	2002	2003	2004	2002	2003	2004	2002	2003	2004	2002	2003	2004
Table 3 Transactions in assets and liabilities												
3 **Change in net worth from transactns....**	−42.83	−47.55	−52.26	−32.20	−31.02	−26.34	−5.63	−11.57	−8.56	−80.66	−90.14	−87.16
31 **Net acquisition of nonfinancial assets...**	.21	.05	−.02	−.03	−.32	−1.26	−1.27	−3.32	−4.68	−1.09	−3.59	−5.96
311 Fixed assets........................	.27	.13	.06	—	−.29	−1.23	—	−2.05	−3.41	.27	−2.21	−4.58
3111 Buildings and structures...........	....	....	....	—	....	....	—	....	....	....	....	....
3112 Machinery and equipment...........	....	....	....	—	....	....	—	....	....	....	....	....
3113 Other fixed assets.................	....	....	....	—	....	....	—	....	....	....	....	....
312 Inventories.......................	—	—	—	—	—	—	.05	.05	.05	.05	.05	.05
313 Valuables.........................	—	—	—	—	—	—	—	—	—	—	—	—
314 Nonproduced assets...............	−.06	−.08	−.08	−.03	—	−.03	−1.32	−1.32	−1.32	−1.41	−1.43	−1.43
3141 Land.............................	....	....	....	....	....	....	....	....	....	....	....	....
3142 Subsoil assets....................	....	....	....	—	....	....	....	....	....	....	....	....
3143 Other naturally occurring assets...	....	....	....	—	....	....	....	....	....	....	....	....
3144 Intangible nonproduced assets......	....	....	....	—	....	....	....	....	....	....	....	....
32 **Net acquisition of financial assets.........**	....	....	....	....	....	....	....	....	....	−20.76	4.74	−7.12
321 Domestic...........................	....	....	....	....	....	....	....	....	....	....	....	....
3212 Currency and deposits.............	....	....	....	....	....	....	....	....	....	−8.90	−6.40	−4.06
3213 Securities other than shares.......	....	....	....	....	....	....	....	....	....	−2.02	.85	.27
3214 Loans.............................	....	....	....	....	....	....	....	....	....	.05	—	−5.26
3215 Shares and other equity...........	....	....	....	....	....	....	....	....	....	−9.01	−4.44	−5.26
3216 Insurance technical reserves........	....	....	....	....	....	....	....	....	....	.02	.01	.02
3217 Financial derivatives..............	....	....	....	....	....	....	....	....	....	....	....	....
3218 Other accounts receivable.........	....	....	....	....	....	....	....	....	....	5.71	15.46	9.01
322 Foreign............................	....	....	....	....	....	....	....	....	....	....	....	....
3222 Currency and deposits.............	....	....	....	....	....	....	....	....	....	−6.66	−.29	−1.78
3223 Securities other than shares.......	....	....	....	....	....	....	....	....	....	....	....	....
3224 Loans.............................	....	....	....	....	....	....	....	....	....	.06	−.44	−.06
3225 Shares and other equity...........	....	....	....	....	....	....	....	....	....	....	....	....
3226 Insurance technical reserves........	....	....	....	....	....	....	....	....	....	....	....	....
3227 Financial derivatives..............	....	....	....	....	....	....	....	....	....	....	....	....
3228 Other accounts receivable.........	....	....	....	....	....	....	....	....	....	....	....	....
323 Monetary gold and SDRs...........	....	....	....	....	....	....	....	....	....	—	—	—
33 **Net incurrence of liabilities...................**	....	....	....	....	....	....	....	....	....	56.69	86.17	72.95
331 Domestic...........................	....	....	....	....	....	....	....	....	....	....	....	....
3312 Currency and deposits.............	....	....	....	....	....	....	....	....	....	−2.57	.76	.43
3313 Securities other than shares.......	....	....	....	....	....	....	....	....	....	67.37	75.25	71.83
3314 Loans.............................	....	....	....	....	....	....	....	....	....	−10.39	6.73	1.81
3316 Insurance technical reserves........	....	....	....	....	....	....	....	....	....	....	....	....
3317 Financial derivatives..............	....	....	....	....	....	....	....	....	....	....	....	....
3318 Other accounts payable...........	....	....	....	....	....	....	....	....	....	3.83	−.05	−.04
332 Foreign............................	....	....	....	....	....	....	....	....	....	....	....	....
3322 Currency and deposits.............	....	....	....	....	....	....	....	....	....	....	....	....
3323 Securities other than shares.......	....	....	....	....	....	....	....	....	....	....	....	....
3324 Loans.............................	....	....	....	....	....	....	....	....	....	−1.55	3.49	−1.08
3326 Insurance technical reserves........	....	....	....	....	....	....	....	....	....	....	....	....
3327 Financial derivatives..............	....	....	....	....	....	....	....	....	....	....	....	....
3328 Other accounts payable...........	....	....	....	....	....	....	....	....	....	....	....	....
Table 4 Holding gains in assets and liabilities												
Table 5 Other changes in the volume of assets and liabilities												
Table 6 Balance sheet												
6 **Net worth.................................**	....	....	....	....	....	....	....	....	....	....	....	....
61 **Nonfinancial assets.....................**	....	....	....	....	....	....	....	....	....	....	....	....
611 Fixed assets.......................	....	....	....	....	....	....	....	....	....	....	....	....
6111 Buildings and structures...........	....	....	....	....	....	....	....	....	....	....	....	....
6112 Machinery and equipment...........	....	....	....	....	....	....	....	....	....	....	....	....
6113 Other fixed assets.................	....	....	....	....	....	....	....	....	....	....	....	....
612 Inventories.......................	....	....	....	....	....	....	....	....	....	....	....	....
613 Valuables.........................	....	....	....	....	....	....	....	....	....	....	....	....
614 Nonproduced assets...............	....	....	....	....	....	....	....	....	....	....	....	....
6141 Land.............................	....	....	....	....	....	....	....	....	....	....	....	....
6142 Subsoil assets....................	....	....	....	....	....	....	....	....	....	....	....	....
6143 Other naturally occurring assets...	....	....	....	....	....	....	....	....	....	....	....	....
6144 Intangible nonproduced assets......	....	....	....	....	....	....	....	....	....	....	....	....

In Billions of Euros / Year Ending December 31 / Noncash Reporter

		Central Government			State Government			Local Government			General Government		
		2002	2003	2004	2002	2003	2004	2002	2003	2004	2002	2003	2004
62	**Financial assets**	....	....	....	....	....	....	....	....	....	303.60	307.60	296.10
621	Domestic	....	....	....	....	....	....	....	....	....	....	....	....
6212	Currency and deposits	....	....	....	....	....	....	....	....	....	150.89	143.69	138.90
6213	Securities other than shares	....	....	....	....	....	....	....	....	....	11.30	12.40	13.40
6214	Loans	....	....	....	....	....	....	....	....	....	31.22	31.61	22.25
6215	Shares and other equity	....	....	....	....	....	....	....	....	....	82.80	86.80	85.50
6216	Insurance technical reserves	....	....	....	....	....	....	....	....	....	.60	.60	.60
6217	Financial derivatives	....	....	....	....	....	....	....	....	....	....	....	....
6218	Other accounts receivable	....	....	....	....	....	....	....	....	....	....	....	....
622	Foreign	....	....	....	....	....	....	....	....	....	....	....	....
6222	Currency and deposits	....	....	....	....	....	....	....	....	....	....	....	....
6223	Securities other than shares	....	....	....	....	....	....	....	....	....	3.91	10.41	9.31
6224	Loans	....	....	....	....	....	....	....	....	....	....	....	....
6225	Shares and other equity	....	....	....	....	....	....	....	....	....	22.88	22.09	26.15
6226	Insurance technical reserves	....	....	....	....	....	....	....	....	....	....	....	....
6227	Financial derivatives	....	....	....	....	....	....	....	....	....	....	....	....
6228	Other accounts receivable	....	....	....	....	....	....	....	....	....	....	....	....
623	Monetary gold and SDRs	....	....	....	....	....	....	....	....	....	....	....	....
63	**Liabilities**	....	....	....	....	....	....	....	....	....	1,323.40	1,399.70	1,499.20
631	Domestic	....	....	....	....	....	....	....	....	....	....	....	....
6312	Currency and deposits	....	....	....	....	....	....	....	....	....	3.80	4.50	5.00
6313	Securities other than shares	....	....	....	....	....	....	....	....	....	885.80	951.20	1,049.50
6314	Loans	....	....	....	....	....	....	....	....	....	421.45	428.50	425.61
6316	Insurance technical reserves	....	....	....	....	....	....	....	....	....	....	....	....
6317	Financial derivatives	....	....	....	....	....	....	....	....	....	....	....	....
6318	Other accounts payable	....	....	....	....	....	....	....	....	....	3.80	3.80	3.70
632	Foreign	....	....	....	....	....	....	....	....	....	....	....	....
6322	Currency and deposits	....	....	....	....	....	....	....	....	....	....	....	....
6323	Securities other than shares	....	....	....	....	....	....	....	....	....	....	....	....
6324	Loans	....	....	....	....	....	....	....	....	....	8.55	11.70	15.29
6326	Insurance technical reserves	....	....	....	....	....	....	....	....	....	....	....	....
6327	Financial derivatives	....	....	....	....	....	....	....	....	....	....	....	....
6328	Other accounts payable	....	....	....	....	....	....	....	....	....	....	....	....
Memorandum items:													
6M2	Net financial worth	....	....	....	....	....	....	....	....	....	−1,019.80	−1,092.10	−1,203.10
6M3	Debt at market value	....	....	....	....	....	....	....	....	....	....	....	....
6M4	Debt at nominal value	....	....	....	....	....	....	....	....	....	....	....	....
6M5	Arrears	....	....	....	....	....	....	....	....	....	....	....	....
6M6	Obligations for social security benefits	....	....	....	....	....	....	....	....	....	....	....	....
6M7	Contingent liabilities	....	....	....	....	....	....	....	....	....	....	....	....
6M8	Uncapitalized military weapons, systems	....	....	....	....	....	....	....	....	....	....	....	....
Table 7 Outlays by functions of govt.													
7	**Total outlays**	684.81	700.44	691.46	290.64	290.85	287.69	156.04	158.84	159.84	1,030.76	1,046.81	1,038.04
701	**General public services**	....	....	....	73.82	75.29	74.75	24.60	23.67	22.83	....	....	....
7017	Public debt transactions	40.10	40.40	39.18	18.55	19.46	19.46	4.50	5.02	4.57	....	....	....
7018	General transfers between levels of govt	....	....	....	....	....	....	....	....	....	62.88	64.57	62.91
702	**Defense**	....	....	....	—	—	—	—	—	—	....	....	....
703	**Public order and safety**	....	....	....	26.36	26.01	26.08	7.26	7.21	7.22	....	....	....
704	**Economic affairs**	....	....	....	32.83	32.70	31.70	18.84	18.78	18.42	....	....	....
7042	Agriculture, forestry, fishing, and hunting	....	....	....	....	....	....	....	....	....	....	....	....
7043	Fuel and energy	....	....	....	....	....	....	....	....	....	....	....	....
7044	Mining, manufacturing, and construction	....	....	....	....	....	....	....	....	....	....	....	....
7045	Transport	....	....	....	....	....	....	....	....	....	....	....	....
7046	Communication	....	....	....	....	....	....	....	....	....	....	....	....
705	**Environmental protection**	....	....	....	1.65	1.70	1.59	9.37	9.29	9.50	....	....	....
706	**Housing and community amenities**	....	....	....	8.80	9.26	8.92	10.75	10.80	10.56	....	....	....
707	**Health**	....	....	....	4.36	5.09	4.04	2.95	3.12	3.15	....	....	....
7072	Outpatient services	....	....	....	....	....	....	....	....	....	....	....	....
7073	Hospital services	....	....	....	....	....	....	....	....	....	....	....	....
7074	Public health services	....	....	....	....	....	....	....	....	....	....	....	....
708	**Recreation, culture, and religion**	....	....	....	4.98	4.94	4.88	10.44	10.49	10.43	....	....	....

In Billions of Euros / Year Ending December 31 / Noncash Reporter

		Central Government			State Government			Local Government			General Government		
		2002	2003	2004	2002	2003	2004	2002	2003	2004	2002	2003	2004
709	**Education**....................................	....	....	....	71.29	69.71	68.73	25.37	26.24	26.28	....	....	....
7091	Pre-primary and primary education...............	....	....	....	....	....	....	....	....	....	....	....	....
7092	Secondary education....................	....	....	....	....	....	....	....	....	....	....	....	....
7094	Tertiary education.....................	....	....	....	....	....	....	....	....	....	....	....	....
710	**Social protection**.......................	....	....	....	66.55	66.15	67.00	46.46	49.24	51.45	....	....	....
7	Statistical discrepancy: Total outlays..............	....	....	....	—	—	—	—	—	—	....	....	....

**Table 8   Transactions in financial assets
and liabilities by sector**

In Billions of Cedis / Year Ending December 31 / Cash Reporter

		Budgetary Central Government			Central Government			Local Government			General Government		
		2002p	2003p	2004p	2002	2003	2004	2002	2003	2004	2002	2003	2004
Statement of government operations													
Statement of other economic flows													
Balance sheet													
6	*Net worth*	....	....	....	....	....	....	....	....	....	....	....	....
61	Nonfinancial assets	....	....	....	....	....	....	....	....	....	....	....	....
62	Financial assets	....	....	....	....	....	....	....	....	....	....	....	....
63	Liabilities	....	....	....	....	....	....	....	....	....	....	....	....
Statement of sources and uses of cash													
1	Cash receipts from operating activities	10,324	16,862	24,078	....	....	....	....	....	....	....	....	....
11	Taxes	8,547	13,380	17,862	....	....	....	....	....	....	....	....	....
12	Social contributions	—	—	—	....	....	....	....	....	....	....	....	....
13	Grants	1,525	3,119	5,080	....	....	....	....	....	....	....	....	....
14	Other receipts	252	363	1,136	....	....	....	....	....	....	....	....	....
2	Cash payments for operating activities	9,787	12,302	16,696	....	....	....	....	....	....	....	....	....
21	Compensation of employees	4,500	6,073	7,483	....	....	....	....	....	....	....	....	....
22	Purchases of goods and services	....	....	....	....	....	....	....	....	....	....	....	....
24	Interest	2,999	3,633	3,472	....	....	....	....	....	....	....	....	....
25	Subsidies	....	....	....	....	....	....	....	....	....	....	....	....
26	Grants	....	....	....	....	....	....	....	....	....	....	....	....
27	Social benefits	386	560	785	....	....	....	....	....	....	....	....	....
28	Other payments	—	—	—	....	....	....	....	....	....	....	....	....
CIO	*Net cash inflow from oper. activities*	*538*	*4,560*	*7,382*	....	....	....	....	....	....	....	....	....
31.1	Purchases of nonfinancial assets	2,991	6,303	9,705	....	....	....	....	....	....	....	....	....
31.2	Sales of nonfinancial assets	—	—	—	....	....	....	....	....	....	....	....	....
31	Net cash outflow from investments in nonfinancial assets	2,991	6,303	9,705	....	....	....	....	....	....	....	....	....
CSD	*Cash surplus/deficit*	*−2,453*	*−1,743*	*−2,323*	....	....	....	....	....	....	....	....	....
32x	Net acquisition of fin assets, excl. cash	−2	35	176	....	....	....	....	....	....	....	....	....
321x	Domestic	−2	35	176	....	....	....	....	....	....	....	....	....
322x	Foreign	—	—	—	....	....	....	....	....	....	....	....	....
323	Monetary gold and SDRs	—	—	—	....	....	....	....	....	....	....	....	....
33	Net incurrence of liabilities	....	....	....	....	....	....	....	....	....	....	....	....
331	Domestic	....	....	....	....	....	....	....	....	....	....	....	....
332	Foreign	461	2,384	2,611	....	....	....	....	....	....	....	....	....
NFB	Net cash inflow from fin. activities	....	....	....	....	....	....	....	....	....	....	....	....
NCB	*Net change in the stock of cash*	....	....	....	....	....	....	....	....	....	....	....	....
Table 1 Revenue													
1	**Revenue**	**10,324**	**16,862**	**24,078**	....	....	....	....	....	....	....	....	....
11	**Taxes**	**8,547**	**13,380**	**17,862**	....	....	....	....	....	....	....	....	....
111	Taxes on income, profits, & capital gains	2,795	4,091	5,344	....	....	....	....	....	....	....	....	....
1111	Individuals	929	1,535	1,908	....	....	....	....	....	....	....	....	....
1112	Corporations and other enterprises	1,334	1,866	2,626	....	....	....	....	....	....	....	....	....
112	Taxes on payroll and workforce	—	—	—	....	....	....	....	....	....	....	....	....
113	Taxes on property	—	—	—	....	....	....	....	....	....	....	....	....
114	Taxes on goods and services	2,159	3,203	5,194	....	....	....	....	....	....	....	....	....
1141	General taxes on goods and services	710	1,023	1,460	....	....	....	....	....	....	....	....	....
1142	Excises	368	474	615	....	....	....	....	....	....	....	....	....
115	Taxes on int'l. trade and transactions	3,593	5,467	6,865	....	....	....	....	....	....	....	....	....
116	Other taxes	—	617	459	....	....	....	....	....	....	....	....	....
12	**Social contributions**	—	—	—	....	....	....	....	....	....	....	....	....
121	Social security contributions	—	—	—	....	....	....	....	....	....	....	....	....
122	Other social contributions	—	—	—	....	....	....	....	....	....	....	....	....
13	**Grants**	**1,525**	**3,119**	**5,080**	....	....	....	....	....	....	....	....	....
131	From foreign governments	....	....	....	....	....	....	....	....	....	....	....	....
132	From international organizations	....	....	....	....	....	....	....	....	....	....	....	....
133	From other general government units	....	....	....	....	....	....	....	....	....	....	....	....
14	**Other revenue**	**252**	**363**	**1,136**	....	....	....	....	....	....	....	....	....
Table 2 Expense by economic type													
2	**Expense**	**9,787**	**12,302**	**16,696**	....	....	....	....	....	....	....	....	....
21	**Compensation of employees**	**4,500**	**6,073**	**7,483**	....	....	....	....	....	....	....	....	....
211	Wages and salaries	4,197	5,661	6,988	....	....	....	....	....	....	....	....	....
212	Social contributions	303	412	495	....	....	....	....	....	....	....	....	....
22	**Use of goods and services**	....	....	....	....	....	....	....	....	....	....	....	....
23	**Consumption of fixed capital**	....	....	....	....	....	....	....	....	....	....	....	....
24	Interest	2,999	3,633	3,472	....	....	....	....	....	....	....	....	....
25	**Subsidies**	....	....	....	....	....	....	....	....	....	....	....	....

		Budgetary Central Government			Central Government			Local Government			General Government		
		2002p	2003p	2004p	2002	2003	2004	2002	2003	2004	2002	2003	2004
26	**Grants**........................	....	....	....	....	....	....	....	....	....	....	....	....
261	To foreign govenments.................	....	....	....	....	....	....	....	....	....	....	....	....
262	To international organizations..........	....	....	....	....	....	....	....	....	....	....	....	....
263	To other general government units....	....	....	....	....	....	....	....	....	....	....	....	....
2631	Current........................	....	....	....	....	....	....	....	....	....	....	....	....
2632	Capital........................	....	....	....	....	....	....	....	....	....	....	....	....
27	**Social benefits**...................	386	560	785	....	....	....	....	....	....	....	....	....
28	**Other expense**...................	—	—	—	....	....	....	....	....	....	....	....	....
281	Property expense other than interest....	—	—	—	....	....	....	....	....	....	....	....	....
282	Miscellaneous other expense.........	—	—	—	....	....	....	....	....	....	....	....	....
2821	Current........................	—	—	—	....	....	....	....	....	....	....	....	....
2822	Capital........................	—	—	—	....	....	....	....	....	....	....	....	....
Table 3	**Transactions in assets and liabilities**												
3	**Change in net worth from transactns....**	....	....	....	....	....	....	....	....	....	....	....	....
31	**Net acquisition of nonfinancial assets...**	2,991	6,303	9,705	....	....	....	....	....	....	....	....	....
311	Fixed assets....................	....	....	....	....	....	....	....	....	....	....	....	....
3111	Buildings and structures...........	....	....	....	....	....	....	....	....	....	....	....	....
3112	Machinery and equipment.........	....	....	....	....	....	....	....	....	....	....	....	....
3113	Other fixed assets..............	....	....	....	....	....	....	....	....	....	....	....	....
312	Inventories....................	....	....	....	....	....	....	....	....	....	....	....	....
313	Valuables.....................	....	....	....	....	....	....	....	....	....	....	....	....
314	Nonproduced assets.............	....	....	....	....	....	....	....	....	....	....	....	....
3141	Land.........................	....	....	....	....	....	....	....	....	....	....	....	....
3142	Subsoil assets.................	....	....	....	....	....	....	....	....	....	....	....	....
3143	Other naturally occurring assets....	....	....	....	....	....	....	....	....	....	....	....	....
3144	Intangible nonproduced assets.....	....	....	....	....	....	....	....	....	....	....	....	....
32	**Net acquisition of financial assets........**	....	....	....	....	....	....	....	....	....	....	....	....
321	Domestic.....................	....	....	....	....	....	....	....	....	....	....	....	....
3212	Currency and deposits............	....	....	....	....	....	....	....	....	....	....	....	....
3213	Securities other than shares.......	....	....	....	....	....	....	....	....	....	....	....	....
3214	Loans........................	....	....	....	....	....	....	....	....	....	....	....	....
3215	Shares and other equity..........	....	....	....	....	....	....	....	....	....	....	....	....
3216	Insurance technical reserves.......	....	....	....	....	....	....	....	....	....	....	....	....
3217	Financial derivatives.............	....	....	....	....	....	....	....	....	....	....	....	....
3218	Other accounts receivable.........	....	....	....	....	....	....	....	....	....	....	....	....
322	Foreign......................	....	....	....	....	....	....	....	....	....	....	....	....
3222	Currency and deposits............	....	....	....	....	....	....	....	....	....	....	....	....
3223	Securities other than shares.......	....	....	....	....	....	....	....	....	....	....	....	....
3224	Loans........................	....	....	....	....	....	....	....	....	....	....	....	....
3225	Shares and other equity..........	....	....	....	....	....	....	....	....	....	....	....	....
3226	Insurance technical reserves.......	....	....	....	....	....	....	....	....	....	....	....	....
3227	Financial derivatives.............	....	....	....	....	....	....	....	....	....	....	....	....
3228	Other accounts receivable.........	....	....	....	....	....	....	....	....	....	....	....	....
323	Monetary gold and SDRs..........	....	....	....	....	....	....	....	....	....	....	....	....
33	**Net incurrence of liabilities...................**	....	....	....	....	....	....	....	....	....	....	....	....
331	Domestic.....................	....	....	....	....	....	....	....	....	....	....	....	....
3312	Currency and deposits............	....	....	....	....	....	....	....	....	....	....	....	....
3313	Securities other than shares.......	....	....	....	....	....	....	....	....	....	....	....	....
3314	Loans........................	....	....	....	....	....	....	....	....	....	....	....	....
3316	Insurance technical reserves.......	....	....	....	....	....	....	....	....	....	....	....	....
3317	Financial derivatives.............	....	....	....	....	....	....	....	....	....	....	....	....
3318	Other accounts payable...........	....	....	....	....	....	....	....	....	....	....	....	....
332	Foreign......................	461	2,384	2,611	....	....	....	....	....	....	....	....	....
3322	Currency and deposits............	....	....	....	....	....	....	....	....	....	....	....	....
3323	Securities other than shares.......	....	....	....	....	....	....	....	....	....	....	....	....
3324	Loans........................	....	....	....	....	....	....	....	....	....	....	....	....
3326	Insurance technical reserves.......	....	....	....	....	....	....	....	....	....	....	....	....
3327	Financial derivatives.............	....	....	....	....	....	....	....	....	....	....	....	....
3328	Other accounts payable...........	....	....	....	....	....	....	....	....	....	....	....	....

In Billions of Cedis / Year Ending December 31 / Cash Reporter

	Budgetary Central Government			Central Government			Local Government			General Government		
	2002p	2003p	2004p	2002	2003	2004	2002	2003	2004	2002	2003	2004
Table 4 Holding gains in assets and liabilities												
Table 5 Other changes in the volume of assets and liabilities												
Table 6 Balance sheet												
Table 7 Outlays by functions of govt.												
7 **Total outlays**........................	12,778	18,605	26,401	....	....	....	....	....	....	....	....	....
701 **General public services**..........................	8,510	13,217	19,178	....	....	....	....	....	....	....	....	....
7017 Public debt transactions..........................	2,999	3,633	3,472	....	....	....	....	....	....	....	....	....
7018 General transfers between levels of govt......	....	....	....	....	....	....	....	....	....	....	....	....
702 **Defense**........................	293	462	507	....	....	....	....	....	....	....	....	....
703 **Public order and safety**........................	564	772	995	....	....	....	....	....	....	....	....	....
704 **Economic affairs**........................	271	417	599	....	....	....	....	....	....	....	....	....
7042 Agriculture, forestry, fishing, and hunting.....	130	172	219	....	....	....	....	....	....	....	....	....
7043 Fuel and energy..........................	30	13	5	....	....	....	....	....	....	....	....	....
7044 Mining, manufacturing, and construction.....	....	....	....	....	....	....	....	....	....	....	....	....
7045 Transport..........................	87	200	322	....	....	....	....	....	....	....	....	....
7046 Communication..........................	....	....	....	....	....	....	....	....	....	....	....	....
705 **Environmental protection**..........................	....	....	....	....	....	....	....	....	....	....	....	....
706 **Housing and community amenities**........	65	61	81	....	....	....	....	....	....	....	....	....
707 **Health**..........................	670	957	1,023	....	....	....	....	....	....	....	....	....
7072 Outpatient services..........................	....	....	....	....	....	....	....	....	....	....	....	....
7073 Hospital services..........................	....	....	....	....	....	....	....	....	....	....	....	....
7074 Public health services..........................	....	....	....	....	....	....	....	....	....	....	....	....
708 **Recreation, culture, and religion**...........	26	23	33	....	....	....	....	....	....	....	....	....
709 **Education**..........................	2,315	3,103	4,019	....	....	....	....	....	....	....	....	....
7091 Pre-primary and primary education...........	....	....	....	....	....	....	....	....	....	....	....	....
7092 Secondary education..........................	....	....	....	....	....	....	....	....	....	....	....	....
7094 Tertiary education..........................	....	....	....	....	....	....	....	....	....	....	....	....
710 **Social protection**..........................	36	38	66	....	....	....	....	....	....	....	....	....
7 Statistical discrepancy: Total outlays...........	28	−445	−100	....	....	....	....	....	....	....	....	....
Table 8 Transactions in financial assets and liabilities by sector												
82 **Net acquisition of financial assets**........	....	....	....	....	....	....	....	....	....	....	....	....
821 Domestic..........................	....	....	....	....	....	....	....	....	....	....	....	....
8211 General government..........................	....	....	....	....	....	....	....	....	....	....	....	....
8212 Central bank..........................	....	....	....	....	....	....	....	....	....	....	....	....
8213 Other depository corporations..........................	....	....	....	....	....	....	....	....	....	....	....	....
8214 Financial corporations n.e.c..........................	....	....	....	....	....	....	....	....	....	....	....	....
8215 Nonfinancial corporations..........................	....	....	....	....	....	....	....	....	....	....	....	....
8216 Households & NPIs serving households......	....	....	....	....	....	....	....	....	....	....	....	....
822 Foreign..........................	....	....	....	....	....	....	....	....	....	....	....	....
8221 General government..........................	....	....	....	....	....	....	....	....	....	....	....	....
8227 International organizations..........................	....	....	....	....	....	....	....	....	....	....	....	....
8228 Financial corporations other than international organizations...........	....	....	....	....	....	....	....	....	....	....	....	....
8229 Other nonresidents..........................	....	....	....	....	....	....	....	....	....	....	....	....
823 Monetary gold and SDRs..........................	....	....	....	....	....	....	....	....	....	....	....	....
83 **Net incurrence of liabilities**....................	....	....	....	....	....	....	....	....	....	....	....	....
831 Domestic..........................	....	....	....	....	....	....	....	....	....	....	....	....
8311 General government..........................	....	....	....	....	....	....	....	....	....	....	....	....
8312 Central bank..........................	....	....	....	....	....	....	....	....	....	....	....	....
8313 Other depository corporations..........................	....	....	....	....	....	....	....	....	....	....	....	....
8314 Financial corporations n.e.c..........................	....	....	....	....	....	....	....	....	....	....	....	....
8315 Nonfinancial corporations..........................	....	....	....	....	....	....	....	....	....	....	....	....
8316 Households & NPIs serving households......	....	....	....	....	....	....	....	....	....	....	....	....
832 Foreign..........................	461	2,384	2,611	....	....	....	....	....	....	....	....	....
8321 General government..........................	....	....	....	....	....	....	....	....	....	....	....	....
8327 International organizations..........................	....	....	....	....	....	....	....	....	....	....	....	....
8328 Financial corporations other than international organizations..............	....	....	....	....	....	....	....	....	....	....	....	....
8329 Other nonresidents..........................	....	....	....	....	....	....	....	....	....	....	....	....

In Millions of Euros / Year Ending December 31 / Noncash Reporter

	Budgetary Central Government			Central Government			Local Government			General Government		
	1998	1999	2000	1998	1999	2000	1998	1999	2000	1998	1999	2000
Statement of government operations												
1 Revenue............................	35,488	39,906	42,705	48,636	54,285	57,882	2,761	3,177	3,348	49,702	55,474	59,375
2 Expense............................	37,597	41,107	42,972	48,203	52,605	55,130	1,893	2,119	2,265	48,401	52,736	55,540
GOB *Gross operating balance*................	*−2,085*	*−1,176*	*−242*	*506*	*1,757*	*2,831*	*870*	*1,060*	*1,086*	*1,376*	*2,817*	*3,917*
NOB *Net operating balance*................	*−2,109*	*−1,201*	*−267*	*433*	*1,680*	*2,752*	*868*	*1,058*	*1,083*	*1,301*	*2,738*	*3,835*
31 Net acquisition of nonfinancial assets...........	3,068	3,780	4,005	3,162	3,902	4,114	801	979	1,024	3,963	4,881	5,138
NLB *Net lending/borrowing*................	*−5,177*	*−4,981*	*−4,272*	*−2,729*	*−2,222*	*−1,362*	*67*	*79*	*59*	*−2,662*	*−2,143*	*−1,303*
32 Net acquisition of financial assets..........	....	....	....	....	....	....	....	....	....	....	....	....
33 Net incurrence of liabilities.................	....	....	....	....	....	....	....	....	....	....	....	....
NLB Statistical discrepancy................	....	....	....	....	....	....	....	....	....	....	....	....
Statement of other economic flows												
Balance sheet												
Statement of sources and uses of cash												
Table 1 Revenue												
1 **Revenue**................................	†35,488	39,906	42,705	†48,636	54,285	57,882	†2,761	3,177	3,348	†49,702	55,474	59,375
11 **Taxes**................................	†25,664	28,975	31,249	†25,995	29,367	31,682	†340	378	402	†26,335	29,745	32,084
111 Taxes on income, profits, & capital gains......	†9,882	11,139	12,285	†9,882	11,139	12,285	†—	—	—	†9,882	11,139	12,285
1111 Individuals................................	†6,000	6,630	7,369	†6,000	6,630	7,369	†—	—	—	†6,000	6,630	7,369
1112 Corporations and other enterprises.............	†3,412	3,897	4,206	†3,412	3,897	4,206	†—	—	—	†3,412	3,897	4,206
112 Taxes on payroll and workforce..............	†—	—	—	†—	—	—	†—	—	—	†—	—	—
113 Taxes on property.............	†792	1,501	1,696	†931	1,661	1,871	†197	217	226	†1,128	1,878	2,097
114 Taxes on goods and services.............	†14,394	15,758	16,531	†14,586	15,990	16,789	†139	157	172	†14,725	16,147	16,961
1141 General taxes on goods and services.........	†7,787	8,720	9,771	†7,906	8,832	9,899	†11	11	11	†7,917	8,843	9,910
1142 Excises.............	†4,328	4,393	4,199	†4,328	4,393	4,199	†—	—	—	†4,328	4,393	4,199
115 Taxes on int'l. trade and transactions...........	†−11	−39	54	†−11	−39	54	†4	4	4	†−7	−35	58
116 Other taxes.............	†607	616	683	†607	616	683	†—	—	—	†607	616	683
12 **Social contributions**................	†3,138	3,317	3,315	†14,782	16,135	16,648	†—	—	—	†14,782	16,135	16,648
121 Social security contributions................	†880	626	643	†12,520	13,440	13,972	†—	—	—	†12,520	13,440	13,972
122 Other social contributions.............	†2,258	2,691	2,672	†2,262	2,695	2,676	†—	—	—	†2,262	2,695	2,676
13 **Grants**................................	†1,627	2,146	2,396	†652	956	1,351	†1,040	1,314	1,344	†464	792	1,186
131 From foreign governments................	†—	—	—	†—	—	—	†—	—	—	†—	—	—
132 From international organizations................	†392	725	884	†437	771	1,162	†27	21	24	†464	792	1,186
133 From other general government units..........	†1,235	1,421	1,512	†215	185	189	†1,013	1,293	1,320	†—	—	—
14 **Other revenue**................	†5,059	5,468	5,745	†7,207	7,827	8,201	†1,381	1,485	1,602	†8,121	8,802	9,457
Table 2 Expense by economic type												
2 **Expense**................................	†37,597	41,107	42,972	†48,203	52,605	55,130	†1,893	2,119	2,265	†48,401	52,736	55,540
21 **Compensation of employees**................	†9,417	10,391	10,846	†11,735	12,857	13,351	†927	1,027	1,096	†12,662	13,884	14,447
211 Wages and salaries................	†7,001	7,471	7,961	†9,132	9,741	10,268	†836	916	977	†9,968	10,657	11,245
212 Social contributions................	†2,416	2,920	2,885	†2,603	3,116	3,083	†91	111	119	†2,694	3,227	3,202
22 **Use of goods and services**................	†3,448	3,478	3,938	†4,705	4,841	5,382	†641	727	795	†5,346	5,568	6,177
23 **Consumption of fixed capital**................	†24	25	25	†73	77	79	†2	2	3	†75	79	82
24 **Interest**................................	†9,730	10,210	10,236	†9,776	10,241	10,273	†30	42	42	†9,339	9,773	9,969
25 **Subsidies**................................	†153	222	220	†153	222	220	†—	—	—	†153	222	220
26 **Grants**................................	†8,094	9,090	9,715	†1,766	2,006	2,127	†216	184	189	†754	712	807
261 To foreign governments................	†—	—	—	†—	—	—	†—	—	—	†—	—	—
262 To international organizations................	†754	712	807	†754	712	807	†—	—	—	†754	712	807
263 To other general government units.............	†7,340	8,378	8,908	†1,012	1,294	1,320	†216	184	189	†—	—	—
2631 Current................................	†7,250	8,028	8,454	†1,004	1,285	1,312	†168	184	189	†—	—	—
2632 Capital................................	†90	350	454	†8	9	8	†48	—	—	†—	—	—
27 **Social benefits**................	†3,927	4,291	4,437	†17,177	18,904	20,098	†−22	−21	−22	†17,155	18,883	20,076
28 **Other expense**................	†2,804	3,400	3,555	†2,818	3,457	3,600	†99	158	162	†2,917	3,615	3,762
281 Property expense other than interest...........	†—	—	—	†—	—	—	†2	3	3	†2	3	3
282 Miscellaneous other expense................	†2,804	3,400	3,555	†2,818	3,457	3,600	†97	155	159	†2,915	3,612	3,759
2821 Current................................	†557	644	688	†571	701	733	†37	31	36	†608	732	769
2822 Capital................................	†2,247	2,756	2,867	†2,247	2,756	2,867	†60	124	123	†2,307	2,880	2,990

In Millions of Euros / Year Ending December 31 / Noncash Reporter

	Budgetary Central Government			Central Government			Local Government			General Government		
	1998	1999	2000	1998	1999	2000	1998	1999	2000	1998	1999	2000
Table 3 Transactions in assets and liabilities												
3 **Change in net worth from transactns....**	†–2,109	–1,201	–267	†433	1,680	2,752	†868	1,058	1,083	†1,301	2,738	3,835
31 **Net acquisition of nonfinancial assets...**	†3,068	3,780	4,005	†3,162	3,902	4,114	†801	979	1,024	†3,963	4,881	5,138
311 Fixed assets...............................	†2,946	3,571	3,870	†3,024	3,676	3,963	†771	951	997	†3,795	4,627	4,960
3111 Buildings and structures.................	....	....	....	....	....	....	....	....	....	....	....	....
3112 Machinery and equipment..................	....	....	....	....	....	....	....	....	....	....	....	....
3113 Other fixed assets.......................	....	....	....	....	....	....	....	....	....	....	....	....
312 Inventories...............................	†—	—	—	†—	—	—	†—	—	—	†—	—	—
313 Valuables.................................	†—	—	—	†—	—	—	†—	—	—	†—	—	—
314 Nonproduced assets........................	†122	209	135	†138	226	151	†16	28	27	†168	254	178
3141 Land......................................	....	....	....	....	....	....	....	....	....	....	....	....
3142 Subsoil assets............................	....	....	....	....	....	....	....	....	....	....	....	....
3143 Other naturally occurring assets.........	....	....	....	....	....	....	....	....	....	....	....	....
3144 Intangible nonproduced assets............	....	....	....	....	....	....	....	....	....	....	....	....
32 **Net acquisition of financial assets........**	....	....	....	....	....	....	....	....	....	....	....	....
321 Domestic...................................	....	....	....	....	....	....	....	....	....	....	....	....
3212 Currency and deposits....................	....	....	....	....	....	....	....	....	....	....	....	....
3213 Securities other than shares............	....	....	....	....	....	....	....	....	....	....	....	....
3214 Loans...................................	....	....	....	....	....	....	....	....	....	....	....	....
3215 Shares and other equity.................	....	....	....	....	....	....	....	....	....	....	....	....
3216 Insurance technical reserves............	....	....	....	....	....	....	....	....	....	....	....	....
3217 Financial derivatives...................	....	....	....	....	....	....	....	....	....	....	....	....
3218 Other accounts receivable...............	....	....	....	....	....	....	....	....	....	....	....	....
322 Foreign...................................	....	....	....	....	....	....	....	....	....	....	....	....
3222 Currency and deposits...................	....	....	....	....	....	....	....	....	....	....	....	....
3223 Securities other than shares............	....	....	....	....	....	....	....	....	....	....	....	....
3224 Loans...................................	....	....	....	....	....	....	....	....	....	....	....	....
3225 Shares and other equity.................	....	....	....	....	....	....	....	....	....	....	....	....
3226 Insurance technical reserves............	....	....	....	....	....	....	....	....	....	....	....	....
3227 Financial derivatives...................	....	....	....	....	....	....	....	....	....	....	....	....
3228 Other accounts receivable...............	....	....	....	....	....	....	....	....	....	....	....	....
323 Monetary gold and SDRs....................	....	....	....	....	....	....	....	....	....	....	....	....
33 **Net incurrence of liabilities...................**	....	....	....	....	....	....	....	....	....	....	....	....
331 Domestic...................................	....	....	....	....	....	....	....	....	....	....	....	....
3312 Currency and deposits...................	....	....	....	....	....	....	....	....	....	....	....	....
3313 Securities other than shares............	....	....	....	....	....	....	....	....	....	....	....	....
3314 Loans...................................	....	....	....	....	....	....	....	....	....	....	....	....
3316 Insurance technical reserves............	....	....	....	....	....	....	....	....	....	....	....	....
3317 Financial derivatives...................	....	....	....	....	....	....	....	....	....	....	....	....
3318 Other accounts payable..................	....	....	....	....	....	....	....	....	....	....	....	....
332 Foreign...................................	....	....	....	....	....	....	....	....	....	....	....	....
3322 Currency and deposits...................	....	....	....	....	....	....	....	....	....	....	....	....
3323 Securities other than shares............	....	....	....	....	....	....	....	....	....	....	....	....
3324 Loans...................................	....	....	....	....	....	....	....	....	....	....	....	....
3326 Insurance technical reserves............	....	....	....	....	....	....	....	....	....	....	....	....
3327 Financial derivatives...................	....	....	....	....	....	....	....	....	....	....	....	....
3328 Other accounts payable..................	....	....	....	....	....	....	....	....	....	....	....	....
Table 4 Holding gains in assets and liabilities												
Table 5 Other changes in the volume of assets and liabilities												
Table 6 Balance sheet												
Table 7 Outlays by functions of govt.												
7 Total outlays.......................	†40,665	44,887	46,977	†51,365	56,507	59,244	†2,694	3,098	3,289	†52,364	57,617	60,678
701 **General public services.........................**	....	....	....	....	....	....	....	....	....	†10,944	12,293	....
7017 Public debt transactions...............	†9,730	10,210	10,236	†9,776	10,241	10,273	†30	42	42	†9,339	9,773	9,969
7018 General transfers between levels of govt.....	....	....	....	....	....	....	....	....	....	....	....	....
702 **Defense...**	....	....	....	....	....	....	....	....	....	†3,422	3,684	....
703 **Public order and safety.........................**	....	....	....	....	....	....	....	....	....	†1,190	1,325	....
704 **Economic affairs.................................**	....	....	....	....	....	....	....	....	....	†219	244	....
7042 Agriculture, forestry, fishing, and hunting......	....	....	....	....	....	....	....	....	....	....	....	....
7043 Fuel and energy.........................	....	....	....	....	....	....	....	....	....	....	....	....
7044 Mining, manufacturing, and construction.....	....	....	....	....	....	....	....	....	....	....	....	....
7045 Transport...............................	....	....	....	....	....	....	....	....	....	....	....	....
7046 Communication...........................	....	....	....	....	....	....	....	....	....	....	....	....

In Millions of Euros / Year Ending December 31 / Noncash Reporter

		Budgetary Central Government			Central Government			Local Government			General Government		
		1998	1999	2000	1998	1999	2000	1998	1999	2000	1998	1999	2000
705	**Environmental protection**....................	....	....	....	....	....	....	....	....	....	†543	643	....
706	**Housing and community amenities**........	....	....	....	....	....	....	....	....	....	†369	227	....
707	**Health**...	....	....	....	....	....	....	....	....	....	†4,350	4,651	....
7072	Outpatient services..................................	....	....	....	....	....	....	....	....	....	....	....	....
7073	Hospital services.....................................	....	....	....	....	....	....	....	....	....	....	....	....
7074	Public health services..............................	....	....	....	....	....	....	....	....	....	....	....	....
708	**Recreation, culture, and religion**...........	....	....	....	....	....	....	....	....	....	†374	429	....
709	**Education**......................................	....	....	....	....	....	....	....	....	....	†4,391	4,884	....
7091	Pre-primary and primary education..............	....	....	....	....	....	....	....	....	....	....	....	....
7092	Secondary education................................	....	....	....	....	....	....	....	....	....	....	....	....
7094	Tertiary education...................................	....	....	....	....	....	....	....	....	....	....	....	....
710	**Social protection**.............................	....	....	....	....	....	....	....	....	....	†20,663	22,817	....
7	Statistical discrepancy: Total outlays............	....	....	....	....	....	....	....	....	....	†—	—	....

Table 8 Transactions in financial assets and liabilities by sector

Guatemala 258

In Millions of Quetzales / Year Ending December 31 / Cash Reporter

	Budgetary Central Government			Central Government			Local Government			General Government		
	2002	2003	2004	2002	2003	2004	2002	2003	2004	2002	2003	2004
Statement of government operations												
Statement of other economic flows												
Balance sheet												
6 *Net worth*...............................	....	....	....	....	....	....	....	....	....	....	....	....
61 Nonfinancial assets............	....	....	....	....	....	....	....	....	....	....	....	....
62 Financial assets.................	....	....	....	....	....	....	....	....	....	....	....	....
63 Liabilities.........................	29,890.9	36,046.4	41,489.2	....	....	....	....	....	....	....	....	....
Statement of sources and uses of cash												
1 Cash receipts from operating activities....	20,715.6	21,694.4	23,389.1	....	....	....	....	....	....	....	....	....
11 Taxes.............................	19,346.7	20,317.7	22,001.0	....	....	....	....	....	....	....	....	....
12 Social contributions............	468.6	504.7	539.7	....	....	....	....	....	....	....	....	....
13 Grants...........................	414.9	377.1	312.1	....	....	....	....	....	....	....	....	....
14 Other receipts..................	525.4	494.9	536.4	....	....	....	....	....	....	....	....	....
2 Cash payments for operating activities....	20,758.7	24,968.6	24,128.9	....	....	....	....	....	....	....	....	....
21 Compensation of employees......	6,413.0	6,751.9	6,783.9	....	....	....	....	....	....	....	....	....
22 Purchases of goods and services...	3,013.9	3,405.7	2,884.0	....	....	....	....	....	....	....	....	....
24 Interest.........................	2,191.5	2,207.4	2,547.1	....	....	....	....	....	....	....	....	....
25 Subsidies........................	8.2	242.3	179.2	....	....	....	....	....	....	....	....	....
26 Grants...........................	2,707.4	2,961.2	3,099.3	....	....	....	....	....	....	....	....	....
27 Social benefits..................	2,710.7	1,883.5	1,738.6	....	....	....	....	....	....	....	....	....
28 Other payments.................	3,714.0	7,516.5	6,897.0	....	....	....	....	....	....	....	....	....
CIO *Net cash inflow from oper. activities*.....	−43.1	−3,274.2	−739.8	....	....	....	....	....	....	....	....	....
31.1 Purchases of nonfinancial assets....	1,509.2	1,241.8	1,253.3	....	....	....	....	....	....	....	....	....
31.2 Sales of nonfinancial assets.......	.1	—	.6	....	....	....	....	....	....	....	....	....
31 Net cash outflow from investments in nonfinancial assets............	1,509.1	1,241.8	1,252.6	....	....	....	....	....	....	....	....	....
CSD *Cash surplus/deficit*...............	−1,552.2	−4,516.0	−1,992.4	....	....	....	....	....	....	....	....	....
32x Net acquisition of fin assets, excl. cash....	217.5	49.8	87.6	....	....	....	....	....	....	....	....	....
321x Domestic......................	217.5	49.8	87.6	....	....	....	....	....	....	....	....	....
322x Foreign........................	—	—	—	....	....	....	....	....	....	....	....	....
323 Monetary gold and SDRs.........	—	—	—	....	....	....	....	....	....	....	....	....
33 Net incurrence of liabilities........	640.7	5,846.7	5,425.0	....	....	....	....	....	....	....	....	....
331 Domestic........................	−1,111.0	2,867.3	1,804.1	....	....	....	....	....	....	....	....	....
332 Foreign.........................	1,751.6	2,979.4	3,620.8	....	....	....	....	....	....	....	....	....
NFB Net cash inflow from fin. activities....	423.2	5,796.9	5,337.4	....	....	....	....	....	....	....	....	....
NCB *Net change in the stock of cash*.....	−1,129.0	1,280.9	3,344.9	....	....	....	....	....	....	....	....	....
Table 1 Revenue												
1 **Revenue**........................	**20,715.6**	**21,694.4**	**23,389.1**	....	....	....	....	....	....	....	....	....
11 **Taxes**...........................	**19,346.7**	**20,317.7**	**22,001.0**	....	....	....	....	....	....	....	....	....
111 Taxes on income, profits, & capital gains...	5,453.8	5,601.1	5,739.6	....	....	....	....	....	....	....	....	....
1111 Individuals....................	486.7	323.8	346.8	....	....	....	....	....	....	....	....	....
1112 Corporations and other enterprises....	2,182.3	2,501.9	3,312.0	....	....	....	....	....	....	....	....	....
112 Taxes on payroll and workforce.....	—	—	—	....	....	....	....	....	....	....	....	....
113 Taxes on property...............	8.9	8.7	9.1	....	....	....	....	....	....	....	....	....
114 Taxes on goods and services.....	11,435.2	12,146.1	13,535.9	....	....	....	....	....	....	....	....	....
1141 General taxes on goods and services....	8,618.4	9,288.6	10,482.3	....	....	....	....	....	....	....	....	....
1142 Excises.......................	2,249.9	2,244.0	2,445.6	....	....	....	....	....	....	....	....	....
115 Taxes on int'l. trade and transactions....	2,264.1	2,385.0	2,428.1	....	....	....	....	....	....	....	....	....
116 Other taxes.....................	184.7	176.8	288.4	....	....	....	....	....	....	....	....	....
12 **Social contributions**...........	**468.6**	**504.7**	**539.7**	....	....	....	....	....	....	....	....	....
121 Social security contributions......	—	—	—	....	....	....	....	....	....	....	....	....
122 Other social contributions........	468.6	504.7	539.7	....	....	....	....	....	....	....	....	....
13 **Grants**.........................	**414.9**	**377.1**	**312.1**	....	....	....	....	....	....	....	....	....
131 From foreign governments........	414.9	377.1	302.1	....	....	....	....	....	....	....	....	....
132 From international organizations....	—	—	9.9	....	....	....	....	....	....	....	....	....
133 From other general government units....	—	—	—	....	....	....	....	....	....	....	....	....
14 **Other revenue**.................	**525.4**	**494.9**	**536.4**	....	....	....	....	....	....	....	....	....
Table 2 Expense by economic type												
2 **Expense**........................	**20,758.7**	**24,968.6**	**24,128.9**	....	....	....	....	....	....	....	....	....
21 **Compensation of employees**.....	**6,413.0**	**6,751.9**	**6,783.9**	....	....	....	....	....	....	....	....	....
211 Wages and salaries.............	6,311.2	6,648.2	6,615.9	....	....	....	....	....	....	....	....	....
212 Social contributions............	101.8	103.7	168.0	....	....	....	....	....	....	....	....	....
22 **Use of goods and services**......	**3,013.9**	**3,405.7**	**2,884.0**	....	....	....	....	....	....	....	....	....
23 **Consumption of fixed capital**....	....	....	....	....	....	....	....	....	....	....	....	....
24 **Interest**........................	**2,191.5**	**2,207.4**	**2,547.1**	....	....	....	....	....	....	....	....	....
25 **Subsidies**......................	**8.2**	**242.3**	**179.2**	....	....	....	....	....	....	....	....	....

		Budgetary Central Government			Central Government			Local Government			General Government		
		2002	2003	2004	2002	2003	2004	2002	2003	2004	2002	2003	2004
26	**Grants**..............................	**2,707.4**	**2,961.2**	**3,099.3**	....	....	....	....	....	....	....	....	....
261	To foreign govenments......................	533.9	742.4	820.1	....	....	....	....	....	....	....	....	....
262	To international organizations.............	—	—	—	....	....	....	....	....	....	....	....	....
263	To other general government units.............	2,173.5	2,218.8	2,279.2	....	....	....	....	....	....	....	....	....
2631	Current...............................	—	—	—	....	....	....	....	....	....	....	....	....
2632	Capital...............................	2,173.5	2,218.8	2,279.2	....	....	....	....	....	....	....	....	....
27	**Social benefits**...................	**2,710.7**	**1,883.5**	**1,738.6**	....	....	....	....	....	....	...	....	....
28	**Other expense**....................	**3,714.0**	**7,516.5**	**6,897.0**	....	....	....	....	....	....	...	....	....
281	Property expense other than interest.............	—	—	—	....	....	....	....	....	....	....	....	....
282	Miscellaneous other expense..................	3,714.0	7,516.5	6,897.0	....	....	....	....	....	....	....	....	....
2821	Current...............................	2,156.2	4,861.0	4,269.2	....	....	....	....	....	....	....	....	....
2822	Capital...............................	1,557.9	2,655.6	2,627.8	....	....	....	....	....	....	....	....	....

Table 3   Transactions in assets and liabilities

		2002	2003	2004	2002	2003	2004	2002	2003	2004	2002	2003	2004
3	**Change in net worth from transactns....**	....	....	....	....	....	....	....	....	....	....	....	....
31	**Net acquisition of nonfinancial assets....**	**1,509.1**	**1,241.8**	**1,252.6**	....	....	....	....	....	....	....	....	....
311	Fixed assets..............................	1,454.7	1,223.2	1,250.2	....	....	....	....	....	....	....	....	....
3111	Buildings and structures..................	....	1,162.1	1,188.2	....	....	....	....	....	....	....	....	....
3112	Machinery and equipment......................	....	59.3	59.2	....	....	....	....	....	....	....	....	....
3113	Other fixed assets.........................	....	1.8	2.9	....	....	....	....	....	....	....	....	....
312	Inventories...............................	—	—	—	....	....	....	....	....	....	....	....	....
313	Valuables...............................	—	—	—	....	....	....	....	....	....	....	....	....
314	Nonproduced assets..........................	54.4	18.7	2.4	....	....	....	....	....	....	....	....	....
3141	Land..................................	54.4	18.7	2.4	....	....	....	....	....	....	....	....	....
3142	Subsoil assets............................	—	—	—	....	....	....	....	....	....	....	....	....
3143	Other naturally occurring assets................	—	—	—	....	....	....	....	....	....	....	....	....
3144	Intangible nonproduced assets.................	—	—	—	....	....	....	....	....	....	....	....	....
32	**Net acquisition of financial assets.........**	**−911.5**	**1,330.7**	**3,432.6**	....	....	....	....	....	....	....	....	....
321	Domestic..................................	....	....	....	....	....	....	....	....	....	....	....	....
3212	Currency and deposits........................	....	....	....	....	....	....	....	....	....	....	....	....
3213	Securities other than shares..................	....	....	....	....	....	....	....	....	....	....	....	....
3214	Loans.................................	....	....	....	....	....	....	....	....	....	....	....	....
3215	Shares and other equity.......................	....	....	....	....	....	....	....	....	....	....	....	....
3216	Insurance technical reserves..................	....	....	....	....	....	....	....	....	....	....	....	....
3217	Financial derivatives........................	....	....	....	....	....	....	....	....	....	....	....	....
3218	Other accounts receivable....................	....	....	....	....	....	....	....	....	....	....	....	....
322	Foreign.................................	....	....	....	....	....	....	....	....	....	....	....	....
3222	Currency and deposits........................	....	....	....	....	....	....	....	....	....	....	....	....
3223	Securities other than shares..................	....	....	....	....	....	....	....	....	....	....	....	....
3224	Loans.................................	....	....	....	....	....	....	....	....	....	....	....	....
3225	Shares and other equity.......................	....	....	....	....	....	....	....	....	....	....	....	....
3226	Insurance technical reserves..................	....	....	....	....	....	....	....	....	....	....	....	....
3227	Financial derivatives........................	....	....	....	....	....	....	....	....	....	....	....	....
3228	Other accounts receivable....................	....	....	....	....	....	....	....	....	....	....	....	....
323	Monetary gold and SDRs..................	—	—	—	....	....	....	....	....	....	....	....	....
33	**Net incurrence of liabilities...................**	**640.7**	**5,846.7**	**5,425.0**	....	....	....	....	....	....	....	....	....
331	Domestic..................................	−1,111.0	2,867.3	1,804.1	....	....	....	....	....	....	....	....	....
3312	Currency and deposits........................	—	—	—	....	....	....	....	....	....	....	....	....
3313	Securities other than shares..................	−1,111.0	2,867.3	1,804.1	....	....	....	....	....	....	....	....	....
3314	Loans.................................	—	—	—	....	....	....	....	....	....	....	....	....
3316	Insurance technical reserves..................	—	—	—	....	....	....	....	....	....	....	....	....
3317	Financial derivatives........................	—	—	—	....	....	....	....	....	....	....	....	....
3318	Other accounts payable.......................	....	....	....	....	....	....	....	....	....	....	....	....
332	Foreign.................................	1,751.6	2,979.4	3,620.8	....	....	....	....	....	....	....	....	....
3322	Currency and deposits........................	—	—	—	....	....	....	....	....	....	....	....	....
3323	Securities other than shares..................	—	—	—	....	....	....	....	....	....	....	....	....
3324	Loans.................................	1,751.6	2,979.4	3,620.8	....	....	....	....	....	....	....	....	....
3326	Insurance technical reserves..................	—	—	—	....	....	....	....	....	....	....	....	....
3327	Financial derivatives........................	—	—	—	....	....	....	....	....	....	....	....	....
3328	Other accounts payable.......................	....	....	....	....	....	....	....	....	....	....	....	....

Guatemala   258

In Millions of Quetzales / Year Ending December 31 / Cash Reporter

	Budgetary Central Government			Central Government			Local Government			General Government		
	2002	2003	2004	2002	2003	2004	2002	2003	2004	2002	2003	2004
Table 4 Holding gains in assets and liabilities												
Table 5 Other changes in the volume of assets and liabilities												
Table 6 Balance sheet												
6 Net worth....................	....	....	....	....	....	....	....	....	....	....	....	....
61 **Nonfinancial assets.....................**	....	....	....	....	....	....	....	....	....	....	....	....
611 Fixed assets...............	....	....	....	....	....	....	....	....	....	....	....	....
6111 Buildings and structures..................	....	....	....	....	....	....	....	....	....	....	....	....
6112 Machinery and equipment.................	....	....	....	....	....	....	....	....	....	....	....	....
6113 Other fixed assets...............	....	....	....	....	....	....	....	....	....	....	....	....
612 Inventories...............	....	....	....	....	....	....	....	....	....	....	....	....
613 Valuables...................	....	....	....	....	....	....	....	....	....	....	....	....
614 Nonproduced assets...............	....	....	....	....	....	....	....	....	....	....	....	....
6141 Land...............	....	....	....	....	....	....	....	....	....	....	....	....
6142 Subsoil assets...............	....	....	....	....	....	....	....	....	....	....	....	....
6143 Other naturally occurring assets.........	....	....	....	....	....	....	....	....	....	....	....	....
6144 Intangible nonproduced assets.........	....	....	....	....	....	....	....	....	....	....	....	....
62 **Financial assets.....................**	....	....	....	....	....	....	....	....	....	....	....	....
621 Domestic..................	....	....	....	....	....	....	....	....	....	....	....	....
6212 Currency and deposits...............	....	....	....	....	....	....	....	....	....	....	....	....
6213 Securities other than shares...............	....	....	....	....	....	....	....	....	....	....	....	....
6214 Loans...............	....	....	....	....	....	....	....	....	....	....	....	....
6215 Shares and other equity...............	....	....	....	....	....	....	....	....	....	....	....	....
6216 Insurance technical reserves............	....	....	....	....	....	....	....	....	....	....	....	....
6217 Financial derivatives...............	....	....	....	....	....	....	....	....	....	....	....	....
6218 Other accounts receivable............	....	....	....	....	....	....	....	....	....	....	....	....
622 Foreign...............	....	....	....	....	....	....	....	....	....	....	....	....
6222 Currency and deposits...............	....	....	....	....	....	....	....	....	....	....	....	....
6223 Securities other than shares...............	....	....	....	....	....	....	....	....	....	....	....	....
6224 Loans...............	....	....	....	....	....	....	....	....	....	....	....	....
6225 Shares and other equity...............	....	....	....	....	....	....	....	....	....	....	....	....
6226 Insurance technical reserves............	....	....	....	....	....	....	....	....	....	....	....	....
6227 Financial derivatives...............	....	....	....	....	....	....	....	....	....	....	....	....
6228 Other accounts receivable............	....	....	....	....	....	....	....	....	....	....	....	....
623 Monetary gold and SDRs...............	....	....	....	....	....	....	....	....	....	....	....	....
63 **Liabilities.....................**	29,890.9	36,046.4	41,489.2	....	....	....	....	....	....	....	....	....
631 Domestic..................	8,169.2	11,036.5	12,840.6	....	....	....	....	....	....	....	....	....
6312 Currency and deposits...............	....	....	....	....	....	....	....	....	....	....	....	....
6313 Securities other than shares...............	....	....	....	....	....	....	....	....	....	....	....	....
6314 Loans...............	....	....	....	....	....	....	....	....	....	....	....	....
6316 Insurance technical reserves............	....	....	....	....	....	....	....	....	....	....	....	....
6317 Financial derivatives...............	....	....	....	....	....	....	....	....	....	....	....	....
6318 Other accounts payable............	....	....	....	....	....	....	....	....	....	....	....	....
632 Foreign...............	21,721.7	25,009.9	28,648.6	....	....	....	....	....	....	....	....	....
6322 Currency and deposits...............	....	....	....	....	....	....	....	....	....	....	....	....
6323 Securities other than shares...............	....	....	....	....	....	....	....	....	....	....	....	....
6324 Loans...............	....	....	....	....	....	....	....	....	....	....	....	....
6326 Insurance technical reserves............	....	....	....	....	....	....	....	....	....	....	....	....
6327 Financial derivatives...............	....	....	....	....	....	....	....	....	....	....	....	....
6328 Other accounts payable............	....	....	....	....	....	....	....	....	....	....	....	....
Memorandum items:												
6M2 Net financial worth...............	....	....	....	....	....	....				....	....	....
6M3 Debt at market value...............	....	....	....	....	....	....				....	....	....
6M4 Debt at nominal value...............	....	....	....	....	....	....				....	....	....
6M5 Arrears...............	....	....	....	....	....	....				....	....	....
6M6 Obligations for social security benefits............	....	....	....	....	....	....				....	....	....
6M7 Contingent liabilities...............	....	....	....	....	....	....				....	....	....
6M8 Uncapitalized military weapons, systems........	....	....	....	....	....	....				....	....	....
Table 7 Outlays by functions of govt.												
7 **Total outlays...........................**	22,270.4	26,210.9	25,382.2	....	....	....	....	....	....	....	....	....
701 **General public services........................**	4,643.6	5,819.7	7,301.6	....	....	....	....	....	....	....	....	....
7017 Public debt transactions...............	2,191.5	2,207.4	2,547.1	....	....	....	....	....	....	....	....	....
7018 General transfers between levels of govt......	....	....	2,279.2	....	....	....	....	....	....	....	....	....
702 **Defense..........................**	1,057.3	1,235.1	775.4	....	....	....	....	....	....	....	....	....
703 **Public order and safety........................**	2,247.5	2,725.1	2,630.1	....	....	....	....	....	....	....	....	....

		Budgetary Central Government			Central Government			Local Government			General Government		
		2002	2003	2004	2002	2003	2004	2002	2003	2004	2002	2003	2004
704	**Economic affairs**..............................	**5,033.0**	**6,265.3**	**6,077.4**	....	....	....	....	....	....	....	....	....
7042	Agriculture, forestry, fishing, and hunting.....	613.2	859.3	829.5	....	....	....	....	....	....	....	....	....
7043	Fuel and energy...........................	30.6	29.1	21.1	....	....	....	....	....	....	....	....	....
7044	Mining, manufacturing, and construction.....	270.3	150.7	133.5	....	....	....	....	....	....	....	....	....
7045	Transport..................................	2,131.1	2,167.3	2,380.8	....	....	....	....	....	....	....	....	....
7046	Communication............................	85.5	73.9	63.4	....	....	....	....	....	....	....	....	....
705	**Environmental protection**....................	**169.0**	**204.7**	**186.6**	....	....	....	....	....	....	....	....	....
706	**Housing and community amenities**........	**3,051.8**	**2,948.3**	**1,250.7**	....	....	....	....	....	....	....	....	....
707	**Health**......................................	**1,638.1**	**1,830.4**	**1,799.9**	....	....	....	....	....	....	....	....	....
7072	Outpatient services........................	1,261.0	1,388.5	1,423.9	....	....	....	....	....	....	....	....	....
7073	Hospital services...........................	377.1	442.0	376.0	....	....	....	....	....	....	....	....	....
7074	Public health services......................	—	—	—	....	....	....	....	....	....	....	....	....
708	**Recreation, culture, and religion**...........	**356.3**	**395.2**	**399.9**	....	....	....	....	....	....	....	....	....
709	**Education**..................................	**3,973.7**	**4,625.1**	**4,794.7**	....	....	....	....	....	....	....	....	....
7091	Pre-primary and primary education..............	2,464.6	2,458.4	283.4	....	....	....	....	....	....	....	....	....
7092	Secondary education.......................	471.0	918.6	2,876.4	....	....	....	....	....	....	....	....	....
7094	Tertiary education..........................	595.8	605.6	1,035.9	....	....	....	....	....	....	....	....	....
710	**Social protection**...........................	**100.0**	**162.0**	**166.0**	....	....	....	....	....	....	....	....	....
7	Statistical discrepancy: Total outlays.............	—	—	—	....	....	....	....	....	....	....	....	....

Table 8 Transactions in financial assets and liabilities by sector

		Budgetary Central Government			Central Government			Local Government			General Government		
82	**Net acquisition of financial assets**.........	**−911.5**	**1,330.7**	**3,432.6**	....	....	....	....	....	....	....	....	....
821	Domestic....................................	....	....	....	....	....	....	....	....	....	....	....	....
8211	General government........................	....	....	....	....	....	....	....	....	....	....	....	....
8212	Central bank...............................	....	....	....	....	....	....	....	....	....	....	....	....
8213	Other depository corporations..............	....	....	....	....	....	....	....	....	....	....	....	....
8214	Financial corporations n.e.c................	....	....	....	....	....	....	....	....	....	....	....	....
8215	Nonfinancial corporations..................	....	....	....	....	....	....	....	....	....	....	....	....
8216	Households & NPIs serving households......	....	....	....	....	....	....	....	....	....	....	....	....
822	Foreign......................................	....	....	....	....	....	....	....	....	....	....	....	....
8221	General government........................	....	....	....	....	....	....	....	....	....	....	....	....
8227	International organizations..................	....	....	....	....	....	....	....	....	....	....	....	....
8228	Financial corporations other than international organizations.............	....	....	....	....	....	....	....	....	....	....	....	....
8229	Other nonresidents.........................	....	....	....	....	....	....	....	....	....	....	....	....
823	Monetary gold and SDRs....................	—	—	—	....	....	....	....	....	....	....	....	....
83	**Net incurrence of liabilities**...................	**640.7**	**5,846.7**	**5,425.0**	....	....	....	....	....	....	....	....	....
831	Domestic....................................	−1,111.0	2,867.3	1,804.1	....	....	....	....	....	....	....	....	....
8311	General government........................	34.0	1,118.1	2,323.8	....	....	....	....	....	....	....	....	....
8312	Central bank...............................	—	—	—	....	....	....	....	....	....	....	....	....
8313	Other depository corporations..............	−76.9	1,941.8	825.3	....	....	....	....	....	....	....	....	....
8314	Financial corporations n.e.c................	—	—	—	....	....	....	....	....	....	....	....	....
8315	Nonfinancial corporations..................	−1,068.1	−192.6	−1,344.9	....	....	....	....	....	....	....	....	....
8316	Households & NPIs serving households......	—	—	—	....	....	....	....	....	....	....	....	....
832	Foreign......................................	1,751.6	2,979.4	3,620.8	....	....	....	....	....	....	....	....	....
8321	General government........................	291.3	−741.4	557.1	....	....	....	....	....	....	....	....	....
8327	International organizations..................	1,879.9	1,346.7	467.9	....	....	....	....	....	....	....	....	....
8328	Financial corporations other than international organizations.............	—	—	—	....	....	....	....	....	....	....	....	....
8329	Other nonresidents.........................	−419.6	2,374.1	2,595.9	....	....	....	....	....	....	....	....	....

2005, International Monetary Fund: *Government Finance Statistics Yearbook*

Guinea 656

In Millions of Francs / Year Ending December 31 / Cash Reporter

		Budgetary Central Government			Central Government			Local Government			General Government		
		1997	1998	1999f	1997	1998	1999	1997	1998	1999	1997	1998	1999
Statement of government operations													
Statement of other economic flows													
Balance sheet													
Statement of sources and uses of cash													
1	Cash receipts from operating activities	....	603,574	895,400	....	....	....	....	....	....	....	....	....
11	Taxes	....	463,842	534,450	....	....	....	....	....	....	....	....	....
12	Social contributions	....	3,270	5,260	....	....	....	....	....	....	....	....	....
13	Grants	....	106,481	320,500	....	....	....	....	....	....	....	....	....
14	Other receipts	....	29,981	35,190	....	....	....	....	....	....	....	....	....
2	Cash payments for operating activities	....	535,191	646,560	....	....	....	....	....	....	....	....	....
21	Compensation of employees	....	181,203	192,200	....	....	....	....	....	....	....	....	....
22	Purchases of goods and services	....	89,402	99,300	....	....	....	....	....	....	....	....	....
24	Interest	....	149,125	208,150	....	....	....	....	....	....	....	....	....
25	Subsidies	....	33,580	43,600	....	....	....	....	....	....	....	....	....
26	Grants	....	—	—	....	....	....	....	....	....	....	....	....
27	Social benefits	....	16,630	32,900	....	....	....	....	....	....	....	....	....
28	Other payments	....	6,316	4,050	....	....	....	....	....	....	....	....	....
CIO	*Net cash inflow from oper. activities*	....	*68,383*	*248,840*	....	....	....	....	....	....	....	....	....
31.1	Purchases of nonfinancial assets	....	257,363	363,500	....	....	....	....	....	....	....	....	....
31.2	Sales of nonfinancial assets	....	200	—	....	....	....	....	....	....	....	....	....
31	Net cash outflow from investments in nonfinancial assets	....	257,163	363,500	....	....	....	....	....	....	....	....	....
CSD	*Cash surplus/deficit*	....	*−188,780*	*−114,660*	....	....	....	....	....	....	....	....	....
32x	Net acquisition of fin assets, excl. cash	....	3,870	1,650	....	....	....	....	....	....	....	....	....
321x	Domestic	....	3,870	1,650	....	....	....	....	....	....	....	....	....
322x	Foreign	....	—	—	....	....	....	....	....	....	....	....	....
323	Monetary gold and SDRs	....	—	—	....	....	....	....	....	....	....	....	....
33	Net incurrence of liabilities	....	195,920	125,730	....	....	....	....	....	....	....	....	....
331	Domestic	....	−2,610	8,250	....	....	....	....	....	....	....	....	....
332	Foreign	....	198,530	117,480	....	....	....	....	....	....	....	....	....
NFB	Net cash inflow from fin. activities	....	192,050	124,080	....	....	....	....	....	....	....	....	....
NCB	*Net change in the stock of cash*	....	*3,270*	*9,420*	....	....	....	....	....	....	....	....	....
Table 1 Revenue													
1	**Revenue**	....	603,574	895,400	....	....	....	....	....	....	....	....	....
11	**Taxes**	....	463,842	534,450	....	....	....	....	....	....	....	....	....
111	Taxes on income, profits, & capital gains	....	49,176	54,553	....	....	....	....	....	....	....	....	....
1111	Individuals	....	29,641	35,815	....	....	....	....	....	....	....	....	....
1112	Corporations and other enterprises	....	18,053	15,988	....	....	....	....	....	....	....	....	....
112	Taxes on payroll and workforce	....	4,365	4,505	....	....	....	....	....	....	....	....	....
113	Taxes on property	....	9,410	16,305	....	....	....	....	....	....	....	....	....
114	Taxes on goods and services	....	27,132	29,525	....	....	....	....	....	....	....	....	....
1141	General taxes on goods and services	....	26,521	28,925	....	....	....	....	....	....	....	....	....
1142	Excises	....	611	600	....	....	....	....	....	....	....	....	....
115	Taxes on int'l. trade and transactions	....	373,652	429,170	....	....	....	....	....	....	....	....	....
116	Other taxes	....	107	392	....	....	....	....	....	....	....	....	....
12	**Social contributions**	....	**3,270**	**5,260**	....	....	....	....	....	....	....	....	....
121	Social security contributions	....	3,270	3,500	....	....	....	....	....	....	....	....	....
122	Other social contributions	....	—	1,760	....	....	....	....	....	....	....	....	....
13	**Grants**	....	106,481	320,500	....	....	....	....	....	....	....	....	....
131	From foreign governments	....	106,481	320,500	....	....	....	....	....	....	....	....	....
132	From international organizations	....	—	—	....	....	....	....	....	....	....	....	....
133	From other general government units	....	—	—	....	....	....	....	....	....	....	....	....
14	**Other revenue**	....	**29,981**	**35,190**	....	....	....	....	....	....	....	....	....
Table 2 Expense by economic type													
2	**Expense**	....	535,191	646,560	....	....	....	....	....	....	....	....	....
21	**Compensation of employees**	....	181,203	192,200	....	....	....	....	....	....	....	....	....
211	Wages and salaries	....	181,203	190,440	....	....	....	....	....	....	....	....	....
212	Social contributions	....	—	1,760	....	....	....	....	....	....	....	....	....
22	**Use of goods and services**	....	89,402	99,300	....	....	....	....	....	....	....	....	....
23	**Consumption of fixed capital**	....	....	....	....	....	....	....	....	....	....	....	....
24	**Interest**	....	149,125	208,150	....	....	....	....	....	....	....	....	....
25	**Subsidies**	....	33,580	43,600	....	....	....	....	....	....	....	....	....

In Millions of Francs / Year Ending December 31 / Cash Reporter

		Budgetary Central Government			Central Government			Local Government			General Government		
		1997	1998	1999f	1997	1998	1999	1997	1998	1999	1997	1998	1999
26	**Grants**...............................	....	—	—	....	....	....	....	....	....	....	....	....
261	To foreign govenments....................	....	—	—	....	....	....	....	....	....	....	....	....
262	To international organizations..............	....	—	—	....	....	....	....	....	....	....	....	....
263	To other general government units..........	....	—	—	....	....	....	....	....	....	....	....	....
2631	Current..................................	....	—	—	....	....	....	....	....	....	....	....	....
2632	Capital..................................	....	—	—	....	....	....	....	....	....	....	....	....
27	**Social benefits**........................	....	16,630	32,900	....	....	....	....	....	....	....	....	....
28	**Other expense**..........................	....	6,316	4,050	....	....	....	....	....	....	....	....	....
281	Property expense other than interest..........	....	—	—	....	....	....	....	....	....	....	....	....
282	Miscellaneous other expense................	....	6,316	4,050	....	....	....	....	....	....	....	....	....
2821	Current..................................	....	—	—	....	....	....	....	....	....	....	....	....
2822	Capital..................................	....	6,316	4,050	....	....	....	....	....	....	....	....	....
Table 3	**Transactions in assets and liabilities**												
3	**Change in net worth from transactns....**	....	....	....	....	....	....	....	....	....	....	....	....
31	**Net acquisition of nonfinancial assets...**	....	257,163	363,500	....	....	....	....	....	....	....	....	....
311	Fixed assets..............................	....	257,363	363,500	....	....	....	....	....	....	....	....	....
3111	Buildings and structures.................	....	....	....	....	....	....	....	....	....	....	....	....
3112	Machinery and equipment.................	....	....	....	....	....	....	....	....	....	....	....	....
3113	Other fixed assets......................	....	....	....	....	....	....	....	....	....	....	....	....
312	Inventories..............................	....	—	—	....	....	....	....	....	....	....	....	....
313	Valuables................................	....	—	—	....	....	....	....	....	....	....	....	....
314	Nonproduced assets.......................	....	−200	—	....	....	....	....	....	....	....	....	....
3141	Land....................................	....	....	—	....	....	....	....	....	....	....	....	....
3142	Subsoil assets..........................	....	....	—	....	....	....	....	....	....	....	....	....
3143	Other naturally occurring assets..............	....	....	—	....	....	....	....	....	....	....	....	....
3144	Intangible nonproduced assets...........	....	....	—	....	....	....	....	....	....	....	....	....
32	**Net acquisition of financial assets.........**	....	7,140	11,070	....	....	....	....	....	....	....	....	....
321	Domestic.................................	....	3,870	1,650	....	....	....	....	....	....	....	....	....
3212	Currency and deposits....................	....	—	—	....	....	....	....	....	....	....	....	....
3213	Securities other than shares.............	....	....	....	....	....	....	....	....	....	....	....	....
3214	Loans...................................	....	....	....	....	....	....	....	....	....	....	....	....
3215	Shares and other equity..................	....	....	....	....	....	....	....	....	....	....	....	....
3216	Insurance technical reserves.............	....	....	....	....	....	....	....	....	....	....	....	....
3217	Financial derivatives....................	....	....	....	....	....	....	....	....	....	....	....	....
3218	Other accounts receivable................	....	....	....	....	....	....	....	....	....	....	....	....
322	Foreign..................................	....	3,270	9,420	....	....	....	....	....	....	....	....	....
3222	Currency and deposits....................	....	3,270	9,420	....	....	....	....	....	....	....	....	....
3223	Securities other than shares.............	....	—	—	....	....	....	....	....	....	....	....	....
3224	Loans...................................	....	—	—	....	....	....	....	....	....	....	....	....
3225	Shares and other equity..................	....	—	—	....	....	....	....	....	....	....	....	....
3226	Insurance technical reserves.............	....	—	—	....	....	....	....	....	....	....	....	....
3227	Financial derivatives....................	....	—	—	....	....	....	....	....	....	....	....	....
3228	Other accounts receivable................	....	....	....	....	....	....	....	....	....	....	....	....
323	Monetary gold and SDRs.................	....	—	—	....	....	....	....	....	....	....	....	....
33	**Net incurrence of liabilities...................**	....	195,920	125,730	....	....	....	....	....	....	....	....	....
331	Domestic.................................	....	−2,610	8,250	....	....	....	....	....	....	....	....	....
3312	Currency and deposits....................	....	—	−14,750	....	....	....	....	....	....	....	....	....
3313	Securities other than shares.............	....	11,490	—	....	....	....	....	....	....	....	....	....
3314	Loans...................................	....	−14,100	23,000	....	....	....	....	....	....	....	....	....
3316	Insurance technical reserves.............	....	—	—	....	....	....	....	....	....	....	....	....
3317	Financial derivatives....................	....	—	—	....	....	....	....	....	....	....	....	....
3318	Other accounts payable...................	....	....	....	....	....	....	....	....	....	....	....	....
332	Foreign..................................	....	198,530	117,480	....	....	....	....	....	....	....	....	....
3322	Currency and deposits....................	....	—	—	....	....	....	....	....	....	....	....	....
3323	Securities other than shares.............	....	151,450	124,480	....	....	....	....	....	....	....	....	....
3324	Loans...................................	....	47,080	−7,000	....	....	....	....	....	....	....	....	....
3326	Insurance technical reserves.............	....	—	—	....	....	....	....	....	....	....	....	....
3327	Financial derivatives....................	....	—	—	....	....	....	....	....	....	....	....	....
3328	Other accounts payable...................	....	....	....	....	....	....	....	....	....	....	....	....

2005, International Monetary Fund: *Government Finance Statistics Yearbook*

In Millions of Francs / Year Ending December 31 / Cash Reporter

	Budgetary Central Government			Central Government			Local Government			General Government		
	1997	1998	1999f	1997	1998	1999	1997	1998	1999	1997	1998	1999
Table 4 Holding gains in assets and liabilities												
Table 5 Other changes in the volume of assets and liabilities												
Table 6 Balance sheet												
Table 7 Outlays by functions of govt.												
7 Total outlays	....	792,554	1,010,060	....	....	....	....	....	....	....	....	....
701 **General public services**	....	....	....	....	....	....	....	....	....	....	....	....
7017 Public debt transactions	....	149,125	208,150	....	....	....	....	....	....	....	....	....
7018 General transfers between levels of govt.	....	....	....	....	....	....	....	....	....	....	....	....
702 **Defense**	....	....	....	....	....	....	....	....	....	....	....	....
703 **Public order and safety**	....	....	....	....	....	....	....	....	....	....	....	....
704 **Economic affairs**	....	....	....	....	....	....	....	....	....	....	....	....
7042 Agriculture, forestry, fishing, and hunting	....	....	....	....	....	....	....	....	....	....	....	....
7043 Fuel and energy	....	....	....	....	....	....	....	....	....	....	....	....
7044 Mining, manufacturing, and construction	....	....	....	....	....	....	....	....	....	....	....	....
7045 Transport	....	....	....	....	....	....	....	....	....	....	....	....
7046 Communication	....	....	....	....	....	....	....	....	....	....	....	....
705 **Environmental protection**	....	....	....	....	....	....	....	....	....	....	....	....
706 **Housing and community amenities**	....	....	....	....	....	....	....	....	....	....	....	....
707 **Health**	....	....	....	....	....	....	....	....	....	....	....	....
7072 Outpatient services	....	....	....	....	....	....	....	....	....	....	....	....
7073 Hospital services	....	....	....	....	....	....	....	....	....	....	....	....
7074 Public health services	....	....	....	....	....	....	....	....	....	....	....	....
708 **Recreation, culture, and religion**	....	....	....	....	....	....	....	....	....	....	....	....
709 **Education**	....	....	....	....	....	....	....	....	....	....	....	....
7091 Pre-primary and primary education	....	....	....	....	....	....	....	....	....	....	....	....
7092 Secondary education	....	....	....	....	....	....	....	....	....	....	....	....
7094 Tertiary education	....	....	....	....	....	....	....	....	....	....	....	....
710 **Social protection**	....	....	....	....	....	....	....	....	....	....	....	....
7 Statistical discrepancy: Total outlays	....	....	....	....	....	....	....	....	....	....	....	....
Table 8 Transactions in financial assets and liabilities by sector												
82 **Net acquisition of financial assets**	....	7,140	11,070	....	....	....	....	....	....	....	....	....
821 Domestic	....	3,870	1,650	....	....	....	....	....	....	....	....	....
8211 General government	....	—	—	....	....	....	....	....	....	....	....	....
8212 Central bank	....	—	—	....	....	....	....	....	....	....	....	....
8213 Other depository corporations	....	—	—	....	....	....	....	....	....	....	....	....
8214 Financial corporations n.e.c.	....	—	—	....	....	....	....	....	....	....	....	....
8215 Nonfinancial corporations	....	3,870	1,650	....	....	....	....	....	....	....	....	....
8216 Households & NPIs serving households	....	—	—	....	....	....	....	....	....	....	....	....
822 Foreign	....	3,270	9,420	....	....	....	....	....	....	....	....	....
8221 General government	....	....	....	....	....	....	....	....	....	....	....	....
8227 International organizations	....	....	....	....	....	....	....	....	....	....	....	....
8228 Financial corporations other than international organizations	....	....	....	....	....	....	....	....	....	....	....	....
8229 Other nonresidents	....	....	....	....	....	....	....	....	....	....	....	....
823 Monetary gold and SDRs	....	—	—	....	....	....	....	....	....	....	....	....
83 **Net incurrence of liabilities**	....	195,920	125,730	....	....	....	....	....	....	....	....	....
831 Domestic	....	−2,610	8,250	....	....	....	....	....	....	....	....	....
8311 General government	....	....	....	....	....	....	....	....	....	....	....	....
8312 Central bank	....	....	....	....	....	....	....	....	....	....	....	....
8313 Other depository corporations	....	....	....	....	....	....	....	....	....	....	....	....
8314 Financial corporations n.e.c.	....	....	....	....	....	....	....	....	....	....	....	....
8315 Nonfinancial corporations	....	....	....	....	....	....	....	....	....	....	....	....
8316 Households & NPIs serving households	....	....	....	....	....	....	....	....	....	....	....	....
832 Foreign	....	198,530	117,480	....	....	....	....	....	....	....	....	....
8321 General government	....	—	—	....	....	....	....	....	....	....	....	....
8327 International organizations	....	198,530	124,480	....	....	....	....	....	....	....	....	....
8328 Financial corporations other than international organizations	....	—	—	....	....	....	....	....	....	....	....	....
8329 Other nonresidents	....	—	−7,000	....	....	....	....	....	....	....	....	....

Hungary   944

In Billions of Forint / Year Ending December 31 / Noncash Reporter

	Budgetary Central Government			Central Government			Local Government			General Government		
	2001	2002	2003p	2001	2002	2003p	2001	2002	2003p	2001	2002	2003p
Statement of government operations												
1 Revenue..........	4,017.0	4,375.6	4,919.7	5,707.5	6,338.1	6,961.5	1,806.0	2,072.6	2,393.9	6,592.6	7,377.6	8,111.8
2 Expense..........	4,202.0	5,194.1	5,482.9	5,968.6	7,161.8	7,764.5	1,578.2	1,859.4	2,117.2	6,625.9	7,988.1	8,638.2
GOB *Gross operating balance*..........	*−185.0*	*−818.4*	*−563.2*	*−261.1*	*−823.7*	*−803.0*	*227.8*	*213.2*	*276.6*	*−33.3*	*−610.5*	*−526.4*
NOB *Net operating balance*..........	....	....	....	405.6	619.8	349.4	258.6	337.3	282.8	664.3	957.0	632.3
31 Net acquisition of nonfinancial assets..........	303.2	588.3	281.8	405.6	619.8	349.4	258.6	337.3	282.8	664.3	957.0	632.3
NLB *Net lending/borrowing*..........	*−488.2*	*−1,406.7*	*−844.9*	*−666.7*	*−1,443.4*	*−1,152.4*	*−30.8*	*−124.1*	*−6.2*	*−697.5*	*−1,567.5*	*−1,158.7*
32 Net acquisition of financial assets..........	288.8	−23.6	186.1	306.1	−103.2	−78.8	105.6	−16.5	−18.8	392.1	−106.8	−64.7
33 Net incurrence of liabilities..........	992.4	1,333.7	1,084.0	1,031.6	1,315.5	1,053.1	56.9	101.3	5.8	1,068.8	1,429.7	1,091.8
NLB Statistical discrepancy..........	−215.5	49.4	−52.9	−58.8	24.7	20.5	79.6	6.3	−18.3	20.8	31.0	2.2
Statement of other economic flows												
4 *Change in net worth from holding gains*..........	....	....	....	....	....	....	....	....	....	....	....	....
41 Nonfinancial assets..........	....	....	....	....	....	....	....	....	....	....	....	....
42 Financial assets..........	....	....	....	−290.3	....	298.7	....	....	....	....	....	....
43 Liabilities..........	....	....	....	−74.3	....	−169.2	....	....	....	....	....	....
5 *Change in net worth from other volume changes*..........	....	....	....	....	....	....	....	....	....	....	....	....
51 Nonfinancial assets..........	....	....	....	....	....	....	....	....	....	....	....	....
52 Financial assets..........	....	....	....	−.1	....	4.3	....	....	....	....	....	....
53 Liabilities..........	....	....	....	.1	....	—	....	....	....	....	....	....
Balance sheet												
6 *Net worth*..........	....	....	....	....	....	....	....	....	....	....	....	....
61 Nonfinancial assets..........	....	....	....	....	....	....	....	....	....	....	....	....
62 Financial assets..........	....	....	....	3,080.8	2,558.7	2,782.9	....	....	....	....	....	....
63 Liabilities..........	....	....	....	8,906.4	10,060.1	10,944.0	....	....	....	....	....	....
Statement of sources and uses of cash												
1 Cash receipts from operating activities..........	4,022.1	4,318.3	4,884.6	5,618.0	6,148.2	6,664.3	1,800.3	2,072.6	2,386.5	6,497.7	7,187.7	7,807.2
11 Taxes..........	3,253.5	3,542.9	4,056.7	3,295.6	3,590.8	4,110.8	604.5	686.7	813.8	3,900.2	4,277.5	4,924.5
12 Social contributions..........	—	—	—	1,897.5	2,130.0	2,301.9				1,897.5	2,130.0	2,301.9
13 Grants..........	399.0	411.3	437.5	33.0	37.8	−209.4	869.0	1,044.7	1,246.0	−18.7	49.4	−206.9
14 Other receipts..........	369.6	364.1	390.4	391.9	389.5	461.1	326.8	341.2	326.7	718.7	730.8	787.8
2 Cash payments for operating activities..........	4,133.2	5,331.5	5,386.3	5,862.1	7,252.8	7,477.6	1,539.3	1,846.1	2,147.6	6,480.8	8,065.7	8,381.6
21 Compensation of employees..........	741.9	921.6	1,065.9	781.4	966.6	1,115.3	807.8	1,003.1	1,270.8	1,589.2	1,969.6	2,386.0
22 Purchases of goods and services..........	490.7	525.4	580.9	523.8	554.7	614.2	513.5	588.3	617.3	1,037.3	1,143.0	1,231.5
24 Interest..........	715.4	728.4	802.4	715.9	728.8	802.7	9.5	10.0	12.7	725.4	738.9	815.4
25 Subsidies..........	301.8	427.1	388.4	383.2	529.8	501.6	35.6	41.4	32.3	418.9	571.2	533.9
26 Grants..........	1,018.5	1,252.5	1,343.9	841.3	951.8	942.3	3.2	4.0	8.8	−76.0	−77.3	−292.4
27 Social benefits..........	478.8	579.2	667.4	2,164.1	2,587.7	2,919.4	103.1	111.8	115.6	2,267.2	2,699.5	3,035.0
28 Other payments..........	386.0	897.3	537.5	452.3	933.5	582.1	66.6	87.4	90.1	518.8	1,020.9	672.1
CIO *Net cash inflow from oper. activities*.....	*−111.1*	*−1,013.1*	*−501.8*	*−244.1*	*−1,104.6*	*−813.3*	*261.0*	*226.6*	*238.9*	*16.9*	*−878.0*	*−574.4*
31.1 Purchases of nonfinancial assets..........	316.9	378.1	275.2	331.0	384.1	283.2	340.0	420.3	367.6	671.1	804.3	650.8
31.2 Sales of nonfinancial assets..........	13.7	9.0	5.9	15.4	10.3	10.4	81.4	83.0	93.0	96.8	93.3	103.4
31 Net cash outflow from investments in nonfinancial assets..........	303.2	369.1	269.3	315.6	373.8	272.9	258.6	337.3	274.6	574.3	711.0	547.5
CSD *Cash surplus/deficit*..........	*−414.4*	*−1,382.2*	*−771.1*	*−559.7*	*−1,478.4*	*−1,086.2*	*2.4*	*−110.7*	*−35.7*	*−557.4*	*−1,589.1*	*−1,121.9*
32x Net acquisition of fin assets, excl. cash..........	....	....	....	....	....	....	....	....	....	....	....	....
321x Domestic..........	....	....	....	....	....	....	....	....	....	....	....	....
322x Foreign..........	....	....	....	....	....	....	....	....	....	....	....	....
323 Monetary gold and SDRs..........	....	....	....	....	....	....	....	....	....	....	....	....
33 Net incurrence of liabilities..........	....	....	....	....	....	....	....	....	....	....	....	....
331 Domestic..........	....	....	....	....	....	....	....	....	....	....	....	....
332 Foreign..........	....	....	....	....	....	....	....	....	....	....	....	....
NFB Net cash inflow from fin. activities..........	....	....	....	....	....	....	....	....	....	....	....	....
NCB *Net change in the stock of cash*..........	*184.5*	*−336.3*	*43.2*	*184.5*	*−336.3*	*43.2*	*53.6*	*25.3*	*−12.6*	*238.2*	*−311.0*	*30.5*
Table 1 Revenue												
1 **Revenue**..........	**4,017.0**	**4,375.6**	**4,919.7**	**5,707.5**	**6,338.1**	**6,961.5**	**1,806.0**	**2,072.6**	**2,393.9**	**6,592.6**	**7,377.6**	**8,111.8**
11 **Taxes**..........	**3,266.5**	**3,606.2**	**4,062.9**	**3,307.6**	**3,656.6**	**4,117.4**	**604.5**	**686.7**	**813.8**	**3,912.2**	**4,343.3**	**4,931.2**
111 Taxes on income, profits, & capital gains..........	1,205.8	1,355.4	1,328.2	1,205.8	1,355.4	1,328.2	288.8	335.6	405.4	1,494.7	1,690.9	1,733.7
1111 Individuals..........	854.0	958.8	914.6	854.0	958.8	914.6	286.4	333.0	405.4	1,140.4	1,291.8	1,320.0
1112 Corporations and other enterprises..........	351.9	396.6	413.7	351.9	396.6	413.7	—	—	—	351.9	396.6	413.7
112 Taxes on payroll and workforce..........	—	—	—	18.5	21.3	22.8	1.2	1.2	1.1	19.6	22.5	24.0
113 Taxes on property..........	35.6	40.3	52.9	35.6	40.3	52.9	70.7	79.6	100.4	106.3	119.9	153.3
114 Taxes on goods and services..........	1,856.2	2,032.0	2,490.4	1,856.2	2,032.0	2,490.4	243.8	270.4	306.8	2,100.0	2,302.4	2,797.2
1141 General taxes on goods and services..........	1,230.2	1,340.9	1,681.9	1,230.2	1,340.9	1,681.9	226.5	252.6	272.0	1,456.7	1,593.5	1,953.9
1142 Excises..........	541.6	597.6	662.7	541.6	597.6	662.7	—	—	—	541.6	597.6	662.7

In Billions of Forint / Year Ending December 31 / Noncash Reporter

		Budgetary Central Government			Central Government			Local Government			General Government		
		2001	2002	2003p	2001	2002	2003p	2001	2002	2003p	2001	2002	2003p
115	Taxes on int'l. trade and transactions...........	125.0	129.3	132.6	125.0	129.3	132.6	—	—	—	125.0	129.3	132.6
116	Other taxes........................	43.8	49.1	58.8	66.5	78.2	90.5	—	—	—	66.5	78.2	90.5
12	**Social contributions.............................**	—	—	—	1,925.8	2,159.1	2,309.7	—	—	—	1,925.8	2,159.1	2,309.7
121	Social security contributions................	—	—	—	1,925.8	2,159.1	2,309.7	—	—	—	1,925.8	2,159.1	2,309.7
122	Other social contributions.................	—	—	—	—	—	—	—	—	—	—	—	—
13	**Grants..**	380.9	367.1	506.6	48.7	23.4	37.5	910.5	1,028.2	1,231.9	38.6	18.4	25.9
131	From foreign governments.................	—	—	—	—	—	—	—	—	—	—	—	—
132	From international organizations..............	35.2	18.5	25.9	35.2	18.5	25.9	3.3	—	—	38.6	18.5	25.9
133	From other general government units...........	345.6	348.6	480.7	13.5	4.9	11.6	907.1	1,028.2	1,231.9	—	—	—
14	**Other revenue................................**	369.7	402.4	350.2	425.4	499.0	496.9	291.0	357.7	348.2	716.1	856.7	845.1

Table 2   Expense by economic type

		Budgetary Central Government			Central Government			Local Government			General Government		
2	**Expense..............................**	4,202.0	5,194.1	5,482.9	5,968.6	7,161.8	7,764.5	1,578.2	1,859.4	2,117.2	6,625.9	7,988.1	8,638.2
21	**Compensation of employees.................**	756.9	948.4	1,070.4	796.8	996.8	1,123.9	846.7	1,019.5	1,232.4	1,643.4	2,016.2	2,356.3
211	Wages and salaries........................	565.7	718.9	814.7	582.2	740.9	840.7	618.4	756.4	924.9	1,200.5	1,497.3	1,765.6
212	Social contributions.......................	191.2	229.4	255.6	214.6	255.9	283.2	228.3	263.1	307.5	442.9	519.0	590.7
22	**Use of goods and services.....................**	490.7	521.6	580.6	527.7	559.9	618.9	513.5	585.8	621.7	1,041.2	1,145.7	1,240.6
23	**Consumption of fixed capital................**	....	....	....	....	....	....	....	....	....	....	....	....
24	**Interest..**	722.2	677.1	749.7	717.2	679.1	761.6	9.5	9.5	12.2	726.4	688.7	773.8
25	**Subsidies......................................**	323.2	427.1	396.3	404.6	529.8	509.6	35.6	41.4	32.3	440.3	571.2	541.9
26	**Grants..**	1,100.5	1,347.2	1,541.0	907.1	1,028.2	1,231.9	13.5	4.9	11.6	—	—	—
261	To foreign govenments..................	—	—	—	—	—	—	—	—	—	—	—	—
262	To international organizations................	—	—	—	—	—	—	—	—	—	—	—	—
263	To other general government units..............	1,100.5	1,347.2	1,541.0	907.1	1,028.2	1,231.9	13.5	4.9	11.6	—	—	—
2631	Current..............................	824.3	1,124.1	1,348.8	727.4	889.5	1,157.7	10.2	2.4	10.5	—	—	—
2632	Capital...............................	276.1	223.1	192.2	179.7	138.7	74.2	3.3	2.5	1.1	—	—	—
27	**Social benefits..............................**	494.6	579.2	662.7	2,185.7	2,598.5	2,915.3	103.1	111.8	115.6	2,288.9	2,710.3	3,031.0
28	**Other expense...............................**	313.9	693.5	482.1	429.3	769.5	603.2	56.3	86.6	91.4	485.7	856.1	694.6
281	Property expense other than interest..........	—	—	—	—	—	—	—	—	—	—	—	—
282	Miscellaneous other expense......................	313.9	693.5	482.1	429.3	769.5	603.2	56.3	86.6	91.4	485.7	856.1	694.6
2821	Current...............................	112.3	141.5	259.4	146.3	178.5	327.0	22.4	35.0	37.5	168.7	213.6	364.5
2822	Capital...............................	201.6	552.0	222.7	283.1	590.9	276.2	33.9	51.6	53.9	317.0	642.5	330.1

Table 3   Transactions in assets and liabilities

		Budgetary Central Government			Central Government			Local Government			General Government		
3	**Change in net worth from transactns....**	....	....	....	....	....	....	....	....	....	....	....	....
31	**Net acquisition of nonfinancial assets...**	303.2	588.3	281.8	405.6	619.8	349.4	258.6	337.3	282.8	664.3	957.0	632.3
311	Fixed assets..............................	289.3	567.7	280.8	391.7	599.2	348.4	269.2	348.5	302.7	660.9	947.6	651.1
3111	Buildings and structures...................	145.0	361.7	144.4	145.0	170.7	200.1	238.8	301.4	259.3	383.8	472.1	459.3
3112	Machinery and equipment.....................	94.7	122.3	120.4	94.7	122.3	120.1	34.7	43.0	45.8	129.4	165.3	165.9
3113	Other fixed assets.......................	49.7	83.7	15.9	152.1	306.2	28.3	−4.4	4.1	−2.4	147.7	310.2	25.9
312	Inventories................................	—	—	—	—	—	—	—	—	—	—	—	—
313	Valuables.................................	—	—	—	—	—	—	—	—	—	—	—	—
314	Nonproduced assets........................	13.9	20.6	1.0	13.9	20.6	1.0	−10.5	−11.2	−19.8	3.4	9.4	−18.8
3141	Land..................................	—	—	1.0	—	—	1.0	−14.1	−16.2	−19.8	−14.1	−16.2	−18.8
3142	Subsoil assets..........................	—	—	—	—	—	—	—	—	—	—	—	—
3143	Other naturally occurring assets............	—	—	—	—	—	—	—	—	—	—	—	—
3144	Intangible nonproduced assets...............	13.9	20.6	—	13.9	20.6	—	3.6	5.0	—	17.5	25.6	—
32	**Net acquisition of financial assets........**	288.8	−23.6	186.1	306.1	−103.2	−78.8	105.6	−16.5	−18.8	392.1	−106.8	−64.7
321	Domestic..............................	300.4	−19.8	232.8	317.8	−99.5	−32.1	105.6	−16.5	−18.8	403.8	−103.1	−18.0
3212	Currency and deposits.....................	184.5	−336.3	43.2	184.5	−336.3	43.2	53.6	25.3	−12.6	238.2	−311.0	30.5
3213	Securities other than shares...............	−46.5	11.5	19.3	1.4	−1.5	.9	16.5	−52.8	−20.7	6.4	−17.1	.7
3214	Loans..................................	17.8	139.3	235.6	−21.4	19.3	−18.3	3.1	12.5	.6	−23.0	2.4	−1.9
3215	Shares and other equity..................	156.2	154.8	−107.2	155.3	154.8	−107.2	27.8	−.3	9.3	183.1	154.4	−97.9
3216	Insurance technical reserves...............	—	—	—	—	—	—	—	—	—	—	—	—
3217	Financial derivatives.....................	−53.5	−62.2	.3	−53.5	−62.2	.3	—	—	—	−53.5	−62.2	.3
3218	Other accounts receivable.................	42.0	73.1	41.6	51.4	126.4	49.0	4.7	−1.2	4.7	52.7	130.5	50.3
322	Foreign..............................	−11.7	−3.7	−46.7	−11.7	−3.7	−46.7	—	—	—	−11.7	−3.7	−46.7
3222	Currency and deposits.....................	—	—	—	—	—	—	—	—	—	—	—	—
3223	Securities other than shares...............	—	—	—	—	—	—	—	—	—	—	—	—
3224	Loans..................................	−13.7	−5.1	−44.5	−13.7	−5.1	−44.5	—	—	—	−13.7	−5.1	−44.5
3225	Shares and other equity..................	2.1	1.4	−2.1	2.1	1.4	−2.1	—	—	—	2.1	1.4	−2.1
3226	Insurance technical reserves...............	—	—	—	—	—	—	—	—	—	—	—	—
3227	Financial derivatives.....................	—	—	—	—	—	—	—	—	—	—	—	—
3228	Other accounts receivable.................	—	—	—	—	—	—	—	—	—	—	—	—
323	Monetary gold and SDRs..................	—	—	—	....	....	....	....	....	....	....	....	....

In Billions of Forint / Year Ending December 31 / Noncash Reporter

		Budgetary Central Government			Central Government			Local Government			General Government		
		2001	2002	2003p	2001	2002	2003p	2001	2002	2003p	2001	2002	2003p
33	Net incurrence of liabilities....................	**992.4**	**1,333.7**	**1,084.0**	**1,031.6**	**1,315.5**	**1,053.1**	**56.9**	**101.3**	**5.8**	**1,068.8**	**1,429.7**	**1,091.8**
331	Domestic................................	429.4	495.3	78.3	468.5	477.1	47.4	41.8	80.9	15.1	490.7	570.9	95.3
3312	Currency and deposits....................	8.3	−6.1	2.5	1.8	.4	−2.1	—	—	—	1.8	.4	−2.1
3313	Securities other than shares...............	422.1	683.4	855.9	470.1	670.4	837.5	.6	2.4	−.3	459.2	709.9	857.6
3314	Loans..	−246.6	72.9	−713.9	−246.0	54.8	−716.8	20.8	71.9	18.6	−230.0	97.3	−682.4
3316	Insurance technical reserves...............	—	—	—	—	—	—	—	—	—	—	—	—
3317	Financial derivatives......................	−66.4	−51.3	−35.8	−66.4	−51.3	−35.8	—	—	—	−66.4	−51.3	−35.8
3318	Other accounts payable....................	312.0	−203.5	−30.5	309.1	−197.1	−35.4	20.4	6.6	−3.2	326.1	−185.3	−42.0
332	Foreign...................................	563.0	838.4	1,005.7	563.0	838.4	1,005.7	15.1	20.3	−9.3	578.1	858.7	996.4
3322	Currency and deposits....................												
3323	Securities other than shares...............	589.1	718.2	946.8	589.1	718.2	946.8	—	—	−20.7	589.2	718.2	926.1
3324	Loans..	−26.1	120.2	58.9	−26.1	120.2	58.9	15.1	20.3	11.4	−11.0	140.5	70.4
3326	Insurance technical reserves...............	—	—	—	—	—	—	—	—	—	—	—	—
3327	Financial derivatives......................	—	—	—	—	—	—	—	—	—	—	—	—
3328	Other accounts payable....................	—	—	—	—	—	—	—	—	—	—	—	—
Table 4	**Holding gains in assets and liabilities**												
4	Change in net worth from hold. gains...	....	....	....	....	....	....	....	....	....	....	....	....
41	Nonfinancial assets...........................	....	....	....	....	....	....	....	....	....	....	....	....
411	Fixed assets...............................	....	....	....	....	....	....	....	....	....	....	....	....
412	Inventories................................	....	....	....	....	....	....	....	....	....	....	....	....
413	Valuables..................................	....	....	....	....	....	....	....	....	....	....	....	....
414	Nonproduced assets........................	....	....	....	....	....	....	....	....	....	....	....	....
42	Financial assets...............................	....	....	....	−290.3	....	298.7	....	....	....	....	....	....
421	Domestic..................................	....	....	....	−293.0	....	291.5	....	....	....	....	....	....
422	Foreign...................................	....	....	....	2.7	....	7.2	....	....	....	....	....	....
423	Monetary gold and SDRs..................	....	....	....	—	....	—	....	....	....	....	....	....
43	Liabilities....................................	....	....	....	−74.3	....	−169.2	....	....	....	....	....	....
431	Domestic..................................	....	....	....	−29.0	....	−121.1	....	....	....	....	....	....
432	Foreign...................................	....	....	....	−45.3	....	−48.1	....	....	....	....	....	....
Table 5	**Other changes in the volume of assets and liabilities**												
5	Change in net worth from vol. chngs.....	....	....	....	....	....	....	....	....	....	....	....	....
51	Nonfinancial assets...........................	....	....	....	....	....	....	....	....	....	....	....	....
511	Fixed assets...............................	....	....	....	....	....	....	....	....	....	....	....	....
512	Inventories................................	....	....	....	....	....	....	....	....	....	....	....	....
513	Valuables..................................	....	....	....	....	....	....	....	....	....	....	....	....
514	Nonproduced assets........................	....	....	....	....	....	....	....	....	....	....	....	....
52	Financial assets...............................	....	....	....	−.1	....	4.3	....	....	....	....	....	....
521	Domestic..................................	....	....	....	—	....	—	....	....	....	....	....	....
522	Foreign...................................	....	....	....	−.1	....	4.3	....	....	....	....	....	....
523	Monetary gold and SDRs..................	....	....	....	—	....	—	....	....	....	....	....	....
53	Liabilities....................................	....	....	....	.1	....	—	....	....	....	....	....	....
531	Domestic..................................	....	....	....	—	....	—	....	....	....	....	....	....
532	Foreign...................................	....	....	....	.1	....	—	....	....	....	....	....	....
Table 6	**Balance sheet**												
6	Net worth..................................	....	....	....	....	....	....	....	....	....	....	....	....
61	Nonfinancial assets...........................	....	....	....	....	....	....	....	....	....	....	....	....
611	Fixed assets...............................	....	....	....	....	....	....	....	....	....	....	....	....
6111	Buildings and structures...................	....	....	....	....	....	....	....	....	....	....	....	....
6112	Machinery and equipment.................	....	....	....	....	....	....	....	....	....	....	....	....
6113	Other fixed assets.........................	....	....	....	....	....	....	....	....	....	....	....	....
612	Inventories................................	....	....	....	....	....	....	....	....	....	....	....	....
613	Valuables..................................	....	....	....	....	....	....	....	....	....	....	....	....
614	Nonproduced assets........................	....	....	....	....	....	....	....	....	....	....	....	....
6141	Land......................................	....	....	....	....	....	....	....	....	....	....	....	....
6142	Subsoil assets.............................	....	....	....	....	....	....	....	....	....	....	....	....
6143	Other naturally occurring assets...........	....	....	....	....	....	....	....	....	....	....	....	....
6144	Intangible nonproduced assets.............	....	....	....	....	....	....	....	....	....	....	....	....

In Billions of Forint / Year Ending December 31 / Noncash Reporter

		Budgetary Central Government			Central Government			Local Government			General Government		
		2001	2002	2003p	2001	2002	2003p	2001	2002	2003p	2001	2002	2003p
62	**Financial assets**	....	....	....	**3,080.8**	**2,558.7**	**2,782.9**	....	....	....	....	....	....
621	Domestic	....	....	....	2,956.3	2,449.1	2,708.5	....	....	....	....	....	....
6212	Currency and deposits	....	....	....	469.2	121.2	172.2	....	....	....	....	....	....
6213	Securities other than shares	....	....	....	1.6	.1	1.0	....	....	....	....	....	....
6214	Loans	....	....	....	116.6	145.9	127.7	....	....	....	....	....	....
6215	Shares and other equity	....	....	....	1,295.9	1,384.4	1,634.1	....	....	....	....	....	....
6216	Insurance technical reserves	....	....	....	—	—	—	....	....	....	....	....	....
6217	Financial derivatives	....	....	....	316.5	119.3	46.4	....	....	....	....	....	....
6218	Other accounts receivable	....	....	....	756.5	678.1	727.1	....	....	....	....	....	....
622	Foreign	....	....	....	124.5	109.6	74.4	....	....	....	....	....	....
6222	Currency and deposits	....	....	....	—	—	—	....	....	....	....	....	....
6223	Securities other than shares	....	....	....	—	—	—	....	....	....	....	....	....
6224	Loans	....	....	....	98.6	85.1	54.2	....	....	....	....	....	....
6225	Shares and other equity	....	....	....	25.9	24.5	20.2	....	....	....	....	....	....
6226	Insurance technical reserves	....	....	....				....	....	....	....	....	....
6227	Financial derivatives	....	....	....				....	....	....	....	....	....
6228	Other accounts receivable	....	....	....	—	—	—	....	....	....	....	....	....
623	Monetary gold and SDRs	....	....	....	—	—	—	....	....	....	....	....	....
63	**Liabilities**	....	....	....	**8,906.4**	**10,060.1**	**10,944.0**	....	....	....	....	....	....
631	Domestic	....	....	....	6,510.3	6,894.9	6,821.2	....	....	....	....	....	....
6312	Currency and deposits	....	....	....	1.8	2.1	.1	....	....	....	....	....	....
6313	Securities other than shares	....	....	....	4,337.2	5,045.8	5,658.8	....	....	....	....	....	....
6314	Loans	....	....	....	1,560.5	1,499.2	820.8	....	....	....	....	....	....
6316	Insurance technical reserves	....	....	....	—	—	—	....	....	....	....	....	....
6317	Financial derivatives	....	....	....	108.2	54.0	83.0	....	....	....	....	....	....
6318	Other accounts payable	....	....	....	502.5	293.8	258.4	....	....	....	....	....	....
632	Foreign	....	....	....	2,396.1	3,165.1	4,122.8	....	....	....	....	....	....
6322	Currency and deposits	....	....	....	—	—	—	....	....	....	....	....	....
6323	Securities other than shares	....	....	....	2,045.2	2,731.0	3,598.1	....	....	....	....	....	....
6324	Loans	....	....	....	351.0	434.2	524.7	....	....	....	....	....	....
6326	Insurance technical reserves	....	....	....	—	—	—	....	....	....	....	....	....
6327	Financial derivatives	....	....	....	—	—	—	....	....	....	....	....	....
6328	Other accounts payable	....	....	....	—	—	—	....	....	....	....	....	....
Memorandum items:													
6M2	Net financial worth	....	....	....	−5,825.6	−7,501.4	−8,161.1	....	....	....	....	....	....
6M3	Debt at market value	....	....	....	8,295.6	9,712.2	10,602.5	....	....	....	....	....	....
6M4	Debt at nominal value	....	....	....	7,918.5	9,457.2	10,812.5	....	....	....	....	....	....
6M5	Arrears	....	....	....	....	....	....	....	....	....	....	....	....
6M6	Obligations for social security benefits	....	....	....	....	....	....	....	....	....	....	....	....
6M7	Contingent liabilities	....	....	....	997.4	921.7	1,221.0	....	....	....	....	....	....
6M8	Uncapitalized military weapons, systems	....	....	....	12.9	....	....	....	....	....	....	....	....
Table 7 Outlays by functions of govt.													
7	**Total outlays**	**4,505.2**	**5,782.3**	**5,764.6**	**6,374.2**	**7,781.6**	**8,113.9**	**1,836.8**	**2,196.7**	**2,400.1**	**7,290.1**	**8,945.1**	**9,270.5**
701	**General public services**	**2,282.3**	**2,609.6**	....	**2,210.9**	**2,188.0**	....	**245.9**	**332.3**	....	**1,536.0**	**1,487.2**	....
7017	Public debt transactions	722.2	677.1	749.7	717.2	679.1	761.6	9.5	9.5	12.2	726.4	688.7	773.8
7018	General transfers between levels of govt	1,106.2	1,539.2		907.4	1,028.8		13.5	4.9		—	.5	
702	**Defense**	**194.3**	**231.5**	....	**194.3**	**231.5**	....	**.7**	**.8**	....	**194.9**	**232.3**	....
703	**Public order and safety**	**287.3**	**333.0**	....	**287.3**	**333.0**	....	**24.2**	**26.3**	....	**311.5**	**359.3**	....
704	**Economic affairs**	**669.2**	**1,335.8**	....	**794.3**	**1,599.3**	....	**112.7**	**157.0**	....	**907.0**	**1,756.3**	....
7042	Agriculture, forestry, fishing, and hunting	254.2	347.6	....	254.2	347.6	....	12.8	15.9	....	267.0	363.5	....
7043	Fuel and energy	3.1	4.7	....	3.1	4.7	....	—	—	....	3.1	4.7	....
7044	Mining, manufacturing, and construction	9.7	9.1	....	9.7	9.1	....	30.6	41.1	....	40.4	50.2	....
7045	Transport	26.3	410.0	....	118.9	631.2	....	54.9	83.9	....	173.8	715.1	....
7046	Communication	17.8	21.0	....	17.8	21.0	....	1.1	1.3	....	18.9	22.2	....
705	**Environmental protection**	**25.3**	**29.9**	....	**30.9**	**40.4**	....	**112.8**	**124.0**	....	**143.7**	**164.4**	....
706	**Housing and community amenities**	**43.1**	**33.8**	....	**43.1**	**33.8**	....	**169.8**	**194.5**	....	**212.9**	**228.2**	....
707	**Health**	**111.1**	**135.3**	....	**385.1**	**453.3**	....	**304.5**	**354.5**	....	**689.6**	**807.7**	....
7072	Outpatient services	—	.2	....	64.8	74.9	....	81.0	90.4	....	145.9	165.2	....
7073	Hospital services	74.2	90.8	....	74.2	90.8	....	214.2	252.7	....	288.4	343.5	....
7074	Public health services	34.0	41.0	....	34.0	41.0	....	1.7	1.8	....	35.7	42.8	....
708	**Recreation, culture, and religion**	**134.1**	**141.0**	....	**134.1**	**141.0**	....	**93.1**	**107.8**	....	**227.2**	**248.8**	....

In Billions of Forint / Year Ending December 31 / Noncash Reporter

		Budgetary Central Government			Central Government			Local Government			General Government		
		2001	2002	2003p	2001	2002	2003p	2001	2002	2003p	2001	2002	2003p
709	**Education**................................	**335.2**	**402.0**	....	**343.0**	**407.4**	....	**535.5**	**631.9**	....	**878.5**	**1,039.3**	....
7091	Pre-primary and primary education...............	6.8	7.6	....	6.8	7.6	....	292.0	354.2	....	298.8	361.7	....
7092	Secondary education..................................	44.0	55.2	....	51.8	60.6	....	42.8	49.6	....	94.6	110.2	....
7094	Tertiary education.....................................	46.3	59.1	....	54.0	64.5	....	41.4	49.0	....	95.5	113.5	....
710	**Social protection**....................................	**423.3**	**530.3**	....	**1,951.3**	**2,353.8**	....	**237.5**	**267.6**	....	**2,188.8**	**2,621.5**	....
7	Statistical discrepancy: Total outlays...............	—	—	....	—	—	....	—	—	....	—	—	....
Table 8 Transactions in financial assets and liabilities by sector													
82	**Net acquisition of financial assets**.........	**288.8**	**−23.6**	**186.1**	**306.1**	**−103.2**	**−78.8**	**105.6**	**−16.5**	**−18.8**	**392.1**	**−106.8**	**−64.7**
821	Domestic......................................	300.4	−19.8	232.8	317.8	−99.5	−32.1	105.6	−16.5	−18.8	403.8	−103.1	−18.0
8211	General government.......................	−4.7	156.0	263.1	3.7	28.4	−10.4	15.9	−41.4	−22.5	—	—	—
8212	Central bank................................	303.9	−342.2	47.3	303.9	−342.2	47.3	5.6	−16.4	.1	309.5	−358.6	47.4
8213	Other depository corporations..................	−16.4	49.6	−19.1	−16.4	49.6	−19.1	49.5	30.4	−8.4	33.1	80.0	−27.5
8214	Financial corporations n.e.c.....................	2.6	−10.9	1.1	2.6	−10.9	1.1	6.9	−.4	.2	9.5	−11.3	1.3
8215	Nonfinancial corporations.......................	15.0	127.6	−59.7	23.9	175.5	−51.1	30.0	10.3	11.2	54.0	185.9	−39.9
8216	Households & NPIs serving households......	—	—	—	—	—	—	−2.2	.9	.7	−2.2	.9	.7
822	Foreign.......................................	−11.7	−3.7	−46.7	−11.7	−3.7	−46.7	—	—	—	−11.7	−3.7	−46.7
8221	General government.......................	—	—	—	—	—	—	—	—	—	—	—	—
8227	International organizations.....................	—	—	—	—	—	—	—	—	—	—	—	—
8228	Financial corporations other than international organizations..............	—	—	—	—	—	—	—	—	—	—	—	—
8229	Other nonresidents....................	−11.7	−3.7	−46.7	−11.7	−3.7	−46.7	—	—	—	−11.7	−3.7	−46.7
823	Monetary gold and SDRs....................												
83	**Net incurrence of liabilities**...................	**992.4**	**1,333.7**	**1,084.0**	**1,031.6**	**1,315.5**	**1,053.1**	**56.9**	**101.3**	**5.8**	**1,068.8**	**1,429.7**	**1,091.8**
831	Domestic......................................	429.4	495.3	78.3	468.5	477.1	47.4	41.8	80.9	15.1	490.7	570.9	95.3
8311	General government.......................	−25.9	−20.5	10.3	13.3	−38.8	−20.5	6.3	25.8	−12.3	—	—	—
8312	Central bank................................	−329.0	−526.1	−606.0	−329.0	−526.1	−606.0	—	—	—	−329.0	−526.1	−606.0
8313	Other depository corporations..................	373.1	422.4	30.8	373.1	422.4	30.8	16.1	43.2	27.1	389.1	465.7	57.9
8314	Financial corporations n.e.c.....................	311.4	486.9	439.1	311.4	486.9	439.1	.5	1.3	6.6	311.9	488.2	445.7
8315	Nonfinancial corporations.......................	43.5	51.1	120.1	43.5	51.1	120.1	5.6	10.4	5.0	49.0	61.5	125.1
8316	Households & NPIs serving households......	56.4	81.5	83.9	56.4	81.5	83.9	13.3	.2	−11.2	69.6	81.7	72.7
832	Foreign.......................................	563.0	838.4	1,005.7	563.0	838.4	1,005.7	15.1	20.3	−9.3	578.1	858.7	996.4
8321	General government.......................	—	—	—	—	—	—	—	—	—	—	—	—
8327	International organizations.....................	—	—	—	—	—	—	—	—	—	—	—	—
8328	Financial corporations other than international organizations..............	—	—	—	—	—	—	—	—	—	—	—	—
8329	Other nonresidents....................	563.0	838.4	1,005.7	563.0	838.4	1,005.7	15.1	20.3	−9.3	578.1	858.7	996.4

In Millions of Kronur / Year Ending December 31 / Noncash Reporter

	Budgetary Central Government			Central Government			Local Government			General Government		
	2000	2001	2002	2000	2001	2002	2000	2001	2002	2000	2001	2002
Statement of government operations												
1 Revenue	227,563	246,444	258,363	227,831	247,073	259,012	79,287	91,659	99,639	300,069	329,517	348,932
2 Expense	210,147	238,130	260,322	208,218	236,703	259,449	71,298	83,259	91,505	272,466	310,747	341,236
GOB *Gross operating balance*	*27,196*	*18,699*	*9,184*	*29,393*	*20,755*	*10,706*	*11,672*	*12,535*	*12,956*	*41,065*	*33,290*	*23,662*
NOB *Net operating balance*	*17,417*	*8,314*	*-1,959*	*19,614*	*10,370*	*-438*	*7,989*	*8,400*	*8,134*	*27,603*	*18,770*	*7,696*
31 Net acquisition of nonfinancial assets	1,082	3,757	2,782	1,082	3,757	2,782	10,262	13,742	12,518	11,344	17,498	15,300
NLB *Net lending/borrowing*	*16,335*	*4,557*	*-4,741*	*18,532*	*6,613*	*-3,220*	*-2,273*	*-5,341*	*-4,384*	*16,259*	*1,272*	*-7,603*
32 Net acquisition of financial assets	6,544	37,140	-5,519	8,659	41,869	-3,877	1,730	3,719	946	10,671	45,699	-3,608
33 Net incurrence of liabilities	-9,791	32,583	-778	-9,872	35,256	-658	4,003	9,060	5,329	-5,588	44,427	3,995
NLB Statistical discrepancy	—	—	—	—	—	—	—	—	—	—	—	—
Statement of other economic flows												
4 *Change in net worth from holding gains*	....	....	....	....	....	....	*6,981*	*24,065*	*21,869*	....	....	....
41 Nonfinancial assets	....	....	....	....	....	....	12,180	27,820	....	....	....	....
42 Financial assets	5,893	16,070	11,058	5,906	16,087	11,064	-385	840	....	5,474	16,866	....
43 Liabilities	28,515	51,333	-11,032	28,515	51,333	-11,032	4,814	4,595	....	33,282	55,866	....
5 *Change in net worth from other volume changes*	....	....	....	....	....	....	—	*5,206*	*23,706*	....	....	....
51 Nonfinancial assets	....	....	....	....	....	....	—	—	....	....	....	....
52 Financial assets	-10,118	-1,078	-8,782	-12,339	-1,078	-8,810	—	5,206	....	-12,339	4,128	....
53 Liabilities	10,375	-5,383	11,152	10,375	-5,383	11,152	—	—	....	10,375	-5,383	....
Balance sheet												
6 *Net worth*	....	....	....	....	....	....	*122,774*	*160,446*	*214,155*	....	....	....
61 Nonfinancial assets	....	....	....	....	....	....	176,592	218,154	175,048	....	....	....
62 Financial assets	214,559	266,690	263,446	215,774	272,652	271,029	26,515	36,280	86,706	241,542	308,234	356,387
63 Liabilities	412,948	491,481	490,823	413,376	494,583	494,045	80,333	93,988	47,599	492,962	587,873	540,296
Statement of sources and uses of cash												
Table 1 Revenue												
1 **Revenue**	**227,563**	**246,444**	**258,363**	**227,831**	**247,073**	**259,012**	**79,287**	**91,659**	**99,639**	**300,069**	**329,517**	**348,932**
11 **Taxes**	**178,139**	**189,778**	**197,026**	**178,139**	**189,778**	**197,026**	**59,445**	**67,613**	**75,323**	**237,584**	**257,391**	**272,350**
111 Taxes on income, profits, & capital gains	57,652	67,045	69,430	57,652	67,045	69,430	45,980	54,163	59,524	103,632	121,208	128,954
1111 Individuals	43,476	51,703	54,207	43,476	51,703	54,207	45,965	54,148	59,509	89,440	105,851	113,716
1112 Corporations and other enterprises	9,222	9,132	8,397	9,222	9,132	8,397	15	15	15	9,237	9,147	8,412
112 Taxes on payroll and workforce	—	—	—	—	—	—				—	—	—
113 Taxes on property	9,841	10,563	10,990	9,841	10,563	10,990	12,737	12,529	14,775	22,578	23,092	25,765
114 Taxes on goods and services	107,421	108,421	113,330	107,421	108,421	113,330	—	—	—	107,421	108,421	113,330
1141 General taxes on goods and services	71,184	74,048	78,272	71,184	74,048	78,272	—	—	—	71,184	74,048	78,272
1142 Excises	23,582	21,440	21,652	23,582	21,440	21,652	—	—	—	23,582	21,440	21,652
115 Taxes on int'l. trade and transactions	2,712	3,034	2,476	2,712	3,034	2,476	—	—	—	2,712	3,034	2,476
116 Other taxes	513	714	800	513	714	800	728	921	1,024	1,241	1,635	1,824
12 **Social contributions**	**20,047**	**22,296**	**23,904**	**20,047**	**22,296**	**23,904**	**—**	**—**	**—**	**20,047**	**22,296**	**23,904**
121 Social security contributions	20,047	22,296	23,904	20,047	22,296	23,904	—	—	—	20,047	22,296	23,904
122 Other social contributions	—	—	—	—	—	—	—	—	—	—	—	—
13 **Grants**	**26**	**—**	**—**	**26**	**—**	**—**	**7,050**	**9,215**	**9,719**	**26**	**—**	**—**
131 From foreign governments	26	—	—	26	—	—	—	—	—	26	—	—
132 From international organizations	—	—	—	—	—	—	—	—	—	—	—	—
133 From other general government units	—	—	—	—	—	—	7,050	9,215	9,719	—	—	—
14 **Other revenue**	**29,351**	**34,371**	**37,432**	**29,619**	**34,999**	**38,081**	**12,793**	**14,831**	**14,597**	**42,412**	**49,831**	**52,678**
Table 2 Expense by economic type												
2 **Expense**	**210,147**	**238,130**	**260,322**	**208,218**	**236,703**	**259,449**	**71,298**	**83,259**	**91,505**	**272,466**	**310,747**	**341,236**
21 **Compensation of employees**	**56,937**	**63,620**	**72,432**	**60,809**	**67,296**	**76,875**	**36,122**	**41,849**	**47,353**	**96,931**	**109,145**	**124,228**
211 Wages and salaries	51,086	55,547	63,331	54,606	58,889	67,371	31,032	35,952	40,647	85,637	94,842	108,018
212 Social contributions	5,852	8,072	9,100	6,204	8,407	9,504	5,090	5,897	6,706	11,294	14,303	16,210
22 **Use of goods and services**	**38,598**	**46,031**	**50,433**	**50,489**	**58,622**	**64,242**	**20,540**	**22,367**	**24,616**	**71,029**	**80,989**	**88,858**
23 **Consumption of fixed capital**	**9,779**	**10,385**	**11,143**	**9,779**	**10,385**	**11,143**	**3,683**	**4,134**	**4,822**	**13,462**	**14,520**	**15,965**
24 **Interest**	**19,665**	**23,128**	**21,891**	**19,665**	**23,128**	**21,891**	**3,096**	**5,439**	**4,043**	**22,761**	**28,568**	**25,934**
25 **Subsidies**	**9,721**	**10,779**	**11,235**	**9,721**	**10,779**	**11,235**	**1,845**	**2,065**	**2,468**	**11,566**	**12,844**	**13,703**
26 **Grants**	**52,841**	**55,658**	**61,647**	**7,600**	**9,939**	**10,406**	**—**	**—**	**—**	**550**	**724**	**688**
261 To foreign governments	—	—	—	—	—	—	—	—	—	—	—	—
262 To international organizations	550	724	688	550	724	688	—	—	—	550	724	688
263 To other general government units	52,291	54,934	60,960	7,050	9,215	9,719	—	—	—	—	—	—
2631 Current	50,790	52,798	58,403	5,549	7,079	7,162	—	—	—	—	—	—
2632 Capital	1,501	2,136	2,556	1,501	2,136	2,556	—	—	—	—	—	—

In Millions of Kronur / Year Ending December 31 / Noncash Reporter

		Budgetary Central Government			Central Government			Local Government			General Government		
		2000	2001	2002	2000	2001	2002	2000	2001	2002	2000	2001	2002
27	Social benefits.........................	699	12,557	14,994	28,248	40,581	47,111	3,053	3,674	3,967	31,301	44,256	51,078
28	Other expense..........................	21,906	15,972	16,546	21,906	15,972	16,546	2,959	3,729	4,236	24,865	19,701	20,782
281	Property expense other than interest...........	—	—	—	—	—	—	—	—	—	—	—	—
282	Miscellaneous other expense................	21,906	15,972	16,546	21,906	15,972	16,546	2,959	3,729	4,236	24,865	19,701	20,782
2821	Current.................................	14,257	7,452	7,810	14,257	7,452	7,810	1,116	1,344	1,451	15,373	8,795	9,260
2822	Capital.................................	7,648	8,520	8,737	7,648	8,520	8,737	1,843	2,386	2,785	9,491	10,906	11,522

Table 3   Transactions in assets and liabilities

		Budgetary Central Government			Central Government			Local Government			General Government		
3	**Change in net worth from transactns....**	17,417	8,314	−1,959	19,614	10,370	−438	7,989	8,400	8,134	27,603	18,770	7,696
31	**Net acquisition of nonfinancial assets...**	1,082	3,757	2,782	1,082	3,757	2,782	10,262	13,742	12,518	11,344	17,498	15,300
311	Fixed assets............................	1,082	3,757	2,782	1,082	3,757	2,782	10,262	13,742	12,518	11,344	17,498	15,300
3111	Buildings and structures..............	....	....	....	....	....	....	....	....	....	....	....	....
3112	Machinery and equipment.............	993	−259	−350	993	−259	−350	....	....	....	....	....	....
3113	Other fixed assets...................	....	....	....	....	....	....	....	....	....	....	....	....
312	Inventories...........................	—	—	—	—	—	—	—	—	—	—	—	—
313	Valuables.............................	—	—	—	—	—	—	—	—	—	—	—	—
314	Nonproduced assets....................	—	—	—	—	—	—	—	—	—	—	—	—
3141	Land................................	—	—	—	—	—	—	—	—	—	—	—	—
3142	Subsoil assets.......................	—	—	—	—	—	—	—	—	—	—	—	—
3143	Other naturally occurring assets......	—	—	—	—	—	—	—	—	—	—	—	—
3144	Intangible nonproduced assets.........	—	—	—	—	—	—	—	—	—	—	—	—
32	**Net acquisition of financial assets........**	6,544	37,140	−5,519	8,659	41,869	−3,877	1,730	3,719	946	10,671	45,699	−3,608
321	Domestic..............................	7,255	37,235	−5,309	9,371	41,964	−3,667	1,730	3,719	946	11,382	45,794	−3,398
3212	Currency and deposits.................	2,166	1,655	−825	2,176	2,088	−281	−104	1,285	336	2,072	3,373	55
3213	Securities other than shares..........	—	—	—	—	—	—	—	—	—	—	—	—
3214	Loans................................	−3,293	12,611	−11,310	−3,450	12,447	−11,374	−434	640	43	−3,603	13,198	−12,007
3215	Shares and other equity...............	2,888	11,279	−11,534	2,888	11,279	−11,534	—	1,773	—	2,888	13,052	−11,534
3216	Insurance technical reserves..........	—	—	—	—	—	—	—	—	—	—	—	—
3217	Financial derivatives.................	—	—	—	—	—	—	—	—	—	—	—	—
3218	Other accounts receivable.............	5,494	11,690	18,359	7,758	16,151	19,521	2,268	21	567	10,026	16,171	20,088
322	Foreign...............................	−711	−95	−210	−711	−95	−210	—	—	—	−711	−95	−210
3222	Currency and deposits.................	−872	−267	−353	−872	−267	−353	—	—	—	−872	−267	−353
3223	Securities other than shares..........	—	—	—	—	—	—	—	—	—	—	—	—
3224	Loans................................	—	—	—	—	—	—	—	—	—	—	—	—
3225	Shares and other equity...............	161	172	143	161	172	143	—	—	—	161	172	143
3226	Insurance technical reserves..........	—	—	—	—	—	—	—	—	—	—	—	—
3227	Financial derivatives.................	—	—	—	—	—	—	—	—	—	—	—	—
3228	Other accounts receivable.............	—	—	—	—	—	—	—	—	—	—	—	—
323	Monetary gold and SDRs................	—	—	—	—	—	—	—	—	—	—	—	—
33	**Net incurrence of liabilities...................**	−9,791	32,583	−778	−9,872	35,256	−658	4,003	9,060	5,329	−5,588	44,427	3,995
331	Domestic..............................	−18,007	−1,351	−11,285	−18,089	1,322	−11,165	3,362	5,824	1,016	−14,446	7,257	−10,825
3312	Currency and deposits.................	—	—	—	—	—	—	—	—	—	—	—	—
3313	Securities other than shares..........	−10,946	1,895	3,374	−10,946	1,895	3,374	—	—	—	−10,946	1,895	3,374
3314	Loans................................	−5,453	5,812	−415	−5,453	5,812	−415	497	1,992	1,261	−4,674	7,915	170
3316	Insurance technical reserves..........	743	−12,229	−9,212	743	−12,229	−9,212	2,360	2,900	—	3,103	−9,329	−9,212
3317	Financial derivatives.................	—	—	—	—	—	—	—	—	—	—	—	—
3318	Other accounts payable................	−2,352	3,171	−5,032	−2,434	5,844	−4,912	505	932	−245	−1,929	6,776	−5,157
332	Foreign...............................	8,217	33,934	10,507	8,217	33,934	10,507	641	3,236	4,313	8,858	37,170	14,820
3322	Currency and deposits.................	—	—	—	—	—	—	—	—	—	—	—	—
3323	Securities other than shares..........	—	—	—	—	—	—	—	—	—	—	—	—
3324	Loans................................	8,217	33,934	10,507	8,217	33,934	10,507	641	3,236	4,313	8,858	37,170	14,820
3326	Insurance technical reserves..........	—	—	—	—	—	—	—	—	—	—	—	—
3327	Financial derivatives.................	—	—	—	—	—	—	—	—	—	—	—	—
3328	Other accounts payable................	—	—	—	—	—	—	—	—	—	—	—	—

Table 4   Holding gains in assets and liabilities

		Budgetary Central Government			Central Government			Local Government			General Government		
4	**Change in net worth from hold. gains...**	....	....	....	....	....	....	6,981	24,065	21,869	....	....	....
41	**Nonfinancial assets..........................**	....	....	....	....	....	....	12,180	27,820	....	....	....	....
411	Fixed assets............................	....	....	....	....	....	....	....	....	....	....	....	....
412	Inventories...........................	....	....	....	....	....	....	....	....	....	....	....	....
413	Valuables.............................	....	....	....	....	....	....	....	....	....	....	....	....
414	Nonproduced assets....................	....	....	....	....	....	....	....	....	....	....	....	....
42	**Financial assets...........................**	5,893	16,070	11,058	5,906	16,087	11,064	−385	840	....	5,474	16,866	....
421	Domestic..............................	5,387	15,695	10,559	5,399	15,712	10,565	−385	840	....	4,967	16,491	....
422	Foreign...............................	507	375	499	507	375	499	—	—	....	507	375	....
423	Monetary gold and SDRs................	—	—	—	—	—	—	—	—	....	—	—	....

In Millions of Kronur / Year Ending December 31 / Noncash Reporter

		Budgetary Central Government			Central Government			Local Government			General Government		
		2000	2001	2002	2000	2001	2002	2000	2001	2002	2000	2001	2002
43	Liabilities	28,515	51,333	−11,032	28,515	51,333	−11,032	4,814	4,595	....	33,282	55,866	....
431	Domestic	15,543	26,303	15,760	15,543	26,303	15,760	3,724	3,362	....	19,220	29,603	....
432	Foreign	12,972	25,030	−26,792	12,972	25,030	−26,792	1,090	1,233	....	14,062	26,263	....

Table 5   Other changes in the volume of assets and liabilities

		Budgetary Central Government			Central Government			Local Government			General Government		
5	Change in net worth from vol. chngs.	....	....	....	....	....	....	—	5,206	23,706	....	....	....
51	Nonfinancial assets	....	....	....	....	....	....	—	—	....	....	....	....
511	Fixed assets	....	....	....	....	....	....	—	—	....	....	....	....
512	Inventories	....	....	....	....	....	....	—	—	....	....	....	....
513	Valuables	....	....	....	....	....	....	—	—	....	....	....	....
514	Nonproduced assets	....	....	....	....	....	....	—	—	....	....	....	....
52	Financial assets	−10,118	−1,078	−8,782	−12,339	−1,078	−8,810	—	5,206	....	−12,339	4,128	....
521	Domestic	−10,118	−1,078	−8,782	−12,339	−1,078	−8,810	—	5,206	....	−12,339	4,128	....
522	Foreign	—	—	—	—	—	—	—	—	....	—	—	....
523	Monetary gold and SDRs	—	—	—	—	—	—	—	—	....	—	—	....
53	Liabilities	10,375	−5,383	11,152	10,375	−5,383	11,152	—	—	....	10,375	−5,383	....
531	Domestic	10,375	−5,383	11,152	10,375	−5,383	11,152	—	—	....	10,375	−5,383	
532	Foreign	—	—	—	—	—	—	—	—	....			

Table 6   Balance sheet

		Budgetary Central Government			Central Government			Local Government			General Government		
6	Net worth	....	....	....	....	....	....	122,774	160,446	214,155	....	....	....
61	Nonfinancial assets	....	....	....	....	....	....	176,592	218,154	175,048	....	....	....
611	Fixed assets	....	....	....	....	....	....				....	....	....
6111	Buildings and structures	....	....	....	....	....	....				....	....	....
6112	Machinery and equipment	13,671	15,606	8,693	13,671	15,606	8,693						
6113	Other fixed assets	....	....	....	....	....	....						
612	Inventories	....	....	....	....	....	....						
613	Valuables	....	....	....	....	....	....						
614	Nonproduced assets	....	....	....	....	....	....						
6141	Land	....	....	....	....	....	....						
6142	Subsoil assets	....	....	....	....	....	....						
6143	Other naturally occurring assets	....	....	....	....	....	....						
6144	Intangible nonproduced assets	....	....	....	....	....	....				....		
62	Financial assets	214,559	266,690	263,446	215,774	272,652	271,029	26,515	36,280	86,706	241,542	308,234	356,387
621	Domestic	209,411	261,261	257,728	210,626	267,223	265,311	26,515	36,280	86,706	236,394	302,805	350,669
6212	Currency and deposits	14,920	16,574	15,749	15,274	17,361	17,080	2,627	3,912	4,338	17,901	21,273	21,418
6213	Securities other than shares	—	—	—	—	—	—	—	—	—	—	—	—
6214	Loans	70,920	93,049	80,875	71,269	93,251	81,019	6,595	6,074	6,882	77,117	98,627	86,553
6215	Shares and other equity	71,420	88,821	84,814	71,420	88,821	84,814	—	9,620	57,010	71,420	98,441	141,824
6216	Insurance technical reserves	—	—	—	—	—	—	—	—	—	—	—	—
6217	Financial derivatives	—	—	—	—	—	—	—	—	—	—	—	—
6218	Other accounts receivable	52,151	62,817	76,290	52,663	67,791	82,398	17,293	16,674	18,476	69,956	84,465	100,874
622	Foreign	5,148	5,429	5,718	5,148	5,429	5,718	—	—	—	5,148	5,429	5,718
6222	Currency and deposits	1,911	1,472	719	1,911	1,472	719	—	—	—	1,911	1,472	719
6223	Securities other than shares	—	—	—	—	—	—	—	—	—	—	—	—
6224	Loans	—	—	—	—	—	—	—	—	—	—	—	—
6225	Shares and other equity	3,238	3,957	4,999	3,238	3,957	4,999	—	—	—	3,238	3,957	4,999
6226	Insurance technical reserves	—	—	—	—	—	—	—	—	—	—	—	—
6227	Financial derivatives	—	—	—	—	—	—	—	—	—	—	—	—
6228	Other accounts receivable	—	—	—	—	—	—	—	—	—	—	—	—
623	Monetary gold and SDRs	—	—	—	—	—	—	—	—	—	—	—	—
63	Liabilities	412,948	491,481	490,823	413,376	494,583	494,045	80,333	93,988	47,599	492,962	587,873	540,296
631	Domestic	273,623	293,192	308,819	274,051	296,294	312,041	66,755	75,941	37,602	340,059	371,537	348,295
6312	Currency and deposits	—	—	—	—	—	—	—	—	—	—	—	—
6313	Securities other than shares	64,077	69,868	74,146	64,077	69,868	74,146	—	—	—	64,077	69,868	74,146
6314	Loans	8,878	16,195	15,804	8,878	16,195	15,804	32,321	34,690	30,021	40,452	50,187	44,477
6316	Insurance technical reserves	163,007	167,746	183,231	163,007	167,746	183,231	24,130	30,015	—	187,137	197,761	183,231
6317	Financial derivatives	—	—	—	—	—	—	—	—	—	—	—	—
6318	Other accounts payable	37,661	39,383	35,638	38,090	42,485	38,860	10,304	11,236	7,581	48,394	53,721	46,441
632	Foreign	139,325	198,289	182,004	139,325	198,289	182,004	13,578	18,047	9,997	152,903	216,336	192,001
6322	Currency and deposits	—	—	—	—	—	—	—	—	—	—	—	—
6323	Securities other than shares	—	—	—	—	—	—	—	—	—	—	—	—
6324	Loans	139,325	198,289	182,004	139,325	198,289	182,004	13,578	18,047	9,997	152,903	216,336	192,001
6326	Insurance technical reserves	—	—	—	—	—	—	—	—	—	—	—	—
6327	Financial derivatives	—	—	—	—	—	—	—	—	—	—	—	—
6328	Other accounts payable	—	—	—	—	—	—	—	—	—	—	—	—

In Millions of Kronur / Year Ending December 31 / Noncash Reporter

	Budgetary Central Government			Central Government			Local Government			General Government		
	2000	2001	2002	2000	2001	2002	2000	2001	2002	2000	2001	2002
Memorandum items:												
6M2 Net financial worth	−198,389	−224,791	−227,377	−197,602	−221,931	−223,016	−53,818	−57,708	39,107	−251,420	−279,639	−183,909
6M3 Debt at market value	....	....	....	....	....	....	....	....	....	....	....	....
6M4 Debt at nominal value	....	....	....	....	....	....	....	....	....	....	....	....
6M5 Arrears	....	....	....	....	....	....	....	....	....	....	....	....
6M6 Obligations for social security benefits	....	....	....	....	....	....	....	....	....	....	....	....
6M7 Contingent liabilities	....	....	....	....	....	....	....	....	....	....	....	....
6M8 Uncapitalized military weapons, systems	....	....	....	....	....	....	....	....	....	....	....	....
Table 7 Outlays by functions of govt.												
7 **Total outlays**	211,229	241,887	263,104	209,300	240,460	262,231	81,560	97,001	104,023	283,810	328,245	356,535
701 **General public services**	41,146	47,849	48,434	41,146	47,849	48,434	7,162	11,639	12,482	45,081	56,034	57,273
7017 Public debt transactions	19,665	23,128	21,891	19,665	23,128	21,891	3,096	5,439	4,043	22,761	28,568	25,934
7018 General transfers between levels of govt.	....	....	....	....	....	....	....	....	....	....	....	....
702 **Defense**	—	—	—	—	—	—	....	....	....	....	....	....
703 **Public order and safety**	10,460	11,507	12,881	10,460	11,507	12,881	1,951	2,090	2,241	11,990	13,444	14,962
704 **Economic affairs**	34,948	41,833	41,090	34,992	41,876	41,198	11,278	14,335	15,373	44,555	52,759	52,931
7042 Agriculture, forestry, fishing, and hunting	12,418	14,299	16,168	12,418	14,299	16,168	290	326	350	12,705	14,620	16,511
7043 Fuel and energy	....	....	....	....	....	....	....	....	....	....	....	....
7044 Mining, manufacturing, and construction	....	....	....	....	....	....	....	....	....	....	....	....
7045 Transport	14,842	17,902	18,014	14,842	17,902	18,014	9,255	12,384	13,281	22,620	27,167	28,006
7046 Communication	....	....	....	....	....	....	....	....	....	....	....	....
705 **Environmental protection**	....	....	....	....	....	....	....	....	....	....	....	....
706 **Housing and community amenities**	1,732	1,972	2,383	1,732	1,972	2,383	4,402	6,126	6,569	5,315	7,924	8,770
707 **Health**	52,880	59,027	69,154	52,488	58,588	68,812	887	966	1,036	53,358	60,476	70,821
7072 Outpatient services	....	....	....	....	....	....	....	....	....	....	....	....
7073 Hospital services	....	....	....	....	....	....	....	....	....	....	....	....
7074 Public health services	....	....	....	....	....	....	....	....	....	....	....	....
708 **Recreation, culture, and religion**	7,091	7,650	8,227	7,091	7,650	8,227	12,781	13,772	14,769	19,677	21,622	23,207
709 **Education**	18,942	23,211	26,048	19,002	23,266	26,106	25,272	28,841	30,929	44,081	51,256	56,137
7091 Pre-primary and primary education	....	....	....	....	....	....	....	....	....	....	....	....
7092 Secondary education	....	....	....	....	....	....	....	....	....	....	....	....
7094 Tertiary education	....	....	....	....	....	....	....	....	....	....	....	....
710 **Social protection**	44,029	48,838	54,888	42,389	47,752	54,190	17,826	19,232	20,624	59,752	64,729	72,436
7 Statistical discrepancy: Total outlays	—	—	—	—	—	—	—	—	—	—	—	—
Table 8 Transactions in financial assets and liabilities by sector												
82 **Net acquisition of financial assets**	6,544	37,140	−5,519	8,659	41,869	−3,877	1,730	3,719	946	10,671	45,699	−3,608
821 Domestic	7,255	37,235	−5,309	9,371	41,964	−3,667	1,730	3,719	946	11,382	45,794	−3,398
8211 General government	....	....	....	....	....	....	....	....	....	....	....	....
8212 Central bank	....	....	....	....	....	....	....	....	....	....	....	....
8213 Other depository corporations	....	....	....	....	....	....	....	....	....	....	....	....
8214 Financial corporations n.e.c.	....	....	....	....	....	....	....	....	....	....	....	....
8215 Nonfinancial corporations	....	....	....	....	....	....	....	....	....	....	....	....
8216 Households & NPIs serving households	....	....	....	....	....	....	....	....	....	....	....	....
822 Foreign	−711	−95	−210	−711	−95	−210	—	—	—	−711	−95	−210
8221 General government	....	....	....	....	....	....	—	—	—	....	....	....
8227 International organizations	....	....	....	....	....	....	—	—	—	....	....	....
8228 Financial corporations other than international organizations	....	....	....	....	....	....	—	—	—	....	....	....
8229 Other nonresidents	....	....	....	....	....	....	—	—	—	....	....	....
823 Monetary gold and SDRs	—	—	—	—	—	—	—	—	—	—	—	—
83 **Net incurrence of liabilities**	−9,791	32,583	−778	−9,872	35,256	−658	4,003	9,060	5,329	−5,588	44,427	3,995
831 Domestic	−18,007	−1,351	−11,285	−18,089	1,322	−11,165	3,362	5,824	1,016	−14,446	7,257	−10,825
8311 General government	....	....	....	....	....	....	....	....	....	....	....	....
8312 Central bank	....	....	....	....	....	....	....	....	....	....	....	....
8313 Other depository corporations	....	....	....	....	....	....	....	....	....	....	....	....
8314 Financial corporations n.e.c.	....	....	....	....	....	....	....	....	....	....	....	....
8315 Nonfinancial corporations	....	....	....	....	....	....	....	....	....	....	....	....
8316 Households & NPIs serving households	....	....	....	....	....	....	....	....	....	....	....	....
832 Foreign	8,217	33,934	10,507	8,217	33,934	10,507	641	3,236	4,313	8,858	37,170	14,820
8321 General government	....	....	....	....	....	....	....	....	....	....	....	....
8327 International organizations	....	....	....	....	....	....	....	....	....	....	....	....
8328 Financial corporations other than international organizations	....	....	....	....	....	....	....	....	....	....	....	....
8329 Other nonresidents	....	....	....	....	....	....	....	....	....	....	....	....

India 534

In Billions of Rupees / Year Beginning April 1 / Cash Reporter

	Central Government			State Government			Local Government			General Government		
	2002	2003p	2004f	2002	2003	2004	2002	2003	2004	2002	2003	2004
Statement of government operations												
Statement of other economic flows												
Balance sheet												
6 *Net worth*...................................	....	....	....	....	....	....	....	....	....	....	....	....
61 Nonfinancial assets...................	....	....	....	....	....	....	....	....	....	....	....	....
62 Financial assets........................	....	....	....	....	....	....	....	....	....	....	....	....
63 Liabilities................................	15,609.3	17,162.7	20,432.3	....	....	....	....	....	....	....	....	....
Statement of sources and uses of cash												
1 Cash receipts from operating activities.........	2,908.7	3,323.6	3,941.4	....	....	....	....	....	....	4,189.8	....	....
11 Taxes..	2,162.7	2,549.2	3,177.3	....	....	....	....	....	....	3,514.7	....	....
12 Social contributions.................	6.8	12.3	13.6	....	....	....	....	....	....	6.8	....	....
13 Grants......................................	18.7	28.6	36.0	....	....	....	....	....	....	18.7	....	....
14 Other receipts..........................	720.5	733.5	714.6	....	....	....	....	....	....	649.6	....	....
2 Cash payments for operating activities.........	4,001.4	4,365.3	4,928.6	....	....	....	....	....	....	5,718.3	....	....
21 Compensation of employees.................	388.8	427.0	486.9	....	....	....	....	....	....	1,455.4	....	....
22 Purchases of goods and services...............	465.1	530.2	720.1	....	....	....	....	....	....	707.9	....	....
24 Interest...................................	1,148.0	1,211.9	1,257.7	....	....	....	....	....	....	1,455.4	....	....
25 Subsidies................................	....	....	....	....	....	....	....	....	....	....	....	....
26 Grants......................................	....	....	....	....	....	....	....	....	....	....	....	....
27 Social benefits.........................	....	....	....	....	....	....	....	....	....	....	....	....
28 Other payments........................	....	....	....	....	....	....	....	....	....	....	....	....
CIO *Net cash inflow from oper. activities.....*	*−1,092.7*	*−1,041.7*	*−987.2*	....	....	....	....	....	....	*−1,528.5*	....	....
31.1 Purchases of nonfinancial assets.................	106.8	126.0	176.2	....	....	....	....	....	....	431.3	....	....
31.2 Sales of nonfinancial assets........................	37.6	152.3	47.6	....	....	....	....	....	....	38.2	....	....
31 Net cash outflow from investments in nonfinancial assets.................	69.2	−26.3	128.6	....	....	....	....	....	....	393.1	....	....
CSD *Cash surplus/deficit*.................................	*−1,162.0*	*−1,015.4*	*−1,115.8*	....	....	....	....	....	....	*−1,921.6*	....	....
32x Net acquisition of fin assets, excl. cash...........	118.6	−159.5	231.8	....	....	....	....	....	....	310.5	....	....
321x Domestic................................	110.5	−165.3	227.6	....	....	....	....	....	....	....	....	....
322x Foreign................................	8.1	5.8	4.2	....	....	....	....	....	....	....	....	....
323 Monetary gold and SDRs................	—	—	—	....	....	....	....	....	....	—	....	....
33 Net incurrence of liabilities..........................	1,261.7	958.2	1,211.6	....	....	....	....	....	....	....	....	....
331 Domestic................................	1,381.1	1,075.3	1,130.8	....	....	....	....	....	....	....	....	....
332 Foreign................................	−119.3	−117.0	80.8	....	....	....	....	....	....	....	....	....
NFB Net cash inflow from fin. activities.................	1,143.1	1,117.7	979.8	....	....	....	....	....	....	....	....	....
NCB *Net change in the stock of cash............*	*−18.8*	*102.3*	*−136.0*	....	....	....	....	....	....	....	....	....
Table 1 Revenue												
1 **Revenue**..	**2,908.7**	**3,323.6**	**3,941.4**	....	....	....	....	....	....	**4,189.8**	....	....
11 **Taxes**..	**2,162.7**	**2,549.2**	**3,177.3**	....	....	....	....	....	....	**3,514.7**	....	....
111 Taxes on income, profits, & capital gains......	827.6	1,032.6	1,393.7	....	....	....	....	....	....	827.6	....	....
1111 Individuals................................	368.7	402.7	509.3	....	....	....	....	....	....	368.7	....	....
1112 Corporations and other enterprises............	461.7	629.9	884.4	....	....	....	....	....	....	461.7	....	....
112 Taxes on payroll and workforce...............	—	—	—	....	....	....	....	....	....	—	....	....
113 Taxes on property......................	1.9	1.8	1.8	....	....	....	....	....	....	17.2	....	....
114 Taxes on goods and services.................	882.9	1,021.4	1,239.4	....	....	....	....	....	....	2,084.8	....	....
1141 General taxes on goods and services...........	4.6	4.1	4.3	....	....	....	....	....	....	....	....	....
1142 Excises................................	824.2	924.9	1,093.1	....	....	....	....	....	....	....	....	....
115 Taxes on int'l. trade and transactions...........	448.5	493.5	542.5	....	....	....	....	....	....	583.5	....	....
116 Other taxes............................	1.7	—	—	....	....	....	....	....	....	1.7	....	....
12 **Social contributions**........................	**6.8**	**12.3**	**13.6**	....	....	....	....	....	....	**6.8**	....	....
121 Social security contributions.................	—	—	—	....	....	....	....	....	....	—	....	....
122 Other social contributions.................	6.8	12.3	13.6	....	....	....	....	....	....	6.8	....	....
13 **Grants**..	**18.7**	**28.6**	**36.0**	....	....	....	....	....	....	**18.7**	....	....
131 From foreign governments..................	18.7	28.6	36.0	....	....	....	....	....	....	18.7	....	....
132 From international organizations.............	—	—	—	....	....	....	....	....	....	....	....	....
133 From other general government units..........	—	—	—	....	....	....	....	....	....	—	....	....
14 **Other revenue**...............................	**720.5**	**733.5**	**714.6**	....	....	....	....	....	....	**649.6**	....	....
Table 2 Expense by economic type												
2 **Expense**..	**4,001.4**	**4,365.3**	**4,928.6**	....	....	....	....	....	....	**5,718.3**	....	....
21 **Compensation of employees**.................	**388.8**	**427.0**	**486.9**	....	....	....	....	....	....	**1,455.4**	....	....
211 Wages and salaries.......................	388.8	427.0	486.9	....	....	....	....	....	....	1,455.4	....	....
212 Social contributions.....................	—	—	—	....	....	....	....	....	....	—	....	....
22 **Use of goods and services**.................	**465.1**	**530.2**	**720.1**	....	....	....	....	....	....	**707.9**	....	....
23 **Consumption of fixed capital**.................	....	....	....	....	....	....	....	....	....	....	....	....
24 **Interest**..	**1,148.0**	**1,211.9**	**1,257.7**	....	....	....	....	....	....	**1,455.4**	....	....
25 **Subsidies**..	....	....	....	....	....	....	....	....	....	....	....	....

In Billions of Rupees / Year Beginning April 1 / Cash Reporter

		Central Government			State Government			Local Government			General Government		
		2002	2003p	2004f	2002	2003	2004	2002	2003	2004	2002	2003	2004
26	**Grants**........................	....	....	....	....	....	....	....	....	....	....	....	....
261	To foreign govenments.............	....	....	....	....	....	....	....	....	....	....	....	....
262	To international organizations........	....	....	....	....	....	....	....	....	....	....	....	....
263	To other general government units.........	1,118.6	1,264.6	1,564.2	....	....	....	....	....	....	....	....	....
2631	Current............................	846.2	983.6	1,219.5	....	....	....	....	....	....	....	....	....
2632	Capital............................	272.4	281.0	344.7	....	....	....	....	....	....	....	....	....
27	**Social benefits**..................	....	....	....	....	....	....	....	....	....	....	....	....
28	**Other expense**...................	....	....	....	....	....	....	....	....	....	....	....	....
281	Property expense other than interest...........	....	....	....	....	....	....	....	....	....	....	....	....
282	Miscellaneous other expense...........	....	....	....	....	....	....	....	....	....	....	....	....
2821	Current............................	....	....	....	....	....	....	....	....	....	....	....	....
2822	Capital............................	....	....	....	....	....	....	....	....	....	....	....	....

Table 3   Transactions in assets and liabilities

		Central Government			State Government			Local Government			General Government		
		2002	2003p	2004f	2002	2003	2004	2002	2003	2004	2002	2003	2004
3	**Change in net worth from transactns....**	....	....	....	....	....	....	....	....	....	....	....	....
31	**Net acquisition of nonfinancial assets...**	69.2	−26.3	128.6	....	....	....	....	....	....	393.1	....	....
311	Fixed assets........................	101.9	120.9	169.8	....	....	....	....	....	....	....	....	....
3111	Buildings and structures.............	....	....	....	....	....	....	....	....	....	....	....	....
3112	Machinery and equipment.............	....	....	....	....	....	....	....	....	....	....	....	....
3113	Other fixed assets...................	....	....	....	....	....	....	....	....	....	....	....	....
312	Inventories.........................	−1.1	−2.2	−1.3	....	....	....	....	....	....	....	....	....
313	Valuables..........................	—	—	—	....	....	....	....	....	....	....	....	....
314	Nonproduced assets.................	−31.5	−145.0	−40.0	....	....	....	....	....	....	....	....	....
3141	Land..............................	....	....	....	....	....	....	....	....	....	....	....	....
3142	Subsoil assets......................	....	....	....	....	....	....	....	....	....	....	....	....
3143	Other naturally occurring assets.......	....	....	....	....	....	....	....	....	....	....	....	....
3144	Intangible nonproduced assets.........	....	....	....	....	....	....	....	....	....	....	....	....
32	**Net acquisition of financial assets.........**	99.7	−57.2	95.8	....	....	....	....	....	....	....	....	....
321	Domestic...........................	91.7	−63.0	91.6	....	....	....	....	....	....	....	....	....
3212	Currency and deposits...............	−18.8	102.3	−136.0	....	....	....	....	....	....	....	....	....
3213	Securities other than shares.........	....	....	....	....	....	....	....	....	....	....	....	....
3214	Loans..............................	....	....	....	....	....	....	....	....	....	....	....	....
3215	Shares and other equity.............	....	....	....	....	....	....	....	....	....	....	....	....
3216	Insurance technical reserves.........	....	....	....	....	....	....	....	....	....	....	....	....
3217	Financial derivatives................	....	....	....	....	....	....	....	....	....	....	....	....
3218	Other accounts receivable............	....	....	....	....	....	....	....	....	....	....	....	....
322	Foreign............................	8.1	5.8	4.2	....	....	....	....	....	....	....	....	....
3222	Currency and deposits...............	....	....	....	....	....	....	....	....	....	....	....	....
3223	Securities other than shares.........	....	....	....	....	....	....	....	....	....	....	....	....
3224	Loans..............................	....	....	....	....	....	....	....	....	....	....	....	....
3225	Shares and other equity.............	....	....	....	....	....	....	....	....	....	....	....	....
3226	Insurance technical reserves.........	....	....	....	....	....	....	....	....	....	....	....	....
3227	Financial derivatives................	....	....	....	....	....	....	....	....	....	....	....	....
3228	Other accounts receivable............	....	....	....	....	....	....	....	....	....	....	....	....
323	Monetary gold and SDRs.............	—	—	—	....	....	....	....	....	....	....	....	....
33	**Net incurrence of liabilities...................**	1,261.7	958.2	1,211.6	....	....	....	....	....	....	....	....	....
331	Domestic...........................	1,381.1	1,075.3	1,130.8	....	....	....	....	....	....	....	....	....
3312	Currency and deposits...............	313.9	245.5	227.2	....	....	....	....	....	....	....	....	....
3313	Securities other than shares.........	975.9	858.0	905.0	....	....	....	....	....	....	....	....	....
3314	Loans..............................	91.2	−28.2	−1.4	....	....	....	....	....	....	....	....	....
3316	Insurance technical reserves.........	—	....	....	....	....	....	....	....	....	....	....	....
3317	Financial derivatives................	—	—	—	....	....	....	....	....	....	....	....	....
3318	Other accounts payable..............	....	....	....	....	....	....	....	....	....	....	....	....
332	Foreign............................	−119.3	−117.0	80.8	....	....	....	....	....	....	....	....	....
3322	Currency and deposits...............	....	....	....	....	....	....	....	....	....	....	....	....
3323	Securities other than shares.........	....	....	....	....	....	....	....	....	....	....	....	....
3324	Loans..............................	....	....	....	....	....	....	....	....	....	....	....	....
3326	Insurance technical reserves.........	....	....	....	....	....	....	....	....	....	....	....	....
3327	Financial derivatives................	....	....	....	....	....	....	....	....	....	....	....	....
3328	Other accounts payable..............	....	....	....	....	....	....	....	....	....	....	....	....

In Billions of Rupees / Year Beginning April 1 / Cash Reporter

	Central Government			State Government			Local Government			General Government		
	2002	2003p	2004f	2002	2003	2004	2002	2003	2004	2002	2003	2004
Table 4 Holding gains in assets and liabilities												
Table 5 Other changes in the volume of assets and liabilities												
Table 6 Balance sheet												
6 Net worth..........................	....	....	....	....	....	....	....	....	....	....	....	....
61 Nonfinancial assets..........................	....	....	....	....	....	....	....	....	....	....	....	....
611 Fixed assets..........................	....	....	....	....	....	....	....	....	....	....	....	....
6111 Buildings and structures..........................	....	....	....	....	....	....	....	....	....	....	....	....
6112 Machinery and equipment..........................	....	....	....	....	....	....	....	....	....	....	....	....
6113 Other fixed assets..........................	....	....	....	....	....	....	....	....	....	....	....	....
612 Inventories..........................	....	....	....	....	....	....	....	....	....	....	....	....
613 Valuables..........................	....	....	....	....	....	....	....	....	....	....	....	....
614 Nonproduced assets..........................	....	....	....	....	....	....	....	....	....	....	....	....
6141 Land..........................	....	....	....	....	....	....	....	....	....	....	....	....
6142 Subsoil assets..........................	....	....	....	....	....	....	....	....	....	....	....	....
6143 Other naturally occurring assets..........................	....	....	....	....	....	....	....	....	....	....	....	....
6144 Intangible nonproduced assets..........................	....	....	....	....	....	....	....	....	....	....	....	....
62 **Financial assets**..........................	....	....	....	....	....	....	....	....	....	....	....	....
621 Domestic..........................	....	....	....	....	....	....	....	....	....	....	....	....
6212 Currency and deposits..........................	....	....	....	....	....	....	....	....	....	....	....	....
6213 Securities other than shares..........................	....	....	....	....	....	....	....	....	....	....	....	....
6214 Loans..........................	....	....	....	....	....	....	....	....	....	....	....	....
6215 Shares and other equity..........................	....	....	....	....	....	....	....	....	....	....	....	....
6216 Insurance technical reserves..........................	....	....	....	....	....	....	....	....	....	....	....	....
6217 Financial derivatives..........................	....	....	....	....	....	....	....	....	....	....	....	....
6218 Other accounts receivable..........................	....	....	....	....	....	....	....	....	....	....	....	....
622 Foreign..........................	....	....	....	....	....	....	....	....	....	....	....	....
6222 Currency and deposits..........................	....	....	....	....	....	....	....	....	....	....	....	....
6223 Securities other than shares..........................	....	....	....	....	....	....	....	....	....	....	....	....
6224 Loans..........................	....	....	....	....	....	....	....	....	....	....	....	....
6225 Shares and other equity..........................	....	....	....	....	....	....	....	....	....	....	....	....
6226 Insurance technical reserves..........................	....	....	....	....	....	....	....	....	....	....	....	....
6227 Financial derivatives..........................	....	....	....	....	....	....	....	....	....	....	....	....
6228 Other accounts receivable..........................	....	....	....	....	....	....	....	....	....	....	....	....
623 Monetary gold and SDRs..........................	....	....	....	....	....	....	....	....	....	....	....	....
63 **Liabilities**..........................	**15,609.3**	**17,162.7**	**20,432.3**	....	....	....	....	....	....	....	....	....
631 Domestic..........................	15,013.2	16,688.7	19,881.4	....	....	....	....	....	....	....	....	....
6312 Currency and deposits..........................	....	....	....	....	....	....	....	....	....	....	....	....
6313 Securities other than shares..........................	....	....	....	....	....	....	....	....	....	....	....	....
6314 Loans..........................	....	....	....	....	....	....	....	....	....	....	....	....
6316 Insurance technical reserves..........................	....	....	....	....	....	....	....	....	....	....	....	....
6317 Financial derivatives..........................	....	....	....	....	....	....	....	....	....	....	....	....
6318 Other accounts payable..........................	....	....	....	....	....	....	....	....	....	....	....	....
632 Foreign..........................	596.1	474.1	550.8	....	....	....	....	....	....	....	....	....
6322 Currency and deposits..........................	....	....	....	....	....	....	....	....	....	....	....	....
6323 Securities other than shares..........................	....	....	....	....	....	....	....	....	....	....	....	....
6324 Loans..........................	....	....	....	....	....	....	....	....	....	....	....	....
6326 Insurance technical reserves..........................	....	....	....	....	....	....	....	....	....	....	....	....
6327 Financial derivatives..........................	....	....	....	....	....	....	....	....	....	....	....	....
6328 Other accounts payable..........................	....	....	....	....	....	....	....	....	....	....	....	....
Memorandum items:												
6M2 Net financial worth..........................	....	....	....	....	....	....	....	....	....	....	....	....
6M3 Debt at market value..........................	....	....	....	....	....	....	....	....	....	....	....	....
6M4 Debt at nominal value..........................	....	....	....	....	....	....	....	....	....	....	....	....
6M5 Arrears..........................	....	....	....	....	....	....	....	....	....	....	....	....
6M6 Obligations for social security benefits..........................	....	....	....	....	....	....	....	....	....	....	....	....
6M7 Contingent liabilities..........................	....	....	....	....	....	....	....	....	....	....	....	....
6M8 Uncapitalized military weapons, systems..........................	....	....	....	....	....	....	....	....	....	....	....	....
Table 7 Outlays by functions of govt.												
7 **Total outlays**..........................	**4,108.2**	**4,491.2**	**5,104.8**	....	....	....	....	....	....	**6,149.6**	....	....
701 **General public services**..........................	**2,462.5**	**2,723.2**	**3,027.2**	....	....	....	....	....	....	**2,549.8**	....	....
7017 Public debt transactions..........................	1,148.0	1,211.9	1,257.7	....	....	....	....	....	....	1,455.4	....	....
7018 General transfers between levels of govt.	....	....	....	....	....	....	....	....	....	....	....	....
702 **Defense**..........................	**555.7**	**602.1**	**769.0**	....	....	....	....	....	....	**562.8**	....	....
703 **Public order and safety**..........................	....	....	....	....	....	....	....	....	....	....	....	....

		Central Government			State Government			Local Government			General Government		
		2002	2003p	2004f	2002	2003	2004	2002	2003	2004	2002	2003	2004
704	**Economic affairs**.....................	**697.8**	**755.3**	**904.0**	....	....	....	....	....	....	**1,461.0**	....	....
7042	Agriculture, forestry, fishing, and hunting......	168.7	180.1	214.4	....	....	....	....	....	....	486.2	....	....
7043	Fuel and energy....................	137.3	139.1	128.0	....	....	....	....	....	....	....	....	....
7044	Mining, manufacturing, and construction.....	—	—	—	....	....	....	....	....	....	....	....	....
7045	Transport........................	101.3	100.7	123.4	....	....	....	....	....	....	255.1	....	....
7046	Communication....................	....	....	....	....	....	....	....	....	....	....	....	....
705	**Environmental protection**...................	....	....	....	....	....	....	....	....	....	....	....	....
706	**Housing and community amenities**........	**233.8**	**237.0**	**212.4**	....	....	....	....	....	....	**192.0**	....	....
707	**Health**........................	**64.2**	**67.6**	**78.0**	....	....	....	....	....	....		....	....
7072	Outpatient services..................	....	....	....	....	....	....	....	....	....	....	....	....
7073	Hospital services....................	....	....	....	....	....	....	....	....	....	....	....	....
7074	Public health services..................	....	....	....	....	....	....	....	....	....	....	....	....
708	**Recreation, culture, and religion**......	....	....	....	....	....	....	....	....	....	....	....	....
709	**Education**......................	**94.2**	**106.1**	**114.1**	....	....	....	....	....	....	**851.2**	....	....
7091	Pre-primary and primary education.............	....	....	....	....	....	....	....	....	....	....	....	....
7092	Secondary education..................	....	....	....	....	....	....	....	....	....	....	....	....
7094	Tertiary education...................	....	....	....	....	....	....	....	....	....	....	....	....
710	**Social protection**.....................	....	....	....	....	....	....	....	....	....	....	....	....
7	Statistical discrepancy: Total outlays.............	—	—	—	....	....	....	....	....	....	—	....	....
Table 8	**Transactions in financial assets and liabilities by sector**												
82	**Net acquisition of financial assets**........	**99.7**	**−57.2**	**95.8**	....	....	....	....	....	....	....	....	....
821	Domestic......................	91.7	−63.0	91.6	....	....	....	....	....	....	....	....	....
8211	General government........................	−7.2	−328.9	37.9	....	....	....	....	....	....	....	....	....
8212	Central bank.......................	....	....	....	....	....	....	....	....	....	....	....	....
8213	Other depository corporations..................	....	....	....	....	....	....	....	....	....	....	....	....
8214	Financial corporations n.e.c.......................	....	....	....	....	....	....	....	....	....	....	....	....
8215	Nonfinancial corporations.....................	....	....	....	....	....	....	....	....	....	....	....	....
8216	Households & NPIs serving households......	....	....	....	....	....	....	....	....	....	....	....	....
822	Foreign.........................	8.1	5.8	4.2	....	....	....	....	....	....	....	....	....
8221	General government........................	....	....	....	....	....	....	....	....	....	....	....	....
8227	International organizations.......................	....	....	....	....	....	....	....	....	....	....	....	....
8228	Financial corporations other than international organizations...............	....	....	....	....	....	....	....	....	....	....	....	....
8229	Other nonresidents.....................	....	....	....	....	....	....	....	....	....	....	....	....
823	Monetary gold and SDRs.....	—	—	—	....	....	....	....	....	....	....	....	....
83	**Net incurrence of liabilities**....................	**1,261.7**	**958.2**	**1,211.6**	....	....	....	....	....	....	....	....	....
831	Domestic......................	1,381.1	1,075.3	1,130.8	....	....	....	....	....	....	....	....	....
8311	General government........................	....	....	....	....	....	....	....	....	....	....	....	....
8312	Central bank.......................	....	....	....	....	....	....	....	....	....	....	....	....
8313	Other depository corporations..................	....	....	....	....	....	....	....	....	....	....	....	....
8314	Financial corporations n.e.c.......................	....	....	....	....	....	....	....	....	....	....	....	....
8315	Nonfinancial corporations.....................	....	....	....	....	....	....	....	....	....	....	....	....
8316	Households & NPIs serving households......	....	....	....	....	....	....	....	....	....	....	....	....
832	Foreign.........................	−119.3	−117.0	80.8	....	....	....	....	....	....	....	....	....
8321	General government........................	−61.3	−91.3	36.0	....	....	....	....	....	....	....	....	....
8327	International organizations.......................	−58.1	−25.7	44.7	....	....	....	....	....	....	....	....	....
8328	Financial corporations other than international organizations.............	—	—	—	....	....	....	....	....	....	....	....	....
8329	Other nonresidents.....................	—	—	—	....	....	....	....	....	....	....	....	....

		Budgetary Central Government			Central Government			Local Government			General Government		
		2002	2003	2004p	2002	2003	2004p	2002	2003	2004	2002	2003	2004
Statement of government operations													
Statement of other economic flows													
Balance sheet													
6	*Net worth*....................	....	....	....	....	....	....	....	....	....	....	....	....
61	Nonfinancial assets................	....	....	....	....	....	....	....	....	....	....	....	....
62	Financial assets....................	....	....	....	....	....	....	....	....	....	....	....	....
63	Liabilities..........................	587,070	598,412	660,333	587,070	598,412	660,333	....	....	....	....	....	....
Statement of sources and uses of cash													
1	Cash receipts from operating activities..........	298,518	341,377	400,590	317,807	349,306	421,918	....	....	....	....	....	....
11	Taxes..........................	215,468	249,404	283,093	215,468	249,404	283,093	....	....	....	....	....	....
12	Social contributions..................	—	—	—	19,152	10,862	11,612	....	....	....	....	....	....
13	Grants..........................	—	468	278	—	468	278	....	....	....	....	....	....
14	Other receipts....................	83,051	91,505	117,219	83,188	88,572	126,936	....	....	....	....	....	....
2	Cash payments for operating activities..........	280,429	307,934	363,608	286,273	327,382	386,937	....	....	....	....	....	....
21	Compensation of employees..................	21,259	47,662	49,270	21,259	47,662	49,270	....	....	....	....	....	....
22	Purchases of goods and services................	26,129	30,033	29,580	26,129	30,033	29,580	....	....	....	....	....	....
24	Interest..........................	81,122	65,351	62,486	81,122	65,351	62,486	....	....	....	....	....	....
25	Subsidies..........................	40,006	43,899	91,617	40,006	43,899	91,617	....	....	....	....	....	....
26	Grants..........................	97,591	120,314	130,045	97,591	120,314	130,045	....	....	....	....	....	....
27	Social benefits....................	14,121	—	—	19,965	19,447	23,329	....	....	....	....	....	....
28	Other payments....................	201	676	611	201	676	611	....	....	....	....	....	....
CIO	*Net cash inflow from oper. activities.....*	*23,311*	*30,823*	*55,028*	*31,535*	*21,924*	*34,981*	....	....	....	....	....	....
31.1	Purchases of nonfinancial assets..................	35,206	68,571	60,368	36,910	68,571	60,368	....	....	....	....	....	....
31.2	Sales of nonfinancial assets..........................	10	19	22	10	19	22	....	....	....	....	....	....
31	Net cash outflow from investments in nonfinancial assets..........................	35,196	68,552	60,346	36,900	68,552	60,346	....	....	....	....	....	....
CSD	*Cash surplus/deficit.*................	*−11,885*	*−37,729*	*−5,319*	*−5,365*	*−46,627*	*−25,365*	....	....	....	....	....	....
32x	Net acquisition of fin assets, excl. cash..........	—	—	—	−4,627	2,447	—	....	....	....	....	....	....
321x	Domestic..........................	—	—	—	−4,627	2,447	—	....	....	....	....	....	....
322x	Foreign..........................	—	—	—	—	—	—	....	....	....	....	....	....
323	Monetary gold and SDRs..................	—	—	—	—	—	—	....	....	....	....	....	....
33	Net incurrence of liabilities..................	−2,462	−6,710	−9,733	−389	−6,585	−10,108	....	....	....	....	....	....
331	Domestic..........................	—	—	—	2,073	125	−375	....	....	....	....	....	....
332	Foreign..........................	−2,462	−6,710	−9,733	−2,462	−6,710	−9,733	....	....	....	....	....	....
NFB	Net cash inflow from fin. activities..................	−2,462	−6,710	−9,733	4,237	−9,031	−10,108	....	....	....	....	....	....
NCB	*Net change in the stock of cash.*............	*−14,347*	*−44,438*	*−15,052*	*−1,128*	*−55,659*	*−35,474*	....	....	....	....	....	....
Table 1 Revenue													
1	**Revenue**..........................	**298,518**	**341,377**	**400,590**	**317,807**	**349,306**	**421,918**	....	....	....	....	....	....
11	**Taxes**..........................	**215,468**	**249,404**	**283,093**	**215,468**	**249,404**	**283,093**	....	....	....	....	....	....
111	Taxes on income, profits, & capital gains......	101,874	115,016	118,923	101,874	115,016	118,923	....	....	....	....	....	....
1111	Individuals..........................	25,545	96,053	95,700	25,545	96,053	95,700	....	....	....	....	....	....
1112	Corporations and other enterprises............	70,870	18,963	23,224	70,870	18,963	23,224	....	....	....	....	....	....
112	Taxes on payroll and workforce................	—	—	—	—	—	—	....	....	....	....	....	....
113	Taxes on property....................	9,252	12,518	14,652	9,252	12,518	14,652	....	....	....	....	....	....
114	Taxes on goods and services..................	93,705	110,688	135,167	93,705	110,688	135,167	....	....	....	....	....	....
1141	General taxes on goods and services..........	65,153	77,081	98,683	65,153	77,081	98,683	....	....	....	....	....	....
1142	Excises..........................	23,189	26,277	29,173	23,189	26,277	29,173	....	....	....	....	....	....
115	Taxes on int'l. trade and transactions...........	10,575	11,114	12,742	10,575	11,114	12,742	....	....	....	....	....	....
116	Other taxes....................	62	69	1,609	62	69	1,609	....	....	....	....	....	....
12	**Social contributions**..................	—	—	—	**19,152**	**10,862**	**11,612**	....	....	....	....	....	....
121	Social security contributions..................	—	—	—	19,152	10,862	11,612	....	....	....	....	....	....
122	Other social contributions..................	—	—	—	—	—	—	....	....	....	....	....	....
13	**Grants**..........................	—	**468**	**278**	—	**468**	**278**	....	....	....	....	....	....
131	From foreign governments..................	—	—	—	—	—	—	....	....	....	....	....	....
132	From international organizations................	—	468	278	—	468	278	....	....	....	....	....	....
133	From other general government units..........	—	—	—	—	—	—	....	....	....	....	....	....
14	**Other revenue**..........................	**83,051**	**91,505**	**117,219**	**83,188**	**88,572**	**126,936**	....	....	....	....	....	....
Table 2 Expense by economic type													
2	**Expense**..........................	**280,429**	**307,934**	**363,608**	**286,273**	**327,382**	**386,937**	....	....	....	....	....	....
21	**Compensation of employees**..................	**21,259**	**47,662**	**49,270**	**21,259**	**47,662**	**49,270**	....	....	....	....	....	....
211	Wages and salaries....................	21,259	47,662	49,270	21,259	47,662	49,270	....	....	....	....	....	....
212	Social contributions....................	—	—	—	—	—	—	....	....	....	....	....	....
22	**Use of goods and services**....................	**26,129**	**30,033**	**29,580**	**26,129**	**30,033**	**29,580**	....	....	....	....	....	....
23	**Consumption of fixed capital**................	....	....	....	....	....	....	....	....	....	....	....	....
24	**Interest**..........................	**81,122**	**65,351**	**62,486**	**81,122**	**65,351**	**62,486**	....	....	....	....	....	....
25	**Subsidies**..........................	**40,006**	**43,899**	**91,617**	**40,006**	**43,899**	**91,617**	....	....	....	....	....	....

	Budgetary Central Government			Central Government			Local Government			General Government		
	2002	2003	2004p	2002	2003	2004p	2002	2003	2004	2002	2003	2004
26 **Grants**...............................	**97,591**	**120,314**	**130,045**	**97,591**	**120,314**	**130,045**	....	....	....	....	....	....
261 To foreign govenments....................	—	—	—	—	—	—	....	....	....	....	....	....
262 To international organizations.................	—	—	—	—	—	—	....	....	....	....	....	....
263 To other general government units..............	97,591	120,314	130,045	97,591	120,314	130,045	....	....	....	....	....	....
2631 Current.................................	97,591	120,314	130,045	97,591	120,314	130,045	....	....	....	....	....	....
2632 Capital.................................	—	—	—	—	—	—	....	....	....	....	....	....
27 **Social benefits**.......................	**14,121**	**—**	**—**	**19,965**	**19,447**	**23,329**	....	....	....	....	....	....
28 **Other expense**........................	**201**	**676**	**611**	**201**	**676**	**611**	....	....	....	....	....	....
281 Property expense other than interest...........	—	—	—	—	—	—	....	....	....	....	....	....
282 Miscellaneous other expense..................	201	676	611	201	676	611	....	....	....	....	....	....
2821 Current.................................	—	—	—	—	—	—	....	....	....	....	....	....
2822 Capital.................................	201	676	611	201	676	611	....	....	....	....	....	....

Table 3 Transactions in assets and liabilities

	Budgetary Central Government			Central Government			Local Government			General Government		
	2002	2003	2004p	2002	2003	2004p	2002	2003	2004	2002	2003	2004
3 **Change in net worth from transactns....**	....	....	....	....	....	....	....	....	....	....	....	....
31 **Net acquisition of nonfinancial assets...**	**35,196**	**68,552**	**60,346**	**36,900**	**68,552**	**60,346**	....	....	....	....	....	....
311 Fixed assets..............................	35,196	68,552	60,346	36,900	68,552	60,346	....	....	....	....	....	....
3111 Buildings and structures.................	....	....	....	....	....	....	....	....	....	....	....	....
3112 Machinery and equipment.................	....	....	....	....	....	....	....	....	....	....	....	....
3113 Other fixed assets.....................	....	....	....	....	....	....	....	....	....	....	....	....
312 Inventories.............................	—	—	—	—	—	—	....	....	....	....	....	....
313 Valuables..............................	—	—	—	—	—	—	....	....	....	....	....	....
314 Nonproduced assets.......................	—	—	—	—	—	—	....	....	....	....	....	....
3141 Land.................................	—	—	—	—	—	—	....	....	....	....	....	....
3142 Subsoil assets........................	—	—	—	—	—	—	....	....	....	....	....	....
3143 Other naturally occurring assets................	—	—	—	—	—	—	....	....	....	....	....	....
3144 Intangible nonproduced assets..............	—	—	—	—	—	—	....	....	....	....	....	....
32 **Net acquisition of financial assets.........**	**−14,347**	**−44,438**	**−15,052**	**−5,755**	**−53,212**	**−35,474**	....	....	....	....	....	....
321 Domestic...............................	−14,347	−44,438	−15,052	−5,755	−53,212	−35,474	....	....	....	....	....	....
3212 Currency and deposits...................	−14,347	−44,438	−15,052	−1,128	−55,659	−35,474	....	....	....	....	....	....
3213 Securities other than shares..............	—	—	—	....	....	—	....	....	....	....	....	....
3214 Loans...............................	—	—	—	....	....	—	....	....	....	....	....	....
3215 Shares and other equity.................	—	—	—	....	....	—	....	....	....	....	....	....
3216 Insurance technical reserves..............	—	—	—	....	....	—	....	....	....	....	....	....
3217 Financial derivatives...................	—	—	—	....	....	—	....	....	....	....	....	....
3218 Other accounts receivable...............	....	....	....	....	....	....	....	....	....	....	....	....
322 Foreign................................	—	—	—	—	—	—	....	....	....	....	....	....
3222 Currency and deposits...................	—	—	—	—	—	—	....	....	....	....	....	....
3223 Securities other than shares..............	—	—	—	—	—	—	....	....	....	....	....	....
3224 Loans...............................	—	—	—	—	—	—	....	....	....	....	....	....
3225 Shares and other equity.................	—	—	—	—	—	—	....	....	....	....	....	....
3226 Insurance technical reserves..............	—	—	—	—	—	—	....	....	....	....	....	....
3227 Financial derivatives...................	—	—	—	—	—	—	....	....	....	....	....	....
3228 Other accounts receivable...............	....	....	....	....	....	....	....	....	....	....	....	....
323 Monetary gold and SDRs....................	—	—	—	—	—	—	....	....	....	....	....	....
33 **Net incurrence of liabilities...................**	**−2,462**	**−6,710**	**−9,733**	**−389**	**−6,585**	**−10,108**	....	....	....	....	....	....
331 Domestic...............................	—	—	—	2,073	125	−375	....	....	....	....	....	....
3312 Currency and deposits...................	—	—	—	2,073	125	−375	....	....	....	....	....	....
3313 Securities other than shares..............	—	—	—	—	—	—	....	....	....	....	....	....
3314 Loans...............................	—	—	—	—	—	—	....	....	....	....	....	....
3316 Insurance technical reserves..............	—	—	—	—	—	—	....	....	....	....	....	....
3317 Financial derivatives...................	—	—	—	—	—	—	....	....	....	....	....	....
3318 Other accounts payable..................	....	....	....	....	....	....	....	....	....	....	....	....
332 Foreign................................	−2,462	−6,710	−9,733	−2,462	−6,710	−9,733	....	....	....	....	....	....
3322 Currency and deposits...................	—	—	—	—	—	—	....	....	....	....	....	....
3323 Securities other than shares..............	—	—	—	—	—	—	....	....	....	....	....	....
3324 Loans...............................	−2,462	−6,710	−9,733	−2,462	−6,710	−9,733	....	....	....	....	....	....
3326 Insurance technical reserves..............	—	—	—	—	—	—	....	....	....	....	....	....
3327 Financial derivatives...................	—	—	—	—	—	—	....	....	....	....	....	....
3328 Other accounts payable..................	....	....	....	....	....	....	....	....	....	....	....	....

In Billions of Rupiah / Year Beginning April 1 / Cash Reporter

		Budgetary Central Government			Central Government			Local Government			General Government		
		2002	2003	2004p	2002	2003	2004p	2002	2003	2004	2002	2003	2004
Table 4	**Holding gains in assets and liabilities**												
Table 5	**Other changes in the volume of assets and liabilities**												
Table 6	**Balance sheet**												
6	**Net worth**	....	....	....	....	....	....	....	....	....	....	....	....
61	**Nonfinancial assets**	....	....	....	....	....	....	....	....	....	....	....	....
611	Fixed assets	....	....	....	....	....	....	....	....	....	....	....	....
6111	Buildings and structures	....	....	....	....	....	....						
6112	Machinery and equipment	....	....	....	....	....							
6113	Other fixed assets	....	....	....	....								
612	Inventories	....	....	....	....								
613	Valuables	....	....	....	....	....							
614	Nonproduced assets	....	....	....	....								
6141	Land	....	....	....									
6142	Subsoil assets	....	....	....									
6143	Other naturally occurring assets	....	....	....									
6144	Intangible nonproduced assets	....	....	....	....	....							
62	**Financial assets**	....	....	....	....	....	....	....	....	....	....	....	....
621	Domestic	....	....	....	....	....							....
6212	Currency and deposits	....	....	....	....								
6213	Securities other than shares	....	....	....	....								
6214	Loans	....	....	....									
6215	Shares and other equity	....	....	....	....								
6216	Insurance technical reserves	....	....	....									
6217	Financial derivatives	....	....	....									
6218	Other accounts receivable	....	....	....	....								
622	Foreign	....	....	....	....								
6222	Currency and deposits	....	....	....									
6223	Securities other than shares	....	....	....									
6224	Loans	....	....	....									
6225	Shares and other equity	....	....	....									
6226	Insurance technical reserves	....	....	....									
6227	Financial derivatives	....	....	....									
6228	Other accounts receivable	....	....	....	....								
623	Monetary gold and SDRs	....	....	....	....								
63	**Liabilities**	587,070	598,412	660,333	587,070	598,412	660,333	....	....	....	....	....	....
631	Domestic	—	—	—	—	—	—	....	....	....	....	....	....
6312	Currency and deposits	—	—	—	—	—	—	....	....	....	....	....	....
6313	Securities other than shares	—	—	—	—	—	—	....	....	....	....	....	....
6314	Loans	—	—	—	—	—	—	....	....	....	....	....	....
6316	Insurance technical reserves	—	—	—	—	—	—	....	....	....	....	....	....
6317	Financial derivatives	—	—	—	—	—	—	....	....	....	....	....	....
6318	Other accounts payable	....	....	....	....	....	....	....	....	....	....	....	....
632	Foreign	587,070	598,412	660,333	587,070	598,412	660,333	....	....	....	....	....	....
6322	Currency and deposits	....	....	....	....	....	....	....	....	....	....	....	....
6323	Securities other than shares	....	....	....	....	....	....	....	....	....	....	....	....
6324	Loans	....	....	....	....	....	....	....	....	....	....	....	....
6326	Insurance technical reserves	....	....	....	....	....	....	....	....	....	....	....	....
6327	Financial derivatives	....	....	....	....	....	....	....	....	....	....	....	....
6328	Other accounts payable	....	....	....	....	....	....	....	....	....	....	....	....
Memorandum items:													
6M2	Net financial worth	....	....		....	....		....	....	....	....	....	....
6M3	Debt at market value	....	....		....	....		....	....	....	....	....	....
6M4	Debt at nominal value	....	....		....	....		....	....	....	....	....	....
6M5	Arrears	....	....		....	....		....	....	....	....	....	....
6M6	Obligations for social security benefits	....	....		....	....		....	....	....	....	....	....
6M7	Contingent liabilities	....	....		....	....		....	....	....	....	....	....
6M8	Uncapitalized military weapons, systems	....	....		....	....		....	....	....	....	....	....
Table 7	**Outlays by functions of govt.**												
7	**Total outlays**	315,634	376,505	423,976	323,182	395,952	447,305	....	....	....	....	....	....
701	**General public services**	238,126	279,036	331,296	238,126	279,036	331,296	....	....	....	....	....	....
7017	Public debt transactions	81,122	65,351	62,486	81,122	65,351	62,486	....	....	....	....	....	....
7018	General transfers between levels of govt	....	....	....	....	....	....	....	....	....	....	....	....
702	**Defense**	19,418	26,975	29,466	19,418	26,975	29,466	....	....	....	....	....	....
703	**Public order and safety**	2,167	3,018	3,124	2,167	3,018	3,124	....	....	....	....	....	....

In Billions of Rupiah / Year Beginning April 1 / Cash Reporter

	Budgetary Central Government			Central Government			Local Government			General Government		
	2002	2003	2004p	2002	2003	2004p	2002	2003	2004	2002	2003	2004
704 **Economic affairs**................................	**16,744**	**29,709**	**27,857**	**18,448**	**29,709**	**27,857**	....	....	....	....	....	....
7042 Agriculture, forestry, fishing, and hunting.....	7,345	11,461	10,959	9,048	11,461	10,959	....	....	....	....	....	....
7043 Fuel and energy..................................	1,536	3,896	2,047	1,536	3,896	2,047	....	....	....	....	....	....
7044 Mining, manufacturing, and construction.....	828	1,299	3,330	828	1,299	3,330	....	....	....	....	....	....
7045 Transport.......................................	5,460	9,784	8,820	5,460	9,784	8,820	....	....	....	....	....	....
7046 Communication..................................	....	....	....	....	....	....	....	....	....	....	....	....
705 **Environmental protection**....................	....	....	....	....	....	....	....	....	....	....	....	....
706 **Housing and community amenities**.......	**4,550**	**4,971**	**3,784**	**4,550**	**4,971**	**3,784**	....	....	....	....	....	....
707 **Health**...	**3,747**	**7,316**	**6,174**	**3,747**	**7,316**	**6,174**	....	....	....	....	....	....
7072 Outpatient services..............................	—	....	....	—	....	....	....	....	....	....	....	....
7073 Hospital services................................	2,410	....	....	2,410	....	....	....	....	....	....	....	....
7074 Public health services..........................	....	....	....	....	....	....	....	....	....	....	....	....
708 **Recreation, culture, and religion**...........	**2,299**	**2,742**	**2,619**	**2,299**	**2,742**	**2,619**	....	....	....	....	....	....
709 **Education**......................................	**13,264**	**20,887**	**17,741**	**13,264**	**20,887**	**17,741**	....	....	....	....	....	....
7091 Pre-primary and primary education.............	....	....	....	....	....	....	....	....	....	....	....	....
7092 Secondary education............................	7,871	....	....	7,871	....	....	....	....	....	....	....	....
7094 Tertiary education..............................	4,629	....	....	4,629	....	....	....	....	....	....	....	....
710 **Social protection**...............................	**15,320**	**1,853**	**1,916**	**21,164**	**21,300**	**25,245**	....	....	....	....	....	....
7 Statistical discrepancy: Total outlays.............	—	—	—	—	—	—	....	....	....	....	....	....

Table 8 Transactions in financial assets and liabilities by sector

	Budgetary Central Government			Central Government			Local Government			General Government		
	2002	2003	2004p	2002	2003	2004p	2002	2003	2004	2002	2003	2004
82 **Net acquisition of financial assets**........	**−14,347**	**−44,438**	**−15,052**	**−5,755**	**−53,212**	**−35,474**	....	....	....	....	....	....
821 Domestic....................................	−14,347	−44,438	−15,052	−5,755	−53,212	−35,474	....	....	....	....	....	....
8211 General government........................	—	—	—	700	—	—	....	....	....	....	....	....
8212 Central bank..............................	....	....	....	....	....	....	....	....	....	....	....	....
8213 Other depository corporations...............	....	....	....	....	....	....	....	....	....	....	....	....
8214 Financial corporations n.e.c.................	....	....	....	....	....	....	....	....	....	....	....	....
8215 Nonfinancial corporations..................	—	—	—	3,967	—	—	....	....	....	....	....	....
8216 Households & NPIs serving households......	....	....	....	....	....	....	....	....	....	....	....	....
822 Foreign.......................................	—	—	—	—	—	—	....	....	....	....	....	....
8221 General government........................	—	—	—	—	—	—	....	....	....	....	....	....
8227 International organizations..................	—	—	—	—	—	—	....	....	....	....	....	....
8228 Financial corporations other than international organizations............	—	—	—	—	—	—	....	....	....	....	....	....
8229 Other nonresidents..........................	—	—	—	—	—	—	....	....	....	....	....	....
823 Monetary gold and SDRs....................	—	—	—	—	—	—	....	....	....	....	....	....
83 **Net incurrence of liabilities**...............	**−2,462**	**−6,710**	**−9,733**	**−389**	**−6,585**	**−10,108**	....	....	....	....	....	....
831 Domestic....................................	—	—	—	2,073	125	−375	....	....	....	....	....	....
8311 General government........................	—	—	—	....	....	....	....	....	....	....	....	....
8312 Central bank..............................	—	—	—	....	....	....	....	....	....	....	....	....
8313 Other depository corporations...............	—	—	—	....	....	....	....	....	....	....	....	....
8314 Financial corporations n.e.c.................	—	—	—	....	....	....	....	....	....	....	....	....
8315 Nonfinancial corporations..................	—	—	—	....	....	....	....	....	....	....	....	....
8316 Households & NPIs serving households......	—	—	—	....	....	....	....	....	....	....	....	....
832 Foreign.......................................	−2,462	−6,710	−9,733	−2,462	−6,710	−9,733	....	....	....	....	....	....
8321 General government........................	4,681	4,052	−5,207	4,681	4,052	−5,207	....	....	....	....	....	....
8327 International organizations..................	−1,968	−7,661	−3,395	−1,968	−7,661	−3,395	....	....	....	....	....	....
8328 Financial corporations other than international organizations.............	—	—	—	—	—	—	....	....	....	....	....	....
8329 Other nonresidents..........................	−5,175	−3,100	−1,131	−5,175	−3,100	−1,131	....	....	....	....	....	....

In Billions of Rials / Year Beginning March 21 / Cash Reporter

	Budgetary Central Government			Central Government			Local Government			General Government		
	2003	2004p	2005f	2003	2004p	2005f	2003	2004p	2005f	2003	2004p	2005f
Statement of government operations												
Statement of other economic flows												
Balance sheet												
Statement of sources and uses of cash												
1 Cash receipts from operating activities	256,491	342,995	430,538	302,749	406,876	527,365	24,464	29,161	36,592	324,968	434,651	562,222
11 Taxes	65,106	84,456	130,160	65,439	84,663	131,744	16,627	20,783	26,083	82,066	105,446	157,827
12 Social contributions	—	—	—	40,663	53,139	64,849	—	—	—	40,663	53,139	64,849
13 Grants	—	—	—	—	—	—	2,244	1,387	1,736	—	—	—
14 Other receipts	191,385	258,539	300,377	196,646	269,075	330,772	5,592	6,991	8,773	202,239	276,065	339,545
2 Cash payments for operating activities	173,749	225,320	248,241	216,090	284,348	339,398	8,201	10,637	12,233	222,047	293,598	349,895
21 Compensation of employees	91,414	118,513	135,221	97,195	128,883	163,200	3,777	4,899	5,634	....	....	....
22 Purchases of goods and services	24,478	32,276	36,963	25,800	34,695	43,617	1,681	2,180	2,507	....	....	....
24 Interest	2,220	3,226	4,634	2,220	3,226	4,634	—	—	—	2,220	3,226	4,634
25 Subsidies	33,615	42,881	43,961	33,615	42,881	43,961	....	....	....	....	....	....
26 Grants	3,509	5,551	2,168	3,509	5,551	2,168	....	....	....	....	....	....
27 Social benefits	2,945	2,582	7,142	38,028	48,819	63,667	....	....	....	....	....	....
28 Other payments	15,567	20,292	18,152	15,723	20,292	18,152	....	....	....	....	....	....
CIO *Net cash inflow from oper. activities*	*82,742*	*117,675*	*182,297*	*86,658*	*122,529*	*187,967*	*16,262*	*18,523*	*24,360*	*102,921*	*141,052*	*212,327*
31.1 Purchases of nonfinancial assets	65,532	70,532	120,423	69,449	75,386	126,093	11,364	11,705	17,557	80,812	87,091	143,651
31.2 Sales of nonfinancial assets	878	4,044	2,077	878	4,044	2,077	—	—	—	878	4,044	2,077
31 Net cash outflow from investments in nonfinancial assets	64,655	66,489	118,346	68,571	71,343	124,016	11,364	11,705	17,557	79,935	83,047	141,574
CSD *Cash surplus/deficit*	*18,087*	*51,186*	*63,951*	*18,087*	*51,186*	*63,951*	*4,898*	*6,819*	*6,802*	*22,986*	*58,005*	*70,753*
32x Net acquisition of fin assets, excl. cash	1,406	4,402	−17,823	1,406	4,402	−17,823	—	—	—	1,406	4,402	−17,823
321x Domestic	1,406	4,402	−17,823	1,406	4,402	−17,823	—	—	—	1,406	4,402	−17,823
322x Foreign	—	—	—	—	—	—	—	—	—	—	—	—
323 Monetary gold and SDRs	—	—	—	—	—	—	—	—	—	—	—	—
33 Net incurrence of liabilities	11,127	−8,531	−29,691	11,127	−8,531	−29,691	—	—	—	11,127	−8,531	−29,691
331 Domestic	31,002	16,473	9,601	31,002	16,473	9,601	—	—	—	31,002	16,473	9,601
332 Foreign	−19,875	−25,004	−39,292	−19,875	−25,004	−39,292	—	—	—	−19,875	−25,004	−39,292
NFB Net cash inflow from fin. activities	9,721	−12,933	−11,869	9,721	−12,933	−11,869	—	—	—	9,721	−12,933	−11,869
NCB *Net change in the stock of cash*	*27,809*	*38,253*	*52,082*	*27,809*	*38,253*	*52,082*	*4,898*	*6,819*	*6,802*	*32,707*	*45,072*	*58,885*
Table 1 Revenue												
1 **Revenue**	256,491	342,995	430,538	302,749	406,876	527,365	24,464	29,161	36,592	324,968	434,651	562,222
11 **Taxes**	65,106	84,456	130,160	65,439	84,663	131,744	16,627	20,783	26,083	82,066	105,446	157,827
111 Taxes on income, profits, & capital gains	29,384	37,801	74,525	29,607	37,927	74,868	—	—	—	29,607	37,927	74,868
1111 Individuals	8,984	11,727	14,650	9,109	11,789	14,798	—	—	—	9,109	11,789	14,798
1112 Corporations and other enterprises	20,376	26,027	59,825	20,473	26,092	60,019	—	—	—	20,473	26,092	60,019
112 Taxes on payroll and workforce	—	—	—	—	—	—	—	—	—	—	—	—
113 Taxes on property	2,650	4,096	6,955	2,687	4,114	7,025	—	—	—	2,687	4,114	7,025
114 Taxes on goods and services	10,671	9,472	11,000	10,744	9,520	12,111	3,865	4,831	6,063	14,608	14,351	18,174
1141 General taxes on goods and services	4,184	6,455	7,620	4,244	6,486	7,699	—	—	—	4,244	6,486	7,699
1142 Excises	208	241	300	208	241	1,300	3,865	4,831	6,063	4,072	5,071	7,363
115 Taxes on int'l. trade and transactions	22,401	33,087	37,680	22,401	33,087	37,680	—	—	—	22,401	33,087	37,680
116 Other taxes	—	—	—	—	—	14	12,762	15,953	20,021	12,762	15,967	20,081
12 **Social contributions**	—	—	—	40,663	53,139	64,849	—	—	—	40,663	53,139	64,849
121 Social security contributions	—	—	—	40,663	53,139	64,849	—	—	—	40,663	53,139	64,849
122 Other social contributions	—	—	—	—	—	—	—	—	—	—	—	—
13 **Grants**	—	—	—	—	—	—	2,244	1,387	1,736	—	—	—
131 From foreign governments	—	—	—	—	—	—	—	—	—	—	—	—
132 From international organizations	—	—	—	—	—	—	—	—	—	—	—	—
133 From other general government units	—	—	—	—	—	—	2,244	1,387	1,736	—	—	—
14 **Other revenue**	191,385	258,539	300,377	196,646	269,075	330,772	5,592	6,991	8,773	202,239	276,065	339,545
Table 2 Expense by economic type												
2 **Expense**	173,749	225,320	248,241	216,090	284,348	339,398	8,201	10,637	12,233	222,047	293,598	349,895
21 **Compensation of employees**	91,414	118,513	135,221	97,195	128,883	163,200	3,777	4,899	5,634	....	....	....
211 Wages and salaries	78,264	105,139	119,176	84,045	115,509	147,154	....	....	....	....	....	....
212 Social contributions	13,150	13,374	16,046	13,150	13,374	16,046	....	....	....	....	....	....
22 **Use of goods and services**	24,478	32,276	36,963	25,800	34,695	43,617	1,681	2,180	2,507	....	....	....
23 **Consumption of fixed capital**	....	....	....	....	....	....	....	....	....	....	....	....
24 **Interest**	2,220	3,226	4,634	2,220	3,226	4,634	—	—	—	2,220	3,226	4,634
25 **Subsidies**	33,615	42,881	43,961	33,615	42,881	43,961	....	....	....	....	....	....

Iran, Islamic Republic of   429

In Billions of Rials / Year Beginning March 21 / Cash Reporter

		Budgetary Central Government			Central Government			Local Government			General Government		
		2003	2004p	2005f	2003	2004p	2005f	2003	2004p	2005f	2003	2004p	2005f
26	Grants..............................	3,509	5,551	2,168	3,509	5,551	2,168	....	....	....	....	....	....
261	To foreign govenments.................	87	847	300	87	847	300	....	....	....	....	....	....
262	To international organizations............	17	84	29	17	84	29	....	....	....	....	....	....
263	To other general government units........	3,404	4,620	1,839	3,404	4,620	1,839	....	....	....	....	....	....
2631	Current...........................	3,404	4,620	1,839	3,404	4,620	1,839	....	....	....	....	....	....
2632	Capital............................	—	—	—	—	—	—	....	....	....	....	....	....
27	Social benefits........................	2,945	2,582	7,142	38,028	48,819	63,667	....	....	....	....	....	....
28	Other expense.........................	15,567	20,292	18,152	15,723	20,292	18,152	....	....	....	....	....	....
281	Property expense other than interest.........	—	—	—	—	—	—	....	....	....	....	....	....
282	Miscellaneous other expense..............	15,567	20,292	18,152	15,723	20,292	18,152	....	....	....	....	....	....
2821	Current...........................	15,542	20,232	18,012	15,698	20,232	18,012	....	....	....	....	....	....
2822	Capital............................	25	60	140	25	60	140	....	....	....	....	....	....

Table 3 Transactions in assets and liabilities

		Budgetary Central Government			Central Government			Local Government			General Government		
		2003	2004p	2005f	2003	2004p	2005f	2003	2004p	2005f	2003	2004p	2005f
3	Change in net worth from transactns....	....	....	....	....	....	....	....	....	....	....	....	....
31	Net acquisition of nonfinancial assets...	64,655	66,489	118,346	68,571	71,343	124,016	11,364	11,705	17,557	79,935	83,047	141,574
311	Fixed assets...........................	55,824	57,883	95,901	59,668	62,642	101,461	11,364	11,705	17,557	71,032	74,347	119,018
3111	Buildings and structures...............	37,245	39,042	69,651	39,218	41,483	72,483	11,080	11,412	17,118	50,298	52,895	89,601
3112	Machinery and equipment...............	18,626	20,759	23,370	20,495	23,076	26,099	284	293	439	20,779	23,369	26,538
3113	Other fixed assets....................	–46	–1,917	2,880	–46	–1,917	2,880	—	—	—	–46	–1,917	2,880
312	Inventories............................	43	45	563	43	45	563	—	—	—	43	45	563
313	Valuables..............................	—	—	—	—	—	—	—	—	—	—	—	—
314	Nonproduced assets.....................	8,788	8,561	21,883	8,861	8,656	21,993	—	—	—	8,861	8,656	21,993
3141	Land................................	1,794	1,838	2,033	1,867	1,933	2,143	—	—	—	1,867	1,933	2,143
3142	Subsoil assets........................	—	—	—	—	—	—	—	—	—	—	—	—
3143	Other naturally occurring assets........	—	—	—	—	—	—	—	—	—	—	—	—
3144	Intangible nonproduced assets..........	6,994	6,723	19,850	6,994	6,723	19,850	—	—	—	6,994	6,723	19,850
32	Net acquisition of financial assets........	29,214	42,655	34,259	29,214	42,655	34,259	4,898	6,819	6,803	34,113	49,474	41,062
321	Domestic..............................	17,644	17,954	2,687	17,644	17,954	2,687	4,898	6,819	6,803	22,543	24,773	9,490
3212	Currency and deposits..................	16,239	13,552	20,510	16,239	13,552	20,510	4,898	6,819	6,803	21,137	20,371	27,312
3213	Securities other than shares............	....	....	....	....	....	....				....	....	....
3214	Loans..............................	....	....	....	....	....	....				....	....	....
3215	Shares and other equity...............	....	....	....	....	....	....				....	....	....
3216	Insurance technical reserves...........	....	....	....	....	....	....				....	....	....
3217	Financial derivatives.................	....	....	....	....	....	....				....	....	....
3218	Other accounts receivable..............	....	....	....	....	....	....		....	....	....	....	....
322	Foreign...............................	11,570	24,701	31,572	11,570	24,701	31,572	—	—	—	11,570	24,701	31,572
3222	Currency and deposits..................	11,570	24,701	31,572	11,570	24,701	31,572	—	—	—	11,570	24,701	31,572
3223	Securities other than shares............	—	—	—	—	—	—	—	—	—	—	—	—
3224	Loans..............................	—	—	—	—	—	—	—	—	—	—	—	—
3225	Shares and other equity...............	—	—	—	—	—	—	—	—	—	—	—	—
3226	Insurance technical reserves...........	—	—	—	—	—	—	—	—	—	—	—	—
3227	Financial derivatives.................	—	—	—	—	—	—	—	—	—	—	—	—
3228	Other accounts receivable..............	—	—	—	—	—	—	—	—	—	—	—	—
323	Monetary gold and SDRs.................	—	—	—	—	—	—	—	—	—	—	—	—
33	Net incurrence of liabilities..................	11,127	–8,531	–29,691	11,127	–8,531	–29,691	—	—	—	11,127	–8,531	–29,691
331	Domestic..............................	31,002	16,473	9,601	31,002	16,473	9,601	—	—	—	31,002	16,473	9,601
3312	Currency and deposits..................	....	....	....	....	....	....	—	—	—	....	....	....
3313	Securities other than shares............	....	....	....	....	....	....	—	—	—	....	....	....
3314	Loans..............................	....	....	....	....	....	....	—	—	—	....	....	....
3316	Insurance technical reserves...........	....	....	....	....	....	....	—	—	—	....	....	....
3317	Financial derivatives.................	....	....	....	....	....	....	—	—	—	....	....	....
3318	Other accounts payable................	....	....	....	....	....	....	....	....	—	....	....	....
332	Foreign...............................	–19,875	–25,004	–39,292	–19,875	–25,004	–39,292	—	—	—	–19,875	–25,004	–39,292
3322	Currency and deposits..................	—	—	—	—	—	—	—	—	—	—	—	—
3323	Securities other than shares............	—	—	—	—	—	—	—	—	—	—	—	—
3324	Loans..............................	–19,875	–25,004	–39,292	–19,875	–25,004	–39,292	—	—	—	–19,875	–25,004	–39,292
3326	Insurance technical reserves...........	—	—	—	—	—	—	—	—	—	—	—	—
3327	Financial derivatives.................	—	—	—	—	—	—	—	—	—	—	—	—
3328	Other accounts payable................	....	....	....	....	....	....				....	....	....

2005, International Monetary Fund: *Government Finance Statistics Yearbook*

In Billions of Rials / Year Beginning March 21 / Cash Reporter

	Budgetary Central Government			Central Government			Local Government			General Government		
	2003	2004p	2005f	2003	2004p	2005f	2003	2004p	2005f	2003	2004p	2005f
Table 4 Holding gains in assets and liabilities												
Table 5 Other changes in the volume of assets and liabilities												
Table 6 Balance sheet												
Table 7 Outlays by functions of govt.												
7 Total outlays	238,404	291,809	366,587	284,661	355,690	463,415	19,565	22,342	29,790	301,982	376,646	491,468
701 General public services	31,399	36,537	38,728	31,446	36,589	38,742	—	—	—	31,446	36,589	38,742
7017 Public debt transactions	2,220	3,226	4,634	2,220	3,226	4,634	—	—	—	2,220	3,226	4,634
7018 General transfers between levels of govt.	....	....	....	....	....	....	....	....	....	....	....	....
702 Defense	33,998	46,191	46,816	34,955	48,264	55,667	—	—	—	34,955	48,264	55,667
703 Public order and safety	18,101	18,963	23,155	18,101	18,963	23,196	—	—	—	18,101	18,963	23,196
704 Economic affairs	53,908	71,394	96,120	54,106	71,730	98,162	8,955	10,734	13,656	63,061	82,463	111,817
7042 Agriculture, forestry, fishing, and hunting	7,084	10,972	17,733	7,084	10,972	17,733	....	....	....	....	....	....
7043 Fuel and energy	5,318	15,045	22,732	5,318	15,045	22,732	....	....	....	....	....	....
7044 Mining, manufacturing, and construction	5,864	5,502	6,919	5,866	5,504	6,919	....	....	....	....	....	....
7045 Transport	13,198	11,207	19,457	13,198	11,207	19,457	....	....	....	....	....	....
7046 Communication	208	1,455	1,592	208	1,455	1,592	....	....	....	....	....	....
705 Environmental protection	2,457	2,255	6,890	2,457	2,255	6,894	408	339	979	2,865	2,594	7,873
706 Housing and community amenities	19,389	19,168	29,575	19,389	19,168	29,575	3,221	2,882	4,202	20,366	20,663	32,040
707 Health	17,825	19,061	26,137	20,929	25,224	42,653	—	—	—	20,929	25,224	42,653
7072 Outpatient services	11,506	12,199	8,283	13,862	15,644	8,312	—	—	—	13,862	15,644	8,312
7073 Hospital services	260	353	560	260	353	1,889	—	—	—	260	353	1,889
7074 Public health services	5,908	6,264	6,001	6,200	6,613	7,277	—	—	—	6,200	6,613	7,277
708 Recreation, culture, and religion	7,538	10,471	12,472	7,558	10,472	12,605	1,252	1,574	1,772	8,810	12,046	14,377
709 Education	19,305	22,455	22,066	20,572	24,573	26,443	—	—	—	20,572	24,573	26,443
7091 Pre-primary and primary education	282	475	246	282	475	246	—	—	—	282	475	246
7092 Secondary education	209	304	351	209	304	351	—	—	—	209	304	351
7094 Tertiary education	11,514	12,176	8,684	12,226	13,425	8,817	—	—	—	12,226	13,425	8,817
710 Social protection	34,485	45,315	64,629	75,148	98,454	129,478	5,729	6,813	9,182	80,876	105,267	138,660
7 Statistical discrepancy: Total outlays	—	—	—	—	—	—	—	—	—	—	—	—
Table 8 Transactions in financial assets and liabilities by sector												
82 Net acquisition of financial assets	29,214	42,655	34,259	29,214	42,655	34,259	4,898	6,819	6,803	34,113	49,474	41,062
821 Domestic	17,644	17,954	2,687	17,644	17,954	2,687	4,898	6,819	6,803	22,543	24,773	9,490
8211 General government	....	....	....	....	....	....	....	....	....	....	....	....
8212 Central bank	....	....	....	....	....	....	....	....	....	....	....	....
8213 Other depository corporations	....	....	....	....	....	....	....	....	....	....	....	....
8214 Financial corporations n.e.c.	....	....	....	....	....	....	....	....	....	....	....	....
8215 Nonfinancial corporations	....	....	....	....	....	....	....	....	....	....	....	....
8216 Households & NPIs serving households	....	....	....	....	....	....	....	....	....	....	....	....
822 Foreign	11,570	24,701	31,572	11,570	24,701	31,572	—	—	—	11,570	24,701	31,572
8221 General government	....	....	....	....	....	....	—	—	—	....	....	....
8227 International organizations	....	....	....	....	....	....	—	—	—	....	....	....
8228 Financial corporations other than international organizations	....	....	....	....	....	....	—	—	—	....	....	....
8229 Other nonresidents	....	....	....	....	....	....	—	—	—	....	....	....
823 Monetary gold and SDRs	—	—	—	—	—	—	....	....	....	....	....	....
83 Net incurrence of liabilities	11,127	−8,531	−29,691	11,127	−8,531	−29,691	—	—	—	11,127	−8,531	−29,691
831 Domestic	31,002	16,473	9,601	31,002	16,473	9,601	—	—	—	31,002	16,473	9,601
8311 General government	....	....	....	....	....	....	—	—	—	....	....	....
8312 Central bank	....	....	....	....	....	....	—	—	—	....	....	....
8313 Other depository corporations	....	....	....	....	....	....	—	—	—	....	....	....
8314 Financial corporations n.e.c.	....	....	....	....	....	....	—	—	—	....	....	....
8315 Nonfinancial corporations	....	....	....	....	....	....	—	—	—	....	....	....
8316 Households & NPIs serving households	....	....	....	....	....	....	—	—	—	....	....	....
832 Foreign	−19,875	−25,004	−39,292	−19,875	−25,004	−39,292	—	—	—	−19,875	−25,004	−39,292
8321 General government	....	....	....	....	....	....	—	—	—	....	....	....
8327 International organizations	....	....	....	....	....	....	—	—	—	....	....	....
8328 Financial corporations other than international organizations	....	....	....	....	....	....	—	—	—	....	....	....
8329 Other nonresidents	....	....	....	....	....	....	—	—	—	....	....	....

		Budgetary Central Government			Central Government			Local Government			General Government		
		2002	2003	2004p	2002	2003	2004p	2002	2003	2004p	2002	2003	2004p
Statement of government operations													
1	Revenue..........	191,501	175,831	182,529	237,604	224,094	232,024	34,955	34,807	34,326	254,100	241,235	249,379
2	Expense..........	211,160	210,423	211,383	254,724	253,942	255,432	32,674	32,457	32,298	268,939	268,733	270,759
GOB	*Gross operating balance.........*	*−17,440*	*−32,895*	*−27,066*	*−12,762*	*−26,040*	*−19,327*	*5,242*	*5,900*	*5,770*	*−7,520*	*−20,140*	*−13,557*
NOB	*Net operating balance.........*	*−19,659*	*−34,592*	*−28,854*	*−17,120*	*−29,848*	*−23,408*	*2,281*	*2,350*	*2,028*	*−14,839*	*−27,498*	*−21,380*
31	Net acquisition of nonfinancial assets..........	1,026	1,869	1,429	1,847	2,548	1,685	4,273	3,551	3,543	6,120	6,099	5,228
NLB	*Net lending/borrowing.........*	*−20,685*	*−36,461*	*−30,283*	*−18,967*	*−32,396*	*−25,093*	*−1,992*	*−1,201*	*−1,515*	*−20,959*	*−33,597*	*−26,608*
32	Net acquisition of financial assets...........	....	....	....	....	....	....	....	....	....	....	....	....
33	Net incurrence of liabilities...........	....	....	....	....	....	....	....	....	....	....	....	....
NLB	Statistical discrepancy...........	....	....	....	....	....	....	....	....	....	....	....	....
Statement of other economic flows													
Balance sheet													
Statement of sources and uses of cash													
1	Cash receipts from operating activities..........	180,495	172,925	175,928	226,598	221,188	225,423	34,428	34,259	33,761	242,567	237,781	242,213
11	Taxes..........	146,699	143,464	150,067	147,279	143,882	150,423	12,892	13,039	13,431	160,171	156,921	163,854
12	Social contributions..........	—	—	—	31,377	32,298	32,940	—	—	—	31,377	32,298	32,940
13	Grants..........	19,238	17,203	13,619	20,320	17,790	14,205	14,362	14,141	13,583	16,406	14,450	10,997
14	Other receipts..........	14,558	12,258	12,242	27,622	27,218	27,855	7,174	7,079	6,747	34,613	34,112	34,422
2	Cash payments for operating activities..........	199,065	200,348	199,661	240,490	241,756	241,417	29,186	28,359	27,991	251,217	252,449	252,437
21	Compensation of employees..........	35,445	34,822	35,281	55,224	53,591	55,122	12,057	11,234	11,299	67,281	64,825	66,421
22	Purchases of goods and services..........	41,885	39,706	37,356	70,048	70,369	67,616	8,774	9,159	8,772	78,822	79,528	76,388
24	Interest..........	26,118	31,558	32,427	22,758	27,949	28,654	1,471	1,382	1,420	24,046	29,146	29,894
25	Subsidies..........	3,706	4,645	4,717	3,730	4,653	4,726	—	—	—	3,730	4,653	4,726
26	Grants..........	62,270	60,061	58,267	16,211	14,436	13,881	3,915	3,340	3,208	1,850	295	298
27	Social benefits..........	18,246	18,661	18,288	59,061	57,931	56,043	574	27	28	59,635	57,958	56,071
28	Other payments..........	11,395	10,895	13,325	13,458	12,827	15,375	2,395	3,217	3,264	15,853	16,044	18,639
CIO	*Net cash inflow from oper. activities.....*	*−18,570*	*−27,423*	*−23,733*	*−13,892*	*−20,568*	*−15,994*	*5,242*	*5,900*	*5,770*	*−8,650*	*−14,668*	*−10,224*
31.1	Purchases of nonfinancial assets..........	....	....	....	....	....	....	....	....	....	....	....	....
31.2	Sales of nonfinancial assets..........	....	....	....	....	....	....	....	....	....	....	....	....
31	Net cash outflow from investments in nonfinancial assets..........	3,245	3,566	3,217	6,205	6,356	5,766	7,234	7,101	7,285	13,439	13,457	13,051
CSD	*Cash surplus/deficit..........*	*−21,815*	*−30,989*	*−26,950*	*−20,098*	*−26,924*	*−21,760*	*−1,991*	*−1,201*	*−1,515*	*−22,089*	*−28,125*	*−23,275*
32x	Net acquisition of fin assets, excl. cash..........	....	....	....	....	....	....	....	....	....	....	....	....
321x	Domestic..........	....	....	....	....	....	....	....	....	....	....	....	....
322x	Foreign..........	....	....	....	....	....	....	....	....	....	....	....	....
323	Monetary gold and SDRs..........	....	....	....	....	....	....	....	....	....	....	....	....
33	Net incurrence of liabilities..........	....	....	....	....	....	....	....	....	....	....	....	....
331	Domestic..........	....	....	....	....	....	....	....	....	....	....	....	....
332	Foreign..........	....	....	....	....	....	....	....	....	....	....	....	....
NFB	Net cash inflow from fin. activities..........	....	....	....	....	....	....	....	....	....	....	....	....
NCB	*Net change in the stock of cash..........*	....	....	....	....	....	....	....	....	....	....	....	....
Table 1 Revenue													
1	**Revenue..........**	**191,501**	**175,831**	**182,529**	**237,604**	**224,094**	**232,024**	**34,955**	**34,807**	**34,326**	**254,100**	**241,235**	**249,379**
11	**Taxes..........**	**146,899**	**143,889**	**150,523**	**147,479**	**144,307**	**150,879**	**13,419**	**13,587**	**13,996**	**160,898**	**157,894**	**164,875**
111	Taxes on income, profits, & capital gains.....	67,545	65,238	67,444	67,545	65,238	67,444	—	—	—	67,545	65,238	67,444
1111	Individuals..........	50,632	45,218	45,035	50,632	45,218	45,035	—	—	—	50,632	45,218	45,035
1112	Corporations and other enterprises..........	11,431	13,188	15,200	11,431	13,188	15,200	—	—	—	11,431	13,188	15,200
112	Taxes on payroll and workforce..........	9,378	9,179	9,679	9,378	9,179	9,679	—	—	—	9,378	9,179	9,679
113	Taxes on property..........	1,864	1,776	2,612	2,444	2,194	2,968	12,581	12,854	13,240	15,025	15,048	16,208
114	Taxes on goods and services..........	65,853	65,517	68,311	65,853	65,517	68,311	838	733	756	66,691	66,250	69,067
1141	General taxes on goods and services..........	55,742	54,692	56,748	55,742	54,692	56,748	—	—	—	55,742	54,692	56,748
1142	Excises..........	7,697	8,277	8,829	7,697	8,277	8,829	—	—	—	7,697	8,277	8,829
115	Taxes on int'l. trade and transactions..........	1,398	1,376	1,594	1,398	1,376	1,594	—	—	—	1,398	1,376	1,594
116	Other taxes..........	861	803	883	861	803	883	—	—	—	861	803	883
12	**Social contributions..........**	**6,271**	**6,134**	**6,391**	**37,648**	**38,432**	**39,331**	**—**	**—**	**—**	**37,648**	**38,432**	**39,331**
121	Social security contributions..........	—	—	—	31,377	32,298	32,940	—	—	—	31,377	32,298	32,940
122	Other social contributions..........	6,271	6,134	6,391	6,271	6,134	6,391	—	—	—	6,271	6,134	6,391
13	**Grants..........**	**19,238**	**17,203**	**13,619**	**20,320**	**17,790**	**14,205**	**14,362**	**14,141**	**13,583**	**16,406**	**14,450**	**10,997**
131	From foreign governments..........	16,406	14,450	10,997	16,406	14,450	10,997	—	—	—	16,406	14,450	10,997
132	From international organizations..........	—	—	—	—	—	—	—	—	—	—	—	—
133	From other general government units..........	2,832	2,753	2,622	3,914	3,340	3,208	14,362	14,141	13,583	—	—	—
14	**Other revenue..........**	**19,093**	**8,605**	**11,996**	**32,157**	**23,565**	**27,609**	**7,174**	**7,079**	**6,747**	**39,148**	**30,459**	**34,176**

In Millions of New Sheqalim / Year Ending December 31 / Noncash Reporter

	Budgetary Central Government			Central Government			Local Government			General Government		
	2002	2003	2004p	2002	2003	2004p	2002	2003	2004p	2002	2003	2004p
Table 2 Expense by economic type												
2 **Expense**...	**211,160**	**210,423**	**211,383**	**254,724**	**253,942**	**255,432**	**32,674**	**32,457**	**32,298**	**268,939**	**268,733**	**270,759**
21 **Compensation of employees**.................	**42,165**	**41,136**	**42,302**	**61,944**	**59,905**	**62,143**	**12,584**	**11,782**	**11,864**	**74,528**	**71,687**	**74,007**
211 Wages and salaries...........................	32,305	32,287	33,119	48,957	48,744	50,515	11,326	11,099	11,176	60,283	59,843	61,691
212 Social contributions........................	9,860	8,849	9,183	12,987	11,161	11,628	1,258	683	688	14,245	11,844	12,316
22 **Use of goods and services**....................	**41,885**	**39,706**	**37,356**	**70,048**	**70,369**	**67,616**	**8,774**	**9,159**	**8,772**	**78,822**	**79,528**	**76,388**
23 **Consumption of fixed capital**...............	**2,219**	**1,697**	**1,788**	**4,358**	**3,808**	**4,081**	**2,961**	**3,550**	**3,742**	**7,319**	**7,358**	**7,823**
24 **Interest**..	**28,638**	**32,982**	**34,690**	**25,278**	**29,373**	**30,917**	**1,471**	**1,382**	**1,420**	**26,566**	**30,570**	**32,157**
25 **Subsidies**...	**3,706**	**4,645**	**4,717**	**3,730**	**4,653**	**4,726**	—	—	—	**3,730**	**4,653**	**4,726**
26 **Grants**...	**62,270**	**60,061**	**58,267**	**16,211**	**14,436**	**13,881**	**3,915**	**3,340**	**3,208**	**1,850**	**295**	**298**
261 To foreign governents.....................	1,810	166	184	1,810	166	184	—	—	—	1,810	166	184
262 To international organizations............	40	129	114	40	129	114	—	—	—	40	129	114
263 To other general government units...........	60,420	59,766	57,969	14,361	14,141	13,583	3,915	3,340	3,208	—	—	—
2631 Current..	57,434	56,809	55,525	11,931	11,702	11,481	3,860	3,287	3,158	—	—	—
2632 Capital...	2,986	2,957	2,444	2,430	2,439	2,102	55	53	50	—	—	—
27 **Social benefits**....................................	**18,246**	**18,661**	**18,288**	**59,061**	**57,931**	**56,043**	**574**	**27**	**28**	**59,635**	**57,958**	**56,071**
28 **Other expense**....................................	**12,031**	**11,535**	**13,975**	**14,094**	**13,467**	**16,025**	**2,395**	**3,217**	**3,264**	**16,489**	**16,684**	**19,289**
281 Property expense other than interest...........	—	—	—	—	—	—	—	—	—	—	—	—
282 Miscellaneous other expense......................	12,031	11,535	13,975	14,094	13,467	16,025	2,395	3,217	3,264	16,489	16,684	19,289
2821 Current..	5,303	5,299	5,506	7,313	7,189	7,511	2,265	3,037	3,104	9,578	10,226	10,615
2822 Capital...	6,728	6,236	8,469	6,781	6,278	8,514	130	180	160	6,911	6,458	8,674
Table 3 Transactions in assets and liabilities												
3 **Change in net worth from transactns....**	**−19,659**	**−34,592**	**−28,854**	**−17,120**	**−29,848**	**−23,408**	**2,281**	**2,350**	**2,028**	**−14,839**	**−27,498**	**−21,380**
31 **Net acquisition of nonfinancial assets...**	**1,026**	**1,869**	**1,429**	**1,847**	**2,548**	**1,685**	**4,273**	**3,551**	**3,543**	**6,120**	**6,099**	**5,228**
311 Fixed assets....................................	981	1,809	1,364	1,802	2,488	1,620	4,218	3,501	3,493	6,020	5,989	5,113
3111 Buildings and structures......................	834	1,907	1,560	1,532	3,011	2,321	3,585	3,893	3,961	5,117	6,904	6,282
3112 Machinery and equipment......................	147	−98	−196	270	−523	−701	633	−392	−468	903	−915	−1,169
3113 Other fixed assets.............................	—	—	—	—	—	—	—	—	—	—	—	—
312 Inventories.....................................	—	—	—	—	—	—	—	—	—	—	—	—
313 Valuables.......................................	—	—	—	—	—	—	—	—	—	—	—	—
314 Nonproduced assets...........................	45	60	65	45	60	65	55	50	50	100	110	115
3141 Land...	45	60	65	45	60	65	55	50	50	100	110	115
3142 Subsoil assets.................................	—	—	—	—	—	—	—	—	—	—	—	—
3143 Other naturally occurring assets.............	—	—	—	—	—	—	—	—	—	—	—	—
3144 Intangible nonproduced assets.............	—	—	—	—	—	—	—	—	—	—	—	—
32 **Net acquisition of financial assets.........**	....	....	....	....	....	....	....	....	....	....	....	....
321 Domestic..	....	....	....	....	....	....	....	....	....	....	....	....
3212 Currency and deposits......................	....	....	....	....	....	....	....	....	....	....	....	....
3213 Securities other than shares...............	....	....	....	....	....	....	....	....	....	....	....	....
3214 Loans..	....	....	....	....	....	....	....	....	....	....	....	....
3215 Shares and other equity.....................	....	....	....	....	....	....	....	....	....	....	....	....
3216 Insurance technical reserves...............	....	....	....	....	....	....	....	....	....	....	....	....
3217 Financial derivatives.........................	....	....	....	....	....	....	....	....	....	....	....	....
3218 Other accounts receivable..................	....	....	....	....	....	....	....	....	....	....	....	....
322 Foreign...	....	....	....	....	....	....	....	....	....	....	....	....
3222 Currency and deposits......................	....	....	....	....	....	....	....	....	....	....	....	....
3223 Securities other than shares...............	....	....	....	....	....	....	....	....	....	....	....	....
3224 Loans..	....	....	....	....	....	....	....	....	....	....	....	....
3225 Shares and other equity.....................	....	....	....	....	....	....	....	....	....	....	....	....
3226 Insurance technical reserves...............	....	....	....	....	....	....	....	....	....	....	....	....
3227 Financial derivatives.........................	....	....	....	....	....	....	....	....	....	....	....	....
3228 Other accounts receivable..................	....	....	....	....	....	....	....	....	....	....	....	....
323 Monetary gold and SDRs......................	....	....	....	....	....	....	....	....	....	....	....	....
33 **Net incurrence of liabilities...................**	....	....	....	....	....	....	....	....	....	....	....	....
331 Domestic..	....	....	....	....	....	....	....	....	....	....	....	....
3312 Currency and deposits......................	....	....	....	....	....	....	....	....	....	....	....	....
3313 Securities other than shares...............	....	....	....	....	....	....	....	....	....	....	....	....
3314 Loans..	....	....	....	....	....	....	....	....	....	....	....	....
3316 Insurance technical reserves...............	....	....	....	....	....	....	....	....	....	....	....	....
3317 Financial derivatives.........................	....	....	....	....	....	....	....	....	....	....	....	....
3318 Other accounts payable.....................	....	....	....	....	....	....	....	....	....	....	....	....

In Millions of New Sheqalim / Year Ending December 31 / Noncash Reporter

		Budgetary Central Government			Central Government			Local Government			General Government		
		2002	2003	2004p	2002	2003	2004p	2002	2003	2004p	2002	2003	2004p
332	Foreign..............................	....	....	....	....	....	....	....	....	....	....	....	....
3322	Currency and deposits..............	....	....	....	....	....	....	....	....	....	....	....	....
3323	Securities other than shares.......	....	....	....	....	....	....	....	....	....	....	....	....
3324	Loans...............................	....	....	....	....	....	....	....	....	....	....	....	....
3326	Insurance technical reserves.......	....	....	....	....	....	....	....	....	....	....	....	....
3327	Financial derivatives..............	....	....	....	....	....	....	....	....	....	....	....	....
3328	Other accounts payable.............	....	....	....	....	....	....	....	....	....	....	....	....

Table 4 Holding gains in assets and liabilities

Table 5 Other changes in the volume of assets and liabilities

Table 6 Balance sheet

Table 7 Outlays by functions of govt.

		Budgetary Central Government			Central Government			Local Government			General Government		
		2002	2003	2004p	2002	2003	2004p	2002	2003	2004p	2002	2003	2004p
7	**Total outlays**...............	212,186	212,292	212,812	256,571	256,490	257,116	36,947	36,008	35,841	275,059	274,832	275,987
701	**General public services**.........	....	43,169	45,333	....	39,670	41,758	....	6,394	6,288	....	41,922	44,008
7017	Public debt transactions...........	28,638	32,982	34,690	25,278	29,373	30,917	1,471	1,382	1,420	26,566	30,570	32,157
7018	General transfers between levels of govt......	....	5,343	5,198	....	3,810	3,710	....	148	148	....	1	—
702	**Defense**.........................	....	48,359	45,804	....	48,394	45,831	....	220	217	....	48,534	45,970
703	**Public order and safety**.........	....	8,956	9,685	....	8,948	9,677	....	776	759	....	9,681	10,396
704	**Economic affairs**................	....	13,696	14,218	....	13,883	14,302	....	4,044	3,707	....	16,464	16,746
7042	Agriculture, forestry, fishing, and hunting.....	....	....	....	....	....	....	....	....	....	....	....	....
7043	Fuel and energy....................	....	....	....	....	....	....	....	....	....	....	....	....
7044	Mining, manufacturing, and construction.....	....	....	....	....	....	....	....	....	....	....	....	....
7045	Transport..........................	....	....	....	....	....	....	....	....	....	....	....	....
7046	Communication......................	....	....	....	....	....	....	....	....	....	....	....	....
705	**Environmental protection**........	....	632	655	....	631	655	....	4,155	4,366	....	4,638	4,890
706	**Housing and community amenities**......	....	3,904	3,191	....	3,867	3,205	....	1,134	923	....	4,958	4,088
707	**Health**..........................	....	16,509	16,604	....	32,540	33,353	....	237	243	....	32,713	33,534
7072	Outpatient services................	....	....	....	....	....	....	....	....	....	....	....	....
7073	Hospital services..................	....	....	....	....	....	....	....	....	....	....	....	....
7074	Public health services.............	....	....	....	....	....	....	....	....	....	....	....	....
708	**Recreation, culture, and religion**........	....	2,492	2,539	....	5,043	4,682	....	3,723	3,722	....	8,022	7,663
709	**Education**.......................	....	31,734	33,075	....	37,255	39,446	....	10,617	10,968	....	41,052	43,778
7091	Pre-primary and primary education....	....	....	....	....	....	....	....	....	....	....	....	....
7092	Secondary education................	....	....	....	....	....	....	....	....	....	....	....	....
7094	Tertiary education.................	....	....	....	....	....	....	....	....	....	....	....	....
710	**Social protection**...............	....	42,841	41,708	....	66,259	64,207	....	4,708	4,648	....	66,848	64,914
7	Statistical discrepancy: Total outlays..............	....	—	—	....	—	—	....	—	—	....	—	—

Table 8 Transactions in financial assets and liabilities by sector

In Billions of Euros / Year Ending December 31 / Noncash Reporter

	Budgetary Central Government			Central Government			Local Government			General Government		
	2001	2002	2003	2001	2002	2003	2001	2002	2003	2001	2002	2003
Statement of government operations												
1　Revenue	308.00	310.31	319.09	463.95	472.72	492.53	180.45	184.22	196.92	563.12	577.75	606.95
2　Expense	340.30	343.97	348.33	492.55	502.31	520.23	169.72	177.53	184.51	580.99	600.65	622.23
GOB　*Gross operating balance*	*−28.12*	*−29.30*	*−24.62*	*−22.27*	*−23.09*	*−21.16*	*20.01*	*16.58*	*23.12*	*−2.26*	*−6.51*	*1.97*
NOB　*Net operating balance*	*−32.30*	*−33.67*	*−29.24*	*−28.60*	*−29.59*	*−27.70*	*10.73*	*6.69*	*12.42*	*−17.87*	*−22.90*	*−15.28*
31　Net acquisition of nonfinancial assets	1.02	1.20	2.36	.74	−7.40	1.59	13.89	14.83	15.61	14.63	7.43	17.20
NLB　*Net lending/borrowing*	*−33.32*	*−34.87*	*−31.59*	*−29.33*	*−22.19*	*−29.28*	*−3.16*	*−8.14*	*−3.19*	*−32.49*	*−30.33*	*−32.47*
32　Net acquisition of financial assets	....	....	....	5.17	7.97	−59.37	3.48	2.43	3.41	8.65	10.41	−55.96
33　Net incurrence of liabilities	....	....	....	41.09	30.57	−28.52	2.39	12.80	6.53	43.48	43.37	−21.99
NLB　Statistical discrepancy	....	....	....	−6.59	−.41	−1.57	4.26	−2.23	.08	−2.34	−2.63	−1.49
Statement of other economic flows												
Balance sheet												
Statement of sources and uses of cash												
Table 1　Revenue												
1　**Revenue**	**308.00**	**310.31**	**319.09**	**463.95**	**472.72**	**492.53**	**180.45**	**184.22**	**196.92**	**563.12**	**577.75**	**606.95**
11　**Taxes**	**283.65**	**285.45**	**297.22**	**283.56**	**285.18**	**297.33**	**77.38**	**82.52**	**89.41**	**360.25**	**367.07**	**386.10**
111　Taxes on income, profits, & capital gains	164.18	157.31	152.11	164.09	157.04	152.22	15.92	19.00	21.72	179.32	175.40	173.31
1111　Individuals	121.30	120.68	119.90	121.30	120.68	119.90	14.44	17.06	19.68	135.74	137.74	139.58
1112　Corporations and other enterprises	34.86	30.92	27.13	34.86	30.92	27.13	1.36	1.77	1.87	36.22	32.70	29.00
112　Taxes on payroll and workforce	—	—	—	—	—	—	—	—	—	—	—	—
113　Taxes on property	5.85	8.20	6.91	5.85	8.20	6.91	11.22	12.24	12.78	17.07	20.44	19.69
114　Taxes on goods and services	109.44	115.06	116.74	109.44	115.06	116.74	49.67	50.40	52.03	159.11	165.47	168.77
1141　General taxes on goods and services	69.55	74.90	73.86	69.55	74.90	73.86	3.29	2.22	2.40	72.84	77.12	76.25
1142　Excises	32.46	32.52	34.64	32.46	32.52	34.64	6.26	6.00	6.29	38.71	38.52	40.93
115　Taxes on int'l. trade and transactions	−.02	−.03	−.03	−.02	−.03	−.03	—	—	—	−.02	−.03	−.03
116　Other taxes	4.19	4.91	21.48	4.19	4.91	21.48	.57	.88	2.87	4.76	5.79	24.36
12　**Social contributions**	**2.30**	**2.12**	**2.07**	**152.88**	**160.24**	**169.91**	**1.03**	**1.09**	**1.12**	**153.91**	**161.33**	**171.03**
121　Social security contributions	—	—	—	149.83	157.48	167.20	—	—	—	149.83	157.48	167.20
122　Other social contributions	2.30	2.12	2.07	3.05	2.76	2.70	1.03	1.09	1.12	4.08	3.84	3.83
13　**Grants**	**3.33**	**2.99**	**2.48**	**1.44**	**1.06**	**1.50**	**78.74**	**77.16**	**82.52**	**1.82**	**2.03**	**4.53**
131　From foreign governments	.12	.06	.19	.24	.62	1.12	1.05	.95	2.34	1.29	1.57	3.45
132　From international organizations	.01	.10	.09	.02	.10	.11	.51	.36	.97	.53	.46	1.08
133　From other general government units	3.19	2.83	2.20	1.18	.34	.28	77.18	75.85	79.21	—	—	—
14　**Other revenue**	**18.73**	**19.75**	**17.34**	**26.08**	**26.24**	**23.79**	**23.30**	**23.46**	**23.87**	**47.15**	**47.33**	**45.29**
Table 2　Expense by economic type												
2　**Expense**	**340.30**	**343.97**	**348.33**	**492.55**	**502.31**	**520.23**	**169.72**	**177.53**	**184.51**	**580.99**	**600.65**	**622.23**
21　**Compensation of employees**	**71.61**	**74.58**	**80.47**	**76.45**	**79.58**	**85.50**	**54.64**	**56.84**	**58.11**	**131.08**	**136.42**	**143.61**
211　Wages and salaries	48.09	49.95	53.22	51.27	53.35	56.65	41.38	43.18	44.16	92.65	96.53	100.81
212　Social contributions	23.53	24.63	27.25	25.18	26.23	28.85	13.25	13.67	13.95	38.43	39.89	42.80
22　**Use of goods and services**	**13.78**	**12.11**	**14.69**	**19.85**	**18.75**	**21.57**	**42.49**	**44.66**	**47.46**	**62.34**	**63.41**	**69.02**
23　**Consumption of fixed capital**	**4.18**	**4.37**	**4.62**	**6.33**	**6.50**	**6.54**	**9.28**	**9.90**	**10.71**	**15.61**	**16.39**	**17.24**
24　**Interest**	**76.64**	**72.25**	**67.27**	**77.47**	**72.32**	**67.78**	**4.56**	**4.52**	**4.52**	**79.80**	**74.47**	**69.93**
25　**Subsidies**	**6.83**	**5.54**	**5.77**	**7.05**	**5.69**	**5.95**	**7.62**	**7.95**	**8.56**	**14.67**	**13.64**	**14.51**
26　**Grants**	**148.50**	**154.56**	**156.87**	**84.22**	**86.16**	**90.84**	**1.18**	**.34**	**.28**	**7.04**	**10.31**	**11.63**
261　To foreign govenments	—	—	—	—	—	—	—	—	—	—	—	—
262　To international organizations	6.71	9.94	11.23	7.04	10.31	11.63	—	—	—	7.04	10.31	11.63
263　To other general government units	141.79	144.61	145.64	77.18	75.85	79.21	1.18	.34	.28	—	—	—
2631　Current	122.17	125.82	123.81	62.43	62.21	62.08	.40	.34	.28	—	—	—
2632　Capital	19.62	18.80	21.83	14.75	13.64	17.14	.78	—	—	—	—	—
27　**Social benefits**	**3.96**	**3.63**	**3.73**	**200.87**	**212.39**	**222.55**	**32.72**	**34.73**	**34.92**	**233.59**	**247.12**	**257.47**
28　**Other expense**	**14.81**	**16.94**	**14.91**	**20.31**	**20.92**	**19.50**	**17.22**	**18.60**	**19.95**	**36.85**	**38.88**	**38.82**
281　Property expense other than interest	—	—	—	—	—	—	.06	.06	.06	.06	.06	.07
282　Miscellaneous other expense	14.81	16.94	14.91	20.31	20.92	19.50	17.17	18.54	19.89	36.80	38.82	38.75
2821　Current	8.92	10.09	9.94	11.40	11.95	11.59	9.27	9.90	10.68	19.99	21.22	21.63
2822　Capital	5.89	6.84	4.97	8.92	8.96	7.91	7.90	8.64	9.21	16.81	17.61	17.12

In Billions of Euros / Year Ending December 31 / Noncash Reporter

	Budgetary Central Government			Central Government			Local Government			General Government		
	2001	2002	2003	2001	2002	2003	2001	2002	2003	2001	2002	2003
Table 3 Transactions in assets and liabilities												
3 Change in net worth from transactns....	....	....	....	−35.19	−30.00	−29.27	14.98	4.46	12.50	−20.20	−25.53	−16.77
31 Net acquisition of nonfinancial assets...	1.02	1.20	2.36	.74	−7.40	1.59	13.89	14.83	15.61	14.63	7.43	17.20
311 Fixed assets............................	1.02	1.20	2.36	.67	−7.48	1.50	13.68	14.63	15.46	14.35	7.15	16.96
3111 Buildings and structures..............	....	....	....	....	....	....	....	....	....	....	....	....
3112 Machinery and equipment.............	....	....	....	....	....	....	....	....	....	....	....	....
3113 Other fixed assets.....................	....	....	....	....	....	....	....	....	....	....	....	....
312 Inventories...........................	—	—	—	—	—	—	—	—	—	—	—	—
313 Valuables.............................	—	—	—	—	—	—	—	—	—	—	—	—
314 Nonproduced assets...................	—	—	—	.07	.08	.09	.21	.20	.15	.28	.28	.24
3141 Land................................	—	—	—	....	....	....	....	....	....	....	....	....
3142 Subsoil assets.......................	—	—	—	....	....	....	....	....	....	....	....	....
3143 Other naturally occurring assets.....	—	—	—	....	....	....	....	....	....	....	....	....
3144 Intangible nonproduced assets........	—	—	—	....	....	....	....	....	....	....	....	....
32 Net acquisition of financial assets........	....	....	....	5.17	7.97	−59.37	3.48	2.43	3.41	8.65	10.41	−55.96
321 Domestic.............................	....	....	....	....	....	....	....	....	....	....	....	....
3212 Currency and deposits...............	....	....	....	....	....	....	....	....	....	....	....	....
3213 Securities other than shares..........	....	....	....	....	....	....	....	....	....	....	....	....
3214 Loans...............................	....	....	....	....	....	....	....	....	....	....	....	....
3215 Shares and other equity.............	....	....	....	....	....	....	....	....	....	....	....	....
3216 Insurance technical reserves.........	....	....	....	....	....	....	....	....	....	....	....	....
3217 Financial derivatives.................	....	....	....	....	....	....	....	....	....	....	....	....
3218 Other accounts receivable............	....	....	....	....	....	....	....	....	....	....	....	....
322 Foreign..............................	....	....	....	....	....	....	....	....	....	....	....	....
3222 Currency and deposits...............	....	....	....	....	....	....	....	....	....	....	....	....
3223 Securities other than shares..........	....	....	....	....	....	....	....	....	....	....	....	....
3224 Loans...............................	....	....	....	....	....	....	....	....	....	....	....	....
3225 Shares and other equity.............	....	....	....	....	....	....	....	....	....	....	....	....
3226 Insurance technical reserves.........	....	....	....	....	....	....	....	....	....	....	....	....
3227 Financial derivatives.................	....	....	....	....	....	....	....	....	....	....	....	....
3228 Other accounts receivable............	....	....	....	....	....	....	....	....	....	....	....	....
323 Monetary gold and SDRs..............	....	....	....	—	—	—	—	—	—	—	—	—
33 Net incurrence of liabilities..................	....	....	....	41.09	30.57	−28.52	2.39	12.80	6.53	43.48	43.37	−21.99
331 Domestic.............................	....	....	....	....	....	....	....	....	....	....	....	....
3312 Currency and deposits...............	....	....	....	....	....	....	....	....	....	....	....	....
3313 Securities other than shares..........	....	....	....	....	....	....	....	....	....	....	....	....
3314 Loans...............................	....	....	....	....	....	....	....	....	....	....	....	....
3316 Insurance technical reserves.........	....	....	....	....	....	....	....	....	....	....	....	....
3317 Financial derivatives.................	....	....	....	....	....	....	....	....	....	....	....	....
3318 Other accounts payable..............	....	....	....	....	....	....	....	....	....	....	....	....
332 Foreign..............................	....	....	....	....	....	....	....	....	....	....	....	....
3322 Currency and deposits...............	....	....	....	....	....	....	....	....	....	....	....	....
3323 Securities other than shares..........	....	....	....	....	....	....	....	....	....	....	....	....
3324 Loans...............................	....	....	....	....	....	....	....	....	....	....	....	....
3326 Insurance technical reserves.........	....	....	....	....	....	....	....	....	....	....	....	....
3327 Financial derivatives.................	....	....	....	....	....	....	....	....	....	....	....	....
3328 Other accounts payable..............	....	....	....	....	....	....	....	....	....	....	....	....
Table 4 Holding gains in assets and liabilities												
Table 5 Other changes in the volume of assets and liabilities												
Table 6 Balance sheet												
Table 7 Outlays by functions of govt.												
7 Total outlays............................	341.32	345.17	350.69	493.28	494.91	521.81	183.61	192.36	200.12	595.62	608.08	639.42
701 General public services.................	150.94	153.22	149.33	150.97	153.21	149.28	24.18	24.42	25.29	117.80	117.24	117.88
7017 Public debt transactions..............	76.64	72.25	67.27	77.47	72.32	67.78	4.56	4.52	4.52	79.80	74.47	69.93
7018 General transfers between levels of govt......	....	....	....	....	....	....	....	....	....	....	....	....
702 Defense..............................	14.17	15.68	17.55	14.17	15.68	17.55	.01	.01	.01	14.18	15.69	17.56
703 Public order and safety...............	21.04	22.03	24.14	21.04	22.03	24.14	3.03	3.16	3.26	23.96	25.02	27.25
704 Economic affairs......................	30.14	27.61	28.25	23.26	20.84	20.43	27.48	28.97	30.83	48.94	48.34	49.35
7042 Agriculture, forestry, fishing, and hunting.....	....	....	....	....	....	....	....	....	....	....	....	....
7043 Fuel and energy......................	....	....	....	....	....	....	....	....	....	....	....	....
7044 Mining, manufacturing, and construction.....	....	....	....	....	....	....	....	....	....	....	....	....
7045 Transport............................	....	....	....	....	....	....	....	....	....	....	....	....
7046 Communication......................	....	....	....	....	....	....	....	....	....	....	....	....

In Billions of Euros / Year Ending December 31 / Noncash Reporter

	Budgetary Central Government			Central Government			Local Government			General Government		
	2001	2002	2003	2001	2002	2003	2001	2002	2003	2001	2002	2003
705 **Environmental protection**......................	1.76	1.73	2.05	1.76	1.73	2.05	9.68	10.12	10.36	10.37	10.78	11.02
706 **Housing and community amenities**........	1.03	1.37	1.16	.46	−7.70	.42	9.78	10.30	10.76	9.80	1.83	10.59
707 **Health**..	15.24	9.24	15.81	15.45	9.34	15.93	76.43	80.48	82.96	78.19	81.91	84.40
7072 Outpatient services................................	....	....	....	....	....	....	....	....	....	....	....	....
7073 Hospital services....................................	....	....	....	....	....	....	....	....	....	....	....	....
7074 Public health services.............................	....	....	....	....	....	....	....	....	....	....	....	....
708 **Recreation, culture, and religion**...........	8.93	9.31	8.77	8.93	9.31	8.77	6.56	6.74	7.07	15.04	15.58	15.35
709 **Education**...	48.37	49.90	53.02	48.37	49.90	53.02	18.59	19.60	20.69	61.38	63.52	67.79
7091 Pre-primary and primary education.............	....	....	....	....	....	....	....	....	....	....	....	....
7092 Secondary education................................	....	....	....	....	....	....	....	....	....	....	....	....
7094 Tertiary education...................................	....	....	....	....	....	....	....	....	....	....	....	....
710 **Social protection**.................................	54.81	59.29	56.49	208.87	220.57	230.24	7.86	8.56	8.89	215.96	228.18	238.24
7 Statistical discrepancy: Total outlays..............	−5.11	−4.20	−5.87	—	—	—	—	—	—	—	—	—

Table 8   Transactions in financial assets and liabilities by sector

	Budgetary Central Government			Central Government			Local Government			General Government		
82 **Net acquisition of financial assets**.........	....	....	....	5.17	7.97	−59.37	3.48	2.43	3.41	8.65	10.41	−55.96
821 Domestic..	....	....	....	....	....	....	....	....	....	....	....	....
8211 General government.................................	....	....	....	....	....	....	....	....	....	....	....	....
8212 Central bank..	....	....	....	....	....	....	....	....	....	....	....	....
8213 Other depository corporations...................	....	....	....	....	....	....	....	....	....	....	....	....
8214 Financial corporations n.e.c......................	....	....	....	....	....	....	....	....	....	....	....	....
8215 Nonfinancial corporations.........................	....	....	....	....	....	....	....	....	....	....	....	....
8216 Households & NPIs serving households......	....	....	....	....	....	....	....	....	....	....	....	....
822 Foreign...	....	....	....	....	....	....	....	....	....	....	....	....
8221 General government.................................	....	....	....	....	....	....	....	....	....	....	....	....
8227 International organizations........................	....	....	....	....	....	....	....	....	....	....	....	....
8228 Financial corporations other than international organizations..............	....	....	....	....	....	....	....	....	....	....	....	....
8229 Other nonresidents.................................	....	....	....	....	....	....	....	....	....	....	....	....
823 Monetary gold and SDRs...........................	....	....	....	—	—	—	....	....	....	—	—	—
83 **Net incurrence of liabilities**...................	....	....	....	41.09	30.57	−28.52	2.39	12.80	6.53	43.48	43.37	−21.99
831 Domestic..	....	....	....	....	....	....	....	....	....	....	....	....
8311 General government.................................	....	....	....	....	....	....	....	....	....	....	....	....
8312 Central bank..	....	....	....	....	....	....	....	....	....	....	....	....
8313 Other depository corporations...................	....	....	....	....	....	....	....	....	....	....	....	....
8314 Financial corporations n.e.c......................	....	....	....	....	....	....	....	....	....	....	....	....
8315 Nonfinancial corporations.........................	....	....	....	....	....	....	....	....	....	....	....	....
8316 Households & NPIs serving households......	....	....	....	....	....	....	....	....	....	....	....	....
832 Foreign...	....	....	....	....	....	....	....	....	....	....	....	....
8321 General government.................................	....	....	....	....	....	....	....	....	....	....	....	....
8327 International organizations........................	....	....	....	....	....	....	....	....	....	....	....	....
8328 Financial corporations other than international organizations..............	....	....	....	....	....	....	....	....	....	....	....	....
8329 Other nonresidents.................................	....	....	....	....	....	....	....	....	....	....	....	....

In Millions of Dollars / Year Ending March 31 / Cash Reporter

	Budgetary Central Government			Central Government			Local Government			General Government		
	2001	2002	2003	2001	2002	2003	2001	2002	2003	2001	2002	2003
Statement of government operations												
Statement of other economic flows												
Balance sheet												
6 *Net worth*................	....	....	....	....	....	....	....	....	....	....	....	....
61 Nonfinancial assets................	....	....	....	....	....	....	....	....	....	....	....	....
62 Financial assets................	....	....	....	....	....	....	....	....	....	....	....	....
63 Liabilities................	....	....	....	497,083	601,241	693,886	....	....	....	....	....	....
Statement of sources and uses of cash												
1 Cash receipts from operating activities..........	108,719	118,266	131,088	120,350	131,282	153,195	....	....	2,288	....	....	155,483
11 Taxes................	90,985	103,126	....	90,985	103,126	....	....	....	2,287	....	....	....
12 Social contributions................	—	—	—	4,583	5,117	10,255	....	....	—	....	....	10,255
13 Grants................	1,941	—	—	1,941	—	222	....	....	—	....	....	222
14 Other receipts................	15,792	15,140	....	22,840	23,038	....	....	....	1	....	....	....
2 Cash payments for operating activities..........	121,983	145,944	182,831	132,403	158,334	196,483	....	....	2,835	....	....	199,317
21 Compensation of employees................	43,030	56,491	60,463	44,247	57,818	62,313	....	....	127	....	....	62,440
22 Purchases of goods and services................	19,588	....	19,747	22,543	....	25,306	....	....	2,553	....	....	27,859
24 Interest................	51,550	60,738	90,741	51,550	60,738	90,741	....	....	—	....	....	90,741
25 Subsidies................	—	—	—	—	—	—	....	....	—	....	....	—
26 Grants................	1,295	169	—	—	—	—	....	....	—	....	....	....
27 Social benefits................	—	—	—	1,852	1,830	3,000	....	....	—	....	....	3,000
28 Other payments................	6,520	....	11,880	12,211	....	15,123	....	....	155	....	....	15,278
CIO *Net cash inflow from oper. activities*.....	−13,265	−27,677	−51,743	−12,053	−27,053	−43,287	....	....	−547	....	....	−43,834
31.1 Purchases of nonfinancial assets................	1,594	2,592	2,592	1,825	3,298	3,005	....	....	....	....	....	....
31.2 Sales of nonfinancial assets................	—	—	—	—	—	—	....	....	....	....	....	....
31 Net cash outflow from investments in nonfinancial assets................	1,594	2,592	2,592	1,825	3,298	3,005	....	....	....	....	....	....
CSD *Cash surplus/deficit*................	−14,859	−30,269	−54,335	−13,878	−30,351	−46,292	....	....	....	....	....	....
32x Net acquisition of fin assets, excl. cash........	....	....	....	....	....	....	....	....	....	....	....	....
321x Domestic................	....	....	....	....	....	....	....	....	....	....	....	....
322x Foreign................	....	....	....	....	....	....	....	....	....	....	....	....
323 Monetary gold and SDRs................	....	....	....	....	....	....	....	....	....	....	....	....
33 Net incurrence of liabilities................	....	....	....	....	....	....	....	....	....	....	....	....
331 Domestic................	....	....	....	....	....	....	....	....	....	....	....	....
332 Foreign................	....	....	....	....	....	....	....	....	....	....	....	....
NFB Net cash inflow from fin. activities................	....	....	....	....	....	....	....	....	....	....	....	....
NCB *Net change in the stock of cash*............	....	....	....	....	....	....	....	....	....	....	....	....
Table 1 Revenue												
1 **Revenue**................	**108,719**	**118,266**	**131,088**	**120,350**	**131,282**	**153,195**	....	....	**2,288**	....	....	**155,483**
11 **Taxes**................	**90,985**	**103,126**	....	**90,985**	**103,126**	....	....	....	**2,287**	....	....	....
111 Taxes on income, profits, & capital gains.....	35,495	39,046	....	35,495	39,046	....	....	....	—	....	....	....
1111 Individuals................	19,750	22,256	....	19,750	22,256	....	....	....	—	....	....	....
1112 Corporations and other enterprises............	6,680	7,809	10,015	6,680	7,809	10,015	....	....	—	....	....	10,015
112 Taxes on payroll and workforce................	—	—	—	—	—	....	....	....	—	....	....	....
113 Taxes on property................	—	—	—	—	—	—	....	....	1,414	....	....	1,414
114 Taxes on goods and services................	38,561	44,315	....	38,561	44,315	....	....	....	872	....	....	....
1141 General taxes on goods and services.........	34,625	40,070	36,508	34,625	40,070	36,508	....	....	—	....	....	36,508
1142 Excises................	—	—	....	—	—	....	....	....	—	....	....	....
115 Taxes on int'l. trade and transactions.........	8,501	10,150	14,086	8,501	10,150	14,086	....	....	—	....	....	14,086
116 Other taxes................	8,428	9,615	....	8,428	9,615	....	....	....	—	....	....	....
12 **Social contributions**................	**—**	**—**	**—**	**4,583**	**5,117**	**10,255**	....	....	**—**	....	....	**10,255**
121 Social security contributions................	—	—	—	—	—	10,255	....	....	—	....	....	10,255
122 Other social contributions................	—	—	—	4,583	5,117	—	....	....	—	....	....	—
13 **Grants**................	**1,941**	**—**	**—**	**1,941**	**—**	**222**	....	....	**—**	....	....	**222**
131 From foreign governments................	1,941	—	—	1,941	—	—	....	....	—	....	....	—
132 From international organizations................	—	—	—	—	—	222	....	....	—	....	....	222
133 From other general government units..........	—	—	—	—	—	—	....	....	—	....	....	—
14 **Other revenue**................	**15,792**	**15,140**	....	**22,840**	**23,038**	....	....	....	**1**	....	....	....
Table 2 Expense by economic type												
2 **Expense**................	**121,983**	**145,944**	**182,831**	**132,403**	**158,334**	**196,483**	....	....	**2,835**	....	....	**199,317**
21 **Compensation of employees**................	**43,030**	**56,491**	**60,463**	**44,247**	**57,818**	**62,313**	....	....	**127**	....	....	**62,440**
211 Wages and salaries................	42,588	51,496	....	43,805	52,823	....	....	....	....	....	....	....
212 Social contributions................	442	4,995	....	442	4,995	....	....	....	....	....	....	....
22 **Use of goods and services**................	**19,588**	....	**19,747**	**22,543**	....	**25,306**	....	....	**2,553**	....	....	**27,859**
23 **Consumption of fixed capital**................	....	....	....	....	....	....	....	....	....	....	....	....
24 **Interest**................	**51,550**	**60,738**	**90,741**	**51,550**	**60,738**	**90,741**	....	....	**—**	....	....	**90,741**
25 **Subsidies**................	**—**	**—**	**—**	**—**	**—**	**—**	....	....	**—**	....	....	**—**

		Budgetary Central Government			Central Government			Local Government			General Government		
		2001	2002	2003	2001	2002	2003	2001	2002	2003	2001	2002	2003
26	Grants................................	1,295	169	—	—	—	—	....	....	—	....	....	—
261	To foreign govenments............	—	—	—	—	—	—	....	....	—	....	....	—
262	To international organizations.........	—	—	—	—	—	—	....	....	—	....	....	—
263	To other general government units.......	1,295	169	—	—	—	—	....	....	—	....	....	—
2631	Current....................	1,295	169	—	—	—	—	....	....	—	....	....	—
2632	Capital.....................	—	—	—	—	—	—	....	....	—	....	....	—
27	**Social benefits................**	—	—	—	1,852	1,830	3,000	....	....	—	....	....	3,000
28	**Other expense...................**	6,520	....	11,880	12,211	....	15,123	....	....	155	...	....	15,278
281	Property expense other than interest...........	—	....	—	—	....	89	....	....	—	....	....	89
282	Miscellaneous other expense..........	6,520	....	11,880	12,211	....	15,034	....	....	155	....	....	15,189
2821	Current..........................	—	....	5,815	—	....	5,815	....	....	155	....	....	5,970
2822	Capital............................	6,520	....	6,065	12,211	....	9,219	....	....	—	....	....	9,219

Table 3   Transactions in assets and liabilities

3	**Change in net worth from transactns....**	....	....	....	....	....	....	....	....	....	....	....	....
31	**Net acquisition of nonfinancial assets...**	1,594	2,592	2,592	1,825	3,298	3,005	....	....	....	....	....	....
311	Fixed assets...........................	452	1,322	1,322	589	1,784	1,626	....	....	....	....	....	....
3111	Buildings and structures................	....	....	....	....	....	....	....	....	....	....	....	....
3112	Machinery and equipment............	....	....	....	....	....	....	....	....	....	....	....	....
3113	Other fixed assets.....................	....	....	....	....	....	....	....	....	....	....	....	....
312	Inventories............................	—	—	—	—	—	—	....	....	....	....	....	....
313	Valuables.............................	—	—	—	—	—	—	....	....	....	....	....	....
314	Nonproduced assets...............	1,141	1,270	1,270	1,236	1,514	1,379	....	....	....	....	....	....
3141	Land.................................	....	....	....	....	....	....	....	....	....	....	....	....
3142	Subsoil assets.......................	....	....	....	....	....	....	....	....	....	....	....	....
3143	Other naturally occurring assets.......	....	....	....	....	....	....	....	....	....	....	....	....
3144	Intangible nonproduced assets..........	....	....	....	....	....	....	....	....	....	....	....	....
32	**Net acquisition of financial assets.........**	....	....	....	....	....	....	....	....	....	....	....	....
321	Domestic.............................	....	....	....	....	....	....	....	....	....	....	....	....
3212	Currency and deposits...............	....	....	....	....	....	....	....	....	....	....	....	....
3213	Securities other than shares............	....	....	....	....	....	....	....	....	....	....	....	....
3214	Loans...............................	....	....	....	....	....	....	....	....	....	....	....	....
3215	Shares and other equity...............	....	....	....	....	....	....	....	....	....	....	....	....
3216	Insurance technical reserves..........	....	....	....	....	....	....	....	....	....	....	....	....
3217	Financial derivatives.................	....	....	....	....	....	....	....	....	....	....	....	....
3218	Other accounts receivable.............	....	....	....	....	....	....	....	....	....	....	....	....
322	Foreign...............................	....	....	....	....	....	....	....	....	....	....	....	....
3222	Currency and deposits...............	....	....	....	....	....	....	....	....	....	....	....	....
3223	Securities other than shares...........	....	....	....	....	....	....	....	....	....	....	....	....
3224	Loans................................	....	....	....	....	....	....	....	....	....	....	....	....
3225	Shares and other equity...............	....	....	....	....	....	....	....	....	....	....	....	....
3226	Insurance technical reserves...........	....	....	....	....	....	....	....	....	....	....	....	....
3227	Financial derivatives.................	....	....	....	....	....	....	....	....	....	....	....	....
3228	Other accounts receivable.............	....	....	....	....	....	....	....	....	....	....	....	....
323	Monetary gold and SDRs.............	....	....	....	....	....	....	....	....	....	....	....	....
33	**Net incurrence of liabilities...................**	....	....	....	....	....	....	....	....	....	....	....	....
331	Domestic.............................	....	....	....	....	....	....	....	....	....	....	....	....
3312	Currency and deposits...............	....	....	....	....	....	....	....	....	....	....	....	....
3313	Securities other than shares...........	....	....	....	....	....	....	....	....	....	....	....	....
3314	Loans...............................	....	....	....	....	....	....	....	....	....	....	....	....
3316	Insurance technical reserves..........	....	....	....	....	....	....	....	....	....	....	....	....
3317	Financial derivatives.................	....	....	....	....	....	....	....	....	....	....	....	....
3318	Other accounts payable...............	....	....	....	....	....	....	....	....	....	....	....	....
332	Foreign...............................	....	....	....	....	....	....	....	....	....	....	....	....
3322	Currency and deposits...............	....	....	....	....	....	....	....	....	....	....	....	....
3323	Securities other than shares...........	....	....	....	....	....	....	....	....	....	....	....	....
3324	Loans...............................	....	....	....	....	....	....	....	....	....	....	....	....
3326	Insurance technical reserves...........	....	....	....	....	....	....	....	....	....	....	....	....
3327	Financial derivatives.................	....	....	....	....	....	....	....	....	....	....	....	....
3328	Other accounts payable...............	....	....	....	....	....	....	....	....	....	....	....	....

In Millions of Dollars / Year Ending March 31 / Cash Reporter

	Budgetary Central Government			Central Government			Local Government			General Government		
	2001	2002	2003	2001	2002	2003	2001	2002	2003	2001	2002	2003
Table 4 Holding gains in assets and liabilities												
Table 5 Other changes in the volume of assets and liabilities												
Table 6 Balance sheet												
6 Net worth......	....	....	....	....	....	....	....	....	....	....	....	....
61 Nonfinancial assets......	....	....	....	....	....	....	....	....	....	....	....	....
611 Fixed assets......	....	....	....	....	....	....	....	....	....	....	....	....
6111 Buildings and structures......	....	....	....	....	....	....	....	....	....	....	....	....
6112 Machinery and equipment......	....	....	....	....	....	....	....	....	....	....	....	....
6113 Other fixed assets......	....	....	....	....	....	....	....	....	....	....	....	....
612 Inventories......	....	....	....	....	....	....	....	....	....	....	....	....
613 Valuables......	....	....	....	....	....	....	....	....	....	....	....	....
614 Nonproduced assets......	....	....	....	....	....	....	....	....	....	....	....	....
6141 Land......	....	....	....	....	....	....	....	....	....	....	....	....
6142 Subsoil assets......	....	....	....	....	....	....	....	....	....	....	....	....
6143 Other naturally occurring assets......	....	....	....	....	....	....	....	....	....	....	....	....
6144 Intangible nonproduced assets......	....	....	....	....	....	....	....	....	....	....	....	....
62 Financial assets......	....	....	....	....	....	....	....	....	....	....	....	....
621 Domestic......	....	....	....	....	....	....	....	....	....	....	....	....
6212 Currency and deposits......	....	....	....	....	....	....	....	....	....	....	....	....
6213 Securities other than shares......	....	....	....	....	....	....	....	....	....	....	....	....
6214 Loans......	....	....	....	....	....	....	....	....	....	....	....	....
6215 Shares and other equity......	....	....	....	....	....	....	....	....	....	....	....	....
6216 Insurance technical reserves......	....	....	....	....	....	....	....	....	....	....	....	....
6217 Financial derivatives......	....	....	....	....	....	....	....	....	....	....	....	....
6218 Other accounts receivable......	....	....	....	....	....	....	....	....	....	....	....	....
622 Foreign......	....	....	....	....	....	....	....	....	....	....	....	....
6222 Currency and deposits......	....	....	....	....	....	....	....	....	....	....	....	....
6223 Securities other than shares......	....	....	....	....	....	....	....	....	....	....	....	....
6224 Loans......	....	....	....	....	....	....	....	....	....	....	....	....
6225 Shares and other equity......	....	....	....	....	....	....	....	....	....	....	....	....
6226 Insurance technical reserves......	....	....	....	....	....	....	....	....	....	....	....	....
6227 Financial derivatives......	....	....	....	....	....	....	....	....	....	....	....	....
6228 Other accounts receivable......	....	....	....	....	....	....	....	....	....	....	....	....
623 Monetary gold and SDRs......	....	....	....				....	....	....	....	....	....
63 Liabilities......	....	....	....	497,083	601,241	693,886	....	....	....	....	....	....
631 Domestic......	....	....	....	300,202	366,158	417,571	....	....	....	....	....	....
6312 Currency and deposits......	....	....	....	....	....	....	....	....	....	....	....	....
6313 Securities other than shares......	....	....	....	....	....	....	....	....	....	....	....	....
6314 Loans......	....	....	....	....	....	....	....	....	....	....	....	....
6316 Insurance technical reserves......	....	....	....	....	....	....	....	....	....	....	....	....
6317 Financial derivatives......	....	....	....	....	....	....	....	....	....	....	....	....
6318 Other accounts payable......	....	....	....	....	....	....	....	....	....	....	....	....
632 Foreign......	....	....	....	196,881	235,083	276,314	....	....	....	....	....	....
6322 Currency and deposits......	....	....	....	....	....	....	....	....	....	....	....	....
6323 Securities other than shares......	....	....	....	....	....	....	....	....	....	....	....	....
6324 Loans......	....	....	....	....	....	....	....	....	....	....	....	....
6326 Insurance technical reserves......	....	....	....	....	....	....	....	....	....	....	....	....
6327 Financial derivatives......	....	....	....	....	....	....	....	....	....	....	....	....
6328 Other accounts payable......	....	....	....	....	....	....	....	....	....	....	....	....
Memorandum items:												
6M2 Net financial worth......	....	....	....	....	....	....	....	....	....	....	....	....
6M3 Debt at market value......	....	....	....	....	....	....	....	....	....	....	....	....
6M4 Debt at nominal value......	....	....	....	....	....	....	....	....	....	....	....	....
6M5 Arrears......	....	....	....	....	....	....	....	....	....	....	....	....
6M6 Obligations for social security benefits......	....	....	....	....	....	....	....	....	....	....	....	....
6M7 Contingent liabilities......	....	....	....	....	....	....	....	....	....	....	....	....
6M8 Uncapitalized military weapons, systems......	....	....	....	....	....	....	....	....	....	....	....	....
Table 7 Outlays by functions of govt.												
7 **Total outlays**......	**123,577**	**148,535**	**185,422**	**134,228**	**161,632**	**199,487**	....	....	....	....	....	....
701 **General public services**......	**65,252**	**77,898**	**107,590**	....	....	....	....	....	....	....	....	....
7017 Public debt transactions......	51,550	60,738	90,741	51,550	60,738	90,741	....	....	....	....	....	....
7018 General transfers between levels of govt......	....	....	16,849	....	....	....	....	....	....	....	....	....
702 **Defense**......	**2,212**	**2,936**	**3,244**	....	....	....	....	....	....	....	....	....
703 **Public order and safety**......	**10,693**	**12,965**	**13,776**	....	....	....	....	....	....	....	....	....

In Millions of Dollars / Year Ending March 31 / Cash Reporter

		Budgetary Central Government			Central Government			Local Government			General Government		
		2001	2002	2003	2001	2002	2003	2001	2002	2003	2001	2002	2003
704	**Economic affairs**.....................	**11,258**	**7,901**	**8,857**	....	....	....	....	....	....	....	....	....
7042	Agriculture, forestry, fishing, and hunting.....	2,291	2,793	2,748	....	....	....	....	....	....	....	....	....
7043	Fuel and energy.............................	250	321	878	....	....	....	....	....	....	....	....	....
7044	Mining, manufacturing, and construction.....	1,229	961	963	....	....	....	....	....	....	....	....	....
7045	Transport.................................	3,577	3,534	3,986	....	....	....	....	....	....	....	....	....
7046	Communication............................	....	293	282	....	....	....	....	....	....	....	....	....
705	**Environmental protection**....................	—	—	**368**	....	....	....	....	....	....	....	....	....
706	**Housing and community amenities**........	**2,741**	**3,588**	**3,460**	....	....	....	....	....	....	....	....	....
707	**Health**.................................	**8,222**	**11,310**	**11,763**	....	....	....	....	....	....	....	....	....
7072	Outpatient services...........................	—	—	—	....	....	....	....	....	....	....	....	....
7073	Hospital services...........................	8,222	11,310	11,763	....	....	....	....	....	....	....	....	....
7074	Public health services......................	—	—	—	....	....	....	....	....	....	....	....	....
708	**Recreation, culture, and religion**...........	**276**	**313**	—	....	....	....	....	....	....	....	....	....
709	**Education**..............................	**21,628**	**23,179**	**29,184**	....	....	....	....	....	....	....	....	....
7091	Pre-primary and primary education.............	....	....	....	....	....	....	....	....	....	....	....	....
7092	Secondary education..........................	....	....	....	....	....	....	....	....	....	....	....	....
7094	Tertiary education...........................	....	....	....	....	....	....	....	....	....	....	....	....
710	**Social protection**..........................	**1,295**	**5,854**	**4,589**	....	....	....	....	....	....	....	....	....
7	Statistical discrepancy: Total outlays..............	—	2,591	2,592	....	....	....	....	....	....	....	....	....

Table 8   Transactions in financial assets and liabilities by sector

In Billions of Yen / Year Beginning April 1 / Noncash Reporter

	Budgetary Central Government			Central Government			Local Government			General Government		
	2001	2002	2003	2001	2002	2003	2001	2002	2003	2001	2002	2003p
Statement of government operations												
1 Revenue....................	....	....	....	....	....	....	....	....	....	157,408	148,763	149,435
2 Expense....................	....	....	....	....	....	....	....	....	....	175,436	176,918	176,797
GOB *Gross operating balance..................*	....	....	....	....	....	....	....	....	....	*−5,349*	*−14,898*	*−13,647*
NOB *Net operating balance..................*	....	....	....	....	....	....	....	....	....	*−18,028*	*−28,155*	*−27,362*
31 Net acquisition of nonfinancial assets...........	....	....	....	....	....	....	....	....	....	15,319	12,838	10,184
NLB *Net lending/borrowing..................*	....	....	....	....	....	....	....	....	....	*−33,347*	*−40,992*	*−37,546*
32 Net acquisition of financial assets..................	....	....	....	....	....	....	....	....	....	7,871	9,787	32,305
33 Net incurrence of liabilities..................	....	....	....	....	....	....	....	....	....	43,048	39,335	67,263
NLB Statistical discrepancy..................	....	....	....	....	....	....	....	....	....	−1,830	11,444	2,587
Statement of other economic flows												
4 *Change in net worth from holding gains..................*	....	....	....	....	....	....	....	....	....	*−15,451*	*−24,608*	*5,243*
41 Nonfinancial assets..................	....	....	....	....	....	....	....	....	....	−20,827	−17,431	−11,836
42 Financial assets..................	....	....	....	....	....	....	....	....	....	5,382	−5,070	1,580
43 Liabilities..................	....	....	....	....	....	....	....	....	....	5	2,107	−15,499
5 *Change in net worth from other volume changes..................*	....	....	....	....	....	....	....	....	....	*1,189*	*715*	*2,926*
51 Nonfinancial assets..................	....	....	....	....	....	....	....	....	....	−209	−189	−252
52 Financial assets..................	....	....	....	....	....	....	....	....	....	—	—	—
53 Liabilities..................	....	....	....	....	....	....	....	....	....	−1,398	−904	−3,177
Balance sheet												
6 *Net worth..................*	....	....	....	....	....	....	....	....	....	*144,167*	*107,244*	*80,552*
61 Nonfinancial assets..................	....	....	....	....	....	....	....	....	....	470,756	463,606	459,077
62 Financial assets..................	....	....	....	....	....	....	....	....	....	426,590	432,831	441,280
63 Liabilities..................	....	....	....	....	....	....	....	....	....	753,179	789,193	819,805
Statement of sources and uses of cash												
1 Cash receipts from operating activities..........	....	....	....	....	....	....	....	....	....	157,408	148,763	149,435
11 Taxes..................	....	....	....	....	....	....	....	....	....	87,850	80,667	78,983
12 Social contributions..................	....	....	....	....	....	....	....	....	....	51,720	51,706	51,837
13 Grants..................	....	....	....	....	....	....	....	....	....	360	—	1
14 Other receipts..................	....	....	....	....	....	....	....	....	....	17,478	16,390	18,614
2 Cash payments for operating activities..........	....	....	....	....	....	....	....	....	....	133,035	133,690	132,428
21 Compensation of employees..................	....	....	....	....	....	....	....	....	....	32,754	32,053	31,602
22 Purchases of goods and services..................	....	....	....	....	....	....	....	....	....	17,270	17,621	17,470
24 Interest..................	....	....	....	....	....	....	....	....	....	15,754	14,874	13,874
25 Subsidies..................	....	....	....	....	....	....	....	....	....	4,111	3,969	3,910
26 Grants..................	....	....	....	....	....	....	....	....	....	329	297	373
27 Social benefits..................	....	....	....	....	....	....	....	....	....	52,649	54,157	54,815
28 Other payments..................	....	....	....	....	....	....	....	....	....	10,167	10,719	10,386
CIO *Net cash inflow from oper. activities.....*	....	....	....	....	....	....	....	....	....	*24,373*	*15,074*	*17,007*
31.1 Purchases of nonfinancial assets..................	....	....	....	....	....	....				....	....	....
31.2 Sales of nonfinancial assets..................	....	....	....	....	....	....				....	....	....
31 Net cash outflow from investments in nonfinancial assets..................	....	....	....	....	....	....	....	....	....	15,282	12,816	10,170
CSD *Cash surplus/deficit..................*	....	....	....	....	....	....	....	....	....	*9,091*	*2,258*	*6,837*
32x Net acquisition of fin assets, excl. cash..........	....	....	....	....	....	....	....	....	....	....	....	....
321x Domestic..................	....	....	....	....	....	....	....	....	....	....	....	....
322x Foreign..................	....	....	....	....	....	....	....	....	....	....	....	....
323 Monetary gold and SDRs..................	....	....	....	....	....	....	....	....	....	....	....	....
33 Net incurrence of liabilities..................	....	....	....	....	....	....	....	....	....	....	....	....
331 Domestic..................	....	....	....	....	....	....	....	....	....	....	....	....
332 Foreign..................	....	....	....	....	....	....	....	....	....	....	....	....
NFB Net cash inflow from fin. activities..................	....	....	....	....	....	....	....	....	....	....	....	....
NCB *Net change in the stock of cash..................*	....	....	....	....	....	....	....	....	....	....	....	....
Table 1 Revenue												
1 **Revenue..................**	....	....	....	....	....	....	....	....	....	**157,408**	**148,763**	**149,435**
11 **Taxes..................**	....	....	....	....	....	....	....	....	....	**87,850**	**80,667**	**78,983**
111 Taxes on income, profits, & capital gains......	....	....	....	....	....	....	....	....	....	41,330	35,378	34,292
1111 Individuals..................	....	....	....	....	....	....	....	....	....	....	....	....
1112 Corporations and other enterprises..........	....	....	....	....	....	....	....	....	....	....	....	....
112 Taxes on payroll and workforce..................	....	....	....	....	....	....	....	....	....	....	....	....
113 Taxes on property..................	....	....	....	....	....	....	....	....	....	....	....	....
114 Taxes on goods and services..................	....	....	....	....	....	....	....	....	....	....	....	....
1141 General taxes on goods and services..........	....	....	....	....	....	....	....	....	....	....	....	....
1142 Excises..................	....	....	....	....	....	....	....	....	....	....	....	....

In Billions of Yen / Year Beginning April 1 / Noncash Reporter

	Budgetary Central Government			Central Government			Local Government			General Government		
	2001	2002	2003	2001	2002	2003	2001	2002	2003	2001	2002	2003p
115 Taxes on int'l. trade and transactions...........	....	....	....	....	....	....	....	....	....	....	....	....
116 Other taxes......................................	....	....	....	....	....	....	....	....	....	....	....	....
12 **Social contributions.............................**	....	....	....	....	....	....	....	....	....	51,720	51,706	51,837
121 Social security contributions......................	....	....	....	....	....	....	....	....	....	48,958	48,938	48,870
122 Other social contributions.........................	....	....	....	....	....	....	....	....	....	2,762	2,769	2,967
13 **Grants..**	....	....	....	....	....	....	....	....	....	360	—	1
131 From foreign governments.........................	....	....	....	....	....	....	....	....	....	....	....	....
132 From international organizations.................	....	....	....	....	....	....	....	....	....	....	....	....
133 From other general government units...........	....	....	....	....	....	....	....	....	....	—	—	—
14 **Other revenue....................................**	....	....	....	....	....	....	....	....	....	17,478	16,390	18,614
Table 2 Expense by economic type												
2 **Expense...**	....	....	....	....	....	....	....	....	....	175,436	176,918	176,797
21 **Compensation of employees..................**	....	....	....	....	....	....	....	....	....	32,754	32,053	31,602
211 Wages and salaries.................................	....	....	....	....	....	....	....	....	....	....	....	....
212 Social contributions...............................	....	....	....	....	....	....	....	....	....	....	....	....
22 **Use of goods and services.....................**	....	....	....	....	....	....	....	....	....	17,270	17,621	17,470
23 **Consumption of fixed capital................**	....	....	....	....	....	....	....	....	....	12,679	13,257	13,715
24 **Interest..**	....	....	....	....	....	....	....	....	....	15,754	14,874	13,874
25 **Subsidies..**	....	....	....	....	....	....	....	....	....	4,111	3,969	3,910
26 **Grants...**	....	....	....	....	....	....	....	....	....	329	297	373
261 To foreign governments............................	....	....	....	....	....	....	....	....	....	....	....	....
262 To international organizations.....................	....	....	....	....	....	....	....	....	....	....	....	....
263 To other general government units...............	....	....	....	....	....	....	....	....	....	—	—	—
2631 Current..	....	....	....	....	....	....	....	....	....	—	—	—
2632 Capital...	....	....	....	....	....	....	....	....	....	—	—	—
27 **Social benefits...................................**	....	....	....	....	....	....	....	....	....	82,371	84,129	85,469
28 **Other expense....................................**	....	....	....	....	....	....	....	....	....	10,167	10,719	10,386
281 Property expense other than interest............	....	....	....	....	....	....	....	....	....	320	329	326
282 Miscellaneous other expense......................	....	....	....	....	....	....	....	....	....	9,847	10,390	10,060
2821 Current..	....	....	....	....	....	....	....	....	....	5,053	5,074	5,185
2822 Capital...	....	....	....	....	....	....	....	....	....	4,794	5,316	4,875
Table 3 Transactions in assets and liabilities												
3 **Change in net worth from transactns....**	....	....	....	....	....	....	....	....	....	−19,858	−16,711	−24,774
31 **Net acquisition of nonfinancial assets...**	....	....	....	....	....	....	....	....	....	15,319	12,838	10,184
311 Fixed assets.......................................	....	....	....	....	....	....	....	....	....	11,662	9,653	7,315
3111 Buildings and structures.......................	....	....	....	....	....	....	....	....	....	....	....	....
3112 Machinery and equipment......................	....	....	....	....	....	....	....	....	....	....	....	....
3113 Other fixed assets.............................	....	....	....	....	....	....	....	....	....	....	....	....
312 Inventories..	....	....	....	....	....	....	....	....	....	37	22	14
313 Valuables..	....	....	....	....	....	....	....	....	....	—	—	—
314 Nonproduced assets...............................	....	....	....	....	....	....	....	....	....	3,621	3,163	2,855
3141 Land..	....	....	....	....	....	....	....	....	....	3,621	3,163	2,855
3142 Subsoil assets..................................	....	....	....	....	....	....	....	....	....	—	—	—
3143 Other naturally occurring assets.............	....	....	....	....	....	....	....	....	....	....	....	....
3144 Intangible nonproduced assets................	....	....	....	....	....	....	....	....	....	—	—	—
32 **Net acquisition of financial assets.........**	....	....	....	....	....	....	....	....	....	7,871	9,787	32,305
321 Domestic...	....	....	....	....	....	....	....	....	....	....	....	....
3212 Currency and deposits.........................	....	....	....	....	....	....	....	....	....	....	....	....
3213 Securities other than shares..................	....	....	....	....	....	....	....	....	....	....	....	....
3214 Loans..	....	....	....	....	....	....	....	....	....	....	....	....
3215 Shares and other equity.......................	....	....	....	....	....	....	....	....	....	....	....	....
3216 Insurance technical reserves..................	....	....	....	....	....	....	....	....	....	....	....	....
3217 Financial derivatives...........................	....	....	....	....	....	....	....	....	....	....	....	....
3218 Other accounts receivable.....................	....	....	....	....	....	....	....	....	....	....	....	....
322 Foreign..	....	....	....	....	....	....	....	....	....	....	....	....
3222 Currency and deposits.........................	....	....	....	....	....	....	....	....	....	....	....	....
3223 Securities other than shares..................	....	....	....	....	....	....	....	....	....	....	....	....
3224 Loans..	....	....	....	....	....	....	....	....	....	....	....	....
3225 Shares and other equity.......................	....	....	....	....	....	....	....	....	....	....	....	....
3226 Insurance technical reserves..................	....	....	....	....	....	....	....	....	....	....	....	....
3227 Financial derivatives...........................	....	....	....	....	....	....	....	....	....	....	....	....
3228 Other accounts receivable.....................	....	....	....	....	....	....	....	....	....	....	....	....
323 Monetary gold and SDRs...........................	....	....	....	....	....	....	....	....	....	....	....	....

In Billions of Yen / Year Beginning April 1 / Noncash Reporter

		Budgetary Central Government			Central Government			Local Government			General Government		
		2001	2002	2003	2001	2002	2003	2001	2002	2003	2001	2002	2003p
33	**Net incurrence of liabilities**..........	....	....	....	....	....	....	....	....	....	43,048	39,335	67,263
331	Domestic..........	....	....	....	....	....	....	....	....	....	....	....	....
3312	Currency and deposits..........	....	....	....	....	....	....	....	....	....	....	....	....
3313	Securities other than shares..........	....	....	....	....	....	....	....	....	....	....	....	....
3314	Loans..........	....	....	....	....	....	....	....	....	....	....	....	....
3316	Insurance technical reserves..........	....	....	....	....	....	....	....	....	....	....	....	....
3317	Financial derivatives..........	....	....	....	....	....	....	....	....	....	....	....	....
3318	Other accounts payable..........	....	....	....	....	....	....	....	....	....	....	....	....
332	Foreign..........	....	....	....	....	....	....	....	....	....	....	....	....
3322	Currency and deposits..........	....	....	....	....	....	....	....	....	....	....	....	....
3323	Securities other than shares..........	....	....	....	....	....	....	....	....	....	....	....	....
3324	Loans..........	....	....	....	....	....	....	....	....	....	....	....	....
3326	Insurance technical reserves..........	....	....	....	....	....	....	....	....	....	....	....	....
3327	Financial derivatives..........	....	....	....	....	....	....	....	....	....	....	....	....
3328	Other accounts payable..........	....	....	....	....	....	....	....	....	....	....	....	....
Table 4	**Holding gains in assets and liabilities**												
4	**Change in net worth from hold. gains**...	....	....	....	....	....	....	....	....	....	−15,451	−24,608	5,243
41	**Nonfinancial assets**..........	....	....	....	....	....	....	....	....	....	−20,827	−17,431	−11,836
411	Fixed assets..........	....	....	....	....	....	....	....	....	....	−5,097	−4,456	622
412	Inventories..........	....	....	....	....	....	....	....	....	....	−453	−157	−69
413	Valuables..........	....	....	....	....	....	....	....	....	....	—	—	—
414	Nonproduced assets..........	....	....	....	....	....	....	....	....	....	−15,278	−12,818	−12,389
42	**Financial assets**..........	....	....	....	....	....	....	....	....	....	5,382	−5,070	1,580
421	Domestic..........	....	....	....	....	....	....	....	....	....	....	....	....
422	Foreign..........	....	....	....	....	....	....	....	....	....	....	....	....
423	Monetary gold and SDRs..........	....	....	....	....	....	....	....	....	....	....	....	....
43	**Liabilities**..........	....	....	....	....	....	....	....	....	....	5	2,107	−15,499
431	Domestic..........	....	....	....	....	....	....	....	....	....	....	....	....
432	Foreign..........	....	....	....	....	....	....	....	....	....	....	....	....
Table 5	**Other changes in the volume of assets and liabilities**												
5	**Change in net worth from vol. chngs**.....	....	....	....	....	....	....	....	....	....	1,189	715	2,926
51	**Nonfinancial assets**..........	....	....	....	....	....	....	....	....	....	−209	−189	−252
511	Fixed assets..........	....	....	....	....	....	....	....	....	....	−209	−189	−252
512	Inventories..........	....	....	....	....	....	....	....	....	....	—	—	—
513	Valuables..........	....	....	....	....	....	....	....	....	....	—	—	—
514	Nonproduced assets..........	....	....	....	....	....	....	....	....	....	—	—	—
52	**Financial assets**..........	....	....	....	....	....	....	....	....	....	—	—	—
521	Domestic..........	....	....	....	....	....	....	....	....	....	....	....	....
522	Foreign..........	....	....	....	....	....	....	....	....	....	....	....	....
523	Monetary gold and SDRs..........	....	....	....	....	....	....	....	....	....	....	....	....
53	**Liabilities**..........	....	....	....	....	....	....	....	....	....	−1,398	−904	−3,177
531	Domestic..........	....	....	....	....	....	....	....	....	....	....	....	....
532	Foreign..........	....	....	....	....	....	....	....	....	....	....	....	....
Table 6	**Balance sheet**												
6	**Net worth**..........	....	....	....	....	....	....	....	....	....	144,167	107,244	80,552
61	**Nonfinancial assets**..........	....	....	....	....	....	....	....	....	....	470,756	463,606	459,077
611	Fixed assets..........	....	....	....	....	....	....	....	....	....	323,900	323,962	326,483
6111	Buildings and structures..........	....	....	....	....	....	....	....	....	....	....		....
6112	Machinery and equipment..........	....	....	....	....	....	....	....	....	....	....		....
6113	Other fixed assets..........	....	....	....	....	....	....	....	....	....	....		....
612	Inventories..........	....	....	....	....	....	....	....	....	....	4,529	4,394	4,351
613	Valuables..........	....	....	....	....	....	....	....	....	....	—	—	—
614	Nonproduced assets..........	....	....	....	....	....	....	....	....	....	142,327	135,250	128,243
6141	Land..........	....	....	....	....	....	....	....	....	....	142,327	135,250	128,243
6142	Subsoil assets..........	....	....	....	....	....	....	....	....	....	—	—	—
6143	Other naturally occurring assets..........	....	....	....	....	....	....	....	....	....	—	—	—
6144	Intangible nonproduced assets..........	....	....	....	....	....	....	....	....	....	—	—	—

In Billions of Yen / Year Beginning April 1 / Noncash Reporter

	Budgetary Central Government			Central Government			Local Government			General Government		
	2001	2002	2003	2001	2002	2003	2001	2002	2003	2001	2002	2003p
62 **Financial assets**............	....	....	....	....	....	....	....	....	....	426,590	432,831	441,280
621 Domestic............	....	....	....	....	....	....	....	....	....	....	....	....
6212 Currency and deposits............	....	....	....	....	....	....	....	....	....	....	....	....
6213 Securities other than shares............	....	....	....	....	....	....	....	....	....	....	....	....
6214 Loans............	....	....	....	....	....	....	....	....	....	....	....	....
6215 Shares and other equity............	....	....	....	....	....	....	....	....	....	....	....	....
6216 Insurance technical reserves............	....	....	....	....	....	....	....	....	....	....	....	....
6217 Financial derivatives............	....	....	....	....	....	....	....	....	....	....	....	....
6218 Other accounts receivable............	....	....	....	....	....	....	....	....	....	....	....	....
622 Foreign............	....	....	....	....	....	....	....	....	....	....	....	....
6222 Currency and deposits............	....	....	....	....	....	....	....	....	....	....	....	....
6223 Securities other than shares............	....	....	....	....	....	....	....	....	....	....	....	....
6224 Loans............	....	....	....	....	....	....	....	....	....	....	....	....
6225 Shares and other equity............	....	....	....	....	....	....	....	....	....	....	....	....
6226 Insurance technical reserves............	....	....	....	....	....	....	....	....	....	....	....	....
6227 Financial derivatives............	....	....	....	....	....	....	....	....	....	....	....	....
6228 Other accounts receivable............	....	....	....	....	....	....	....	....	....	....	....	....
623 Monetary gold and SDRs............	....	....	....	....	....	....	....	....	....	....	....	....
63 **Liabilities**............	....	....	....	....	....	....	....	....	....	753,179	789,193	819,805
631 Domestic............	....	....	....	....	....	....	....	....	....	....	....	....
6312 Currency and deposits............	....	....	....	....	....	....	....	....	....	....	....	....
6313 Securities other than shares............	....	....	....	....	....	....	....	....	....	....	....	....
6314 Loans............	....	....	....	....	....	....	....	....	....	....	....	....
6316 Insurance technical reserves............	....	....	....	....	....	....	....	....	....	....	....	....
6317 Financial derivatives............	....	....	....	....	....	....	....	....	....	....	....	....
6318 Other accounts payable............	....	....	....	....	....	....	....	....	....	....	....	....
632 Foreign............	....	....	....	....	....	....	....	....	....	....	....	....
6322 Currency and deposits............	....	....	....	....	....	....	....	....	....	....	....	....
6323 Securities other than shares............	....	....	....	....	....	....	....	....	....	....	....	....
6324 Loans............	....	....	....	....	....	....	....	....	....	....	....	....
6326 Insurance technical reserves............	....	....	....	....	....	....	....	....	....	....	....	....
6327 Financial derivatives............	....	....	....	....	....	....	....	....	....	....	....	....
6328 Other accounts payable............	....	....	....	....	....	....	....	....	....	....	....	....
Memorandum items:												
6M2 Net financial worth............	....	....	....	....	....	....	....	....	....	−326,589	−356,362	−378,525
6M3 Debt at market value............	....	....	....	....	....	....	....	....	....	....	....	....
6M4 Debt at nominal value............	....	....	....	....	....	....	....	....	....	....	....	....
6M5 Arrears............	....	....	....	....	....	....	....	....	....	....	....	....
6M6 Obligations for social security benefits............	....	....	....	....	....	....	....	....	....	....	....	....
6M7 Contingent liabilities............	....	....	....	....	....	....	....	....	....	....	....	....
6M8 Uncapitalized military weapons, systems........	....	....	....	....	....	....	....	....	....	....	....	....
Table 7 Outlays by functions of govt.												
7 **Total outlays**............	....	....	....	....	....	....	....	....	....	190,754	189,756	186,981
701 **General public services**............	....	....	....	....	....	....	....	....	....	27,328	27,930	27,031
7017 Public debt transactions............	....	....	....	....	....	....	....	....	....	15,754	14,874	13,874
7018 General transfers between levels of govt......	....	....	....	....	....	....	....	....	....	—	—	—
702 **Defense**............	....	....	....	....	....	....	....	....	....	4,871	4,824	4,851
703 **Public order and safety**............	....	....	....	....	....	....	....	....	....	7,079	7,038	7,012
704 **Economic affairs**............	....	....	....	....	....	....	....	....	....	23,335	22,364	21,183
7042 Agriculture, forestry, fishing, and hunting.....	....	....	....	....	....	....	....	....	....	....	....	....
7043 Fuel and energy............	....	....	....	....	....	....	....	....	....	....	....	....
7044 Mining, manufacturing, and construction.....	....	....	....	....	....	....	....	....	....	....	....	....
7045 Transport............	....	....	....	....	....	....	....	....	....	....	....	....
7046 Communication............	....	....	....	....	....	....	....	....	....	....	....	....
705 **Environmental protection**............	....	....	....	....	....	....	....	....	....	8,385	7,897	7,022
706 **Housing and community amenities**........	....	....	....	....	....	....	....	....	....	4,116	3,785	3,556
707 **Health**............	....	....	....	....	....	....	....	....	....	33,397	33,312	33,931
7072 Outpatient services............	....	....	....	....	....	....	....	....	....	....	....	....
7073 Hospital services............	....	....	....	....	....	....	....	....	....	....	....	....
7074 Public health services............	....	....	....	....	....	....	....	....	....	....	....	....
708 **Recreation, culture, and religion**............	....	....	....	....	....	....	....	....	....	911	856	831

In Billions of Yen / Year Beginning April 1 / Noncash Reporter

	Budgetary Central Government			Central Government			Local Government			General Government		
	2001	2002	2003	2001	2002	2003	2001	2002	2003	2001	2002	2003p
709 **Education**..............	....	....	....	....	....	....	....	....	....	20,688	20,318	20,155
7091 Pre-primary and primary education.............	....	....	....	....	....	....	....	....	....	....	....	....
7092 Secondary education....................	....	....	....	....	....	....	....	....	....	....	....	....
7094 Tertiary education..........................	....	....	....	....	....	....	....	....	....	....	....	....
710 **Social protection**......................	....	....	....	....	....	....	....	....	....	57,024	58,268	58,556
7 Statistical discrepancy: Total outlays.............	....	....	....	....	....	....	....	....	....	3,621	3,163	2,855
Table 8 Transactions in financial assets and liabilities by sector												
82 **Net acquisition of financial assets**.........	....	....	....	....	....	....	....	....	....	7,871	9,787	32,305
821 Domestic.........................	....	....	....	....	....	....	....	....	....	....	....	....
8211 General government...........................	....	....	....	....	....	....	....	....	....	....	....	....
8212 Central bank.................................	....	....	....	....	....	....	....	....	....	....	....	....
8213 Other depository corporations....................	....	....	....	....	....	....	....	....	....	....	....	....
8214 Financial corporations n.e.c......................	....	....	....	....	....	....	....	....	....	....	....	....
8215 Nonfinancial corporations.....................	....	....	....	....	....	....	....	....	....	....	....	....
8216 Households & NPIs serving households......	....	....	....	....	....	....	....	....	....	....	....	....
822 Foreign.......................	....	....	....	....	....	....	....	....	....	....	....	....
8221 General government...........................	....	....	....	....	....	....	....	....	....	....	....	....
8227 International organizations......................	....	....	....	....	....	....	....	....	....	....	....	....
8228 Financial corporations other than international organizations..............	....	....	....	....	....	....	....	....	....	....	....	....
8229 Other nonresidents.....................	....	....	....	....	....	....	....	....	....	....	....	....
823 Monetary gold and SDRs................	....	....	....	....	....	....	....	....	....	....	....	....
83 **Net incurrence of liabilities**....................	....	....	....	....	....	....	....	....	....	43,048	39,335	67,263
831 Domestic.........................	....	....	....	....	....	....	....	....	....	....	....	....
8311 General government...........................	....	....	....	....	....	....	....	....	....	....	....	....
8312 Central bank.................................	....	....	....	....	....	....	....	....	....	....	....	....
8313 Other depository corporations....................	....	....	....	....	....	....	....	....	....	....	....	....
8314 Financial corporations n.e.c......................	....	....	....	....	....	....	....	....	....	....	....	....
8315 Nonfinancial corporations.....................	....	....	....	....	....	....	....	....	....	....	....	....
8316 Households & NPIs serving households......	....	....	....	....	....	....	....	....	....	....	....	....
832 Foreign.......................	....	....	....	....	....	....	....	....	....	....	....	....
8321 General government...........................	....	....	....	....	....	....	....	....	....	....	....	....
8327 International organizations......................	....	....	....	....	....	....	....	....	....	....	....	....
8328 Financial corporations other than international organizations..............	....	....	....	....	....	....	....	....	....	....	....	....
8329 Other nonresidents.....................	....	....	....	....	....	....	....	....	....	....	....	....

In Millions of Dinars / Year Ending December 31 / Cash Reporter

	Budgetary Central Government			Central Government			Local Government			General Government		
	2002	2003	2004p	2002	2003	2004	2002	2003	2004	2002	2003	2004
Statement of government operations												
Statement of other economic flows												
Balance sheet												
6 *Net worth*..............................	....	....	....	....	....	....	....	....	....	....	....	....
61 Nonfinancial assets.................	....	....	....	....	....	....	....	....	....	....	....	....
62 Financial assets......................	....	....	....	....	....	....	....	....	....	....	....	....
63 Liabilities..............................	5,779.9	6,427.6	7,202.7	....	....	....	....	....	....	....	....	....
Statement of sources and uses of cash												
1 Cash receipts from operating activities...........	1,943.0	2,364.2	2,754.6	....	....	....	....	....	....	....	....	....
11 Taxes.................................	1,187.7	1,316.9	1,698.7	....	....	....	....	....	....	....	....	....
12 Social contributions...............	18.0	19.0	18.3	....	....	....	....	....	....	....	....	....
13 Grants...............................	266.7	683.9	667.1	....	....	....	....	....	....	....	....	....
14 Other receipts......................	470.7	344.4	370.5	....	....	....	....	....	....	....	....	....
2 Cash payments for operating activities...........	1,925.2	2,130.0	2,600.2	....	....	....	....	....	....	....	....	....
21 Compensation of employees......	1,290.7	1,436.3	1,500.9	....	....	....	....	....	....	....	....	....
22 Purchases of goods and services........	104.0	123.2	155.7	....	....	....	....	....	....	....	....	....
24 Interest..............................	176.7	170.7	161.1	....	....	....	....	....	....	....	....	....
25 Subsidies............................	135.8	145.5	308.2	....	....	....	....	....	....	....	....	....
26 Grants...............................	59.2	81.3	85.8	....	....	....	....	....	....	....	....	....
27 Social benefits......................	16.7	18.4	70.7	....	....	....	....	....	....	....	....	....
28 Other payments.....................	142.1	154.6	317.9	....	....	....	....	....	....	....	....	....
CIO *Net cash inflow from oper. activities.....*	*17.8*	*234.2*	*154.4*	....	....	....	....	....	....	....	....	....
31.1 Purchases of nonfinancial assets..................	234.6	260.5	270.9	....	....	....	....	....	....	....	....	....
31.2 Sales of nonfinancial assets........................	4.5	3.0	—	....	....	....	....	....	....	....	....	....
31 Net cash outflow from investments in nonfinancial assets..................	230.2	257.5	270.9	....	....	....	....	....	....	....	....	....
CSD *Cash surplus/deficit............................*	*−212.4*	*−23.3*	*−116.5*	....	....	....	....	....	....	....	....	....
32x Net acquisition of fin assets, excl. cash..........	−11.2	19.9	—	....	....	....	....	....	....	....	....	....
321x Domestic.......................	−11.2	19.9	—	....	....	....	....	....	....	....	....	....
322x Foreign.........................	—	—	—	....	....	....	....	....	....	....	....	....
323 Monetary gold and SDRs.......	—	—	—	....	....	....	....	....	....	....	....	....
33 Net incurrence of liabilities........................	†203.0	−132.9	6.0	....	....	....	....	....	....	....	....	....
331 Domestic.........................	†231.0	141.2	248.2	....	....	....	....	....	....	....	....	....
332 Foreign...........................	†−28.0	−274.1	−242.2	....	....	....	....	....	....	....	....	....
NFB Net cash inflow from fin. activities.................	214.3	−152.7	6.0	....	....	....	....	....	....	....	....	....
NCB *Net change in the stock of cash............*	*1.9*	*−176.1*	*−110.6*	....	....	....	....	....	....	....	....	....
Table 1 Revenue												
1 **Revenue**..	**1,943.0**	**2,364.2**	**2,754.6**	....	....	....	....	....	....	....	....	....
11 **Taxes**..	**1,187.7**	**1,316.9**	**1,698.7**	....	....	....	....	....	....	....	....	....
111 Taxes on income, profits, & capital gains......	196.2	195.4	217.9	....	....	....	....	....	....	....	....	....
1111 Individuals...........................	54.2	62.7	70.9	....	....	....	....	....	....	....	....	....
1112 Corporations and other enterprises...........	137.0	128.3	147.0	....	....	....	....	....	....	....	....	....
112 Taxes on payroll and workforce...................	24.9	30.3	40.2	....	....	....	....	....	....	....	....	....
113 Taxes on property...................	71.1	82.0	125.3	....	....	....	....	....	....	....	....	....
114 Taxes on goods and services................	554.5	671.8	895.0	....	....	....	....	....	....	....	....	....
1141 General taxes on goods and services...	525.9	643.0	856.2	....	....	....	....	....	....	....	....	....
1142 Excises...........................	—	—	—	....	....	....	....	....	....	....	....	....
115 Taxes on int'l. trade and transactions..........	256.7	247.4	309.9	....	....	....	....	....	....	....	....	....
116 Other taxes.........................	84.3	90.1	110.5	....	....	....	....	....	....	....	....	....
12 **Social contributions**...........................	**18.0**	**19.0**	**18.3**	....	....	....	....	....	....	....	....	....
121 Social security contributions.......................	18.0	19.0	18.3	....	....	....	....	....	....	....	....	....
122 Other social contributions...................	—	—	—	....	....	....	....	....	....	....	....	....
13 **Grants**..	**266.7**	**683.9**	**667.1**	....	....	....	....	....	....	....	....	....
131 From foreign governments.....................	245.0	655.5	667.1	....	....	....	....	....	....	....	....	....
132 From international organizations..................	21.7	28.4	—	....	....	....	....	....	....	....	....	....
133 From other general government units.............	—	—	—	....	....	....	....	....	....	....	....	....
14 **Other revenue**..................................	**470.7**	**344.4**	**370.5**	....	....	....	....	....	....	....	....	....
Table 2 Expense by economic type												
2 **Expense**..	**1,925.2**	**2,130.0**	**2,600.2**	....	....	....	....	....	....	....	....	....
21 **Compensation of employees**.................	**1,290.7**	**1,436.3**	**1,500.9**	....	....	....	....	....	....	....	....	....
211 Wages and salaries........................	970.5	1,090.7	1,123.6	....	....	....	....	....	....	....	....	....
212 Social contributions......................	320.2	345.6	377.4	....	....	....	....	....	....	....	....	....
22 **Use of goods and services**.....................	**104.0**	**123.2**	**155.7**	....	....	....	....	....	....	....	....	....
23 **Consumption of fixed capital**.................	....	....	....	....	....	....	....	....	....	....	....	....
24 **Interest**..	**176.7**	**170.7**	**161.1**	....	....	....	....	....	....	....	....	....
25 **Subsidies**......................................	**135.8**	**145.5**	**308.2**	....	....	....	....	....	....	....	....	....

In Millions of Dinars / Year Ending December 31 / Cash Reporter

		Budgetary Central Government			Central Government			Local Government			General Government		
		2002	2003	2004p	2002	2003	2004	2002	2003	2004	2002	2003	2004
26	Grants.........................	**59.2**	**81.3**	**85.8**	....	....	....	....	....	....	....	....	....
261	To foreign govenments................	1.4	....	1.8	....	....	....	....	....	....	....	....	....
262	To international organizations...........	—	....	—	....	....	....	....	....	....	....	....	....
263	To other general government units.....	57.8	....	84.0	....	....	....	....	....	....	....	....	....
2631	Current..................	57.8	....	68.0	....	....	....	....	....	....	....	....	....
2632	Capital..................	—	....	16.0	....	....	....	....	....	....	....	....	....
27	Social benefits.......................	**16.7**	**18.4**	**70.7**	....	....	....	....	....	....	....	....	....
28	Other expense......................	**142.1**	**154.6**	**317.9**	....	....	....	....	....	....	....	....	....
281	Property expense other than interest...........	—	....	—	....	....	....	....	....	....	....	....	....
282	Miscellaneous other expense.................	142.1	154.6	317.9	....	....	....	....	....	....	....	....	....
2821	Current..................	—	—	47.0	....	....	....	....	....	....	....	....	....
2822	Capital..................	142.1	154.6	270.9	....	....	....	....	....	....	....	....	....

Table 3 Transactions in assets and liabilities

		Budgetary Central Government			Central Government			Local Government			General Government		
3	**Change in net worth from transactns....**	....	....	....	....	....	....	....	....	....	....	....	....
31	**Net acquisition of nonfinancial assets...**	230.2	257.5	270.9	....	....	....	....	....	....	....	....	....
311	Fixed assets........................	211.2	226.5	234.5	....	....	....	....	....	....	....	....	....
3111	Buildings and structures..........................	175.8	....	189.3	....	....	....	....	....	....	....	....	....
3112	Machinery and equipment..................	28.5	....	37.3	....	....	....	....	....	....	....	....	....
3113	Other fixed assets..................	6.9	....	7.9	....	....	....	....	....	....	....	....	....
312	Inventories................	11.5	12.0	13.1	....	....	....	....	....	....	....	....	....
313	Valuables.....................	—	—	—	....	....	....	....	....	....	....	....	....
314	Nonproduced assets................	7.5	19.0	23.4	....	....	....	....	....	....	....	....	....
3141	Land.....................	....	....	23.4	....	....	....	....	....	....	....	....	....
3142	Subsoil assets..................	....	....	—	....	....	....	....	....	....	....	....	....
3143	Other naturally occurring assets............	....	....	—	....	....	....	....	....	....	....	....	....
3144	Intangible nonproduced assets.................	....	....	—	....	....	....	....	....	....	....	....	....
32	**Net acquisition of financial assets.........**	−9.4	−156.3	−110.6	....	....	....	....	....	....	....	....	....
321	Domestic....................	−11.2	....	—	....	....	....	....	....	....	....	....	....
3212	Currency and deposits.................	—	....	—	....	....	....	....	....	....	....	....	....
3213	Securities other than shares.................	....	....	—	....	....	....	....	....	....	....	....	....
3214	Loans....................	....	....	—	....	....	....	....	....	....	....	....	....
3215	Shares and other equity..................	....	....	—	....	....	....	....	....	....	....	....	....
3216	Insurance technical reserves.................	—	—	—	....	....	....	....	....	....	....	....	....
3217	Financial derivatives.................	—	—	—	....	....	....	....	....	....	....	....	....
3218	Other accounts receivable.................	....	....	....	....	....	....	....	....	....	....	....	....
322	Foreign....................	1.9	....	−110.6	....	....	....	....	....	....	....	....	....
3222	Currency and deposits.................	1.9	....	−110.6	....	....	....	....	....	....	....	....	....
3223	Securities other than shares.................	—	....	—	....	....	....	....	....	....	....	....	....
3224	Loans....................	....	....	—	....	....	....	....	....	....	....	....	....
3225	Shares and other equity..................	—	....	—	....	....	....	....	....	....	....	....	....
3226	Insurance technical reserves.................	—	—	—	....	....	....	....	....	....	....	....	....
3227	Financial derivatives.................	—	—	—	....	....	....	....	....	....	....	....	....
3228	Other accounts receivable.................	....	....	....	....	....	....	....	....	....	....	....	....
323	Monetary gold and SDRs..................	—	—	—	....	....	....	....	....	....	....	....	....
33	**Net incurrence of liabilities...................**	†203.0	−132.9	6.0	....	....	....	....	....	....	....	....	....
331	Domestic....................	†231.0	141.2	248.2	....	....	....	....	....	....	....	....	....
3312	Currency and deposits.................	....	....	....	....	....	....	....	....	....	....	....	....
3313	Securities other than shares.................	†234.5	189.0	....	....	....	....	....	....	....	....	....	....
3314	Loans....................	†106.2	....	....	....	....	....	....	....	....	....	....	....
3316	Insurance technical reserves.................	—	—	—	....	....	....	....	....	....	....	....	....
3317	Financial derivatives.................	—	—	—	....	....	....	....	....	....	....	....	....
3318	Other accounts payable.................	....	....	....	....	....	....	....	....	....	....	....	....
332	Foreign....................	†−28.0	−274.1	−242.2	....	....	....	....	....	....	....	....	....
3322	Currency and deposits.................	†—	—	—	....	....	....	....	....	....	....	....	....
3323	Securities other than shares.................	†—	—	—	....	....	....	....	....	....	....	....	....
3324	Loans....................	†−28.0	−274.1	−242.2	....	....	....	....	....	....	....	....	....
3326	Insurance technical reserves.................	†—	—	—	....	....	....	....	....	....	....	....	....
3327	Financial derivatives.................	†—	—	—	....	....	....	....	....	....	....	....	....
3328	Other accounts payable.................	....	....	....	....	....	....	....	....	....	....	....	....

In Millions of Dinars / Year Ending December 31 / Cash Reporter

	Budgetary Central Government			Central Government			Local Government			General Government		
	2002	2003	2004p	2002	2003	2004	2002	2003	2004	2002	2003	2004
Table 4 Holding gains in assets and liabilities												
Table 5 Other changes in the volume of assets and liabilities												
Table 6 Balance sheet												
6 Net worth	....	....	....	....	....	....	....	....	....	....	....	....
61 Nonfinancial assets	....	....	....	....	....	....	....	....	....	....	....	....
611 Fixed assets	....	....	....	....	....	....	....	....	....	....	....	....
6111 Buildings and structures	....	....	....	....	....	....	....	....	....	....	....	....
6112 Machinery and equipment	....	....	....	....	....	....	....	....	....	....	....	....
6113 Other fixed assets	....	....	....	....	....	....	....	....	....	....	....	....
612 Inventories	....	....	....	....	....	....	....	....	....	....	....	....
613 Valuables	....	....	....	....	....	....	....	....	....	....	....	....
614 Nonproduced assets	....	....	....	....	....	....	....	....	....	....	....	....
6141 Land	....	....	....	....	....	....	....	....	....	....	....	....
6142 Subsoil assets	....	....	....	....	....	....	....	....	....	....	....	....
6143 Other naturally occurring assets	....	....	....	....	....	....	....	....	....	....	....	....
6144 Intangible nonproduced assets	....	....	....	....	....	....	....	....	....	....	....	....
62 Financial assets	....	....	....	....	....	....	....	....	....	....	....	....
621 Domestic	....	....	....	....	....	....	....	....	....	....	....	....
6212 Currency and deposits	....	....	....	....	....	....	....	....	....	....	....	....
6213 Securities other than shares	....	....	....	....	....	....	....	....	....	....	....	....
6214 Loans	....	....	....	....	....	....	....	....	....	....	....	....
6215 Shares and other equity	....	....	....	....	....	....	....	....	....	....	....	....
6216 Insurance technical reserves	....	....	....	....	....	....	....	....	....	....	....	....
6217 Financial derivatives	....	....	....	....	....	....	....	....	....	....	....	....
6218 Other accounts receivable	....	....	....	....	....	....	....	....	....	....	....	....
622 Foreign	....	....	....	....	....	....	....	....	....	....	....	....
6222 Currency and deposits	....	....	....	....	....	....	....	....	....	....	....	....
6223 Securities other than shares	....	....	....	....	....	....	....	....	....	....	....	....
6224 Loans	....	....	....	....	....	....	....	....	....	....	....	....
6225 Shares and other equity	....	....	....	....	....	....	....	....	....	....	....	....
6226 Insurance technical reserves	....	....	....	....	....	....	....	....	....	....	....	....
6227 Financial derivatives	....	....	....	....	....	....	....	....	....	....	....	....
6228 Other accounts receivable	....	....	....	....	....	....	....	....	....	....	....	....
623 Monetary gold and SDRs	....	....	....	....	....	....	....	....	....	....	....	....
63 Liabilities	5,779.9	6,427.6	7,202.7	....	....	....	....	....	....	....	....	....
631 Domestic	1,288.8	1,521.4	1,954.8	....	....	....	....	....	....	....	....	....
6312 Currency and deposits	....	....	....	....	....	....	....	....	....	....	....	....
6313 Securities other than shares	....	....	....	....	....	....	....	....	....	....	....	....
6314 Loans	....	....	....	....	....	....	....	....	....	....	....	....
6316 Insurance technical reserves	....	....	....	....	....	....	....	....	....	....	....	....
6317 Financial derivatives	....	....	....	....	....	....	....	....	....	....	....	....
6318 Other accounts payable	....	....	....	....	....	....	....	....	....	....	....	....
632 Foreign	4,491.1	4,906.2	5,247.9	....	....	....	....	....	....	....	....	....
6322 Currency and deposits	....	....	....	....	....	....	....	....	....	....	....	....
6323 Securities other than shares	....	....	....	....	....	....	....	....	....	....	....	....
6324 Loans	....	....	....	....	....	....	....	....	....	....	....	....
6326 Insurance technical reserves	....	....	....	....	....	....	....	....	....	....	....	....
6327 Financial derivatives	....	....	....	....	....	....	....	....	....	....	....	....
6328 Other accounts payable	....	....	....	....	....	....	....	....	....	....	....	....
Memorandum items:												
6M2 Net financial worth	....	....	....	....	....	....	....	....	....	....	....	....
6M3 Debt at market value	....	....	....	....	....	....	....	....	....	....	....	....
6M4 Debt at nominal value	....	....	....	....	....	....	....	....	....	....	....	....
6M5 Arrears	....	....	....	....	....	....	....	....	....	....	....	....
6M6 Obligations for social security benefits	....	....	....	....	....	....	....	....	....	....	....	....
6M7 Contingent liabilities	....	....	....	....	....	....	....	....	....	....	....	....
6M8 Uncapitalized military weapons, systems	....	....	....	....	....	....	....	....	....	....	....	....
Table 7 Outlays by functions of govt.												
7 Total outlays	2,155.4	2,387.6	2,871.2	....	....	....	....	....	....	....	....	....
701 General public services	655.3	730.6	1,217.3	....	....	....	....	....	....	....	....	....
7017 Public debt transactions	176.7	170.7	161.1	....	....	....	....	....	....	....	....	....
7018 General transfers between levels of govt	....	....	....	....	....	....	....	....	....	....	....	....
702 Defense	439.0	517.6	425.0	....	....	....	....	....	....	....	....	....
703 Public order and safety	184.7	211.6	261.1	....	....	....	....	....	....	....	....	....

In Millions of Dinars / Year Ending December 31 / Cash Reporter

		Budgetary Central Government			Central Government			Local Government			General Government		
		2002	2003	2004p	2002	2003	2004	2002	2003	2004	2002	2003	2004
704	**Economic affairs**.....................	**80.0**	**77.0**	**133.5**	....	....	....	....	....	....	....	....	....
7042	Agriculture, forestry, fishing, and hunting.....	25.6	25.1	73.1	....	....	....	....	....	....	....	....	....
7043	Fuel and energy.........................	5.4	1.0	20.7	....	....	....	....	....	....	....	....	....
7044	Mining, manufacturing, and construction.....	19.7	4.1	16.4	....	....	....	....	....	....	....	....	....
7045	Transport.........................	29.3	14.8	15.4	....	....	....	....	....	....	....	....	....
7046	Communication.........................	—	5.8	7.8	....	....	....	....	....	....	....	....	....
705	**Environmental protection**.....................	**75.3**	**87.2**	**36.2**	....	....	....	....	....	....	....	....	....
706	**Housing and community amenities**........	**54.1**	**58.9**	**63.5**	....	....	....	....	....	....	....	....	....
707	**Health**.....................	**233.9**	**246.3**	**279.8**	....	....	....	....	....	....	....	....	....
7072	Outpatient services.....................	38.3	....	41.6	....	....	....	....	....	....	....	....	....
7073	Hospital services.....................	157.3	....	188.3	....	....	....	....	....	....	....	....	....
7074	Public health services.....................	38.5	....	50.0	....	....	....	....	....	....	....	....	....
708	**Recreation, culture, and religion**............	**37.3**	**45.8**	**52.5**	....	....	....	....	....	....	....	....	....
709	**Education**.....................	**330.4**	**355.4**	**377.0**	....	....	....	....	....	....	....	....	....
7091	Pre-primary and primary education.............	19.1	....	292.0	....	....	....	....	....	....	....	....	....
7092	Secondary education.....................	253.3	....	5.6	....	....	....	....	....	....	....	....	....
7094	Tertiary education.....................	58.0	....	79.4	....	....	....	....	....	....	....	....	....
710	**Social protection**.....................	**65.4**	**57.2**	**48.8**	....	....	....	....	....	....	....	....	....
7	Statistical discrepancy: Total outlays..............	—	—	−23.3	....	....	....	....	....	....	....	....	....

Table 8 Transactions in financial assets and liabilities by sector

		Budgetary Central Government			Central Government			Local Government			General Government		
82	**Net acquisition of financial assets**........	**−9.4**	**−156.3**	**−110.6**	....	....	....	....	....	....	....	....	....
821	Domestic.........................	−11.2	....	—	....	....	....	....	....	....	....	....	....
8211	General government.....................	....	....	....	....	....	....	....	....	....	....	....	....
8212	Central bank.........................	....	....	....	....	....	....	....	....	....	....	....	....
8213	Other depository corporations.....................	....	....	....	....	....	....	....	....	....	....	....	....
8214	Financial corporations n.e.c.....................	....	....	....	....	....	....	....	....	....	....	....	....
8215	Nonfinancial corporations.....................	....	....	....	....	....	....	....	....	....	....	....	....
8216	Households & NPIs serving households......	....	....	....	....	....	....	....	....	....	....	....	....
822	Foreign.........................	1.9	....	−110.6	....	....	....	....	....	....	....	....	....
8221	General government.....................	....	....	....	....	....	....	....	....	....	....	....	....
8227	International organizations.....................	....	....	....	....	....	....	....	....	....	....	....	....
8228	Financial corporations other than international organizations.............	....	....	....	....	....	....	....	....	....	....	....	....
8229	Other nonresidents.....................	....	....	....	....	....	....	....	....	....	....	....	....
823	Monetary gold and SDRs.....................	—	—	—	....	....	....	....	....	....	....	....	....
83	**Net incurrence of liabilities**...................	**†203.0**	**−132.9**	**6.0**	....	....	....	....	....	....	....	....	....
831	Domestic.........................	†231.0	141.2	248.2	....	....	....	....	....	....	....	....	....
8311	General government.....................	....	....	....	....	....	....	....	....	....	....	....	....
8312	Central bank.........................	....	....	....	....	....	....	....	....	....	....	....	....
8313	Other depository corporations.....................	....	....	....	....	....	....	....	....	....	....	....	....
8314	Financial corporations n.e.c.....................	....	....	....	....	....	....	....	....	....	....	....	....
8315	Nonfinancial corporations.....................	....	....	....	....	....	....	....	....	....	....	....	....
8316	Households & NPIs serving households......	....	....	....	....	....	....	....	....	....	....	....	....
832	Foreign.........................	†−28.0	−274.1	−242.2	....	....	....	....	....	....	....	....	....
8321	General government.....................	†−109.4	−86.3	....	....	....	....	....	....	....	....	....	....
8327	International organizations.....................	†51.8	−156.4	....	....	....	....	....	....	....	....	....	....
8328	Financial corporations other than international organizations.............	†—	—	....	....	....	....	....	....	....	....	....	....
8329	Other nonresidents.....................	†29.6	−31.5	....	....	....	....	....	....	....	....	....	....

Kazakhstan 916

In Billions of Tenge / Year Ending December 31 / Cash Reporter

		Budgetary Central Government			Central Government			Local Government			General Government		
		2002	2003	2004	2002	2003	2004	2002	2003	2004	2002	2003	2004
Statement of government operations													
Statement of other economic flows													
Balance sheet													
6	*Net worth*	....	....	....	....	....	....	....	....	....	....	....	....
61	Nonfinancial assets	....	....	....	....	....	....	....	....	....	....	....	....
62	Financial assets	....	....	....	....	....	....	....	....	....	....	....	....
63	Liabilities	....	....	....	579.90	609.59	....	....	....	....	....	....	....
Statement of sources and uses of cash													
1	Cash receipts from operating activities	....	....	....	548.83	700.37	955.68	375.56	472.36	587.87	798.36	992.06	1,267.64
11	Taxes	....	....	....	458.23	603.40	816.46	294.56	343.86	369.68	752.78	947.25	1,186.14
12	Social contributions	....	....	....	—	—	—	—	—	—	—	—	—
13	Grants	....	....	....	49.06	57.63	66.67	76.78	122.93	209.06	—	—	—
14	Other receipts	....	....	....	41.54	39.35	72.55	4.22	5.58	9.13	45.57	44.81	81.50
2	Cash payments for operating activities	....	....	....	479.25	640.48	825.97	317.55	367.18	472.96	670.77	826.99	1,023.02
21	Compensation of employees	....	....	....	46.55	50.06	74.88	105.45	120.85	162.53	152.00	170.91	237.41
22	Purchases of goods and services	....	....	....	132.68	163.79	202.93	114.02	138.24	180.79	246.70	302.03	383.72
24	Interest	....	....	....	38.35	34.34	34.12	.87	1.17	1.03	39.03	35.40	34.97
25	Subsidies	....	....	....	3.04	7.47	9.47	11.54	14.82	20.71	14.58	22.30	30.19
26	Grants	....	....	....	77.48	124.05	210.74	49.06	57.63	66.67	.70	1.13	1.68
27	Social benefits	....	....	....	163.01	197.97	228.92	27.59	27.31	26.32	190.60	225.28	255.24
28	Other payments	....	....	....	18.14	62.79	64.91	9.01	7.16	14.90	27.15	69.95	79.81
CIO	*Net cash inflow from oper. activities*	....	....	....	*69.58*	*59.90*	*129.71*	*58.01*	*105.17*	*114.91*	*127.59*	*165.07*	*244.62*
31.1	Purchases of nonfinancial assets	....	....	....	62.38	94.33	122.92	67.92	105.65	142.00	130.30	199.98	264.91
31.2	Sales of nonfinancial assets	....	....	....	5.94	6.26	6.18	3.55	6.25	12.92	9.49	12.50	19.10
31	Net cash outflow from investments in nonfinancial assets	....	....	....	56.44	88.08	116.74	64.37	99.40	129.08	120.81	187.48	245.82
CSD	*Cash surplus/deficit*	....	....	....	*13.14*	*−28.18*	*12.97*	*−6.36*	*5.77*	*−14.17*	*6.78*	*−22.41*	*−1.20*
32x	Net acquisition of fin assets, excl. cash	....	....	....	−.92	21.21	25.02	1.52	−1.44	−3.36	.45	20.38	10.41
321x	Domestic	....	....	....	−1.19	19.92	24.75	1.52	−1.44	−3.36	.18	19.10	10.13
322x	Foreign	....	....	....	.27	1.29	.27	—	—	—	.27	1.29	.27
323	Monetary gold and SDRs	....	....	....	—	—	—	—	—	—	—	—	—
33	Net incurrence of liabilities	....	....	....	−14.42	58.41	14.84	−.29	−.89	8.47	−15.33	58.14	12.29
331	Domestic	....	....	....	37.50	51.14	64.21	−.29	−.89	8.47	36.59	50.87	61.66
332	Foreign	....	....	....	−51.92	7.28	−49.37	—	—	—	−51.92	7.28	−49.37
NFB	Net cash inflow from fin. activities	....	....	....	−13.51	37.20	−10.18	−1.81	.55	11.83	−15.78	37.76	1.89
NCB	*Net change in the stock of cash*	....	....	....	*−.36*	*9.03*	*2.79*	*−8.17*	*6.33*	*−2.34*	*−9.00*	*15.35*	*.69*

Table 1 Revenue

		Budgetary Central Government			Central Government			Local Government			General Government		
		2002	2003	2004	2002	2003	2004	2002	2003	2004	2002	2003	2004
1	**Revenue**	....	....	....	548.83	700.37	955.68	375.56	472.36	587.87	798.36	992.06	1,267.64
11	**Taxes**	....	....	....	458.23	603.40	816.46	294.56	343.86	369.68	752.78	947.25	1,186.14
111	Taxes on income, profits, & capital gains	....	....	....	209.05	272.63	382.81	77.38	93.28	98.53	286.44	365.91	481.35
1111	Individuals	....	....	....	—	—	—	77.38	93.28	98.53	77.38	93.28	98.53
1112	Corporations and other enterprises	....	....	....	209.05	272.63	382.81	—	—	—	209.05	272.63	382.81
112	Taxes on payroll and workforce	....	....	....	—	—	—	133.85	157.68	168.00	133.85	157.68	168.00
113	Taxes on property	....	....	....	—	—	—	35.28	33.06	37.87	35.28	33.06	37.87
114	Taxes on goods and services	....	....	....	208.45	286.04	381.74	44.72	54.52	58.93	253.17	340.56	440.68
1141	General taxes on goods and services	....	....	....	166.41	222.16	234.79	9.52	9.18	8.17	175.94	231.34	242.96
1142	Excises	....	....	....	4.09	6.02	8.42	21.35	20.97	21.49	25.44	26.99	29.91
115	Taxes on int'l. trade and transactions	....	....	....	38.60	42.49	50.34	—	—	—	38.60	42.49	50.34
116	Other taxes	....	....	....	2.12	2.24	1.56	3.33	5.31	6.34	5.44	7.55	7.90
12	**Social contributions**	....	....	....	—	—	—	—	—	—	—	—	—
121	Social security contributions	....	....	....	—	—	—	—	—	—	—	—	—
122	Other social contributions	....	....	....	—	—	—	—	—	—	—	—	—
13	**Grants**	....	....	....	49.06	57.63	66.67	76.78	122.93	209.06	—	—	—
131	From foreign governments	....	....	....	—	—	—	—	—	—	—	—	—
132	From international organizations	....	....	....	—	—	—	—	—	—	—	—	—
133	From other general government units	....	....	....	49.06	57.63	66.67	76.78	122.93	209.06	—	—	—
14	**Other revenue**	....	....	....	41.54	39.35	72.55	4.22	5.58	9.13	45.57	44.81	81.50

Table 2 Expense by economic type

		Budgetary Central Government			Central Government			Local Government			General Government		
		2002	2003	2004	2002	2003	2004	2002	2003	2004	2002	2003	2004
2	**Expense**	....	....	....	479.25	640.48	825.97	317.55	367.18	472.96	670.77	826.99	1,023.02
21	**Compensation of employees**	....	....	....	46.55	50.06	74.88	105.45	120.85	162.53	152.00	170.91	237.41
211	Wages and salaries	....	....	....	42.84	45.85	69.72	90.81	103.98	142.00	133.65	149.83	211.72
212	Social contributions	....	....	....	3.72	4.22	5.16	14.63	16.86	20.53	18.35	21.08	25.69
22	**Use of goods and services**	....	....	....	132.68	163.79	202.93	114.02	138.24	180.79	246.70	302.03	383.72
23	**Consumption of fixed capital**	....	....	....	....	....	....	....	....	....	....	....	....
24	**Interest**	....	....	....	38.35	34.34	34.12	.87	1.17	1.03	39.03	35.40	34.97
25	**Subsidies**	....	....	....	3.04	7.47	9.47	11.54	14.82	20.71	14.58	22.30	30.19

In Billions of Tenge / Year Ending December 31 / Cash Reporter

	Budgetary Central Government			Central Government			Local Government			General Government		
	2002	2003	2004	2002	2003	2004	2002	2003	2004	2002	2003	2004
26 Grants..................................	....	....	....	77.48	124.05	210.74	49.06	57.63	66.67	.70	1.13	1.68
261 To foreign govenments...............	....	....	....	—	—	—	—	—	—	—	—	—
262 To international organizations........	....	....	....	.70	1.13	1.68	—	—	—	.70	1.13	1.68
263 To other general government units.......	....	....	....	76.78	122.93	209.06	49.06	57.63	66.67	—	—	—
2631 Current.............................	....	....	....	63.55	84.56	145.14	49.06	57.63	66.67	—	—	—
2632 Capital.............................	....	....	....	13.23	38.37	63.92	—	—	—	—	—	—
27 Social benefits.........................	....	....	....	163.01	197.97	228.92	27.59	27.31	26.32	190.60	225.28	255.24
28 Other expense.........................	....	....	....	18.14	62.79	64.91	9.01	7.16	14.90	27.15	69.95	79.81
281 Property expense other than interest............	....			—	—	—	—	—	—	—	—	—
282 Miscellaneous other expense............	....			18.14	62.79	64.91	9.01	7.16	14.90	27.15	69.95	79.81
2821 Current..............................	....	....	....	14.59	16.32	12.49	.22	.39	.20	14.81	16.71	12.69
2822 Capital..............................	....	....	....	3.55	46.47	52.42	8.79	6.77	14.70	12.34	53.24	67.12

Table 3 Transactions in assets and liabilities

	Budgetary Central Government			Central Government			Local Government			General Government		
	2002	2003	2004	2002	2003	2004	2002	2003	2004	2002	2003	2004
3 Change in net worth from transactns....	....	....	....	....	....	....	....	....	....	....	....	....
31 Net acquisition of nonfinancial assets...	....	....	....	56.44	88.08	116.74	64.37	99.40	129.08	120.81	187.48	245.82
311 Fixed assets.............................	....	....	....	55.94	86.92	112.84	67.80	105.49	141.64	123.74	192.41	254.48
3111 Buildings and structures.............	....	....	....	....	71.54	91.72	....	94.30	126.10	....	165.84	217.82
3112 Machinery and equipment............	....	....	....	....	15.38	21.12	....	11.19	15.54	....	26.57	36.66
3113 Other fixed assets....................	....	....	....	....	—	—	....	—	—	....	—	—
312 Inventories.............................	....	....	....	−.07	.19	1.37	—	—	—	−.07	.19	1.37
313 Valuables..............................	....	....	....	—	—	—	—	—	—	—	—	—
314 Nonproduced assets....................	....	....	....	.57	.97	2.53	−3.43	−6.09	−12.57	−2.86	−5.12	−10.03
3141 Land................................	....	....	....	—	—	1.07	−3.44	−6.12	−12.68	−3.44	−6.12	−11.61
3142 Subsoil assets.......................	....	....	....	—	—	—	—	—	—	—	—	—
3143 Other naturally occurring assets.....	....	....	....	—	—	—	—	—	—	—	—	—
3144 Intangible nonproduced assets.......	....	....	....	.57	.97	1.46	.01	.04	.12	.58	1.00	1.58
32 Net acquisition of financial assets........	....	....	....	−1.28	30.23	27.81	−6.65	4.89	−5.70	−8.55	35.73	11.10
321 Domestic..............................	....	....	....	−1.55	28.95	27.54	−6.65	4.89	−5.70	−8.82	34.45	10.83
3212 Currency and deposits...............	....	....	....	−.36	9.03	2.79	−8.17	6.33	−2.34	−9.00	15.35	.69
3213 Securities other than shares.........	....	....	....	—	—	—	—	—	—	—	—	—
3214 Loans...............................	....	....	....	17.57	22.39	29.96	2.10	−.53	−1.48	19.52	22.47	17.22
3215 Shares and other equity.............	....	....	....	−18.75	−2.47	−5.21	−.59	−.91	−1.88	−19.34	−3.38	−7.09
3216 Insurance technical reserves.........	....	....	....	—	—	—	—	—	—	—	—	—
3217 Financial derivatives.................	....	....	....	—	—	—	—	—	—	—	—	—
3218 Other accounts receivable...........	....	....	....	.27	1.29	.27	....	—	....	.27	1.29	.27
322 Foreign...............................	....	....	....	—	—	—	—	—	—	—	—	—
3222 Currency and deposits...............	....	....	....	—	—	—	—	—	—	—	—	—
3223 Securities other than shares.........	....	....	....	—	1.03	—	—	—	—	—	1.03	—
3224 Loans...............................	....	....	....	.27	.26	.27	—	—	—	.27	.26	.27
3225 Shares and other equity.............	....	....	....	—	—	—	—	—	—	—	—	—
3226 Insurance technical reserves.........	....	....	....	—	—	—	—	—	—	—	—	—
3227 Financial derivatives.................	....	....	....	....	....	....	....	....	....	....	....	....
3228 Other accounts receivable...........	....	....	....	—	—	—	—	—	—	—	—	—
323 Monetary gold and SDRs...............	....	....	....	−14.42	58.41	14.84	−.29	−.89	8.47	−15.33	58.14	12.29
33 Net incurrence of liabilities..................	....	....	....	37.50	51.14	64.21	−.29	−.89	8.47	36.59	50.87	61.66
331 Domestic..............................	....	....	....	—	—	—	—	—	—	—	—	—
3312 Currency and deposits...............	....	....	....	37.83	51.14	64.21	2.34	4.69	8.47	39.56	55.83	61.66
3313 Securities other than shares.........	....	....	....	−.33	—	—	−2.63	−5.58	—	−2.96	−4.96	—
3314 Loans...............................	....	....	....	—	—	—	—	—	—	—	—	—
3316 Insurance technical reserves.........	....	....	....	—	—	—	—	—	—	—	—	—
3317 Financial derivatives.................	....	....	....	....	....	....	....	....	....	....	....	....
3318 Other accounts payable..............	....	....	....	−51.92	7.28	−49.37	—	—	—	−51.92	7.28	−49.37
332 Foreign...............................	....	....	....	—	—	—	—	—	—	—	—	—
3322 Currency and deposits...............	....	....	....	−54.09	—	−39.93	—	—	—	−54.09	—	−39.93
3323 Securities other than shares.........	....	....	....	2.17	7.28	−9.44	—	—	—	2.17	7.28	−9.44
3324 Loans...............................	....	....	....	—	—	—	—	—	—	—	—	—
3326 Insurance technical reserves.........	....	....	....	—	—	—	—	—	—	—	—	—
3327 Financial derivatives.................	....	....	....	....	....	....	....	....	....	....	....	....
3328 Other accounts payable..............	....	....	....									

Kazakhstan 916

In Billions of Tenge / Year Ending December 31 / Cash Reporter

	Budgetary Central Government			Central Government			Local Government			General Government		
	2002	2003	2004	2002	2003	2004	2002	2003	2004	2002	2003	2004
Table 4 Holding gains in assets and liabilities												
Table 5 Other changes in the volume of assets and liabilities												
Table 6 Balance sheet												
6 Net worth....................	....	....	....	....	....	....	....	....	....	....	....	....
61 Nonfinancial assets....................	....	....	....	....	....	....	....	....	....	....	....	....
611 Fixed assets....................	....	....	....	....	....	....	....	....	....	....	....	....
6111 Buildings and structures....................	....	....	....	....	....	....	....	....	....	....	....	....
6112 Machinery and equipment....................	....	....	....	....	....	....	....	....	....	....	....	....
6113 Other fixed assets....................	....	....	....	....	....	....	....	....	....	....	....	....
612 Inventories....................	....	....	....	....	....	....	....	....	....	....	....	....
613 Valuables....................	....	....	....	....	....	....	....	....	....	....	....	....
614 Nonproduced assets....................	....	....	....	....	....	....	....	....	....	....	....	....
6141 Land....................	....	....	....	....	....	....	....	....	....	....	....	....
6142 Subsoil assets....................	....	....	....	....	....	....	....	....	....	....	....	....
6143 Other naturally occurring assets....................	....	....	....	....	....	....	....	....	....	....	....	....
6144 Intangible nonproduced assets....................	....	....	....	....	....	....	....	....	....	....	....	....
62 **Financial assets**....................	....	....	....	....	....	....	....	....	....	....	....	....
621 Domestic....................	....	....	....	....	....	....	....	....	....	....	....	....
6212 Currency and deposits....................	....	....	....	....	....	....	....	....	....	....	....	....
6213 Securities other than shares....................	....	....	....	....	....	....	....	....	....	....	....	....
6214 Loans....................	....	....	....	....	....	....	....	....	....	....	....	....
6215 Shares and other equity....................	....	....	....	....	....	....	....	....	....	....	....	....
6216 Insurance technical reserves....................	....	....	....	....	....	....	....	....	....	....	....	....
6217 Financial derivatives....................	....	....	....	....	....	....	....	....	....	....	....	....
6218 Other accounts receivable....................	....	....	....	....	....	....	....	....	....	....	....	....
622 Foreign....................	....	....	....	....	....	....	....	....	....	....	....	....
6222 Currency and deposits....................	....	....	....	....	....	....	....	....	....	....	....	....
6223 Securities other than shares....................	....	....	....	....	....	....	....	....	....	....	....	....
6224 Loans....................	....	....	....	....	....	....	....	....	....	....	....	....
6225 Shares and other equity....................	....	....	....	....	....	....	....	....	....	....	....	....
6226 Insurance technical reserves....................	....	....	....	....	....	....	....	....	....	....	....	....
6227 Financial derivatives....................	....	....	....	....	....	....	....	....	....	....	....	....
6228 Other accounts receivable....................	....	....	....	....	....	....	....	....	....	....	....	....
623 Monetary gold and SDRs....................	....	....	....	....	....	....	....	....	....	....	....	....
63 **Liabilities**....................	....	....	....	579.90	609.59	....	....	....	....	....	....	....
631 Domestic....................	....	....	....	121.80	166.37	....	....	....	....	....	....	....
6312 Currency and deposits....................	....	....	....	—	—	....	....	....	....	....	....	....
6313 Securities other than shares....................	....	....	....	108.46	165.65	....	....	....	....	....	....	....
6314 Loans....................	....	....	....	13.34	.72	....	....	....	....	....	....	....
6316 Insurance technical reserves....................	....	....	....	—	—	....	....	....	....	....	....	....
6317 Financial derivatives....................	....	....	....	—	—	....	....	....	....	....	....	....
6318 Other accounts payable....................	....	....	....	....	....	....	....	....	....	....	....	....
632 Foreign....................	....	....	....	458.09	443.22	....	....	....	....	....	....	....
6322 Currency and deposits....................	....	....	....	—	—	....	....	....	....	....	....	....
6323 Securities other than shares....................	....	....	....	101.14	—	....	....	....	....	....	....	....
6324 Loans....................	....	....	....	356.95	443.22	....	....	....	....	....	....	....
6326 Insurance technical reserves....................	....	....	....	—	—	....	....	....	....	....	....	....
6327 Financial derivatives....................	....	....	....	—	—	....	....	....	....	....	....	....
6328 Other accounts payable....................	....	....	....	....	....	....	....	....	....	....	....	....
Memorandum items:												
6M2 Net financial worth....................	....	....	....	....	....	....	....	....	....	....	....	....
6M3 Debt at market value....................	....	....	....	....	....	....	....	....	....	....	....	....
6M4 Debt at nominal value....................	....	....	....	....	....	....	....	....	....	....	....	....
6M5 Arrears....................	....	....	....	....	....	....	....	....	....	....	....	....
6M6 Obligations for social security benefits....................	....	....	....	....	....	....	....	....	....	....	....	....
6M7 Contingent liabilities....................	....	....	....	....	....	....	....	....	....	....	....	....
6M8 Uncapitalized military weapons, systems....................	....	....	....	....	....	....	....	....	....	....	....	....
Table 7 Outlays by functions of govt.												
7 Total outlays....................	....	....	....	541.63	734.81	948.89	385.47	472.83	614.95	801.07	1,026.97	1,287.93
701 General public services....................	....	....	....	156.55	240.38	290.50	62.59	111.01	117.51	97.14	199.62	199.79
7017 Public debt transactions....................	....	....	....	38.35	34.34	34.12	.87	1.17	1.03	39.03	35.40	34.97
7018 General transfers between levels of govt......	....	....	....	....	....	....	....	....	....	....	....	....
702 Defense....................	....	....	....	30.90	40.44	48.24	6.81	7.15	10.05	37.71	47.48	58.01
703 Public order and safety....................	....	....	....	61.12	73.82	94.79	16.62	17.77	24.49	77.74	91.59	118.56

	Budgetary Central Government			Central Government			Local Government			General Government		
	2002	2003	2004	2002	2003	2004	2002	2003	2004	2002	2003	2004
704 **Economic affairs**........................	....	....	....	89.43	109.91	167.88	58.67	33.67	48.90	144.06	137.48	196.13
7042 Agriculture, forestry, fishing, and hunting.....	....	....	....	23.64	40.37	58.94	2.08	4.50	4.99	25.59	42.74	63.87
7043 Fuel and energy.........................	....	....	....	2.66	8.49	24.88	—	.78	9.13	2.66	8.49	25.32
7044 Mining, manufacturing, and construction.....	....	....	....	5.42	1.39	1.60	1.29	2.50	.76	6.71	3.90	2.35
7045 Transport...............................	....	....	....	38.73	57.99	81.15	16.24	23.15	34.03	54.97	78.15	103.27
7046 Communication..........................	....	....	....	.51	1.67	1.32	—	2.73	—	.51	4.21	1.32
705 **Environmental protection**...............	....	....	....	1.63	2.67	5.43	1.55	2.54	3.59	3.18	4.46	8.16
706 **Housing and community amenities**.......	....	....	....	—	10.32	26.28	24.73	34.54	67.56	24.73	34.54	69.06
707 **Health**.................................	....	....	....	12.02	19.10	29.22	59.10	74.11	107.07	71.12	89.78	131.18
7072 Outpatient services......................	....	....	....	....	—	—	....	13.24	20.01	....	13.24	20.01
7073 Hospital services........................	....	....	....	.60	1.04	1.94	15.69	17.63	45.72	16.29	18.27	47.66
7074 Public health services...................	....	....	....	....	18.07	27.28	....	43.23	41.34	....	58.27	63.51
708 **Recreation, culture, and religion**.........	....	....	....	8.14	12.88	18.99	14.69	20.91	28.37	22.83	33.79	43.95
709 **Education**..............................	....	....	....	16.45	23.24	34.57	104.70	130.98	167.36	121.14	148.99	190.75
7091 Pre-primary and primary education............	....	....	....	—	5.95	6.68	3.88	115.76	148.26	3.88	117.75	150.39
7092 Secondary education.....................	....	....	....	2.88	4.79	12.02	96.61	15.21	19.10	99.49	18.74	24.49
7094 Tertiary education.......................	....	....	....	11.89	12.49	15.87	—	—	—	11.89	12.49	15.87
710 **Social protection**.......................	....	....	....	165.39	202.04	233.00	36.03	40.14	40.04	201.42	239.23	272.33
7 Statistical discrepancy: Total outlays..............	....	....	....	—	—	—	—	—	—	—	—	—

Table 8 Transactions in financial assets and liabilities by sector

	Budgetary Central Government			Central Government			Local Government			General Government		
	2002	2003	2004	2002	2003	2004	2002	2003	2004	2002	2003	2004
82 **Net acquisition of financial assets**........	....	....	....	−1.28	30.23	27.81	−6.65	4.89	−5.70	−8.55	35.73	11.10
821 Domestic...............................	....	....	....	−1.55	28.95	27.54	−6.65	4.89	−5.70	−8.82	34.45	10.83
8211 General government....................	....	....	....	.60	9.03	2.79	.01	6.33	−2.34	—	15.36	.68
8212 Central bank...........................	....	....	....	—	—	—	−8.18	—	—	−8.18	—	—
8213 Other depository corporations...................	....	....	....	−.36	22.39	29.96	—	−.53	−1.48	−.36	22.47	17.23
8214 Financial corporations n.e.c................	....	....	....	—	−2.47	−5.21	—	−.91	−1.88	—	−3.38	−7.09
8215 Nonfinancial corporations................	....	....	....	−4.27	—	—	1.47	—	—	−2.80	—	—
8216 Households & NPIs serving households......	....	....	....	2.48	—	—	.05	—	—	2.53	—	—
822 Foreign................................	....	....	....	.27	1.29	.27	—	—	—	.27	1.29	.27
8221 General government....................	....	....	....	—	—	—	—	—	—	—	—	—
8227 International organizations................	....	....	....	.27	.26	.27	—	—	—	.27	.26	.27
8228 Financial corporations other than international organizations...............	....	....	....	—	—	—	—	—	—	—	—	—
8229 Other nonresidents.....................	....	....	....	—	1.03	—	—	—	—	—	1.03	—
823 Monetary gold and SDRs.................	....	....	....	—	—	—	—	—	—	—	—	—
83 **Net incurrence of liabilities**................	....	....	....	−14.42	58.41	14.84	−.29	−.89	8.47	−15.33	58.14	12.29
831 Domestic...............................	....	....	....	37.50	51.14	64.21	−.29	−.89	8.47	36.59	50.87	61.66
8311 General government....................	....	....	....	—	51.14	—	.62	−.89	—	—	50.87	—
8312 Central bank...........................	....	....	....	—	—	—	—	—	—	—	—	—
8313 Other depository corporations...................	....	....	....	37.83	—	64.21	2.34	—	8.47	40.17	—	61.66
8314 Financial corporations n.e.c................	....	....	....	−.33	—	—	−3.25	—	—	−3.58	—	—
8315 Nonfinancial corporations................	....	....	....	—	—	—	—	—	—	—	—	—
8316 Households & NPIs serving households......	....	....	....	—	—	—	—	—	—	—	—	—
832 Foreign................................	....	....	....	−51.92	7.28	−49.37	—	—	—	−51.92	7.28	−49.37
8321 General government....................	....	....	....	1.33	13.02	10.14	—	—	—	1.33	13.02	10.14
8327 International organizations................	....	....	....	3.56	−2.64	−15.52	—	—	—	3.56	−2.64	−15.52
8328 Financial corporations other than international organizations...............	....	....	....	−2.72	−3.11	−4.06	—	—	—	−2.72	−3.11	−4.06
8329 Other nonresidents.....................	....	....	....	−54.09	—	−39.93	—	—	—	−54.09	—	−39.93

Kenya   664

In Millions of Shillings / Year Ending June 30 / Cash Reporter

	Budgetary Central Government			Central Government			Local Government			General Government		
	2000	2001	2002	2000	2001	2002	2000	2001	2002	2000	2001	2002
Statement of government operations												
Statement of other economic flows												
Balance sheet												
Statement of sources and uses of cash												
1 Cash receipts from operating activities..........	218,443	234,436	204,004	....	....	....	....	....	....	....	....	....
11 Taxes..	181,924	179,064	178,434	....	....	....	....	....	....	....	....	....
12 Social contributions...............................	451	424	460	....	....	....	....	....	....	....	....	....
13 Grants...	24,080	6,823	14,942	....	....	....	....	....	....	....	....	....
14 Other receipts.......................................	11,989	48,126	10,168	....	....	....	....	....	....	....	....	....
2 Cash payments for operating activities..........	188,417	196,563	213,980	....	....	....	....	....	....	....	....	....
21 Compensation of employees.....................	96,345	110,418	100,364	....	....	....	....	....	....	....	....	....
22 Purchases of goods and services................	56,540	44,851	67,939	....	....	....	....	....	....	....	....	....
24 Interest..	24,425	29,851	36,631	....	....	....	....	....	....	....	....	....
25 Subsidies..	1,780	4,424	—	....	....	....	....	....	....	....	....	....
26 Grants..	4,643	1,218	1,432	....	....	....	....	....	....	....	....	....
27 Social benefits.......................................	581	1,040	620	....	....	....	....	....	....	....	....	....
28 Other payments.....................................	4,102	4,761	6,994	....	....	....	....	....	....	....	....	....
CIO *Net cash inflow from oper. activities.....*	*30,026*	*37,873*	*−9,976*	....	....	....	....	....	....	....	....	....
31.1 Purchases of nonfinancial assets..................	9,617	17,233	14,918	....	....	....	....	....	....	....	....	....
31.2 Sales of nonfinancial assets.......................	15	—	31	....	....	....	....	....	....	....	....	....
31 Net cash outflow from investments in nonfinancial assets.............................	9,602	17,233	14,888	....	....	....	....	....	....	....	....	....
CSD *Cash surplus/deficit.............................*	*20,424*	*20,640*	*−24,864*	....	....	....	....	....	....	....	....	....
32x Net acquisition of fin assets, excl. cash........	14,132	10,923	−5,465	....	....	....	....	....	....	....	....	....
321x Domestic..	14,132	10,923	−5,465	....	....	....	....	....	....	....	....	....
322x Foreign..	—	—	—	....	....	....	....	....	....	....	....	....
323 Monetary gold and SDRs.........................	—	—	—	....	....	....	....	....	....	....	....	....
33 Net incurrence of liabilities.......................	13,113	....	4,002	....	....	....	....	....	....	....	....	....
331 Domestic..	624	....	46,922	....	....	....	....	....	....	....	....	....
332 Foreign..	12,489	....	−42,920	....	....	....	....	....	....	....	....	....
NFB Net cash inflow from fin. activities.............	−1,019	....	9,467	....	....	....	....	....	....	....	....	....
NCB *Net change in the stock of cash.............*	*19,406*	....	*−15,396*	....	....	....	....	....	....	....	....	....
Table 1 Revenue												
1 **Revenue..**	218,443	234,436	204,004	....	....	....	....	....	....	....	....	....
11 **Taxes...**	181,924	179,064	178,434	....	....	....	....	....	....	....	....	....
111 Taxes on income, profits, & capital gains......	55,689	58,958	70,140	....	....	....	....	....	....	....	....	....
1111 Individuals...	27,495	30,903	34,400	....	....	....	....	....	....	....	....	....
1112 Corporations and other enterprises............	—	—	—	....	....	....	....	....	....	....	....	....
112 Taxes on payroll and workforce..................	—	—	—	....	....	....	....	....	....	....	....	....
113 Taxes on property...................................	73	89	72	....	....	....	....	....	....	....	....	....
114 Taxes on goods and services......................	87,994	92,002	101,462	....	....	....	....	....	....	....	....	....
1141 General taxes on goods and services..........	50,221	50,872	56,135	....	....	....	....	....	....	....	....	....
1142 Excises..	36,599	39,980	44,043	....	....	....	....	....	....	....	....	....
115 Taxes on int'l. trade and transactions..........	37,444	27,302	5,919	....	....	....	....	....	....	....	....	....
116 Other taxes..	723	712	842	....	....	....	....	....	....	....	....	....
12 **Social contributions...........................**	451	424	460	....	....	....	....	....	....	....	....	....
121 Social security contributions.....................	451	424	460	....	....	....	....	....	....	....	....	....
122 Other social contributions.......................	—	—	—	....	....	....	....	....	....	....	....	....
13 **Grants..**	24,080	6,823	14,942	....	....	....	....	....	....	....	....	....
131 From foreign governments.......................	....	....	....	....	....	....	....	....	....	....	....	....
132 From international organizations.................	12,444	....	....	....	....	....	....	....	....	....	....	....
133 From other general government units..........	....	....	....	....	....	....	....	....	....	....	....	....
14 **Other revenue...................................**	11,989	48,126	10,168	....	....	....	....	....	....	....	....	....
Table 2 Expense by economic type												
2 **Expense..**	188,417	196,563	213,980	....	....	....	....	....	....	....	....	....
21 **Compensation of employees.................**	96,345	110,418	100,364	....	....	....	....	....	....	....	....	....
211 Wages and salaries..................................	90,021	101,788	98,469	....	....	....	....	....	....	....	....	....
212 Social contributions................................	6,324	8,630	1,895	....	....	....	....	....	....	....	....	....
22 **Use of goods and services....................**	56,540	44,851	67,939	....	....	....	....	....	....	....	....	....
23 **Consumption of fixed capital................**	....	....	....	....	....	....	....	....	....	....	....	....
24 **Interest...**	24,425	29,851	36,631	....	....	....	....	....	....	....	....	....
25 **Subsidies...**	1,780	4,424	—	....	....	....	....	....	....	....	....	....

Kenya   664

In Millions of Shillings / Year Ending June 30 / Cash Reporter

	Budgetary Central Government			Central Government			Local Government			General Government		
	2000	2001	2002	2000	2001	2002	2000	2001	2002	2000	2001	2002
26 Grants....................................	4,643	1,218	1,432	....	....	....	....	....	....	....	....	....
261 To foreign govenments..............	—	—	—	....	....	....	....	....	....	....	....	....
262 To international organizations........	—	198	723	....	....	....	....	....	....	....	....	....
263 To other general government units..............	4,643	1,021	710	....	....	....	....	....	....	....	....	....
2631 Current...........................	4,643	1,021	710	....	....	....	....	....	....	....	....	....
2632 Capital.............................	—	—	—	....	....	....	....	....	....	....	....	....
27 **Social benefits**....................	581	1,040	620	....	....	....	....	....	....	....	....	....
28 **Other expense**.....................	4,102	4,761	6,994	....	....	....	....	....	....	....	....	....
281 Property expense other than interest...........	—	—	—	....	....	....	....	....	....	....	....	....
282 Miscellaneous other expense..............	4,102	4,761	6,994	....	....	....	....	....	....	....	....	....
2821 Current...........................	3,644	4,464	5,804	....	....	....	....	....	....	....	....	....
2822 Capital.............................	458	297	1,189	....	....	....	....	....	....	....	....	....

Table 3   Transactions in assets and liabilities

	Budgetary Central Government			Central Government			Local Government			General Government		
3 **Change in net worth from transactns....**	....	....	....	....	....	....	....	....	....	....	....	....
31 **Net acquisition of nonfinancial assets...**	9,602	17,233	14,888	....	....	....	....	....	....	....	....	....
311 Fixed assets.............................	9,602	17,233	14,888	....	....	....	....	....	....	....	....	....
3111 Buildings and structures..............	5,892	8,388	9,465	....	....	....	....	....	....	....	....	....
3112 Machinery and equipment.......................	3,710	8,845	5,423	....	....	....	....	....	....	....	....	....
3113 Other fixed assets.....................	—	—	—	....	....	....	....	....	....	....	....	....
312 Inventories.............................	—	—	—	....	....	....	....	....	....	....	....	....
313 Valuables.............................	—	—	—	....	....	....	....	....	....	....	....	....
314 Nonproduced assets.............................	—	—	—	....	....	....	....	....	....	....	....	....
3141 Land................................	—	—	—	....	....	....	....	....	....	....	....	....
3142 Subsoil assets.....................	—	—	—	....	....	....	....	....	....	....	....	....
3143 Other naturally occurring assets..............	—	—	—	....	....	....	....	....	....	....	....	....
3144 Intangible nonproduced assets........	—	—	—	....	....	....	....	....	....	....	....	....
32 **Net acquisition of financial assets.........**	33,538	10,923	−20,862	....	....	....	....	....	....	....	....	....
321 Domestic.............................	33,538	10,923	−20,862	....	....	....	....	....	....	....	....	....
3212 Currency and deposits.................	19,406	—	−15,396	....	....	....	....	....	....	....	....	....
3213 Securities other than shares............	—	—	—	....	....	....	....	....	....	....	....	....
3214 Loans...............................	4,586	4,719	−5,467	....	....	....	....	....	....	....	....	....
3215 Shares and other equity................	9,546	6,204	2	....	....	....	....	....	....	....	....	....
3216 Insurance technical reserves..............	—	—	—	....	....	....	....	....	....	....	....	....
3217 Financial derivatives.....................	—	—	—	....	....	....	....	....	....	....	....	....
3218 Other accounts receivable........	....	....	....	....	....	....	....	....	....	....	....	....
322 Foreign.............................	—	—	—	....	....	....	....	....	....	....	....	....
3222 Currency and deposits.................	—	—	—	....	....	....	....	....	....	....	....	....
3223 Securities other than shares............	—	—	—	....	....	....	....	....	....	....	....	....
3224 Loans...............................	—	—	—	....	....	....	....	....	....	....	....	....
3225 Shares and other equity................	—	—	—	....	....	....	....	....	....	....	....	....
3226 Insurance technical reserves..............	—	—	—	....	....	....	....	....	....	....	....	....
3227 Financial derivatives.....................	—	—	—	....	....	....	....	....	....	....	....	....
3228 Other accounts receivable........	....	....	....	....	....	....	....	....	....	....	....	....
323 Monetary gold and SDRs............	—	—	—	....	....	....	....	....	....	....	....	....
33 **Net incurrence of liabilities...................**	13,113	....	4,002	....	....	....	....	....	....	....	....	....
331 Domestic.............................	624	....	46,922	....	....	....	....	....	....	....	....	....
3312 Currency and deposits.................	—	....	—	....	....	....	....	....	....	....	....	....
3313 Securities other than shares............	—	....	—	....	....	....	....	....	....	....	....	....
3314 Loans...............................	624	....	46,922	....	....	....	....	....	....	....	....	....
3316 Insurance technical reserves..............	—	....	—	....	....	....	....	....	....	....	....	....
3317 Financial derivatives.....................	—	....	—	....	....	....	....	....	....	....	....	....
3318 Other accounts payable................	....	....	....	....	....	....	....	....	....	....	....	....
332 Foreign.............................	12,489	....	−42,920	....	....	....	....	....	....	....	....	....
3322 Currency and deposits.................	—	....	—	....	....	....	....	....	....	....	....	....
3323 Securities other than shares............	—	....	—	....	....	....	....	....	....	....	....	....
3324 Loans...............................	12,489	....	−42,920	....	....	....	....	....	....	....	....	....
3326 Insurance technical reserves..............	—	....	—	....	....	....	....	....	....	....	....	....
3327 Financial derivatives.....................	—	....	—	....	....	....	....	....	....	....	....	....
3328 Other accounts payable................	....	....	....	....	....	....	....	....	....	....	....	....

2005, International Monetary Fund: *Government Finance Statistics Yearbook*

In Millions of Shillings / Year Ending June 30 / Cash Reporter

	Budgetary Central Government			Central Government			Local Government			General Government		
	2000	2001	2002	2000	2001	2002	2000	2001	2002	2000	2001	2002
Table 4 Holding gains in assets and liabilities												
Table 5 Other changes in the volume of assets and liabilities												
Table 6 Balance sheet												
Table 7 Outlays by functions of govt.												
7 Total outlays.........	198,019	213,796	228,868	....	....	....	....	....	....	....	....	....
701 General public services.........	67,406	66,196	83,040	....	....	....	....	....	....	....	....	....
7017 Public debt transactions.........	24,425	29,851	36,631	....	....	....	....	....	....	....	....	....
7018 General transfers between levels of govt......	2,260	2,935	2,747	....	....	....	....	....	....	....	....	....
702 Defense.........	16,847	19,035	17,605	....	....	....	....	....	....	....	....	....
703 Public order and safety.........	13,615	17,001	18,233	....	....	....	....	....	....	....	....	....
704 Economic affairs.........	35,734	33,938	34,628	....	....	....	....	....	....	....	....	....
7042 Agriculture, forestry, fishing, and hunting.....	9,536	10,671	10,488	....	....	....	....	....	....	....	....	....
7043 Fuel and energy.........	11,097	8,447	10,205	....	....	....	....	....	....	....	....	....
7044 Mining, manufacturing, and construction.....	39	46	69	....	....	....	....	....	....	....	....	....
7045 Transport.........	10,791	10,052	8,324	....	....	....	....	....	....	....	....	....
7046 Communication.........	—	—	—	....	....	....	....	....	....	....	....	....
705 Environmental protection.........	1,302	1,585	1,358	....	....	....	....	....	....	....	....	....
706 Housing and community amenities........	6,039	5,842	1,420	....	....	....	....	....	....	....	....	....
707 Health.........	10,744	13,966	13,757	....	....	....	....	....	....	....	....	....
7072 Outpatient services.........	1,604	2,134	1,808	....	....	....	....	....	....	....	....	....
7073 Hospital services.........	7,306	9,269	10,755	....	....	....	....	....	....	....	....	....
7074 Public health services.........	1,174	757	13	....	....	....	....	....	....	....	....	....
708 Recreation, culture, and religion.........	1,136	720	76	....	....	....	....	....	....	....	....	....
709 Education.........	51,616	57,771	67,191	....	....	....	....	....	....	....	....	....
7091 Pre-primary and primary education.........	1,145	1,367	3,649	....	....	....	....	....	....	....	....	....
7092 Secondary education.........	1,618	2,043	1,728	....	....	....	....	....	....	....	....	....
7094 Tertiary education.........	8,345	9,092	9,780	....	....	....	....	....	....	....	....	....
710 Social protection.........	12,548	8,755	19,116	....	....	....	....	....	....	....	....	....
7 Statistical discrepancy: Total outlays.........	−18,967	−11,011	−27,554	....	....	....	....	....	....	....	....	....
Table 8 Transactions in financial assets and liabilities by sector												
82 Net acquisition of financial assets.........	33,538	10,923	−20,862	....	....	....	....	....	....	....	....	....
821 Domestic.........	33,538	10,923	−20,862	....	....	....	....	....	....	....	....	....
8211 General government.........	....	....	−5,466	....	....	....	....	....	....	....	....	....
8212 Central bank.........	....	....	....	....	....	....	....	....	....	....	....	....
8213 Other depository corporations.........	....	....	....	....	....	....	....	....	....	....	....	....
8214 Financial corporations n.e.c.........	....	....	....	....	....	....	....	....	....	....	....	....
8215 Nonfinancial corporations.........	....	....	....	....	....	....	....	....	....	....	....	....
8216 Households & NPIs serving households......	....	....	....	....	....	....	....	....	....	....	....	....
822 Foreign.........	—	—	—	....	....	....	....	....	....	....	....	....
8221 General government.........	—	—	—	....	....	....	....	....	....	....	....	....
8227 International organizations.........	—	—	—	....	....	....	....	....	....	....	....	....
8228 Financial corporations other than international organizations.........	—	—	—	....	....	....	....	....	....	....	....	....
8229 Other nonresidents.........	—	—	—	....	....	....	....	....	....	....	....	....
823 Monetary gold and SDRs.........	—	—	—	....	....	....	....	....	....	....	....	....
83 Net incurrence of liabilities.........	13,113	....	4,002	....	....	....	....	....	....	....	....	....
831 Domestic.........	624	....	46,922	....	....	....	....	....	....	....	....	....
8311 General government.........	....	....	....	....	....	....	....	....	....	....	....	....
8312 Central bank.........	....	....	....	....	....	....	....	....	....	....	....	....
8313 Other depository corporations.........	....	....	....	....	....	....	....	....	....	....	....	....
8314 Financial corporations n.e.c.........	....	....	....	....	....	....	....	....	....	....	....	....
8315 Nonfinancial corporations.........	....	....	....	....	....	....	....	....	....	....	....	....
8316 Households & NPIs serving households......	....	....	....	....	....	....	....	....	....	....	....	....
832 Foreign.........	12,489	....	−42,920	....	....	....	....	....	....	....	....	....
8321 General government.........	....	....	....	....	....	....	....	....	....	....	....	....
8327 International organizations.........	....	....	....	....	....	....	....	....	....	....	....	....
8328 Financial corporations other than international organizations.........	....	....	....	....	....	....	....	....	....	....	....	....
8329 Other nonresidents.........	....	....	....	....	....	....	....	....	....	....	....	....

		Budgetary Central Government			Central Government			Local Government			General Government		
		1999	2000	2001	1999	2000	2001	1999	2000	2001	1999	2000	2001
Statement of government operations													
Statement of other economic flows													
Balance sheet													
Statement of sources and uses of cash													
1	Cash receipts from operating activities..........	86,648	105,927	107,918	106,006	134,647	141,864	....	....	....	....	....	....
11	Taxes..	75,658	92,935	95,793	75,658	92,935	95,793	....	....	....	....	....	....
12	Social contributions............................	160	166	213	12,168	17,922	21,102	....	....	....	....	....	....
13	Grants..	—	—	—	—	—	—	....	....	....	....	....	....
14	Other receipts....................................	10,830	12,827	11,911	18,180	23,791	24,969	....	....	....	....	....	....
2	Cash payments for operating activities..........	73,851	81,792	95,774	87,807	100,293	115,462	....	....	....	....	....	....
21	Compensation of employees......................	10,055	11,028	12,277	10,058	11,150	12,393	....	....	....	....	....	....
22	Purchases of goods and services..................	9,463	12,766	12,872	9,714	13,557	13,830	....	....	....	....	....	....
24	Interest..	1,133	1,123	1,150	5,884	6,888	7,198	....	....	....	....	....	....
25	Subsidies..	426	325	528	432	329	534	....	....	....	....	....	....
26	Grants..	35,251	37,741	46,877	35,467	37,750	46,890	....	....	....	....	....	....
27	Social benefits....................................	5,249	5,777	7,750	12,335	15,496	17,035	....	....	....	....	....	....
28	Other payments...................................	12,274	13,032	14,321	13,917	15,122	17,581	....	....	....	....	....	....
CIO	*Net cash inflow from oper. activities.....*	*23,590*	*23,007*	*10,582*	*18,200*	*34,355*	*26,402*	....	....	....	....	....	....
31.1	Purchases of nonfinancial assets..................	12,090	8,749	9,767	12,484	9,305	9,945	....	....	....	....	....	....
31.2	Sales of nonfinancial assets......................	793	491	678	1,306	1,339	1,274	....	....	....	....	....	....
31	Net cash outflow from investments in nonfinancial assets......................	11,297	8,258	9,090	11,178	7,966	8,671	....	....	....	....	....	....
CSD	*Cash surplus/deficit.............................*	*12,293*	*14,749*	*1,493*	*7,022*	*26,389*	*17,731*	....	....	....	....	....	....
32x	Net acquisition of fin assets, excl. cash..........	10,670	12,411	3,947	19,752	19,841	10,077	....	....	....	....	....	....
321x	Domestic..	10,670	12,411	3,947	19,629	19,747	9,926	....	....	....	....	....	....
322x	Foreign..	—	—	—	122	94	150	....	....	....	....	....	....
323	Monetary gold and SDRs..........................	—	—	—	—	—	—	....	....	....	....	....	....
33	Net incurrence of liabilities......................	951	−400	−434	15,090	−5,923	−14,728	....	....	....	....	....	....
331	Domestic..	−24	16	—	14,116	−5,508	−14,294	....	....	....	....	....	....
332	Foreign..	975	−415	−434	975	−415	−434	....	....	....	....	....	....
NFB	Net cash inflow from fin. activities................	−9,719	−12,810	−4,381	−4,661	−25,764	−24,805	....	....	....	....	....	....
NCB	*Net change in the stock of cash.............*	*2,574*	*1,939*	*−2,888*	*2,360*	*625*	*−7,074*	....	....	....	....	....	....
Table 1 Revenue													
1	**Revenue.......................................**	**86,648**	**105,927**	**107,918**	**106,006**	**134,647**	**141,864**	....	....	....	....	....	....
11	**Taxes...**	**75,658**	**92,935**	**95,793**	**75,658**	**92,935**	**95,793**	....	....	....	....	....	....
111	Taxes on income, profits, & capital gains......	25,220	35,387	35,638	25,220	35,387	35,638	....	....	....	....	....	....
1111	Individuals..	15,855	17,509	18,663	15,855	17,509	18,663	....	....	....	....	....	....
1112	Corporations and other enterprises...........	9,365	17,878	16,975	9,365	17,878	16,975	....	....	....	....	....	....
112	Taxes on payroll and workforce..................	—	—	—	—	—	—	....	....	....	....	....	....
113	Taxes on property..................................	3,272	4,262	2,920	3,272	4,262	2,920	....	....	....	....	....	....
114	Taxes on goods and services......................	33,607	38,020	43,818	33,607	38,020	43,818	....	....	....	....	....	....
1141	General taxes on goods and services..........	20,369	23,212	25,835	20,369	23,212	25,835	....	....	....	....	....	....
1142	Excises..	12,047	13,351	16,637	12,047	13,351	16,637	....	....	....	....	....	....
115	Taxes on int'l. trade and transactions..........	4,687	5,800	5,923	4,687	5,800	5,923	....	....	....	....	....	....
116	Other taxes..	8,871	9,465	7,494	8,871	9,465	7,494	....	....	....	....	....	....
12	**Social contributions..............................**	**160**	**166**	**213**	**12,168**	**17,922**	**21,102**	....	....	....	....	....	....
121	Social security contributions......................	—	—	—	12,008	14,798	17,538	....	....	....	....	....	....
122	Other social contributions........................	160	166	213	160	3,124	3,564	....	....	....	....	....	....
13	**Grants...**	—	—	—	—	—	—	....	....	....	....	....	....
131	From foreign governments........................	—	—	—	—	—	—	....	....	....	....	....	....
132	From international organizations..................	—	—	—	—	—	—	....	....	....	....	....	....
133	From other general government units...........	—	—	—	—	—	—	....	....	....	....	....	....
14	**Other revenue....................................**	**10,830**	**12,827**	**11,911**	**18,180**	**23,791**	**24,969**	....	....	....	....	....	....
Table 2 Expense by economic type													
2	**Expense...**	**73,851**	**81,792**	**95,774**	**87,807**	**100,293**	**115,462**	....	....	....	....	....	....
21	**Compensation of employees..................**	**10,055**	**11,028**	**12,277**	**10,058**	**11,150**	**12,393**	....	....	....	....	....	....
211	Wages and salaries................................	10,055	11,028	12,277	10,058	11,150	12,393	....	....	....	....	....	....
212	Social contributions...............................	—	—	—	—	—	—	....	....	....	....	....	....
22	**Use of goods and services......................**	**9,463**	**12,766**	**12,872**	**9,714**	**13,557**	**13,830**	....	....	....	....	....	....
23	**Consumption of fixed capital................**	....	....	....	....	....	....	....	....	....	....	....	....
24	**Interest...**	**1,133**	**1,123**	**1,150**	**5,884**	**6,888**	**7,198**	....	....	....	....	....	....
25	**Subsidies..**	**426**	**325**	**528**	**432**	**329**	**534**	....	....	....	....	....	....

		Budgetary Central Government			Central Government			Local Government			General Government		
		1999	2000	2001	1999	2000	2001	1999	2000	2001	1999	2000	2001
26	**Grants**........................	**35,251**	**37,741**	**46,877**	**35,467**	**37,750**	**46,890**	....	....	....	....	....	....
261	To foreign govenments.........	350	416	484	350	416	485	....	....	....	....	....	....
262	To international organizations....	29	22	25	29	22	25	....	....	....	....	....	....
263	To other general government units....	34,872	37,302	46,368	35,088	37,312	46,380	....	....	....	....	....	....
2631	Current..................	25,428	28,328	36,250	25,640	28,338	36,262	....	....	....	....	....	....
2632	Capital..................	9,445	8,974	10,118	9,448	8,974	10,118	....	....	....	....	....	....
27	**Social benefits**..............	**5,249**	**5,777**	**7,750**	**12,335**	**15,496**	**17,035**	....	....	....	....	....	....
28	**Other expense**................	**12,274**	**13,032**	**14,321**	**13,917**	**15,122**	**17,581**	....	....	....	....	....	....
281	Property expense other than interest...........	—	—	—	—	—	—	....	....	....	....	....	....
282	Miscellaneous other expense..........	12,274	13,032	14,321	13,917	15,122	17,581	....	....	....	....	....	....
2821	Current..................	8,915	8,787	9,297	10,547	10,512	12,199	....	....	....	....	....	....
2822	Capital..................	3,359	4,244	5,024	3,370	4,610	5,383	....	....	....	....	....	....
	Table 3 Transactions in assets and liabilities												
3	**Change in net worth from transactns....**	....	....	....	....	....	....	....	....	....	....	....	....
31	**Net acquisition of nonfinancial assets...**	**11,297**	**8,258**	**9,090**	**11,178**	**7,966**	**8,671**	....	....	....	....	....	....
311	Fixed assets..............	10,592	7,317	8,314	10,648	7,348	8,377	....	....	....	....	....	....
3111	Buildings and structures..........	....	....	....	....	....	....	....	....	....	....	....	....
3112	Machinery and equipment..........	....	....	....	....	....	....	....	....	....	....	....	....
3113	Other fixed assets...........	....	....	....	....	....	....	....	....	....	....	....	....
312	Inventories..................	—	—	—	−190	−263	−473	....	....	....	....	....	....
313	Valuables..................	—	—	—	—	—	—	....	....	....	....	....	....
314	Nonproduced assets..........	705	941	776	719	882	767	....	....	....	....	....	....
3141	Land..................	....	....	....	....	....	....	....	....	....	....	....	....
3142	Subsoil assets..............	....	....	....	....	....	....	....	....	....	....	....	....
3143	Other naturally occurring assets....	....	....	....	....	....	....	....	....	....	....	....	....
3144	Intangible nonproduced assets.......	....	....	....	....	....	....	....	....	....	....	....	....
32	**Net acquisition of financial assets........**	**13,243**	**14,350**	**1,059**	**22,112**	**20,465**	**3,003**	....	....	....	....	....	....
321	Domestic..................	13,243	14,350	1,059	21,990	20,371	2,853	....	....	....	....	....	....
3212	Currency and deposits..........	2,574	1,939	−2,888	2,360	625	−7,074	....	....	....	....	....	....
3213	Securities other than shares..........	....	....	....	....	....	....	....	....	....	....	....	....
3214	Loans..................	....	....	....	....	....	....	....	....	....	....	....	....
3215	Shares and other equity..........	....	....	....	....	....	....	....	....	....	....	....	....
3216	Insurance technical reserves..........	....	....	....	....	....	....	....	....	....	....	....	....
3217	Financial derivatives..........	....	....	....	....	....	....	....	....	....	....	....	....
3218	Other accounts receivable..........	....	....	....	....	....	....	....	....	....	....	....	....
322	Foreign..................	—	—	—	122	94	150	....	....	....	....	....	....
3222	Currency and deposits..........	—	—	—	....	....	....	....	....	....	....	....	....
3223	Securities other than shares..........	—	—	—	....	....	....	....	....	....	....	....	....
3224	Loans..................	—	—	—	....	....	....	....	....	....	....	....	....
3225	Shares and other equity..........	—	—	—	....	....	....	....	....	....	....	....	....
3226	Insurance technical reserves..........	—	—	—	....	....	....	....	....	....	....	....	....
3227	Financial derivatives..........	—	—	—	....	....	....	....	....	....	....	....	....
3228	Other accounts receivable..........	—	—	....	....	....	....	....	....	....	....	....	....
323	Monetary gold and SDRs..........	—	—	—	—	—	—	....	....	....	....	....	....
33	**Net incurrence of liabilities...................**	**951**	**−400**	**−434**	**15,090**	**−5,923**	**−14,728**	....	....	....	....	....	....
331	Domestic..................	−24	16	—	14,116	−5,508	−14,294	....	....	....	....	....	....
3312	Currency and deposits..........							....	....	....	....	....	....
3313	Securities other than shares..........	—	—	—	—	—	—	....	....	....	....	....	....
3314	Loans..................	−24	16	—	14,116	−5,508	−14,294	....	....	....	....	....	....
3316	Insurance technical reserves..........	—	—	—	—	—	—	....	....	....	....	....	....
3317	Financial derivatives..........	—	—	—	—	—	—	....	....	....	....	....	....
3318	Other accounts payable..........	....	....	....	....	....	....	....	....	....	....	....	....
332	Foreign..................	975	−415	−434	975	−415	−434	....	....	....	....	....	....
3322	Currency and deposits..........	—	—	—	—	—	—	....	....	....	....	....	....
3323	Securities other than shares..........	—	—	—	—	—	—	....	....	....	....	....	....
3324	Loans..................	975	−415	−434	975	−415	−434	....	....	....	....	....	....
3326	Insurance technical reserves..........	—	—	—	—	—	—	....	....	....	....	....	....
3327	Financial derivatives..........	—	—	—	—	—	—	....	....	....	....	....	....
3328	Other accounts payable..........	....	....	....	....	....	....	....	....	....	....	....	....

	Budgetary Central Government			Central Government			Local Government			General Government		
	1999	2000	2001	1999	2000	2001	1999	2000	2001	1999	2000	2001
Table 4 **Holding gains in assets and liabilities**												
Table 5 **Other changes in the volume of assets and liabilities**												
Table 6 **Balance sheet**												
Table 7 **Outlays by functions of govt.**												
7 Total outlays.............	85,941	90,541	105,541	100,291	109,597	125,406	....	....	....	....	....	....
701 General public services.................	15,364	18,799	23,935	19,409	23,286	31,635	....	....	....	....	....	....
7017 Public debt transactions..................	1,133	1,123	1,150	5,884	6,888	7,198	....	....	....	....	....	....
7018 General transfers between levels of govt......	....	....	....	....	....	....	....	....	....	....	....	....
702 Defense..........................	13,213	14,388	15,494	13,213	14,400	15,702	....	....	....	....	....	....
703 Public order and safety..................	5,861	5,794	6,217	5,861	5,794	6,331	....	....	....	....	....	....
704 Economic affairs....................	24,542	22,747	23,980	26,177	25,909	26,983	....	....	....	....	....	....
7042 Agriculture, forestry, fishing, and hunting.....	....	....	....	....	....	....	....	....	....	....	....	....
7043 Fuel and energy...................	....	....	....	....	....	....	....	....	....	....	....	....
7044 Mining, manufacturing, and construction.....	....	....	....	....	....	....	....	....	....	....	....	....
7045 Transport....................	....	....	....	....	....	....	....	....	....	....	....	....
7046 Communication..................	....	....	....	....	....	....	....	....	....	....	....	....
705 Environmental protection................	....	....	....	....	....	....	....	....	....	....	....	....
706 Housing and community amenities........	1,371	1,010	1,404	2,311	1,747	2,740	....	....	....	....	....	....
707 Health................	791	661	555	791	680	555	....	....	....	....	....	....
7072 Outpatient services................	....	....	....	....	....	....	....	....	....	....	....	....
7073 Hospital services................	239	94	88	239	94	88	....	....	....	....	....	....
7074 Public health services................	....	....	....	....	....	....	....	....	....	....	....	....
708 Recreation, culture, and religion..........	881	925	1,179	893	1,014	1,272	....	....	....	....	....	....
709 Education...................	16,732	18,276	21,629	16,733	18,276	22,218	....	....	....	....	....	....
7091 Pre-primary and primary education.............	....	....	....	....	....	....	....	....	....	....	....	....
7092 Secondary education...............	....	....	....	....	....	....	....	....	....	....	....	....
7094 Tertiary education................	2,003	1,908	2,256	2,003	1,908	2,256	....	....	....	....	....	....
710 Social protection.................	7,187	7,941	11,148	14,903	18,492	17,969	....	....	....	....	....	....
7 Statistical discrepancy: Total outlays.............	—	—	—	—	—	—	....	....	....	....	....	....
Table 8 **Transactions in financial assets and liabilities by sector**												
82 Net acquisition of financial assets........	13,243	14,350	1,059	22,112	20,465	3,003	....	....	....	....	....	....
821 Domestic................	13,243	14,350	1,059	21,990	20,371	2,853	....	....	....	....	....	....
8211 General government.................	1,145	608	90	2,071	608	175	....	....	....	....	....	....
8212 Central bank.................	....	....	....	....	....	....	....	....	....	....	....	....
8213 Other depository corporations............	....	....	....	....	....	....	....	....	....	....	....	....
8214 Financial corporations n.e.c.............	....	....	....	....	....	....	....	....	....	....	....	....
8215 Nonfinancial corporations.............	....	....	....	....	....	....	....	....	....	....	....	....
8216 Households & NPIs serving households......	....	....	....	....	....	....	....	....	....	....	....	....
822 Foreign.................	—	—	—	122	94	150	....	....	....	....	....	....
8221 General government.................	—	—	—	....	....	....	....	....	....	....	....	....
8227 International organizations.................	—	—	—	....	....	....	....	....	....	....	....	....
8228 Financial corporations other than international organizations.............	—	—	—	....	....	....	....	....	....	....	....	....
8229 Other nonresidents.................	—	—	—	....	....	....	....	....	....	....	....	....
823 Monetary gold and SDRs.................	—	—	—	—	—	—	....	....	....	....	....	....
83 Net incurrence of liabilities.................	951	−400	−434	15,090	−5,923	−14,728	....	....	....	....	....	....
831 Domestic.................	−24	16	—	14,116	−5,508	−14,294	....	....	....	....	....	....
8311 General government.................	....	....	....	....	....	....	....	....	....	....	....	....
8312 Central bank.................	....	....	—	....	....	....	....	....	....	....	....	....
8313 Other depository corporations.............	....	....	—	....	....	....	....	....	....	....	....	....
8314 Financial corporations n.e.c.............	....	....	—	....	....	....	....	....	....	....	....	....
8315 Nonfinancial corporations.............	....	....	—	....	....	....	....	....	....	....	....	....
8316 Households & NPIs serving households......	....	....	—	....	....	....	....	....	....	....	....	....
832 Foreign.................	975	−415	−434	975	−415	−434	....	....	....	....	....	....
8321 General government.................	....	....	....	....	....	....	....	....	....	....	....	....
8327 International organizations.................	....	....	....	....	....	....	....	....	....	....	....	....
8328 Financial corporations other than international organizations.............	....	....	....	....	....	....	....	....	....	....	....	....
8329 Other nonresidents.................	....	....	....	....	....	....	....	....	....	....	....	....

Kuwait 443

In Millions of Dinars / Year Ending June 30 / Cash Reporter

		Budgetary Central Government			Extrabudgetary Accounts			Central Government			General Government		
		2001	2002	2003	2001	2002	2003	2001	2002	2003	2001	2002	2003
	Statement of government operations												
	Statement of other economic flows												
	Balance sheet												
	Statement of sources and uses of cash												
1	Cash receipts from operating activities	....	6,038	6,719	....	28	49	....	6,066	6,768	....	6,066	6,768
11	Taxes	....	135	187	....	—	—	....	135	187	....	135	187
12	Social contributions	....	—	—	....	—	—	....	—	—	....	—	—
13	Grants	....	—	—	....	—	—	....	—	—	....	—	—
14	Other receipts	....	5,903	6,532	....	28	49	....	5,931	6,581	....	5,931	6,581
2	Cash payments for operating activities	....	4,330	4,889	....	470	502	....	4,800	5,391	....	4,800	5,391
21	Compensation of employees	....	1,427	1,512	....	282	313	....	1,709	1,825	....	1,709	1,825
22	Purchases of goods and services	....	1,124	1,350	....	72	86	....	1,196	1,436	....	1,196	1,436
24	Interest	....	31	18	....	—	—	....	31	18	....	31	18
25	Subsidies	....	649	775	....	51	35	....	700	810	....	700	810
26	Grants	....	82	63	....	—	—	....	82	63	....	82	63
27	Social benefits	....	510	558	....	—	—	....	510	558	....	510	558
28	Other payments	....	507	613	....	65	68	....	572	681	....	572	681
CIO	*Net cash inflow from oper. activities*	....	*1,708*	*1,830*	....	*−442*	*−453*	....	*1,266*	*1,377*	....	*1,266*	*1,377*
31.1	Purchases of nonfinancial assets	....	485	610	....	—	—	....	485	610	....	485	610
31.2	Sales of nonfinancial assets	....	26	37	....	—	—	....	26	37	....	26	37
31	Net cash outflow from investments in nonfinancial assets	....	459	573	....	—	—	....	459	573	....	459	573
CSD	*Cash surplus/deficit*	....	*1,249*	*1,257*	....	*−442*	*−453*	....	*807*	*804*	....	*807*	*804*
32x	Net acquisition of fin. assets, excl. cash	....	....	....	....	....	....	....	....	....	....	....	....
321x	Domestic	....	....	....	....	....	....	....	....	....	....	....	....
322x	Foreign	....	....	....	....	....	....	....	....	....	....	....	....
323	Monetary gold and SDRs	....	....	....	....	....	....	....	....	....	....	....	....
33	Net incurrence of liabilities	....	....	....	....	....	....	....	....	....	....	....	....
331	Domestic	....	....	....	....	....	....	....	....	....	....	....	....
332	Foreign	....	....	....	....	....	....	....	....	....	....	....	....
NFB	Net cash inflow from fin. activities	....	....	....	....	....	....	....	....	....	....	....	....
NCB	*Net change in the stock of cash*	....	....	....	....	....	....	....	....	....	....	....	....
Table 1	**Revenue**												
1	**Revenue**	....	**6,038**	**6,719**	....	**28**	**49**	....	**6,066**	**6,768**	....	**6,066**	**6,768**
11	**Taxes**	....	**135**	**187**	....	**—**	**—**	....	**135**	**187**	....	**135**	**187**
111	Taxes on income, profits, & capital gains	....	26	30	....	—	—	....	26	30	....	26	30
1111	Individuals	....	—	—	....	—	—	....	—	—	....	—	—
1112	Corporations and other enterprises	....	26	30	....	—	—	....	26	30	....	26	30
112	Taxes on payroll and workforce	....	—	—	....	—	—	....	—	—	....	—	—
113	Taxes on property	....	8	10	....	—	—	....	8	10	....	8	10
114	Taxes on goods and services	....	—	—	....	—	—	....	—	—	....	—	—
1141	General taxes on goods and services	....	—	—	....	—	—	....	—	—	....	—	—
1142	Excises	....	—	—	....	—	—	....	—	—	....	—	—
115	Taxes on int'l. trade and transactions	....	101	147	....	—	—	....	101	147	....	101	147
116	Other taxes	....	—	—	....	—	—	....	—	—	....	—	—
12	**Social contributions**	....	**—**	**—**	....	**—**	**—**	....	**—**	**—**	....	**—**	**—**
121	Social security contributions	....	—	—	....	—	—	....	—	—	....	—	—
122	Other social contributions	....	—	—	....	—	—	....	—	—	....	—	—
13	**Grants**	....	**—**	**—**	....	**—**	**—**	....			....		
131	From foreign governments	....	—	—	....	—	—	....	—	—	....	—	—
132	From international organizations	....	—	—	....	—	—	....	—	—	....	—	—
133	From other general government units	....	—	—	....	—	—	....	—	—	....	—	—
14	**Other revenue**	....	**5,903**	**6,532**	....	**28**	**49**	....	**5,931**	**6,581**	....	**5,931**	**6,581**
Table 2	**Expense by economic type**												
2	**Expense**	....	**4,330**	**4,889**	....	**470**	**502**	....	**4,800**	**5,391**	....	**4,800**	**5,391**
21	**Compensation of employees**	....	**1,427**	**1,512**	....	**282**	**313**	....	**1,709**	**1,825**	....	**1,709**	**1,825**
211	Wages and salaries	....	1,297	1,395	....	261	289	....	1,558	1,684	....	1,558	1,684
212	Social contributions	....	130	117	....	21	24	....	151	141	....	151	141
22	**Use of goods and services**	....	**1,124**	**1,350**	....	**72**	**86**	....	**1,196**	**1,436**	....	**1,196**	**1,436**
23	**Consumption of fixed capital**	....	....	....	....	....	....	....	....	....	....	....	....
24	**Interest**	....	**31**	**18**	....	**—**	**—**	....	**31**	**18**	....	**31**	**18**
25	**Subsidies**	....	**649**	**775**	....	**51**	**35**	....	**700**	**810**	....	**700**	**810**

Kuwait 443

In Millions of Dinars / Year Ending June 30 / Cash Reporter

	Budgetary Central Government			Extrabudgetary Accounts			Central Government			General Government		
	2001	2002	2003	2001	2002	2003	2001	2002	2003	2001	2002	2003
26 Grants	....	82	63	....	—	—	....	82	63	....	82	63
261 To foreign govenments	....	82	63	....	—	—	....	82	63	....	82	63
262 To international organizations	....	—	—	....	—	—	....	—	—	....	—	—
263 To other general government units	....	—	—	....	—	—	....	—	—	....	—	—
2631 Current	....	—	—	....	—	—	....	—	—	....	—	—
2632 Capital	....	—	—	....	—	—	....	—	—	....	—	—
27 Social benefits	....	510	558	....	—	—	....	510	558	....	510	558
28 Other expense	....	507	613	....	65	68	....	572	681	....	572	681
281 Property expense other than interest	....	—	—	....	—	—	....	—	—	....	—	—
282 Miscellaneous other expense	....	507	613	....	65	68	....	572	681	....	572	681
2821 Current	....	—	—	....	—	—	....	—	—	....	—	—
2822 Capital	....	507	613	....	65	68	....	572	681	....	572	681

Table 3 Transactions in assets and liabilities

	Budgetary Central Government			Extrabudgetary Accounts			Central Government			General Government		
	2001	2002	2003	2001	2002	2003	2001	2002	2003	2001	2002	2003
3 Change in net worth from transactns	....	....	....	....	....	—	....	459	573	....	459	573
31 Net acquisition of nonfinancial assets	....	459	573	....	—	—	....	459	573	....	459	573
311 Fixed assets	....	437	562	....	—	—	....	437	562	....	437	562
3111 Buildings and structures	....	413	522	....	—	—	....	413	522	....	413	522
3112 Machinery and equipment	....	24	41	....	—	—	....	24	41	....	24	41
3113 Other fixed assets	....	—	—	....	—	—	....	—	—	....	—	—
312 Inventories	....	—	—	....	—	—	....	—	—	....	—	—
313 Valuables	....	—	—	....	—	—	....	—	—	....	—	—
314 Nonproduced assets	....	22	11	....	—	—	....	22	11	....	22	11
3141 Land	....	22	11	....	—	—	....	22	11	....	22	11
3142 Subsoil assets	....	—	—	....	—	—						
3143 Other naturally occurring assets	....	—	—	....	—	—						
3144 Intangible nonproduced assets	....	—	—	....	—	—						
32 Net acquisition of financial assets	....	....	....	....	....	....	....	....	....	....	....	....
321 Domestic	....	....	....	....	....	....	....	....	....	....	....	....
3212 Currency and deposits	....	....	....	....	....	....	....	....	....	....	....	....
3213 Securities other than shares	....	....	....	....	....	....	....	....	....	....	....	....
3214 Loans	....	....	....	....	....	....	....	....	....	....	....	....
3215 Shares and other equity	....	....	....	....	....	....	....	....	....	....	....	....
3216 Insurance technical reserves	....	....	....	....	....	....	....	....	....	....	....	....
3217 Financial derivatives	....	....	....	....	....	....	....	....	....	....	....	....
3218 Other accounts receivable	....	....	....	....	....	....	....	....	....	....	....	....
322 Foreign	....	....	....	....	....	....	....	....	....	....	....	....
3222 Currency and deposits	....	....	....	....	....	....	....	....	....	....	....	....
3223 Securities other than shares	....	....	....	....	....	....	....	....	....	....	....	....
3224 Loans	....	....	....	....	....	....	....	....	....	....	....	....
3225 Shares and other equity	....	....	....	....	....	....	....	....	....	....	....	....
3226 Insurance technical reserves	....	....	....	....	....	....	....	....	....	....	....	....
3227 Financial derivatives	....	....	....	....	....	....	....	....	....	....	....	....
3228 Other accounts receivable	....	....	....	....	....	....	....	....	....	....	....	....
323 Monetary gold and SDRs	....	....	....	....	....	....	....	....	....	....	....	....
33 Net incurrence of liabilities	....	....	....	....	....	....	....	....	....	....	....	....
331 Domestic	....	....	....	....	....	....	....	....	....	....	....	....
3312 Currency and deposits	....	....	....	....	....	....	....	....	....	....	....	....
3313 Securities other than shares	....	....	....	....	....	....	....	....	....	....	....	....
3314 Loans	....	....	....	....	....	....	....	....	....	....	....	....
3316 Insurance technical reserves	....	....	....	....	....	....	....	....	....	....	....	....
3317 Financial derivatives	....	....	....	....	....	....	....	....	....	....	....	....
3318 Other accounts payable	....	....	....	....	....	....	....	....	....	....	....	....
332 Foreign	....	....	....	....	....	....	....	....	....	....	....	....
3322 Currency and deposits	....	....	....	....	....	....	....	....	....	....	....	....
3323 Securities other than shares	....	....	....	....	....	....	....	....	....	....	....	....
3324 Loans	....	....	....	....	....	....	....	....	....	....	....	....
3326 Insurance technical reserves	....	....	....	....	....	....	....	....	....	....	....	....
3327 Financial derivatives	....	....	....	....	....	....	....	....	....	....	....	....
3328 Other accounts payable	....	....	....	....	....	....	....	....	....	....	....	....

In Millions of Dinars / Year Ending June 30 / Cash Reporter

	Budgetary Central Government			Extrabudgetary Accounts			Central Government			General Government		
	2001	2002	2003	2001	2002	2003	2001	2002	2003	2001	2002	2003
Table 4 Holding gains in assets and liabilities												
Table 5 Other changes in the volume of assets and liabilities												
Table 6 Balance sheet												
Table 7 Outlays by functions of govt.												
7 Total outlays.....................	....	4,789	5,462	....	470	502	....	5,259	5,964	....	5,259	5,964
701 General public services................	....	399	481	....	65	70	....	464	551	....	464	551
7017 Public debt transactions............	....	31	18	....	—	—	....	31	18	....	31	18
7018 General transfers between levels of govt......	....	....	....	....	....	....	....	....	....	....	....	....
702 Defense...............................	....	882	950	....	—	—	....	882	950	....	882	950
703 Public order and safety...............	....	439	476	....	37	40	....	476	516	....	476	516
704 Economic affairs.......................	....	553	734	....	36	36	....	589	770	....	589	770
7042 Agriculture, forestry, fishing, and hunting.....	....	—	—	....	36	36	....	36	36	....	36	36
7043 Fuel and energy......................	....	513	653	....	—	—	....	513	653	....	513	653
7044 Mining, manufacturing, and construction.....	....	18	15	....	—	—	....	18	15	....	18	15
7045 Transport...........................	....	—	66	....	—	—	....	—	66	....	—	66
7046 Communication.....................	....	22	61	....	—	—	....	22	61	....	22	61
705 Environmental protection...............	....	—	—	....	5	6	....	5	6	....	5	6
706 Housing and community amenities.......	....	262	331	....	85	91	....	347	422	....	347	422
707 Health..............................	....	333	371	....	—	—	....	333	371	....	333	371
7072 Outpatient services................	....	....	....	....	—	—	....	....	....	....	....	....
7073 Hospital services..................	....	....	....	....	—	—	....	....	....	....	....	....
7074 Public health services..............	....	....	....	....	—	—	....	....	....	....	....	....
708 Recreation, culture, and religion..........	....	141	156	....	28	33	....	169	189	....	169	189
709 Education...........................	....	509	531	....	201	212	....	710	743	....	710	743
7091 Pre-primary and primary education............	....	....	....	....	....	....	....	....	....	....	....	....
7092 Secondary education..................	....	....	....	....	....	....	....	....	....	....	....	....
7094 Tertiary education...................	....	....	....	....	....	....	....	....	....	....	....	....
710 Social protection.....................	....	812	859	....	13	14	....	825	873	....	825	873
7 Statistical discrepancy: Total outlays............	....	459	573	....	—	—	....	459	573	....	459	573
Table 8 Transactions in financial assets and liabilities by sector												

In Millions of Soms / Year Ending December 31 / Cash Reporter

	Budgetary Central Government			Central Government			Local Government			General Government		
	1999	2000	2001	1999	2000	2001	1999	2000	2001	1999	2000	2001
Statement of government operations												
Statement of other economic flows												
Balance sheet												
6 *Net worth*	....	....	....	....	....	....	....	....	....	....	....	....
61 Nonfinancial assets	....	....	....	....	....	....	....	....	....	....	....	....
62 Financial assets	....	....	....	....	....	....	....	....	....	....	....	....
63 Liabilities	64,699.8	74,857.3	73,389.0	....	....	....	....	....	....	....	....	....
Statement of sources and uses of cash												
1 Cash receipts from operating activities	8,004.1	9,864.7	12,482.1	....	....	....	2,823.3	3,335.5	4,166.6	....	....	....
11 Taxes	5,954.0	7,675.5	9,187.9	....	....	....	1,053.7	1,286.6	1,490.5	....	....	....
12 Social contributions	—	—	—	....	....	....				....	....	....
13 Grants	278.8	608.2	622.0	....	....	....	1,414.5	1,625.2	2,212.7	....	....	....
14 Other receipts	1,771.2	1,581.0	2,672.3	....	....	....	355.1	423.7	463.5	....	....	....
2 Cash payments for operating activities	8,643.9	10,328.2	11,643.4	....	....	....	2,705.7	3,254.2	3,874.7	....	....	....
21 Compensation of employees	3,271.6	3,823.5	4,728.0	....	....	....	1,747.5	1,903.4	2,192.0	....	....	....
22 Purchases of goods and services	3,368.6	4,081.3	3,945.9	....	....	....	861.2	1,147.1	1,357.9	....	....	....
24 Interest	743.0	940.6	1,045.5	....	....	....	—	—	—	....	....	....
25 Subsidies	322.9	446.2	574.2	....	....	....	....	....	....	....	....	....
26 Grants	300.0	150.0	—	....	....	....	....	....	....	....	....	....
27 Social benefits	637.8	886.6	1,349.8	....	....	....	....	....	....	....	....	....
28 Other payments	—	—	—	....	....	....	....	....	....	....	....	....
CIO *Net cash inflow from oper. activities*	*−639.8*	*−463.5*	*838.7*	....	....	....	*117.6*	*81.3*	*291.9*	....	....	....
31.1 Purchases of nonfinancial assets	967.6	1,433.1	1,455.4	....	....	....	123.6	199.8	204.7	....	....	....
31.2 Sales of nonfinancial assets	148.5	23.6	57.1	....	....	....	.7	3.5	.1	....	....	....
31 Net cash outflow from investments in nonfinancial assets	819.1	1,409.5	1,398.3	....	....	....	122.9	196.3	204.6	....	....	....
CSD *Cash surplus/deficit*	*−1,458.9*	*−1,873.0*	*−559.6*	....	....	....	*−5.3*	*−115.0*	*87.3*	....	....	....
32x Net acquisition of fin assets, excl. cash	−299.5	−453.1	−843.1	....	....	....	−19.7	−46.5	−48.5	....	....	....
321x Domestic	−299.5	−453.1	−843.1	....	....	....	....	....	....	....	....	....
322x Foreign	—	—	—	....	....	....	....	....	....	....	....	....
323 Monetary gold and SDRs	—	—	—	....	....	....	—	—	—	....	....	....
33 Net incurrence of liabilities	....	....	....	....	....	....	....	....	....	....	....	....
331 Domestic	....	....	....	....	....	....	....	....	....	....	....	....
332 Foreign	....	....	....	....	....	....	....	....	....	....	....	....
NFB Net cash inflow from fin. activities	....	....	....	....	....	....	....	....	....	....	....	....
NCB *Net change in the stock of cash*	....	....	....	....	....	....	....	....	....	....	....	....
Table 1 Revenue												
1 **Revenue**	**8,004.1**	**9,864.7**	**12,482.1**	....	....	....	**2,823.3**	**3,335.5**	**4,166.6**	....	....	....
11 **Taxes**	**5,954.0**	**7,675.5**	**9,187.9**	....	....	....	**1,053.7**	**1,286.6**	**1,490.5**	....	....	....
111 Taxes on income, profits, & capital gains	1,150.6	1,379.5	2,008.5	....	....	....	424.5	487.6	703.0	....	....	....
1111 Individuals	546.2	753.8	960.9	....	....	....	193.5	263.8	336.3	....	....	....
1112 Corporations and other enterprises	567.6	572.8	993.7	....	....	....	....	....	....	....	....	....
112 Taxes on payroll and workforce	—	—	—	....	....	....	—	—	—	....	....	....
113 Taxes on property	.1	.2	—	....	....	....	.1	.2	—	....	....	....
114 Taxes on goods and services	4,496.7	6,020.7	6,878.0	....	....	....	627.2	797.4	787.5	....	....	....
1141 General taxes on goods and services	2,439.7	3,208.1	4,526.5	....	....	....	....	....	....	....	....	....
1142 Excises	1,252.6	1,518.4	1,102.6	....	....	....	....	....	....	....	....	....
115 Taxes on int'l. trade and transactions	306.6	275.1	301.4	....	....	....	....	....	....	....	....	....
116 Other taxes	—	—	—	....	....	....	1.9	1.4	—	....	....	....
12 **Social contributions**	—	—	—	....	....	....	—	—	—	....	....	....
121 Social security contributions	—	—	—	....	....	....	....	....	....	....	....	....
122 Other social contributions	—	—	—	....	....	....	....	....	....	....	....	....
13 **Grants**	**278.8**	**608.2**	**622.0**	....	....	....	**1,414.5**	**1,625.2**	**2,212.7**	....	....	....
131 From foreign governments	278.8	608.2	622.0	....	....	....	—	—	—	....	....	....
132 From international organizations	—	—	—	....	....	....	—	—	—	....	....	....
133 From other general government units	—	—	—	....	....	....	1,414.5	1,625.2	2,212.7	....	....	....
14 **Other revenue**	**1,771.2**	**1,581.0**	**2,672.3**	....	....	....	**355.1**	**423.7**	**463.5**	....	....	....
Table 2 Expense by economic type												
2 **Expense**	**8,643.9**	**10,328.2**	**11,643.4**	....	....	....	**2,705.7**	**3,254.2**	**3,874.7**	....	....	....
21 **Compensation of employees**	**3,271.6**	**3,823.5**	**4,728.0**	....	....	....	**1,747.5**	**1,903.4**	**2,192.0**	....	....	....
211 Wages and salaries	2,544.6	3,055.5	3,838.9	....	....	....	1,747.5	1,903.4	2,192.0	....	....	....
212 Social contributions	727.0	768.0	889.1	....	....	....	—	—	—	....	....	....
22 **Use of goods and services**	**3,368.6**	**4,081.3**	**3,945.9**	....	....	....	**861.2**	**1,147.1**	**1,357.9**	....	....	....
23 **Consumption of fixed capital**	....	....	....	....	....	....	....	....	....	....	....	....
24 **Interest**	**743.0**	**940.6**	**1,045.5**	....	....	....	....	....	....	....	....	....
25 **Subsidies**	**322.9**	**446.2**	**574.2**	....	....	....	....	....	....	....	....	....

		Budgetary Central Government			Central Government			Local Government			General Government		
		1999	2000	2001	1999	2000	2001	1999	2000	2001	1999	2000	2001
26	**Grants**............................	300.0	150.0	—	....	....	....	....	....	....	....	....	....
261	To foreign govenments..................	—	—	—	....	....	....	....	....	....	....	....	....
262	To international organizations..............	—	—	—	....	....	....	....	....	....	....	....	....
263	To other general government units..............	300.0	150.0	—	....	....	....	33.7	86.7	122.5	....	....	....
2631	Current.........................	300.0	150.0	—	....	....	....	33.7	86.7	122.5	....	....	....
2632	Capital.........................	—	—	—	....	....	....	—	—	—	....	....	....
27	**Social benefits**.........................	637.8	886.6	1,349.8	....	....	....	....	....	....	....	....	....
28	**Other expense**........................	—	—	—	....	....	....	....	....	....	....	....	....
281	Property expense other than interest...........	—	—	—	....	....	....	....	....	....	....	....	....
282	Miscellaneous other expense..................	—	—	—	....	....	....	....	....	....	....	....	....
2821	Current.........................	—	—	—	....	....	....	....	....	....	....	....	....
2822	Capital.........................	—	—	—	....	....	....	....	....	....	....	....	....

Table 3 Transactions in assets and liabilities

		Budgetary Central Government			Central Government			Local Government			General Government		
		1999	2000	2001	1999	2000	2001	1999	2000	2001	1999	2000	2001
3	**Change in net worth from transactns....**	....	....	....	....	....	....	....	....	....	....	....	....
31	**Net acquisition of nonfinancial assets...**	819.1	1,409.5	1,398.3	....	....	....	122.9	196.3	204.6	....	....	....
311	Fixed assets............................	908.9	1,280.7	1,183.3	....	....	....	....	....	....	....	....	....
3111	Buildings and structures....................	....	....	....	....	....	....	....	....	....	....	....	....
3112	Machinery and equipment..................	....	....	....	....	....	....	....	....	....	....	....	....
3113	Other fixed assets.........................	....	....	....	....	....	....	....	....	....	....	....	....
312	Inventories................................	−89.8	128.8	215.0	....	....	....	....	....	....	....	....	....
313	Valuables.................................	—	—	—	....	....	....	....	....	....	....	....	....
314	Nonproduced assets.......................	—	—	—	....	....	....	....	....	....	....	....	....
3141	Land....................................	—	—	—	....	....	....	....	....	....	....	....	....
3142	Subsoil assets............................	—	—	—	....	....	....	....	....	....	....	....	....
3143	Other naturally occurring assets............	—	—	—	....	....	....	....	....	....	....	....	....
3144	Intangible nonproduced assets..................	—	—	—	....	....	....	....	....	....	....	....	....
32	**Net acquisition of financial assets........**	....	....	....	....	....	....	....	....	....	....	....	....
321	Domestic.................................	....	....	....	....	....	....	....	....	....	....	....	....
3212	Currency and deposits.....................	....	....	....	....	....	....	....	....	....	....	....	....
3213	Securities other than shares..................	....	....	....	....	....	....	....	....	....	....	....	....
3214	Loans....................................	....	....	....	....	....	....	....	....	....	....	....	....
3215	Shares and other equity....................	....	....	....	....	....	....	....	....	....	....	....	....
3216	Insurance technical reserves.................	....	....	....	....	....	....	....	....	....	....	....	....
3217	Financial derivatives.......................	....	....	....	....	....	....	....	....	....	....	....	....
3218	Other accounts receivable..................	....	....	....	....	....	....	....	....	....	....	....	....
322	Foreign..................................	....	....	....	....	....	....	....	....	....	....	....	....
3222	Currency and deposits.....................	....	....	....	....	....	....	....	....	....	....	....	....
3223	Securities other than shares.................	....	....	....	....	....	....	....	....	....	....	....	....
3224	Loans....................................	....	....	....	....	....	....	....	....	....	....	....	....
3225	Shares and other equity....................	....	....	....	....	....	....	....	....	....	....	....	....
3226	Insurance technical reserves.................	....	....	....	....	....	....	....	....	....	....	....	....
3227	Financial derivatives.......................	....	....	....	....	....	....	....	....	....	....	....	....
3228	Other accounts receivable..................	....	....	....	....	....	....	....	....	....	....	....	....
323	Monetary gold and SDRs...................	....	....	....	....	....	....	....	....	....	....	....	....
33	**Net incurrence of liabilities...................**	....	....	....	....	....	....	....	....	....	....	....	....
331	Domestic.................................	....	....	....	....	....	....	....	....	....	....	....	....
3312	Currency and deposits.....................	....	....	....	....	....	....	....	....	....	....	....	....
3313	Securities other than shares.................	....	....	....	....	....	....	....	....	....	....	....	....
3314	Loans....................................	....	....	....	....	....	....	....	....	....	....	....	....
3316	Insurance technical reserves.................	....	....	....	....	....	....	....	....	....	....	....	....
3317	Financial derivatives.......................	....	....	....	....	....	....	....	....	....	....	....	....
3318	Other accounts payable.....................	....	....	....	....	....	....	....	....	....	....	....	....
332	Foreign..................................	....	....	....	....	....	....	....	....	....	....	....	....
3322	Currency and deposits.....................	....	....	....	....	....	....	....	....	....	....	....	....
3323	Securities other than shares.................	....	....	....	....	....	....	....	....	....	....	....	....
3324	Loans....................................	....	....	....	....	....	....	....	....	....	....	....	....
3326	Insurance technical reserves.................	....	....	....	....	....	....	....	....	....	....	....	....
3327	Financial derivatives.......................	....	....	....	....	....	....	....	....	....	....	....	....
3328	Other accounts payable.....................	....	....	....	....	....	....	....	....	....	....	....	....

Kyrgyz Republic   917

In Millions of Soms / Year Ending December 31 / Cash Reporter

	Budgetary Central Government			Central Government			Local Government			General Government		
	1999	2000	2001	1999	2000	2001	1999	2000	2001	1999	2000	2001
Table 4 Holding gains in assets and liabilities												
Table 5 Other changes in the volume of assets and liabilities												
Table 6 Balance sheet												
6 Net worth....................	....	....	....	....	....	....	....	....	....	....	....	....
61 **Nonfinancial assets**.....................	....	....	....	....	....	....	....	....	....	....	....	....
611 Fixed assets........................	....	....	....	....	....	....	....	....	....	....	....	....
6111 Buildings and structures.................	....	....	....	....	....	....	....	....	....	....	....	....
6112 Machinery and equipment..................	....	....	....	....	....	....	....	....	....	....	....	....
6113 Other fixed assets.....................	....	....	....	....	....	....	....	....	....	....	....	....
612 Inventories...........................	....	....	....	....	....	....	....	....	....	....	....	....
613 Valuables.............................	....	....	....	....	....	....	....	....	....	....	....	....
614 Nonproduced assets...................	....	....	....	....	....	....	....	....	....	....	....	....
6141 Land...............................	....	....	....	....	....	....	....	....	....	....	....	....
6142 Subsoil assets.....................	....	....	....	....	....	....	....	....	....	....	....	....
6143 Other naturally occurring assets......	....	....	....	....	....	....	....	....	....	....	....	....
6144 Intangible nonproduced assets........	....	....	....	....	....	....	....	....	....	....	....	....
62 **Financial assets**.........................	....	....	....	....	....	....	....	....	....	....	....	....
621 Domestic.............................	....	....	....	....	....	....	....	....	....	....	....	....
6212 Currency and deposits.................	....	....	....	....	....	....	....	....	....	....	....	....
6213 Securities other than shares.........	....	....	....	....	....	....	....	....	....	....	....	....
6214 Loans................................	....	....	....	....	....	....	....	....	....	....	....	....
6215 Shares and other equity..............	....	....	....	....	....	....	....	....	....	....	....	....
6216 Insurance technical reserves.........	....	....	....	....	....	....	....	....	....	....	....	....
6217 Financial derivatives................	....	....	....	....	....	....	....	....	....	....	....	....
6218 Other accounts receivable............	....	....	....	....	....	....	....	....	....	....	....	....
622 Foreign..............................	....	....	....	....	....	....	....	....	....	....	....	....
6222 Currency and deposits.................	....	....	....	....	....	....	....	....	....	....	....	....
6223 Securities other than shares.........	....	....	....	....	....	....	....	....	....	....	....	....
6224 Loans................................	....	....	....	....	....	....	....	....	....	....	....	....
6225 Shares and other equity..............	....	....	....	....	....	....	....	....	....	....	....	....
6226 Insurance technical reserves.........	....	....	....	....	....	....	....	....	....	....	....	....
6227 Financial derivatives................	....	....	....	....	....	....	....	....	....	....	....	....
6228 Other accounts receivable............	....	....	....	....	....	....	....	....	....	....	....	....
623 Monetary gold and SDRs...............	....	....	....	....	....	....	....	....	....	....	....	....
63 **Liabilities**..............................	64,699.8	74,857.3	73,389.0	....	....	....	....	....	....	....	....	....
631 Domestic.............................	5,322.9	6,484.1	6,665.4	....	....	....	....	....	....	....	....	....
6312 Currency and deposits.................	....	....	....	....	....	....	....	....	....	....	....	....
6313 Securities other than shares.........	....	....	....	....	....	....	....	....	....	....	....	....
6314 Loans................................	....	....	....	....	....	....	....	....	....	....	....	....
6316 Insurance technical reserves.........	....	....	....	....	....	....	....	....	....	....	....	....
6317 Financial derivatives................	....	....	....	....	....	....	....	....	....	....	....	....
6318 Other accounts payable...............	....	....	....	....	....	....	....	....	....	....	....	....
632 Foreign..............................	59,376.9	68,373.2	66,723.6	....	....	....	....	....	....	....	....	....
6322 Currency and deposits.................	....	....	....	....	....	....	....	....	....	....	....	....
6323 Securities other than shares.........	....	....	....	....	....	....	....	....	....	....	....	....
6324 Loans................................	....	....	....	....	....	....	....	....	....	....	....	....
6326 Insurance technical reserves.........	....	....	....	....	....	....	....	....	....	....	....	....
6327 Financial derivatives................	....	....	....	....	....	....	....	....	....	....	....	....
6328 Other accounts payable...............	....	....	....	....	....	....	....	....	....	....	....	....
Memorandum items:												
6M2 Net financial worth..................	....	....	....	....	....	....	....	....	....	....	....	....
6M3 Debt at market value.................	....	....	....	....	....	....	....	....	....	....	....	....
6M4 Debt at nominal value................	....	....	....	....	....	....	....	....	....	....	....	....
6M5 Arrears..............................	....	....	....	....	....	....	....	....	....	....	....	....
6M6 Obligations for social security benefits...........	....	....	....	....	....	....	....	....	....	....	....	....
6M7 Contingent liabilities...............	....	....	....	....	....	....	....	....	....	....	....	....
6M8 Uncapitalized military weapons, systems........	....	....	....	....	....	....	....	....	....	....	....	....
Table 7 Outlays by functions of govt.												
7 **Total outlays**......................	9,611.5	11,761.3	13,098.8	....	....	....	2,829.3	3,454.0	4,079.4	....	....	....
701 **General public services**.....................	2,106.3	2,830.3	3,202.7	....	....	....	241.0	411.8	503.4	....	....	....
7017 Public debt transactions.............	743.0	940.6	1,045.5	....	....	....	—	—	—	....	....	....
7018 General transfers between levels of govt......	....	....	....	....	....	....	....	....	....	....	....	....
702 **Defense**...............................	844.3	1,137.5	980.6	....	....	....	11.1	17.0	19.6	....	....	....
703 **Public order and safety**.....................	464.6	744.1	752.0	....	....	....	31.4	35.6	36.7	....	....	....

2005, International Monetary Fund: *Government Finance Statistics Yearbook*

In Millions of Soms / Year Ending December 31 / Cash Reporter

		Budgetary Central Government			Central Government			Local Government			General Government		
		1999	2000	2001	1999	2000	2001	1999	2000	2001	1999	2000	2001
704	**Economic affairs**	1,108.7	1,342.7	1,423.1	....	....	....	74.1	82.9	74.6	....	....	....
7042	Agriculture, forestry, fishing, and hunting	388.8	476.1	606.9	....	....	....	49.4	52.6	35.5	....	....	....
7043	Fuel and energy	76.6	23.0	243.9	....	....	....	—	—	—	....	....	....
7044	Mining, manufacturing, and construction	81.1	330.3	103.2	....	....	....	2.5	13.0	3.5	....	....	....
7045	Transport	523.3	464.9	419.6	....	....	....	9.6	3.0	26.5	....	....	....
7046	Communication	....	....	....	....	....	....	....	....	....	....	....	....
705	**Environmental protection**	....	....	....	....	....	....	....	....	....	....	....	....
706	**Housing and community amenities**	464.7	666.5	800.9	....	....	....	185.4	255.5	324.5	....	....	....
707	**Health**	1,125.4	1,295.9	1,379.0	....	....	....	771.7	869.2	949.7	....	....	....
7072	Outpatient services	....	....	147.1	....	....	....	....	....	....	....	....	....
7073	Hospital services	....	....	915.7	....	....	....	....	....	....	....	....	....
7074	Public health services	....	....	....	....	....	....	....	....	....	....	....	....
708	**Recreation, culture, and religion**	308.1	337.3	295.0	....	....	....	87.4	117.1	119.9	....	....	....
709	**Education**	1,991.3	2,293.1	2,847.6	....	....	....	1,353.5	1,553.3	1,921.5	....	....	....
7091	Pre-primary and primary education	....	....	....	....	....	....	....	....	....	....	....	....
7092	Secondary education	....	....	2,036.8	....	....	....	....	....	....	....	....	....
7094	Tertiary education	....	....	490.3	....	....	....	....	....	....	....	....	....
710	**Social protection**	1,198.1	1,113.9	1,417.9	....	....	....	73.8	111.6	129.4	....	....	....
7	Statistical discrepancy: Total outlays	—	—	—	....	....	....	—	—	—	....	....	....

Table 8 Transactions in financial assets and liabilities by sector

		Budgetary Central Government			Central Government			Local Government			General Government		
82	**Net acquisition of financial assets**	....	....	....	....	....	....	....	....	....	....	....	....
821	Domestic	....	....	....	....	....	....	....	....	....	....	....	....
8211	General government	11.8	12.1	16.0	....	....	....	....	83.3	....	....	....	....
8212	Central bank	....	....	....	....	....	....	....	....	....	....	....	....
8213	Other depository corporations	....	....	....	....	....	....	....	....	....	....	....	....
8214	Financial corporations n.e.c.	....	....	....	....	....	....	....	....	....	....	....	....
8215	Nonfinancial corporations	−311.3	−465.2	−859.1	....	....	....	....	....	....	....	....	....
8216	Households & NPIs serving households	....	....	....	....	....	....	....	....	....	....	....	....
822	Foreign	....	....	....	....	....	....	....	....	....	....	....	....
8221	General government	....	....	....	....	....	....	....	....	....	....	....	....
8227	International organizations	....	....	....	....	....	....	....	....	....	....	....	....
8228	Financial corporations other than international organizations	....	....	....	....	....	....	....	....	....	....	....	....
8229	Other nonresidents	....	....	....	....	....	....	....	....	....	....	....	....
823	Monetary gold and SDRs	....	....	....	....	....	....	....	....	....	....	....	....
83	**Net incurrence of liabilities**	....	....	....	....	....	....	....	....	....	....	....	....
831	Domestic	....	....	....	....	....	....	....	....	....	....	....	....
8311	General government	....	....	....	....	....	....	....	....	....	....	....	....
8312	Central bank	....	....	....	....	....	....	....	....	....	....	....	....
8313	Other depository corporations	....	....	....	....	....	....	....	....	....	....	....	....
8314	Financial corporations n.e.c.	....	....	....	....	....	....	....	....	....	....	....	....
8315	Nonfinancial corporations	....	....	....	....	....	....	....	....	....	....	....	....
8316	Households & NPIs serving households	....	....	....	....	....	....	....	....	....	....	....	....
832	Foreign	....	....	....	....	....	....	....	....	....	....	....	....
8321	General government	....	....	....	....	....	....	....	....	....	....	....	....
8327	International organizations	....	....	....	....	....	....	....	....	....	....	....	....
8328	Financial corporations other than international organizations	....	....	....	....	....	....	....	....	....	....	....	....
8329	Other nonresidents	....	....	....	....	....	....	....	....	....	....	....	....

Latvia   941

In Millions of Lats / Year Ending December 31 / Cash Reporter

	Budgetary Central Government			Central Government			Local Government			General Government		
	2002	2003	2004	2002	2003	2004	2002	2003	2004	2002	2003	2004
Statement of government operations												
Statement of other economic flows												
Balance sheet												
Statement of sources and uses of cash												
1 Cash receipts from operating activities..........	†818.5	937.6	†1,419.2	1,529.2	1,715.5	2,056.5	507.1	580.2	680.3	1,872.2	2,107.4	2,522.2
11 Taxes....................	†622.7	705.9	†1,011.9	790.6	901.4	1,011.9	279.1	319.3	373.4	1,069.7	1,220.7	1,385.3
12 Social contributions...............	†—	—	†—	528.8	561.9	641.2	—	—	—	528.8	561.9	641.2
13 Grants....................	†29.1	50.7	†154.9	28.1	51.1	154.9	161.1	168.7	211.0	28.1	50.0	154.4
14 Other receipts..............	†166.7	181.0	†252.4	181.8	201.1	248.5	66.9	92.2	95.9	245.7	274.8	341.3
2 Cash payments for operating activities..........	†908.8	1,029.8	†1,501.7	1,597.1	1,735.7	2,064.1	499.5	551.5	612.4	1,932.6	2,098.9	2,461.9
21 Compensation of employees................	†245.7	280.5	†330.7	249.6	284.0	335.4	247.1	279.3	319.0	496.7	563.3	654.4
22 Purchases of goods and services....................	†165.4	198.5	†251.8	191.1	227.5	257.5	133.9	153.5	175.8	324.9	380.3	433.3
24 Interest....................	†44.3	47.0	†52.0	44.3	47.0	50.0	5.5	7.2	7.7	46.7	51.3	54.6
25 Subsidies....................	†35.7	45.3	†37.6	42.1	52.8	37.6	.3	.7	.9	42.4	53.5	38.5
26 Grants....................	†222.8	240.8	†225.2	161.1	164.3	210.6	—	—	.9	—	—	—
27 Social benefits....................	†81.3	91.1	†94.9	591.9	613.0	659.8	18.7	19.6	21.8	610.6	632.6	681.6
28 Other payments....................	†113.7	126.6	†509.5	317.2	347.1	513.2	94.1	91.2	86.3	411.3	417.9	599.5
CIO *Net cash inflow from oper. activities.....*	*†–90.3*	*–92.2*	*†–82.5*	*–67.9*	*–20.2*	*–7.6*	*7.6*	*28.7*	*67.9*	*–60.3*	*8.5*	*60.3*
31.1 Purchases of nonfinancial assets....................	†19.8	33.5	†62.5	37.1	60.5	62.5	52.4	53.1	75.1	89.5	113.6	137.6
31.2 Sales of nonfinancial assets....................	†.1	—	†—	.1	—	—	1.8	—	—	1.8	—	—
31 Net cash outflow from investments in nonfinancial assets....................	†19.8	33.5	†62.5	37.0	60.5	62.5	50.6	53.1	75.1	87.7	113.6	137.6
CSD *Cash surplus/deficit....................*	*†–110.1*	*–125.7*	*†–145.0*	*–104.9*	*–80.7*	*–70.1*	*–43.1*	*–24.4*	*–7.2*	*–148.0*	*–105.1*	*–77.3*
32x Net acquisition of fin assets, excl. cash..........	....	....	†–20.5	–5.7	–10.1	11.1	.7	—	–.4	–17.5	–21.2	1.1
321x Domestic....................	....	....	†–20.5	–5.7	–10.1	11.1	.7	—	–.4	–17.5	–21.2	1.1
322x Foreign....................	....	....	†—	—	—	—	—	—	—	—	—	—
323 Monetary gold and SDRs....................	....	....	†—	—	—	—	—	—	—	—	—	—
33 Net incurrence of liabilities....................	....	....	†145.6	58.8	60.2	153.5	43.8	29.2	–2.4	90.1	78.3	141.5
331 Domestic....................	....	....	†19.0	51.2	105.1	26.9	43.8	29.2	–2.2	82.5	123.2	15.1
332 Foreign....................	....	....	†126.6	7.6	–44.9	126.6	—	—	–.2	7.6	–44.9	126.4
NFB Net cash inflow from fin. activities....................	....	....	†166.1	64.6	70.3	142.4	43.1	29.2	–2.0	107.6	99.5	140.4
NCB *Net change in the stock of cash....................*	....	....	*†21.1*	*–40.4*	*–10.4*	*72.3*	*—*	*4.8*	*–9.2*	*–40.4*	*–5.6*	*63.1*
Table 1 Revenue												
1 **Revenue......................**	**†818.5**	**937.6**	**†1,419.2**	**1,529.2**	**1,715.5**	**2,056.5**	**507.1**	**580.2**	**680.3**	**1,872.2**	**2,107.4**	**2,522.2**
11 **Taxes......................**	**†622.7**	**705.9**	**†1,011.9**	**790.6**	**901.4**	**1,011.9**	**279.1**	**319.3**	**373.4**	**1,069.7**	**1,220.7**	**1,385.3**
111 Taxes on income, profits, & capital gains......	†109.7	93.9	†251.4	200.8	197.6	251.4	228.5	263.5	311.9	429.2	461.1	563.3
1111 Individuals....................	†—	—	†123.6	91.1	103.7	123.6	228.5	263.5	311.9	319.5	367.2	435.5
1112 Corporations and other enterprises....................	†109.7	93.9	†127.8	109.7	93.9	127.8	—	—	—	109.7	93.9	127.8
112 Taxes on payroll and workforce....................	†—	—	†—	—	—	—	—	—	—	—	—	—
113 Taxes on property....................	†—	—	†—	—	—	—	46.7	51.8	56.8	46.7	51.8	56.8
114 Taxes on goods and services....................	†497.9	593.2	†737.3	566.1	677.2	737.3	1.8	1.9	2.5	567.9	679.1	739.8
1141 General taxes on goods and services..........	†383.0	459.2	†486.7	383.0	459.2	486.7	—	—	—	383.0	459.2	486.7
1142 Excises....................	†114.9	134.0	†236.9	177.5	212.1	236.9	—	—	—	177.5	212.1	236.9
115 Taxes on int'l. trade and transactions..........	†15.1	18.8	†17.1	15.1	18.8	17.1	—	—	—	15.1	18.8	17.1
116 Other taxes....................	†—	—	†6.1	8.6	7.8	6.1	2.2	2.1	2.2	10.8	9.9	8.3
12 **Social contributions....................**	**†—**	**—**	**†—**	**528.8**	**561.9**	**641.2**	**—**	**—**	**—**	**528.8**	**561.9**	**641.2**
121 Social security contributions....................	†—	—	†—	528.8	561.9	641.2	—	—	—	528.8	561.9	641.2
122 Other social contributions....................	†—	—	†—	—	—	—	—	—	—	—	—	—
13 **Grants....................**	**†29.1**	**50.7**	**†154.9**	**28.1**	**51.1**	**154.9**	**161.1**	**168.7**	**211.0**	**28.1**	**50.0**	**154.4**
131 From foreign governments....................	†27.9	50.7	†154.0	28.1	51.1	154.0	—	4.4	.4	28.1	50.0	154.4
132 From international organizations....................	†—	—	†—	—	—	—	—	—	—	—	—	—
133 From other general government units..........	†1.2	—	†.9	—	—	.9	161.1	164.3	210.6	—	—	—
14 **Other revenue....................**	**†166.7**	**181.0**	**†252.4**	**181.8**	**201.1**	**248.5**	**66.9**	**92.2**	**95.9**	**245.7**	**274.8**	**341.3**
Table 2 Expense by economic type												
2 **Expense....................**	**†908.8**	**1,029.8**	**†1,501.7**	**1,597.1**	**1,735.7**	**2,064.1**	**499.5**	**551.5**	**612.4**	**1,932.6**	**2,098.9**	**2,461.9**
21 **Compensation of employees....................**	**†245.7**	**280.5**	**†330.7**	**249.6**	**284.0**	**335.4**	**247.1**	**279.3**	**319.0**	**496.7**	**563.3**	**654.4**
211 Wages and salaries....................	†193.5	228.0	†268.8	196.6	230.9	272.6	197.1	226.1	258.6	393.7	457.0	531.2
212 Social contributions....................	†52.2	52.5	†61.9	53.0	53.1	62.8	50.0	53.2	60.4	103.0	106.3	123.2
22 **Use of goods and services....................**	**†165.4**	**198.5**	**†251.8**	**191.1**	**227.5**	**257.5**	**133.9**	**153.5**	**175.8**	**324.9**	**380.3**	**433.3**
23 **Consumption of fixed capital................**	....	....	....	....	....	....	....	....	....	....	....	....
24 **Interest....................**	**†44.3**	**47.0**	**†52.0**	**44.3**	**47.0**	**50.0**	**5.5**	**7.2**	**7.7**	**46.7**	**51.3**	**54.6**
25 **Subsidies....................**	**†35.7**	**45.3**	**†37.6**	**42.1**	**52.8**	**37.6**	**.3**	**.7**	**.9**	**42.4**	**53.5**	**38.5**

In Millions of Lats / Year Ending December 31 / Cash Reporter

		Budgetary Central Government			Central Government			Local Government			General Government		
		2002	2003	2004	2002	2003	2004	2002	2003	2004	2002	2003	2004
26	Grants	†222.8	240.8	†225.2	161.1	164.3	210.6	—	—	.9	—	—	—
261	To foreign govenments	†—	—	†—	—	—	—	—	—	—	—	—	—
262	To international organizations	†—	—	†—	—	—	—	—	—	—	—	—	—
263	To other general government units	†222.8	240.8	†225.2	161.1	164.3	210.6	—	—	.9	—	—	—
2631	Current	†210.8	240.6	†225.2	150.0	164.2	210.6	—	—	.9	—	—	—
2632	Capital	†11.9	.2	†—	11.1	.1	—	—	—	—	—	—	—
27	Social benefits	†81.3	91.1	†94.9	591.9	613.0	659.8	18.7	19.6	21.8	610.6	632.6	681.6
28	Other expense	†113.7	126.6	†509.5	317.2	347.1	513.2	94.1	91.2	86.3	411.3	417.9	599.5
281	Property expense other than interest	†—	—	†.5	—	—	.5	—	—	—	—	—	.5
282	Miscellaneous other expense	†113.7	126.6	†509.0	317.2	347.1	512.7	94.1	91.2	86.3	411.3	417.9	599.0
2821	Current	†58.8	65.1	†423.1	252.8	279.9	424.9	.9	37.8	48.3	253.6	308.4	473.2
2822	Capital	†54.9	61.5	†85.9	64.4	67.2	87.8	93.2	53.4	38.0	157.6	109.5	125.8

Table 3   Transactions in assets and liabilities

		Budgetary Central Government			Central Government			Local Government			General Government		
3	Change in net worth from transactns	....	....	....	....	....	....	....	....	....	....	....	....
31	Net acquisition of nonfinancial assets	†19.8	33.5	†62.5	37.0	60.5	62.5	50.6	53.1	75.1	87.7	113.6	137.6
311	Fixed assets	†18.6	30.6	†57.9	35.8	57.0	57.9	48.9	52.0	74.5	84.7	109.0	132.4
3111	Buildings and structures	†5.6	13.3	†41.8	21.5	38.7	41.8	−1.8	52.0	74.5	19.8	90.7	116.3
3112	Machinery and equipment	†11.8	17.3	†16.1	12.9	18.3	16.1	—	—	—	12.9	18.3	16.1
3113	Other fixed assets	†1.2	—	†—	1.4	—	—	50.7	—	—	52.0	—	—
312	Inventories	†—	—	†—	—	—	—	—	—	—	—	—	—
313	Valuables	†—	—	†—	—	.1	—	—	—	—	—	.1	—
314	Nonproduced assets	†1.2	2.9	†4.6	1.3	3.4	4.6	1.7	1.1	.6	3.0	4.5	5.2
3141	Land	†.3	.1	†.2	.4	.6	.2	1.7	1.1	.6	2.1	1.7	.8
3142	Subsoil assets	†—	—	†—	—	—	—	—	—	—	—	—	—
3143	Other naturally occurring assets	†—	—	†—	—	—	—	—	—	—	—	—	—
3144	Intangible nonproduced assets	†.9	2.8	†4.4	.9	2.8	4.4	—	—	—	.9	2.8	4.4
32	Net acquisition of financial assets	....	....	†.6	−46.1	−20.5	83.4	.7	4.8	−9.6	−57.9	−26.8	64.2
321	Domestic	....	....	†−6.9	−42.5	−27.4	75.9	3.5	5.1	−9.6	−51.5	−33.4	56.7
3212	Currency and deposits	....	....	†13.6	−36.8	−17.3	64.8	2.8	5.1	−9.2	−34.0	−12.2	55.6
3213	Securities other than shares	....	....	†—	—	—	—	—	—	—	—	—	—
3214	Loans	....	....	†−20.5	−5.7	−10.1	11.1	.7	—	−.4	−17.5	−21.2	1.1
3215	Shares and other equity	....	....	†—	—	—	—	—	—	—	—	—	—
3216	Insurance technical reserves	....	....	†—	—	—	—	—	—	—	—	—	—
3217	Financial derivatives	....	....	†—	—	—	—	—	—	—	—	—	—
3218	Other accounts receivable	....	....	....	....	....	....	....	....	....	....	....	....
322	Foreign	....	....	†7.5	−3.6	6.9	7.5	−2.8	−.3	—	−6.4	6.6	7.5
3222	Currency and deposits	....	....	†7.5	−3.6	6.9	7.5	−2.8	−.3	—	−6.4	6.6	7.5
3223	Securities other than shares	....	....	†—	—	—	—	—	—	—	—	—	—
3224	Loans	....	....	†—	—	—	—	—	—	—	—	—	—
3225	Shares and other equity	....	....	†—	—	—	—	—	—	—	—	—	—
3226	Insurance technical reserves	....	....	†—	—	—	—	—	—	—	—	—	—
3227	Financial derivatives	....	....	†—	—	—	—	—	—	—	—	—	—
3228	Other accounts receivable	....	....	....	....	....	....	....	....	....	....	....	....
323	Monetary gold and SDRs	....	....	†—	....	....	....	....	....	....	....	....	....
33	Net incurrence of liabilities	....	....	†145.6	58.8	60.2	153.5	43.8	29.2	−2.4	90.1	78.3	141.5
331	Domestic	....	....	†19.0	51.2	105.1	26.9	43.8	29.2	−2.2	82.5	123.2	15.1
3312	Currency and deposits	....	....	†—	15.7	−12.7	—	—	—	—	—	−12.7	—
3313	Securities other than shares	....	....	†43.3	35.6	82.3	43.3	—	—	—	35.6	82.3	43.3
3314	Loans	....	....	†−24.3	—	35.5	−16.4	43.9	29.2	−2.2	31.4	53.6	−28.2
3316	Insurance technical reserves	....	....	†—	—	—	—	—	—	—	—	—	—
3317	Financial derivatives	....	....	†—	—	—	—	—	—	—	—	—	—
3318	Other accounts payable	....	....	....	....	....	....	....	....	....	....	....	....
332	Foreign	....	....	†126.6	7.6	−44.9	126.6	—	—	−.2	7.6	−44.9	126.4
3322	Currency and deposits	....	....	†—	—	—	—	—	—	—	—	—	—
3323	Securities other than shares	....	....	†—	—	—	—	—	—	—	—	—	—
3324	Loans	....	....	†126.6	7.6	−44.9	126.6	—	—	−.2	7.6	−44.9	126.4
3326	Insurance technical reserves	....	....	†—	—	—	—	—	—	—	—	—	—
3327	Financial derivatives	....	....	†—	—	—	—	—	—	—	—	—	—
3328	Other accounts payable	....	....	....	....	....	....	....	....	....	....	....	....

In Millions of Lats / Year Ending December 31 / Cash Reporter

	Budgetary Central Government			Central Government			Local Government			General Government		
	2002	2003	2004	2002	2003	2004	2002	2003	2004	2002	2003	2004
Table 4 Holding gains in assets and liabilities												
Table 5 Other changes in the volume of assets and liabilities												
Table 6 Balance sheet												
Table 7 Outlays by functions of govt.												
7 Total outlays..........	†928.6	1,063.3	†1,564.2	1,634.1	1,796.2	2,126.6	550.2	604.6	687.5	2,020.2	2,212.5	2,599.5
701 General public services..........	†323.8	344.4	†475.2	327.5	347.1	473.2	77.3	93.8	104.6	261.3	288.8	406.6
7017 Public debt transactions..........	†44.3	47.0	†52.0	44.3	47.0	50.0	5.5	7.2	7.7	46.7	51.3	54.6
7018 General transfers between levels of govt......	†279.5	297.4	†423.2	283.2	300.1	423.2	71.8	86.6	96.9	214.6	237.5	352.0
702 Defense..........	†67.6	80.5	†91.4	67.3	80.3	91.3	.1	.1	.1	67.4	79.5	90.1
703 Public order and safety..........	†123.0	145.8	†154.8	123.1	145.9	154.8	6.8	7.9	8.9	129.9	153.8	163.7
704 Economic affairs..........	†95.4	123.8	†290.4	166.0	211.2	290.4	27.7	35.2	41.7	173.3	221.6	303.0
7042 Agriculture, forestry, fishing, and hunting.....	†77.4	105.6	†162.3	77.9	106.6	162.3	1.8	2.5	3.0	79.7	109.1	161.3
7043 Fuel and energy..........	†.1	.1	†.1	.1	.1	.1	3.8	1.3	1.5	3.8	1.4	1.6
7044 Mining, manufacturing, and construction.....	†.9	.8	†1.4	.9	1.4	1.4	—	—	.1	.9	1.4	1.5
7045 Transport..........	†17.1	17.3	†126.6	87.1	103.1	126.6	22.1	31.4	37.1	88.9	109.7	138.6
7046 Communication..........	....	....	....	....	....	....	....	....	....	....	....	....
705 Environmental protection..........	....	....	....	....	....	....	....	....	....	....	....	....
706 Housing and community amenities........	†8.1	14.5	†30.9	17.6	20.6	30.9	91.3	93.3	104.7	108.9	113.3	135.0
707 Health..........	†86.3	95.6	†234.1	180.1	200.8	234.1	7.3	6.3	11.6	187.4	207.1	245.7
7072 Outpatient services..........	....	....	....	....	....	....	....	....	....	....	....	....
7073 Hospital services..........	....	....	....	....	....	....	....	....	....	....	....	....
7074 Public health services..........	....	....	....	....	....	....	....	....	....	....	....	....
708 Recreation, culture, and religion..........	†31.1	32.6	†45.7	42.0	43.8	45.7	37.1	44.8	50.2	78.8	88.4	95.1
709 Education..........	†106.6	118.3	†129.7	106.4	117.4	129.7	260.2	278.4	311.8	366.6	386.2	429.9
7091 Pre-primary and primary education..........	....	....	....	....	....	....	....	....	....	....	....	....
7092 Secondary education..........	....	....	....	....	....	....	....	....	....	....	....	....
7094 Tertiary education..........	....	....	....	....	....	....	....	....	....	....	....	....
710 Social protection..........	†86.6	107.8	†112.0	604.3	629.1	676.5	42.4	44.8	53.9	646.7	673.8	730.4
7 Statistical discrepancy: Total outlays..........	†—	—	†—	—	—	—	—	—	—	—	—	—
Table 8 Transactions in financial assets and liabilities by sector												
82 Net acquisition of financial assets........	....	....	†.6	−46.1	−20.5	83.4	.7	4.8	−9.6	−57.9	−26.8	64.2
821 Domestic..........	....	....	†−6.9	−42.5	−27.4	75.9	3.5	5.1	−9.6	−51.5	−33.4	56.7
8211 General government..........	....	....	†−20.5	12.5	−11.2	11.1	—	−9.7	1.3	—	−32.0	2.8
8212 Central bank..........	....	....	†−32.5	−57.9	11.4	18.7	—	—	—	−57.9	11.4	18.7
8213 Other depository corporations..........	....	....	†46.1	—	−27.6	46.1	—	14.8	−10.5	—	−12.8	35.6
8214 Financial corporations n.e.c..........	....	....	†—	21.1	—	—	2.8	—	—	23.9	—	—
8215 Nonfinancial corporations..........	....	....	†—	—	—	—	—	—	−.4	—	—	−.4
8216 Households & NPIs serving households......	....	....	†—	−18.2	—	—	.7	—	—	−17.5	—	—
822 Foreign..........	....	....	†7.5	−3.6	6.9	7.5	−2.8	−.3	—	−6.4	6.6	7.5
8221 General government..........	....	....	†7.5	—	6.9	7.5	—	−.3	—	—	6.6	7.5
8227 International organizations..........	....	....	†—	−3.6	—	—	−2.8	—	—	−6.4	—	—
8228 Financial corporations other than international organizations..........	....	....	†—	—	—	—	—	—	—	—	—	—
8229 Other nonresidents..........	....	....	†—	—	—	—	—	—	—	—	—	—
823 Monetary gold and SDRs..........	....	....	†—	—	—	—	—	—	—	—	—	—
83 Net incurrence of liabilities..........	....	....	†145.6	58.8	60.2	153.5	43.8	29.2	−2.4	90.1	78.3	141.5
831 Domestic..........	....	....	†19.0	51.2	105.1	26.9	43.8	29.2	−2.2	82.5	123.2	15.1
8311 General government..........	....	....	†−7.9	—	−4.5	—	24.1	−28.0	−12.1	11.6	−43.6	−21.7
8312 Central bank..........	....	....	†30.4	51.0	−1.5	30.4	—	—	—	51.0	−1.5	30.4
8313 Other depository corporations..........	....	....	†−3.5	—	111.1	−3.5	—	57.2	9.9	—	168.3	6.4
8314 Financial corporations n.e.c..........	....	....	†—	.3	—	—	19.7	—	—	19.9	—	—
8315 Nonfinancial corporations..........	....	....	†—	—	—	—	—	—	—	—	—	—
8316 Households & NPIs serving households......	....	....	†—	—	—	—	—	—	—	—	—	—
832 Foreign..........	....	....	†126.6	7.6	−44.9	126.6	—	—	−.2	7.6	−44.9	126.4
8321 General government..........	....	....	†−2.5	—	−24.9	−2.5	—	—	—	—	−24.9	−2.5
8327 International organizations..........	....	....	†−.7	7.6	−46.7	−.7	—	—	−.2	7.6	−46.7	−.9
8328 Financial corporations other than international organizations..........	....	....	†−1.2	—	−.1	−1.2	—	—	—	—	−.1	−1.2
8329 Other nonresidents..........	....	....	†131.0	—	26.8	131.0	—	—	—	—	26.8	131.0

In Billions of Pounds / Year Ending December 31 / Noncash Reporter

	Budgetary Central Government			Central Government			Local Government			General Government		
	2001	2002	2003p	2001	2002	2003	2001	2002	2003	2001	2002	2003
Statement of government operations												
1 Revenue	4,260	5,385	6,181	....	....	....	....	....	....	....	....	....
2 Expense	7,719	8,186	9,226	....	....	....	....	....	....	....	....	....
GOB *Gross operating balance*	–3,459	–2,800	–3,045	....	....	....	....	....	....	....	....	....
NOB *Net operating balance*	....	....	....	....	....	....	....	....	....	....	....	....
31 Net acquisition of nonfinancial assets	545	870	967	....	....	....	....	....	....	....	....	....
NLB *Net lending/borrowing*	–4,003	–3,670	–4,012	....	....	....	....	....	....	....	....	....
32 Net acquisition of financial assets	814	314	–394	....	....	....	....	....	....	....	....	....
33 Net incurrence of liabilities	4,817	3,984	3,618	....	....	....	....	....	....	....	....	....
NLB Statistical discrepancy	—	—	—	....	....	....	....	....	....	....	....	....
Statement of other economic flows												
Balance sheet												
Statement of sources and uses of cash												
Table 1 Revenue												
1 **Revenue**	**4,260**	**5,385**	**6,181**	....	....	....	....	....	....	....	....	....
11 **Taxes**	**3,160**	**4,166**	**4,655**	....	....	....	....	....	....	....	....	....
111 Taxes on income, profits, & capital gains	494	590	610	....	....	....	....	....	....	....	....	....
1111 Individuals	....	....	....	....	....	....	....	....	....	....	....	....
1112 Corporations and other enterprises	....	....	....	....	....	....	....	....	....	....	....	....
112 Taxes on payroll and workforce	132	137	174	....	....	....	....	....	....	....	....	....
113 Taxes on property	274	300	321	....	....	....	....	....	....	....	....	....
114 Taxes on goods and services	1,213	2,356	2,858	....	....	....	....	....	....	....	....	....
1141 General taxes on goods and services	—	993	1,323	....	....	....	....	....	....	....	....	....
1142 Excises	836	1,031	1,170	....	....	....	....	....	....	....	....	....
115 Taxes on int'l. trade and transactions	857	596	475	....	....	....	....	....	....	....	....	....
116 Other taxes	191	189	218	....	....	....	....	....	....	....	....	....
12 **Social contributions**	**74**	**75**	**73**	....	....	....	....	....	....	....	....	....
121 Social security contributions	—	—	—	....	....	....	....	....	....	....	....	....
122 Other social contributions	74	75	73	....	....	....	....	....	....	....	....	....
13 **Grants**	—	—	—	....	....	....	....	....	....	....	....	....
131 From foreign governments	—	—	—	....	....	....	....	....	....	....	....	....
132 From international organizations	—	—	—	....	....	....	....	....	....	....	....	....
133 From other general government units	—	—	—	....	....	....	....	....	....	....	....	....
14 **Other revenue**	**1,025**	**1,144**	**1,453**	....	....	....	....	....	....	....	....	....
Table 2 Expense by economic type												
2 **Expense**	**7,719**	**8,186**	**9,225**	....	....	....	....	....	....	....	....	....
21 **Compensation of employees**	**2,594**	**2,666**	**2,757**	....	....	....	....	....	....	....	....	....
211 Wages and salaries	2,448	2,508	2,600	....	....	....	....	....	....	....	....	....
212 Social contributions	146	158	157	....	....	....	....	....	....	....	....	....
22 **Use of goods and services**	**237**	**233**	**243**	....	....	....	....	....	....	....	....	....
23 **Consumption of fixed capital**	....	....	....	....	....	....	....	....	....	....	....	....
24 **Interest**	**4,091**	**4,366**	**4,942**	....	....	....	....	....	....	....	....	....
25 **Subsidies**	**15**	**17**	**259**	....	....	....	....	....	....	....	....	....
26 **Grants**	**5**	**4**	**71**	....	....	....	....	....	....	....	....	....
261 To foreign govenments	—	—	—	....	....	....	....	....	....	....	....	....
262 To international organizations	5	4	5	....	....	....	....	....	....	....	....	....
263 To other general government units	—	—	66	....	....	....	....	....	....	....	....	....
2631 Current	—	—	66	....	....	....	....	....	....	....	....	....
2632 Capital	—	—	—	....	....	....	....	....	....	....	....	....
27 **Social benefits**	**627**	**702**	**733**	....	....	....	....	....	....	....	....	....
28 **Other expense**	**148**	**198**	**220**	....	....	....	....	....	....	....	....	....
281 Property expense other than interest	18	16	12	....	....	....	....	....	....	....	....	....
282 Miscellaneous other expense	131	182	208	....	....	....	....	....	....	....	....	....
2821 Current	131	182	208	....	....	....	....	....	....	....	....	....
2822 Capital	—	—	—	....	....	....	....	....	....	....	....	....

In Billions of Pounds / Year Ending December 31 / Noncash Reporter

	Budgetary Central Government			Central Government			Local Government			General Government		
	2001	2002	2003p	2001	2002	2003	2001	2002	2003	2001	2002	2003
Table 3 Transactions in assets and liabilities												
3 Change in net worth from transactns....	....	....	....	....	....	....	....	....	....	....	....	....
31 **Net acquisition of nonfinancial assets...**	**545**	**870**	**967**	....	....	....	....	....	....	....	....	....
311 Fixed assets.............................	528	849	960	....	....	....	....	....	....	....	....	....
3111 Buildings and structures..........................	463	757	872	....	....	....	....	....	....	....	....	....
3112 Machinery and equipment......................	46	55	49	....	....	....	....	....	....	....	....	....
3113 Other fixed assets............................	18	38	40	....	....	....	....	....	....	....	....	....
312 Inventories.................................	—	—	—	....	....	....	....	....	....	....	....	....
313 Valuables..................................	—	—	—	....	....	....	....	....	....	....	....	....
314 Nonproduced assets.......................	17	21	7	....	....	....	....	....	....	....	....	....
3141 Land....................................	17	21	7	....	....	....	....	....	....	....	....	....
3142 Subsoil assets..........................	—	—	—	....	....	....	....	....	....	....	....	....
3143 Other naturally occurring assets.................	—	—	—	....	....	....	....	....	....	....	....	....
3144 Intangible nonproduced assets..................	—	—	—	....	....	....	....	....	....	....	....	....
32 **Net acquisition of financial assets........**	**814**	**314**	**−394**	....	....	....	....	....	....	....	....	....
321 Domestic..................................	814	314	3	....	....	....	....	....	....	....	....	....
3212 Currency and deposits........................	814	314	−277	....	....	....	....	....	....	....	....	....
3213 Securities other than shares....................	—	—	—	....	....	....	....	....	....	....	....	....
3214 Loans...................................	—	—	—	....	....	....	....	....	....	....	....	....
3215 Shares and other equity.......................	—	—	280	....	....	....	....	....	....	....	....	....
3216 Insurance technical reserves....................	—	—	—	....	....	....	....	....	....	....	....	....
3217 Financial derivatives........................	—	—	—	....	....	....	....	....	....	....	....	....
3218 Other accounts receivable.....................	—	—	—	....	....	....	....	....	....	....	....	....
322 Foreign...................................	—	—	−397	....	....	....	....	....	....	....	....	....
3222 Currency and deposits........................	—	—	−397	....	....	....	....	....	....	....	....	....
3223 Securities other than shares....................	—	—	—	....	....	....	....	....	....	....	....	....
3224 Loans...................................	—	—	—	....	....	....	....	....	....	....	....	....
3225 Shares and other equity.......................	—	—	—	....	....	....	....	....	....	....	....	....
3226 Insurance technical reserves....................	—	—	—	....	....	....	....	....	....	....	....	....
3227 Financial derivatives........................	—	—	—	....	....	....	....	....	....	....	....	....
3228 Other accounts receivable.....................	—	—	—	....	....	....	....	....	....	....	....	....
323 Monetary gold and SDRs....................	—	—	—	....	....	....	....	....	....	....	....	....
33 **Net incurrence of liabilities...................**	**4,817**	**3,984**	**3,618**	....	....	....	....	....	....	....	....	....
331 Domestic..................................	1,249	−3,472	1,562	....	....	....	....	....	....	....	....	....
3312 Currency and deposits........................	165	−631	−27	....	....	....	....	....	....	....	....	....
3313 Securities other than shares....................	1,109	−2,838	1,623	....	....	....	....	....	....	....	....	....
3314 Loans...................................	−25	−3	−16	....	....	....	....	....	....	....	....	....
3316 Insurance technical reserves....................	—	—	—	....	....	....	....	....	....	....	....	....
3317 Financial derivatives........................	—	—	—	....	....	....	....	....	....	....	....	....
3318 Other accounts payable.......................	—	—	−18	....	....	....	....	....	....	....	....	....
332 Foreign...................................	3,568	7,456	2,056	....	....	....	....	....	....	....	....	....
3322 Currency and deposits........................	—	—	—	....	....	....	....	....	....	....	....	....
3323 Securities other than shares....................	3,550	7,385	1,030	....	....	....	....	....	....	....	....	....
3324 Loans...................................	18	72	1,026	....	....	....	....	....	....	....	....	....
3326 Insurance technical reserves....................	—	—	—	....	....	....	....	....	....	....	....	....
3327 Financial derivatives........................	—	—	—	....	....	....	....	....	....	....	....	....
3328 Other accounts payable.......................	—	—	—	....	....	....	....	....	....	....	....	....
Table 4 Holding gains in assets and liabilities												
Table 5 Other changes in the volume of assets and liabilities												
Table 6 Balance sheet												
Table 7 Outlays by functions of govt.												
7 **Total outlays....................**	**8,263**	**9,056**	**10,192**	....	....	....	....	....	....	....	....	....
701 **General public services.........................**	**5,265**	**5,576**	**6,244**	....	....	....	....	....	....	....	....	....
7017 Public debt transactions......................	4,091	4,366	4,942	....	....	....	....	....	....	....	....	....
7018 General transfers between levels of govt......	1,174	1,210	1,302	....	....	....	....	....	....	....	....	....
702 **Defense.................................**	**971**	**932**	**927**	....	....	....	....	....	....	....	....	....
703 **Public order and safety.........................**	**345**	**395**	**398**	....	....	....	....	....	....	....	....	....
704 **Economic affairs..............................**	**515**	**808**	**1,138**	....	....	....	....	....	....	....	....	....
7042 Agriculture, forestry, fishing, and hunting......	22	34	29	....	....	....	....	....	....	....	....	....
7043 Fuel and energy............................	5	6	184	....	....	....	....	....	....	....	....	....
7044 Mining, manufacturing, and construction.....	234	200	4	....	....	....	....	....	....	....	....	....
7045 Transport.................................	182	215	196	....	....	....	....	....	....	....	....	....
7046 Communication...........................	11	12	11	....	....	....	....	....	....	....	....	....

		Budgetary Central Government			Central Government			Local Government			General Government		
		2001	2002	2003p	2001	2002	2003	2001	2002	2003	2001	2002	2003
705	**Environmental protection**...................	5	9	19	....	....	....	....	....	....	....	....	....
706	**Housing and community amenities**........	40	73	67	....	....	....	....	....	....	....	....	....
707	**Health**..	251	298	351	....	....	....	....	....	....	....	....	....
7072	Outpatient services............................	....	....	....	....	....	....	....	....	....	....	....	....
7073	Hospital services...............................	181	216	272	....	....	....	....	....	....	....	....	....
7074	Public health services.........................	....	....	....	....	....	....	....	....	....	....	....	....
708	**Recreation, culture, and religion**...........	50	59	52	....	....	....	....	....	....	....	....	....
709	**Education**.......................................	700	728	780	....	....	....	....	....	....	....	....	....
7091	Pre-primary and primary education..............	350	348	399	....	....	....	....	....	....	....	....	....
7092	Secondary education............................	133	143	147	....	....	....	....	....	....	....	....	....
7094	Tertiary education..............................	218	237	234	....	....	....	....	....	....	....	....	....
710	**Social protection**..............................	122	178	216	....	....	....	....	....	....	....	....	....
7	Statistical discrepancy: Total outlays.............	—	—	—	....	....	....	....	....	....	....	....	....

Table 8   Transactions in financial assets and liabilities by sector

		Budgetary Central Government			Central Government			Local Government			General Government		
82	**Net acquisition of financial assets**........	814	314	−394	....	....	....	....	....	....	....	....	....
821	Domestic..	814	314	3	....	....	....	....	....	....	....	....	....
8211	General government............................	....	....	—	....	....	....	....	....	....	....	....	....
8212	Central bank....................................	....	....	−277	....	....	....	....	....	....	....	....	....
8213	Other depository corporations...................	....	....	—	....	....	....	....	....	....	....	....	....
8214	Financial corporations n.e.c...................	....	....	—	....	....	....	....	....	....	....	....	....
8215	Nonfinancial corporations......................	....	....	280	....	....	....	....	....	....	....	....	....
8216	Households & NPIs serving households......	....	....	—	....	....	....	....	....	....	....	....	....
822	Foreign...	—	—	−397	....	....	....	....	....	....	....	....	....
8221	General government............................	—	—	....	....	....	....	....	....	....	....	....	....
8227	International organizations.....................	—	—	....	....	....	....	....	....	....	....	....	....
8228	Financial corporations other than international organizations..............	—	—	....	....	....	....	....	....	....	....	....	....
8229	Other nonresidents..............................	—	—	....	....	....	....	....	....	....	....	....	....
823	Monetary gold and SDRs.......................	—	—	—	....	....	....	....	....	....	....	....	....
83	**Net incurrence of liabilities**...................	4,817	3,984	3,618	....	....	....	....	....	....	....	....	....
831	Domestic..	1,249	−3,472	1,562	....	....	....	....	....	....	....	....	....
8311	General government............................	491	−465	−650	....	....	....	....	....	....	....	....	....
8312	Central bank....................................	4,524	−5,528	7,850	....	....	....	....	....	....	....	....	....
8313	Other depository corporations...................	−2,906	1,382	−4,602	....	....	....	....	....	....	....	....	....
8314	Financial corporations n.e.c...................	9	16	−23	....	....	....	....	....	....	....	....	....
8315	Nonfinancial corporations......................	—	—	—	....	....	....	....	....	....	....	....	....
8316	Households & NPIs serving households......	−869	1,123	−1,013	....	....	....	....	....	....	....	....	....
832	Foreign...	3,568	7,456	2,056	....	....	....	....	....	....	....	....	....
8321	General government............................	−14	32	872	....	....	....	....	....	....	....	....	....
8327	International organizations.....................	94	141	251	....	....	....	....	....	....	....	....	....
8328	Financial corporations other than international organizations..............	−61	−101	−97	....	....	....	....	....	....	....	....	....
8329	Other nonresidents..............................	3,550	7,385	1,030	....	....	....	....	....	....	....	....	....

In Millions of Maloti / Year Beginning April 1 / Cash Reporter

	Budgetary Central Government			Extrabudgetary Accounts			Central Government			General Government		
	2002	2003	2004	2002	2003	2004	2002	2003p	2004p	2002	2003p	2004p
Statement of government operations												
Statement of other economic flows												
Balance sheet												
Statement of sources and uses of cash												
1 Cash receipts from operating activities...........	....	....	....	....	....	....	3,331	3,617	4,455	3,331	3,617	4,455
11 Taxes...	....	....	....	....	....	....	2,576	2,888	3,687	2,576	2,888	3,687
12 Social contributions.................................	....	....	....	....	....	....	—	—	—	—	—	—
13 Grants..	....	....	....	....	....	....	296	178	245	296	178	245
14 Other receipts...	....	....	....	....	....	....	459	552	523	459	552	523
2 Cash payments for operating activities...........	....	....	....	....	....	....	2,982	3,026	3,220	2,982	3,026	3,220
21 Compensation of employees.......................	....	....	....	....	....	....	1,082	1,123	1,219	1,082	1,123	1,219
22 Purchases of goods and services.................	....	....	....	....	....	....	1,065	936	996	1,065	936	996
24 Interest..	....	....	....	....	....	....	220	216	167	220	216	167
25 Subsidies...	....	....	....	....	....	....	509	631	623	509	631	623
26 Grants..	....	....	....	....	....	....	—	—	—	—	—	—
27 Social benefits..	....	....	....	....	....	....	105	119	215	105	119	215
28 Other payments.......................................	....	....	....	....	....	....	—	—	—	—	—	—
CIO *Net cash inflow from oper. activities.....*	....	....	....	....	....	....	*349*	*591*	*1,235*	*349*	*591*	*1,235*
31.1 Purchases of nonfinancial assets..................	....	....	....	....	....	....	631	539	788	631	539	788
31.2 Sales of nonfinancial assets.......................	....	....	....	....	....	....	—	—	—	—	—	—
31 Net cash outflow from investments in nonfinancial assets.....................................	....	....	....	....	....	....	631	539	788	631	539	788
CSD *Cash surplus/deficit....................*	....	....	....	....	....	....	*−282*	*53*	*447*	*−282*	*53*	*447*
32x Net acquisition of fin assets, excl. cash...........	....	....	....	....	....	....	−32	−10	....	−32	−10	....
321x Domestic...	....	....	....	....	....	....	−32	−10	....	−32	−10	....
322x Foreign..	....	....	....	....	....	....	—	—	....	—	—	....
323 Monetary gold and SDRs...........................	....	....	....	....	....	....	—	—	....	—	—	....
33 Net incurrence of liabilities..........................	....	....	....	....	....	....	....	....	....	....	....	....
331 Domestic...	....	....	....	....	....	....	....	....	....	....	....	....
332 Foreign..	....	....	....	....	....	....	....	....	....	....	....	....
NFB Net cash inflow from fin. activities...............	....	....	....	....	....	....	....	....	....	....	....	....
NCB *Net change in the stock of cash..............*	....	....	....	....	....	....	....	....	....	....	....	....
Table 1 Revenue												
1 **Revenue...**	....	....	....	....	....	....	3,331	3,617	4,455	3,331	3,617	4,455
11 **Taxes..**	....	....	....	....	....	....	2,576	2,887	3,687	2,576	2,887	3,687
111 Taxes on income, profits, & capital gains......	....	....	....	....	....	....	663	852	902	663	852	902
1111 Individuals...	....	....	....	....	....	....	404	494	544	404	494	544
1112 Corporations and other enterprises.............	....	....	....	....	....	....	143	237	247	143	237	247
112 Taxes on payroll and workforce....................	....	....	....	....	....	....	—	—	—	—	—	—
113 Taxes on property.....................................	....	....	....	....	....	....	—	—	—	—	—	—
114 Taxes on goods and services......................	....	....	....	....	....	....	436	603	762	436	603	762
1141 General taxes on goods and services..........	....	....	....	....	....	....	344	519	762	344	519	762
1142 Excises...	....	....	....	....	....	....	86	81	—	86	81	—
115 Taxes on int'l. trade and transactions............	....	....	....	....	....	....	1,470	1,422	2,012	1,470	1,422	2,012
116 Other taxes...	....	....	....	....	....	....	6	11	10	6	11	10
12 **Social contributions.....................**	....	....	....	....	....	....	—	—	—	—	—	—
121 Social security contributions........................	....	....	....	....	....	....	—	—	—	—	—	—
122 Other social contributions..........................	....	....	....	....	....	....	—	—	—	—	—	—
13 **Grants.....................................**	....	....	....	....	....	....	296	178	245	296	178	245
131 From foreign governments.........................	....	....	....	....	....	....	296	178	245	296	178	245
132 From international organizations..................	....	....	....	....	....	....	—	—	—	—	—	—
133 From other general government units...........	....	....	....	....	....	....	—	—	—	—	—	—
14 **Other revenue.............................**	....	....	....	....	....	....	459	552	523	459	552	523
Table 2 Expense by economic type												
2 **Expense..**	....	....	....	....	....	....	2,982	3,026	3,220	2,982	3,026	3,220
21 **Compensation of employees.................**	....	....	....	....	....	....	1,082	1,123	1,219	1,082	1,123	1,219
211 Wages and salaries.................................	....	....	....	....	....	....	1,082	1,123	1,219	1,082	1,123	1,219
212 Social contributions.................................	....	....	....	....	....	....	—	—	—	—	—	—
22 **Use of goods and services......................**	....	....	....	....	....	....	1,065	936	996	1,065	936	996
23 **Consumption of fixed capital.................**	....	....	....	....	....	....	....	....	....	....	....	....
24 **Interest..**	....	....	....	....	....	....	220	216	167	220	216	167
25 **Subsidies..**	....	....	....	....	....	....	509	631	623	509	631	623

In Millions of Maloti / Year Beginning April 1 / Cash Reporter

	Budgetary Central Government			Extrabudgetary Accounts			Central Government			General Government		
	2002	2003	2004	2002	2003	2004	2002	2003p	2004p	2002	2003p	2004p
26 **Grants**.................................	....	....	....	....	....	....	—	—	—	—	—	—
261 To foreign governents......................	....	....	....	....	....	....	—	—	—	—	—	—
262 To international organizations..............	....	....	....	....	....	....	—	—	—	—	—	—
263 To other general government units..............	....	....	....	....	....	....	—	—	—	—	—	—
2631 Current.........................	....	....	....	....	....	....	—	—	—	—	—	—
2632 Capital.........................	....	....	....	....	....	....	—	—	—	—	—	—
27 **Social benefits**.........................	....	....	....	....	....	....	105	119	215	105	119	215
28 **Other expense**.........................	....	....	....	....	....	....	—	—	—	—	—	—
281 Property expense other than interest...........	....	....	....	....	....	....	—	—	—	—	—	—
282 Miscellaneous other expense..................	....	....	....	....	....	....	—	—	—	—	—	—
2821 Current.........................	....	....	....	....	....	....	—	—	—	—	—	—
2822 Capital.........................	....	....	....	....	....	....	—	—	—	—	—	—

Table 3 Transactions in assets and liabilities

	Budgetary Central Government			Extrabudgetary Accounts			Central Government			General Government		
	2002	2003	2004	2002	2003	2004	2002	2003p	2004p	2002	2003p	2004p
3 **Change in net worth from transactns....**	....	....	....	....	....	....	....	....	....	....	....	....
31 **Net acquisition of nonfinancial assets...**	....	....	....	....	....	....	631	539	788	631	539	788
311 Fixed assets................................	....	....	....	....	....	....	631	539	788	631	539	788
3111 Buildings and structures...............	....	....	....	....	....	....	....	....	....	....	....	....
3112 Machinery and equipment................	....	....	....	....	....	....	....	....	....	....	....	....
3113 Other fixed assets..................	....	....	....	....	....	....	....	....	....	....	....	....
312 Inventories..............................	....	....	....	....	....	....	—	—	—	—	—	—
313 Valuables...............................	....	....	....	....	....	....	—	—	—	—	—	—
314 Nonproduced assets.....................	....	....	....	....	....	....	—	—	—	—	—	—
3141 Land...............................	....	....	....	....	....	....	—	—	—	—	—	—
3142 Subsoil assets...................	....	....	....	....	....	....	—	—	—	—	—	—
3143 Other naturally occurring assets..................	....	....	....	....	....	....	—	—	—	—	—	—
3144 Intangible nonproduced assets...........	....	....	....	....	....	....	—	—	—	—	—	—
32 **Net acquisition of financial assets.........**	....	....	....	....	....	....	....	....	....	....	....	....
321 Domestic................................	....	....	....	....	....	....	....	....	....	....	....	....
3212 Currency and deposits...............	....	....	....	....	....	....	....	....	....	....	....	....
3213 Securities other than shares..............	....	....	....	....	....	....	....	....	....	....	....	....
3214 Loans.............................	....	....	....	....	....	....	....	....	....	....	....	....
3215 Shares and other equity...............	....	....	....	....	....	....	....	....	....	....	....	....
3216 Insurance technical reserves................	....	....	....	....	....	....	....	....	....	....	....	....
3217 Financial derivatives...................	....	....	....	....	....	....	....	....	....	....	....	....
3218 Other accounts receivable...............	....	....	....	....	....	....	....	....	....	....	....	....
322 Foreign.................................	....	....	....	....	....	....	....	....	....	....	....	....
3222 Currency and deposits...............	....	....	....	....	....	....	....	....	....	....	....	....
3223 Securities other than shares..............	....	....	....	....	....	....	....	....	....	....	....	....
3224 Loans.............................	....	....	....	....	....	....	....	....	....	....	....	....
3225 Shares and other equity...............	....	....	....	....	....	....	....	....	....	....	....	....
3226 Insurance technical reserves................	....	....	....	....	....	....	....	....	....	....	....	....
3227 Financial derivatives...................	....	....	....	....	....	....	....	....	....	....	....	....
3228 Other accounts receivable...............	....	....	....	....	....	....	....	....	....	....	....	....
323 Monetary gold and SDRs...................	....	....	....	....	....	....	....	....	....	....	....	....
33 **Net incurrence of liabilities................**	....	....	....	....	....	....	....	....	....	....	....	....
331 Domestic................................	....	....	....	....	....	....	....	....	....	....	....	....
3312 Currency and deposits...............	....	....	....	....	....	....	....	....	....	....	....	....
3313 Securities other than shares..............	....	....	....	....	....	....	....	....	....	....	....	....
3314 Loans.............................	....	....	....	....	....	....	....	....	....	....	....	....
3316 Insurance technical reserves................	....	....	....	....	....	....	....	....	....	....	....	....
3317 Financial derivatives...................	....	....	....	....	....	....	....	....	....	....	....	....
3318 Other accounts payable...............	....	....	....	....	....	....	....	....	....	....	....	....
332 Foreign.................................	....	....	....	....	....	....	....	....	....	....	....	....
3322 Currency and deposits...............	....	....	....	....	....	....	....	....	....	....	....	....
3323 Securities other than shares..............	....	....	....	....	....	....	....	....	....	....	....	....
3324 Loans.............................	....	....	....	....	....	....	....	....	....	....	....	....
3326 Insurance technical reserves................	....	....	....	....	....	....	....	....	....	....	....	....
3327 Financial derivatives...................	....	....	....	....	....	....	....	....	....	....	....	....
3328 Other accounts payable...............	....	....	....	....	....	....	....	....	....	....	....	....

	Budgetary Central Government			Extrabudgetary Accounts			Central Government			General Government		
	2002	2003	2004	2002	2003	2004	2002	2003p	2004p	2002	2003p	2004p
Table 4 Holding gains in assets and liabilities												
Table 5 Other changes in the volume of assets and liabilities												
Table 6 Balance sheet												
Table 7 Outlays by functions of govt.												
7 Total outlays....................	....	....	....	....	....	....	3,613	3,564	4,009	3,613	3,564	4,009
701 **General public services...................**	....	....	....	....	....	....	507	502	722	507	502	722
7017 Public debt transactions.................	....	....	....	....	....	....	220	216	167	220	216	167
7018 General transfers between levels of govt......	....	....	....	....	....	....	35	35	101	35	35	101
702 **Defense.................................**	....	....	....	....	....	....	209	207	201	209	207	201
703 **Public order and safety...................**	....	....	....	....	....	....	317	314	415	317	314	415
704 **Economic affairs...........................**	....	....	....	....	....	....	297	294	305	297	294	305
7042 Agriculture, forestry, fishing, and hunting.....	....	....	....	....	....	....	138	137	122	138	137	122
7043 Fuel and energy........................	....	....	....	....	....	....	6	6	18	6	6	18
7044 Mining, manufacturing, and construction.....	....	....	....	....	....	....	40	40	89	40	40	89
7045 Transport......	....	....	....	....	....	....	94	93	55	94	93	55
7046 Communication....................	....	....	....	....	....	....	19	19	22	19	19	22
705 **Environmental protection....................**	....	....	....	....	....	....	....	....	....	....	....	....
706 **Housing and community amenities........**	....	....	....	....	....	....	62	61	78	62	61	78
707 **Health................................**	....	....	....	....	....	....	228	225	247	228	225	247
7072 Outpatient services.....................	....	....	....	....	....	....	....	....	....	....	....	....
7073 Hospital services.......................	....	....	....	....	....	....	....	....	....	....	....	....
7074 Public health services...................	....	....	....	....	....	....	....	....	....	....	....	....
708 **Recreation, culture, and religion...........**	....	....	....	....	....	....	49	48	13	49	48	13
709 **Education................................**	....	....	....	....	....	....	867	859	995	867	859	995
7091 Pre-primary and primary education............	....	....	....	....	....	....	....	....	....	....	....	....
7092 Secondary education.....................	....	....	....	....	....	....	....	....	....	....	....	....
7094 Tertiary education........................	....	....	....	....	....	....	....	....	....	....	....	....
710 **Social protection.........................**	....	....	....	....	....	....	141	139	243	141	139	243
7 Statistical discrepancy: Total outlays..............	....	....	....	....	....	....	937	914	788	937	914	788
Table 8 Transactions in financial assets and liabilities by sector												

In Millions of Litai / Year Ending December 31 / Noncash Reporter

	Budgetary Central Government 2002	2003	2004p	Central Government 2002	2003	2004p	Local Government 2002	2003	2004	General Government 2002	2003	2004p
Statement of government operations												
1 Revenue......	9,227	10,053	10,894	14,849	16,069	17,961	3,677	3,730	4,329	16,466	17,726	19,938
2 Expense......	9,529	10,004	11,087	14,772	15,684	17,817	3,549	3,667	4,021	16,261	17,277	19,487
GOB *Gross operating balance*......	*74*	*456*	*221*	*474*	*806*	*581*	*351*	*291*	*552*	*825*	*1,097*	*1,133*
NOB *Net operating balance*......	*−302*	*49*	*−194*	*77*	*385*	*144*	*128*	*63*	*308*	*205*	*448*	*451*
31 Net acquisition of nonfinancial assets......	669	926	1,054	774	1,079	1,132	107	58	216	881	1,137	1,348
NLB *Net lending/borrowing*......	*−970*	*−877*	*−1,248*	*−697*	*−694*	*−989*	*21*	*5*	*92*	*−676*	*−689*	*−897*
32 Net acquisition of financial assets......	178	−139	−352	305	−566	−814	−17	30	69	358	−493	−646
33 Net incurrence of liabilities......	1,148	738	896	1,002	129	175	−38	25	−23	1,034	196	251
NLB Statistical discrepancy......	—	—	—	—	—	—	—	—	—	—	—	—
Statement of other economic flows												
Balance sheet												
6 *Net worth*......	....	....	....	....	....	....	....	....	....	....	....	....
61 Nonfinancial assets......	....	....	....	....	....	....	....	....	....	....	....	....
62 Financial assets......	....	3,055	2,432	....	4,876	4,151	....	124	269	....	4,825	4,347
63 Liabilities......	....	15,093	15,067	....	15,075	14,605	....	614	521	....	15,515	15,053
Statement of sources and uses of cash												
1 Cash receipts from operating activities......	9,127	10,027	10,753	14,757	16,043	17,849	3,677	3,730	4,249	16,374	17,699	19,826
11 Taxes......	7,805	8,563	9,223	8,926	9,700	10,492	1,450	1,499	1,744	10,376	11,199	12,236
12 Social contributions......	—	—	—	4,465	4,824	5,759	—	—	—	4,465	4,824	5,759
13 Grants......	301	389	560	301	389	560	2,056	2,071	2,271	301	389	560
14 Other receipts......	1,020	1,076	970	1,065	1,130	1,038	170	160	233	1,232	1,288	1,271
2 Cash payments for operating activities......	9,106	9,513	10,497	14,364	15,318	17,225	3,326	3,439	3,776	15,630	16,684	18,729
21 Compensation of employees......	2,638	2,790	3,115	2,718	2,885	3,268	2,050	2,105	2,278	4,768	4,990	5,545
22 Purchases of goods and services......	2,115	2,378	2,021	2,185	2,489	2,170	611	693	789	2,797	3,182	2,959
24 Interest......	680	662	608	690	670	614	24	18	16	710	685	630
25 Subsidies......	102	142	260	102	142	308	23	23	33	126	164	341
26 Grants......	2,710	2,634	2,720	2,059	2,073	2,604	—	—	—	3	3	332
27 Social benefits......	577	605	756	6,306	6,733	7,230	592	585	571	6,898	7,317	7,802
28 Other payments......	284	303	1,016	304	328	1,032	25	15	90	329	343	1,121
CIO *Net cash inflow from oper. activities*......	*21*	*514*	*256*	*393*	*724*	*624*	*351*	*291*	*472*	*744*	*1,015*	*1,096*
31.1 Purchases of nonfinancial assets......	1,052	1,341	1,529	1,188	1,531	1,647	386	378	576	1,574	1,910	2,223
31.2 Sales of nonfinancial assets......	8	8	61	29	31	77	56	92	116	85	123	193
31 Net cash outflow from investments in nonfinancial assets......	1,044	1,333	1,469	1,160	1,500	1,570	330	286	461	1,489	1,786	2,030
CSD *Cash surplus/deficit*......	*−1,023*	*−819*	*−1,212*	*−767*	*−776*	*−946*	*21*	*5*	*12*	*−745*	*−771*	*−934*
32x Net acquisition of fin assets, excl. cash......	−40	−142	−132	−325	−929	−337	−41	−23	−84	−296	−909	−402
321x Domestic......	−40	−159	−178	−325	−946	−383	−41	−23	−84	−296	−926	−448
322x Foreign......	—	17	46	—	17	46	—	—	—	—	17	46
323 Monetary gold and SDRs......	—	—	—	—	—	—	—	—	—	—	—	—
33 Net incurrence of liabilities......	1,140	662	800	1,019	273	178	−38	25	57	1,051	340	254
331 Domestic......	725	123	415	605	−249	−189	−21	32	53	653	−175	−117
332 Foreign......	415	540	385	415	522	367	−17	−7	4	397	514	371
NFB Net cash inflow from fin. activities......	1,180	805	932	1,344	1,201	515	2	47	141	1,347	1,249	656
NCB *Net change in the stock of cash*......	*157*	*−15*	*−280*	*578*	*425*	*−431*	*24*	*52*	*153*	*602*	*478*	*−278*
Table 1 Revenue												
1 **Revenue**......	**9,227**	**10,053**	**10,894**	**14,849**	**16,069**	**17,961**	**3,677**	**3,730**	**4,329**	**16,466**	**17,726**	**19,938**
11 **Taxes**......	**7,885**	**8,593**	**9,366**	**9,005**	**9,731**	**10,635**	**1,450**	**1,499**	**1,744**	**10,455**	**11,230**	**12,379**
111 Taxes on income, profits, & capital gains......	1,690	2,231	2,783	2,711	3,295	3,990	1,159	1,221	1,439	3,870	4,515	5,429
1111 Individuals......	1,432	1,446	1,614	2,452	2,510	2,821	1,115	1,221	1,439	3,568	3,731	4,260
1112 Corporations and other enterprises......	258	785	1,169	258	785	1,169	44	—	—	302	785	1,169
112 Taxes on payroll and workforce......	—	—	—	18	20	22	—	—	—	18	20	22
113 Taxes on property......	—	—	—	—	—	—	254	247	248	254	247	248
114 Taxes on goods and services......	6,062	6,217	6,502	6,144	6,270	6,542	37	31	57	6,181	6,301	6,599
1141 General taxes on goods and services......	4,212	4,238	4,458	4,294	4,291	4,498	—	—	—	4,294	4,291	4,498
1142 Excises......	1,750	1,872	1,905	1,750	1,872	1,905	—	—	—	1,750	1,872	1,905
115 Taxes on int'l. trade and transactions......	133	146	81	133	146	81	—	—	—	133	146	81
116 Other taxes......	—	—	—	—	—	—	—	—	—	—	—	—
12 **Social contributions**......	—	—	—	**4,493**	**4,851**	**5,746**	—	—	—	**4,493**	**4,851**	**5,746**
121 Social security contributions......	—	—	—	4,493	4,851	5,746	—	—	—	4,493	4,851	5,746
122 Other social contributions......	—	—	—	—	—	—	—	—	—	—	—	—
13 **Grants**......	**301**	**389**	**560**	**301**	**389**	**560**	**2,056**	**2,071**	**2,351**	**301**	**389**	**560**
131 From foreign governments......	—	—	—	—	—	—	—	—	—	—	—	—
132 From international organizations......	301	389	560	301	389	560	—	—	—	301	389	560
133 From other general government units......	—	—	—	—	—	—	2,056	2,071	2,351	—	—	—
14 **Other revenue**......	**1,041**	**1,071**	**968**	**1,050**	**1,098**	**1,020**	**170**	**160**	**233**	**1,217**	**1,256**	**1,253**

	Budgetary Central Government			Central Government			Local Government			General Government		
	2002	2003	2004p	2002	2003	2004p	2002	2003	2004	2002	2003	2004p
Table 2 Expense by economic type												
2 Expense................................	9,529	10,004	11,087	14,772	15,684	17,817	3,549	3,667	4,021	16,261	17,277	19,487
21 Compensation of employees..................	2,638	2,790	3,115	2,718	2,885	3,268	2,050	2,105	2,278	4,768	4,990	5,545
211 Wages and salaries........................	2,064	2,175	2,425	2,125	2,248	2,544	1,563	1,610	1,743	3,688	3,857	4,287
212 Social contributions......................	574	615	690	593	638	723	487	496	535	1,080	1,133	1,258
22 Use of goods and services....................	2,115	2,378	2,021	2,187	2,488	2,167	611	693	789	2,798	3,182	2,956
23 Consumption of fixed capital..............	376	407	415	397	421	437	223	228	245	620	649	682
24 Interest.................................	688	699	602	698	706	608	24	18	16	719	722	624
25 Subsidies................................	102	142	353	102	142	401	23	23	33	126	164	434
26 Grants..................................	2,710	2,634	2,800	2,059	2,073	2,684	—	—	—	3	3	332
261 To foreign govenments................	3	3	—	3	3	—	—	—	—	3	3	—
262 To international organizations.............	—	—	332	—	—	332	—	—	—	—	—	332
263 To other general government units.............	2,708	2,632	2,468	2,056	2,071	2,351	—	—	—	—	—	—
2631 Current..............................	2,589	2,557	2,278	2,045	2,044	2,179	—	—	—	—	—	—
2632 Capital..............................	119	75	190	12	27	172	—	—	—	—	—	—
27 Social benefits...........................	577	605	756	6,263	6,586	7,199	592	585	571	6,856	7,171	7,770
28 Other expense...........................	323	350	1,025	348	382	1,055	25	15	90	373	397	1,144
281 Property expense other than interest............	—	—	—	—	—	—	—	—	—	—	—	—
282 Miscellaneous other expense................	323	350	1,025	348	382	1,055	25	15	90	373	397	1,144
2821 Current..............................	244	289	1,008	244	289	1,009	25	15	73	268	304	1,082
2822 Capital..............................	80	61	17	104	93	46	1	—	16	105	93	63
Table 3 Transactions in assets and liabilities												
3 Change in net worth from transactns....	−302	49	−194	77	385	144	128	63	308	205	448	451
31 Net acquisition of nonfinancial assets...	669	926	1,054	774	1,079	1,132	107	58	216	881	1,137	1,348
311 Fixed assets.............................	628	917	1,084	733	1,070	1,163	119	81	218	853	1,151	1,381
3111 Buildings and structures................	....	....	....	....	....	....	....	....	....	....	....	....
3112 Machinery and equipment.............	....	....	....	....	....	....	....	....	....	....	....	....
3113 Other fixed assets.....................	....	....	....	....	....	....	....	....	....	....	....	....
312 Inventories.............................	39	8	15	39	8	15	—	—	—	39	8	15
313 Valuables...............................	—	—	—	—	—	—	—	—	—	—	—	—
314 Nonproduced assets....................	2	1	−46	2	1	−46	−13	−23	−2	−11	−22	−48
3141 Land.................................	2	1	−46	2	1	−46	−13	−23	−2	−11	−22	−48
3142 Subsoil assets.........................	—	—	—	—	—	—	—	—	—	—	—	—
3143 Other naturally occurring assets........	—	—	—	—	—	—	—	—	—	—	—	—
3144 Intangible nonproduced assets..........	—	—	—	—	—	—	—	—	—	—	—	—
32 Net acquisition of financial assets........	178	−139	−352	305	−566	−814	−17	30	69	358	−493	−646
321 Domestic...............................	178	−156	−398	305	−582	−860	−17	30	69	358	−510	−692
3212 Currency and deposits.................	157	−15	−280	578	425	−431	24	52	153	602	478	−278
3213 Securities other than shares............	—	—	—	—	—	—	—	—	—	—	—	—
3214 Loans................................	−80	−168	−277	−103	−143	−248	—	—	3	−34	−101	−147
3215 Shares and other equity................	—	—	18	−263	−892	−293	−40	−23	−87	−303	−914	−380
3216 Insurance technical reserves............	—	—	—	—	—	—	—	—	—	—	—	—
3217 Financial derivatives...................	—	—	—	—	—	—	—	—	—	—	—	—
3218 Other accounts receivable..............	100	26	141	93	27	112	—	—	—	93	27	112
322 Foreign................................	—	17	46	—	17	46	—	—	—	—	17	46
3222 Currency and deposits.................	—	—	—	—	—	—	—	—	—	—	—	—
3223 Securities other than shares............	—	—	—	—	—	—	—	—	—	—	—	—
3224 Loans................................	—	17	−17	—	17	−17	—	—	—	—	17	−17
3225 Shares and other equity................	—	—	—	—	—	—	—	—	—	—	—	—
3226 Insurance technical reserves............	—	—	—	—	—	—	—	—	—	—	—	—
3227 Financial derivatives...................	—	—	—	—	—	—	—	—	—	—	—	—
3228 Other accounts receivable..............	—	—	63	—	—	63	—	—	—	—	—	63
323 Monetary gold and SDRs...............	—	—	—	—	—	—	—	—	—	—	—	—
33 Net incurrence of liabilities..................	1,148	738	896	1,002	129	175	−38	25	−23	1,034	196	251
331 Domestic...............................	720	156	491	574	−436	−211	−21	32	−27	622	−361	−140
3312 Currency and deposits.................	−8	89	−732	−70	−250	−975	—	—	—	−70	−250	−975
3313 Securities other than shares............	837	455	−73	837	318	−84	—	—	—	837	318	−84
3314 Loans................................	−135	−468	637	−188	−438	223	−21	32	−27	−140	−363	294
3316 Insurance technical reserves............	—	—	—	—	—	—	—	—	—	—	—	—
3317 Financial derivatives...................	—	—	—	—	—	—	—	—	—	—	—	—
3318 Other accounts payable................	26	79	659	−5	−67	625	—	—	—	−5	−67	625

In Millions of Litai / Year Ending December 31 / Noncash Reporter

		Budgetary Central Government			Central Government			Local Government			General Government		
		2002	2003	2004p	2002	2003	2004p	2002	2003	2004	2002	2003	2004p
332	Foreign..................................	429	583	405	429	565	387	−17	−7	4	412	557	391
3322	Currency and deposits..............	—	—	−1	—	—	−1	—	—	—	—	—	−1
3323	Securities other than shares......	687	609	1,252	687	609	1,252	—	—	—	687	609	1,252
3324	Loans.....................................	−272	−30	−858	−272	−48	−876	−17	−7	4	−289	−56	−871
3326	Insurance technical reserves.......	—	—	—	—	—	—	—	—	—	—	—	—
3327	Financial derivatives.................	—	—	—	—	—	—	—	—	—	—	—	—
3328	Other accounts payable.............	14	4	11	14	4	11	—	—	—	14	4	11

Table 4 Holding gains in assets and liabilities

Table 5 Other changes in the volume of assets and liabilities

Table 6 Balance sheet

		Budgetary Central Government			Central Government			Local Government			General Government		
		2002	2003	2004p	2002	2003	2004p	2002	2003	2004	2002	2003	2004p
6	**Net worth.....................**	....	....	....	....	....	....	....	....	....	....	....	....
61	**Nonfinancial assets.............**	....	....	....	....	....	....	....	....	....	....	....	....
611	Fixed assets..........................	....	....	....	....	....	....	....	....	....	....	....	....
6111	Buildings and structures.........	....	....	....	....	....	....	....	....	....	....	....	....
6112	Machinery and equipment........	....	....	....	....	....	....	....	....	....	....	....	....
6113	Other fixed assets..................	....	....	....	....	....	....	....	....	....	....	....	....
612	Inventories............................	....	....	....	....	....	....	....	....	....	....	....	....
613	Valuables..............................	....	....	....	....	....	....	....	....	....	....	....	....
614	Nonproduced assets................	....	....	....	....	....	....	....	....	....	....	....	....
6141	Land.....................................	....	....	....	....	....	....	....	....	....	....	....	....
6142	Subsoil assets........................	....	....	....	....	....	....	....	....	....	....	....	....
6143	Other naturally occurring assets..	....	....	....	....	....	....	....	....	....	....	....	....
6144	Intangible nonproduced assets....	....	....	....	....	....	....	....	....	....	....	....	....
62	**Financial assets.................**	....	3,055	2,432	....	4,876	4,151	....	124	269	....	4,825	4,347
621	Domestic...............................	....	3,038	2,432	....	4,859	4,151	....	124	269	....	4,808	4,347
6212	Currency and deposits.............	....	604	306	....	2,607	2,170	....	123	265	....	2,729	2,435
6213	Securities other than shares......	....	—	—	....	—	—	....	—	—	....	—	—
6214	Loans...................................	....	2,434	2,126	....	2,239	1,968	....	1	4	....	2,066	1,899
6215	Shares and other equity...........	....	—	—	....	13	13	....	—	—	....	13	13
6216	Insurance technical reserves......	....	—	—	....	—	—	....	—	—	....	—	—
6217	Financial derivatives...............	....	—	—	....	—	—	....	—	—	....	—	—
6218	Other accounts receivable........	....	—	—	....	—	—	....	—	—	....	—	—
622	Foreign................................	....	17	—	....	17	—	....	—	—	....	17	—
6222	Currency and deposits.............	....	—	—	....	—	—	....	—	—	....	—	—
6223	Securities other than shares......	....	—	—	....	—	—	....	—	—	....	—	—
6224	Loans...................................	....	17	—	....	17	—	....	—	—	....	17	—
6225	Shares and other equity...........	....	—	—	....	—	—	....	—	—	....	—	—
6226	Insurance technical reserves......	....	—	—	....	—	—	....	—	—	....	—	—
6227	Financial derivatives...............	....	—	—	....	—	—	....	—	—	....	—	—
6228	Other accounts receivable........	....	—	—	....	—	—	....	—	—	....	—	—
623	Monetary gold and SDRs..........	....	—	—	....	—	—	....	—	—	....	—	—
63	**Liabilities..........................**	....	15,093	15,067	....	15,075	14,605	....	614	521	....	15,515	15,053
631	Domestic...............................	....	7,776	7,588	....	7,704	7,127	....	591	492	....	8,120	7,546
6312	Currency and deposits.............	....	4,087	3,226	....	4,087	3,226	....	—	—	....	4,087	3,226
6313	Securities other than shares......	....	3,600	3,566	....	3,463	3,418	....	—	—	....	3,463	3,418
6314	Loans...................................	....	90	797	....	154	483	....	591	492	....	570	902
6316	Insurance technical reserves......	....	—	—	....	—	—	....	—	—	....	—	—
6317	Financial derivatives...............	....	—	—	....	—	—	....	—	—	....	—	—
6318	Other accounts payable............	....	—	—	....	—	—	....	—	—	....	—	—
632	Foreign................................	....	7,317	7,479	....	7,371	7,479	....	23	29	....	7,395	7,508
6322	Currency and deposits.............	....	—	—	....	—	—	....	—	—	....	—	—
6323	Securities other than shares......	....	5,063	6,228	....	5,063	6,228	....	—	—	....	5,063	6,228
6324	Loans...................................	....	2,255	1,251	....	2,309	1,251	....	23	29	....	2,332	1,280
6326	Insurance technical reserves......	....	—	—	....	—	—	....	—	—	....	—	—
6327	Financial derivatives...............	....	—	—	....	—	—	....	—	—	....	—	—
6328	Other accounts payable............	....	—	—	....	—	—	....	—	—	....	—	—

In Millions of Litai / Year Ending December 31 / Noncash Reporter

	Budgetary Central Government			Central Government			Local Government			General Government		
	2002	2003	2004p	2002	2003	2004p	2002	2003	2004	2002	2003	2004p
Memorandum items:												
6M2 Net financial worth............................	....	−12,039	−12,635	....	−10,199	−10,454	....	−490	−252	....	−10,689	−10,706
6M3 Debt at market value............................	....	....	....	....	....	....	....	....	....	....	....	....
6M4 Debt at nominal value............................	11,092	11,624	12,176	11,270	11,606	11,714	518	614	521	11,591	12,046	12,162
6M5 Arrears..	....	....	....	....	....	....	....	....	....	....	....	....
6M6 Obligations for social security benefits....	—	—	—	....	....	....	—	—	—	....	....	....
6M7 Contingent liabilities............................	....	1,323	1,206	....	1,323	1,206	....	33	45	....	1,356	1,251
6M8 Uncapitalized military weapons, systems........	....	....	....	....	....	....	....	....	....	....	....	....
Table 7 Outlays by functions of govt.												
7 **Total outlays..........**	**10,197**	**10,931**	**12,141**	**15,546**	**16,763**	**18,950**	**3,655**	**3,725**	**4,237**	**17,142**	**18,415**	**20,835**
701 **General public services...................**	**4,400**	**4,477**	**4,605**	**3,754**	**3,951**	**4,531**	**287**	**318**	**268**	**1,981**	**2,196**	**2,447**
7017 Public debt transactions.......................	688	699	602	698	706	608	24	18	16	719	722	624
7018 General transfers between levels of govt......	2,708	2,632	2,468	2,056	2,071	2,351	—	—	—	—	—	—
702 **Defense..........................**	**779**	**802**	**828**	**875**	**891**	**894**	**2**	**2**	**8**	**877**	**894**	**902**
703 **Public order and safety...................**	**1,002**	**1,054**	**1,124**	**1,016**	**1,088**	**1,127**	**32**	**33**	**32**	**1,048**	**1,121**	**1,160**
704 **Economic affairs........................**	**1,750**	**2,107**	**2,111**	**1,769**	**2,148**	**2,170**	**253**	**268**	**221**	**2,023**	**2,416**	**2,391**
7042 Agriculture, forestry, fishing, and hunting.....	652	869	708	653	872	708	53	56	64	705	927	771
7043 Fuel and energy..................................	19	26	68	25	45	129	112	108	11	138	153	140
7044 Mining, manufacturing, and construction.....	98	113	19	98	113	19	—	—	13	98	113	32
7045 Transport..	834	986	1,082	834	987	1,082	86	87	37	919	1,075	1,119
7046 Communication.....................................	13	15	31	13	15	31	—	—	1	13	15	33
705 **Environmental protection...............**	**33**	**96**	**152**	**33**	**96**	**152**	**15**	**—**	**127**	**48**	**96**	**278**
706 **Housing and community amenities........**	**—**	**—**	**—**	**1**	**1**	**−5**	**358**	**329**	**283**	**359**	**329**	**278**
707 **Health....................................**	**176**	**181**	**721**	**2,031**	**2,084**	**2,808**	**22**	**29**	**72**	**2,053**	**2,113**	**2,880**
7072 Outpatient services........................	4	4	43	382	392	516	—	—	4	382	392	520
7073 Hospital services............................	8	8	42	1,028	1,106	1,573	6	12	15	1,034	1,118	1,588
7074 Public health services......................	46	48	45	47	52	69	4	4	7	51	56	76
708 **Recreation, culture, and religion...........**	**257**	**287**	**347**	**259**	**289**	**346**	**176**	**191**	**269**	**435**	**480**	**614**
709 **Education...............................**	**1,160**	**1,228**	**1,382**	**1,163**	**1,238**	**1,386**	**2,034**	**2,081**	**2,308**	**3,196**	**3,319**	**3,694**
7091 Pre-primary and primary education..............	1	1	347	4	3	349	400	411	608	404	414	957
7092 Secondary education............................	386	405	67	386	414	69	1,415	1,462	1,432	1,800	1,876	1,501
7094 Tertiary education............................	659	700	688	659	700	688	—	—	—	659	700	688
710 **Social protection..........................**	**640**	**698**	**871**	**4,646**	**4,976**	**5,542**	**476**	**473**	**649**	**5,122**	**5,450**	**6,191**
7 Statistical discrepancy: Total outlays..............	—	—	—	—	—	—	—	—	—	—	—	—
Table 8 Transactions in financial assets and liabilities by sector												
82 **Net acquisition of financial assets..........**	**178**	**−139**	**−352**	**305**	**−566**	**−814**	**−17**	**30**	**69**	**358**	**−493**	**−646**
821 Domestic...	178	−156	−398	305	−582	−860	−17	30	69	358	−510	−692
8211 General government............................	−48	−73	−135	−70	−43	−99	—	—	—	—	—	—
8212 Central bank..................................	188	−13	−275	525	281	−743	—	—	—	525	281	−743
8213 Other depository corporations................	−31	−2	−6	53	144	313	24	52	153	77	197	465
8214 Financial corporations n.e.c.................	—	—	—	—	—	—	—	—	—	—	—	—
8215 Nonfinancial corporations...................	67	−40	44	−196	−936	−276	−41	−23	−84	−236	−959	−360
8216 Households & NPIs serving households......	2	−29	−26	−7	−29	−55	—	—	—	−7	−29	−55
822 Foreign...	—	17	46	—	17	46	—	—	—	—	17	46
8221 General government............................	—	—	—	—	—	—	—	—	—	—	—	—
8227 International organizations..................	—	17	46	—	17	46	—	—	—	—	17	46
8228 Financial corporations other than international organizations..............	—	—	—	—	—	—	—	—	—	—	—	—
8229 Other nonresidents...........................	—	—	—	—	—	—	—	—	—	—	—	—
823 Monetary gold and SDRs......................	—	—	—	—	—	—	—	—	—	—	—	—
83 **Net incurrence of liabilities...................**	**1,148**	**738**	**896**	**1,002**	**129**	**175**	**−38**	**25**	**−23**	**1,034**	**196**	**251**
831 Domestic...	720	156	491	574	−436	−211	−21	32	−27	622	−361	−140
8311 General government............................	—	135	385	—	—	—	−70	−43	−99	—	—	—
8312 Central bank..................................	−94	−84	−55	−94	−84	−55	—	—	—	−94	−84	−55
8313 Other depository corporations................	301	−350	−208	248	−322	−248	48	75	71	296	−247	−177
8314 Financial corporations n.e.c.................	—	57	211	—	57	211	—	—	—	—	57	211
8315 Nonfinancial corporations...................	216	281	735	227	281	732	—	—	—	227	281	732
8316 Households & NPIs serving households......	297	117	−577	194	−368	−851	—	—	—	194	−368	−851
832 Foreign...	429	583	405	429	565	387	−17	−7	4	412	557	391
8321 General government............................	−75	−47	−89	−75	−47	−89	—	—	—	−75	−47	−89
8327 International organizations..................	−78	−92	−336	−78	−92	−336	—	—	—	−78	−92	−336
8328 Financial corporations other than international organizations............	581	726	831	581	708	813	−17	−7	4	564	701	817
8329 Other nonresidents...........................	—	−5	−1	—	−5	−1	—	—	—	—	−5	−1

In Millions of Euros / Year Ending December 31 / Noncash Reporter

	Budgetary Central Government			Central Government			Local Government			General Government		
	2002	2003p	2004p	2002	2003p	2004p	2002	2003p	2004p	2002	2003p	2004p
Statement of government operations												
1 Revenue	6,888	7,126	7,697	9,652	10,018	10,728	1,434	1,483	1,484	10,445	10,836	11,458
2 Expense	6,550	7,100	7,917	8,755	9,539	10,427	1,119	1,178	1,254	9,233	10,051	10,927
GOB *Gross operating balance*	*564*	*271*	*47*	*1,137*	*738*	*581*	*505*	*508*	*450*	*1,642*	*1,246*	*1,031*
NOB *Net operating balance*	*338*	*26*	*−220*	*897*	*480*	*301*	*315*	*305*	*230*	*1,212*	*785*	*531*
31 Net acquisition of nonfinancial assets	447	433	433	446	425	428	286	311	262	732	736	689
NLB *Net lending/borrowing*	*−109*	*−407*	*−652*	*451*	*55*	*−127*	*29*	*−6*	*−31*	*480*	*49*	*−158*
32 Net acquisition of financial assets	−68	−199	−284	439	358	−24	−6	133	−86	433	491	−110
33 Net incurrence of liabilities	85	−183	221	56	−130	183	38	180	−96	93	48	86
NLB Statistical discrepancy	−43	392	148	−68	433	−80	−73	−40	41	−140	394	−38
Statement of other economic flows												
4 *Change in net worth from holding gains*	....	....	....	....	....	....	....	....	....	....	....	....
41 Nonfinancial assets	....	....	....	....	....	....	....	....	....	....	....	....
42 Financial assets	−15	339	320	−41	341	309	19	4	2	−22	346	311
43 Liabilities	−46	−9	−11	−40	−10	−9	—	—	—	−40	−10	−9
5 *Change in net worth from other volume changes*	....	....	....	....	....	....	....	....	....	....	....	....
51 Nonfinancial assets	....	....	....	....	....	....	....	....	....	....	....	....
52 Financial assets	−19	—	—	−19	—	—				−19		
53 Liabilities	—	—	—							—		
Balance sheet												
6 *Net worth*	....	....	....	....	....	....	....	....	....	....	....	....
61 Nonfinancial assets	....	....	....	....	....	....	....	....	....	....	....	....
62 Financial assets	8,442	8,582	8,618	13,235	13,934	14,218	1,140	1,277	1,193	14,371	15,208	15,408
63 Liabilities	1,372	1,180	1,389	1,118	978	1,152	516	695	599	1,592	1,631	1,708
Statement of sources and uses of cash												
Table 1 Revenue												
1 **Revenue**	**6,888**	**7,126**	**7,697**	**9,652**	**10,018**	**10,728**	**1,434**	**1,483**	**1,484**	**10,445**	**10,836**	**11,458**
11 **Taxes**	**6,083**	**6,338**	**6,794**	**6,083**	**6,338**	**6,794**	**573**	**586**	**502**	**6,656**	**6,924**	**7,296**
111 Taxes on income, profits, & capital gains	2,920	3,035	2,938	2,920	3,035	2,938	535	548	459	3,454	3,583	3,397
1111 Individuals	1,528	1,690	1,825	1,528	1,690	1,825	—	—	—	1,528	1,690	1,825
1112 Corporations and other enterprises	1,391	1,345	1,113	1,391	1,345	1,113	535	548	459	1,926	1,892	1,571
112 Taxes on payroll and workforce	—	—	—	—	—	—	—	—	—	—	—	—
113 Taxes on property	344	339	352	344	339	352	30	29	34	374	369	385
114 Taxes on goods and services	2,807	2,952	3,491	2,807	2,952	3,491	8	9	10	2,815	2,960	3,501
1141 General taxes on goods and services	1,278	1,383	1,643	1,278	1,383	1,643	—	—	—	1,278	1,383	1,643
1142 Excises	1,051	1,113	1,332	1,051	1,113	1,332	—	—	—	1,051	1,113	1,332
115 Taxes on int'l. trade and transactions	—	—	—	—	—	—	—	—	—	—	—	—
116 Other taxes	12	12	13	12	12	13	—	—	—	12	12	13
12 **Social contributions**	**248**	**273**	**297**	**2,811**	**2,997**	**3,163**	**4**	**4**	**4**	**2,814**	**3,001**	**3,167**
121 Social security contributions	63	63	49	2,614	2,775	2,903	—	—	—	2,614	2,775	2,903
122 Other social contributions	185	210	247	196	222	259	4	4	4	200	226	263
13 **Grants**	**84**	**85**	**110**	**76**	**80**	**92**	**568**	**591**	**667**	**4**	**6**	**5**
131 From foreign governments	—	—	—	—	—	—	—	—	—	—	—	—
132 From international organizations	4	6	5	4	6	5	—	—	—	4	6	5
133 From other general government units	80	79	105	72	74	87	568	591	667	—	—	—
14 **Other revenue**	**473**	**429**	**497**	**682**	**603**	**680**	**289**	**303**	**312**	**971**	**906**	**991**
Table 2 Expense by economic type												
2 **Expense**	**6,550**	**7,100**	**7,917**	**8,755**	**9,539**	**10,427**	**1,119**	**1,178**	**1,254**	**9,233**	**10,051**	**10,927**
21 **Compensation of employees**	**1,400**	**1,496**	**1,642**	**1,464**	**1,564**	**1,713**	**464**	**492**	**527**	**1,928**	**2,056**	**2,240**
211 Wages and salaries	1,152	1,214	1,316	1,202	1,268	1,373	388	411	443	1,590	1,679	1,816
212 Social contributions	248	281	325	262	296	340	76	81	84	338	377	424
22 **Use of goods and services**	**498**	**524**	**571**	**519**	**548**	**593**	**275**	**295**	**308**	**794**	**843**	**900**
23 **Consumption of fixed capital**	**226**	**245**	**266**	**240**	**259**	**280**	**190**	**203**	**219**	**430**	**462**	**500**
24 **Interest**	**73**	**76**	**60**	**62**	**59**	**43**	**18**	**17**	**16**	**80**	**76**	**59**
25 **Subsidies**	**341**	**359**	**400**	**341**	**359**	**401**	**40**	**35**	**33**	**381**	**394**	**434**
26 **Grants**	**2,728**	**2,919**	**3,274**	**685**	**731**	**953**	**73**	**74**	**87**	**118**	**141**	**287**
261 To foreign govenments	—	—	—	—	—	—	—	—	—	—	—	—
262 To international organizations	112	137	282	117	140	286	1	1	1	118	141	287
263 To other general government units	2,615	2,782	2,992	568	591	667	72	74	87	—	—	—
2631 Current	2,537	2,704	2,910	492	514	587	72	74	87	—	—	—
2632 Capital	78	79	82	76	77	80	—	—	—	—	—	—

In Millions of Euros / Year Ending December 31 / Noncash Reporter

		Budgetary Central Government			Central Government			Local Government			General Government		
		2002	2003p	2004p	2002	2003p	2004p	2002	2003p	2004p	2002	2003p	2004p
27	Social benefits..............	473	545	595	4,628	5,079	5,330	15	16	18	4,643	5,095	5,348
28	Other expense.................	812	935	1,110	817	940	1,114	43	44	45	860	984	1,159
281	Property expense other than interest...........	—	—	—	—	—	—	—	—	—	—	—	—
282	Miscellaneous other expense.............	812	935	1,110	817	940	1,114	43	44	45	860	984	1,159
2821	Current.................	522	610	665	523	610	665	34	36	39	557	646	704
2822	Capital.................	290	326	445	294	330	448	9	8	7	303	338	455

Table 3 Transactions in assets and liabilities

		2002	2003p	2004p	2002	2003p	2004p	2002	2003p	2004p	2002	2003p	2004p
3	Change in net worth from transactns....	294	417	–71	829	913	221	242	265	271	1,073	1,179	494
31	Net acquisition of nonfinancial assets...	447	433	433	446	425	428	286	311	262	732	736	689
311	Fixed assets.................	450	432	438	449	424	433	280	310	264	728	734	696
3111	Buildings and structures.............	....	....	....	....	....	....	....	....	....	....	....	....
3112	Machinery and equipment.............	....	....	....	....	....	....	....	....	....	....	....	....
3113	Other fixed assets.............	....	....	....	....	....	....	....	....	....	....	....	....
312	Inventories.................	—	—	—	—	—	—	—	—	—	—	—	—
313	Valuables.................	1	1	1	1	1	1	—	—	1	1	1	1
314	Nonproduced assets.............	–3	—	–6	–3	—	–6	6	1	–3	3	1	–9
3141	Land.................	....	....	....	....	....	....	....	....	....	....	....	....
3142	Subsoil assets.................	....	....	....	....	....	....	....	....	....	....	....	....
3143	Other naturally occurring assets.................	....	....	....	....	....	....	....	....	....	....	....	....
3144	Intangible nonproduced assets.................	....	....	....	....	....	....	....	....	....	....	....	....
32	Net acquisition of financial assets.........	–68	–199	–284	439	358	–24	–6	133	–86	433	491	–110
321	Domestic.................	–68	–22	–215	439	544	49	–6	133	–86	433	678	–37
3212	Currency and deposits.............	–126	43	–151	387	679	241	–8	132	–87	378	811	154
3213	Securities other than shares.............	43	–70	–113	83	–106	–177	—	—	—	83	–106	–177
3214	Loans.................	2	1	1	–44	–33	–63	1	1	1	–42	–32	–62
3215	Shares and other equity.............	13	4	48	13	4	48	1	1	—	14	4	48
3216	Insurance technical reserves.............	—	—	—	—	—	—	—	—	—	—	—	—
3217	Financial derivatives.............	—	—	—	—	—	—	—	—	—	—	—	—
3218	Other accounts receivable.............	—	—	—	—	—	—	—	—	—	—	—	—
322	Foreign.................	—	–177	–69	—	–186	–73	—	—	—	—	–186	–73
3222	Currency and deposits.............	—	—	—	—	—	—	—	—	—	—	—	—
3223	Securities other than shares.............	—	–177	–69	—	–186	–73	—	—	—	—	–186	–73
3224	Loans.................	—	—	—	—	—	—	—	—	—	—	—	—
3225	Shares and other equity.............	—	—	—	—	—	—	—	—	—	—	—	—
3226	Insurance technical reserves.............	—	—	—	—	—	—	—	—	—	—	—	—
3227	Financial derivatives.............	—	—	—	—	—	—	—	—	—	—	—	—
3228	Other accounts receivable.............	—	—	—	—	—	—	—	—	—	—	—	—
323	Monetary gold and SDRs.............	—	—	—	—	—	—	—	—	—	—	—	—
33	Net incurrence of liabilities..................	85	–183	221	56	–130	183	38	180	–96	93	48	86
331	Domestic.................	83	–182	264	54	–129	226	38	180	–96	91	50	129
3312	Currency and deposits.............	40	24	22	40	24	22	—	—	—	40	24	22
3313	Securities other than shares.............	–57	–206	—	–57	–197	—	—	—	–25	–57	–197	–25
3314	Loans.................	100	—	242	71	44	204	38	180	–71	108	222	131
3316	Insurance technical reserves.............	—	—	—	—	—	—	—	—	—	—	—	—
3317	Financial derivatives.............	—	—	—	—	—	—	—	—	—	—	—	—
3318	Other accounts payable.............	—	—	—	—	—	—	—	—	—	—	—	—
332	Foreign.................	2	–1	–43	2	–1	–43	—	—	—	2	–1	–43
3322	Currency and deposits.............	—	—	—	—	—	—	—	—	—	—	—	—
3323	Securities other than shares.............	—	—	—	—	—	—	—	—	—	—	—	—
3324	Loans.................	2	–1	–43	2	–1	–43	—	—	—	2	–1	–43
3326	Insurance technical reserves.............	—	—	—	—	—	—	—	—	—	—	—	—
3327	Financial derivatives.............	—	—	—	—	—	—	—	—	—	—	—	—
3328	Other accounts payable.............	—	—	—	—	—	—	—	—	—	—	—	—

Table 4 Holding gains in assets and liabilities

		2002	2003p	2004p	2002	2003p	2004p	2002	2003p	2004p	2002	2003p	2004p
4	Change in net worth from hold. gains...	....	....	....	....	....	....	....	....	....	....	....	....
41	Nonfinancial assets.............................	....	....	....	....	....	....	....	....	....	....	....	....
411	Fixed assets.................	....	....	....	....	....	....	....	....	....	....	....	....
412	Inventories.................	....	....	....	....	....	....	....	....	....	....	....	....
413	Valuables.................	....	....	....	....	....	....	....	....	....	....	....	....
414	Nonproduced assets.................	....	....	....	....	....	....	....	....	....	....	....	....
42	Financial assets..............................	–15	339	320	–41	341	309	19	4	2	–22	346	311
421	Domestic.................	–50	347	355	–70	350	346	19	4	2	–51	354	348
422	Foreign.................	36	–9	–35	29	–8	–37	—	—	—	29	–8	–37
423	Monetary gold and SDRs.............	—	—	—	—	—	—	—	—	—	—	—	—

In Millions of Euros / Year Ending December 31 / Noncash Reporter

		Budgetary Central Government			Central Government			Local Government			General Government		
		2002	2003p	2004p	2002	2003p	2004p	2002	2003p	2004p	2002	2003p	2004p
43	**Liabilities**	−46	−9	−11	−40	−10	−9	—	—	—	−40	−10	−9
431	Domestic	−46	−9	−11	−40	−10	−9	—	—	—	−40	−10	−9
432	Foreign	—	—	—	—	—	—	—	—	—	—	—	—
Table 5	**Other changes in the volume of assets and liabilities**												
5	**Change in net worth from vol. chngs**	....	....	....	....	....	....	....	....	....	....	....	....
51	**Nonfinancial assets**	....	....	....	....	....	....	....	....	....	....	....	....
511	Fixed assets	....	....	....	....	....	....	....	....	....	....	....	....
512	Inventories	....	....	....	....	....	....	....	....	....	....	....	....
513	Valuables	....	....	....	....	....	....	....	....	....	....	....	....
514	Nonproduced assets	....	....	....	....	....	....	....	....	....	....	....	....
52	**Financial assets**	−19	—	—	−19	—	—	—	—	—	−19	—	—
521	Domestic	−19	—	—	−19	—	—	—	—	—	−19	—	—
522	Foreign	—	—	—	—	—	—	—	—	—	—	—	—
523	Monetary gold and SDRs	—	—	—	—	—	—	—	—	—	—	—	—
53	**Liabilities**	—	—	—	—	—	—	—	—	—	—	—	—
531	Domestic	—	—	—	—	—	—	—	—	—	—	—	—
532	Foreign	—	—	—	—	—	—	—	—	—	—	—	—
Table 6	**Balance sheet**												
6	**Net worth**	....	....	....	....	....	....	....	....	....	....	....	....
61	**Nonfinancial assets**	....	....	....	....	....	....	....	....	....	....	....	....
611	Fixed assets	....	....	....	....	....	....	....	....	....	....	....	....
6111	Buildings and structures	....	....	....	....	....	....	....	....	....	....	....	....
6112	Machinery and equipment	....	....	....	....	....	....	....	....	....	....	....	....
6113	Other fixed assets	....	....	....	....	....	....	....	....	....	....	....	....
612	Inventories	....	....	....	....	....	....	....	....	....	....	....	....
613	Valuables	....	....	....	....	....	....	....	....	....	....	....	....
614	Nonproduced assets	....	....	....	....	....	....	....	....	....	....	....	....
6141	Land	....	....	....	....	....	....	....	....	....	....	....	....
6142	Subsoil assets	....	....	....	....	....	....	....	....	....	....	....	....
6143	Other naturally occurring assets	....	....	....	....	....	....	....	....	....	....	....	....
6144	Intangible nonproduced assets	....	....	....	....	....	....	....	....	....	....	....	....
62	**Financial assets**	8,442	8,582	8,618	13,235	13,934	14,218	1,140	1,277	1,193	14,371	15,208	15,408
621	Domestic	7,776	8,101	8,241	12,455	13,349	13,744	1,140	1,277	1,193	13,591	14,623	14,934
6212	Currency and deposits	2,464	2,507	2,356	6,239	6,919	7,159	616	747	661	6,855	7,666	7,820
6213	Securities other than shares	664	614	499	994	909	720	—	—	—	994	909	720
6214	Loans	39	40	41	604	571	508	42	43	44	642	610	549
6215	Shares and other equity	4,610	4,940	5,345	4,618	4,951	5,357	482	487	488	5,100	5,438	5,845
6216	Insurance technical reserves	—	—	—	—	—	—	—	—	—	—	—	—
6217	Financial derivatives	—	—	—	—	—	—	—	—	—	—	—	—
6218	Other accounts receivable	—	—	—	—	—	—	—	—	—	—	—	—
622	Foreign	666	480	377	780	585	474	—	—	—	780	585	474
6222	Currency and deposits	—	—	—	—	—	—	—	—	—	—	—	—
6223	Securities other than shares	666	480	377	780	585	474	—	—	—	780	585	474
6224	Loans	—	—	—	—	—	—	—	—	—	—	—	—
6225	Shares and other equity	—	—	—	—	—	—	—	—	—	—	—	—
6226	Insurance technical reserves	—	—	—	—	—	—	—	—	—	—	—	—
6227	Financial derivatives	—	—	—	—	—	—	—	—	—	—	—	—
6228	Other accounts receivable	—	—	—	—	—	—	—	—	—	—	—	—
623	Monetary gold and SDRs	—	—	—	—	—	—	—	—	—	—	—	—
63	**Liabilities**	1,372	1,180	1,389	1,118	978	1,152	516	695	599	1,592	1,631	1,708
631	Domestic	1,327	1,136	1,389	1,073	935	1,152	516	695	599	1,547	1,587	1,708
6312	Currency and deposits	58	82	104	58	82	104	—	—	—	58	82	104
6313	Securities other than shares	635	420	409	538	332	324	25	25	—	563	357	324
6314	Loans	634	634	875	476	520	724	491	671	599	926	1,148	1,279
6316	Insurance technical reserves	1	1	1	1	1	1	—	—	—	1	1	1
6317	Financial derivatives	—	—	—	—	—	—	—	—	—	—	—	—
6318	Other accounts payable	—	—	—	—	—	—	—	—	—	—	—	—
632	Foreign	45	43	—	45	43	—	—	—	—	45	43	—
6322	Currency and deposits	—	—	—	—	—	—	—	—	—	—	—	—
6323	Securities other than shares	—	—	—	—	—	—	—	—	—	—	—	—
6324	Loans	45	43	—	45	43	—	—	—	—	45	43	—
6326	Insurance technical reserves	—	—	—	—	—	—	—	—	—	—	—	—
6327	Financial derivatives	—	—	—	—	—	—	—	—	—	—	—	—
6328	Other accounts payable	—	—	—	—	—	—	—	—	—	—	—	—

In Millions of Euros / Year Ending December 31 / Noncash Reporter

	Budgetary Central Government			Central Government			Local Government			General Government		
	2002	2003p	2004p	2002	2003p	2004p	2002	2003p	2004p	2002	2003p	2004p
Memorandum items:												
6M2 Net financial worth................	7,070	7,402	7,229	12,117	12,956	13,066	624	582	593	12,779	13,577	13,701
6M3 Debt at market value................	....	....	....	....	....	....	....	....	....	....	....	....
6M4 Debt at nominal value...............	....	....	....	....	....	....	....	....	....	....	....	....
6M5 Arrears......................................	....	....	....	....	....	....	....	....	....	....	....	....
6M6 Obligations for social security benefits...........	....	....	....	....	....	....	....	....	....	....	....	....
6M7 Contingent liabilities..................	....	....	....	....	....	....	....	....	....	....	....	....
6M8 Uncapitalized military weapons, systems........	....	....	....	....	....	....	....	....	....	....	....	....
Table 7 Outlays by functions of govt.												
7 **Total outlays**..............................	6,997	7,533	8,350	9,201	9,963	10,855	1,405	1,489	1,516	9,965	10,787	11,616
701 **General public services**..............	1,311	1,369	1,613	1,311	1,369	1,613	260	285	308	1,571	1,654	1,921
7017 Public debt transactions................	73	76	60	62	59	43	18	17	16	80	76	59
7018 General transfers between levels of govt......	....	....	....	....	....	....	....	....	....	....	....	....
702 **Defense**...................................	68	73	76	68	73	76	—	—	—	68	73	76
703 **Public order and safety**..............	243	252	268	243	252	268	24	24	26	267	275	295
704 **Economic affairs**......................	904	931	1,033	904	931	1,033	288	290	258	1,193	1,221	1,291
7042 Agriculture, forestry, fishing, and hunting.....	....	....	....	....	....	....	....	....	....	....	....	....
7043 Fuel and energy..........................	....	....	....	....	....	....	....	....	....	....	....	....
7044 Mining, manufacturing, and construction.....	....	....	....	....	....	....	....	....	....	....	....	....
7045 Transport....................................	....	....	....	....	....	....	....	....	....	....	....	....
7046 Communication...........................	....	....	....	....	....	....	....	....	....	....	....	....
705 **Environmental protection**............	117	135	147	117	135	147	158	167	167	274	302	315
706 **Housing and community amenities**......	158	126	152	158	126	152	101	112	110	258	238	262
707 **Health**....................................	80	114	150	1,116	1,234	1,403	5	4	3	1,121	1,238	1,406
7072 Outpatient services......................	....	....	....	....	....	....	....	....	....	....	....	....
7073 Hospital services.........................	....	....	....	....	....	....	....	....	....	....	....	....
7074 Public health services..................	....	....	....	....	....	....	....	....	....	....	....	....
708 **Recreation, culture, and religion**..........	260	352	372	260	352	372	184	196	191	444	548	563
709 **Education**.................................	949	998	1,130	949	998	1,130	316	347	380	1,265	1,345	1,510
7091 Pre-primary and primary education...........	....	....	....	....	....	....	....	....	....	....	....	....
7092 Secondary education....................	....	....	....	....	....	....	....	....	....	....	....	....
7094 Tertiary education.......................	....	....	....	....	....	....	....	....	....	....	....	....
710 **Social protection**......................	2,907	3,183	3,408	6,142	6,709	7,020	69	65	71	6,212	6,774	7,091
7 Statistical discrepancy: Total outlays...	—	—	—	-2,067	-2,215	-2,360	—	—	—	-2,708	-2,880	-3,114
Table 8 Transactions in financial assets and liabilities by sector												
82 **Net acquisition of financial assets**........	-68	-199	-284	439	358	-24	-6	133	-86	433	491	-110
821 Domestic...................................	-68	-22	-215	439	544	49	-6	133	-86	433	678	-37
8211 General government....................	—	—	—	-2	-1	-1	1	1	1	—	—	—
8212 Central bank.............................	—	—	—	—	—	—	—	—	—	—	—	—
8213 Other depository corporations......	—	—	—	—	—	—	—	—	—	—	—	—
8214 Financial corporations n.e.c...........	-126	-23	-221	437	581	110	-8	132	-87	429	712	23
8215 Nonfinancial corporations.............	58	1	6	21	-9	-29	1	1	—	21	-8	-30
8216 Households & NPIs serving households......	—	—	—	-17	-26	-30	—	—	—	-17	-26	-30
822 Foreign.....................................	—	-177	-69	—	-186	-73	—	—	—	—	-186	-73
8221 General government....................	—	....	....	—	....	....	—	—	—	—	....	....
8227 International organizations.............	—	....	....	—	....	....	—	—	—	—	....	....
8228 Financial corporations other than international organizations.........	—	—	—	—	—	—	—	—	—	—	—	—
8229 Other nonresidents.....................	—	—	—	—	—	—	—	—	—	—	—	—
823 Monetary gold and SDRs...............	—	—	—	—	—	—	—	—	—	—	—	—
83 **Net incurrence of liabilities**..............	85	-183	221	56	-130	183	38	180	-96	93	48	86
831 Domestic...................................	83	-182	264	54	-129	226	38	180	-96	91	50	129
8311 General government....................	31	-10	6	2	1	1	—	—	—	—	—	—
8312 Central bank.............................	—	—	—	—	—	—	—	—	—	—	—	—
8313 Other depository corporations......	—	—	—	—	—	—	—	—	—	—	—	—
8314 Financial corporations n.e.c...........	52	-172	258	52	-130	225	39	180	-96	91	50	129
8315 Nonfinancial corporations.............	—	—	—	—	—	—	—	—	—	—	—	—
8316 Households & NPIs serving households......	—	—	—	—	—	—	—	—	—	—	—	—
832 Foreign.....................................	2	-1	-43	2	-1	-43	—	—	—	2	-1	-43
8321 General government....................	....	....	....	....	....	....	—	—	—	....	....	....
8327 International organizations.............	....	....	....	....	....	....	—	—	—	....	....	....
8328 Financial corporations other than international organizations............	....	....	....	....	....	....	—	—	—	....	....	....
8329 Other nonresidents.....................	....	....	....	....	....	....	—	—	—	....	....	....

In Billions of Francs / Year Ending December 31 / Noncash Reporter

	Budgetary Central Government			Central Government			Local Government			General Government		
	2002	2003	2004	2002	2003	2004	2002	2003	2004	2002	2003	2004
Statement of government operations												
1 Revenue......	....	....	....	2,895.0	5,163.3	8,283.9	....	....	....	....	....	....
2 Expense......	....	....	....	2,838.0	3,803.7	5,138.0	....	....	....	....	....	....
GOB *Gross operating balance*......	....	....	....	*57.0*	*1,359.5*	*3,145.9*	....	....	....	....	....	....
NOB *Net operating balance*......	....	....	....	....	....	....	....	....	....	....	....	....
31 Net acquisition of nonfinancial assets......	....	....	....	1,393.5	2,609.4	4,982.8	....	....	....	....	....	....
NLB *Net lending/borrowing*......	....	....	....	*−1,336.5*	*−1,249.9*	*−1,836.9*	....	....	....	....	....	....
32 Net acquisition of financial assets......	....	....	....	69.6	481.9	462.5	....	....	....	....	....	....
33 Net incurrence of liabilities......	....	....	....	1,406.1	1,731.8	2,299.4	....	....	....	....	....	....
NLB Statistical discrepancy......	....	....	....	—	—	—	....	....	....	....	....	....
Statement of other economic flows												
Balance sheet												
Statement of sources and uses of cash												
1 Cash receipts from operating activities......	....	....	....	2,895.0	5,163.3	8,283.9	....	....	....	....	....	....
11 Taxes......	....	....	....	2,304.2	3,392.4	4,435.6	....	....	....	....	....	....
12 Social contributions......	....	....	....	—	—	—	....	....	....	....	....	....
13 Grants......	....	....	....	492.0	1,538.7	3,355.5	....	....	....	....	....	....
14 Other receipts......	....	....	....	98.9	232.2	492.7	....	....	....	....	....	....
2 Cash payments for operating activities......	....	....	....	2,752.3	3,729.4	5,089.0	....	....	....	....	....	....
21 Compensation of employees......	....	....	....	1,380.0	1,827.1	2,000.2	....	....	....	....	....	....
22 Purchases of goods and services......	....	....	....	435.8	688.8	687.2	....	....	....	....	....	....
24 Interest......	....	....	....	364.8	565.8	1,197.4	....	....	....	....	....	....
25 Subsidies......	....	....	....	278.4	453.1	550.8	....	....	....	....	....	....
26 Grants......	....	....	....	—	—	—	....	....	....	....	....	....
27 Social benefits......	....	....	....	—	—	—	....	....	....	....	....	....
28 Other payments......	....	....	....	293.3	194.7	653.4	....	....	....	....	....	....
CIO *Net cash inflow from oper. activities*......	....	....	....	*142.7*	*1,433.9*	*3,194.9*	....	....	....	....	....	....
31.1 Purchases of nonfinancial assets......	....	....	....	1,287.7	2,470.8	4,923.0	....	....	....	....	....	....
31.2 Sales of nonfinancial assets......	....	....	....	52.3	48.0	107.3	....	....	....	....	....	....
31 Net cash outflow from investments in nonfinancial assets......	....	....	....	1,235.4	2,422.8	4,815.7	....	....	....	....	....	....
CSD *Cash surplus/deficit*......	....	....	....	*−1,092.8*	*−988.9*	*−1,620.8*	....	....	....	....	....	....
32x Net acquisition of fin assets, excl. cash......	....	....	....	....	477.4	530.3	....	....	....	....	....	....
321x Domestic......	....	....	....	....	477.4	530.3	....	....	....	....	....	....
322x Foreign......	....	....	....	—	—	—	....	....	....	....	....	....
323 Monetary gold and SDRs......	....	....	....	—	—	—	....	....	....	....	....	....
33 Net incurrence of liabilities......	....	....	....	....	1,731.8	2,299.4	....	....	....	....	....	....
331 Domestic......	....	....	....	....	731.9	−291.6	....	....	....	....	....	....
332 Foreign......	....	....	....	957.5	999.9	2,591.0	....	....	....	....	....	....
NFB Net cash inflow from fin. activities......	....	....	....	818.8	1,254.4	1,769.1	....	....	....	....	....	....
NCB *Net change in the stock of cash*......	....	....	....	*−274.0*	*135.5*	*131.7*	....	....	....	....	....	....
Table 1 Revenue												
1 **Revenue**......	....	....	....	**2,895.0**	**5,163.3**	**8,283.9**	....	....	....	....	....	....
11 **Taxes**......	....	....	....	**2,304.1**	**3,392.4**	**4,435.6**	....	....	....	....	....	....
111 Taxes on income, profits, & capital gains......	....	....	....	527.5	370.5	514.8	....	....	....	....	....	....
1111 Individuals......	....	....	....	208.8	48.2	60.4	....	....	....	....	....	....
1112 Corporations and other enterprises......	....	....	....	215.6	317.1	449.4	....	....	....	....	....	....
112 Taxes on payroll and workforce......	....	....	....	—	180.0	245.4	....	....	....	....	....	....
113 Taxes on property......	....	....	....	27.2	62.5	94.7	....	....	....	....	....	....
114 Taxes on goods and services......	....	....	....	689.7	1,037.1	1,324.9	....	....	....	....	....	....
1141 General taxes on goods and services......	....	....	....	575.9	639.7	921.2	....	....	....	....	....	....
1142 Excises......	....	....	....	102.3	177.8	185.5	....	....	....	....	....	....
115 Taxes on int'l. trade and transactions......	....	....	....	1,043.6	1,713.2	2,224.6	....	....	....	....	....	....
116 Other taxes......	....	....	....	16.1	29.2	31.3	....	....	....	....	....	....
12 **Social contributions**......	....	....	....	—	—	—	....	....	....	....	....	....
121 Social security contributions......	....	....	....	—	—	—	....	....	....	....	....	....
122 Other social contributions......	....	....	....	—	—	—	....	....	....	....	....	....
13 **Grants**......	....	....	....	492.0	1,538.7	3,355.5	....	....	....	....	....	....
131 From foreign governments......	....	....	....	492.0	1,538.7	3,355.5	....	....	....	....	....	....
132 From international organizations......	....	....	....	—	—	—	....	....	....	....	....	....
133 From other general government units......	....	....	....	—	—	—	....	....	....	....	....	....
14 **Other revenue**......	....	....	....	**98.9**	**232.2**	**492.7**	....	....	....	....	....	....

In Billions of Francs / Year Ending December 31 / Noncash Reporter

	Budgetary Central Government			Central Government			Local Government			General Government		
	2002	2003	2004	2002	2003	2004	2002	2003	2004	2002	2003	2004
Table 2 Expense by economic type												
2 **Expense**...............	....	....	....	2,838.0	3,803.7	5,138.0	....	....	....	....	....	....
21 **Compensation of employees**...............	....	....	....	1,380.0	1,827.1	2,000.2	....	....	....	....	....	....
211 Wages and salaries...............	....	....	....	1,380.0	1,827.1	2,000.2	....	....	....	....	....	....
212 Social contributions...............	....	....	....	—	—	—	....	....	....	....	....	....
22 **Use of goods and services**...............	....	....	....	514.8	745.2	735.3	....	....	....	....	....	....
23 **Consumption of fixed capital**...............	....	....	....	....	....	....	....	....	....	....	....	....
24 **Interest**...............	....	....	....	364.8	565.8	1,197.4	....	....	....	....	....	....
25 **Subsidies**...............	....	....	....	285.0	470.9	551.7	....	....	....	....	....	....
26 **Grants**...............	....	....	....	—	—	—	....	....	....	....	....	....
261 To foreign govenments...............	....	....	....	—	—	—	....	....	....	....	....	....
262 To international organizations...............	....	....	....	—	—	—	....	....	....	....	....	....
263 To other general government units...............	....	....	....	—	—	—	....	....	....	....	....	....
2631 Current...............	....	....	....	—	—	—	....	....	....	....	....	....
2632 Capital...............	....	....	....	—	—	—	....	....	....	....	....	....
27 **Social benefits**...............	....	....	....	—	—	—	....	....	....	....	....	....
28 **Other expense**...............	....	....	....	293.4	194.7	653.4	....	....	....	....	....	....
281 Property expense other than interest...............	....	....	....	—	—	—	....	....	....	....	....	....
282 Miscellaneous other expense...............	....	....	....	293.4	194.7	653.4	....	....	....	....	....	....
2821 Current...............	....	....	....	293.4	194.7	653.4	....	....	....	....	....	....
2822 Capital...............	....	....	....	—	—	—	....	....	....	....	....	....
Table 3 Transactions in assets and liabilities												
3 **Change in net worth from transactns**....	....	....	....	....	....	....	....	....	....	....	....	....
31 **Net acquisition of nonfinancial assets**...	....	....	....	1,393.5	2,609.4	4,982.8	....	....	....	....	....	....
311 Fixed assets...............	....	....	....	1,445.8	2,657.4	5,090.1	....	....	....	....	....	....
3111 Buildings and structures...............	....	....	....	....	....	....	....	....	....	....	....	....
3112 Machinery and equipment...............	....	....	....	....	....	....	....	....	....	....	....	....
3113 Other fixed assets...............	....	....	....	....	....	....	....	....	....	....	....	....
312 Inventories...............	....	....	....	−52.3	−48.0	−107.3	....	....	....	....	....	....
313 Valuables...............	....	....	....	—	—	—	....	....	....	....	....	....
314 Nonproduced assets...............	....	....	....	—	—	—	....	....	....	....	....	....
3141 Land...............	....	....	....	—	—	—	....	....	....	....	....	....
3142 Subsoil assets...............	....	....	....	—	—	—	....	....	....	....	....	....
3143 Other naturally occurring assets...............	....	....	....	—	—	—	....	....	....	....	....	....
3144 Intangible nonproduced assets...............	....	....	....	—	—	—	....	....	....	....	....	....
32 **Net acquisition of financial assets**........	....	....	....	69.6	481.9	462.5	....	....	....	....	....	....
321 Domestic...............	....	....	....	69.6	481.9	462.5	....	....	....	....	....	....
3212 Currency and deposits...............	....	....	....	−274.0	135.5	131.7	....	....	....	....	....	....
3213 Securities other than shares...............	....	....	....	—	—	—	....	....	....	....	....	....
3214 Loans...............	....	....	....	212.6	239.9	315.8	....	....	....	....	....	....
3215 Shares and other equity...............	....	....	....	—	—	—	....	....	....	....	....	....
3216 Insurance technical reserves...............	....	....	....	—	—	—	....	....	....	....	....	....
3217 Financial derivatives...............	....	....	....	—	—	—	....	....	....	....	....	....
3218 Other accounts receivable...............	....	....	....	131.0	106.5	15.0	....	....	....	....	....	....
322 Foreign...............	....	....	....	—	—	—	....	....	....	....	....	....
3222 Currency and deposits...............	....	....	....	—	—	—	....	....	....	....	....	....
3223 Securities other than shares...............	....	....	....	—	—	—	....	....	....	....	....	....
3224 Loans...............	....	....	....	—	—	—	....	....	....	....	....	....
3225 Shares and other equity...............	....	....	....	—	—	—	....	....	....	....	....	....
3226 Insurance technical reserves...............	....	....	....	—	—	—	....	....	....	....	....	....
3227 Financial derivatives...............	....	....	....	—	—	—	....	....	....	....	....	....
3228 Other accounts receivable...............	....	....	....	—	—	—	....	....	....	....	....	....
323 Monetary gold and SDRs...............	....	....	....	—	—	—	....	....	....	....	....	....
33 **Net incurrence of liabilities**...............	....	....	....	1,406.1	1,731.8	2,299.4	....	....	....	....	....	....
331 Domestic...............	....	....	....	448.6	731.9	−291.6	....	....	....	....	....	....
3312 Currency and deposits...............	....	....	....	135.4	156.0	86.7	....	....	....	....	....	....
3313 Securities other than shares...............	....	....	....	−71.8	422.6	539.6	....	....	....	....	....	....
3314 Loans...............	....	....	....	385.0	153.4	−917.9	....	....	....	....	....	....
3316 Insurance technical reserves...............	....	....	....	—	—	—	....	....	....	....	....	....
3317 Financial derivatives...............	....	....	....	—	—	—	....	....	....	....	....	....
3318 Other accounts payable...............	....	....	....	—	—	—	....	....	....	....	....	....

In Billions of Francs / Year Ending December 31 / Noncash Reporter

		Budgetary Central Government			Central Government			Local Government			General Government		
		2002	2003	2004	2002	2003	2004	2002	2003	2004	2002	2003	2004
332	Foreign.................................	....	....	....	957.5	999.9	2,591.0	....	....	....	....	....	....
3322	Currency and deposits...................	....	....	....	—	—	—	....	....	....	....	....	....
3323	Securities other than shares.............	....	....	....	—	—	—	....	....	....	....	....	....
3324	Loans.................................	....	....	....	957.5	999.9	2,591.0	....	....	....	....	....	....
3326	Insurance technical reserves.............	....	....	....				....	....	....	....	....	....
3327	Financial derivatives...................	....	....	....				....	....	....	....	....	....
3328	Other accounts payable.................	....	....	....	—	—	—	....	....	....	....	....	....

Table 4   Holding gains in assets and liabilities

Table 5   Other changes in the volume of assets and liabilities

Table 6   Balance sheet

Table 7   Outlays by functions of govt.

		Budgetary Central Government			Central Government			Local Government			General Government		
7	**Total outlays**.................................	....	....	....	**4,283.5**	**6,413.2**	**10,120.7**	....	....	....	....	....	....
701	**General public services**.................	....	....	....	**1,778.0**	**2,886.0**	**4,050.5**	....	....	....	....	....	....
7017	Public debt transactions.................	....	....	....	364.8	565.8	1,197.4	....	....	....	....	....	....
7018	General transfers between levels of govt......	....	....	....	1,413.3	2,320.2	2,853.1	....	....	....	....	....	....
702	**Defense**.................................	....	....	....	—	**449.1**	**508.8**	....	....	....	....	....	....
703	**Public order and safety**.................	....	....	....	**366.4**	**162.7**	**185.4**	....	....	....	....	....	....
704	**Economic affairs**.................	....	....	....	**636.4**	**1,384.3**	**3,133.4**	....	....	....	....	....	....
7042	Agriculture, forestry, fishing, and hunting.....	....	....	....	181.8	414.8	736.9	....	....	....	....	....	....
7043	Fuel and energy.........................	....	....	....	69.7	136.6	394.0	....	....	....	....	....	....
7044	Mining, manufacturing, and construction.....	....	....	....	291.4	627.7	1,498.5	....	....	....	....	....	....
7045	Transport.............................	....	....	....	74.4	166.7	469.1	....	....	....	....	....	....
7046	Communication.........................	....	....	....	....	....	....	....	....	....	....	....	....
705	**Environmental protection**.................	....	....	....	**168.7**	**3.9**	**—**	....	....	....	....	....	....
706	**Housing and community amenities**........	....	....	....	—	—	—	....	....	....	....	....	....
707	**Health**.................................	....	....	....	**344.7**	**418.2**	**760.7**	....	....	....	....	....	....
7072	Outpatient services.....................	....	....	....	....	....	....	....	....	....	....	....	....
7073	Hospital services.......................	....	....	....	....	....	....	....	....	....	....	....	....
7074	Public health services...................	....	....	....	....	....	....	....	....	....	....	....	....
708	**Recreation, culture, and religion**............	....	....	....	**22.8**	**7.0**	**10.7**	....	....	....	....	....	....
709	**Education**.................................	....	....	....	**885.4**	**1,032.3**	**1,344.9**	....	....	....	....	....	....
7091	Pre-primary and primary education...............	....	....	....	698.0	881.8	1,155.1	....	....	....	....	....	....
7092	Secondary education.....................	....	....	....	—	150.5	189.8	....	....	....	....	....	....
7094	Tertiary education.......................	....	....	....	187.4	—	—	....	....	....	....	....	....
710	**Social protection**.................................	....	....	....	**81.1**	**69.7**	**126.3**	....	....	....	....	....	....
7	Statistical discrepancy: Total outlays..............	....	....	....	....	....	....	....	....	....	....	....	....

Table 8   Transactions in financial assets and liabilities by sector

		Budgetary Central Government			Central Government			Local Government			General Government		
82	**Net acquisition of financial assets**........	....	....	....	**69.6**	**481.9**	**462.5**	....	....	....	....	....	....
821	Domestic.................................	....	....	....	69.6	481.9	462.5	....	....	....	....	....	....
8211	General government.......................	....	....	....	....	....	....	....	....	....	....	....	....
8212	Central bank.............................	....	....	....	....	....	....	....	....	....	....	....	....
8213	Other depository corporations.............	....	....	....	....	....	....	....	....	....	....	....	....
8214	Financial corporations n.e.c...............	....	....	....	....	....	....	....	....	....	....	....	....
8215	Nonfinancial corporations.................	....	....	....	....	....	....	....	....	....	....	....	....
8216	Households & NPIs serving households......	....	....	....	....	....	....	....	....	....	....	....	....
822	Foreign.................................	....	....	....	—	—	—	....	....	....	....	....	....
8221	General government.......................	....	....	....	—	—	—	....	....	....	....	....	....
8227	International organizations.................	....	....	....	—	—	—	....	....	....	....	....	....
8228	Financial corporations other than international organizations.............	....	....	....	—	—	—	....	....	....	....	....	....
8229	Other nonresidents.......................	....	....	....	—	—	—	....	....	....	....	....	....
823	Monetary gold and SDRs.................	....	....	....	—	—	—	....	....	....	....	....	....
83	**Net incurrence of liabilities**.................	....	....	....	**1,406.1**	**1,731.8**	**2,299.4**	....	....	....	....	....	....
831	Domestic.................................	....	....	....	448.6	731.9	−291.6	....	....	....	....	....	....
8311	General government.......................	....	....	....	....	....	....	....	....	....	....	....	....
8312	Central bank.............................	....	....	....	....	....	....	....	....	....	....	....	....
8313	Other depository corporations.............	....	....	....	....	....	....	....	....	....	....	....	....
8314	Financial corporations n.e.c...............	....	....	....	....	....	....	....	....	....	....	....	....
8315	Nonfinancial corporations.................	....	....	....	....	....	....	....	....	....	....	....	....
8316	Households & NPIs serving households......	....	....	....	....	....	....	....	....	....	....	....	....

Madagascar   674

In Billions of Francs / Year Ending December 31 / Noncash Reporter

		Budgetary Central Government			Central Government			Local Government			General Government		
		2002	2003	2004	2002	2003	2004	2002	2003	2004	2002	2003	2004
832	Foreign...............................	....	....	....	957.5	999.9	2,591.0	....	....	....	....	....	....
8321	General government....................	....	....	....	....	....	....	....	....	....	....	....	....
8327	International organizations........................	....	....	....	....	....	....	....	....	....	....	....	....
8328	Financial corporations other than international organizations.............	....	....	....	....	....	....	....	....	....	....	....	....
8329	Other nonresidents...................................	....	....	....	....	....	....	....	....	....	....	....	....

2005, International Monetary Fund: *Government Finance Statistics Yearbook*

In Millions of Ringgit / Year Ending December 31 / Cash Reporter

		Central Government			State Government			Local Government			General Government		
		2001	2002	2003p	2001	2002	2003p	2001	2002	2003p	2001	2002	2003p
	Statement of government operations												
	Statement of other economic flows												
	Balance sheet												
	Statement of sources and uses of cash												
1	Cash receipts from operating activities..........	84,445	88,412	93,610	7,071	8,233	9,148	3,812	4,081	5,178	92,338	96,723	102,970
11	Taxes...	62,968	68,059	69,470	1,111	1,236	1,297	2,162	2,285	2,440	66,241	71,579	73,207
12	Social contributions.................................	—	—	—	—	—	—	—	—	—	—	—	—
13	Grants..	—	—	—	2,307	3,198	3,200	681	803	1,763	—	—	—
14	Other receipts..................................	21,477	20,354	24,140	3,653	3,799	4,651	969	993	975	26,097	25,143	29,763
2	Cash payments for operating activities..........	65,463	83,550	79,366	5,484	5,289	6,263	2,777	2,945	3,286	70,733	87,780	83,949
21	Compensation of employees.....................	20,548	23,788	23,511	1,732	1,903	2,047	....	....	....	....	....	....
22	Purchases of goods and services..................	15,535	17,467	20,599	1,517	1,889	1,785	....	....	....	....	....	....
24	Interest...	10,797	10,573	9,870	....	....	....	....	....	....	....	....	....
25	Subsidies...	14,678	13,210	15,672	....	....	....	....	....	....	....	....	....
26	Grants..	2,718	3,707	4,665	270	294	298	—	—	—	—	—	—
27	Social benefits...................................	4,788	5,502	4,603	....	....	....	....	....	....	....	....	....
28	Other payments..................................	319	415	445	....	....	....	....	....	....	....	....	....
CIO	*Net cash inflow from oper. activities.....*	*18,982*	*4,862*	*14,244*	*1,587*	*2,944*	*2,885*	*1,035*	*1,136*	*1,893*	*21,604*	*8,943*	*19,021*
31.1	Purchases of nonfinancial assets.................	29,201	27,744	31,349	3,830	3,670	5,200	2,176	2,322	2,508	35,207	33,736	39,057
31.2	Sales of nonfinancial assets.....................	131	177	144	755	866	896	5	16	8	891	1,059	1,048
31	Net cash outflow from investments in nonfinancial assets.................	29,070	27,567	31,205	3,075	2,804	4,304	2,171	2,306	2,500	34,317	32,676	38,009
CSD	*Cash surplus/deficit.............................*	*−10,088*	*−22,705*	*−16,961*	*−1,488*	*140*	*−1,420*	*−1,136*	*−1,170*	*−607*	*−12,712*	*−23,734*	*−18,988*
32x	Net acquisition of fin assets, excl. cash....	....	....	....	....	....	....	....	....	....	....	....	....
321x	Domestic......................................	....	....	....	....	....	....	....	....	....	....	....	....
322x	Foreign..	....	....	....	....	....	....	....	....	....	....	....	....
323	Monetary gold and SDRs........................	....	....	....	....	....	....	....	....	....	....	....	....
33	Net incurrence of liabilities....................	....	....	....	....	....	....	....	....	....	....	....	....
331	Domestic......................................	....	....	....	....	....	....	....	....	....	....	....	....
332	Foreign..	....	....	....	....	....	....	....	....	....	....	....	....
NFB	Net cash inflow from fin. activities..........	....	....	....	....	....	....	....	....	....	....	....	....
NCB	*Net change in the stock of cash............*	....	....	....	....	....	....	....	....	....	....	....	....

Table 1   Revenue

		2001	2002	2003p	2001	2002	2003p	2001	2002	2003p	2001	2002	2003p
1	**Revenue......................................**	**84,445**	**88,412**	**93,610**	**7,071**	**8,233**	**9,148**	**3,812**	**4,081**	**5,178**	**92,338**	**96,723**	**102,970**
11	**Taxes...**	**62,968**	**68,059**	**69,470**	**1,111**	**1,236**	**1,297**	**2,162**	**2,285**	**2,440**	**66,241**	**71,579**	**73,207**
111	Taxes on income, profits, & capital gains......	40,134	42,236	44,390	—	—	—	....	....	....	....	....	....
1111	Individuals..................................	9,436	9,889	10,370	—	—	—	....	....	....	....	....	....
1112	Corporations and other enterprises...........	30,628	32,278	33,947	—	—	—	....	....	....	....	....	....
112	Taxes on payroll and workforce...............	—	—	—	—	—	—	....	....	....	....	....	....
113	Taxes on property.............................	229	320	211	1,012	1,106	1,156	....	....	....	....	....	....
114	Taxes on goods and services..................	17,919	20,232	20,060	99	130	141	....	....	....	....	....	....
1141	General taxes on goods and services.........	7,356	9,244	8,514	....	....	....	....	....	....	....	....	....
1142	Excises......................................	4,130	4,745	4,933	....	....	....	....	....	....	....	....	....
115	Taxes on int'l. trade and transactions.........	4,284	4,793	5,232	—	—	—	....	....	....	....	....	....
116	Other taxes...................................	403	477	−423	—	—	—	....	....	....	....	....	....
12	**Social contributions.........................**	—	—	—	—	—	—	—	—	—	—	—	—
121	Social security contributions.................	—	—	—	—	—	—	—	—	—	—	—	—
122	Other social contributions....................	—	—	—	—	—	—	—	—	—	—	—	—
13	**Grants.......................................**	—	—	—	2,307	3,198	3,200	681	803	1,763	—	—	—
131	From foreign governments.....................	—	—	—	—	—	—	—	—	—	—	—	—
132	From international organizations................	—	—	—	—	—	—	—	—	—	—	—	—
133	From other general government units..........	—	—	—	2,307	3,198	3,200	681	803	1,763	—	—	—
14	**Other revenue................................**	21,477	20,354	24,140	3,653	3,799	4,651	969	993	975	26,097	25,143	29,763

Table 2   Expense by economic type

		2001	2002	2003p	2001	2002	2003p	2001	2002	2003p	2001	2002	2003p
2	**Expense......................................**	**65,463**	**83,550**	**79,366**	**5,484**	**5,289**	**6,263**	**2,777**	**2,945**	**3,286**	**70,733**	**87,780**	**83,949**
21	**Compensation of employees.................**	**20,548**	**23,788**	**23,511**	**1,732**	**1,903**	**2,047**	....	....	....	....	....	....
211	Wages and salaries............................	20,215	23,431	23,135	1,732	1,903	2,047	....	....	....	....	....	....
212	Social contributions..........................	332	357	376	—	—	—	....	....	....	....	....	....
22	**Use of goods and services...................**	**15,535**	**17,467**	**20,599**	**1,517**	**1,889**	**1,785**	....	....	....	....	....	....
23	**Consumption of fixed capital...............**	....	....	....	....	....	....	....	....	....	....	....	....
24	**Interest......................................**	**10,797**	**10,573**	**9,870**	....	....	....	....	....	....	....	....	....
25	**Subsidies.....................................**	**14,678**	**13,210**	**15,672**	....	....	....	....	....	....	....	....	....

In Millions of Ringgit / Year Ending December 31 / Cash Reporter

	Central Government			State Government			Local Government			General Government		
	2001	2002	2003p	2001	2002	2003p	2001	2002	2003p	2001	2002	2003p
26 **Grants**.....................	2,718	3,707	4,665	270	294	298	—	—	—	—	—	—
261 To foreign govenments............	—	—	—	—	—	—	—	—	—	—	—	—
262 To international organizations.........	—	—	—	—	—	—	—	—	—	—	—	—
263 To other general government units..............	2,718	3,707	4,665	270	294	298	—	—	—	—	—	—
2631 Current..................	2,090	2,622	2,694	91	95	108	—	—	—	—	—	—
2632 Capital...................	628	1,085	1,971	179	199	190	—	—	—	—	—	—
27 **Social benefits**.....................	4,788	5,502	4,603	....	....	....	....	....	....	....	....	....
28 **Other expense**.....................	319	415	445	....	....	....	....	....	....	....	....	....
281 Property expense other than interest...........	—	—	—	....	....	....	....	....	....	....	....	....
282 Miscellaneous other expense..................	319	415	445	....	....	....	....	....	....	....	....	....
2821 Current..................	—	—	—	....	....	....	....	....	....	....	....	....
2822 Capital...................	319	415	445	....	....	....	....	....	....	....	....	....

Table 3   Transactions in assets and liabilities

	Central Government			State Government			Local Government			General Government		
	2001	2002	2003p	2001	2002	2003p	2001	2002	2003p	2001	2002	2003p
3 **Change in net worth from transactns....**	....	....	....	....	....	....	....	....	....	....	....	....
31 **Net acquisition of nonfinancial assets...**	29,070	27,567	31,205	3,075	2,804	4,304	2,171	2,306	2,500	34,317	32,676	38,009
311 Fixed assets..................	....	....	....	....	....	....	....	....	....	....	....	....
3111 Buildings and structures............	....	....	....	....	....	....	....	....	....	....	....	....
3112 Machinery and equipment.........	....	....	....	....	....	....	....	....	....	....	....	....
3113 Other fixed assets............	....	....	....	....	....	....	....	....	....	....	....	....
312 Inventories..............	....	....	....	—	—	—	—	—	—	....	....	....
313 Valuables................	—	—	—	—	—	—	—	—	—	—	—	—
314 Nonproduced assets..............	....	....	....	....	....	....	....	....	....	....	....	....
3141 Land...........	....	....	....	....	....	....	....	....	....	....	....	....
3142 Subsoil assets............	....	....	....	....	....	....	....	....	....	....	....	....
3143 Other naturally occurring assets.............	....	....	....	....	....	....	....	....	....	....	....	....
3144 Intangible nonproduced assets.........	....	....	....	....	....	....	....	....	....	....	....	....
32 **Net acquisition of financial assets.........**	....	....	....	....	....	....	....	....	....	....	....	....
321 Domestic...............	....	....	....	....	....	....	....	....	....	....	....	....
3212 Currency and deposits..........	....	....	....	....	....	....	....	....	....	....	....	....
3213 Securities other than shares............	....	....	....	....	....	....	....	....	....	....	....	....
3214 Loans..............	....	....	....	....	....	....	....	....	....	....	....	....
3215 Shares and other equity..............	....	....	....	....	....	....	....	....	....	....	....	....
3216 Insurance technical reserves............	....	....	....	....	....	....	....	....	....	....	....	....
3217 Financial derivatives............	....	....	....	....	....	....	....	....	....	....	....	....
3218 Other accounts receivable............	....	....	....	....	....	....	....	....	....	....	....	....
322 Foreign............	....	....	....	....	....	....	....	....	....	....	....	....
3222 Currency and deposits..........	....	....	....	....	....	....	....	....	....	....	....	....
3223 Securities other than shares...........	....	....	....	....	....	....	....	....	....	....	....	....
3224 Loans..............	....	....	....	....	....	....	....	....	....	....	....	....
3225 Shares and other equity............	....	....	....	....	....	....	....	....	....	....	....	....
3226 Insurance technical reserves............	....	....	....	....	....	....	....	....	....	....	....	....
3227 Financial derivatives............	....	....	....	....	....	....	....	....	....	....	....	....
3228 Other accounts receivable...........	....	....	....	....	....	....	....	....	....	....	....	....
323 Monetary gold and SDRs........	....	....	....	....	....	....	....	....	....	....	....	....
33 **Net incurrence of liabilities...................**	....	....	....	....	....	....	....	....	....	...	....	....
331 Domestic...............	....	....	....	....	....	....	....	....	....	....	....	....
3312 Currency and deposits..........	....	....	....	....	....	....	....	....	....	....	....	....
3313 Securities other than shares...........	....	....	....	....	....	....	....	....	....	....	....	....
3314 Loans...............	....	....	....	....	....	....	....	....	....	....	....	....
3316 Insurance technical reserves............	....	....	....	....	....	....	....	....	....	....	....	....
3317 Financial derivatives............	....	....	....	....	....	....	....	....	....	....	....	....
3318 Other accounts payable............	....	....	....	....	....	....	....	....	....	....	....	....
332 Foreign............	....	....	....	....	....	....	....	....	....	....	....	....
3322 Currency and deposits..........	....	....	....	....	....	....	....	....	....	....	....	....
3323 Securities other than shares...........	....	....	....	....	....	....	....	....	....	....	....	....
3324 Loans..............	....	....	....	....	....	....	....	....	....	....	....	....
3326 Insurance technical reserves............	....	....	....	....	....	....	....	....	....	....	....	....
3327 Financial derivatives............	....	....	....	....	....	....	....	....	....	....	....	....
3328 Other accounts payable............	....	....	....	....	....	....	....	....	....	....	....	....

In Millions of Ringgit / Year Ending December 31 / Cash Reporter

	Central Government			State Government			Local Government			General Government		
	2001	2002	2003p	2001	2002	2003p	2001	2002	2003p	2001	2002	2003p
Table 4 Holding gains in assets and liabilities												
Table 5 Other changes in the volume of assets and liabilities												
Table 6 Balance sheet												
Table 7 Outlays by functions of govt.												
7 Total outlays..........................	94,533	111,117	110,571	8,559	8,093	10,567	4,948	5,251	5,785	105,050	120,456	121,958
701 **General public services**.........................	....	....	....	....	....	....	....	....	....	....	....	....
7017 Public debt transactions......................	10,797	10,573	9,870	....	....	....	....	....	....	....	....	....
7018 General transfers between levels of govt......	....	....	....	....	....	....	....	....	....	....	....	....
702 **Defense**....................................	....	....	....	....	....	....	....	....	....	....	....	....
703 **Public order and safety**......................	....	....	....	....	....	....	....	....	....	....	....	....
704 **Economic affairs**.............................	....	....	....	....	....	....	....	....	....	....	....	....
7042 Agriculture, forestry, fishing, and hunting.....	....	....	....	....	....	....	....	....	....	....	....	....
7043 Fuel and energy.............................	....	....	....	....	....	....	....	....	....	....	....	....
7044 Mining, manufacturing, and construction.....	....	....	....	....	....	....	....	....	....	....	....	....
7045 Transport...................................	....	....	....	....	....	....	....	....	....	....	....	....
7046 Communication.............................	....	....	....	....	....	....	....	....	....	....	....	....
705 **Environmental protection**....................	....	....	....	....	....	....	....	....	....	....	....	....
706 **Housing and community amenities**........	....	....	....	....	....	....	....	....	....	....	....	....
707 **Health**...................................	....	....	....	....	....	....	....	....	....	....	....	....
7072 Outpatient services.........................	....	....	....	....	....	....	....	....	....	....	....	....
7073 Hospital services...........................	....	....	....	....	....	....	....	....	....	....	....	....
7074 Public health services.......................	....	....	....	....	....	....	....	....	....	....	....	....
708 **Recreation, culture, and religion**............	....	....	....	....	....	....	....	....	....	....	....	....
709 **Education**.................................	....	....	....	....	....	....	....	....	....	....	....	....
7091 Pre-primary and primary education............	....	....	....	....	....	....	....	....	....	....	....	....
7092 Secondary education........................	....	....	....	....	....	....	....	....	....	....	....	....
7094 Tertiary education..........................	....	....	....	....	....	....	....	....	....	....	....	....
710 **Social protection**..........................	....	....	....	....	....	....	....	....	....	....	....	....
7 Statistical discrepancy: Total outlays..............	....	....	....	....	....	....	....	....	....	....	....	....
Table 8 Transactions in financial assets and liabilities by sector												

Maldives 556

In Millions of Rufiyaa / Year Ending December 31 / Cash Reporter

	Budgetary Central Government			Extrabudgetary Accounts			Central Government			General Government		
	2003	2004p	2005f	2003	2004	2005	2003	2004p	2005f	2003	2004p	2005f
Statement of government operations												
Statement of other economic flows												
Balance sheet												
6 *Net worth*................	....	....	....	....	....	....	....	....	....	....	....	....
61 Nonfinancial assets.............	....	....	....	....	....	....	....	....	....	....	....	....
62 Financial assets................	....	....	....	....	....	....	....	....	....	....	....	....
63 Liabilities..................	4,087.6	4,284.5	4,676.5	....	....	....	4,087.6	4,284.5	4,676.5	4,087.6	4,284.5	4,676.5
Statement of sources and uses of cash												
1 Cash receipts from operating activities...........	3,060.4	3,376.9	4,181.3	....	....	....	3,060.4	3,376.9	4,181.3	3,060.4	3,376.9	4,181.3
11 Taxes.................	1,268.7	1,638.1	1,877.5	....	....	....	1,268.7	1,638.1	1,877.5	1,268.7	1,638.1	1,877.5
12 Social contributions...............	—	—	—	....	....	....	123.6	74.5	82.6	123.6	74.5	82.6
13 Grants............	123.6	74.5	82.6	....	....	....	1,668.1	1,664.3	2,221.2	1,668.1	1,664.3	2,221.2
14 Other receipts................	1,668.1	1,664.3	2,221.2	....	....	....	2,345.7	2,657.9	3,475.1	2,345.7	2,657.9	3,475.1
2 Cash payments for operating activities...........	2,345.7	2,657.9	3,475.1	....	....	....	564.1	695.2	1,034.4	564.1	695.2	1,034.4
21 Compensation of employees........	564.1	695.2	1,034.4	....	....	....	1,610.6	1,778.3	2,230.0	1,610.6	1,778.3	2,230.0
22 Purchases of goods and services......	1,610.6	1,778.3	2,230.0	....	....	....	135.2	134.8	140.0	135.2	134.8	140.0
24 Interest.................	135.2	134.8	140.0	....	....	....	35.8	49.6	70.7	35.8	49.6	70.7
25 Subsidies................	35.8	49.6	70.7	....	....	....	—	—	—	—	—	—
26 Grants..................	—	—	—	....	....	....	—	—	—	—	—	—
27 Social benefits................	—	—	—	....	....	....	—	—	—	—	—	—
28 Other payments...............	—	—	—	....	....	....	714.7	719.0	706.2	714.7	719.0	706.2
CIO *Net cash inflow from oper. activities.....*	*714.7*	*719.0*	*706.2*	....	....	....	1,206.2	1,100.2	1,267.8	1,206.2	1,100.2	1,267.8
31.1 Purchases of nonfinancial assets...............	1,206.2	1,100.2	1,267.8	....	....	....	27.5	18.3	26.0	27.5	18.3	26.0
31.2 Sales of nonfinancial assets.............	27.5	18.3	26.0	....	....	....						
31 Net cash outflow from investments in nonfinancial assets.............	1,178.7	1,081.9	1,241.8	....	....	....	1,178.7	1,081.9	1,241.8	1,178.7	1,081.9	1,241.8
CSD *Cash surplus/deficit.............*	*−464.0*	*−362.9*	*−535.6*	*....*	*....*	*....*	*−464.0*	*−362.9*	*−535.6*	*−464.0*	*−362.9*	*−535.6*
32x Net acquisition of fin assets, excl. cash...........	−163.7	−192.8	−106.7	....	....	....	−163.7	−192.8	−106.7	−163.7	−192.8	−106.7
321x Domestic.............	−163.7	−196.6	−110.5	....	....	....	−163.7	−196.6	−110.5	−163.7	−196.6	−110.5
322x Foreign................	—	3.8	3.8	....	....	....	—	3.8	3.8	—	3.8	3.8
323 Monetary gold and SDRs................	—	—	—	....	....	....						
33 Net incurrence of liabilities...............	283.2	216.6	435.4	....	....	....	283.2	216.6	435.4	283.2	216.6	435.4
331 Domestic..................	−136.0	−188.8	27.8	....	....	....	−136.0	−188.8	27.8	−136.0	−188.8	27.8
332 Foreign..................	419.2	405.4	407.6	....	....	....	419.2	405.4	407.6	419.2	405.4	407.6
NFB Net cash inflow from fin. activities.............	446.9	409.4	542.1	....	....	....	446.9	409.4	542.1	446.9	409.4	542.1
NCB *Net change in the stock of cash.............*	*−17.1*	*46.5*	*6.5*	....	....	....	*−17.1*	*46.5*	*6.5*	*−17.1*	*46.5*	*6.5*
Table 1 Revenue												
1 **Revenue**........................	**3,060.4**	**3,376.9**	**4,181.3**	....	....	....	**3,060.4**	**3,376.9**	**4,181.3**	**3,060.4**	**3,376.9**	**4,181.3**
11 **Taxes**....................	**1,268.7**	**1,638.1**	**1,877.5**	....	....	....	**1,268.7**	**1,638.1**	**1,877.5**	**1,268.7**	**1,638.1**	**1,877.5**
111 Taxes on income, profits, & capital gains......	46.2	48.6	68.6	....	....	....	46.2	48.6	68.6	46.2	48.6	68.6
1111 Individuals...............	—	—	—	....	....	....						
1112 Corporations and other enterprises............	46.2	48.6	68.6	....	....	....	46.2	48.6	68.6	46.2	48.6	68.6
112 Taxes on payroll and workforce...............	—	—	—	....	....	....						
113 Taxes on property.................	—	.5	.5	....	....	....	—	.5	.5	—	.5	.5
114 Taxes on goods and services...............	394.8	451.4	598.9	....	....	....	394.8	451.4	598.9	394.8	451.4	598.9
1141 General taxes on goods and services.........	—	—	—	....	....	....	—	—	—	—	—	—
1142 Excises..................	—	—	—	....	....	....						
115 Taxes on int'l. trade and transactions...............	817.1	1,126.7	1,193.9	....	....	....	817.1	1,126.7	1,193.9	817.1	1,126.7	1,193.9
116 Other taxes.................	10.6	10.9	15.6	....	....	....	10.6	10.9	15.6	10.6	10.9	15.6
12 **Social contributions**.............	—	—	—	....	....	....	—	—	—	—	—	—
121 Social security contributions.............	—	—	—	....	....	....						
122 Other social contributions...............	—	—	—	....	....	....	—	—	—	—	—	—
13 **Grants**..................	**123.6**	**74.5**	**82.6**	....	....	....	**123.6**	**74.5**	**82.6**	**123.6**	**74.5**	**82.6**
131 From foreign governments.............	123.6	74.5	82.6	....	....	....	123.6	74.5	82.6	123.6	74.5	82.6
132 From international organizations................	—	—	—	....	....	....	—	—	—	—	—	—
133 From other general government units........	—	—	—	....	....	....						
14 **Other revenue**................	**1,668.1**	**1,664.3**	**2,221.2**	....	....	....	**1,668.1**	**1,664.3**	**2,221.2**	**1,668.1**	**1,664.3**	**2,221.2**
Table 2 Expense by economic type												
2 **Expense**..................	**2,345.7**	**2,657.9**	**3,475.1**	....	....	....	**2,345.7**	**2,657.9**	**3,475.1**	**2,345.7**	**2,657.9**	**3,475.1**
21 **Compensation of employees**..................	**564.1**	**695.2**	**1,034.4**	....	....	....	**564.1**	**695.2**	**1,034.4**	**564.1**	**695.2**	**1,034.4**
211 Wages and salaries...............	564.1	695.2	1,034.4	....	....	....	564.1	695.2	1,034.4	564.1	695.2	1,034.4
212 Social contributions...............	—	—	—	....	....	....						
22 **Use of goods and services**..................	**1,610.6**	**1,778.3**	**2,230.0**	....	....	....	**1,610.6**	**1,778.3**	**2,230.0**	**1,610.6**	**1,778.3**	**2,230.0**
23 **Consumption of fixed capital**..........	....	....	....	....	....	....				....	....	....
24 **Interest**.................	**135.2**	**134.8**	**140.0**	....	....	....	**135.2**	**134.8**	**140.0**	**135.2**	**134.8**	**140.0**
25 **Subsidies**..................	**35.8**	**49.6**	**70.7**	....	....	....	**35.8**	**49.6**	**70.7**	**35.8**	**49.6**	**70.7**

		Budgetary Central Government			Extrabudgetary Accounts			Central Government			General Government		
		2003	2004p	2005f	2003	2004	2005	2003	2004p	2005f	2003	2004p	2005f
26	**Grants**..................................	—	—	—	....	....	....	—	—	—	—	—	—
261	To foreign govenments.....................	—	—	—	....	....	....	—	—	—	—	—	—
262	To international organizations..............	—	—	—	....	....	....	—	—	—	—	—	—
263	To other general government units..........	—	—	—	....	....	....	—	—	—	—	—	—
2631	Current..................................	—	—	—	....	....	....	—	—	—	—	—	—
2632	Capital..................................	—	—	—	....	....	....	—	—	—	—	—	—
27	**Social benefits**............................	—	—	—	....	....	....	—	—	—	—	—	—
28	**Other expense**.............................	—	—	—	....	....	....	—	—	—	—	—	—
281	Property expense other than interest........	—	—	—	....	....	....	—	—	—	—	—	—
282	Miscellaneous other expense................	—	—	—	....	....	....	—	—	—	—	—	—
2821	Current..................................	—	—	—	....	....	....	—	—	—	—	—	—
2822	Capital..................................	—	—	—	....	....	....	—	—	—	—	—	—

Table 3   Transactions in assets and liabilities

		Budgetary Central Government			Extrabudgetary Accounts			Central Government			General Government		
		2003	2004p	2005f	2003	2004	2005	2003	2004p	2005f	2003	2004p	2005f
3	**Change in net worth from transactns....**	....	....	....	....	....	....	....	....	....	....	....	....
31	**Net acquisition of nonfinancial assets...**	**1,178.7**	**1,081.9**	**1,241.8**	....	....	....	**1,178.7**	**1,081.9**	**1,241.8**	**1,178.7**	**1,081.9**	**1,241.8**
311	Fixed assets.............................	1,178.7	1,081.9	1,241.8	....	....	....	1,178.7	1,081.9	1,241.8	1,178.7	1,081.9	1,241.8
3111	Buildings and structures..............	....	....	....	....	....	....	....	....	....	....	....	....
3112	Machinery and equipment..............	....	....	....	....	....	....	....	....	....	....	....	....
3113	Other fixed assets....................	....	....	....	....	....	....	....	....	....	....	....	....
312	Inventories..............................	—	—	—	....	....	....	—	—	—	—	—	—
313	Valuables................................	—	—	—	....	....	....	—	—	—	—	—	—
314	Nonproduced assets......................	—	—	—	....	....	....	—	—	—	—	—	—
3141	Land..................................	—	—	—	....	....	....	—	—	—	—	—	—
3142	Subsoil assets........................	—	—	—	....	....	....	—	—	—	—	—	—
3143	Other naturally occurring assets......	—	—	—	....	....	....	—	—	—	—	—	—
3144	Intangible nonproduced assets.........	—	—	—	....	....	....	—	—	—	—	—	—
32	**Net acquisition of financial assets........**	**−180.8**	**−146.3**	**−100.2**	....	....	....	**−180.8**	**−146.3**	**−100.2**	**−180.8**	**−146.3**	**−100.2**
321	Domestic.................................	−180.8	−150.1	−104.0	....	....	....	−180.8	−150.1	−104.0	−180.8	−150.1	−104.0
3212	Currency and deposits.................	−17.1	46.5	6.5	....	....	....	−17.1	46.5	6.5	−17.1	46.5	6.5
3213	Securities other than shares..........	....	....	....	....	....	....	....	....	....	....	....	....
3214	Loans.................................	....	....	....	....	....	....	....	....	....	....	....	....
3215	Shares and other equity...............	....	....	....	....	....	....	....	....	....	....	....	....
3216	Insurance technical reserves..........	—	—	—	....	....	....	—	—	—	—	—	—
3217	Financial derivatives.................	—	—	—	....	....	....	—	—	—	—	—	—
3218	Other accounts receivable.............	....	....	....	....	....	....	....	....	....	....	....	....
322	Foreign..................................	—	3.8	3.8	....	....	....	—	3.8	3.8	—	3.8	3.8
3222	Currency and deposits.................	—	—	—	....	....	....	—	—	—	—	—	—
3223	Securities other than shares..........	—	....	....	....	....	....	—	....	....	—	....	....
3224	Loans.................................	—	....	....	....	....	....	—	....	....	—	....	....
3225	Shares and other equity...............	—	....	....	....	....	....	—	....	....	—	....	....
3226	Insurance technical reserves..........	—	—	—	....	....	....	—	—	—	—	—	—
3227	Financial derivatives.................	—	—	—	....	....	....	—	—	—	—	—	—
3228	Other accounts receivable.............	....	....	....	....	....	....	....	....	....	....	....	....
323	Monetary gold and SDRs..................	....	....	....	....	....	....	....	....	....	....	....	....
33	**Net incurrence of liabilities...................**	**283.2**	**216.6**	**435.4**	....	....	....	**283.2**	**216.6**	**435.4**	**283.2**	**216.6**	**435.4**
331	Domestic.................................	−136.0	−188.8	27.8	....	....	....	−136.0	−188.8	27.8	−136.0	−188.8	27.8
3312	Currency and deposits.................	—	—	—	....	....	....	—	—	—	—	—	—
3313	Securities other than shares..........	—	—	—	....	....	....	—	—	—	—	—	—
3314	Loans.................................	−136.0	−188.8	27.8	....	....	....	−136.0	−188.8	27.8	−136.0	−188.8	27.8
3316	Insurance technical reserves..........	—	—	—	....	....	....	—	—	—	—	—	—
3317	Financial derivatives.................	—	—	—	....	....	....	—	—	—	—	—	—
3318	Other accounts payable................	....	....	....	....	....	....	....	....	....	....	....	....
332	Foreign..................................	419.2	405.4	407.6	....	....	....	419.2	405.4	407.6	419.2	405.4	407.6
3322	Currency and deposits.................	—	—	—	....	....	....	—	—	—	—	—	—
3323	Securities other than shares..........	—	—	—	....	....	....	—	—	—	—	—	—
3324	Loans.................................	419.2	405.4	407.6	....	....	....	419.2	405.4	407.6	419.2	405.4	407.6
3326	Insurance technical reserves..........	—	—	—	....	....	....	—	—	—	—	—	—
3327	Financial derivatives.................	—	—	—	....	....	....	—	—	—	—	—	—
3328	Other accounts payable................	....	....	....	....	....	....	....	....	....	....	....	....

In Millions of Rufiyaa / Year Ending December 31 / Cash Reporter

	Budgetary Central Government			Extrabudgetary Accounts			Central Government			General Government		
	2003	2004p	2005f	2003	2004	2005	2003	2004p	2005f	2003	2004p	2005f
Table 4 Holding gains in assets and liabilities												
Table 5 Other changes in the volume of assets and liabilities												
Table 6 Balance sheet												
6 Net worth..................................	....	....	....	....	....	....	....	....	....	....	....	....
61 Nonfinancial assets...................	....	....	....	....	....	....	....	....	....	....	....	....
611 Fixed assets............................	....	....	....	....	....	....	....	....	....	....	....	....
6111 Buildings and structures............	....	....	....	....	....	....	....	....	....	....	....	....
6112 Machinery and equipment..........	....	....	....	....	....	....	....	....	....	....	....	....
6113 Other fixed assets....................	....	....	....	....	....	....	....	....	....	....	....	....
612 Inventories..............................	....	....	....	....	....	....	....	....	....	....	....	....
613 Valuables...............................	....	....	....	....	....	....	....	....	....	....	....	....
614 Nonproduced assets..................	....	....	....	....	....	....	....	....	....	....	....	....
6141 Land....................................	....	....	....	....	....	....	....	....	....	....	....	....
6142 Subsoil assets........................	....	....	....	....	....	....	....	....	....	....	....	....
6143 Other naturally occurring assets...	....	....	....	....	....	....	....	....	....	....	....	....
6144 Intangible nonproduced assets.....	....	....	....	....	....	....	....	....	....	....	....	....
62 Financial assets........................	....	....	....	....	....	....	....	....	....	....	....	....
621 Domestic...............................	....	....	....	....	....	....	....	....	....	....	....	....
6212 Currency and deposits..............	....	....	....	....	....	....	....	....	....	....	....	....
6213 Securities other than shares........	....	....	....	....	....	....	....	....	....	....	....	....
6214 Loans..................................	....	....	....	....	....	....	....	....	....	....	....	....
6215 Shares and other equity............	....	....	....	....	....	....	....	....	....	....	....	....
6216 Insurance technical reserves........	....	....	....	....	....	....	....	....	....	....	....	....
6217 Financial derivatives.................	....	....	....	....	....	....	....	....	....	....	....	....
6218 Other accounts receivable..........	....	....	....	....	....	....	....	....	....	....	....	....
622 Foreign.................................	....	....	....	....	....	....	....	....	....	....	....	....
6222 Currency and deposits..............	....	....	....	....	....	....	....	....	....	....	....	....
6223 Securities other than shares........	....	....	....	....	....	....	....	....	....	....	....	....
6224 Loans..................................	....	....	....	....	....	....	....	....	....	....	....	....
6225 Shares and other equity............	....	....	....	....	....	....	....	....	....	....	....	....
6226 Insurance technical reserves........	....	....	....	....	....	....	....	....	....	....	....	....
6227 Financial derivatives.................	....	....	....	....	....	....	....	....	....	....	....	....
6228 Other accounts receivable..........	....	....	....	....	....	....	....	....	....	....	....	....
623 Monetary gold and SDRs...........	....	....	....	....	....	....	....	....	....	....	....	....
63 **Liabilities**............................	**4,087.6**	**4,284.5**	**4,676.5**	....	....	....	**4,087.6**	**4,284.5**	**4,676.5**	**4,087.6**	**4,284.5**	**4,676.5**
631 Domestic...............................	1,464.7	1,256.2	1,240.6	....	....	....	1,464.7	1,256.2	1,240.6	1,464.7	1,256.2	1,240.6
6312 Currency and deposits..............	....	....	....	....	....	....	....	....	....	....	....	....
6313 Securities other than shares........	....	....	....	....	....	....	....	....	....	....	....	....
6314 Loans..................................	....	....	....	....	....	....	....	....	....	....	....	....
6316 Insurance technical reserves........	....	....	....	....	....	....	....	....	....	....	....	....
6317 Financial derivatives.................	....	....	....	....	....	....	....	....	....	....	....	....
6318 Other accounts payable............	....	....	....	....	....	....	....	....	....	....	....	....
632 Foreign.................................	2,622.9	3,028.3	3,435.9	....	....	....	2,622.9	3,028.3	3,435.9	2,622.9	3,028.3	3,435.9
6322 Currency and deposits..............	....	....	....	....	....	....	....	....	....	....	....	....
6323 Securities other than shares........	....	....	....	....	....	....	....	....	....	....	....	....
6324 Loans..................................	....	....	....	....	....	....	....	....	....	....	....	....
6326 Insurance technical reserves........	....	....	....	....	....	....	....	....	....	....	....	....
6327 Financial derivatives.................	....	....	....	....	....	....	....	....	....	....	....	....
6328 Other accounts payable............	....	....	....	....	....	....	....	....	....	....	....	....
Memorandum items:												
6M2 Net financial worth..................	....	....	....	....	....	....	....	....	....	....	....	....
6M3 Debt at market value...............	....	....	....	....	....	....	....	....	....	....	....	....
6M4 Debt at nominal value..............	....	....	....	....	....	....	....	....	....	....	....	....
6M5 Arrears.................................	....	....	....	....	....	....	....	....	....	....	....	....
6M6 Obligations for social security benefits........	....	....	....	....	....	....	....	....	....	....	....	....
6M7 Contingent liabilities.................	....	....	....	....	....	....	....	....	....	....	....	....
6M8 Uncapitalized military weapons, systems........	....	....	....	....	....	....	....	....	....	....	....	....
Table 7 Outlays by functions of govt.												
7 **Total outlays**....................	**3,551.9**	**3,758.1**	**4,742.9**	....	....	....	**3,551.9**	**3,758.1**	**4,742.9**	**3,551.9**	**3,758.1**	**4,742.9**
701 **General public services**.............	**808.0**	**919.9**	**1,213.0**	....	....	....	**808.0**	**919.9**	**1,213.0**	**808.0**	**919.9**	**1,213.0**
7017 Public debt transactions............	135.2	134.8	140.0	....	....	....	135.2	134.8	140.0	135.2	134.8	140.0
7018 General transfers between levels of govt......	....	....	....	....	....	....	....	....	....	....	....	....
702 **Defense**...............................	**441.9**	**374.1**	**526.4**	....	....	....	**441.9**	**374.1**	**526.4**	**441.9**	**374.1**	**526.4**
703 **Public order and safety**..............	**90.2**	**120.5**	**199.7**	....	....	....	**90.2**	**120.5**	**199.7**	**90.2**	**120.5**	**199.7**

In Millions of Rufiyaa / Year Ending December 31 / Cash Reporter

		Budgetary Central Government			Extrabudgetary Accounts			Central Government			General Government		
		2003	2004p	2005f	2003	2004	2005	2003	2004p	2005f	2003	2004p	2005f
704	**Economic affairs**	**544.2**	**596.8**	**818.5**	....	....	....	**544.2**	**596.8**	**818.5**	**544.2**	**596.8**	**818.5**
7042	Agriculture, forestry, fishing, and hunting	26.2	32.4	94.0	....	....	....	26.2	32.4	94.0	26.2	32.4	94.0
7043	Fuel and energy	30.0	8.8	31.7	....	....	....	30.0	8.8	31.7	30.0	8.8	31.7
7044	Mining, manufacturing, and construction	—	—	—	....	....	....	—	—	—	—	—	—
7045	Transport	447.3	453.9	526.3	....	....	....	447.3	453.9	526.3	447.3	453.9	526.3
7046	Communication	....	....	....	....	....	....	....	....	....	....	....	....
705	**Environmental protection**	—	—	—	....	....	....	—	—	—	—	—	—
706	**Housing and community amenities**	**439.4**	**424.2**	**313.2**	....	....	....	**439.4**	**424.2**	**313.2**	**439.4**	**424.2**	**313.2**
707	**Health**	**363.3**	**423.9**	**533.4**	....	....	....	**363.3**	**423.9**	**533.4**	**363.3**	**423.9**	**533.4**
7072	Outpatient services	83.0	99.3	130.4	....	....	....	83.0	99.3	130.4	83.0	99.3	130.4
7073	Hospital services	182.6	221.3	252.5	....	....	....	182.6	221.3	252.5	182.6	221.3	252.5
7074	Public health services	....	....	....	....	....	....	....	....	....	....	....	....
708	**Recreation, culture, and religion**	—	—	—	....	....	....	—	—	—	—	—	—
709	**Education**	**723.6**	**736.6**	**970.0**	....	....	....	**723.6**	**736.6**	**970.0**	**723.6**	**736.6**	**970.0**
7091	Pre-primary and primary education	....	....	....	....	....	....	....	....	....	....	....	....
7092	Secondary education	522.7	488.9	684.9	....	....	....	522.7	488.9	684.9	522.7	488.9	684.9
7094	Tertiary education	47.3	64.3	82.4	....	....	....	47.3	64.3	82.4	47.3	64.3	82.4
710	**Social protection**	**141.3**	**162.1**	**168.7**	....	....	....	**141.3**	**162.1**	**168.7**	**141.3**	**162.1**	**168.7**
7	Statistical discrepancy: Total outlays	—	—	—	....	....	....	—	—	—	—	—	—

Table 8   Transactions in financial assets and liabilities by sector

		Budgetary Central Government			Extrabudgetary Accounts			Central Government			General Government		
82	**Net acquisition of financial assets**	**−180.8**	**−146.3**	**−100.2**	....	....	....	**−180.8**	**−146.3**	**−100.2**	**−180.8**	**−146.3**	**−100.2**
821	Domestic	−180.8	−150.1	−104.0	....	....	....	−180.8	−150.1	−104.0	−180.8	−150.1	−104.0
8211	General government	−163.7	−196.6	−110.5	....	....	....	−163.7	−196.6	−110.5	−163.7	−196.6	−110.5
8212	Central bank	−17.1	46.5	6.5	....	....	....	−17.1	46.5	6.5	−17.1	46.5	6.5
8213	Other depository corporations	—	—	—	....	....	....	—	—	—	—	—	—
8214	Financial corporations n.e.c.	—	—	—	....	....	....	—	—	—	—	—	—
8215	Nonfinancial corporations	—	—	—	....	....	....	—	—	—	—	—	—
8216	Households & NPIs serving households	—	—	—	....	....	....	—	—	—	—	—	—
822	Foreign	—	3.8	3.8	....	....	....	—	3.8	3.8	—	3.8	3.8
8221	General government	....	....	....	....	....	....	....	....	....	....	....	....
8227	International organizations	....	....	....	....	....	....	....	....	....	....	....	....
8228	Financial corporations other than international organizations	....	....	....	....	....	....	....	....	....	....	....	....
8229	Other nonresidents	....	....	....	....	....	....	....	....	....	....	....	....
823	Monetary gold and SDRs	—	—	—	....	....	....	—	—	—	....	....	....
83	**Net incurrence of liabilities**	**283.2**	**216.6**	**435.4**	....	....	....	**283.2**	**216.6**	**435.4**	**283.2**	**216.6**	**435.4**
831	Domestic	−136.0	−188.8	27.8	....	....	....	−136.0	−188.8	27.8	−136.0	−188.8	27.8
8311	General government	....	....	....	....	....	....	....	....	....	....	....	....
8312	Central bank	....	....	....	....	....	....	....	....	....	....	....	....
8313	Other depository corporations	....	....	....	....	....	....	....	....	....	....	....	....
8314	Financial corporations n.e.c.	....	....	....	....	....	....	....	....	....	....	....	....
8315	Nonfinancial corporations	....	....	....	....	....	....	....	....	....	....	....	....
8316	Households & NPIs serving households	....	....	....	....	....	....	....	....	....	....	....	....
832	Foreign	419.2	405.4	407.6	....	....	....	419.2	405.4	407.6	419.2	405.4	407.6
8321	General government	23.6	62.0	130.4	....	....	....	23.6	62.0	130.4	23.6	62.0	130.4
8327	International organizations	145.8	141.6	269.5	....	....	....	145.8	141.6	269.5	145.8	141.6	269.5
8328	Financial corporations other than international organizations	—	—	—	....	....	....	—	—	—	—	—	—
8329	Other nonresidents	249.8	201.8	7.7	....	....	....	249.8	201.8	7.7	249.8	201.8	7.7

Malta 181

In Millions of Liri / Year Ending December 31 / Cash Reporter

	Budgetary Central Government			Extrabudgetary Accounts			Central Government			General Government		
	1999	2000	2001	1999	2000	2001	1999	2000	2001	1999	2000	2001
Statement of government operations												
Statement of other economic flows												
Balance sheet												
6 **Net worth**......	....	....	....	....	....	....	....	....	....	....	....	....
61 Nonfinancial assets........	....	....	....	....	....	....	....	....	....	....	....	....
62 Financial assets........	....	....	....	....	....	....	....	....	....	....	....	....
63 Liabilities........	839.85	924.97	1,012.69	....	....	....	839.85	924.97	1,012.69	839.85	924.97	1,012.69
Statement of sources and uses of cash												
1 Cash receipts from operating activities.......	491.55	532.76	575.93	....	....	....	491.55	532.76	575.93	491.55	532.76	575.93
11 Taxes........	329.99	371.84	409.22	....	....	....	329.99	371.84	409.22	329.99	371.84	409.22
12 Social contributions........	82.76	94.97	104.11	....	....	....	82.76	94.97	104.11	82.76	94.97	104.11
13 Grants........	9.68	9.55	1.39	....	....	....	9.68	9.55	1.39	9.68	9.55	1.39
14 Other receipts........	69.11	56.39	61.20	....	....	....	69.11	56.39	61.20	69.11	56.39	61.20
2 Cash payments for operating activities........	515.97	560.45	619.52	....	....	....	515.97	560.45	619.52	515.97	560.45	619.52
21 Compensation of employees........	166.88	177.08	202.36	....	....	....	166.88	177.08	202.36	166.88	177.08	202.36
22 Purchases of goods and services........	47.16	57.70	58.19	....	....	....	47.16	57.70	58.19	47.16	57.70	58.19
24 Interest........	52.07	56.44	60.68	....	....	....	52.07	56.44	60.68	52.07	56.44	60.68
25 Subsidies........	21.11	29.65	45.45	....	....	....	21.11	29.65	45.45	21.11	29.65	45.45
26 Grants........	6.12	11.96	12.45	....	....	....	6.12	11.96	12.45	6.12	11.96	12.45
27 Social benefits........	209.63	219.35	235.89	....	....	....	209.63	219.35	235.89	209.63	219.35	235.89
28 Other payments........	12.99	8.26	4.49	....	....	....	12.99	8.26	4.49	12.99	8.26	4.49
CIO **Net cash inflow from oper. activities....**	−24.42	−27.69	−43.59	....	....	....	−24.42	−27.69	−43.59	−24.42	−27.69	−43.59
31.1 Purchases of nonfinancial assets........	65.84	63.93	57.21	....	....	....	65.84	63.93	57.21	65.84	63.93	57.21
31.2 Sales of nonfinancial assets........	1.02	2.21	2.07	....	....	....	1.02	2.21	2.07	1.02	2.21	2.07
31 Net cash outflow from investments in nonfinancial assets	64.82	61.71	55.14	....	....	....	64.82	61.71	55.14	64.82	61.71	55.14
CSD **Cash surplus/deficit........**	−89.24	−89.40	−98.73	....	....	....	−89.24	−89.40	−98.73	−89.24	−89.40	−98.73
32x Net acquisition of fin assets, excl. cash........	—	—	—	....	....	....	—	—	—	—	—	—
321x Domestic........	—	—	—	....	....	....	—	—	—	—	—	—
322x Foreign........	—	—	—	....	....	....	—	—	—	—	—	—
323 Monetary gold and SDRs........	—	—	—	....	....	....	—	—	—	—	—	—
33 Net incurrence of liabilities........	77.76	87.29	87.22	....	....	....	77.76	87.29	87.22	77.76	87.29	87.22
331 Domestic........	79.92	92.39	86.09	....	....	....	79.92	92.39	86.09	79.92	92.39	86.09
332 Foreign........	−2.16	−5.10	1.13	....	....	....	−2.16	−5.10	1.13	−2.16	−5.10	1.13
NFB Net cash inflow from fin. activities........	77.76	87.29	87.22	....	....	....	77.76	87.29	87.22	77.76	87.29	87.22
NCB **Net change in the stock of cash........**	−11.48	−2.11	−11.51	....	....	....	−11.48	−2.11	−11.51	−11.48	−2.11	−11.51
Table 1 Revenue												
1 **Revenue........**	491.55	532.76	575.93	....	....	....	491.55	532.76	575.93	491.55	532.76	575.93
11 **Taxes........**	329.99	371.84	409.22	....	....	....	329.99	371.84	409.22	329.99	371.84	409.22
111 Taxes on income, profits, & capital gains......	125.74	146.66	163.25	....	....	....	125.74	146.66	163.25	125.74	146.66	163.25
1111 Individuals........	62.70	72.96	91.89	....	....	....	62.70	72.96	91.89	62.70	72.96	91.89
1112 Corporations and other enterprises........	55.93	64.67	61.24	....	....	....	55.93	64.67	61.24	55.93	64.67	61.24
112 Taxes on payroll and workforce........	—	—	—	....	....	....						
113 Taxes on property........	12.62	13.40	15.61	....	....	....	12.62	13.40	15.61	12.62	13.40	15.61
114 Taxes on goods and services........	169.93	190.84	208.91	....	....	....	169.93	190.84	208.91	169.93	190.84	208.91
1141 General taxes on goods and services........	82.72	102.58	114.67	....	....	....	82.72	102.58	114.67	82.72	102.58	114.67
1142 Excises........	43.97	42.76	48.66	....	....	....	43.97	42.76	48.66	43.97	42.76	48.66
115 Taxes on int'l. trade and transactions........	21.31	20.82	21.46	....	....	....	21.31	20.82	21.46	21.31	20.82	21.46
116 Other taxes........	.39	.13	—	....	....	....	.39	.13	—	.39	.13	—
12 **Social contributions........**	82.76	94.97	104.11	....	....	....	82.76	94.97	104.11	82.76	94.97	104.11
121 Social security contributions........	82.76	94.97	104.11	....	....	....	82.76	94.97	104.11	82.76	94.97	104.11
122 Other social contributions........	—	—	—	....	....	....						
13 **Grants........**	9.68	9.55	1.39	....	....	....	9.68	9.55	1.39	9.68	9.55	1.39
131 From foreign governments........	9.68	9.55	1.39	....	....	....	9.68	9.55	1.39	9.68	9.55	1.39
132 From international organizations........	—	—	—	....	....	....	—	—	—	—	—	—
133 From other general government units........				....	....	....	—	—	—	—	—	—
14 **Other revenue........**	69.11	56.39	61.20	....	....	....	69.11	56.39	61.20	69.11	56.39	61.20
Table 2 Expense by economic type												
2 **Expense........**	515.97	560.45	619.52	....	....	....	515.97	560.45	619.52	515.97	560.45	619.52
21 **Compensation of employees........**	166.88	177.08	202.36	....	....	....	166.88	177.08	202.36	166.88	177.08	202.36
211 Wages and salaries........	166.88	177.08	202.36	....	....	....	166.88	177.08	202.36	166.88	177.08	202.36
212 Social contributions........				....	....	....	—	—	—	—	—	—
22 **Use of goods and services........**	47.16	57.70	58.19	....	....	....	47.16	57.70	58.19	47.16	57.70	58.19
23 **Consumption of fixed capital........**	....	....	....	....	....	....	....	....	....	....	....	....
24 **Interest........**	52.07	56.44	60.68	....	....	....	52.07	56.44	60.68	52.07	56.44	60.68
25 **Subsidies........**	21.11	29.65	45.45	....	....	....	21.11	29.65	45.45	21.11	29.65	45.45

In Millions of Liri / Year Ending December 31 / Cash Reporter

		Budgetary Central Government			Extrabudgetary Accounts			Central Government			General Government		
		1999	2000	2001	1999	2000	2001	1999	2000	2001	1999	2000	2001
26	**Grants**............................	**6.12**	**11.96**	**12.45**	....	....	....	**6.12**	**11.96**	**12.45**	**6.12**	**11.96**	**12.45**
261	To foreign govenments......................	.35	.51	1.20	....	....	....	.35	.51	1.20	.35	.51	1.20
262	To international organizations...................	—	—	—	....	....	....	—	—	—	—	—	—
263	To other general government units............	5.77	11.45	11.26	....	....	....	5.77	11.45	11.26	5.77	11.45	11.26
2631	Current...........................	5.77	11.45	11.26	....	....	....	5.77	11.45	11.26	5.77	11.45	11.26
2632	Capital...........................	—	—	—	....	....	....	—	—	—	—	—	—
27	**Social benefits**.......................	**209.63**	**219.35**	**235.89**	....	....	....	**209.63**	**219.35**	**235.89**	**209.63**	**219.35**	**235.89**
28	**Other expense**........................	**12.99**	**8.26**	**4.49**	....	....	....	**12.99**	**8.26**	**4.49**	**12.99**	**8.26**	**4.49**
281	Property expense other than interest............	—	—	—	....	....	....	—	—	—	—	—	—
282	Miscellaneous other expense...................	12.99	8.26	4.49	....	....	....	12.99	8.26	4.49	12.99	8.26	4.49
2821	Current...........................	—	—	—	....	....	....	—	—	—	—	—	—
2822	Capital...........................	12.99	8.26	4.49	....	....	....	12.99	8.26	4.49	12.99	8.26	4.49

Table 3 Transactions in assets and liabilities

		Budgetary Central Government			Extrabudgetary Accounts			Central Government			General Government		
		1999	2000	2001	1999	2000	2001	1999	2000	2001	1999	2000	2001
3	**Change in net worth from transactns....**	....	....	....	....	....	....	....	....	....	....	....	....
31	**Net acquisition of nonfinancial assets...**	**64.82**	**61.71**	**55.14**	....	....	....	**64.82**	**61.71**	**55.14**	**64.82**	**61.71**	**55.14**
311	Fixed assets.................................	65.84	63.93	57.04	....	....	....	65.84	63.93	57.04	65.84	63.93	57.04
3111	Buildings and structures...................	....	....	....	....	....	....	....	....	....	....	....	....
3112	Machinery and equipment.................	....	....	....	....	....	....	....	....	....	....	....	....
3113	Other fixed assets......................	....	....	....	....	....	....	....	....	....	....	....	....
312	Inventories................................	—	—	—	....	....	....	—	—	—	—	—	—
313	Valuables.................................	—	—	—	....	....	....	—	—	—	—	—	—
314	Nonproduced assets......................	−1.02	−2.21	−1.90	....	....	....	−1.02	−2.21	−1.90	−1.02	−2.21	−1.90
3141	Land..................................	....	....	....	....	....	....	....	....	....	....	....	....
3142	Subsoil assets...........................	....	....	....	....	....	....	....	....	....	....	....	....
3143	Other naturally occurring assets...........	....	....	....	....	....	....	....	....	....	....	....	....
3144	Intangible nonproduced assets.................	....	....	....	....	....	....	....	....	....	....	....	....
32	**Net acquisition of financial assets........**	**−11.48**	**−2.11**	**−11.51**	....	....	....	**−11.48**	**−2.11**	**−11.51**	**−11.48**	**−2.11**	**−11.51**
321	Domestic..................................	−13.76	−2.55	−9.58	....	....	....	−13.76	−2.55	−9.58	−13.76	−2.55	−9.58
3212	Currency and deposits...................	−13.76	−2.55	−9.58	....	....	....	−13.76	−2.55	−9.58	−13.76	−2.55	−9.58
3213	Securities other than shares...........	—	—	—	....	....	....	—	—	—	—	—	—
3214	Loans.................................	—	—	—	....	....	....	—	—	—	—	—	—
3215	Shares and other equity.................	—	—	—	....	....	....	—	—	—	—	—	—
3216	Insurance technical reserves............	—	—	—	....	....	....	—	—	—	—	—	—
3217	Financial derivatives...................	—	—	—	....	....	....	—	—	—	—	—	—
3218	Other accounts receivable...............	....	....	....	....	....	....	....	....	....	....	....	....
322	Foreign...................................	2.28	.45	−1.93	....	....	....	2.28	.45	−1.93	2.28	.45	−1.93
3222	Currency and deposits...................	2.28	.45	−1.93	....	....	....	2.28	.45	−1.93	2.28	.45	−1.93
3223	Securities other than shares...........	—	—	—	....	....	....	—	—	—	—	—	—
3224	Loans.................................	—	—	—	....	....	....	—	—	—	—	—	—
3225	Shares and other equity.................	—	—	—	....	....	....	—	—	—	—	—	—
3226	Insurance technical reserves............	—	—	—	....	....	....	—	—	—	—	—	—
3227	Financial derivatives...................	—	—	—	....	....	....	—	—	—	—	—	—
3228	Other accounts receivable...............	....	....	....	....	....	....	....	....	....	....	....	....
323	Monetary gold and SDRs...................	—	—	—	....	....	....	—	—	—	—	—	—
33	**Net incurrence of liabilities...................**	**77.76**	**87.29**	**87.22**	....	....	....	**77.76**	**87.29**	**87.22**	**77.76**	**87.29**	**87.22**
331	Domestic..................................	79.92	92.39	86.09	....	....	....	79.92	92.39	86.09	79.92	92.39	86.09
3312	Currency and deposits...................	−.50	−.50	−.50	....	....	....	−.50	−.50	−.50	−.50	−.50	−.50
3313	Securities other than shares...........	80.42	92.89	86.60	....	....	....	80.42	92.89	86.60	80.42	92.89	86.60
3314	Loans.................................	—	—	—	....	....	....	—	—	—	—	—	—
3316	Insurance technical reserves............	—	—	—	....	....	....	—	—	—	—	—	—
3317	Financial derivatives...................	—	—	—	....	....	....	—	—	—	—	—	—
3318	Other accounts payable...................	....	....	....	....	....	....	....	....	....	....	....	....
332	Foreign...................................	−2.16	−5.10	1.13	....	....	....	−2.16	−5.10	1.13	−2.16	−5.10	1.13
3322	Currency and deposits...................	—	—	—	....	....	....	—	—	—	—	—	—
3323	Securities other than shares...........	—	—	—	....	....	....	—	—	—	—	—	—
3324	Loans.................................	−2.16	−5.10	1.13	....	....	....	−2.16	−5.10	1.13	−2.16	−5.10	1.13
3326	Insurance technical reserves............	—	—	—	....	....	....	—	—	—	—	—	—
3327	Financial derivatives...................	—	—	—	....	....	....	—	—	—	—	—	—
3328	Other accounts payable...................	....	....	....	....	....	....	....	....	....	....	....	....

	Budgetary Central Government			Extrabudgetary Accounts			Central Government			General Government		
	1999	2000	2001	1999	2000	2001	1999	2000	2001	1999	2000	2001
Table 4 Holding gains in assets and liabilities												
Table 5 Other changes in the volume of assets and liabilities												
Table 6 Balance sheet												
6 Net worth....................	....	....	....	....	....	....	....	....	....	....	....	....
61 Nonfinancial assets................	....	....	....	....	....	....	....	....	....	....	....	....
611 Fixed assets..................	....	....	....	....	....	....	....	....	....	....	....	....
6111 Buildings and structures........	....	....	....	....	....	....	....	....	....	....	....	....
6112 Machinery and equipment.......	....	....	....	....	....	....	....	....	....	....	....	....
6113 Other fixed assets............	....	....	....	....	....	....	....	....	....	....	....	....
612 Inventories.................	....	....	....	....	....	....	....	....	....	....	....	....
613 Valuables..................	....	....	....	....	....	....	....	....	....	....	....	....
614 Nonproduced assets............	....	....	....	....	....	....	....	....	....	....	....	....
6141 Land...................	....	....	....	....	....	....	....	....	....	....	....	....
6142 Subsoil assets.............	....	....	....	....	....	....	....	....	....	....	....	....
6143 Other naturally occurring assets...	....	....	....	....	....	....	....	....	....	....	....	....
6144 Intangible nonproduced assets....	....	....	....	....	....	....	....	....	....	....	....	....
62 Financial assets.................	....	....	....	....	....	....	....	....	....	....	....	....
621 Domestic..................	....	....	....	....	....	....	....	....	....	....	....	....
6212 Currency and deposits........	....	....	....	....	....	....	....	....	....	....	....	....
6213 Securities other than shares....	....	....	....	....	....	....	....	....	....	....	....	....
6214 Loans..................	....	....	....	....	....	....	....	....	....	....	....	....
6215 Shares and other equity........	....	....	....	....	....	....	....	....	....	....	....	....
6216 Insurance technical reserves.....	....	....	....	....	....	....	....	....	....	....	....	....
6217 Financial derivatives.........	....	....	....	....	....	....	....	....	....	....	....	....
6218 Other accounts receivable......	....	....	....	....	....	....	....	....	....	....	....	....
622 Foreign...................	....	....	....	....	....	....	....	....	....	....	....	....
6222 Currency and deposits........	....	....	....	....	....	....	....	....	....	....	....	....
6223 Securities other than shares....	....	....	....	....	....	....	....	....	....	....	....	....
6224 Loans..................	....	....	....	....	....	....	....	....	....	....	....	....
6225 Shares and other equity........	....	....	....	....	....	....	....	....	....	....	....	....
6226 Insurance technical reserves.....	....	....	....	....	....	....	....	....	....	....	....	....
6227 Financial derivatives.........	....	....	....	....	....	....	....	....	....	....	....	....
6228 Other accounts receivable......	....	....	....	....	....	....	....	....	....	....	....	....
623 Monetary gold and SDRs........	....	....	....	....	....	....	....	....	....	....	....	....
63 **Liabilities**.................	**839.85**	**924.97**	**1,012.69**	....	....	....	**839.85**	**924.97**	**1,012.69**	**839.85**	**924.97**	**1,012.69**
631 Domestic..................	795.50	885.72	972.31	....	....	....	795.50	885.72	972.31	795.50	885.72	972.31
6312 Currency and deposits........	....	....	....	....	....	....	....	....	....	....	....	....
6313 Securities other than shares....	....	....	....	....	....	....	....	....	....	....	....	....
6314 Loans..................	....	....	....	....	....	....	....	....	....	....	....	....
6316 Insurance technical reserves.....	....	....	....	....	....	....	....	....	....	....	....	....
6317 Financial derivatives.........	....	....	....	....	....	....	....	....	....	....	....	....
6318 Other accounts payable........	....	....	....	....	....	....	....	....	....	....	....	....
632 Foreign...................	44.35	39.25	40.38	....	....	....	44.35	39.25	40.38	44.35	39.25	40.38
6322 Currency and deposits........	....	....	....	....	....	....	....	....	....	....	....	....
6323 Securities other than shares....	....	....	....	....	....	....	....	....	....	....	....	....
6324 Loans..................	....	....	....	....	....	....	....	....	....	....	....	....
6326 Insurance technical reserves.....	....	....	....	....	....	....	....	....	....	....	....	....
6327 Financial derivatives.........	....	....	....	....	....	....	....	....	....	....	....	....
6328 Other accounts payable........	....	....	....	....	....	....	....	....	....	....	....	....
Memorandum items:												
6M2 Net financial worth...........	....	....	....	....	....	....	....	....	....	....	....	....
6M3 Debt at market value..........	....	....	....	....	....	....	....	....	....	....	....	....
6M4 Debt at nominal value.........	....	....	....	....	....	....	....	....	....	....	....	....
6M5 Arrears..................	....	....	....	....	....	....	....	....	....	....	....	....
6M6 Obligations for social security benefits...	....	....	....	....	....	....	....	....	....	....	....	....
6M7 Contingent liabilities..........	....	....	....	....	....	....	....	....	....	....	....	....
6M8 Uncapitalized military weapons, systems....	....	....	....	....	....	....	....	....	....	....	....	....
Table 7 Outlays by functions of govt.												
7 **Total outlays**.................	**581.80**	**624.38**	**676.72**	....	....	....	**581.80**	**624.38**	**676.72**	**581.80**	**624.38**	**676.72**
701 **General public services**..............	**81.70**	**97.87**	**109.80**	....	....	....	**81.70**	**97.87**	**109.80**	**81.70**	**97.87**	**109.80**
7017 Public debt transactions........	52.07	56.44	60.68	....	....	....	52.07	56.44	60.68	52.07	56.44	60.68
7018 General transfers between levels of govt....	29.63	41.43	49.12	....	....	....	29.63	41.43	49.12	29.63	41.43	49.12
702 **Defense**..................	**10.32**	**10.23**	**11.07**	....	....	....	**10.32**	**10.23**	**11.07**	**10.32**	**10.23**	**11.07**
703 **Public order and safety**................	**21.18**	**24.14**	**26.83**	....	....	....	**21.18**	**24.14**	**26.83**	**21.18**	**24.14**	**26.83**

Malta 181

In Millions of Liri / Year Ending December 31 / Cash Reporter

		Budgetary Central Government			Extrabudgetary Accounts			Central Government			General Government		
		1999	2000	2001	1999	2000	2001	1999	2000	2001	1999	2000	2001
704	**Economic affairs**	95.56	84.34	91.44	....	....	....	95.56	84.34	91.44	95.56	84.34	91.44
7042	Agriculture, forestry, fishing, and hunting	....	....	....	....	....	....	....	....	....	....	....	....
7043	Fuel and energy	....	....	....	....	....	....	....	....	....	....	....	....
7044	Mining, manufacturing, and construction	....	....	....	....	....	....	....	....	....	....	....	....
7045	Transport	....	....	....	....	....	....	....	....	....	....	....	....
7046	Communication	....	....	....	....	....	....	....	....	....	....	....	....
705	**Environmental protection**	7.52	7.97	8.58	....	....	....	7.52	7.97	8.58	7.52	7.97	8.58
706	**Housing and community amenities**	17.87	16.03	16.07	....	....	....	17.87	16.03	16.07	17.87	16.03	16.07
707	**Health**	59.45	75.79	81.80	....	....	....	59.45	75.79	81.80	59.45	75.79	81.80
7072	Outpatient services	....	....	....	....	....	....	....	....	....	....	....	....
7073	Hospital services	....	....	....	....	....	....	....	....	....	....	....	....
7074	Public health services	....	....	....	....	....	....	....	....	....	....	....	....
708	**Recreation, culture, and religion**	9.56	10.74	10.02	....	....	....	9.56	10.74	10.02	9.56	10.74	10.02
709	**Education**	68.94	76.52	86.47	....	....	....	68.94	76.52	86.47	68.94	76.52	86.47
7091	Pre-primary and primary education	....	....	....	....	....	....	....	....	....	....	....	....
7092	Secondary education	....	....	....	....	....	....	....	....	....	....	....	....
7094	Tertiary education	....	....	....	....	....	....	....	....	....	....	....	....
710	**Social protection**	209.71	220.74	234.65	....	....	....	209.71	220.74	234.65	209.71	220.74	234.65
7	Statistical discrepancy: Total outlays	—	—	—	....	....	....	—	—	—	—	—	—

Table 8   Transactions in financial assets and liabilities by sector

82	**Net acquisition of financial assets**	−11.48	−2.11	−11.51	....	....	....	−11.48	−2.11	−11.51	−11.48	−2.11	−11.51
821	Domestic	−13.76	−2.55	−9.58	....	....	....	−13.76	−2.55	−9.58	−13.76	−2.55	−9.58
8211	General government	—	—	—	....	....	....	—	—	—	—	—	—
8212	Central bank	....	....	....	....	....	....	....	....	....	....	....	....
8213	Other depository corporations	....	....	....	....	....	....	....	....	....	....	....	....
8214	Financial corporations n.e.c.	....	....	....	....	....	....	....	....	....	....	....	....
8215	Nonfinancial corporations	—	—	—	....	....	....	....	....	....	....	....	....
8216	Households & NPIs serving households	....	....	....	....	....	....	—	—	—	—	—	—
822	Foreign	2.28	.45	−1.93	....	....	....	2.28	.45	−1.93	2.28	.45	−1.93
8221	General government	....	....	....	....	....	....	....	....	....	....	....	....
8227	International organizations	....	....	....	....	....	....	....	....	....	....	....	....
8228	Financial corporations other than international organizations	....	....	....	....	....	....	....	....	....	....	....	....
8229	Other nonresidents	....	....	....	....	....	....	....	....	....	....	....	....
823	Monetary gold and SDRs	—	—	—	....	....	....	—	—	—	—	—	—
83	**Net incurrence of liabilities**	77.76	87.29	87.22	....	....	....	77.76	87.29	87.22	77.76	87.29	87.22
831	Domestic	79.92	92.39	86.09	....	....	....	79.92	92.39	86.09	79.92	92.39	86.09
8311	General government	....	....	....	....	....	....	....	....	....	....	....	....
8312	Central bank	....	....	....	....	....	....	....	....	....	....	....	....
8313	Other depository corporations	....	....	....	....	....	....	....	....	....	....	....	....
8314	Financial corporations n.e.c.	....	....	....	....	....	....	....	....	....	....	....	....
8315	Nonfinancial corporations	....	....	....	....	....	....	....	....	....	....	....	....
8316	Households & NPIs serving households	....	....	....	....	....	....	....	....	....	....	....	....
832	Foreign	−2.16	−5.10	1.13	....	....	....	−2.16	−5.10	1.13	−2.16	−5.10	1.13
8321	General government	.99	−5.14	−2.93	....	....	....	.99	−5.14	−2.93	.99	−5.14	−2.93
8327	International organizations	−2.91	1.31	5.26	....	....	....	−2.91	1.31	5.26	−2.91	1.31	5.26
8328	Financial corporations other than international organizations	—	—	—	....	....	....	—	—	—	—	—	—
8329	Other nonresidents	−.24	−1.27	−1.21	....	....	....	−.24	−1.27	−1.21	−.24	−1.27	−1.21

2005, International Monetary Fund: *Government Finance Statistics Yearbook*   299

In Millions of Rupees / Year Ending June 30 / Cash Reporter

	Central Government			State Government			Local Government			General Government		
	2002	2003	2004	2002	2003	2004	2002	2003	2004	2002	2003	2004
Statement of government operations												
Statement of other economic flows												
Balance sheet												
6 *Net worth*.........	....	....	....	....	....	....	....	....	....	....	....	....
61 Nonfinancial assets.........	....	....	....	....	....	....	....	....	....	....	....	....
62 Financial assets.........	....	....	....	....	....	....	....	....	....	....	....	....
63 Liabilities.........	†57,757	72,605	70,669	....	....	....	....	....	....	....	....	....
Statement of sources and uses of cash												
1 Cash receipts from operating activities..........	†27,772	32,919	36,621		794	1,089	1,499	1,589	1,827	†28,357	33,545	37,265
11 Taxes.........	†21,768	26,121	29,380	....	—	1	416	454	464	†22,183	26,576	29,844
12 Social contributions.........	†1,228	1,256	1,394		—	—	—	—	—	†1,228	1,256	1,394
13 Grants.........	†317	363	618		787	1,073	914	969	1,200	†317	363	618
14 Other receipts.........	†4,460	5,180	5,230	....	6	15	169	165	164	†4,629	5,351	5,408
2 Cash payments for operating activities.........	†28,578	31,727	35,961		461	658	1,258	1,315	1,527	†28,922	31,746	35,874
21 Compensation of employees.........	†11,084	11,901	13,887		304	445	673	755	856	†11,757	12,959	15,188
22 Purchases of goods and services.........	†3,741	4,048	4,353		67	102	417	424	512	†4,158	4,538	4,966
24 Interest.........	†3,533	4,440	5,078	....	—	—	9	9	8	†3,542	4,448	5,086
25 Subsidies.........	†1,313	1,311	955	....	—	2	—	—	—	†1,313	1,311	957
26 Grants.........	†1,025	1,914	2,410	....	—	—	—	—	—	†111	158	138
27 Social benefits.........	†7,302	7,176	8,087		59	81	159	114	143	†7,462	7,349	8,310
28 Other payments.........	†580	936	1,192		32	28	—	14	9	†580	983	1,229
CIO *Net cash inflow from oper. activities*.....	*†–806*	*1,193*	*660*	....	*333*	*431*	*241*	*274*	*300*	*†–565*	*1,799*	*1,391*
31.1 Purchases of nonfinancial assets.........	†4,431	6,245	5,941		252	397	200	261	359	†4,631	6,758	6,697
31.2 Sales of nonfinancial assets.........	†130	—	72	....	—	—	—	—	—	†130	—	72
31 Net cash outflow from investments in nonfinancial assets.........	†4,302	6,245	5,870	....	252	397	200	261	359	†4,501	6,758	6,626
CSD *Cash surplus/deficit*.........	*†–5,108*	*–5,053*	*–5,209*	....	*80*	*34*	*42*	*13*	*–59*	*†–5,066*	*–4,959*	*–5,234*
32x Net acquisition of fin assets, excl. cash.........	†500	959	439	....	—	—	—	—	—	†500	959	439
321x Domestic.........	†500	957	439	....	—	—	—	—	—	†500	957	439
322x Foreign.........	†—	2	—	....	—	—	—	—	—	†—	2	—
323 Monetary gold and SDRs.........	†—			....	—	—	—	—	—	†—		
33 Net incurrence of liabilities.........	†10,449	12,909	–3,172	....	—	–34	–42	–13	59	†10,407	12,896	–3,147
331 Domestic.........	†9,419	12,822	–2,704	....	—	–34	–42	–13	59	†9,377	12,809	–2,679
332 Foreign.........	†1,030	87	–468	....	—	—	—	—	—	†1,030	87	–468
NFB Net cash inflow from fin. activities.........	†9,949	11,950	–3,610	....	—	–34	–42	–13	59	†9,907	11,937	–3,585
NCB *Net change in the stock of cash*.........	*†4,841*	*6,897*	*–8,820*	....	*80*	....	....	....	....	....	....	....
Table 1 Revenue												
1 **Revenue**.........	**†27,772**	**32,919**	**36,621**	....	**794**	**1,089**	**1,499**	**1,589**	**1,827**	**†28,357**	**33,545**	**37,265**
11 **Taxes**.........	**†21,768**	**26,121**	**29,380**	....	**—**	**1**	**416**	**454**	**464**	**†22,183**	**26,576**	**29,844**
111 Taxes on income, profits, & capital gains......	†3,494	4,014	4,669	....	—	—	—	—	—	†3,494	4,014	4,669
1111 Individuals.........	†1,619	1,859	2,265	....	—	—	—	—	—	†1,619	1,859	2,265
1112 Corporations and other enterprises.........	†1,875	2,155	2,405	....	—	—	—	—	—	†1,875	2,155	2,405
112 Taxes on payroll and workforce.........	†163	172	183	....	—	—	—	—	—	†163	172	183
113 Taxes on property.........	†1,299	1,375	1,469	....	—	—	217	230	244	†1,515	1,605	1,713
114 Taxes on goods and services.........	†10,906	14,027	15,660	....	—	1	199	224	219	†11,105	14,252	15,880
1141 General taxes on goods and services.........	†7,053	9,812	11,191	....	—	—	—	—	—	†7,053	9,812	11,191
1142 Excises.........	†2,299	2,332	2,408	....	—	—	—	—	—	†2,299	2,332	2,408
115 Taxes on int'l. trade and transactions.........	†5,893	6,523	7,385	....	—	—	—	—	—	†5,893	6,523	7,385
116 Other taxes.........	†13	12	13	....	—	—	—	—	—	†13	12	13
12 **Social contributions**.........	**†1,228**	**1,256**	**1,394**	....	**—**	**—**	**—**	**—**	**—**	**†1,228**	**1,256**	**1,394**
121 Social security contributions.........	†1,097	1,121	1,232	....	—	—	—	—	—	†1,097	1,121	1,232
122 Other social contributions.........	†131	135	162	....	—	—	—	—	—	†131	135	162
13 **Grants**.........	**†317**	**363**	**618**	....	**787**	**1,073**	**914**	**969**	**1,200**	**†317**	**363**	**618**
131 From foreign governments.........	†8	9	157	....	—	—	—	—	—	†8	9	157
132 From international organizations.........	†309	354	461	....	—	—	—	—	—	†309	354	461
133 From other general government units.........	†—	—	—	....	787	1,073	914	969	1,200	†—	—	—
14 **Other revenue**.........	**†4,460**	**5,180**	**5,230**	....	**6**	**15**	**169**	**165**	**164**	**†4,629**	**5,351**	**5,408**
Table 2 Expense by economic type												
2 **Expense**.........	**†28,578**	**31,727**	**35,961**	....	**461**	**658**	**1,258**	**1,315**	**1,527**	**†28,922**	**31,746**	**35,874**
21 **Compensation of employees**.........	**†11,084**	**11,901**	**13,887**	....	**304**	**445**	**673**	**755**	**856**	**†11,757**	**12,959**	**15,188**
211 Wages and salaries.........	†10,781	11,706	13,667	....	304	445	....	755	856	....	12,764	14,968
212 Social contributions.........	†303	195	220	....	—	—	....	—	—	....	195	220
22 **Use of goods and services**.........	**†3,741**	**4,048**	**4,353**	....	**67**	**102**	**417**	**424**	**512**	**†4,158**	**4,538**	**4,966**
23 **Consumption of fixed capital**.........	....	....	....	....	....	....	....	....	....	....	....	....
24 **Interest**.........	**†3,533**	**4,440**	**5,078**	....	**—**	**—**	**9**	**9**	**8**	**†3,542**	**4,448**	**5,086**
25 **Subsidies**.........	**†1,313**	**1,311**	**955**	....	**—**	**2**	**—**	**—**	**—**	**†1,313**	**1,311**	**957**

In Millions of Rupees / Year Ending June 30 / Cash Reporter

	Central Government			State Government			Local Government			General Government		
	2002	**2003**	**2004**	**2002**	**2003**	**2004**	**2002**	**2003**	**2004**	**2002**	**2003**	**2004**
26 **Grants**....................................	†1,025	1,914	2,410	....	—	—	—	—	—	†111	158	138
261 To foreign govenments........................	†111	158	138	....	—	—	—	—	—	†111	158	138
262 To international organizations................	†—	—	—	....	—	—	—	—	—	†—	—	—
263 To other general government units...........	†914	1,757	2,273	....	—	—	—	—	—	†—	—	—
2631 Current.....................................	†851	1,424	1,763	....	—	—	—	—	—	†—	—	—
2632 Capital.....................................	†63	333	510	....	—	—	—	—	—	†—	—	—
27 **Social benefits**..........................	†7,302	7,176	8,087	....	59	81	159	114	143	†7,462	7,349	8,310
28 **Other expense**...........................	†580	936	1,192	....	32	28	—	14	9	†580	983	1,229
281 Property expense other than interest...........	†—	—	—	....	—	—	—	—	—	†—	—	—
282 Miscellaneous other expense...................	†580	936	1,192	....	32	28	—	14	9	†580	983	1,229
2821 Current.....................................	†—	424	520	....	17	28	—	14	9	†—	455	557
2822 Capital.....................................	†580	513	672	....	15	—	—	—	—	†580	528	672

Table 3 Transactions in assets and liabilities

	Central Government			State Government			Local Government			General Government		
	2002	**2003**	**2004**	**2002**	**2003**	**2004**	**2002**	**2003**	**2004**	**2002**	**2003**	**2004**
3 **Change in net worth from transactns....**	....	....	....	....	....	....	....	....	....	....	....	....
31 **Net acquisition of nonfinancial assets...**	†4,302	6,245	5,870	....	252	397	200	261	359	†4,501	6,758	6,626
311 Fixed assets.................................	†4,106	6,081	5,772	....	252	397	199	261	359	†4,305	6,594	6,528
3111 Buildings and structures...................	....	....	....	....	....	....	....	....	....	....	....	....
3112 Machinery and equipment..................	....	....	....	....	....	....	....	....	....	....	....	....
3113 Other fixed assets.........................	....	....	....	....	....	....	....	....	....	....	....	....
312 Inventories..................................	†—	—	—	....	—	—	—	—	—	†—	—	—
313 Valuables...................................	†—	—	—	....	—	—	—	—	—	†—	—	—
314 Nonproduced assets.........................	†196	164	97	....	—	—	1	—	—	†197	164	97
3141 Land.......................................	†196	164	97	....	—	—	1	—	—	†197	164	97
3142 Subsoil assets.............................	†—	—	—	....	—	—	—	—	—	†—	—	—
3143 Other naturally occurring assets............	†—	—	—	....	—	—	—	—	—	†—	—	—
3144 Intangible nonproduced assets..............	†—	—	—	....	—	—	—	—	—	†—	—	—
32 **Net acquisition of financial assets.........**	†5,341	7,856	−8,381	....	80	—	—	—	—	†5,341	7,937	−8,381
321 Domestic....................................	†5,189	7,854	−8,381	....	80	—	—	—	—	†5,189	7,935	−8,381
3212 Currency and deposits.....................	†4,689	6,897	−8,820	....	80	—	—	—	—	†4,689	6,978	−8,820
3213 Securities other than shares...............	†—	—	—	....	—	—	—	—	—	†—	—	—
3214 Loans.....................................	†130	328	450	....	—	—	—	—	—	†130	328	450
3215 Shares and other equity...................	†371	629	−11	....	—	—	—	—	—	†371	629	−11
3216 Insurance technical reserves...............	†—	—	—	....	—	—	—	—	—	†—	—	—
3217 Financial derivatives......................	†—	—	—	....	—	—	—	—	—	†—	—	—
3218 Other accounts receivable.................	....	....	....	....	—	—	—	—	—	....	....	....
322 Foreign.....................................	†152	2	—	....	—	—	—	—	—	†152	2	....
3222 Currency and deposits.....................	†152	—	—	....	—	—	—	—	—	†152	—	—
3223 Securities other than shares...............	†—	—	—	....	—	—	—	—	—	†—	—	—
3224 Loans.....................................	†—	—	—	....	—	—	—	—	—	†—	—	—
3225 Shares and other equity...................	†—	2	—	....	—	—	—	—	—	†—	2	—
3226 Insurance technical reserves...............	†—	—	—	....	—	—	—	—	—	†—	—	—
3227 Financial derivatives......................	†—	—	—	....	—	—	—	—	—	†—	—	—
3228 Other accounts receivable.................	....	....	....	....	—	—	—	—	—	....	....	....
323 Monetary gold and SDRs....................	†—	—	—	....	—	—	—	—	—	†—	....	....
33 **Net incurrence of liabilities..................**	†10,449	12,909	−3,172	....	—	−34	−42	−13	59	†10,407	12,896	−3,147
331 Domestic....................................	†9,419	12,822	−2,704	....	—	−34	−42	−13	59	†9,377	12,809	−2,679
3312 Currency and deposits.....................	†124	287	−4,551	....	—	−34	−42	−13	59	†82	275	−4,526
3313 Securities other than shares...............	†9,567	12,595	384	....	—	—	—	—	—	†9,567	12,595	384
3314 Loans.....................................	†−272	−61	1,463	....	—	—	—	—	—	†−272	−61	1,463
3316 Insurance technical reserves...............	†—	—	—	....	—	—	—	—	—	†—	—	—
3317 Financial derivatives......................	†—	—	—	....	—	—	—	—	—	†—	—	—
3318 Other accounts payable....................	....	—	—	....	—	—	—	—	—	†—	—	—
332 Foreign.....................................	†1,030	87	−468	....	—	—	—	—	—	†1,030	87	−468
3322 Currency and deposits.....................	†—	—	—	....	—	—	—	—	—	†—	—	—
3323 Securities other than shares...............	†−40	163	−312	....	—	—	—	—	—	†−40	163	−312
3324 Loans.....................................	†1,070	−76	−156	....	—	—	—	—	—	†1,070	−76	−156
3326 Insurance technical reserves...............	†—	—	—	....	—	—	—	—	—	†—	—	—
3327 Financial derivatives......................	†—	—	—	....	—	—	—	—	—	†—	—	—
3328 Other accounts payable....................	....	....	....	....	—	—	—	—	—	....	....	....

In Millions of Rupees / Year Ending June 30 / Cash Reporter

	Central Government			State Government			Local Government			General Government		
	2002	2003	2004	2002	2003	2004	2002	2003	2004	2002	2003	2004
Table 4 Holding gains in assets and liabilities												
Table 5 Other changes in the volume of assets and liabilities												
Table 6 Balance sheet												
6 Net worth....................	....	....	....	....	....	....	....	....	....	....	....	....
61 Nonfinancial assets....................	....	....	....	....	....	....	....	....	....	....	....	....
611 Fixed assets....................	....	....	....	....	....	....	....	....	....	....	....	....
6111 Buildings and structures....................	....	....	....	....	....	....	....	....	....	....	....	....
6112 Machinery and equipment....................	....	....	....	....	....	....	....	....	....	....	....	....
6113 Other fixed assets....................	....	....	....	....	....	....	....	....	....	....	....	....
612 Inventories....................	....	....	....	....	....	....	....	....	....	....	....	....
613 Valuables....................	....	....	....	....	....	....	....	....	....	....	....	....
614 Nonproduced assets....................	....	....	....	....	....	....	....	....	....	....	....	....
6141 Land....................	....	....	....	....	....	....	....	....	....	....	....	....
6142 Subsoil assets....................	....	....	....	....	....	....	....	....	....	....	....	....
6143 Other naturally occurring assets....................	....	....	....	....	....	....	....	....	....	....	....	....
6144 Intangible nonproduced assets....................	....	....	....	....	....	....	....	....	....	....	....	....
62 **Financial assets**....................	....	....	....	....	....	....	....	....	....	....	....	....
621 Domestic....................	....	....	....	....	....	....	....	....	....	....	....	....
6212 Currency and deposits....................	....	....	....	....	....	....	....	....	....	....	....	....
6213 Securities other than shares....................	....	....	....	....	....	....	....	....	....	....	....	....
6214 Loans....................	....	....	....	....	....	....	....	....	....	....	....	....
6215 Shares and other equity....................	....	....	....	....	....	....	....	....	....	....	....	....
6216 Insurance technical reserves....................	....	....	....	....	....	....	....	....	....	....	....	....
6217 Financial derivatives....................	....	....	....	....	....	....	....	....	....	....	....	....
6218 Other accounts receivable....................	....	....	....	....	....	....	....	....	....	....	....	....
622 Foreign....................	....	....	....	....	....	....	....	....	....	....	....	....
6222 Currency and deposits....................	....	....	....	....	....	....	....	....	....	....	....	....
6223 Securities other than shares....................	....	....	....	....	....	....	....	....	....	....	....	....
6224 Loans....................	....	....	....	....	....	....	....	....	....	....	....	....
6225 Shares and other equity....................	....	....	....	....	....	....	....	....	....	....	....	....
6226 Insurance technical reserves....................	....	....	....	....	....	....	....	....	....	....	....	....
6227 Financial derivatives....................	....	....	....	....	....	....	....	....	....	....	....	....
6228 Other accounts receivable....................	....	....	....	....	....	....	....	....	....	....	....	....
623 Monetary gold and SDRs....................	....	....	....	....	....	....	....	....	....	....	....	....
63 **Liabilities**....................	†57,757	72,605	70,669	....	....	....	....	....	....	....	....	....
631 Domestic....................	†48,973	63,531	62,224	....	....	....	....	....	....	....	....	....
6312 Currency and deposits....................	†580	600	688	....	....	....	....	....	....	....	....	....
6313 Securities other than shares....................	†48,393	62,931	61,536	....	....	....	....	....	....	....	....	....
6314 Loans....................	†—	—	—	....	....	....	....	....	....	....	....	....
6316 Insurance technical reserves....................	†—	—	—	....	....	....	....	....	....	....	....	....
6317 Financial derivatives....................	†—	—	—	....	....	....	....	....	....	....	....	....
6318 Other accounts payable....................	....	....	....	....	....	....	....	....	....	....	....	....
632 Foreign....................	†8,785	9,074	8,445	....	....	....	....	....	....	....	....	....
6322 Currency and deposits....................	†—	—	—	....	....	....	....	....	....	....	....	....
6323 Securities other than shares....................	†320	524	125	....	....	....	....	....	....	....	....	....
6324 Loans....................	†8,465	8,550	8,320	....	....	....	....	....	....	....	....	....
6326 Insurance technical reserves....................	†—	—	—	....	....	....	....	....	....	....	....	....
6327 Financial derivatives....................	†—	—	—	....	....	....	....	....	....	....	....	....
6328 Other accounts payable....................	....	....	....	....	....	....	....	....	....	....	....	....
Memorandum items:												
6M2 Net financial worth....................	....	....	....	....	....	....	....	....	....	....	....	....
6M3 Debt at market value....................	....	....	....	....	....	....	....	....	....	....	....	....
6M4 Debt at nominal value....................	....	....	....	....	....	....	....	....	....	....	....	....
6M5 Arrears....................	....	....	....	....	....	....	....	....	....	....	....	....
6M6 Obligations for social security benefits....................	....	....	....	....	....	....	....	....	....	....	....	....
6M7 Contingent liabilities....................	....	....	....	....	....	....	....	....	....	....	....	....
6M8 Uncapitalized military weapons, systems....................	....	....	....	....	....	....	....	....	....	....	....	....
Table 7 Outlays by functions of govt.												
7 **Total outlays**....................	†33,010	37,972	41,831	....	713	1,055	1,458	1,576	1,886	†33,553	38,504	42,499
701 **General public services**....................	†7,388	9,303	10,691	....	101	148	339	392	407	†6,813	8,039	8,973
7017 Public debt transactions....................	†3,533	4,440	5,078	—	—	—	9	9	8	†3,542	4,448	5,086
7018 General transfers between levels of govt......	†914	1,757	2,273	—	—	—	—	—	—	†	—	—
702 **Defense**....................	†270	299	308	....	—	—	—	—	—	†270	299	308
703 **Public order and safety**....................	†2,509	2,897	3,550	....	12	19	—	—	—	†2,509	2,909	3,569

2005, International Monetary Fund: *Government Finance Statistics Yearbook*

		Central Government			State Government			Local Government			General Government		
		2002	2003	2004	2002	2003	2004	2002	2003	2004	2002	2003	2004
704	**Economic affairs**	†3,926	4,518	4,453	....	181	260	332	365	419	†4,258	5,063	5,132
7042	Agriculture, forestry, fishing, and hunting	†1,313	1,324	1,677	....	66	103	—	—	—	†1,313	1,390	1,780
7043	Fuel and energy	†44	34	35	....	—	—	—	—	—	†44	34	35
7044	Mining, manufacturing, and construction	†193	195	218	....	—	—	190	215	293	†384	410	510
7045	Transport	†864	1,104	1,001	....	93	144	141	150	126	†1,005	1,347	1,271
7046	Communication	†191	167	67	....	—	—	—	—	—	†191	167	67
705	**Environmental protection**	†1,246	1,602	1,616	....	—	35	210	230	247	†1,456	1,832	1,897
706	**Housing and community amenities**	†2,009	1,723	1,375	....	136	167	304	303	525	†2,314	2,162	2,067
707	**Health**	†2,892	3,177	3,773	....	78	130	—	—	—	†2,892	3,255	3,903
7072	Outpatient services	....	....	....	....	....	....	—	—	—	....	....	....
7073	Hospital services	....	....	....	....	....	....	—	—	—	....	....	....
7074	Public health services	....	....	....	....	....	....	—	—	—	....	....	....
708	**Recreation, culture, and religion**	†497	835	796	....	14	50	148	159	159	†645	1,008	1,005
709	**Education**	†5,114	5,997	6,619	....	130	162	13	15	12	†5,127	6,143	6,792
7091	Pre-primary and primary education	....	....	....	....	....	....	....	....	....	....	....	....
7092	Secondary education	....	....	....	....	....	....	....	....	....	....	....	....
7094	Tertiary education	....	....	....	....	....	....	....	....	....	....	....	....
710	**Social protection**	†7,157	7,621	8,650	....	61	84	111	113	118	†7,268	7,795	8,852
7	Statistical discrepancy: Total outlays	†—	—	—	....	—	—	—	—	—	†—		

Table 8 Transactions in financial assets and liabilities by sector

		Central Government			State Government			Local Government			General Government		
		2002	2003	2004	2002	2003	2004	2002	2003	2004	2002	2003	2004
82	**Net acquisition of financial assets**	†5,341	7,856	−8,381	....	80	—	—	—	—	†5,341	7,937	−8,381
821	Domestic	†5,189	7,854	−8,381	....	80	—	—	—	—	†5,189	7,935	−8,381
8211	General government	†3,925	....	−8,820	....	....	—	—	—	—	†3,925	....	−8,820
8212	Central bank	†—	....	—	....	....	—	—	—	—	†—	....	—
8213	Other depository corporations	†346	....	—	....	....	—	—	—	—	†346	....	—
8214	Financial corporations n.e.c.	†500	....	24	....	....	—	—	—	—	†500	....	24
8215	Nonfinancial corporations	†418	....	414	....	....	—	—	—	—	†418	....	414
8216	Households & NPIs serving households	†—	....	—	....	....	—	—	—	—	†—	....	—
822	Foreign	†152	2	—	....	—	—	—	—	—	†152	2	—
8221	General government	†—	—	—	....	—	—	—	—	—	†—	—	—
8227	International organizations	†—	—	—	....	—	—	—	—	—	†—	—	—
8228	Financial corporations other than international organizations	†152	2	—	....	—	—	—	—	—	†152	2	—
8229	Other nonresidents	†—	—	—	....	—	—	—	—	—	†—	—	—
823	Monetary gold and SDRs	†—	—	—	....	—	—	—	—	—	†—	—	—
83	**Net incurrence of liabilities**	†10,449	12,909	−3,172	....	—	−34	−42	−13	59	†10,407	12,896	−3,147
831	Domestic	†9,419	12,822	−2,704	....	—	−34	−42	−13	59	†9,377	12,809	−2,679
8311	General government	†−607	163	1,062	....	—	—	....	....	—			1,062
8312	Central bank	†−431	−1,026	−122	....	—	—	....	....	—			−122
8313	Other depository corporations	†6,999	10,388	5,356	....	—	−34	....	....	59			5,381
8314	Financial corporations n.e.c.	†2,764	2,891	−3,871	....	—	—	....	....	—			−3,871
8315	Nonfinancial corporations	†694	406	−5,129	....	—	—	....	....	—			−5,129
8316	Households & NPIs serving households	†—	—	—	....	—	—	....	....	—			—
832	Foreign	†1,030	87	−468	....	—	—	—	—	—	†1,030	87	−468
8321	General government	†58	−9	322	....	—	—	—	—	—	†58	−9	322
8327	International organizations	†1,018	−58	−473	....	—	—	—	—	—	†1,018	−58	−473
8328	Financial corporations other than international organizations	†−46	154	−318	....	—	—	—	—	—	†−46	154	−318
8329	Other nonresidents	†—	—	—	....	—	—	—	—	—	†—	—	—

In Millions of Pesos / Year Ending December 31 / Cash Reporter

	Central Government			State Government			Local Government			General Government		
	1998	1999	2000	1998	1999	2000	1998	1999	2000	1998	1999	2000
Statement of government operations												
Statement of other economic flows												
Balance sheet												
6 *Net worth*..............................	....	....	....	....	....	....	....	....	....	....	....	....
61 Nonfinancial assets..................	....	....	....	....	....	....	....	....	....	....	....	....
62 Financial assets.......................	....	....	....	....	....	....	....	....	....	....	....	....
63 Liabilities...............................	1,069,946	1,175,528	1,276,451	....	....	....	....	....	....			
Statement of sources and uses of cash												
1 Cash receipts from operating activities...........	501,019	634,057	810,620	246,289	311,017	391,057	46,048	64,180	77,884	....	....	....
11 Taxes..................................	392,295	493,975	640,777	101,160	123,325	161,172	31,610	40,316	45,464	....	....	....
12 Social contributions.................	58,046	69,015	84,931	—	—	—	—	—	—	....	....	....
13 Grants.................................	—	—	—	119,427	155,071	199,383	5,608	12,833	21,259	....	....	....
14 Other receipts.......................	50,678	71,067	84,912	25,702	32,621	30,502	8,830	11,031	11,161	....	....	....
2 Cash payments for operating activities...........	536,882	686,485	848,763	216,357	268,776	342,811	31,745	42,737	53,521	....	....	....
21 Compensation of employees..................	95,340	122,994	145,061	....	....	....	....	....	....	....	....	....
22 Purchases of goods and services..................	40,655	49,948	66,789									
24 Interest................................	82,917	115,894	113,161	5,046	6,277	7,381	552	626	445			
25 Subsidies..............................	....	....	....	....	....	....	....	....	....			
26 Grants.................................	....	....	....	....	....	....	....	....	....			
27 Social benefits.......................	....	....	....									
28 Other payments......................	....	....	....	....								
CIO *Net cash inflow from oper. activities*.....	*−35,863*	*−52,428*	*−38,143*	*29,932*	*42,241*	*48,246*	*14,303*	*21,443*	*24,363*	....	....	....
31.1 Purchases of nonfinancial assets..................	27,108	25,652	27,012	28,359	35,465	42,875	12,054	19,757	23,048			
31.2 Sales of nonfinancial assets..................	212	392	811	741	655	904	433	558	900			
31 Net cash outflow from investments in nonfinancial assets..................	26,896	25,260	26,201	27,618	34,810	41,971	11,621	19,199	22,148			
CSD *Cash surplus/deficit*..............	*−67,091*	*−69,786*	*−66,483*	*2,314*	*7,431*	*6,275*	*2,682*	*2,244*	*2,215*	....	....	....
32x Net acquisition of fin assets, excl. cash...........	−11,500	1,503	2,423	—	—	—	—	—	—	....	....	....
321x Domestic..............................	−11,500	1,503	2,423	—	—	—	—	—	—			
322x Foreign...............................	—	—	—	—	—	—	—	—	—			
323 Monetary gold and SDRs............	—	—	—	—	—	—	—	—	—			
33 Net incurrence of liabilities............	....	....	....	....	....	....	....	....	....	....	....	....
331 Domestic..............................	....	....	....	....								
332 Foreign...............................	22,226	8,243	−41,036	....	....	....						
NFB Net cash inflow from fin. activities...........	....	....	....	....	....	....	....	....	....			
NCB *Net change in the stock of cash*.............	....	....	....	....	....	....	....	....	....			
Table 1 Revenue												
1 **Revenue**........................	**501,019**	**634,057**	**810,620**	**246,289**	**311,017**	**391,057**	**46,048**	**64,180**	**77,884**	....	....	....
11 **Taxes**.............................	**392,295**	**493,975**	**640,777**	**101,160**	**123,325**	**161,172**	**31,610**	**40,316**	**45,464**	....	....	....
111 Taxes on income, profits, & capital gains......	181,749	231,498	276,548	15	—	2	—	3	—	....	....	....
1111 Individuals............................	—	—	—	—	—	—	—	—	—	....	....	....
1112 Corporations and other enterprises............	—	—	—	—	—	—	—	—	—	....	....	....
112 Taxes on payroll and workforce...........	—	—	—	—	—	—	—	—	—	....	....	....
113 Taxes on property....................	—	—	—	5,048	5,738	7,097	4,709	5,760	6,946	....	....	....
114 Taxes on goods and services...................	294,764	366,616	503,622	933	1,029	1,336	905	785	202	....	....	....
1141 General taxes on goods and services.........	119,871	151,184	189,606	....	....	....	....	....	....	....	....	....
1142 Excises..............................	78,824	110,117	86,163	....	....	....	....	....	....	....	....	....
115 Taxes on int'l. trade and transactions...........	21,489	27,304	32,865	....	....	....	....	....	....	....	....	....
116 Other taxes..........................	7,871	9,228	5,878	7,551	9,619	12,049	31	36	868	....	....	....
12 **Social contributions**.....................	**58,046**	**69,015**	**84,931**	**—**	**—**	**—**	**—**	**—**	**—**	....	....	....
121 Social security contributions..................	58,046	69,015	84,931	—	—	—	—	—	—	....	....	....
122 Other social contributions.............	—	—	—	—	—	—	—	—	—	....	....	....
13 **Grants**...........................	**—**	**—**	**—**	**119,427**	**155,071**	**199,383**	**5,608**	**12,833**	**21,259**	....	....	....
131 From foreign governments................	—	—	—	—	—	—	—	—	—	....	....	....
132 From international organizations..................	—	—	—	—	—	—	—	—	—	....	....	....
133 From other general government units...........	—	—	—	119,427	155,071	199,383	5,608	12,833	21,259	....	....	....
14 **Other revenue**...........................	**50,678**	**71,067**	**84,912**	**25,702**	**32,621**	**30,502**	**8,830**	**11,031**	**11,161**	....	....	....
Table 2 Expense by economic type												
2 **Expense**........................	**536,882**	**686,485**	**848,763**	**216,357**	**268,776**	**342,811**	**31,745**	**42,737**	**53,521**	....	....	....
21 **Compensation of employees**..................	**95,340**	**122,994**	**145,061**	....	....	....	....	....	....	....	....	....
211 Wages and salaries..................	95,340	122,994	145,061	....	....	....	....	....	....	....	....	....
212 Social contributions..................	—	—	—	....	....	....	....	....	....	....	....	....
22 **Use of goods and services**....................	**40,655**	**49,948**	**66,789**	....	....	....	....	....	....	....	....	....
23 **Consumption of fixed capital**.................	....	....	....	....	....	....	....	....	....	....	....	....
24 **Interest**.............................	**82,917**	**115,894**	**113,161**	**5,046**	**6,277**	**7,381**	**552**	**626**	**445**	....	....	....
25 **Subsidies**..........................	....	....	....	....	....	....	....	....	....	....	....	....

		Central Government			State Government			Local Government			General Government		
		1998	1999	2000	1998	1999	2000	1998	1999	2000	1998	1999	2000
26	**Grants**...............	....	....	....	....	....	....	....	....	....	....	....	....
261	To foreign govenments...............	....	....	....	....	....	....	....	....	....	....	....	....
262	To international organizations............	....	....	....	....	....	....	....	....	....	....	....	....
263	To other general government units............	....	....	....	37,300	109,285	186,974	2,486	5,245	8,943	....	....	....
2631	Current...............	....	....	....	37,300	109,285	186,974	2,486	5,245	8,943	....	....	....
2632	Capital...............	....	....	....	—	—	—	—	—	—	....	....	....
27	**Social benefits**...............	....	....	....	....	....	....	....	....	....	....	....	....
28	**Other expense**...............	....	....	....	....	....	....	....	....	....	....	....	....
281	Property expense other than interest............	....	....	....	....	....	....	....	....	....	....	....	....
282	Miscellaneous other expense............	....	....	....	....	....	....	....	....	....	....	....	....
2821	Current...............	....	....	....	....	....	....	....	....	....	....	....	....
2822	Capital...............	....	....	....	....	....	....	....	....	....	....	....	....

Table 3   Transactions in assets and liabilities

		Central Government			State Government			Local Government			General Government		
3	**Change in net worth from transactns....**	....	....	....	....	....	....	....	....	....	....	....	....
31	**Net acquisition of nonfinancial assets...**	26,896	25,260	26,201	27,618	34,810	41,971	11,621	19,199	22,148	....	....	....
311	Fixed assets...............	26,896	25,260	26,201	....	....	....	....	....	....	....	....	....
3111	Buildings and structures............	....	....	....	....	....	....	....	....	....	....	....	....
3112	Machinery and equipment............	....	....	....	....	....	....	....	....	....	....	....	....
3113	Other fixed assets............	....	....	....	....	....	....	....	....	....	....	....	....
312	Inventories...............	—	—	—	....	....	....	....	....	....	....	....	....
313	Valuables...............	—	—	—	....	....	....	....	....	....	....	....	....
314	Nonproduced assets............	—	—	—	....	....	....	....	....	....	....	....	....
3141	Land...............	—	—	—	....	....	....	....	....	....	....	....	....
3142	Subsoil assets............	—	—	—	....	....	....	....	....	....	....	....	....
3143	Other naturally occurring assets............	—	—	—	....	....	....	....	....	....	....	....	....
3144	Intangible nonproduced assets............	—	—	—	....	....	....	....	....	....	....	....	....
32	**Net acquisition of financial assets........**	....	....	....	....	....	....	....	....	....	....	....	....
321	Domestic...............	....	....	....	....	....	....	....	....	....	....	....	....
3212	Currency and deposits............	....	....	....	....	....	....	....	....	....	....	....	....
3213	Securities other than shares............	....	....	....	....	....	....	....	....	....	....	....	....
3214	Loans...............	....	....	....	....	....	....	....	....	....	....	....	....
3215	Shares and other equity............	....	....	....	....	....	....	....	....	....	....	....	....
3216	Insurance technical reserves............	....	....	....	....	....	....	....	....	....	....	....	....
3217	Financial derivatives............	....	....	....	....	....	....	....	....	....	....	....	....
3218	Other accounts receivable............	....	....	....	....	....	....	....	....	....	....	....	....
322	Foreign...............	1,708	1,948	7,468	....	....	....	....	....	....	....	....	....
3222	Currency and deposits............	1,708	1,948	7,468	....	....	....	....	....	....	....	....	....
3223	Securities other than shares............	—	—	—	....	....	....	....	....	....	....	....	....
3224	Loans...............	—	—	—	....	....	....	....	....	....	....	....	....
3225	Shares and other equity............	—	—	—	....	....	....	....	....	....	....	....	....
3226	Insurance technical reserves............	—	—	—	....	....	....	....	....	....	....	....	....
3227	Financial derivatives............	—	—	—	....	....	....	....	....	....	....	....	....
3228	Other accounts receivable............	....	....	....	....	....	....	....	....	....	....	....	....
323	Monetary gold and SDRs............	—	—	—	....	....	....	....	....	....	....	....	....
33	**Net incurrence of liabilities............**	....	....	....	....	....	....	....	....	....	....	....	....
331	Domestic...............	....	....	....	....	....	....	....	....	....	....	....	....
3312	Currency and deposits............	....	....	....	....	....	....	....	....	....	....	....	....
3313	Securities other than shares............	....	....	....	....	....	....	....	....	....	....	....	....
3314	Loans...............	....	....	....	....	....	....	....	....	....	....	....	....
3316	Insurance technical reserves............	....	....	....	....	....	....	....	....	....	....	....	....
3317	Financial derivatives............	....	....	....	....	....	....	....	....	....	....	....	....
3318	Other accounts payable............	....	....	....	....	....	....	....	....	....	....	....	....
332	Foreign...............	22,226	8,243	−41,036	....	....	....	....	....	....	....	....	....
3322	Currency and deposits............	....	....	....	....	....	....	....	....	....	....	....	....
3323	Securities other than shares............	....	....	....	....	....	....	....	....	....	....	....	....
3324	Loans...............	....	....	....	....	....	....	....	....	....	....	....	....
3326	Insurance technical reserves............	....	....	....	....	....	....	....	....	....	....	....	....
3327	Financial derivatives............	....	....	....	....	....	....	....	....	....	....	....	....
3328	Other accounts payable............	....	....	....	....	....	....	....	....	....	....	....	....

In Millions of Pesos / Year Ending December 31 / Cash Reporter

	Central Government			State Government			Local Government			General Government		
	1998	1999	2000	1998	1999	2000	1998	1999	2000	1998	1999	2000
Table 4 Holding gains in assets and liabilities												
Table 5 Other changes in the volume of assets and liabilities												
Table 6 Balance sheet												
6 Net worth............................	....	....	....	....	....	....	....	....	....	....	....	....
61 **Nonfinancial assets**...............	....	....	....	....	....	....	....	....	....	....	....	....
611 Fixed assets........................	....	....	....	....	....	....	....	....	....	....	....	....
6111 Buildings and structures............	....	....	....	....	....	....	....	....	....	....	....	....
6112 Machinery and equipment............	....	....	....	....	....	....	....	....	....	....	....	....
6113 Other fixed assets..................	....	....	....	....	....	....	....	....	....	....	....	....
612 Inventories.........................	....	....	....	....	....	....	....	....	....	....	....	....
613 Valuables..........................	....	....	....	....	....	....	....	....	....	....	....	....
614 Nonproduced assets................	....	....	....	....	....	....	....	....	....	....	....	....
6141 Land.............................	....	....	....	....	....	....	....	....	....	....	....	....
6142 Subsoil assets.....................	....	....	....	....	....	....	....	....	....	....	....	....
6143 Other naturally occurring assets.....	....	....	....	....	....	....	....	....	....	....	....	....
6144 Intangible nonproduced assets.......	....	....	....	....	....	....	....	....	....	....	....	....
62 **Financial assets**...................	....	....	....	....	....	....	....	....	....	....	....	....
621 Domestic...........................	....	....	....	....	....	....	....	....	....	....	....	....
6212 Currency and deposits..............	....	....	....	....	....	....	....	....	....	....	....	....
6213 Securities other than shares........	....	....	....	....	....	....	....	....	....	....	....	....
6214 Loans.............................	....	....	....	....	....	....	....	....	....	....	....	....
6215 Shares and other equity............	....	....	....	....	....	....	....	....	....	....	....	....
6216 Insurance technical reserves........	....	....	....	....	....	....	....	....	....	....	....	....
6217 Financial derivatives...............	....	....	....	....	....	....	....	....	....	....	....	....
6218 Other accounts receivable..........	....	....	....	....	....	....	....	....	....	....	....	....
622 Foreign............................	....	....	....	....	....	....	....	....	....	....	....	....
6222 Currency and deposits..............	....	....	....	....	....	....	....	....	....	....	....	....
6223 Securities other than shares........	....	....	....	....	....	....	....	....	....	....	....	....
6224 Loans.............................	....	....	....	....	....	....	....	....	....	....	....	....
6225 Shares and other equity............	....	....	....	....	....	....	....	....	....	....	....	....
6226 Insurance technical reserves........	....	....	....	....	....	....	....	....	....	....	....	....
6227 Financial derivatives...............	....	....	....	....	....	....	....	....	....	....	....	....
6228 Other accounts receivable..........	....	....	....	....	....	....	....	....	....	....	....	....
623 Monetary gold and SDRs.............	....	....	....	....	....	....	....	....	....	....	....	....
63 **Liabilities**.........................	**1,069,946**	**1,175,528**	**1,276,451**	....	....	....	....	....	....	....	....	....
631 Domestic...........................	378,256	506,389	675,107	....	....	....	....	....	....	....	....	....
6312 Currency and deposits..............	....	....	....	....	....	....	....	....	....	....	....	....
6313 Securities other than shares........	....	....	....	....	....	....	....	....	....	....	....	....
6314 Loans.............................	....	....	....	....	....	....	....	....	....	....	....	....
6316 Insurance technical reserves........	....	....	....	....	....	....	....	....	....	....	....	....
6317 Financial derivatives...............	....	....	....	....	....	....	....	....	....	....	....	....
6318 Other accounts payable............	....	....	....	....	....	....	....	....	....	....	....	....
632 Foreign............................	691,690	669,139	601,344	....	....	....	....	....	....	....	....	....
6322 Currency and deposits..............	....	....	....	....	....	....	....	....	....	....	....	....
6323 Securities other than shares........	....	....	....	....	....	....	....	....	....	....	....	....
6324 Loans.............................	....	....	....	....	....	....	....	....	....	....	....	....
6326 Insurance technical reserves........	....	....	....	....	....	....	....	....	....	....	....	....
6327 Financial derivatives...............	....	....	....	....	....	....	....	....	....	....	....	....
6328 Other accounts payable............	....	....	....	....	....	....	....	....	....	....	....	....
Memorandum items:												
6M2 Net financial worth.................	....	....	....	....	....	....	....	....	....	....	....	....
6M3 Debt at market value................	....	....	....	....	....	....	....	....	....	....	....	....
6M4 Debt at nominal value...............	....	....	....	....	....	....	....	....	....	....	....	....
6M5 Arrears............................	....	....	....	....	....	....	....	....	....	....	....	....
6M6 Obligations for social security benefits....	....	....	....	....	....	....	....	....	....	....	....	....
6M7 Contingent liabilities................	....	....	....	....	....	....	....	....	....	....	....	....
6M8 Uncapitalized military weapons, systems.......	....	....	....	....	....	....	....	....	....	....	....	....
Table 7 Outlays by functions of govt.												
7 **Total outlays**.....................	**563,990**	**712,137**	**875,775**	**243,004**	**301,906**	**382,638**	**43,799**	**62,494**	**76,569**	....	....	....
701 **General public services**..........	**197,587**	**265,138**	**335,966**	....	....	....	....	....	....	....	....	....
7017 Public debt transactions............	82,917	115,894	113,161	5,046	6,277	7,381	552	626	445	....	....	....
7018 General transfers between levels of govt......	....	....	....	....	....	....	....	....	....	....	....	....
702 **Defense**.........................	**19,823**	**23,275**	**26,586**	....	....	....	....	....	....	....	....	....
703 **Public order and safety**..........	**11,164**	**19,881**	**23,832**	....	....	....	....	....	....	....	....	....

In Millions of Pesos / Year Ending December 31 / Cash Reporter

		Central Government			State Government			Local Government			General Government		
		1998	1999	2000	1998	1999	2000	1998	1999	2000	1998	1999	2000
704	**Economic affairs**.....................	**63,799**	**64,707**	**71,025**	....	....	....	....	....	....	....	....	....
7042	Agriculture, forestry, fishing, and hunting.....	22,955	22,401	23,715	....	....	....	....	....	....	....	....	....
7043	Fuel and energy..........................	8,690	10,760	11,997	....	....	....	....	....	....	....	....	....
7044	Mining, manufacturing, and construction.....	3,180	1,816	1,982	....	....	....	....	....	....	....	....	....
7045	Transport..................................	17,376	18,588	20,344	....	....	....	....	....	....	....	....	....
7046	Communication............................	....	....	....	....	....	....	....	....	....	....	....	....
705	**Environmental protection**..................	....	....	....	....	....	....	....	....	....	....	....	....
706	**Housing and community amenities**........	**34,101**	**45,850**	**60,633**	....	....	....	....	....	....	....	....	....
707	**Health**....................................	**24,548**	**30,052**	**43,387**	....	....	....	....	....	....	....	....	....
7072	Outpatient services.......................	....	....	....	....	....	....	....	....	....	....	....	....
7073	Hospital services..........................	....	....	....	....	....	....	....	....	....	....	....	....
7074	Public health services.....................	....	....	....	....	....	....	....	....	....	....	....	....
708	**Recreation, culture, and religion**...........	**3,667**	**4,759**	**4,885**	....	....	....	....	....	....	....	....	....
709	**Education**.................................	**150,762**	**181,870**	**216,548**	....	....	....	....	....	....	....	....	....
7091	Pre-primary and primary education............	....	....	....	....	....	....	....	....	....	....	....	....
7092	Secondary education........................	....	....	....	....	....	....	....	....	....	....	....	....
7094	Tertiary education.........................	....	....	....	....	....	....	....	....	....	....	....	....
710	**Social protection**..........................	**116,024**	**150,758**	**176,175**	....	....	....	....	....	....	....	....	....
7	Statistical discrepancy: Total outlays....	−57,485	−74,153	−83,262	....	....	....	....	....	....	....	....	....

Table 8 Transactions in financial assets and liabilities by sector

		Central Government			State Government			Local Government			General Government		
82	**Net acquisition of financial assets**........	....	....	....	....	....	....	....	....	....	....	....	....
821	Domestic.................................	....	....	....	....	....	....	....	....	....	....	....	....
8211	General government........................	....	....	....	....	....	....	....	....	....	....	....	....
8212	Central bank.............................	....	....	....	....	....	....	....	....	....	....	....	....
8213	Other depository corporations................	....	....	....	....	....	....	....	....	....	....	....	....
8214	Financial corporations n.e.c..................	....	....	....	....	....	....	....	....	....	....	....	....
8215	Nonfinancial corporations...................	....	....	....	....	....	....	....	....	....	....	....	....
8216	Households & NPIs serving households......	....	....	....	....	....	....	....	....	....	....	....	....
822	Foreign...................................	1,708	1,948	7,468	....	....	....	....	....	....	....	....	....
8221	General government........................	....	....	....	....	....	....	....	....	....	....	....	....
8227	International organizations...................	....	....	....	....	....	....	....	....	....	....	....	....
8228	Financial corporations other than international organizations..............	....	....	....	....	....	....	....	....	....	....	....	....
8229	Other nonresidents........................	....	....	....	....	....	....	....	....	....	....	....	....
823	Monetary gold and SDRs...................	—	—	—	....	....	....	....	....	....	....	....	....
83	**Net incurrence of liabilities**.................	....	....	....	....	....	....	....	....	....	....	....	....
831	Domestic.................................	....	....	....	....	....	....	....	....	....	....	....	....
8311	General government........................	....	....	....	....	....	....	....	....	....	....	....	....
8312	Central bank.............................	....	....	....	....	....	....	....	....	....	....	....	....
8313	Other depository corporations................	....	....	....	....	....	....	....	....	....	....	....	....
8314	Financial corporations n.e.c..................	....	....	....	....	....	....	....	....	....	....	....	....
8315	Nonfinancial corporations...................	....	....	....	....	....	....	....	....	....	....	....	....
8316	Households & NPIs serving households......	....	....	....	....	....	....	....	....	....	....	....	....
832	Foreign...................................	22,226	8,243	−41,036	....	....	....	....	....	....	....	....	....
8321	General government........................	14,305	−39,852	−22,166	....	....	....	....	....	....	....	....	....
8327	International organizations...................	4,417	−2,235	7,482	....	....	....	....	....	....	....	....	....
8328	Financial corporations other than international organizations..............	—	—	—	....	....	....	....	....	....	....	....	....
8329	Other nonresidents........................	3,930	48,790	50,424	....	....	....	....	....	....	....	....	....

Moldova 921

In Millions of Lei / Year Ending December 31 / Cash Reporter

	Budgetary Central Government			Central Government			Local Government			General Government		
	2002	2003	2004	2002	2003	2004	2002	2003	2004	2002	2003	2004
Statement of government operations												
Statement of other economic flows												
Balance sheet												
Statement of sources and uses of cash												
1 Cash receipts from operating activities...........	†3,371	4,565	5,625	†5,663	7,377	9,372	†2,437	2,894	2,945	†7,376	9,411	11,383
11 Taxes..........	†2,906	4,053	5,240	†2,906	4,053	5,240	†1,119	1,671	1,663	†4,024	5,723	6,902
12 Social contributions..............	†—	—	—	†1,644	1,978	2,493	†—	—	—	†1,644	1,978	2,493
13 Grants.................	†69	—	152	†69	—	152	†728	861	869	†73	1	125
14 Other receipts.............	†396	512	234	†1,044	1,346	1,488	†590	362	413	†1,635	1,709	1,863
2 Cash payments for operating activities...........	....	3,914	5,470	....	6,136	8,675	....	2,307	2,443	....	7,583	10,184
21 Compensation of employees..................	†833	1,008	1,005	†1,029	1,257	1,309	†1,086	1,366	1,161	†2,115	2,623	2,470
22 Purchases of goods and services..................	†617	430	474	†862	497	1,535	†652	354	322	†1,514	851	1,856
24 Interest.................	†486	580	773	†486	580	773	....	9	5	....	588	777
25 Subsidies..................	....	—	281	....	—	335	....	—	414	....	—	711
26 Grants...............	†1,095	1,249	2,015	†724	860	909	†—	—	30	†—	—	43
27 Social benefits..............	†138	167	245	†1,986	2,341	3,016	†—	—	76	†1,986	2,341	3,092
28 Other payments..............	....	480	677	....	601	799	....	578	436	....	1,179	1,235
CIO *Net cash inflow from oper. activities.....*	....	*651*	*155*	....	*1,241*	*697*	....	*587*	*502*	....	*1,828*	*1,198*
31.1 Purchases of nonfinancial assets..................	....	392	327	....	708	573	....	482	496	....	1,190	1,069
31.2 Sales of nonfinancial assets..................	....	9	15	....	15	19	....	13	18	....	29	36
31 Net cash outflow from investments in nonfinancial assets..................	....	383	312	....	693	554	....	469	479	....	1,161	1,033
CSD *Cash surplus/deficit..................*	*†-184*	*268*	*-157*	*†41*	*548*	*142*	*†77*	*119*	*23*	*†119*	*667*	*166*
32x Net acquisition of fin assets, excl. cash..........	....	....	—	....	....	—	....	....	—	....	....	—
321x Domestic..........	....	....	—	....	....	—	....	....	—	....	....	—
322x Foreign..........	....	....	—	....	....	—	....	....	—	....	....	—
323 Monetary gold and SDRs..........	†—	—	—	†—	—	—	†—	—	—	†—	—	—
33 Net incurrence of liabilities..................	....	....	177	....	....	177	....	....	59	....	....	236
331 Domestic..................	....	....	779	....	....	779	....	....	59	....	....	838
332 Foreign..................	....	....	-602	....	....	-602	....	....	—	....	....	-602
NFB Net cash inflow from fin. activities..........	†166	-329	177	†166	-329	177	†48	-74	59	†214	-403	236
NCB *Net change in the stock of cash..........*	*†-18*	*-62*	*21*	*†208*	*219*	*319*	*†125*	*45*	*83*	*†333*	*264*	*402*
Table 1 Revenue												
1 **Revenue......**	**†3,371**	**4,565**	**5,625**	**†5,663**	**7,377**	**9,372**	**†2,437**	**2,894**	**2,945**	**†7,376**	**9,411**	**11,383**
11 **Taxes......**	**†2,906**	**4,053**	**5,240**	**†2,906**	**4,053**	**5,240**	**†1,119**	**1,671**	**1,663**	**†4,024**	**5,723**	**6,902**
111 Taxes on income, profits, & capital gains......	†140	212	282	†140	212	282	†755	989	1,294	†895	1,201	1,576
1111 Individuals..........	†2	3	3	†2	3	3	†465	609	793	†467	612	797
1112 Corporations and other enterprises...........	†138	209	279	†138	209	279	†290	380	501	†428	589	780
112 Taxes on payroll and workforce..........	†—	—	—	†—	—	—	†—	—	—	†—	—	—
113 Taxes on property..........	†—	—	—	†—	—	—	†—	199	225	†—	199	225
114 Taxes on goods and services..........	†2,378	3,364	4,462	†2,378	3,364	4,462	†364	483	143	†2,742	3,847	4,605
1141 General taxes on goods and services..........	†1,688	2,382	3,412	†1,688	2,382	3,412	†346	410	16	†2,034	2,792	3,428
1142 Excises..........	†654	883	900	†654	883	900	†4	5	11	†658	888	910
115 Taxes on int'l. trade and transactions..........	†333	477	496	†333	477	496	†—	—	—	†333	477	496
116 Other taxes..........	†54	—	—	†54	—	—	†—	—	—	†54	—	—
12 **Social contributions......**	**†—**	**—**	**—**	**†1,644**	**1,978**	**2,493**	**†—**	**—**	**—**	**†1,644**	**1,978**	**2,493**
121 Social security contributions..........	†—	—	—	†1,644	1,978	2,493	†—	—	—	†1,644	1,978	2,493
122 Other social contributions..........	†—	—	—	†—	—	—	†—	—	—	†—	—	—
13 **Grants......**	**†69**	**—**	**152**	**†69**	**—**	**152**	**†728**	**861**	**869**	**†73**	**1**	**125**
131 From foreign governments..........	†69	—	16	†69	—	16	†4	1	3	†73	1	19
132 From international organizations..........	†—	—	106	†—	—	106	†—	—	—	†—	—	106
133 From other general government units..........	†—	—	30	†—	—	30	†724	860	866	†—	—	—
14 **Other revenue......**	**†396**	**512**	**234**	**†1,044**	**1,346**	**1,488**	**†590**	**362**	**413**	**†1,635**	**1,709**	**1,863**
Table 2 Expense by economic type												
2 **Expense......**	....	**3,914**	**5,470**	....	**6,136**	**8,675**	....	**2,307**	**2,443**	....	**7,583**	**10,184**
21 **Compensation of employees......**	**†833**	**1,008**	**1,005**	**†1,029**	**1,257**	**1,309**	**†1,086**	**1,366**	**1,161**	**†2,115**	**2,623**	**2,470**
211 Wages and salaries..........	†716	861	851	†874	1,061	1,093	†854	1,084	913	†1,728	2,144	2,006
212 Social contributions..........	†117	147	154	†155	196	216	†232	282	248	†387	479	464
22 **Use of goods and services......**	**†617**	**430**	**474**	**†862**	**497**	**1,535**	**†652**	**354**	**322**	**†1,514**	**851**	**1,856**
23 **Consumption of fixed capital......**	....	....	....	....	....	....	....	....	....	....	....	....
24 **Interest......**	**†486**	**580**	**773**	**†486**	**580**	**773**	....	**9**	**5**	....	**588**	**777**
25 **Subsidies......**	....	**—**	**281**	....	**—**	**335**	....	**—**	**414**	....	**—**	**711**

	Budgetary Central Government			Central Government			Local Government			General Government		
	2002	2003	2004	2002	2003	2004	2002	2003	2004	2002	2003	2004
26 Grants	†1,095	1,249	2,015	†724	860	909	†—	—	30	†—	—	43
261 To foreign governments	†—	—	—	†—	—	—	†—			†—		
262 To international organizations	†—	—	42	†—	—	43	†—	—	—	†—		43
263 To other general government units	†1,095	1,249	1,973	†724	860	866	†—	—	30	†—	—	
2631 Current	†1,095	1,249	1,861	†724	860	754	†—	—	30	†—	—	
2632 Capital	†—	—	112	†—	—	112	†—	—	—	†—	—	
27 Social benefits	†138	167	245	†1,986	2,341	3,016	†—	—	76	†1,986	2,341	3,092
28 Other expense	....	480	677	....	601	799	....	578	436	....	1,179	1,235
281 Property expense other than interest	....	86	—	....	144	—	....	74	—	....	218	—
282 Miscellaneous other expense	....	394	677	....	458	799	....	504	436	....	962	1,235
2821 Current	....	394	677	....	458	799	....	504	436	....	962	1,235
2822 Capital		—			—		....		—	....		—

Table 3 Transactions in assets and liabilities

	Budgetary Central Government			Central Government			Local Government			General Government		
	2002	2003	2004	2002	2003	2004	2002	2003	2004	2002	2003	2004
3 Change in net worth from transactns	....	....	....	....	....	....	....	....	....	....	....	....
31 Net acquisition of nonfinancial assets	....	383	312	....	693	554	....	469	479	....	1,161	1,033
311 Fixed assets	....	143	68	....	236	139	....	155	228	....	390	367
3111 Buildings and structures	....	....	....	....	....	....	....	....	....	....	....	....
3112 Machinery and equipment	....	....	....	....	....	....	....	....	....	....	....	....
3113 Other fixed assets	....	....	....	....	....	....	....	....	....	....	....	....
312 Inventories	....	240	243	....	457	415	....	314	251	....	771	666
313 Valuables	....	—	—	....	—	—	....	—	—	....	—	—
314 Nonproduced assets	....			....			....			....		
3141 Land	....			....			....			....		
3142 Subsoil assets	....			....			....			....		
3143 Other naturally occurring assets	....			....			....			....		
3144 Intangible nonproduced assets	....	—	—	....	—	—	....	—	—	....		
32 Net acquisition of financial assets	....	....	21	....	....	319	....	....	83	....		402
321 Domestic	....	....	21	....	....	319	....	....	83	....		402
3212 Currency and deposits	†−18	−62	21	†208	219	319	†125	45	83	†333	264	402
3213 Securities other than shares	....		—	....		—	....			....		
3214 Loans	....		—	....		—	....			....		
3215 Shares and other equity	....		—	....		—	....			....		
3216 Insurance technical reserves	....		—	....		—	....			....		
3217 Financial derivatives	....		—	....		—	....			....		
3218 Other accounts receivable	....		....	....		....	....		....	....		....
322 Foreign	....		—	....		—	....		—	....		
3222 Currency and deposits	†—	—	—	†—	—	—	†—	—	—	†—	—	—
3223 Securities other than shares	....		—	....		—	....		—	....		
3224 Loans	....		—	....		—	....		—	....		
3225 Shares and other equity	....		—	....		—	....		—	....		
3226 Insurance technical reserves	....		—	....		—	....		—	....		
3227 Financial derivatives	....		—	....		—	....		—	....		
3228 Other accounts receivable	....		....	....		....	....		....	....		....
323 Monetary gold and SDRs	†—	—	—	†—	—	—	†—	—		†—		
33 Net incurrence of liabilities	....	....	177	....	....	177	....	....	59	....	....	236
331 Domestic	....	....	779	....	....	779	....		59	....		838
3312 Currency and deposits	....	....	—	....	....	—	....		—	....		
3313 Securities other than shares	....	....	200	....	....	200	....		—	....		200
3314 Loans	....	....	562	....	....	562	....		59	....		621
3316 Insurance technical reserves	....	....	—	....	....	—	....		—	....		
3317 Financial derivatives	....	....	—	....	....	—	....		—	....		
3318 Other accounts payable	....	....	....	....	....	....	....		....	....		....
332 Foreign	....	....	−602	....	....	−602	....		—	....		−602
3322 Currency and deposits	....	....	—	....	....	—	....		—	....		
3323 Securities other than shares	....	....	—	....	....	—	....		—	....		
3324 Loans	....	....	−602	....	....	−602	....		—	....		−602
3326 Insurance technical reserves	....	....	—	....	....	—	....		—	....		
3327 Financial derivatives	....	....	—	....	....	—	....		—	....		
3328 Other accounts payable	....	....	....	....	....	....	....		....	....		....

In Millions of Lei / Year Ending December 31 / Cash Reporter

	Budgetary Central Government			Central Government			Local Government			General Government		
	2002	2003	2004	2002	2003	2004	2002	2003	2004	2002	2003	2004
Table 4 Holding gains in assets and liabilities												
Table 5 Other changes in the volume of assets and liabilities												
Table 6 Balance sheet												
6 Net worth.........	....	....	....	....	....	....	....	....	....	....	....	....
61 **Nonfinancial assets**...............	....	....	6,445	....	....	7,256	....	....	12,136	....	....	19,393
611 Fixed assets.......................	....	....	5,967	....	....	6,655	....	....	12,000	....	....	18,655
6111 Buildings and structures.........	....	....	4,039	....	....	4,261	....	....	10,359	....	....	14,620
6112 Machinery and equipment........	....	....	1,062	....	....	1,360	....	....	560	....	....	1,920
6113 Other fixed assets...............	....	....	867	....	....	1,034	....	....	1,081	....	....	2,115
612 Inventories.....................	....	....	478	....	....	601	....	....	136	....	....	738
613 Valuables.......................	....	....	—	....	....	—	....	....	—	....	....	—
614 Nonproduced assets.............	....	....	—	....	....	—	....	....	—	....	....	—
6141 Land.........................	....	....	—	....	....	—	....	....	—	....	....	—
6142 Subsoil assets.................	....	....	—	....	....	—	....	....	—	....	....	—
6143 Other naturally occurring assets...	....	....	—	....	....	—	....	....	—	....	....	—
6144 Intangible nonproduced assets...	....	....	—	....	....	—	....	....	—	....	....	—
62 **Financial assets**...............	....	....	33	....	....	1,136	....	....	338	....	....	1,474
621 Domestic......................	....	....	33	....	....	1,136	....	....	338	....	....	1,474
6212 Currency and deposits.........	....	....	33	....	....	1,136	....	....	338	....	....	1,474
6213 Securities other than shares......	....	....		....	....		....	....		....	....	.
6214 Loans.........................	....	....	—	....	....	—	....	....	—	....	....	—
6215 Shares and other equity.........	....	....	—	....	....	—	....	....	—	....	....	—
6216 Insurance technical reserves......	....	....	—	....	....	—	....	....	—	....	....	—
6217 Financial derivatives...........	....	....	—	....	....	—	....	....	—	....	....	—
6218 Other accounts receivable.......	....	....	....	....	....	....	....	....	....	....	....	....
622 Foreign.......................	....	....	—	....	....	—	....	....	—	....	....	—
6222 Currency and deposits.........	....	....	—	....	....	—	....	....	—	....	....	—
6223 Securities other than shares......	....	....	—	....	....	—	....	....	—	....	....	—
6224 Loans.........................	....	....	—	....	....	—	....	....	—	....	....	—
6225 Shares and other equity.........	....	....	—	....	....	—	....	....	—	....	....	—
6226 Insurance technical reserves......	....	....	—	....	....	—	....	....	—	....	....	—
6227 Financial derivatives...........	....	....	—	....	....	—	....	....	—	....	....	—
6228 Other accounts receivable.......	....	....	....	....	....	....	....	....	....	....	....	....
623 Monetary gold and SDRs.......	....	....	....	....	....	....	....	....	....	....	....	....
63 **Liabilities**..................	†12,910	13,705	16,642	†13,434	14,509	16,642	†338	292	94	†13,772	14,802	16,736
631 Domestic......................	†2,898	2,933	3,714	†3,423	3,737	3,714	†338	292	94	†3,761	4,030	3,808
6312 Currency and deposits.........	†77	12	—	†601	817	—	†210	255	—	†811	1,072	—
6313 Securities other than shares......	†1,077	1,176	1,376	†1,077	1,176	1,376	†—	—	—	†1,077	1,176	1,376
6314 Loans.........................	†1,744	1,744	2,338	†1,744	1,744	2,338	†129	38	94	†1,873	1,782	2,432
6316 Insurance technical reserves......	†—	—	—	†—	—	—	†—	—	—	†—	—	—
6317 Financial derivatives...........	†—	—	—	†—	—	—	†—	—	—	†—	—	—
6318 Other accounts payable.........	....	....	....	....	....	....	....	....	....	....	....	....
632 Foreign.......................	†10,012	10,772	12,928	†10,012	10,772	12,928	†—	—	—	†10,012	10,772	12,928
6322 Currency and deposits.........	†—	—	—	†—	—	—	†—	—	—	†—	—	—
6323 Securities other than shares......	†—	—	—	†—	—	—	†—	—	—	†—	—	—
6324 Loans.........................	†10,012	10,772	12,928	†10,012	10,772	12,928	†—	—	—	†10,012	10,772	12,928
6326 Insurance technical reserves......	†—	—	—	†—	—	—	†—	—	—	†—	—	—
6327 Financial derivatives...........	†—	—	—	†—	—	—	†—	—	—	†—	—	—
6328 Other accounts payable.........	....	....	....	....	....	....	....	....	....	....	....	....
Memorandum items:												
6M2 Net financial worth.............	....	....	−16,609	....	....	−15,506	....	....	244	....	....	−15,262
6M3 Debt at market value...........	....	....	....	....	....	....	....	....	....	....	....	....
6M4 Debt at nominal value..........	....	....	....	....	....	....	....	....	....	....	....	....
6M5 Arrears........................	....	....	....	....	....	....	....	....	....	....	....	....
6M6 Obligations for social security benefits..	....	....	....	....	....	....	....	....	....	....	....	....
6M7 Contingent liabilities...........	....	....	....	....	....	....	....	....	....	....	....	....
6M8 Uncapitalized military weapons, systems...	....	....	....	....	....	....	....	....	....	....	....	....
Table 7 Outlays by functions of govt.												
7 **Total outlays**..............	†3,556	4,297	5,782	†5,622	6,829	9,229	†2,360	2,776	2,921	†7,257	8,744	11,217
701 **General public services**.........	†1,670	2,100	2,591	†1,835	2,279	1,765	†457	532	933	†1,567	1,952	1,802
7017 Public debt transactions........	†486	580	773	†486	580	773	....	9	5	....	588	777
7018 General transfers between levels of govt...	†724	861	1,973	†724	860	866	†—	—	30	†—	—	—
702 **Defense**......................	†95	115	116	†110	115	133	†1	2	3	†111	117	137
703 **Public order and safety**...........	†394	429	440	†469	526	543	†91	89	97	†560	615	639

Moldova   921

In Millions of Lei / Year Ending December 31 / Cash Reporter

		Budgetary Central Government			Central Government			Local Government			General Government		
		2002	2003	2004	2002	2003	2004	2002	2003	2004	2002	2003	2004
704	**Economic affairs**.....................	†177	203	316	†197	228	367	†60	62	91	†256	290	458
7042	Agriculture, forestry, fishing, and hunting.....	†79	94	162	†96	115	210	†30	28	38	†126	143	248
7043	Fuel and energy....................	†2	2	14	†2	2	14	†1	1	1	†3	3	14
7044	Mining, manufacturing, and construction.....	†6	6	8	†8	10	11	†5	6	6	†13	15	18
7045	Transport....................	†91	101	133	†91	101	133	†24	27	46	†115	128	179
7046	Communication....................	†—	—	—	†—	—	−1	†—	—	—	†—	—	−1
705	**Environmental protection**.....................	†10	11	14	†21	35	49	†—	—	—	†21	36	49
706	**Housing and community amenities**........	†1	1	3	†1	1	3	†144	227	355	†145	228	358
707	**Health**....................	†263	313	943	†340	422	1,928	†530	575	53	†870	996	1,981
7072	Outpatient services....................	†9	....	4	†19	....	4	†181	190	—	†200	....	4
7073	Hospital services....................	†152	....	5	†193	....	5	†334	413	—	†526	....	5
7074	Public health services....................	....	....	934	....	....	1,919	....	4	53	....	....	1,971
708	**Recreation, culture, and religion**...........	†66	86	105	†74	102	72	†73	89	99	†146	190	171
709	**Education**....................	†287	355	414	†494	627	737	†953	1,143	1,178	†1,447	1,770	1,914
7091	Pre-primary and primary education....................	....	....	—	....	....	—	....	267	303	....	....	303
7092	Secondary education....................	....	....	306	....	....	390	....	....	875	....	....	1,265
7094	Tertiary education....................	†119	....	108	†308	....	347	....	....	—	†308	....	347
710	**Social protection**....................	†594	686	841	†2,083	2,495	3,632	†52	57	114	†2,135	2,552	3,708
7	Statistical discrepancy: Total outlays.............	†—	—	—	†—	—	—	†—	—	—	†—	—	—

Table 8   Transactions in financial assets and liabilities by sector

		Budgetary Central Government			Central Government			Local Government			General Government		
		2002	2003	2004	2002	2003	2004	2002	2003	2004	2002	2003	2004
82	**Net acquisition of financial assets**.........	....	....	21	....	....	319	....	....	83	....	....	402
821	Domestic...................	....	....	21	....	....	319	....	....	83	....	....	402
8211	General government...................	....	....	21	....	....	319	....	....	83	....	....	402
8212	Central bank....................	....	....	—	....	....	—	....	....	—	....	....	—
8213	Other depository corporations....................	....	....	—	....	....	—	....	....	—	....	....	—
8214	Financial corporations n.e.c....................	....	....	—	....	....	—	....	....	—	....	....	—
8215	Nonfinancial corporations....................	....	....	—	....	....	—	....	....	—	....	....	—
8216	Households & NPIs serving households......	....	....		....	....		....	....		....	....	
822	Foreign....................	....	....	—	....	....	—	....	....	—	....	....	—
8221	General government....................	....	....	—	....	....	—	....	....	—	....	....	—
8227	International organizations....................	....	....	—	....	....	—	....	....	—	....	....	—
8228	Financial corporations other than international organizations....................	....	....	—	....	....	—	....	....	—	....	....	—
8229	Other nonresidents....................	....	....	—	....	....	—	....	....	—	....	....	—
823	Monetary gold and SDRs....................	†—	—	—	†—	—	—	†—	—	—	†—	—	—
83	**Net incurrence of liabilities**...................	....	....	177	....	....	177	....	....	59	....	....	236
831	Domestic....................	....	....	779	....	....	779	....	....	59	....	....	838
8311	General government....................	....	....	—	....	....	—	....	....	—	....	....	—
8312	Central bank....................	....	....	594	....	....	594	....	....	—	....	....	594
8313	Other depository corporations....................	....	....	168	....	....	168	....	....	59	....	....	227
8314	Financial corporations n.e.c....................	....	....	17	....	....	17	....	....	—	....	....	17
8315	Nonfinancial corporations....................	....	....	—	....	....	—	....	....	—	....	....	—
8316	Households & NPIs serving households......	....	....	—	....	....	—	....	....	—	....	....	—
832	Foreign....................	....	....	−602	....	....	−602	....	....	—	....	....	−602
8321	General government....................	....	....	—	....	....	—	....	....	—	....	....	—
8327	International organizations....................	....	....	−78	....	....	−78	....	....	—	....	....	−78
8328	Financial corporations other than international organizations..............	....	....	−523	....	....	−523	....	....	—	....	....	−523
8329	Other nonresidents....................	....	....	—	....	....	—	....	....	—	....	....	—

Mongolia 948

In Billions of Togrogs / Year Ending December 31 / Noncash Reporter

	Budgetary Central Government			Central Government			Local Government			General Government		
	2001	2002	2003p	2001	2002	2003p	2001	2002	2003p	2001	2002	2003p
Statement of government operations												
1 Revenue...........	....	....	478.43	....	....	576.69	....	....	50.36	....	....	599.95
2 Expense...........	....	....	422.59	....	....	449.96	....	....	42.99	....	....	465.85
GOB *Gross operating balance...........*	....	....	*55.84*	....	....	*126.73*	....	....	*7.37*	....	....	*134.10*
NOB *Net operating balance...........*	....	....	....	....	....	....	....	....	....	....	....	....
31 Net acquisition of nonfinancial assets...........	....	....	40.02	....	....	133.71	....	....	5.30	....	....	139.01
NLB *Net lending/borrowing...........*	....	....	*15.82*	....	....	*−6.98*	....	....	*2.07*	....	....	*−4.91*
32 Net acquisition of financial assets...........	....	....	103.34	....	....	53.60	....	....	3.60	....	....	54.86
33 Net incurrence of liabilities...........	....	....	90.98	....	....	65.13	....	....	.42	....	....	63.22
NLB Statistical discrepancy...........	....	....	−3.50	....	....	−4.60	....	....	1.10	....	....	−3.40
Statement of other economic flows												
Balance sheet												
6 *Net worth...........*	....	....	*667.28*	*626.63*	*632.85*	*908.57*	....	....	*119.95*	....	....	*1,028.52*
61 Nonfinancial assets...........	....	....	985.93	679.94	763.26	1,235.96	....	....	70.83	....	....	1,306.79
62 Financial assets...........	....	....	1,327.44	1,015.50	1,103.00	1,423.50	....	....	54.44	....	....	1,477.94
63 Liabilities...........	....	....	1,646.09	1,068.81	1,233.41	1,750.89	17.49	....	5.32	....	....	1,756.21
Statement of sources and uses of cash												
1 Cash receipts from operating activities...........	295.49	†318.12	478.43	363.02	403.22	....	160.28	176.40	50.36	....	489.77	....
11 Taxes...........	199.48	†207.30	329.94	204.08	207.30	....	69.81	79.96	23.75	....	287.27	....
12 Social contributions...........	—	†—		61.31	69.92	....	—	—	—	....	54.93	....
13 Grants...........	9.18	†10.78	36.52	9.18	19.31	....	73.90	74.87	12.25	....	19.31	....
14 Other receipts...........	86.84	†100.04	111.97	88.46	106.69	....	16.57	21.56	14.35	....	128.26	....
2 Cash payments for operating activities...........	229.10	†282.32	422.59	306.93	336.44	....	150.82	156.35	42.99	....	402.93	....
21 Compensation of employees...........	35.47	†55.23	132.43	35.47	47.81	....	70.88	79.27	10.01	....	112.10	....
22 Purchases of goods and services...........	84.77	†80.66	149.61	88.93	87.93	....	77.76	76.00	16.77	....	163.93	....
24 Interest...........	16.45	†20.04	17.65	16.45	20.04	....	.07	—	—	....	20.04	....
25 Subsidies...........	5.45	†8.64	8.49	5.45	8.64	....	....	.15	.89	....	8.79	....
26 Grants...........	60.08	†94.49	85.49	69.59	75.49	....	....	—	14.86	....	.62	....
27 Social benefits...........	23.08	†17.35	28.93	87.23	90.62	....	....	—	.47	....	90.62	....
28 Other payments...........	3.80	†5.90	—	3.80	5.90	....	....	.92	—	....	6.82	....
CIO *Net cash inflow from oper. activities.....*	*31.84*	*†35.81*	*55.84*	*56.09*	*66.78*	....	*9.46*	*20.05*	*7.37*	....	*86.83*	....
31.1 Purchases of nonfinancial assets...........	36.16	†62.98	40.02	46.65	86.18	....	8.51	13.47	7.35	....	99.65	....
31.2 Sales of nonfinancial assets...........	4.40	†—	—	4.40	—	....	1.35	—	2.05	....	—	....
31 Net cash outflow from investments in nonfinancial assets...........	31.76	†62.98	40.02	42.25	86.18	....	7.17	13.47	5.30	....	99.65	....
CSD *Cash surplus/deficit...........*	*.08*	*†−27.17*	*15.82*	*13.84*	*−19.40*	....	*2.29*	*6.57*	*2.07*	....	*−12.82*	....
32x Net acquisition of fin assets, excl. cash...........	59.66	†39.61	70.25	59.66	30.44	....	—	−6.90	1.92	....	37.04	....
321x Domestic...........	59.66	†39.31	78.05	59.66	30.14	....	—	−6.90	1.92	....	36.74	....
322x Foreign...........	—	†.30	−7.81	—	.30	....	—	—	—	....	.30	....
323 Monetary gold and SDRs...........	—	†—		—	—	....				....		....
33 Net incurrence of liabilities...........	55.02	†65.45	90.98	55.02	66.55	....	—	−14.69	.42	....	65.36	....
331 Domestic...........	−14.59	†−16.78	190.74	−14.59	−15.67	....	—	−14.69	.42	....	−16.86	....
332 Foreign...........	69.61	†82.22	−99.76	69.61	82.22	....	—	—	—	....	82.22	....
NFB Net cash inflow from fin. activities...........	−4.65	†25.83	20.74	−4.65	36.11	....	—	−7.78	−1.50	....	28.32	....
NCB *Net change in the stock of cash...........*	*−4.56*	*†−1.34*	*33.10*	*9.19*	*16.71*	*58.72*	*2.29*	*−1.21*	*1.68*	....	*15.50*	*60.40*
Table 1 Revenue												
1 **Revenue...........**	**295.49**	**†318.12**	**478.43**	**363.02**	**403.22**	**†576.69**	**160.28**	**176.40**	**50.36**	....	**489.77**	**†599.95**
11 **Taxes...........**	**199.48**	**†207.30**	**329.94**	**204.08**	**207.30**	**†329.94**	**69.81**	**79.96**	**23.75**	....	**287.27**	**†353.70**
111 Taxes on income, profits, & capital gains......	27.88	†45.96	93.09	27.88	45.96	†93.09	37.28	25.50	4.49	....	71.46	†97.58
1111 Individuals...........	—	†—	24.31	—	—	†24.31	20.68	25.49	4.49	....	25.49	†28.80
1112 Corporations and other enterprises...........	27.88	†45.96	68.78	27.88	45.96	†68.78	16.61	.01	—	....	45.97	†68.78
112 Taxes on payroll and workforce...........	—	†—		—	—	†—	—	—	—	....	—	†—
113 Taxes on property...........	.37	†.15	—	.37	.15	†—	1.27	2.58	12.66	....	2.73	†12.66
114 Taxes on goods and services...........	140.74	†136.60	204.20	145.34	136.60	†204.20	20.24	51.89	5.76	....	188.48	†209.96
1141 General taxes on goods and services...........	99.82	†76.56	121.87	99.82	76.56	†121.87	....	37.01	—	....	113.57	†121.87
1142 Excises...........	40.06	†54.32	58.58	40.06	54.32	†58.58	....	3.44	—	....	57.76	†58.58
115 Taxes on int'l. trade and transactions...........	27.02	†24.59	32.65	27.02	24.59	†32.65	—	—	—	....	24.59	†32.65
116 Other taxes...........	3.48	†—		3.48	—	†—	11.01	—	.84	....	—	†.84
12 **Social contributions...........**	—	†—	—	61.31	69.92	†90.84	—	—	—	....	54.93	†90.84
121 Social security contributions...........	—	†—	—	61.31	69.92	†90.84	—	—	—	....	54.93	†90.84
122 Other social contributions...........	—	†—	—	—	—	†—	—	—	—	....	—	†—
13 **Grants...........**	**9.18**	**†10.78**	**36.52**	**9.18**	**19.31**	**†23.58**	**73.90**	**74.87**	**12.25**	....	**19.31**	**†8.73**
131 From foreign governments...........	9.18	†6.93	8.66	9.18	19.31	†8.66	—	—	—	....	19.31	†8.66
132 From international organizations...........	—	†—	—	—	—	†.06	—	—	—	....	—	†.06
133 From other general government units...........	—	†3.85	27.86	—	—	†14.86	73.90	74.87	12.25	....	—	†.01
14 **Other revenue...........**	**86.84**	**†100.04**	**111.97**	**88.46**	**106.69**	**†132.33**	**16.57**	**21.56**	**14.35**	....	**128.26**	**†146.68**

Mongolia 948

In Billions of Togrogs / Year Ending December 31 / Noncash Reporter

		Budgetary Central Government			Central Government			Local Government			General Government		
		2001	2002	2003p	2001	2002	2003p	2001	2002	2003p	2001	2002	2003p
Table 2	**Expense by economic type**												
2	**Expense**	229.10	†282.32	422.59	306.93	336.44	†449.96	150.82	156.35	42.99	....	402.93	†465.85
21	**Compensation of employees**	35.47	†55.23	132.43	35.47	47.81	†132.91	70.88	79.27	10.01	....	112.10	†142.92
211	Wages and salaries	35.47	†47.29	108.93	35.47	47.81	†109.33	70.88	64.29	8.01	....	112.10	†117.34
212	Social contributions	—	†7.94	23.50	—	—	†23.59	....	14.99	2.00	....	—	†25.58
22	**Use of goods and services**	84.77	†80.66	149.61	88.93	87.93	†161.47	77.76	76.00	16.77	....	163.93	†178.23
23	**Consumption of fixed capital**	....	....	....	....	....	....	....	....	....	....	....	....
24	**Interest**	16.45	†20.04	17.65	16.45	20.04	†17.65	.07	—	—	....	20.04	†17.65
25	**Subsidies**	5.45	†8.64	8.49	5.45	8.64	†8.49	....	.15	.89	....	8.79	†9.38
26	**Grants**	60.08	†94.49	85.49	69.59	75.49	†12.97	....	—	14.86	....	.62	†.73
261	To foreign governments	.69	†—	—	.69	—	†—	....	—	—	....	—	†—
262	To international organizations	—	†.62	.72	—	.62	†.72	....	—	—	....	.62	†.72
263	To other general government units	59.39	†93.88	84.78	68.90	74.87	†12.25	2.11	—	14.86	....	—	†.01
2631	Current	59.39	†93.88	41.68	68.90	74.87	†12.25	2.11	—	14.86	....	—	†.01
2632	Capital	—	†—	43.10	—	—	†—	—	—	—	....	—	†—
27	**Social benefits**	23.08	†17.35	28.93	87.23	90.62	†116.34	....	—	.47	....	90.62	†116.81
28	**Other expense**	3.80	†5.90	—	3.80	5.90	†.13	....	.92	—	....	6.82	†.13
281	Property expense other than interest	—	—	—	—	—	†—	....	—	—	....	—	†—
282	Miscellaneous other expense	3.80	†5.90	—	3.80	5.90	†.13	....	.92	—	....	6.82	†.13
2821	Current	—	†5.90	—	—	5.90	†.13	....	.92	—	....	6.82	†.13
2822	Capital	3.80	†—	—	3.80	—	†—	....	—	—	....	—	†—
Table 3	**Transactions in assets and liabilities**												
3	**Change in net worth from transactns**	....	....	....	....	....	....	....	....	....	....	....	....
31	**Net acquisition of nonfinancial assets**	31.76	†62.98	40.02	42.25	86.18	†133.71	7.17	13.47	5.30	....	99.65	†139.01
311	Fixed assets	27.79	†59.52	36.79	38.28	79.93	†94.84	....	13.42	5.30	....	93.35	†100.14
3111	Buildings and structures	....	†41.59	32.40	....	47.08	†91.72	....	7.43	5.05	....	54.51	†96.77
3112	Machinery and equipment	....	†11.15	2.95	....	25.97	†1.13	....	5.84	.25	....	31.81	†1.38
3113	Other fixed assets	....	†6.78	1.44	....	6.89	†1.99	....	.15	—	....	7.04	†1.99
312	Inventories	2.36	†.86	2.37	2.36	3.66	†38.01	....	.03	—	....	3.68	†38.01
313	Valuables	—	†.05	—	—	.05	†—	....	.02	—	....	.06	†—
314	Nonproduced assets	1.61	†2.55	.86	1.61	2.55	†.87	....	.01	—	....	2.55	†.87
3141	Land	....	†—		....	....		....	....		....	....	†—
3142	Subsoil assets	....	†1.30	—	....	1.30	†—	....	—	—	....	1.30	†—
3143	Other naturally occurring assets	....	†.56	.63	....	.56	†.63	....	.01	—	....	.57	†.63
3144	Intangible nonproduced assets	....	†.69	.23	....	.69	†.22	....	—	—	....	.69	†.22
32	**Net acquisition of financial assets**	55.10	†38.27	103.34	68.86	47.15	†53.60	2.29	−8.11	3.60	....	52.54	†54.86
321	Domestic	57.48	†38.83	111.15	71.24	47.50	†61.41	2.29	−8.11	3.60	....	52.89	†62.67
3212	Currency and deposits	−2.19	†−.48	33.10	11.57	17.36	†58.72	2.29	−1.21	1.68	....	16.15	†60.40
3213	Securities other than shares	....	†—	—	....	.23	†—	—	—	—	....	.23	†—
3214	Loans	....	†54.48	89.61	....	45.08	†19.59	—	−5.53	1.92	....	53.05	†19.17
3215	Shares and other equity	....	†−15.17	−11.56	....	−15.17	†−11.56	—	−1.37	—	....	−16.54	†−11.56
3216	Insurance technical reserves	—	†—	—	....	—	†—	—	—	—	....	—	†—
3217	Financial derivatives	—	†—	—	....	—	†—	—	—	—	....	—	†—
3218	Other accounts receivable	....	....	....	....	....	....	....	....	....	....	....	....
322	Foreign	−2.38	†−.56	−7.81	−2.38	−.35	†−7.81	—	—	—	....	−.35	†−7.81
3222	Currency and deposits	−2.38	†−.86	—	−2.38	−.65	†—	—	—	—	....	−.65	†—
3223	Securities other than shares	—	†—	—	—	—	†—	—	—	—	....	—	†—
3224	Loans	—	†—	—	—	—	†—	—	—	—	....	—	†—
3225	Shares and other equity	—	†.30	−7.81	—	.30	†−7.81	—	—	—	....	.30	†−7.81
3226	Insurance technical reserves	—	†—	—	—	—	†—	—	—	—	....	—	†—
3227	Financial derivatives	—	†—	—	—	—	†—	—	—	—	....	—	†—
3228	Other accounts receivable	....	....	....	....	....	....	....	....	....	....	....	....
323	Monetary gold and SDRs	—	†—	—	—	—	†—	....	....	....	....	....	....
33	**Net incurrence of liabilities**	55.02	†65.45	90.98	55.02	66.55	†65.13	—	−14.69	.42	....	65.36	†63.22
331	Domestic	−14.59	†−16.78	190.74	−14.59	−15.67	†164.89	—	−14.69	.42	....	−16.86	†162.98
3312	Currency and deposits	5.57	†—	—	5.57	—	†—	—	—	—	....	—	†—
3313	Securities other than shares	−20.16	†−13.93	19.55	−20.16	−13.93	†19.55	—	—	—	....	−13.93	†19.55
3314	Loans	—	†−2.84	171.19	—	−1.74	†136.47	—	−14.69	.42	....	−2.93	†134.55
3316	Insurance technical reserves	—	†—	—	—	—	†—	—	—	—	....	—	†—
3317	Financial derivatives	—	†—	—	—	—	†—	—	—	—	....	—	†—
3318	Other accounts payable	....	....	....	....	....	....	....	....	....	....	....	....

In Billions of Togrogs / Year Ending December 31 / Noncash Reporter

		Budgetary Central Government			Central Government			Local Government			General Government		
		2001	2002	2003p	2001	2002	2003p	2001	2002	2003p	2001	2002	2003p
332	Foreign..............................	69.61	†82.22	−99.76	69.61	82.22	†−99.76	—	—	—	....	82.22	†−99.76
3322	Currency and deposits.................		†—	—		—	†—	—	—	—	....	—	†—
3323	Securities other than shares............	—	†—	58.45	—	—	†58.45	—	—	—	....	—	†58.45
3324	Loans.................................	69.61	†82.22	−158.21	69.61	82.22	†−158.21	—	—	—	....	82.22	†−158.21
3326	Insurance technical reserves.........	—	†—	—	—	—	†—	—	—	—	....	—	†—
3327	Financial derivatives................	—	†—	—	—	—	†—	—	—	—	....	—	†—
3328	Other accounts payable................	....	....	....	....	....	....	....	....	....	....	....	....

Table 4 Holding gains in assets and liabilities

Table 5 Other changes in the volume of assets and liabilities

Table 6 Balance sheet

		Budgetary Central Government			Central Government			Local Government			General Government		
6	**Net worth**..........................	....	....	667.28	626.63	632.85	908.57	....	....	119.95	....	....	1,028.52
61	**Nonfinancial assets**...............	....	....	985.93	679.94	763.26	1,235.96	....	....	70.83	....	....	1,306.79
611	Fixed assets.........................	....	....	929.78	625.12	704.75	1,072.05	....	....	68.54	....	....	1,140.59
6111	Buildings and structures.............	....	....	613.52	385.28	432.36	752.79	....	....	36.00	....	....	788.79
6112	Machinery and equipment..........	....	....	283.17	195.27	221.24	284.99	....	....	24.17	....	....	309.16
6113	Other fixed assets...................	....	....	33.09	44.57	51.15	34.26	....	....	8.37	....	....	42.64
612	Inventories..........................	....	....	55.97	53.09	56.75	163.72	....	....	2.25	....	....	165.97
613	Valuables............................	....	....	—	1.72	1.77	—	....	....	—	....	....	—
614	Nonproduced assets..................	....	....	.18	—	—	.19	....	....	.03	....	....	.23
6141	Land.................................	....	....	—	—	—	—	....	....	—	....	....	—
6142	Subsoil assets.......................	....	....	—	—	—	—	....	....	—	....	....	—
6143	Other naturally occurring assets......	....	....	—	—	—	—	....	....	—	....	....	—
6144	Intangible nonproduced assets........	....	....	.18	—	—	.19	....	....	.03	....	....	.23
62	**Financial assets**...................	....	....	1,327.44	1,015.50	1,103.00	1,423.50	....	....	54.44	....	....	1,477.94
621	Domestic.............................	....	....	1,327.44	1,008.31	1,096.34	1,423.50	....	....	54.44	....	....	1,477.94
6212	Currency and deposits.................	....	....	88.71	43.42	60.78	158.88	....	....	4.09	....	....	162.96
6213	Securities other than shares..........	....	....	—	.77	1.01	—	....	....	—	....	....	—
6214	Loans.................................	....	....	928.08	402.19	486.63	928.08	....	....	3.30	....	....	931.38
6215	Shares and other equity..............	....	....	310.65	506.42	490.95	310.65	....	....	47.05	....	....	357.70
6216	Insurance technical reserves.........	....	....	—	—	—	—	....	....	—	....	....	—
6217	Financial derivatives................	....	....	—	—	—	—	....	....	—	....	....	—
6218	Other accounts receivable............	....	....	....	55.51	56.97	....	....	....	....	....	....	....
622	Foreign..............................	....	....	—	7.19	6.67	—	....	....	—	....	....	—
6222	Currency and deposits.................	....	....	—	4.67	4.10	—	....	....	—	....	....	—
6223	Securities other than shares..........	....	....	—	—	—	—	....	....	—	....	....	—
6224	Loans.................................	....	....	—	—	—	—	....	....	—	....	....	—
6225	Shares and other equity..............	....	....	—	2.51	2.57	—	....	....	—	....	....	—
6226	Insurance technical reserves.........	....	....	—	—	—	—	....	....	—	....	....	—
6227	Financial derivatives................	....	....	—	—	—	—	....	....	—	....	....	—
6228	Other accounts receivable............	....	....	—	—	—	—	....	....	—	....	....	—
623	Monetary gold and SDRs...............	....	....	—	—	—	—	....	....	—	....	....	—
63	**Liabilities**........................	....	....	1,646.09	1,068.81	1,233.41	1,750.89	17.49	....	5.32	....	....	1,756.21
631	Domestic.............................	....	....	210.60	187.55	174.92	315.40	17.49	....	5.32	....	....	320.72
6312	Currency and deposits.................	....	....	—	—	—	—	....	....	—	....	....	—
6313	Securities other than shares..........	....	....	50.39	77.40	63.47	50.39	....	....	—	....	....	50.39
6314	Loans.................................	....	....	160.22	92.38	93.84	244.55	....	....	5.32	....	....	249.88
6316	Insurance technical reserves.........	....	....	—	—	—	—	....	....	—	....	....	—
6317	Financial derivatives................	....	....	—	—	—	—	....	....	—	....	....	—
6318	Other accounts payable................	....	....	....	17.77	17.61	....	....	....	....	....	....	....
632	Foreign..............................	....	....	1,435.49	881.26	1,058.49	1,435.49	—	....	—	....	....	1,435.49
6322	Currency and deposits.................	....	....	—	—	—	—	....	....	—	....	....	—
6323	Securities other than shares..........	....	....	58.45	—	—	58.45	—	....	—	....	....	58.45
6324	Loans.................................	....	....	1,377.04	881.26	1,058.49	1,377.04	—	....	—	....	....	1,377.04
6326	Insurance technical reserves.........	....	....	—	—	—	—	....	....	—	....	....	—
6327	Financial derivatives................	....	....	—	—	—	—	....	....	—	....	....	—
6328	Other accounts payable................	....	....	....	—	—	....	....	....	—	....	....	....

Mongolia   948

In Billions of Togrogs / Year Ending December 31 / Noncash Reporter

	Budgetary Central Government			Central Government			Local Government			General Government		
	2001	2002	2003p	2001	2002	2003p	2001	2002	2003p	2001	2002	2003p
Memorandum items:												
6M2 Net financial worth	....	....	–318.65	–53.51	–130.41	–327.39	....	....	49.12	....	....	–278.28
6M3 Debt at market value	....	....	....	....	....	....	....	....	....	....	....	....
6M4 Debt at nominal value	....	....	....	....	....	....	....	....	....	....	....	....
6M5 Arrears	....	....	....	....	....	....	....	....	....	....	....	....
6M6 Obligations for social security benefits	....	....	....	....	....	....	....	....	....	....	....	....
6M7 Contingent liabilities	....	....	....	....	....	....	....	....	....	....	....	....
6M8 Uncapitalized military weapons, systems	....	....	....	....	....	....	....	....	....	....	....	....
Table 7 Outlays by functions of govt.												
7 **Total outlays**	**265.26**	**†345.30**	**462.61**	**353.58**	**422.62**	**†583.67**	**159.34**	**169.82**	**48.29**	....	**502.59**	**†604.87**
701 **General public services**	**118.44**	**†157.29**	....	**118.44**	**137.03**	....	**27.57**	**28.44**	....	....	**88.94**	....
7017 Public debt transactions	16.45	†20.04	17.65	16.45	20.04	17.65	.07	—	—	....	20.04	17.65
7018 General transfers between levels of govt.	....	†93.88	....	....	74.87	....	....	—	....	....	—	....
702 **Defense**	**25.38**	**†26.49**	....	**25.38**	**24.91**	....	**—**	**—**	....	....	**24.91**	....
703 **Public order and safety**	**15.40**	**†16.18**	....	**15.40**	**16.69**	....	**13.35**	**13.55**	....	....	**29.76**	....
704 **Economic affairs**	**39.01**	**†65.79**	....	**49.50**	**89.61**	....	**5.57**	**6.88**	....	....	**95.88**	....
7042 Agriculture, forestry, fishing, and hunting	10.37	†12.15	....	10.37	13.68	....	1.29	1.49	....	....	15.07	....
7043 Fuel and energy	11.07	†14.86	....	11.07	17.17	....	.14	.12	....	....	17.28	....
7044 Mining, manufacturing, and construction	2.11	†3.69	....	2.11	3.57	....	—	....	....	....	3.57	....
7045 Transport	12.19	†30.92	....	22.69	30.87	....	.56	.91	....	....	31.78	....
7046 Communication	....	†.15	....	....	20.40	....	....	....	....	....	20.40	....
705 **Environmental protection**	....	**†1.60**	....	....	**1.47**	....	....	**—**	....	....	**1.47**	....
706 **Housing and community amenities**	**1.80**	**†1.08**	....	**1.80**	**1.08**	....	**5.28**	**6.49**	....	....	**7.57**	....
707 **Health**	**19.31**	**†18.41**	....	**30.19**	**19.70**	....	**33.78**	**35.87**	....	....	**52.54**	....
7072 Outpatient services	....	†14.27	....	—	15.86	....	....	35.87	....	....	48.70	....
7073 Hospital services	15.61	†—	....	16.07	—	....	....	—	....	....	—	....
7074 Public health services	....	†4.14	....	....	3.84	....	....	....	....	....	3.84	....
708 **Recreation, culture, and religion**	**8.67**	**†9.65**	....	**8.67**	**9.10**	....	**6.38**	**7.31**	....	....	**15.88**	....
709 **Education**	**27.18**	**†28.52**	....	**27.18**	**26.61**	....	**66.52**	**70.22**	....	....	**88.23**	....
7091 Pre-primary and primary education	....	†6.03	....	....	5.63	....	....	70.22	....	....	67.25	....
7092 Secondary education	3.84	†16.21	....	3.84	15.12	....	....	—	....	....	15.12	....
7094 Tertiary education	14.04	†6.28	....	14.04	5.86	....	....	—	....	....	5.86	....
710 **Social protection**	**17.15**	**†20.28**	....	**84.09**	**96.41**	....	**.88**	**1.07**	....	....	**97.40**	....
7 Statistical discrepancy: Total outlays	—	—	....	—	—	....	—	—	....	....	—	....
Table 8 Transactions in financial assets and liabilities by sector												
82 **Net acquisition of financial assets**	**55.10**	**†38.27**	**103.34**	**68.86**	**47.15**	**†53.60**	**2.29**	**–8.11**	**3.60**	....	**52.54**	**†54.86**
821 Domestic	57.48	†38.83	111.15	71.24	47.50	†61.41	2.29	–8.11	3.60	....	52.89	†62.67
8211 General government	—	†–2.73	35.14	—	–22.37	†–34.88	—	—	1.92	....	–8.87	†–35.30
8212 Central bank	....	†—	39.11	....	—	†56.89	....	—	1.68	....	—	†58.57
8213 Other depository corporations	....	†–15.64	12.52	....	2.19	†20.37	....	–1.21	—	....	.99	†20.37
8214 Financial corporations n.e.c.	....	†—	—	....	—	†—	....	....	—	....	—	†—
8215 Nonfinancial corporations	56.56	†57.21	21.14	56.56	67.68	†15.81	....	–6.90	—	....	60.77	†15.81
8216 Households & NPIs serving households	....	†—	3.23	....	—	†3.23	....	....	—	....	—	†3.23
822 Foreign	–2.38	†–.56	–7.81	–2.38	–.35	†–7.81	—	—	—	....	–.35	†–7.81
8221 General government	....	†—	—	....	—	†—	—	—	—	....	—	†—
8227 International organizations	....	†.30	—	....	.30	†—	—	—	—	....	.30	†—
8228 Financial corporations other than international organizations	....	†–.86	–7.81	....	–.65	†–7.81	—	—	—	....	–.65	†–7.81
8229 Other nonresidents	....	†—		....	—	†—	—	—	—	....	—	†—
823 Monetary gold and SDRs	—	†—	—	—	—	†—	—	—	—	....	—	†—
83 **Net incurrence of liabilities**	**55.02**	**†65.45**	**90.98**	**55.02**	**66.55**	**†65.13**	**—**	**–14.69**	**.42**	....	**65.36**	**†63.22**
831 Domestic	–14.59	†–16.78	190.74	–14.59	–15.67	†164.89	—	–14.69	.42	....	–16.86	†162.98
8311 General government	....	†—	1.92	....	—	†–32.81	—	–13.50	.42	....	—	†–34.73
8312 Central bank	....	†–2.18	169.28	....	–2.18	†169.28	—	—	—	....	–2.18	†169.28
8313 Other depository corporations	....	†–13.34	19.55	....	–13.34	†19.55	—	—	—	....	–13.34	†19.55
8314 Financial corporations n.e.c.	....	†—	—	....	—	†—	....	....	—	....	—	†—
8315 Nonfinancial corporations	....	†–1.26	—	....	–.15	†8.88	—	–1.19	—	....	–1.34	†8.88
8316 Households & NPIs serving households	....	†—	—	....	—	†—	—	—	—	....	—	†—
832 Foreign	69.61	†82.22	–99.76	69.61	82.22	†–99.76	—	—	—	....	82.22	†–99.76
8321 General government	4.65	†35.35	—	4.65	35.35	†—	—	—	—	....	35.35	†—
8327 International organizations	64.96	†46.87	—	64.96	46.87	†—	—	—	—	....	46.87	†—
8328 Financial corporations other than international organizations	—	†—	—	—	—	†—	—	—	—	....	—	†—
8329 Other nonresidents	—	†—	–99.76	—	—	†–99.76	—	—	—	....	—	†–99.76

In Millions of Dirhams / Year Ending December 31 / Cash Reporter

	Budgetary Central Government			Central Government			Local Government			General Government		
	1997	1998	1999	1997	1998	1999	1997	1998	1999	1997	1998	1999
Statement of government operations												
Statement of other economic flows												
Balance sheet												
6 *Net worth*.................	....	....	....	....	....	....	....	....	....	....	....	....
61 Nonfinancial assets.................	....	....	....	....	....	....	....	....	....	....	....	....
62 Financial assets.................	....	....	....	....	....	....	....	....	....	....	....	....
63 Liabilities.................	240,420	245,676	251,507	240,420	245,676	251,507	....	....	....	....	....	....
Statement of sources and uses of cash												
1 Cash receipts from operating activities........	82,347	87,052	93,474	89,777	95,436	102,436	....	....	....	....	....	....
11 Taxes.................	72,375	76,953	81,118	72,375	76,953	81,118	....	....	....	....	....	....
12 Social contributions.................	—	—	—	7,430	8,384	8,962	....	....	....	....	....	....
13 Grants.................	—	—	—	—	—	—	....	....	....	....	....	....
14 Other receipts.................	9,972	10,099	12,356	9,972	10,099	12,356	....	....	....	....	....	....
2 Cash payments for operating activities........	78,974	85,087	89,230	86,608	93,694	98,559	....	....	....	....	....	....
21 Compensation of employees.................	34,813	37,883	40,486	34,813	37,883	40,486	....	....	....	....	....	....
22 Purchases of goods and services.................	10,644	13,382	11,630	10,644	13,382	11,630	....	....	....	....	....	....
24 Interest.................	16,667	16,680	16,904	16,667	16,680	16,904	....	....	....	....	....	....
25 Subsidies.................	2,095	2,322	3,606	2,095	2,322	3,606	....	....	....	....	....	....
26 Grants.................	5,074	5,354	6,721	5,074	5,354	6,721	....	....	....	....	....	....
27 Social benefits.................	5,358	6,017	5,435	12,992	14,624	14,764	....	....	....	....	....	....
28 Other payments.................	4,323	3,449	4,448	4,323	3,449	4,448	....	....	....	....	....	....
CIO *Net cash inflow from oper. activities.....*	*3,191*	*3,462*	*4,919*	*3,169*	*1,742*	*3,877*	....	....	....	....	....	....
31.1 Purchases of nonfinancial assets.................	10,668	13,183	13,929	10,668	13,183	13,929	....	....	....	....	....	....
31.2 Sales of nonfinancial assets.................	5,338	1,891	785	5,338	1,891	785	....	....	....	....	....	....
31 Net cash outflow from investments in nonfinancial assets.................	5,330	11,292	13,144	5,330	11,292	13,144	....	....	....	....	....	....
CSD *Cash surplus/deficit.................*	*−2,139*	*−7,830*	*−8,225*	*−2,161*	*−9,550*	*−9,267*	....	....	....	....	....	....
32x Net acquisition of fin assets, excl. cash........	40	−2,221	−762	40	−2,221	−762	....	....	....	....	....	....
321x Domestic.................	40	−2,221	−762	40	−2,221	−762	....	....	....	....	....	....
322x Foreign.................	—	—	—	—	—	—	....	....	....	....	....	....
323 Monetary gold and SDRs.................	—	—	—	—	—	—	....	....	....	....	....	....
33 Net incurrence of liabilities.................	−1,331	151	3,059	−1,331	151	3,059	....	....	....	....	....	....
331 Domestic.................	3,301	6,333	8,250	3,301	6,333	8,250	....	....	....	....	....	....
332 Foreign.................	−4,632	−6,182	−5,191	−4,632	−6,182	−5,191	....	....	....	....	....	....
NFB Net cash inflow from fin. activities.................	−1,371	2,372	3,821	−1,371	2,372	3,821	....	....	....	....	....	....
NCB *Net change in the stock of cash.............*	*−3,510*	*−5,458*	*−4,404*	*−3,532*	*−7,178*	*−5,446*	....	....	....	....	....	....
Table 1 Revenue												
1 **Revenue.................**	**82,347**	**87,052**	**93,474**	**89,777**	**95,436**	**102,436**	....	....	....	....	....	....
11 **Taxes.................**	**72,375**	**76,953**	**81,118**	**72,375**	**76,953**	**81,118**	....	....	....	....	....	....
111 Taxes on income, profits, & capital gains.....	19,785	21,285	24,625	19,785	21,285	24,625	....	....	....	....	....	....
1111 Individuals.................	9,380	10,252	11,432	9,380	10,252	11,432	....	....	....	....	....	....
1112 Corporations and other enterprises............	7,327	7,523	9,484	7,327	7,523	9,484	....	....	....	....	....	....
112 Taxes on payroll and workforce.................	—	—	—	—	—	—	....	....	....	....	....	....
113 Taxes on property.................	1,748	1,806	1,964	1,748	1,806	1,964	....	....	....	....	....	....
114 Taxes on goods and services.................	35,739	37,506	37,177	35,739	37,506	37,177	....	....	....	....	....	....
1141 General taxes on goods and services..........	18,083	19,699	19,144	18,083	19,699	19,144	....	....	....	....	....	....
1142 Excises.................	14,390	14,796	15,071	14,390	14,796	15,071	....	....	....	....	....	....
115 Taxes on int'l. trade and transactions..........	14,239	15,438	16,293	14,239	15,438	16,293	....	....	....	....	....	....
116 Other taxes.................	864	918	1,059	864	918	1,059	....	....	....	....	....	....
12 **Social contributions.................**	**—**	**—**	**—**	**7,430**	**8,384**	**8,962**	....	....	....	....	....	....
121 Social security contributions.................	—	—	—	4,920	5,127	5,322	....	....	....	....	....	....
122 Other social contributions.................	—	—	—	2,510	3,257	3,640	....	....	....	....	....	....
13 **Grants.................**	**—**	**—**	**—**	**—**	**—**	**—**	....	....	....	....	....	....
131 From foreign governments.................	—	—	—	—	—	—	....	....	....	....	....	....
132 From international organizations.................	—	—	—	—	—	—	....	....	....	....	....	....
133 From other general government units..........	—	—	—	—	—	—	....	....	....	....	....	....
14 **Other revenue.................**	**9,972**	**10,099**	**12,356**	**9,972**	**10,099**	**12,356**	....	....	....	....	....	....
Table 2 Expense by economic type												
2 **Expense.................**	**78,974**	**85,087**	**89,230**	**86,608**	**93,694**	**98,559**	....	....	....	....	....	....
21 **Compensation of employees.................**	**34,813**	**37,883**	**40,486**	**34,813**	**37,883**	**40,486**	....	....	....	....	....	....
211 Wages and salaries.................	34,813	37,883	40,486	34,813	37,883	40,486	....	....	....	....	....	....
212 Social contributions.................	—	—	—	—	—	—	....	....	....	....	....	....
22 **Use of goods and services.................**	**10,644**	**13,382**	**11,630**	**10,644**	**13,382**	**11,630**	....	....	....	....	....	....
23 **Consumption of fixed capital.................**	....	....	....	....	....	....	....	....	....	....	....	....
24 **Interest.................**	**16,667**	**16,680**	**16,904**	**16,667**	**16,680**	**16,904**	....	....	....	....	....	....
25 **Subsidies.................**	**2,095**	**2,322**	**3,606**	**2,095**	**2,322**	**3,606**	....	....	....	....	....	....

In Millions of Dirhams / Year Ending December 31 / Cash Reporter

		Budgetary Central Government			Central Government			Local Government			General Government		
		1997	1998	1999	1997	1998	1999	1997	1998	1999	1997	1998	1999
26	Grants....................	5,074	5,354	6,721	5,074	5,354	6,721	....	....	....	....	....	....
261	To foreign govenments............	—	—	—	—	—	—	....	....	....	....	....	....
262	To international organizations........	—	—	—	—	—	—	....	....	....	....	....	....
263	To other general government units........	5,074	5,354	6,721	5,074	5,354	6,721	....	....	....	....	....	....
2631	Current............	—	—	—	—	—	—	....	....	....	....	....	....
2632	Capital............	5,074	5,354	6,721	5,074	5,354	6,721	....	....	....	....	....	....
27	Social benefits................	5,358	6,017	5,435	12,992	14,624	14,764	....	....	....	....	....	....
28	Other expense................	4,323	3,449	4,448	4,323	3,449	4,448	....	....	....	....	....	....
281	Property expense other than interest........	—	—	—	—	—	—	....	....	....	....	....	....
282	Miscellaneous other expense........	4,323	3,449	4,448	4,323	3,449	4,448	....	....	....	....	....	....
2821	Current............	—	—	—	—	—	—	....	....	....	....	....	....
2822	Capital............	4,323	3,449	4,448	4,323	3,449	4,448	....	....	....	....	....	....
Table 3	**Transactions in assets and liabilities**												
3	Change in net worth from transactns....	....	....	....	....	....	....	....	....	....	....	....	....
31	Net acquisition of nonfinancial assets...	5,330	11,292	13,144	5,330	11,292	13,144	....	....	....	....	....	....
311	Fixed assets........	5,459	11,521	12,838	5,459	11,521	12,838	....	....	....	....	....	....
3111	Buildings and structures........	....	....	....	....	....	....	....	....	....	....	....	....
3112	Machinery and equipment........	....	....	....	....	....	....	....	....	....	....	....	....
3113	Other fixed assets........	....	....	....	....	....	....	....	....	....	....	....	....
312	Inventories........	—	—	—	—	—	—	....	....	....	....	....	....
313	Valuables........	—	—	—	—	—	—	....	....	....	....	....	....
314	Nonproduced assets........	−129	−229	306	−129	−229	306	....	....	....	....	....	....
3141	Land........	....	....	....	....	....	....	....	....	....	....	....	....
3142	Subsoil assets........	....	....	....	....	....	....	....	....	....	....	....	....
3143	Other naturally occurring assets........	....	....	....	....	....	....	....	....	....	....	....	....
3144	Intangible nonproduced assets........	....	....	....	....	....	....	....	....	....	....	....	....
32	Net acquisition of financial assets........	−3,470	−7,679	−5,166	−3,492	−9,399	−6,208	....	....	....	....	....	....
321	Domestic........	−3,470	−7,679	−5,166	−3,492	−9,399	−6,208	....	....	....	....	....	....
3212	Currency and deposits........	−3,510	−5,458	−4,404	−3,532	−7,178	−5,446	....	....	....	....	....	....
3213	Securities other than shares........	....	....	....	....	....	....	....	....	....	....	....	....
3214	Loans........	....	....	....	....	....	....	....	....	....	....	....	....
3215	Shares and other equity........	....	....	....	....	....	....	....	....	....	....	....	....
3216	Insurance technical reserves........	....	....	....	....	....	....	....	....	....	....	....	....
3217	Financial derivatives........	....	....	....	....	....	....	....	....	....	....	....	....
3218	Other accounts receivable........	....	....	....	....	....	....	....	....	....	....	....	....
322	Foreign........	—	—	—	—	—	—	....	....	....	....	....	....
3222	Currency and deposits........	—	—	—	—	—	—	....	....	....	....	....	....
3223	Securities other than shares........	—	—	—	—	—	—	....	....	....	....	....	....
3224	Loans........	—	—	—	—	—	—	....	....	....	....	....	....
3225	Shares and other equity........	—	—	—	—	—	—	....	....	....	....	....	....
3226	Insurance technical reserves........	—	—	—	—	—	—	....	....	....	....	....	....
3227	Financial derivatives........	—	—	—	—	—	—	....	....	....	....	....	....
3228	Other accounts receivable........	....	....	....	....	....	....	....	....	....	....	....	....
323	Monetary gold and SDRs........							....	....	....	....	....	....
33	Net incurrence of liabilities................	−1,331	151	3,059	−1,331	151	3,059	....	....	....	....	....	....
331	Domestic........	3,301	6,333	8,250	3,301	6,333	8,250	....	....	....	....	....	....
3312	Currency and deposits........	−57	−900	−5,738	−57	−900	−5,738	....	....	....	....	....	....
3313	Securities other than shares........	6,541	7,457	13,511	6,541	7,457	13,511	....	....	....	....	....	....
3314	Loans........	−3,183	−224	477	−3,183	−224	477	....	....	....	....	....	....
3316	Insurance technical reserves........	—	—	—	—	—	—	....	....	....	....	....	....
3317	Financial derivatives........	—	—	—	—	—	—	....	....	....	....	....	....
3318	Other accounts payable........	....	....	....	....	....	....	....	....	....	....	....	....
332	Foreign........	−4,632	−6,182	−5,191	−4,632	−6,182	−5,191	....	....	....	....	....	....
3322	Currency and deposits........	—	—	—	—	—	—	....	....	....	....	....	....
3323	Securities other than shares........	−4,632	−6,182	−5,191	−4,632	−6,182	−5,191	....	....	....	....	....	....
3324	Loans........	—	—	—	—	—	—	....	....	....	....	....	....
3326	Insurance technical reserves........	—	—	—	—	—	—	....	....	....	....	....	....
3327	Financial derivatives........	—	—	—	—	—	—	....	....	....	....	....	....
3328	Other accounts payable........	....	....	....	....	....	....	....	....	....	....	....	....

Morocco   686

In Millions of Dirhams / Year Ending December 31 / Cash Reporter

		Budgetary Central Government			Central Government			Local Government			General Government		
		1997	1998	1999	1997	1998	1999	1997	1998	1999	1997	1998	1999
Table 4	**Holding gains in assets and liabilities**												
Table 5	**Other changes in the volume of assets and liabilities**												
Table 6	**Balance sheet**												
6	Net worth	....	....	....	....	....	....	....	....	....	....	....	....
61	Nonfinancial assets	....	....	....	....	....	....	....	....	....	....	....	....
611	Fixed assets	....	....	....	....	....	....	....	....	....	....	....	....
6111	Buildings and structures	....	....	....	....	....	....	....	....	....	....	....	....
6112	Machinery and equipment	....	....	....	....	....	....	....	....	....	....	....	....
6113	Other fixed assets	....	....	....	....	....	....	....	....	....	....	....	....
612	Inventories	....	....	....	....	....	....	....	....	....	....	....	....
613	Valuables	....	....	....	....	....	....	....	....	....	....	....	....
614	Nonproduced assets	....	....	....	....	....	....	....	....	....	....	....	....
6141	Land	....	....	....	....	....	....	....	....	....	....	....	....
6142	Subsoil assets	....	....	....	....	....	....	....	....	....	....	....	....
6143	Other naturally occurring assets	....	....	....	....	....	....	....	....	....	....	....	....
6144	Intangible nonproduced assets	....	....	....	....	....	....	....	....	....	....	....	....
62	Financial assets	....	....	....	....	....	....	....	....	....	....	....	....
621	Domestic	....	....	....	....	....	....	....	....	....	....	....	....
6212	Currency and deposits	....	....	....	....	....	....	....	....	....	....	....	....
6213	Securities other than shares	....	....	....	....	....	....	....	....	....	....	....	....
6214	Loans	....	....	....	....	....	....	....	....	....	....	....	....
6215	Shares and other equity	....	....	....	....	....	....	....	....	....	....	....	....
6216	Insurance technical reserves	....	....	....	....	....	....	....	....	....	....	....	....
6217	Financial derivatives	....	....	....	....	....	....	....	....	....	....	....	....
6218	Other accounts receivable	....	....	....	....	....	....	....	....	....	....	....	....
622	Foreign	....	....	....	....	....	....	....	....	....	....	....	....
6222	Currency and deposits	....	....	....	....	....	....	....	....	....	....	....	....
6223	Securities other than shares	....	....	....	....	....	....	....	....	....	....	....	....
6224	Loans	....	....	....	....	....	....	....	....	....	....	....	....
6225	Shares and other equity	....	....	....	....	....	....	....	....	....	....	....	....
6226	Insurance technical reserves	....	....	....	....	....	....	....	....	....	....	....	....
6227	Financial derivatives	....	....	....	....	....	....	....	....	....	....	....	....
6228	Other accounts receivable	....	....	....	....	....	....	....	....	....	....	....	....
623	Monetary gold and SDRs	....	....	....	....	....	....	....	....	....	....	....	....
63	**Liabilities**	240,420	245,676	251,507	240,420	245,676	251,507	....	....	....	....	....	....
631	Domestic	106,192	115,364	124,297	106,192	115,364	124,297	....	....	....	....	....	....
6312	Currency and deposits	....	....	....	....	....	....	....	....	....	....	....	....
6313	Securities other than shares	....	....	....	....	....	....	....	....	....	....	....	....
6314	Loans	....	....	....	....	....	....	....	....	....	....	....	....
6316	Insurance technical reserves	....	....	....	....	....	....	....	....	....	....	....	....
6317	Financial derivatives	....	....	....	....	....	....	....	....	....	....	....	....
6318	Other accounts payable	....	....	....	....	....	....	....	....	....	....	....	....
632	Foreign	134,228	130,312	127,210	134,228	130,312	127,210	....	....	....	....	....	....
6322	Currency and deposits	....	....	....	....	....	....	....	....	....	....	....	....
6323	Securities other than shares	....	....	....	....	....	....	....	....	....	....	....	....
6324	Loans	....	....	....	....	....	....	....	....	....	....	....	....
6326	Insurance technical reserves	....	....	....	....	....	....	....	....	....	....	....	....
6327	Financial derivatives	....	....	....	....	....	....	....	....	....	....	....	....
6328	Other accounts payable	....	....	....	....	....	....	....	....	....	....	....	....
Memorandum items:													
6M2	Net financial worth	....	....	....	....	....	....	....	....	....	....	....	....
6M3	Debt at market value	....	....	....	....	....	....	....	....	....	....	....	....
6M4	Debt at nominal value	....	....	....	....	....	....	....	....	....	....	....	....
6M5	Arrears	....	....	....	....	....	....	....	....	....	....	....	....
6M6	Obligations for social security benefits	....	....	....	....	....	....	....	....	....	....	....	....
6M7	Contingent liabilities	....	....	....	....	....	....	....	....	....	....	....	....
6M8	Uncapitalized military weapons, systems	....	....	....	....	....	....	....	....	....	....	....	....
Table 7	**Outlays by functions of govt.**												
7	**Total outlays**	89,642	98,270	103,159	97,276	106,877	112,488	....	....	....	....	....	....
701	**General public services**	41,299	41,616	45,563	41,299	41,616	45,563	....	....	....	....	....	....
7017	Public debt transactions	16,667	16,680	16,904	16,667	16,680	16,904						
7018	General transfers between levels of govt	....	....	....	....	....	....						
702	**Defense**	11,328	15,618	14,530	11,328	15,618	14,530	....	....	....	....	....	....
703	**Public order and safety**	6,867	7,567	7,817	6,867	7,567	7,817	....	....	....	....	....	....

In Millions of Dirhams / Year Ending December 31 / Cash Reporter

	Budgetary Central Government			Central Government			Local Government			General Government		
	1997	1998	1999	1997	1998	1999	1997	1998	1999	1997	1998	1999
704 **Economic affairs**.....................	9,266	9,951	9,070	9,266	9,951	9,070	....	....	....	....	....	....
7042 Agriculture, forestry, fishing, and hunting.....	4,234	4,730	4,016	4,234	4,730	4,016	....	....	....	....	....	....
7043 Fuel and energy.........................	444	413	441	444	413	441	....	....	....	....	....	....
7044 Mining, manufacturing, and construction.....	—	—	—	—	—	—	....	....	....	....	....	....
7045 Transport.................................	3,598	3,665	3,882	3,598	3,665	3,882	....	....	....	....	....	....
7046 Communication.........................	....	....	....	....	....	....	....	....	....	....	....	....
705 **Environmental protection**....................	—	—	—				....	....	....	....	....	....
706 **Housing and community amenities**.......	383	265	505	383	265	505	....	....	....	....	....	....
707 **Health**...	2,925	3,407	3,627	2,925	3,407	3,627	....	....	....	....	....	....
7072 Outpatient services...........................	....	....	....	....	....	....	....	....	....	....	....	....
7073 Hospital services...............................	....	....	....	....	....	....	....	....	....	....	....	....
7074 Public health services........................	....	....	....	....	....	....	....	....	....	....	....	....
708 **Recreation, culture, and religion**...........	800	850	913	800	850	913	....	....	....	....	....	....
709 **Education**..	16,266	18,419	20,003	16,266	18,419	20,003	....	....	....	....	....	....
7091 Pre-primary and primary education.............	....	....	....	....	....	....	....	....	....	....	....	....
7092 Secondary education...........................	....	....	....	....	....	....	....	....	....	....	....	....
7094 Tertiary education..............................	....	....	....	....	....	....	....	....	....	....	....	....
710 **Social protection**.............................	508	577	1,131	8,142	9,184	10,460	....	....	....	....	....	....
7 Statistical discrepancy: Total outlays..............	—	—	—	—	—	—	....	....	....	....	....	....

Table 8   Transactions in financial assets and liabilities by sector

	Budgetary Central Government			Central Government			Local Government			General Government		
82 **Net acquisition of financial assets**........	−3,470	−7,679	−5,166	−3,492	−9,399	−6,208	....	....	....	....	....	....
821 Domestic.................................	−3,470	−7,679	−5,166	−3,492	−9,399	−6,208	....	....	....	....	....	....
8211 General government...........................	....	....	....	....	....	....	....	....	....	....	....	....
8212 Central bank................................	....	....	....	....	....	....	....	....	....	....	....	....
8213 Other depository corporations...................	....	....	....	....	....	....	....	....	....	....	....	....
8214 Financial corporations n.e.c.................	....	....	....	....	....	....	....	....	....	....	....	....
8215 Nonfinancial corporations.........................	....	....	....	....	....	....	....	....	....	....	....	....
8216 Households & NPIs serving households......	....	....	....	....	....	....	....	....	....	....	....	....
822 Foreign...................................	—	—	—	—	—	—	....	....	....	....	....	....
8221 General government...........................	—	—	—	—	—	—	....	....	....	....	....	....
8227 International organizations....................	—	—	—	—	—	—	....	....	....	....	....	....
8228 Financial corporations other than international organizations..............	—	—	—	—	—	—						
8229 Other nonresidents...........................	—	—	—	—	—	—	....	....	....	....	....	....
823 Monetary gold and SDRs.........................	—	—	—	—	—	—	....	....	....	....	....	....
83 **Net incurrence of liabilities**..................	−1,331	151	3,059	−1,331	151	3,059	....	....	....	....	....	....
831 Domestic.................................	3,301	6,333	8,250	3,301	6,333	8,250	....	....	....	....	....	....
8311 General government...........................	....	....	....	....	....	....	....	....	....	....	....	....
8312 Central bank................................	....	....	....	....	....	....	....	....	....	....	....	....
8313 Other depository corporations...................	....	....	....	....	....	....	....	....	....	....	....	....
8314 Financial corporations n.e.c.................	....	....	....	....	....	....	....	....	....	....	....	....
8315 Nonfinancial corporations.........................	....	....	....	....	....	....	....	....	....	....	....	....
8316 Households & NPIs serving households......	....	....	....	....	....	....	....	....	....	....	....	....
832 Foreign...................................	−4,632	−6,182	−5,191	−4,632	−6,182	−5,191	....	....	....	....	....	....
8321 General government...........................	−4,812	−7,100	−7,109	−4,812	−7,100	−7,109	....	....	....	....	....	....
8327 International organizations....................	180	918	1,918	180	918	1,918	....	....	....	....	....	....
8328 Financial corporations other than international organizations..............	—	—	—	—	—	—						
8329 Other nonresidents...........................	—	—	—	—	—	—	....	....	....	....	....	....

Myanmar 518

In Millions of Kyats / Year Beginning April 1 / Cash Reporter

		Budgetary Central Government			Central Government			Local Government			General Government		
		2000	2001	2002	2000	2001	2002	2000	2001	2002	2000	2001	2002
Statement of government operations													
Statement of other economic flows													
Balance sheet													
Statement of sources and uses of cash													
1	Cash receipts from operating activities........	....	....	....	134,293	162,534	279,377	....	....	....	....	....	....
11	Taxes........	....	....	....	75,727	80,094	112,564	....	....	....	....	....	....
12	Social contributions........	....	....	....	—	—	—	....	....	....	....	....	....
13	Grants........	....	....	....	242	288	358	....	....	....	....	....	....
14	Other receipts........	....	....	....	58,324	82,152	166,455	....	....	....	....	....	....
2	Cash payments for operating activities........	....	....	....	....	....	....	....	....	....	....	....	....
21	Compensation of employees........	....	....	....	....	....	....	....	....	....	....	....	....
22	Purchases of goods and services........	....	....	....	....	....	....	....	....	....	....	....	....
24	Interest........	....	....	....	....	....	....	....	....	....	....	....	....
25	Subsidies........	....	....	....	....	....	....	....	....	....	....	....	....
26	Grants........	....	....	....	....	....	....	....	....	....	....	....	....
27	Social benefits........	....	....	....	....	....	....	....	....	....	....	....	....
28	Other payments........	....	....	....	....	....	....	....	....	....	....	....	....
CIO	*Net cash inflow from oper. activities.....*	....	....	....	....	....	....	....	....	....	....	....	....
31.1	Purchases of nonfinancial assets........	....	....	....	....	....	....	....	....	....	....	....	....
31.2	Sales of nonfinancial assets........	....	....	....	257	2,242	632	....	....	....	....	....	....
31	Net cash outflow from investments in nonfinancial assets........	....	....	....	....	....	....	....	....	....	....	....	....
CSD	*Cash surplus/deficit........*	....	....	....	*−86,705*	*−106,595*	*−73,380*	....	....	....	....	....	....
32x	Net acquisition of fin assets, excl. cash........	....	....	....	−127	−696	−704	....	....	....	....	....	....
321x	Domestic........	....	....	....	....	....	....	....	....	....	....	....	....
322x	Foreign........	....	....	....	....	....	....	....	....	....	....	....	....
323	Monetary gold and SDRs........	....	....	....	....	....	....	....	....	....	....	....	....
33	Net incurrence of liabilities........	....	....	....	....	....	....	....	....	....	....	....	....
331	Domestic........	....	....	....	....	....	....	....	....	....	....	....	....
332	Foreign........	....	....	....	....	....	....	....	....	....	....	....	....
NFB	Net cash inflow from fin. activities........	....	....	....	....	....	....	....	....	....	....	....	....
NCB	*Net change in the stock of cash........*	....	....	....	....	....	....	....	....	....	....	....	....
Table 1 Revenue													
1	**Revenue........**	....	....	....	**134,293**	**162,534**	**279,377**	....	....	....	....	....	....
11	**Taxes........**	....	....	....	**75,727**	**80,094**	**112,564**	....	....	....	....	....	....
111	Taxes on income, profits, & capital gains......	....	....	....	26,140	28,287	45,589	....	....	....	....	....	....
1111	Individuals........	....	....	....	26,140	28,287	45,589	....	....	....	....	....	....
1112	Corporations and other enterprises........	....	....	....	—	—	—	....	....	....	....	....	....
112	Taxes on payroll and workforce........	....	....	....	—	—	—	....	....	....	....	....	....
113	Taxes on property........	....	....	....	—	—	—	....	....	....	....	....	....
114	Taxes on goods and services........	....	....	....	44,101	45,506	61,680	....	....	....	....	....	....
1141	General taxes on goods and services........	....	....	....	32,961	32,460	46,782	....	....	....	....	....	....
1142	Excises........	....	....	....	285	291	345	....	....	....	....	....	....
115	Taxes on int'l. trade and transactions........	....	....	....	5,486	6,301	5,295	....	....	....	....	....	....
116	Other taxes........	....	....	....	—	—	—	....	....	....	....	....	....
12	**Social contributions........**	....	....	....	—	—	—	....	....	....	....	....	....
121	Social security contributions........	....	....	....	—	—	—	....	....	....	....	....	....
122	Other social contributions........	....	....	....	—	—	—	....	....	....	....	....	....
13	**Grants........**	....	....	....	**242**	**288**	**358**	....	....	....	....	....	....
131	From foreign governments........	....	....	....	242	288	358	....	....	....	....	....	....
132	From international organizations........	....	....	....	—	—	—	....	....	....	....	....	....
133	From other general government units........	....	....	....	—	—	—	....	....	....	....	....	....
14	**Other revenue........**	....	....	....	**58,324**	**82,152**	**166,455**	....	....	....	....	....	....

2005, International Monetary Fund: *Government Finance Statistics Yearbook*

In Millions of Kyats / Year Beginning April 1 / Cash Reporter

	Budgetary Central Government			Central Government			Local Government			General Government		
	2000	2001	2002	2000	2001	2002	2000	2001	2002	2000	2001	2002
Table 2 Expense by economic type												
Table 3 Transactions in assets and liabilities												
Table 4 Holding gains in assets and liabilities												
Table 5 Other changes in the volume of assets and liabilities												
Table 6 Balance sheet												
Table 7 Outlays by functions of govt.												
7 Total outlays.........................	....	....	....	221,255	271,371	353,389	....	....	....	....	....	....
701 **General public services.........................**	....	....	....	44,910	75,684	82,572	....	....	....	....	....	....
7017 Public debt transactions........................	....	....	....	....	....	....	....	....	....	....	....	....
7018 General transfers between levels of govt......	....	....	....	....	....	....	....	....	....	....	....	....
702 **Defense..**	....	....	....	63,453	64,015	76,082	....	....	....	....	....	....
703 **Public order and safety.........................**	....	....	....	—	—	—	....	....	....	....	....	....
704 **Economic affairs.....................................**	....	....	....	66,132	78,117	111,058	....	....	....	....	....	....
7042 Agriculture, forestry, fishing, and hunting.....	....	....	....	38,447	25,917	37,004	....	....	....	....	....	....
7043 Fuel and energy....................................	....	....	....	44	1,219	6,906	....	....	....	....	....	....
7044 Mining, manufacturing, and construction.....	....	....	....	617	1,022	642	....	....	....	....	....	....
7045 Transport..	....	....	....	25,917	48,789	65,041	....	....	....	....	....	....
7046 Communication.......................................	....	....	....	....	....	....	....	....	....	....	....	....
705 **Environmental protection.........................**	....	....	....	—	—	—	....	....	....	....	....	....
706 **Housing and community amenities........**	....	....	....	366	1,526	3,543	....	....	....	....	....	....
707 **Health..**	....	....	....	7,388	8,818	18,852	....	....	....	....	....	....
7072 Outpatient services................................	....	....	....	....	....	....	....	....	....	....	....	....
7073 Hospital services...................................	....	....	....	....	....	....	....	....	....	....	....	....
7074 Public health services............................	....	....	....	....	....	....	....	....	....	....	....	....
708 **Recreation, culture, and religion...........**	....	....	....	2,668	1,646	2,382	....	....	....	....	....	....
709 **Education...**	....	....	....	31,345	35,266	51,711	....	....	....	....	....	....
7091 Pre-primary and primary education..............	....	....	....	....	....	....	....	....	....	....	....	....
7092 Secondary education..............................	....	....	....	17,600	18,392	19,357	....	....	....	....	....	....
7094 Tertiary education..................................	....	....	....	11,818	13,766	28,666	....	....	....	....	....	....
710 **Social protection...................................**	....	....	....	4,993	6,299	7,189	....	....	....	....	....	....
7 Statistical discrepancy: Total outlays..............	....	....	....	—	—	—	....	....	....	....	....	....
Table 8 Transactions in financial assets and liabilities by sector												

Namibia   728

In Millions of Dollars / Year Beginning April 1 / Cash Reporter

		Budgetary Central Government			Central Government			Local Government			General Government		
		2001	2002	2003	2001	2002	2003	2001	2002	2003	2001	2002	2003
Statement of government operations													
Statement of other economic flows													
Balance sheet													
Statement of sources and uses of cash													
1	Cash receipts from operating activities...........	8,953	10,349	9,532	....	....	....	....	....	....	....	....	....
11	Taxes..	8,163	9,326	8,757	....	....	....	....	....	....	....	....	....
12	Social contributions.............................	45	53	60	....	....	....	....	....	....	....	....	....
13	Grants...	58	34	34	....	....	....	....	....	....	....	....	....
14	Other receipts....................................	687	936	681	....	....	....	....	....	....	....	....	....
2	Cash payments for operating activities...........	8,724	9,474	10,526	....	....	....	....	....	....	....	....	....
21	Compensation of employees.....................	4,328	4,709	5,117	....	....	....	....	....	....	....	....	....
22	Purchases of goods and services.................	2,531	2,719	2,902	....	....	....	....	....	....	....	....	....
24	Interest...	586	823	864	....	....	....	....	....	....	....	....	....
25	Subsidies...	....	....	154	....	....	....	....	....	....	....	....	....
26	Grants...	....	....	—	....	....	....	....	....	....	....	....	....
27	Social benefits...................................	949	1,024	1,280	....	....	....	....	....	....	....	....	....
28	Other payments..................................	....	....	208	....	....	....	....	....	....	....	....	....
CIO	*Net cash inflow from oper. activities.....*	*228*	*875*	*−994*	....	....	....	....	....	....	....	....	....
31.1	Purchases of nonfinancial assets.................	1,077	1,183	1,306	....	....	....	....	....	....	....	....	....
31.2	Sales of nonfinancial assets......................	—	—	—	....	....	....	....	....	....	....	....	....
31	Net cash outflow from investments in nonfinancial assets..........................	1,077	1,183	1,306	....	....	....	....	....	....	....	....	....
CSD	*Cash surplus/deficit........................*	*−849*	*−308*	*−2,300*	....	....	....	....	....	....	....	....	....
32x	Net acquisition of fin assets, excl. cash........	456	634	387	....	....	....	....	....	....	....	....	....
321x	Domestic..	456	634	387	....	....	....	....	....	....	....	....	....
322x	Foreign..	—	—	—	....	....	....	....	....	....	....	....	....
323	Monetary gold and SDRs.........................	—	—	—	....	....	....	....	....	....	....	....	....
33	Net incurrence of liabilities.....................	−6,105	−8,625	−6,793	....	....	....	....	....	....	....	....	....
331	Domestic..	−6,085	−8,609	−6,759	....	....	....	....	....	....	....	....	....
332	Foreign..	−20	−16	−35	....	....	....	....	....	....	....	....	....
NFB	Net cash inflow from fin. activities.............	−6,562	−9,258	−7,180	....	....	....	....	....	....	....	....	....
NCB	*Net change in the stock of cash.............*	*−7,411*	*−9,566*	*−9,480*	....	....	....	....	....	....	....	....	....
Table 1 Revenue													
1	**Revenue...**	**8,953**	**10,349**	**9,532**	....	....	....	....	....	....	....	....	....
11	**Taxes...**	**8,163**	**9,326**	**8,757**	....	....	....	....	....	....	....	....	....
111	Taxes on income, profits, & capital gains......	3,282	4,437	3,612	....	....	....	....	....	....	....	....	....
1111	Individuals.....................................	1,938	2,316	2,405	....	....	....	....	....	....	....	....	....
1112	Corporations and other enterprises............	1,343	2,121	1,208	....	....	....	....	....	....	....	....	....
112	Taxes on payroll and workforce.................	—	—	—	....	....	....	....	....	....	....	....	....
113	Taxes on property...............................	64	79	75	....	....	....	....	....	....	....	....	....
114	Taxes on goods and services....................	2,108	2,136	1,951	....	....	....	....	....	....	....	....	....
1141	General taxes on goods and services..........	1,938	2,009	1,756	....	....	....	....	....	....	....	....	....
1142	Excises...	58	−7	64	....	....	....	....	....	....	....	....	....
115	Taxes on int'l. trade and transactions...........	2,641	2,598	3,036	....	....	....	....	....	....	....	....	....
116	Other taxes.......................................	68	76	83	....	....	....	....	....	....	....	....	....
12	**Social contributions.........................**	**45**	**53**	**60**	....	....	....	....	....	....	....	....	....
121	Social security contributions....................	—	—	—	....	....	....	....	....	....	....	....	....
122	Other social contributions......................	45	53	60	....	....	....	....	....	....	....	....	....
13	**Grants...**	**58**	**34**	**34**	....	....	....	....	....	....	....	....	....
131	From foreign governments......................	....	....	34	....	....	....	....	....	....	....	....	....
132	From international organizations.................	....	....	—	....	....	....	....	....	....	....	....	....
133	From other general government units..........	....	....	—	....	....	....	....	....	....	....	....	....
14	**Other revenue.................................**	**687**	**936**	**681**	....	....	....	....	....	....	....	....	....
Table 2 Expense by economic type													
2	**Expense...**	**8,724**	**9,474**	**10,526**	....	....	....	....	....	....	....	....	....
21	**Compensation of employees................**	**4,328**	**4,709**	**5,117**	....	....	....	....	....	....	....	....	....
211	Wages and salaries..............................	4,328	4,709	5,117	....	....	....	....	....	....	....	....	....
212	Social contributions.............................	—	—	—	....	....	....	....	....	....	....	....	....
22	**Use of goods and services.....................**	**2,531**	**2,719**	**2,902**	....	....	....	....	....	....	....	....	....
23	**Consumption of fixed capital................**	....	....	....	....	....	....	....	....	....	....	....	....
24	**Interest...**	**586**	**823**	**864**	....	....	....	....	....	....	....	....	....
25	**Subsidies...**	....	....	**154**	....	....	....	....	....	....	....	....	....

2005, International Monetary Fund: *Government Finance Statistics Yearbook*

In Millions of Dollars / Year Beginning April 1 / Cash Reporter

	Budgetary Central Government			Central Government			Local Government			General Government		
	2001	2002	2003	2001	2002	2003	2001	2002	2003	2001	2002	2003
26 Grants.................................	....	....	—	....	....	....	....	....	....	....	....	....
261 To foreign govenments................	....	....	—	....	....	....	....	....	....	....	....	....
262 To international organizations..........	....	....	—	....	....	....	....	....	....	....	....	....
263 To other general government units.....	....	....	—	....	....	....	....	....	....	....	....	....
2631 Current..................................	....	....	—	....	....	....	....	....	....	....	....	....
2632 Capital...................................	....	....	—	....	....	....	....	....	....	....	....	....
27 Social benefits........................	949	1,024	1,280	....	....	....	....	....	....	....	....	....
28 Other expense.........................	....	....	208	....	....	....	....	....	....	....	....	....
281 Property expense other than interest.....	....	....	—	....	....	....	....	....	....	....	....	....
282 Miscellaneous other expense............	....	....	208	....	....	....	....	....	....	....	....	....
2821 Current..................................	....	....	208	....	....	....	....	....	....	....	....	....
2822 Capital...................................	....	....	—	....	....	....	....	....	....	....	....	....

Table 3 Transactions in assets and liabilities

	Budgetary Central Government			Central Government			Local Government			General Government		
	2001	2002	2003	2001	2002	2003	2001	2002	2003	2001	2002	2003
3 Change in net worth from transactns....	....	....	....	....	....	....	....	....	....	....	....	....
31 Net acquisition of nonfinancial assets...	1,077	1,183	1,306	....	....	....	....	....	....	....	....	....
311 Fixed assets...............................	1,055	1,156	1,299	....	....	....	....	....	....	....	....	....
3111 Buildings and structures...............	726	866	1,000	....	....	....	....	....	....	....	....	....
3112 Machinery and equipment.............	330	290	299	....	....	....	....	....	....	....	....	....
3113 Other fixed assets......................	—	—	—	....	....	....	....	....	....	....	....	....
312 Inventories...............................	—	—	—	....	....	....	....	....	....	....	....	....
313 Valuables.................................	—	—	—	....	....	....	....	....	....	....	....	....
314 Nonproduced assets.....................	22	27	7	....	....	....	....	....	....	....	....	....
3141 Land....................................	22	27	7	....	....	....	....	....	....	....	....	....
3142 Subsoil assets.........................	—	—	—	....	....	....	....	....	....	....	....	....
3143 Other naturally occurring assets......	—	—	—	....	....	....	....	....	....	....	....	....
3144 Intangible nonproduced assets........	—	—	—	....	....	....	....	....	....	....	....	....
32 Net acquisition of financial assets........	−6,954	−8,933	−9,093	....	....	....	....	....	....	....	....	....
321 Domestic.................................	−6,954	−8,933	−9,093	....	....	....	....	....	....	....	....	....
3212 Currency and deposits................	−7,411	−9,566	−9,480	....	....	....	....	....	....	....	....	....
3213 Securities other than shares..........	—	—	—	....	....	....	....	....	....	....	....	....
3214 Loans..................................	96	63	−13	....	....	....	....	....	....	....	....	....
3215 Shares and other equity..............	361	571	400	....	....	....	....	....	....	....	....	....
3216 Insurance technical reserves.........	—	—	—	....	....	....	....	....	....	....	....	....
3217 Financial derivatives..................	—	—	—	....	....	....	....	....	....	....	....	....
3218 Other accounts receivable............	....	....	....	....	....	....	....	....	....	....	....	....
322 Foreign..................................	....	....	....	....	....	....	....	....	....	....	....	....
3222 Currency and deposits................	—	—	—	....	....	....	....	....	....	....	....	....
3223 Securities other than shares..........	—	—	—	....	....	....	....	....	....	....	....	....
3224 Loans..................................	—	—	—	....	....	....	....	....	....	....	....	....
3225 Shares and other equity..............	—	—	—	....	....	....	....	....	....	....	....	....
3226 Insurance technical reserves.........	—	—	—	....	....	....	....	....	....	....	....	....
3227 Financial derivatives..................	—	—	—	....	....	....	....	....	....	....	....	....
3228 Other accounts receivable............	—	—	—	....	....	....	....	....	....	....	....	....
323 Monetary gold and SDRs...............	—	—	—	....	....	....	....	....	....	....	....	....
33 Net incurrence of liabilities.................	−6,105	−8,625	−6,793	....	....	....	....	....	....	....	....	....
331 Domestic.................................	−6,085	−8,609	−6,759	....	....	....	....	....	....	....	....	....
3312 Currency and deposits................	—	—	—	....	....	....	....	....	....	....	....	....
3313 Securities other than shares..........	....	....	—	....	....	....	....	....	....	....	....	....
3314 Loans..................................	−6,571	−9,117	−7,312	....	....	....	....	....	....	....	....	....
3316 Insurance technical reserves.........	....	....	....	....	....	....	....	....	....	....	....	....
3317 Financial derivatives..................	....	....	....	....	....	....	....	....	....	....	....	....
3318 Other accounts payable...............	....	....	....	....	....	....	....	....	....	....	....	....
332 Foreign..................................	−20	−16	−35	....	....	....	....	....	....	....	....	....
3322 Currency and deposits................	—	—	—	....	....	....	....	....	....	....	....	....
3323 Securities other than shares..........	—	—	—	....	....	....	....	....	....	....	....	....
3324 Loans..................................	−20	−16	−35	....	....	....	....	....	....	....	....	....
3326 Insurance technical reserves.........	—	—	—	....	....	....	....	....	....	....	....	....
3327 Financial derivatives..................	—	—	—	....	....	....	....	....	....	....	....	....
3328 Other accounts payable...............	....	....	....	....	....	....	....	....	....	....	....	....

	Budgetary Central Government			Central Government			Local Government			General Government		
	2001	2002	2003	2001	2002	2003	2001	2002	2003	2001	2002	2003
Table 4 Holding gains in assets and liabilities												
Table 5 Other changes in the volume of assets and liabilities												
Table 6 Balance sheet												
Table 7 Outlays by functions of govt.												
7 **Total outlays**..................................	**9,802**	**10,657**	**11,832**	....	....	....	....	....	....	....	....	....
701 **General public services**.........................	**2,277**	**2,818**	**2,739**	....	....	....	....	....	....	....	....	....
7017 Public debt transactions..........................	587	824	864	....	....	....	....	....	....	....	....	....
7018 General transfers between levels of govt.....	....	....	....	....	....	....	....	....	....	....	....	....
702 **Defense**...	**926**	**956**	**993**	....	....	....	....	....	....	....	....	....
703 **Public order and safety**.........................	**975**	**1,044**	**1,173**	....	....	....	....	....	....	....	....	....
704 **Economic affairs**................................	**931**	**1,106**	**1,266**	....	....	....	....	....	....	....	....	....
7042 Agriculture, forestry, fishing, and hunting.....	540	613	632	....	....	....	....	....	....	....	....	....
7043 Fuel and energy..................................	36	40	36	....	....	....	....	....	....	....	....	....
7044 Mining, manufacturing, and construction.....	45	39	48	....	....	....	....	....	....	....	....	....
7045 Transport.......................................	73	105	154	....	....	....	....	....	....	....	....	....
7046 Communication.................................	....	....	....	....	....	....	....	....	....	....	....	....
705 **Environmental protection**.......................	....	....	—	....	....	....	....	....	....	....	....	....
706 **Housing and community amenities**........	**828**	**955**	**1,005**	....	....	....	....	....	....	....	....	....
707 **Health**..	**981**	**1,128**	**1,237**	....	....	....	....	....	....	....	....	....
7072 Outpatient services.............................	....	....	....	....	....	....	....	....	....	....	....	....
7073 Hospital services...............................	....	....	....	....	....	....	....	....	....	....	....	....
7074 Public health services..........................	....	....	....	....	....	....	....	....	....	....	....	....
708 **Recreation, culture, and religion**...........	**249**	**234**	**279**	....	....	....	....	....	....	....	....	....
709 **Education**.......................................	**2,328**	**2,384**	**2,643**	....	....	....	....	....	....	....	....	....
7091 Pre-primary and primary education...........	1,164	1,224	1,328	....	....	....	....	....	....	....	....	....
7092 Secondary education...........................	476	468	477	....	....	....	....	....	....	....	....	....
7094 Tertiary education.............................	361	366	465	....	....	....	....	....	....	....	....	....
710 **Social protection**..............................	**807**	**774**	**909**	....	....	....	....	....	....	....	....	....
7 Statistical discrepancy: Total outlays..............	−501	−742	−413	....	....	....	....	....	....	....	....	....
Table 8 Transactions in financial assets and liabilities by sector												
82 **Net acquisition of financial assets**.........	**−6,954**	**−8,933**	**−9,093**	....	....	....	....	....	....	....	....	....
821 Domestic..	−6,954	−8,933	−9,093	....	....	....	....	....	....	....	....	....
8211 General government............................	....	....	....	....	....	....	....	....	....	....	....	....
8212 Central bank...................................	....	....	....	....	....	....	....	....	....	....	....	....
8213 Other depository corporations.................	....	....	....	....	....	....	....	....	....	....	....	....
8214 Financial corporations n.e.c..................	....	....	....	....	....	....	....	....	....	....	....	....
8215 Nonfinancial corporations....................	....	....	....	....	....	....	....	....	....	....	....	....
8216 Households & NPIs serving households......	....	....	....	....	....	....	....	....	....	....	....	....
822 Foreign...	—	—	—	....	....	....	....	....	....	....	....	....
8221 General government............................	—	—	—	....	....	....	....	....	....	....	....	....
8227 International organizations....................	—	—	—	....	....	....	....	....	....	....	....	....
8228 Financial corporations other than international organizations...............	—	—	—	....	....	....	....	....	....	....	....	....
8229 Other nonresidents............................	—	—	—	....	....	....	....	....	....	....	....	....
823 Monetary gold and SDRs........................	—	—	—	....	....	....	....	....	....	....	....	....
83 **Net incurrence of liabilities**....................	**−6,105**	**−8,625**	**−6,793**	....	....	....	....	....	....	....	....	....
831 Domestic..	−6,085	−8,609	−6,759	....	....	....	....	....	....	....	....	....
8311 General government............................	....	....	....	....	....	....	....	....	....	....	....	....
8312 Central bank...................................	....	....	....	....	....	....	....	....	....	....	....	....
8313 Other depository corporations.................	....	....	....	....	....	....	....	....	....	....	....	....
8314 Financial corporations n.e.c..................	....	....	....	....	....	....	....	....	....	....	....	....
8315 Nonfinancial corporations....................	....	....	....	....	....	....	....	....	....	....	....	....
8316 Households & NPIs serving households......	....	....	....	....	....	....	....	....	....	....	....	....
832 Foreign...	−20	−16	−35	....	....	....	....	....	....	....	....	....
8321 General government............................	....	....	....	....	....	....	....	....	....	....	....	....
8327 International organizations....................	....	....	....	....	....	....	....	....	....	....	....	....
8328 Financial corporations other than international organizations...............	....	....	....	....	....	....	....	....	....	....	....	....
8329 Other nonresidents............................	....	....	....	....	....	....	....	....	....	....	....	....

2005, International Monetary Fund: *Government Finance Statistics Yearbook*

In Millions of Rupees / Year Ending July 15 / Cash Reporter

	Budgetary Central Government			Central Government			Local Government			General Government		
	2002	2003	2004p	2002	2003	2004p	2002	2003	2004	2002	2003	2004
Statement of government operations												
Statement of other economic flows												
Balance sheet												
6 *Net worth*.....	....	....	....	....	....	....	....	....	....	....	....	....
61 Nonfinancial assets.....	....	....	....	....	....	....	....	....	....	....	....	....
62 Financial assets.....	....	....	....	....	....	....	....	....	....	....	....	....
63 Liabilities.....	293,747	308,079	328,232	293,747	308,079	328,232	....	....	....	....	....	....
Statement of sources and uses of cash												
1 Cash receipts from operating activities.....	54,941	65,018	71,307	54,941	65,018	71,307	....	....	....	....	....	....
11 Taxes.....	39,331	42,587	47,979	39,331	42,587	47,979	....	....	....	....	....	....
12 Social contributions.....	—	—	—	—	—	—	....	....	....	....	....	....
13 Grants.....	6,686	11,339	11,458	6,686	11,339	11,458	....	....	....	....	....	....
14 Other receipts.....	8,924	11,092	11,870	8,924	11,092	11,870	....	....	....	....	....	....
2 Cash payments for operating activities.....	....	....	....	....	....	....	....	....	....	....	....	....
21 Compensation of employees.....	....	....	....	....	....	....	....	....	....	....	....	....
22 Purchases of goods and services.....	....	....	....	....	....	....	....	....	....	....	....	....
24 Interest.....	5,770	6,622	8,364	5,770	6,622	8,364	....	....	....	....	....	....
25 Subsidies.....	....	....	....	....	....	....	....	....	....	....	....	....
26 Grants.....	....	....	....	....	....	....	....	....	....	....	....	....
27 Social benefits.....	....	....	....	....	....	....	....	....	....	....	....	....
28 Other payments.....	....	....	....	....	....	....	....	....	....	....	....	....
CIO *Net cash inflow from oper. activities*.....	....	....	....	....	....	....	....	....	....	....	....	....
31.1 Purchases of nonfinancial assets.....	....	....	....	....	....	....	....	....	....	....	....	....
31.2 Sales of nonfinancial assets.....	71	791	546	71	791	546	....	....	....	....	....	....
31 Net cash outflow from investments in nonfinancial assets.....	....	....	....	....	....	....	....	....	....	....	....	....
CSD *Cash surplus/deficit*.....	−18,382	−8,415	−10,542	−18,382	−8,415	−10,542	....	....	....	....	....	....
32x Net acquisition of fin assets, excl. cash.....	−1,876	−1,538	−1,550	−1,876	−1,538	−1,550	....	....	....	....	....	....
321x Domestic.....	−1,876	−1,538	−1,550	−1,876	−1,538	−1,550	....	....	....	....	....	....
322x Foreign.....	—	—	—	—	—	—	....	....	....	....	....	....
323 Monetary gold and SDRs.....	—	—	—	—	—	—	....	....	....	....	....	....
33 Net incurrence of liabilities.....	9,264	3,867	7,288	9,264	3,867	7,288	....	....	....	....	....	....
331 Domestic.....	6,316	4,817	579	6,316	4,817	579	....	....	....	....	....	....
332 Foreign.....	2,948	−950	6,709	2,948	−950	6,709	....	....	....	....	....	....
NFB Net cash inflow from fin. activities.....	11,140	5,405	8,838	11,140	5,405	8,838	....	....	....	....	....	....
NCB *Net change in the stock of cash*.....	−7,242	−3,011	−1,704	−7,242	−3,011	−1,704	....	....	....	....	....	....
Table 1 Revenue												
1 **Revenue**.....	**54,941**	**65,018**	**71,307**	**54,941**	**65,018**	**71,307**	....	....	....	....	....	....
11 **Taxes**.....	**39,331**	**42,587**	**47,979**	**39,331**	**42,587**	**47,979**	....	....	....	....	....	....
111 Taxes on income, profits, & capital gains.....	8,068	6,879	8,094	8,068	6,879	8,094	....	....	....	....	....	....
1111 Individuals.....	2,897	—	—	2,897	—	—	....	....	....	....	....	....
1112 Corporations and other enterprises.....	4,355	5,550	6,771	4,355	5,550	6,771	....	....	....	....	....	....
112 Taxes on payroll and workforce.....	836	1,253	1,390	836	1,253	1,390	....	....	....	....	....	....
113 Taxes on property.....	1,134	1,414	1,900	1,134	1,414	1,900	....	....	....	....	....	....
114 Taxes on goods and services.....	16,634	18,804	21,151	16,634	18,804	21,151	....	....	....	....	....	....
1141 General taxes on goods and services.....	11,964	13,460	14,302	11,964	13,460	14,302	....	....	....	....	....	....
1142 Excises.....	3,807	4,785	6,166	3,807	4,785	6,166	....	....	....	....	....	....
115 Taxes on int'l. trade and transactions.....	12,659	14,236	15,444	12,659	14,236	15,444	....	....	....	....	....	....
116 Other taxes.....	—	—	—	—	—	—	....	....	....	....	....	....
12 **Social contributions**.....	—	—	—	—	—	—	....	....	....	....	....	....
121 Social security contributions.....	—	—	—	—	—	—	....	....	....	....	....	....
122 Other social contributions.....	—	—	—	—	—	—	....	....	....	....	....	....
13 **Grants**.....	**6,686**	**11,339**	**11,458**	**6,686**	**11,339**	**11,458**	....	....	....	....	....	....
131 From foreign governments.....	6,686	11,339	11,458	6,686	11,339	11,458	....	....	....	....	....	....
132 From international organizations.....	—	—	—	—	—	—	....	....	....	....	....	....
133 From other general government units.....	—	—	—	—	—	—	....	....	....	....	....	....
14 **Other revenue**.....	**8,924**	**11,092**	**11,870**	**8,924**	**11,092**	**11,870**	....	....	....	....	....	....
Table 2 Expense by economic type												
2 **Expense**.....	....	....	....	....	....	....	....	....	....	....	....	....
21 **Compensation of employees**.....	....	....	....	....	....	....	....	....	....	....	....	....
211 Wages and salaries.....	....	....	....	....	....	....	....	....	....	....	....	....
212 Social contributions.....	....	....	....	....	....	....	....	....	....	....	....	....
22 **Use of goods and services**.....	....	....	....	....	....	....	....	....	....	....	....	....
23 **Consumption of fixed capital**.....	....	....	....	....	....	....	....	....	....	....	....	....
24 Interest.....	5,770	6,622	8,364	5,770	6,622	8,364	....	....	....	....	....	....
25 **Subsidies**.....	....	....	....	....	....	....	....	....	....	....	....	....

In Millions of Rupees / Year Ending July 15 / Cash Reporter

		Budgetary Central Government			Central Government			Local Government			General Government		
		2002	2003	2004p	2002	2003	2004p	2002	2003	2004	2002	2003	2004
26	**Grants**................................	....	....	....	....	....	....	....	....	....	....	....	....
261	To foreign govenments................	....	....	....	....	....	....	....	....	....	....	....	....
262	To international organizations..............	....	....	....	....	....	....	....	....	....	....	....	....
263	To other general government units..........	....	....	....	....	....	....	....	....	....	....	....	....
2631	Current.............................	....	....	....	....	....	....	....	....	....	....	....	....
2632	Capital..............................	....	....	....	....	....	....	....	....	....	....	....	....
27	**Social benefits**........................	....	....	....	....	....	....	....	....	....	....	....	....
28	**Other expense**........................	....	....	....	....	....	....	....	....	....	....	....	....
281	Property expense other than interest..........	....	....	....	....	....	....	....	....	....	....	....	....
282	Miscellaneous other expense...............	....	....	....	....	....	....	....	....	....	....	....	....
2821	Current.............................	....	....	....	....	....	....	....	....	....	....	....	....
2822	Capital..............................	....	....	....	....	....	....	....	....	....	....	....	....

Table 3 Transactions in assets and liabilities

		Budgetary Central Government			Central Government			Local Government			General Government		
		2002	2003	2004p	2002	2003	2004p	2002	2003	2004	2002	2003	2004
3	**Change in net worth from transactns....**	....	....	....	....	....	....	....	....	....	....	....	....
31	**Net acquisition of nonfinancial assets...**	....	....	....	....	....	....	....	....	....	....	....	....
311	Fixed assets...........................	....	....	....	....	....	....	....	....	....	....	....	....
3111	Buildings and structures...............	....	....	....	....	....	....	....	....	....	....	....	....
3112	Machinery and equipment...............	....	....	....	....	....	....	....	....	....	....	....	....
3113	Other fixed assets....................	....	....	....	....	....	....	....	....	....	....	....	....
312	Inventories............................	....	....	....	....	....	....	....	....	....	....	....	....
313	Valuables.............................	....	....	....	....	....	....	....	....	....	....	....	....
314	Nonproduced assets....................	....	....	....	....	....	....	....	....	....	....	....	....
3141	Land................................	....	....	....	....	....	....	....	....	....	....	....	....
3142	Subsoil assets.......................	....	....	....	....	....	....	....	....	....	....	....	....
3143	Other naturally occurring assets..........	....	....	....	....	....	....	....	....	....	....	....	....
3144	Intangible nonproduced assets..................	....	....	....	....	....	....	....	....	....	....	....	....
32	**Net acquisition of financial assets........**	−9,118	−4,548	−3,254	−9,118	−4,548	−3,254	....	....	....	....	....	....
321	Domestic.............................	−9,118	−4,548	−3,254	−9,118	−4,548	−3,254	....	....	....	....	....	....
3212	Currency and deposits..............	−7,242	−3,011	−1,704	−7,242	−3,011	−1,704	....	....	....	....	....	....
3213	Securities other than shares...........	....	....	....	....	....	....	....	....	....	....	....	....
3214	Loans.............................	....	....	....	....	....	....	....	....	....	....	....	....
3215	Shares and other equity...............	....	....	....	....	....	....	....	....	....	....	....	....
3216	Insurance technical reserves...........	....	....	....	....	....	....	....	....	....	....	....	....
3217	Financial derivatives.................	....	....	....	....	....	....	....	....	....	....	....	....
3218	Other accounts receivable.............	....	....	....	....	....	....	....	....	....	....	....	....
322	Foreign...............................	—	—	—	—	—	—	....	....	....	....	....	....
3222	Currency and deposits...............	—	—	—	—	—	—	....	....	....	....	....	....
3223	Securities other than shares...........	—	—	—	—	—	—	....	....	....	....	....	....
3224	Loans.............................	—	—	—	—	—	—	....	....	....	....	....	....
3225	Shares and other equity...............	—	—	—	—	—	—	....	....	....	....	....	....
3226	Insurance technical reserves...........	—	—	—	—	—	—	....	....	....	....	....	....
3227	Financial derivatives.................	—	—	—	—	—	—	....	....	....	....	....	....
3228	Other accounts receivable.............	....	....	....	....	....	....	....	....	....	....	....	....
323	Monetary gold and SDRs.............	—	—	—	—	—	—	....	....	....	....	....	....
33	**Net incurrence of liabilities....................**	9,264	3,867	7,288	9,264	3,867	7,288	....	....	....	....	....	....
331	Domestic.............................	6,316	4,817	579	6,316	4,817	579	....	....	....	....	....	....
3312	Currency and deposits..............	—	—	—	—	—	—	....	....	....	....	....	....
3313	Securities other than shares...........	6,316	4,817	579	6,316	4,817	579	....	....	....	....	....	....
3314	Loans.............................	—	—	—	—	—	—	....	....	....	....	....	....
3316	Insurance technical reserves...........	—	—	—	—	—	—	....	....	....	....	....	....
3317	Financial derivatives.................	—	—	—	—	—	—	....	....	....	....	....	....
3318	Other accounts payable...............	....	....	....	....	....	....	....	....	....	....	....	....
332	Foreign...............................	2,948	−950	6,709	2,948	−950	6,709	....	....	....	....	....	....
3322	Currency and deposits...............	—	—	—	—	—	—	....	....	....	....	....	....
3323	Securities other than shares...........	—	—	—	—	—	—	....	....	....	....	....	....
3324	Loans.............................	2,948	−950	6,709	2,948	−950	6,709	....	....	....	....	....	....
3326	Insurance technical reserves...........	—	—	—	—	—	—	....	....	....	....	....	....
3327	Financial derivatives.................	—	—	—	—	—	—	....	....	....	....	....	....
3328	Other accounts payable...............	....	....	....	....	....	....	....	....	....	....	....	....

In Millions of Rupees / Year Ending July 15 / Cash Reporter

	Budgetary Central Government			Central Government			Local Government			General Government		
	2002	2003	2004p	2002	2003	2004p	2002	2003	2004	2002	2003	2004
Table 4 Holding gains in assets and liabilities												
Table 5 Other changes in the volume of assets and liabilities												
Table 6 Balance sheet												
6 Net worth......................................	....	....	....	....	....	....	....	....	....	....	....	....
61 **Nonfinancial assets**..............................	....	....	....	....	....	....	....	....	....	....	....	....
611 Fixed assets..	....	....	....	....	....	....	....	....	....	....	....	....
6111 Buildings and structures....................	....	....	....	....	....	....	....	....	....			
6112 Machinery and equipment......................	....	....	....	....	....	....	....	....	....			
6113 Other fixed assets............................	....	....	....	....	....	....	....	....	....			
612 Inventories......................................	....	....	....	....	....	....	....	....	....			
613 Valuables.......................................	....	....	....	....	....	....	....	....	....			
614 Nonproduced assets............................	....	....	....	....	....	....	....	....	....			
6141 Land..	....	....	....	....	....	....	....	....	....			
6142 Subsoil assets.................................	....	....	....	....	....	....	....	....	....			
6143 Other naturally occurring assets............	....	....	....	....	....	....	....	....	....			
6144 Intangible nonproduced assets..............	....	....	....	....	....	....	....	....	....			
62 **Financial assets**.............................	....	....	....	....	....	....	....	....	....	....	....	....
621 Domestic.......................................	....	....	....	....	....	....	....	....	....	....	....	
6212 Currency and deposits.......................	....	....	....	....	....	....	....	....	....			
6213 Securities other than shares..............	....	....	....	....	....	....	....	....	....			
6214 Loans..	....	....	....	....	....	....	....	....	....			
6215 Shares and other equity....................	....	....	....	....	....	....	....	....	....			
6216 Insurance technical reserves...............	....	....	....	....	....	....	....	....	....			
6217 Financial derivatives.......................	....	....	....	....	....	....	....	....	....			
6218 Other accounts receivable..................	....	....	....	....	....	....	....	....	....			
622 Foreign..	....	....	....	....	....	....	....	....	....			
6222 Currency and deposits.......................	....	....	....	....	....	....	....	....	....			
6223 Securities other than shares..............	....	....	....	....	....	....	....	....	....			
6224 Loans..	....	....	....	....	....	....	....	....	....			
6225 Shares and other equity....................	....	....	....	....	....	....	....	....	....			
6226 Insurance technical reserves...............	....	....	....	....	....	....	....	....	....			
6227 Financial derivatives.......................	....	....	....	....	....	....	....	....	....			
6228 Other accounts receivable..................	....	....	....	....	....	....	....	....	....			
623 Monetary gold and SDRs.......................	....	....	....	....	....	....	....	....	....			
63 **Liabilities**....................................	**293,747**	**308,079**	**328,232**	**293,747**	**308,079**	**328,232**	....	....	....	....	....	....
631 Domestic.......................................	73,621	84,645	83,021	73,621	84,645	83,021	....	....	....	....	....	....
6312 Currency and deposits.......................	....	....	....	....	....	....	....	....	....			
6313 Securities other than shares..............	....	....	....	....	....	....	....	....	....			
6314 Loans..	....	....	....	....	....	....	....	....	....			
6316 Insurance technical reserves...............	....	....	....	....	....	....	....	....	....			
6317 Financial derivatives.......................	....	....	....	....	....	....	....	....	....			
6318 Other accounts payable......................	....	....	....	....	....	....	....	....	....			
632 Foreign..	220,126	223,433	245,211	220,126	223,433	245,211	....	....	....			
6322 Currency and deposits.......................	....	....	....	....	....	....	....	....	....			
6323 Securities other than shares..............	....	....	....	....	....	....	....	....	....			
6324 Loans..	....	....	....	....	....	....	....	....	....			
6326 Insurance technical reserves...............	....	....	....	....	....	....	....	....	....			
6327 Financial derivatives.......................	....	....	....	....	....	....	....	....	....			
6328 Other accounts payable......................	....	....	....	....	....	....	....	....	....			
Memorandum items:												
6M2 Net financial worth...........................							....	....	....			
6M3 Debt at market value..........................	....	....	....	....	....	....	....	....	....			
6M4 Debt at nominal value.........................	....	....	....	....	....	....	....	....	....			
6M5 Arrears..	....	....	....	....	....	....	....	....	....			
6M6 Obligations for social security benefits...........	....	....	....	....	....	....	....	....	....			
6M7 Contingent liabilities........................	....	....	....	....	....	....	....	....	....			
6M8 Uncapitalized military weapons, systems........	....	....	....	....	....	....	....	....	....			
Table 7 Outlays by functions of govt.												
7 Total outlays..................................	**73,394**	**74,225**	**82,394**	**73,394**	**74,225**	**82,394**	....	....	....	....	....	....
701 **General public services**........................	**18,092**	**18,644**	**20,233**	**18,092**	**18,644**	**20,233**	....	....	....	....	....	....
7017 Public debt transactions.....................	5,770	6,622	8,364	5,770	6,622	8,364	....	....	....	....	....	....
7018 General transfers between levels of govt......	....	....	....	....	....	....	....	....	....	....	....	....
702 **Defense**..	**5,860**	**7,382**	**8,382**	**5,860**	**7,382**	**8,382**	....	....	....	....	....	....
703 **Public order and safety**........................	**6,625**	**6,813**	**6,891**	**6,625**	**6,813**	**6,891**	....	....	....	....	....	....

In Millions of Rupees / Year Ending July 15 / Cash Reporter

	Budgetary Central Government			Central Government			Local Government			General Government		
	2002	2003	2004p	2002	2003	2004p	2002	2003	2004	2002	2003	2004
704 **Economic affairs**............................	19,127	17,420	20,332	19,127	17,420	20,332	....	....	....	....	....	....
7042 Agriculture, forestry, fishing, and hunting.....	4,335	3,616	3,836	4,335	3,616	3,836	....	....	....	....	....	....
7043 Fuel and energy............................	4,405	3,913	5,795	4,405	3,913	5,795	....	....	....	....	....	....
7044 Mining, manufacturing, and construction......	820	790	567	820	790	567	....	....	....	....	....	....
7045 Transport......................................	4,841	5,499	5,030	4,841	5,499	5,030	....	....	....	....	....	....
7046 Communication............................	....	....	....	....	....	....	....	....	....	....	....	....
705 **Environmental protection**..................	—	—	—				....	....	....	....	....	....
706 **Housing and community amenities**........	3,256	3,177	3,617	3,256	3,177	3,617	....	....	....	....	....	....
707 **Health**..	3,857	3,652	4,399	3,857	3,652	4,399	....	....	....	....	....	....
7072 Outpatient services............................	....	....	....	....	....	....	....	....	....	....	....	....
7073 Hospital services..............................	....	....	....	....	....	....	....	....	....	....	....	....
7074 Public health services........................	....	....	....	....	....	....	....	....	....	....	....	....
708 **Recreation, culture, and religion**............	—	—	—	—	—	—	....	....	....	....	....	....
709 **Education**.....................................	13,050	13,242	14,397	13,050	13,242	14,397	....	....	....	....	....	....
7091 Pre-primary and primary education..............	....	....	....	....	....	....	....	....	....	....	....	....
7092 Secondary education........................	....	....	....	....	....	....	....	....	....	....	....	....
7094 Tertiary education..............................	....	....	....	....	....	....	....	....	....	....	....	....
710 **Social protection**............................	3,527	3,897	4,142	3,527	3,897	4,142	....	....	....	....	....	....
7 Statistical discrepancy: Total outlays..............	—	—	—	—	—	—	....	....	....	....	....	....

Table 8 Transactions in financial assets and liabilities by sector

	Budgetary Central Government			Central Government			Local Government			General Government		
	2002	2003	2004p	2002	2003	2004p	2002	2003	2004	2002	2003	2004
82 **Net acquisition of financial assets**........	–9,118	–4,548	–3,254	–9,118	–4,548	–3,254	....	....	....	....	....	....
821 Domestic.....................................	–9,118	–4,548	–3,254	–9,118	–4,548	–3,254	....	....	....	....	....	....
8211 General government..............................	....	–1,538	–1,550	....	–1,538	–1,550	....	....	....	....	....	....
8212 Central bank..............................	....	....	....	....	....	....	....	....	....	....	....	....
8213 Other depository corporations....................	....	....	....	....	....	....	....	....	....	....	....	....
8214 Financial corporations n.e.c....................	....	....	....	....	....	....	....	....	....	....	....	....
8215 Nonfinancial corporations......................	....	....	....	....	....	....	....	....	....	....	....	....
8216 Households & NPIs serving households......	....	....	....	....	....	....	....	....	....	....	....	....
822 Foreign..	—	—	—	—	—	—	....	....	....	....	....	....
8221 General government..............................	—	—	—	—	—	—	....	....	....	....	....	....
8227 International organizations......................	—	—	—	—	—	—	....	....	....	....	....	....
8228 Financial corporations other than international organizations....	—	—	—	—	—	—	....	....	....	....	....	....
8229 Other nonresidents..............................	—	—	—	—	—	—	....	....	....	....	....	....
823 Monetary gold and SDRs......................	—	—	—	—	—	—	....	....	....	....	....	....
83 **Net incurrence of liabilities**....................	9,264	3,867	7,288	9,264	3,867	7,288	....	....	....	....	....	....
831 Domestic.....................................	6,316	4,817	579	6,316	4,817	579	....	....	....	....	....	....
8311 General government..............................	....	....	....	....	....	....	....	....	....	....	....	....
8312 Central bank..............................	....	....	....	....	....	....	....	....	....	....	....	....
8313 Other depository corporations....................	....	....	....	....	....	....	....	....	....	....	....	....
8314 Financial corporations n.e.c....................	....	....	....	....	....	....	....	....	....	....	....	....
8315 Nonfinancial corporations......................	....	....	....	....	....	....	....	....	....	....	....	....
8316 Households & NPIs serving households......	....	....	....	....	....	....	....	....	....	....	....	....
832 Foreign..	2,948	–950	6,709	2,948	–950	6,709	....	....	....	....	....	....
8321 General government..............................	....	....	....	....	....	....	....	....	....	....	....	....
8327 International organizations......................	....	....	....	....	....	....	....	....	....	....	....	....
8328 Financial corporations other than international organizations..............	....	....	....	....	....	....	....	....	....	....	....	....
8329 Other nonresidents..............................	....	....	....	....	....	....	....	....	....	....	....	....

Netherlands   138

In Millions of Euros / Year Ending December 31 / Noncash Reporter

	Budgetary Central Government			Central Government			Local Government			General Government		
	2002	2003p	2004p	2002	2003p	2004p	2002	2003p	2004p	2002	2003p	2004p
Statement of government operations												
1 Revenue.....................	120,421	119,101	123,576	181,928	184,831	192,220	72,790	77,370	77,084	204,928	208,369	216,548
2 Expense......................	122,780	130,466	130,672	186,356	196,084	198,680	72,870	76,492	77,942	209,436	218,744	223,866
GOB *Gross operating balance*..........	*1,492*	*−7,288*	*−2,944*	*−429*	*−7,031*	*−2,162*	*7,323*	*8,548*	*6,994*	*6,894*	*1,517*	*4,832*
NOB *Net operating balance*.............	*−2,359*	*−11,365*	*−7,096*	*−4,428*	*−11,253*	*−6,460*	*−80*	*878*	*−858*	*−4,508*	*−10,375*	*−7,318*
31 Net acquisition of nonfinancial assets.............	2,585	2,317	1,578	2,595	2,330	1,590	2,175	2,349	1,261	4,770	4,679	2,851
NLB *Net lending/borrowing*..........	*−4,944*	*−13,682*	*−8,674*	*−7,023*	*−13,583*	*−8,050*	*−2,255*	*−1,471*	*−2,119*	*−9,278*	*−15,054*	*−10,169*
32 Net acquisition of financial assets.................	2,947	2,224	−1,110	1,768	2,888	−3,943	−1,225	−1,484	−1,762	528	−192	−5,791
33 Net incurrence of liabilities.................	7,891	15,906	7,564	8,791	16,471	4,107	1,030	−13	357	9,806	14,862	4,378
NLB Statistical discrepancy................	—	—	—	—	—	—	—	—	—	—	—	—
Statement of other economic flows												
Balance sheet												
6 *Net worth*...............	....	....	....	....	....	....	....	....	....	....	....	....
61 Nonfinancial assets................	....	....	....	....	....	....	....	....	....	....	....	....
62 Financial assets................	66,240	69,715	68,667	74,652	79,562	78,349	44,216	43,782	42,099	118,091	122,575	119,632
63 Liabilities................	232,383	245,655	256,129	229,434	243,936	253,123	51,744	51,525	51,968	280,401	294,692	304,275
Statement of sources and uses of cash												
Table 1 Revenue												
1 **Revenue**................	**120,421**	**119,101**	**123,576**	**181,928**	**184,831**	**192,220**	**72,790**	**77,370**	**77,084**	**204,928**	**208,369**	**216,548**
11 **Taxes**................	**104,769**	**103,201**	**106,256**	**104,769**	**103,201**	**106,256**	**6,512**	**7,033**	**7,534**	**111,281**	**110,234**	**113,790**
111 Taxes on income, profits, & capital gains......	47,286	44,615	44,499	47,286	44,615	44,499	—	—	—	47,286	44,615	44,499
1111 Individuals................	31,856	31,187	29,469	31,856	31,187	29,469	—	—	—	31,856	31,187	29,469
1112 Corporations and other enterprises..........	15,430	13,428	15,030	15,430	13,428	15,030	—	—	—	15,430	13,428	15,030
112 Taxes on payroll and workforce..................	541	425	405	541	425	405	—	—	—	541	425	405
113 Taxes on property................	5,407	4,975	5,331	5,407	4,975	5,331	2,905	3,162	3,376	8,312	8,137	8,707
114 Taxes on goods and services..................	50,435	52,112	54,785	50,435	52,112	54,785	3,607	3,871	4,158	54,042	55,983	58,943
1141 General taxes on goods and services.........	35,074	36,513	38,101	35,074	36,513	38,101	—	—	—	35,074	36,513	38,101
1142 Excises................	11,560	11,813	12,784	11,560	11,813	12,784	—	—	—	11,560	11,813	12,784
115 Taxes on int'l. trade and transactions..........	1,100	1,074	1,236	1,100	1,074	1,236	—	—	—	1,100	1,074	1,236
116 Other taxes................	—	—	—	—	—	—	—	—	—	—	—	—
12 **Social contributions**................	**2,252**	**2,203**	**2,332**	**64,044**	**68,100**	**70,997**	**2,305**	**2,272**	**2,417**	**66,349**	**70,372**	**73,414**
121 Social security contributions................	—	—	—	61,718	65,822	68,574	—	—	—	61,718	65,822	68,574
122 Other social contributions................	2,252	2,203	2,332	2,326	2,278	2,423	2,305	2,272	2,417	4,631	4,550	4,840
13 **Grants**................	**1,426**	**1,408**	**1,378**	**464**	**475**	**553**	**49,714**	**53,711**	**52,613**	**420**	**397**	**442**
131 From foreign governments................	—	—	—	—	—	—	—	—	—	—	—	—
132 From international organizations................	368	374	355	368	374	355	52	23	87	420	397	442
133 From other general government units..........	1,058	1,034	1,023	96	101	198	49,662	53,688	52,526			
14 **Other revenue**................	**11,974**	**12,289**	**13,610**	**12,651**	**13,055**	**14,414**	**14,259**	**14,354**	**14,520**	**26,878**	**27,366**	**28,902**
Table 2 Expense by economic type												
2 **Expense**................	**122,780**	**130,466**	**130,672**	**186,356**	**196,084**	**198,680**	**72,870**	**76,492**	**77,942**	**209,436**	**218,744**	**223,866**
21 **Compensation of employees**................	**14,097**	**14,690**	**14,806**	**15,835**	**16,576**	**16,731**	**29,764**	**31,450**	**32,316**	**45,599**	**48,026**	**49,047**
211 Wages and salaries................	10,161	10,645	10,416	11,551	12,159	11,939	22,777	24,013	24,171	34,328	36,172	36,110
212 Social contributions................	3,936	4,045	4,390	4,284	4,417	4,792	6,987	7,437	8,145	11,271	11,854	12,937
22 **Use of goods and services**................	**12,321**	**12,499**	**12,097**	**13,737**	**13,924**	**13,724**	**19,333**	**20,390**	**20,813**	**33,070**	**34,314**	**34,537**
23 **Consumption of fixed capital**................	**3,851**	**4,077**	**4,152**	**3,999**	**4,222**	**4,298**	**7,403**	**7,670**	**7,852**	**11,402**	**11,892**	**12,150**
24 **Interest**................	**11,459**	**10,894**	**10,762**	**11,164**	**10,686**	**10,588**	**1,917**	**2,094**	**2,114**	**13,049**	**12,737**	**12,670**
25 **Subsidies**................	**3,625**	**3,315**	**2,963**	**4,088**	**3,756**	**4,190**	**2,813**	**2,899**	**2,705**	**6,901**	**6,655**	**6,895**
26 **Grants**................	**64,075**	**71,367**	**71,982**	**55,687**	**59,683**	**59,374**	**96**	**101**	**198**	**6,025**	**5,995**	**6,848**
261 To foreign governments................	—	—	—	—	—	—	—	—	—	—	—	—
262 To international organizations................	6,025	5,995	6,848	6,025	5,995	6,848	—	—	—	6,025	5,995	6,848
263 To other general government units................	58,050	65,372	65,134	49,662	53,688	52,526	96	101	198	—	—	—
2631 Current................	55,802	62,304	62,087	47,414	50,620	49,479	89	97	83	—	—	—
2632 Capital................	2,248	3,068	3,047	2,248	3,068	3,047	7	4	115	—	—	—
27 **Social benefits**................	**10,811**	**10,984**	**11,336**	**79,288**	**84,597**	**87,201**	**8,751**	**9,082**	**9,238**	**88,039**	**93,679**	**96,439**
28 **Other expense**................	**2,541**	**2,640**	**2,574**	**2,558**	**2,640**	**2,574**	**2,793**	**2,806**	**2,706**	**5,351**	**5,446**	**5,280**
281 Property expense other than interest............	16	16	15	16	16	15	5	4	3	21	20	18
282 Miscellaneous other expense................	2,525	2,624	2,559	2,542	2,624	2,559	2,788	2,802	2,703	5,330	5,426	5,262
2821 Current................	1,463	1,475	1,518	1,463	1,475	1,518	1,009	1,033	1,044	2,472	2,508	2,562
2822 Capital................	1,062	1,149	1,041	1,079	1,149	1,041	1,779	1,769	1,659	2,858	2,918	2,700

In Millions of Euros / Year Ending December 31 / Noncash Reporter

	Budgetary Central Government			Central Government			Local Government			General Government		
	2002	2003p	2004p	2002	2003p	2004p	2002	2003p	2004p	2002	2003p	2004p
Table 3 Transactions in assets and liabilities												
3 Change in net worth from transactns....	−2,359	−11,365	−7,096	−4,428	−11,253	−6,460	−80	878	−858	−4,508	−10,375	−7,318
31 Net acquisition of nonfinancial assets...	2,585	2,317	1,578	2,595	2,330	1,590	2,175	2,349	1,261	4,770	4,679	2,851
311 Fixed assets..............	2,412	2,228	1,329	2,424	2,243	1,343	2,599	1,960	1,722	5,023	4,203	3,065
3111 Buildings and structures............	....	....	....	....	....	....	....	....	....	....	....	....
3112 Machinery and equipment...........	....	....	....	....	....	....	....	....	....	....	....	....
3113 Other fixed assets............	....	....	....	....	....	....	....	....	....	....	....	....
312 Inventories............	2	—	—	2	—	—	—	—	—	2	—	—
313 Valuables.............	—	—	—	—	—	—	17	16	14	17	16	14
314 Nonproduced assets............	171	89	249	169	87	247	−441	373	−475	−272	460	−228
3141 Land............	....	....	....	....	....	....	....	....	....	....	....	....
3142 Subsoil assets............	....	....	....	....	....	....	....	....	....	....	....	....
3143 Other naturally occurring assets...	....	....	....	....	....	....	....	....	....	....	....	....
3144 Intangible nonproduced assets.....	....	....	....	....	....	....	....	....	....	....	....	....
32 Net acquisition of financial assets........	2,947	2,224	−1,110	1,768	2,888	−3,943	−1,225	−1,484	−1,762	528	−192	−5,791
321 Domestic..............	2,947	2,224	−1,110	1,768	2,888	−3,943	−1,225	−1,484	−1,762	528	−192	−5,791
3212 Currency and deposits.............	−165	412	290	−402	1,028	529	−325	−1,109	52	−723	−79	581
3213 Securities other than shares..........	3	—	—	−224	167	—	20	−11	—	−209	165	—
3214 Loans.............	3,226	1,731	−55	627	−450	−126	−1,006	−1,996	−879	−393	−2,446	−1,052
3215 Shares and other equity............	125	−1,797	−1,534	277	−1,942	−1,500	−480	−1,052	−145	−203	−2,994	−1,645
3216 Insurance technical reserves...........	—	—	—	—	—	—	—	—	—	—	—	—
3217 Financial derivatives............	—	—	—	—	—	—	—	—	—	—	—	—
3218 Other accounts receivable............	−242	1,878	189	1,490	4,085	−2,846	566	2,684	−790	2,056	5,162	−3,675
322 Foreign.............	....	....	....	....	....	....	....	....	....	....	....	....
3222 Currency and deposits.............	....	....	....	....	....	....	....	....	....	....	....	....
3223 Securities other than shares...........	....	....	....	....	....	....	....	....	....	....	....	....
3224 Loans.............	....	....	....	....	....	....	....	....	....	....	....	....
3225 Shares and other equity............	....	....	....	....	....	....	....	....	....	....	....	....
3226 Insurance technical reserves............	....	....	....	....	....	....	....	....	....	....	....	....
3227 Financial derivatives............	....	....	....	....	....	....	....	....	....	....	....	....
3228 Other accounts receivable............	....	....	....	....	....	....	....	....	....	....	....	....
323 Monetary gold and SDRs............	—	—	—	—	—	—	—	—	—	—	—	—
33 Net incurrence of liabilities...................	7,891	15,906	7,564	8,791	16,471	4,107	1,030	−13	357	9,806	14,862	4,378
331 Domestic..............	7,891	15,906	7,564	8,791	16,471	4,107	1,030	−13	357	9,806	14,862	4,378
3312 Currency and deposits.............	22	37	−30	23	37	−30	—	—	—	27	39	−30
3313 Securities other than shares..........	8,117	14,449	12,134	8,357	14,345	12,134	−48	−139	−293	8,304	14,215	11,841
3314 Loans.............	669	−1,798	−2,824	−1,121	−2,227	−4,699	1,054	508	580	−81	−1,719	−4,166
3316 Insurance technical reserves............	—	—	—	—	—	—	—	—	—	—	—	—
3317 Financial derivatives............	—	—	—	—	—	—	—	—	—	—	—	—
3318 Other accounts payable............	−917	3,218	−1,716	1,532	4,316	−3,298	24	−382	70	1,556	2,327	−3,267
332 Foreign.............	....	....	....	....	....	....	....	....	....	....	....	....
3322 Currency and deposits.............	....	....	....	....	....	....	....	....	....	....	....	....
3323 Securities other than shares...........	....	....	....	....	....	....	....	....	....	....	....	....
3324 Loans.............	....	....	....	....	....	....	....	....	....	....	....	....
3326 Insurance technical reserves............	....	....	....	....	....	....	....	....	....	....	....	....
3327 Financial derivatives............	....	....	....	....	....	....	....	....	....	....	....	....
3328 Other accounts payable............	....	....	....	....	....	....	....	....	....	....	....	....
Table 4 Holding gains in assets and liabilities												
Table 5 Other changes in the volume of assets and liabilities												
Table 6 Balance sheet												
6 Net worth...............	....	....	....	....	....	....	....	....	....	....	....	....
61 Nonfinancial assets.................	....	....	....	....	....	....	....	....	....	....	....	....
611 Fixed assets................	....	....	....	....	....	....	....	....	....	....	....	....
6111 Buildings and structures............	....	....	....	....	....	....	....	....	....	....	....	....
6112 Machinery and equipment...........	....	....	....	....	....	....	....	....	....	....	....	....
6113 Other fixed assets............	....	....	....	....	....	....	....	....	....	....	....	....
612 Inventories............	....	....	....	....	....	....	....	....	....	....	....	....
613 Valuables............	....	....	....	....	....	....	....	....	....	....	....	....
614 Nonproduced assets............	....	....	....	....	....	....	....	....	....	....	....	....
6141 Land............	....	....	....	....	....	....	....	....	....	....	....	....
6142 Subsoil assets............	....	....	....	....	....	....	....	....	....	....	....	....
6143 Other naturally occurring assets.........	....	....	....	....	....	....	....	....	....	....	....	....
6144 Intangible nonproduced assets...........	....	....	....	....	....	....	....	....	....	....	....	....

In Millions of Euros / Year Ending December 31 / Noncash Reporter

	Budgetary Central Government			Central Government			Local Government			General Government		
	2002	2003p	2004p	2002	2003p	2004p	2002	2003p	2004p	2002	2003p	2004p
62 Financial assets.........................	66,240	69,715	68,667	74,652	79,562	78,349	44,216	43,782	42,099	118,091	122,575	119,632
621 Domestic...........................	66,240	69,715	68,667	74,652	79,562	78,349	44,216	43,782	42,099	118,091	122,575	119,632
6212 Currency and deposits..............	2,145	2,529	2,819	2,586	3,586	4,115	8,671	7,362	7,439	11,245	10,938	11,544
6213 Securities other than shares........	43	—	—	537	661	661	777	768	768	552	674	674
6214 Loans................................	13,163	14,658	14,587	10,845	10,159	11,683	18,018	15,890	15,011	28,860	26,045	26,643
6215 Shares and other equity...........	36,813	36,225	34,976	37,408	36,735	35,520	5,191	5,289	5,192	42,599	42,024	40,712
6216 Insurance technical reserves.......	—	—	—	—	—	—	—	—	—	—	—	—
6217 Financial derivatives...............	—	—	—	—	—	—	—	—	—	—	—	—
6218 Other accounts receivable.........	14,076	16,303	16,285	23,276	28,421	26,370	11,559	14,473	13,689	34,835	42,894	40,059
622 Foreign............................	....	....	....	....	....	....	....	....	....	....	....	....
6222 Currency and deposits..............	....	....	....	....	....	....	....	....	....	....	....	....
6223 Securities other than shares........	....	....	....	....	....	....	....	....	....	....	....	....
6224 Loans................................	....	....	....	....	....	....	....	....	....	....	....	....
6225 Shares and other equity...........	....	....	....	....	....	....	....	....	....	....	....	....
6226 Insurance technical reserves.......	....	....	....	....	....	....	....	....	....	....	....	....
6227 Financial derivatives...............	....	....	....	....	....	....	....	....	....	....	....	....
6228 Other accounts receivable.........	....	....	....	....	....	....	....	....	....	....	....	....
623 Monetary gold and SDRs...........	—	—	—	—	—	—	....	....	....	....	....	....
63 Liabilities...............................	232,383	245,655	256,129	229,434	243,936	253,123	51,744	51,525	51,968	280,401	294,692	304,275
631 Domestic...........................	232,383	245,655	256,129	229,434	243,936	253,123	51,744	51,525	51,968	280,401	294,692	304,275
6312 Currency and deposits..............	684	719	689	683	718	688	—	—	—	671	708	678
6313 Securities other than shares........	199,048	211,116	226,175	198,958	210,922	225,981	2,262	2,166	1,879	200,458	212,333	227,105
6314 Loans................................	21,311	19,299	16,461	9,781	7,340	4,293	36,515	36,857	37,519	46,293	44,193	41,761
6316 Insurance technical reserves.......	—	—	—	—	—	—	—	—	—	—	—	—
6317 Financial derivatives...............	—	—	—	—	—	—	—	—	—	—	—	—
6318 Other accounts payable...........	11,340	14,521	12,804	20,012	24,956	22,161	12,967	12,502	12,570	32,979	37,458	34,731
632 Foreign............................	....	....	....	....	....	....	....	....	....	....	....	....
6322 Currency and deposits..............	....	....	....	....	....	....	....	....	....	....	....	....
6323 Securities other than shares........	....	....	....	....	....	....	....	....	....	....	....	....
6324 Loans................................	....	....	....	....	....	....	....	....	....	....	....	....
6326 Insurance technical reserves.......	....	....	....	....	....	....	....	....	....	....	....	....
6327 Financial derivatives...............	....	....	....	....	....	....	....	....	....	....	....	....
6328 Other accounts payable...........	....	....	....	....	....	....	....	....	....	....	....	....
Memorandum items:												
6M2 Net financial worth.................	−166,143	−175,940	−187,462	−154,782	−164,374	−174,774	−7,528	−7,743	−9,869	−162,310	−172,117	−184,643
6M3 Debt at market value..............	....	....	....	....	....	....	....	....	....	....	....	....
6M4 Debt at nominal value.............	....	....	....	....	....	....	....	....	....	....	....	....
6M5 Arrears.............................	....	....	....	....	....	....	....	....	....	....	....	....
6M6 Obligations for social security benefits..........	....	....	....	....	....	....	....	....	....	....	....	....
6M7 Contingent liabilities................	....	....	....	....	....	....	....	....	....	....	....	....
6M8 Uncapitalized military weapons, systems.......	....	....	....	....	....	....	....	....	....	....	....	....

Table 7 Outlays by functions of govt.

	2002	2003p	2004p	2002	2003p	2004p	2002	2003p	2004p	2002	2003p	2004p
7 Total outlays........................	125,365	132,783	132,250	188,951	198,414	200,270	75,045	78,841	79,203	214,206	223,423	226,717
701 General public services......................	40,397	43,181	41,153	40,100	42,971	40,962	11,507	13,344	12,882	35,185	37,192	36,591
7017 Public debt transactions...............	11,459	10,894	10,762	11,164	10,686	10,588	1,917	2,094	2,114	13,049	12,737	12,670
7018 General transfers between levels of govt......	....	....	....	....	....	....	....	....	....	....	....	....
702 Defense...............................	7,107	7,149	7,195	7,107	7,149	7,195	—	—	—	7,107	7,149	7,195
703 Public order and safety......................	7,258	7,752	8,076	7,258	7,752	8,076	4,253	4,548	4,735	7,794	8,309	8,690
704 Economic affairs......................	12,857	13,032	13,202	12,857	13,032	13,202	13,243	13,064	12,338	24,738	24,664	24,145
7042 Agriculture, forestry, fishing, and hunting.....	....	....	....	....	....	....	....	....	....	....	....	....
7043 Fuel and energy......................	....	....	....	....	....	....	....	....	....	....	....	....
7044 Mining, manufacturing, and construction......	....	....	....	....	....	....	....	....	....	....	....	....
7045 Transport...........................	....	....	....	....	....	....	....	....	....	....	....	....
7046 Communication......................	....	....	....	....	....	....	....	....	....	....	....	....
705 Environmental protection.....................	906	871	755	906	871	755	3,172	3,387	3,359	3,950	4,162	4,034
706 Housing and community amenities........	1,156	1,128	1,331	1,156	1,128	1,331	4,742	4,894	5,199	5,801	5,926	6,436
707 Health................................	562	737	716	18,420	19,656	20,774	989	1,318	1,458	19,318	20,764	22,061
7072 Outpatient services....................	....	....	....	....	....	....	....	....	....	....	....	....
7073 Hospital services.....................	....	....	....	....	....	....	....	....	....	....	....	....
7074 Public health services.................	....	....	....	....	....	....	....	....	....	....	....	....
708 Recreation, culture, and religion............	1,758	1,679	1,654	1,758	1,679	1,654	5,458	5,642	5,671	6,894	6,963	6,990

		Budgetary Central Government			Central Government			Local Government			General Government		
		2002	2003p	2004p	2002	2003p	2004p	2002	2003p	2004p	2002	2003p	2004p
709	**Education**.............................	20,692	21,646	22,315	20,692	21,646	22,315	18,886	19,880	20,723	23,764	24,895	25,841
7091	Pre-primary and primary education............	....	....	....	....	....	....	....	....	....	....	....	....
7092	Secondary education...............................	....	....	....	....	....	....	....	....	....	....	....	....
7094	Tertiary education.................................	....	....	....	....	....	....	....	....	....	....	....	....
710	**Social protection**...........................	32,672	35,608	35,853	78,697	82,530	84,006	12,795	12,764	12,838	79,655	83,399	84,734
7	Statistical discrepancy: Total outlays...............	—	—	—	—	—	—	—	—	—	—	—	—

Table 8   Transactions in financial assets and liabilities by sector

		Budgetary Central Government			Central Government			Local Government			General Government		
82	**Net acquisition of financial assets**........	2,947	2,224	−1,110	1,768	2,888	−3,943	−1,225	−1,484	−1,762	528	−192	−5,791
821	Domestic.................................	2,947	2,224	−1,110	1,768	2,888	−3,943	−1,225	−1,484	−1,762	528	−192	−5,791
8211	General government...........................	....	....	....	....	....	....	....	....	....	....	....	....
8212	Central bank.................................	....	....	....	....	....	....	....	....	....	....	....	....
8213	Other depository corporations...................	....	....	....	....	....	....	....	....	....	....	....	....
8214	Financial corporations n.e.c.....................	....	....	....	....	....	....	....	....	....	....	....	....
8215	Nonfinancial corporations......................	....	....	....	....	....	....	....	....	....	....	....	....
8216	Households & NPIs serving households......	....	....	....	....	....	....	....	....	....	....	....	....
822	Foreign...................................	....	....	....	....	....	....	....	....	....	....	....	....
8221	General government...........................	....	....	....	....	....	....	....	....	....	....	....	....
8227	International organizations.....................	....	....	....	....	....	....	....	....	....	....	....	....
8228	Financial corporations other than international organizations.............	....	....	....	....	....	....	....	....	....	....	....	....
8229	Other nonresidents...........................	....	....	....	....	....	....	....	....	....	....	....	....
823	Monetary gold and SDRs.....................	—		—	—		—		—		—	—	—
83	**Net incurrence of liabilities**...................	7,891	15,906	7,564	8,791	16,471	4,107	1,030	−13	357	9,806	14,862	4,378
831	Domestic.................................	7,891	15,906	7,564	8,791	16,471	4,107	1,030	−13	357	9,806	14,862	4,378
8311	General government...........................	....	....	....	....	....	....	....	....	....	....	....	....
8312	Central bank.................................	....	....	....	....	....	....	....	....	....	....	....	....
8313	Other depository corporations...................	....	....	....	....	....	....	....	....	....	....	....	....
8314	Financial corporations n.e.c.....................	....	....	....	....	....	....	....	....	....	....	....	....
8315	Nonfinancial corporations......................	....	....	....	....	....	....	....	....	....	....	....	....
8316	Households & NPIs serving households......	....	....	....	....	....	....	....	....	....	....	....	....
832	Foreign...................................	....	....	....	....	....	....	....	....	....	....	....	....
8321	General government...........................	....	....	....	....	....	....	....	....	....	....	....	....
8327	International organizations.....................	....	....	....	....	....	....	....	....	....	....	....	....
8328	Financial corporations other than international organizations.............	....	....	....	....	....	....	....	....	....	....	....	....
8329	Other nonresidents...........................	....	....	....	....	....	....	....	....	....	....	....	....

New Zealand 196

In Millions of Dollars / Year Ending June 30 / Noncash Reporter

		Budgetary Central Government			Central Government			Local Government			General Government		
		2002	2003	2004p	2002	2003	2004p	2002	2003p	2004p	2002	2003p	2004p
Statement of government operations													
1	Revenue	39,951	43,717	46,722	45,182	49,786	53,421	4,140	4,570	5,051	....	53,829	57,858
2	Expense	36,817	39,809	41,214	41,535	45,110	47,042	3,792	4,025	4,377	....	48,607	50,806
GOB	*Gross operating balance*	*3,922*	*4,613*	*6,245*	*5,151*	*6,401*	*8,256*	*1,118*	*1,374*	*1,563*	....	*7,775*	*9,820*
NOB	*Net operating balance*	*3,134*	*3,907*	*5,508*	*3,646*	*4,677*	*6,378*	*348*	*545*	*674*	....	*5,222*	*7,052*
31	Net acquisition of nonfinancial assets	689	−90	136	1,443	624	895	1,501	660	924	....	1,284	1,819
NLB	*Net lending/borrowing*	*2,445*	*3,998*	*5,372*	*2,203*	*4,053*	*5,484*	*−1,153*	*−115*	*−251*	....	*3,938*	*5,233*
32	Net acquisition of financial assets	2,043	5,035	3,738	2,701	6,449	4,544	....	....	....	....	....	....
33	Net incurrence of liabilities	−402	1,037	−1,635	497	2,396	−940	....	....	....	....	....	....
NLB	Statistical discrepancy	—	—	—	—	—	—	....	....	....	....	....	....
Statement of other economic flows													
4	*Change in net worth from holding gains*	*1,291*	*975*	*4,763*	*3,358*	*309*	*5,344*	....	....	*2,995*	....	....	*8,411*
41	Nonfinancial assets	1,685	1,828	1,029	4,064	2,550	3,900	....	1,664	2,909	....	4,214	6,809
42	Financial assets	−80	−789	3,417	13	668	480	....	....	....	....	....	....
43	Liabilities	313	64	−317	718	2,909	−964	....	....	....	....	....	....
5	*Change in net worth from other volume changes*	—	*−36*	*1,459*	*600*	*1,068*	*6*	....	—	—	....	*1,068*	*6*
51	Nonfinancial assets	—	−13,759	—	—	1,650	253	....	—	—	....	1,650	253
52	Financial assets	—	13,722	1,459	600	−582	−189	....	—	—	....	−582	−189
53	Liabilities	—	—	—	—	—	59	....	—	—	....	—	59
Balance sheet													
6	*Net worth*	....	*20,913*	*32,626*	*21,513*	*20,826*	*32,626*	....	*55,868*	*59,537*	....	*76,694*	*92,163*
61	Nonfinancial assets	....	16,066	17,231	28,088	45,764	50,811	....	52,393	56,226	....	98,156	107,038
62	Financial assets	....	50,233	58,847	37,733	44,778	49,616	....	6,512	6,562	....	51,290	56,178
63	Liabilities	....	45,386	43,452	44,307	69,715	67,801	....	3,037	3,251	....	72,752	71,052
Statement of sources and uses of cash													
1	Cash receipts from operating activities	39,396	42,762	45,628	43,922	49,309	52,692	....	4,644	4,803	....	53,425	56,881
11	Taxes	37,000	40,241	43,269	38,606	42,153	45,556	....	2,683	2,755	....	44,746	48,213
12	Social contributions	−119	21	18	479	617	117	....	—	—	....	617	117
13	Grants	—	—	—	—	—	1	....	436	515	....	—	1
14	Other receipts	2,515	2,499	2,341	4,836	6,538	7,018	....	1,524	1,532	....	8,063	8,550
2	Cash payments for operating activities	35,746	38,053	40,111	39,150	42,776	44,295	....	3,348	3,494	....	45,596	47,175
21	Compensation of employees	....	2,772	3,341	....	10,430	11,621	....	924	1,026	....	11,354	12,647
22	Purchases of goods and services	....	5,101	7,808	....	12,973	12,634	....	1,920	1,976	....	14,893	14,610
24	Interest	2,447	2,343	2,247	2,320	2,231	2,258	....	143	143	....	2,375	2,400
25	Subsidies	—	—	—	—	—	—	....	217	270	....	217	270
26	Grants	9,802	13,766	12,465	—	436	515	....	—	—	....	—	—
27	Social benefits	13,709	14,071	14,250	14,298	16,042	16,142	....	—	—	....	16,042	16,142
28	Other payments	—	—	—	—	663	1,125	....	143	78	....	715	1,105
CIO	*Net cash inflow from oper. activities*	*3,650*	*4,708*	*5,517*	*4,772*	*6,533*	*8,398*	....	*1,296*	*1,309*	....	*7,829*	*9,706*
31.1	Purchases of nonfinancial assets	1,329	1,170	1,683	2,499	2,917	3,609	....	1,573	1,617	....	4,490	5,225
31.2	Sales of nonfinancial assets	104	112	157	148	180	216	....	192	133	....	372	349
31	Net cash outflow from investments in nonfinancial assets	1,225	1,058	1,526	2,350	2,736	3,392	....	1,381	1,484	....	4,117	4,876
CSD	*Cash surplus/deficit*	*2,425*	*3,651*	*3,991*	*2,421*	*3,797*	*5,006*	....	*−85*	*−175*	....	*3,712*	*4,831*
32x	Net acquisition of fin assets, excl. cash	399	−190	4,408	199	11	5,058	....	1,774	1,514	....	1,785	6,572
321x	Domestic	−1,547	1,129	4,512	−1,757	1,268	5,163	....	1,774	1,514	....	3,042	6,677
322x	Foreign	2,004	−1,321	−104	2,013	−1,260	−105	....	—	—	....	−1,260	−105
323	Monetary gold and SDRs	−58	3	—	−58	3	—	....	—	—	....	3	—
33	Net incurrence of liabilities	−3,271	−3,570	−1,336	−3,275	−3,564	−1,351	....	1,946	1,679	....	−1,619	328
331	Domestic	−3,248	−3,560	−682	−3,248	−3,560	−682	....	1,946	1,679	....	−1,614	997
332	Foreign	−23	−11	−655	−27	−5	−669	....	—	—	....	−5	−669
NFB	Net cash inflow from fin. activities	−3,670	−3,381	−5,744	−3,473	−3,575	−6,409	....	172	164	....	−3,403	−6,245
NCB	*Net change in the stock of cash*	*−1,245*	*270*	*−1,754*	*−1,052*	*221*	*−1,403*	....	*87*	*−11*	....	*308*	*−1,414*
Table 1 Revenue													
1	**Revenue**	**39,951**	**43,717**	**46,722**	**45,182**	**49,786**	**53,421**	**4,140**	**4,570**	**5,051**	....	**53,829**	**57,858**
11	**Taxes**	**36,540**	**40,287**	**43,085**	**38,132**	**42,264**	**45,221**	**2,328**	**2,588**	**2,907**	....	**44,761**	**48,029**
111	Taxes on income, profits, & capital gains	23,891	26,518	28,298	23,598	26,358	28,160	—	—	—	....	26,358	28,160
1111	Individuals	19,163	20,837	21,722	19,163	20,837	21,722	—	—	—	....	20,837	21,722
1112	Corporations and other enterprises	4,728	5,680	6,576	4,435	5,521	6,438	—	—	—	....	5,521	6,438
112	Taxes on payroll and workforce	—	—	—	—	—	—	—	—	—	....	—	—
113	Taxes on property	1	1	2	1	1	2	2,301	2,561	2,878	....	2,471	2,782
114	Taxes on goods and services	11,317	12,286	13,264	13,203	14,423	15,538	27	27	28	....	14,450	15,566
1141	General taxes on goods and services	7,996	8,738	9,718	7,996	8,738	9,718	—	—	—	....	8,738	9,718
1142	Excises	2,141	2,310	2,242	2,141	2,310	2,242	27	27	28	....	2,337	2,270

		Budgetary Central Government			Central Government			Local Government			General Government		
		2002	2003	2004p	2002	2003	2004p	2002	2003p	2004p	2002	2003p	2004p
115	Taxes on int'l. trade and transactions............	1,330	1,482	1,520	1,330	1,482	1,520	—	—	—	....	1,482	1,520
116	Other taxes..........................	—	—	—	—	—	—	—	—	—	....	—	—
12	**Social contributions......................**	**−95**	**21**	**14**	**24**	**132**	**113**	**—**	**—**	**—**	**....**	**132**	**113**
121	Social security contributions........................	—	—	—	—	—	—	—	—	—	....	—	—
122	Other social contributions........................	−95	21	14	24	132	113	—	—	—	....	132	113
13	**Grants........................**	**110**	**113**	**112**	**—**	**—**	**—**	**444**	**436**	**515**	**....**	**—**	**—**
131	From foreign governments........................	—	—	—	—	—	—	—	—	—	....	—	—
132	From international organizations.................	—	—	—	—	—	—	—	—	—	....	—	—
133	From other general government units..........	110	113	112	—	—	—	444	436	515	....	—	—
14	**Other revenue........................**	**3,396**	**3,296**	**3,512**	**7,026**	**7,390**	**8,087**	**1,368**	**1,546**	**1,629**	**....**	**8,936**	**9,716**

Table 2   Expense by economic type

		Budgetary Central Government			Central Government			Local Government			General Government		
2	**Expense........................**	**36,817**	**39,809**	**41,214**	**41,535**	**45,110**	**47,042**	**3,792**	**4,025**	**4,377**	**....**	**48,607**	**50,806**
21	**Compensation of employees................**	**3,855**	**3,745**	**4,072**	**11,356**	**10,915**	**11,939**	**884**	**947**	**1,030**	**....**	**11,862**	**12,968**
211	Wages and salaries........................	3,334	2,772	3,223	10,518	10,429	11,536	864	926	1,008	....	11,354	12,544
212	Social contributions........................	521	973	849	838	486	402	20	21	21	....	507	424
22	**Use of goods and services................**	**3,923**	**5,161**	**5,152**	**11,380**	**12,533**	**12,448**	**1,774**	**1,884**	**2,033**	**....**	**14,417**	**14,481**
23	**Consumption of fixed capital................**	**788**	**706**	**738**	**1,505**	**1,724**	**1,878**	**770**	**829**	**890**	**....**	**2,553**	**2,767**
24	**Interest........................**	**2,513**	**2,633**	**2,500**	**2,192**	**2,494**	**2,519**	**141**	**140**	**142**	**....**	**2,634**	**2,660**
25	**Subsidies........................**	**115**	**113**	**110**	**115**	**113**	**110**	**—**	**217**	**270**	**....**	**331**	**380**
26	**Grants........................**	**12,569**	**14,025**	**15,033**	**381**	**695**	**779**	**—**	**—**	**—**	**....**	**258**	**264**
261	To foreign govenments........................	223	230	237	223	230	237	—	—	—	....	230	237
262	To international organizations...................	30	28	26	30	28	26	—	—	—	....	28	26
263	To other general government units..............	12,316	13,766	14,770	128	436	515	—	—	—	....	—	—
2631	Current........................	12,316	13,766	14,770	128	351	382	—	—	—	....	—	—
2632	Capital........................	—	—	—	—	86	134	—	—	—	....	—	—
27	**Social benefits........................**	**13,054**	**13,256**	**13,609**	**14,324**	**15,802**	**16,245**	**—**	**—**	**—**	**....**	**15,802**	**16,245**
28	**Other expense........................**	**—**	**171**	**—**	**283**	**834**	**1,125**	**224**	**8**	**13**	**....**	**751**	**1,040**
281	Property expense other than interest............	—	—	—	—	10	28	—	—	—	....	10	28
282	Miscellaneous other expense........................	—	171	—	283	824	1,097	224	8	13	....	741	1,011
2821	Current........................	—	171	—	283	824	1,097	224	5	6	....	738	1,004
2822	Capital........................	—	—	—	—	—	—	—	3	7	....	3	7

Table 3   Transactions in assets and liabilities

		Budgetary Central Government			Central Government			Local Government			General Government		
3	**Change in net worth from transactns....**	**3,134**	**3,907**	**5,508**	**3,646**	**4,677**	**6,378**	**348**	**545**	**674**	**....**	**5,222**	**7,052**
31	**Net acquisition of nonfinancial assets...**	**689**	**−90**	**136**	**1,443**	**624**	**895**	**1,501**	**660**	**924**	**....**	**1,284**	**1,819**
311	Fixed assets........................	607	−240	348	2,645	908	715	1,420	604	845	....	1,511	1,560
3111	Buildings and structures........................	354	−153	33	1,926	850	354	1,280	576	792	....	1,426	1,146
3112	Machinery and equipment........................	42	−118	301	356	303	230	140	6	45	....	310	275
3113	Other fixed assets........................	211	31	14	363	−246	131	—	21	8	....	−224	140
312	Inventories........................	92	−4	4	119	−22	16	—	—	1	....	−22	16
313	Valuables........................	—	—	—	—	—	—	—	—	—	....	—	—
314	Nonproduced assets........................	−10	154	−217	−1,322	−262	164	81	57	78	....	−205	242
3141	Land........................	−478	118	−190	−1,788	−300	182	81	57	78	....	−243	261
3142	Subsoil assets........................	—	—	—	—	—	—	—	—	—	....	—	—
3143	Other naturally occurring assets...........	−2	−1	−27	−2	−1	−27	—	—	—	....	−1	−27
3144	Intangible nonproduced assets.................	469	37	—	468	39	8	—	—	—	....	39	8
32	**Net acquisition of financial assets........**	**2,043**	**5,035**	**3,738**	**2,701**	**6,449**	**4,544**	**....**	**....**	**....**	**....**	**....**	**....**
321	Domestic........................	3,301	4,365	769	4,550	4,846	−955	....	....	....	....	....	....
3212	Currency and deposits........................	293	270	−1,753	495	221	−1,433	....	....	....	....	....	....
3213	Securities other than shares........................	277	1,658	−941	526	64	−795	....	....	....	....	....	....
3214	Loans........................	1,105	835	2,040	862	637	970	....	....	....	....	....	....
3215	Shares and other equity........................	1,191	666	247	1,807	2,317	−889	....	....	....	....	....	....
3216	Insurance technical reserves........................	—	—	—	—	—	—	....	....	....	....	....	....
3217	Financial derivatives........................	—	—	—	—	—	—	....	....	....	....	....	....
3218	Other accounts receivable........................	434	937	1,176	859	1,607	1,192	....	....	....	....	....	....
322	Foreign........................	−1,258	669	2,969	−1,849	1,602	5,499	....	....	....	....	....	....
3222	Currency and deposits........................	−1,538	—	—	−1,547	—	30	....	....	....	....	....	....
3223	Securities other than shares........................	—	647	685	—	630	1,328	....	....	....	....	....	....
3224	Loans........................	—	—	—	—	—	—	....	....	....	....	....	....
3225	Shares and other equity........................	280	22	2,285	−302	972	4,142	....	....	....	....	....	....
3226	Insurance technical reserves........................	—	—	—	—	—	—	....	....	....	....	....	....
3227	Financial derivatives........................	—	—	—	—	—	—	....	....	....	....	....	....
3228	Other accounts receivable........................	—	—	—	—	—	—	....	....	....	....	....	....
323	Monetary gold and SDRs........................	—	—	—	—	—	—	....	....	....	....	....	....

In Millions of Dollars / Year Ending June 30 / Noncash Reporter

		Budgetary Central Government			Central Government			Local Government			General Government		
		2002	2003	2004p	2002	2003	2004p	2002	2003p	2004p	2002	2003p	2004p
33	**Net incurrence of liabilities...**	−402	1,037	−1,635	497	2,396	−940	....	....	....	....	....	....
331	Domestic...	973	753	−1,067	1,805	2,159	−526	....	....	....	....	....	....
3312	Currency and deposits...	—	13	—	—	13	—	....	....	....	....	....	....
3313	Securities other than shares...	1,000	−11	−1,000	1,388	−40	−1,664	....	....	....	....	....	....
3314	Loans...	—	—	—	—	93	—	....	....	....	....	....	....
3316	Insurance technical reserves...	−230	−3	−1	−80	500	523	....	....	....	....	....	....
3317	Financial derivatives...	—	—	—	—	—	—	....	....	....	....	....	....
3318	Other accounts payable...	203	755	−67	498	1,593	615	....	....	....	....	....	....
332	Foreign...	−1,375	284	−567	−1,308	236	−414	....	....	....	....	....	....
3322	Currency and deposits...	−1,375	−60	−5	−1,308	−108	−4	....	....	....	....	....	....
3323	Securities other than shares...	—	344	−563	—	344	−410	....	....	....	....	....	....
3324	Loans...	—	—	—	—	—	—	....	....	....	....	....	....
3326	Insurance technical reserves...	—	—	—	—	—	—	....	....	....	....	....	....
3327	Financial derivatives...	—	—	—	—	—	—	....	....	....	....	....	....
3328	Other accounts payable...	—	—	—	—	—	—	....	....	....	....	....	....

Table 4   Holding gains in assets and liabilities

		2002	2003	2004p	2002	2003	2004p	2002	2003p	2004p	2002	2003p	2004p
4	**Change in net worth from hold. gains...**	1,291	975	4,763	3,358	309	5,344	....	....	2,995	....	....	8,411
41	**Nonfinancial assets...**	1,685	1,828	1,029	4,064	2,550	3,900	....	1,664	2,909	....	4,214	6,809
411	Fixed assets...	834	190	291	1,512	600	1,753	....	1,096	2,500	....	1,695	4,254
412	Inventories...	—	—	—	—	—	—	....	—	—	....	—	—
413	Valuables...	—	—	—	—	—	—	....	—	—	....	—	—
414	Nonproduced assets...	851	1,638	738	2,552	1,951	2,147	....	568	409	....	2,519	2,556
42	**Financial assets...**	−80	−789	3,417	13	668	480	....	....	....	....	....	....
421	Domestic...	−80	−789	3,703	13	668	789	....	....	....	....	....	....
422	Foreign...	—	—	−286	—	—	−308	....	....	....	....	....	....
423	Monetary gold and SDRs...	—	—	—	—	—	—	....	....	....	....	....	....
43	**Liabilities...**	313	64	−317	718	2,909	−964	....	....	....	....	....	....
431	Domestic...	231	4	—	703	2,801	−647	....	....	....	....	....	....
432	Foreign...	82	60	−317	15	108	−317	....	....	....	....	....	....

Table 5   Other changes in the volume of assets and liabilities

		2002	2003	2004p	2002	2003	2004p	2002	2003p	2004p	2002	2003p	2004p
5	**Change in net worth from vol. chngs...**	—	−36	1,459	600	1,068	6	....	—	—	....	1,068	6
51	**Nonfinancial assets...**	—	−13,759	—	—	1,650	253	....	—	—	....	1,650	253
511	Fixed assets...	—	−11,945	—	—	3,238	91	....	—	—	....	3,238	91
512	Inventories...	—	—	—	—	—	132	....	—	—	....	—	132
513	Valuables...	—	—	—	—	—	—	....	—	—	....	—	—
514	Nonproduced assets...	—	−1,814	—	—	−1,588	30	....	—	—	....	−1,588	30
52	**Financial assets...**	—	13,722	1,459	600	−582	−189	....	—	—	....	−582	−189
521	Domestic...	—	13,722	1,459	600	−582	−189	....	—	—	....	−582	−189
522	Foreign...	—	—	—	—	—	—	....	—	—	....	—	—
523	Monetary gold and SDRs...	—	—	—	—	—	—	....	—	—	....	—	—
53	**Liabilities...**	—	—	—	—	—	59	....	—	—	....	—	59
531	Domestic...	—	—	—	—	—	59	....	—	—	....	—	59
532	Foreign...	—	—	—	—	—	—	....	—	—	....	—	—

Table 6   Balance sheet

		2002	2003	2004p	2002	2003	2004p	2002	2003p	2004p	2002	2003p	2004p
6	**Net worth...**	....	20,913	32,626	21,513	20,826	32,626	....	55,868	59,537	....	76,694	92,163
61	**Nonfinancial assets...**	....	16,066	17,231	28,088	45,764	50,811	....	52,393	56,226	....	98,156	107,038
611	Fixed assets...	....	12,150	12,789	24,145	37,606	40,165	....	48,161	51,507	....	85,767	91,672
6111	Buildings and structures...	....	7,972	8,310	20,052	30,139	32,241	....	46,947	50,229	....	77,086	82,470
6112	Machinery and equipment...	....	788	1,095	938	2,506	2,793	....	687	679	....	3,193	3,471
6113	Other fixed assets...	....	3,390	3,385	3,156	4,961	5,132	....	526	599	....	5,487	5,731
612	Inventories...	....	274	278	278	391	540	....	19	19	....	410	559
613	Valuables...	....	—	—	—	—	—	....	—	—	....	—	—
614	Nonproduced assets...	....	3,642	4,163	3,664	7,766	10,106	....	4,213	4,700	....	11,979	14,806
6141	Land...	....	2,928	3,557	2,883	7,037	9,478	....	4,213	4,700	....	11,250	14,179
6142	Subsoil assets...	....	—	—	—	—	—	....	—	—	....	—	—
6143	Other naturally occurring assets...	....	312	251	332	312	251	....	—	—	....	312	251
6144	Intangible nonproduced assets...	....	402	356	449	417	377	....	—	—	....	417	377

In Millions of Dollars / Year Ending June 30 / Noncash Reporter

	Budgetary Central Government			Central Government			Local Government			General Government		
	2002	2003	2004p	2002	2003	2004p	2002	2003p	2004p	2002	2003p	2004p
62 Financial assets	....	50,233	58,847	37,733	44,778	49,616	....	6,512	6,562	....	51,290	56,178
621 Domestic	....	43,746	49,676	29,966	35,946	35,594	....	6,512	6,562	....	42,459	42,156
6212 Currency and deposits	....	3,553	1,799	2,655	5,444	4,027	....	1,137	936	....	6,581	4,963
6213 Securities other than shares	....	3,298	2,288	−298	6,605	6,127	....	980	682	....	7,585	6,809
6214 Loans	....	6,554	8,288	5,720	5,839	6,502	....	385	357	....	6,224	6,859
6215 Shares and other equity	....	23,411	29,458	15,614	9,589	9,473	....	3,393	3,630	....	12,982	13,103
6216 Insurance technical reserves	....	—	—	—	—	—	....	—	—	....	—	—
6217 Financial derivatives	....	—	—	—	—	—	....	—	—	....	—	—
6218 Other accounts receivable	....	6,931	7,843	6,274	8,470	9,465	....	617	957	....	9,088	10,422
622 Foreign	....	6,487	9,171	7,768	8,831	14,022	....	—	—	....	8,831	14,022
6222 Currency and deposits	....	14	13	6,542	14	21	....	—	—	....	14	21
6223 Securities other than shares	....	5,226	5,625	—	5,404	6,446	....	—	—	....	5,404	6,446
6224 Loans	....	—	—	—	—	—	....	—	—	....	—	—
6225 Shares and other equity	....	1,248	3,533	1,226	3,413	7,555	....	—	—	....	3,413	7,555
6226 Insurance technical reserves	....	—	—	—	—	—	....	—	—	....	—	—
6227 Financial derivatives	....	—	—	—	—	—	....	—	—	....	—	—
6228 Other accounts receivable	....	—	—	—	—	—	....	—	—	....	—	—
623 Monetary gold and SDRs	....	....	....	....	....	....	....	....	....	....	....	....
63 Liabilities	....	45,386	43,452	44,307	69,715	67,801	....	3,037	3,251	....	72,752	71,052
631 Domestic	....	38,689	37,639	37,954	63,018	61,836	....	3,037	3,251	....	66,055	65,087
6312 Currency and deposits	....	88	88	75	88	88	....	68	122	....	156	209
6313 Securities other than shares	....	31,724	30,725	31,736	29,420	27,756	....	—	—	....	29,420	27,756
6314 Loans	....	—	—	—	—	—	....	1,974	2,027	....	1,974	2,027
6316 Insurance technical reserves	....	1	—	—	23,012	22,888	....	—	—	....	23,012	22,888
6317 Financial derivatives	....	—	—	—	—	—	....	—	—	....	—	—
6318 Other accounts payable	....	6,877	6,827	6,144	10,498	11,104	....	995	1,103	....	11,493	12,206
632 Foreign	....	6,697	5,813	6,353	6,697	5,966	....	—	—	....	6,697	5,966
6322 Currency and deposits	....	—	—	6,353	—	—	....	—	—	....	—	—
6323 Securities other than shares	....	6,697	5,813	—	6,697	5,966	....	—	—	....	6,697	5,966
6324 Loans	....	—	—	—	—	—	....	—	—	....	—	—
6326 Insurance technical reserves	....	—	—	—	—	—	....	—	—	....	—	—
6327 Financial derivatives	....	—	—	—	—	—	....	—	—	....	—	—
6328 Other accounts payable	....	—	—	—	—	—	....	—	—	....	—	—
Memorandum items:												
6M2 Net financial worth	....	4,847	15,395	−6,574	−24,938	−18,185	....	3,475	3,311	....	−21,462	−14,875
6M3 Debt at market value	....	....	....	....	....	....	....	....	....	....	....	....
6M4 Debt at nominal value	....	....	....	....	....	....	....	....	....	....	....	....
6M5 Arrears	....	....	....	....	....	....	....	....	....	....	....	....
6M6 Obligations for social security benefits	....	....	....	....	....	....	....	....	....	....	....	....
6M7 Contingent liabilities	....	....	....	....	....	....	....	....	....	....	....	....
6M8 Uncapitalized military weapons, systems	....	....	....	....	....	....	....	....	....	....	....	....
Table 7 Outlays by functions of govt.												
7 Total outlays	37,506	39,719	41,350	42,978	45,733	47,937	5,293	4,686	5,302	....	49,891	52,624
701 General public services	....	....	3,646	....	....	3,572	....	887	995	....	....	4,559
7017 Public debt transactions	2,513	2,633	2,500	2,192	2,494	2,519	141	140	142	....	2,634	2,660
7018 General transfers between levels of govt	....	....	−10	....	....	—	....	—	—	....	....	—
702 Defense	....	....	1,287	....	....	1,285	....	29	34	....	....	1,315
703 Public order and safety	....	....	1,876	....	....	2,076	....	—	—	....	....	2,067
704 Economic affairs	....	....	3,398	....	....	3,311	....	1,365	1,554	....	....	4,347
7042 Agriculture, forestry, fishing, and hunting	....	....	361	....	....	863	....	16	14	....	....	877
7043 Fuel and energy	....	....	88	....	....	117	....	—	—	....	....	117
7044 Mining, manufacturing, and construction	....	....	—	....	....	—	....	—	—	....	....	—
7045 Transport	....	....	1,465	....	....	1,583	....	1,349	1,540	....	....	2,605
7046 Communication	....	....	—	....	....	—	....	—	—	....	....	—
705 Environmental protection	....	....	−190	....	....	−203	....	973	1,115	....	....	912
706 Housing and community amenities	....	....	78	....	....	767	....	369	430	....	....	1,121
707 Health	....	....	8,093	....	....	8,336	....	—	—	....	....	8,336
7072 Outpatient services	....	....	8,093	....	....	8,329	....	—	—	....	....	8,329
7073 Hospital services	....	....	....	....	....	....	....	—	—	....	....	—
7074 Public health services	....	....	—	....	....	6	....	—	—	....	....	6
708 Recreation, culture, and religion	....	....	661	....	....	1,667	....	1,057	966	....	....	2,632

In Millions of Dollars / Year Ending June 30 / Noncash Reporter

		Budgetary Central Government			Central Government			Local Government			General Government		
		2002	2003	2004p	2002	2003	2004p	2002	2003p	2004p	2002	2003p	2004p
709	**Education**....................	....	....	**7,580**	....	....	**9,864**	....	—	—	....	....	**9,864**
7091	Pre-primary and primary education..............	....	....	2,877	....	....	3,105	....	—	—	....	....	3,105
7092	Secondary education....................	....	....	1,954	....	....	2,281	....	—	—	....	....	2,281
7094	Tertiary education....................	....	....	2,574	....	....	4,218	....	—	—	....	....	4,218
710	**Social protection**....................	....	....	**14,921**	....	....	**17,264**	....	5	208	....	....	**17,471**
7	Statistical discrepancy: Total outlays..............	....	....	—	....	....	—	....	....	....	....	....	—

Table 8   Transactions in financial assets and liabilities by sector

		Budgetary Central Government			Central Government			Local Government			General Government		
82	**Net acquisition of financial assets**........	**2,043**	**5,035**	**3,738**	**2,701**	**6,449**	**4,544**	....	....	....	....	....
821	Domestic....................	3,301	4,365	769	4,550	4,846	−955	....	....	....	....	....	....
8211	General government....................	....	....	....	....	....	....	....	....	....	....	....	....
8212	Central bank....................	....	....	....	....	....	....	....	....	....	....	....	....
8213	Other depository corporations....................	....	....	....	....	....	....	....	....	....	....	....	....
8214	Financial corporations n.e.c....................	....	....	....	....	....	....	....	....	....	....	....	....
8215	Nonfinancial corporations....................	....	....	....	....	....	....	....	....	....	....	....	....
8216	Households & NPIs serving households......	....	....	....	....	....	....	....	....	....	....	....	....
822	Foreign....................	−1,258	669	2,969	−1,849	1,602	5,499	....	....	....	....	....	....
8221	General government....................	....	....	....	....	....	....	....	....	....	....	....	....
8227	International organizations....................	....	....	....	....	....	....	....	....	....	....	....	....
8228	Financial corporations other than international organizations..............	....	....	....	....	....	....	....	....	....	....	....	....
8229	Other nonresidents....................	....	....	....	....	....	....	....	....	....	....	....	....
823	Monetary gold and SDRs....................	—	—	—	....	....	....	....	....	....	....	....	....
83	**Net incurrence of liabilities**....................	**−402**	**1,037**	**−1,635**	**497**	**2,396**	**−940**	....	....	....	....	....	....
831	Domestic....................	973	753	−1,067	1,805	2,159	−526	....	....	....	....	....	....
8311	General government....................	....	....	....	....	....	....	....	....	....	....	....	....
8312	Central bank....................	....	....	....	....	....	....	....	....	....	....	....	....
8313	Other depository corporations....................	....	....	....	....	....	....	....	....	....	....	....	....
8314	Financial corporations n.e.c....................	....	....	....	....	....	....	....	....	....	....	....	....
8315	Nonfinancial corporations....................	....	....	....	....	....	....	....	....	....	....	....	....
8316	Households & NPIs serving households......	....	....	....	....	....	....	....	....	....	....	....	....
832	Foreign....................	−1,375	284	−567	−1,308	236	−414	....	....	....	....	....	....
8321	General government....................	....	....	....	....	....	....	....	....	....	....	....	....
8327	International organizations....................	....	....	....	....	....	....	....	....	....	....	....	....
8328	Financial corporations other than international organizations..............	....	....	....	....	....	....	....	....	....	....	....	....
8329	Other nonresidents....................	....	....	....	....	....	....	....	....	....	....	....	....

Nicaragua   278

In millions of Cordobas / Year Ending December 31 / Cash Reporter

		Budgetary Central Government			Central Government			Local Government			General Government		
		2002	2003p	2004p	2002	2003p	2004p	2002	2003	2004	2002	2003	2004
Statement of government operations													
Statement of other economic flows													
Balance sheet													
Statement of sources and uses of cash													
1	Cash receipts from operating activities..........	10,086	12,230	14,609	12,537	14,970	17,837	....	....	....	....	....	....
11	Taxes...	7,739	9,422	11,253	7,739	9,422	11,253	....	....	....	....	....	....
12	Social contributions.............................	—	—	—	2,217	2,468	2,874	....	....	....	....	....	....
13	Grants...	1,522	2,079	2,374	1,524	2,079	2,374	....	....	....	....	....	....
14	Other receipts....................................	824	729	983	1,057	1,001	1,337	....	....	....	....	....	....
2	Cash payments for operating activities..........	9,085	10,573	11,932	11,044	12,711	14,332	....	....	....	....	....	....
21	Compensation of employees......................	3,444	3,834	4,178	3,591	3,976	4,327	....	....	....	....	....	....
22	Purchases of goods and services.................	1,333	1,246	1,468	1,893	1,882	2,219	....	....	....	....	....	....
24	Interest...	1,287	1,919	1,478	1,287	1,919	1,478	....	....	....	....	....	....
25	Subsidies..	—	—	—	—	—	—	....	....	....	....	....	....
26	Grants...	2,504	3,050	4,240	2,504	3,050	4,240	....	....	....	....	....	....
27	Social benefits....................................	157	223	227	1,405	1,581	1,725	....	....	....	....	....	....
28	Other payments...................................	361	300	340	363	303	343	....	....	....	....	....	....
CIO	*Net cash inflow from oper. activities.....*	*1,001*	*1,657*	*2,678*	*1,493*	*2,259*	*3,505*	....	....	....	....	....	....
31.1	Purchases of nonfinancial assets.................	2,442	3,427	4,268	2,473	3,431	4,278	....	....	....	....	....	....
31.2	Sales of nonfinancial assets......................	26	6	15	26	6	15	....	....	....	....	....	....
31	Net cash outflow from investments in nonfinancial assets...........................	2,416	3,420	4,253	2,448	3,425	4,263	....	....	....	....	....	....
CSD	*Cash surplus/deficit.....*	*−1,416*	*−1,764*	*−1,575*	*−954*	*−1,166*	*−758*	....	....	....	....	....	....
32x	Net acquisition of fin assets, excl. cash..........	....	....	....	....	....	....	....	....	....	....	....	....
321x	Domestic..	....	....	....	....	....	....	....	....	....	....	....	....
322x	Foreign..	....	....	....	....	....	....	....	....	....	....	....	....
323	Monetary gold and SDRs..........................	....	....	....	....	....	....	....	....	....	....	....	....
33	Net incurrence of liabilities......................	....	....	....	....	....	....	....	....	....	....	....	....
331	Domestic..	....	....	....	....	....	....	....	....	....	....	....	....
332	Foreign..	....	....	....	....	....	....	....	....	....	....	....	....
NFB	Net cash inflow from fin. activities...............	....	....	....	....	....	....	....	....	....	....	....	....
NCB	*Net change in the stock of cash.............*	....	....	....	....	....	....	....	....	....	....	....	....
Table 1 Revenue													
1	**Revenue**...	**10,086**	**12,230**	**14,609**	**12,537**	**14,970**	**17,837**	....	....	....	....	....	....
11	**Taxes**...	**7,739**	**9,422**	**11,253**	**7,739**	**9,422**	**11,253**	....	....	....	....	....	....
111	Taxes on income, profits, & capital gains.....	1,610	2,448	3,176	1,610	2,448	3,176	....	....	....	....	....	....
1111	Individuals.....................................	....	....	....	....	....	....	....	....	....	....	....	....
1112	Corporations and other enterprises...........	....	....	....	....	....	....	....	....	....	....	....	....
112	Taxes on payroll and workforce.................	—	—	—	—	—	—	....	....	....	....	....	....
113	Taxes on property...............................	2	—	1	2	—	1	....	....	....	....	....	....
114	Taxes on goods and services....................	5,473	6,333	7,377	5,473	6,333	7,377	....	....	....	....	....	....
1141	General taxes on goods and services..........	3,356	3,813	4,575	3,356	3,813	4,575	....	....	....	....	....	....
1142	Excises..	2,117	2,520	2,802	2,117	2,520	2,802	....	....	....	....	....	....
115	Taxes on int'l. trade and transactions..........	642	628	684	642	628	684	....	....	....	....	....	....
116	Other taxes......................................	12	13	15	12	13	15	....	....	....	....	....	....
12	**Social contributions**.............................	—	—	—	**2,217**	**2,468**	**2,874**	....	....	....	....	....	....
121	Social security contributions.....................	—	—	—	2,217	2,468	2,874	....	....	....	....	....	....
122	Other social contributions.......................	—	—	—	—	—	—	....	....	....	....	....	....
13	**Grants**...	**1,522**	**2,079**	**2,374**	**1,524**	**2,079**	**2,374**	....	....	....	....	....	....
131	From foreign governments.......................	1,522	2,079	2,374	1,522	2,079	2,374	....	....	....	....	....	....
132	From international organizations.................	—	—	—	—	—	—	....	....	....	....	....	....
133	From other general government units..........	—	—	—	2	—	—	....	....	....	....	....	....
14	**Other revenue**.....................................	**824**	**729**	**983**	**1,057**	**1,001**	**1,337**	....	....	....	....	....	....
Table 2 Expense by economic type													
2	**Expense**..	**9,085**	**10,573**	**11,932**	**11,044**	**12,711**	**14,332**	....	....	....	....	....	....
21	**Compensation of employees**.................	**3,444**	**3,834**	**4,178**	**3,591**	**3,976**	**4,327**	....	....	....	....	....	....
211	Wages and salaries..............................	3,162	3,533	3,836	3,295	3,660	3,970	....	....	....	....	....	....
212	Social contributions.............................	282	301	342	296	316	357	....	....	....	....	....	....
22	**Use of goods and services**....................	**1,333**	**1,246**	**1,468**	**1,893**	**1,882**	**2,219**	....	....	....	....	....	....
23	**Consumption of fixed capital**...............	....	....	....	....	....	....	....	....	....	....	....	....
24	**Interest**..	**1,287**	**1,919**	**1,478**	**1,287**	**1,919**	**1,478**	....	....	....	....	....	....
25	**Subsidies**..	—	—	—	—	—	—	....	....	....	....	....	....

In millions of Cordobas / Year Ending December 31 / Cash Reporter

	Budgetary Central Government			Central Government			Local Government			General Government		
	2002	2003p	2004p	2002	2003p	2004p	2002	2003	2004	2002	2003	2004
26 Grants..................	2,504	3,050	4,240	2,504	3,050	4,240	....	....	....	....	....	....
261 To foreign govenments................	—	50	48	—	50	48	....	....	....	....	....	....
262 To international organizations............	55	—	—	55	—	—	....	....	....	....	....	....
263 To other general government units..........	2,450	3,000	4,192	2,450	3,000	4,192	....	....	....	....	....	....
2631 Current..................	1,165	1,269	1,660	1,165	1,269	1,660	....	....	....	....	....	....
2632 Capital..................	1,285	1,731	2,532	1,285	1,731	2,532	....	....	....	....	....	....
27 Social benefits................	157	223	227	1,405	1,581	1,725	....	....	....	....	....	....
28 Other expense................	361	300	340	363	303	343	....	....	....	....	....	....
281 Property expense other than interest...........	—	—	—	—	—	—	....	....	....	....	....	....
282 Miscellaneous other expense................	361	300	340	363	303	343	....	....	....	....	....	....
2821 Current..................	180	135	197	183	138	201	....	....	....	....	....	....
2822 Capital..................	181	166	142	181	166	142	....	....	....	....	....	....
Table 3 Transactions in assets and liabilities												
3 Change in net worth from transactns....	....	....	....	....	....	....	....	....	....	....	....	....
31 Net acquisition of nonfinancial assets...	2,416	3,420	4,253	2,448	3,425	4,263	....	....	....	....	....	....
311 Fixed assets................	2,416	3,420	4,253	2,448	3,425	4,263	....	....	....	....	....	....
3111 Buildings and structures.........	....	....	....	....	....	....	....	....	....	....	....	....
3112 Machinery and equipment........	....	....	....	....	....	....	....	....	....	....	....	....
3113 Other fixed assets........	....	....	....	....	....	....	....	....	....	....	....	....
312 Inventories................	—	—	—	—	—	—	....	....	....	....	....	....
313 Valuables................	—	—	—	—	—	—	....	....	....	....	....	....
314 Nonproduced assets................	—	—	—	—	—	—	....	....	....	....	....	....
3141 Land................	—	—	—	—	—	—	....	....	....	....	....	....
3142 Subsoil assets................	—	—	—	—	—	—	....	....	....	....	....	....
3143 Other naturally occurring assets........	—	—	—	—	—	—	....	....	....	....	....	....
3144 Intangible nonproduced assets........	—	—	—	—	—	—	....	....	....	....	....	....
32 Net acquisition of financial assets........	....	....	....	....	....	....	....	....	....	....	....	....
321 Domestic................	....	....	....	....	....	....	....	....	....	....	....	....
3212 Currency and deposits........	....	....	....	....	....	....	....	....	....	....	....	....
3213 Securities other than shares........	....	....	....	....	....	....	....	....	....	....	....	....
3214 Loans................	....	....	....	....	....	....	....	....	....	....	....	....
3215 Shares and other equity........	....	....	....	....	....	....	....	....	....	....	....	....
3216 Insurance technical reserves........	....	....	....	....	....	....	....	....	....	....	....	....
3217 Financial derivatives........	....	....	....	....	....	....	....	....	....	....	....	....
3218 Other accounts receivable........	....	....	....	....	....	....	....	....	....	....	....	....
322 Foreign................	....	....	....	....	....	....	....	....	....	....	....	....
3222 Currency and deposits........	....	....	....	....	....	....	....	....	....	....	....	....
3223 Securities other than shares........	....	....	....	....	....	....	....	....	....	....	....	....
3224 Loans................	....	....	....	....	....	....	....	....	....	....	....	....
3225 Shares and other equity........	....	....	....	....	....	....	....	....	....	....	....	....
3226 Insurance technical reserves........	....	....	....	....	....	....	....	....	....	....	....	....
3227 Financial derivatives........	....	....	....	....	....	....	....	....	....	....	....	....
3228 Other accounts receivable........	....	....	....	....	....	....	....	....	....	....	....	....
323 Monetary gold and SDRs........	....	....	....	....	....	....	....	....	....	....	....	....
33 Net incurrence of liabilities................	....	....	....	....	....	....	....	....	....	....	....	....
331 Domestic................	....	....	....	....	....	....	....	....	....	....	....	....
3312 Currency and deposits........	....	....	....	....	....	....	....	....	....	....	....	....
3313 Securities other than shares........	....	....	....	....	....	....	....	....	....	....	....	....
3314 Loans................	....	....	....	....	....	....	....	....	....	....	....	....
3316 Insurance technical reserves........	....	....	....	....	....	....	....	....	....	....	....	....
3317 Financial derivatives........	....	....	....	....	....	....	....	....	....	....	....	....
3318 Other accounts payable........	....	....	....	....	....	....	....	....	....	....	....	....
332 Foreign................	....	....	....	....	....	....	....	....	....	....	....	....
3322 Currency and deposits........	....	....	....	....	....	....	....	....	....	....	....	....
3323 Securities other than shares........	....	....	....	....	....	....	....	....	....	....	....	....
3324 Loans................	....	....	....	....	....	....	....	....	....	....	....	....
3326 Insurance technical reserves........	....	....	....	....	....	....	....	....	....	....	....	....
3327 Financial derivatives........	....	....	....	....	....	....	....	....	....	....	....	....
3328 Other accounts payable........	....	....	....	....	....	....	....	....	....	....	....	....

	Budgetary Central Government			Central Government			Local Government			General Government		
	2002	2003p	2004p	2002	2003p	2004p	2002	2003	2004	2002	2003	2004
Table 4 Holding gains in assets and liabilities												
Table 5 Other changes in the volume of assets and liabilities												
Table 6 Balance sheet												
Table 7 Outlays by functions of govt.												
7 Total outlays.............................	11,501	13,994	16,184	13,491	16,136	18,595	....	....	....	....	....	....
701 General public services..........................	....	....	....	....	....	....	....	....	....	....	....	....
7017 Public debt transactions.....................	1,287	1,919	1,478	1,287	1,919	1,478	....	....	....	....	....	....
7018 General transfers between levels of govt......	....	....	....	....	....	....	....	....	....	....	....	....
702 Defense..	....	....	....	....	....	....	....	....	....	....	....	....
703 Public order and safety.........................	....	....	....	....	....	....	....	....	....	....	....	....
704 Economic affairs..................................	....	....	....	....	....	....	....	....	....	....	....	....
7042 Agriculture, forestry, fishing, and hunting.....	....	....	....	....	....	....	....	....	....	....	....	....
7043 Fuel and energy...................................	....	....	....	....	....	....	....	....	....	....	....	....
7044 Mining, manufacturing, and construction.....	....	....	....	....	....	....	....	....	....	....	....	....
7045 Transport...	....	....	....	....	....	....	....	....	....	....	....	....
7046 Communication....................................	....	....	....	....	....	....	....	....	....	....	....	....
705 Environmental protection......................	....	....	....	....	....	....	....	....	....	....	....	....
706 Housing and community amenities........	....	....	....	....	....	....	....	....	....	....	....	....
707 Health..	....	....	....	....	....	....	....	....	....	....	....	....
7072 Outpatient services..............................	....	....	....	....	....	....	....	....	....	....	....	....
7073 Hospital services.................................	....	....	....	....	....	....	....	....	....	....	....	....
7074 Public health services..........................	....	....	....	....	....	....	....	....	....	....	....	....
708 Recreation, culture, and religion............	....	....	....	....	....	....	....	....	....	....	....	....
709 Education..	....	....	....	....	....	....	....	....	....	....	....	....
7091 Pre-primary and primary education.............	....	....	....	....	....	....	....	....	....	....	....	....
7092 Secondary education............................	....	....	....	....	....	....	....	....	....	....	....	....
7094 Tertiary education................................	....	....	....	....	....	....	....	....	....	....	....	....
710 Social protection.................................	....	....	....	....	....	....	....	....	....	....	....	....
7 Statistical discrepancy: Total outlays.............	....	....	....	....	....	....	....	....	....	....	....	....
Table 8 Transactions in financial assets and liabilities by sector												

In Billions of Kroner / Year Ending December 31 / Noncash Reporter

	Budgetary Central Government			Central Government			Local Government			General Government		
	2002	2003p	2004p	2002	2003p	2004p	2002	2003p	2004p	2002	2003p	2004p
Statement of government operations												
1 Revenue......	671.79	680.23	762.60	728.26	739.45	831.90	224.64	223.98	231.59	855.06	880.65	976.96
2 Expense......	682.71	688.35	727.31	584.71	602.45	627.37	214.21	226.83	230.52	702.22	747.42	771.00
GOB *Gross operating balance.....*	*4.32*	*7.67*	*51.61*	*158.77*	*152.80*	*220.84*	*25.18*	*13.26*	*17.77*	*182.81*	*165.13*	*238.96*
NOB *Net operating balance.....*	*−10.91*	*−8.13*	*35.30*	*143.55*	*137.00*	*204.53*	*10.43*	*−2.85*	*1.07*	*152.84*	*133.23*	*205.95*
31 Net acquisition of nonfinancial assets.....	−3.26	−4.30	−5.22	3.53	3.97	4.91	8.41	10.45	8.12	11.94	14.42	13.03
NLB *Net lending/borrowing.....*	*−7.65*	*−3.83*	*40.52*	*140.01*	*133.03*	*199.62*	*2.02*	*−13.30*	*−7.05*	*140.89*	*118.81*	*192.92*
32 Net acquisition of financial assets.....	−14.03	48.04	....	231.64	265.38	....	5.81	.50	....	237.33	271.20	....
33 Net incurrence of liabilities.....	9.87	49.60	....	108.17	143.80	....	−1.67	16.70	....	106.37	165.82	....
NLB Statistical discrepancy.....	−16.25	2.27	....	−16.54	−11.45	....	5.46	−2.90	....	−9.93	−13.43	....
Statement of other economic flows												
4 *Change in net worth from*												
holding gains.....	....	....	....	....	....	....	....	....	....	....	....	....
41 Nonfinancial assets.....	....	....	....	....	....	....	....	....	....	....	....	....
42 Financial assets.....	5.70	3.76	....	−149.44	121.90	....	1.77	—	....	−147.67	121.90	....
43 Liabilities.....	—	—	....	....	....	....	....	....	....	....	....	....
5 *Change in net worth from*												
other volume changes.....	....	....	....	....	....	....	....	....	....	....	....	....
51 Nonfinancial assets.....	....	....	....	....	....	....	....	....	....	....	....	....
52 Financial assets.....	2.06	—	....	2.06	—	....	—	—	....	2.06	—	....
53 Liabilities.....	—	7.40	....	2.90	7.40	....	−2.90	—	....	—	7.40	....
Balance sheet												
6 *Net worth.....*	*659.08*	*668.25*	....	*1,402.34*	*1,652.79*	....	*341.71*	*358.08*	....	*1,744.05*	*2,010.87*	....
61 Nonfinancial assets.....	296.30	310.67	....	296.30	310.67	....	364.94	397.50	....	661.23	708.17	....
62 Financial assets.....	691.40	743.19	....	1,544.12	1,931.41	....	150.33	150.83	....	1,677.47	2,070.57	....
63 Liabilities.....	328.61	385.61	....	438.08	589.28	....	173.56	190.26	....	594.66	767.87	....
Statement of sources and uses of cash												
1 Cash receipts from operating activities.....	664.92	680.54	725.49	721.38	739.77	794.78	229.59	221.47	228.54	853.13	878.46	936.79
11 Taxes.....	415.85	421.87	449.58	417.50	423.71	451.52	90.88	96.94	101.36	508.38	520.65	552.87
12 Social contributions.....	135.83	142.71	149.87	148.52	155.22	163.15	—	—	—	148.52	155.22	163.15
13 Grants.....	1.04	2.55	1.69	.56	.64	.86	97.34	82.14	85.68	.05	—	—
14 Other receipts.....	112.20	113.41	124.35	154.81	160.20	179.26	41.36	42.39	41.51	196.17	202.59	220.77
2 Cash payments for operating activities.....	670.55	669.50	708.03	572.55	583.60	608.09	199.47	210.72	213.82	675.32	712.45	735.02
21 Compensation of employees.....	46.62	42.28	45.28	91.11	94.09	100.41	119.99	126.98	130.05	211.10	221.07	230.46
22 Purchases of goods and services.....	51.11	44.82	46.55	70.59	67.10	72.18	40.30	42.93	44.53	110.89	110.02	116.71
24 Interest.....	17.24	18.61	16.79	18.20	20.36	17.67	9.55	8.43	7.30	27.74	28.79	24.98
25 Subsidies.....	24.28	22.09	22.99	30.71	29.25	29.96	5.98	6.13	5.50	36.69	35.37	35.46
26 Grants.....	296.75	284.64	310.30	108.32	93.64	99.24	1.67	2.26	2.04	13.28	14.04	14.39
27 Social benefits.....	226.20	248.81	256.12	241.34	265.62	274.36	14.83	16.42	18.46	256.17	282.04	292.81
28 Other payments.....	8.35	8.25	10.00	12.30	13.55	14.26	7.15	7.57	5.94	19.45	21.12	20.21
CIO *Net cash inflow from oper. activities.....*	*−5.63*	*11.04*	*17.47*	*148.83*	*156.17*	*186.70*	*30.12*	*10.75*	*14.72*	*177.80*	*166.01*	*201.77*
31.1 Purchases of nonfinancial assets.....	12.54	11.95	12.19	19.46	20.45	22.45	25.87	28.61	27.07	45.33	49.06	49.51
31.2 Sales of nonfinancial assets.....	.57	.46	1.10	.70	.69	1.23	2.72	2.05	2.25	3.42	2.73	3.48
31 Net cash outflow from investments												
in nonfinancial assets.....	11.97	11.49	11.09	18.76	19.76	21.22	23.15	26.56	24.82	41.91	46.32	46.04
CSD *Cash surplus/deficit.....*	*−17.59*	*−.45*	*6.38*	*130.07*	*136.41*	*165.48*	*6.96*	*−15.80*	*−10.10*	*135.89*	*119.69*	*155.73*
32x Net acquisition of fin assets, excl. cash.....	10.84	−10.90	....	260.29	209.28	....	6.64	5.30	....	265.66	218.98	....
321x Domestic.....	10.77	−11.85	....	58.72	−64.17	....	7.83	2.01	....	65.28	−57.76	....
322x Foreign.....	.07	.96	....	201.56	273.46	....	−1.19	3.28	....	200.38	276.74	....
323 Monetary gold and SDRs.....	—	—	—	—	—	—	—	—	—	—	—	—
33 Net incurrence of liabilities.....	9.87	49.60	....	108.17	143.80	....	−1.67	16.70	....	106.37	165.82	....
331 Domestic.....	12.08	39.33	....	25.22	36.10	....	3.78	15.24	....	28.87	56.66	....
332 Foreign.....	−2.21	10.28	....	82.95	107.70	....	−5.45	1.46	....	77.50	109.15	....
NFB Net cash inflow from fin. activities.....	−.97	60.50	....	−152.12	−65.49	....	−8.31	11.40	....	−159.29	−53.17	....
NCB *Net change in the stock of cash.....*	*−18.56*	*60.05*	....	*−22.05*	*70.92*	....	*−1.35*	*−4.41*	....	*−23.40*	*66.52*	....
Table 1 Revenue												
1 **Revenue.....**	**671.79**	**680.23**	**762.60**	**728.26**	**739.45**	**831.90**	**224.64**	**223.98**	**231.59**	**855.06**	**880.65**	**976.96**
11 **Taxes.....**	**426.37**	**421.24**	**486.30**	**428.02**	**423.08**	**488.23**	**85.94**	**99.45**	**104.41**	**513.96**	**522.53**	**592.64**
111 Taxes on income, profits, & capital gains.....	212.75	204.88	257.86	212.86	205.02	258.01	75.68	88.73	92.97	288.54	293.75	350.97
1111 Individuals.....	88.20	79.24	87.40	88.20	79.24	87.40	75.68	88.73	92.97	163.89	167.97	180.37
1112 Corporations and other enterprises.....	124.54	125.63	170.46	124.66	125.78	170.60	—	—	—	124.66	125.78	170.60
112 Taxes on payroll and workforce.....	—	—	—	—	—	—	—	—	—	—	—	—
113 Taxes on property.....	8.03	8.52	10.11	8.03	8.53	10.12	8.11	8.66	9.24	16.14	17.18	19.35
114 Taxes on goods and services.....	203.99	206.00	216.34	205.52	207.70	218.13	2.15	2.06	2.20	207.67	209.76	220.32
1141 General taxes on goods and services.....	135.28	135.30	143.08	135.67	135.67	143.45	—	—	—	135.67	135.67	143.45
1142 Excises.....	40.30	42.43	41.27	40.35	42.46	41.24	—	—	—	40.35	42.46	41.24

		Budgetary Central Government			Central Government			Local Government			General Government		
		2002	2003p	2004p	2002	2003p	2004p	2002	2003p	2004p	2002	2003p	2004p
115	Taxes on int'l. trade and transactions...........	1.61	1.74	1.90	1.61	1.74	1.90	—	—	—	1.61	1.74	1.90
116	Other taxes.....................................	—	.09	.08	—	.09	.08	—	—	—	—	.09	.08
12	**Social contributions**...........................	**138.41**	**143.03**	**150.26**	**151.10**	**155.53**	**163.55**	**—**	**—**	**—**	**151.10**	**155.53**	**163.55**
121	Social security contributions....................	138.41	143.03	150.26	151.10	155.53	163.55	—	—	—	151.10	155.53	163.55
122	Other social contributions......................	—	—	—	—	—	—	—	—	—	—	—	—
13	**Grants**..	**1.04**	**2.55**	**1.69**	**.56**	**.64**	**.86**	**97.34**	**82.14**	**85.68**	**.05**	**—**	**—**
131	From foreign governments.......................	—	—	—	—	—	—	—	—	—	—	—	—
132	From international organizations.................	.05	—	—	.05	—	—	—	—	—	.05	—	—
133	From other general government units...........	.99	2.55	1.69	.50	.64	.85	97.34	82.14	85.68	—	—	—
14	**Other revenue**..................................	**105.97**	**113.41**	**124.35**	**148.58**	**160.21**	**179.26**	**41.36**	**42.39**	**41.51**	**189.95**	**202.59**	**220.77**

Table 2 Expense by economic type

		2002	2003p	2004p	2002	2003p	2004p	2002	2003p	2004p	2002	2003p	2004p
2	**Expense**..	**682.71**	**688.35**	**727.31**	**584.71**	**602.45**	**627.37**	**214.21**	**226.83**	**230.52**	**702.22**	**747.42**	**771.00**
21	**Compensation of employees**..................	**44.72**	**42.28**	**45.28**	**89.21**	**94.09**	**100.41**	**119.99**	**126.98**	**130.05**	**209.20**	**221.07**	**230.46**
211	Wages and salaries.............................	33.92	32.90	35.32	69.78	74.33	78.96	91.55	96.89	99.23	161.33	171.22	178.19
212	Social contributions............................	10.81	9.38	9.96	19.43	19.75	21.45	28.44	30.10	30.82	47.87	49.85	52.28
22	**Use of goods and services**.....................	**46.78**	**44.82**	**46.55**	**66.26**	**67.10**	**72.18**	**40.30**	**42.93**	**44.53**	**106.56**	**110.02**	**116.71**
23	**Consumption of fixed capital**.................	**15.23**	**15.79**	**16.31**	**15.23**	**15.79**	**16.31**	**14.74**	**16.11**	**16.70**	**29.97**	**31.91**	**33.01**
24	**Interest**...	**17.24**	**18.61**	**16.79**	**18.20**	**20.36**	**17.67**	**9.55**	**8.43**	**7.30**	**27.74**	**28.79**	**24.98**
25	**Subsidies**.......................................	**24.28**	**22.09**	**22.99**	**30.71**	**29.25**	**29.96**	**5.98**	**6.13**	**5.50**	**36.69**	**35.37**	**35.46**
26	**Grants**..	**296.75**	**284.64**	**310.30**	**108.32**	**93.64**	**99.24**	**1.67**	**2.26**	**2.04**	**13.28**	**14.04**	**14.39**
261	To foreign governents..........................	6.54	5.46	5.53	6.54	5.55	5.67	—	—	—	6.54	5.55	5.67
262	To international organizations..................	6.37	7.95	8.19	6.74	8.48	8.72	—	—	—	6.74	8.48	8.72
263	To other general government units.............	283.83	271.23	296.59	95.03	79.60	84.85	1.67	2.26	2.04	—	—	—
2631	Current......................................	281.72	269.98	295.54	92.92	79.60	83.81	1.67	2.26	2.04	—	—	—
2632	Capital.......................................	2.12	1.25	1.04	2.12	—	1.04	—	—	—	—	—	—
27	**Social benefits**.................................	**226.20**	**248.81**	**256.12**	**241.34**	**265.62**	**274.36**	**14.83**	**16.42**	**18.46**	**256.17**	**282.04**	**292.81**
28	**Other expense**..................................	**11.51**	**11.32**	**12.97**	**15.46**	**16.61**	**17.24**	**7.15**	**7.57**	**5.94**	**22.61**	**24.18**	**23.18**
281	Property expense other than interest...........	—	—	—	—	—	—	—	—	—	—	—	—
282	Miscellaneous other expense....................	11.51	11.32	12.97	15.46	16.61	17.24	7.15	7.57	5.94	22.61	24.18	23.18
2821	Current......................................	7.12	7.19	8.97	10.05	11.46	13.09	7.15	7.57	5.94	17.20	19.03	19.03
2822	Capital.......................................	4.39	4.12	4.01	5.41	5.15	4.15	—	—	—	5.41	5.15	4.15

Table 3 Transactions in assets and liabilities

		2002	2003p	2004p	2002	2003p	2004p	2002	2003p	2004p	2002	2003p	2004p
3	**Change in net worth from transactns....**	**−27.16**	**−5.86**	**35.30**	**127.01**	**125.55**	**204.53**	**15.89**	**−5.75**	**1.07**	**142.90**	**119.80**	**205.95**
31	**Net acquisition of nonfinancial assets...**	**−3.26**	**−4.30**	**−5.22**	**3.53**	**3.97**	**4.91**	**8.41**	**10.45**	**8.12**	**11.94**	**14.42**	**13.03**
311	Fixed assets....................................	−3.04	−4.06	−4.27	2.77	4.39	6.00	9.78	11.23	9.42	12.55	15.62	15.42
3111	Buildings and structures.....................	−.77	−1.45	−1.64	2.51	4.61	1.50	....	....	....	....	....	....
3112	Machinery and equipment....................	−1.06	−1.60	−1.53	1.48	.79	5.59	....	....	....	....	....	....
3113	Other fixed assets...........................	−1.21	−1.01	−1.10	−1.21	−1.01	−1.10	....	....	....	....	....	....
312	Inventories.....................................	—	—	—	—	—	—	—	—	—	—	—	—
313	Valuables.......................................	—	—	—	—	—	—	—	—	—	—	—	—
314	Nonproduced assets.............................	−.22	−.24	−.95	.76	−.42	−1.09	−1.37	−.78	−1.30	−.61	−1.21	−2.39
3141	Land...	−.22	−.24	−.95	.76	−.42	−1.09	−1.37	−.78	−1.30	−.61	−1.21	−2.39
3142	Subsoil assets................................	—	—	—	—	—	—	—	—	—	—	—	—
3143	Other naturally occurring assets..............	—	—	—	—	—	—	—	—	—	—	—	—
3144	Intangible nonproduced assets................	—	—	—	—	—	—	—	—	—	—	—	—
32	**Net acquisition of financial assets**	**−14.03**	**48.04**	**....**	**231.64**	**265.38**	**....**	**5.81**	**.50**	**....**	**237.33**	**271.20**	**....**
321	Domestic.......................................	−14.10	47.02	....	30.08	−18.43	....	7.00	−2.79	....	36.95	−15.90	....
3212	Currency and deposits.......................	−18.58	59.99	....	−11.94	60.57	....	−1.35	−4.41	....	−13.29	56.16	....
3213	Securities other than shares.................	.42	−.16	....	−2.18	−1.58	....	5.39	.62	....	1.72	.16	....
3214	Loans.......................................	13.34	1.94	....	13.50	1.29	....	1.57	−1.45	....	15.06	−.20	....
3215	Shares and other equity.....................	−15.59	−3.51	....	29.78	−71.58	....	2.22	4.54	....	31.99	−67.04	....
3216	Insurance technical reserves.................	—	—	....	—	—	....	—	—	....	—	—	....
3217	Financial derivatives........................	—	—	....	—	—	....	—	—	....	—	—	....
3218	Other accounts receivable...................	6.30	−11.24	....	.92	−7.13	....	−.83	−2.09	....	1.46	−4.98	....
322	Foreign..	.07	1.02	....	201.56	283.81	....	−1.19	3.29	....	200.38	287.10	....
3222	Currency and deposits.......................	.01	.06	....	−10.11	10.35	....	—	—	....	−10.11	10.36	....
3223	Securities other than shares.................	−.42	1.03	....	43.83	89.11	....	—	.06	....	43.83	89.17	....
3224	Loans.......................................	.20	1.59	....	66.81	102.88	....	—	.20	....	66.81	103.08	....
3225	Shares and other equity.....................	−1.26	.76	....	99.38	81.72	....	.07	−.04	....	99.45	81.68	....
3226	Insurance technical reserves.................	—	—	....	—	—	....	—	—	....	—	—	....
3227	Financial derivatives........................	—	—	....	—	—	....	—	—	....	—	—	....
3228	Other accounts receivable...................	1.53	−2.42	....	1.66	−.25	....	−1.26	3.07	....	.41	2.82	....
323	Monetary gold and SDRs......................	—	—	....	—	—	....	—	—	....	—	—	....

In Billions of Kroner / Year Ending December 31 / Noncash Reporter

		Budgetary Central Government			Central Government			Local Government			General Government		
		2002	2003p	2004p	2002	2003p	2004p	2002	2003p	2004p	2002	2003p	2004p
33	**Net incurrence of liabilities**	**9.87**	**49.60**	....	**108.17**	**143.80**	....	**−1.67**	**16.70**	....	**106.37**	**165.82**	....
331	Domestic	12.08	39.33	....	25.22	36.10	....	3.78	15.24	....	28.87	56.66	....
3312	Currency and deposits	—	—	....	—	—	....	—	—	....	—	—	....
3313	Securities other than shares	6.51	34.42	....	8.18	34.83	....	−1.15	5.65	....	5.54	40.53	....
3314	Loans	9.36	−.71	....	4.87	−1.89	....	9.37	11.35	....	14.23	9.43	....
3316	Insurance technical reserves	—	—	....	—	—	....	—	—	....	—	—	....
3317	Financial derivatives	—	—	....	—	—	....	—	—	....	—	—	....
3318	Other accounts payable	−3.79	5.63	....	12.18	3.16	....	−4.44	−1.76	....	9.11	6.70	....
332	Foreign	−2.21	10.28	....	82.95	107.70	....	−5.45	1.46	....	77.50	109.15	....
3322	Currency and deposits	—	—	....	—	—	....	—	—	....	—	—	....
3323	Securities other than shares	1.12	6.88	....	1.12	6.88	....	−.77	.98	....	.35	7.85	....
3324	Loans	−.11	.88	....	85.10	97.72	....	−2.45	−3.25	....	82.64	94.47	....
3326	Insurance technical reserves	—	—	....	—	—	....	—	—	....	—	—	....
3327	Financial derivatives	—	—	....	—	—	....	—	—	....	—	—	....
3328	Other accounts payable	−3.22	2.52	....	−3.27	3.10	....	−2.23	3.73	....	−5.50	6.83	....
Table 4	**Holding gains in assets and liabilities**												
4	**Change in net worth from hold. gains**	....	....	....	....	....	....	....	....	....	....	....	....
41	**Nonfinancial assets**	....	....	....	....	....	....	....	....	....	....	....	....
411	Fixed assets	....	....	....	....	....	....	....	....	....	....	....	....
412	Inventories	....	....	....	....	....	....	....	....	....	....	....	....
413	Valuables	....	....	....	....	....	....	....	....	....	....	....	....
414	Nonproduced assets	....	....	....	....	....	....	....	....	....	....	....	....
42	**Financial assets**	**5.70**	**3.76**	....	**−149.44**	**121.90**	....	**1.77**	**—**	....	**−147.67**	**121.90**	....
421	Domestic	4.42	4.26	....	−41.42	74.85	....	1.77	—	....	−39.65	74.85	....
422	Foreign	1.28	−.50	....	−108.02	47.05	....	—	—	....	−108.02	47.05	....
423	Monetary gold and SDRs	—	—	....	—	—	....	—	—	....	—	—	....
43	**Liabilities**	—	—	....	—	—	....	—	—	....	—	—	....
431	Domestic	—	—	....	—	—	....	—	—	....	—	—	....
432	Foreign	—	—	....	—	—	....	—	—	....	—	—	....
Table 5	**Other changes in the volume of assets and liabilities**												
5	**Change in net worth from vol. chngs**	....	....	....	....	....	....	....	....	....	....	....	....
51	**Nonfinancial assets**	....	....	....	....	....	....	....	....	....	....	....	....
511	Fixed assets	....	....	....	....	....	....	....	....	....	....	....	....
512	Inventories	....	....	....	....	....	....	....	....	....	....	....	....
513	Valuables	....	....	....	....	....	....	....	....	....	....	....	....
514	Nonproduced assets	....	....	....	....	....	....	....	....	....	....	....	....
52	**Financial assets**	**2.06**	**—**	....	**2.06**	**—**	....	**—**	**—**	....	**2.06**	**—**	....
521	Domestic	2.06	—	....	2.06	—	....	—	—	....	2.06	—	....
522	Foreign	—	—	....	—	—	....	—	—	....	—	—	....
523	Monetary gold and SDRs	—	—	....	—	—	....	—	—	....	—	—	....
53	**Liabilities**	**—**	**7.40**	....	**2.90**	**7.40**	....	**−2.90**	**—**	....	**—**	**7.40**	....
531	Domestic	—	7.40	....	2.90	7.40	....	−2.90	—	....	—	7.40	....
532	Foreign	—	—	....	—	—	....	—	—	....	—	—	....
Table 6	**Balance sheet**												
6	**Net worth**	**659.08**	**668.25**	....	**1,402.34**	**1,652.79**	....	**341.71**	**358.08**	....	**1,744.05**	**2,010.87**	....
61	**Nonfinancial assets**	**296.30**	**310.67**	....	**296.30**	**310.67**	....	**364.94**	**397.50**	....	**661.23**	**708.17**	....
611	Fixed assets	296.30	310.67	....	296.30	310.67	....	364.94	397.50	....	661.23	708.17	....
6111	Buildings and structures	....	....	....	....	....	....	....	....	....	....	....	....
6112	Machinery and equipment	....	....	....	....	....	....	....	....	....	....	....	....
6113	Other fixed assets	....	....	....	....	....	....	....	....	....	....	....	....
612	Inventories	—	—	....	—	—	....	—	—	....	—	—	....
613	Valuables	—	—	....	—	—	....	—	—	....	—	—	....
614	Nonproduced assets	—	—	....	—	—	....	—	—	....	—	—	....
6141	Land	—	—	....	—	—	....	—	—	....	—	—	....
6142	Subsoil assets	—	—	....	—	—	....	—	—	....	—	—	....
6143	Other naturally occurring assets	—	—	....	—	—	....	—	—	....	—	—	....
6144	Intangible nonproduced assets	—	—	....	—	—	....	—	—	....	—	—	....

In Billions of Kroner / Year Ending December 31 / Noncash Reporter

		Budgetary Central Government			Central Government			Local Government			General Government		
		2002	2003p	2004p	2002	2003p	2004p	2002	2003p	2004p	2002	2003p	2004p
62	Financial assets	691.40	743.19	....	1,544.12	1,931.41	....	150.33	150.83	....	1,677.47	2,070.57	....
621	Domestic	676.04	727.32	....	710.38	766.80	....	147.67	144.88	....	841.07	900.02	....
6212	Currency and deposits	79.77	139.76	....	96.11	156.68	....	42.20	37.79	....	138.31	194.47	....
6213	Securities other than shares	1.03	.87	....	24.53	22.95	....	13.85	14.47	....	35.76	35.92	....
6214	Loans	219.23	221.18	....	221.85	223.14	....	38.51	37.05	....	260.20	260.00	....
6215	Shares and other equity	214.43	215.18	....	212.49	215.75	....	40.03	44.57	....	252.52	260.33	....
6216	Insurance technical reserves	—	—	....	—	—	....	—	—	....	—	—	....
6217	Financial derivatives	—	—	....	—	—	....	—	—	....	—	—	....
6218	Other accounts receivable	161.58	150.34	....	155.41	148.29	....	13.08	10.99	....	154.29	149.30	....
622	Foreign	15.36	15.88	....	833.74	1,164.60	....	2.66	5.95	....	836.40	1,170.55	....
6222	Currency and deposits	.30	.36	....	10.18	20.53	....	—	.01	....	10.18	20.54	....
6223	Securities other than shares	8.12	9.14	....	402.37	491.48	....	.04	.09	....	402.41	491.58	....
6224	Loans	3.15	4.74	....	191.61	294.48	....	—	.21	....	191.61	294.69	....
6225	Shares and other equity	1.38	1.64	....	228.20	356.97	....	.07	.03	....	228.27	357.00	....
6226	Insurance technical reserves	—	—	....	—	—	....	—	—	....	—	—	....
6227	Financial derivatives	—	—	....	—	—	....	—	—	....	—	—	....
6228	Other accounts receivable	2.42	—	....	1.39	1.13	....	2.54	5.61	....	3.93	6.75	....
623	Monetary gold and SDRs	—	—	....	—	—	....	—	—	....	—	—	....
63	Liabilities	328.61	385.61	....	438.08	589.28	....	173.56	190.26	....	594.66	767.87	....
631	Domestic	269.92	316.64	....	175.04	218.53	....	164.96	180.19	....	323.01	387.07	....
6312	Currency and deposits	—	—	....	—	—	....	—	—	....	—	—	....
6313	Securities other than shares	118.12	152.53	....	112.49	147.33	....	27.25	32.90	....	137.12	177.65	....
6314	Loans	124.71	131.39	....	34.53	40.04	....	110.02	121.36	....	144.39	161.21	....
6316	Insurance technical reserves	—	—	....	—	—	....	—	—	....	—	—	....
6317	Financial derivatives	—	—	....	—	—	....	—	—	....	—	—	....
6318	Other accounts payable	27.10	32.72	....	28.01	31.17	....	27.69	25.93	....	41.50	48.20	....
632	Foreign	58.69	68.97	....	263.05	370.74	....	8.60	10.06	....	271.65	380.81	....
6322	Currency and deposits	—	—	....	—	—	....	—	—	....	—	—	....
6323	Securities other than shares	60.27	67.15	....	60.27	67.15	....	1.43	2.41	....	61.70	69.56	....
6324	Loans	.31	1.19	....	204.61	302.33	....	.96	−2.29	....	205.57	300.04	....
6326	Insurance technical reserves	—	—	....	—	—	....	—	—	....	—	—	....
6327	Financial derivatives	—	—	....	—	—	....	—	—	....	—	—	....
6328	Other accounts payable	−1.89	.63	....	−1.83	1.27	....	6.21	9.94	....	4.38	11.21	....
Memorandum items:													
6M2	Net financial worth	362.78	357.58	....	1,106.04	1,342.13	....	−23.23	−39.43	....	1,082.81	1,302.70	....
6M3	Debt at market value	....	....	....	....	....	....	....	....	....	....	....	....
6M4	Debt at nominal value	....	....	....	....	....	....	....	....	....	....	....	....
6M5	Arrears	....	....	....	....	....	....	....	....	....	....	....	....
6M6	Obligations for social security benefits	....	....	....	....	....	....	....	....	....	....	....	....
6M7	Contingent liabilities	....	....	....	....	....	....	....	....	....	....	....	....
6M8	Uncapitalized military weapons, systems	....	....	....	....	....	....	....	....	....	....	....	....

Table 7 Outlays by functions of govt.

		2002	2003p	2004p	2002	2003p	2004p	2002	2003p	2004p	2002	2003p	2004p
7	**Total outlays**	679.44	684.05	722.09	588.24	606.42	632.28	222.62	237.28	238.64	714.17	761.84	784.03
701	**General public services**	238.80	214.85	227.66	125.28	106.69	105.81	27.29	26.62	23.25	76.47	77.58	73.31
7017	Public debt transactions	17.24	18.61	16.79	18.20	20.36	17.67	9.55	8.43	7.30	27.74	28.79	24.98
7018	General transfers between levels of govt	191.78	166.20	178.91	75.95	55.39	56.23	.07	.05	−.03	.15	.31	.62
702	**Defense**	30.97	30.35	30.53	31.08	30.54	30.67	—	—	—	31.08	30.54	30.67
703	**Public order and safety**	15.38	16.03	16.11	15.38	15.96	16.11	2.25	2.37	2.62	17.60	18.29	18.69
704	**Economic affairs**	57.59	55.06	56.75	59.73	61.44	62.64	12.69	12.37	13.53	70.52	68.94	70.62
7042	Agriculture, forestry, fishing, and hunting	15.87	15.23	15.79	15.85	15.51	15.86	—	—	—	15.85	15.51	15.86
7043	Fuel and energy	2.93	2.93	2.92	1.43	1.45	1.46	—	—	—	1.43	1.45	1.46
7044	Mining, manufacturing, and construction	2.10	.50	.12	1.75	1.66	.29	—	—	—	1.71	1.65	.28
7045	Transport	20.33	21.05	22.96	22.32	23.25	25.92	10.63	10.61	11.27	31.95	32.91	35.89
7046	Communication	.21	.23	.25	.21	.23	.25	—	—	—	.21	.23	.25
705	**Environmental protection**	2.18	2.04	2.05	2.16	2.09	2.11	6.61	7.24	8.52	8.61	9.22	10.47
706	**Housing and community amenities**	1.29	.94	1.07	1.29	.94	1.08	4.61	11.78	7.00	5.84	12.66	8.02
707	**Health**	83.36	88.89	95.84	87.64	94.10	102.72	37.87	39.58	39.52	121.30	129.31	134.74
7072	Outpatient services	8.98	10.04	10.06	9.01	9.88	10.08	6.54	6.97	7.48	15.30	16.61	17.27
7073	Hospital services	25.52	4.39	3.32	60.73	63.76	72.09	29.29	30.52	29.99	87.20	91.53	99.46
7074	Public health services	4.46	4.73	8.02	2.66	3.29	6.83	2.04	2.10	2.06	3.55	4.00	4.30
708	**Recreation, culture, and religion**	5.99	6.26	6.56	7.00	7.47	7.86	11.69	12.42	12.89	17.82	18.88	19.77

		Budgetary Central Government			Central Government			Local Government			General Government		
		2002	2003p	2004p	2002	2003p	2004p	2002	2003p	2004p	2002	2003p	2004p
709	**Education**............................	**33.58**	**36.49**	**35.64**	**36.11**	**40.27**	**39.55**	**62.19**	**68.11**	**68.79**	**94.77**	**105.14**	**106.56**
7091	Pre-primary and primary education..............	2.69	2.41	2.06	2.69	2.41	2.06	39.21	43.06	43.57	39.80	43.63	44.09
7092	Secondary education................................	4.51	5.25	7.09	4.51	5.25	7.09	16.57	18.11	18.23	20.83	23.12	25.11
7094	Tertiary education..................................	23.39	25.85	24.55	25.95	29.65	28.48	—	—	—	25.75	29.48	28.48
710	**Social protection**................................	**210.30**	**233.15**	**249.88**	**222.57**	**246.92**	**263.73**	**57.43**	**56.79**	**62.53**	**270.15**	**291.27**	**311.18**
7	Statistical discrepancy: Total outlays.............	—	—	—	—	—	—	—	—	—	—	—	—

Table 8   Transactions in financial assets and liabilities by sector

		Budgetary Central Government			Central Government			Local Government			General Government		
82	**Net acquisition of financial assets**.........	**−14.03**	**48.04**	....	**231.64**	**265.38**	....	**5.81**	**.50**	....	**237.33**	**271.20**	....
821	Domestic...................................	−14.10	47.02	....	30.08	−18.43	....	7.00	−2.79	....	36.95	−15.90	....
8211	General government...............................	10.81	−2.39	....	−.58	−2.02	....	.71	−3.30	....	—	—	....
8212	Central bank.......................................	—	—	....	—	—	....	—	—	....	—	—	....
8213	Other depository corporations..................	−8.50	61.64	....	−5.61	67.67	....	7.95	−1.54	....	2.34	66.13	....
8214	Financial corporations n.e.c....................	—	—	....	—	—	....	—	—	....	—	—	....
8215	Nonfinancial corporations.......................	−10.24	−7.11	....	39.06	−79.02	....	−1.38	.44	....	37.68	−78.58	....
8216	Households & NPIs serving households......	−6.17	−5.12	....	−2.80	−5.06	....	−.27	1.61	....	−3.07	−3.45	....
822	Foreign...	.07	1.02	....	201.56	283.81	....	−1.19	3.29	....	200.38	287.10	....
8221	General government...............................	....	....	....	....	....	....	....	....	....	....	....	....
8227	International organizations.....................	....	....	....	....	....	....	....	....	....	....	....	....
8228	Financial corporations other than international organizations.............	....	....	....	....	....	....	....	....	....	....	....	....
8229	Other nonresidents...............................	....	....	....	....	....	....	....	....	....	....	....	....
823	Monetary gold and SDRs........................	—	—	....	—	—	....	—	—	....	—	—	....
83	**Net incurrence of liabilities**..................	**9.87**	**49.60**	....	**108.17**	**143.80**	....	**−1.67**	**16.70**	....	**106.37**	**165.82**	....
831	Domestic...................................	12.08	39.33	....	25.22	36.10	....	3.78	15.24	....	28.87	56.66	....
8311	General government...............................	−4.20	−5.41	....	−2.19	−3.30	....	2.32	−2.02	....	—	—	....
8312	Central bank.......................................	—	—	....	—	—	....	—	—	....	—	—	....
8313	Other depository corporations..................	18.40	37.94	....	18.59	31.09	....	6.36	14.40	....	24.95	45.49	....
8314	Financial corporations n.e.c....................	—	—	....	—	—	....	—	—	....	—	—	....
8315	Nonfinancial corporations.......................	−2.99	4.34	....	5.07	6.07	....	−1.06	1.59	....	4.02	7.66	....
8316	Households & NPIs serving households......	.86	2.46	....	3.75	2.24	....	−3.85	1.27	....	−.10	3.51	....
832	Foreign...	−2.21	10.28	....	82.95	107.70	....	−5.45	1.46	....	77.50	109.15	....
8321	General government...............................	....	....	....	....	....	....	....	....	....	....	....	....
8327	International organizations.....................	....	....	....	....	....	....	....	....	....	....	....	....
8328	Financial corporations other than international organizations.............	....	....	....	....	....	....	....	....	....	....	....	....
8329	Other nonresidents...............................	....	....	....	....	....	....	....	....	....	....	....	....

In Millions of Rials / Year Ending December 31 / Cash Reporter

	Budgetary Central Government			Extrabudgetary Accounts			Central Government			General Government		
	1999	2000	2001	1999	2000	2001	1999	2000	2001	1999	2000	2001
Statement of government operations												
Statement of other economic flows												
Balance sheet												
6 *Net worth*................	....	....	....	....	....	....	....	....	....	....	....	....
61 Nonfinancial assets............	....	....	....	....	....	....	....	....	....	....	....	....
62 Financial assets............	....	....	....	....	....	....	....	....	....	....	....	....
63 Liabilities............	1,611.5	1,456.9	1,523.9	....	....	....	....	....	....	....	....	....
Statement of sources and uses of cash												
1 Cash receipts from operating activities............	1,400.1	1,839.7	2,073.5	....	....	....	....	....	....	....	....	....
11 Taxes............	403.9	547.1	566.7	....	....	....	....	....	....	....	....	....
12 Social contributions............	—	—	—	....	....	....	....	....	....	....	....	....
13 Grants............	5.6	13.2	2.9	....	....	....	....	....	....	....	....	....
14 Other receipts............	990.6	1,279.4	1,503.9	....	....	....	....	....	....	....	....	....
2 Cash payments for operating activities............	1,714.3	2,000.5	2,065.4	....	....	....	....	....	....	....	....	....
21 Compensation of employees............	569.6	670.9	650.8	....	....	....	....	....	....	....	....	....
22 Purchases of goods and services............	849.1	1,006.6	1,120.2	....	....	....	....	....	....	....	....	....
24 Interest............	98.8	107.1	94.3	....	....	....	....	....	....	....	....	....
25 Subsidies............	56.2	67.7	60.7	....	....	....	....	....	....	....	....	....
26 Grants............	95.1	99.2	79.5	....	....	....	....	....	....	....	....	....
27 Social benefits............	43.7	48.3	59.9	....	....	....	....	....	....	....	....	....
28 Other payments............	1.8	.7	—	....	....	....	....	....	....	....	....	....
CIO *Net cash inflow from oper. activities.....*	*−314.2*	*−160.8*	*8.1*	....	....	....	....	....	....	....	....	....
31.1 Purchases of nonfinancial assets............	145.1	179.0	229.7	....	....	....	....	....	....	....	....	....
31.2 Sales of nonfinancial assets............	7.3	4.7	6.6	....	....	....	....	....	....	....	....	....
31 Net cash outflow from investments in nonfinancial assets............	137.8	174.3	223.1	....	....	....	....	....	....	....	....	....
CSD *Cash surplus/deficit............*	*−452.0*	*−335.1*	*−215.0*	....	....	....	....	....	....	....	....	....
32x Net acquisition of fin assets, excl. cash............	22.1	28.1	109.1	....	....	....	....	....	....	....	....	....
321x Domestic............	19.8	27.5	88.9	....	....	....	....	....	....	....	....	....
322x Foreign............	2.3	.6	20.2	....	....	....	....	....	....	....	....	....
323 Monetary gold and SDRs............	—	—	—	....	....	....	....	....	....	....	....	....
33 Net incurrence of liabilities............	22.4	−154.7	67.0	....	....	....	....	....	....	....	....	....
331 Domestic............	132.7	−101.2	231.4	....	....	....	....	....	....	....	....	....
332 Foreign............	−110.3	−53.5	−164.4	....	....	....	....	....	....	....	....	....
NFB Net cash inflow from fin. activities............	.3	−182.8	−42.1	....	....	....	....	....	....	....	....	....
NCB *Net change in the stock of cash............*	*−451.7*	*−517.9*	*−257.1*	....	....	....	....	....	....	....	....	....
Table 1 Revenue												
1 **Revenue............**	**1,400.1**	**1,839.7**	**2,073.5**	....	....	....	....	....	....	....	....	....
11 **Taxes............**	**403.9**	**547.1**	**566.7**	....	....	....	....	....	....	....	....	....
111 Taxes on income, profits, & capital gains......	257.0	436.4	437.2	....	....	....	....	....	....	....	....	....
1111 Individuals............	—	—	—	....	....	....	....	....	....	....	....	....
1112 Corporations and other enterprises............	253.0	432.4	432.7	....	....	....	....	....	....	....	....	....
112 Taxes on payroll and workforce............	38.0	36.8	38.7	....	....	....	....	....	....	....	....	....
113 Taxes on property............	4.3	4.4	6.1	....	....	....	....	....	....	....	....	....
114 Taxes on goods and services............	23.4	23.4	26.1	....	....	....	....	....	....	....	....	....
1141 General taxes on goods and services............	—	—	—	....	....	....	....	....	....	....	....	....
1142 Excises............	—	—	—	....	....	....	....	....	....	....	....	....
115 Taxes on int'l. trade and transactions............	80.3	46.1	58.6	....	....	....	....	....	....	....	....	....
116 Other taxes............	.9	—	—	....	....	....	....	....	....	....	....	....
12 **Social contributions............**	**—**	**—**	**—**	....	....	....	....	....	....	....	....	....
121 Social security contributions............	—	—	—	....	....	....	....	....	....	....	....	....
122 Other social contributions............	—	—	—	....	....	....	....	....	....	....	....	....
13 **Grants............**	**5.6**	**13.2**	**2.9**	....	....	....	....	....	....	....	....	....
131 From foreign governments............	5.6	13.2	2.9	....	....	....	....	....	....	....	....	....
132 From international organizations............	—	—	—	....	....	....	....	....	....	....	....	....
133 From other general government units............	—	—	—	....	....	....	....	....	....	....	....	....
14 **Other revenue............**	**990.6**	**1,279.4**	**1,503.9**	....	....	....	....	....	....	....	....	....
Table 2 Expense by economic type												
2 **Expense............**	**1,714.3**	**2,000.5**	**2,065.4**	....	....	....	....	....	....	....	....	....
21 **Compensation of employees............**	**569.6**	**670.9**	**650.8**	....	....	....	....	....	....	....	....	....
211 Wages and salaries............	553.2	604.9	626.4	....	....	....	....	....	....	....	....	....
212 Social contributions............	16.4	66.0	24.4	....	....	....	....	....	....	....	....	....
22 **Use of goods and services............**	**849.1**	**1,006.6**	**1,120.2**	....	....	....	....	....	....	....	....	....
23 **Consumption of fixed capital............**	....	....	....	....	....	....	....	....	....	....	....	....
24 **Interest............**	**98.8**	**107.1**	**94.3**	....	....	....	....	....	....	....	....	....
25 **Subsidies............**	**56.2**	**67.7**	**60.7**	....	....	....	....	....	....	....	....	....

In Millions of Rials / Year Ending December 31 / Cash Reporter

	Budgetary Central Government			Extrabudgetary Accounts			Central Government			General Government		
	1999	2000	2001	1999	2000	2001	1999	2000	2001	1999	2000	2001
26 **Grants**....................................	**95.1**	**99.2**	**79.5**	....	....	....	....	....	....	....	....	....
261 To foreign govenments....................	15.5	14.2	6.6	....	....	....	....	....	....	....	....	....
262 To international organizations....................	—	—	—	....	....	....	....	....	....	....	....	....
263 To other general government units..............	79.6	85.0	72.9	....	....	....	....	....	....	....	....	....
2631 Current....................................	—	—	—	....	....	....	....	....	....	....	....	....
2632 Capital....................................	79.6	85.0	72.9	....	....	....	....	....	....	....	....	....
27 **Social benefits**....................................	**43.7**	**48.3**	**59.9**	....	....	....	....	....	....	....	....	....
28 **Other expense**....................................	**1.8**	**.7**	**—**	....	....	....	....	....	....	....	....	....
281 Property expense other than interest............	—	—	—	....	....	....	....	....	....	....	....	....
282 Miscellaneous other expense....................	1.8	.7	—	....	....	....	....	....	....	....	....	....
2821 Current....................................	—	—	—	....	....	....	....	....	....	....	....	....
2822 Capital....................................	1.8	.7	—	....	....	....	....	....	....	....	....	....

Table 3   Transactions in assets and liabilities

	Budgetary Central Government			Extrabudgetary Accounts			Central Government			General Government		
	1999	2000	2001	1999	2000	2001	1999	2000	2001	1999	2000	2001
3 **Change in net worth from transactns....**	....	....	....	....	....	....	....	....	....	....	....	....
31 **Net acquisition of nonfinancial assets...**	**137.8**	**174.3**	**223.1**	....	....	....	....	....	....	....	....	....
311 Fixed assets....................................	141.6	177.4	227.1	....	....	....	....	....	....	....	....	....
3111 Buildings and structures....................	....	....	....	....	....	....	....	....	....	....	....	....
3112 Machinery and equipment....................	....	....	....	....	....	....	....	....	....	....	....	....
3113 Other fixed assets....................	....	....	....	....	....	....	....	....	....	....	....	....
312 Inventories....................................	—	—	—	....	....	....	....	....	....	....	....	....
313 Valuables....................................	—	—	—	....	....	....	....	....	....	....	....	....
314 Nonproduced assets....................	−3.8	−3.1	−4.0	....	....	....	....	....	....	....	....	....
3141 Land....................................	....	....	....	....	....	....	....	....	....	....	....	....
3142 Subsoil assets....................	....	....	....	....	....	....	....	....	....	....	....	....
3143 Other naturally occurring assets....................	....	....	....	....	....	....	....	....	....	....	....	....
3144 Intangible nonproduced assets....................	....	....	....	....	....	....	....	....	....	....	....	....
32 **Net acquisition of financial assets.........**	**−429.6**	**−489.8**	**−148.0**	....	....	....	....	....	....	....	....	....
321 Domestic....................................	46.8	−150.3	233.9	....	....	....	....	....	....	....	....	....
3212 Currency and deposits....................	27.0	−177.8	145.0	....	....	....	....	....	....	....	....	....
3213 Securities other than shares....................	....	....	....	....	....	....	....	....	....	....	....	....
3214 Loans....................................	....	....	....	....	....	....	....	....	....	....	....	....
3215 Shares and other equity....................	....	....	....	....	....	....	....	....	....	....	....	....
3216 Insurance technical reserves....................	....	....	....	....	....	....	....	....	....	....	....	....
3217 Financial derivatives....................	....	....	....	....	....	....	....	....	....	....	....	....
3218 Other accounts receivable....................	....	....	....	....	....	....	....	....	....	....	....	....
322 Foreign....................................	−476.4	−339.5	−381.9	....	....	....	....	....	....	....	....	....
3222 Currency and deposits....................	−478.7	−340.1	−402.1	....	....	....	....	....	....	....	....	....
3223 Securities other than shares....................	....	....	....	....	....	....	....	....	....	....	....	....
3224 Loans....................................	....	....	....	....	....	....	....	....	....	....	....	....
3225 Shares and other equity....................	....	....	....	....	....	....	....	....	....	....	....	....
3226 Insurance technical reserves....................	....	....	....	....	....	....	....	....	....	....	....	....
3227 Financial derivatives....................	....	....	....	....	....	....	....	....	....	....	....	....
3228 Other accounts receivable....................	....	....	....	....	....	....	....	....	....	....	....	....
323 Monetary gold and SDRs....................	—	—	—	....	....	....	....	....	....	....	....	....
33 **Net incurrence of liabilities..................**	**22.4**	**−154.7**	**67.0**	....	....	....	....	....	....	....	....	....
331 Domestic....................................	132.7	−101.2	231.4	....	....	....	....	....	....	....	....	....
3312 Currency and deposits....................	—	—	—	....	....	....	....	....	....	....	....	....
3313 Securities other than shares....................	82.8	−106.2	117.6	....	....	....	....	....	....	....	....	....
3314 Loans....................................	49.9	5.0	113.8	....	....	....	....	....	....	....	....	....
3316 Insurance technical reserves....................	—	—	—	....	....	....	....	....	....	....	....	....
3317 Financial derivatives....................	—	—	—	....	....	....	....	....	....	....	....	....
3318 Other accounts payable....................	....	....	....	....	....	....	....	....	....	....	....	....
332 Foreign....................................	−110.3	−53.5	−164.4	....	....	....	....	....	....	....	....	....
3322 Currency and deposits....................	....	....	....	....	....	....	....	....	....	....	....	....
3323 Securities other than shares....................	4.7	−10.3	6.1	....	....	....	....	....	....	....	....	....
3324 Loans....................................	−115.0	−43.2	−170.5	....	....	....	....	....	....	....	....	....
3326 Insurance technical reserves....................	—	—	—	....	....	....	....	....	....	....	....	....
3327 Financial derivatives....................	—	—	—	....	....	....	....	....	....	....	....	....
3328 Other accounts payable....................	....	....	....	....	....	....	....	....	....	....	....	....

In Millions of Rials / Year Ending December 31 / Cash Reporter

	Budgetary Central Government			Extrabudgetary Accounts			Central Government			General Government		
	1999	2000	2001	1999	2000	2001	1999	2000	2001	1999	2000	2001
Table 4 Holding gains in assets and liabilities												
Table 5 Other changes in the volume of assets and liabilities												
Table 6 Balance sheet												
6 **Net worth**.....................	....	....	....	....	....	....	....	....	....	....	....	....
61 **Nonfinancial assets**.....................	....	....	....	....	....	....	....	....	....	....	....	....
611 Fixed assets.....................	....	....	....	....	....	....	....	....	....	....	....	....
6111 Buildings and structures.....................	....	....	....	....	....	....	....	....	....	....	....	....
6112 Machinery and equipment.....................	....	....	....	....	....	....	....	....	....	....	....	....
6113 Other fixed assets.....................	....	....	....	....	....	....	....	....	....	....	....	....
612 Inventories.....................	....	....	....	....	....	....	....	....	....	....	....	....
613 Valuables.....................	....	....	....	....	....	....	....	....	....	....	....	....
614 Nonproduced assets.....................	....	....	....	....	....	....	....	....	....	....	....	....
6141 Land.....................	....	....	....	....	....	....	....	....	....	....	....	....
6142 Subsoil assets.....................	....	....	....	....	....	....	....	....	....	....	....	....
6143 Other naturally occurring assets.....................	....	....	....	....	....	....	....	....	....	....	....	....
6144 Intangible nonproduced assets.....................	....	....	....	....	....	....	....	....	....	....	....	....
62 **Financial assets**.....................	....	....	....	....	....	....	....	....	....	....	....	....
621 Domestic.....................	....	....	....	....	....	....	....	....	....	....	....	....
6212 Currency and deposits.....................	....	....	....	....	....	....	....	....	....	....	....	....
6213 Securities other than shares.....................	....	....	....	....	....	....	....	....	....	....	....	....
6214 Loans.....................	....	....	....	....	....	....	....	....	....	....	....	....
6215 Shares and other equity.....................	....	....	....	....	....	....	....	....	....	....	....	....
6216 Insurance technical reserves.....................	....	....	....	....	....	....	....	....	....	....	....	....
6217 Financial derivatives.....................	....	....	....	....	....	....	....	....	....	....	....	....
6218 Other accounts receivable.....................	....	....	....	....	....	....	....	....	....	....	....	....
622 Foreign.....................	....	....	....	....	....	....	....	....	....	....	....	....
6222 Currency and deposits.....................	....	....	....	....	....	....	....	....	....	....	....	....
6223 Securities other than shares.....................	....	....	....	....	....	....	....	....	....	....	....	....
6224 Loans.....................	....	....	....	....	....	....	....	....	....	....	....	....
6225 Shares and other equity.....................	....	....	....	....	....	....	....	....	....	....	....	....
6226 Insurance technical reserves.....................	....	....	....	....	....	....	....	....	....	....	....	....
6227 Financial derivatives.....................	....	....	....	....	....	....	....	....	....	....	....	....
6228 Other accounts receivable.....................	....	....	....	....	....	....	....	....	....	....	....	....
623 Monetary gold and SDRs.....................	....	....	....	....	....	....	....	....	....	....	....	....
63 **Liabilities**.....................	**1,611.5**	**1,456.9**	**1,523.9**	....	....	....	....	....	....	....	....	....
631 Domestic.....................	493.1	392.1	623.4	....	....	....	....	....	....	....	....	....
6312 Currency and deposits.....................	....	....	....	....	....	....	....	....	....	....	....	....
6313 Securities other than shares.....................	....	....	....	....	....	....	....	....	....	....	....	....
6314 Loans.....................	....	....	....	....	....	....	....	....	....	....	....	....
6316 Insurance technical reserves.....................	....	....	....	....	....	....	....	....	....	....	....	....
6317 Financial derivatives.....................	....	....	....	....	....	....	....	....	....	....	....	....
6318 Other accounts payable.....................	....	....	....	....	....	....	....	....	....	....	....	....
632 Foreign.....................	1,118.4	1,064.8	900.5	....	....	....	....	....	....	....	....	....
6322 Currency and deposits.....................	....	....	....	....	....	....	....	....	....	....	....	....
6323 Securities other than shares.....................	....	....	....	....	....	....	....	....	....	....	....	....
6324 Loans.....................	....	....	....	....	....	....	....	....	....	....	....	....
6326 Insurance technical reserves.....................	....	....	....	....	....	....	....	....	....	....	....	....
6327 Financial derivatives.....................	....	....	....	....	....	....	....	....	....	....	....	....
6328 Other accounts payable.....................	....	....	....	....	....	....	....	....	....	....	....	....
Memorandum items:												
6M2 Net financial worth.....................	....	....	....	....	....	....	....	....	....	....	....	....
6M3 Debt at market value.....................	....	....	....	....	....	....	....	....	....	....	....	....
6M4 Debt at nominal value.....................	....	....	....	....	....	....	....	....	....	....	....	....
6M5 Arrears.....................	....	....	....	....	....	....	....	....	....	....	....	....
6M6 Obligations for social security benefits.....................	....	....	....	....	....	....	....	....	....	....	....	....
6M7 Contingent liabilities.....................	....	....	....	....	....	....	....	....	....	....	....	....
6M8 Uncapitalized military weapons, systems.....................	....	....	....	....	....	....	....	....	....	....	....	....
Table 7 Outlays by functions of govt.												
7 **Total outlays**.....................	**1,859.4**	**2,179.5**	**2,295.1**	....	....	....	....	....	....	....	....	....
701 **General public services**.....................	**261.5**	**295.9**	**304.2**	....	....	....	....	....	....	....	....	....
7017 Public debt transactions.....................	98.8	107.1	94.3	....	....	....	....	....	....	....	....	....
7018 General transfers between levels of govt.....				....	....	....	....	....	....	....	....	....
702 **Defense**.....................	**598.7**	**705.3**	**810.4**	....	....	....	....	....	....	....	....	....
703 **Public order and safety**.....................	**109.3**	**127.2**	**135.3**	....	....	....	....	....	....	....	....	....

In Millions of Rials / Year Ending December 31 / Cash Reporter

		Budgetary Central Government			Extrabudgetary Accounts			Central Government			General Government		
		1999	2000	2001	1999	2000	2001	1999	2000	2001	1999	2000	2001
704	**Economic affairs**............................	**205.6**	**226.4**	**210.8**	....	....	....	....	....	....	....	....	....
7042	Agriculture, forestry, fishing, and hunting.....	23.3	23.3	21.8	....	....	....	....	....	....	....	....	....
7043	Fuel and energy....................................	126.7	124.9	121.0	....	....	....	....	....	....	....	....	....
7044	Mining, manufacturing, and construction.....	1.8	.7	.8	....	....	....	....	....	....	....	....	....
7045	Transport..	30.9	45.2	33.9	....	....	....	....	....	....	....	....	....
7046	Communication....................................	....	....	....	....	....	....	....	....	....	....	....	....
705	**Environmental protection**....................	....	....	....	....	....	....	....	....	....	....	....	....
706	**Housing and community amenities**........	**104.6**	**126.4**	**146.5**	....	....	....	....	....	....	....	....	....
707	**Health**..	**138.5**	**149.8**	**152.6**	....	....	....	....	....	....	....	....	....
7072	Outpatient services..............................	....	....	....	....	....	....	....	....	....	....	....	....
7073	Hospital services..................................	....	....	....	....	....	....	....	....	....	....	....	....
7074	Public health services...........................	....	....	....	....	....	....	....	....	....	....	....	....
708	**Recreation, culture, and religion**...........	**37.9**	**39.4**	**41.0**	....	....	....	....	....	....	....	....	....
709	**Education**..	**292.2**	**330.7**	**365.8**	....	....	....	....	....	....	....	....	....
7091	Pre-primary and primary education...........	....	....	....	....	....	....	....	....	....	....	....	....
7092	Secondary education.............................	....	....	....	....	....	....	....	....	....	....	....	....
7094	Tertiary education................................	....	....	....	....	....	....	....	....	....	....	....	....
710	**Social protection**................................	**111.1**	**178.4**	**128.5**	....	....	....	....	....	....	....	....	....
7	Statistical discrepancy: Total outlays.............	—	—	—	....	....	....	....	....	....	....	....	....

Table 8   Transactions in financial assets and liabilities by sector

		Budgetary Central Government			Extrabudgetary Accounts			Central Government			General Government		
		1999	2000	2001	1999	2000	2001	1999	2000	2001	1999	2000	2001
82	**Net acquisition of financial assets**.........	**−429.6**	**−489.8**	**−148.0**	....	....	....	....	....	....	....	....	....
821	Domestic................................	46.8	−150.3	233.9	....	....	....	....	....	....	....	....	....
8211	General government.............................	2.9	4.0	20.0	....	....	....	....	....	....	....	....	....
8212	Central bank......................................	....	....	....	....	....	....	....	....	....	....	....	....
8213	Other depository corporations..................	....	....	....	....	....	....	....	....	....	....	....	....
8214	Financial corporations n.e.c....................	....	....	....	....	....	....	....	....	....	....	....	....
8215	Nonfinancial corporations.......................	1.2	.8	.6	....	....	....	....	....	....	....	....	....
8216	Households & NPIs serving households......	....	....	....	....	....	....	....	....	....	....	....	....
822	Foreign................................	−476.4	−339.5	−381.9	....	....	....	....	....	....	....	....	....
8221	General government..............................	....	....	....	....	....	....	....	....	....	....	....	....
8227	International organizations......................	....	....	....	....	....	....	....	....	....	....	....	....
8228	Financial corporations other than international organizations..............	....	....	....	....	....	....	....	....	....	....	....	....
8229	Other nonresidents...............................	....	....	....	....	....	....	....	....	....	....	....	....
823	Monetary gold and SDRs.........................	—	—	—	....	....	....	....	....	....	....	....	....
83	**Net incurrence of liabilities**..................	**22.4**	**−154.7**	**67.0**	....	....	....	....	....	....	....	....	....
831	Domestic................................	132.7	−101.2	231.4	....	....	....	....	....	....	....	....	....
8311	General government.............................	....	....	....	....	....	....	....	....	....	....	....	....
8312	Central bank......................................	....	....	....	....	....	....	....	....	....	....	....	....
8313	Other depository corporations..................	....	....	....	....	....	....	....	....	....	....	....	....
8314	Financial corporations n.e.c....................	....	....	....	....	....	....	....	....	....	....	....	....
8315	Nonfinancial corporations.......................	....	....	....	....	....	....	....	....	....	....	....	....
8316	Households & NPIs serving households......	....	....	....	....	....	....	....	....	....	....	....	....
832	Foreign................................	−110.3	−53.5	−164.4	....	....	....	....	....	....	....	....	....
8321	General government.............................	−1.4	9.5	−15.5	....	....	....	....	....	....	....	....	....
8327	International organizations......................	31.9	−.5	6.4	....	....	....	....	....	....	....	....	....
8328	Financial corporations other than international organizations..............	—	—	—	....	....	....	....	....	....	....	....	....
8329	Other nonresidents...............................	−140.8	−62.5	−155.3	....	....	....	....	....	....	....	....	....

Pakistan 564

In Billions of Rupees / Year Ending June 30 / Cash Reporter

		Central Government			State Government			Local Government			General Government		
		2004	2005	2006f	2004	2005	2006	2004	2005	2006	2004	2005	2006
Statement of government operations													
Statement of other economic flows													
Balance sheet													
Statement of sources and uses of cash													
1	Cash receipts from operating activities	795.47	863.44	949.40	....	....	....	....	....	....	....	....	....
11	Taxes	580.11	624.27	732.64	....	....	....	....	....	....	....	....	....
12	Social contributions	—	—	—	....	....	....	....	....	....	....	....	....
13	Grants	34.48	18.56	22.00	....	....	....	....	....	....	....	....	....
14	Other receipts	180.88	220.61	194.76	....	....	....	....	....	....	....	....	....
2	Cash payments for operating activities	814.19	950.52	1,045.49	....	....	....	....	....	....	....	....	....
21	Compensation of employees	37.31	42.19	48.85	....	....	....	....	....	....	....	....	....
22	Purchases of goods and services	251.84	345.72	337.80	....	....	....	....	....	....	....	....	....
24	Interest	317.72	274.72	301.35	....	....	....	....	....	....	....	....	....
25	Subsidies	43.53	51.36	72.34	....	....	....	....	....	....	....	....	....
26	Grants	163.79	236.54	285.15	....	....	....	....	....	....	....	....	....
27	Social benefits	—	—	—	....	....	....	....	....	....	....	....	....
28	Other payments	—	—	—	....	....	....	....	....	....	....	....	....
CIO	*Net cash inflow from oper. activities*	*–18.72*	*–87.08*	*–96.10*	....	....	....	....	....	....	....	....	....
31.1	Purchases of nonfinancial assets	91.36	121.10	198.68	....	....	....	....	....	....	....	....	....
31.2	Sales of nonfinancial assets	—	—	—	....	....	....	....	....	....	....	....	....
31	Net cash outflow from investments in nonfinancial assets	91.36	121.10	198.68	....	....	....	....	....	....	....	....	....
CSD	*Cash surplus/deficit*	*–110.08*	*–208.17*	*–294.78*	....	....	....	....	....	....	....	....	....
32x	Net acquisition of fin assets, excl. cash	....	....	....	....	....	....	....	....	....	....	....	....
321x	Domestic	....	....	....	....	....	....	....	....	....	....	....	....
322x	Foreign	....	....	....	....	....	....	....	....	....	....	....	....
323	Monetary gold and SDRs	....	....	....	....	....	....	....	....	....	....	....	....
33	Net incurrence of liabilities	....	....	....	....	....	....	....	....	....	....	....	....
331	Domestic	....	....	....	....	....	....	....	....	....	....	....	....
332	Foreign	....	....	....	....	....	....	....	....	....	....	....	....
NFB	Net cash inflow from fin. activities	....	....	....	....	....	....	....	....	....	....	....	....
NCB	*Net change in the stock of cash*	....	....	....	....	....	....	....	....	....	....	....	....
Table 1 Revenue													
1	**Revenue**	**795.47**	**863.44**	**949.40**	....	....	....	....	....	....	....	....	....
11	**Taxes**	**580.11**	**624.27**	**732.64**	....	....	....	....	....	....	....	....	....
111	Taxes on income, profits, & capital gains	160.90	176.93	211.40	....	....	....	....	....	....	....	....	....
1111	Individuals	23.20	....	....	....	....	....	....	....	....	....	....	....
1112	Corporations and other enterprises	131.44	....	....	....	....	....	....	....	....	....	....	....
112	Taxes on payroll and workforce	—	—	—	....	....	....	....	....	....	....	....	....
113	Taxes on property	.60	—	4.00	....	....	....	....	....	....	....	....	....
114	Taxes on goods and services	261.90	294.20	353.40	....	....	....	....	....	....	....	....	....
1141	General taxes on goods and services	218.40	235.53	294.00	....	....	....	....	....	....	....	....	....
1142	Excises	43.50	58.67	59.40	....	....	....	....	....	....	....	....	....
115	Taxes on int'l. trade and transactions	86.60	117.24	121.20	....	....	....	....	....	....	....	....	....
116	Other taxes	70.11	35.89	42.64	....	....	....	....	....	....	....	....	....
12	**Social contributions**	—	—	—	....	....	....	....	....	....	....	....	....
121	Social security contributions	—	—	—	....	....	....	....	....	....	....	....	....
122	Other social contributions	—	—	—	....	....	....	....	....	....	....	....	....
13	**Grants**	**34.48**	**18.56**	**22.00**	....	....	....	....	....	....	....	....	....
131	From foreign governments	34.48	18.56	22.00	....	....	....	....	....	....	....	....	....
132	From international organizations	—	—	—	....	....	....	....	....	....	....	....	....
133	From other general government units	—	—	—	....	....	....	....	....	....	....	....	....
14	**Other revenue**	**180.88**	**220.61**	**194.76**	....	....	....	....	....	....	....	....	....
Table 2 Expense by economic type													
2	**Expense**	**814.19**	**950.52**	**1,045.49**	....	....	....	....	....	....	....	....	....
21	**Compensation of employees**	**37.31**	**42.19**	**48.85**	....	....	....	....	....	....	....	....	....
211	Wages and salaries	37.31	42.19	48.85	....	....	....	....	....	....	....	....	....
212	Social contributions	—	—	—	....	....	....	....	....	....	....	....	....
22	**Use of goods and services**	**251.84**	**345.72**	**337.80**	....	....	....	....	....	....	....	....	....
23	**Consumption of fixed capital**	....	....	....	....	....	....	....	....	....	....	....	....
24	**Interest**	**317.72**	**274.72**	**301.35**	....	....	....	....	....	....	....	....	....
25	**Subsidies**	**43.53**	**51.36**	**72.34**	....	....	....	....	....	....	....	....	....

2005, International Monetary Fund: *Government Finance Statistics Yearbook*

		Central Government			State Government			Local Government			General Government		
		2004	2005	2006f	2004	2005	2006	2004	2005	2006	2004	2005	2006
26	**Grants**...............................	163.79	236.54	285.15	....	....	....	....	....	....	....	....	....
261	To foreign govenments..................	—	—	—	....	....	....	....	....	....	....	....	....
262	To international organizations..................	—	—	—	....	....	....	....	....	....	....	....	....
263	To other general government units..............	163.79	236.54	285.15	....	....	....	....	....	....	....	....	....
2631	Current..................	163.79	236.54	285.15	....	....	....	....	....	....	....	....	....
2632	Capital..................	—	—	—	....	....	....	....	....	....	....	....	....
27	**Social benefits**..................	—	—	—	....	....	....	....	....	....	....	....	....
28	**Other expense**..................	—	—	—	....	....	....	....	....	....	....	....	....
281	Property expense other than interest............	—	—	—	....	....	....	....	....	....	....	....	....
282	Miscellaneous other expense..................	—	—	—	....	....	....	....	....	....	....	....	....
2821	Current..................	—	—	—	....	....	....	....	....	....	....	....	....
2822	Capital..................	—	—	—	....	....	....	....	....	....	....	....	....

Table 3   Transactions in assets and liabilities

		Central Government			State Government			Local Government			General Government		
3	**Change in net worth from transactns....**	....	....	....	....	....	....	....	....	....	....	....	....
31	**Net acquisition of nonfinancial assets...**	91.36	121.10	198.68	....	....	....	....	....	....	....	....	....
311	Fixed assets..................	91.36	121.10	198.68	....	....	....	....	....	....	....	....	....
3111	Buildings and structures..................	....	....	....	....	....	....	....	....	....	....	....	....
3112	Machinery and equipment..................	....	....	....	....	....	....	....	....	....	....	....	....
3113	Other fixed assets..................	....	....	....	....	....	....	....	....	....	....	....	....
312	Inventories..................	—	—	—	....	....	....	....	....	....	....	....	....
313	Valuables..................	—	—	—	....	....	....	....	....	....	....	....	....
314	Nonproduced assets..................	—	—	—	....	....	....	....	....	....	....	....	....
3141	Land..................	—	—	—	....	....	....	....	....	....	....	....	....
3142	Subsoil assets..................	—	—	—	....	....	....	....	....	....	....	....	....
3143	Other naturally occurring assets..................	—	—	—	....	....	....	....	....	....	....	....	....
3144	Intangible nonproduced assets..................	—	—	—	....	....	....	....	....	....	....	....	....
32	**Net acquisition of financial assets.........**	....	....	....	....	....	....	....	....	....	....	....	....
321	Domestic..................	....	....	....	....	....	....	....	....	....	....	....	....
3212	Currency and deposits..................	....	....	....	....	....	....	....	....	....	....	....	....
3213	Securities other than shares..................	....	....	....	....	....	....	....	....	....	....	....	....
3214	Loans..................	....	....	....	....	....	....	....	....	....	....	....	....
3215	Shares and other equity..................	....	....	....	....	....	....	....	....	....	....	....	....
3216	Insurance technical reserves..................	....	....	....	....	....	....	....	....	....	....	....	....
3217	Financial derivatives..................	....	....	....	....	....	....	....	....	....	....	....	....
3218	Other accounts receivable..................	....	....	....	....	....	....	....	....	....	....	....	....
322	Foreign..................	....	....	....	....	....	....	....	....	....	....	....	....
3222	Currency and deposits..................	....	....	....	....	....	....	....	....	....	....	....	....
3223	Securities other than shares..................	....	....	....	....	....	....	....	....	....	....	....	....
3224	Loans..................	....	....	....	....	....	....	....	....	....	....	....	....
3225	Shares and other equity..................	....	....	....	....	....	....	....	....	....	....	....	....
3226	Insurance technical reserves..................	....	....	....	....	....	....	....	....	....	....	....	....
3227	Financial derivatives..................	....	....	....	....	....	....	....	....	....	....	....	....
3228	Other accounts receivable..................	....	....	....	....	....	....	....	....	....	....	....	....
323	Monetary gold and SDRs..................	....	....	....	....	....	....	....	....	....	....	....	....
33	**Net incurrence of liabilities...................**	....	....	....	....	....	....	....	....	....	....	....	....
331	Domestic..................	....	....	....	....	....	....	....	....	....	....	....	....
3312	Currency and deposits..................	....	....	....	....	....	....	....	....	....	....	....	....
3313	Securities other than shares..................	....	....	....	....	....	....	....	....	....	....	....	....
3314	Loans..................	....	....	....	....	....	....	....	....	....	....	....	....
3316	Insurance technical reserves..................	....	....	....	....	....	....	....	....	....	....	....	....
3317	Financial derivatives..................	....	....	....	....	....	....	....	....	....	....	....	....
3318	Other accounts payable..................	....	....	....	....	....	....	....	....	....	....	....	....
332	Foreign..................	....	....	....	....	....	....	....	....	....	....	....	....
3322	Currency and deposits..................	....	....	....	....	....	....	....	....	....	....	....	....
3323	Securities other than shares..................	....	....	....	....	....	....	....	....	....	....	....	....
3324	Loans..................	....	....	....	....	....	....	....	....	....	....	....	....
3326	Insurance technical reserves..................	....	....	....	....	....	....	....	....	....	....	....	....
3327	Financial derivatives..................	....	....	....	....	....	....	....	....	....	....	....	....
3328	Other accounts payable..................	....	....	....	....	....	....	....	....	....	....	....	....

In Billions of Rupees / Year Ending June 30 / Cash Reporter

	Central Government			State Government			Local Government			General Government		
	2004	2005	2006f	2004	2005	2006	2004	2005	2006	2004	2005	2006
Table 4 Holding gains in assets and liabilities												
Table 5 Other changes in the volume of assets and liabilities												
Table 6 Balance sheet												
Table 7 Outlays by functions of govt.												
7 **Total outlays**................................	**905.55**	**1,071.62**	**1,244.17**	....	....	....	....	....	....	....	....	....
701 **General public services**.........................	**601.83**	**722.68**	**845.24**	....	....	....	....	....	....	....	....	....
7017 Public debt transactions..............................	317.72	274.72	301.35	....	....	....	....	....	....	....	....	....
7018 General transfers between levels of govt......	....	....	....	....	....	....	....	....	....	....	....	....
702 **Defense**..	**180.54**	**211.72**	**223.50**	....	....	....	....	....	....	....	....	....
703 **Public order and safety**.........................	**15.39**	**18.42**	**21.95**	....	....	....	....	....	....	....	....	....
704 **Economic affairs**...................................	**76.73**	**87.46**	**107.58**	....	....	....	....	....	....	....	....	....
7042 Agriculture, forestry, fishing, and hunting.....	18.99	3.05	....	....	....	....	....	....	....	....	....	....
7043 Fuel and energy...	1.64	.27	....	....	....	....	....	....	....	....	....	....
7044 Mining, manufacturing, and construction.....	9.50	.45	....	....	....	....	....	....	....	....	....	....
7045 Transport...	5.69	6.94	....	....	....	....	....	....	....	....	....	....
7046 Communication..	.17	.65	....	....	....	....	....	....	....	....	....	....
705 **Environmental protection**......................	**.14**	**.08**	**.18**	....	....	....	....	....	....	....	....	....
706 **Housing and community amenities**........	**2.98**	**2.30**	**4.76**	....	....	....	....	....	....	....	....	....
707 **Health**..	**7.12**	**8.12**	**13.12**	....	....	....	....	....	....	....	....	....
7072 Outpatient services.....................................	—	....	....	....	....	....	....	....	....	....	....	....
7073 Hospital services...	2.83	....	....	....	....	....	....	....	....	....	....	....
7074 Public health services.................................	3.65	....	....	....	....	....	....	....	....	....	....	....
708 **Recreation, culture, and religion**...........	**2.30**	**2.75**	**3.02**	....	....	....	....	....	....	....	....	....
709 **Education**...	**17.00**	**15.98**	**21.52**	....	....	....	....	....	....	....	....	....
7091 Pre-primary and primary education.............	1.40	2.90	....	....	....	....	....	....	....	....	....	....
7092 Secondary education...................................	1.66	1.89	....	....	....	....	....	....	....	....	....	....
7094 Tertiary education.......................................	....	7.60	....	....	....	....	....	....	....	....	....	....
710 **Social protection**.....................................	**1.52**	**2.12**	**3.31**	....	....	....	....	....	....	....	....	....
7 Statistical discrepancy: Total outlays...............	—	—	—	....	....	....	....	....	....	....	....	....
Table 8 Transactions in financial assets and liabilities by sector												

In Millions of Balboas / Year Ending December 31 / Cash Reporter

	Budgetary Central Government			Central Government			Local Government			General Government		
	1999	2000	2001	1999	2000	2001	1999	2000	2001	1999	2000	2001
Statement of government operations												
Statement of other economic flows												
Balance sheet												
Statement of sources and uses of cash												
1 Cash receipts from operating activities	1,907.7	1,935.6	1,964.0	2,668.1	2,705.0	3,041.0	....	....	....	....	....	....
11 Taxes	1,265.5	1,185.8	1,093.4	1,265.5	1,185.8	1,093.4	....	....	....	....	....	....
12 Social contributions	—	—	—	472.1	497.8	594.9	....	....	....	....	....	....
13 Grants	6.8	17.8	23.5	6.8	17.8	23.5	....	....	....	....	....	....
14 Other receipts	635.4	732.0	847.0	923.7	1,003.6	1,329.2	....	....	....	....	....	....
2 Cash payments for operating activities	1,486.6	1,529.0	1,620.3	2,442.5	2,567.7	2,736.0	....	....	....	....	....	....
21 Compensation of employees	640.6	633.5	683.9	942.4	942.2	1,014.0	....	....	....	....	....	....
22 Purchases of goods and services	239.4	267.6	282.8	373.3	388.3	450.5	....	....	....	....	....	....
24 Interest	478.8	554.2	586.9	481.0	556.3	587.3	....	....	....	....	....	....
25 Subsidies	80.1	39.2	43.9	80.1	39.2	43.9	....	....	....	....	....	....
26 Grants	5.9	3.9	7.4	5.9	3.9	8.1	....	....	....	....	....	....
27 Social benefits	28.9	14.6	15.4	546.9	621.8	632.3	....	....	....	....	....	....
28 Other payments	12.9	16.0	—	12.9	16.0	—	....	....	....	....	....	....
CIO *Net cash inflow from oper. activities*	*69.3*	*–43.9*	*424.2*	*225.6*	*137.3*	*304.9*	....	....	....	....	....	....
31.1 Purchases of nonfinancial assets	153.1	187.2	168.2	208.4	236.2	198.4	....	....	....	....	....	....
31.2 Sales of nonfinancial assets	3.2	1.2	.9	3.2	1.2	.9	....	....	....	....	....	....
31 Net cash outflow from investments in nonfinancial assets	149.9	186.0	167.3	205.2	235.0	197.5	....	....	....	....	....	....
CSD *Cash surplus/deficit*	*–80.6*	*–229.9*	*256.9*	*20.4*	*–97.7*	*107.4*	....	....	....	....	....	....
32x Net acquisition of fin assets, excl. cash	–29.0	–18.1	—	–14.0	–127.9	13.7	....	....	....	....	....	....
321x Domestic	–29.0	–18.1	—	–14.0	–127.9	13.7	....	....	....	....	....	....
322x Foreign	—	—	—	—	—	—	....	....	....	....	....	....
323 Monetary gold and SDRs	—	—	—	—	—	—	....	....	....	....	....	....
33 Net incurrence of liabilities	....	....	....	....	....	....	....	....	....	....	....	....
331 Domestic	....	....	....	....	....	....	....	....	....	....	....	....
332 Foreign	....	....	....	....	....	....	....	....	....	....	....	....
NFB Net cash inflow from fin. activities	....	....	....	....	....	....	....	....	....	....	....	....
NCB *Net change in the stock of cash*	....	....	....	....	....	....	....	....	....	....	....	....
Table 1 Revenue												
1 **Revenue**	**1,907.7**	**1,935.6**	**1,964.0**	**2,668.1**	**2,705.0**	**3,041.0**	....	....	....	....	....	....
11 **Taxes**	**1,265.5**	**1,185.8**	**1,093.4**	**1,265.5**	**1,185.8**	**1,093.4**	....	....	....	....	....	....
111 Taxes on income, profits, & capital gains	508.4	494.2	454.1	508.4	494.2	454.1	....	....	....	....	....	....
1111 Individuals	21.7	20.3	28.2	21.7	20.3	28.2	....	....	....	....	....	....
1112 Corporations and other enterprises	186.8	155.2	124.3	186.8	155.2	124.3	....	....	....	....	....	....
112 Taxes on payroll and workforce	—	—	—	—	—	—	....	....	....	....	....	....
113 Taxes on property	41.5	33.9	42.0	41.5	33.9	42.0	....	....	....	....	....	....
114 Taxes on goods and services	....	....	270.8	....	....	270.8	....	....	....	....	....	....
1141 General taxes on goods and services	....	....	66.7	....	....	66.7	....	....	....	....	....	....
1142 Excises	....	....	138.0	....	....	138.0	....	....	....	....	....	....
115 Taxes on int'l. trade and transactions	....	....	260.7	....	....	260.7	....	....	....	....	....	....
116 Other taxes	69.6	77.8	65.7	69.6	77.8	65.7	....	....	....	....	....	....
12 **Social contributions**	—	—	—	472.1	497.8	594.9	....	....	....	....	....	....
121 Social security contributions	—	—	—	472.1	497.8	594.9	....	....	....	....	....	....
122 Other social contributions	—	—	—	—	—	—	....	....	....	....	....	....
13 **Grants**	6.8	17.8	23.5	6.8	17.8	23.5	....	....	....	....	....	....
131 From foreign governments	6.8	17.8	23.5	6.8	17.8	23.5	....	....	....	....	....	....
132 From international organizations	—	—	—	—	—	—	....	....	....	....	....	....
133 From other general government units	—	—	—	—	—	—	....	....	....	....	....	....
14 **Other revenue**	**635.4**	**732.0**	**847.0**	**923.7**	**1,003.6**	**1,329.2**	....	....	....	....	....	....
Table 2 Expense by economic type												
2 **Expense**	**1,486.6**	**1,529.0**	**1,620.3**	**2,442.5**	**2,567.7**	**2,736.0**	....	....	....	....	....	....
21 **Compensation of employees**	**640.6**	**633.5**	**683.9**	**942.4**	**942.2**	**1,014.0**	....	....	....	....	....	....
211 Wages and salaries	640.6	633.5	683.9	942.4	942.2	1,014.0	....	....	....	....	....	....
212 Social contributions	....	....	....	....	....	....	....	....	....	....	....	....
22 **Use of goods and services**	**239.4**	**267.6**	**282.8**	**373.3**	**388.3**	**450.5**	....	....	....	....	....	....
23 **Consumption of fixed capital**	....	....	....	....	....	....	....	....	....	....	....	....
24 **Interest**	**478.8**	**554.2**	**586.9**	**481.0**	**556.3**	**587.3**	....	....	....	....	....	....
25 **Subsidies**	**80.1**	**39.2**	**43.9**	**80.1**	**39.2**	**43.9**	....	....	....	....	....	....

In Millions of Balboas / Year Ending December 31 / Cash Reporter

	Budgetary Central Government			Central Government			Local Government			General Government		
	1999	2000	2001	1999	2000	2001	1999	2000	2001	1999	2000	2001
26 Grants...........................	5.9	3.9	7.4	5.9	3.9	8.1	....	....	....	....	....	....
261 To foreign govenments...............	5.9	3.9	7.4	5.9	3.9	8.1	....	....	....	....	....	....
262 To international organizations..............	—	—	—	....	....	....	....	....	....	....	....	....
263 To other general government units.............	—	—	—	—	—	—	....	....	....	....	....	....
2631 Current.............................	—	—	—	—	—	—	....	....	....	....	....	....
2632 Capital.............................	—	—	—	—	—	—	....	....	....	....	....	....
27 Social benefits....................	28.9	14.6	15.4	546.9	621.8	632.3	....	....	....	....	....	....
28 Other expense.....................	12.9	16.0	—	12.9	16.0	—	....	....	....	....	....	....
281 Property expense other than interest...........	—	—	—	—	—	—	....	....	....	....	....	....
282 Miscellaneous other expense...................	12.9	16.0	—	12.9	16.0	—	....	....	....	....	....	....
2821 Current.............................	—	—	—	—	—	—	....	....	....	....	....	....
2822 Capital.............................	12.9	16.0	—	12.9	16.0	—	....	....	....	....	....	....

Table 3 Transactions in assets and liabilities

	Budgetary Central Government			Central Government			Local Government			General Government		
	1999	2000	2001	1999	2000	2001	1999	2000	2001	1999	2000	2001
3 Change in net worth from transactns....	....	....	....	....	....	....	....	....	....	....	....	....
31 Net acquisition of nonfinancial assets...	149.9	186.0	167.3	205.2	235.0	197.5	....	....	....	....	....	....
311 Fixed assets.............................	149.9	186.0	166.8	205.2	235.0	197.0	....	....	....	....	....	....
3111 Buildings and structures.................	....	....	....	....	....	....	....	....	....	....	....	....
3112 Machinery and equipment.................	....	....	....	....	....	....	....	....	....	....	....	....
3113 Other fixed assets.....................	....	....	....	....	....	....	....	....	....	....	....	....
312 Inventories.............................	—	—	—	—	—	—	....	....	....	....	....	....
313 Valuables.............................	—	—	—	—	—	—	....	....	....	....	....	....
314 Nonproduced assets.....................	—	—	.5	—	—	.5	....	....	....	....	....	....
3141 Land.................................	—	—	....	—	—	....	....	....	....	....	....	....
3142 Subsoil assets.....................	—	—	....	—	—	....	....	....	....	....	....	....
3143 Other naturally occurring assets.........	—	—	....	—	—	....	....	....	....	....	....	....
3144 Intangible nonproduced assets.............	—	—	....	—	—	....	....	....	....	....	....	....
32 Net acquisition of financial assets.........	....	....	....	....	....	....	....	....	....	....	....	....
321 Domestic.............................	....	....	....	....	....	....	....	....	....	....	....	....
3212 Currency and deposits...................	....	....	....	....	....	....	....	....	....	....	....	....
3213 Securities other than shares.............	....	....	....	....	....	....	....	....	....	....	....	....
3214 Loans.............................	....	....	....	....	....	....	....	....	....	....	....	....
3215 Shares and other equity.................	....	....	....	....	....	....	....	....	....	....	....	....
3216 Insurance technical reserves.............	....	....	....	....	....	....	....	....	....	....	....	....
3217 Financial derivatives...................	....	....	....	....	....	....	....	....	....	....	....	....
3218 Other accounts receivable...............	....	....	....	....	....	....	....	....	....	....	....	....
322 Foreign.............................	....	....	....	....	....	....	....	....	....	....	....	....
3222 Currency and deposits...................	....	....	....	....	....	....	....	....	....	....	....	....
3223 Securities other than shares.............	....	....	....	....	....	....	....	....	....	....	....	....
3224 Loans.............................	....	....	....	....	....	....	....	....	....	....	....	....
3225 Shares and other equity.................	....	....	....	....	....	....	....	....	....	....	....	....
3226 Insurance technical reserves.............	....	....	....	....	....	....	....	....	....	....	....	....
3227 Financial derivatives...................	....	....	....	....	....	....	....	....	....	....	....	....
3228 Other accounts receivable...............	....	....	....	....	....	....	....	....	....	....	....	....
323 Monetary gold and SDRs...............	....	....	....	....	....	....	....	....	....	....	....	....
33 Net incurrence of liabilities...................	....	....	....	....	....	....	....	....	....	....	....	....
331 Domestic.............................	....	....	....	....	....	....	....	....	....	....	....	....
3312 Currency and deposits...................	....	....	....	....	....	....	....	....	....	....	....	....
3313 Securities other than shares.............	....	....	....	....	....	....	....	....	....	....	....	....
3314 Loans.............................	....	....	....	....	....	....	....	....	....	....	....	....
3316 Insurance technical reserves.............	....	....	....	....	....	....	....	....	....	....	....	....
3317 Financial derivatives...................	....	....	....	....	....	....	....	....	....	....	....	....
3318 Other accounts payable.................	....	....	....	....	....	....	....	....	....	....	....	....
332 Foreign.............................	....	....	....	....	....	....	....	....	....	....	....	....
3322 Currency and deposits...................	....	....	....	....	....	....	....	....	....	....	....	....
3323 Securities other than shares.............	....	....	....	....	....	....	....	....	....	....	....	....
3324 Loans.............................	....	....	....	....	....	....	....	....	....	....	....	....
3326 Insurance technical reserves.............	....	....	....	....	....	....	....	....	....	....	....	....
3327 Financial derivatives...................	....	....	....	....	....	....	....	....	....	....	....	....
3328 Other accounts payable.................	....	....	....	....	....	....	....	....	....	....	....	....

In Millions of Balboas / Year Ending December 31 / Cash Reporter

	Budgetary Central Government			Central Government			Local Government			General Government		
	1999	2000	2001	1999	2000	2001	1999	2000	2001	1999	2000	2001
Table 4 Holding gains in assets and liabilities												
Table 5 Other changes in the volume of assets and liabilities												
Table 6 Balance sheet												
Table 7 Outlays by functions of govt.												
7 **Total outlays**...................	**1,639.7**	**1,716.2**	**1,788.5**	**2,650.9**	**2,803.9**	**2,934.4**	....	....	....	....	....	....
701 **General public services**..................	**690.0**	**763.9**	**807.9**	**692.2**	**766.0**	**808.3**	....	....	....	....	....	....
7017 Public debt transactions...............	478.8	554.2	586.9	481.0	556.3	587.3	....	....	....	....	....	....
7018 General transfers between levels of govt......	....	....	....	....	....	....	....	....	....	....	....	....
702 **Defense**..................................	—	—	—	—	—	—	....	....	....	....	....	....
703 **Public order and safety**.......................	**211.2**	**199.4**	**195.6**	**211.2**	**199.4**	**195.6**	....	....	....	....	....	....
704 **Economic affairs**..............................	**189.2**	**177.5**	**158.2**	**208.2**	**196.1**	**175.9**	....	....	....	....	....	....
7042 Agriculture, forestry, fishing, and hunting.....	47.4	37.6	62.5	53.3	42.6	68.1	....	....	....	....	....	....
7043 Fuel and energy............................	....	....	.7	....	....	.7	....	....	....	....	....	....
7044 Mining, manufacturing, and construction.....	3.3	4.1	1.8	3.3	4.1	1.8	....	....	....	....	....	....
7045 Transport.................................	106.9	92.4	56.9	106.9	92.4	56.9	....	....	....	....	....	....
7046 Communication............................	....	....	....	....	....	....	....	....	....	....	....	....
705 **Environmental protection**....................	....	—	—	....	—	—	....	....	....	....	....	....
706 **Housing and community amenities**........	**76.8**	**80.6**	**107.5**	**95.0**	**80.6**	**107.5**	....	....	....	....	....	....
707 **Health**...................................	**169.8**	**179.1**	**175.9**	**470.2**	**482.1**	**527.5**	....	....	....	....	....	....
7072 Outpatient services........................	....	—	....	....	—	....	....	....	....	....	....	....
7073 Hospital services..........................	167.4	178.9	173.4	467.8	481.9	525.0	....	....	....	....	....	....
7074 Public health services.....................	....	—	....	....	—	....	....	....	....	....	....	....
708 **Recreation, culture, and religion**...........	**9.7**	**9.5**	**21.8**	**28.0**	**27.9**	**39.2**	....	....	....	....	....	....
709 **Education**...............................	**286.3**	**299.1**	**311.8**	**450.1**	**465.4**	**476.7**	....	....	....	....	....	....
7091 Pre-primary and primary education.............	....	....	....	....	....	....	....	....	....	....	....	....
7092 Secondary education.......................	235.4	255.6	271.2	235.4	255.6	271.2	....	....	....	....	....	....
7094 Tertiary education.........................	—	—	—	125.6	128.4	127.6	....	....	....	....	....	....
710 **Social protection**...........................	**6.7**	**7.1**	**9.8**	**496.0**	**586.4**	**603.7**	....	....	....	....	....	....
7 Statistical discrepancy: Total outlays...............	—	—	—	—	—	—	....	....	....	....	....	....
Table 8 Transactions in financial assets and liabilities by sector												

		Budgetary Central Government			Central Government			Local Government			General Government		
		2000	2001	2002p	2000	2001	2002	2000	2001	2002	2000	2001	2002
Statement of government operations													
Statement of other economic flows													
Balance sheet													
6	*Net worth*...............	....	....	....	....	....	....	....	....	....	....	....	....
61	Nonfinancial assets...............	....	....	....	....	....	....	....	....	....	....	....	....
62	Financial assets...............	....	....	....	....	....	....	....	....	....	....	....	....
63	Liabilities...............	5,621.6	7,097.3	8,127.9	....	....	....	....	....	....	....	....	....
Statement of sources and uses of cash													
1	Cash receipts from operating activities...........	2,764.2	2,835.4	2,666.3	....	....	....	....	....	....	....	....	....
11	Taxes...............	1,847.5	2,567.5	2,449.2	....	....	....	....	....	....	....	....	....
12	Social contributions...............	4.9	4.0	4.4	....	....	....	....	....	....	....	....	....
13	Grants...............	405.7	111.2	47.6	....	....	....	....	....	....	....	....	....
14	Other receipts...............	506.2	152.7	165.1	....	....	....	....	....	....	....	....	....
2	Cash payments for operating activities...........	2,925.3	2,799.0	2,575.2	....	....	....	....	....	....	....	....	....
21	Compensation of employees...............	731.5	736.0	715.4	....	....	....	....	....	....	....	....	....
22	Purchases of goods and services...............	1,086.9	1,025.1	906.8	....	....	....	....	....	....	....	....	....
24	Interest...............	406.3	419.6	530.7	....	....	....	....	....	....	....	....	....
25	Subsidies...............	.4	—	.1	....	....	....	....	....	....	....	....	....
26	Grants...............	654.0	576.3	398.1	....	....	....	....	....	....	....	....	....
27	Social benefits...............	46.3	42.0	24.0	....	....	....	....	....	....	....	....	....
28	Other payments...............	—	—	—	....	....	....	....	....	....	....	....	....
CIO	*Net cash inflow from oper. activities*.....	−161.1	36.4	91.1	....	....	....	....	....	....	....	....	....
31.1	Purchases of nonfinancial assets...............	123.1	169.6	355.1	....	....	....	....	....	....	....	....	....
31.2	Sales of nonfinancial assets...............	100.9	.6	.2	....	....	....	....	....	....	....	....	....
31	Net cash outflow from investments in nonfinancial assets...............	22.2	168.9	354.9	....	....	....	....	....	....	....	....	....
CSD	*Cash surplus/deficit*...............	−183.3	−132.5	−263.8	....	....	....	....	....	....	....	....	....
32x	Net acquisition of fin assets, excl. cash...........	−1.6	—	—	....	....	....	....	....	....	....	....	....
321x	Domestic...............	−1.6	—	—	....	....	....	....	....	....	....	....	....
322x	Foreign...............	—	—	—	....	....	....	....	....	....	....	....	....
323	Monetary gold and SDRs...............	—	—	—	....	....	....	....	....	....	....	....	....
33	Net incurrence of liabilities...............	339.6	427.8	316.8	....	....	....	....	....	....	....	....	....
331	Domestic...............	159.7	118.2	572.1	....	....	....	....	....	....	....	....	....
332	Foreign...............	179.9	309.6	−255.3	....	....	....	....	....	....	....	....	....
NFB	Net cash inflow from fin. activities...............	341.2	427.8	316.8	....	....	....	....	....	....	....	....	....
NCB	*Net change in the stock of cash*.............	157.9	295.2	53.0	....	....	....	....	....	....	....	....	....
Table 1 Revenue													
1	**Revenue**...............	**2,764.2**	**2,835.4**	**2,666.3**	....	....	....	....	....	....	....	....	....
11	**Taxes**...............	**1,847.5**	**2,567.5**	**2,449.2**	....	....	....	....	....	....	....	....	....
111	Taxes on income, profits, & capital gains......	862.9	1,567.9	1,322.2	....	....	....	....	....	....	....	....	....
1111	Individuals...............	330.4	....	689.8	....	....	....	....	....	....	....	....	....
1112	Corporations and other enterprises...............	530.2	....	632.4	....	....	....	....	....	....	....	....	....
112	Taxes on payroll and workforce...............	—	—	—	....	....	....	....	....	....	....	....	....
113	Taxes on property...............	—	—	—	....	....	....	....	....	....	....	....	....
114	Taxes on goods and services...............	255.1	342.5	342.8	....	....	....	....	....	....	....	....	....
1141	General taxes on goods and services...........	....	....	....	....	....	....	....	....	....	....	....	....
1142	Excises...............	....	....	....	....	....	....	....	....	....	....	....	....
115	Taxes on int'l. trade and transactions...............	669.8	592.1	704.5	....	....	....	....	....	....	....	....	....
116	Other taxes...............	59.6	65.1	79.8	....	....	....	....	....	....	....	....	....
12	**Social contributions**...............	**4.9**	**4.0**	**4.4**	....	....	....	....	....	....	....	....	....
121	Social security contributions...............	—	—	—	....	....	....	....	....	....	....	....	....
122	Other social contributions...............	4.9	4.0	4.4	....	....	....	....	....	....	....	....	....
13	**Grants**...............	**405.7**	**111.2**	**47.6**	....	....	....	....	....	....	....	....	....
131	From foreign governments...............	390.3	111.0	46.7	....	....	....	....	....	....	....	....	....
132	From international organizations...............	15.4	.2	.9	....	....	....	....	....	....	....	....	....
133	From other general government units...........	—	—	—	....	....	....	....	....	....	....	....	....
14	**Other revenue**...............	**506.2**	**152.7**	**165.1**	....	....	....	....	....	....	....	....	....
Table 2 Expense by economic type													
2	**Expense**...............	**2,925.3**	**2,799.0**	**2,575.2**	....	....	....	....	....	....	....	....	....
21	**Compensation of employees**...............	**731.5**	**736.0**	**715.4**	....	....	....	....	....	....	....	....	....
211	Wages and salaries...............	731.5	736.0	715.4	....	....	....	....	....	....	....	....	....
212	Social contributions...............	—	—	—	....	....	....	....	....	....	....	....	....
22	**Use of goods and services**...............	**1,086.9**	**1,025.1**	**906.8**	....	....	....	....	....	....	....	....	....
23	**Consumption of fixed capital**...............	....	....	....	....	....	....	....	....	....	....	....	....
24	**Interest**...............	**406.3**	**419.6**	**530.7**	....	....	....	....	....	....	....	....	....
25	**Subsidies**...............	**.4**	**—**	**.1**	....	....	....	....	....	....	....	....	....

In Millions of Kina / Year Ending December 31 / Cash Reporter

	Budgetary Central Government			Central Government			Local Government			General Government		
	2000	2001	2002p	2000	2001	2002	2000	2001	2002	2000	2001	2002
26 Grants................................	654.0	576.3	398.1	....	....	....	....	....	....	....	....	....
261 To foreign governments..............	—	—	—	....	....	....	....	....	....	....	....	....
262 To international organizations........	—	—	—	....	....	....	....	....	....	....	....	....
263 To other general government units..........	654.0	576.3	398.1	....	....	....	....	....	....	....	....	....
2631 Current...........	653.4	572.0	393.6	....	....	....	....	....	....	....	....	....
2632 Capital............	.6	4.3	4.6	....	....	....	....	....	....	....	....	....
27 Social benefits....................	46.3	42.0	24.0	....	....	....	....	....	....	....	....	....
28 Other expense....................	—	—	—	....	....	....	....	....	....	....	....	....
281 Property expense other than interest..........	—	—	—	....	....	....	....	....	....	....	....	....
282 Miscellaneous other expense.............	—	—	—	....	....	....	....	....	....	....	....	....
2821 Current.............	—	—	—	....	....	....	....	....	....	....	....	....
2822 Capital.............	—	—	—	....	....	....	....	....	....	....	....	....
Table 3 Transactions in assets and liabilities												
3 Change in net worth from transactns....	....	....	....	....	....	....	....	....	....	....	....	....
31 Net acquisition of nonfinancial assets...	22.2	168.9	354.9	....	....	....	....	....	....	....	....	....
311 Fixed assets..............	45.9	168.1	352.7	....	....	....	....	....	....	....	....	....
3111 Buildings and structures............	....	....	....	....	....	....	....	....	....	....	....	....
3112 Machinery and equipment............	....	....	....	....	....	....	....	....	....	....	....	....
3113 Other fixed assets............	....	....	....	....	....	....	....	....	....	....	....	....
312 Inventories...........	—	—	—	....	....	....	....	....	....	....	....	....
313 Valuables...........	—	—	—	....	....	....	....	....	....	....	....	....
314 Nonproduced assets............	−23.7	.9	2.2	....	....	....	....	....	....	....	....	....
3141 Land...........	....	....	....	....	....	....	....	....	....	....	....	....
3142 Subsoil assets...........	....	....	....	....	....	....	....	....	....	....	....	....
3143 Other naturally occurring assets...........	....	....	....	....	....	....	....	....	....	....	....	....
3144 Intangible nonproduced assets...........	....	....	....	....	....	....	....	....	....	....	....	....
32 Net acquisition of financial assets........	156.3	295.2	53.0	....	....	....	....	....	....	....	....	....
321 Domestic...........	156.3	295.2	53.0	....	....	....	....	....	....	....	....	....
3212 Currency and deposits...........	157.9	295.2	53.0	....	....	....	....	....	....	....	....	....
3213 Securities other than shares...........	....	—	—	....	....	....	....	....	....	....	....	....
3214 Loans...........	....	—	—	....	....	....	....	....	....	....	....	....
3215 Shares and other equity...........	....	—	—	....	....	....	....	....	....	....	....	....
3216 Insurance technical reserves...........	—	—	—	....	....	....	....	....	....	....	....	....
3217 Financial derivatives...........	—	—	—	....	....	....	....	....	....	....	....	....
3218 Other accounts receivable...........	....	....	....	....	....	....	....	....	....	....	....	....
322 Foreign...........	—	—	—	....	....	....	....	....	....	....	....	....
3222 Currency and deposits...........	—	—	—	....	....	....	....	....	....	....	....	....
3223 Securities other than shares...........	—	—	—	....	....	....	....	....	....	....	....	....
3224 Loans...........	—	—	—	....	....	....	....	....	....	....	....	....
3225 Shares and other equity...........	—	—	—	....	....	....	....	....	....	....	....	....
3226 Insurance technical reserves...........	—	—	—	....	....	....	....	....	....	....	....	....
3227 Financial derivatives...........	—	—	—	....	....	....	....	....	....	....	....	....
3228 Other accounts receivable...........	....	....	....	....	....	....	....	....	....	....	....	....
323 Monetary gold and SDRs...........	—	—	—	....	....	....	....	....	....	....	....	....
33 Net incurrence of liabilities................	339.6	427.8	316.8	....	....	....	....	....	....	....	....	....
331 Domestic...........	159.7	118.2	572.1	....	....	....	....	....	....	....	....	....
3312 Currency and deposits...........	—	—	—	....	....	....	....	....	....	....	....	....
3313 Securities other than shares...........	211.1	154.3	....	....	....	....	....	....	....	....	....	....
3314 Loans...........	−51.4	−36.1	....	....	....	....	....	....	....	....	....	....
3316 Insurance technical reserves...........	—	—	—	....	....	....	....	....	....	....	....	....
3317 Financial derivatives...........	—	—	—	....	....	....	....	....	....	....	....	....
3318 Other accounts payable...........	....	....	....	....	....	....	....	....	....	....	....	....
332 Foreign...........	179.9	309.6	−255.3	....	....	....	....	....	....	....	....	....
3322 Currency and deposits...........	—	—	—	....	....	....	....	....	....	....	....	....
3323 Securities other than shares...........	—	—	—	....	....	....	....	....	....	....	....	....
3324 Loans...........	179.9	309.6	−255.3	....	....	....	....	....	....	....	....	....
3326 Insurance technical reserves...........	—	—	—	....	....	....	....	....	....	....	....	....
3327 Financial derivatives...........	—	—	—	....	....	....	....	....	....	....	....	....
3328 Other accounts payable...........	....	....	....	....	....	....	....	....	....	....	....	....

Papua New Guinea   853

In Millions of Kina / Year Ending December 31 / Cash Reporter

	Budgetary Central Government			Central Government			Local Government			General Government		
	2000	2001	2002p	2000	2001	2002	2000	2001	2002	2000	2001	2002
Table 4 Holding gains in assets and liabilities												
Table 5 Other changes in the volume of assets and liabilities												
Table 6 Balance sheet												
6 Net worth..........	....	....	....	....	....	....	....	....	....	....	....	....
61 Nonfinancial assets..........	....	....	....	....	....	....	....	....	....	....	....	....
611 Fixed assets..........	....	....	....	....	....	....	....	....	....	....	....	....
6111 Buildings and structures..........	....	....	....	....	....	....	....	....	....	....	....	....
6112 Machinery and equipment..........	....	....	....	....	....	....	....	....	....	....	....	....
6113 Other fixed assets..........	....	....	....	....	....	....	....	....	....	....	....	....
612 Inventories..........	....	....	....	....	....	....	....	....	....	....	....	....
613 Valuables..........	....	....	....	....	....	....	....	....	....	....	....	....
614 Nonproduced assets..........	....	....	....	....	....	....	....	....	....	....	....	....
6141 Land..........	....	....	....	....	....	....	....	....	....	....	....	....
6142 Subsoil assets..........	....	....	....	....	....	....	....	....	....	....	....	....
6143 Other naturally occurring assets..........	....	....	....	....	....	....	....	....	....	....	....	....
6144 Intangible nonproduced assets..........	....	....	....	....	....	....	....	....	....	....	....	....
62 Financial assets..........	....	....	....	....	....	....	....	....	....	....	....	....
621 Domestic..........	....	....	....	....	....	....	....	....	....	....	....	....
6212 Currency and deposits..........	....	....	....	....	....	....	....	....	....	....	....	....
6213 Securities other than shares..........	....	....	....	....	....	....	....	....	....	....	....	....
6214 Loans..........	....	....	....	....	....	....	....	....	....	....	....	....
6215 Shares and other equity..........	....	....	....	....	....	....	....	....	....	....	....	....
6216 Insurance technical reserves..........	....	....	....	....	....	....	....	....	....	....	....	....
6217 Financial derivatives..........	....	....	....	....	....	....	....	....	....	....	....	....
6218 Other accounts receivable..........	....	....	....	....	....	....	....	....	....	....	....	....
622 Foreign..........	....	....	....	....	....	....	....	....	....	....	....	....
6222 Currency and deposits..........	....	....	....	....	....	....	....	....	....	....	....	....
6223 Securities other than shares..........	....	....	....	....	....	....	....	....	....	....	....	....
6224 Loans..........	....	....	....	....	....	....	....	....	....	....	....	....
6225 Shares and other equity..........	....	....	....	....	....	....	....	....	....	....	....	....
6226 Insurance technical reserves..........	....	....	....	....	....	....	....	....	....	....	....	....
6227 Financial derivatives..........	....	....	....	....	....	....	....	....	....	....	....	....
6228 Other accounts receivable..........	....	....	....	....	....	....	....	....	....	....	....	....
623 Monetary gold and SDRs..........	....	....	....	....	....	....	....	....	....	....	....	....
63 Liabilities..........	**5,621.6**	**7,097.3**	**8,127.9**	....	....	....	....	....	....	....	....	....
631 Domestic..........	1,783.3	2,115.1	2,530.5	....	....	....	....	....	....	....	....	....
6312 Currency and deposits..........	....	....	....	....	....	....	....	....	....	....	....	....
6313 Securities other than shares..........	....	....	....	....	....	....	....	....	....	....	....	....
6314 Loans..........	....	....	....	....	....	....	....	....	....	....	....	....
6316 Insurance technical reserves..........	....	....	....	....	....	....	....	....	....	....	....	....
6317 Financial derivatives..........	....	....	....	....	....	....	....	....	....	....	....	....
6318 Other accounts payable..........	....	....	....	....	....	....	....	....	....	....	....	....
632 Foreign..........	3,838.3	4,982.2	5,597.4	....	....	....	....	....	....	....	....	....
6322 Currency and deposits..........	....	....	....	....	....	....	....	....	....	....	....	....
6323 Securities other than shares..........	....	....	....	....	....	....	....	....	....	....	....	....
6324 Loans..........	....	....	....	....	....	....	....	....	....	....	....	....
6326 Insurance technical reserves..........	....	....	....	....	....	....	....	....	....	....	....	....
6327 Financial derivatives..........	....	....	....	....	....	....	....	....	....	....	....	....
6328 Other accounts payable..........	....	....	....	....	....	....	....	....	....	....	....	....
Memorandum items:												
6M2 Net financial worth..........	....	....	....	....	....	....	....	....	....	....	....	....
6M3 Debt at market value..........	....	....	....	....	....	....	....	....	....	....	....	....
6M4 Debt at nominal value..........	....	....	....	....	....	....	....	....	....	....	....	....
6M5 Arrears..........	....	....	....	....	....	....	....	....	....	....	....	....
6M6 Obligations for social security benefits..........	....	....	....	....	....	....	....	....	....	....	....	....
6M7 Contingent liabilities..........	....	....	....	....	....	....	....	....	....	....	....	....
6M8 Uncapitalized military weapons, systems..........	....	....	....	....	....	....	....	....	....	....	....	....
Table 7 Outlays by functions of govt.												
7 Total outlays..........	**3,047.4**	**2,968.3**	**3,052.4**	....	....	....	....	....	....	....	....	....
701 General public services..........	**1,414.0**	**1,396.7**	**1,821.8**	....	....	....	....	....	....	....	....	....
7017 Public debt transactions..........	406.3	419.6	530.7	....	....	....	....	....	....	....	....	....
7018 General transfers between levels of govt.	....	....	....	....	....	....	....	....	....	....	....	....
702 Defense..........	**93.5**	**82.7**	**72.0**	....	....	....	....	....	....	....	....	....
703 Public order and safety..........	**204.8**	**239.1**	**227.6**	....	....	....	....	....	....	....	....	....

2005, International Monetary Fund: *Government Finance Statistics Yearbook*

In Millions of Kina / Year Ending December 31 / Cash Reporter

		Budgetary Central Government			Central Government			Local Government			General Government		
		2000	2001	2002p	2000	2001	2002	2000	2001	2002	2000	2001	2002
704	**Economic affairs**....................	**538.4**	**456.1**	**369.5**	....	....	....	....	....	....	....	....	....
7042	Agriculture, forestry, fishing, and hunting.....	80.0	67.3	51.0	....	....	....	....	....	....	....	....	....
7043	Fuel and energy....................	10.3	14.3	17.8	....	....	....	....	....	....	....	....	....
7044	Mining, manufacturing, and construction.....	15.2	16.2	16.5	....	....	....	....	....	....	....	....	....
7045	Transport.....................	104.3	73.5	219.7	....	....	....	....	....	....	....	....	....
7046	Communication.....................	....	....	....	....	....	....	....	....	....	....	....	....
705	**Environmental protection**.....................	....	....	....	....	....	....	....	....	....	....	....	....
706	**Housing and community amenities**........	**68.6**	**21.4**	**10.7**	....	....	....	....	....	....	....	....	....
707	**Health**................	**158.3**	**225.7**	**174.0**	....	....	....	....	....	....	....	....	....
7072	Outpatient services....................	19.1	49.8	22.5	....	....	....	....	....	....	....	....	....
7073	Hospital services....................	72.6	121.3	133.5	....	....	....	....	....	....	....	....	....
7074	Public health services....................	....	....	....	....	....	....	....	....	....	....	....	....
708	**Recreation, culture, and religion**...........	**16.4**	**21.0**	**26.0**	....	....	....	....	....	....	....	....	....
709	**Education**.................	**501.3**	**480.7**	**305.7**	....	....	....	....	....	....	....	....	....
7091	Pre-primary and primary education.............	....	....	....	....	....	....	....	....	....	....	....	....
7092	Secondary education................	51.9	63.7	117.6	....	....	....	....	....	....	....	....	....
7094	Tertiary education....................	123.0	113.8	173.7	....	....	....	....	....	....	....	....	....
710	**Social protection**................	**52.1**	**45.0**	**45.1**	....	....	....	....	....	....	....	....	....
7	Statistical discrepancy: Total outlays.............	—	—	—	....	....	....	....	....	....	....	....	....

Table 8   Transactions in financial assets and liabilities by sector

		Budgetary Central Government			Central Government			Local Government			General Government		
		2000	2001	2002p	2000	2001	2002	2000	2001	2002	2000	2001	2002
82	**Net acquisition of financial assets**........	**156.3**	**295.2**	**53.0**	....	....	....	....	....	....	....	....	....
821	Domestic.....................	156.3	295.2	53.0	....	....	....	....	....	....	....	....	....
8211	General government....................	—	—	—	....	....	....	....	....	....	....	....	....
8212	Central bank....................	....	....	....	....	....	....	....	....	....	....	....	....
8213	Other depository corporations....................	....	....	....	....	....	....	....	....	....	....	....	....
8214	Financial corporations n.e.c....................	....	....	....	....	....	....	....	....	....	....	....	....
8215	Nonfinancial corporations....................	−.1	....	....	....	....	....	....	....	....	....	....	....
8216	Households & NPIs serving households....	....	....	....	....	....	....	....	....	....	....	....	....
822	Foreign....................	—	—	—	....	....	....	....	....	....	....	....	....
8221	General government....................	—	—	—	....	....	....	....	....	....	....	....	....
8227	International organizations....................	—	—	—	....	....	....	....	....	....	....	....	....
8228	Financial corporations other than international organizations.............	—	—	—	....	....	....	....	....	....	....	....	....
8229	Other nonresidents....................	—	—	—	....	....	....	....	....	....	....	....	....
823	Monetary gold and SDRs....................	—	—	—	....	....	....	....	....	....	....	....	....
83	**Net incurrence of liabilities**..................	**339.6**	**427.8**	**316.8**	....	....	....	....	....	....	....	....	....
831	Domestic....................	159.7	118.2	572.1	....	....	....	....	....	....	....	....	....
8311	General government....................	....	....	....	....	....	....	....	....	....	....	....	....
8312	Central bank....................	....	....	....	....	....	....	....	....	....	....	....	....
8313	Other depository corporations....................	....	....	....	....	....	....	....	....	....	....	....	....
8314	Financial corporations n.e.c....................	....	....	....	....	....	....	....	....	....	....	....	....
8315	Nonfinancial corporations....................	....	....	....	....	....	....	....	....	....	....	....	....
8316	Households & NPIs serving households......	....	....	....	....	....	....	....	....	....	....	....	....
832	Foreign....................	179.9	309.6	−255.3	....	....	....	....	....	....	....	....	....
8321	General government....................	—	—	....	....	....	....	....	....	....	....	....	....
8327	International organizations....................	125.8	232.0	....	....	....	....	....	....	....	....	....	....
8328	Financial corporations other than international organizations.............	—	—	....	....	....	....	....	....	....	....	....	....
8329	Other nonresidents....................	54.1	77.6	....	....	....	....	....	....	....	....	....	....

Paraguay 288

	Budgetary Central Government			Central Government			Local Government			General Government		
	2002	2003	2004	2002	2003	2004	2002	2003	2004	2002	2003	2004
Statement of government operations												
Statement of other economic flows												
Balance sheet												
Statement of sources and uses of cash												
1 Cash receipts from operating activities...........	5,078.1	6,065.6	7,648.5	....	....	....	....	....	....	....	....	....
11 Taxes...................................	2,920.8	3,676.4	4,929.2	....	....	....	....	....	....	....	....	....
12 Social contributions.....................	339.7	369.4	439.7	....	....	....	....	....	....	....	....	....
13 Grants..................................	195.1	163.3	222.6	....	....	....	....	....	....	....	....	....
14 Other receipts..........................	1,622.5	1,856.4	2,057.0	....	....	....	....	....	....	....	....	....
2 Cash payments for operating activities...........	4,918.7	5,215.1	5,702.6	....	....	....	....	....	....	....	....	....
21 Compensation of employees...............	2,581.8	2,724.0	2,983.5	....	....	....	....	....	....	....	....	....
22 Purchases of goods and services..........	395.1	417.6	465.6	....	....	....	....	....	....	....	....	....
24 Interest................................	438.2	478.8	474.2	....	....	....	....	....	....	....	....	....
25 Subsidies...............................	—	—	—	....	....	....	....	....	....	....	....	....
26 Grants..................................	499.0	593.4	612.8	....	....	....	....	....	....	....	....	....
27 Social benefits.........................	983.3	991.0	1,008.0	....	....	....	....	....	....	....	....	....
28 Other payments.........................	21.4	10.2	158.6	....	....	....	....	....	....	....	....	....
CIO *Net cash inflow from oper. activities.....*	*159.4*	*850.5*	*2,014.9*	....	....	....	....	....	....	....	....	....
31.1 Purchases of nonfinancial assets..........	1,112.5	1,085.7	1,318.3	....	....	....	....	....	....	....	....	....
31.2 Sales of nonfinancial assets.............	1.7	.9	1.8	....	....	....	....	....	....	....	....	....
31 Net cash outflow from investments in nonfinancial assets..................	1,110.7	1,084.8	1,316.6	....	....	....	....	....	....	....	....	....
CSD *Cash surplus/deficit....................*	*−951.4*	*−234.3*	*698.3*	....	....	....	....	....	....	....	....	....
32x Net acquisition of fin assets, excl. cash...........	−6.5	−89.1	−29.2	....	....	....	....	....	....	....	....	....
321x Domestic..............................	−16.0	−94.4	−31.3	....	....	....	....	....	....	....	....	....
322x Foreign...............................	9.5	5.3	2.1	....	....	....	....	....	....	....	....	....
323 Monetary gold and SDRs.................	—	—	—	....	....	....	....	....	....	....	....	....
33 Net incurrence of liabilities...............	1,018.0	378.8	−614.5	....	....	....	....	....	....	....	....	....
331 Domestic..............................	771.2	−152.9	−533.8	....	....	....	....	....	....	....	....	....
332 Foreign...............................	246.8	531.8	−80.6	....	....	....	....	....	....	....	....	....
NFB Net cash inflow from fin. activities.................	1,024.5	468.0	−585.2	....	....	....	....	....	....	....	....	....
NCB *Net change in the stock of cash............*	*29.3*	*390.3*	*113.1*	....	....	....	....	....	....	....	....	....
Table 1 Revenue												
1 **Revenue........................**	**5,078.1**	**6,065.6**	**7,648.5**	....	....	....	....	....	....	....	....	....
11 **Taxes.........................**	**2,920.8**	**3,676.4**	**4,929.2**	....	....	....	....	....	....	....	....	....
111 Taxes on income, profits, & capital gains......	584.7	623.9	880.2	....	....	....	....	....	....	....	....	....
1111 Individuals............................	—	—	—	....	....	....	....	....	....	....	....	....
1112 Corporations and other enterprises...........	584.7	623.9	880.2	....	....	....	....	....	....	....	....	....
112 Taxes on payroll and workforce.................				....	....	....	....	....	....	....	....	....
113 Taxes on property..........................	.5	.1	.1	....	....	....	....	....	....	....	....	....
114 Taxes on goods and services.................	1,791.1	2,278.4	2,952.4	....	....	....	....	....	....	....	....	....
1141 General taxes on goods and services..........	1,252.5	1,570.3	1,939.0	....	....	....	....	....	....	....	....	....
1142 Excises..............................	533.9	704.7	1,012.6	....	....	....	....	....	....	....	....	....
115 Taxes on int'l. trade and transactions...........	487.5	665.1	904.0	....	....	....	....	....	....	....	....	....
116 Other taxes..............................	57.0	109.0	192.6	....	....	....	....	....	....	....	....	....
12 **Social contributions......................**	**339.7**	**369.4**	**439.7**	....	....	....	....	....	....	....	....	....
121 Social security contributions.................	—	—	—	....	....	....	....	....	....	....	....	....
122 Other social contributions...................	339.7	369.4	439.7	....	....	....	....	....	....	....	....	....
13 **Grants..............................**	**195.1**	**163.3**	**222.6**	....	....	....	....	....	....	....	....	....
131 From foreign governments..................	48.6	47.6	33.3	....	....	....	....	....	....	....	....	....
132 From international organizations.................	—	—	—	....	....	....	....	....	....	....	....	....
133 From other general government units..........	146.5	115.7	189.4	....	....	....	....	....	....	....	....	....
14 **Other revenue........................**	**1,622.5**	**1,856.4**	**2,057.0**	....	....	....	....	....	....	....	....	....
Table 2 Expense by economic type												
2 **Expense.........................**	**4,918.7**	**5,215.1**	**5,702.6**	....	....	....	....	....	....	....	....	....
21 **Compensation of employees.................**	**2,581.8**	**2,724.0**	**2,983.5**	....	....	....	....	....	....	....	....	....
211 Wages and salaries......................	2,581.8	2,724.0	2,983.5	....	....	....	....	....	....	....	....	....
212 Social contributions.....................	—	—	—	....	....	....	....	....	....	....	....	....
22 **Use of goods and services.................**	**395.1**	**417.6**	**465.6**	....	....	....	....	....	....	....	....	....
23 **Consumption of fixed capital................**	....	....	....	....	....	....	....	....	....	....	....	....
24 **Interest.........................**	**438.2**	**478.8**	**474.2**	....	....	....	....	....	....	....	....	....
25 **Subsidies.........................**	—	—	—	....	....	....	....	....	....	....	....	....

In Billions of Guaranies / Year Ending December 31 / Cash Reporter

		Budgetary Central Government			Central Government			Local Government			General Government		
		2002	2003	2004	2002	2003	2004	2002	2003	2004	2002	2003	2004
26	**Grants**..................................	**499.0**	**593.4**	**612.8**	....	....	....	....	....	....	....	....	....
261	To foreign govenments......................	10.3	9.0	13.6	....	....	....	....	....	....	....	....	....
262	To international organizations..................	—	—	—	....	....	....	....	....	....	....	....	....
263	To other general government units..............	488.7	584.5	599.1	....	....	....	....	....	....	....	....	....
2631	Current.................................	346.2	370.8	429.3	....	....	....	....	....	....	....	....	....
2632	Capital.................................	142.6	213.6	169.9	....	....	....	....	....	....	....	....	....
27	**Social benefits**..........................	**983.3**	**991.0**	**1,008.0**	....	....	....	....	....	....	....	....	....
28	**Other expense**..........................	**21.4**	**10.2**	**158.6**	....	....	....	....	....	....	....	....	....
281	Property expense other than interest...........	—	—	—	....	....	....	....	....	....	....	....	....
282	Miscellaneous other expense..................	21.4	10.2	158.6	....	....	....	....	....	....	....	....	....
2821	Current.................................	—	—	—	....	....	....	....	....	....	....	....	....
2822	Capital.................................	21.4	10.2	158.6	....	....	....	....	....	....	....	....	....

Table 3 Transactions in assets and liabilities

		Budgetary Central Government			Central Government			Local Government			General Government		
3	**Change in net worth from transactns....**	....	....	....	....	....	....	....	....	....	....	....	....
31	**Net acquisition of nonfinancial assets...**	**1,110.7**	**1,084.8**	**1,316.6**	....	....	....	....	....	....	....	....	....
311	Fixed assets..............................	1,109.5	1,084.1	1,314.7	....	....	....	....	....	....	....	....	....
3111	Buildings and structures..................	....	....	....	....	....	....	....	....	....	....	....	....
3112	Machinery and equipment.................	....	....	....	....	....	....	....	....	....	....	....	....
3113	Other fixed assets.......................	....	....	....	....	....	....	....	....	....	....	....	....
312	Inventories...............................	—	—	—	....	....	....	....	....	....	....	....	....
313	Valuables................................	—	—	—	....	....	....	....	....	....	....	....	....
314	Nonproduced assets........................	1.2	.7	1.8	....	....	....	....	....	....	....	....	....
3141	Land...................................	....	....	....	....	....	....	....	....	....	....	....	....
3142	Subsoil assets...........................	....	....	....	....	....	....	....	....	....	....	....	....
3143	Other naturally occurring assets............	....	....	....	....	....	....	....	....	....	....	....	....
3144	Intangible nonproduced assets..............	....	....	....	....	....	....	....	....	....	....	....	....
32	**Net acquisition of financial assets.........**	**22.8**	**301.2**	**83.8**	....	....	....	....	....	....	....	....	....
321	Domestic.................................	13.3	295.9	81.8	....	....	....	....	....	....	....	....	....
3212	Currency and deposits....................	29.3	390.3	113.1	....	....	....	....	....	....	....	....	....
3213	Securities other than shares...............	....	....	—	....	....	....	....	....	....	....	....	....
3214	Loans..................................	....	....	—	....	....	....	....	....	....	....	....	....
3215	Shares and other equity..................	....	....	−31.3	....	....	....	....	....	....	....	....	....
3216	Insurance technical reserves..............	....	....	—	....	....	....	....	....	....	....	....	....
3217	Financial derivatives.....................	....	....	—	....	....	....	....	....	....	....	....	....
3218	Other accounts receivable.................	....	....	....	....	....	....	....	....	....	....	....	....
322	Foreign..................................	9.5	5.3	2.1	....	....	....	....	....	....	....	....	....
3222	Currency and deposits....................	....	....	—	....	....	....	....	....	....	....	....	....
3223	Securities other than shares...............	....	....	—	....	....	....	....	....	....	....	....	....
3224	Loans..................................	....	....	—	....	....	....	....	....	....	....	....	....
3225	Shares and other equity..................	....	....	2.1	....	....	....	....	....	....	....	....	....
3226	Insurance technical reserves..............	....	....	—	....	....	....	....	....	....	....	....	....
3227	Financial derivatives.....................	....	....	—	....	....	....	....	....	....	....	....	....
3228	Other accounts receivable.................	....	....	....	....	....	....	....	....	....	....	....	....
323	Monetary gold and SDRs....................	—	—	—	....	....	....	....	....	....	....	....	....
33	**Net incurrence of liabilities...................**	**1,018.0**	**378.8**	**−614.5**	....	....	....	....	....	....	....	....	....
331	Domestic.................................	771.2	−152.9	−533.8	....	....	....	....	....	....	....	....	....
3312	Currency and deposits....................	473.7	−96.8	−407.5	....	....	....	....	....	....	....	....	....
3313	Securities other than shares...............	297.5	−56.2	−125.2	....	....	....	....	....	....	....	....	....
3314	Loans..................................	—	—	−1.1	....	....	....	....	....	....	....	....	....
3316	Insurance technical reserves..............	—	—	—	....	....	....	....	....	....	....	....	....
3317	Financial derivatives.....................	—	—	—	....	....	....	....	....	....	....	....	....
3318	Other accounts payable...................	....	....	....	....	....	....	....	....	....	....	....	....
332	Foreign..................................	246.8	531.8	−80.6	....	....	....	....	....	....	....	....	....
3322	Currency and deposits....................	—	—	—	....	....	....	....	....	....	....	....	....
3323	Securities other than shares...............	—	—	—	....	....	....	....	....	....	....	....	....
3324	Loans..................................	246.8	531.8	−80.6	....	....	....	....	....	....	....	....	....
3326	Insurance technical reserves..............	—	—	—	....	....	....	....	....	....	....	....	....
3327	Financial derivatives.....................	—	—	—	....	....	....	....	....	....	....	....	....
3328	Other accounts payable...................	....	....	....	....	....	....	....	....	....	....	....	....

In Billions of Guaranies / Year Ending December 31 / Cash Reporter

	Budgetary Central Government			Central Government			Local Government			General Government		
	2002	2003	2004	2002	2003	2004	2002	2003	2004	2002	2003	2004
Table 4 Holding gains in assets and liabilities												
Table 5 Other changes in the volume of assets and liabilities												
Table 6 Balance sheet												
Table 7 Outlays by functions of govt.												
7 **Total outlays**............................	6,029.5	6,299.8	7,019.2	....	....	....	....	....	....	....	....	....
701 **General public services**.........................	....	....	....	....	....	....	....	....	....	....	....	....
7017 Public debt transactions........................	438.2	478.8	474.2	....	....	....	....	....	....	....	....	....
7018 General transfers between levels of govt......	....	....	....	....	....	....	....	....	....	....	....	....
702 **Defense**..	....	....	....	....	....	....	....	....	....	....	....	....
703 **Public order and safety**........................	....	....	....	....	....	....	....	....	....	....	....	....
704 **Economic affairs**...............................	....	....	....	....	....	....	....	....	....	....	....	....
7042 Agriculture, forestry, fishing, and hunting.....	....	....	....	....	....	....	....	....	....	....	....	....
7043 Fuel and energy.................................	....	....	....	....	....	....	....	....	....	....	....	....
7044 Mining, manufacturing, and construction.....	....	....	....	....	....	....	....	....	....	....	....	....
7045 Transport...	....	....	....	....	....	....	....	....	....	....	....	....
7046 Communication..................................	....	....	....	....	....	....	....	....	....	....	....	....
705 **Environmental protection**......................	....	....	....	....	....	....	....	....	....	....	....	....
706 **Housing and community amenities**........	....	....	....	....	....	....	....	....	....	....	....	....
707 **Health**..	....	....	....	....	....	....	....	....	....	....	....	....
7072 Outpatient services.............................	....	....	....	....	....	....	....	....	....	....	....	....
7073 Hospital services................................	....	....	....	....	....	....	....	....	....	....	....	....
7074 Public health services..........................	....	....	....	....	....	....	....	....	....	....	....	....
708 **Recreation, culture, and religion**...........	....	....	....	....	....	....	....	....	....	....	....	....
709 **Education**..	....	....	....	....	....	....	....	....	....	....	....	....
7091 Pre-primary and primary education.............	....	....	....	....	....	....	....	....	....	....	....	....
7092 Secondary education............................	....	....	....	....	....	....	....	....	....	....	....	....
7094 Tertiary education...............................	....	....	....	....	....	....	....	....	....	....	....	....
710 **Social protection**...............................	....	....	....	....	....	....	....	....	....	....	....	....
7 Statistical discrepancy: Total outlays............	....	....	....	....	....	....	....	....	....	....	....	....
Table 8 Transactions in financial assets and liabilities by sector												
82 **Net acquisition of financial assets**........	22.8	301.2	83.8	....	....	....	....	....	....	....	....	....
821 Domestic.......................................	13.3	295.9	81.8	....	....	....	....	....	....	....	....	....
8211 General government............................	−6.5	−65.2	−12.7	....	....	....	....	....	....	....	....	....
8212 Central bank...................................	....	....	....	....	....	....	....	....	....	....	....	....
8213 Other depository corporations.................	....	....	....	....	....	....	....	....	....	....	....	....
8214 Financial corporations n.e.c...................	....	....	−18.6	....	....	....	....	....	....	....	....	....
8215 Nonfinancial corporations.....................	—	—	....	....	....	....	....	....	....	....	....	....
8216 Households & NPIs serving households......	....	....	....	....	....	....	....	....	....	....	....	....
822 Foreign...	9.5	5.3	2.1	....	....	....	....	....	....	....	....	....
8221 General government............................	....	....	—	....	....	....	....	....	....	....	....	....
8227 International organizations.....................	....	....	2.1	....	....	....	....	....	....	....	....	....
8228 Financial corporations other than international organizations.............	....	....	—	....	....	....	....	....	....	....	....	....
8229 Other nonresidents.............................	....	....	—	....	....	....	....	....	....	....	....	....
823 Monetary gold and SDRs.......................	—	—	—	....	....	....	....	....	....	....	....	....
83 **Net incurrence of liabilities**....................	1,018.0	378.8	−614.5	....	....	....	....	....	....	....	....	....
831 Domestic.......................................	771.2	−152.9	−533.8	....	....	....	....	....	....	....	....	....
8311 General government............................	....	....	....	....	....	....	....	....	....	....	....	....
8312 Central bank...................................	....	....	....	....	....	....	....	....	....	....	....	....
8313 Other depository corporations.................	....	....	....	....	....	....	....	....	....	....	....	....
8314 Financial corporations n.e.c...................	....	....	....	....	....	....	....	....	....	....	....	....
8315 Nonfinancial corporations.....................	....	....	....	....	....	....	....	....	....	....	....	....
8316 Households & NPIs serving households......	....	....	....	....	....	....	....	....	....	....	....	....
832 Foreign...	246.8	531.8	−80.6	....	....	....	....	....	....	....	....	....
8321 General government............................	139.2	123.4	−33.3	....	....	....	....	....	....	....	....	....
8327 International organizations.....................	121.4	421.3	−35.0	....	....	....	....	....	....	....	....	....
8328 Financial corporations other than international organizations.............	—	—	—	....	....	....	....	....	....	....	....	....
8329 Other nonresidents.............................	−13.9	−13.0	−12.3	....	....	....	....	....	....	....	....	....

In millions of Nuevos Soles / Year Ending December 31 / Cash Reporter

	Central Government			State Government			Local Government			General Government		
	2002p	2003p	2004p	2002p	2003p	2004p	2002p	2003p	2004p	2002p	2003p	2004p
Statement of government operations												
Statement of other economic flows												
Balance sheet												
Statement of sources and uses of cash												
1 Cash receipts from operating activities...........	32,606	35,672	39,468	6,114	6,649	8,060	4,266	4,798	5,448	34,619	37,650	41,810
11 Taxes...............	24,062	27,405	31,144	—	—	—	536	584	685	24,597	27,989	31,828
12 Social contributions..................	3,320	3,504	3,738	—	—	—	—	—	—	3,320	3,504	3,738
13 Grants.......................	309	362	254	5,769	6,387	7,776	2,316	2,763	3,099	309	362	254
14 Other receipts.......................	4,915	4,402	4,333	345	262	285	1,415	1,451	1,664	6,393	5,796	5,989
2 Cash payments for operating activities...........	33,940	36,304	39,492	5,525	6,115	7,090	2,663	2,942	3,277	33,760	35,891	38,691
21 Compensation of employees.................	7,693	8,309	8,360	3,874	4,203	4,994	698	824	853	12,264	13,335	14,206
22 Purchases of goods and services.................	7,189	7,590	8,368	580	628	686	1,470	1,544	1,597	9,238	9,762	10,651
24 Interest...............	4,098	4,427	4,716	—	—	—	92	84	84	4,190	4,511	4,800
25 Subsidies...............	—	—	—	—	—	—	—	—	—	—	—	—
26 Grants...............	8,085	9,150	10,875	—	—	—	—	—	—	—	—	—
27 Social benefits...............	6,083	6,081	6,410	1,036	1,166	1,250	—	—	—	7,119	7,247	7,660
28 Other payments...............	792	747	763	36	119	161	404	490	743	948	1,037	1,374
CIO *Net cash inflow from oper. activities.....*	*−1,334*	*−632*	*−23*	*589*	*534*	*971*	*1,603*	*1,856*	*2,171*	*859*	*1,759*	*3,118*
31.1 Purchases of nonfinancial assets.................	2,959	3,117	3,088	579	518	821	1,488	1,607	1,930	5,026	5,242	5,839
31.2 Sales of nonfinancial assets.......................	1,503	181	389	—	—	—	—	—	—	1,503	181	389
31 Net cash outflow from investments in nonfinancial assets...............	1,456	2,936	2,699	579	518	821	1,488	1,607	1,930	3,523	5,061	5,449
CSD *Cash surplus/deficit.............................*	*−2,790*	*−3,568*	*−2,722*	*11*	*16*	*150*	*116*	*249*	*241*	*−2,664*	*−3,303*	*−2,331*
32x Net acquisition of fin assets, excl. cash........	6,191	5,023	5,918	—	—	—	—	—	—	6,191	5,023	5,918
321x Domestic..............................	—	985	1,404	—	—	—	—	—	—	—	985	1,404
322x Foreign..............................	6,191	4,038	4,515	—	—	—	—	—	—	6,191	4,038	4,515
323 Monetary gold and SDRs..................	—	—	—	—	—	—	—	—	—	—	—	—
33 Net incurrence of liabilities..................	10,915	9,127	10,832	5	8	15	—	—	—	10,920	9,136	10,847
331 Domestic..................	733	1,712	2,494	—	—	—	—	—	—	733	1,712	2,494
332 Foreign..................	10,182	7,416	8,338	5	8	15	—	—	—	10,187	7,424	8,353
NFB Net cash inflow from fin. activities..........	4,724	4,104	4,914	5	8	15	—	—	—	4,730	4,112	4,929
NCB *Net change in the stock of cash.............*	*1,935*	*537*	*2,192*	*16*	*24*	*165*	*116*	*249*	*241*	*2,066*	*810*	*2,598*
Table 1 Revenue												
1 **Revenue........................**	**32,606**	**35,672**	**39,468**	**6,114**	**6,649**	**8,060**	**4,266**	**4,798**	**5,448**	**34,619**	**37,650**	**41,810**
11 **Taxes........................**	**24,062**	**27,405**	**31,144**	**—**	**—**	**—**	**536**	**584**	**685**	**24,597**	**27,989**	**31,828**
111 Taxes on income, profits, & capital gains......	6,413	8,397	9,429	—	—	—	—	—	—	6,413	8,397	9,429
1111 Individuals..............................	2,694	3,094	3,309	—	—	—	—	—	—	2,694	3,094	3,309
1112 Corporations and other enterprises...........	3,719	5,303	6,120	—	—	—	—	—	—	3,719	5,303	6,120
112 Taxes on payroll and workforce.................	18	9	7	—	—	—	—	—	—	18	9	7
113 Taxes on property.......................	—	—	—	—	—	—	420	437	511	420	437	511
114 Taxes on goods and services.......................	16,889	18,732	20,786	—	—	—	34	55	67	16,923	18,787	20,852
1141 General taxes on goods and services..........	12,613	14,110	16,206	—	—	—	—	—	—	12,613	14,110	16,206
1142 Excises..............................	4,276	4,622	4,579	—	—	—	—	—	—	4,276	4,622	4,579
115 Taxes on int'l. trade and transactions..........	2,483	2,550	2,744	—	—	—	—	—	—	2,483	2,550	2,744
116 Other taxes..............................	1,228	883	1,640	—	—	—	81	92	107	1,309	974	1,747
12 **Social contributions............................**	**3,320**	**3,504**	**3,738**	**—**	**—**	**—**	**—**	**—**	**—**	**3,320**	**3,504**	**3,738**
121 Social security contributions.................	3,320	3,504	3,738	—	—	—	—	—	—	3,320	3,504	3,738
122 Other social contributions.................	—	—	—	—	—	—	—	—	—	—	—	—
13 **Grants............................**	**309**	**362**	**254**	**5,769**	**6,387**	**7,776**	**2,316**	**2,763**	**3,099**	**309**	**362**	**254**
131 From foreign governments..........................	309	362	254	—	—	—	—	—	—	309	362	254
132 From international organizations.................	—	—	—	—	—	—	—	—	—	—	—	—
133 From other general government units..........	—	—	—	5,769	6,387	7,776	2,316	2,763	3,099	—	—	—
14 **Other revenue...............................**	**4,915**	**4,402**	**4,333**	**345**	**262**	**285**	**1,415**	**1,451**	**1,664**	**6,393**	**5,796**	**5,989**
Table 2 Expense by economic type												
2 **Expense........................**	**33,940**	**36,304**	**39,492**	**5,525**	**6,115**	**7,090**	**2,663**	**2,942**	**3,277**	**33,760**	**35,891**	**38,691**
21 **Compensation of employees..................**	**7,693**	**8,309**	**8,360**	**3,874**	**4,203**	**4,994**	**698**	**824**	**853**	**12,264**	**13,335**	**14,206**
211 Wages and salaries..........................	7,147	7,692	7,750	3,591	3,883	4,701	698	824	853	11,436	12,399	13,305
212 Social contributions..........................	546	616	609	283	319	292	—	—	—	829	936	902
22 **Use of goods and services....................**	**7,189**	**7,590**	**8,368**	**580**	**628**	**686**	**1,470**	**1,544**	**1,597**	**9,238**	**9,762**	**10,651**
23 **Consumption of fixed capital...............**	....	....	....	....	....	....	....	....	....	....	....	....
24 **Interest.......................**	**4,098**	**4,427**	**4,716**	**—**	**—**	**—**	**92**	**84**	**84**	**4,190**	**4,511**	**4,800**
25 **Subsidies.......................**	**—**	**—**	**—**	**—**	**—**	**—**	**—**	**—**	**—**	**—**	**—**	**—**

In millions of Nuevos Soles / Year Ending December 31 / Cash Reporter

		Central Government			State Government			Local Government			General Government		
		2002p	2003p	2004p	2002p	2003p	2004p	2002p	2003p	2004p	2002p	2003p	2004p
26	**Grants**	**8,085**	**9,150**	**10,875**	—	—	—	—	—	—	—	—	—
261	To foreign govenments	—	—	—	—	—	—	—	—	—	—	—	—
262	To international organizations	—	—	—	—	—	—	—	—	—	—	—	—
263	To other general government units	8,085	9,150	10,875	—	—	—	—	—	—	—	—	—
2631	Current	7,688	8,716	10,336	—	—	—	—	—	—	—	—	—
2632	Capital	397	434	539	—	—	—	—	—	—	—	—	—
27	**Social benefits**	**6,083**	**6,081**	**6,410**	**1,036**	**1,166**	**1,250**	—	—	—	**7,119**	**7,247**	**7,660**
28	**Other expense**	**792**	**747**	**763**	**36**	**119**	**161**	**404**	**490**	**743**	**948**	**1,037**	**1,374**
281	Property expense other than interest	—	—	—	—	—	—	—	—	—	—	—	—
282	Miscellaneous other expense	792	747	763	36	119	161	404	490	743	948	1,037	1,374
2821	Current	405	394	434	24	46	61	358	427	674	504	548	877
2822	Capital	386	353	329	12	72	100	46	63	69	444	489	497

Table 3 Transactions in assets and liabilities

		Central Government			State Government			Local Government			General Government		
3	Change in net worth from transactns	....	....	....	....	....	....	....	....	....	....	....	....
31	**Net acquisition of nonfinancial assets**	**1,456**	**2,936**	**2,699**	**579**	**518**	**821**	**1,488**	**1,607**	**1,930**	**3,523**	**5,061**	**5,449**
311	Fixed assets	1,456	2,936	2,699	579	518	821	1,488	1,607	1,930	3,523	5,061	5,449
3111	Buildings and structures	1,456	2,936	2,699	579	518	821	1,488	1,607	1,930	3,523	5,061	5,449
3112	Machinery and equipment	—	—	—	—	—	—	—	—	—	—	—	—
3113	Other fixed assets	—	—	—	—	—	—	—	—	—	—	—	—
312	Inventories	—	—	—	—	—	—	—	—	—	—	—	—
313	Valuables	—	—	—	—	—	—	—	—	—	—	—	—
314	Nonproduced assets	—	—	—	—	—	—	—	—	—	—	—	—
3141	Land	—	—	—	—	—	—	—	—	—	—	—	—
3142	Subsoil assets	—	—	—	—	—	—	—	—	—	—	—	—
3143	Other naturally occurring assets	—	—	—	—	—	—	—	—	—	—	—	—
3144	Intangible nonproduced assets	—	—	—	—	—	—	—	—	—	—	—	—
32	**Net acquisition of financial assets**	**8,125**	**5,560**	**8,110**	**16**	**24**	**165**	**116**	**249**	**241**	**8,257**	**5,833**	**8,517**
321	Domestic	1,935	817	3,373	16	24	165	116	249	241	2,066	1,090	3,780
3212	Currency and deposits	1,935	−168	1,970	16	24	165	116	249	241	2,066	105	2,376
3213	Securities other than shares	—	985	1,404	—	—	—	—	—	—	—	985	1,404
3214	Loans	—	—	—	—	—	—	—	—	—	—	—	—
3215	Shares and other equity	—	—	—	—	—	—	—	—	—	—	—	—
3216	Insurance technical reserves	—	—	—	—	—	—	—	—	—	—	—	—
3217	Financial derivatives	—	—	—	—	—	—	—	—	—	—	—	—
3218	Other accounts receivable	....	....	....	....	....	....	....	....	....	....	....	....
322	Foreign	6,191	4,743	4,737	—	—	—	—	—	—	6,191	4,743	4,737
3222	Currency and deposits	—	705	222	—	—	—	—	—	—	—	705	222
3223	Securities other than shares	3,252	153	228	—	—	—	—	—	—	3,252	153	228
3224	Loans	2,938	3,885	4,286	—	—	—	—	—	—	2,938	3,885	4,286
3225	Shares and other equity	—	—	—	—	—	—	—	—	—	—	—	—
3226	Insurance technical reserves	—	—	—	—	—	—	—	—	—	—	—	—
3227	Financial derivatives	—	—	—	—	—	—	—	—	—	—	—	—
3228	Other accounts receivable	....									....		
323	Monetary gold and SDRs												
33	**Net incurrence of liabilities**	**10,915**	**9,127**	**10,832**	**5**	**8**	**15**	—	—	—	**10,920**	**9,136**	**10,847**
331	Domestic	733	1,712	2,494	—	—	—	—	—	—	733	1,712	2,494
3312	Currency and deposits	—	—	—	—	—	—	—	—	—	—	—	—
3313	Securities other than shares	733	1,712	2,494	—	—	—	—	—	—	733	1,712	2,494
3314	Loans	—	—	—	—	—	—	—	—	—	—	—	—
3316	Insurance technical reserves	—	—	—	—	—	—	—	—	—	—	—	—
3317	Financial derivatives	—	—	—	—	—	—	—	—	—	—	—	—
3318	Other accounts payable	....	....	....	....	....	....	....	....	....	....	....	....
332	Foreign	10,182	7,416	8,338	5	8	15	—	—	—	10,187	7,424	8,353
3322	Currency and deposits	—	—	—	—	—	—	—	—	—	—	—	—
3323	Securities other than shares	6,639	4,336	4,416	—	—	—	—	—	—	6,639	4,336	4,416
3324	Loans	3,543	3,080	3,922	5	8	15	—	—	—	3,549	3,088	3,937
3326	Insurance technical reserves	—	—	—	—	—	—	—	—	—	—	—	—
3327	Financial derivatives	—	—	—	—	—	—	—	—	—	—	—	—
3328	Other accounts payable	....	....	....	....	....	....	....	....	....	....	....	....

	Central Government			State Government			Local Government			General Government		
	2002p	2003p	2004p	2002p	2003p	2004p	2002p	2003p	2004p	2002p	2003p	2004p
Table 4 Holding gains in assets and liabilities												
Table 5 Other changes in the volume of assets and liabilities												
Table 6 Balance sheet												
Table 7 Outlays by functions of govt.												
7 Total outlays....................	35,396	39,240	42,191	6,104	6,633	7,910	4,151	4,549	5,207	37,282	40,953	44,141
701 **General public services....................**	....	....	....	....	....	....	....	....	....	....	....	....
7017 Public debt transactions.............................	4,098	4,427	4,716	—	—	—	92	84	84	4,190	4,511	4,800
7018 General transfers between levels of govt......	....	....	....	....	....	....	....	....	....	....	....	....
702 **Defense...**	....	....	....	....	....	....	....	....	....	....	....	....
703 **Public order and safety........................**	....	....	....	....	....	....	....	....	....	....	....	....
704 **Economic affairs..................................**	....	....	....	....	....	....	....	....	....	....	....	....
7042 Agriculture, forestry, fishing, and hunting.....	....	....	....	....	....	....	....	....	....	....	....	....
7043 Fuel and energy...............................	....	....	....	....	....	....	....	....	....	....	....	....
7044 Mining, manufacturing, and construction.....	....	....	....	....	....	....	....	....	....	....	....	....
7045 Transport..	....	....	....	....	....	....	....	....	....	....	....	....
7046 Communication.....................................	....	....	....	....	....	....	....	....	....	....	....	....
705 **Environmental protection....................**	....	....	....	....	....	....	....	....	....	....	....	....
706 **Housing and community amenities.......**	....	....	....	....	....	....	....	....	....	....	....	....
707 **Health...**	....	....	....	....	....	....	....	....	....	....	....	....
7072 Outpatient services..................................	....	....	....	....	....	....	....	....	....	....	....	....
7073 Hospital services...................................	....	....	....	....	....	....	....	....	....	....	....	....
7074 Public health services..............................	....	....	....	....	....	....	....	....	....	....	....	....
708 **Recreation, culture, and religion...........**	....	....	....	....	....	....	....	....	....	....	....	....
709 **Education...**	....	....	....	....	....	....	....	....	....	....	....	....
7091 Pre-primary and primary education............	....	....	....	....	....	....	....	....	....	....	....	....
7092 Secondary education................................	....	....	....	....	....	....	....	....	....	....	....	....
7094 Tertiary education...................................	....	....	....	....	....	....	....	....	....	....	....	....
710 **Social protection..................................**	....	....	....	....	....	....	....	....	....	....	....	....
7 Statistical discrepancy: Total outlays..............	....	....	....	....	....	....	....	....	....	....	....	....
Table 8 Transactions in financial assets and liabilities by sector												
82 **Net acquisition of financial assets........**	8,125	5,560	8,110	16	24	165	116	249	241	8,257	5,833	8,517
821 Domestic...	1,935	817	3,373	16	24	165	116	249	241	2,066	1,090	3,780
8211 General government.................................	....	....	—	....	....	—	....	....	—	....	....	—
8212 Central bank...	....	....	—	....	....	—	....	....	—	....	....	—
8213 Other depository corporations...................	....	....	—	....	....	—	....	....	—	....	....	—
8214 Financial corporations n.e.c.....................	....	....	1,970	....	....	165	....	....	241	....	....	2,376
8215 Nonfinancial corporations........................	....	....	1,404	....	....	—	....	....	—	....	....	1,404
8216 Households & NPIs serving households......	....	....	—	....	....	—	....	....	—	....	....	—
822 Foreign..	6,191	4,743	4,737	—	—	—	—	—	—	6,191	4,743	4,737
8221 General government.................................	....	....	—	—	—	—	—	—	—	....	....	—
8227 International organizations........................	....	....	4,286	—	—	—	—	—	—	....	....	4,286
8228 Financial corporations other than international organizations............	....	....	222	—	—	—	—	—	—	....	....	222
8229 Other nonresidents.................................	....	....	228	—	—	—	—	—	—	....	....	228
823 Monetary gold and SDRs.........................	—	—	—	—	—	—	—	—	—	—	—	—
83 **Net incurrence of liabilities..................**	10,915	9,127	10,832	5	8	15	—	—	—	10,920	9,136	10,847
831 Domestic...	733	1,712	2,494	—	—	—	—	—	—	733	1,712	2,494
8311 General government.................................	....	....	—	—	—	—	—	—	—	....	....	—
8312 Central bank...	....	....	—	—	—	—	—	—	—	....	....	—
8313 Other depository corporations...................	....	....	—	—	—	—	—	—	—	....	....	—
8314 Financial corporations n.e.c.....................	....	....	—	—	—	—	—	—	—	....	....	—
8315 Nonfinancial corporations........................	....	....	2,494	—	—	—	—	—	—	....	....	2,494
8316 Households & NPIs serving households......	....	....	—	—	—	—	—	—	—	....	....	—
832 Foreign..	10,182	7,416	8,338	5	8	15	—	—	—	10,187	7,424	8,353
8321 General government.................................	....	....	—	....	....	—	—	—	—	....	....	—
8327 International organizations........................	....	....	3,922	....	....	15	—	—	—	....	....	3,937
8328 Financial corporations other than international organizations............	....	....	—	....	....	—	—	—	—	....	....	—
8329 Other nonresidents.................................	....	....	4,416	....	....	—	—	—	—	....	....	4,416

Philippines 566

In Billions of Pesos / Year Ending December 31 / Cash Reporter

		Budgetary Central Government			Central Government			Local Government			General Government		
		2002	2003	2004p	2002	2003	2004p	2002	2003	2004p	2002	2003	2004p
Statement of government operations													
Statement of other economic flows													
Balance sheet													
6	*Net worth*	....	....	....	....	....	....	....	....	....	....	....	....
61	Nonfinancial assets	....	....	....	....	....	....	....	....	....	....	....	....
62	Financial assets	....	....	....	....	....	....	....	....	....	....	....	....
63	Liabilities	2,635.30	3,081.30	3,397.10	2,622.70	3,052.60	3,321.20	33.70	43.90	49.20	2,655.70	3,094.40	3,369.50
Statement of sources and uses of cash													
1	Cash receipts from operating activities	569.68	628.71	701.96	....	....	....	....	....	....	....	....	....
11	Taxes	496.37	537.36	598.01	....	....	....	....	....	....	....	....	....
12	Social contributions	—	—	—	....	....	....	....	....	....	....	....	....
13	Grants	1.05	1.20	.07	....	....	....	....	....	....	....	....	....
14	Other receipts	72.25	90.15	103.87	....	....	....	....	....	....	....	....	....
2	Cash payments for operating activities	....	....	....	....	....	....	....	....	....	....	....	....
21	Compensation of employees	....	....	....	....	....	....	....	....	....	....	....	....
22	Purchases of goods and services	....	....	....	....	....	....	....	....	....	....	....	....
24	Interest	200.72	241.83	278.43	....	....	....	....	....	....	....	....	....
25	Subsidies	....	....	....	....	....	....	....	....	....	....	....	....
26	Grants	....	....	....	....	....	....	....	....	....	....	....	....
27	Social benefits	....	....	....	....	....	....	....	....	....	....	....	....
28	Other payments	....	....	....	....	....	....	....	....	....	....	....	....
CIO	*Net cash inflow from oper. activities*	....	....	....	....	....	....	....	....	....	....	....	....
31.1	Purchases of nonfinancial assets	....	....	....	....	....	....	....	....	....	....	....	....
31.2	Sales of nonfinancial assets	.59	.57	.42	....	....	....	....	....	....	....	....	....
31	Net cash outflow from investments in nonfinancial assets	....	....	....	....	....	....	....	....	....	....	....	....
CSD	*Cash surplus/deficit*	*−218.96*	*−204.97*	*−196.68*	....	....	....	....	....	....	....	....	....
32x	Net acquisition of fin assets, excl. cash	59.90	55.47	99.19	....	....	....	....	....	....	....	....	....
321x	Domestic	59.90	55.47	99.19	....	....	....	....	....	....	....	....	....
322x	Foreign	—	—	—	....	....	....	....	....	....	....	....	....
323	Monetary gold and SDRs	—	—	—	....	....	....	....	....	....	....	....	....
33	Net incurrence of liabilities	277.16	286.21	276.46	....	....	....	....	....	....	....	....	....
331	Domestic	163.04	132.07	190.71	....	....	....	....	....	....	....	....	....
332	Foreign	114.11	154.14	85.75	....	....	....	....	....	....	....	....	....
NFB	Net cash inflow from fin. activities	217.25	230.74	177.27	....	....	....	....	....	....	....	....	....
NCB	*Net change in the stock of cash*	*−1.71*	*25.77*	*−19.41*	....	....	....	....	....	....	....	....	....
Table 1 Revenue													
1	**Revenue**	569.68	628.71	701.96	....	....	....	....	....	....	....	....	....
11	**Taxes**	496.37	537.36	598.01	....	....	....	....	....	....	....	....	....
111	Taxes on income, profits, & capital gains	226.50	245.30	278.21	....	....	....	....	....	....	....	....	....
1111	Individuals	86.44	90.29	100.92	....	....	....	....	....	....	....	....	....
1112	Corporations and other enterprises	100.76	114.61	131.17	....	....	....	....	....	....	....	....	....
112	Taxes on payroll and workforce	—	—	—	....	....	....	....	....	....	....	....	....
113	Taxes on property	.53	.70	.75	....	....	....	....	....	....	....	....	....
114	Taxes on goods and services	152.32	162.55	174.80	....	....	....	....	....	....	....	....	....
1141	General taxes on goods and services	65.93	81.28	80.22	....	....	....	....	....	....	....	....	....
1142	Excises	57.00	56.91	59.53	....	....	....	....	....	....	....	....	....
115	Taxes on int'l. trade and transactions	96.84	106.85	122.98	....	....	....	....	....	....	....	....	....
116	Other taxes	20.19	21.97	21.27	....	....	....	....	....	....	....	....	....
12	**Social contributions**	—	—	—	....	....	....	....	....	....	....	....	....
121	Social security contributions	—	—	—	....	....	....	....	....	....	....	....	....
122	Other social contributions	—	—	—	....	....	....	....	....	....	....	....	....
13	**Grants**	1.05	1.20	.07	....	....	....	....	....	....	....	....	....
131	From foreign governments	1.05	1.20	.07	....	....	....	....	....	....	....	....	....
132	From international organizations	—	—	—	....	....	....	....	....	....	....	....	....
133	From other general government units	—	—	—	....	....	....	....	....	....	....	....	....
14	**Other revenue**	72.25	90.15	103.87	....	....	....	....	....	....	....	....	....
Table 2 Expense by economic type													
2	**Expense**	....	....	....	....	....	....	....	....	....	....	....	....
21	**Compensation of employees**	....	....	....	....	....	....	....	....	....	....	....	....
211	Wages and salaries	....	....	....	....	....	....	....	....	....	....	....	....
212	Social contributions	....	....	....	....	....	....	....	....	....	....	....	....
22	**Use of goods and services**	....	....	....	....	....	....	....	....	....	....	....	....
23	**Consumption of fixed capital**	....	....	....	....	....	....	....	....	....	....	....	....
24	Interest	200.72	241.83	278.43	....	....	....	....	....	....	....	....	....
25	Subsidies	....	....	....	....	....	....	....	....	....	....	....	....

2005, International Monetary Fund: *Government Finance Statistics Yearbook*

		Budgetary Central Government			Central Government			Local Government			General Government		
		2002	2003	2004p	2002	2003	2004p	2002	2003	2004p	2002	2003	2004p
26	**Grants**............................	....	....	....	....	....	....	....	....	....	....	....	....
261	To foreign govenments.................	....	....	....	....	....	....	....	....	....	....	....	....
262	To international organizations..............	....	....	....	....	....	....	....	....	....	....	....	....
263	To other general government units.............	....	....	....	....	....	....	....	....	....	....	....	....
2631	Current.............................	....	....	....	....	....	....	....	....	....	....	....	....
2632	Capital.............................	....	....	....	....	....	....	....	....	....	....	....	....
27	**Social benefits**......................	....	....	....	....	....	....	....	....	....	....	....	....
28	**Other expense**.......................	....	....	....	....	....	....	....	....	....	....	....	....
281	Property expense other than interest...........	....	....	....	....	....	....	....	....	....	....	....	....
282	Miscellaneous other expense..............	....	....	....	....	....	....	....	....	....	....	....	....
2821	Current..............................	....	....	....	....	....	....	....	....	....	....	....	....
2822	Capital..............................	....	....	....	....	....	....	....	....	....	....	....	....
Table 3	**Transactions in assets and liabilities**												
3	**Change in net worth from transactns....**	....	....	....	....	....	....	....	....	....	....	....	....
31	**Net acquisition of nonfinancial assets...**	....	....	....	....	....	....	....	....	....	....	....	....
311	Fixed assets...........................	....	....	....	....	....	....	....	....	....	....	....	....
3111	Buildings and structures................	....	....	....	....	....	....	....	....	....	....	....	....
3112	Machinery and equipment...............	....	....	....	....	....	....	....	....	....	....	....	....
3113	Other fixed assets.....................	....	....	....	....	....	....	....	....	....	....	....	....
312	Inventories............................	....	....	....	....	....	....	....	....	....	....	....	....
313	Valuables.............................	....	....	....	....	....	....	....	....	....	....	....	....
314	Nonproduced assets....................	....	....	....	....	....	....	....	....	....	....	....	....
3141	Land..............................	....	....	....	....	....	....	....	....	....	....	....	....
3142	Subsoil assets.......................	....	....	....	....	....	....	....	....	....	....	....	....
3143	Other naturally occurring assets.........	....	....	....	....	....	....	....	....	....	....	....	....
3144	Intangible nonproduced assets..............	....	....	....	....	....	....	....	....	....	....	....	....
32	**Net acquisition of financial assets........**	**58.20**	**81.24**	**79.78**	....	....	....	....	....	....	....	....	....
321	Domestic.............................	58.20	81.24	79.78	....	....	....	....	....	....	....	....	....
3212	Currency and deposits.................	−1.71	25.77	−19.41	....	....	....	....	....	....	....	....	....
3213	Securities other than shares..............	38.63	24.61	77.07	....	....	....	....	....	....	....	....	....
3214	Loans..............................	17.76	23.19	16.82	....	....	....	....	....	....	....	....	....
3215	Shares and other equity.................	3.52	7.68	5.30	....	....	....	....	....	....	....	....	....
3216	Insurance technical reserves.............	—	—	—	....	....	....	....	....	....	....	....	....
3217	Financial derivatives...................	—	—	—	....	....	....	....	....	....	....	....	....
3218	Other accounts receivable...............	....	....	....	....	....	....	....	....	....	....	....	....
322	Foreign..............................	—	—	—	....	....	....	....	....	....	....	....	....
3222	Currency and deposits.................	—	—	—	....	....	....	....	....	....	....	....	....
3223	Securities other than shares.............	—	—	—	....	....	....	....	....	....	....	....	....
3224	Loans..............................	—	—	—	....	....	....	....	....	....	....	....	....
3225	Shares and other equity.................	—	—	—	....	....	....	....	....	....	....	....	....
3226	Insurance technical reserves.............	—	—	—	....	....	....	....	....	....	....	....	....
3227	Financial derivatives...................	—	—	—	....	....	....	....	....	....	....	....	....
3228	Other accounts receivable...............	....	....	....	....	....	....	....	....	....	....	....	....
323	Monetary gold and SDRs.................	—	—	—	....	....	....	....	....	....	....	....	....
33	**Net incurrence of liabilities.............**	**277.16**	**286.21**	**276.46**	....	....	....	....	....	....	....	....	....
331	Domestic.............................	163.04	132.07	190.71	....	....	....	....	....	....	....	....	....
3312	Currency and deposits.................	2.37	1.48	34.99	....	....	....	....	....	....	....	....	....
3313	Securities other than shares..............	152.29	119.02	132.82	....	....	....	....	....	....	....	....	....
3314	Loans..............................	8.39	11.57	22.90	....	....	....	....	....	....	....	....	....
3316	Insurance technical reserves.............	—	—	—	....	....	....	....	....	....	....	....	....
3317	Financial derivatives...................	—	—	—	....	....	....	....	....	....	....	....	....
3318	Other accounts payable.................	....	....	....	....	....	....	....	....	....	....	....	....
332	Foreign..............................	114.11	154.14	85.75	....	....	....	....	....	....	....	....	....
3322	Currency and deposits.................	—	—	—	....	....	....	....	....	....	....	....	....
3323	Securities other than shares.............	109.38	143.33	108.78	....	....	....	....	....	....	....	....	....
3324	Loans..............................	4.73	10.81	−23.03	....	....	....	....	....	....	....	....	....
3326	Insurance technical reserves.............	—	—	—	....	....	....	....	....	....	....	....	....
3327	Financial derivatives...................	—	—	—	....	....	....	....	....	....	....	....	....
3328	Other accounts payable.................	....	....	....	....	....	....	....	....	....	....	....	....

Philippines   566

In Billions of Pesos / Year Ending December 31 / Cash Reporter

	Budgetary Central Government			Central Government			Local Government			General Government		
	2002	2003	2004p	2002	2003	2004p	2002	2003	2004p	2002	2003	2004p
Table 4 Holding gains in assets and liabilities												
Table 5 Other changes in the volume of assets and liabilities												
Table 6 Balance sheet												
6 Net worth.................................	....	....	....	....	....	....	....	....	....	....	....	....
61 Nonfinancial assets............................	....	....	....	....	....	....	....	....	....	....	....	....
611 Fixed assets............................	....	....	....	....	....	....	....	....	....	....	....	....
6111 Buildings and structures...................	....	....	....	....	....	....	....	....	....	....	....	....
6112 Machinery and equipment....................	....	....	....	....	....	....	....	....	....	....	....	....
6113 Other fixed assets......................	....	....	....	....	....	....	....	....	....	....	....	....
612 Inventories................................	....	....	....	....	....	....	....	....	....	....	....	....
613 Valuables................................	....	....	....	....	....	....	....	....	....	....	....	....
614 Nonproduced assets.....................	....	....	....	....	....	....	....	....	....	....	....	....
6141 Land......................................	....	....	....	....	....	....	....	....	....	....	....	....
6142 Subsoil assets........................	....	....	....	....	....	....	....	....	....	....	....	....
6143 Other naturally occurring assets................	....	....	....	....	....	....	....	....	....	....	....	....
6144 Intangible nonproduced assets..................	....	....	....	....	....	....	....	....	....	....	....	....
62 **Financial assets**............................	....	....	....	....	....	....	....	....	....	....	....	....
621 Domestic................................	....	....	....	....	....	....	....	....	....	....	....	....
6212 Currency and deposits...................	....	....	....	....	....	....	....	....	....	....	....	....
6213 Securities other than shares..............	....	....	....	....	....	....	....	....	....	....	....	....
6214 Loans...................................	....	....	....	....	....	....	....	....	....	....	....	....
6215 Shares and other equity.................	....	....	....	....	....	....	....	....	....	....	....	....
6216 Insurance technical reserves...............	....	....	....	....	....	....	....	....	....	....	....	....
6217 Financial derivatives..................	....	....	....	....	....	....	....	....	....	....	....	....
6218 Other accounts receivable................	....	....	....	....	....	....	....	....	....	....	....	....
622 Foreign................................	....	....	....	....	....	....	....	....	....	....	....	....
6222 Currency and deposits...................	....	....	....	....	....	....	....	....	....	....	....	....
6223 Securities other than shares..............	....	....	....	....	....	....	....	....	....	....	....	....
6224 Loans...................................	....	....	....	....	....	....	....	....	....	....	....	....
6225 Shares and other equity.................	....	....	....	....	....	....	....	....	....	....	....	....
6226 Insurance technical reserves...............	....	....	....	....	....	....	....	....	....	....	....	....
6227 Financial derivatives..................	....	....	....	....	....	....	....	....	....	....	....	....
6228 Other accounts receivable................	....	....	....	....	....	....	....	....	....	....	....	....
623 Monetary gold and SDRs................	....	....	....	....	....	....	....	....	....	....	....	....
63 **Liabilities**............................	2,635.30	3,081.30	3,397.10	2,622.70	3,052.60	3,321.20	33.70	43.90	49.20	2,655.70	3,094.40	3,369.50
631 Domestic................................	1,291.00	1,430.80	1,589.50	1,211.30	1,341.60	1,465.10	33.70	43.90	49.20	1,244.30	1,383.40	1,513.40
6312 Currency and deposits...................	....	....	....	....	....	....	....	....	....	....	....	....
6313 Securities other than shares..............	....	....	....	....	....	....	....	....	....	....	....	....
6314 Loans...................................	....	....	....	....	....	....	....	....	....	....	....	....
6316 Insurance technical reserves...............	....	....	....	....	....	....	....	....	....	....	....	....
6317 Financial derivatives..................	....	....	....	....	....	....	....	....	....	....	....	....
6318 Other accounts payable................	....	....	....	....	....	....	....	....	....	....	....	....
632 Foreign................................	1,344.30	1,650.50	1,807.60	1,411.40	1,711.00	1,856.10	—	—	—	1,411.40	1,711.00	1,856.10
6322 Currency and deposits...................	....	....	....	....	....	....	—	—	—	....	....	....
6323 Securities other than shares..............	....	....	....	....	....	....	—	—	—	....	....	....
6324 Loans...................................	....	....	....	....	....	....	—	—	—	....	....	....
6326 Insurance technical reserves...............	....	....	....	....	....	....	—	—	—	....	....	....
6327 Financial derivatives..................	....	....	....	....	....	....	—	—	—	....	....	....
6328 Other accounts payable................	....	....	....	....	....	....	....	....	....	....	....	....
Memorandum items:												
6M2 Net financial worth................	....	....	....	....	....	....	....	....	....	....	....	....
6M3 Debt at market value................	....	....	....	....	....	....	....	....	....	....	....	....
6M4 Debt at nominal value................	....	....	....	....	....	....	....	....	....	....	....	....
6M5 Arrears................................	....	....	....	....	....	....	....	....	....	....	....	....
6M6 Obligations for social security benefits...........	....	....	....	....	....	....	....	....	....	....	....	....
6M7 Contingent liabilities................	....	....	....	....	....	....	....	....	....	....	....	....
6M8 Uncapitalized military weapons, systems........	....	....	....	....	....	....	....	....	....	....	....	....
Table 7 Outlays by functions of govt.												
7 **Total outlays**.................................	788.63	833.68	898.64	....	....	....	....	....	....	....	....	....
701 **General public services**........................	406.73	437.51	512.60	....	....	....	....	....	....	....	....	....
7017 Public debt transactions...................	200.72	241.83	278.43	....	....	....	....	....	....	....	....	....
7018 General transfers between levels of govt......	....	....	....	....	....	....	....	....	....	....	....	....
702 **Defense**..............................	41.98	44.44	43.85	....	....	....	....	....	....	....	....	....
703 **Public order and safety**........................	51.05	52.57	53.21	....	....	....	....	....	....	....	....	....

2005, International Monetary Fund: *Government Finance Statistics Yearbook*

		Budgetary Central Government			Central Government			Local Government			General Government		
		2002	2003	2004p	2002	2003	2004p	2002	2003	2004p	2002	2003	2004p
704	**Economic affairs**	**103.77**	**109.78**	**96.17**	....	....	....	....	....	....	....	....	....
7042	Agriculture, forestry, fishing, and hunting	37.82	39.68	32.04	....	....	....	....	....	....	....	....	....
7043	Fuel and energy	1.37	1.10	2.00	....	....	....	....	....	....	....	....	....
7044	Mining, manufacturing, and construction	.16	.16	.15	....	....	....	....	....	....	....	....	....
7045	Transport	64.41	68.84	61.99	....	....	....	....	....	....	....	....	....
7046	Communication	....	....	....	....	....	....	....	....	....	....	....	....
705	**Environmental protection**	—	—	—	....	....	....	....	....	....	....	....	....
706	**Housing and community amenities**	**2.08**	**3.11**	**2.61**	....	....	....	....	....	....	....	....	....
707	**Health**	**14.52**	**12.40**	**12.88**	....	....	....	....	....	....	....	....	....
7072	Outpatient services	....	....	....	....	....	....	....	....	....	....	....	....
7073	Hospital services	....	....	....	....	....	....	....	....	....	....	....	....
7074	Public health services	....	....	....	....	....	....	....	....	....	....	....	....
708	**Recreation, culture, and religion**	**5.69**	**6.18**	**5.94**	....	....	....	....	....	....	....	....	....
709	**Education**	**128.79**	**128.61**	**133.01**	....	....	....	....	....	....	....	....	....
7091	Pre-primary and primary education	....	....	....	....	....	....	....	....	....	....	....	....
7092	Secondary education	....	....	....	....	....	....	....	....	....	....	....	....
7094	Tertiary education	....	....	....	....	....	....	....	....	....	....	....	....
710	**Social protection**	**34.01**	**39.10**	**38.38**	....	....	....	....	....	....	....	....	....
7	Statistical discrepancy: Total outlays	—	—	—	....	....	....	....	....	....	....	....	....

Table 8   Transactions in financial assets and liabilities by sector

		Budgetary Central Government			Central Government			Local Government			General Government		
82	**Net acquisition of financial assets**	**58.20**	**81.24**	**79.78**	....	....	....	....	....	....	....	....	....
821	Domestic	58.20	81.24	79.78	....	....	....	....	....	....	....	....	....
8211	General government	....	....	....	....	....	....	....	....	....	....	....	....
8212	Central bank	....	....	....	....	....	....	....	....	....	....	....	....
8213	Other depository corporations	....	....	....	....	....	....	....	....	....	....	....	....
8214	Financial corporations n.e.c.	....	....	....	....	....	....	....	....	....	....	....	....
8215	Nonfinancial corporations	....	....	....	....	....	....	....	....	....	....	....	....
8216	Households & NPIs serving households	....	....	....	....	....	....	....	....	....	....	....	....
822	Foreign	—	—	—	....	....	....	....	....	....	....	....	....
8221	General government	—	—	—	....	....	....	....	....	....	....	....	....
8227	International organizations	—	—	—	....	....	....	....	....	....	....	....	....
8228	Financial corporations other than international organizations	—	—	—	....	....	....	....	....	....	....	....	....
8229	Other nonresidents	—	—	—	....	....	....	....	....	....	....	....	....
823	Monetary gold and SDRs	—	—	—	....	....	....	....	....	....	....	....	....
83	**Net incurrence of liabilities**	**277.16**	**286.21**	**276.46**	....	....	....	....	....	....	....	....	....
831	Domestic	163.04	132.07	190.71	....	....	....	....	....	....	....	....	....
8311	General government	....	....	....	....	....	....	....	....	....	....	....	....
8312	Central bank	....	....	....	....	....	....	....	....	....	....	....	....
8313	Other depository corporations	....	....	....	....	....	....	....	....	....	....	....	....
8314	Financial corporations n.e.c.	....	....	....	....	....	....	....	....	....	....	....	....
8315	Nonfinancial corporations	....	....	....	....	....	....	....	....	....	....	....	....
8316	Households & NPIs serving households	....	....	....	....	....	....	....	....	....	....	....	....
832	Foreign	114.11	154.14	85.75	....	....	....	....	....	....	....	....	....
8321	General government	....	....	....	....	....	....	....	....	....	....	....	....
8327	International organizations	−9.18	−6.26	−11.36	....	....	....	....	....	....	....	....	....
8328	Financial corporations other than international organizations	....	....	....	....	....	....	....	....	....	....	....	....
8329	Other nonresidents	....	....	....	....	....	....	....	....	....	....	....	....

In Millions of Zlotys / Year Ending December 31 / Noncash Reporter

	Budgetary Central Government			Central Government			Local Government			General Government		
	2001	2002	2003	2001	2002	2003	2001	2002	2003	2001	2002	2003
Statement of government operations												
1 Revenue......	143,721	143,303	153,224	249,799	248,163	286,963	115,286	116,218	87,771	318,943	318,562	329,794
2 Expense......	182,061	186,905	204,955	277,339	278,031	320,312	105,471	109,691	78,742	336,668	341,903	354,114
GOB *Gross operating balance......*	*−28,160*	*−33,101*	*−39,244*	*−16,889*	*−18,476*	*−20,003*	*9,855*	*6,748*	*9,477*	*−7,034*	*−11,728*	*−10,526*
NOB *Net operating balance......*	*−38,340*	*−43,602*	*−51,731*	*−27,540*	*−29,868*	*−33,349*	*9,815*	*6,527*	*9,029*	*−17,725*	*−23,341*	*−24,320*
31 Net acquisition of nonfinancial assets......	−7,196	−5,677	−6,487	−5,801	−4,175	−5,435	12,020	11,620	10,370	6,219	7,445	4,935
NLB *Net lending/borrowing......*	*−31,144*	*−37,925*	*−45,244*	*−21,739*	*−25,693*	*−27,914*	*−2,205*	*−5,093*	*−1,341*	*−23,944*	*−30,786*	*−29,255*
32 Net acquisition of financial assets......	−7,840	−3,217	1,052	2,876	11,107	5,100	1,405	−997	2,374	4,262	10,069	7,516
33 Net incurrence of liabilities......	23,304	34,708	46,296	24,615	36,799	33,014	3,610	4,096	3,715	28,206	40,854	36,771
NLB Statistical discrepancy......	—	—	—	—	—	—	—	—	—	—	—	—
Statement of other economic flows												
Balance sheet												
6 *Net worth......*	....	....	....	....	....	....	....	....	....	....	....	....
61 Nonfinancial assets......	....	....	....	....	....	....	....	....	....	....	....	....
62 Financial assets......	....	....	....	....	....	....	....	....	....	....	....	....
63 Liabilities......	†268,529	331,059	372,814	†256,971	313,027	352,530	†12,471	15,615	16,691	†265,568	324,661	365,883
Statement of sources and uses of cash												
Table 1 Revenue												
1 **Revenue......**	†143,721	143,303	153,224	†249,799	248,163	286,963	†115,286	116,218	87,771	†318,943	318,562	329,794
11 **Taxes......**	†123,626	134,812	140,307	†124,640	135,866	141,299	†20,318	22,890	22,458	†144,714	158,506	163,450
111 Taxes on income, profits, & capital gains......	†36,744	39,326	39,841	†37,061	39,627	40,117	†10,230	10,274	10,304	†47,291	49,899	50,403
1111 Individuals......	†23,506	24,217	25,733	†23,704	24,453	26,065	†9,480	9,425	9,519	†33,184	33,878	35,584
1112 Corporations and other enterprises......	†13,238	15,109	14,108	†13,357	15,174	14,052	†750	849	785	†14,107	16,021	14,819
112 Taxes on payroll and workforce......	†—	—	—	†—	—	—	†—	—	—	†—	—	—
113 Taxes on property......	†—	55	251	†11	67	268	†9,419	10,681	11,198	†9,289	10,602	11,268
114 Taxes on goods and services......	†82,811	90,892	96,463	†83,494	91,634	97,162	†668	1,925	953	†84,059	93,466	98,024
1141 General taxes on goods and services......	†53,228	57,656	60,315	†53,855	58,331	60,936	†—	—	2	†53,760	58,240	60,847
1142 Excises......	†28,894	31,523	34,388	†28,948	31,583	34,450	†—	—	—	†28,948	31,583	34,450
115 Taxes on int'l. trade and transactions......	†4,060	3,806	3,751	†4,060	3,806	3,751	†—	—	—	†4,060	3,806	3,751
116 Other taxes......	†11	733	1	†14	732	1	†1	10	3	†15	733	4
12 **Social contributions......**	†—	—	—	†89,204	88,894	115,208	†26,739	25,750	—	†115,943	114,644	115,208
121 Social security contributions......	†—	—	—	†89,204	88,894	115,208	†26,739	25,750	—	†115,943	114,644	115,208
122 Other social contributions......	†—	—	—	†—	—	—	†—	—	—	†—	—	—
13 **Grants......**	†4,397	1,076	1,352	†3,954	603	1,254	†45,830	45,494	44,262	†3,936	585	1,223
131 From foreign governments......	†3,936	585	1,186	†3,936	585	1,186	†—	—	—	†3,936	585	1,186
132 From international organizations......	†—	—	—	†—	—	37	†—	—	—	†—	—	37
133 From other general government units......	†461	491	166	†18	18	31	†45,830	45,494	44,262	†—	—	—
14 **Other revenue......**	†15,698	7,415	11,565	†32,001	22,800	29,202	†22,399	22,084	21,051	†54,350	44,827	49,913
Table 2 Expense by economic type												
2 **Expense......**	†182,061	186,905	204,955	†277,339	278,031	320,312	†105,471	109,691	78,742	†336,668	341,903	354,114
21 **Compensation of employees......**	†18,925	19,577	23,618	†30,713	32,079	39,162	†43,477	42,915	39,956	†74,190	74,994	79,118
211 Wages and salaries......	†15,598	16,331	20,296	†23,387	24,595	30,852	†36,164	36,356	33,254	†59,551	60,951	64,106
212 Social contributions......	†3,327	3,246	3,322	†7,326	7,484	8,310	†7,313	6,559	6,702	†14,639	14,043	15,012
22 **Use of goods and services......**	†10,199	10,597	12,221	†20,183	20,860	42,826	†50,070	54,238	23,858	†70,253	75,098	66,680
23 **Consumption of fixed capital......**	†10,180	10,501	12,487	†10,651	11,392	13,346	†40	221	448	†10,691	11,613	13,794
24 **Interest......**	†23,124	22,643	23,488	†22,070	21,814	22,031	†817	902	825	†22,886	22,715	22,855
25 **Subsidies......**	†4,712	3,234	3,672	†5,896	4,469	4,709	†1,707	1,239	988	†7,603	5,708	5,697
26 **Grants......**	†94,433	101,756	110,339	†46,113	45,800	44,649	†18	18	32	†283	306	388
261 To foreign governments......	†—	—	—	†—	—	—	†—	—	—	†—	—	—
262 To international organizations......	†283	306	387	†283	306	387	†—	—	1	†283	306	388
263 To other general government units......	†94,150	101,450	109,952	†45,830	45,494	44,262	†18	18	31	†—	—	—
2631 Current......	†91,435	98,812	99,324	†43,706	43,415	42,072	†18	18	14	†—	—	—
2632 Capital......	†2,715	2,638	10,628	†2,124	2,079	2,190	†—	—	17	†—	—	—
27 **Social benefits......**	†13,122	13,566	14,227	†130,618	132,759	144,044	†4,632	5,064	4,969	†135,250	137,823	149,013
28 **Other expense......**	†7,366	5,031	4,903	†11,095	8,858	9,545	†4,710	5,094	7,666	†15,512	13,646	16,569
281 Property expense other than interest......	†—	—	—	†—	—	—	†—	—	—	†—	—	—
282 Miscellaneous other expense......	†7,366	5,031	4,903	†11,095	8,858	9,545	†4,710	5,094	7,666	†15,512	13,646	16,569
2821 Current......	†6,050	2,977	3,562	†7,721	5,691	8,051	†3,463	3,927	6,354	†10,891	9,312	13,763
2822 Capital......	†1,316	2,054	1,341	†3,374	3,167	1,494	†1,247	1,167	1,312	†4,621	4,334	2,806

In Millions of Zlotys / Year Ending December 31 / Noncash Reporter

	Budgetary Central Government			Central Government			Local Government			General Government		
	2001	2002	2003	2001	2002	2003	2001	2002	2003	2001	2002	2003
Table 3 Transactions in assets and liabilities												
3 Change in net worth from transactns....	†−38,340	−43,602	−51,731	†−27,540	−29,868	−33,349	†9,815	6,527	9,029	†−17,725	−23,341	−24,320
31 Net acquisition of nonfinancial assets...	†−7,196	−5,677	−6,487	†−5,801	−4,175	−5,435	†12,020	11,620	10,370	†6,219	7,445	4,935
311 Fixed assets..............................	†−7,196	−5,677	−6,487	†−5,801	−4,042	−5,256	†12,020	11,620	10,369	†6,219	7,578	5,113
3111 Buildings and structures...............	....	4,824	....	....	7,350	....	....	—	....	....	7,350	....
3112 Machinery and equipment..............	....	....	....	....	....	....	....	....	....	....	....	....
3113 Other fixed assets......................	....	....	....	....	....	....	....	....	....	....	....	....
312 Inventories..............................	†—	—	—	†—	−133	−179	†—	—	1	†—	−133	−178
313 Valuables..............................	†—	—	—	†—	—	—	†—	—	—	†—	—	—
314 Nonproduced assets....................	†—	—	—	†—	—	—	†—	—	—	†—	—	—
3141 Land..................................	†—	—	—	†—	—	—	†—	—	—	†—	—	—
3142 Subsoil assets........................	†—	—	—	†—	—	—	†—	—	—	†—	—	—
3143 Other naturally occurring assets.......	†—	—	—	†—	—	—	†—	—	—	†—	—	—
3144 Intangible nonproduced assets........	†—	—	—	†—	—	—	†—	—	—	†—	—	—
32 Net acquisition of financial assets........	†−7,840	−3,217	1,052	†2,876	11,107	5,100	†1,405	−997	2,374	†4,262	10,069	7,516
321 Domestic..............................	†−8,918	−2,649	−695	†1,798	11,675	3,353	†1,405	−997	2,374	†3,184	10,637	5,769
3212 Currency and deposits..................	†−299	−692	2,666	†1,348	3,767	1,257	†1,559	−1,002	2,331	†2,907	2,765	3,588
3213 Securities other than shares...........	†—	—	—	†—	—	—	†—	—	22	†—	—	22
3214 Loans................................	†15	−73	−5	†625	438	350	†−449	408	−226	†157	805	166
3215 Shares and other equity...............	†−6,490	−2,392	−3,217	†−3,220	2,026	2,101	†42	−422	155	†−3,178	1,604	2,256
3216 Insurance technical reserves..........	†—	—	—	†—	—	—	†—	—	—	†—	—	—
3217 Financial derivatives..................	†—	—	—	†—	—	—	†—	—	—	†—	—	—
3218 Other accounts receivable.............	†−2,144	508	−139	†3,045	5,444	−355	†253	19	92	†3,298	5,463	−263
322 Foreign..............................	†1,078	−568	1,747	†1,078	−568	1,747	†—	—	—	†1,078	−568	1,747
3222 Currency and deposits..................	†952	−690	615	†952	−690	615	†—	—	—	†952	−690	615
3223 Securities other than shares...........	†—	—	—	†—	—	—	†—	—	—	†—	—	—
3224 Loans................................	†91	100	151	†91	100	151	†—	—	—	†91	100	151
3225 Shares and other equity...............	†35	29	167	†35	29	167	†—	—	—	†35	29	167
3226 Insurance technical reserves..........	†—	—	—	†—	—	—	†—	—	—	†—	—	—
3227 Financial derivatives..................	†—	—	—	†—	—	—	†—	—	—	†—	—	—
3228 Other accounts receivable.............	†—	−7	814	†—	−7	814	†—	—	—	†—	−7	814
323 Monetary gold and SDRs..............	†—	—	—	†—	—	—	†—	—	—	†—	—	—
33 Net incurrence of liabilities.................	†23,304	34,708	46,296	†24,615	36,799	33,014	†3,610	4,096	3,715	†28,206	40,854	36,771
331 Domestic..............................	†36,814	32,268	43,141	†38,125	34,359	29,859	†3,562	3,887	3,467	†41,668	38,205	33,368
3312 Currency and deposits..................	†—	—	—	†—	—	16	†—	—	—	†—	—	16
3313 Securities other than shares...........	†36,298	38,348	41,359	†29,992	31,859	33,689	†789	621	426	†30,781	32,480	34,115
3314 Loans................................	†1,246	−1,341	−3,308	†5,012	911	−436	†2,553	2,149	1,330	†7,546	3,019	936
3316 Insurance technical reserves..........	†—	—	—	†—	—	—	†—	—	—	†—	—	—
3317 Financial derivatives..................	†—	—	—	†—	—	—	†—	—	—	†—	—	—
3318 Other accounts payable...............	†−730	−4,739	5,090	†3,121	1,589	−3,410	†220	1,117	1,711	†3,341	2,706	−1,699
332 Foreign..............................	†−13,510	2,440	3,155	†−13,510	2,440	3,155	†48	209	248	†−13,462	2,649	3,403
3322 Currency and deposits..................	†—	—	—	†—	—	—	†—	—	—	†—	—	—
3323 Securities other than shares...........	†3,013	4,821	8,563	†3,013	4,821	8,563	†−8	17	23	†3,005	4,838	8,586
3324 Loans................................	†−13,012	−2,379	−5,408	†−13,012	−2,379	−5,408	†56	192	225	†−12,956	−2,187	−5,183
3326 Insurance technical reserves..........	†—	—	—	†—	—	—	†—	—	—	†—	—	—
3327 Financial derivatives..................	†—	—	—	†—	—	—	†—	—	—	†—	—	—
3328 Other accounts payable...............	†−3,511	−2	—	†−3,511	−2	—	†—	—	—	†−3,511	−2	—
Table 4 Holding gains in assets and liabilities												
Table 5 Other changes in the volume of assets and liabilities												
Table 6 Balance sheet												
6 Net worth..............................	....	....	....	....	....	....	....	....	....	....	....	....
61 Nonfinancial assets.....................	....	....	....	....	....	....	....	....	....	....	....	....
611 Fixed assets..........................	....	....	....	....	....	....	....	....	....	....	....	....
6111 Buildings and structures...............	....	....	....	....	....	....	....	....	....	....	....	....
6112 Machinery and equipment..............	....	....	....	....	....	....	....	....	....	....	....	....
6113 Other fixed assets......................	....	....	....	....	....	....	....	....	....	....	....	....
612 Inventories..............................	....	....	....	....	....	....	....	....	....	....	....	....
613 Valuables..............................	....	....	....	....	....	....	....	....	....	....	....	....
614 Nonproduced assets....................	....	....	....	....	....	....	....	....	....	....	....	....
6141 Land..................................	....	....	....	....	....	....	....	....	....	....	....	....
6142 Subsoil assets........................	....	....	....	....	....	....	....	....	....	....	....	....
6143 Other naturally occurring assets.......	....	....	....	....	....	....	....	....	....	....	....	....
6144 Intangible nonproduced assets........	....	....	....	....	....	....	....	....	....	....	....	....

In Millions of Zlotys / Year Ending December 31 / Noncash Reporter

		Budgetary Central Government			Central Government			Local Government			General Government		
		2001	2002	2003	2001	2002	2003	2001	2002	2003	2001	2002	2003
62	Financial assets............................	....	....	....	....	....	....	....	....	....	....	....	....
621	Domestic.....................................	....	....	....	....	....	....	....	....	....	....	....	....
6212	Currency and deposits.................	....	....	....	....	....	....	....	....	....	....	....	....
6213	Securities other than shares.........	....	....	....	....	....	....	....	....	....	....	....	....
6214	Loans..	....	....	....	....	....	....	....	....	....	....	....	....
6215	Shares and other equity................	....	....	....	....	....	....	....	....	....	....	....	....
6216	Insurance technical reserves.........	....	....	....	....	....	....	....	....	....	....	....	....
6217	Financial derivatives.....................	....	....	....	....	....	....	....	....	....	....	....	....
6218	Other accounts receivable.............	....	....	....	....	....	....	....	....	....	....	....	....
622	Foreign.......................................	....	....	....	....	....	....	....	....	....	....	....	....
6222	Currency and deposits.................	....	....	....	....	....	....	....	....	....	....	....	....
6223	Securities other than shares.........	....	....	....	....	....	....	....	....	....	....	....	....
6224	Loans..	....	....	....	....	....	....	....	....	....	....	....	....
6225	Shares and other equity................	....	....	....	....	....	....	....	....	....	....	....	....
6226	Insurance technical reserves.........	....	....	....	....	....	....	....	....	....	....	....	....
6227	Financial derivatives.....................	....	....	....	....	....	....	....	....	....	....	....	....
6228	Other accounts receivable.............	....	....	....	....	....	....	....	....	....	....	....	....
623	Monetary gold and SDRs..............	....	....	....	....	....	....	....	....	....	....	....	....
63	Liabilities...................................	†268,529	331,059	372,814	†256,971	313,027	352,530	†12,471	15,615	16,691	†265,568	324,661	365,883
631	Domestic.....................................	†180,615	224,614	247,995	†169,052	206,574	227,699	†12,194	15,129	15,956	†177,372	217,722	240,317
6312	Currency and deposits.................	†—	—	—	†—	8	24	†69	28	25	†62	33	48
6313	Securities other than shares.........	†155,566	203,240	232,763	†141,312	180,749	204,400	†1,552	2,241	2,654	†142,857	182,980	207,035
6314	Loans..	†25,049	21,374	15,232	†27,740	25,817	23,275	†10,573	12,861	13,277	†34,453	34,710	33,234
6316	Insurance technical reserves.........	†—	—	—	†—	—	—	†—	—	—	†—	—	—
6317	Financial derivatives.....................	†—	—	—	†—	—	—	†—	—	—	†—	—	—
6318	Other accounts payable................	....	....	....	....	....	....	....	....	....	....	....	....
632	Foreign.......................................	†87,914	106,445	124,819	†87,919	106,453	124,831	†277	486	735	†88,196	106,939	125,566
6322	Currency and deposits.................	†—	—	—	†—	—	—	†—	—	—	†—	—	—
6323	Securities other than shares.........	†22,307	30,306	44,809	†22,307	30,306	44,809	†123	140	164	†22,430	30,446	44,973
6324	Loans..	†65,607	76,139	80,010	†65,612	76,147	80,022	†154	346	571	†65,766	76,493	80,593
6326	Insurance technical reserves.........	†—	—	—	†—	—	—	†—	—	—	†—	—	—
6327	Financial derivatives.....................	†—	—	—	†—	—	—	†—	—	—	†—	—	—
6328	Other accounts payable................	†—	—	—	†—	—	—	†—	—	—	†—	—	—
Memorandum items:													
6M2	Net financial worth......................	....	....	....	....	....	....	....	....	....	†265,568	324,661	365,883
6M3	Debt at market value....................	†268,529	331,059	372,814	†256,971	313,027	352,530	†12,471	15,615	16,691	†278,988	321,089	369,377
6M4	Debt at nominal value...................	†282,305	325,698	375,532	†270,391	309,455	356,024	†12,471	15,615	16,691	†278,988	321,089	369,377
6M5	Arrears.......................................	†859	414	330	†974	685	569	†923	1,094	652	†1,555	1,372	980
6M6	Obligations for social security benefits..	....	....	....	....	....	....	....	....	....	....	....	....
6M7	Contingent liabilities....................	....	....	....	....	....	....	....	....	....	....	....	....
6M8	Uncapitalized military weapons, systems......	....	....	....	....	....	....	....	....	....	....	....	....
Table 7	**Outlays by functions of govt.**												
7	**Total outlays.............................**	†174,865	181,228	198,468	†271,538	273,856	314,877	†117,491	121,311	89,112	†342,887	349,348	359,049
701	**General public services...............**	†85,020	93,872	38,704	†37,852	39,047	39,272	†8,981	9,301	9,919	†42,008	43,321	43,428
7017	Public debt transactions................	†23,124	22,643	23,488	†22,070	21,814	22,031	†817	902	825	†22,886	22,715	22,855
7018	General transfers between levels of govt......	†53,813	61,469	4,764	†4,793	5,002	4,764	†14	13	—	†—	—	—
702	**Defense.....................................**	†8,943	9,190	10,186	†9,472	9,497	10,595	†26	25	34	†9,400	9,409	10,498
703	**Public order and safety.............**	†12,862	10,434	14,636	†13,037	10,556	14,791	†4,868	5,074	1,810	†13,751	11,156	15,472
704	**Economic affairs.......................**	†13,242	12,695	16,338	†17,017	16,669	18,749	†14,328	14,044	12,446	†26,702	25,980	26,374
7042	Agriculture, forestry, fishing, and hunting.....	†2,148	2,267	4,743	†5,047	4,806	5,469	†1,014	1,121	1,106	†5,594	5,463	5,994
7043	Fuel and energy...........................	†1,959	1,171	901	†1,959	1,194	896	†49	99	107	†1,988	1,269	1,003
7044	Mining, manufacturing, and construction.....	†558	531	1,222	†682	578	1,170	†526	235	252	†1,108	690	1,160
7045	Transport....................................	†7,707	7,825	8,583	†8,399	8,474	9,300	†11,633	11,946	10,150	†16,048	16,355	15,532
7046	Communication............................	†99	84	75	†99	84	73	†194	191	—	†293	275	73
705	**Environmental protection.............**	†231	484	324	†873	1,204	1,114	†6,402	7,165	6,134	†7,195	8,296	6,652
706	**Housing and community amenities........**	†3,236	2,208	2,069	†4,407	3,406	2,528	†6,472	7,073	7,892	†10,235	9,667	10,319
707	**Health.......................................**	†4,028	4,131	3,659	†31,247	35,316	33,460	†3,570	1,990	1,889	†32,093	36,176	34,408
7072	Outpatient services......................	†198	86	39	....	....	....	†354	371	169	....	....	....
7073	Hospital services.........................	†502	1,268	710	....	....	....	†1,443	1,068	1,286	....	....	....
7074	Public health services..................	†492	1,755	1,018	....	....	....	†1,773	550	370	....	....	....
708	**Recreation, culture, and religion...........**	†1,367	1,135	1,236	†2,039	1,726	1,904	†4,485	4,576	4,255	†6,235	6,061	5,901

In Millions of Zlotys / Year Ending December 31 / Noncash Reporter

	Budgetary Central Government			Central Government			Local Government			General Government		
	2001	2002	2003	2001	2002	2003	2001	2002	2003	2001	2002	2003
709 Education............................	†25,479	26,168	33,071	†34,756	36,016	36,822	†32,480	33,408	34,888	†44,605	46,294	46,980
7091 Pre-primary and primary education..........	†36	127	56	†46	137	101	†22,686	23,878	24,140	....	....	24,196
7092 Secondary education.........................	†359	391	475	†359	391	423	†7,076	6,761	7,297	....	....	7,620
7094 Tertiary education...........................	†877	999	6,814	†10,322	10,795	10,852	†518	583	33	....	....	7,620
710 Social protection.........................	†20,457	20,911	78,245	†120,838	120,419	155,642	†35,879	38,655	9,845	†150,663	152,988	159,017
7 Statistical discrepancy: Total outlays..............	†—	—	—	†—	—	—	†—	—	—	†—	—	—

Table 8 Transactions in financial assets and liabilities by sector

	Budgetary Central Government			Central Government			Local Government			General Government		
	2001	2002	2003	2001	2002	2003	2001	2002	2003	2001	2002	2003
82 Net acquisition of financial assets........	†−7,840	−3,217	1,052	†2,876	11,107	5,100	†1,405	−997	2,374	†4,262	10,069	7,516
821 Domestic................................	†−8,918	−2,649	−695	†1,798	11,675	3,353	†1,405	−997	2,374	†3,184	10,637	5,769
8211 General government........................	†−959	−382	−143	†19	41	....	†—	—	....	†—	—	....
8212 Central bank...............................	†−299	−692	3,834	†−299	6,662	....	†—	−1,002	....	†−299	5,660	....
8213 Other depository corporations..............	†—	—	....	†4,240	2,805	....	†1,559	—	....	†5,799	2,805	....
8214 Financial corporations n.e.c..............	†—	—	....	†—	—	....	†—	—	....	†—	—	....
8215 Nonfinancial corporations.................	†−7,660	−1,897	−2,999	†−8,615	−2,929	....	†−154	−14	....	†−8,769	−2,943	....
8216 Households & NPIs serving households......	†—	322	....	†6,453	5,095	....	†—	19	....	†6,453	5,114	....
822 Foreign..................................	†1,078	−568	1,747	†1,078	−568	1,747	†—	—	—	†1,078	−568	1,747
8221 General government........................	†91	162	116	†91	162	116	†—	—	—	†91	162	116
8227 International organizations...............	†35	29	35	†35	29	35	†—	—	—	†35	29	35
8228 Financial corporations other than international organizations..............	†952	−690	....	†952	−690	....	†—	—	—	†952	−690	....
8229 Other nonresidents........................	†—	−69	....	†—	−69	....	†—	—	—	†—	−69	....
823 Monetary gold and SDRs.................	†—	—	—	†—	—	—	†—	—	—	†—	—	—
83 Net incurrence of liabilities................	†23,304	34,708	46,296	†24,615	36,799	33,014	†3,610	4,096	3,715	†28,206	40,854	36,771
831 Domestic................................	†36,814	32,268	43,141	†38,125	34,359	29,859	†3,562	3,887	3,467	†41,668	38,205	33,368
8311 General government........................	†6,306	6,489	....	†—	—	....	†19	41	....	†—	—	....
8312 Central bank...............................	†7,606	−11,996	−8,130	†7,606	−4,679	....	†—	−1,002	....	†7,606	−5,681	....
8313 Other depository corporations..............	†20,652	40,113	43,336	†27,137	40,075	....	†3,159	3,258	....	†30,296	43,333	....
8314 Financial corporations n.e.c..............	†—	—	....	†—	521	....	†—	—	....	†—	521	....
8315 Nonfinancial corporations.................	†−770	−1,361	2,817	†−3,411	−6,915	....	†229	100	....	†−3,182	−6,815	....
8316 Households & NPIs serving households......	†3,020	−977	−7	†6,793	5,357	....	†155	1,490	....	†6,948	6,847	....
832 Foreign..................................	†−13,510	2,440	3,155	†−13,510	2,440	3,155	†48	209	248	†−13,462	2,649	3,403
8321 General government........................	†−13,648	−4,207	−5,794	†−13,648	−4,207	−5,794	†—	—	—	†−13,648	−4,207	−5,794
8327 International organizations...............	†−2,663	677	1,882	†−2,663	677	1,882	†—	209	248	†−2,663	886	2,130
8328 Financial corporations other than international organizations..............	†−1,021	−4,196	−9,620	†−1,021	−4,196	−9,620	†−8	—	—	†−1,029	−4,196	−9,620
8329 Other nonresidents........................	†3,822	10,166	16,687	†3,822	10,166	16,687	†56	—	—	†3,878	10,166	16,687

In Millions of Euros / Year Ending December 31 / Noncash Reporter

	Budgetary Central Government			Central Government			Local Government			General Government		
	2000	2001	2002	2000	2001	2002	2000	2001	2002	2000	2001	2002
Statement of government operations												
1 Revenue..	32,942	33,913	35,788	44,878	46,890	50,850	6,505	7,361	7,763	48,849	51,363	55,561
2 Expense...	35,397	37,748	39,750	47,266	51,022	53,762	5,748	6,383	7,148	50,480	54,517	57,858
GOB *Gross operating balance*.....................	−1,429	−2,830	−3,039	−1,319	−3,057	−1,973	2,089	2,513	2,423	770	−544	450
NOB *Net operating balance*......................	−2,455	−3,834	−3,961	−2,388	−4,131	−2,912	756	978	615	−1,632	−3,153	−2,297
31 Net acquisition of nonfinancial assets...........	557	775	−63	579	801	−3	1,226	1,482	1,223	1,805	2,283	1,219
NLB *Net lending/borrowing*......................	−3,012	−4,610	−3,898	−2,968	−4,933	−2,908	−470	−504	−608	−3,437	−5,437	−3,516
32 Net acquisition of financial assets.................	−1,306	1,232	2,100	−1,107	1,201	2,788	102	99	341	−1,000	1,262	2,588
33 Net incurrence of liabilities...........................	1,706	5,812	5,996	1,861	6,105	5,694	572	603	949	2,437	6,669	6,102
NLB Statistical discrepancy...........................	—	29	2	—	29	2	—	—	—	—	29	2
Statement of other economic flows												
Balance sheet												
6 *Net worth*......................................	....	....	....	....	....	....	....	....	....	....	....	....
61 Nonfinancial assets...............................	....	....	....	....	....	....	....	....	....	....	....	....
62 Financial assets.....................................	....	....	....	....	....	....	....	....	....	39,544	47,291	48,208
63 Liabilities..	....	....	....	....	....	....	....	....	....	70,900	79,951	87,213
Statement of sources and uses of cash												
Table 1 Revenue												
1 **Revenue**.......................................	**32,942**	**33,913**	**35,788**	**44,878**	**46,890**	**50,850**	**6,505**	**7,361**	**7,763**	**48,849**	**51,363**	**55,561**
11 **Taxes**..	**25,750**	**26,502**	**28,452**	**26,281**	**27,067**	**29,074**	**2,524**	**2,552**	**2,816**	**28,805**	**29,619**	**31,890**
111 Taxes on income, profits, & capital gains......	11,109	11,153	11,450	11,109	11,153	11,450	573	587	637	11,682	11,740	12,087
1111 Individuals.....................................	6,745	7,173	7,230	6,745	7,173	7,230	202	197	229	6,947	7,370	7,459
1112 Corporations and other enterprises............	4,364	3,980	4,220	4,364	3,980	4,220	371	390	408	4,735	4,370	4,628
112 Taxes on payroll and workforce..................	—	—	—	—	—	—	—	—	1	—	—	1
113 Taxes on property...................................	102	90	104	102	90	104	509	538	606	611	627	710
114 Taxes on goods and services......................	13,683	14,343	15,900	14,214	14,908	16,522	1,424	1,410	1,555	15,638	16,318	18,077
1141 General taxes on goods and services.........	8,314	8,631	9,327	8,748	9,114	9,851	493	482	521	9,241	9,597	10,373
1142 Excises..	3,354	3,622	4,115	3,354	3,622	4,115	108	112	136	3,462	3,734	4,250
115 Taxes on int'l. trade and transactions...........	1	—	1	1	—	1	—	—	—	1	—	1
116 Other taxes..	856	917	998	856	917	998	18	17	18	874	933	1,015
12 **Social contributions**.........................	**1,088**	**1,163**	**1,180**	**13,546**	**14,592**	**15,654**	**62**	**73**	**95**	**13,608**	**14,665**	**15,749**
121 Social security contributions.......................	108	120	122	12,557	13,539	14,580	5	5	6	12,561	13,544	14,586
122 Other social contributions.........................	981	1,043	1,057	989	1,053	1,074	57	67	89	1,047	1,120	1,163
13 **Grants**..	**1,779**	**2,992**	**2,454**	**613**	**1,794**	**2,290**	**2,516**	**3,521**	**3,685**	**596**	**2,427**	**2,923**
131 From foreign governments.........................	—	1	1	—	1	1	—	—	—	—	1	1
132 From international organizations.................	244	1,318	1,462	595	1,775	2,265	1	652	657	596	2,427	2,923
133 From other general government units...........	1,534	1,674	991	18	19	24	2,516	2,869	3,028	—	—	—
14 **Other revenue**.................................	**4,325**	**3,256**	**3,703**	**4,438**	**3,437**	**3,832**	**1,402**	**1,215**	**1,167**	**5,839**	**4,652**	**4,999**
Table 2 Expense by economic type												
2 **Expense**...	**35,397**	**37,748**	**39,750**	**47,266**	**51,022**	**53,762**	**5,748**	**6,383**	**7,148**	**50,480**	**54,517**	**57,858**
21 **Compensation of employees**.................	**14,868**	**15,763**	**16,755**	**15,159**	**16,100**	**17,167**	**2,167**	**2,400**	**2,603**	**17,326**	**18,500**	**19,770**
211 Wages and salaries..............................	11,500	12,357	12,942	11,779	12,676	13,328	1,901	2,106	2,266	13,680	14,783	15,594
212 Social contributions...............................	3,368	3,405	3,813	3,380	3,423	3,839	266	294	337	3,646	3,717	4,176
22 **Use of goods and services**....................	**3,601**	**3,797**	**3,758**	**3,720**	**3,918**	**3,912**	**1,374**	**1,405**	**1,601**	**5,095**	**5,322**	**5,512**
23 **Consumption of fixed capital**................	**1,026**	**1,005**	**922**	**1,069**	**1,074**	**939**	**1,333**	**1,535**	**1,809**	**2,401**	**2,609**	**2,747**
24 **Interest**..	**3,685**	**3,840**	**3,952**	**3,670**	**3,818**	**3,814**	**92**	**135**	**129**	**3,761**	**3,953**	**3,943**
25 **Subsidies**......................................	**1,028**	**1,233**	**1,201**	**1,151**	**1,464**	**1,719**	**87**	**121**	**162**	**1,238**	**1,585**	**1,881**
26 **Grants**..	**5,289**	**5,786**	**6,849**	**2,778**	**3,249**	**3,425**	**18**	**20**	**24**	**262**	**381**	**397**
261 To foreign govenments..........................	—	3	2	—	3	2	—	1	—	—	4	3
262 To international organizations...................	262	377	395	262	377	395	—	—	—	262	377	395
263 To other general government units..............	5,027	5,406	6,452	2,516	2,869	3,028	18	19	24	—	—	—
2631 Current.......................................	3,781	3,893	5,116	1,288	1,398	1,712	10	14	17	—	—	—
2632 Capital..	1,247	1,513	1,336	1,227	1,471	1,316	8	5	7	—	—	—
27 **Social benefits**...............................	**2,947**	**3,266**	**3,438**	**16,068**	**17,536**	**19,126**	**158**	**185**	**210**	**16,226**	**17,721**	**19,336**
28 **Other expense**................................	**2,953**	**3,057**	**2,874**	**3,651**	**3,864**	**3,661**	**520**	**582**	**610**	**4,171**	**4,445**	**4,271**
281 Property expense other than interest...........	—	—	—	—	—	—	1	2	1	1	2	1
282 Miscellaneous other expense.....................	2,953	3,057	2,874	3,651	3,864	3,660	519	580	609	4,170	4,444	4,269
2821 Current.......................................	1,584	1,600	1,781	2,222	2,348	2,554	280	288	295	2,502	2,636	2,848
2822 Capital..	1,369	1,457	1,093	1,429	1,516	1,107	239	292	314	1,668	1,808	1,421

In Millions of Euros / Year Ending December 31 / Noncash Reporter

	Budgetary Central Government			Central Government			Local Government			General Government		
	2000	2001	2002	2000	2001	2002	2000	2001	2002	2000	2001	2002
Table 3 Transactions in assets and liabilities												
3 Change in net worth from transactns....	−2,455	−3,805	−3,959	−2,388	−4,102	−2,909	756	978	615	−1,632	−3,124	−2,295
31 Net acquisition of nonfinancial assets...	557	775	−63	579	801	−3	1,226	1,482	1,223	1,805	2,283	1,219
311 Fixed assets................................	846	786	648	868	811	708	1,175	1,467	1,154	2,043	2,279	1,861
3111 Buildings and structures.................	....	....	....	....	....	....	....	....	....	....	....	....
3112 Machinery and equipment...............	....	....	....	....	....	....	....	....	....	....	....	....
3113 Other fixed assets.........................	....	....	....	....	....	....	....	....	....	....	....	....
312 Inventories.....................................	—	—	—	—	—	—	—	—	—			
313 Valuables.......................................	—	—	—	—	—	—	—	—	—	—		—
314 Nonproduced assets.......................	−289	−11	−711	−289	−10	−711	51	15	69	−238	4	−642
3141 Land..	....	....	....	....	....	....	....	....	....	....	....	....
3142 Subsoil assets..............................	....	....	....	....	....	....	....	....	....	....	....	....
3143 Other naturally occurring assets.......	....	....	....	....	....	....	....	....	....	....	....	....
3144 Intangible nonproduced assets.........	....	....	....	....	....	....	....	....	....	....	....	....
32 Net acquisition of financial assets.........	−1,306	1,232	2,100	−1,107	1,201	2,788	102	99	341	−1,000	1,262	2,588
321 Domestic......................................	−1,825	520	2,263	−1,620	699	2,372	103	84	354	−1,513	744	2,185
3212 Currency and deposits....................	−884	−2,167	1,133	−691	−1,904	1,264	2	86	265	−690	−1,872	1,564
3213 Securities other than shares...........	183	85	164	95	−162	540	2	−2	6	150	−101	−28
3214 Loans...	—	−11	185	—	−9	183	—	—	—	—	−9	183
3215 Shares and other equity..................	−1,247	−25	651	−1,240	−38	610	70	8	65	−1,170	−30	674
3216 Insurance technical reserves...........	1	1	—	1	1	—	—	—	—	1	1	—
3217 Financial derivatives......................	—	—	—	—	—	—	—	—	—	—	—	—
3218 Other accounts receivable..............	121	2,638	131	215	2,811	−225	29	−8	18	196	2,756	−209
322 Foreign..	520	711	−163	514	502	415	−1	16	−13	513	518	402
3222 Currency and deposits....................	10	59	10	10	59	10	—	—	—	10	60	10
3223 Securities other than shares...........	126	464	−132	120	255	190	−1	15	−13	119	270	177
3224 Loans...	162	162	98	162	162	98	—	—	—	162	162	98
3225 Shares and other equity..................	139	−50	−140	139	−50	−58	—	—	—	139	−50	−58
3226 Insurance technical reserves...........	—	—	—	—	—	—	—	—	—	—	—	—
3227 Financial derivatives......................	−197	−109	−195	−197	−109	−195	—	—	—	−197	−109	−195
3228 Other accounts receivable..............	279	185	196	279	185	371	—	—	—	279	185	371
323 Monetary gold and SDRs.................	—	—	—	—	—	—	—	—	—	—	—	—
33 Net incurrence of liabilities..................	1,706	5,812	5,996	1,861	6,105	5,694	572	603	949	2,437	6,669	6,102
331 Domestic......................................	−867	2,240	1,899	−856	2,533	1,597	578	511	845	−273	3,004	1,900
3312 Currency and deposits....................	1,190	1,148	1,049	1,190	1,148	1,049	—	—	—	1,190	1,094	1,084
3313 Securities other than shares...........	−1,445	1,278	2,043	−1,445	1,278	2,043	18	56	−33	−1,373	1,397	1,436
3314 Loans...	−223	285	−150	−248	440	−330	318	569	673	70	1,009	343
3316 Insurance technical reserves...........	—	—	—	—	—	—	—	—	—	—	—	—
3317 Financial derivatives......................	—	—	—	—	—	—	—	—	—	—	—	—
3318 Other accounts payable..................	−390	−471	−1,043	−353	−333	−1,166	241	−114	205	−160	−495	−963
332 Foreign..	2,573	3,572	4,097	2,716	3,572	4,097	−6	93	105	2,710	3,665	4,202
3322 Currency and deposits....................	−54	23	−35	−54	23	−35	—	—	—	−54	23	−35
3323 Securities other than shares...........	2,663	3,886	4,017	2,663	3,886	4,017	—	—	—	2,663	3,886	4,017
3324 Loans...	−136	−336	115	−136	−336	115	−6	93	105	−142	−244	219
3326 Insurance technical reserves...........	—	—	—	—	—	—	—	—	—	—	—	—
3327 Financial derivatives......................	—	—	—	—	—	—	—	—	—	—	—	—
3328 Other accounts payable..................	100	—	—	243	—	—	—	—	—	243	—	—
Table 4 Holding gains in assets and liabilities												
Table 5 Other changes in the volume of assets and liabilities												
Table 6 Balance sheet												
6 Net worth......................................	....	....	....	....	....	....	....	....	....	....	....	....
61 Nonfinancial assets........................	....	....	....	....	....	....	....	....	....	....	....	....
611 Fixed assets..................................	....	....	....	....	....	....	....	....	....	....	....	....
6111 Buildings and structures.................	....	....	....	....	....	....	....	....	....	....	....	....
6112 Machinery and equipment...............	....	....	....	....	....	....	....	....	....	....	....	....
6113 Other fixed assets.........................	....	....	....	....	....	....	....	....	....	....	....	....
612 Inventories.....................................	....	....	....	....	....	....	....	....	....	....	....	....
613 Valuables.......................................	....	....	....	....	....	....	....	....	....	....	....	....
614 Nonproduced assets.......................	....	....	....	....	....	....	....	....	....	....	....	....
6141 Land..	....	....	....	....	....	....	....	....	....	....	....	....
6142 Subsoil assets..............................	....	....	....	....	....	....	....	....	....	....	....	....
6143 Other naturally occurring assets.......	....	....	....	....	....	....	....	....	....	....	....	....
6144 Intangible nonproduced assets........	....	....	....	....	....	....	....	....	....	....	....	....

In Millions of Euros / Year Ending December 31 / Noncash Reporter

	Budgetary Central Government			Central Government			Local Government			General Government		
	2000	2001	2002	2000	2001	2002	2000	2001	2002	2000	2001	2002
62 **Financial assets**........................	....	....	....	....	....	....	....	....	....	**39,544**	**47,291**	**48,208**
621 Domestic........................	....	....	....	....	....	....	....	....	....	37,097	41,866	42,818
6212 Currency and deposits...........	....	....	....	....	....	....	....	....	....	8,183	6,352	7,916
6213 Securities other than shares......	....	....	....	....	....	....	....	....	....	175	−54	125
6214 Loans....................	....	....	....	....	....	....	....	....	....	80	73	256
6215 Shares and other equity..........	....	....	....	....	....	....	....	....	....	17,612	21,729	20,789
6216 Insurance technical reserves......	....	....	....	....	....	....	....	....	....	9	10	11
6217 Financial derivatives.............	....	....	....	....	....	....	....	....	....	−353	—	—
6218 Other accounts receivable........	....	....	....	....	....	....	....	....	....	11,392	13,755	13,721
622 Foreign........................	....	....	....	....	....	....	....	....	....	2,447	5,425	5,390
6222 Currency and deposits...........	....	....	....	....	....	....	....	....	....	32	93	100
6223 Securities other than shares......	....	....	....	....	....	....	....	....	....	900	1,569	1,652
6224 Loans....................	....	....	....	....	....	....	....	....	....	711	2,421	2,272
6225 Shares and other equity..........	....	....	....	....	....	....	....	....	....	143	332	335
6226 Insurance technical reserves......	....	....	....	....	....	....	....	....	....	—	—	—
6227 Financial derivatives.............	....	....	....	....	....	....	....	....	....	353	429	79
6228 Other accounts receivable........	....	....	....	....	....	....	....	....	....	307	581	952
623 Monetary gold and SDRs...........	....	....	....	....	....	....	....	....	....	—	—	—
63 **Liabilities**..........................	....	....	....	....	....	....	....	....	....	**70,900**	**79,951**	**87,213**
631 Domestic........................	....	....	....	....	....	....	....	....	....	39,515	44,650	46,729
6312 Currency and deposits...........	....	....	....	....	....	....	....	....	....	14,131	15,128	15,909
6313 Securities other than shares......	....	....	....	....	....	....	....	....	....	20,163	22,563	24,225
6314 Loans....................	....	....	....	....	....	....	....	....	....	2,284	3,417	3,850
6316 Insurance technical reserves......	....	....	....	....	....	....	....	....	....	—	—	—
6317 Financial derivatives.............	....	....	....	....	....	....	....	....	....	2,937	3,543	2,745
6318 Other accounts payable..........	....	....	....	....	....	....	....	....	....	31,385	35,301	40,485
632 Foreign........................	....	....	....	....	....	....	....	....	....	35	58	23
6322 Currency and deposits...........	....	....	....	....	....	....	....	....	....	29,071	33,186	38,422
6323 Securities other than shares......	....	....	....	....	....	....	....	....	....	2,035	1,814	1,797
6324 Loans....................	....	....	....	....	....	....	....	....	....	—	—	—
6326 Insurance technical reserves......	....	....	....	....	....	....	....	....	....	—	—	—
6327 Financial derivatives.............	....	....	....	....	....	....	....	....	....	243	243	243
6328 Other accounts payable..........	....	....	....	....	....	....	....	....	....			
Memorandum items:												
6M2 Net financial worth.............	....	....	....	....	....	....	....	....	....	−31,355	−32,660	−39,005
6M3 Debt at market value...........	....	....	....	....	....	....	....	....	....	....	....	....
6M4 Debt at nominal value..........	....	....	....	....	....	....	....	....	....	....	....	....
6M5 Arrears....................	....	....	....	....	....	....	....	....	....	....	....	....
6M6 Obligations for social security benefits...........	....	....	....	....	....	....	....	....	....	....	....	....
6M7 Contingent liabilities.............	....	....	....	....	....	....	....	....	....	....	....	....
6M8 Uncapitalized military weapons, systems.......	....	....	....	....	....	....	....	....	....	....	....	....

Table 7 Outlays by functions of govt.

	Budgetary Central Government			Central Government			Local Government			General Government		
	2000	2001	2002	2000	2001	2002	2000	2001	2002	2000	2001	2002
7 **Total outlays**..................	35,954	38,523	39,686	47,845	51,823	53,758	6,974	7,865	8,371	52,286	56,800	59,077
701 **General public services**..............	....	11,730	12,486	....	9,175	8,928	....	1,822	2,188	7,510	8,109	8,063
7017 Public debt transactions.............	....	3,840	3,952	....	3,818	3,814	....	135	129	3,763	3,953	3,943
7018 General transfers between levels of govt......	....	....	....	....	....	....	....	....	....	—	....	....
702 **Defense**........................	....	1,847	1,743	....	1,847	1,743	....	—	—	2,131	1,847	1,743
703 **Public order and safety**......................	....	2,201	2,430	....	2,201	2,430	....	114	119	2,212	2,315	2,549
704 **Economic affairs**...................	....	4,510	3,855	....	4,742	4,379	....	2,053	2,017	6,172	6,795	6,396
7042 Agriculture, forestry, fishing, and hunting....	....	....	....	....	....	....	....	....	....	1,073	....	....
7043 Fuel and energy................	....	....	....	....	....	....	....	....	....	33	....	....
7044 Mining, manufacturing, and construction......	....	....	....	....	....	....	....	....	....	1,039	....	....
7045 Transport....................	....	....	....	....	....	....	....	....	....	2,303	....	....
7046 Communication..................	....	....	....	....	....	....	....	....	....	10	....	....
705 **Environmental protection**..............	....	193	177	....	193	177	....	635	651	798	828	828
706 **Housing and community amenities**........	....	113	84	....	110	87	....	1,103	1,033	1,149	1,213	1,120
707 **Health**........................	....	8,280	8,556	....	8,294	8,573	....	358	454	7,746	8,652	9,027
7072 Outpatient services..............	....	....	....	....	....	....	....	....	....	1,673	....	....
7073 Hospital services..............	....	....	....	....	....	....	....	....	....	4,254	....	....
7074 Public health services...........	....	....	....	....	....	....	....	....	....	12	....	....
708 **Recreation, culture, and religion**............	....	557	560	....	569	566	....	901	980	1,301	1,470	1,546

In Millions of Euros / Year Ending December 31 / Noncash Reporter

		Budgetary Central Government			Central Government			Local Government			General Government		
		2000	2001	2002	2000	2001	2002	2000	2001	2002	2000	2001	2002
709	**Education**..........	....	7,834	8,417	....	7,834	8,417	....	686	729	7,985	8,520	9,146
7091	Pre-primary and primary education..........	....	....	....	....	....	....	....	....	....	1,514	....	....
7092	Secondary education..........	....	....	....	....	....	....	....	....	....	3,893	....	....
7094	Tertiary education..........	....	....	....	....	....	....	....	....	....	1,470	....	....
710	**Social protection**..........	....	1,257	1,378	....	16,857	18,459	....	194	201	15,282	17,051	18,660
7	Statistical discrepancy: Total outlays..........	—	—	—	—	—	—	—	—	—	—	—	—

Table 8 Transactions in financial assets and liabilities by sector

		2000	2001	2002	2000	2001	2002	2000	2001	2002	2000	2001	2002
82	**Net acquisition of financial assets**..........	−1,306	1,232	2,100	−1,107	1,201	2,788	102	99	341	−1,000	1,262	2,588
821	Domestic..........	−1,825	520	2,263	−1,620	699	2,372	103	84	354	−1,513	744	2,185
8211	General government..........	....	....	....	....	....	....	....	....	....	....	....	....
8212	Central bank..........	....	....	....	....	....	....	....	....	....	....	....	....
8213	Other depository corporations..........	....	....	....	....	....	....	....	....	....	....	....	....
8214	Financial corporations n.e.c.........	....	....	....	....	....	....	....	....	....	....	....	....
8215	Nonfinancial corporations..........	....	....	....	....	....	....	....	....	....	....	....	....
8216	Households & NPIs serving households......	....	....	....	....	....	....	....	....	....	....	....	....
822	Foreign..........	520	711	−163	514	502	415	−1	16	−13	513	518	402
8221	General government..........	....	....	....	....	....	....	....	....	....	....	....	....
8227	International organizations..........	....	....	....	....	....	....	....	....	....	....	....	....
8228	Financial corporations other than international organizations..........	....	....	....	....	....	....	....	....	....	....	....	....
8229	Other nonresidents..........	....	....	....	....	....	....	....	....	....	....	....	....
823	Monetary gold and SDRs..........	—	—	—	—	—	—						....
83	**Net incurrence of liabilities**..........	1,706	5,812	5,996	1,861	6,105	5,694	572	603	949	2,437	6,669	6,102
831	Domestic..........	−867	2,240	1,899	−856	2,533	1,597	578	511	845	−273	3,004	1,900
8311	General government..........	....	....	....	....	....	....	....	....	....	....	....	....
8312	Central bank..........	....	....	....	....	....	....	....	....	....	....	....	....
8313	Other depository corporations..........	....	....	....	....	....	....	....	....	....	....	....	....
8314	Financial corporations n.e.c.........	....	....	....	....	....	....	....	....	....	....	....	....
8315	Nonfinancial corporations..........	....	....	....	....	....	....	....	....	....	....	....	....
8316	Households & NPIs serving households......	....	....	....	....	....	....	....	....	....	....	....	....
832	Foreign..........	2,573	3,572	4,097	2,716	3,572	4,097	−6	93	105	2,710	3,665	4,202
8321	General government..........	....	....	....	....	....	....	....	....	....	....	....	....
8327	International organizations..........	....	....	....	....	....	....	....	....	....	....	....	....
8328	Financial corporations other than international organizations..........	....	....	....	....	....	....	....	....	....	....	....	....
8329	Other nonresidents..........	....	....	....	....	....	....	....	....	....	....	....	....

In Billions of Lei / Year Ending December 31 / Noncash Reporter

		Budgetary Central Government			Central Government			Local Government			General Government		
		2000	2001	2002p	2000	2001	2002p	2000	2001	2002p	2000	2001	2002p
Statement of government operations													
1	Revenue......	....	....	193,631	....	....	395,467	....	....	100,234	....	....	489,289
2	Expense......	....	....	209,516	....	....	392,470	....	....	91,206	....	....	477,263
GOB	*Gross operating balance......*	....	....	*−15,885*	....	....	*2,997*	....	....	*9,028*	....	....	*12,025*
NOB	*Net operating balance......*	....	....	....	....	....	....	....	....	....	....	....	....
31	Net acquisition of nonfinancial assets......	....	....	25,011	....	....	32,916	....	....	9,462	....	....	42,378
NLB	*Net lending/borrowing......*	....	....	*−40,895*	....	....	*−29,919*	....	....	*−434*	....	....	*−30,353*
32	Net acquisition of financial assets......	....	....	16,395	....	....	9,194	....	....	8	....	....	9,202
33	Net incurrence of liabilities......	....	....	41,100	....	....	31,765	....	....	276	....	....	32,041
NLB	Statistical discrepancy......	....	....	16,190	....	....	7,348	....	....	166	....	....	7,513
Statement of other economic flows													
Balance sheet													
Statement of sources and uses of cash													
1	Cash receipts from operating activities......	120,186	147,080	†188,038	237,694	312,534	389,865	35,264	74,432	99,233	....	....	482,686
11	Taxes......	113,070	126,302	†161,387	120,875	137,200	173,169	24,459	59,320	82,801	....	....	255,970
12	Social contributions......	416	9,585	†6,650	88,762	128,918	163,367	—	—	—	....	....	163,367
13	Grants......	461	271	†4,950	880	1,345	4,950	5,975	8,119	6,413	....	....	4,950
14	Other receipts......	6,240	10,922	†15,050	27,177	45,071	48,378	4,830	6,994	10,020	....	....	58,398
2	Cash payments for operating activities......	127,993	152,388	†208,529	260,763	331,537	392,304	30,038	67,091	89,752	....	....	475,643
21	Compensation of employees......	35,483	27,568	†32,374	53,489	50,979	61,971	6,931	32,449	42,878	....	....	104,849
22	Purchases of goods and services......	14,006	20,603	†39,464	43,821	65,602	83,381	13,529	20,843	26,411	....	....	109,792
24	Interest......	32,299	35,150	†36,598	32,446	35,763	34,581	35	70	148	....	....	34,728
25	Subsidies......	13,706	12,670	†19,952	13,734	12,743	22,142	....	....	7,729	....	....	29,870
26	Grants......	2,982	5,894	†14,540	12,178	13,726	4,625	....	....	2,387	....	....	599
27	Social benefits......	19,998	37,670	†28,808	89,423	134,434	140,487	....	....	5,292	....	....	145,780
28	Other payments......	9,519	12,834	†36,793	15,672	18,289	45,118	....	....	4,907	....	....	50,025
CIO	*Net cash inflow from oper. activities.....*	*−7,807*	*−5,308*	*†−20,491*	*−23,069*	*−19,003*	*−2,438*	*5,226*	*7,341*	*9,481*	....	....	*7,043*
31.1	Purchases of nonfinancial assets......	3,299	5,953	†25,081	13,228	23,300	33,012	5,242	7,579	10,295	....	....	43,308
31.2	Sales of nonfinancial assets......	121	83	†70	347	131	97	152	451	834	....	....	930
31	Net cash outflow from investments in nonfinancial assets......	3,178	5,870	†25,011	12,881	23,169	32,916	5,090	7,127	9,462	....	....	42,378
CSD	*Cash surplus/deficit......*	*−10,985*	*−11,178*	*†−45,502*	*−35,950*	*−42,172*	*−35,354*	*136*	*213*	*19*	....	....	*−35,335*
32x	Net acquisition of fin assets, excl. cash......	−187	−1,245	†16,395	−4,180	−6,762	9,194	−439	−138	8	....	....	9,202
321x	Domestic......	−187	−1,245	†16,395	−4,180	−6,762	9,194	....	....	8	....	....	9,202
322x	Foreign......	—	—	†—	—	—	—	....	....	—	....	....	—
323	Monetary gold and SDRs......	—	—	†—	—	—	—	....	....	—	....	....	—
33	Net incurrence of liabilities......	....	....	†41,100	....	....	31,765	....	....	276	....	....	32,041
331	Domestic......	....	....	†15,344	....	....	6,169	....	....	426	....	....	6,596
332	Foreign......	....	....	†25,757	....	....	25,596	....	....	−150	....	....	25,445
NFB	Net cash inflow from fin. activities......	....	....	†24,706	....	....	22,571	....	....	268	....	....	22,839
NCB	*Net change in the stock of cash......*	....	....	*†−20,796*	....	....	*−12,783*	....	....	*287*	....	....	*−12,496*

Table 1   Revenue

		Budgetary Central Government			Central Government			Local Government			General Government		
1	**Revenue......**	**120,186**	**147,080**	**†193,631**	**237,694**	**312,534**	**†395,467**	**35,264**	**74,432**	**†100,234**	....	....	**†489,289**
11	**Taxes......**	**113,070**	**126,302**	**†167,095**	**120,875**	**137,200**	**†177,842**	**24,459**	**59,320**	**†83,801**	....	....	**†261,643**
111	Taxes on income, profits, & capital gains......	31,057	32,055	†36,685	31,057	32,055	†36,685	19,106	29,986	†41,970	....	....	†78,655
1111	Individuals......	11,110	9,235	†1,217	11,110	9,235	†1,217	18,531	29,134	†41,036	....	....	†42,253
1112	Corporations and other enterprises......	19,944	22,447	†35,467	19,944	22,447	†35,467	....	....	†230	....	....	†35,697
112	Taxes on payroll and workforce......	—	—	†4	—	—	†4	—	—	†—	....	....	†4
113	Taxes on property......	—	—	†1,910	—	—	†1,910	3,955	5,971	†8,486	....	....	†10,396
114	Taxes on goods and services......	71,944	82,941	†118,314	79,111	93,796	†129,060	582	22,707	†33,345	....	....	†162,405
1141	General taxes on goods and services......	50,439	51,793	†78,773	50,439	51,793	†83,148	....	....	†32,046	....	....	†115,194
1142	Excises......	20,636	29,457	†35,473	26,964	40,312	†41,507	....	....	†—	....	....	†41,507
115	Taxes on int'l. trade and transactions......	8,702	9,562	†10,038	9,052	9,562	†10,038	—	—	†—	....	....	†10,038
116	Other taxes......	1,367	1,745	†144	1,656	1,787	†144	817	656	†—	....	....	†144
12	**Social contributions......**	**416**	**9,585**	**†6,535**	**88,762**	**128,918**	**†164,297**	**—**	**—**	**†—**	....	....	**†164,297**
121	Social security contributions......	416	9,585	†6,535	88,762	128,918	†163,747	—	—	†—	....	....	†163,747
122	Other social contributions......	—	—	†—	—	—	†550	—	—	†—	....	....	†550
13	**Grants......**	**461**	**271**	**†4,950**	**880**	**1,345**	**†4,950**	**5,975**	**8,119**	**†6,413**	....	....	**†4,950**
131	From foreign governments......	461	271	†—	880	1,345	†—	147	346	†—	....	....	†—
132	From international organizations......	—	—	†4,950	—	—	†4,950	—	—	†—	....	....	†4,950
133	From other general government units......	—	—	†—	—	—	†—	5,828	7,773	†6,413	....	....	†—
14	**Other revenue......**	**6,240**	**10,922**	**†15,050**	**27,177**	**45,071**	**†48,379**	**4,830**	**6,994**	**†10,020**	....	....	**†58,399**

In Billions of Lei / Year Ending December 31 / Noncash Reporter

	Budgetary Central Government			Central Government			Local Government			General Government		
	2000	2001	2002p	2000	2001	2002p	2000	2001	2002p	2000	2001	2002p
Table 2 Expense by economic type												
2 **Expense**...................................	**127,993**	**152,388**	**†209,516**	**260,763**	**331,537**	**†392,470**	**30,038**	**67,091**	**†91,206**	....	....	**†477,263**
21 **Compensation of employees**..................	**35,483**	**27,568**	**†32,289**	**53,489**	**50,979**	**†61,734**	**6,931**	**32,449**	**†43,096**	....	....	**†104,829**
211 Wages and salaries................	29,417	23,134	†26,926	43,037	40,868	†49,454	6,931	32,449	†32,721	....	....	†82,175
212 Social contributions..............	6,066	4,434	†5,362	10,452	10,111	†12,279	—	—	†10,375	....	....	†22,654
22 **Use of goods and services**..............	**14,006**	**20,603**	**†41,492**	**43,821**	**65,602**	**†84,736**	**13,529**	**20,843**	**†27,640**	....	....	**†112,376**
23 **Consumption of fixed capital**................	....	....	....	....	....	....	....	....	....	....	....	....
24 **Interest**................................	**32,299**	**35,150**	**†35,096**	**32,446**	**35,763**	**†33,084**	**35**	**70**	**†155**	....	....	**†33,238**
25 **Subsidies**................................	**13,706**	**12,670**	**†19,952**	**13,734**	**12,743**	**†22,142**	....	....	**†7,729**	....	....	**†29,870**
26 **Grants**..................................	**2,982**	**5,894**	**†14,540**	**12,178**	**13,726**	**†4,625**	....	....	**†2,387**	....	....	**†599**
261 To foreign govenments..............	272	591	†—	272	591	†—	....	....	†—	....	....	†—
262 To international organizations.........	—	—	†599	—	—	†599	....	....	†—	....	....	†599
263 To other general government units............	2,710	5,303	†13,941	11,906	13,135	†4,026	133	—	†2,387	....	....	†—
2631 Current..............................	2,710	5,303	†12,106	11,906	13,135	†74	133	—	†2,387	....	....	†—
2632 Capital...............................			†1,835			†3,951	—	—	†—	....	....	†—
27 **Social benefits**...........................	**19,998**	**37,670**	**†28,808**	**89,423**	**134,434**	**†140,487**	....	....	**†5,292**	....	....	**†145,780**
28 **Other expense**...........................	**9,519**	**12,834**	**†37,338**	**15,672**	**18,289**	**†45,664**	....	....	**†4,907**	....	....	**†50,571**
281 Property expense other than interest...........	—	—	†—				....	....	†—	....	....	†—
282 Miscellaneous other expense............	9,519	12,834	†37,338	15,672	18,289	†45,664	....	....	†4,907	....	....	†50,571
2821 Current..............................	—	—	†19,080	—	—	†22,568	....	....	†2,164	....	....	†24,732
2822 Capital...............................	9,519	12,834	†18,259	15,672	18,289	†23,096	....	....	†2,743	....	....	†25,838
Table 3 Transactions in assets and liabilities												
3 **Change in net worth from transactns....**	....	....	....	....	....	....	....	....	....	....	....	....
31 **Net acquisition of nonfinancial assets...**	**3,178**	**5,870**	**†25,011**	**12,881**	**23,169**	**†32,916**	**5,090**	**7,127**	**†9,462**	....	....	**†42,378**
311 Fixed assets.......................	3,191	5,870	†24,354	12,893	23,170	†32,260	....	....	†9,462	....	....	†41,722
3111 Buildings and structures.............	....	....	....	....	....	....	....	....	....	....	....	....
3112 Machinery and equipment..............	....	....	....	....	....	....	....	....	....	....	....	....
3113 Other fixed assets...................	....	....	....	....	....	....	....	....	....	....	....	....
312 Inventories.........................	−13	−1	†656	−13	−1	†656	....	....	†—	....	....	†656
313 Valuables...........................	—	—	†—	—	—	†—	....	....	†—	....	....	†—
314 Nonproduced assets....................	—	—	†—	—	—	†—	....	....	†—	....	....	†—
3141 Land................................	—	—	†—	—	—	†—	....	....	†—	....	....	†—
3142 Subsoil assets......................	—	—	†—	—	—	†—	....	....	†—	....	....	†—
3143 Other naturally occurring assets......	—	—	†—	—	—	†—	....	....	†—	....	....	†—
3144 Intangible nonproduced assets........	—	—	†—	—	—	†—	....	....	†—	....	....	†—
32 **Net acquisition of financial assets........**	....	....	**†16,395**	....	....	**†9,194**	....	....	**†8**	....	....	**†9,202**
321 Domestic..........................	....	....	†16,395	....	....	†9,194	....	....	†8	....	....	†9,202
3212 Currency and deposits...............	....	....	†−20,796	....	....	†−12,783	....	....	†287	....	....	†−12,496
3213 Securities other than shares.........	....	....	†—	....	....	†—	....	....	†—	....	....	†—
3214 Loans..............................	....	....	†−70	....	....	†550	....	....	†8	....	....	†557
3215 Shares and other equity.............	....	....	†—	....	....	†−7,820	....	....	†—	....	....	†−7,820
3216 Insurance technical reserves.........	....	....	†—	....	....	†—	....	....	†—	....	....	†—
3217 Financial derivatives...............	....	....	†—	....	....	†—	....	....	†—	....	....	†—
3218 Other accounts receivable...........	....	....	†37,261	....	....	†29,248	....	....	†−287	....	....	†28,961
322 Foreign...........................	—	—	†—	—	—	†—	....	....	†—	....	....	†—
3222 Currency and deposits...............	—	—	†—	—	—	†—	....	....	†—	....	....	†—
3223 Securities other than shares.........	—	—	†—	—	—	†—	....	....	†—	....	....	†—
3224 Loans..............................	—	—	†—	—	—	†—	....	....	†—	....	....	†—
3225 Shares and other equity.............	—	—	†—	—	—	†—	....	....	†—	....	....	†—
3226 Insurance technical reserves.........	—	—	†—	—	—	†—	....	....	†—	....	....	†—
3227 Financial derivatives...............	—	—	†—	—	—	†—	....	....	†—	....	....	†—
3228 Other accounts receivable...........	....	....	†—	....	....	†—	....	....	†—	....	....	†—
323 Monetary gold and SDRs............	—	—	†—	—	—	†—	....	....	†—	....	....	†—
33 **Net incurrence of liabilities...................**	....	....	**†41,100**	....	....	**†31,765**	....	....	**†276**	....	....	**†32,041**
331 Domestic..........................	....	....	†15,344	....	....	†6,169	....	....	†426	....	....	†6,596
3312 Currency and deposits...............	....	....	†—	....	....	†—	....	....	†—	....	....	†—
3313 Securities other than shares.........	....	....	†15,344	....	....	†15,344	....	....	†107	....	....	†15,450
3314 Loans..............................	....	....	†—	....	....	†−9,174	....	....	†320	....	....	†−8,855
3316 Insurance technical reserves.........	....	....	†—	....	....	†—	....	....	†—	....	....	†—
3317 Financial derivatives...............	....	....	†—	....	....	†—	....	....	†—	....	....	†—
3318 Other accounts payable..............	....	....	†—	....	....	†—	....	....	†—	....	....	†—

In Billions of Lei / Year Ending December 31 / Noncash Reporter

		Budgetary Central Government			Central Government			Local Government			General Government		
		2000	2001	2002p	2000	2001	2002p	2000	2001	2002p	2000	2001	2002p
332	Foreign	....	....	†25,757	....	....	†25,596	....	....	†−150	....	....	†25,445
3322	Currency and deposits	....	....	†—	....	....	†—	....	....	†—	....	....	†—
3323	Securities other than shares	....	....	†14,562	....	....	†14,562	....	....	†—	....	....	†14,562
3324	Loans	....	....	†11,195	....	....	†11,034	....	....	†−150	....	....	†10,884
3326	Insurance technical reserves	....	....	†—	....	....	†—	....	....	†—	....	....	†—
3327	Financial derivatives	....	....	†—	....	....	†—	....	....	†—	....	....	†—
3328	Other accounts payable	....	....	†—	....	....	†—	....	....	†—	....	....	†—

Table 4 Holding gains in assets and liabilities

Table 5 Other changes in the volume of assets and liabilities

Table 6 Balance sheet

Table 7 Outlays by functions of govt.

		Budgetary Central Government			Central Government			Local Government			General Government		
		2000	2001	2002p	2000	2001	2002p	2000	2001	2002p	2000	2001	2002p
7	**Total outlays**	131,172	158,258	†234,526	273,643	354,706	†425,386	35,128	74,219	†100,667	....	....	†519,641
701	**General public services**	45,010	51,960	†56,747	55,602	64,525	†55,241	6,308	7,801	†10,397	....	....	†61,613
7017	Public debt transactions	32,299	35,150	†35,096	32,446	35,763	†33,084	35	70	†155	....	....	†33,238
7018	General transfers between levels of govt	....	....	†3,265	....	....	†4,026	....	....	†—	....	....	†—
702	**Defense**	10,502	12,792	†20,908	13,548	18,056	†21,458	—		†—	....	....	†21,458
703	**Public order and safety**	14,690	20,652	†30,599	19,496	25,239	†34,556	562	886	†1,163	....	....	†35,719
704	**Economic affairs**	22,946	29,372	†58,908	38,404	49,286	†68,002	8,619	12,122	†12,152	....	....	†80,154
7042	Agriculture, forestry, fishing, and hunting	9,019	9,784	†11,932	9,256	11,818	†14,817	218	496	†728	....	....	†15,545
7043	Fuel and energy	3,066	4,105	†2,086	5,427	7,169	†6,111	—	—	†—	....	....	†6,111
7044	Mining, manufacturing, and construction	1,024	1,669	†6,935	1,198	1,671	†6,939	—	—	†—	....	....	†6,939
7045	Transport	8,489	11,930	†23,829	17,791	25,332	†27,646	7,840	11,235	†6,740	....	....	†34,386
7046	Communication	....	....	†8	....	....	†677	....	....	†—	....	....	†677
705	**Environmental protection**	....	....	†1,699	....	....	†1,895	....	....	†—	....	....	†1,895
706	**Housing and community amenities**	1,817	3,435	†8,873	2,139	6,626	†8,376	10,697	16,146	†23,976	....	....	†29,966
707	**Health**	2,824	4,739	†8,983	35,331	54,839	†59,337	59	83	†424	....	....	†59,761
7072	Outpatient services	1,056	2,857	†—	10,142	12,177	†16,237	....	....	†—	....	....	†16,237
7073	Hospital services	646	—	†4,083	20,571	25,574	†34,247	....	....	†—	....	....	†34,247
7074	Public health services	....	....	†4,900	....	....	†8,007	....	....	†424	....	....	†8,430
708	**Recreation, culture, and religion**	1,929	2,262	†4,284	3,246	4,007	†6,366	2,351	3,638	†5,852	....	....	†12,218
709	**Education**	19,659	9,206	†14,441	28,967	20,862	†27,900	2,570	27,038	†34,989	....	....	†62,890
7091	Pre-primary and primary education	....	....	†206	....	....	†206	....	....	†23,459	....	....	†23,665
7092	Secondary education	11,999	308	†1,504	14,015	1,263	†1,520	....	....	†11,300	....	....	†12,819
7094	Tertiary education	4,157	5,566	†8,051	9,741	14,112	†19,518	....	....	†1	....	....	†19,518
710	**Social protection**	11,915	23,923	†29,154	77,258	111,396	†142,350	4,116	6,957	†12,547	....	....	†154,898
7	Statistical discrepancy: Total outlays	−121	−83	†−70	−347	−131	†−97	−152	−451	†−833	....	....	†−930

Table 8 Transactions in financial assets and liabilities by sector

		Budgetary Central Government			Central Government			Local Government			General Government		
		2000	2001	2002p	2000	2001	2002p	2000	2001	2002p	2000	2001	2002p
82	**Net acquisition of financial assets**	....	....	†16,395	....	....	†9,194	....	....	†8	....	....	†9,202
821	Domestic	....	....	†16,395	....	....	†9,194	....	....	†8	....	....	†9,202
8211	General government	—	—	....	—	—	....	....	....	....	....	....	....
8212	Central bank	....	....	....	....	....	....	....	....	....	....	....	....
8213	Other depository corporations	....	....	....	....	....	....	....	....	....	....	....	....
8214	Financial corporations n.e.c.	....	....	....	....	....	....	....	....	....	....	....	....
8215	Nonfinancial corporations	−187	−1,246	†−70	−4,181	−7,589	†452	....	....	....	....	....	†452
8216	Households & NPIs serving households	....	....	....	....	....	....	....	....	....	....	....	....
822	Foreign	—	—	†—	—	—	†—	....	....	†—	....	....	†—
8221	General government	—	—	†—	—	—	†—	....	....	†—	....	....	†—
8227	International organizations	—	—	†—	—	—	†—	....	....	†—	....	....	†—
8228	Financial corporations other than international organizations	—	—	†—	—	—	†—	....	....	†—	....	....	†—
8229	Other nonresidents	—	—	†—	—	—	†—	....	....	†—	....	....	†—
823	Monetary gold and SDRs	—	—	†—	—	—	†—	....	....	†—	....	....	†—
83	**Net incurrence of liabilities**	....	....	†41,100	....	....	†31,765	....	....	†276	....	....	†32,041
831	Domestic	....	....	†15,344	....	....	†6,169	....	....	†426	....	....	†6,596
8311	General government	....	....	....	....	....	....	....	....	....	....	....	....
8312	Central bank	....	....	....	....	....	....	....	....	....	....	....	....
8313	Other depository corporations	....	....	....	....	....	....	....	....	....	....	....	....
8314	Financial corporations n.e.c.	....	....	....	....	....	....	....	....	....	....	....	....
8315	Nonfinancial corporations	....	....	....	....	....	....	....	....	....	....	....	....
8316	Households & NPIs serving households	....	....	....	....	....	....	....	....	....	....	....	....

In Billions of Lei / Year Ending December 31 / Noncash Reporter

		Budgetary Central Government			Central Government			Local Government			General Government		
		2000	2001	2002p	2000	2001	2002p	2000	2001	2002p	2000	2001	2002p
832	Foreign..................................	....	....	†25,757	....	....	†25,596	....	....	†−150	....	....	†25,445
8321	General government...............................	....	....	†−1,445	....	....	†−1,445	....	....	†—	....	....	†−1,445
8327	International organizations......................	....	....	†11,607	....	....	†11,447	....	....	†−135	....	....	†11,312
8328	Financial corporations other than international organizations..............	....	....	†13,912	....	....	†13,912	....	....	†−16	....	....	†13,896
8329	Other nonresidents.....................	....	....	†1,683	....	....	†1,683	....	....	†—	....	....	†1,683

Russian Federation 922

In Billions of Rubles / Year Ending December 31 / Noncash Reporter

	Budgetary Central Government			Central Government			Local Government			General Government		
	2002	2003	2004	2002	2003	2004	2002	2003	2004	2002	2003	2004
Statement of government operations												
1 Revenue..........	†2,220.9	2,579.9	3,410.4	†3,436.7	3,644.5	4,607.7	†2,268.4	2,017.5	2,610.5	†5,385.1	5,313.5	6,772.8
2 Expense..........	†1,339.3	2,102.9	2,659.7	†2,440.7	3,044.0	3,673.4	†1,888.9	1,654.9	2,138.0	†4,009.7	4,350.5	5,365.9
GOB *Gross operating balance*..........	*†881.7*	*477.0*	*1,015.1*	*†996.0*	*600.5*	*1,198.7*	*†379.5*	*362.5*	*603.4*	*†1,375.5*	*963.0*	*1,802.1*
NOB *Net operating balance*..........	....	....	*750.7*	....	....	....	....	....	*472.6*	....	....	....
31 Net acquisition of nonfinancial assets..........	†171.3	238.2	−40.1	†235.3	308.9	35.1	†393.0	404.2	385.5	†628.4	713.1	420.6
NLB *Net lending/borrowing*..........	*†710.4*	*238.7*	*790.8*	*†760.6*	*291.6*	*899.2*	*†−13.5*	*−41.6*	*87.1*	*†747.1*	*250.0*	*986.3*
32 Net acquisition of financial assets..........	†52.0	−132.8	562.5	†102.3	−79.9	670.9	†12.1	−21.5	158.1	†102.3	−107.7	828.1
33 Net incurrence of liabilities..........	†−658.4	−371.5	−228.3	†−658.4	−371.5	−228.3	†25.6	20.2	71.0	†−644.8	−357.7	−158.2
NLB Statistical discrepancy..........	†—	—	—	†—	—	—	†—	—	—	†—	—	—
Statement of other economic flows												
4 *Change in net worth from holding gains*..........	*−88.2*	*−389.9*	*−18.9*	*−88.2*	....	....	*−6.5*	*53.0*	*−1.2*	*−94.7*	....	....
41 Nonfinancial assets..........	—	—	—	—	....	....	—	—	—	—	....	....
42 Financial assets..........	102.9	−441.5	−105.2	102.9	....	....	—	54.4	.3	102.9	....	....
43 Liabilities..........	191.1	−51.6	−86.4	191.1	....	....	6.5	1.4	1.5	197.6	....	....
5 *Change in net worth from other volume changes*..........	*−490.9*	*3,770.1*	*3,487.1*	*−463.7*	....	....	*−34.1*	*1,685.3*	*−529.4*	*−497.7*	....	....
51 Nonfinancial assets..........	−32.6	3,828.0	3,382.1	−19.7	....	....	−38.3	1,716.3	−299.5	−58.1	....	....
52 Financial assets..........	95.2	29.5	185.3	121.1	....	....	4.4	.8	31.1	127.0	....	....
53 Liabilities..........	553.5	87.4	80.3	565.1	....	....	.1	31.7	261.1	566.7	....	....
Balance sheet												
6 *Net worth*..........	*†501.9*	*4,359.0*	*8,826.1*	*†1,089.8*	....	....	*†1,503.7*	*3,604.5*	*3,539.8*	*†2,593.5*	....	....
61 Nonfinancial assets..........	†1,032.6	5,098.9	8,705.3	†1,372.8	....	....	†1,493.2	3,613.7	3,737.8	†2,866.1	....	....
62 Financial assets..........	†3,881.6	3,336.8	3,965.0	†4,195.7	....	....	†239.9	273.5	370.9	†4,387.4	....	....
63 Liabilities..........	†4,412.3	4,076.6	3,844.3	†4,478.7	....	....	†229.9	282.7	568.9	†4,660.0	....	....
Statement of sources and uses of cash												
1 Cash receipts from operating activities..........	2,202.0	2,585.3	3,377.5	3,393.8	3,647.2	4,513.4	2,252.1	2,028.5	2,554.6	5,326.0	5,327.5	6,626.1
11 Taxes..........	1,481.7	1,775.7	2,240.9	1,474.7	1,753.7	2,180.0	1,103.9	1,231.1	1,690.4	2,578.7	2,979.7	3,866.7
12 Social contributions..........	340.4	365.5	437.9	1,275.3	1,107.8	1,258.9	—	—	—	1,275.3	1,107.8	1,258.9
13 Grants..........	.9	1.1	30.9	.9	1.1	30.9	318.3	341.8	407.3	—	—	—
14 Other receipts..........	379.0	443.0	667.7	642.9	784.5	1,043.6	829.9	455.6	456.9	1,472.0	1,239.9	1,500.5
2 Cash payments for operating activities..........	1,818.8	2,127.1	2,431.2	2,923.6	3,072.0	3,386.9	1,898.1	1,656.3	1,981.7	4,501.9	4,380.1	4,926.8
21 Compensation of employees..........	318.0	418.5	520.0	411.9	548.7	655.0	483.5	518.1	670.5	895.3	1,066.8	1,325.5
22 Purchases of goods and services..........	395.0	479.1	552.4	498.1	603.0	869.6	728.2	360.3	473.4	1,226.3	963.3	1,343.0
24 Interest..........	229.6	220.9	204.7	229.6	220.9	204.7	14.1	20.0	25.6	243.0	240.7	230.3
25 Subsidies..........	35.2	135.1	49.6	41.3	139.2	50.8	513.1	546.9	509.5	554.4	686.1	560.3
26 Grants..........	318.3	701.4	903.9	318.3	341.9	407.3	.9	1.0	30.9	—	—	—
27 Social benefits..........	510.8	157.0	180.8	1,404.0	1,194.7	1,235.9	149.3	179.5	245.0	1,553.4	1,374.2	1,480.8
28 Other payments..........	11.9	15.0	19.8	20.5	23.6	−36.5	9.0	30.5	26.9	29.5	49.0	−13.2
CIO *Net cash inflow from oper. activities*..........	*383.2*	*458.2*	*946.2*	*470.1*	*575.2*	*1,126.5*	*353.9*	*372.2*	*572.8*	*824.1*	*947.4*	*1,699.4*
31.1 Purchases of nonfinancial assets..........	246.7	256.2	268.8	324.4	325.3	339.8	409.2	403.9	515.7	733.6	729.3	855.5
31.2 Sales of nonfinancial assets..........	20.0	−4.3	31.5	20.0	−4.3	31.5	23.4	13.8	14.0	43.4	9.5	45.5
31 Net cash outflow from investments in nonfinancial assets..........	226.7	260.5	237.3	304.4	329.7	308.3	385.8	390.2	501.7	690.2	719.8	810.0
CSD *Cash surplus/deficit*..........	*156.6*	*197.8*	*709.0*	*165.7*	*245.5*	*818.2*	*−31.9*	*−17.9*	*71.1*	*133.8*	*227.6*	*889.3*
32x Net acquisition of fin assets, excl. cash..........	−17.0	−76.7	−63.5	−58.1	−81.7	−62.6	−2.0	49.9	−35.3	−72.1	−38.2	−98.8
321x Domestic..........	−4.4	−61.6	−64.1	−45.5	−66.6	−63.1	−2.0	49.9	−35.3	−59.5	−23.1	−99.3
322x Foreign..........	−12.6	−15.1	.6	−12.6	−15.1	.6	—	—	—	−12.6	−15.1	.6
323 Monetary gold and SDRs..........	—	—	—	—	—	—						
33 Net incurrence of liabilities..........	−104.6	−291.2	−148.0	−104.6	−291.2	−148.0	39.5	53.8	87.0	−77.1	−243.8	−61.9
331 Domestic..........	105.7	−.2	69.3	105.7	−.1	69.3	43.5	57.2	90.1	137.2	50.7	158.5
332 Foreign..........	−210.3	−291.1	−217.3	−210.3	−291.1	−217.3	−4.0	−3.4	−3.2	−214.3	−294.5	−220.5
NFB Net cash inflow from fin. activities..........	−87.6	−214.5	−84.5	−46.5	−209.5	−85.4	41.5	3.8	122.2	−5.0	−205.6	36.8
NCB *Net change in the stock of cash*..........	*69.0*	*−16.8*	*624.5*	*119.3*	*36.0*	*732.8*	*9.6*	*−14.1*	*193.4*	*128.9*	*21.9*	*926.1*
Table 1 Revenue												
1 **Revenue**..........	**†2,220.9**	**2,579.9**	**3,410.4**	**†3,436.7**	**3,644.5**	**4,607.7**	**†2,268.4**	**2,017.5**	**2,610.5**	**†5,385.1**	**5,313.5**	**6,772.8**
11 **Taxes**..........	**†1,481.7**	**1,775.7**	**2,270.9**	**†1,476.7**	**1,758.5**	**2,253.4**	**†1,105.4**	**1,231.1**	**1,715.3**	**†2,582.1**	**2,985.3**	**3,966.5**
111 Taxes on income, profits, & capital gains..........	†179.7	183.4	222.6	†174.7	166.3	205.1	†674.8	873.4	1,312.9	†849.5	1,035.4	1,515.8
1111 Individuals..........	†—	—	—	†—	—	—	†373.8	455.7	574.5	†373.8	455.7	574.5
1112 Corporations and other enterprises..........	†179.7	173.3	222.6	†174.7	152.6	197.8	†301.1	397.6	688.2	†475.7	545.8	883.8
112 Taxes on payroll and workforce..........	†—	—	—	†—	—	—	†—	—	—	†—	—	—
113 Taxes on property..........	†5.0	1.9	.1	†5.0	1.9	.1	†150.8	187.8	212.8	†155.7	189.7	212.9
114 Taxes on goods and services..........	†971.2	1,137.3	1,188.2	†971.2	1,137.3	1,188.2	†272.1	164.8	179.4	†1,243.3	1,302.1	1,367.5
1141 General taxes on goods and services..........	†752.7	882.1	1,069.7	†752.7	882.1	1,069.7	†50.1	56.4	6.2	†802.7	938.4	1,075.9
1142 Excises..........	†216.4	252.5	117.2	†216.4	252.5	117.2	†49.2	95.3	164.4	†265.6	347.8	281.6

In Billions of Rubles / Year Ending December 31 / Noncash Reporter

		Budgetary Central Government			Central Government			Local Government			General Government		
		2002	2003	2004	2002	2003	2004	2002	2003	2004	2002	2003	2004
115	Taxes on int'l. trade and transactions	†325.6	452.8	859.7	†325.6	452.8	859.7	†1.5	—	—	†327.1	452.8	859.7
116	Other taxes	†.3	.2	.3	†.3	.2	.3	†6.2	5.1	10.3	†6.5	5.3	10.6
12	**Social contributions**	†340.4	365.5	442.9	†1,275.3	1,107.8	1,263.9	†—	—	—	†1,275.3	1,107.8	1,263.9
121	Social security contributions	†340.4	365.5	442.9	†1,275.3	1,107.8	1,263.9	†—	—	—	†1,275.3	1,107.8	1,263.9
122	Other social contributions	†—	—	—	†—	—	—	†—	—	—	†—	—	—
13	**Grants**	†.9	1.1	35.9	†.9	1.1	35.9	†318.3	341.8	407.3	†—	—	—
131	From foreign governments	†—	—	—	†—	—	—	†—	—	—	†—	—	—
132	From international organizations	†—	—	—	†—	—	—	†—	—	—	†—	—	—
133	From other general government units	†.9	1.1	35.9	†.9	1.1	35.9	†318.3	341.8	407.3	†—	—	—
14	**Other revenue**	†397.9	437.6	660.6	†683.7	777.0	1,054.5	†844.7	444.5	487.9	†1,527.7	1,220.4	1,542.3

Table 2 Expense by economic type

		2002	2003	2004	2002	2003	2004	2002	2003	2004	2002	2003	2004
2	**Expense**	†1,339.3	2,102.9	2,659.7	†2,440.7	3,044.0	3,673.4	†1,888.9	1,654.9	2,138.0	†4,009.7	4,350.5	5,365.9
21	**Compensation of employees**	†320.0	419.5	518.5	†412.9	548.4	651.0	†483.9	531.7	662.5	†896.8	1,080.1	1,313.5
211	Wages and salaries	†273.2	363.8	449.3	†348.2	470.0	556.6	†365.6	404.7	505.6	†713.8	874.7	1,062.2
212	Social contributions	†46.8	55.7	69.2	†64.7	78.3	94.4	†118.3	127.0	156.9	†183.1	205.4	251.3
22	**Use of goods and services**	†364.6	460.9	538.6	†465.2	582.7	848.4	†729.5	359.0	472.1	†1,194.7	941.7	1,320.5
23	**Consumption of fixed capital**	....	....	264.4	....	....	....	....	....	130.9	....	....	1,320.5
24	**Interest**	†222.6	218.5	185.9	†222.6	218.5	185.9	†14.1	20.0	25.6	†236.0	237.3	211.5
25	**Subsidies**	†35.4	135.1	49.1	†41.7	139.0	50.4	†513.2	547.0	510.4	†554.8	686.0	560.8
26	**Grants**	†318.3	701.3	903.9	†318.3	341.8	407.3	†.9	1.1	35.9	†—	—	—
261	To foreign governments	†—	—	—	†—	—	—	†—	—	—	†—	—	—
262	To international organizations	†—	—	—	†—	—	—	†—	—	—	†—	—	—
263	To other general government units	†318.3	701.3	903.9	†318.3	341.8	407.3	†.9	1.1	35.9	†—	—	—
2631	Current	†318.0	701.0	833.3	†318.0	341.5	336.7	†.9	1.1	35.9	†—	—	—
2632	Capital	†.2	.4	70.6	†.2	.4	70.6	†—	—	—	†—	—	—
27	**Social benefits**	†70.1	156.5	179.3	†963.1	1,194.1	1,234.2	†138.2	170.3	296.5	†1,101.3	1,364.4	1,530.7
28	**Other expense**	†8.3	11.1	20.0	†16.9	19.6	31.9	†9.0	25.7	4.1	†26.0	41.1	33.8
281	Property expense other than interest	†—	—	—	†—	—	—	†—	—	—	†—	—	—
282	Miscellaneous other expense	†8.3	11.1	20.0	†16.9	19.6	31.9	†9.0	25.7	4.1	†26.0	41.1	33.8
2821	Current	†—	10.9	16.3	†7.2	19.4	28.2	†—	25.7	4.1	†7.2	40.8	30.1
2822	Capital	†8.3	.2	3.7	†9.7	.2	3.7	†9.0	—	—	†18.7	.2	3.7

Table 3 Transactions in assets and liabilities

		2002	2003	2004	2002	2003	2004	2002	2003	2004	2002	2003	2004
3	**Change in net worth from transactns**	....	....	750.7	....	....	....	....	....	472.6	....	....	....
31	**Net acquisition of nonfinancial assets**	†171.3	238.2	−40.1	†235.3	308.9	35.1	†393.0	404.2	385.5	†628.4	713.1	420.6
311	Fixed assets	†109.3	137.8	−118.4	†136.3	170.3	−85.1	†255.0	283.0	242.7	†391.2	453.2	157.7
3111	Buildings and structures	....	106.2	106.2	....	124.2	118.9	....	218.4	306.4	....	342.6	425.4
3112	Machinery and equipment	....	31.3	39.3	....	45.7	53.4	....	64.6	67.0	....	110.3	120.4
3113	Other fixed assets	....	.3	−263.9	....	.4	−257.4	....	—	−130.7	....	.4	−388.1
312	Inventories	†78.5	92.4	104.4	†115.6	130.6	146.2	†149.3	121.2	142.7	†264.9	251.8	289.0
313	Valuables	†−14.6	8.1	−26.0	†−14.6	8.1	−26.0	†—	—	—	†−14.6	8.1	−26.0
314	Nonproduced assets	†−2.0	—	—	†−2.0	—	—	†−11.3	—	—	†−13.2	—	—
3141	Land	....			....			....			....		
3142	Subsoil assets	....			....			....			....		
3143	Other naturally occurring assets	....			....			....			....		
3144	Intangible nonproduced assets	....			....			....			....		
32	**Net acquisition of financial assets**	†52.0	−132.8	562.5	†102.3	−79.9	670.9	†12.1	−21.5	158.1	†102.3	−107.7	828.1
321	Domestic	†64.6	−116.8	558.9	†114.9	−63.9	667.3	†12.1	−21.5	158.1	†115.0	−91.8	824.5
3212	Currency and deposits	†69.0	−16.8	624.5	†119.3	36.0	732.8	†9.6	−14.1	193.4	†128.9	21.9	926.1
3213	Securities other than shares	†—	—	—	†—	—	—	†—	—	—	†—	—	—
3214	Loans	†4.1	−6.0	3.6	†4.1	−5.9	3.6	†12.1	19.0	−1.9	†4.2	6.7	.7
3215	Shares and other equity	†−8.5	−94.1	−69.2	†−8.5	−94.1	−69.1	†−9.6	−26.4	−33.3	†−18.1	−120.4	−102.4
3216	Insurance technical reserves	†—	—	—	†—	—	—	†—	—	—	†—	—	—
3217	Financial derivatives	†—	—	—	†—	—	—	†—	—	—	†—	—	—
3218	Other accounts receivable	†—	—	—	†—	—	—	†—	—	—	†—	—	—
322	Foreign	†−12.6	−16.0	3.6	†−12.6	−16.0	3.6	†—	—	—	†−12.6	−16.0	3.6
3222	Currency and deposits	†—	—	—	†—	—	—	†—	—	—	†—	—	—
3223	Securities other than shares	†—	—	—	†—	—	—	†—	—	—	†—	—	—
3224	Loans	†−12.6	−16.0	3.6	†−12.6	−16.0	3.6	†—	—	—	†−12.6	−16.0	3.6
3225	Shares and other equity	†—	—	—	†—	—	—	†—	—	—	†—	—	—
3226	Insurance technical reserves	†—	—	—	†—	—	—	†—	—	—	†—	—	—
3227	Financial derivatives	†—	—	—	†—	—	—	†—	—	—	†—	—	—
3228	Other accounts receivable	†—	—	—	†—	—	—	†—	—	—	†—	—	—
323	Monetary gold and SDRs	†—	—	—	†—	—	—	†—	—	—	†—	—	—

In Billions of Rubles / Year Ending December 31 / Noncash Reporter

		Budgetary Central Government			Central Government			Local Government			General Government		
		2002	2003	2004	2002	2003	2004	2002	2003	2004	2002	2003	2004
33	Net incurrence of liabilities..................	†−658.4	−371.5	−228.3	†−658.4	−371.5	−228.3	†25.6	20.2	71.0	†−644.8	−357.7	−158.2
331	Domestic............................	†−448.0	−80.5	−11.0	†−448.0	−80.4	−11.0	†29.6	23.6	74.2	†−430.4	−63.2	62.3
3312	Currency and deposits.............	†—	—	—	†—	—	—	†—	—	—	†—	—	—
3313	Securities other than shares........	†129.0	25.9	96.1	†129.0	25.9	96.1	†17.2	41.9	94.8	†146.2	67.8	190.9
3314	Loans...............................	†−23.2	—	—	†−23.2	—	—	†26.3	18.8	4.0	†−8.9	12.4	3.1
3316	Insurance technical reserves........	†—	—	—	†—	—	—	†—	—	—	†—	—	—
3317	Financial derivatives...............	†—	—	—	†—	—	—	†—	—	—	†—	—	—
3318	Other accounts payable.............	†−553.8	−106.4	−107.1	†−553.8	−106.4	−107.1	†−13.9	−37.1	−24.5	†−567.7	−143.5	−131.7
332	Foreign...........................	†−210.3	−291.1	−217.3	†−210.3	−291.1	−217.3	†−4.0	−3.4	−3.2	†−214.3	−294.5	−220.5
3322	Currency and deposits.............	†—	—	—	†—	—	—	†—	—	—	†—	—	—
3323	Securities other than shares........	†—	—	—	†—	—	—	†—	—	—	†—	—	—
3324	Loans...............................	†−210.3	−291.1	−217.3	†−210.3	−291.1	−217.3	†−4.0	−3.4	−3.2	†−214.3	−294.5	−220.5
3326	Insurance technical reserves........	†—	—	—	†—	—	—	†—	—	—	†—	—	—
3327	Financial derivatives...............	†—	—	—	†—	—	—	†—	—	—	†—	—	—
3328	Other accounts payable.............	†—	—	—	†—	—	—	†—	—	—	†—	—	—

Table 4 Holding gains in assets and liabilities

		Budgetary Central Government			Central Government			Local Government			General Government		
4	Change in net worth from hold. gains...	−88.2	−389.9	−18.9	−88.2	....	....	−6.5	53.0	−1.2	−94.7	....	....
41	Nonfinancial assets.........................	—	—	—	—	....	....	—	—	—	—	....	....
411	Fixed assets......................	—	—	—	—	....	....	—	—	—	—	....	....
412	Inventories.......................	—	—	—	—	....	....	—	—	—	—	....	....
413	Valuables.........................	—	—	—	—	....	....	—	—	—	—	....	....
414	Nonproduced assets................	—	—	—	—	....	....	—	—	—	—	....	....
42	Financial assets...........................	102.9	−441.5	−105.2	102.9	....	....	—	54.4	.3	102.9	....	....
421	Domestic.........................	.4	26.0	52.3	.4	....	....	—	54.4	.3	.4	....	....
422	Foreign...........................	102.5	−467.6	−157.5	102.5	....	....	—	—	—	102.5	....	....
423	Monetary gold and SDRs............	—	—	—	—	....	....	—	—	—	—	....	....
43	Liabilities................................	191.1	−51.6	−86.4	191.1	....	....	6.5	1.4	1.5	197.6	....	....
431	Domestic.........................	—	—	—	—	....	....	—	—	—	—	....	....
432	Foreign...........................	191.1	−51.6	−86.4	191.1	....	....	6.5	1.4	1.5	197.6	....	....

Table 5 Other changes in the volume of assets and liabilities

		Budgetary Central Government			Central Government			Local Government			General Government		
5	Change in net worth from vol. chngs.....	−490.9	3,770.1	3,487.1	−463.7	....	....	−34.1	1,685.3	−529.4	−497.7	....	....
51	Nonfinancial assets.........................	−32.6	3,828.0	3,382.1	−19.7	....	....	−38.3	1,716.3	−299.5	−58.1	....	....
511	Fixed assets......................	16.6	3,164.1	1,731.9	31.2	....	....	44.4	1,630.0	−160.8	75.6	....	....
512	Inventories.......................	−65.7	671.9	1,624.2	−67.4	....	....	−94.0	86.3	−138.7	−161.5	....	....
513	Valuables.........................	14.6	−8.1	26.0	14.6	....	....	11.3	—	—	14.6	....	....
514	Nonproduced assets................	2.0	—	—	2.0	....	....	—	—	—	13.2	....	....
52	Financial assets...........................	95.2	29.5	185.3	121.1	....	....	4.4	.8	31.1	127.0	....	....
521	Domestic.........................	95.2	29.5	185.3	121.1	....	....	4.4	.8	31.1	127.0	....	....
522	Foreign...........................	—	—	—	—	....	....	—	—	—	—	....	....
523	Monetary gold and SDRs............	—	—	—	—	....	....	—	—	—	—	....	....
53	Liabilities................................	553.5	87.4	80.3	565.1	....	....	.1	31.7	261.1	566.7	....	....
531	Domestic.........................	553.5	87.6	80.3	565.1	....	....	.1	31.7	261.1	566.7	....	....
532	Foreign...........................	—	−.2	—	—	....	....	—	—	—	—	....	....

Table 6 Balance sheet

		Budgetary Central Government			Central Government			Local Government			General Government		
6	Net worth...........................	†501.9	4,359.0	8,826.1	†1,089.8	....	....	†1,503.7	3,604.5	3,539.8	†2,593.5	....	....
61	Nonfinancial assets.........................	†1,032.6	5,098.9	8,705.3	†1,372.8	....	96.1	†1,493.2	3,613.7	3,737.8	†2,866.1	....	....
611	Fixed assets......................	†992.4	4,294.4	6,976.7	†1,151.6	....	....	†1,241.3	3,154.4	3,703.8	†2,392.9	....	....
6111	Buildings and structures.............	†960.2	4,252.3	6,923.5	†1,104.5	....	....	†1,151.7	3,068.0	3,238.4	†2,256.2	....	....
6112	Machinery and equipment.............	†26.0	31.3	39.3	†38.4	....	....	†77.3	64.6	416.3	†115.7	....	....
6113	Other fixed assets...................	†6.3	10.8	14.0	†8.6	....	....	†12.3	21.7	49.1	†20.9	....	....
612	Inventories........................	†40.2	804.5	1,728.6	†221.3	....	....	†251.9	459.3	34.0	†473.2	....	....
613	Valuables.........................	†—	—	—	†—	....	....	†—	—	—	†—	....	....
614	Nonproduced assets................	†—	—	—	†—	....	....	†—	—	—	†—	....	....
6141	Land.............................	†—	—	—	†—	....	....	†—	—	—	†—	....	....
6142	Subsoil assets.....................	†—	—	—	†—	....	....	†—	—	—	†—	....	....
6143	Other naturally occurring assets.......	†—	—	—	†—	....	....	†—	—	—	†—	....	....
6144	Intangible nonproduced assets........	†—	—	—	†—	....	....	†—	—	—	†—	....	....

In Billions of Rubles / Year Ending December 31 / Noncash Reporter

		Budgetary Central Government			Central Government			Local Government			General Government		
		2002	2003	2004	2002	2003	2004	2002	2003	2004	2002	2003	2004
62	**Financial assets**.....................	†3,881.6	3,336.8	3,965.0	†4,195.7	....	....	†239.9	273.5	370.9	†4,387.4	....	....
621	Domestic......................	†859.9	798.7	1,580.8	†1,174.0	....	....	†239.9	273.5	370.9	†1,365.8	....	....
6212	Currency and deposits.........	†268.8	281.5	952.6	†477.7	....	....	†106.5	128.6	231.2	†584.2	....	....
6213	Securities other than shares......	†—	—	—	†4.1	....	....	†—	—	—	†4.1	....	....
6214	Loans..............................	†327.5	275.6	337.7	†327.5	....	....	†133.4	145.0	139.7	†412.7	....	....
6215	Shares and other equity.........	†45.3	45.2	1.5	†46.6	....	....	†—	—	—	†46.6	....	....
6216	Insurance technical reserves......	†—	—	—	†—	....	....	†—	—	—	†—	....	....
6217	Financial derivatives.............	†—	—	—	†—	....	....	†—	—	—	†—	....	....
6218	Other accounts receivable........	†218.4	196.3	289.0	†318.2	....	....	†—	—	—	†318.2	....	....
622	Foreign........................	†3,021.7	2,538.1	2,384.2	†3,021.7	....	....	†—	—	—	†3,021.7	....	....
6222	Currency and deposits.........	†—	—	—	†—	....	....	†—	—	—	†—	....	....
6223	Securities other than shares......	†—	—	—	†—	....	....	†—	—	—	†—	....	....
6224	Loans..............................	†3,021.7	2,538.1	2,384.2	†3,021.7	....	....	†—	—	—	†3,021.7	....	....
6225	Shares and other equity.........	†—	—	—	†—	....	....	†—	—	—	†—	....	....
6226	Insurance technical reserves......	†—	—	—	†—	....	....	†—	—	—	†—	....	....
6227	Financial derivatives.............	†—	—	—	†—	....	....	†—	—	—	†—	....	....
6228	Other accounts receivable........	†—	—	—	†—	....	....	†—	—	—	†—	....	....
623	Monetary gold and SDRs.........	†—	—	—	†—	....	....	†—	—	—	†—	....	....
63	**Liabilities**...................	†4,412.3	4,076.6	3,844.3	†4,478.7	....	....	†229.5	282.7	568.9	†4,660.0	....	....
631	Domestic......................	†727.1	734.2	833.3	†793.5	....	....	†193.9	249.1	537.0	†939.2	....	....
6312	Currency and deposits.........	†—	—	—	†—	....	....	†—	—	—	†—	....	....
6313	Securities other than shares......	†671.3	681.5	756.8	†671.3	....	....	†35.0	77.3	124.9	†706.3	....	....
6314	Loans..............................	†−23.2	—	—	†−23.2	....	....	†91.3	105.7	362.0	†19.9	....	....
6316	Insurance technical reserves......	†—	—	—	†—	....	....	†—	—	—	†—	....	....
6317	Financial derivatives.............	†—	—	—	†—	....	....	†—	—	—	†—	....	....
6318	Other accounts payable..........	†79.0	52.8	76.5	†145.4	....	....	†67.6	66.2	50.2	†213.0	....	....
632	Foreign........................	†3,685.2	3,342.4	3,011.0	†3,685.2	....	....	†35.6	33.6	31.9	†3,720.8	....	....
6322	Currency and deposits.........	†—	—	—	†—	....	....	†—	—	—	†—	....	....
6323	Securities other than shares......	†—	—	—	†—	....	....	†—	—	—	†—	....	....
6324	Loans..............................	†3,685.2	3,342.4	3,011.0	†3,685.2	....	....	†35.6	33.6	31.9	†3,720.8	....	....
6326	Insurance technical reserves......	†—	—	—	†—	....	....	†—	—	—	†—	....	....
6327	Financial derivatives.............	†—	—	—	†—	....	....	†—	—	—	†—	....	....
6328	Other accounts payable..........	†—	—	—	†—	....	....	†—	—	—	†—	....	....
	Memorandum items:												
6M2	Net financial worth...........	†−530.8	−739.8	120.7	†−283.0	....	....	†10.4	−9.2	−198.0	†−272.6	....	....
6M3	Debt at market value...........	....	....	....	....	....	....	....	....	....	....	....	....
6M4	Debt at nominal value...........	....	....	....	....	....	....	....	....	....	....	....	....
6M5	Arrears.....................	....	....	....	....	....	....	....	....	....	....	....	....
6M6	Obligations for social security benefits........	....	....	....	....	....	....	....	....	....	....	....	....
6M7	Contingent liabilities...........	....	....	....	....	....	....	....	....	....	....	....	....
6M8	Uncapitalized military weapons, systems.......	....	....	....	....	....	....	....	....	....	....	....	....
	Table 7 Outlays by functions of govt.												
7	**Total outlays**.....................	†1,530.6	2,336.8	2,619.6	†2,696.0	3,348.6	3,708.5	†2,305.3	2,072.9	2,523.4	†4,681.4	5,073.0	5,786.5
701	**General public services**..................	†687.6	1,237.0	1,266.7	†936.8	1,177.3	1,081.0	†851.5	355.6	483.4	†1,468.5	1,184.5	1,119.0
7017	Public debt transactions..................	†222.6	218.5	185.9	†222.6	218.5	185.9	†14.1	20.0	25.6	†236.0	237.3	211.5
7018	General transfers between levels of govt......	†318.3	701.3	903.9	†318.3	341.8	407.3	†.9	1.1	35.9	†—	....	....
702	**Defense**....................	†314.9	381.8	446.4	†314.9	381.8	446.4	†.3	.4	.5	†315.2	382.2	446.9
703	**Public order and safety**..................	†196.2	273.4	355.7	†196.2	273.4	355.7	†56.3	78.5	96.4	†252.5	351.8	452.1
704	**Economic affairs**.....................	†147.3	163.8	188.4	†147.3	163.8	188.4	†440.1	515.1	562.2	†587.4	678.8	750.6
7042	Agriculture, forestry, fishing, and hunting.....	†27.3	31.8	35.3	†27.3	31.8	35.3	†28.3	34.1	43.8	†55.7	65.9	79.1
7043	Fuel and energy.....................	†22.4	22.3	20.6	†22.4	22.3	20.6	†5.6	5.4	5.4	†28.0	27.7	26.0
7044	Mining, manufacturing, and construction.....	†52.9	59.8	75.5	†52.9	59.8	75.5	†213.5	260.6	311.6	†266.3	320.3	387.1
7045	Transport.....................	†44.0	48.2	54.6	†44.0	48.2	54.6	†188.4	209.6	192.3	†232.4	257.8	246.9
7046	Communication.....................	†.7	1.7	2.5	†.7	1.7	2.5	†2.0	2.4	5.5	†2.7	4.1	8.0
705	**Environmental protection**..................	†9.7	11.3	12.4	†9.7	11.3	12.4	†9.3	7.8	6.7	†19.0	19.1	19.1
706	**Housing and community amenities**........	†—	—	—	†—	—	—	†221.9	254.1	291.7	†221.9	254.1	291.7
707	**Health**.....................	†29.5	38.2	46.0	†29.5	38.2	46.0	†210.0	201.5	242.4	†239.5	239.7	288.3
7072	Outpatient services.....................	....	....	....	....	....	....	....	....	....	....	....	....
7073	Hospital services.....................	....	....	....	....	....	....	....	....	....	....	....	....
7074	Public health services.....................	....	....	....	....	....	....	....	....	....	....	....	....
708	**Recreation, culture, and religion**...........	†20.0	28.7	76.4	†20.0	28.7	76.4	†58.8	71.7	88.1	†78.8	100.4	164.5

Russian Federation 922

In Billions of Rubles / Year Ending December 31 / Noncash Reporter

	Budgetary Central Government			Central Government			Local Government			General Government		
	2002	2003	2004	2002	2003	2004	2002	2003	2004	2002	2003	2004
709 **Education**	†81.6	100.4	121.4	†81.6	100.4	121.4	†326.8	381.3	466.8	†408.5	481.7	588.2
7091 Pre-primary and primary education	†1.9	2.4	1.7	†1.9	2.4	1.7	†275.6	306.3	388.1	†277.5	308.7	389.8
7092 Secondary education	†18.5	21.5	24.3	†18.5	21.5	24.3	†8.3	8.9	11.2	†26.7	30.4	35.5
7094 Tertiary education	†56.4	71.3	89.1	†56.4	71.3	89.1	†15.0	17.8	22.8	†71.4	89.1	111.9
710 **Social protection**	†43.8	102.3	106.0	†960.0	1,173.8	1,380.7	†130.2	216.1	285.3	†1,090.3	1,389.9	1,666.0
7 Statistical discrepancy: Total outlays	†—	—	—	†—	—	—	†—	−9.2	—	†—	−9.2	—

Table 8 Transactions in financial assets and liabilities by sector

	Budgetary Central Government			Central Government			Local Government			General Government		
	2002	2003	2004	2002	2003	2004	2002	2003	2004	2002	2003	2004
82 **Net acquisition of financial assets**	†52.0	−132.8	562.5	†102.3	−79.9	670.9	†12.1	−21.5	158.1	†102.3	−107.7	828.1
821 Domestic	†64.6	−116.8	558.9	†114.9	−63.9	667.3	†12.1	−21.5	158.1	†115.0	−91.8	824.5
8211 General government	†12.0	−.6	−3.6	†12.0	−.6	−3.6	†—	7.0	.9	†—	—	−2.7
8212 Central bank	....	....	....	....	....	....	....	....	....	†−5.7	−11.9	−3.8
8213 Other depository corporations	†−5.7	−11.9	−3.8	†−5.7	−11.9	−3.8	†—	—	—	....	....	....
8214 Financial corporations n.e.c.	....	....	....	....	....	....	....	....	....	....	....	....
8215 Nonfinancial corporations	†−.3	−.4	−.6	†−.3	−.4	−.6	†−.3	.6	.7	†−.6	.2	.1
8216 Households & NPIs serving households	....	....	....	....	....	....	....	....	....	....	....	....
822 Foreign	†−12.6	−16.0	3.6	†−12.6	−16.0	3.6	†—	—	—	†−12.6	−16.0	3.6
8221 General government	†−12.6	−16.0	3.6	†−12.6	−16.0	3.6	†—	—	—	†−12.6	−16.0	3.6
8227 International organizations	†—	—	—	†—	—	—	†—	—	—	†—	—	—
8228 Financial corporations other than international organizations	†—	—	—	†—	—	—	†—	—	—	†—	—	—
8229 Other nonresidents	†—	—	—	†—	—	—	†—	—	—	†—	—	—
823 Monetary gold and SDRs												
83 **Net incurrence of liabilities**	†−658.4	−371.5	−228.3	†−658.4	−371.5	−228.3	†25.6	20.2	71.0	†−644.8	−357.7	−158.2
831 Domestic	†−448.0	−80.5	−11.0	†−448.0	−80.4	−11.0	†29.6	23.6	74.2	†−430.4	−63.2	62.3
8311 General government	....	....	....	....	....	....	....	....	....	....	....	....
8312 Central bank	....	....	....	....	....	....	....	....	....	....	....	....
8313 Other depository corporations	....	....	....	....	....	....	....	....	....	....	....	....
8314 Financial corporations n.e.c.	....	....	....	....	....	....	....	....	....	....	....	....
8315 Nonfinancial corporations	....	....	....	....	....	....	....	....	....	....	....	....
8316 Households & NPIs serving households	....	....	....	....	....	....	....	....	....	....	....	....
832 Foreign	†−210.3	−291.1	−217.3	†−210.3	−291.1	−217.3	†−4.0	−3.4	−3.2	†−214.3	−294.5	−220.5
8321 General government	†−134.0	−115.0	−102.1	†−134.0	−115.0	−102.1	†—	—	—	†−134.0	−115.0	−102.1
8327 International organizations	†−56.5	−71.0	−61.7	†−56.5	−71.0	−61.7	†—	—	—	†−56.5	−71.0	−61.7
8328 Financial corporations other than international organizations	†−.2	−51.5	−53.3	†−.2	−51.5	−53.3	†—	−4.1	−1.0	†−.2	−55.7	−54.4
8329 Other nonresidents	†−19.6	−53.5	−.1	†−19.6	−53.5	−.1	†−4.0	.7	−2.1	†−23.6	−52.8	−2.3

2005, International Monetary Fund: *Government Finance Statistics Yearbook*

In Millions of Dollars / Year Ending December 31 / Cash Reporter

	Budgetary Central Government			Extrabudgetary Accounts			Central Government			General Government		
	2001	2002	2003	2001	2002	2003	2001	2002	2003	2001	2002	2003
Statement of government operations												
Statement of other economic flows												
Balance sheet												
Statement of sources and uses of cash												
1 Cash receipts from operating activities	....	....	322.1	....	....	....	....	....	372.9	....	....	372.9
11 Taxes	....	....	234.1	....	....	....	....	....	234.1	....	....	234.2
12 Social contributions	....	....	—	....	....	....	....	....	48.0	....	....	48.0
13 Grants	....	....	.4	....	....	....	....	....	.4	....	....	.4
14 Other receipts	....	....	87.6	....	....	....	....	....	90.4	....	....	90.3
2 Cash payments for operating activities	....	....	333.2	....	....	....	....	....	360.6	....	....	360.6
21 Compensation of employees	....	....	144.1	....	....	....	....	....	148.0	....	....	148.0
22 Purchases of goods and services	....	....	71.0	....	....	....	....	....	73.5	....	....	73.5
24 Interest	....	....	74.5	....	....	....	....	....	74.5	....	....	74.5
25 Subsidies	....	....	—	....	....	....	....	....	—	....	....	—
26 Grants	....	....	14.0	....	....	....	....	....	14.0	....	....	14.0
27 Social benefits	....	....	17.8	....	....	....	....	....	38.4	....	....	38.4
28 Other payments	....	....	11.8	....	....	....	....	....	12.2	....	....	12.2
CIO *Net cash inflow from oper. activities*	....	....	*−11.1*	....	....	....	....	....	*12.3*	....	....	*12.3*
31.1 Purchases of nonfinancial assets	....	....	58.4	....	....	....	....	....	58.4	....	....	58.4
31.2 Sales of nonfinancial assets	....	....	2.0	....	....	....	....	....	2.0	....	....	2.0
31 Net cash outflow from investments in nonfinancial assets	....	....	56.5	....	....	....	....	....	56.5	....	....	56.4
CSD *Cash surplus/deficit*	....	....	*−67.5*	....	....	....	....	....	*−44.2*	....	....	*−44.1*
32x Net acquisition of fin assets, excl. cash	....	....	....	....	....	....	....	....	....	....	....	....
321x Domestic	....	....	....	....	....	....	....	....	....	....	....	....
322x Foreign	....	....	....	....	....	....	....	....	....	....	....	....
323 Monetary gold and SDRs	....	....	....	....	....	....	....	....	....	....	....	....
33 Net incurrence of liabilities	....	....	....	....	....	....	....	....	....	....	....	....
331 Domestic	....	....	....	....	....	....	....	....	....	....	....	....
332 Foreign	....	....	....	....	....	....	....	....	....	....	....	....
NFB Net cash inflow from fin. activities	....	....	....	....	....	....	....	....	....	....	....	....
NCB *Net change in the stock of cash*	....	....	....	....	....	....	....	....	....	....	....	....
Table 1 Revenue												
1 **Revenue**	....	....	**322.1**	....	....	....	....	....	**372.9**	....	....	**372.9**
11 **Taxes**	....	....	**234.1**	....	....	....	....	....	**234.1**	....	....	**234.1**
111 Taxes on income, profits, & capital gains	....	....	42.7	....	....	....	....	....	42.7	....	....	42.7
1111 Individuals	....	....	.8	....	....	....	....	....	.8	....	....	.8
1112 Corporations and other enterprises	....	....	41.9	....	....	....	....	....	41.9	....	....	41.9
112 Taxes on payroll and workforce	....	....	21.3	....	....	....	....	....	21.3	....	....	21.3
113 Taxes on property	....	....	5.2	....	....	....	....	....	5.2	....	....	5.2
114 Taxes on goods and services	....	....	31.5	....	....	....	....	....	31.5	....	....	31.5
1141 General taxes on goods and services	....	....	2.1	....	....	....	....	....	2.1	....	....	2.1
1142 Excises	....	....	3.1	....	....	....	....	....	3.1	....	....	3.1
115 Taxes on int'l. trade and transactions	....	....	116.6	....	....	....	....	....	116.6	....	....	116.6
116 Other taxes	....	....	16.7	....	....	....	....	....	16.7	....	....	16.7
12 **Social contributions**	....	....	**—**	....	....	....	....	....	**48.0**	....	....	**48.0**
121 Social security contributions	....	....	—	....	....	....	....	....	48.0	....	....	48.0
122 Other social contributions	....	....	—	....	....	....	....	....	—	....	....	—
13 **Grants**	....	....	**.4**	....	....	....	....	....	**.4**	....	....	**.4**
131 From foreign governments	....	....	.4	....	....	....	....	....	.4	....	....	.4
132 From international organizations	....	....	—	....	....	....	....	....	—	....	....	—
133 From other general government units	....	....	—	....	....	....	....	....	—	....	....	—
14 **Other revenue**	....	....	**87.6**	....	....	....	....	....	**90.4**	....	....	**90.4**
Table 2 Expense by economic type												
2 **Expense**	....	....	**333.2**	....	....	....	....	....	**360.6**	....	....	**360.6**
21 **Compensation of employees**	....	....	**144.1**	....	....	....	....	....	**148.0**	....	....	**148.0**
211 Wages and salaries	....	....	129.4	....	....	....	....	....	133.3	....	....	133.3
212 Social contributions	....	....	14.7	....	....	....	....	....	14.7	....	....	14.7
22 **Use of goods and services**	....	....	**71.0**	....	....	....	....	....	**73.5**	....	....	**73.5**
23 **Consumption of fixed capital**	....	....	....	....	....	....	....	....	....	....	....	....
24 **Interest**	....	....	**74.4**	....	....	....	....	....	**74.4**	....	....	**74.4**
25 **Subsidies**	....	....	**—**	....	....	....	....	....	**—**	....	....	**—**

St. Kitts and Nevis   361

In Millions of Dollars / Year Ending December 31 / Cash Reporter

	Budgetary Central Government			Extrabudgetary Accounts			Central Government			General Government		
	2001	2002	2003	2001	2002	2003	2001	2002	2003	2001	2002	2003
26 **Grants**....................	....	....	**14.0**	....	....	....	....	....	**14.0**	....	....	**14.0**
261 To foreign govenments.....................	....	....	—	....	....	....	....	....	—	....	....	—
262 To international organizations....................	....	....	—	....	....	....	....	....	—	....	....	—
263 To other general government units..............	....	....	14.0	....	....	....	....	....	14.0	....	....	14.0
2631 Current.....................	....	....	14.0	....	....	....	....	....	14.0	....	....	14.0
2632 Capital.....................	....	....	—	....	....	....	....	....	—	....	....	—
27 **Social benefits**....................	....	....	**17.8**	....	....	....	....	....	**38.4**	....	....	**38.4**
28 **Other expense**....................	....	....	**11.8**	....	....	....	....	....	**12.2**	....	....	**12.2**
281 Property expense other than interest..........	....	....	—	....	....	....	....	....	—	....	....	—
282 Miscellaneous other expense.....................	....	....	11.8	....	....	....	....	....	12.2	....	....	12.2
2821 Current.....................	....	....	11.8	....	....	....	....	....	11.8	....	....	11.8
2822 Capital.....................	....	....	—	....	....	....	....	....	.5	....	....	.5

Table 3 Transactions in assets and liabilities

	Budgetary Central Government			Extrabudgetary Accounts			Central Government			General Government		
3 **Change in net worth from transactns....**	....	....	....	....	....	....	....	....	....	....	....	....
31 **Net acquisition of nonfinancial assets...**	....	....	**56.5**	....	....	....	....	....	....	....	....	....
311 Fixed assets...................	....	....	58.4	....	....	....	....	....	....	....	....	....
3111 Buildings and structures...............	....	....	....	....	....	....	....	....	....	....	....	....
3112 Machinery and equipment..........	....	....	....	....	....	....	....	....	....	....	....	....
3113 Other fixed assets...............	....	....	−.3	....	....	....	....	....	....	....	....	....
312 Inventories...................	....	....	—	....	....	....	....	....	....	....	....	....
313 Valuables....................	....	....	—	....	....	....	....	....	....	....	....	....
314 Nonproduced assets.................	....	....	−2.0	....	....	....	....	....	....	....	....	....
3141 Land...................	....	....	−2.0	....	....	....	....	....	....	....	....	....
3142 Subsoil assets................	....	....	—	....	....	....	....	....	....	....	....	....
3143 Other naturally occurring assets..............	....	....	—	....	....	....	....	....	....	....	....	....
3144 Intangible nonproduced assets..........	....	....	—	....	....	....	....	....	....	....	....	....
32 **Net acquisition of financial assets.........**	....	....	....	....	....	....	....	....	....	....	....	....
321 Domestic....................	....	....	....	....	....	....	....	....	....	....	....	....
3212 Currency and deposits.....................	....	....	....	....	....	....	....	....	....	....	....	....
3213 Securities other than shares...................	....	....	....	....	....	....	....	....	....	....	....	....
3214 Loans.....................	....	....	....	....	....	....	....	....	....	....	....	....
3215 Shares and other equity...................	....	....	....	....	....	....	....	....	....	....	....	....
3216 Insurance technical reserves...................	....	....	....	....	....	....	....	....	....	....	....	....
3217 Financial derivatives...................	....	....	....	....	....	....	....	....	....	....	....	....
3218 Other accounts receivable...................	....	....	....	....	....	....	....	....	....	....	....	....
322 Foreign....................	....	....	....	....	....	....	....	....	....	....	....	....
3222 Currency and deposits.....................	....	....	....	....	....	....	....	....	....	....	....	....
3223 Securities other than shares...................	....	....	....	....	....	....	....	....	....	....	....	....
3224 Loans.....................	....	....	....	....	....	....	....	....	....	....	....	....
3225 Shares and other equity...................	....	....	....	....	....	....	....	....	....	....	....	....
3226 Insurance technical reserves...................	....	....	....	....	....	....	....	....	....	....	....	....
3227 Financial derivatives...................	....	....	....	....	....	....	....	....	....	....	....	....
3228 Other accounts receivable...................	....	....	....	....	....	....	....	....	....	....	....	....
323 Monetary gold and SDRs.....................	....	....	....	....	....	....	....	....	....	....	....	....
33 **Net incurrence of liabilities....................**	....	....	....	....	....	....	....	....	....	....	....	....
331 Domestic....................	....	....	....	....	....	....	....	....	....	....	....	....
3312 Currency and deposits.....................	....	....	....	....	....	....	....	....	....	....	....	....
3313 Securities other than shares...................	....	....	....	....	....	....	....	....	....	....	....	....
3314 Loans.....................	....	....	....	....	....	....	....	....	....	....	....	....
3316 Insurance technical reserves...................	....	....	....	....	....	....	....	....	....	....	....	....
3317 Financial derivatives...................	....	....	....	....	....	....	....	....	....	....	....	....
3318 Other accounts payable.....................	....	....	....	....	....	....	....	....	....	....	....	....
332 Foreign....................	....	....	....	....	....	....	....	....	....	....	....	....
3322 Currency and deposits.....................	....	....	....	....	....	....	....	....	....	....	....	....
3323 Securities other than shares...................	....	....	....	....	....	....	....	....	....	....	....	....
3324 Loans.....................	....	....	....	....	....	....	....	....	....	....	....	....
3326 Insurance technical reserves...................	....	....	....	....	....	....	....	....	....	....	....	....
3327 Financial derivatives...................	....	....	....	....	....	....	....	....	....	....	....	....
3328 Other accounts payable.....................	....	....	....	....	....	....	....	....	....	....	....	....

2005, International Monetary Fund: *Government Finance Statistics Yearbook*

	Budgetary Central Government			Extrabudgetary Accounts			Central Government			General Government		
	2001	2002	2003	2001	2002	2003	2001	2002	2003	2001	2002	2003
Table 4 Holding gains in assets and liabilities												
Table 5 Other changes in the volume of assets and liabilities												
Table 6 Balance sheet												
Table 7 Outlays by functions of govt.												
7 **Total outlays**.....................	....	....	**389.6**	....	....	....	....	....	....	....	....	....
701 **General public services**..................	....	....	**74.4**	....	....	....	....	....	....	....	....	....
7017 Public debt transactions...................	....	....	74.4	....	....	....	....	....	....	....	....	....
7018 General transfers between levels of govt......	....	....	....	....	....	....	....	....	....	....	....	....
702 **Defense**................................	....	....	**3.7**	....	....	....	....	....	....	....	....	....
703 **Public order and safety**..................	....	....	**20.8**	....	....	....	....	....	....	....	....	....
704 **Economic affairs**.......................	....	....	**46.8**	....	....	....	....	....	....	....	....	....
7042 Agriculture, forestry, fishing, and hunting.....	....	....	2.2	....	....	....	....	....	....	....	....	....
7043 Fuel and energy...........................	....	....	28.9	....	....	....	....	....	....	....	....	....
7044 Mining, manufacturing, and construction.....	....	....	.4	....	....	....	....	....	....	....	....	....
7045 Transport.................................	....	....	6.8	....	....	....	....	....	....	....	....	....
7046 Communication............................	....	....	8.5	....	....	....	....	....	....	....	....	....
705 **Environmental protection**................	....	....	—	....	....	....	....	....	....	....	....	....
706 **Housing and community amenities**.......	....	....	**2.8**	....	....	....	....	....	....	....	....	....
707 **Health**................................	....	....	**22.4**	....	....	....	....	....	....	....	....	....
7072 Outpatient services........................	....	....	....	....	....	....	....	....	....	....	....	....
7073 Hospital services..........................	....	....	....	....	....	....	....	....	....	....	....	....
7074 Public health services......................	....	....	....	....	....	....	....	....	....	....	....	....
708 **Recreation, culture, and religion**..........	....	....	**5.7**	....	....	....	....	....	....	....	....	....
709 **Education**.............................	....	....	**33.7**	....	....	....	....	....	....	....	....	....
7091 Pre-primary and primary education.............	....	....	13.0	....	....	....	....	....	....	....	....	....
7092 Secondary education.......................	....	....	11.1	....	....	....	....	....	....	....	....	....
7094 Tertiary education.........................	....	....	9.6	....	....	....	....	....	....	....	....	....
710 **Social protection**.......................	....	....	**.2**	....	....	....	....	....	....	....	....	....
7 Statistical discrepancy: Total outlays..............	....	....	179.3	....	....	....	....	....	....	....	....	....
Table 8 Transactions in financial assets and liabilities by sector												

In Millions of Dollars / Year Ending December 31 / Cash Reporter

	Budgetary Central Government			Central Government			Local Government			General Government		
	2002	2003	2004	2002	2003	2004	2002	2003	2004	2002	2003	2004p
Statement of government operations												
Statement of other economic flows												
Balance sheet												
Statement of sources and uses of cash												
1 Cash receipts from operating activities	....	....	....	....	....	....	....	....	....	334.9	352.6	376.3
11 Taxes	....	....	....	....	....	....	....	....	....	264.8	266.0	266.3
12 Social contributions	....	....	....	....	....	....	....	....	....	18.8	20.2	21.9
13 Grants	....	....	....	....	....	....	....	....	....	10.5	15.7	40.6
14 Other receipts	....	....	....	....	....	....	....	....	....	40.8	50.7	47.5
2 Cash payments for operating activities	....	....	....	....	....	....	....	....	....	....	....	....
21 Compensation of employees	....	....	....	....	....	....	....	....	....	....	....	....
22 Purchases of goods and services	....	....	....	....	....	....	....	....	....	....	....	....
24 Interest	....	....	....	....	....	....	....	....	....	....	....	....
25 Subsidies	....	....	....	....	....	....	....	....	....	....	....	....
26 Grants	....	....	....	....	....	....	....	....	....	....	....	....
27 Social benefits	....	....	....	....	....	....	....	....	....	....	....	....
28 Other payments	....	....	....	....	....	....	....	....	....	....	....	....
CIO *Net cash inflow from oper. activities*	....	....	....	....	....	....	....	....	....	....	....	....
31.1 Purchases of nonfinancial assets	....	....	....	....	....	....	....	....	....	....	....	....
31.2 Sales of nonfinancial assets	....	....	....	....	....	....	....	....	....	....	....	....
31 Net cash outflow from investments in nonfinancial assets	....	....	....	....	....	....	....	....	....	34.9	29.0	15.5
CSD *Cash surplus/deficit*	....	....	....	....	....	....	....	....	....			
32x Net acquisition of fin assets, excl. cash	....	....	....	....	....	....	....	....	....			
321x Domestic	....	....	....	....	....	....	....	....	....			
322x Foreign	....	....	....	....	....	....	....	....	....			
323 Monetary gold and SDRs	....	....	....	....	....	....	....	....	....			
33 Net incurrence of liabilities	....	....	....	....	....	....	....	....	....			
331 Domestic	....	....	....	....	....	....	....	....	....			
332 Foreign	....	....	....	....	....	....	....	....	....			
NFB Net cash inflow from fin. activities	....	....	....	....	....	....	....	....	....			
NCB *Net change in the stock of cash*	....	....	....	....	....	....	....	....	....			
Table 1 Revenue												
1 **Revenue**	....	....	....	....	....	....	....	....	....	334.9	352.6	376.3
11 **Taxes**	....	....	....	....	....	....	....	....	....	264.8	266.0	266.3
111 Taxes on income, profits, & capital gains	....	....	....	....	....	....	....	....	....	87.8	77.0	78.5
1111 Individuals	....	....	....	....	....	....	....	....	....	35.0	35.2	38.5
1112 Corporations and other enterprises	....	....	....	....	....	....	....	....	....	45.2	38.1	35.4
112 Taxes on payroll and workforce	....	....	....	....	....	....	....	....	....	—	—	—
113 Taxes on property	....	....	....	....	....	....	....	....	....	2.5	2.7	2.4
114 Taxes on goods and services	....	....	....	....	....	....	....	....	....	47.8	53.2	61.0
1141 General taxes on goods and services	....	....	....	....	....	....	....	....	....	—	—	—
1142 Excises	....	....	....	....	....	....	....	....	....	1.8	1.9	2.0
115 Taxes on int'l. trade and transactions	....	....	....	....	....	....	....	....	....	126.7	133.1	124.4
116 Other taxes	....	....	....	....	....	....	....	....	....	—	—	—
12 **Social contributions**	....	....	....	....	....	....	....	....	....	18.8	20.2	21.9
121 Social security contributions	....	....	....	....	....	....	....	....	....	18.8	20.2	21.9
122 Other social contributions	....	....	....	....	....	....	....	....	....	—	—	—
13 **Grants**	....	....	....	....	....	....	....	....	....	10.5	15.7	40.6
131 From foreign governments	....	....	....	....	....	....	....	....	....	10.5	8.2	17.2
132 From international organizations	....	....	....	....	....	....	....	....	....	—	7.5	23.4
133 From other general government units	....	....	....	....	....	....	....	....	....	—	—	—
14 **Other revenue**	....	....	....	....	....	....	....	....	....	40.8	50.7	47.5

In Millions of Dollars / Year Ending December 31 / Cash Reporter

	Budgetary Central Government			Central Government			Local Government			General Government		
	2002	2003	2004	2002	2003	2004	2002	2003	2004	2002	2003	2004p
Table 2 Expense by economic type												
Table 3 Transactions in assets and liabilities												
Table 4 Holding gains in assets and liabilities												
Table 5 Other changes in the volume of assets and liabilities												
Table 6 Balance sheet												
Table 7 Outlays by functions of govt.												
7 **Total outlays**	....	....	....	....	....	....	....	....	....	300.0	323.6	360.8
701 **General public services**	....	....	....	....	....	....	....	....	....	98.2	140.0	161.8
7017 Public debt transactions	....	....	....	....	....	....	....	....	....	....	....	....
7018 General transfers between levels of govt.	....	....	....	....	....	....	....	....	....	....	....	....
702 **Defense**	....	....	....	....	....	....	....	....	....	....	....	....
703 **Public order and safety**	....	....	....	....	....	....	....	....	....	—	—	—
704 **Economic affairs**	....	....	....	....	....	....	....	....	....	26.8	25.9	30.1
7042 Agriculture, forestry, fishing, and hunting	....	....	....	....	....	....	....	....	....	35.3	30.5	32.1
7043 Fuel and energy	....	....	....	....	....	....	....	....	....	9.5	7.7	9.7
7044 Mining, manufacturing, and construction	....	....	....	....	....	....	....	....	....	—	—	—
7045 Transport	....	....	....	....	....	....	....	....	....	14.7	15.0	18.2
7046 Communication	....	....	....	....	....	....	....	....	....	8.6	7.8	4.2
705 **Environmental protection**	....	....	....	....	....	....	....	....	....	4.4	4.6	4.4
706 **Housing and community amenities**	....	....	....	....	....	....	....	....	....	5.6	5.0	5.5
707 **Health**	....	....	....	....	....	....	....	....	....	40.3	34.7	38.0
7072 Outpatient services	....	....	....	....	....	....	....	....	....	8.7	8.6	9.3
7073 Hospital services	....	....	....	....	....	....	....	....	....	26.6	25.7	28.2
7074 Public health services	....	....	....	....	....	....	....	....	....	.4	.4	.5
708 **Recreation, culture, and religion**	....	....	....	....	....	....	....	....	....	.7	.8	.7
709 **Education**	....	....	....	....	....	....	....	....	....	52.5	45.1	50.7
7091 Pre-primary and primary education	....	....	....	....	....	....	....	....	....	28.1	28.0	30.4
7092 Secondary education	....	....	....	....	....	....	....	....	....	12.3	12.7	14.8
7094 Tertiary education	....	....	....	....	....	....	....	....	....	4.5	4.4	5.5
710 **Social protection**	....	....	....	....	....	....	....	....	....	36.2	37.0	37.5
7 Statistical discrepancy: Total outlays	....	....	....	....	....	....	....	....	....	—	—	—
Table 8 Transactions in financial assets and liabilities by sector												

In Thousands of Euros / Year Ending December 31 / Noncash Reporter

	Budgetary Central Government			Extrabudgetary Accounts			Central Government			General Government		
	2000	2001	2002	2000	2001	2002	2000	2001	2002	2000	2001	2002
Statement of government operations												
1 Revenue............................	....	....	274,679	....	....	93,778	....	....	438,922	....	....	438,922
2 Expense............................	....	....	281,456	....	....	83,780	....	....	436,881	....	....	436,881
GOB *Gross operating balance................*	....	....	*450*	....	....	*14,572*	....	....	*15,043*	....	....	*15,043*
NOB *Net operating balance................*	....	....	*−6,777*	....	....	*9,998*	....	....	*2,040*	....	....	*2,040*
31 Net acquisition of nonfinancial assets...........	....	....	7,495	....	....	−16,966	....	....	−10,018	....	....	−10,018
NLB *Net lending/borrowing........................*	....	....	*−14,272*	....	....	*26,964*	....	....	*12,058*	....	....	*12,058*
32 Net acquisition of financial assets...............	....	....	30,510	....	....	17,240	....	....	−7,227	....	....	−7,227
33 Net incurrence of liabilities...................	....	....	34,865	....	....	195	....	....	−19,285	....	....	−19,285
NLB Statistical discrepancy...................	....	....	9,918	....	....	−9,918	....	....	—	....	....	—
Statement of other economic flows												
Balance sheet												
6 *Net worth.................................*	....	....	*125,986*	....	....	*70,726*	....	....	*196,712*	....	....	*196,712*
61 Nonfinancial assets...................	....	....	197,747	....	....	44,462	....	....	247,660	....	....	247,660
62 Financial assets...................	....	....	108,820	....	....	57,637	....	....	103,780	....	....	103,780
63 Liabilities...................	....	....	180,581	....	....	31,373	....	....	154,728	....	....	154,728
Statement of sources and uses of cash												
Table 1 Revenue												
1 **Revenue................**	....	....	**274,679**	....	....	**93,778**	....	....	**438,922**	....	....	**438,922**
11 **Taxes................**	....	....	**217,894**	....	....	**2,000**	....	....	**219,894**	....	....	**219,894**
111 Taxes on income, profits, & capital gains......	....	....	100,255	....	....	2,000	....	....	102,255	....	....	102,255
1111 Individuals................	....	....	91,249	....	....	2,000	....	....	93,249	....	....	93,249
1112 Corporations and other enterprises...........	....	....	9,006	....	....	—	....	....	9,006	....	....	9,006
112 Taxes on payroll and workforce.................	....	....	—	....	....		....	....	—	....	....	
113 Taxes on property.................	....	....	11,072	....	....		....	....	11,072	....	....	11,072
114 Taxes on goods and services.................	....	....	101,647	....	....	—	....	....	101,647	....	....	101,647
1141 General taxes on goods and services........	....	....	56,848	....	....	—	....	....	56,848	....	....	56,848
1142 Excises.................	....	....	16,275	....	....	—	....	....	16,275	....	....	16,275
115 Taxes on int'l. trade and transactions...........	....	....	4,435	....	....	—	....	....	4,435	....	....	4,435
116 Other taxes.................	....	....	485	....	....	—	....	....	485	....	....	485
12 **Social contributions................**	....	....	**—**	....	....	**—**	....	....	**94,358**	....	....	**94,358**
121 Social security contributions.................	....	....	—	....	....	—	....	....	92,792	....	....	92,792
122 Other social contributions.................	....	....	—	....	....	—	....	....	1,566	....	....	1,566
13 **Grants................**	....	....	**5,724**	....	....	**17,782**	....	....	**4,648**	....	....	**4,648**
131 From foreign governments.................	....	....	4,648	....	....	—	....	....	4,648	....	....	4,648
132 From international organizations.................	....	....	—	....	....	—	....	....	—	....	....	—
133 From other general government units.........	....	....	1,076	....	....	17,782	....	....	—	....	....	—
14 **Other revenue................**	....	....	**51,061**	....	....	**73,995**	....	....	**120,021**	....	....	**120,021**
Table 2 Expense by economic type												
2 **Expense................**	....	....	**281,456**	....	....	**83,780**	....	....	**436,881**	....	....	**436,881**
21 **Compensation of employees................**	....	....	**80,809**	....	....	**24,675**	....	....	**148,489**	....	....	**148,489**
211 Wages and salaries.................	....	....	68,654	....	....	24,243	....	....	128,017	....	....	128,017
212 Social contributions.................	....	....	12,155	....	....	432	....	....	20,472	....	....	20,472
22 **Use of goods and services................**	....	....	**34,747**	....	....	**50,055**	....	....	**79,310**	....	....	**79,310**
23 **Consumption of fixed capital................**	....	....	**7,226**	....	....	**4,574**	....	....	**13,002**	....	....	**13,002**
24 **Interest................**	....	....	**9,046**	....	....	**348**	....	....	**9,895**	....	....	**9,895**
25 **Subsidies................**	....	....	**8,668**	....	....	**—**	....	....	**8,668**	....	....	**8,668**
26 **Grants................**	....	....	**98,918**	....	....	**3**	....	....	**2**	....	....	**2**
261 To foreign governments.................	....	....	—	....	....	—	....	....	—	....	....	—
262 To international organizations.................	....	....	—	....	....	—	....	....	2	....	....	2
263 To other general government units............	....	....	98,918	....	....	3	....	....	—	....	....	—
2631 Current.................	....	....	81,136	....	....	3	....	....	—	....	....	—
2632 Capital.................	....	....	17,782	....	....	—	....	....	—	....	....	—
27 **Social benefits................**	....	....	**11,679**	....	....	**—**	....	....	**118,312**	....	....	**118,312**
28 **Other expense................**	....	....	**30,363**	....	....	**4,125**	....	....	**59,203**	....	....	**59,203**
281 Property expense other than interest...........	....	....	—	....	....	—	....	....	748	....	....	748
282 Miscellaneous other expense.................	....	....	30,363	....	....	4,125	....	....	58,455	....	....	58,455
2821 Current.................	....	....	28,221	....	....	4,125	....	....	56,313	....	....	56,313
2822 Capital.................	....	....	2,142	....	....	—	....	....	2,142	....	....	2,142

In Thousands of Euros / Year Ending December 31 / Noncash Reporter

		Budgetary Central Government			Extrabudgetary Accounts			Central Government			General Government		
		2000	2001	2002	2000	2001	2002	2000	2001	2002	2000	2001	2002
Table 3	**Transactions in assets and liabilities**												
3	**Change in net worth from transactns....**	....	....	**3,141**	....	....	**80**	....	....	**2,040**	....	....	**2,040**
31	**Net acquisition of nonfinancial assets...**	....	....	**7,495**	....	....	**−16,966**	....	....	**−10,018**	....	....	**−10,018**
311	Fixed assets........	....	....	2,568	....	....	−16,994	....	....	−14,799	....	....	−14,799
3111	Buildings and structures........	....	....	4,029	....	....	−742	....	....	3,287	....	....	3,287
3112	Machinery and equipment........	....	....	−1,322	....	....	−15,501	....	....	−17,298	....	....	−17,298
3113	Other fixed assets........	....	....	−139	....	....	−751	....	....	−788	....	....	−788
312	Inventories........	....	....	3,089	....	....	28	....	....	2,943	....	....	2,943
313	Valuables........	....	....	−1,282	....	....	—	....	....	−1,282	....	....	−1,282
314	Nonproduced assets........	....	....	3,121	....	....	—	....	....	3,121	....	....	3,121
3141	Land........	....	....	—	....	....	—	....	....	—	....	....	—
3142	Subsoil assets........	....	....	—	....	....	—	....	....	—	....	....	—
3143	Other naturally occurring assets........	....	....	3,121	....	....	—	....	....	3,121	....	....	3,121
3144	Intangible nonproduced assets........	....	....	—	....	....	—	....	....	—	....	....	—
32	**Net acquisition of financial assets......**	....	....	**30,510**	....	....	**17,240**	....	....	**−7,227**	....	....	**−7,227**
321	Domestic........	....	....	41,755	....	....	17,240	....	....	1,308	....	....	1,308
3212	Currency and deposits........	....	....	48,098	....	....	19,421	....	....	36,607	....	....	36,607
3213	Securities other than shares........	....	....	649	....	....	255	....	....	904	....	....	904
3214	Loans........	....	....	—	....	....	—	....	....	—	....	....	—
3215	Shares and other equity........	....	....	—	....	....	—	....	....	—	....	....	—
3216	Insurance technical reserves........	....	....	—	....	....	—	....	....	—	....	....	—
3217	Financial derivatives........	....	....	—	....	....	—	....	....	—	....	....	—
3218	Other accounts receivable........	....	....	−6,992	....	....	−2,435	....	....	−36,202	....	....	−36,202
322	Foreign........	....	....	−11,245	....	....	—	....	....	−8,536	....	....	−8,536
3222	Currency and deposits........	....	....	—	....	....	—	....	....	—	....	....	—
3223	Securities other than shares........	....	....	—	....	....	—	....	....	—	....	....	—
3224	Loans........	....	....	−1,162	....	....	—	....	....	−1,162	....	....	−1,162
3225	Shares and other equity........	....	....	—	....	....	—	....	....	—	....	....	—
3226	Insurance technical reserves........	....	....	—	....	....	—	....	....	—	....	....	—
3227	Financial derivatives........	....	....	—	....	....	—	....	....	—	....	....	—
3228	Other accounts receivable........	....	....	−10,083	....	....	—	....	....	−7,374	....	....	−7,374
323	Monetary gold and SDRs........	....	....	—	....	....	—	....	....	—	....	....	—
33	**Net incurrence of liabilities........**	....	....	**34,865**	....	....	**195**	....	....	**−19,285**	....	....	**−19,285**
331	Domestic........	....	....	35,381	....	....	195	....	....	−42,448	....	....	−42,448
3312	Currency and deposits........	....	....	—	....	....	—	....	....	—	....	....	—
3313	Securities other than shares........	....	....	—	....	....	—	....	....	—	....	....	—
3314	Loans........	....	....	−13,277	....	....	−191	....	....	−13,468	....	....	−13,468
3316	Insurance technical reserves........	....	....	—	....	....	—	....	....	—	....	....	—
3317	Financial derivatives........	....	....	—	....	....	—	....	....	—	....	....	—
3318	Other accounts payable........	....	....	48,658	....	....	386	....	....	−28,979	....	....	−28,979
332	Foreign........	....	....	−517	....	....	—	....	....	23,163	....	....	23,163
3322	Currency and deposits........	....	....	—	....	....	—	....	....	—	....	....	—
3323	Securities other than shares........	....	....	—	....	....	—	....	....	—	....	....	—
3324	Loans........	....	....	−517	....	....	—	....	....	23,163	....	....	23,163
3326	Insurance technical reserves........	....	....	—	....	....	—	....	....	—	....	....	—
3327	Financial derivatives........	....	....	—	....	....	—	....	....	—	....	....	—
3328	Other accounts payable........	....	....	—	....	....	—	....	....	—	....	....	—
Table 4	**Holding gains in assets and liabilities**												
Table 5	**Other changes in the volume of assets and liabilities**												
Table 6	**Balance sheet**												
6	**Net worth........**	....	....	**125,986**	....	....	**70,726**	....	....	**196,712**	....	....	**196,712**
61	**Nonfinancial assets........**	....	....	**197,747**	....	....	**44,462**	....	....	**247,660**	....	....	**247,660**
611	Fixed assets........	....	....	151,969	....	....	42,329	....	....	198,154	....	....	198,154
6111	Buildings and structures........	....	....	125,289	....	....	5,456	....	....	130,781	....	....	130,781
6112	Machinery and equipment........	....	....	26,101	....	....	35,623	....	....	65,322	....	....	65,322
6113	Other fixed assets........	....	....	579	....	....	1,250	....	....	2,051	....	....	2,051
612	Inventories........	....	....	30,454	....	....	2,133	....	....	34,182	....	....	34,182
613	Valuables........	....	....	4,739	....	....	—	....	....	4,739	....	....	4,739
614	Nonproduced assets........	....	....	10,586	....	....	—	....	....	10,586	....	....	10,586
6141	Land........	....	....	—	....	....	—	....	....	—	....	....	—
6142	Subsoil assets........	....	....	—	....	....	—	....	....	—	....	....	—
6143	Other naturally occurring assets........	....	....	10,586	....	....	—	....	....	10,586	....	....	10,586
6144	Intangible nonproduced assets........	....	....	—	....	....	—	....	....	—	....	....	—

In Thousands of Euros / Year Ending December 31 / Noncash Reporter

		Budgetary Central Government			Extrabudgetary Accounts			Central Government			General Government		
		2000	2001	2002	2000	2001	2002	2000	2001	2002	2000	2001	2002
62	**Financial assets**................	....	....	**108,820**	....	....	**57,637**	....	....	**103,780**	....	....	**103,780**
621	Domestic.........................	....	....	102,474	....	....	57,637	....	....	81,008	....	....	81,008
6212	Currency and deposits..........	....	....	48,382	....	....	42,376	....	....	101,702	....	....	101,702
6213	Securities other than shares.....	....	....	27,757	....	....	1,913	....	....	29,670	....	....	29,670
6214	Loans...........................	....	....	—	....	....	2	....	....	2	....	....	2
6215	Shares and other equity..........	....	....	—	....	....	—	....	....	—	....	....	—
6216	Insurance technical reserves......	....	....	—	....	....	—	....	....	—	....	....	—
6217	Financial derivatives.............	....	....	—	....	....	—	....	....	—	....	....	—
6218	Other accounts receivable........	....	....	26,335	....	....	13,346	....	....	−50,366	....	....	−50,366
622	Foreign..........................	....	....	6,346	....	....	—	....	....	22,772	....	....	22,772
6222	Currency and deposits...........	....	....	—	....	....	—	....	....	—	....	....	—
6223	Securities other than shares......	....	....	—	....	....	—	....	....	—	....	....	—
6224	Loans...........................	....	....	—	....	....	—	....	....	—	....	....	—
6225	Shares and other equity..........	....	....	—	....	....	—	....	....	—	....	....	—
6226	Insurance technical reserves......	....	....	—	....	....	—	....	....	—	....	....	—
6227	Financial derivatives.............	....	....	—	....	....	—	....	....	—	....	....	—
6228	Other accounts receivable........	....	....	6,346	....	....	—	....	....	22,772	....	....	22,772
623	Monetary gold and SDRs..........	....	....	—	....	....	—	....	....	—	....	....	—
63	**Liabilities**...................	....	....	**180,581**	....	....	**31,373**	....	....	**154,728**	....	....	**154,728**
631	Domestic.........................	....	....	177,741	....	....	31,373	....	....	122,702	....	....	122,702
6312	Currency and deposits..........	....	....	—	....	....	—	....	....	—	....	....	—
6313	Securities other than shares......	....	....	—	....	....	—	....	....	—	....	....	—
6314	Loans...........................	....	....	51,508	....	....	428	....	....	51,936	....	....	51,936
6316	Insurance technical reserves......	....	....	—	....	....	—	....	....	—	....	....	—
6317	Financial derivatives.............	....	....	—	....	....	—	....	....	—	....	....	—
6318	Other accounts payable..........	....	....	126,233	....	....	30,945	....	....	70,766	....	....	70,766
632	Foreign..........................	....	....	2,840	....	....	—	....	....	32,026	....	....	32,026
6322	Currency and deposits..........	....	....	—	....	....	—	....	....	—	....	....	—
6323	Securities other than shares......	....	....	—	....	....	—	....	....	—	....	....	—
6324	Loans...........................	....	....	2,840	....	....	—	....	....	2,840	....	....	2,840
6326	Insurance technical reserves......	....	....	—	....	....	—	....	....	—	....	....	—
6327	Financial derivatives.............	....	....	—	....	....	—	....	....	—	....	....	—
6328	Other accounts payable..........	....	....	—	....	....	—	....	....	29,186	....	....	29,186
	Memorandum items:												
6M2	Net financial worth...............	....	....	−71,761	....	....	26,263	....	....	−50,948	....	....	−50,948
6M3	Debt at market value.............	....	....	....									
6M4	Debt at nominal value............	....	....	....									
6M5	Arrears...........................	....	....	....									
6M6	Obligations for social security benefits...........	....	....	....									
6M7	Contingent liabilities..............	....	....	....									
6M8	Uncapitalized military weapons, systems........	....	....	....									
Table 7	**Outlays by functions of govt.**												
7	**Total outlays**...................	....	....	**288,952**	....	....	**66,814**	....	....	**426,864**	....	....	**426,864**
701	**General public services**..................	....	....	**77,110**	....	....	**5,333**	....	....	**61,975**	....	....	**61,975**
7017	Public debt transactions.........	....	....	9,046	....	....	348	....	....	9,895	....	....	9,895
7018	General transfers between levels of govt......	....	....	....	....	....	....	....	....	....			
702	**Defense**.......................	....	....	**—**	....	....		....	....	**—**	....	....	**—**
703	**Public order and safety**........	....	....	**12,569**	....	....	**—**	....	....	**12,569**	....	....	**12,569**
704	**Economic affairs**................	....	....	**28,941**	....	....	**43,641**	....	....	**61,118**	....	....	**61,118**
7042	Agriculture, forestry, fishing, and hunting.....	....	....	3,746	....	....	—	....	....	3,746	....	....	3,746
7043	Fuel and energy.................	....	....	1,275	....	....	18,244	....	....	18,603	....	....	18,603
7044	Mining, manufacturing, and construction.....	....	....	1,118	....	....	—	....	....	1,118	....	....	1,118
7045	Transport........................	....	....	....	....	....	....	....	....	....			
7046	Communication..................	....	....	4,069	....	....	455	....	....	4,524	....	....	4,524
705	**Environmental protection**..................	....	....	**5,687**	....	....	**8,122**	....	....	**13,809**	....	....	**13,809**
706	**Housing and community amenities**.......	....	....	**7,752**	....	....	**2,256**	....	....	**10,008**	....	....	**10,008**
707	**Health**..........................	....	....	**76,663**	....	....	**—**	....	....	**77,424**	....	....	**77,424**
7072	Outpatient services..............	....	....	5,043	....	....		....	....	39,363	....	....	39,363
7073	Hospital services.................	....	....	48,622	....	....	—	....	....	4,729	....	....	4,729
7074	Public health services............	....	....	19,050	....	....	—	....	....	11,140	....	....	11,140
708	**Recreation, culture, and religion**...........	....	....	**10,097**	....	....	**4,606**	....	....	**9,816**	....	....	**9,816**

In Thousands of Euros / Year Ending December 31 / Noncash Reporter

	Budgetary Central Government			Extrabudgetary Accounts			Central Government			General Government		
	2000	2001	2002	2000	2001	2002	2000	2001	2002	2000	2001	2002
709 **Education**.....................	....	....	**39,999**	....	....	**2,853**	....	....	**40,143**	....	....	**40,143**
7091 Pre-primary and primary education..............	....	....	15,110	....	....	—	....	....	15,110	....	....	15,110
7092 Secondary education.................	....	....	9,273	....	....	—	....	....	9,273	....	....	9,273
7094 Tertiary education.................	....	....	2,643	....	....	2,853	....	....	5,226	....	....	5,226
710 **Social protection**.................	....	....	**30,133**	....	....	**3**	....	....	**140,003**	....	....	**140,003**
7 Statistical discrepancy: Total outlays..............	....	....	—	....	....	—	....	....	—	....	....	—

Table 8   Transactions in financial assets and liabilities by sector

	Budgetary Central Government			Extrabudgetary Accounts			Central Government			General Government		
	2000	2001	2002	2000	2001	2002	2000	2001	2002	2000	2001	2002
82 **Net acquisition of financial assets**.........	....	....	**30,510**	....	....	**17,240**	....	....	**−7,227**	....	....	**−7,227**
821 Domestic.................	....	....	41,755	....	....	17,240	....	....	1,308	....	....	1,308
8211 General government.....................	....	....	....	....	....	....	....	....	....	....	....	....
8212 Central bank.....................	....	....	....	....	....	....	....	....	....	....	....	....
8213 Other depository corporations..................	....	....	....	....	....	....	....	....	....	....	....	....
8214 Financial corporations n.e.c................	....	....	....	....	....	....	....	....	....	....	....	....
8215 Nonfinancial corporations..................	....	....	....	....	....	....	....	....	....	....	....	....
8216 Households & NPIs serving households......	....	....	....	....	....	....	....	....	....	....	....	....
822 Foreign.................	....	....	−11,245	....	....	—	....	....	−8,536	....	....	−8,536
8221 General government.....................	....	....	....	....	....	—	....	....	....	....	....	....
8227 International organizations....................	....	....	....	....	....	—	....	....	....	....	....	....
8228 Financial corporations other than international organizations..............	....	....	....	....	....	—	....	....	....	....	....	....
8229 Other nonresidents....................	....	....	....	....	....	—	....	....	....	....	....	....
823 Monetary gold and SDRs....................	....	....	—	....	....	—	....	....	....	....	....	....
83 **Net incurrence of liabilities**..................	....	....	**34,865**	....	....	**195**	....	....	**−19,285**	....	....	**−19,285**
831 Domestic.................	....	....	35,381	....	....	195	....	....	−42,448	....	....	−42,448
8311 General government.....................	....	....	....	....	....	....	....	....	....	....	....	....
8312 Central bank.....................	....	....	....	....	....	....	....	....	....	....	....	....
8313 Other depository corporations..................	....	....	....	....	....	....	....	....	....	....	....	....
8314 Financial corporations n.e.c................	....	....	....	....	....	....	....	....	....	....	....	....
8315 Nonfinancial corporations..................	....	....	....	....	....	....	....	....	....	....	....	....
8316 Households & NPIs serving households......	....	....	....	....	....	....	....	....	....	....	....	....
832 Foreign.................	....	....	−517	....	....	—	....	....	23,163	....	....	23,163
8321 General government.....................	....	....	....	....	....	—	....	....	....	....	....	....
8327 International organizations....................	....	....	....	....	....	—	....	....	....	....	....	....
8328 Financial corporations other than international organizations..............	....	....	....	....	....	—	....	....	....	....	....	....
8329 Other nonresidents....................	....	....	....	....	....	—	....	....	....	....	....	....

In billions of Francs / Year Ending December 31 / Cash Reporter

		Budgetary Central Government			Central Government			Local Government			General Government		
		1999	2000	2001	1999	2000	2001	1999	2000	2001	1999	2000	2001
Statement of government operations													
Statement of other economic flows													
Balance sheet													
6	*Net worth*.....................	....	....	....	....	....	....	....	....	....	....	....	....
61	Nonfinancial assets.................	....	....	....	....	....	....	....	....	....	....	....	....
62	Financial assets...................	....	....	....	....	....	....	....	....	....	....	....	....
63	Liabilities...................	2,648.2	2,456.3	2,461.8	....	....	....	....	....	....	....	....	....
Statement of sources and uses of cash													
1	Cash receipts from operating activities..........	568.4	612.2	663.8	....	....	....	37.0	....	....	....	....	....
11	Taxes...................	491.2	537.4	576.2	....	....	....	14.0	....	....	....	....	....
12	Social contributions...................	—	—	—	....	....	....	.1	....	....	....	....	....
13	Grants...................	61.6	49.9	61.7	....	....	....	9.9	....	....	....	....	....
14	Other receipts...................	15.6	24.9	25.9	....	....	....	12.9	....	....	....	....	....
2	Cash payments for operating activities..........	362.3	425.1	520.4	....	....	....	....	....	....	....	....	....
21	Compensation of employees...................	166.6	175.8	177.3	....	....	....	....	....	....	....	....	....
22	Purchases of goods and services.................	92.7	110.5	130.3	....	....	....	....	....	....	....	....	....
24	Interest...................	42.5	45.3	30.3	....	....	....	....	....	....	....	....	....
25	Subsidies...................	—	—	105.0	....	....	....	....	....	....	....	....	....
26	Grants...................	35.9	66.0	64.5	....	....	....	....	....	....	....	....	....
27	Social benefits...................	13.4	13.5	9.2	....	....	....	....	....	....	....	....	....
28	Other payments...................	—	—	—	....	....	....	....	....	....	....	....	....
CIO	*Net cash inflow from oper. activities*.....	206.1	187.1	143.4	....	....	....	....	....	....	....	....	....
31.1	Purchases of nonfinancial assets...................	234.5	216.1	217.2	....	....	....	....	....	....	....	....	....
31.2	Sales of nonfinancial assets...................	—	—	—	....	....	....	....	....	....	....	....	....
31	Net cash outflow from investments in nonfinancial assets...................	234.5	216.1	217.2	....	....	....	....	....	....	....	....	....
CSD	*Cash surplus/deficit*...................	−28.4	−29.0	−73.8	....	....	....	....	....	....	....	....	....
32x	Net acquisition of fin assets, excl. cash........	5.3	6.9	−4.6	....	....	....	....	....	....	....	....	....
321x	Domestic...................	5.3	6.9	−4.6	....	....	....	....	....	....	....	....	....
322x	Foreign...................	—	—	—	....	....	....	....	....	....	....	....	....
323	Monetary gold and SDRs...................	—	—	—	....	....	....	....	....	....	....	....	....
33	Net incurrence of liabilities...................	−2.6	25.7	100.8	....	....	....	....	....	....	....	....	....
331	Domestic...................	−25.5	8.5	45.9	....	....	....	....	....	....	....	....	....
332	Foreign...................	22.9	17.2	54.9	....	....	....	....	....	....	....	....	....
NFB	Net cash inflow from fin. activities...................	−7.9	18.8	105.4	....	....	....	....	....	....	....	....	....
NCB	*Net change in the stock of cash*...........	−36.3	−10.2	31.6	....	....	....	....	....	....	....	....	....
Table 1 Revenue													
1	**Revenue**	568.4	612.2	663.8	....	....	....	37.0	....	....	....	....	....
11	**Taxes**	491.2	537.4	576.2	....	....	....	14.0	....	....	....	....	....
111	Taxes on income, profits, & capital gains......	107.5	130.1	131.3	....	....	....	—	....	....	....	....	....
1111	Individuals...................	55.3	63.1	63.3	....	....	....	—	....	....	....	....	....
1112	Corporations and other enterprises............	39.1	50.1	48.1	....	....	....	—	....	....	....	....	....
112	Taxes on payroll and workforce...................	—	—	—	....	....	....	—	....	....	....	....	....
113	Taxes on property...................	11.6	11.3	14.1	....	....	....	—	....	....	....	....	....
114	Taxes on goods and services...................	179.7	206.4	200.0	....	....	....	14.0	....	....	....	....	....
1141	General taxes on goods and services...........	....	....	....	....	....	....	....	....	....	....	....	....
1142	Excises...................	....	....	....	....	....	....	....	....	....	....	....	....
115	Taxes on int'l. trade and transactions...........	185.1	180.9	219.8	....	....	....	—	....	....	....	....	....
116	Other taxes...................	7.3	8.7	11.0	....	....	....	—	....	....	....	....	....
12	**Social contributions**	—	—	—	....	....	....	.1	....	....	....	....	....
121	Social security contributions...................	—	—	—	....	....	....		....	....	....	....	....
122	Other social contributions...................	—	—	—	....	....	....	.1	....	....	....	....	....
13	**Grants**	61.6	49.9	61.7	....	....	....	9.9	....	....	....	....	....
131	From foreign governments...................	....	....	....	....	....	....	—	....	....	....	....	....
132	From international organizations...................	....	....	....	....	....	....		....	....	....	....	....
133	From other general government units.........	....	....	....	....	....	....	9.9	....	....	....	....	....
14	**Other revenue**	15.6	24.9	25.9	....	....	....	12.9	....	....	....	....	....
Table 2 Expense by economic type													
2	**Expense**	362.3	425.1	520.4	....	....	....	....	....	....	....	....	....
21	**Compensation of employees**	166.6	175.8	177.3	....	....	....	....	....	....	....	....	....
211	Wages and salaries...................	166.6	175.8	177.3	....	....	....	....	....	....	....	....	....
212	Social contributions...................	....	....	....	....	....	....	....	....	....	....	....	....
22	**Use of goods and services**	92.7	110.5	130.3	....	....	....	....	....	....	....	....	....
23	**Consumption of fixed capital**	....	....	....	....	....	....	....	....	....	....	....	....
24	**Interest**	42.5	45.3	30.3	....	....	....	....	....	....	....	....	....
25	**Subsidies**	—	—	105.0	....	....	....	....	....	....	....	....	....

2005, International Monetary Fund: *Government Finance Statistics Yearbook*

In billions of Francs / Year Ending December 31 / Cash Reporter

		Budgetary Central Government			Central Government			Local Government			General Government		
		1999	2000	2001	1999	2000	2001	1999	2000	2001	1999	2000	2001
26	**Grants**	**35.9**	**66.0**	**64.5**	....	....	....	....	....	....	....	....	....
261	To foreign govenments	—	—	—	....	....	....	....	....	....	....	....	....
262	To international organizations	—	—	—	....	....	....	....	....	....	....	....	....
263	To other general government units	35.9	66.0	64.5	....	....	....	....	....	....	....	....	....
2631	Current	35.9	66.0	64.5	....	....	....	....	....	....	....	....	....
2632	Capital				....	....	....	....	....	....	....	....	....
27	**Social benefits**	**13.4**	**13.5**	**9.2**	....	....	....	....	....	....	....	....	....
28	**Other expense**	**—**	**—**	**—**	....	....	....	....	....	....	....	....	....
281	Property expense other than interest	—	—	—	....	....	....	....	....	....	....	....	....
282	Miscellaneous other expense	—	—	—	....	....	....	....	....	....	....	....	....
2821	Current	—	—	—	....	....	....	....	....	....	....	....	....
2822	Capital	—	—	—	....	....	....	....	....	....	....	....	....

Table 3   Transactions in assets and liabilities

		Budgetary Central Government			Central Government			Local Government			General Government		
		1999	2000	2001	1999	2000	2001	1999	2000	2001	1999	2000	2001
3	**Change in net worth from transactns**	....	....	....	....	....	....	....	....	....	....	....	....
31	**Net acquisition of nonfinancial assets**	**234.5**	**216.1**	**217.2**	....	....	....	....	....	....	....	....	....
311	Fixed assets	....	....	....	....	....	....	....	....	....	....	....	....
3111	Buildings and structures	....	....	....	....	....	....	....	....	....	....	....	....
3112	Machinery and equipment	....	....	....	....	....	....	....	....	....	....	....	....
3113	Other fixed assets	....	....	....	....	....	....	....	....	....	....	....	....
312	Inventories	....	....	....	....	....	....	....	....	....	....	....	....
313	Valuables	....	....	....	....	....	....	....	....	....	....	....	....
314	Nonproduced assets	....	....	....	....	....	....	....	....	....	....	....	....
3141	Land	....	....	....	....	....	....	....	....	....	....	....	....
3142	Subsoil assets	....	....	....	....	....	....	....	....	....	....	....	....
3143	Other naturally occurring assets	....	....	....	....	....	....	....	....	....	....	....	....
3144	Intangible nonproduced assets	....	....	....	....	....	....	....	....	....	....	....	....
32	**Net acquisition of financial assets**	**−31.0**	**−3.3**	**27.0**	....	....	....	....	....	....	....	....	....
321	Domestic	−31.0	−3.3	27.0	....	....	....	....	....	....	....	....	....
3212	Currency and deposits	−36.3	−10.2	31.6	....	....	....	....	....	....	....	....	....
3213	Securities other than shares	—	—	—	....	....	....	....	....	....	....	....	....
3214	Loans	5.3	6.9	−4.6	....	....	....	....	....	....	....	....	....
3215	Shares and other equity	—	—	—	....	....	....	....	....	....	....	....	....
3216	Insurance technical reserves	—	—	—	....	....	....	....	....	....	....	....	....
3217	Financial derivatives	—	—	—	....	....	....	....	....	....	....	....	....
3218	Other accounts receivable	....	....	....	....	....	....	....	....	....	....	....	....
322	Foreign	—	—	—	....	....	....	....	....	....	....	....	....
3222	Currency and deposits	—	—	—	....	....	....	....	....	....	....	....	....
3223	Securities other than shares	—	—	—	....	....	....	....	....	....	....	....	....
3224	Loans	—	—	—	....	....	....	....	....	....	....	....	....
3225	Shares and other equity	—	—	—	....	....	....	....	....	....	....	....	....
3226	Insurance technical reserves	—	—	—	....	....	....	....	....	....	....	....	....
3227	Financial derivatives	—	—	—	....	....	....	....	....	....	....	....	....
3228	Other accounts receivable	....	....	....	....	....	....	....	....	....	....	....	....
323	Monetary gold and SDRs	—	—	—	....	....	....	....	....	....	....	....	....
33	**Net incurrence of liabilities**	**−2.6**	**25.7**	**100.8**	....	....	....	....	....	....	....	....	....
331	Domestic	−25.5	8.5	45.9	....	....	....	....	....	....	....	....	....
3312	Currency and deposits	....	....	....	....	....	....	....	....	....	....	....	....
3313	Securities other than shares	....	....	....	....	....	....	....	....	....	....	....	....
3314	Loans	....	....	....	....	....	....	....	....	....	....	....	....
3316	Insurance technical reserves	....	....	....	....	....	....	....	....	....	....	....	....
3317	Financial derivatives	....	....	....	....	....	....	....	....	....	....	....	....
3318	Other accounts payable	....	....	....	....	....	....	....	....	....	....	....	....
332	Foreign	22.9	17.2	54.9	....	....	....	....	....	....	....	....	....
3322	Currency and deposits	....	....	....	....	....	....	....	....	....	....	....	....
3323	Securities other than shares	....	....	....	....	....	....	....	....	....	....	....	....
3324	Loans	....	....	....	....	....	....	....	....	....	....	....	....
3326	Insurance technical reserves	....	....	....	....	....	....	....	....	....	....	....	....
3327	Financial derivatives	....	....	....	....	....	....	....	....	....	....	....	....
3328	Other accounts payable	....	....	....	....	....	....	....	....	....	....	....	....

	Budgetary Central Government			Central Government			Local Government			General Government		
	1999	2000	2001	1999	2000	2001	1999	2000	2001	1999	2000	2001
Table 4 Holding gains in assets and liabilities												
Table 5 Other changes in the volume of assets and liabilities												
Table 6 Balance sheet												
6 Net worth............................	....	....	....	....	....	....	....	....	....	....	....	....
61 Nonfinancial assets........................	....	....	....	....	....	....	....	....	....	....	....	....
611 Fixed assets..............................	....	....	....	....	....	....	....	....	....	....	....	....
6111 Buildings and structures...........	....	....	....	....	....	....	....	....	....	....	....	....
6112 Machinery and equipment.........	....	....	....	....	....	....	....	....	....	....	....	....
6113 Other fixed assets.................	....	....	....	....	....	....	....	....	....	....	....	....
612 Inventories............................	....	....	....	....	....	....	....	....	....	....	....	....
613 Valuables..............................	....	....	....	....	....	....	....	....	....	....	....	....
614 Nonproduced assets................	....	....	....	....	....	....	....	....	....	....	....	....
6141 Land..................................	....	....	....	....	....	....	....	....	....	....	....	....
6142 Subsoil assets......................	....	....	....	....	....	....	....	....	....	....	....	....
6143 Other naturally occurring assets...............	....	....	....	....	....	....	....	....	....	....	....	....
6144 Intangible nonproduced assets................	....	....	....	....	....	....	....	....	....	....	....	....
62 **Financial assets**........................	....	....	....	....	....	....	....	....	....	....	....	....
621 Domestic..............................	....	....	....	....	....	....	....	....	....	....	....	....
6212 Currency and deposits...........	....	....	....	....	....	....	....	....	....	....	....	....
6213 Securities other than shares....	....	....	....	....	....	....	....	....	....	....	....	....
6214 Loans.................................	....	....	....	....	....	....	....	....	....	....	....	....
6215 Shares and other equity.........	....	....	....	....	....	....	....	....	....	....	....	....
6216 Insurance technical reserves....	....	....	....	....	....	....	....	....	....	....	....	....
6217 Financial derivatives..............	....	....	....	....	....	....	....	....	....	....	....	....
6218 Other accounts receivable......	....	....	....	....	....	....	....	....	....	....	....	....
622 Foreign................................	....	....	....	....	....	....	....	....	....	....	....	....
6222 Currency and deposits...........	....	....	....	....	....	....	....	....	....	....	....	....
6223 Securities other than shares....	....	....	....	....	....	....	....	....	....	....	....	....
6224 Loans.................................	....	....	....	....	....	....	....	....	....	....	....	....
6225 Shares and other equity.........	....	....	....	....	....	....	....	....	....	....	....	....
6226 Insurance technical reserves....	....	....	....	....	....	....	....	....	....	....	....	....
6227 Financial derivatives..............	....	....	....	....	....	....	....	....	....	....	....	....
6228 Other accounts receivable......	....	....	....	....	....	....	....	....	....	....	....	....
623 Monetary gold and SDRs.........	....	....	....	....	....	....	....	....	....	....	....	....
63 **Liabilities**...........................	**2,648.2**	**2,456.3**	**2,461.8**	....	....	....	....	....	....	....	....	....
631 Domestic..............................	289.2	236.5	213.0	....	....	....	....	....	....	....	....	....
6312 Currency and deposits...........	....	....	....	....	....	....	....	....	....	....	....	....
6313 Securities other than shares....	....	....	....	....	....	....	....	....	....	....	....	....
6314 Loans.................................	....	....	....	....	....	....	....	....	....	....	....	....
6316 Insurance technical reserves....	....	....	....	....	....	....	....	....	....	....	....	....
6317 Financial derivatives..............	....	....	....	....	....	....	....	....	....	....	....	....
6318 Other accounts payable.........	....	....	....	....	....	....	....	....	....	....	....	....
632 Foreign................................	2,359.0	2,219.8	2,248.8	....	....	....	....	....	....	....	....	....
6322 Currency and deposits...........	....	....	....	....	....	....	....	....	....	....	....	....
6323 Securities other than shares....	....	....	....	....	....	....	....	....	....	....	....	....
6324 Loans.................................	....	....	....	....	....	....	....	....	....	....	....	....
6326 Insurance technical reserves....	....	....	....	....	....	....	....	....	....	....	....	....
6327 Financial derivatives..............	....	....	....	....	....	....	....	....	....	....	....	....
6328 Other accounts payable.........	....	....	....	....	....	....	....	....	....	....	....	....
Memorandum items:												
6M2 Net financial worth................	....	....	....	....	....	....	....	....	....	....	....	....
6M3 Debt at market value.............	....	....	....	....	....	....	....	....	....	....	....	....
6M4 Debt at nominal value............	....	....	....	....	....	....	....	....	....	....	....	....
6M5 Arrears...............................	....	....	....	....	....	....	....	....	....	....	....	....
6M6 Obligations for social security benefits...........	....	....	....	....	....	....	....	....	....	....	....	....
6M7 Contingent liabilities..............	....	....	....	....	....	....	....	....	....	....	....	....
6M8 Uncapitalized military weapons, systems........	....	....	....	....	....	....	....	....	....	....	....	....
Table 7 Outlays by functions of govt.												
7 **Total outlays**......................	**596.8**	**641.2**	**737.6**	....	....	....	....	....	....	....	....	....
701 **General public services**..................	**177.3**	**219.0**		....	....	....	....	....	....	....	....	....
7017 Public debt transactions.........	42.5	45.3	30.3	....	....	....	....	....	....	....	....	....
7018 General transfers between levels of govt......	....	....	....	....	....	....	....	....	....	....	....	....
702 **Defense**.............................	**46.1**	**47.1**	....	....	....	....	....	....	....	....	....	....
703 **Public order and safety**....................	—	—	....	....	....	....	....	....	....	....	....	....

		Budgetary Central Government			Central Government			Local Government			General Government		
		1999	2000	2001	1999	2000	2001	1999	2000	2001	1999	2000	2001
704	**Economic affairs**............................	13.8	15.5	....	....	....	....	....	....	....	....	....	....
7042	Agriculture, forestry, fishing, and hunting.....	....	....	....	....	....	....	....	....	....	....	....	....
7043	Fuel and energy............................	....	....	....	....	....	....	....	....	....	....	....	....
7044	Mining, manufacturing, and construction.....	....	....	....	....	....	....	....	....	....	....	....	....
7045	Transport....................................	....	....	....	....	....	....	....	....	....	....	....	....
7046	Communication............................	....	....	....	....	....	....	....	....	....	....	....	....
705	**Environmental protection**..................	—	—	....	....	....	....	....	....	....	....	....	....
706	**Housing and community amenities**........	6.6	18.1	....	....	....	....	....	....	....	....	....	....
707	**Health**....................................	16.9	22.2	....	....	....	....	....	....	....	....	....	....
7072	Outpatient services........................	....	....	....	....	....	....	....	....	....	....	....	....
7073	Hospital services..........................	....	....	....	....	....	....	....	....	....	....	....	....
7074	Public health services......................	....	....	....	....	....	....	....	....	....	....	....	....
708	**Recreation, culture, and religion**...........	—	—	....	....	....	....	....	....	....	....	....	....
709	**Education**.................................	90.4	87.9	....	....	....	....	....	....	....	....	....	....
7091	Pre-primary and primary education...........	....	....	....	....	....	....	....	....	....	....	....	....
7092	Secondary education.......................	....	....	....	....	....	....	....	....	....	....	....	....
7094	Tertiary education..........................	....	....	....	....	....	....	....	....	....	....	....	....
710	**Social protection**..........................	—	—	....	....	....	....	....	....	....	....	....	....
7	Statistical discrepancy: Total outlays...........	—	—	....	....	....	....	....	....	....	....	....	....

Table 8 Transactions in financial assets and liabilities by sector

		Budgetary Central Government			Central Government			Local Government			General Government		
82	**Net acquisition of financial assets**........	−31.0	−3.3	27.0	....	....	....	....	....	....	....	....	....
821	Domestic..................................	−31.0	−3.3	27.0	....	....	....	....	....	....	....	....	....
8211	General government.......................	....	....	....	....	....	....	....	....	....	....	....	....
8212	Central bank...............................	....	....	....	....	....	....	....	....	....	....	....	....
8213	Other depository corporations.................	....	....	....	....	....	....	....	....	....	....	....	....
8214	Financial corporations n.e.c...................	....	....	....	....	....	....	....	....	....	....	....	....
8215	Nonfinancial corporations...................	....	....	....	....	....	....	....	....	....	....	....	....
8216	Households & NPIs serving households......	....	....	....	....	....	....	....	....	....	....	....	....
822	Foreign....................................	—	—	—	....	....	....	....	....	....	....	....	....
8221	General government.......................	—	—	—	....	....	....	....	....	....	....	....	....
8227	International organizations..................	—	—	—	....	....	....	....	....	....	....	....	....
8228	Financial corporations other than international organizations.............	—	—	—	....	....	....	....	....	....	....	....	....
8229	Other nonresidents........................	—	—	—	....	....	....	....	....	....	....	....	....
823	Monetary gold and SDRs....................	—	—	—	....	....	....	....	....	....	....	....	....
83	**Net incurrence of liabilities**..................	−2.6	25.7	100.8	....	....	....	....	....	....	....	....	....
831	Domestic..................................	−25.5	8.5	45.9	....	....	....	....	....	....	....	....	....
8311	General government.......................	....	....	....	....	....	....	....	....	....	....	....	....
8312	Central bank...............................	....	....	....	....	....	....	....	....	....	....	....	....
8313	Other depository corporations.................	....	....	....	....	....	....	....	....	....	....	....	....
8314	Financial corporations n.e.c...................	....	....	....	....	....	....	....	....	....	....	....	....
8315	Nonfinancial corporations...................	....	....	....	....	....	....	....	....	....	....	....	....
8316	Households & NPIs serving households......	....	....	....	....	....	....	....	....	....	....	....	....
832	Foreign....................................	22.9	17.2	54.9	....	....	....	....	....	....	....	....	....
8321	General government.......................	....	....	....	....	....	....	....	....	....	....	....	....
8327	International organizations..................	....	....	....	....	....	....	....	....	....	....	....	....
8328	Financial corporations other than international organizations.............	....	....	....	....	....	....	....	....	....	....	....	....
8329	Other nonresidents........................	....	....	....	....	....	....	....	....	....	....	....	....

Serbia and Montenegro 965

In Millions of Dinar / Year Ending December 31 / Cash Reporter

	Central Government			State Government			Local Government			General Government		
	2000	2001	2002	2000	2001	2002	2000	2001	2002	2000	2001	2002
Statement of government operations												
Statement of other economic flows												
Balance sheet												
Statement of sources and uses of cash												
1 Cash receipts from operating activities..........	....	....	368,653	....	....	8,833	....	....	56,300	....	....	425,494
11 Taxes....................	....	....	229,129	....	....	2,479	....	....	45,565	....	....	277,173
12 Social contributions.................	....	....	106,255	....	....	—	....	....	1,664	....	....	107,919
13 Grants.............	....	....	11,414	....	....	6,272	....	....	111	....	....	9,505
14 Other receipts...............	....	....	21,855	....	....	81	....	....	8,960	....	....	30,897
2 Cash payments for operating activities...........	....	....	398,179	....	....	8,747	....	....	....	....	....	....
21 Compensation of employees...............	....	....	53,783	....	....	267	....	....	....	....	....	....
22 Purchases of goods and services..............	....	....	40,399	....	....	944	....	....	....	....	....	....
24 Interest..................	....	....	9,670	....	....	—	....	....	....	....	....	....
25 Subsidies....................	....	....	45,546	....	....	94	....	....	....	....	....	....
26 Grants.................	....	....	24,165	....	....	6,599	....	....	....	....	....	....
27 Social benefits................	....	....	202,570	....	....	43	....	....	....	....	....	....
28 Other payments.................	....	....	22,046	....	....	800	....	....	....	....	....	....
CIO *Net cash inflow from oper. activities.....*	....	....	*−29,526*	....	....	*86*	....	....	....	....	....	....
31.1 Purchases of nonfinancial assets.................	....	....	....	....	....	....	....	....	....	....	....	....
31.2 Sales of nonfinancial assets..............	....	....	....	....	....	....	....	....	....	....	....	....
31 Net cash outflow from investments in nonfinancial assets..............	....	....	....	....	....	....	....	....	....	....	....	....
CSD *Cash surplus/deficit...............*	....	....	....	....	....	....	....	....	....	....	....	....
32x Net acquisition of fin assets, excl. cash..........	....	....	....	....	....	....	....	....	....	....	....	....
321x Domestic....................	....	....	....	....	....	....	....	....	....	....	....	....
322x Foreign....................	....	....	....	....	....	....	....	....	....	....	....	....
323 Monetary gold and SDRs................	....	....	....	....	....	....	....	....	....	....	....	....
33 Net incurrence of liabilities.................	....	....	....	....	....	....	....	....	....	....	....	....
331 Domestic.................	....	....	....	....	....	....	....	....	....	....	....	....
332 Foreign..................	....	....	....	....	....	....	....	....	....	....	....	....
NFB Net cash inflow from fin. activities............	....	....	....	....	....	....	....	....	....	....	....	....
NCB *Net change in the stock of cash.............*	....	....	....	....	....	....	....	....	....	....	....	....
Table 1 Revenue												
1 **Revenue**.........................	....	....	**368,653**	....	....	**8,833**	....	....	**56,300**	....	....	**425,494**
11 **Taxes**....................	....	....	**229,129**	....	....	**2,479**	....	....	**45,565**	....	....	**277,173**
111 Taxes on income, profits, & capital gains......	....	....	48,174	....	....	2,479	....	....	7,721	....	....	58,374
1111 Individuals...................	....	....	44,144	....	....	2,042	....	....	7,721	....	....	53,906
1112 Corporations and other enterprises......	....	....	4,030	....	....	438	....	....	—	....	....	4,468
112 Taxes on payroll and workforce..............	....	....	50	....	....	—	....	....	11,335	....	....	11,385
113 Taxes on property................	....	....	10,410	....	....	—	....	....	8,762	....	....	19,172
114 Taxes on goods and services..............	....	....	142,904	....	....	—	....	....	16,418	....	....	159,322
1141 General taxes on goods and services..........	....	....	91,954	....	....	—	....	....	14,098	....	....	106,052
1142 Excises......................	....	....	46,881	....	....	—	....	....	—	....	....	46,881
115 Taxes on int'l. trade and transactions..........	....	....	24,648	....	....	—	....	....	—	....	....	24,648
116 Other taxes.....................	....	....	2,944	....	....	—	....	....	1,328	....	....	4,272
12 **Social contributions**.............................	....	....	**106,255**	....	....	**—**	....	....	**1,664**	....	....	**107,919**
121 Social security contributions....................	....	....	106,255	....	....	—	....	....	1,664	....	....	107,919
122 Other social contributions...................	....	....	....	....	....	....	....	....	....	....	....	....
13 **Grants**..............................	....	....	**11,414**	....	....	**6,272**	....	....	**111**	....	....	**9,505**
131 From foreign governments.................	....	....	9,389	....	....	—	....	....	111	....	....	9,500
132 From international organizations..............	....	....	2	....	....	2	....	....	—	....	....	5
133 From other general government units...........	....	....	2,022	....	....	6,270	....	....	—	....	....	—
14 **Other revenue**..........................	....	....	**21,855**	....	....	**81**	....	....	**8,960**	....	....	**30,897**
Table 2 Expense by economic type												
2 **Expense**............................	....	....	**398,179**	....	....	**8,747**	....	....	....	....	....	....
21 **Compensation of employees**................	....	....	**53,783**	....	....	**267**	....	....	....	....	....	....
211 Wages and salaries......................	....	....	53,783	....	....	233	....	....	....	....	....	....
212 Social contributions......................	....	....	—	....	....	34	....	....	....	....	....	....
22 **Use of goods and services**......................	....	....	**40,399**	....	....	**944**	....	....	....	....	....	....
23 **Consumption of fixed capital**................	....	....	....	....	....	....	....	....	....	....	....	....
24 **Interest**.............................	....	....	**9,670**	....	....	**—**	....	....	....	....	....	....
25 **Subsidies**.............................	....	....	**45,546**	....	....	**94**	....	....	....	....	....	....

In Millions of Dinar / Year Ending December 31 / Cash Reporter

		Central Government			State Government			Local Government			General Government		
		2000	2001	2002	2000	2001	2002	2000	2001	2002	2000	2001	2002
26	Grants..	....	....	24,165	....	....	6,599	....	....	....	....	....	....
261	To foreign govenments...........................	....	....	—	....	....	—	....	....	....	....	....	....
262	To international organizations....................	....	....	241	....	....	1	....	....	....	....	....	....
263	To other general government units...............	....	....	23,924	....	....	6,598	....	....	....	....	....	....
2631	Current...	....	....	23,924	....	....	6,598	....	....	....	....	....	....
2632	Capital..	....	....	—	....	....	....	....	....	....	....	....	....
27	Social benefits.................................	....	....	202,570	....	....	43	....	....	....	....	....	....
28	Other expense.................................	....	....	22,046	....	....	800	....	....	....	....	....	....
281	Property expense other than interest.............	....	....	507	....	....	—	....	....	....	....	....	....
282	Miscellaneous other expense.....................	....	....	21,539	....	....	800	....	....	....	....	....	....
2821	Current...	....	....	21,539	....	....	800	....	....	....	....	....	....
2822	Capital..	....	....	—	....	....	—	....	....	....	....	....	....

Table 3 Transactions in assets and liabilities													
Table 4 Holding gains in assets and liabilities													
Table 5 Other changes in the volume of assets and liabilities													
Table 6 Balance sheet													
Table 7 Outlays by functions of govt.													
Table 8 Transactions in financial assets and liabilities by sector													

In Millions of Rupees / Year Ending December 31 / Cash Reporter

	Budgetary Central Government			Extrabudgetary Accounts			Central Government			General Government		
	2002	2003	2004	2002	2003	2004	2002	2003	2004p	2002	2003	2004p
Statement of government operations												
Statement of other economic flows												
Balance sheet												
Statement of sources and uses of cash												
1　Cash receipts from operating activities...........	....	....	....	....	....	....	1,607.0	1,755.8	1,894.6	1,607.0	1,755.8	1,894.6
11　Taxes....................................	....	....	....	....	....	....	999.1	1,247.4	1,362.5	999.1	1,247.4	1,362.5
12　Social contributions......................	....	....	....	....	....	....	253.7	269.7	250.4	253.7	269.7	250.4
13　Grants...................................	....	....	....	....	....	....	25.1	12.9	10.9	25.1	12.9	10.9
14　Other receipts...........................	....	....	....	....	....	....	329.1	225.8	270.8	329.1	225.8	270.8
2　Cash payments for operating activities...........	....	....	....	....	....	....	1,810.5	1,372.5	1,737.5	1,810.5	1,372.5	1,737.5
21　Compensation of employees.................	....	....	....	....	....	....	508.4	467.3	488.5	508.4	467.3	488.5
22　Purchases of goods and services.............	....	....	....	....	....	....	447.0	212.9	338.5	447.0	212.9	338.5
24　Interest.................................	....	....	....	....	....	....	307.1	217.6	263.6	307.1	217.6	263.6
25　Subsidies...............................	....	....	....	....	....	....	105.3	120.4	94.2	105.3	120.4	94.2
26　Grants..................................	....	....	....	....	....	....	—	—	—	—	—	—
27　Social benefits..........................	....	....	....	....	....	....	442.4	331.8	525.5	442.4	331.8	525.5
28　Other payments..........................	....	....	....	....	....	....	.3	22.5	27.2	.3	22.5	27.2
CIO　*Net cash inflow from oper. activities.....*	....	....	....	....	....	....	*−203.5*	*383.3*	*157.1*	*−203.5*	*383.3*	*157.1*
31.1　Purchases of nonfinancial assets..................	....	....	....	....	....	....	362.3	96.7	165.8	362.3	96.7	165.8
31.2　Sales of nonfinancial assets..................	....	....	....	....	....	....	16.4	117.2	122.3	16.4	117.2	122.3
31　Net cash outflow from investments in nonfinancial assets..................	....	....	....	....	....	....	345.9	−20.5	43.5	345.9	−20.5	43.5
CSD　*Cash surplus/deficit*....................	....	....	....	....	....	....	*−549.4*	*403.8*	*113.6*	*−549.4*	*403.8*	*113.6*
32x　Net acquisition of fin assets, excl. cash...........	....	....	....	....	....	....	37.3	29.0	202.0	37.3	29.0	202.0
321x　Domestic..............................	....	....	....	....	....	....	37.3	29.0	202.0	37.3	29.0	202.0
322x　Foreign...............................	....	....	....	....	....	....	—	—	—	—	—	—
323　Monetary gold and SDRs.................	....	....	....	....	....	....						
33　Net incurrence of liabilities................	....	....	....	....	....	....	333.5	−1,305.2	−1,186.0	333.5	−1,305.2	−1,186.0
331　Domestic..............................	....	....	....	....	....	....	656.0	−1,319.1	−1,176.3	656.0	−1,319.1	−1,176.3
332　Foreign...............................	....	....	....	....	....	....	−322.5	13.9	−9.7	−322.5	13.9	−9.7
NFB　Net cash inflow from fin. activities.............	....	....	....	....	....	....	296.2	−1,334.2	−1,388.0	296.2	−1,334.2	−1,388.0
NCB　*Net change in the stock of cash............*	....	....	....	....	....	....	*−253.2*	*−930.4*	*−1,274.4*	*−253.2*	*−930.4*	*−1,274.4*
Table 1　Revenue												
1　**Revenue**.................................	....	....	....	....	....	....	**1,607.0**	**1,755.8**	**1,894.6**	**1,607.0**	**1,755.8**	**1,894.6**
11　**Taxes**.................................	....	....	....	....	....	....	**999.1**	**1,247.4**	**1,362.5**	**999.1**	**1,247.4**	**1,362.5**
111　Taxes on income, profits, & capital gains......	....	....	....	....	....	....	253.1	276.6	298.4	253.1	276.6	298.4
1111　Individuals............................	....	....	....	....	....	....	.1	—	—	.1	—	—
1112　Corporations and other enterprises............	....	....	....	....	....	....	253.0	276.6	298.4	253.0	276.6	298.4
112　Taxes on payroll and workforce.............	....	....	....	....	....	....	—	—	—	—	—	—
113　Taxes on property.......................	....	....	....	....	....	....	19.5	1.7	.9	19.5	1.7	.9
114　Taxes on goods and services................	....	....	....	....	....	....	321.5	547.1	686.7	321.5	547.1	686.7
1141　General taxes on goods and services..........	....	....	....	....	....	....	....	....	....	....	....	....
1142　Excises...............................	....	....	....	....	....	....	....	....	....	....	....	....
115　Taxes on int'l. trade and transactions...........	....	....	....	....	....	....	389.8	393.9	351.2	389.8	393.9	351.2
116　Other taxes............................	....	....	....	....	....	....	15.2	28.1	25.3	15.2	28.1	25.3
12　**Social contributions**.....................	....	....	....	....	....	....	**253.7**	**269.7**	**250.4**	**253.7**	**269.7**	**250.4**
121　Social security contributions................	....	....	....	....	....	....	253.7	269.7	250.4	253.7	269.7	250.4
122　Other social contributions................	....	....	....	....	....	....	—	—	—	—	—	—
13　**Grants**.................................	....	....	....	....	....	....	**25.1**	**12.9**	**10.9**	**25.1**	**12.9**	**10.9**
131　From foreign governments.................	....	....	....	....	....	....	25.1	12.9	10.9	25.1	12.9	10.9
132　From international organizations..............	....	....	....	....	....	....	—	—	—	—	—	—
133　From other general government units...........	....	....	....	....	....	....	—	—	—	—	—	—
14　**Other revenue**...........................	....	....	....	....	....	....	**329.1**	**225.8**	**270.8**	**329.1**	**225.8**	**270.8**
Table 2　Expense by economic type												
2　**Expense**................................	....	....	....	....	....	....	**1,810.5**	**1,372.5**	**1,737.5**	**1,810.5**	**1,372.5**	**1,737.5**
21　**Compensation of employees**.................	....	....	....	....	....	....	**508.4**	**467.3**	**488.5**	**508.4**	**467.3**	**488.5**
211　Wages and salaries.......................	....	....	....	....	....	....	....	....	....	....	....	....
212　Social contributions.....................	....	....	....	....	....	....	....	....	....	....	....	....
22　**Use of goods and services**..................	....	....	....	....	....	....	**447.0**	**212.9**	**338.5**	**447.0**	**212.9**	**338.5**
23　**Consumption of fixed capital**...............	....	....	....	....	....	....	....	....	....	....	....	....
24　**Interest**................................	....	....	....	....	....	....	**307.1**	**217.6**	**263.6**	**307.1**	**217.6**	**263.6**
25　**Subsidies**...............................	....	....	....	....	....	....	**105.3**	**120.4**	**94.2**	**105.3**	**120.4**	**94.2**

In Millions of Rupees / Year Ending December 31 / Cash Reporter

		Budgetary Central Government			Extrabudgetary Accounts			Central Government			General Government		
		2002	2003	2004	2002	2003	2004	2002	2003	2004p	2002	2003	2004p
26	**Grants**................................	....	....	....	....	....	....	—	—	—	—	—	—
261	To foreign govenments................	....	....	....	....	....	....	—	—	—	—	—	—
262	To international organizations........	....	....	....	....	....	....	—	—	—	—	—	—
263	To other general government units........	....	....	....	....	....	....	—	—	—	—	—	—
2631	Current................................	....	....	....	....	....	....	—	—	—	—	—	—
2632	Capital................................	....	....	....	....	....	....	—	—	—	—	—	—
27	**Social benefits**........................	....	....	....	....	....	....	442.4	331.8	525.5	442.4	331.8	525.5
28	**Other expense**.........................	....	....	....	....	....	....	.3	22.5	27.2	.3	22.5	27.2
281	Property expense other than interest........	....	....	....	....	....	....						
282	Miscellaneous other expense..........	....	....	....	....	....	....	.3	22.5	27.2	.3	22.5	27.2
2821	Current................................	....	....	....	....	....	....	—	—	—	—	—	—
2822	Capital................................	....	....	....	....	....	....	.3	22.5	27.2	.3	22.5	27.2

Table 3 Transactions in assets and liabilities

		Budgetary Central Government			Extrabudgetary Accounts			Central Government			General Government		
		2002	2003	2004	2002	2003	2004	2002	2003	2004p	2002	2003	2004p
3	**Change in net worth from transactns....**	....	....	....	....	....	....	....	....	....	....	....	....
31	**Net acquisition of nonfinancial assets...**	....	....	....	....	....	....	345.9	−20.5	43.5	345.9	−20.5	43.5
311	Fixed assets...........................	....	....	....	....	....	....	345.9	−20.5	43.5	345.9	−20.5	43.5
3111	Buildings and structures.............	....	....	....	....	....	....	....	....	....	....	....	....
3112	Machinery and equipment............	....	....	....	....	....	....	....	....	....	....	....	....
3113	Other fixed assets...................	....	....	....	....	....	....	....	....	....	....	....	....
312	Inventories............................	....	....	....	....	....	....	—	—	—	—	—	—
313	Valuables..............................	....	....	....	....	....	....	—	—	—	—	—	—
314	Nonproduced assets....................	....	....	....	....	....	....	—	—	—	—	—	—
3141	Land.................................	....	....	....	....	....	....	—	—	—	—	—	—
3142	Subsoil assets.......................	....	....	....	....	....	....	—	—	—	—	—	—
3143	Other naturally occurring assets....	....	....	....	....	....	....	—	—	—	—	—	—
3144	Intangible nonproduced assets.......	....	....	....	....	....	....	—	—	—	—	—	—
32	**Net acquisition of financial assets........**	....	....	....	....	....	....	−215.9	−901.4	−1,072.4	−215.9	−901.4	−1,072.4
321	Domestic...............................	....	....	....	....	....	....	−218.7	−901.4	−1,072.4	−218.7	−901.4	−1,072.4
3212	Currency and deposits................	....	....	....	....	....	....	−256.0	−930.4	−1,274.4	−256.0	−930.4	−1,274.4
3213	Securities other than shares.........	....	....	....	....	....	....	—	—	—	—	—	—
3214	Loans................................	....	....	....	....	....	....	37.3	29.0	202.0	37.3	29.0	202.0
3215	Shares and other equity..............	....	....	....	....	....	....	—	—	—	—	—	—
3216	Insurance technical reserves.........	....	....	....	....	....	....	—	—	—	—	—	—
3217	Financial derivatives................	....	....	....	....	....	....	—	—	—	—	—	—
3218	Other accounts receivable............	....	....	....	....	....	....	....	....	....	....	....	....
322	Foreign...............................	....	....	....	....	....	....	2.8	—	—	2.8	—	—
3222	Currency and deposits................	....	....	....	....	....	....	2.8	—	—	2.8	—	—
3223	Securities other than shares.........	....	....	....	....	....	....						
3224	Loans................................	....	....	....	....	....	....						
3225	Shares and other equity..............	....	....	....	....	....	....						
3226	Insurance technical reserves.........	....	....	....	....	....	....						
3227	Financial derivatives................	....	....	....	....	....	....	—	—	—	—	—	—
3228	Other accounts receivable............	....	....	....	....	....	....	....	....	....	....	....	....
323	Monetary gold and SDRs.................	....	....	....	....	....	....	—	—	—	—	—	—
33	**Net incurrence of liabilities...................**	....	....	....	....	....	....	333.5	−1,305.2	−1,186.0	333.5	−1,305.2	−1,186.0
331	Domestic...............................	....	....	....	....	....	....	656.0	−1,319.1	−1,176.3	656.0	−1,319.1	−1,176.3
3312	Currency and deposits................	....	....	....	....	....	....	—	—	—	—	—	—
3313	Securities other than shares.........	....	....	....	....	....	....	—	—	—	—	—	—
3314	Loans................................	....	....	....	....	....	....	656.0	−1,319.1	−1,176.3	656.0	−1,319.1	−1,176.3
3316	Insurance technical reserves.........	....	....	....	....	....	....	—	—	—	—	—	—
3317	Financial derivatives................	....	....	....	....	....	....	—	—	—	—	—	—
3318	Other accounts payable...............	....	....	....	....	....	....	....	....	....	....	....	....
332	Foreign...............................	....	....	....	....	....	....	−322.5	13.9	−9.7	−322.5	13.9	−9.7
3322	Currency and deposits................	....	....	....	....	....	....						
3323	Securities other than shares.........	....	....	....	....	....	....	—	—	—	—	—	—
3324	Loans................................	....	....	....	....	....	....	−322.5	13.9	−9.7	−322.5	13.9	−9.7
3326	Insurance technical reserves.........	....	....	....	....	....	....	—	—	—	—	—	—
3327	Financial derivatives................	....	....	....	....	....	....	—	—	—	—	—	—
3328	Other accounts payable...............	....	....	....	....	....	....	....	....	....	....	....	....

In Millions of Rupees / Year Ending December 31 / Cash Reporter

	Budgetary Central Government			Extrabudgetary Accounts			Central Government			General Government		
	2002	2003	2004	2002	2003	2004	2002	2003	2004p	2002	2003	2004p
Table 4 Holding gains in assets and liabilities												
Table 5 Other changes in the volume of assets and liabilities												
Table 6 Balance sheet												
Table 7 Outlays by functions of govt.												
7 **Total outlays**	....	....	....	....	....	....	2,156.4	1,352.0	1,781.0	2,156.4	1,352.0	1,781.0
701 **General public services**	....	....	....	....	....	....	770.8	534.6	624.1	770.8	534.6	624.1
7017 Public debt transactions	....	....	....	....	....	....	307.1	217.6	263.6	307.1	217.6	263.6
7018 General transfers between levels of govt.	....	....	....	....	....	....	....	....	....	....	....	....
702 **Defense**	....	....	....	....	....	....	78.8	67.4	86.0	78.8	67.4	86.0
703 **Public order and safety**	....	....	....	....	....	....	81.0	90.3	92.1	81.0	90.3	92.1
704 **Economic affairs**	....	....	....	....	....	....	165.5	135.2	156.5	165.5	135.2	156.5
7042 Agriculture, forestry, fishing, and hunting	....	....	....	....	....	....	35.1	36.3	66.7	35.1	36.3	66.7
7043 Fuel and energy	....	....	....	....	....	....	—	—	—	—	—	—
7044 Mining, manufacturing, and construction	....	....	....	....	....	....	4.0	4.1	2.0	4.0	4.1	2.0
7045 Transport	....	....	....	....	....	....	79.6	111.9	71.8	79.6	111.9	71.8
7046 Communication	....	....	....	....	....	....	....	....	....	....	....	....
705 **Environmental protection**	....	....	....	....	....	....	....	....	....	....	....	....
706 **Housing and community amenities**	....	....	....	....	....	....	54.5	11.7	15.4	54.5	11.7	15.4
707 **Health**	....	....	....	....	....	....	136.6	158.1	174.4	136.6	158.1	174.4
7072 Outpatient services	....	....	....	....	....	....	....	....	....	....	....	....
7073 Hospital services	....	....	....	....	....	....	....	....	....	....	....	....
7074 Public health services	....	....	....	....	....	....	....	....	....	....	....	....
708 **Recreation, culture, and religion**	....	....	....	....	....	....	23.8	27.6	58.3	23.8	27.6	58.3
709 **Education**	....	....	....	....	....	....	211.8	173.1	164.3	211.8	173.1	164.3
7091 Pre-primary and primary education	....	....	....	....	....	....	....	....	....	....	....	....
7092 Secondary education	....	....	....	....	....	....	....	....	....	....	....	....
7094 Tertiary education	....	....	....	....	....	....	....	....	....	....	....	....
710 **Social protection**	....	....	....	....	....	....	302.0	304.0	358.4	302.0	304.0	358.4
7 Statistical discrepancy: Total outlays	....	....	....	....	....	....	331.0	−150.0	51.5	331.0	−150.0	51.5
Table 8 Transactions in financial assets and liabilities by sector												
82 **Net acquisition of financial assets**	....	....	....	....	....	....	−215.9	−901.4	−1,072.4	−215.9	−901.4	−1,072.4
821 Domestic	....	....	....	....	....	....	−218.7	−901.4	−1,072.4	−218.7	−901.4	−1,072.4
8211 General government	....	....	....	....	....	....	—	—	−1,274.4	—	—	−1,274.4
8212 Central bank	....	....	....	....	....	....	....	....	....	....	....	....
8213 Other depository corporations	....	....	....	....	....	....	....	....	....	....	....	....
8214 Financial corporations n.e.c.	....	....	....	....	....	....	....	....	....	....	....	....
8215 Nonfinancial corporations	....	....	....	....	....	....	37.4	29.0	202.0	37.4	29.0	202.0
8216 Households & NPIs serving households	....	....	....	....	....	....	....	....	....	....	....	....
822 Foreign	....	....	....	....	....	....	2.8	—	—	2.8	—	—
8221 General government	....	....	....	....	....	....	—	—	—	—	—	—
8227 International organizations	....	....	....	....	....	....	....	....	....	....	....	....
8228 Financial corporations other than international organizations	....	....	....	....	....	....	—	—	—	—	—	—
8229 Other nonresidents	....	....	....	....	....	....	—	—	—	....	—	—
823 Monetary gold and SDRs	....	....	....	....	....	....	—	—	—	—	—	—
83 **Net incurrence of liabilities**	....	....	....	....	....	....	333.5	−1,305.2	−1,186.0	333.5	−1,305.2	−1,186.0
831 Domestic	....	....	....	....	....	....	656.0	−1,319.1	−1,176.3	656.0	−1,319.1	−1,176.3
8311 General government	....	....	....	....	....	....	....	....	....	....	....	....
8312 Central bank	....	....	....	....	....	....	....	....	....	....	....	....
8313 Other depository corporations	....	....	....	....	....	....	....	....	....	....	....	....
8314 Financial corporations n.e.c.	....	....	....	....	....	....	....	....	....	....	....	....
8315 Nonfinancial corporations	....	....	....	....	....	....	....	....	....	....	....	....
8316 Households & NPIs serving households	....	....	....	....	....	....	....	....	....	....	....	....
832 Foreign	....	....	....	....	....	....	−322.5	13.9	−9.7	−322.5	13.9	−9.7
8321 General government	....	....	....	....	....	....	−.7	−5.5	—	−.7	−5.5	—
8327 International organizations	....	....	....	....	....	....	−3.5	−22.9	−4.7	−3.5	−22.9	−4.7
8328 Financial corporations other than international organizations	....	....	....	....	....	....	....	....	....	....	....	....
8329 Other nonresidents	....	....	....	....	....	....	....	....	....	....	....	....

In Billions of Leones / Year Ending December 31 / Cash Reporter

	Budgetary Central Government			Central Government			Local Government			General Government		
	1997	1998	1999	1997	1998	1999	1997	1998	1999	1997	1998	1999
Statement of government operations												
Statement of other economic flows												
Balance sheet												
6 *Net worth*...................	....	....	....	....	....	....	....	....	....	....	....	....
61 Nonfinancial assets..........	....	....	....	....	....	....	....	....	....	....	....	....
62 Financial assets..........	....	....	....	....	....	....	....	....	....	....	....	....
63 Liabilities..........	994.22	†1,974.19	2,987.64	....	....	....	....	....	....	....	....	....
Statement of sources and uses of cash												
1 Cash receipts from operating activities..........	94.99	†99.66	151.21	....	....	....	....	....	....	....	....	....
11 Taxes..........	82.71	†75.69	82.34	....	....	....	....	....	....	....	....	....
12 Social contributions..........	—	†—	—	....	....	....	....	....	....	....	....	....
13 Grants..........	9.50	†22.46	65.39	....	....	....	....	....	....	....	....	....
14 Other receipts..........	2.79	†1.51	3.48	....	....	....	....	....	....	....	....	....
2 Cash payments for operating activities..........	....	....	....	....	....	....	....	....	....	....	....	....
21 Compensation of employees..........	28.32	†59.68	117.53	....	....	....	....	....	....	....	....	....
22 Purchases of goods and services..........	27.59	†35.21	33.99	....	....	....	....	....	....	....	....	....
24 Interest..........	17.93	†50.64	70.24	....	....	....	....	....	....	....	....	....
25 Subsidies..........	26.19	†.52	—	....	....	....	....	....	....	....	....	....
26 Grants..........	....	....	....	....	....	....	....	....	....	....	....	....
27 Social benefits..........	7.85	†9.36	14.18	....	....	....	....	....	....	....	....	....
28 Other payments..........	....	....	....	....	....	....	....	....	....	....	....	....
CIO *Net cash inflow from oper. activities*.....	....	....	....	....	....	....	....	....	....	....	....	....
31.1 Purchases of nonfinancial assets..........	....	....	....	....	....	....	....	....	....	....	....	....
31.2 Sales of nonfinancial assets..........	—	†—	—	....	....	....	....	....	....	....	....	....
31 Net cash outflow from investments in nonfinancial assets..........	....	....	....	....	....	....	....	....	....	....	....	....
CSD *Cash surplus/deficit*..........	−48.30	†−47.40	−101.67	....	....	....	....	....	....	....	....	....
32x Net acquisition of fin assets, excl. cash..........	—	†.33	.70	....	....	....	....	....	....	....	....	....
321x Domestic..........	—	†.33	.70	....	....	....	....	....	....	....	....	....
322x Foreign..........	—	†—	—	....	....	....	....	....	....	....	....	....
323 Monetary gold and SDRs..........	—	†—	—	....	....	....	....	....	....	....	....	....
33 Net incurrence of liabilities..........	....	....	....	....	....	....	....	....	....	....	....	....
331 Domestic..........	10.76	†50.60	102.79	....	....	....	....	....	....	....	....	....
332 Foreign..........	....	....	....	....	....	....	....	....	....	....	....	....
NFB Net cash inflow from fin. activities..........	....	....	....	....	....	....	....	....	....	....	....	....
NCB *Net change in the stock of cash*..........	....	....	....	....	....	....	....	....	....	....	....	....
Table 1 Revenue												
1 **Revenue**..........	**94.99**	**†99.66**	**151.21**	....	....	....	....	....	....	....	....	....
11 **Taxes**..........	**82.71**	**†75.69**	**82.34**	....	....	....	....	....	....	....	....	....
111 Taxes on income, profits, & capital gains......	14.57	†13.32	22.15	....	....	....	....	....	....	....	....	....
1111 Individuals..........	6.02	†5.82	13.55	....	....	....	....	....	....	....	....	....
1112 Corporations and other enterprises..........	7.85	†6.42	8.43	....	....	....	....	....	....	....	....	....
112 Taxes on payroll and workforce..........	.20	†—	—	....	....	....	....	....	....	....	....	....
113 Taxes on property..........	—	†—	—	....	....	....	....	....	....	....	....	....
114 Taxes on goods and services..........	28.11	†19.53	18.48	....	....	....	....	....	....	....	....	....
1141 General taxes on goods and services..........	2.74	†1.87	.42	....	....	....	....	....	....	....	....	....
1142 Excises..........	21.02	†14.55	15.30	....	....	....	....	....	....	....	....	....
115 Taxes on int'l. trade and transactions..........	39.74	†42.84	41.71	....	....	....	....	....	....	....	....	....
116 Other taxes..........	.09	†—	—	....	....	....	....	....	....	....	....	....
12 **Social contributions**..........	—	†—	—	....	....	....	....	....	....	....	....	....
121 Social security contributions..........	—	†—	—	....	....	....	....	....	....	....	....	....
122 Other social contributions..........	—	†—	—	....	....	....	....	....	....	....	....	....
13 **Grants**..........	**9.50**	**†22.46**	**65.39**	....	....	....	....	....	....	....	....	....
131 From foreign governments..........	9.50	†22.46	65.39	....	....	....	....	....	....	....	....	....
132 From international organizations..........	—	†—	—	....	....	....	....	....	....	....	....	....
133 From other general government units..........	—	†—	—	....	....	....	....	....	....	....	....	....
14 **Other revenue**..........	**2.79**	**†1.51**	**3.48**	....	....	....	....	....	....	....	....	....
Table 2 Expense by economic type												
2 **Expense**..........	....	....	....	....	....	....	....	....	....	....	....	....
21 **Compensation of employees**..........	**28.32**	**†59.68**	**117.53**	....	....	....	....	....	....	....	....	....
211 Wages and salaries..........	28.32	†59.68	117.53	....	....	....	....	....	....	....	....	....
212 Social contributions..........	—	†—	—	....	....	....	....	....	....	....	....	....
22 **Use of goods and services**..........	**27.59**	**†35.21**	**33.99**	....	....	....	....	....	....	....	....	....
23 **Consumption of fixed capital**..........	....	....	....	....	....	....	....	....	....	....	....	....
24 **Interest**..........	**17.93**	**†50.64**	**70.24**	....	....	....	....	....	....	....	....	....
25 **Subsidies**..........	**26.19**	**†.52**	**—**	....	....	....	....	....	....	....	....	....

In Billions of Leones / Year Ending December 31 / Cash Reporter

	Budgetary Central Government			Central Government			Local Government			General Government		
	1997	1998	1999	1997	1998	1999	1997	1998	1999	1997	1998	1999
26 **Grants**................................	....	....	....	....	....	....	....	....	....	....	....	....
261 To foreign govenments............	....	....	....	....	....	....	....	....	....	....	....	....
262 To international organizations......	....	....	....	....	....	....	....	....	....	....	....	....
263 To other general government units......	....	....	....	....	....	....	....	....	....	....	....	....
2631 Current..................	—	†—	—	....	....	....	....	....	....	....	....	....
2632 Capital..................	....	....	....	....	....	....	....	....	....	....	....	....
27 **Social benefits**....................	7.85	†9.36	14.18	....	....	....	....	....	....	....	....	....
28 **Other expense**....................	....	....	....	....	....	....	....	....	....	....	....	....
281 Property expense other than interest...........	....	....	....	....	....	....	....	....	....	....	....	....
282 Miscellaneous other expense............	....	....	....	....	....	....	....	....	....	....	....	....
2821 Current..................	....	....	....	....	....	....	....	....	....	....	....	....
2822 Capital..................	....	....	....	....	....	....	....	....	....	....	....	....
Table 3 Transactions in assets and liabilities												
3 **Change in net worth from transactns....**	....	....	....	....	....	....	....	....	....	....	....	....
31 **Net acquisition of nonfinancial assets...**	....	....	....	....	....	....	....	....	....	....	....	....
311 Fixed assets..................	....	....	....	....	....	....	....	....	....	....	....	....
3111 Buildings and structures..........	....	....	....	....	....	....	....	....	....	....	....	....
3112 Machinery and equipment..........	....	....	....	....	....	....	....	....	....	....	....	....
3113 Other fixed assets..............	....	....	....	....	....	....	....	....	....	....	....	....
312 Inventories..................	....	....	....	....	....	....	....	....	....	....	....	....
313 Valuables..................	....	....	....	....	....	....	....	....	....	....	....	....
314 Nonproduced assets............	....	....	....	....	....	....	....	....	....	....	....	....
3141 Land..................	....	....	....	....	....	....	....	....	....	....	....	....
3142 Subsoil assets..............	....	....	....	....	....	....	....	....	....	....	....	....
3143 Other naturally occurring assets..........	....	....	....	....	....	....	....	....	....	....	....	....
3144 Intangible nonproduced assets............	....	....	....	....	....	....	....	....	....	....	....	....
32 **Net acquisition of financial assets.........**	....	....	....	....	....	....	....	....	....	....	....	....
321 Domestic..................	3.27	†3.15	14.68	....	....	....	....	....	....	....	....	....
3212 Currency and deposits............	3.27	†2.82	13.98	....	....	....	....	....	....	....	....	....
3213 Securities other than shares..........	....	....	....	....	....	....	....	....	....	....	....	....
3214 Loans..................	....	....	....	....	....	....	....	....	....	....	....	....
3215 Shares and other equity..........	....	....	....	....	....	....	....	....	....	....	....	....
3216 Insurance technical reserves..........	....	....	....	....	....	....	....	....	....	....	....	....
3217 Financial derivatives..............	....	....	....	....	....	....	....	....	....	....	....	....
3218 Other accounts receivable..........	....	....	....	....	....	....	....	....	....	....	....	....
322 Foreign..................	....	....	....	....	....	....	....	....	....	....	....	....
3222 Currency and deposits............	....	....	....	....	....	....	....	....	....	....	....	....
3223 Securities other than shares..........	....	....	....	....	....	....	....	....	....	....	....	....
3224 Loans..................	....	....	....	....	....	....	....	....	....	....	....	....
3225 Shares and other equity..........	....	....	....	....	....	....	....	....	....	....	....	....
3226 Insurance technical reserves..........	....	....	....	....	....	....	....	....	....	....	....	....
3227 Financial derivatives..............	....	....	....	....	....	....	....	....	....	....	....	....
3228 Other accounts receivable..........	....	....	....	....	....	....	....	....	....	....	....	....
323 Monetary gold and SDRs..........	—	†—	—	....	....	....	....	....	....	....	....	....
33 **Net incurrence of liabilities...................**	....	....	....	....	....	....	....	....	....	....	....	....
331 Domestic..................	10.76	†50.60	102.79	....	....	....	....	....	....	....	....	....
3312 Currency and deposits............	—	†—'	—	....	....	....	....	....	....	....	....	....
3313 Securities other than shares..........	−.55	†61.89	34.26	....	....	....	....	....	....	....	....	....
3314 Loans..................	11.31	†−11.29	68.53	....	....	....	....	....	....	....	....	....
3316 Insurance technical reserves..........	....	....	....	....	....	....	....	....	....	....	....	....
3317 Financial derivatives..............	....	....	....	....	....	....	....	....	....	....	....	....
3318 Other accounts payable..........	....	....	....	....	....	....	....	....	....	....	....	....
332 Foreign..................	....	....	....	....	....	....	....	....	....	....	....	....
3322 Currency and deposits............	....	....	....	....	....	....	....	....	....	....	....	....
3323 Securities other than shares..........	....	....	....	....	....	....	....	....	....	....	....	....
3324 Loans..................	....	....	....	....	....	....	....	....	....	....	....	....
3326 Insurance technical reserves..........	....	....	....	....	....	....	....	....	....	....	....	....
3327 Financial derivatives..............	....	....	....	....	....	....	....	....	....	....	....	....
3328 Other accounts payable..........	....	....	....	....	....	....	....	....	....	....	....	....

In Billions of Leones / Year Ending December 31 / Cash Reporter

	Budgetary Central Government			Central Government			Local Government			General Government		
	1997	1998	1999	1997	1998	1999	1997	1998	1999	1997	1998	1999
Table 4 Holding gains in assets and liabilities												
Table 5 Other changes in the volume of assets and liabilities												
Table 6 Balance sheet												
6 **Net worth**............................	....	....	....	....	....	....	....	....	....	....	....	....
61 **Nonfinancial assets**...................	....	....	....	....	....	....	....	....	....	....	....	....
611 Fixed assets...............................	....	....	....	....	....	....	....	....	....	....	....	....
6111 Buildings and structures...............	....	....	....	....	....	....	....	....	....	....	....	....
6112 Machinery and equipment.............	....	....	....	....	....	....	....	....	....	....	....	....
6113 Other fixed assets.........................	....	....	....	....	....	....	....	....	....	....	....	....
612 Inventories.................................	....	....	....	....	....	....	....	....	....	....	....	....
613 Valuables....................................	....	....	....	....	....	....	....	....	....	....	....	....
614 Nonproduced assets......................	....	....	....	....	....	....	....	....	....	....	....	....
6141 Land...	....	....	....	....	....	....	....	....	....	....	....	....
6142 Subsoil assets..............................	....	....	....	....	....	....	....	....	....	....	....	....
6143 Other naturally occurring assets.....	....	....	....	....	....	....	....	....	....	....	....	....
6144 Intangible nonproduced assets.......	....	....	....	....	....	....	....	....	....	....	....	....
62 **Financial assets**.........................	....	....	....	....	....	....	....	....	....	....	....	....
621 Domestic....................................	....	....	....	....	....	....	....	....	....	....	....	....
6212 Currency and deposits...................	....	....	....	....	....	....	....	....	....	....	....	....
6213 Securities other than shares...........	....	....	....	....	....	....	....	....	....	....	....	....
6214 Loans..	....	....	....	....	....	....	....	....	....	....	....	....
6215 Shares and other equity.................	....	....	....	....	....	....	....	....	....	....	....	....
6216 Insurance technical reserves..........	....	....	....	....	....	....	....	....	....	....	....	....
6217 Financial derivatives.....................	....	....	....	....	....	....	....	....	....	....	....	....
6218 Other accounts receivable..............	....	....	....	....	....	....	....	....	....	....	....	....
622 Foreign.......................................	....	....	....	....	....	....	....	....	....	....	....	....
6222 Currency and deposits...................	....	....	....	....	....	....	....	....	....	....	....	....
6223 Securities other than shares...........	....	....	....	....	....	....	....	....	....	....	....	....
6224 Loans..	....	....	....	....	....	....	....	....	....	....	....	....
6225 Shares and other equity.................	....	....	....	....	....	....	....	....	....	....	....	....
6226 Insurance technical reserves..........	....	....	....	....	....	....	....	....	....	....	....	....
6227 Financial derivatives.....................	....	....	....	....	....	....	....	....	....	....	....	....
6228 Other accounts receivable..............	....	....	....	....	....	....	....	....	....	....	....	....
623 Monetary gold and SDRs................	....	....	....	....	....	....	....	....	....	....	....	....
63 **Liabilities**.................................	994.22	†1,974.19	2,987.64	....	....	....	....	....	....	....	....	....
631 Domestic....................................	52.37	†133.20	231.67	....	....	....	....	....	....	....	....	....
6312 Currency and deposits...................	....	....	....	....	....	....	....	....	....	....	....	....
6313 Securities other than shares...........	....	....	....	....	....	....	....	....	....	....	....	....
6314 Loans..	....	....	....	....	....	....	....	....	....	....	....	....
6316 Insurance technical reserves..........	....	....	....	....	....	....	....	....	....	....	....	....
6317 Financial derivatives.....................	....	....	....	....	....	....	....	....	....	....	....	....
6318 Other accounts payable.................	....	....	....	....	....	....	....	....	....	....	....	....
632 Foreign.......................................	941.85	†1,840.99	2,755.97	....	....	....	....	....	....	....	....	....
6322 Currency and deposits...................	....	....	....	....	....	....	....	....	....	....	....	....
6323 Securities other than shares...........	....	....	....	....	....	....	....	....	....	....	....	....
6324 Loans..	....	....	....	....	....	....	....	....	....	....	....	....
6326 Insurance technical reserves..........	....	....	....	....	....	....	....	....	....	....	....	....
6327 Financial derivatives.....................	....	....	....	....	....	....	....	....	....	....	....	....
6328 Other accounts payable.................	....	....	....	....	....	....	....	....	....	....	....	....
Memorandum items:												
6M2 Net financial worth.......................	....	....	....	....	....	....	....	....	....	....	....	....
6M3 Debt at market value.....................	....	....	....	....	....	....	....	....	....	....	....	....
6M4 Debt at nominal value....................	....	....	....	....	....	....	....	....	....	....	....	....
6M5 Arrears.......................................	....	....	....	....	....	....	....	....	....	....	....	....
6M6 Obligations for social security benefits............	....	....	....	....	....	....	....	....	....	....	....	....
6M7 Contingent liabilities.....................	....	....	....	....	....	....	....	....	....	....	....	....
6M8 Uncapitalized military weapons, systems........	....	....	....	....	....	....	....	....	....	....	....	....
Table 7 Outlays by functions of govt.												
7 **Total outlays**............................	143.29	†147.05	252.88	....	....	....	....	....	....	....	....	....
701 **General public services**....................	....	....	....	....	....	....	....	....	....	....	....	....
7017 Public debt transactions.................	17.93	†50.64	70.24	....	....	....	....	....	....	....	....	....
7018 General transfers between levels of govt......	....	....	....	....	....	....	....	....	....	....	....	....
702 **Defense**.....................................	....	....	....	....	....	....	....	....	....	....	....	....
703 **Public order and safety**.....................	....	....	....	....	....	....	....	....	....	....	....	....

	Budgetary Central Government			Central Government			Local Government			General Government		
	1997	1998	1999	1997	1998	1999	1997	1998	1999	1997	1998	1999
704 **Economic affairs**............................	....	....	....	....	....	....	....	....	....	....	.....	....
7042 Agriculture, forestry, fishing, and hunting.....	....	....	....	....	....	....	....	....	....	....	....	....
7043 Fuel and energy..................................	....	....	....	....	....	....	....	....	....	....	....	....
7044 Mining, manufacturing, and construction.....	....	....	....	....	....	....	....	....	....	....	....	....
7045 Transport...	....	....	....	....	....	....	....	....	....	....	....	....
7046 Communication..................................	....	....	....	....	....	....	....	....	....	....	....	....
705 **Environmental protection**................	....	....	....	....	....	....	....	....	....	....	....	....
706 **Housing and community amenities**........	....	....	....	....	....	....	....	....	....	....	....	....
707 **Health**...	....	....	....	....	....	....	....	....	....	....	....	....
7072 Outpatient services..............................	....	....	....	....	....	....	....	....	....	....	....	....
7073 Hospital services................................	....	....	....	....	....	....	....	....	....	....	....	....
7074 Public health services...........................	....	....	....	....	....	....	....	....	....	....	....	....
708 **Recreation, culture, and religion**...........	....	....	....	....	....	....	....	....	....	....	....	....
709 **Education**.......................................	....	....	....	....	....	....	....	....	....	....	....	....
7091 Pre-primary and primary education..............	....	....	....	....	....	....	....	....	....	....	....	....
7092 Secondary education.............................	....	....	....	....	....	....	....	....	....	....	....	....
7094 Tertiary education................................	....	....	....	....	....	....	....	....	....	....	....	....
710 **Social protection**..............................	....	....	....	....	....	....	....	....	....	....	....	....
7 Statistical discrepancy: Total outlays.............	....	....	....	....	....	....	....	....	....	....	....	....
Table 8 Transactions in financial assets and liabilities by sector												
82 **Net acquisition of financial assets**.........	....	....	....	....	....	....	....	....	....	....	....	....
821 Domestic..	3.27	†3.15	14.68	....	....	....	....	....	....	....	....	....
8211 General government.............................	....	....	....	....	....	....	....	....	....	....	....	....
8212 Central bank.....................................	....	....	....	....	....	....	....	....	....	....	....	....
8213 Other depository corporations..................	....	....	....	....	....	....	....	....	....	....	....	....
8214 Financial corporations n.e.c....................	....	....	....	....	....	....	....	....	....	....	....	....
8215 Nonfinancial corporations......................	....	....	....	....	....	....	....	....	....	....	....	....
8216 Households & NPIs serving households......	....	....	....	....	....	....	....	....	....	....	....	....
822 Foreign..	....	....	....	....	....	....	....	....	....	....	....	....
8221 General government.............................	....	....	....	....	....	....	....	....	....	....	....	....
8227 International organizations......................	....	....	....	....	....	....	....	....	....	....	....	....
8228 Financial corporations other than international organizations..............	....	....	....	....	....	....	....	....	....	....	....	....
8229 Other nonresidents..............................	....	....	....	....	....	....	....	....	....	....	....	....
823 Monetary gold and SDRs.........................	—	†—	—	....	....	....	....	....	....	....	....	....
83 **Net incurrence of liabilities**..................	....	....	....	....	....	....	....	....	....	....	....	....
831 Domestic..	10.76	†50.60	102.79	....	....	....	....	....	....	....	....	....
8311 General government.............................	....	....	....	....	....	....	....	....	....	....	....	....
8312 Central bank.....................................	....	....	....	....	....	....	....	....	....	....	....	....
8313 Other depository corporations..................	....	....	....	....	....	....	....	....	....	....	....	....
8314 Financial corporations n.e.c....................	....	....	....	....	....	....	....	....	....	....	....	....
8315 Nonfinancial corporations......................	....	....	....	....	....	....	....	....	....	....	....	....
8316 Households & NPIs serving households......	....	....	....	....	....	....	....	....	....	....	....	....
832 Foreign..	....	....	....	....	....	....	....	....	....	....	....	....
8321 General government.............................	....	....	....	....	....	....	....	....	....	....	....	....
8327 International organizations......................	....	....	....	....	....	....	....	....	....	....	....	....
8328 Financial corporations other than international organizations..............	....	....	....	....	....	....	....	....	....	....	....	....
8329 Other nonresidents..............................	....	....	....	....	....	....	....	....	....	....	....	....

In Millions of Dollars / Year Beginning April 1 / Cash Reporter

	Budgetary Central Government			Extrabudgetary Accounts			Central Government			General Government		
	2002	2003	2004	2002	2003	2004	2002	2003	2004	2002	2003	2004
Statement of government operations												
Statement of other economic flows												
Balance sheet												
6 *Net worth*	....	....	....	....	....	....	....	....	....	....	....	....
61 Nonfinancial assets	....	....	....	....	....	....	....	....	....	....	....	....
62 Financial assets	....	....	....	....	....	....	....	....	....	....	....	....
63 Liabilities	176,191	184,731	197,892	—	—	—	176,191	184,731	197,892	176,191	184,731	197,892
Statement of sources and uses of cash												
1 Cash receipts from operating activities	34,225	32,054	35,608	875	992	910	35,100	33,046	36,518	35,100	33,046	36,518
11 Taxes	20,908	21,051	22,429	117	122	134	21,025	21,173	22,563	21,025	21,173	22,563
12 Social contributions	—	—	—	—	—	—	—	—	—	—	—	—
13 Grants	—	—	—	—	—	—	—	—	—	—	—	—
14 Other receipts	13,317	11,003	13,179	758	870	776	14,075	11,873	13,955	14,075	11,873	13,955
2 Cash payments for operating activities	23,037	23,231	24,048	3,716	3,881	3,935	26,753	27,112	27,983	26,753	27,112	27,983
21 Compensation of employees	6,431	6,444	6,816	1,852	1,862	1,890	8,283	8,306	8,706	8,283	8,306	8,706
22 Purchases of goods and services	7,333	7,273	7,627	1,864	2,019	2,045	9,197	9,292	9,672	9,197	9,292	9,672
24 Interest	447	380	291	—	—	—	447	380	291	447	380	291
25 Subsidies	—	—	—	—	—	—	—	—	—	—	—	—
26 Grants	3,909	4,367	4,247	—	—	—	3,909	4,367	4,247	3,909	4,367	4,247
27 Social benefits	4,917	4,767	5,067	—	—	—	4,917	4,767	5,067	4,917	4,767	5,067
28 Other payments	—	—	—	—	—	—	—	—	—	—	—	—
CIO *Net cash inflow from oper. activities*	*6,956*	*4,316*	*7,376*	*1,391*	*1,618*	*1,159*	*8,347*	*5,934*	*8,535*	*8,347*	*5,934*	*8,535*
31.1 Purchases of nonfinancial assets	2,988	2,863	3,127	—	—	—	2,988	2,863	3,127	2,988	2,863	3,127
31.2 Sales of nonfinancial assets	2,192	1,894	2,106	—	—	—	2,192	1,894	2,106	2,192	1,894	2,106
31 Net cash outflow from investments in nonfinancial assets	796	969	1,021	—	—	—	796	969	1,021	796	969	1,021
CSD *Cash surplus/deficit*	*6,160*	*3,347*	*6,355*	*1,391*	*1,618*	*1,159*	*7,551*	*4,965*	*7,514*	*7,551*	*4,965*	*7,514*
32x Net acquisition of fin assets, excl. cash	−1,164	−7,029	−5,306	—	—	—	−1,164	−7,029	−5,306	−1,164	−7,029	−5,306
321x Domestic	−1,164	−7,029	−5,306	—	—	—	−1,164	−7,029	−5,306	−1,164	−7,029	−5,306
322x Foreign	—	—	—	—	—	—	—	—	—	—	—	—
323 Monetary gold and SDRs	—	—	—	—	—	—	—	—	—	—	—	—
33 Net incurrence of liabilities	10,321	12,123	16,781	—	—	—	10,321	12,123	16,781	10,321	12,123	16,781
331 Domestic	10,321	12,123	16,781	—	—	—	10,321	12,123	16,781	10,321	12,123	16,781
332 Foreign	—	—	—	—	—	—	—	—	—	—	—	—
NFB Net cash inflow from fin. activities	11,485	19,152	22,087	—	—	—	11,485	19,152	22,087	11,485	19,152	22,087
NCB *Net change in the stock of cash*	*17,645*	*22,499*	*28,442*	*1,391*	*1,618*	*1,159*	*19,036*	*24,117*	*29,601*	*19,036*	*24,117*	*29,601*
Table 1 Revenue												
1 **Revenue**	**34,225**	**32,054**	**35,608**	**875**	**992**	**910**	**35,100**	**33,046**	**36,518**	**35,100**	**33,046**	**36,518**
11 **Taxes**	**20,908**	**21,051**	**22,429**	**117**	**122**	**134**	**21,025**	**21,173**	**22,563**	**21,025**	**21,173**	**22,563**
111 Taxes on income, profits, & capital gains	10,871	9,783	10,063	—	—	—	10,871	9,783	10,063	10,871	9,783	10,063
1111 Individuals	....	....	....	—	—	—	....	....	....	....	....	....
1112 Corporations and other enterprises	....	....	....	—	—	—	....	....	....	....	....	....
112 Taxes on payroll and workforce	—	—	—	—	—	—	—	—	—	—	—	—
113 Taxes on property	1,308	1,512	2,059	—	—	—	1,308	1,512	2,059	1,308	1,512	2,059
114 Taxes on goods and services	6,385	8,057	8,496	117	122	134	6,502	8,179	8,630	6,502	8,179	8,630
1141 General taxes on goods and services	2,165	2,957	3,470	—	—	—	2,165	2,957	3,470	2,165	2,957	3,470
1142 Excises	874	2,052	2,065	—	—	—	874	2,052	2,065	874	2,052	2,065
115 Taxes on int'l. trade and transactions	701	17	24	—	—	—	701	17	24	701	17	24
116 Other taxes	1,643	1,682	1,787	—	—	—	1,643	1,682	1,787	1,643	1,682	1,787
12 **Social contributions**	**—**	**—**	**—**	**—**	**—**	**—**	**—**	**—**	**—**	**—**	**—**	**—**
121 Social security contributions	—	—	—	—	—	—	—	—	—	—	—	—
122 Other social contributions	—	—	—	—	—	—	—	—	—	—	—	—
13 **Grants**	**—**	**—**	**—**	**—**	**—**	**—**	**—**	**—**	**—**	**—**	**—**	**—**
131 From foreign governments	—	—	—	—	—	—	—	—	—	—	—	—
132 From international organizations	—	—	—	—	—	—	—	—	—	—	—	—
133 From other general government units	—	—	—	—	—	—	—	—	—	—	—	—
14 **Other revenue**	**13,317**	**11,003**	**13,179**	**758**	**870**	**776**	**14,075**	**11,873**	**13,955**	**14,075**	**11,873**	**13,955**
Table 2 Expense by economic type												
2 **Expense**	**23,037**	**23,231**	**24,048**	**3,716**	**3,881**	**3,935**	**26,753**	**27,112**	**27,983**	**26,753**	**27,112**	**27,983**
21 **Compensation of employees**	**6,431**	**6,444**	**6,816**	**1,852**	**1,862**	**1,890**	**8,283**	**8,306**	**8,706**	**8,283**	**8,306**	**8,706**
211 Wages and salaries	6,431	6,444	6,816	1,852	1,862	1,890	8,283	8,306	8,706	8,283	8,306	8,706
212 Social contributions	—	—	—	—	—	—	—	—	—	—	—	—
22 **Use of goods and services**	**7,333**	**7,273**	**7,627**	**1,864**	**2,019**	**2,045**	**9,197**	**9,292**	**9,672**	**9,197**	**9,292**	**9,672**
23 **Consumption of fixed capital**	....	....	....	....	....	....	....	....	....	....	....	....
24 **Interest**	**447**	**380**	**291**	**—**	**—**	**—**	**447**	**380**	**291**	**447**	**380**	**291**
25 **Subsidies**	**—**	**—**	**—**	**—**	**—**	**—**	**—**	**—**	**—**	**—**	**—**	**—**

		Budgetary Central Government			Extrabudgetary Accounts			Central Government			General Government		
		2002	2003	2004	2002	2003	2004	2002	2003	2004	2002	2003	2004
26	**Grants**....................	**3,909**	**4,367**	**4,247**	—	—	—	**3,909**	**4,367**	**4,247**	**3,909**	**4,367**	**4,247**
261	To foreign govenments............	82	80	97	—	—	—	82	80	97	82	80	97
262	To international organizations..........	—	—	—	—	—	—	—	—	—	—	—	—
263	To other general government units...........	3,827	4,287	4,150	—	—	—	3,827	4,287	4,150	3,827	4,287	4,150
2631	Current...........	—	—	—	—	—	—	—	—	—	—	—	—
2632	Capital...........	3,827	4,287	4,150	—	—	—	3,827	4,287	4,150	3,827	4,287	4,150
27	**Social benefits**............	**4,917**	**4,767**	**5,067**	—	—	—	**4,917**	**4,767**	**5,067**	**4,917**	**4,767**	**5,067**
28	**Other expense**............	—	—	—	—	—	—	—	—	—	—	—	—
281	Property expense other than interest...........	—	—	—	—	—	—	—	—	—	—	—	—
282	Miscellaneous other expense...........	—	—	—	—	—	—	—	—	—	—	—	—
2821	Current...........	—	—	—	—	—	—	—	—	—	—	—	—
2822	Capital...........	—	—	—	—	—	—	—	—	—	—	—	—

Table 3 Transactions in assets and liabilities

		Budgetary Central Government			Extrabudgetary Accounts			Central Government			General Government		
3	**Change in net worth from transactns....**	....	....	....	—	....	....	....	....	....	....	....	....
31	**Net acquisition of nonfinancial assets...**	**796**	**969**	**1,021**	—	—	—	**796**	**969**	**1,021**	**796**	**969**	**1,021**
311	Fixed assets...........	2,096	2,184	2,660	—	—	—	2,096	2,184	2,660	2,096	2,184	2,660
3111	Buildings and structures...........	....	....	....	—			....	....	....	....	....	....
3112	Machinery and equipment...........	....	....	....	—			....	....	....	....	....	....
3113	Other fixed assets...........	....	....	....	—			....	....	....	....	....	....
312	Inventories...........	—	—	—	—	—	—	—	—	—	—	—	—
313	Valuables...........	—	—	—	—	—	—	—	—	—	—	—	—
314	Nonproduced assets...........	−1,300	−1,215	−1,639	—	—	—	−1,300	−1,215	−1,639	−1,300	−1,215	−1,639
3141	Land...........	....	....	....				....	....	....	....	....	....
3142	Subsoil assets...........	....	....	....				....	....	....	....	....	....
3143	Other naturally occurring assets...........	....	....	....				....	....	....	....	....	....
3144	Intangible nonproduced assets...........	....	....	....	—		....	....	....	....	....	....	....
32	**Net acquisition of financial assets........**	**16,481**	**15,470**	**23,136**	**1,391**	**1,618**	**1,159**	**17,872**	**17,088**	**24,295**	**17,872**	**17,088**	**24,295**
321	Domestic...........	16,481	15,470	23,136	1,391	1,618	1,159	17,872	17,088	24,295	17,872	17,088	24,295
3212	Currency and deposits...........	17,645	22,499	28,442	1,391	1,618	1,159	19,036	24,117	29,601	19,036	24,117	29,601
3213	Securities other than shares...........	....	....	—				....	....	—	....	....	....
3214	Loans...........	....	....	−5,306	—	—	—	....	....	−5,306	....	....	−5,306
3215	Shares and other equity...........	....	....	—				....	....	—	....	....	....
3216	Insurance technical reserves...........	....	....	—				....	....	—	....	....	....
3217	Financial derivatives...........	....	....	—				....	....	—	....	....	....
3218	Other accounts receivable...........	....	....	....	....	....	....	....	....	....	....	....	....
322	Foreign...........	—	—	—	—	—	—	—	—	—	—	—	—
3222	Currency and deposits...........	—	—	—	—	—	—	—	—	—	—	—	—
3223	Securities other than shares...........	—	—	—	—	—	—	—	—	—	—	—	—
3224	Loans...........	—	—	—	—	—	—	—	—	—	—	—	—
3225	Shares and other equity...........	—	—	—	—	—	—	—	—	—	—	—	—
3226	Insurance technical reserves...........	—	—	—	—	—	—	—	—	—	—	—	—
3227	Financial derivatives...........	—	—	—	—	—	—	—	—	—	—	—	—
3228	Other accounts receivable...........	....	....	....	....	....	....	....	....	....	....	....	....
323	Monetary gold and SDRs...........	—	—	—	—	—	—	—	—	—	—	—	—
33	**Net incurrence of liabilities...................**	**10,321**	**12,123**	**16,781**	—	—	—	**10,321**	**12,123**	**16,781**	**10,321**	**12,123**	**16,781**
331	Domestic...........	10,321	12,123	16,781	—	—	—	10,321	12,123	16,781	10,321	12,123	16,781
3312	Currency and deposits...........	—	—	—	—	—	—	—	—	—	—	—	—
3313	Securities other than shares...........	10,321	12,123	16,781	—	—	—	10,321	12,123	16,781	10,321	12,123	16,781
3314	Loans...........	—	—	—	—	—	—	—	—	—	—	—	—
3316	Insurance technical reserves...........	—	—	—	—	—	—	—	—	—	—	—	—
3317	Financial derivatives...........	—	—	—	—	—	—	—	—	—	—	—	—
3318	Other accounts payable...........	....	....	....	....	....	....	....	....	....	....	....	....
332	Foreign...........	—	—	—	—	—	—	—	—	—	—	—	—
3322	Currency and deposits...........	—	—	—	—	—	—	—	—	—	—	—	—
3323	Securities other than shares...........	—	—	—	—	—	—	—	—	—	—	—	—
3324	Loans...........	—	—	—	—	—	—	—	—	—	—	—	—
3326	Insurance technical reserves...........	—	—	—	—	—	—	—	—	—	—	—	—
3327	Financial derivatives...........	—	—	—	—	—	—	—	—	—	—	—	—
3328	Other accounts payable...........	....	....	....	....	....	....	....	....	....	....	....	....

In Millions of Dollars / Year Beginning April 1 / Cash Reporter

	Budgetary Central Government			Extrabudgetary Accounts			Central Government			General Government		
	2002	2003	2004	2002	2003	2004	2002	2003	2004	2002	2003	2004
Table 4 Holding gains in assets and liabilities												
Table 5 Other changes in the volume of assets and liabilities												
Table 6 Balance sheet												
6 **Net worth**	....	....	....	....	....	....	....	....	....	....	....	....
61 **Nonfinancial assets**	....	....	....	....	....	....	....	....	....	....	....	....
611 Fixed assets	....	....	....	....	....	....	....	....	....	....	....	....
6111 Buildings and structures	....	....	....	....	....	....	....	....	....	....	....	....
6112 Machinery and equipment	....	....	....	....	....	....	....	....	....	....	....	....
6113 Other fixed assets	....	....	....	....	....	....	....	....	....	....	....	....
612 Inventories	....	....	....	....	....	....	....	....	....	....	....	....
613 Valuables	....	....	....	....	....	....	....	....	....	....	....	....
614 Nonproduced assets	....	....	....	....	....	....	....	....	....	....	....	....
6141 Land	....	....	....	....	....	....	....	....	....	....	....	....
6142 Subsoil assets	....	....	....	....	....	....	....	....	....	....	....	....
6143 Other naturally occurring assets	....	....	....	....	....	....	....	....	....	....	....	....
6144 Intangible nonproduced assets	....	....	....	....	....	....	....	....	....	....	....	....
62 **Financial assets**	....	....	....	....	....	....	....	....	....	....	....	....
621 Domestic	....	....	....	....	....	....	....	....	....	....	....	....
6212 Currency and deposits	....	....	....	....	....	....	....	....	....	....	....	....
6213 Securities other than shares	....	....	....	....	....	....	....	....	....	....	....	....
6214 Loans	....	....	....	....	....	....	....	....	....	....	....	....
6215 Shares and other equity	....	....	....	....	....	....	....	....	....	....	....	....
6216 Insurance technical reserves	....	....	....	....	....	....	....	....	....	....	....	....
6217 Financial derivatives	....	....	....	....	....	....	....	....	....	....	....	....
6218 Other accounts receivable	....	....	....	....	....	....	....	....	....	....	....	....
622 Foreign	....	....	....	....	....	....	....	....	....	....	....	....
6222 Currency and deposits	....	....	....	....	....	....	....	....	....	....	....	....
6223 Securities other than shares	....	....	....	....	....	....	....	....	....	....	....	....
6224 Loans	....	....	....	....	....	....	....	....	....	....	....	....
6225 Shares and other equity	....	....	....	....	....	....	....	....	....	....	....	....
6226 Insurance technical reserves	....	....	....	....	....	....	....	....	....	....	....	....
6227 Financial derivatives	....	....	....	....	....	....	....	....	....	....	....	....
6228 Other accounts receivable	....	....	....	....	....	....	....	....	....	....	....	....
623 Monetary gold and SDRs	....	....	....	....	....	....	....	....	....	....	....	....
63 **Liabilities**	**176,191**	**184,731**	**197,892**	—	—	—	**176,191**	**184,731**	**197,892**	**176,191**	**184,731**	**197,892**
631 Domestic	176,191	184,731	197,892	—	—	—	176,191	184,731	197,892	176,191	184,731	197,892
6312 Currency and deposits	....	....	....	—	—	—	....	....	....	....	....	....
6313 Securities other than shares	....	....	....	—	—	—	....	....	....	....	....	....
6314 Loans	....	....	....	—	—	—	....	....	....	....	....	....
6316 Insurance technical reserves	....	....	....	—	—	—	....	....	....	....	....	....
6317 Financial derivatives	....	....	....	—	—	—	....	....	....	....	....	....
6318 Other accounts payable	....	....	....	—	—	—	....	....	....	....	....	....
632 Foreign	—	—	—	—	—	—	—	—	—	—	—	—
6322 Currency and deposits	—	—	—	—	—	—	—	—	—	—	—	—
6323 Securities other than shares	—	—	—	—	—	—	—	—	—	—	—	—
6324 Loans	—	—	—	—	—	—	—	—	—	—	—	—
6326 Insurance technical reserves	—	—	—	—	—	—	—	—	—	—	—	—
6327 Financial derivatives	—	—	—	—	—	—	—	—	—	—	—	—
6328 Other accounts payable	....	....	....	....	....	....	....	....	....	....	....	....
Memorandum items:												
6M2 Net financial worth	....	....	....	....	....	....	....	....	....	....	....	....
6M3 Debt at market value	....	....	....	....	....	....	....	....	....	....	....	....
6M4 Debt at nominal value	....	....	....	....	....	....	....	....	....	....	....	....
6M5 Arrears	....	....	....	....	....	....	....	....	....	....	....	....
6M6 Obligations for social security benefits	....	....	....	....	....	....	....	....	....	....	....	....
6M7 Contingent liabilities	....	....	....	....	....	....	....	....	....	....	....	....
6M8 Uncapitalized military weapons, systems	....	....	....	....	....	....	....	....	....	....	....	....
Table 7 Outlays by functions of govt.												
7 **Total outlays**	26,025	26,094	27,173	3,716	3,881	3,935	29,741	29,975	31,108	29,741	29,975	31,108
701 **General public services**	2,618	2,409	2,810	—	—	—	2,618	2,409	2,810	2,618	2,409	2,810
7017 Public debt transactions	447	380	291	—	—	—	447	380	291	447	380	291
7018 General transfers between levels of govt.	....	....	....	—	—	—	....	....	....	....	....	....
702 **Defense**	8,485	8,533	8,969	—	—	—	8,485	8,533	8,969	8,485	8,533	8,969
703 **Public order and safety**	1,767	1,794	1,914	—	—	—	1,767	1,794	1,914	1,767	1,794	1,914

In Millions of Dollars / Year Beginning April 1 / Cash Reporter

		Budgetary Central Government			Extrabudgetary Accounts			Central Government			General Government		
		2002	2003	2004	2002	2003	2004	2002	2003	2004	2002	2003	2004
704	**Economic affairs**............................	**3,163**	**2,757**	**3,059**	**493**	**440**	**705**	**3,656**	**3,197**	**3,764**	**3,656**	**3,197**	**3,764**
7042	Agriculture, forestry, fishing, and hunting.....	70	74	66	—	—	—	70	74	66	70	74	66
7043	Fuel and energy.................................	—	—	....	—	—	—	—	—	....	—	—	....
7044	Mining, manufacturing, and construction.....	21	19	22	—	—	—	21	19	22	21	19	22
7045	Transport...	1,595	1,463	2,067	—	—	—	1,595	1,463	2,067	1,595	1,463	2,067
7046	Communication.................................	....	....	....	....	....	—	....	....	....	....	....	....
705	**Environmental protection**.................	....	....	....	....	....	....	....	....	....	....	....	....
706	**Housing and community amenities**........	**2,832**	**3,751**	**3,712**	**367**	**586**	**403**	**3,199**	**4,337**	**4,115**	**3,199**	**4,337**	**4,115**
707	**Health**...	**1,662**	**2,366**	**1,790**	—	—	—	**1,662**	**2,366**	**1,790**	**1,662**	**2,366**	**1,790**
7072	Outpatient services.............................	111	98	99	—	—	—	111	98	99	111	98	99
7073	Hospital services................................	1,199	1,605	1,411	—	—	—	1,199	1,605	1,411	1,199	1,605	1,411
7074	Public health services..........................	....	....	....	—	—	—	....	....	....	....	....	....
708	**Recreation, culture, and religion**...........	**1,090**	**26**	**20**	—	**90**	—	**1,090**	**116**	**20**	**1,090**	**116**	**20**
709	**Education**.......................................	**4,096**	**3,810**	**3,892**	**2,856**	**2,765**	**2,827**	**6,952**	**6,575**	**6,719**	**6,952**	**6,575**	**6,719**
7091	Pre-primary and primary education..............	....	....	....	....	....	....	....	....	....	....	....	....
7092	Secondary education............................	3,585	3,311	3,280	—	—	—	3,585	3,311	3,280	3,585	3,311	3,280
7094	Tertiary education...............................	313	310	434	1,783	1,708	1,720	2,096	2,018	2,154	2,096	2,018	2,154
710	**Social protection**.............................	**1,242**	**648**	**1,007**	—	—	—	**1,242**	**648**	**1,007**	**1,242**	**648**	**1,007**
7	Statistical discrepancy: Total outlays..............	−930	—	—	—	—	—	−930	—	—	−930	—	—

Table 8   Transactions in financial assets and liabilities by sector

		Budgetary Central Government			Extrabudgetary Accounts			Central Government			General Government		
82	**Net acquisition of financial assets**.........	**16,481**	**15,470**	**23,136**	**1,391**	**1,618**	**1,159**	**17,872**	**17,088**	**24,295**	**17,872**	**17,088**	**24,295**
821	Domestic...	16,481	15,470	23,136	1,391	1,618	1,159	17,872	17,088	24,295	17,872	17,088	24,295
8211	General government...........................	....	....	....	....	....	....	....	....	....	....	....	....
8212	Central bank....................................	....	....	....	....	....	....	....	....	....	....	....	....
8213	Other depository corporations....................	....	....	....	....	....	....	....	....	....	....	....	....
8214	Financial corporations n.e.c....................	....	....	....	....	....	....	....	....	....	....	....	....
8215	Nonfinancial corporations......................	....	....	....	....	....	....	....	....	....	....	....	....
8216	Households & NPIs serving households......	....	....	....	....	....	....	....	....	....	....	....	....
822	Foreign..	—	—	—	—	—	—	—	—	—	—	—	—
8221	General government...........................	—	—	—	—	—	—	—	—	—	—	—	—
8227	International organizations.....................	—	—	—	—	—	—	—	—	—	—	—	—
8228	Financial corporations other than international organizations.............	—	—	—	—	—	—	—	—	—	—	—	—
8229	Other nonresidents.............................	—	—	—	—	—	—	—	—	—	—	—	—
823	Monetary gold and SDRs.......................	—	—	—	—	—	—	—	—	—	—	—	—
83	**Net incurrence of liabilities**...................	**10,321**	**12,123**	**16,781**	—	—	—	**10,321**	**12,123**	**16,781**	**10,321**	**12,123**	**16,781**
831	Domestic...	10,321	12,123	16,781	—	—	—	10,321	12,123	16,781	10,321	12,123	16,781
8311	General government...........................	....	....	....	—	—	—	....	....	....	....	....	....
8312	Central bank....................................	....	....	....	—	—	—	....	....	....	....	....	....
8313	Other depository corporations....................	....	....	....	—	—	—	....	....	....	....	....	....
8314	Financial corporations n.e.c....................	....	....	....	—	—	—	....	....	....	....	....	....
8315	Nonfinancial corporations......................	....	....	....	—	—	—	....	....	....	....	....	....
8316	Households & NPIs serving households......	....	....	....	—	—	—	....	....	....	....	....	....
832	Foreign..	—	—	—	—	—	—	—	—	—	—	—	—
8321	General government...........................	—	—	—	—	—	—	—	—	—	—	—	—
8327	International organizations.....................	—	—	—	—	—	—	—	—	—	—	—	—
8328	Financial corporations other than international organizations.............	—	—	—	—	—	—	—	—	—	—	—	—
8329	Other nonresidents.............................	—	—	—	—	—	—	—	—	—	—	—	—

		Budgetary Central Government			Central Government			Local Government			General Government		
		2001p	2002p	2003p	2001p	2002p	2003p	2001p	2002p	2003p	2001p	2002p	2003p
Statement of government operations													
1	Revenue	....	....	230.28	....	....	422.55	....	....	87.60	....	....	460.55
2	Expense	....	....	275.57	....	....	442.10	....	....	80.00	....	....	472.50
GOB	*Gross operating balance*	....	....	*–45.30*	....	....	*–19.55*	....	....	*7.60*	....	....	*–11.95*
NOB	*Net operating balance*	....	....	....	....	....	....	....	....	....	....	....	....
31	Net acquisition of nonfinancial assets	....	....	14.31	....	....	19.89	....	....	9.68	....	....	29.57
NLB	*Net lending/borrowing*	....	....	*–59.61*	....	....	*–39.44*	....	....	*–2.08*	....	....	*–41.52*
32	Net acquisition of financial assets	....	....	–19.18	....	....	–6.74	....	....	–.45	....	....	–7.07
33	Net incurrence of liabilities	....	....	38.85	....	....	31.65	....	....	.09	....	....	31.85
NLB	Statistical discrepancy	....	....	1.58	....	....	1.05	....	....	1.54	....	....	2.59
Statement of other economic flows													
4	*Change in net worth from holding gains*	....	....	*–11.22*	....	....	*–11.22*	....	....	*.29*	....	....	*–10.94*
41	Nonfinancial assets	....	....	—	....	....	—	....	....	—	....	....	—
42	Financial assets	....	....	–15.57	....	....	–15.57	....	....	—	....	....	–15.57
43	Liabilities	....	....	–4.35	....	....	–4.35	....	....	–.29	....	....	–4.64
5	*Change in net worth from other volume changes*	....	....	*19.68*	....	....	*20.32*	....	....	*28.62*	....	....	*48.93*
51	Nonfinancial assets	....	....	–2.09	....	....	–20.43	....	....	25.19	....	....	4.76
52	Financial assets	....	....	27.09	....	....	41.55	....	....	8.02	....	....	49.57
53	Liabilities	....	....	5.31	....	....	.80	....	....	4.60	....	....	5.40
Balance sheet													
6	*Net worth*	....	....	*113.37*	*598.24*	*626.43*	*488.62*	*211.38*	*273.76*	*360.61*	*809.62*	*900.19*	*849.23*
61	Nonfinancial assets	....	....	357.75	467.63	429.91	481.06	194.09	249.52	335.57	661.72	679.43	816.63
62	Financial assets	....	....	259.02	608.02	637.03	566.51	35.21	45.38	54.55	641.09	677.71	616.32
63	Liabilities	....	....	503.41	477.42	440.51	558.95	17.92	21.15	29.50	493.20	456.95	583.72
Statement of sources and uses of cash													
1	Cash receipts from operating activities	204.90	336.05	227.16	345.91	379.96	419.31	25.81	55.24	90.52	366.43	405.31	460.22
11	Taxes	165.07	188.84	199.46	166.35	188.84	199.46	14.22	16.89	17.80	180.57	205.74	217.26
12	Social contributions	—	—	—	142.04	158.13	167.56	—	—	—	142.04	158.13	167.56
13	Grants	12.77	123.72	7.74	.17	.05	.19	5.38	30.22	49.43	.26	.38	.22
14	Other receipts	27.05	23.48	19.96	37.34	32.94	52.09	6.21	8.14	23.29	43.56	41.07	75.18
2	Cash payments for operating activities	322.23	248.85	265.06	379.28	424.89	447.19	20.55	44.09	80.03	394.54	439.09	477.62
21	Compensation of employees	65.44	57.35	40.56	68.71	60.81	61.33	7.62	22.55	41.75	76.33	83.36	103.08
22	Purchases of goods and services	35.70	34.44	31.16	42.47	38.97	49.91	8.84	13.59	27.68	51.31	52.55	77.59
24	Interest	20.50	35.52	30.29	30.60	38.36	31.21	1.03	.90	.92	31.63	39.26	31.95
25	Subsidies	15.74	12.74	17.30	18.45	13.81	18.35	1.59	3.39	2.69	20.03	17.20	21.04
26	Grants	127.22	30.15	77.35	5.99	30.64	50.27	.01	—	—	.71	.75	.86
27	Social benefits	48.92	56.13	56.66	185.23	207.55	209.06	.21	.16	—	185.44	207.70	209.06
28	Other payments	8.70	22.53	11.74	27.84	34.75	27.06	1.25	3.52	6.99	29.09	38.27	34.05
CIO	*Net cash inflow from oper. activities*	*–117.33*	*87.20*	*–37.89*	*–33.37*	*–44.93*	*–27.89*	*5.26*	*11.15*	*10.49*	*–28.11*	*–33.78*	*–17.40*
31.1	Purchases of nonfinancial assets	22.62	21.97	14.75	23.55	23.03	20.60	8.08	15.24	12.88	31.63	38.26	33.47
31.2	Sales of nonfinancial assets	.16	.38	.43	1.84	.46	.71	2.53	3.08	3.20	4.37	3.55	3.90
31	Net cash outflow from investments in nonfinancial assets	22.46	21.60	14.31	21.71	22.56	19.89	5.56	12.15	9.68	27.26	34.71	29.57
CSD	*Cash surplus/deficit*	*–139.79*	*65.60*	*–52.21*	*–55.08*	*–67.49*	*–47.78*	*–.29*	*–1.00*	*.81*	*–55.37*	*–68.49*	*–46.97*
32x	Net acquisition of fin assets, excl. cash	5.25	–19.36	–10.31	–30.82	–174.52	–18.95	–.03	–.04	1.49	–32.63	–177.71	–17.35
321x	Domestic	6.95	–5.91	–7.37	–29.12	–161.08	–16.01	–.03	–.04	1.49	–30.93	–164.26	–14.41
322x	Foreign	–1.70	–13.45	–2.94	–1.70	–13.45	–2.94	—	—	—	–1.70	–13.45	–2.94
323	Monetary gold and SDRs	—	—	—	—	—	—	—	—	—	—	—	—
33	Net incurrence of liabilities	146.86	–2.33	45.85	30.35	–17.36	42.19	1.04	2.64	.12	29.60	–17.86	42.43
331	Domestic	144.27	–1.42	48.80	22.42	–5.61	45.15	1.17	3.24	.13	21.80	–5.51	45.39
332	Foreign	2.59	–.91	–2.95	7.93	–11.75	–2.95	–.13	–.60	–.01	7.80	–12.35	–2.97
NFB	Net cash inflow from fin. activities	141.61	17.03	56.16	61.17	157.17	61.15	1.07	2.68	–1.37	62.24	159.85	59.77
NCB	*Net change in the stock of cash*	*1.83*	*82.63*	*3.95*	*6.09*	*89.68*	*13.37*	*.78*	*1.68*	*–.56*	*6.87*	*91.36*	*12.81*
Table 1 Revenue													
1	**Revenue**	**204.90**	**336.05**	**†230.28**	**345.91**	**379.96**	**†422.55**	**25.81**	**55.24**	**†87.60**	**366.43**	**405.31**	**†460.55**
11	**Taxes**	**165.07**	**188.84**	**†200.79**	**166.35**	**188.84**	**†200.79**	**14.22**	**16.89**	**†17.80**	**180.57**	**205.74**	**†218.59**
111	Taxes on income, profits, & capital gains	57.48	67.07	†71.36	57.48	67.07	†71.36	8.40	9.14	†9.38	65.89	76.22	†80.74
1111	Individuals	27.74	29.83	†32.11	27.74	29.83	†32.11	6.89	7.29	†7.80	34.62	37.12	†39.91
1112	Corporations and other enterprises	20.21	27.91	†30.11	20.21	27.91	†30.11	1.52	1.85	†1.58	21.73	29.76	†31.69
112	Taxes on payroll and workforce	—	—	†—	—	—	†—	—	—	†—	—	—	†—
113	Taxes on property	1.64	2.20	†1.49	1.64	2.20	†1.49	3.69	3.72	†3.79	5.33	5.92	†5.28
114	Taxes on goods and services	101.97	115.57	†123.87	103.25	115.57	†123.87	2.13	4.03	†4.63	105.38	119.60	†128.50
1141	General taxes on goods and services	73.57	82.24	†81.71	73.57	82.24	†81.71	—	—	†—	73.57	82.24	†81.71
1142	Excises	28.40	32.00	†40.68	28.40	32.00	†40.68	—	—	†—	28.40	32.00	†40.68

	Budgetary Central Government			Central Government			Local Government			General Government		
	2001p	2002p	2003p	2001p	2002p	2003p	2001p	2002p	2003p	2001p	2002p	2003p
115 Taxes on int'l. trade and transactions...........	3.92	4.00	†4.06	3.92	4.00	†4.06	—	—	†—	3.92	4.00	†4.06
116 Other taxes...........................	.06	—	†—	.06	—	†—	—	—	†—	.06	—	†—
12 **Social contributions.....................**	—	—	**†—**	**142.04**	**158.13**	**†168.64**	**—**	**—**	**†—**	**142.04**	**158.13**	**†168.64**
121 Social security contributions............			†—	142.04	158.13	†168.64	—	—	†—	142.04	158.13	†168.64
122 Other social contributions..............	—	—	†—	—	—	†—	—	—	†—	—	—	†—
13 **Grants............................**	**12.77**	**123.72**	**†10.56**	**.17**	**.05**	**†.19**	**5.38**	**30.22**	**†49.43**	**.26**	**.38**	**†.22**
131 From foreign governments...................	.17	.05	†.05	.17	.05	†.10	.10	.32	†—	.26	.38	†.10
132 From international organizations................	—	—	†—	—	—	†.09	—	—	†.03	—	—	†.12
133 From other general government units..........	12.61	123.67	†10.51	—	—	†—	5.28	29.89	†49.41	—	—	†—
14 **Other revenue.........................**	**27.05**	**23.48**	**†18.93**	**37.34**	**32.94**	**†52.93**	**6.21**	**8.14**	**†20.37**	**43.56**	**41.07**	**†73.10**

Table 2   Expense by economic type

	Budgetary Central Government			Central Government			Local Government			General Government		
2 **Expense..............................**	**322.23**	**248.85**	**†275.57**	**379.28**	**424.89**	**†442.10**	**20.55**	**44.09**	**†80.00**	**394.54**	**439.09**	**†472.50**
21 **Compensation of employees.................**	**65.44**	**57.35**	**†40.26**	**68.71**	**60.81**	**†58.99**	**7.62**	**22.55**	**†44.48**	**76.33**	**83.36**	**†103.47**
211 Wages and salaries.........................	50.36	44.45	†30.43	52.78	47.02	†46.42	6.13	17.72	†31.44	58.91	64.74	†77.87
212 Social contributions.....................	15.09	12.90	†9.84	15.93	13.79	†12.56	1.49	4.83	†13.04	17.42	18.62	†25.60
22 **Use of goods and services.................**	**35.70**	**34.44**	**†30.68**	**42.47**	**38.97**	**†51.70**	**8.84**	**13.59**	**†24.92**	**51.31**	**52.55**	**†76.62**
23 **Consumption of fixed capital...............**	....	....	....	....	....	....	....	....	....	....	....	....
24 **Interest..............................**	**20.50**	**35.52**	**†28.87**	**30.60**	**38.36**	**†29.66**	**1.03**	**.90**	**†.92**	**31.63**	**39.26**	**†30.40**
25 **Subsidies..............................**	**15.74**	**12.74**	**†17.30**	**18.45**	**13.81**	**†18.35**	**1.59**	**3.39**	**†2.69**	**20.03**	**17.20**	**†21.04**
26 **Grants............................**	**127.22**	**30.15**	**†87.96**	**5.99**	**30.64**	**†50.27**	**.01**	**—**	**†—**	**.71**	**.75**	**†.86**
261 To foreign governments..................	.71	.75	†—	.71	.75	†—	—	—	†—	.71	.75	†—
262 To international organizations..............	—	—	†.86	—	—	†.86	—	—	†—	—	—	†.86
263 To other general government units.............	126.51	29.41	†87.10	5.28	29.89	†49.41	—	—	†—	—	—	†—
2631 Current................................	20.66	25.13	†56.16	2.96	25.59	†41.60	—	—	†—	—	—	†—
2632 Capital................................	105.86	4.28	†30.94	2.32	4.30	†7.81	—	—	†—	—	—	†—
27 **Social benefits........................**	**48.92**	**56.13**	**†56.66**	**185.23**	**207.55**	**†209.06**	**.21**	**.16**	**†—**	**185.44**	**207.70**	**†209.06**
28 **Other expense.........................**	**8.70**	**22.53**	**†13.84**	**27.84**	**34.75**	**†24.07**	**1.25**	**3.52**	**†6.99**	**29.09**	**38.27**	**†31.06**
281 Property expense other than interest.........	—	—	†—	—	—	†—	—	—	†—	—	—	†—
282 Miscellaneous other expense..........	8.70	22.53	†13.84	27.84	34.75	†24.07	1.25	3.52	†6.99	29.09	38.27	†31.06
2821 Current...........................	5.00	17.06	†10.14	5.82	17.27	†16.90	.57	1.89	†5.45	6.40	19.16	†22.35
2822 Capital............................	3.70	5.47	†3.70	22.02	17.48	†7.17	.67	1.63	†1.54	22.69	19.11	†8.71

Table 3   Transactions in assets and liabilities

	Budgetary Central Government			Central Government			Local Government			General Government		
3 **Change in net worth from transactns....**	....	....	....	....	....	....	....	....	....	....	....	....
31 **Net acquisition of nonfinancial assets...**	**22.46**	**21.60**	**†14.31**	**21.71**	**22.56**	**†19.89**	**5.56**	**12.15**	**†9.68**	**27.26**	**34.71**	**†29.57**
311 Fixed assets.............................	21.85	20.70	†13.47	22.77	21.74	†19.18	6.60	13.70	†11.43	29.37	35.44	†30.60
3111 Buildings and structures....................	21.85	20.70	....	22.77	21.74	....	6.60	13.70	....	29.37	35.44	....
3112 Machinery and equipment.................	—	—	....	—	—	....	—	—	....	—	—	....
3113 Other fixed assets...................	—	—	†—	—	—	†—	—	—	†—	—	—	†—
312 Inventories.........................	−.01	—	†—	−1.66	—	†—	—	−.01	†—	−1.66	−.01	†—
313 Valuables..........................	—	—	†—	—	—	†—	—	—	†—	—	—	†—
314 Nonproduced assets....................	.62	.90	†.84	.60	.82	†.72	−1.05	−1.54	†−1.75	−.45	−.72	†−1.03
3141 Land..............................	.62	.90	†.84	.60	.82	†.72	−1.05	−1.54	†−1.75	−.45	−.72	†−1.03
3142 Subsoil assets.......................	—	—	†—	—	—	†—	—	—	†—	—	—	†—
3143 Other naturally occurring assets...........	—	—	†—	—	—	†—	—	—	†—	—	—	†—
3144 Intangible nonproduced assets.................	—	—	†—	—	—	†—	—	—	†—	—	—	†—
32 **Net acquisition of financial assets........**	**7.07**	**63.27**	**†−19.18**	**−24.73**	**−84.85**	**†−6.74**	**.75**	**1.64**	**†−.45**	**−25.77**	**−86.35**	**†−7.07**
321 Domestic.............................	8.77	76.72	†−16.24	−23.03	−71.40	†−3.80	.75	1.64	†−.45	−24.07	−72.91	†−4.13
3212 Currency and deposits......................	1.83	82.63	†3.95	6.09	89.68	†13.37	.78	1.68	†−.56	6.87	91.36	†12.81
3213 Securities other than shares...............	—	—	†—	—	—	†—	—	—	†—	—	—	†—
3214 Loans.................................	6.95	−5.91	†−18.00	3.87	−3.46	†−4.27	−.04	.21	†.05	2.04	−6.39	†−4.11
3215 Shares and other equity...............	—	—	†.02	−32.99	−157.62	†−7.02	.01	−.26	†1.57	−32.98	−157.88	†−5.45
3216 Insurance technical reserves...............	—	—	†—	—	—	†—	—	—	†—	—	—	†—
3217 Financial derivatives....................	—	—	†—	—	—	†—	—	—	†—	—	—	†—
3218 Other accounts receivable..............	....	....	†−2.21	....	....	†−5.88	....	....	†−1.50	....	....	†−7.38
322 Foreign..............................	−1.70	−13.45	†−2.94	−1.70	−13.45	†−2.94	—	—	†—	−1.70	−13.45	†−2.94
3222 Currency and deposits....................	—	—	†—	—	—	†—	—	—	†—	—	—	†—
3223 Securities other than shares.................	—	—	†—	—	—	†—	—	—	†—	—	—	†—
3224 Loans...............................	−1.91	−13.55	†−3.03	−1.91	−13.55	†−3.03	—	—	†—	−1.91	−13.55	†−3.03
3225 Shares and other equity..................	.21	.10	†.09	.21	.10	†.09	—	—	†—	.21	.10	†.09
3226 Insurance technical reserves.............	—	—	†—	—	—	†—	—	—	†—	—	—	†—
3227 Financial derivatives....................	—	—	†—	—	—	†—	—	—	†—	—	—	†—
3228 Other accounts receivable................	....	....	†—	....	....	†—	....	....	†—	....	....	†—
323 Monetary gold and SDRs.............	—	—	†—	—	—	†—	—	—	†—	—	—	†—

		Budgetary Central Government			Central Government			Local Government			General Government		
		2001p	2002p	2003p	2001p	2002p	2003p	2001p	2002p	2003p	2001p	2002p	2003p
33	Net incurrence of liabilities	146.86	−2.33	†38.85	30.35	−17.36	†31.65	1.04	2.64	†.09	29.60	−17.86	†31.85
331	Domestic	144.27	−1.42	†41.80	22.42	−5.61	†34.60	1.17	3.24	†3.61	21.80	−5.51	†38.32
3312	Currency and deposits	—	—	†—	—	—	†—	—	—	†—	—	—	†—
3313	Securities other than shares	150.79	−1.42	†45.40	134.38	−4.70	†45.37	.02	.38	†−.41	134.40	−4.32	†44.96
3314	Loans	−6.53	—	†−2.82	−111.96	−.91	†−6.44	1.15	2.86	†4.04	−112.60	−1.18	†−2.28
3316	Insurance technical reserves	—	—	†—	—	—	†—	—	—	†—	—	—	†—
3317	Financial derivatives	—	—	†—	—	—	†—	—	—	†—	—	—	†—
3318	Other accounts payable	....	....	†−.78	....	....	†−4.33	....	....	†−.03	....	....	†−4.36
332	Foreign	2.59	−.91	†−2.95	7.93	−11.75	†−2.95	−.13	−.60	†−3.51	7.80	−12.35	†−6.47
3322	Currency and deposits	—	—	†—	—	—	†—	—	—	†—	—	—	†—
3323	Securities other than shares	—	—	†−.76	—	—	†−.76	—	—	†—	—	—	†−.76
3324	Loans	2.59	−.91	†−2.19	7.93	−11.75	†−2.19	−.13	−.60	†−3.51	7.80	−12.35	†−5.70
3326	Insurance technical reserves	—	—	†—	—	—	†—	—	—	†—	—	—	†—
3327	Financial derivatives	—	—	†—	—	—	†—	—	—	†—	—	—	†—
3328	Other accounts payable	—	—	†—	....	....	†—	....	....	†—	....	....	†—

Table 4   Holding gains in assets and liabilities

4	Change in net worth from hold. gains	....	....	−11.22	....	....	−11.22	....	....	.29	....	....	−10.94
41	Nonfinancial assets	....	....	—	....	....	—	....	....	—	....	....	—
411	Fixed assets	....	....	—	....	....		....	....		....	....	—
412	Inventories	....	....		....	....		....	....		....	....	—
413	Valuables	....	....		....	....		....	....		....	....	
414	Nonproduced assets	....	....	—	....	....		....	....		....	....	
42	Financial assets	....	....	−15.57	....	....	−15.57	....	....	—	....	....	−15.57
421	Domestic	....	....	−2.32			−2.32	....	....	—			−2.32
422	Foreign	....	....	−13.26			−13.26	....	....	—			−13.26
423	Monetary gold and SDRs	....	....	—	....	....		....	....		....	....	
43	Liabilities	....	....	−4.35	....	....	−4.35	....	....	−.29	....	....	−4.64
431	Domestic	....	....	−.13			−.13	....	....	—			−.13
432	Foreign	....	....	−4.23			−4.23	....	....	−.29			−4.51

Table 5   Other changes in the volume of assets and liabilities

5	Change in net worth from vol. chngs	....	....	19.68	....	....	20.32	....	....	28.62	....	....	48.93
51	Nonfinancial assets	....	....	−2.09	....	....	−20.43	....	....	25.19	....	....	4.76
511	Fixed assets	....	....	−.52	....	....	−20.04	....	....	22.19	....	....	2.16
512	Inventories	....	....	−1.54	....	....	−2.27	....	....	.22	....	....	−2.05
513	Valuables	....	....	.07	....	....	.20	....	....	.19	....	....	.39
514	Nonproduced assets	....	....	−.10	....	....	1.68	....	....	2.58	....	....	4.26
52	Financial assets	....	....	27.09	....	....	41.55	....	....	8.02	....	....	49.57
521	Domestic	....	....	27.09	....	....	41.55	....	....	8.02	....	....	49.57
522	Foreign	....	....	−.01	....	....	−.01	....	....	—	....	....	−.01
523	Monetary gold and SDRs	....	....		....	....		....	....	—	....	....	—
53	Liabilities	....	....	5.31	....	....	.80	....	....	4.60	....	....	5.40
531	Domestic	....	....	4.98			.47	....	....	4.49			4.96
532	Foreign	....	....	.33			.33	....	....	.11			.44

Table 6   Balance sheet

6	Net worth	....	....	113.37	598.24	626.43	488.62	211.38	273.76	360.61	809.62	900.19	849.23
61	Nonfinancial assets	....	....	357.75	467.63	429.91	481.06	194.09	249.52	335.57	661.72	679.43	816.63
611	Fixed assets	....	....	326.71	354.13	321.00	428.97	112.87	163.41	240.55	467.01	484.40	669.52
6111	Buildings and structures	....	....	....	....	....	....	....	....	....	....	....	....
6112	Machinery and equipment	....	....	....	....	....	....	....	....	....	....	....	....
6113	Other fixed assets	....	....	....	....	....	....	....	....	....	....	....	....
612	Inventories	....	....	10.87	88.37	86.55	12.21	.59	.86	1.62	88.96	87.41	13.82
613	Valuables	....	....	.07	—	—	.21	—	—	.19	—	—	.40
614	Nonproduced assets	....	....	20.11	25.13	22.37	39.67	80.63	85.26	93.21	105.76	107.62	132.88
6141	Land	....	....	20.11	....	....	39.67	....	....	93.21	....	....	132.88
6142	Subsoil assets	....	....	—	....	....	—	....	....	—	....	....	—
6143	Other naturally occurring assets	....	....	—	....	....	—	....	....	—	....	....	—
6144	Intangible nonproduced assets	....	....	—	....	....	—	....	....	—	....	....	—

Slovak Republic   936

In Billions of Koruny / Year Ending December 31 / Noncash Reporter

	Budgetary Central Government 2001p	2002p	2003p	Central Government 2001p	2002p	2003p	Local Government 2001p	2002p	2003p	General Government 2001p	2002p	2003p
62 Financial assets..........................	....	....	259.02	608.02	637.03	566.51	35.21	45.38	54.55	641.09	677.71	616.32
621 Domestic...............................	....	....	217.60	500.54	579.40	525.09	35.21	45.38	54.55	533.60	620.08	574.90
6212 Currency and deposits..................	....	....	105.59	49.92	135.20	150.88	5.29	14.03	11.89	55.21	149.23	162.77
6213 Securities other than shares..........	....	....	—	4.60	3.96	.37	2.16	1.85	2.28	6.76	5.81	2.65
6214 Loans................................	....	....	17.57	63.02	74.30	57.13	.62	.59	.34	61.50	70.18	52.74
6215 Shares and other equity...............	....	....	49.56	231.54	233.99	163.16	12.89	13.39	21.22	244.43	247.38	184.38
6216 Insurance technical reserves..........	....	....	—	—	—	—	—	—	—	—	—	—
6217 Financial derivatives.................	....	....	—	—	—	—	—	—	—	—	—	—
6218 Other accounts receivable............	....	....	44.88	151.46	131.97	153.55	14.25	15.53	18.81	165.71	147.49	172.36
622 Foreign................................	....	....	41.42	107.49	57.63	41.42	—	—	—	107.49	57.63	41.42
6222 Currency and deposits..................	....	....	—	—	—	—	—	—	—	—	—	—
6223 Securities other than shares..........	....	....	.03	—	—	.03	—	—	—	—	—	.03
6224 Loans................................	....	....	38.36	103.85	54.14	38.36	—	—	—	103.85	54.14	38.36
6225 Shares and other equity...............	....	....	3.04	3.64	3.48	3.04	—	—	—	3.64	3.48	3.04
6226 Insurance technical reserves..........	....	....	—	—	—	—	—	—	—	—	—	—
6227 Financial derivatives.................	....	....	—	—	—	—	—	—	—	—	—	—
6228 Other accounts receivable............	....	....	—	—	—	—	—	—	—	—	—	—
623 Monetary gold and SDRs................	....	....										
63 Liabilities.............................	....	....	503.41	477.42	440.51	558.95	17.92	21.15	29.50	493.20	456.95	583.72
631 Domestic...............................	....	....	399.44	347.20	329.69	454.98	13.43	16.86	28.91	358.48	341.85	479.16
6312 Currency and deposits..................	....	....	—	—	—	—	—	—	—	—	—	—
6313 Securities other than shares..........	....	....	323.62	274.52	274.24	324.19	—	1.35	.72	274.52	275.59	324.91
6314 Loans................................	....	....	64.55	16.16	13.00	74.03	8.23	8.98	13.39	22.24	17.27	82.68
6316 Insurance technical reserves..........	....	....	—	—	—	—	—	—	—	—	—	—
6317 Financial derivatives.................	....	....	—	—	—	—	—	—	—	—	—	—
6318 Other accounts payable................	....	....	11.27	56.52	42.45	56.76	5.20	6.54	14.81	61.72	48.99	71.57
632 Foreign................................	....	....	103.97	130.22	110.82	103.97	4.50	4.28	.59	134.72	115.10	104.56
6322 Currency and deposits..................	....	....	—	—	—	—	—	—	—	—	—	—
6323 Securities other than shares..........	....	....	72.03	79.39	75.30	72.03	—	4.28	—	79.39	79.58	72.03
6324 Loans................................	....	....	31.94	50.83	35.52	31.94	4.50	—	.59	55.33	35.52	32.53
6326 Insurance technical reserves..........	....	....	—	—	—	—	—	—	—	—	—	—
6327 Financial derivatives.................	....	....	—	—	—	—	—	—	—	—	—	—
6328 Other accounts payable................	....	....	—	—	—	—	—	—	—	—	—	—
Memorandum items:												
6M2 Net financial worth....................	....	....	−244.39	130.60	196.52	7.56	17.29	24.24	25.04	147.89	220.76	32.61
6M3 Debt at market value...................	....	....	....	....	....	....	....	....	....	....	....	....
6M4 Debt at nominal value..................	....	....	....	....	....	....	....	....	....	....	....	....
6M5 Arrears................................	....	....	....	....	....	....	....	....	....	....	....	....
6M6 Obligations for social security benefits............	....	....	....	....	....	....	....	....	....	....	....	....
6M7 Contingent liabilities.................	....	....	66.95	....	....	....	....	....	....	....	....	....
6M8 Uncapitalized military weapons, systems........	....	....	....	....	....	....	....	....	....	....	....	....
Table 7 Outlays by functions of govt.												
7 Total outlays...........................	344.69	270.45	†289.89	400.99	447.45	†461.99	26.10	56.24	†89.68	421.80	473.80	†502.07
701 General public services...............	185.18	74.27	†129.34	72.53	78.29	†95.37	8.58	19.87	†13.92	75.82	68.27	†59.69
7017 Public debt transactions..............	20.50	35.52	†28.87	30.60	38.36	†29.66	1.03	.90	†.92	31.63	39.26	†30.40
7018 General transfers between levels of govt......	126.51	29.41	†87.10	5.28	29.89	†49.41	—	—	†—	—	—	†—
702 Defense................................	16.30	17.61	†21.71	16.30	17.61	†21.71	.01	.01	†.01	16.31	17.61	†21.72
703 Public order and safety................	15.94	19.34	†22.79	15.94	19.34	†23.11	.86	.78	†.85	16.79	20.13	†23.96
704 Economic affairs.......................	39.35	38.90	†41.94	61.37	54.38	†47.00	5.12	8.69	†8.87	66.49	63.06	†55.86
7042 Agriculture, forestry, fishing, and hunting.....	11.41	12.36	†11.69	17.03	12.36	†12.65	1.03	.12	†.52	18.06	12.48	†13.17
7043 Fuel and energy.......................	.15	.38	†.39	.57	1.08	†.39	—	.05	†.49	.57	1.14	†.88
7044 Mining, manufacturing, and construction.....	.33	.22	†.21	4.01	.22	†.21	.08	1.43	†1.23	4.08	1.65	†1.44
7045 Transport.............................	5.92	19.55	†20.66	12.23	19.55	†20.97	3.39	6.67	†3.50	15.62	26.22	†24.47
7046 Communication.........................	....	....	†.11	....	....		....	....	†.02	....	....	†.13
705 Environmental protection...............	—	—	†.90	—	—	†3.46	—	—	†5.66	—	—	†9.12
706 Housing and community amenities........	5.12	8.20	†3.44	6.25	8.28	†3.90	11.06	9.72	†9.70	17.31	18.00	†13.60
707 Health.................................	16.79	19.08	†17.76	69.55	74.66	†93.72	.18	.13	†6.86	69.73	74.78	†100.59
7072 Outpatient services...................	—	....	†—	7.94	....	†9.71	....	....	†.68	7.94	....	†10.39
7073 Hospital services.....................	2.75	....	†.05	21.88	....	†37.40	....	....	†6.08	21.88	....	†43.49
7074 Public health services................	....	....	†1.27	....	....	†1.27	....	....	†—	....	....	†1.27
708 Recreation, culture, and religion..........	5.30	7.19	†2.94	6.77	7.19	†5.49	2.28	4.03	†5.04	9.05	11.22	†10.52

In Billions of Koruny / Year Ending December 31 / Noncash Reporter

		Budgetary Central Government			Central Government			Local Government			General Government		
		2001p	2002p	2003p	2001p	2002p	2003p	2001p	2002p	2003p	2001p	2002p	2003p
709	**Education**................................	**36.35**	**38.87**	**†4.60**	**36.35**	**38.87**	**†15.70**	**.08**	**14.09**	**†36.55**	**36.43**	**52.95**	**†52.25**
7091	Pre-primary and primary education.............	....	....	†1.75	....	....	†1.75	....	....	†19.99	....	....	†21.74
7092	Secondary education..........................	....	....	†.71	....	....	†.72	....	....	†11.75	....	....	†12.47
7094	Tertiary education............................	5.91	....	†.11	5.91	....	†10.75	....	....	†.01	5.91	....	†10.75
710	**Social protection**...........................	**24.52**	**47.38**	**†44.89**	**117.78**	**149.30**	**†153.23**	**.46**	**2.02**	**†5.43**	**118.24**	**151.32**	**†158.66**
7	Statistical discrepancy: Total outlays..............	−.16	−.38	†−.43	−1.84	−.46	†−.71	−2.53	−3.08	†−3.20	−4.37	−3.55	†−3.90

Table 8 Transactions in financial assets and liabilities by sector

		Budgetary Central Government			Central Government			Local Government			General Government		
82	**Net acquisition of financial assets**.........	**7.07**	**63.27**	**†−19.18**	**−24.73**	**−84.85**	**†−6.74**	**.75**	**1.64**	**†−.45**	**−25.77**	**−86.35**	**†−7.07**
821	Domestic....................................	8.77	76.72	†−16.24	−23.03	−71.40	†−3.80	.75	1.64	†−.45	−24.07	−72.91	†−4.13
8211	General government..........................	8.11	1.59	†−13.08	1.79	3.14	†−.11	—	—	†—	−24.07	−72.91	†−4.13
8212	Central bank.................................	1.83	82.63	†3.95	1.83	82.63	†6.29	—	—	†—	1.83	82.63	†6.29
8213	Other depository corporations..................	—	−6.00	†−4.92	4.26	1.05	†2.16	.78	1.68	†−.56	5.04	2.73	†1.59
8214	Financial corporations n.e.c...................	—	—	†—	—	—	†—	—	—	†—	—	—	†—
8215	Nonfinancial corporations.....................	−1.17	−1.50	†−2.21	−34.07	−160.83	†−14.44	.01	−.03	†.11	−34.06	−160.86	†−14.33
8216	Households & NPIs serving households......	—	—	†.02	3.17	2.61	†2.31	−.04	−.02	†.01	3.13	2.60	†2.32
822	Foreign....................................	−1.70	−13.45	†−2.94	−1.70	−13.45	†−2.94	—	—	†—	−1.70	−13.45	†−2.94
8221	General government..........................	−1.91	−13.55	†—	−1.91	−13.55	†—	—	—	†—	−1.91	−13.55	†—
8227	International organizations......................	.21	.10	†.09	.21	.10	†.09	—	—	†—	.21	.10	†.09
8228	Financial corporations other than international organizations.............	—	—	†−3.03	—	—	†−3.03	—	—	†—	—	—	†−3.03
8229	Other nonresidents...........................	—	—	†—	—	—	†—	—	—	†—	—	—	†—
823	Monetary gold and SDRs......................	—	—	†—	—	—	†—	—	—	†—	—	—	†—
83	**Net incurrence of liabilities**..................	**146.86**	**−2.33**	**†38.85**	**30.35**	**−17.36**	**†31.65**	**1.04**	**2.64**	**†.09**	**29.60**	**−17.86**	**†31.85**
831	Domestic....................................	144.27	−1.42	†41.80	22.42	−5.61	†34.60	1.17	3.24	†3.61	21.80	−5.51	†38.32
8311	General government..........................	—	—	†—	—	—	†—	1.79	3.14	†−.11	—	—	†—
8312	Central bank.................................	—	—	†—	−.96	−2.02	†−2.37	—	—	†—	−.96	−2.02	†−2.37
8313	Other depository corporations..................	144.27	−1.42	†41.80	32.33	−.31	†40.56	−.62	.10	†3.35	31.72	−.21	†43.91
8314	Financial corporations n.e.c...................	—	—	†—	—	—	†—	—	—	†—	—	—	†—
8315	Nonfinancial corporations.....................	—	—	†—	—	—	†−2.19	—	—	†.37	—	—	†−1.82
8316	Households & NPIs serving households......	—	—	†—	−8.95	−3.28	†−1.40	—	—	†—	−8.95	−3.28	†−1.40
832	Foreign....................................	2.59	−.91	†−2.95	7.93	−11.75	†−2.95	−.13	−.60	†−3.51	7.80	−12.35	†−6.47
8321	General government..........................	—	—	†—	—	—	†—	—	—	†—	—	—	†—
8327	International organizations......................	—	—	†—	—	—	†—	—	—	†.01	—	—	†.01
8328	Financial corporations other than international organizations.............	2.59	−.91	†−2.61	2.59	−.91	†−2.61	—	—	†−3.52	2.59	−.91	†−6.13
8329	Other nonresidents...........................	—	—	†−.34	5.34	−10.84	†−.34	−.13	−.60	†—	5.21	−11.44	†−.34

Slovenia 961

In Billions of Tolars / Year Ending December 31 / Cash Reporter

	Budgetary Central Government 2002	2003	2004	Central Government 2002	2003	2004	Local Government 2002	2003	2004	General Government 2002	2003	2004
Statement of government operations												
Statement of other economic flows												
Balance sheet												
Statement of sources and uses of cash												
1 Cash receipts from operating activities..........	1,163.6	1,382.1	1,504.0	2,089.8	2,376.6	2,566.8	466.5	508.1	571.9	2,333.2	2,639.6	2,873.5
11 Taxes.....................	1,055.8	1,264.3	1,347.1	1,045.6	1,252.1	1,333.7	164.6	178.8	191.4	1,202.8	1,422.4	1,515.6
12 Social contributions.....................	8.2	8.9	9.5	848.1	918.8	984.4	—	—	—	848.1	918.8	984.4
13 Grants.....................	12.9	4.0	44.1	16.3	8.0	48.8	212.4	233.1	252.1	12.9	4.6	45.3
14 Other receipts.....................	86.7	104.9	103.4	179.9	197.8	199.9	89.5	96.1	128.4	269.4	293.9	328.2
2 Cash payments for operating activities.........	1,258.0	1,393.7	1,522.0	2,169.0	2,374.6	2,550.8	403.0	439.0	503.0	2,348.7	2,568.5	2,788.6
21 Compensation of employees.....................	176.9	199.5	212.7	400.9	449.0	483.1	213.6	230.3	251.7	614.5	679.3	734.8
22 Purchases of goods and services...............	140.5	143.4	148.6	345.9	379.8	402.2	118.0	126.0	144.9	464.0	505.8	547.1
24 Interest.....................	80.9	90.0	89.2	83.8	92.9	92.1	.9	1.1	1.0	84.7	94.0	93.1
25 Subsidies.....................	56.7	64.4	64.4	57.0	72.8	77.5	3.8	5.1	4.9	60.8	77.9	82.4
26 Grants.....................	562.5	623.6	726.6	212.9	233.2	293.0	3.4	4.0	3.8	.5	.6	41.1
27 Social benefits.....................	187.4	209.9	224.0	1,008.5	1,075.5	1,141.3	22.3	23.8	48.3	1,030.8	1,099.4	1,189.6
28 Other payments.....................	53.0	63.0	56.3	59.9	71.4	61.6	41.0	48.7	48.3	93.5	111.5	100.3
CIO *Net cash inflow from oper. activities.....*	*−94.4*	*−11.6*	*−17.9*	*−79.1*	*2.0*	*16.0*	*63.6*	*69.1*	*68.9*	*−15.5*	*71.1*	*84.9*
31.1 Purchases of nonfinancial assets..................	46.3	58.8	64.7	71.0	84.5	100.5	83.8	83.3	85.8	154.7	167.8	186.3
31.2 Sales of nonfinancial assets..................	2.1	1.9	2.3	6.2	3.4	4.9	13.0	13.8	18.3	19.1	17.2	23.2
31 Net cash outflow from investments in nonfinancial assets.....................	44.2	56.9	62.5	64.8	81.0	95.6	70.8	69.5	67.5	135.6	150.6	163.1
CSD *Cash surplus/deficit.....*	*−138.6*	*−68.5*	*−80.4*	*−143.9*	*−79.0*	*−79.6*	*−7.2*	*−.4*	*1.4*	*−151.1*	*−79.5*	*−78.2*
32x Net acquisition of fin assets, excl. cash..	−102.3	1.6	9.6	−96.1	−4.6	12.1	−1.8	−.2	−1.4	−97.8	−4.8	10.7
321x Domestic.....................	−102.5	1.5	7.4	−96.2	−5.1	8.8	−1.8	−.2	−1.4	−98.0	−5.3	7.4
322x Foreign.....................	.2	.1	2.2	.2	.5	3.3	—	—	—	.2	.5	3.3
323 Monetary gold and SDRs..................	—	—	—	—	—	—	—	—	—	—	—	—
33 Net incurrence of liabilities.....................	134.5	25.1	78.6	143.3	49.9	93.5	5.6	3.7	5.2	148.9	53.6	98.6
331 Domestic.....................	155.8	36.8	129.2	164.5	60.2	143.8	5.6	3.7	5.2	170.2	63.9	149.0
332 Foreign.....................	−21.3	−11.7	−50.6	−21.2	−10.3	−50.3	—	—	—	−21.2	−10.3	−50.3
NFB Net cash inflow from fin. activities..................	236.8	23.5	69.0	239.4	54.6	81.3	7.4	3.9	6.6	246.8	58.5	88.0
NCB *Net change in the stock of cash.............*	*98.1*	*−45.0*	*−11.4*	*95.4*	*−24.5*	*1.7*	*.2*	*3.4*	*8.0*	*95.6*	*−21.0*	*9.8*

Table 1 Revenue

	2002	2003	2004	2002	2003	2004	2002	2003	2004	2002	2003	2004
1 **Revenue**.............................	**1,163.6**	**1,382.1**	**1,504.0**	**2,089.8**	**2,376.6**	**2,566.8**	**466.5**	**508.1**	**571.9**	**2,333.2**	**2,639.6**	**2,873.5**
11 **Taxes**.............................	**1,055.8**	**1,264.3**	**1,347.1**	**1,045.6**	**1,252.1**	**1,333.7**	**164.6**	**178.8**	**191.4**	**1,202.8**	**1,422.4**	**1,515.6**
111 Taxes on income, profits, & capital gains.....	283.3	336.9	373.0	283.3	336.9	373.0	111.7	123.6	133.9	395.0	460.5	506.9
1111 Individuals.....................	208.1	229.5	248.6	208.1	229.5	248.6	111.7	123.6	133.9	319.8	353.1	382.5
1112 Corporations and other enterprises.....	75.2	107.4	124.4	75.2	107.4	124.4	—	—	—	75.2	107.4	124.4
112 Taxes on payroll and workforce.....	86.5	98.7	108.7	76.3	86.5	95.3	—	—	—	68.9	78.0	85.8
113 Taxes on property.....................	1.8	.3	2.8	1.8	.3	2.8	32.6	34.1	36.7	34.4	34.4	39.5
114 Taxes on goods and services.....	652.5	793.5	835.8	652.5	793.5	835.8	20.2	21.1	20.8	672.7	814.6	856.6
1141 General taxes on goods and services......	423.7	525.9	539.3	423.7	525.9	539.3	—	—	—	423.7	525.9	539.3
1142 Excises.....................	170.9	197.8	217.6	170.9	197.8	217.6	—	—	—	170.9	197.8	217.6
115 Taxes on int'l. trade and transactions..........	31.3	34.7	19.3	31.3	34.7	19.3	—	—	—	31.3	34.7	19.3
116 Other taxes.....................	.3	.2	7.5	.3	.2	7.5	—	—	—	.4	.3	7.5
12 **Social contributions**.............................	**8.2**	**8.9**	**9.5**	**848.1**	**918.8**	**984.4**	**—**	**—**	**—**	**848.1**	**918.8**	**984.4**
121 Social security contributions.....................	8.2	8.9	9.5	848.1	918.8	984.4	—	—	—	848.1	918.8	984.4
122 Other social contributions.....................	—	—	—	—	—	—	—	—	—	—	—	—
13 **Grants**.............................	**12.9**	**4.0**	**44.1**	**16.3**	**8.0**	**48.8**	**212.4**	**233.1**	**252.1**	**12.9**	**4.6**	**45.3**
131 From foreign governments.....................	—	4.0	.3	—	4.0	.3	—	.6	.2	—	4.6	.4
132 From international organizations.....................	12.9	—	43.8	12.9	—	44.8	—	—	.1	12.9	—	44.9
133 From other general government units..........	—	—	—	3.4	4.0	3.8	212.4	232.5	251.9	—	—	—
14 **Other revenue**.............................	**86.7**	**104.9**	**103.4**	**179.9**	**197.8**	**199.9**	**89.5**	**96.1**	**128.4**	**269.4**	**293.9**	**328.2**

Table 2 Expense by economic type

	2002	2003	2004	2002	2003	2004	2002	2003	2004	2002	2003	2004
2 **Expense**.............................	**1,258.0**	**1,393.7**	**1,522.0**	**2,169.0**	**2,374.6**	**2,550.8**	**403.0**	**439.0**	**503.0**	**2,348.7**	**2,568.5**	**2,788.6**
21 **Compensation of employees**..................	**176.9**	**199.5**	**212.7**	**400.9**	**449.0**	**483.1**	**213.6**	**230.3**	**251.7**	**614.5**	**679.3**	**734.8**
211 Wages and salaries.....................	151.9	171.4	179.7	347.0	389.0	411.3	186.4	201.0	215.1	533.4	590.0	626.3
212 Social contributions.....................	25.1	28.1	33.1	54.0	60.0	71.9	27.1	29.3	36.6	81.1	89.3	108.5
22 **Use of goods and services**..................	**140.5**	**143.4**	**148.6**	**345.9**	**379.8**	**402.2**	**118.0**	**126.0**	**144.9**	**464.0**	**505.8**	**547.1**
23 **Consumption of fixed capital**..................	....	....	....	....	....	....	....	....	....	....	....	....
24 **Interest**.............................	**80.9**	**90.0**	**89.2**	**83.8**	**92.9**	**92.1**	**.9**	**1.1**	**1.0**	**84.7**	**94.0**	**93.1**
25 **Subsidies**.............................	**56.7**	**64.4**	**64.4**	**57.0**	**72.8**	**77.5**	**3.8**	**5.1**	**4.9**	**60.8**	**77.9**	**82.4**

In Billions of Tolars / Year Ending December 31 / Cash Reporter

		Budgetary Central Government			Central Government			Local Government			General Government		
		2002	2003	2004	2002	2003	2004	2002	2003	2004	2002	2003	2004
26	**Grants**.................	**562.5**	**623.6**	**726.6**	**212.9**	**233.2**	**293.0**	**3.4**	**4.0**	**3.8**	**.5**	**.6**	**41.1**
261	To foreign govenments..............	.4	.5	—	.4	.5	—				.4	.5	—
262	To international organizations..............	—	.2	41.1	—	.2	41.1	—	—	—		.2	41.1
263	To other general government units..............	562.1	623.0	685.5	212.4	232.5	251.9	3.4	4.0	3.8	—	—	—
2631	Current..............	545.1	605.1	665.6	199.2	220.1	241.0	2.8	3.4	3.6	—	—	—
2632	Capital..............	17.0	17.8	19.9	13.2	12.5	10.9	.6	.6	.2	—	—	—
27	**Social benefits**..............	**187.4**	**209.9**	**224.0**	**1,008.5**	**1,075.5**	**1,141.3**	**22.3**	**23.8**	**48.3**	**1,030.8**	**1,099.4**	**1,189.6**
28	**Other expense**..............	**53.0**	**63.0**	**56.3**	**59.9**	**71.4**	**61.6**	**41.0**	**48.7**	**48.3**	**93.5**	**111.5**	**100.3**
281	Property expense other than interest..............	—	—	—	—	—	—	—	—	—	—	—	—
282	Miscellaneous other expense..............	53.0	63.0	56.3	59.9	71.4	61.6	41.0	48.7	48.3	93.5	111.5	100.3
2821	Current..............	13.0	12.8	14.1	18.6	19.0	17.9	20.0	23.1	26.4	31.2	33.5	34.7
2822	Capital..............	40.0	50.2	42.2	41.3	52.4	43.7	21.0	25.5	21.9	62.3	77.9	65.6
Table 3 Transactions in assets and liabilities													
3	**Change in net worth from transactns....**	....	....	....	....	....	....	....	....	....	....	....	....
31	**Net acquisition of nonfinancial assets...**	**44.2**	**56.9**	**62.5**	**64.8**	**81.0**	**95.6**	**70.8**	**69.5**	**67.5**	**135.6**	**150.6**	**163.1**
311	Fixed assets..............	42.9	55.7	60.8	63.2	79.1	93.5	73.5	72.4	74.9	136.7	151.4	168.4
3111	Buildings and structures..............	30.4	39.1	43.4	36.0	49.6	61.5	62.7	61.2	63.3	98.7	110.8	124.9
3112	Machinery and equipment..............	12.4	16.4	17.1	26.2	28.6	30.8	11.1	11.4	11.4	37.3	39.9	42.2
3113	Other fixed assets..............	.1	.2	.4	1.0	.9	1.2	−.2	−.2	.1	.7	.7	1.3
312	Inventories..............	—	—	—	—	—	—	—	—	—	—	—	—
313	Valuables..............	—	—	—	—	—	—	—	—	—	—	—	—
314	Nonproduced assets..............	1.3	1.2	1.6	1.6	2.0	2.1	−2.7	−2.8	−7.3	−1.1	−.8	−5.2
3141	Land..............	1.3	1.2	1.6	1.3	1.2	1.3	−7.9	−8.1	−7.3	−6.6	−6.9	−6.0
3142	Subsoil assets..............	—	—	—	—	—	—	—	—	—	—	—	—
3143	Other naturally occurring assets..............	—	—	—	.2	.8	.8	5.2	5.2	—	5.4	6.1	.8
3144	Intangible nonproduced assets..............	—	—	—	—	—	—	—	—	—	—	—	—
32	**Net acquisition of financial assets.........**	**−4.2**	**−43.4**	**−1.8**	**−.6**	**−29.1**	**13.9**	**−1.6**	**3.2**	**6.6**	**−2.2**	**−25.9**	**20.4**
321	Domestic..............	−4.3	−43.5	−4.0	−.8	−29.6	10.5	−1.6	3.2	6.6	−2.4	−26.3	17.1
3212	Currency and deposits..............	98.1	−45.0	−11.4	95.4	−24.5	1.7	.2	3.4	8.0	95.6	−21.0	9.8
3213	Securities other than shares..............	—	—	—	—	—	—	—	—	—	—	—	—
3214	Loans..............	3.0	2.6	.1	10.4	−2.1	.7	−1.0	−.8	−.6	9.4	−2.9	.1
3215	Shares and other equity..............	−105.5	−1.1	7.3	−107.7	−3.1	8.1	−.8	.6	−.8	−108.5	−2.5	7.3
3216	Insurance technical reserves..............	—	—	—	1.0	.1	—	—	—	—	1.0	.1	—
3217	Financial derivatives..............	—	—	—	—	—	—	—	—	—	—	—	—
3218	Other accounts receivable..............	....	....	....	....	....	....	....	....	....	....	....	....
322	Foreign..............	.2	.1	2.2	.2	.5	3.3	—	—	—	.2	.5	3.3
3222	Currency and deposits..............	—	—	—	—	—	—	—	—	—	—	—	—
3223	Securities other than shares..............	—	—	—	—	—	—	—	—	—	—	—	—
3224	Loans..............	—	—	—	—	.3	1.1	—	—	—	—	.3	1.1
3225	Shares and other equity..............	.2	.1	2.2	.2	.1	2.2	—	—	—	.2	.1	2.2
3226	Insurance technical reserves..............	—	—	—	—	—	—	—	—	—	—	—	—
3227	Financial derivatives..............	—	—	—	—	—	—	—	—	—	—	—	—
3228	Other accounts receivable..............	....	....	....	....	....	....	....	....	....	....	....	....
323	Monetary gold and SDRs..............	—	—	—	—	—	—	—	—	—	—	—	....
33	**Net incurrence of liabilities...................**	**134.5**	**25.1**	**78.6**	**143.3**	**49.9**	**93.5**	**5.6**	**3.7**	**5.2**	**148.9**	**53.6**	**98.6**
331	Domestic..............	155.8	36.8	129.2	164.5	60.2	143.8	5.6	3.7	5.2	170.2	63.9	149.0
3312	Currency and deposits..............	—	—	—	—	—	—	—	—	—	—	—	—
3313	Securities other than shares..............	157.9	52.5	137.3	157.3	52.0	137.3	—	—	—	157.3	52.0	137.3
3314	Loans..............	−2.2	−15.7	−8.1	7.3	8.2	6.5	5.6	3.7	5.2	12.9	11.9	11.7
3316	Insurance technical reserves..............	—	—	—	—	—	—	—	—	—	—	—	—
3317	Financial derivatives..............	—	—	—	—	—	—	—	—	—	—	—	—
3318	Other accounts payable..............	....	....	....	....	....	....	....	....	....	....	....	....
332	Foreign..............	−21.3	−11.7	−50.6	−21.2	−10.3	−50.3	—	—	—	−21.2	−10.3	−50.3
3322	Currency and deposits..............	—	—	—	—	—	—	—	—	—	—	—	—
3323	Securities other than shares..............	−2.9	−2.6	−51.5	−2.9	−2.6	−51.5	—	—	—	−2.9	−2.6	−51.5
3324	Loans..............	−18.4	−9.1	.8	−18.3	−7.7	1.1	—	—	—	−18.3	−7.7	1.1
3326	Insurance technical reserves..............	—	—	—	—	—	—	—	—	—	—	—	—
3327	Financial derivatives..............	—	—	—	—	—	—	—	—	—	—	—	—
3328	Other accounts payable..............	....	....	....	....	....	....	....	....	....	....	....	....

In Billions of Tolars / Year Ending December 31 / Cash Reporter

	Budgetary Central Government			Central Government			Local Government			General Government		
	2002	2003	2004	2002	2003	2004	2002	2003	2004	2002	2003	2004
Table 4 Holding gains in assets and liabilities												
Table 5 Other changes in the volume of assets and liabilities												
Table 6 Balance sheet												
Table 7 Outlays by functions of govt.												
7 **Total outlays**............................	1,304.4	1,452.5	1,586.7	2,240.0	2,459.1	2,651.3	486.7	522.3	588.8	2,503.5	2,736.3	2,974.9
701 **General public services**.....................	241.9	270.7	319.7	247.5	275.4	325.2	42.2	42.4	43.6	252.7	276.4	331.4
7017 Public debt transactions..........................	80.9	90.0	89.2	83.8	92.9	92.1	.9	1.1	1.0	84.7	94.0	93.1
7018 General transfers between levels of govt.......	36.6	41.6	78.9	36.6	41.6	78.9	—	—	—	—	.6	42.3
702 **Defense**..................................	63.8	72.5	82.5	63.8	72.5	82.5	.8	.7	.8	64.6	73.2	83.2
703 **Public order and safety**......................	95.4	105.0	113.2	95.8	105.4	113.2	6.2	6.7	7.2	101.6	111.7	119.0
704 **Economic affairs**............................	178.0	195.8	218.1	189.1	214.0	237.0	58.5	60.7	60.6	243.0	268.9	290.8
7042 Agriculture, forestry, fishing, and hunting.....	40.0	46.8	63.0	49.0	51.7	73.1	2.9	3.0	3.1	50.9	53.6	74.9
7043 Fuel and energy..............................	7.6	5.5	5.4	8.2	6.0	6.7	.8	.5	.6	8.5	6.4	6.4
7044 Mining, manufacturing, and construction.....	1.9	2.8	1.4	1.9	2.8	1.4	—	—	—	1.9	2.8	1.4
7045 Transport...................................	80.2	88.6	92.0	80.2	99.8	98.5	29.2	30.2	30.5	109.3	129.9	128.9
7046 Communication..............................	2.8	3.3	3.9	2.5	3.2	3.9				2.5	3.2	3.8
705 **Environmental protection**.....................	18.2	22.2	20.5	20.4	23.4	21.7	20.3	24.2	28.0	37.8	45.8	48.2
706 **Housing and community amenities**........	5.4	8.0	8.2	16.2	22.7	8.2	29.1	31.2	35.6	44.2	51.4	40.9
707 **Health**.....................................	13.1	17.3	17.9	328.7	348.8	389.9	66.3	69.6	71.6	344.5	365.1	405.1
7072 Outpatient services...........................	.3	.3	.5	61.7	67.1	89.3	62.7	65.8	68.3	74.0	79.7	101.3
7073 Hospital services.............................	7.3	11.0	10.3	181.8	190.5	200.2	—	—	—	181.6	190.4	200.0
7074 Public health services........................	3.5	3.8	4.6	3.5	3.8	4.6	3.7	3.8	3.3	7.1	7.6	7.8
708 **Recreation, culture, and religion**...........	34.6	37.4	41.2	39.0	41.6	45.7	37.0	38.5	43.2	69.3	73.2	80.7
709 **Education**...................................	250.3	276.2	307.7	271.1	300.2	333.3	205.4	225.7	272.8	364.0	401.2	464.3
7091 Pre-primary and primary education.............	110.3	122.1	138.7	111.0	123.0	139.7	197.1	216.5	262.5	202.3	222.5	268.7
7092 Secondary education..........................	58.6	64.8	69.6	65.2	71.3	76.9	—	—	—	64.2	70.2	75.8
7094 Tertiary education............................	62.8	68.8	73.9	74.9	83.9	91.6	—	—	—	74.8	83.6	91.5
710 **Social protection**............................	403.5	447.3	457.8	968.4	1,055.1	1,094.6	20.9	22.6	25.5	981.8	1,069.3	1,111.2
7 Statistical discrepancy: Total outlays..............	—	—	—	—	—	—	—	—	—	—	—	—
Table 8 Transactions in financial assets and liabilities by sector												
82 **Net acquisition of financial assets**........	−4.2	−43.4	−1.8	−.6	−29.1	13.9	−1.6	3.2	6.6	−2.2	−25.9	20.4
821 Domestic...................................	−4.3	−43.5	−4.0	−.8	−29.6	10.5	−1.6	3.2	6.6	−2.4	−26.3	17.1
8211 General government...........................	....	....	....	....	....	....	....	....	....	....	....	....
8212 Central bank................................	....	....	....	....	....	....	....	....	....	....	....	....
8213 Other depository corporations.................	....	....	....	....	....	....	....	....	....	....	....	....
8214 Financial corporations n.e.c...................	....	....	....	....	....	....	....	....	....	....	....	....
8215 Nonfinancial corporations....................	....	....	....	....	....	....	....	....	....	....	....	....
8216 Households & NPIs serving households......	....	....	....	....	....	....	....	....	....	....	....	....
822 Foreign....................................	.2	.1	2.2	.2	.5	3.3	—	—	—	.2	.5	3.3
8221 General government...........................	....	....	....	....	....	....	—	—	—	....	....	....
8227 International organizations....................	....	....	....	....	....	....	—	—	—	....	....	....
8228 Financial corporations other than international organizations...............	....	....	....	....	....	....	—	—	—	....	....	....
8229 Other nonresidents..........................	....	....	....	....	....	....	—	—	—	....	....	....
823 Monetary gold and SDRs.....................	—	—	—	—	—	—	—	—	—	—	—	—
83 **Net incurrence of liabilities**..................	134.5	25.1	78.6	143.3	49.9	93.5	5.6	3.7	5.2	148.9	53.6	98.6
831 Domestic...................................	155.8	36.8	129.2	164.5	60.2	143.8	5.6	3.7	5.2	170.2	63.9	149.0
8311 General government...........................	....	....	....	....	....	....	....	....	....	....	....	....
8312 Central bank................................	....	....	....	....	....	....	....	....	....	....	....	....
8313 Other depository corporations.................	....	....	....	....	....	....	....	....	....	....	....	....
8314 Financial corporations n.e.c...................	....	....	....	....	....	....	....	....	....	....	....	....
8315 Nonfinancial corporations....................	....	....	....	....	....	....	....	....	....	....	....	....
8316 Households & NPIs serving households......	....	....	....	....	....	....	....	....	....	....	....	....
832 Foreign....................................	−21.3	−11.7	−50.6	−21.2	−10.3	−50.3	—	—	—	−21.2	−10.3	−50.3
8321 General government...........................	....	....	....	....	....	....	—	—	—	....	....	....
8327 International organizations....................	....	....	....	....	....	....	—	—	—	....	....	....
8328 Financial corporations other than international organizations...............	....	....	....	....	....	....	—	—	—	....	....	....
8329 Other nonresidents..........................	....	....	....	....	....	....	—	—	—	....	....	....

In Millions of Rand / Year Beginning April 1 / Noncash Reporter

	Central Government			State Government			Local Government			General Government		
	2002	2003p	2004p	2002	2003p	2004p	2002	2003p	2004p	2002	2003p	2004p
Statement of government operations												
1 Revenue	310,100	328,966	385,209	142,585	167,769	191,029	69,540	83,210	91,393	373,636	401,375	461,430
2 Expense	322,295	350,230	403,575	136,204	160,354	178,662	62,619	73,574	84,609	372,528	405,588	460,644
GOB *Gross operating balance*	−11,953	−21,264	−18,366	6,381	7,415	12,368	6,921	9,636	6,784	1,350	−4,213	786
NOB *Net operating balance*	....	....	....	....	....	....	....	....	....	....	....	....
31 Net acquisition of nonfinancial assets	6,748	7,572	8,371	8,923	9,605	10,067	13,060	14,752	15,173	28,732	31,929	33,611
NLB *Net lending/borrowing*	−18,943	−28,836	−26,738	−2,542	−2,190	2,301	−6,139	−5,116	−8,388	−27,624	−36,142	−32,825
32 Net acquisition of financial assets	1,949	6,476	18,404	−2,542	−2,190	2,300	1,100	34	49	507	4,320	20,754
33 Net incurrence of liabilities	20,891	35,312	45,142	—	—	—	7,239	5,150	8,437	28,131	40,462	53,579
NLB Statistical discrepancy	—	—	—	—	—	—	—	—	—	—	—	—
Statement of other economic flows												
Balance sheet												
6 *Net worth*	....	....	....	....	....	....	....	....	....	....	....	....
61 Nonfinancial assets	....	....	....	....	....	....	....	....	....	....	....	....
62 Financial assets	....	....	....	....	....	....	....	....	....	....	....	....
63 Liabilities	462,645	473,053	506,977	....	....	....	....	....	....	....	....	....
Statement of sources and uses of cash												
1 Cash receipts from operating activities	310,312	328,966	385,209	142,585	167,769	191,029	69,540	83,210	91,393	373,847	401,375	461,430
11 Taxes	283,387	303,726	357,322	1,992	2,189	3,441	17,152	21,589	21,443	302,531	327,504	382,207
12 Social contributions	7,043	8,080	9,413	—	—	—	—	—	—	7,043	8,080	9,413
13 Grants	1,123	1,989	3,412	136,926	161,532	185,146	10,967	15,249	17,935	426	200	291
14 Other receipts	18,759	15,172	15,062	3,667	4,048	2,442	41,421	46,372	52,015	63,848	65,592	69,519
2 Cash payments for operating activities	315,929	350,230	403,575	136,204	160,354	178,662	62,619	73,574	84,609	366,162	405,588	460,644
21 Compensation of employees	48,408	52,042	57,182	73,685	80,964	87,847	17,883	21,646	25,168	139,976	154,652	170,197
22 Purchases of goods and services	39,273	42,382	46,675	23,011	26,018	28,490	42,786	47,744	55,352	105,070	116,144	130,517
24 Interest	46,908	46,464	49,101	7	5	3	777	1,931	1,524	47,692	48,400	50,628
25 Subsidies	6,848	7,188	5,088	971	1,123	1,680	—	—	—	7,819	8,311	6,768
26 Grants	152,286	180,619	209,894	2,864	5,327	7,496	—	—	—	6,560	7,376	11,189
27 Social benefits	9,084	9,124	10,672	28,757	36,215	42,796	—	—	—	37,841	45,339	53,468
28 Other payments	13,122	12,411	24,963	6,909	10,702	10,349	1,173	2,253	2,565	21,204	25,366	37,878
CIO *Net cash inflow from oper. activities*	−5,617	−21,264	−18,366	6,381	7,415	12,368	6,921	9,636	6,784	7,685	−4,213	786
31.1 Purchases of nonfinancial assets	7,452	8,259	9,233	9,008	9,697	10,127	13,100	14,800	15,231	29,560	32,756	34,591
31.2 Sales of nonfinancial assets	477	687	862	85	92	60	40	48	58	602	827	980
31 Net cash outflow from investments in nonfinancial assets	6,975	7,572	8,371	8,923	9,605	10,067	13,060	14,752	15,173	28,958	31,929	33,611
CSD *Cash surplus/deficit*	−12,592	−28,836	−26,738	−2,542	−2,190	2,301	−6,139	−5,116	−8,388	−21,273	−36,142	−32,825
32x Net acquisition of fin assets, excl. cash	−2,584	4,165	−140	298	97	106	−1,403	−2,748	−2,344	−3,689	1,514	−2,377
321x Domestic	−2,584	4,165	−140	298	97	106	−1,403	−2,748	−2,344	−3,689	1,514	−2,377
322x Foreign	—	—	—	—	—	—	—	—	—	—	—	—
323 Monetary gold and SDRs	—	—	—	—	—	—	—	—	—	—	—	—
33 Net incurrence of liabilities	13,051	35,312	45,142	—	—	—	7,239	5,150	8,437	20,290	40,462	53,579
331 Domestic	−258	37,766	39,328	—	—	—	7,239	5,150	8,437	6,981	42,916	47,766
332 Foreign	13,309	−2,455	5,813	—	—	—	—	—	—	13,309	−2,455	5,813
NFB Net cash inflow from fin. activities	15,635	31,147	45,281	−298	−97	−106	8,642	7,898	10,781	23,979	38,948	55,956
NCB *Net change in the stock of cash*	3,043	2,311	18,544	−2,840	−2,287	2,194	2,503	2,782	2,393	2,706	2,806	23,130
Table 1 Revenue												
1 **Revenue**	†310,100	328,966	385,209	142,585	167,769	191,029	69,540	83,210	91,393	†373,636	401,375	461,430
11 **Taxes**	†283,441	303,726	357,322	1,992	2,189	3,441	17,152	21,589	21,443	†302,585	327,504	382,207
111 Taxes on income, profits, & capital gains	†164,566	171,963	195,597	—	—	—	—	—	—	†164,566	171,963	195,597
1111 Individuals	†94,924	99,220	111,910	—	—	—	—	—	—	†94,924	99,220	111,910
1112 Corporations and other enterprises	†69,642	72,743	83,687	—	—	—	—	—	—	†69,642	72,743	83,687
112 Taxes on payroll and workforce	†3,352	3,896	4,442	—	—	—	—	—	—	†3,352	3,896	4,442
113 Taxes on property	†5,085	6,708	9,013	—	—	—	11,678	17,434	15,774	†16,762	24,142	24,787
114 Taxes on goods and services	†99,905	112,901	135,662	1,992	2,189	3,441	321	638	690	†102,219	115,728	139,793
1141 General taxes on goods and services	†70,150	80,682	98,086	....	....	....	—	—	—	....	....	....
1142 Excises	†28,738	31,323	36,741	....	....	....	—	—	—	....	....	....
115 Taxes on int'l. trade and transactions	†8,527	6,905	11,957	—	—	—	—	—	—	†8,527	6,905	11,957
116 Other taxes	†2,005	1,353	652	—	—	—	5,153	3,517	4,979	†7,159	4,870	5,631
12 **Social contributions**	†6,506	8,080	9,413	—	—	—	—	—	—	†6,506	8,080	9,413
121 Social security contributions	†6,506	8,080	9,413	—	—	—	—	—	—	†6,506	8,080	9,413
122 Other social contributions	†—	—	—	—	—	—	—	—	—	†—	—	—
13 **Grants**	†1,123	1,989	3,412	136,926	161,532	185,146	10,967	15,249	17,935	†426	200	291
131 From foreign governments	†426	200	291	—	—	—	—	—	—	†426	200	291
132 From international organizations	†—	—	—	—	—	—	—	—	—	†—	—	—
133 From other general government units	†697	1,789	3,121	136,926	161,532	185,146	10,967	15,249	17,935	†—	—	—
14 **Other revenue**	†19,030	15,172	15,062	3,667	4,048	2,442	41,421	46,372	52,015	†64,118	65,592	69,519

In Millions of Rand / Year Beginning April 1 / Noncash Reporter

	Central Government			State Government			Local Government			General Government		
	2002	2003p	2004p	2002	2003p	2004p	2002	2003p	2004p	2002	2003p	2004p
Table 2 Expense by economic type												
2 Expense	†322,295	350,230	403,575	136,204	160,354	178,662	62,619	73,574	84,609	†372,528	405,588	460,644
21 Compensation of employees	†48,396	52,042	57,182	73,685	80,964	87,847	17,883	21,646	25,168	†139,964	154,652	170,197
211 Wages and salaries	....	....	....	....	....	....	....	....	....	....	....	....
212 Social contributions	....	....	....	....	....	....	....	....	....	....	....	....
22 Use of goods and services	†38,634	42,382	46,675	23,011	26,018	28,490	42,786	47,744	55,352	†104,431	116,144	130,517
23 Consumption of fixed capital	....	....	....	....	....	....	....	....	....	....	....	....
24 Interest	†46,908	46,464	49,101	7	5	3	777	1,931	1,524	†47,692	48,400	50,628
25 Subsidies	†6,848	7,188	5,088	971	1,123	1,680	—	—	—	†7,819	8,311	6,768
26 Grants	†152,286	180,619	209,894	2,864	5,327	7,496	—	—	—	†6,560	7,376	11,189
261 To foreign governments	†6,560	7,376	11,180	—	—	—	—	—	—	†6,560	7,376	11,180
262 To international organizations	†—	—	—	—	—	9	—	—	—	†—	—	9
263 To other general government units	†145,726	173,243	198,714	2,864	5,327	7,488	—	—	—	†—	—	—
2631 Current	†139,564	165,688	190,746	2,352	3,474	6,723	—	—	—	†—	—	—
2632 Capital	†6,162	7,555	7,968	512	1,853	765	—	—	—	†—	—	—
27 Social benefits	†14,943	9,124	10,672	28,757	36,215	42,796	—	—	—	†43,700	45,339	53,468
28 Other expense	†14,038	12,411	24,963	6,909	10,702	10,349	1,173	2,253	2,565	†22,121	25,366	37,878
281 Property expense other than interest	†122	—	20	—	—	42	—	—	—	†122	—	61
282 Miscellaneous other expense	†13,916	12,411	24,944	6,909	10,702	10,307	1,173	2,253	2,565	†21,999	25,366	37,817
2821 Current	†2,504	1,356	8,248	1,654	4,870	5,899	295	898	1,248	†4,453	7,125	15,395
2822 Capital	†11,413	11,055	16,696	5,255	5,832	4,408	878	1,354	1,318	†17,546	18,242	22,422
Table 3 Transactions in assets and liabilities												
3 Change in net worth from transactns	....	....	....	....	....	....	....	....	....	....	....	....
31 Net acquisition of nonfinancial assets	†6,748	7,572	8,371	8,923	9,605	10,067	13,060	14,752	15,173	†28,732	31,929	33,611
311 Fixed assets	†6,685	7,167	8,109	8,923	9,605	10,062	13,060	14,752	15,173	†28,668	31,524	33,344
3111 Buildings and structures	†3,488	3,432	2,413	6,712	7,181	7,537	11,095	12,532	12,888	†21,295	23,145	22,838
3112 Machinery and equipment	†3,204	3,186	1,956	2,211	2,424	2,471	1,965	2,220	2,285	†7,380	7,830	6,711
3113 Other fixed assets	†−7	549	3,741	—	—	54	—	—	—	†−7	549	3,795
312 Inventories	†26	—	—	—	—	—	—	—	—	†26	—	—
313 Valuables	†—	—	—	—	—	—	—	—	—	†—	—	—
314 Nonproduced assets	†37	405	262	—	—	5	—	—	—	†37	405	267
3141 Land	†37	405	261	—	—	5	—	—	—	†37	405	266
3142 Subsoil assets	†—	—	—	—	—	—	—	—	—	†—	—	—
3143 Other naturally occurring assets	†—	—	—	—	—	—	—	—	—	†—	—	—
3144 Intangible nonproduced assets	†—	—	1	—	—	—	—	—	—	†—	—	1
32 Net acquisition of financial assets	†1,949	6,476	18,404	−2,542	−2,190	2,300	1,100	34	49	†507	4,320	20,754
321 Domestic	†1,949	6,476	18,404	−2,542	−2,190	2,300	1,100	34	49	†507	4,320	20,754
3212 Currency and deposits	†3,043	2,311	18,544	−2,840	−2,287	2,194	2,503	2,782	2,393	†2,706	2,806	23,130
3213 Securities other than shares	†3,408	3,856	—	—	—	—	—	—	—	†3,408	3,856	—
3214 Loans	†−3,538	639	−140	298	97	106	−1,403	−2,748	−2,344	†−4,643	−2,012	−2,377
3215 Shares and other equity	†−371	−330	—	—	—	—	—	—	—	†−371	−330	—
3216 Insurance technical reserves	†1	—	—	—	—	—	—	—	—	†1	—	—
3217 Financial derivatives	†76	—	—	—	—	—	—	—	—	†76	—	—
3218 Other accounts receivable	....	....	....	....	....	....	....	....	....	†—	....	....
322 Foreign	†—	—	—	—	—	—	—	—	—	†—	—	—
3222 Currency and deposits	†—	—	—	—	—	—	—	—	—	†—	—	—
3223 Securities other than shares	†—	—	—	—	—	—	—	—	—	†—	—	—
3224 Loans	†—	—	—	—	—	—	—	—	—	†—	—	—
3225 Shares and other equity	†—	—	—	—	—	—	—	—	—	†—	—	—
3226 Insurance technical reserves	†—	—	—	—	—	—	—	—	—	†—	—	—
3227 Financial derivatives	†—	—	—	—	—	—	—	—	—	†—	—	—
3228 Other accounts receivable	....	....	....	....	....	....	....	....	....	†—	....	....
323 Monetary gold and SDRs	†—	—	—	—	—	—	—	—	—			
33 Net incurrence of liabilities	†20,891	35,312	45,142	—	—	—	7,239	5,150	8,437	†28,131	40,462	53,579
331 Domestic	†7,583	37,766	39,328	—	—	—	7,239	5,150	8,437	†14,822	42,916	47,766
3312 Currency and deposits	†1	—	—	—	—	—	—	—	—	†1	—	—
3313 Securities other than shares	†−97	37,878	38,899	—	—	—	—	—	—	†−97	37,878	38,899
3314 Loans	†−97	−111	429	—	—	—	7,239	5,150	8,437	†7,143	5,039	8,867
3316 Insurance technical reserves	†1	—	—	—	—	—	—	—	—	†1	—	—
3317 Financial derivatives	†—	—	—	....	—	—	....	—	—	†—	—	—
3318 Other accounts payable	....	....	....	....	....	....	....	....	....	....	....	....

In Millions of Rand / Year Beginning April 1 / Noncash Reporter

		Central Government			State Government			Local Government			General Government		
		2002	2003p	2004p	2002	2003p	2004p	2002	2003p	2004p	2002	2003p	2004p
332	Foreign..	†13,309	−2,455	5,813	—	—	—	—	—	—	†13,309	−2,455	5,813
3322	Currency and deposits.........................	†—	—	—	—	—	—	—	—	—	†—	—	—
3323	Securities other than shares...............	†10,751	66	−872	—	—	—	—	—	—	†10,751	66	−872
3324	Loans..	†2,558	−2,521	6,685	—	—	—	—	—	—	†2,558	−2,521	6,685
3326	Insurance technical reserves................	†—	—	—	—	—	—	—	—	—	†—	—	—
3327	Financial derivatives...........................	†—	—	—	—	—	—	—	—	—	†—	—	—
3328	Other accounts payable.......................	....	....	....	....	....	....	....	....	....	....	....	....

Table 4   Holding gains in assets and liabilities

Table 5   Other changes in the volume of assets and liabilities

Table 6   Balance sheet

		Central Government			State Government			Local Government			General Government		
6	**Net worth**...................................	....	....	....	....	....	....	....	....	....	....	....	....
61	**Nonfinancial assets**......................	....	....	....	....	....	....	....	....	....	....	....	....
611	Fixed assets.......................................	....	....	....	....	....	....	....	....	....	....	....	....
6111	Buildings and structures......................	....	....	....	....	....	....	....	....	....	....	....	....
6112	Machinery and equipment....................	....	....	....	....	....	....	....	....	....	....	....	....
6113	Other fixed assets...............................	....	....	....	....	....	....	....	....	....	....	....	....
612	Inventories...	....	....	....	....	....	....	....	....	....	....	....	....
613	Valuables...	....	....	....	....	....	....	....	....	....	....	....	....
614	Nonproduced assets............................	....	....	....	....	....	....	....	....	....	....	....	....
6141	Land..	....	....	....	....	....	....	....	....	....	....	....	....
6142	Subsoil assets....................................	....	....	....	....	....	....	....	....	....	....	....	....
6143	Other naturally occurring assets............	....	....	....	....	....	....	....	....	....	....	....	....
6144	Intangible nonproduced assets.............	....	....	....	....	....	....	....	....	....	....	....	....
62	**Financial assets**...........................	....	....	....	....	....	....	....	....	....	....	....	....
621	Domestic..	....	....	....	....	....	....	....	....	....	....	....	....
6212	Currency and deposits.........................	....	....	....	....	....	....	....	....	....	....	....	....
6213	Securities other than shares................	....	....	....	....	....	....	....	....	....	....	....	....
6214	Loans..	....	....	....	....	....	....	....	....	....	....	....	....
6215	Shares and other equity.......................	....	....	....	....	....	....	....	....	....	....	....	....
6216	Insurance technical reserves................	....	....	....	....	....	....	....	....	....	....	....	....
6217	Financial derivatives...........................	....	....	....	....	....	....	....	....	....	....	....	....
6218	Other accounts receivable....................	....	....	....	....	....	....	....	....	....	....	....	....
622	Foreign..	....	....	....	....	....	....	....	....	....	....	....	....
6222	Currency and deposits.........................	....	....	....	....	....	....	....	....	....	....	....	....
6223	Securities other than shares................	....	....	....	....	....	....	....	....	....	....	....	....
6224	Loans..	....	....	....	....	....	....	....	....	....	....	....	....
6225	Shares and other equity.......................	....	....	....	....	....	....	....	....	....	....	....	....
6226	Insurance technical reserves................	....	....	....	....	....	....	....	....	....	....	....	....
6227	Financial derivatives...........................	....	....	....	....	....	....	....	....	....	....	....	....
6228	Other accounts receivable....................	....	....	....	....	....	....	....	....	....	....	....	....
623	Monetary gold and SDRs......................	....	....	....	....	....	....	....	....	....	....	....	....
63	**Liabilities**...................................	462,645	473,053	506,977	....	....	....	....	....	....	....	....	....
631	Domestic..	388,359	408,383	437,572	....	....	....	....	....	....	....	....	....
6312	Currency and deposits.........................	....	....	....	....	....	....	....	....	....	....	....	....
6313	Securities other than shares................	....	....	....	....	....	....	....	....	....	....	....	....
6314	Loans..	....	....	....	....	....	....	....	....	....	....	....	....
6316	Insurance technical reserves................	....	....	....	....	....	....	....	....	....	....	....	....
6317	Financial derivatives...........................	....	....	....	....	....	....	....	....	....	....	....	....
6318	Other accounts payable.......................	....	....	....	....	....	....	....	....	....	....	....	....
632	Foreign..	74,286	64,670	69,405	....	....	....	....	....	....	....	....	....
6322	Currency and deposits.........................	....	....	....	....	....	....	....	....	....	....	....	....
6323	Securities other than shares................	....	....	....	....	....	....	....	....	....	....	....	....
6324	Loans..	....	....	....	....	....	....	....	....	....	....	....	....
6326	Insurance technical reserves................	....	....	....	....	....	....	....	....	....	....	....	....
6327	Financial derivatives...........................	....	....	....	....	....	....	....	....	....	....	....	....
6328	Other accounts payable.......................	....	....	....	....	....	....	....	....	....	....	....	....

In Millions of Rand / Year Beginning April 1 / Noncash Reporter

	Central Government			State Government			Local Government			General Government		
	2002	2003p	2004p	2002	2003p	2004p	2002	2003p	2004p	2002	2003p	2004p
Memorandum items:												
6M2 Net financial worth..........	....	....	....	....	....	....	....	....	....	....	....	....
6M3 Debt at market value...............	....	....	....	....	....	....	....	....	....	....	....	....
6M4 Debt at nominal value.............	....	....	....	....	....	....	....	....	....	....	....	....
6M5 Arrears................................	....	....	....	....	....	....	....	....	....	....	....	....
6M6 Obligations for social security benefits..........	....	....	....	....	....	....	....	....	....	....	....	....
6M7 Contingent liabilities..............	....	....	....	....	....	....	....	....	....	....	....	....
6M8 Uncapitalized military weapons, systems........	....	....	....	....	....	....	....	....	....	....	....	....
Table 7 Outlays by functions of govt.												
7 **Total outlays..............**	†329,043	357,802	411,946	145,127	169,959	188,729	75,680	88,326	99,782	†401,259	437,517	494,256
701 **General public services................**	†201,254	....	....	5,934	....	....	46,668	....	....	†109,765	....	....
7017 Public debt transactions.............	†46,908	46,464	49,101	7	5	3	777	1,931	1,524	†47,692	48,400	50,628
7018 General transfers between levels of govt.	....	....	....	....	....	....	....	....	....	†—	....	....
702 **Defense........................**	†20,674	....	....	—	....	....	—	....	....	†20,674	....	....
703 **Public order and safety....................**	†33,141	....	....	1,285	....	....	—	....	....	†34,426	....	....
704 **Economic affairs....................**	†23,689	....	....	11,321	....	....	19,104	....	....	†54,114	....	....
7042 Agriculture, forestry, fishing, and hunting.....	†3,465	....	....	2,668	....	....	232	....	....	†6,365	....	....
7043 Fuel and energy...............	†976	....	....	8	....	....	18,582	....	....	†19,565	....	....
7044 Mining, manufacturing, and construction.....	†3,021	....	....	148	....	....	—	....	....	†3,169	....	....
7045 Transport.................	†6,158	....	....	6,814	....	....	290	....	....	†13,262	....	....
7046 Communication.............	†987	....	....	—	....	....	—	....	....	†987	....	....
705 **Environmental protection....................**	†1,196	....	....	928	....	....	—	....	....	†2,124	....	....
706 **Housing and community amenities........**	†7,447	....	....	5,878	....	....	9,878	....	....	†19,402	....	....
707 **Health......................**	†7,882	....	....	32,239	....	....	29	....	....	†40,150	....	....
7072 Outpatient services...............	....	....	....	....	....	....	....	....	....	....	....	....
7073 Hospital services.............	....	....	....	....	....	....	....	....	....	....	....	....
7074 Public health services...............	....	....	....	....	....	....	....	....	....	....	....	....
708 **Recreation, culture, and religion............**	†1,561	....	....	1,305	....	....	—	....	....	†2,866	....	....
709 **Education.....................**	†13,105	....	....	53,867	....	....	—	....	....	†66,275	....	....
7091 Pre-primary and primary education...............	†1,188	....	....	....	....	....	....	....	....	....	....	....
7092 Secondary education.................	†15	....	....	....	....	....	....	....	....	....	....	....
7094 Tertiary education...............	†11,902	....	....	....	....	....	....	....	....	....	....	....
710 **Social protection.....................**	†19,095	....	....	32,370	....	....	—	....	....	†51,465	....	....
7 Statistical discrepancy: Total outlays.............	†—	....	....	—	....	....	....	....	....	†—	....	....
Table 8 Transactions in financial assets and liabilities by sector												
82 **Net acquisition of financial assets.........**	†1,949	6,476	18,404	−2,542	−2,190	2,300	1,100	34	49	†507	4,320	20,754
821 Domestic........................	†1,949	6,476	18,404	−2,542	−2,190	2,300	1,100	34	49	†507	4,320	20,754
8211 General government.................	....	....	....	....	....	....	....	....	....	....	....	....
8212 Central bank....................	....	....	....	....	....	....	....	....	....	....	....	....
8213 Other depository corporations..................	....	....	....	....	....	....	....	....	....	....	....	....
8214 Financial corporations n.e.c.................	....	....	....	....	....	....	....	....	....	....	....	....
8215 Nonfinancial corporations..................	....	....	....	....	....	....	....	....	....	....	....	....
8216 Households & NPIs serving households......	....	....	....	....	....	....	....	....	....	....	....	....
822 Foreign.............	†—	—	—	—	—	—	—	—	—	†—	—	—
8221 General government.............	†—	—	—	—	—	—	—	—	—	†—	—	—
8227 International organizations.................	†—	—	—	—	—	—	—	—	—	†—	—	—
8228 Financial corporations other than international organizations.............	†—	—	—	—	—	—	—	—	—	†—	—	—
8229 Other nonresidents.............	†—	—	—	—	—	—	—	—	—	†—	—	—
823 Monetary gold and SDRs.............	†—	—	—	—	—	—	—	—	—	†—	—	—
83 **Net incurrence of liabilities...................**	†20,891	35,312	45,142	—	—	—	7,239	5,150	8,437	†28,131	40,462	53,579
831 Domestic........................	†7,583	37,766	39,328	—	—	—	7,239	5,150	8,437	†14,822	42,916	47,766
8311 General government.................	....	....	....	—	—	—	....	....	....	....	....	....
8312 Central bank....................	....	....	....	—	—	—	....	....	....	....	....	....
8313 Other depository corporations..................	....	....	....	—	—	—	....	....	....	....	....	....
8314 Financial corporations n.e.c.................	....	....	....	—	—	—	....	....	....	....	....	....
8315 Nonfinancial corporations..................	....	....	....	—	—	—	....	....	....	....	....	....
8316 Households & NPIs serving households......	....	....	....	—	—	—	....	....	....	....	....	....
832 Foreign.............	†13,309	−2,455	5,813	—	—	—	—	—	—	†13,309	−2,455	5,813
8321 General government.............	....	....	....	—	—	—	—	—	—	....	....	....
8327 International organizations.................	....	....	....	—	—	—	—	—	—	....	....	....
8328 Financial corporations other than international organizations.............	....	....	....	—	—	—	—	—	—	....	....	....
8329 Other nonresidents.................	....	....	....	—	—	—	—	—	—	....	....	....

Spain   184

In Millions of Euros / Year Ending December 31 / Noncash Reporter

	Central Government			State Government			Local Government			General Government		
	2001	2002p	2003p	2001	2002p	2003p	2001	2002p	2003p	2001	2002p	2003p
Statement of government operations												
1 Revenue	212,571	230,196	245,091	53,191	87,380	97,938	40,009	42,353	44,768	256,042	277,817	296,582
2 Expense	209,402	220,240	231,921	51,414	80,875	90,701	35,726	35,069	36,620	246,813	254,072	268,027
GOB *Gross operating balance*	*8,384*	*9,956*	*13,170*	*4,084*	*6,505*	*7,237*	*6,789*	*7,284*	*8,148*	*19,257*	*23,745*	*28,555*
NOB *Net operating balance*	*3,169*	....	....	*1,777*	....	....	*4,283*	....	....	*9,229*	....	....
31 Net acquisition of nonfinancial assets	2,137	8,049	8,821	5,133	8,240	8,559	4,502	7,900	8,695	11,772	24,189	26,075
NLB *Net lending/borrowing*	*1,032*	*1,907*	*4,349*	*–3,356*	*–1,735*	*–1,322*	*–219*	*–616*	*–547*	*–2,543*	*–444*	*2,480*
32 Net acquisition of financial assets	–2,360	10,760	4,805	–774	2,265	155	619	1,688	545	–2,515	14,713	5,505
33 Net incurrence of liabilities	–3,392	8,853	456	2,582	4,000	1,477	838	2,304	1,092	28	15,157	3,025
NLB Statistical discrepancy	—	—	—	—	—	—	—	—	—	—	—	—
Statement of other economic flows												
Balance sheet												
Statement of sources and uses of cash												
Table 1 Revenue												
1 **Revenue**	212,571	230,196	245,091	53,191	87,380	97,938	40,009	42,353	44,768	256,042	277,817	296,582
11 **Taxes**	105,530	89,914	91,751	17,120	45,625	53,995	20,457	21,203	21,638	142,981	156,742	167,384
111 Taxes on income, profits, & capital gains	54,829	55,156	55,831	5,694	12,793	14,558	3,756	3,941	4,072	64,279	71,890	74,461
1111 Individuals	36,453	....	....	5,435	....	....	2,791	....	....	44,679	....	....
1112 Corporations and other enterprises	17,471	....	....	259	....	....	965	....	....	18,695	....	....
112 Taxes on payroll and workforce	—	—	—	—	—	—	—	—	—	—	—	—
113 Taxes on property	349	151	156	8,308	15,611	18,983	6,042	1,596	1,687	14,573	17,358	20,826
114 Taxes on goods and services	49,737	34,607	35,764	3,094	17,221	20,454	10,514	15,666	15,879	63,345	67,494	72,097
1141 General taxes on goods and services	31,661	24,031	25,795	1,092	12,539	14,681	4,549	3,537	3,757	37,302	40,107	44,233
1142 Excises	15,368	....	....	486	53	....	1,002	185	....	16,856	....	....
115 Taxes on int'l. trade and transactions	29	—	—	1	—	—	2	—	—	32	—	—
116 Other taxes	586	—	—	23	—	—	143	—	—	752	—	—
12 **Social contributions**	87,146	92,540	99,330	170	174	186	214	225	237	87,530	92,939	99,753
121 Social security contributions	81,985	86,995	93,438	2	2	2	—	—	—	81,987	86,997	93,440
122 Other social contributions	5,161	5,545	5,892	168	172	184	214	225	237	5,543	5,942	6,313
13 **Grants**	8,088	35,704	42,008	32,814	37,785	39,551	14,340	15,801	17,396	5,670	7,178	7,740
131 From foreign governments	—	—	—	—	—	—	—	—	—	—	—	—
132 From international organizations	2,086	3,128	2,826	3,042	3,405	4,063	542	645	851	5,670	7,178	7,740
133 From other general government units	6,002	32,576	39,182	29,772	34,380	35,488	13,798	15,156	16,545	—	—	—
14 **Other revenue**	11,807	12,038	12,002	3,087	3,796	4,206	4,998	5,124	5,497	19,861	20,958	21,705
Table 2 Expense by economic type												
2 **Expense**	209,402	220,240	231,921	51,414	80,875	90,701	35,726	35,069	36,620	246,813	254,072	268,027
21 **Compensation of employees**	33,546	36,094	38,664	22,726	23,478	25,198	11,786	12,425	12,977	68,058	71,997	76,839
211 Wages and salaries	23,511	....	....	20,083	....	....	8,889	....	....	52,483	....	....
212 Social contributions	10,035	....	....	2,643	....	....	2,897	....	....	15,575	....	....
22 **Use of goods and services**	12,393	13,951	14,518	5,643	6,151	6,831	9,633	10,491	11,105	27,669	30,593	32,454
23 **Consumption of fixed capital**	5,215	....	....	2,307	....	....	2,506	....	....	10,028	....	....
24 **Interest**	17,287	17,039	16,277	2,209	2,055	2,032	1,112	950	903	20,577	20,044	19,212
25 **Subsidies**	4,006	4,434	4,475	1,820	2,225	2,335	1,220	1,283	1,474	7,046	7,942	8,284
26 **Grants**	37,038	40,323	42,548	6,246	35,101	41,843	6,855	7,238	7,456	567	550	632
261 To foreign governments	—	—	—	—	—	—	—	—	—	—	—	—
262 To international organizations	498	475	547	39	44	53	30	31	32	567	550	632
263 To other general government units	36,540	39,848	42,001	6,207	35,057	41,790	6,825	7,207	7,424	—	—	—
2631 Current	33,772	37,176	39,120	4,082	31,602	38,160	6,677	7,100	7,322	—	—	—
2632 Capital	2,768	2,672	2,881	2,125	3,455	3,630	148	107	102	—	—	—
27 **Social benefits**	91,367	98,866	105,278	932	1,172	1,183	463	478	496	92,762	100,516	106,957
28 **Other expense**	8,550	9,533	10,161	9,531	10,693	11,279	2,151	2,204	2,209	20,106	22,430	23,649
281 Property expense other than interest	1	....	....	1	....	....	6	....	....	8	....	....
282 Miscellaneous other expense	8,549	....	....	9,530	....	....	2,145	....	....	20,098	....	....
2821 Current	4,816	....	....	4,722	....	....	1,408	....	....	10,820	....	....
2822 Capital	3,733	....	....	4,808	....	....	737	....	....	9,278	....	....

	Central Government 2001	2002p	2003p	State Government 2001	2002p	2003p	Local Government 2001	2002p	2003p	General Government 2001	2002p	2003p
Table 3 Transactions in assets and liabilities												
3 Change in net worth from transactns....	3,169	....	....	1,777	....	....	4,283	....	....	9,229	....	....
31 Net acquisition of nonfinancial assets...	2,137	8,049	8,821	5,133	8,240	8,559	4,502	7,900	8,695	11,772	24,189	26,075
311 Fixed assets....................................	1,892	7,775	8,845	4,993	7,998	8,323	4,404	7,794	8,580	11,289	23,567	25,748
3111 Buildings and structures.................	....	....	....	....	....	....	....	....	....	....	....	....
3112 Machinery and equipment...............	....	....	....	....	....	....	....	....	....	....	....	....
3113 Other fixed assets.........................	....	....	....	....	....	....	....	....	....	....	....	....
312 Inventories...................................	—	—	—	—	—	—	—	—	—	—	—	—
313 Valuables.....................................	—	—	—	—	—	—	—	—	—	—	—	—
314 Nonproduced assets.......................	245	274	−24	140	242	236	98	106	115	483	622	327
3141 Land...	....	....	....	....	....	....	....	....	....	....	....	....
3142 Subsoil assets..............................	....	....	....	....	....	....	....	....	....	....	....	....
3143 Other naturally occurring assets.......	....	....	....	....	....	....	....	....	....	....	....	....
3144 Intangible nonproduced assets.........	....	....	....	....	....	....	....	....	....	....	....	....
32 Net acquisition of financial assets........	−2,360	10,760	4,805	−774	2,265	155	619	1,688	545	−2,515	14,713	5,505
321 Domestic.....................................	−2,360	10,760	4,805	−774	2,265	155	619	1,688	545	−2,515	14,713	5,505
3212 Currency and deposits....................	−1,887	4,879	−3,909	−958	2,013	−49	349	1,224	−245	−2,496	8,116	−4,203
3213 Securities other than shares............	809	4,338	3,814	—	—	—	2	4	5	811	4,342	3,819
3214 Loans...	2,217	2,262	2,050	2	−2	—	—	—	—	2,219	2,260	2,050
3215 Shares and other equity.................	−2,840	−833	1,016	82	−256	186	30	−306	122	−2,728	−1,395	1,324
3216 Insurance technical reserves............	—	—	—	—	—	—	—	—	—	—	—	—
3217 Financial derivatives......................	—	—	—	—	—	—	—	—	—	—	—	—
3218 Other accounts receivable...............	−659	114	1,834	100	510	18	238	766	663	−321	1,390	2,515
322 Foreign.......................................	....	....	....	....	....	....	....	....	....	....	....	....
3222 Currency and deposits....................												
3223 Securities other than shares............												
3224 Loans...												
3225 Shares and other equity.................												
3226 Insurance technical reserves............												
3227 Financial derivatives......................												
3228 Other accounts receivable...............												
323 Monetary gold and SDRs.................	—	—	—	—	—	—	—	—	—	—	—	—
33 Net incurrence of liabilities..................	−3,392	8,853	456	2,582	4,000	1,477	838	2,304	1,092	28	15,157	3,025
331 Domestic.....................................	−3,392	8,853	456	2,582	4,000	1,477	838	2,304	1,092	28	15,157	3,025
3312 Currency and deposits....................	−73	1,260	173	—	—	—	—	—	—	−73	1,260	173
3313 Securities other than shares............	4,383	7,472	317	936	3,311	1,753	95	257	−210	5,414	11,040	1,860
3314 Loans...	−3,435	−236	−1,385	1,672	−1,789	−124	491	1,171	1,417	−1,272	−854	−92
3316 Insurance technical reserves............	—	—	—	—	—	—	—	—	—	—	—	—
3317 Financial derivatives......................	—	—	—	—	—	—	—	—	—	—	—	—
3318 Other accounts payable..................	−4,267	357	1,351	−26	2,478	−152	252	876	−115	−4,041	3,711	1,084
332 Foreign.......................................	....	....	....	....	....	....	....	....	....	....	....	....
3322 Currency and deposits....................												
3323 Securities other than shares............												
3324 Loans...												
3326 Insurance technical reserves............												
3327 Financial derivatives......................												
3328 Other accounts payable..................												
Table 4 Holding gains in assets and liabilities												
Table 5 Other changes in the volume of assets and liabilities												
Table 6 Balance sheet												
Table 7 Outlays by functions of govt.												
7 Total outlays........................	211,539	228,289	240,742	56,547	89,115	99,260	40,228	42,969	45,315	258,585	278,261	294,102
701 General public services......................	60,492	....	....	10,828	....	....	14,113	....	....	35,780	....	....
7017 Public debt transactions..................	17,287	17,039	16,277	2,209	2,055	2,032	1,112	950	903	20,577	20,044	19,212
7018 General transfers between levels of govt......	36,540	....	....	6,207	....	....	6,825	....	....			
702 Defense..	7,821	....	....	—	....	....	—	....	....	7,819		
703 Public order and safety......................	8,104	....	....	2,048	....	....	3,828	....	....	13,971		
704 Economic affairs.............................	13,011	....	....	10,450	....	....	4,931	....	....	28,385		
7042 Agriculture, forestry, fishing, and hunting.....	....	....	....	3,002	....	....	399	....	....			
7043 Fuel and energy.............................	....	....	....	114			—	....	....			
7044 Mining, manufacturing, and construction.....	....	....	....	533			54	....	....			
7045 Transport.....................................	....	....	....	3,160			3,381					
7046 Communication..............................	....	....	....	68	....	....	1	....	....			

In Millions of Euros / Year Ending December 31 / Noncash Reporter

	Central Government			State Government			Local Government			General Government		
	2001	2002p	2003p	2001	2002p	2003p	2001	2002p	2003p	2001	2002p	2003p
705 **Environmental protection**...................	516	....	....	1,428	....	....	3,886	....	....	5,822	....	....
706 **Housing and community amenities**........	263	....	....	1,913	....	....	5,051	....	....	7,213	....	....
707 **Health**.................	32,308	....	....	1,880	...:	....	736	....	....	34,906	....	....
7072 Outpatient services............................	....	....	....	....	....	....	....	....	....	....	....	....
7073 Hospital services..............................	23,767	....	....	1,050	....	....	467	....	....	25,269	....	....
7074 Public health services.......................	116	....	....	404	....	....	196	....	....	716		
708 **Recreation, culture, and religion**............	2,530	....	....	2,215	....	....	3,958	....	....	8,700	....	....
709 **Education**.................................	3,442	....	....	23,695	....	....	1,181	....	....	28,313	....	....
7091 Pre-primary and primary education...............	1,318	....	....	7,725	....	....	900	....	....	9,942	....	....
7092 Secondary education............................	1,381	....	....	8,899	....	....	113	....	....	10,393	....	....
7094 Tertiary education.................................	633	....	....	5,161	....	....	57	....	....	5,847	....	....
710 **Social protection**.................................	83,052	....	....	2,090	....	....	2,544	....	....	87,676	....	....
7 Statistical discrepancy: Total outlays..............	—	....	....	—	....	....	—	....	....	—	....	....
Table 8 Transactions in financial assets and liabilities by sector												
82 **Net acquisition of financial assets**........	−2,360	10,760	4,805	−774	2,265	155	619	1,688	545	−2,515	14,713	5,505
821 Domestic...	−2,360	10,760	4,805	−774	2,265	155	619	1,688	545	−2,515	14,713	5,505
8211 General government............................	....	....	....	....	....	....	....	....	....	....	....	....
8212 Central bank.....................................	....	....	....	....	....	....	....	....	....	....	....	....
8213 Other depository corporations...................	....	....	....	....	....	....	....	....	....	....	....	....
8214 Financial corporations n.e.c...................	....	....	....	....	....	....	....	....	....	....	....	....
8215 Nonfinancial corporations.....................	....	....	....	....	....	....	....	....	....	....	....	....
8216 Households & NPIs serving households......	....	....	....	....	....	....	....	....	....	....	....	....
822 Foreign...	....	....	....	....	....	....	....	....	....	....	....	....
8221 General government............................	....	....	....	....	....	....	....	....	....	....	....	....
8227 International organizations.....................	....	....	....	....	....	....	....	....	....	....	....	....
8228 Financial corporations other than international organizations..............	....	....	....	....	....	....	....	....	....	....	....	....
8229 Other nonresidents.............................	....	....	....	....	....	....	....	....	....	....	....	....
823 Monetary gold and SDRs........................	—	—	—	—	—	—	—	—	—	—	—	—
83 **Net incurrence of liabilities**...................	−3,392	8,853	456	2,582	4,000	1,477	838	2,304	1,092	28	15,157	3,025
831 Domestic...	−3,392	8,853	456	2,582	4,000	1,477	838	2,304	1,092	28	15,157	3,025
8311 General government............................	....	....	....	....	....	....	....	....	....	....	....	....
8312 Central bank.....................................	....	....	....	....	....	....	....	....	....	....	....	....
8313 Other depository corporations...................	....	....	....	....	....	....	....	....	....	....	....	....
8314 Financial corporations n.e.c...................	....	....	....	....	....	....	....	....	....	....	....	....
8315 Nonfinancial corporations.....................	....	....	....	....	....	....	....	....	....	....	....	....
8316 Households & NPIs serving households......	....	....	....	....	....	....	....	....	....	....	....	....
832 Foreign...	....	....	....	....	....	....	....	....	....	....	....	....
8321 General government............................	....	....	....	....	....	....	....	....	....	....	....	....
8327 International organizations.....................	....	....	....	....	....	....	....	....	....	....	....	....
8328 Financial corporations other than international organizations..............	....	....	....	....	....	....	....	....	....	....	....	....
8329 Other nonresidents.............................	....	....	....	....	....	....	....	....	....	....	....	....

		Budgetary Central Government			Central Government			Local Government			General Government		
		2000	2001	2002p	2000	2001	2002	2000	2001	2002p	2000	2001	2002
Statement of government operations													
Statement of other economic flows													
Balance sheet													
6	*Net worth*............	....	....	....	....	....	....	....	....	....	....	....	....
61	Nonfinancial assets............	....	....	....	....	....	....	....	....	....	....	....	....
62	Financial assets............	....	....	....	....	....	....	....	....	....	....	....	....
63	Liabilities............	1,218,700	1,452,706	1,669,284	....	....	....	....	....	....	....	....	....
Statement of sources and uses of cash													
1	Cash receipts from operating activities...........	216,389	239,689	266,998	....	....	....	5,505	6,008	6,485	....		
11	Taxes............	182,392	205,839	221,786	....	....	....	5,011	5,533	5,988			
12	Social contributions............	3,620	2,667	2,630	....	....	....	—	—	—			
13	Grants............	5,145	5,500	7,079	....	....	....	—	—	—			
14	Other receipts............	25,232	25,683	35,503	....	....	....	494	475	497			
2	Cash payments for operating activities...........	289,114	335,149	362,362	....	....	....	....	....	....			
21	Compensation of employees............	68,544	78,056	88,804	....	....	....						
22	Purchases of goods and services............	62,221	65,691	50,115	....	....	....						
24	Interest............	71,200	94,307	116,515	....	....	....						
25	Subsidies............	9,377	12,152	21,187	....	....	....						
26	Grants............	9,896	7,536	6,118	....	....	....						
27	Social benefits............	41,306	52,083	53,046	....	....	....						
28	Other payments............	26,570	25,324	26,577	....	....	....						
CIO	*Net cash inflow from oper. activities*.....	*−72,725*	*−95,460*	*−95,364*	....	....	....	....	....	....			
31.1	Purchases of nonfinancial assets............	32,934	36,115	26,501	....	....	....						
31.2	Sales of nonfinancial assets............	38	107	1,345	....	....	....						
31	Net cash outflow from investments in nonfinancial assets............	32,896	36,008	25,156	....	....	....	....	....	....			
CSD	*Cash surplus/deficit*............	*−105,621*	*−131,468*	*−120,520*	....	....	....	....	....	....			
32x	Net acquisition of fin assets, excl. cash............	13,374	6,665	7,811	....	....	....						
321x	Domestic............	13,374	6,665	7,811	....	....	....						
322x	Foreign............	—	—	—	....	....	....						
323	Monetary gold and SDRs............				....	....	....						
33	Net incurrence of liabilities............	120,175	152,429	112,433	....	....	....						
331	Domestic............	119,680	137,891	110,455	....	....	....						
332	Foreign............	495	14,538	1,978	....	....	....						
NFB	Net cash inflow from fin. activities............	106,801	145,764	104,622	....	....	....						
NCB	*Net change in the stock of cash*............	*1,180*	*14,296*	*−15,898*	....	....	....	....	....	....			
Table 1 Revenue													
1	**Revenue**............	**216,389**	**239,689**	**266,998**	....	....	....	**5,505**	**6,008**	**6,485**	....	....	....
11	**Taxes**............	**182,392**	**205,839**	**221,786**	....	....	....	**5,011**	**5,533**	**5,988**	....	....	....
111	Taxes on income, profits, & capital gains......	27,457	34,636	37,619	....	....	....	—	—	—			
1111	Individuals............	11,700	13,962	12,172	....	....	....	—	—	—			
1112	Corporations and other enterprises............	15,757	20,674	13,934	....	....	....	—	—	—			
112	Taxes on payroll and workforce............	—	—	—	....	....	....	—	—	—			
113	Taxes on property............	8,163	8,415	2,511	....	....	....	—	—	—			
114	Taxes on goods and services............	122,802	136,632	149,852	....	....	....	5,011	5,533	5,988			
1141	General taxes on goods and services............	79,140	90,084	95,886	....	....	....	3,705	4,142	4,460			
1142	Excises............	42,655	44,978	52,099	....	....	....	12	20	15			
115	Taxes on int'l. trade and transactions............	23,970	26,156	31,804	....	....	....	—	—	—			
116	Other taxes............	—	—	—	....	....	....	—	—	—			
12	**Social contributions**............	**3,620**	**2,667**	**2,630**	....	....	....	—	—	—	....	....	....
121	Social security contributions............	—	—	—	....	....	....	—	—	—			
122	Other social contributions............	3,620	2,667	2,630	....	....	....	—	—	—			
13	**Grants**............	**5,145**	**5,500**	**7,079**	....	....	....	—	—	—	....	....	....
131	From foreign governments............	5,145	5,500	7,079	....	....	....	—	—	—			
132	From international organizations............	—	—	—	....	....	....	—	—	—			
133	From other general government units............	—	—	—	....	....	....	—	—	—			
14	**Other revenue**............	**25,232**	**25,683**	**35,503**	....	....	....	**494**	**475**	**497**	....	....	....
Table 2 Expense by economic type													
2	**Expense**............	**289,114**	**335,149**	**362,362**	....	....	....	....	....	....	....	....	....
21	**Compensation of employees**............	**68,544**	**78,056**	**88,804**	....	....	....	....	....	....	....	....	....
211	Wages and salaries............	68,544	78,056	88,804	....	....	....	....	....	....	....	....	....
212	Social contributions............	—	—	—	....	....	....	....	....	....	....	....	....
22	**Use of goods and services**............	**62,221**	**65,691**	**50,115**	....	....	....	....	....	....	....	....	....
23	**Consumption of fixed capital**............	....	....	....	....	....	....	....	....	....	....	....	....
24	**Interest**............	**71,200**	**94,307**	**116,515**	....	....	....	....	....	....	....	....	....
25	**Subsidies**............	**9,377**	**12,152**	**21,187**	....	....	....	....	....	....	....	....	....

In Millions of Rupees / Year Ending December 31 / Cash Reporter

		Budgetary Central Government			Central Government			Local Government			General Government		
		2000	2001	2002p	2000	2001	2002	2000	2001	2002p	2000	2001	2002
26	**Grants**...................................	**9,896**	**7,536**	**6,118**	....	....	....	....	....	....	....	....	....
261	To foreign govenments.......................	—	591	—	....	....	....	....	....	....	....	....	....
262	To international organizations...............	254	—	305	....	....	....	....	....	....	....	....	....
263	To other general government units.........	9,642	6,945	5,813	....	....	....	....	....	....	....	....	....
2631	Current..	1,424	694	392	....	....	....	....	....	....	....	....	....
2632	Capital...	8,218	6,251	5,421	....	....	....	....	....	....	....	....	....
27	**Social benefits**..................................	**41,306**	**52,083**	**53,046**	....	....	....	....	....	....	....	....	....
28	**Other expense**..................................	**26,570**	**25,324**	**26,577**	....	....	....	....	....	....	....	....	....
281	Property expense other than interest...........				....	....	....	....	....	....	....	....	....
282	Miscellaneous other expense..................	26,570	25,324	26,577	....	....	....	....	....	....	....	....	....
2821	Current..	—	—	—	....	....	....	....	....	....	....	....	....
2822	Capital...	26,570	25,324	26,577	....	....	....	....	....	....	....	....	....

Table 3   Transactions in assets and liabilities

3	**Change in net worth from transactns....**	....	....	....	....	....	....	....	....	....	....	....	....
31	**Net acquisition of nonfinancial assets...**	**32,896**	**36,008**	**25,156**	....	....	....	....	....	....	....	....	....
311	Fixed assets.......................................	32,896	36,008	25,156	....	....	....	....	....	....	....	....	....
3111	Buildings and structures.....................	....	....	....	....	....	....	....	....	....	....	....	....
3112	Machinery and equipment....................	....	....	....	....	....	....	....	....	....	....	....	....
3113	Other fixed assets.............................	....	....	....	....	....	....	....	....	....	....	....	....
312	Inventories.......................................	—	—	—	....	....	....	....	....	....	....	....	....
313	Valuables...	—	—	—	....	....	....	....	....	....	....	....	....
314	Nonproduced assets............................	—	—	—	....	....	....	....	....	....	....	....	....
3141	Land..	—	—	—	....	....	....	....	....	....	....	....	....
3142	Subsoil assets..................................	—	—	—	....	....	....	....	....	....	....	....	....
3143	Other naturally occurring assets..................	—	—	—	....	....	....	....	....	....	....	....	....
3144	Intangible nonproduced assets.................	—	—	—	....	....	....	....	....	....	....	....	....
32	**Net acquisition of financial assets.........**	**14,554**	**20,961**	**−8,087**	....	....	....	....	....	....	....	....	....
321	Domestic..	14,554	20,961	−8,087	....	....	....	....	....	....	....	....	....
3212	Currency and deposits............................	1,180	14,296	−15,898	....	....	....	....	....	....	....	....	....
3213	Securities other than shares.....................	—	—	—	....	....	....	....	....	....	....	....	....
3214	Loans...	13,775	15,254	13,504	....	....	....	....	....	....	....	....	....
3215	Shares and other equity........................	−401	−8,589	−5,693	....	....	....	....	....	....	....	....	....
3216	Insurance technical reserves...................	—	—	—	....	....	....	....	....	....	....	....	....
3217	Financial derivatives...........................	—	—	—	....	....	....	....	....	....	....	....	....
3218	Other accounts receivable......................	....	....	....	....	....	....	....	....	....	....	....	....
322	Foreign...	—	—	—	....	....	....	....	....	....	....	....	....
3222	Currency and deposits..........................	—	—	—	....	....	....	....	....	....	....	....	....
3223	Securities other than shares...................	—	—	—	....	....	....	....	....	....	....	....	....
3224	Loans...	—	—	—	....	....	....	....	....	....	....	....	....
3225	Shares and other equity........................	—	—	—	....	....	....	....	....	....	....	....	....
3226	Insurance technical reserves...................	—	—	—	....	....	....	....	....	....	....	....	....
3227	Financial derivatives...........................	—	—	—	....	....	....	....	....	....	....	....	....
3228	Other accounts receivable......................	....	....	....	....	....	....	....	....	....	....	....	....
323	Monetary gold and SDRs........................	—	—	—	....	....	....	....	....	....	....	....	....
33	**Net incurrence of liabilities...................**	**120,175**	**152,429**	**112,433**	....	....	....	....	....	....	....	....	....
331	Domestic..	119,680	137,891	110,455	....	....	....	....	....	....	....	....	....
3312	Currency and deposits............................	3,175	719	−816	....	....	....	....	....	....	....	....	....
3313	Securities other than shares.....................	98,545	94,575	152,561	....	....	....	....	....	....	....	....	....
3314	Loans...	17,960	42,597	−41,290	....	....	....	....	....	....	....	....	....
3316	Insurance technical reserves...................	—	—	—	....	....	....	....	....	....	....	....	....
3317	Financial derivatives...........................	—	—	—	....	....	....	....	....	....	....	....	....
3318	Other accounts payable..........................	....	....	....	....	....	....	....	....	....	....	....	....
332	Foreign...	495	14,538	1,978	....	....	....	....	....	....	....	....	....
3322	Currency and deposits..........................	—	—	—	....	....	....	....	....	....	....	....	....
3323	Securities other than shares...................	—	—	—	....	....	....	....	....	....	....	....	....
3324	Loans...	495	14,538	1,978	....	....	....	....	....	....	....	....	....
3326	Insurance technical reserves...................	—	—	—	....	....	....	....	....	....	....	....	....
3327	Financial derivatives...........................	—	—	—	....	....	....	....	....	....	....	....	....
3328	Other accounts payable..........................	....	....	....	....	....	....	....	....	....	....	....	....

	Budgetary Central Government			Central Government			Local Government			General Government		
	2000	2001	2002p	2000	2001	2002	2000	2001	2002p	2000	2001	2002
Table 4 Holding gains in assets and liabilities												
Table 5 Other changes in the volume of assets and liabilities												
Table 6 Balance sheet												
6 Net worth....................................	....	....	....	....	....	....	....	....	....	....	....	....
61 Nonfinancial assets........................	....	....	....	....	....	....	....	....	....	....	....	....
611 Fixed assets.....................................	....	....	....	....	....		....	....	....	....	....	
6111 Buildings and structures.......................	....	....	....	....	....		....	....	....	....	....	
6112 Machinery and equipment.....................	....	....	....	....	....		....	....	....	....	....	
6113 Other fixed assets............................	....	....	....	....	....		....	....	....	....	....	
612 Inventories.....................................	....	....	....	....	....		....	....	....	....	....	
613 Valuables.......................................	....	....	....	....	....		....	....	....	....	....	
614 Nonproduced assets...........................	....	....	....	....	....		....	....	....	....	....	
6141 Land..	....	....	....	....	....		....	....	....	....	....	
6142 Subsoil assets..................................	....	....	....	....	....		....	....	....	....	....	
6143 Other naturally occurring assets............	....	....	....	....	....		....	....	....	....	....	
6144 Intangible nonproduced assets..............	....	....	....	....	....		....	....	....	....	....	
62 Financial assets...........................	....	....	....	....	....		....	....	....	....	....	
621 Domestic.......................................	....	....		....	....		....	....	....	....	....	
6212 Currency and deposits........................	....	....		....	....		....	....	....	....	....	
6213 Securities other than shares.................	....	....		....	....		....	....	....	....	....	
6214 Loans..	....	....		....	....		....	....	....	....	....	
6215 Shares and other equity......................	....	....		....	....		....	....	....	....	....	
6216 Insurance technical reserves.................	....	....		....	....		....	....	....	....	....	
6217 Financial derivatives..........................	....	....		....	....		....	....	....	....	....	
6218 Other accounts receivable....................	....	....		....	....		....	....	....	....	....	
622 Foreign..	....	....		....	....		....	....	....	....	....	
6222 Currency and deposits........................	....	....		....	....		....	....	....	....	....	
6223 Securities other than shares.................	....	....	....	....	....		....	....	....	....	....	
6224 Loans..	....	....	....	....	....		....	....	....	....	....	
6225 Shares and other equity......................	....	....	....	....	....		....	....	....	....	....	
6226 Insurance technical reserves.................	....	....		....	....		....	....	....	....	....	
6227 Financial derivatives..........................	....	....		....	....		....	....	....	....	....	
6228 Other accounts receivable....................	....	....		....	....		....	....	....	....	....	
623 Monetary gold and SDRs.....................	....	....	....	....	....		....	....	....	....	....	
63 Liabilities................................	1,218,700	1,452,706	1,669,284	....	....		....	....	....	....	....	
631 Domestic.......................................	676,660	815,965	948,386	....	....		....	....	....	....	....	
6312 Currency and deposits........................	....	....	....	....	....		....	....	....	....	....	
6313 Securities other than shares.................	....	....	....	....	....		....	....	....	....	....	
6314 Loans..	....	....	....	....	....		....	....	....	....	....	
6316 Insurance technical reserves.................	....	....	....	....	....		....	....	....	....	....	
6317 Financial derivatives..........................	....	....	....	....	....		....	....	....	....	....	
6318 Other accounts payable.......................	....	....	....	....	....		....	....	....	....	....	
632 Foreign..	542,040	636,741	720,898	....	....		....	....	....	....	....	
6322 Currency and deposits........................	....	....	....	....	....		....	....	....	....	....	
6323 Securities other than shares.................	....	....	....	....	....		....	....	....	....	....	
6324 Loans..	....	....	....	....	....		....	....	....	....	....	
6326 Insurance technical reserves.................	....	....	....	....	....		....	....	....	....	....	
6327 Financial derivatives..........................	....	....	....	....	....		....	....	....	....	....	
6328 Other accounts payable.......................	....	....	....	....	....		....	....	....	....	....	
Memorandum items:												
6M2 Net financial worth............................	....	....	....	....	....		....	....	....	....	....	
6M3 Debt at market value..........................	....	....	....	....	....		....	....	....	....	....	
6M4 Debt at nominal value.........................	....	....	....	....	....		....	....	....	....	....	
6M5 Arrears...	....	....	....	....	....		....	....	....	....	....	
6M6 Obligations for social security benefits........	....	....	....	....	....		....	....	....	....	....	
6M7 Contingent liabilities...........................	....	....	....	....	....		....	....	....	....	....	
6M8 Uncapitalized military weapons, systems........	....	....	....	....	....		....	....	....	....	....	
Table 7 Outlays by functions of govt.												
7 Total outlays....................................	322,048	371,264	388,861	....	....	....	....	....	....	....	....	....
701 General public services........................	90,892	129,702	133,679	....	....	....	....	....	....	....	....	....
7017 Public debt transactions......................	71,200	94,307	116,515	....	....	....	....	....	....	....	....	....
7018 General transfers between levels of govt......	....	....	....	....	....	....	....	....	....	....	....	....
702 Defense.......................................	56,915	54,242	49,163	....	....	....	....	....	....	....	....	....
703 Public order and safety.......................	13,859	14,048	14,972	....	....	....	....	....	....	....	....	....

In Millions of Rupees / Year Ending December 31 / Cash Reporter

		Budgetary Central Government			Central Government			Local Government			General Government		
		2000	2001	2002p	2000	2001	2002	2000	2001	2002p	2000	2001	2002
704	**Economic affairs**	**66,751**	**70,745**	**69,261**	....	....	....	....	....	....	....	....	....
7042	Agriculture, forestry, fishing, and hunting	13,851	15,014	15,749	....	....	....	....	....	....	....	....	....
7043	Fuel and energy	1,890	1,944	1,154	....	....	....	....	....	....	....	....	....
7044	Mining, manufacturing, and construction	1,490	743	1,599	....	....	....	....	....	....	....	....	....
7045	Transport	28,468	26,814	26,060	....	....	....	....	....	....	....	....	....
7046	Communication	....	....	....	....	....	....	....	....	....	....	....	....
705	**Environmental protection**	....	....	....	....	....	....	....	....	....	....	....	....
706	**Housing and community amenities**	**5,905**	**10,382**	**11,916**	....	....	....	....	....	....	....	....	....
707	**Health**	**20,696**	**18,772**	**24,946**	....	....	....	....	....	....	....	....	....
7072	Outpatient services	....	....	....	....	....	....	....	....	....	....	....	....
7073	Hospital services	....	....	....	....	....	....	....	....	....	....	....	....
7074	Public health services	....	....	....	....	....	....	....	....	....	....	....	....
708	**Recreation, culture, and religion**	—	—	—	....	....	....	....	....	....	....	....	....
709	**Education**	**30,929**	**28,286**	**37,209**	....	....	....	....	....	....	....	....	....
7091	Pre-primary and primary education	....	....	....	....	....	....	....	....	....	....	....	....
7092	Secondary education	....	....	....	....	....	....	....	....	....	....	....	....
7094	Tertiary education	....	....	....	....	....	....	....	....	....	....	....	....
710	**Social protection**	**36,101**	**45,087**	**47,715**	....	....	....	....	....	....	....	....	....
7	Statistical discrepancy: Total outlays	—	—	—	....	....	....	....	....	....	....	....	....

Table 8   Transactions in financial assets and liabilities by sector

		Budgetary Central Government			Central Government			Local Government			General Government		
82	**Net acquisition of financial assets**	**14,554**	**20,961**	**−8,087**	....	....	....	....	....	....	....	....	....
821	Domestic	14,554	20,961	−8,087	....	....	....	....	....	....	....	....	....
8211	General government	—	—	—	....	....	....	....	....	....	....	....	....
8212	Central bank	....	....	....	....	....	....	....	....	....	....	....	....
8213	Other depository corporations	....	....	....	....	....	....	....	....	....	....	....	....
8214	Financial corporations n.e.c.	....	....	....	....	....	....	....	....	....	....	....	....
8215	Nonfinancial corporations	13,374	7,130	7,130	....	....	....	....	....	....	....	....	....
8216	Households & NPIs serving households	....	....	....	....	....	....	....	....	....	....	....	....
822	Foreign	—	—	—	....	....	....	....	....	....	....	....	....
8221	General government	—	—	—	....	....	....	....	....	....	....	....	....
8227	International organizations	—	—	—	....	....	....	....	....	....	....	....	....
8228	Financial corporations other than international organizations	—	—	—	....	....	....	....	....	....	....	....	....
8229	Other nonresidents	—	—	—	....	....	....	....	....	....	....	....	....
823	Monetary gold and SDRs	—	—	—	....	....	....	....	....	....	....	....	....
83	**Net incurrence of liabilities**	**120,175**	**152,429**	**112,433**	....	....	....	....	....	....	....	....	....
831	Domestic	119,680	137,891	110,455	....	....	....	....	....	....	....	....	....
8311	General government	....	....	....	....	....	....	....	....	....	....	....	....
8312	Central bank	....	....	....	....	....	....	....	....	....	....	....	....
8313	Other depository corporations	....	....	....	....	....	....	....	....	....	....	....	....
8314	Financial corporations n.e.c.	....	....	....	....	....	....	....	....	....	....	....	....
8315	Nonfinancial corporations	....	....	....	....	....	....	....	....	....	....	....	....
8316	Households & NPIs serving households	....	....	....	....	....	....	....	....	....	....	....	....
832	Foreign	495	14,538	1,978	....	....	....	....	....	....	....	....	....
8321	General government	....	....	....	....	....	....	....	....	....	....	....	....
8327	International organizations	....	....	....	....	....	....	....	....	....	....	....	....
8328	Financial corporations other than international organizations	....	....	....	....	....	....	....	....	....	....	....	....
8329	Other nonresidents	....	....	....	....	....	....	....	....	....	....	....	....

Sudan   732

In Millions of Dinars / Year Ending December 31 / Cash Reporter

	Budgetary Central Government			Central Government			Local Government			General Government		
	1997	1998	1999	1997	1998	1999	1997	1998	1999	1997	1998	1999
Statement of government operations												
Statement of other economic flows												
Balance sheet												
6 *Net worth*..............	....	....	....	....	....	....	....	....	....	....	....	....
61 Nonfinancial assets.............	....	....	....	....	....	....	....	....	....	....	....	....
62 Financial assets.............	....	....	....	....	....	....	....	....	....	....	....	....
63 Liabilities.............	....	177,777	233,591	....	....	....	....	....	....	....	....	....
Statement of sources and uses of cash												
1 Cash receipts from operating activities...........	....	162,143	216,803	....	....	....	....	....	....	....	....	....
11 Taxes.............	....	139,998	172,295	....	....	....	....	....	....	....	....	....
12 Social contributions.............	....	—		....	....	....	....	....	....	....	....	....
13 Grants.............	....	—	1,241	....	....	....	....	....	....	....	....	....
14 Other receipts.............	....	22,145	43,267	....	....	....	....	....	....	....	....	....
2 Cash payments for operating activities...........	....	153,009	204,748	....	....	....	....	....	....	....	....	....
21 Compensation of employees.............	....	58,160	83,177	....	....	....	....	....	....	....	....	....
22 Purchases of goods and services.............	....	67,729	84,923	....	....	....	....	....	....	....	....	....
24 Interest.............	....	11,689	20,366	....	....	....	....	....	....	....	....	....
25 Subsidies.............	....	7,556	6,194	....	....	....	....	....	....	....	....	....
26 Grants.............	....	7,153	8,890	....	....	....	....	....	....	....	....	....
27 Social benefits.............	....	722	1,198	....	....	....	....	....	....	....	....	....
28 Other payments.............	....	—		....	....	....	....	....	....	....	....	....
CIO *Net cash inflow from oper. activities.....*	....	*9,134*	*12,055*	....	....	....	....	....	....	....	....	....
31.1 Purchases of nonfinancial assets.............	....	18,120	22,517	....	....	....	....	....	....	....	....	....
31.2 Sales of nonfinancial assets.............	....	—	—	....	....	....	....	....	....	....	....	....
31 Net cash outflow from investments in nonfinancial assets.............	....	18,120	22,517	....	....	....	....	....	....	....	....	....
CSD *Cash surplus/deficit*.............	....	*−8,986*	*−10,462*	....	....	....	....	....	....	....	....	....
32x Net acquisition of fin assets, excl. cash...........	....	....	....	....	....	....	....	....	....	....	....	....
321x Domestic.............	....	281	13,716	....	....	....	....	....	....	....	....	....
322x Foreign.............	....	....	....	....	....	....	....	....	....	....	....	....
323 Monetary gold and SDRs.............	....	—	—	....	....	....	....	....	....	....	....	....
33 Net incurrence of liabilities.............	....	....	....	....	....	....	....	....	....	....	....	....
331 Domestic.............	....	5,917	26,207	....	....	....	....	....	....	....	....	....
332 Foreign.............	....	....	....	....	....	....	....	....	....	....	....	....
NFB Net cash inflow from fin. activities.............	....	....	....	....	....	....	....	....	....	....	....	....
NCB *Net change in the stock of cash*.............	....	....	....	....	....	....	....	....	....	....	....	....
Table 1 Revenue												
1 **Revenue**.............	....	**162,143**	**216,803**	....	....	....	....	....	....	....	....	....
11 **Taxes**.............	....	**139,998**	**172,295**	....	....	....	....	....	....	....	....	....
111 Taxes on income, profits, & capital gains......	....	28,123	31,498	....	....	....	....	....	....	....	....	....
1111 Individuals.............	....	8,513	11,328	....	....	....	....	....	....	....	....	....
1112 Corporations and other enterprises.............	....	19,610	20,170	....	....	....	....	....	....	....	....	....
112 Taxes on payroll and workforce.............	....	—	—	....	....	....	....	....	....	....	....	....
113 Taxes on property.............	....			....	....	....	....	....	....	....	....	....
114 Taxes on goods and services.............	....	65,744	76,050	....	....	....	....	....	....	....	....	....
1141 General taxes on goods and services..........	....	28,748	22,808	....	....	....	....	....	....	....	....	....
1142 Excises.............	....	22,256	37,323	....	....	....	....	....	....	....	....	....
115 Taxes on int'l. trade and transactions...........	....	44,343	62,557	....	....	....	....	....	....	....	....	....
116 Other taxes.............	....	1,788	2,190	....	....	....	....	....	....	....	....	....
12 **Social contributions**.............	....	—	—	....	....	....	....	....	....	....	....	....
121 Social security contributions.............	....	—	—	....	....	....	....	....	....	....	....	....
122 Other social contributions.............	....	—	—	....	....	....	....	....	....	....	....	....
13 **Grants**.............	....	—	1,241	....	....	....	....	....	....	....	....	....
131 From foreign governments.............	....	—	1,241	....	....	....	....	....	....	....	....	....
132 From international organizations.............	....	—	—	....	....	....	....	....	....	....	....	....
133 From other general government units...........	....			....	....	....	....	....	....	....	....	....
14 **Other revenue**.............	....	**22,145**	**43,267**	....	....	....	....	....	....	....	....	....
Table 2 Expense by economic type												
2 **Expense**.............	....	**153,009**	**204,748**	....	....	....	....	....	....	....	....	....
21 **Compensation of employees**.............	....	**58,160**	**83,177**	....	....	....	....	....	....	....	....	....
211 Wages and salaries.............	....	53,432	76,351	....	....	....	....	....	....	....	....	....
212 Social contributions.............	....	4,728	6,826	....	....	....	....	....	....	....	....	....
22 **Use of goods and services**.............	....	**67,729**	**84,923**	....	....	....	....	....	....	....	....	....
23 **Consumption of fixed capital**.............	....	....	....	....	....	....	....	....	....	....	....	....
24 **Interest**.............	....	**11,689**	**20,366**	....	....	....	....	....	....	....	....	....
25 **Subsidies**.............	....	**7,556**	**6,194**	....	....	....	....	....	....	....	....	....

2005, International Monetary Fund: *Government Finance Statistics Yearbook*

Sudan 732

In Millions of Dinars / Year Ending December 31 / Cash Reporter

		Budgetary Central Government			Central Government			Local Government			General Government		
		1997	1998	1999	1997	1998	1999	1997	1998	1999	1997	1998	1999
26	**Grants**	....	7,153	8,890	....	....	....	....	....	....	....	....	....
261	To foreign govenments	....	604	1,145	....	....	....	....	....	....	....	....	....
262	To international organizations	....	—	—	....	....	....	....	....	....	....	....	....
263	To other general government units	....	6,549	7,745	....	....	....	....	....	....	....	....	....
2631	Current	....	6,549	7,745	....	....	....	....	....	....	....	....	....
2632	Capital	....	—	—	....	....	....	....	....	....	....	....	....
27	**Social benefits**	....	722	1,198	....	....	....	....	....	....	....	....	....
28	**Other expense**	....	—	—	....	....	....	....	....	....	....	....	....
281	Property expense other than interest	....			....	....	....	....	....	....	....	....	....
282	Miscellaneous other expense	....	—	—	....	....	....	....	....	....	....	....	....
2821	Current	....	—	—	....	....	....	....	....	....	....	....	....
2822	Capital	....	—	—	....	....	....	....	....	....	....	....	....

Table 3 Transactions in assets and liabilities

		Budgetary Central Government			Central Government			Local Government			General Government		
3	**Change in net worth from transactns**	....	....	....	....	....	....	....	....	....	....	....	....
31	**Net acquisition of nonfinancial assets**	....	18,120	22,517	....	....	....	....	....	....	....	....	....
311	Fixed assets	....	18,120	22,517	....	....	....	....	....	....	....	....	....
3111	Buildings and structures	....	....	....	....	....	....	....	....	....	....	....	....
3112	Machinery and equipment	....	....	....	....	....	....	....	....	....	....	....	....
3113	Other fixed assets	....	....	....	....	....	....	....	....	....	....	....	....
312	Inventories	....	—	—	....	....	....	....	....	....	....	....	....
313	Valuables	....	—	—	....	....	....	....	....	....	....	....	....
314	Nonproduced assets	....	—	—	....	....	....	....	....	....	....	....	....
3141	Land	....	—	—	....	....	....	....	....	....	....	....	....
3142	Subsoil assets	....	—	—	....	....	....	....	....	....	....	....	....
3143	Other naturally occurring assets	....	—	—	....	....	....	....	....	....	....	....	....
3144	Intangible nonproduced assets	....	—	—	....	....	....	....	....	....	....	....	....
32	**Net acquisition of financial assets**	....	....	....	....	....	....	....	....	....	....	....	....
321	Domestic	....	281	19,696	....	....	....	....	....	....	....	....	....
3212	Currency and deposits	....	....	5,980	....	....	....	....	....	....	....	....	....
3213	Securities other than shares	....	....	....	....	....	....	....	....	....	....	....	....
3214	Loans	....	....	....	....	....	....	....	....	....	....	....	....
3215	Shares and other equity	....	....	....	....	....	....	....	....	....	....	....	....
3216	Insurance technical reserves	....	....	....	....	....	....	....	....	....	....	....	....
3217	Financial derivatives	....	....	....	....	....	....	....	....	....	....	....	....
3218	Other accounts receivable	....	....	....	....	....	....	....	....	....	....	....	....
322	Foreign	....	....	....	....	....	....	....	....	....	....	....	....
3222	Currency and deposits	....	....	....	....	....	....	....	....	....	....	....	....
3223	Securities other than shares	....	....	....	....	....	....	....	....	....	....	....	....
3224	Loans	....	....	....	....	....	....	....	....	....	....	....	....
3225	Shares and other equity	....	....	....	....	....	....	....	....	....	....	....	....
3226	Insurance technical reserves	....	....	....	....	....	....	....	....	....	....	....	....
3227	Financial derivatives	....	....	....	....	....	....	....	....	....	....	....	....
3228	Other accounts receivable	....	....	....	....	....	....	....	....	....	....	....	....
323	Monetary gold and SDRs	....	—	—	....	....	....	....	....	....	....	....	....
33	**Net incurrence of liabilities**	....	....	....	....	....	....	....	....	....	....	....	....
331	Domestic	....	5,917	26,207	....	....	....	....	....	....	....	....	....
3312	Currency and deposits	....	—	—	....	....	....	....	....	....	....	....	....
3313	Securities other than shares	....	5,917	26,207	....	....	....	....	....	....	....	....	....
3314	Loans	....	—	—	....	....	....	....	....	....	....	....	....
3316	Insurance technical reserves	....	—	—	....	....	....	....	....	....	....	....	....
3317	Financial derivatives	....	—	—	....	....	....	....	....	....	....	....	....
3318	Other accounts payable	....	....	....	....	....	....	....	....	....	....	....	....
332	Foreign	....	....	....	....	....	....	....	....	....	....	....	....
3322	Currency and deposits	....	....	....	....	....	....	....	....	....	....	....	....
3323	Securities other than shares	....	....	....	....	....	....	....	....	....	....	....	....
3324	Loans	....	....	....	....	....	....	....	....	....	....	....	....
3326	Insurance technical reserves	....	....	....	....	....	....	....	....	....	....	....	....
3327	Financial derivatives	....	....	....	....	....	....	....	....	....	....	....	....
3328	Other accounts payable	....	....	....	....	....	....	....	....	....	....	....	....

	Budgetary Central Government			Central Government			Local Government			General Government		
	1997	1998	1999	1997	1998	1999	1997	1998	1999	1997	1998	1999
Table 4 Holding gains in assets and liabilities												
Table 5 Other changes in the volume of assets and liabilities												
Table 6 Balance sheet												
6 Net worth.....................	....	....	....	....	....	....	....	....	....	....	....	....
61 **Nonfinancial assets**..................	....	....	....	....	....	....	....	....	....	....	....	....
611 Fixed assets.......................	....	....	....	....	....	....	....	....	....	....	....	....
6111 Buildings and structures.............	....	....	....	....	....	....	....	....	....	....	....	....
6112 Machinery and equipment............	....	....	....	....	....	....	....	....	....	....	....	....
6113 Other fixed assets..................	....	....	....	....	....	....	....	....	....	....	....	....
612 Inventories......................	....	....	....	....	....	....	....	....	....	....	....	....
613 Valuables........................	....	....	....	....	....	....	....	....	....	....	....	....
614 Nonproduced assets...............	....	....	....	....	....	....	....	....	....	....	....	....
6141 Land.........................	....	....	....	....	....	....	....	....	....	....	....	....
6142 Subsoil assets....................	....	....	....	....	....	....	....	....	....	....	....	....
6143 Other naturally occurring assets........	....	....	....	....	....	....	....	....	....	....	....	....
6144 Intangible nonproduced assets........	....	....	....	....	....	....	....	....	....	....	....	....
62 **Financial assets**..................	....	....	....	....	....	....	....	....	....	....	....	....
621 Domestic........................	....	....	....	....	....	....	....	....	....	....	....	....
6212 Currency and deposits.............	....	....	....	....	....	....	....	....	....	....	....	....
6213 Securities other than shares.........	....	....	....	....	....	....	....	....	....	....	....	....
6214 Loans.........................	....	....	....	....	....	....	....	....	....	....	....	....
6215 Shares and other equity............	....	....	....	....	....	....	....	....	....	....	....	....
6216 Insurance technical reserves.........	....	....	....	....	....	....	....	....	....	....	....	....
6217 Financial derivatives..............	....	....	....	....	....	....	....	....	....	....	....	....
6218 Other accounts receivable..........	....	....	....	....	....	....	....	....	....	....	....	....
622 Foreign.........................	....	....	....	....	....	....	....	....	....	....	....	....
6222 Currency and deposits.............	....	....	....	....	....	....	....	....	....	....	....	....
6223 Securities other than shares.........	....	....	....	....	....	....	....	....	....	....	....	....
6224 Loans.........................	....	....	....	....	....	....	....	....	....	....	....	....
6225 Shares and other equity............	....	....	....	....	....	....	....	....	....	....	....	....
6226 Insurance technical reserves.........	....	....	....	....	....	....	....	....	....	....	....	....
6227 Financial derivatives..............	....	....	....	....	....	....	....	....	....	....	....	....
6228 Other accounts receivable..........	....	....	....	....	....	....	....	....	....	....	....	....
623 Monetary gold and SDRs.............	....	....	....	....	....	....	....	....	....	....	....	....
63 **Liabilities**.....................	....	**177,777**	**233,591**	....	....	....	....	....	....	....	....	....
631 Domestic........................	....	69,977	81,977	....	....	....	....	....	....	....	....	....
6312 Currency and deposits.............	....	....	....	....	....	....	....	....	....	....	....	....
6313 Securities other than shares.........	....	....	....	....	....	....	....	....	....	....	....	....
6314 Loans.........................	....	....	....	....	....	....	....	....	....	....	....	....
6316 Insurance technical reserves.........	....	....	....	....	....	....	....	....	....	....	....	....
6317 Financial derivatives..............	....	....	....	....	....	....	....	....	....	....	....	....
6318 Other accounts payable............	....	....	....	....	....	....	....	....	....	....	....	....
632 Foreign.........................	....	107,800	151,614	....	....	....	....	....	....	....	....	....
6322 Currency and deposits.............	....	....	....	....	....	....	....	....	....	....	....	....
6323 Securities other than shares.........	....	....	....	....	....	....	....	....	....	....	....	....
6324 Loans.........................	....	....	....	....	....	....	....	....	....	....	....	....
6326 Insurance technical reserves.........	....	....	....	....	....	....	....	....	....	....	....	....
6327 Financial derivatives..............	....	....	....	....	....	....	....	....	....	....	....	....
6328 Other accounts payable............	....	....	....	....	....	....	....	....	....	....	....	....
Memorandum items:												
6M2 Net financial worth...............	....	....	....	....	....	....	....	....	....	....	....	....
6M3 Debt at market value...............	....	....	....	....	....	....	....	....	....	....	....	....
6M4 Debt at nominal value...............	....	....	....	....	....	....	....	....	....	....	....	....
6M5 Arrears........................	....	....	....	....	....	....	....	....	....	....	....	....
6M6 Obligations for social security benefits........	....	....	....	....	....	....	....	....	....	....	....	....
6M7 Contingent liabilities...............	....	....	....	....	....	....	....	....	....	....	....	....
6M8 Uncapitalized military weapons, systems........	....	....	....	....	....	....	....	....	....	....	....	....
Table 7 Outlays by functions of govt.												
7 **Total outlays**.....................	....	**171,129**	**227,265**	....	....	....	....	....	....	....	....	....
701 **General public services**................	....	**102,927**	**124,414**	....	....	....	....	....	....	....	....	....
7017 Public debt transactions............	....	11,689	20,366	....	....	....	....	....	....	....	....	....
7018 General transfers between levels of govt......	....	....	....	....	....	....	....	....	....	....	....	....
702 **Defense**........................	....	**41,396**	**62,528**	....	....	....	....	....	....	....	....	....
703 **Public order and safety**................	....	**13,257**	**17,696**	....	....	....	....	....	....	....	....	....

In Millions of Dinars / Year Ending December 31 / Cash Reporter

		Budgetary Central Government			Central Government			Local Government			General Government		
		1997	1998	1999	1997	1998	1999	1997	1998	1999	1997	1998	1999
704	**Economic affairs**.....................................	....	3,632	2,531	....	....	....	....	....	....	....	....	....
7042	Agriculture, forestry, fishing, and hunting.....	....	1,875	2,073	....	....	....	....	....	....	....	....	....
7043	Fuel and energy..	....	—	—	....	....	....	....	....	....	....	....	....
7044	Mining, manufacturing, and construction.....	....	255	4	....	....	....	....	....	....	....	....	....
7045	Transport...	....	1,014	45	....	....	....	....	....	....	....	....	....
7046	Communication...	....	....	....	....	....	....	....	....	....	....	....	....
705	**Environmental protection**........................	....	....	....	....	....	....	....	....	....	....	....	....
706	**Housing and community amenities**........	....	39	133	....	....	....	....	....	....	....	....	....
707	**Health**..	....	2,085	2,183	....	....	....	....	....	....	....	....	....
7072	Outpatient services.......................................	....	....	....	....	....	....	....	....	....	....	....	....
7073	Hospital services..	....	....	....	....	....	....	....	....	....	....	....	....
7074	Public health services...................................	....	....	....	....	....	....	....	....	....	....	....	....
708	**Recreation, culture, and religion**............	....	342	327	....	....	....	....	....	....	....	....	....
709	**Education**..	....	7,405	17,368	....	....	....	....	....	....	....	....	....
7091	Pre-primary and primary education..............	....	....	....	....	....	....	....	....	....	....	....	....
7092	Secondary education.....................................	....	....	....	....	....	....	....	....	....	....	....	....
7094	Tertiary education...	....	....	....	....	....	....	....	....	....	....	....	....
710	**Social protection**......................................	....	46	85	....	....	....	....	....	....	....	....	....
7	Statistical discrepancy: Total outlays..............	....	—	—	....	....	....	....	....	....	....	....	....

Table 8 Transactions in financial assets and liabilities by sector

		Budgetary Central Government			Central Government			Local Government			General Government		
82	**Net acquisition of financial assets**........	....	....	....	....	....	....	....	....	....	....	....	....
821	Domestic...	....	281	19,696	....	....	....	....	....	....	....	....	....
8211	General government......................................	....	....	....	....	....	....	....	....	....	....	....	....
8212	Central bank...	....	....	....	....	....	....	....	....	....	....	....	....
8213	Other depository corporations......................	....	....	....	....	....	....	....	....	....	....	....	....
8214	Financial corporations n.e.c..........................	....	....	....	....	....	....	....	....	....	....	....	....
8215	Nonfinancial corporations.............................	....	....	....	....	....	....	....	....	....	....	....	....
8216	Households & NPIs serving households......	....	....	....	....	....	....	....	....	....	....	....	....
822	Foreign...	....	....	....	....	....	....	....	....	....	....	....	....
8221	General government......................................	....	....	....	....	....	....	....	....	....	....	....	....
8227	International organizations...........................	....	....	....	....	....	....	....	....	....	....	....	....
8228	Financial corporations other than international organizations..............	....	....	....	....	....	....	....	....	....	....	....	....
8229	Other nonresidents.......................................	....	....	....	....	....	....	....	....	....	....	....	....
823	Monetary gold and SDRs..............................	....	—	—	....	....	....	....	....	....	....	....	....
83	**Net incurrence of liabilities**...................	....	....	....	....	....	....	....	....	....	....	....	....
831	Domestic...	....	5,917	26,207	....	....	....	....	....	....	....	....	....
8311	General government......................................	....	....	....	....	....	....	....	....	....	....	....	....
8312	Central bank...	....	....	....	....	....	....	....	....	....	....	....	....
8313	Other depository corporations......................	....	....	....	....	....	....	....	....	....	....	....	....
8314	Financial corporations n.e.c..........................	....	....	....	....	....	....	....	....	....	....	....	....
8315	Nonfinancial corporations.............................	....	....	....	....	....	....	....	....	....	....	....	....
8316	Households & NPIs serving households......	....	....	....	....	....	....	....	....	....	....	....	....
832	Foreign...	....	....	....	....	....	....	....	....	....	....	....	....
8321	General government......................................	....	....	....	....	....	....	....	....	....	....	....	....
8327	International organizations...........................	....	....	....	....	....	....	....	....	....	....	....	....
8328	Financial corporations other than international organizations..............	....	....	....	....	....	....	....	....	....	....	....	....
8329	Other nonresidents.......................................	....	....	....	....	....	....	....	....	....	....	....	....

In Millions of Emalangeni / Year Beginning April 1 / Cash Reporter

		Budgetary Central Government			Central Government			Local Government			General Government		
		2001	2002	2003	2001	2002	2003	2001	2002	2003	2001	2002	2003
Statement of government operations													
Statement of other economic flows													
Balance sheet													
Statement of sources and uses of cash													
1	Cash receipts from operating activities.........	3,104.3	3,425.5	3,808.9	....	....	....	72.8	79.9	87.2	....	....	....
11	Taxes.....................................	2,785.2	3,107.3	3,591.9	....	....	....	54.1	55.4	69.7	....	....	....
12	Social contributions......................	—	—	—	....	....	....	—	—	—	....	....	....
13	Grants...................................	126.9	163.0	132.3	....	....	....	13.6	13.1	12.2	....	....	....
14	Other receipts............................	192.3	155.1	84.6	....	....	....	5.1	11.5	5.3	....	....	....
2	Cash payments for operating activities........	2,269.7	2,897.5	3,338.7	....	....	....	67.7	63.4	79.2	....	....	....
21	Compensation of employees.................	1,024.3	1,024.3	1,466.1	....	....	....	....	....	....	....	....	....
22	Purchases of goods and services............	144.4	178.0	120.2	....	....	....	....	....	....	....	....	....
24	Interest..................................	102.1	167.0	179.0	....	....	....	....	....	....	....	....	....
25	Subsidies................................	496.3	504.3	718.9	....	....	....	....	....	....	....	....	....
26	Grants...................................	24.0	24.0	19.5	....	....	....	....	....	....	....	....	....
27	Social benefits...........................	—	—	—	....	....	....	....	....	....	....	....	....
28	Other payments...........................	478.6	999.9	835.1	....	....	....	....	....	....	....	....	....
CIO	*Net cash inflow from oper. activities.....*	*834.6*	*528.0*	*470.1*	....	....	....	*5.1*	*16.5*	*8.0*	....	....	....
31.1	Purchases of nonfinancial assets............	....	....	....	....	....	....	....	....	....			
31.2	Sales of nonfinancial assets................	....	....	....	....	....	....	....	....	....			
31	Net cash outflow from investments in nonfinancial assets......................	876.0	981.0	805.3									
CSD	*Cash surplus/deficit....................*	*−41.4*	*−453.0*	*−335.1*	....	....	....	....	....	....	....	....	....
32x	Net acquisition of fin assets, excl. cash.........	....	....	....	....	....	....	....	....	....			
321x	Domestic................................	....	....	....	....	....	....	....	....	....			
322x	Foreign.................................	....	....	....	....	....	....	....	....	....			
323	Monetary gold and SDRs...................	....	....	....	....	....	....	....	....	....			
33	Net incurrence of liabilities................	....	....	....	....	....	....	....	....	....			
331	Domestic................................	....	....	....	....	....	....	....	....	....			
332	Foreign.................................	....	....	....	....	....	....	....	....	....			
NFB	Net cash inflow from fin. activities.........	....	....	....	....	....	....	....	....	....			
NCB	*Net change in the stock of cash............*	....	....	....	....	....	....	....	....	....			

	Table 1 Revenue												
1	**Revenue........................**	**3,104.3**	**3,425.5**	**3,808.9**	....	....	....	**72.8**	**79.9**	**87.2**	....	....	....
11	**Taxes.........................**	**2,785.2**	**3,107.3**	**3,591.9**	....	....	....	**54.1**	**55.4**	**69.7**	....	....	....
111	Taxes on income, profits, & capital gains......	722.1	824.6	1,102.1	....	....	....	—	—	—	....	....	....
1111	Individuals.............................	428.3	491.2	695.3	....	....	....	—	—	—	....	....	....
1112	Corporations and other enterprises...........	267.8	301.3	356.6	....	....	....	—	—	—	....	....	....
112	Taxes on payroll and workforce...............	—	—	—	....	....	....	—	—	—	....	....	....
113	Taxes on property........................	5.5	6.0	9.0	....	....	....	50.2	53.9	65.5	....	....	....
114	Taxes on goods and services...............	515.3	629.0	582.3	....	....	....	4.0	1.5	4.2	....	....	....
1141	General taxes on goods and services.........	407.7	528.6	547.7	....	....	....	....	....	....	....	....	....
1142	Excises................................	90.8	81.9	12.1	....	....	....	....	....	....	....	....	....
115	Taxes on int'l. trade and transactions............	1,532.2	1,640.4	1,890.3	....	....	....	—	—	—	....	....	....
116	Other taxes.............................	10.1	7.3	8.3	....	....	....	—	—	—	....	....	....
12	**Social contributions...............**	**—**	**—**	**—**	....	....	....	**—**	**—**	**—**	....	....	....
121	Social security contributions................	—	—	—	....	....	....	—	—	—	....	....	....
122	Other social contributions.................	—	—	—	....	....	....	—	—	—	....	....	....
13	**Grants.........................**	**126.9**	**163.0**	**132.3**	....	....	....	**13.6**	**13.1**	**12.2**	....	....	....
131	From foreign governments.................	126.9	163.0	132.3	....	....	....	—	—	—	....	....	....
132	From international organizations.............	—	—	—	....	....	....	—	—	—	....	....	....
133	From other general government units..........	—	—	—	....	....	....	13.6	13.1	12.2	....	....	....
14	**Other revenue....................**	**192.3**	**155.1**	**84.6**	....	....	....	**5.1**	**11.5**	**5.3**	....	....	....

	Table 2 Expense by economic type												
2	**Expense.........................**	**2,269.7**	**2,897.5**	**3,338.7**	....	....	....	**67.7**	**63.4**	**79.2**	....	....	....
21	**Compensation of employees...........**	**1,024.3**	**1,024.3**	**1,466.1**	....	....	....	....	....	....	....	....	....
211	Wages and salaries.......................	1,022.0	1,022.0	1,463.5	....	....	....	....	....	....	....	....	....
212	Social contributions......................	2.3	2.3	2.6	....	....	....	....	....	....	....	....	....
22	**Use of goods and services............**	**144.4**	**178.0**	**120.2**	....	....	....	....	....	....	....	....	....
23	**Consumption of fixed capital..........**	....	....	....	....	....	....	....	....	....	....	....	....
24	**Interest.........................**	**102.1**	**167.0**	**179.0**	....	....	....	....	....	....	....	....	....
25	**Subsidies........................**	**496.3**	**504.3**	**718.9**	....	....	....	....	....	....	....	....	....

In Millions of Emalangeni / Year Beginning April 1 / Cash Reporter

		Budgetary Central Government			Central Government			Local Government			General Government		
		2001	2002	2003	2001	2002	2003	2001	2002	2003	2001	2002	2003
26	Grants.........................	24.0	24.0	19.5	....	....	....	....	....	....	....	....	....
261	To foreign govenments....................	—	—	—	....	....	....	....	....	....	....	....	....
262	To international organizations....................	—	—	—	....	....	....	....	....	....	....	....	....
263	To other general government units.............	24.0	24.0	19.5	....	....	....	....	....	....	....	....	....
2631	Current....................	24.0	24.0	19.5	....	....	....	....	....	....	....	....	....
2632	Capital....................	—	—	—	....	....	....	....	....	....	....	....	....
27	Social benefits....................	—	—	—	....	....	....	....	....	....	....	....	....
28	Other expense....................	478.6	999.9	835.1	....	....	....	....	....	....	....	....	....
281	Property expense other than interest............	—	—	—	....	....	....	....	....	....	....	....	....
282	Miscellaneous other expense....................	478.6	999.9	835.1	....	....	....	....	....	....	....	....	....
2821	Current....................	478.5	987.2	796.9	....	....	....	....	....	....	....	....	....
2822	Capital....................	.2	12.7	38.1	....	....	....	....	....	....	....	....	....
Table 3	**Transactions in assets and liabilities**												
3	**Change in net worth from transactns....**	....	....	....	....	....	....	....	....	....	....	....	....
31	**Net acquisition of nonfinancial assets...**	876.0	981.0	805.3	....	....	....	....	....	....	....	....	....
311	Fixed assets....................	876.3	981.4	807.2	....	....	....	....	....	....	....	....	....
3111	Buildings and structures....................	876.3	981.4	807.2	....	....	....	....	....	....	....	....	....
3112	Machinery and equipment....................	—	—	—	....	....	....	....	....	....	....	....	....
3113	Other fixed assets....................	—	—	—	....	....	....	....	....	....	....	....	....
312	Inventories....................	—	—	—	....	....	....	....	....	....	....	....	....
313	Valuables....................	—	—	—	....	....	....	....	....	....	....	....	....
314	Nonproduced assets....................	−.3	−.4	−1.9	....	....	....	....	....	....	....	....	....
3141	Land....................	−.3	−.4	−1.9	....	....	....	....	....	....	....	....	....
3142	Subsoil assets....................	—	—	—	....	....	....	....	....	....	....	....	....
3143	Other naturally occurring assets....................	—	—	—	....	....	....	....	....	....	....	....	....
3144	Intangible nonproduced assets....................	—	—	—	....	....	....	....	....	....	....	....	....
32	**Net acquisition of financial assets........**	....	....	....	....	....	....	....	....	....	....	....	....
321	Domestic....................	....	....	....	....	....	....	....	....	....	....	....	....
3212	Currency and deposits....................	....	....	....	....	....	....	....	....	....	....	....	....
3213	Securities other than shares....................	....	....	....	....	....	....	....	....	....	....	....	....
3214	Loans....................	....	....	....	....	....	....	....	....	....	....	....	....
3215	Shares and other equity....................	....	....	....	....	....	....	....	....	....	....	....	....
3216	Insurance technical reserves....................	....	....	....	....	....	....	....	....	....	....	....	....
3217	Financial derivatives....................	....	....	....	....	....	....	....	....	....	....	....	....
3218	Other accounts receivable....................	....	....	....	....	....	....	....	....	....	....	....	....
322	Foreign....................	....	....	....	....	....	....	....	....	....	....	....	....
3222	Currency and deposits....................	....	....	....	....	....	....	....	....	....	....	....	....
3223	Securities other than shares....................	....	....	....	....	....	....	....	....	....	....	....	....
3224	Loans....................	....	....	....	....	....	....	....	....	....	....	....	....
3225	Shares and other equity....................	....	....	....	....	....	....	....	....	....	....	....	....
3226	Insurance technical reserves....................	....	....	....	....	....	....	....	....	....	....	....	....
3227	Financial derivatives....................	....	....	....	....	....	....	....	....	....	....	....	....
3228	Other accounts receivable....................	....	....	....	....	....	....	....	....	....	....	....	....
323	Monetary gold and SDRs....................	....	....	....	....	....	....	....	....	....	....	....	....
33	**Net incurrence of liabilities...................**	....	....	....	....	....	....	....	....	....	....	....	....
331	Domestic....................	....	....	....	....	....	....	....	....	....	....	....	....
3312	Currency and deposits....................	....	....	....	....	....	....	....	....	....	....	....	....
3313	Securities other than shares....................	....	....	....	....	....	....	....	....	....	....	....	....
3314	Loans....................	....	....	....	....	....	....	....	....	....	....	....	....
3316	Insurance technical reserves....................	....	....	....	....	....	....	....	....	....	....	....	....
3317	Financial derivatives....................	....	....	....	....	....	....	....	....	....	....	....	....
3318	Other accounts payable....................	....	....	....	....	....	....	....	....	....	....	....	....
332	Foreign....................	....	....	....	....	....	....	....	....	....	....	....	....
3322	Currency and deposits....................	....	....	....	....	....	....	....	....	....	....	....	....
3323	Securities other than shares....................	....	....	....	....	....	....	....	....	....	....	....	....
3324	Loans....................	....	....	....	....	....	....	....	....	....	....	....	....
3326	Insurance technical reserves....................	....	....	....	....	....	....	....	....	....	....	....	....
3327	Financial derivatives....................	....	....	....	....	....	....	....	....	....	....	....	....
3328	Other accounts payable....................	....	....	....	....	....	....	....	....	....	....	....	....

In Millions of Emalangeni / Year Beginning April 1 / Cash Reporter

	Budgetary Central Government			Central Government			Local Government			General Government		
	2001	2002	2003	2001	2002	2003	2001	2002	2003	2001	2002	2003
Table 4 Holding gains in assets and liabilities												
Table 5 Other changes in the volume of assets and liabilities												
Table 6 Balance sheet												
Table 7 Outlays by functions of govt.												
7 Total outlays................................	3,145.7	3,878.5	4,144.0	....	....	....	....	....	....	....	....	....
701 **General public services.........................**	....	....	....	....	....	....	....	....	....	....	....	....
7017 Public debt transactions............................	102.1	167.0	179.0	....	....	....	....	....	....	....	....	....
7018 General transfers between levels of govt......	....	....	....	....	....	....	....	....	....	....	....	....
702 **Defense..**	....	....	....	....	....	....	....	....	....	....	....	....
703 **Public order and safety.........................**	....	....	....	....	....	....	....	....	....	....	....	....
704 **Economic affairs..............................**	....	....	....	....	....	....	....	....	....	....	....	....
7042 Agriculture, forestry, fishing, and hunting.....	....	....	....	....	....	....	....	....	....	....	....	....
7043 Fuel and energy...	....	....	....	....	....	....	....	....	....	....	....	....
7044 Mining, manufacturing, and construction.....	....	....	....	....	....	....	....	....	....	....	....	....
7045 Transport..	....	....	....	....	....	....	....	....	....	....	....	....
7046 Communication...	....	....	....	....	....	....	....	....	....	....	....	....
705 **Environmental protection.....................**	....	....	....	....	....	....	....	....	....	....	....	....
706 **Housing and community amenities........**	....	....	....	....	....	....	....	....	....	....	....	....
707 **Health...**	....	....	....	....	....	....	....	....	....	....	....	....
7072 Outpatient services....................................	....	....	....	....	....	....	....	....	....	....	....	....
7073 Hospital services.......................................	....	....	....	....	....	....	....	....	....	....	....	....
7074 Public health services................................	....	....	....	....	....	....	....	....	....	....	....	....
708 **Recreation, culture, and religion...........**	....	....	....	....	....	....	....	....	....	....	....	....
709 **Education..**	....	....	....	....	....	....	....	....	....	....	....	....
7091 Pre-primary and primary education..............	....	....	....	....	....	....	....	....	....	....	....	....
7092 Secondary education.................................	....	....	....	....	....	....	....	....	....	....	....	....
7094 Tertiary education......................................	....	....	....	....	....	....	....	....	....	....	....	....
710 **Social protection...............................**	....	....	....	....	....	....	....	....	....	....	....	....
7 Statistical discrepancy: Total outlays..............	....	....	....	....	....	....	....	....	....	....	....	....
Table 8 Transactions in financial assets and liabilities by sector												

In Billions of Kronor / Year Ending December 31 / Noncash Reporter

	Budgetary Central Government			Central Government			Local Government			General Government		
	2001	2002	2003	2001	2002	2003	2001	2002	2003	2001	2002	2003
Statement of government operations												
1 Revenue	952.6	727.2	768.8	957.2	890.5	933.2	561.4	597.5	627.5	1,398.4	1,361.9	1,432.6
2 Expense	733.5	757.4	796.1	842.4	873.1	913.6	562.9	603.6	631.9	1,285.2	1,350.7	1,417.4
GOB *Gross operating balance*	*242.9*	*−5.5*	*−2.9*	*138.6*	*42.2*	*44.0*	*28.7*	*25.5*	*28.2*	*167.3*	*67.7*	*72.3*
NOB *Net operating balance*	*219.1*	*−30.2*	*−27.3*	*114.8*	*17.4*	*19.6*	*−1.6*	*−6.1*	*−4.4*	*113.2*	*11.2*	*15.2*
31 Net acquisition of nonfinancial assets	6.2	10.0	11.9	6.2	10.0	11.9	3.6	7.3	2.2	9.8	17.4	14.1
NLB *Net lending/borrowing*	*212.9*	*−40.2*	*−39.2*	*108.6*	*7.3*	*7.7*	*−5.1*	*−13.5*	*−6.5*	*103.4*	*−6.1*	*1.1*
32 Net acquisition of financial assets	46.2	−39.8	1.3	−56.6	6.6	64.5	14.8	17.5	10.8	−41.8	47.4	74.7
33 Net incurrence of liabilities	−139.9	−34.9	41.6	−132.1	−31.3	39.4	16.3	32.1	8.0	−115.7	24.0	46.8
NLB Statistical discrepancy	−26.8	35.4	−1.1	−33.1	30.6	17.5	3.6	−1.1	9.3	−29.5	29.5	26.7
Statement of other economic flows												
Balance sheet												
6 *Net worth*	….	….	….	….	….	….	….	….	….	….	….	….
61 Nonfinancial assets	….	….	….	….	….	….	….	….	….	….	….	….
62 Financial assets	….	837.2	….	….	1,396.8	….	….	260.4	….	1,721.0	1,572.6	….
63 Liabilities	….	1,464.5	….	….	1,468.3	….	….	275.4	….	1,650.1	1,659.1	….
Statement of sources and uses of cash												
Table 1 Revenue												
1 **Revenue**	**952.6**	**727.2**	**768.8**	**957.2**	**890.5**	**933.2**	**561.4**	**597.5**	**627.5**	**1,398.4**	**1,361.9**	**1,432.6**
11 **Taxes**	**517.4**	**447.1**	**481.0**	**517.4**	**447.1**	**481.0**	**359.5**	**378.5**	**402.9**	**876.9**	**825.6**	**883.9**
111 Taxes on income, profits, & capital gains	132.5	38.6	48.0	132.5	38.6	48.0	359.5	378.5	402.9	492.0	417.1	450.9
1111 Individuals	48.3	−13.2	−10.7	48.3	−13.2	−10.7	359.5	378.5	402.9	407.8	365.3	392.3
1112 Corporations and other enterprises	84.2	51.7	58.6	84.2	51.7	58.6	—	—	—	84.2	51.7	58.6
112 Taxes on payroll and workforce	62.7	67.2	73.4	62.7	67.2	73.4	—	—	—	62.7	67.2	73.4
113 Taxes on property	32.7	33.4	37.6	32.7	33.4	37.6	—	—	—	32.7	33.4	37.6
114 Taxes on goods and services	286.7	304.6	319.2	286.7	304.6	319.2	—	—	—	286.7	304.6	319.2
1141 General taxes on goods and services	195.2	208.5	219.7	195.2	208.5	219.7	—	—	—	195.2	208.5	219.7
1142 Excises	73.5	77.6	80.3	73.5	77.6	80.3	—	—	—	73.5	77.6	80.3
115 Taxes on int'l. trade and transactions	—	—	—	—	—	—	—	—	—	—	—	—
116 Other taxes	2.9	3.3	2.9	2.9	3.3	2.9	—	—	—	2.9	3.3	2.9
12 **Social contributions**	**207.0**	**213.3**	**214.6**	**343.3**	**352.9**	**357.8**	**7.8**	**9.2**	**10.5**	**351.1**	**362.1**	**368.3**
121 Social security contributions	200.9	206.8	207.4	337.3	346.3	350.5	—	—	—	337.3	346.3	350.5
122 Other social contributions	6.0	6.6	7.3	6.0	6.6	7.3	7.8	9.2	10.5	13.9	15.7	17.8
13 **Grants**	**158.2**	**3.3**	**4.3**	**5.4**	**5.4**	**6.3**	**115.9**	**121.9**	**123.0**	**1.2**	**1.2**	**1.2**
131 From foreign governments	—	—	—	—	—	—	—	—	—	—	—	—
132 From international organizations	.8	.6	.8	.8	.6	.8	.4	.6	.4	1.2	1.2	1.2
133 From other general government units	157.4	2.7	3.5	4.6	4.7	5.5	115.5	121.4	122.6	—	—	—
14 **Other revenue**	**70.1**	**63.5**	**68.9**	**91.2**	**85.2**	**88.1**	**78.0**	**87.9**	**91.1**	**169.2**	**173.0**	**179.2**
Table 2 Expense by economic type												
2 **Expense**	**733.5**	**757.4**	**796.1**	**842.4**	**873.1**	**913.6**	**562.9**	**603.6**	**631.9**	**1,285.2**	**1,350.7**	**1,417.4**
21 **Compensation of employees**	**84.9**	**90.4**	**97.1**	**85.2**	**90.6**	**97.4**	**277.7**	**291.8**	**308.0**	**362.9**	**382.5**	**405.4**
211 Wages and salaries	….	….	67.6	….	….	67.8	….	….	224.4	….	….	292.2
212 Social contributions	….	….	29.5	….	….	29.6	….	….	83.6	….	….	113.2
22 **Use of goods and services**	**104.9**	**100.9**	**105.1**	**107.5**	**103.5**	**107.8**	**181.3**	**162.5**	**168.6**	**288.8**	**266.1**	**276.4**
23 **Consumption of fixed capital**	**23.8**	**24.7**	**24.4**	**23.8**	**24.8**	**24.5**	**30.3**	**31.7**	**32.6**	**54.1**	**56.5**	**57.0**
24 **Interest**	**64.0**	**65.7**	**49.9**	**64.1**	**65.7**	**49.9**	**7.8**	**8.8**	**8.3**	**72.0**	**74.6**	**58.2**
25 **Subsidies**	**23.6**	**25.9**	**25.5**	**23.6**	**25.9**	**25.5**	**11.2**	**10.2**	**11.9**	**34.7**	**36.1**	**37.5**
26 **Grants**	**173.4**	**171.9**	**175.2**	**128.4**	**133.0**	**134.3**	**4.6**	**4.7**	**5.5**	**12.9**	**11.7**	**11.7**
261 To foreign governments	—	—	—	—	—	—	—	—	—	—	—	—
262 To international organizations	12.9	11.7	11.7	12.9	11.7	11.7	—	—	—	12.9	11.7	11.7
263 To other general government units	160.6	160.2	163.6	115.5	121.4	122.6	4.6	4.7	5.5	—	—	—
2631 Current	152.5	158.7	163.6	114.4	119.9	122.6	4.1	4.7	5.5	—	—	—
2632 Capital	8.1	1.5	—	1.1	1.5	—	.5	—	—	—	—	—
27 **Social benefits**	**237.4**	**246.5**	**277.8**	**380.9**	**398.1**	**433.2**	**41.4**	**86.9**	**89.9**	**422.3**	**484.9**	**523.1**
28 **Other expense**	**21.5**	**31.5**	**41.0**	**29.0**	**31.5**	**41.0**	**8.5**	**6.9**	**7.1**	**37.5**	**38.4**	**48.1**
281 Property expense other than interest	—	—	—	—	—	—	.1	.1	.1	.1	.1	.1
282 Miscellaneous other expense	21.5	31.5	41.0	29.0	31.5	41.0	8.5	6.9	7.0	37.4	38.4	48.0
2821 Current	21.1	25.8	31.8	21.1	25.8	31.8	8.4	6.7	6.7	29.5	32.5	38.6
2822 Capital	.4	5.7	9.2	7.9	5.7	9.2	—	.2	.3	7.9	5.9	9.5

Sweden 144

In Billions of Kronor / Year Ending December 31 / Noncash Reporter

	Budgetary Central Government			Central Government			Local Government			General Government		
	2001	2002	2003	2001	2002	2003	2001	2002	2003	2001	2002	2003
Table 3 Transactions in assets and liabilities												
3 **Change in net worth from transactns....**	192.3	5.1	−28.4	81.7	47.9	37.1	2.0	−7.2	4.9	83.7	40.7	42.0
31 **Net acquisition of nonfinancial assets...**	6.2	10.0	11.9	6.2	10.0	11.9	3.6	7.3	2.2	9.8	17.4	14.1
311 Fixed assets............	6.6	10.3	12.1	6.6	10.3	12.1	8.2	9.8	7.0	14.8	20.1	19.1
3111 Buildings and structures...........	....	....	....	....	....	....	....	....	....	....	....	....
3112 Machinery and equipment...........	....	....	....	....	....	....	....	....	....	....	....	....
3113 Other fixed assets...........	....	....	....	....	....	....	....	....	....	....	....	....
312 Inventories............	—	−.1	−.1	—	−.1	−.1	—	—	—	—	−.1	−.1
313 Valuables............	—	—	—	—	—	—	—	—	—	—	—	—
314 Nonproduced assets............	−.4	−.2	−.1	−.4	−.2	−.1	−4.6	−2.5	−4.8	−5.1	−2.7	−4.9
3141 Land............	....	....	....	....	....	....	....	....	....	....	....	....
3142 Subsoil assets............	....	....	....	....	....	....	....	....	....	....	....	....
3143 Other naturally occurring assets............	....	....	....	....	....	....	....	....	....	....	....	....
3144 Intangible nonproduced assets............	....	....	....	....	....	....	....	....	....	....	....	....
32 **Net acquisition of financial assets........**	46.2	−39.8	1.3	−56.6	6.6	64.5	14.8	17.5	10.8	−41.8	47.4	74.7
321 Domestic............	34.2	−39.8	1.3	−281.1	6.6	64.5	14.5	17.5	10.8	−266.7	47.4	74.7
3212 Currency and deposits............	−8.2	−8.3	5.4	4.8	−12.0	−8.2	1.7	−1.6	4.1	6.5	−13.7	−4.1
3213 Securities other than shares............	27.0	−4.3	−11.3	−302.0	−23.7	19.0	2.6	7.1	−3.9	−299.4	6.6	14.1
3214 Loans............	30.9	−3.3	7.9	22.2	−10.9	3.6	2.5	10.8	10.0	24.7	−.1	13.9
3215 Shares and other equity............	−17.8	−21.2	−.7	−7.8	54.9	48.6	−4.2	.5	1.6	−12.0	55.5	50.2
3216 Insurance technical reserves............	....	....	....	....	....	....	....	....	....	....	....	....
3217 Financial derivatives............	—	—	—	—	—	—	—	—	—	—	—	—
3218 Other accounts receivable............	2.4	−2.7	.1	1.6	−1.6	1.6	11.9	.7	−1.1	13.6	−.9	.5
322 Foreign............	12.0	....	....	224.6	....	....	.3	....	....	224.8	....	....
3222 Currency and deposits............	4.1	....	....	5.4	....	....	—	....	....	5.4	....	....
3223 Securities other than shares............	—	....	....	6.5	....	....	—	....	....	6.5	....	....
3224 Loans............	4.4	....	....	4.4	....	....	—	....	....	4.4	....	....
3225 Shares and other equity............	—	....	....	204.7	....	....	.3	....	....	205.0	....	....
3226 Insurance technical reserves............	—	....	....	—	....	....	—	....	....	—	....	....
3227 Financial derivatives............	—	....	....	—	....	....	....	....	....	—	....	....
3228 Other accounts receivable............	3.5	....	....	3.5	....	....	—	....	....	3.5	....	....
323 Monetary gold and SDRs............	—	—	—	—	—	—	—	—	—	—	—	—
33 **Net incurrence of liabilities...................**	−139.9	−34.9	41.6	−132.1	−31.3	39.4	16.3	32.1	8.0	−115.7	24.0	46.8
331 Domestic............	−150.9	−34.9	41.6	−143.1	−31.3	39.4	19.9	32.1	8.0	−123.2	24.0	46.8
3312 Currency and deposits............	4.4	....	2.4	4.4	....	2.4	—	....	—	4.4	....	2.4
3313 Securities other than shares............	−172.8	−9.9	60.3	−172.8	−9.9	60.3	2.3	2.1	3.2	−170.5	15.4	62.6
3314 Loans............	17.5	−31.6	−20.9	24.7	−28.0	−24.3	3.1	25.3	8.1	27.9	−2.7	−16.0
3316 Insurance technical reserves............	—	....	—	—	....	—	.8	....	—	.8	....	—
3317 Financial derivatives............	—	....	—	—	....	—	—	....	—	—	....	—
3318 Other accounts payable............	−.1	2.8	−.3	.5	2.9	1.0	13.7	2.6	−3.2	14.2	5.5	−2.3
332 Foreign............	11.1	....	....	11.1	....	....	−3.6	....	....	7.4	....	....
3322 Currency and deposits............	—	....	....	—	....	....	—	....	....	—	....	....
3323 Securities other than shares............	12.8	....	....	12.8	....	....	−1.8	....	....	11.0	....	....
3324 Loans............	−1.7	....	....	−1.7	....	....	−1.8	....	....	−3.5	....	....
3326 Insurance technical reserves............	—	....	....	—	....	....	—	....	....	—	....	....
3327 Financial derivatives............	—	....	....	—	....	....	....	....	....	—	....	....
3328 Other accounts payable............	—	....	....	—	....	....	....	....	....	—	....	....
Table 4 Holding gains in assets and liabilities												
Table 5 Other changes in the volume of assets and liabilities												
Table 6 Balance sheet												
6 **Net worth............**	....	....	....	....	....	....	....	....	....	....	....	....
61 **Nonfinancial assets............**	....	....	....	....	....	....	....	....	....	....	....	....
611 Fixed assets............	....	....	....	....	....	....	....	....	....	....	....	....
6111 Buildings and structures............	....	....	....	....	....	....	....	....	....	....	....	....
6112 Machinery and equipment............	....	....	....	....	....	....	....	....	....	....	....	....
6113 Other fixed assets............	....	....	....	....	....	....	....	....	....	....	....	....
612 Inventories............	....	....	....	....	....	....	....	....	....	....	....	....
613 Valuables............	....	....	....	....	....	....	....	....	....	....	....	....
614 Nonproduced assets............	....	....	....	....	....	....	....	....	....	....	....	....
6141 Land............	....	....	....	....	....	....	....	....	....	....	....	....
6142 Subsoil assets............	....	....	....	....	....	....	....	....	....	....	....	....
6143 Other naturally occurring assets............	....	....	....	....	....	....	....	....	....	....	....	....
6144 Intangible nonproduced assets............	....	....	....	....	....	....	....	....	....	....	....	....

In Billions of Kronor / Year Ending December 31 / Noncash Reporter

	Budgetary Central Government			Central Government			Local Government			General Government		
	2001	2002	2003	2001	2002	2003	2001	2002	2003	2001	2002	2003
62 **Financial assets**........................	....	**837.2**	....	....	**1,396.8**	....	....	**260.4**	....	**1,721.0**	**1,572.6**	....
621 Domestic............................	....	837.2	....	....	1,396.8	....	....	260.4	....	1,721.0	1,572.6	....
6212 Currency and deposits............	....	9.7	....	....	27.9	....	....	16.4	....	61.8	44.3	....
6213 Securities other than shares.....	....	206.6	....	....	406.7	....	....	41.4	....	377.6	363.6	....
6214 Loans.............................	....	235.1	....	....	239.7	....	....	105.7	....	344.9	345.3	....
6215 Shares and other equity..........	....	329.7	....	....	665.2	....	....	32.3	....	823.5	697.6	....
6216 Insurance technical reserves......	....	—	....	....	—	....	....	—	....	—	—	....
6217 Financial derivatives.............	....	—	....	....	—	....	....	—	....	—	—	....
6218 Other accounts receivable........	....	56.0	....	....	57.2	....	....	64.6	....	113.2	121.8	....
622 Foreign.............................	....	....	....	....	....	....	....	....	....	....	....	....
6222 Currency and deposits............	....	....	....	....	....	....	....	....	....	....	....	....
6223 Securities other than shares.....	....	....	....	....	....	....	....	....	....	....	....	....
6224 Loans.............................	....	....	....	....	....	....	....	....	....	....	....	....
6225 Shares and other equity..........	....	....	....	....	....	....	....	....	....	....	....	....
6226 Insurance technical reserves......	....	....	....	....	....	....	....	....	....	....	....	....
6227 Financial derivatives.............	....	....	....	....	....	....	....	....	....	....	....	....
6228 Other accounts receivable........	....	....	....	....	....	....	....	....	....	....	....	....
623 Monetary gold and SDRs...........	....	....	....	....	....	....	....	....	....	....	....	....
63 **Liabilities**............................	....	**1,464.5**	....	....	**1,468.3**	....	....	**275.4**	....	**1,650.1**	**1,659.1**	....
631 Domestic............................	....	1,464.5	....	....	1,468.3	....	....	275.4	....	1,650.1	1,659.1	....
6312 Currency and deposits............	....	....	....	....	....	....	....	....	....	....	....	....
6313 Securities other than shares.....	....	1,335.1	....	....	1,335.3	....	....	27.5	....	1,280.8	1,278.3	....
6314 Loans.............................	....	68.8	....	....	72.3	....	....	123.6	....	212.0	195.8	....
6316 Insurance technical reserves......	....	....	....	....	....	....	....	....	....	....	....	....
6317 Financial derivatives.............	....	....	....	....	....	....	....	....	....	....	....	....
6318 Other accounts payable..........	....	44.1	....	....	44.2	....	....	115.3	....	137.8	159.5	....
632 Foreign.............................	....	....	....	....	....	....	....	....	....	....	....	....
6322 Currency and deposits............	....	....	....	....	....	....	....	....	....	....	....	....
6323 Securities other than shares.....	....	....	....	....	....	....	....	....	....	....	....	....
6324 Loans.............................	....	....	....	....	....	....	....	....	....	....	....	....
6326 Insurance technical reserves......	....	....	....	....	....	....	....	....	....	....	....	....
6327 Financial derivatives.............	....	....	....	....	....	....	....	....	....	....	....	....
6328 Other accounts payable..........	....	....	....	....	....	....	....	....	....	....	....	....
Memorandum items:												
6M2 Net financial worth...............	....	−627.3	....	....	−71.5	....	....	−15.0	....	70.9	−86.5	....
6M3 Debt at market value.............	....	....	....	....	....	....	....	....	....	....	....	....
6M4 Debt at nominal value............	....	....	....	....	....	....	....	....	....	....	....	....
6M5 Arrears............................	....	....	....	....	....	....	....	....	....	....	....	....
6M6 Obligations for social security benefits...........	....	....	....	....	....	....	....	....	....	....	....	....
6M7 Contingent liabilities..............	....	....	....	....	....	....	....	....	....	....	....	....
6M8 Uncapitalized military weapons, systems........	....	....	....	....	....	....	....	....	....	....	....	....
Table 7 Outlays by functions of govt.												
7 **Total outlays**......................	739.7	767.4	808.0	848.6	883.2	925.5	566.5	610.9	634.0	1,295.0	1,368.0	1,431.4
701 **General public services**....................	196.7	207.8	197.1	196.7	207.9	197.1	68.9	70.3	67.9	192.9	204.9	201.0
7017 Public debt transactions..........	64.0	65.7	49.9	64.1	65.7	49.9	7.8	8.8	8.3	72.0	74.6	58.2
7018 General transfers between levels of govt......	....	....	....	....	....	....	....	....	....	....	....	....
702 **Defense**...............................	50.7	50.2	50.8	50.7	50.2	50.8	.1	.2	.2	50.3	49.9	50.5
703 **Public order and safety**......................	26.4	28.0	28.6	26.4	28.0	28.6	5.7	6.4	6.9	32.0	34.4	35.0
704 **Economic affairs**..........................	70.1	82.7	91.6	70.1	82.7	91.6	31.6	32.8	33.6	100.0	113.7	121.7
7042 Agriculture, forestry, fishing, and hunting.....	....	....	....	....	....	....	....	....	....	....	....	....
7043 Fuel and energy...................	....	....	....	....	....	....	....	....	....	....	....	....
7044 Mining, manufacturing, and construction.....	....	....	....	....	....	....	....	....	....	....	....	....
7045 Transport..........................	....	....	....	....	....	....	....	....	....	....	....	....
7046 Communication....................	....	....	....	....	....	....	....	....	....	....	....	....
705 **Environmental protection**....................	25.1	4.2	4.0	25.1	4.2	4.0	147.1	4.8	4.7	150.6	8.1	8.1
706 **Housing and community amenities**........	6.8	4.9	5.1	6.8	4.9	5.1	20.2	17.0	18.0	26.0	21.7	22.0
707 **Health**................................	63.1	25.6	30.6	63.1	25.6	30.6	120.7	162.8	172.9	174.5	166.2	177.6
7072 Outpatient services................	....	....	....	....	....	....	....	....	....	....	....	....
7073 Hospital services..................	....	....	....	....	....	....	....	....	....	....	....	....
7074 Public health services.............	....	....	....	....	....	....	....	....	....	....	....	....
708 **Recreation, culture, and religion**...........	6.8	6.8	8.2	6.8	6.8	8.2	20.2	20.4	20.6	26.0	26.1	26.5

In Billions of Kronor / Year Ending December 31 / Noncash Reporter

		Budgetary Central Government			Central Government			Local Government			General Government		
		2001	2002	2003	2001	2002	2003	2001	2002	2003	2001	2002	2003
709	**Education**................................	**63.1**	**56.2**	**56.5**	**63.1**	**56.2**	**56.5**	**120.7**	**129.9**	**136.2**	**174.5**	**176.9**	**181.1**
7091	Pre-primary and primary education...............	....	....	....	....	....	....	....	....	....	....	....	....
7092	Secondary education................................	....	....	....	....	....	....	....	....	....	....	....	....
7094	Tertiary education................................	....	....	....	....	....	....	....	....	....	....	....	....
710	**Social protection**................................	**283.5**	**301.0**	**335.6**	**392.5**	**416.7**	**453.0**	**158.3**	**166.4**	**173.2**	**540.8**	**566.1**	**607.6**
7	Statistical discrepancy: Total outlays............	−52.7	—	—	−52.7	—	—	−127.0	—	—	−172.6	—	.3

Table 8   Transactions in financial assets and liabilities by sector

		Budgetary Central Government			Central Government			Local Government			General Government		
		2001	2002	2003	2001	2002	2003	2001	2002	2003	2001	2002	2003
82	**Net acquisition of financial assets**........	**46.2**	**−39.8**	**1.3**	**−56.6**	**6.6**	**64.5**	**14.8**	**17.5**	**10.8**	**−41.8**	**47.4**	**74.7**
821	Domestic...	34.2	−39.8	1.3	−281.1	6.6	64.5	14.5	17.5	10.8	−266.7	47.4	74.7
8211	General government................................	....	....	....	....	....	....	....	....	....	....	....	....
8212	Central bank..	....	....	....	....	....	....	....	....	....	....	....	....
8213	Other depository corporations....................	....	....	....	....	....	....	....	....	....	....	....	....
8214	Financial corporations n.e.c.....................	....	....	....	....	....	....	....	....	....	....	....	....
8215	Nonfinancial corporations........................	....	....	....	....	....	....	....	....	....	....	....	....
8216	Households & NPIs serving households......	....	....	....	....	....	....	....	....	....	....	....	....
822	Foreign..	12.0	....	....	224.6	....	....	.3	....	....	224.8	....	....
8221	General government................................	....	....	....	....	....	....	....	....	....	....	....	....
8227	International organizations.....................	....	....	....	....	....	....	....	....	....	....	....	....
8228	Financial corporations other than international organizations...............	....	....	....	....	....	....	....	....	....	....	....	....
8229	Other nonresidents................................	....	....	....	....	....	....	....	....	....	....	....	....
823	Monetary gold and SDRs.........................	—	—	—	—	—	—	—	—	—	—	—	—
83	**Net incurrence of liabilities**...................	**−139.9**	**−34.9**	**41.6**	**−132.1**	**−31.3**	**39.4**	**16.3**	**32.1**	**8.0**	**−115.7**	**24.0**	**46.8**
831	Domestic...	−150.9	−34.9	41.6	−143.1	−31.3	39.4	19.9	32.1	8.0	−123.2	24.0	46.8
8311	General government................................	....	....	....	....	....	....	....	....	....	....	....	....
8312	Central bank..	....	....	....	....	....	....	....	....	....	....	....	....
8313	Other depository corporations....................	....	....	....	....	....	....	....	....	....	....	....	....
8314	Financial corporations n.e.c.....................	....	....	....	....	....	....	....	....	....	....	....	....
8315	Nonfinancial corporations........................	....	....	....	....	....	....	....	....	....	....	....	....
8316	Households & NPIs serving households......	....	....	....	....	....	....	....	....	....	....	....	....
832	Foreign..	11.1	....	....	11.1	....	....	−3.6	....	....	7.4	....	....
8321	General government................................	....	....	....	....	....	....	....	....	....	....	....	....
8327	International organizations.....................	....	....	....	....	....	....	....	....	....	....	....	....
8328	Financial corporations other than international organizations...............	....	....	....	....	....	....	....	....	....	....	....	....
8329	Other nonresidents................................	....	....	....	....	....	....	....	....	....	....	....	....

	Central Government			State Government			Local Government			General Government		
	2000	2001	2002	2000	2001	2002	2000	2001	2002	2000	2001	2002
Statement of government operations												
Statement of other economic flows												
Balance sheet												
6 *Net worth*..............	....	....	....	....	....	....	....	....	....	....	....	....
61 Nonfinancial assets..................	....	....	....	....	....	....	....	....	....	....	....	....
62 Financial assets........................	....	....	....	....	....	....	....	....	....	....	....	....
63 Liabilities..............................	108,108	106,813	122,923	64,261	69,161	73,408	38,000	38,000	38,500	210,369	213,974	234,831
Statement of sources and uses of cash												
1 Cash receipts from operating activities...........	117,172	81,727	†85,785	60,862	63,203	64,904	41,435	42,372	43,496	179,544	158,720	†165,098
11 Taxes...................................	46,795	43,200	†43,215	28,850	30,174	31,988	20,226	21,056	21,195	95,871	94,430	†96,399
12 Social contributions..................	48,603	32,391	†33,185	—	—	—	—	—	—	48,603	32,391	†33,185
13 Grants...............................	14,536	2,307	†2,350	19,307	20,513	19,475	7,286	7,487	7,262	1,204	1,725	†—
14 Other receipts........................	7,238	3,829	†7,035	12,705	12,516	13,441	13,923	13,829	15,039	33,866	30,174	†35,514
2 Cash payments for operating activities...........	107,684	79,991	†82,475	54,392	58,444	60,486	35,720	36,828	37,535	157,871	146,681	†151,409
21 Compensation of employees.....................	5,405	4,711	†6,050	21,794	23,415	24,379	15,495	15,944	17,040	42,694	44,070	†47,469
22 Purchases of goods and services..................	24,486	6,821	†7,350	6,999	7,652	7,916	8,539	8,906	9,056	40,024	23,379	†24,322
24 Interest..............................	3,664	3,645	†3,901	2,341	2,253	2,065	2,093	2,000	1,889	8,098	7,898	†7,855
25 Subsidies............................	3,999	3,797	†4,200	....	....	8,458	....	....	2,409	....	....	†15,068
26 Grants..............................	25,912	16,740	†17,441	....	....	9,642	....	....	4,374	....	....	†2,370
27 Social benefits.......................	42,194	41,890	†39,397	....	....	—	....	....	—	....	....	†39,397
28 Other payments......................	2,024	2,387	†4,136	....	....	8,026	....	....	2,767	....	....	†14,929
CIO *Net cash inflow from oper. activities.....*	*9,488*	*1,736*	*†3,309*	*6,470*	*4,759*	*4,419*	*5,715*	*5,544*	*5,961*	*21,673*	*12,039*	*†13,690*
31.1 Purchases of nonfinancial assets..................	340	507	†917	4,824	5,173	5,165	4,625	4,771	4,888	9,789	10,451	†10,970
31.2 Sales of nonfinancial assets......................	75	118	†5	201	152	22	564	578	67	840	848	†94
31 Net cash outflow from investments in nonfinancial assets........................	265	389	†912	4,623	5,021	5,143	4,061	4,193	4,820	8,949	9,603	†10,876
CSD *Cash surplus/deficit................................*	*9,223*	*1,347*	*†2,397*	*1,847*	*−262*	*−725*	*1,654*	*1,351*	*1,141*	*12,724*	*2,436*	*†2,814*
32x Net acquisition of fin assets, excl. cash...........	−2,722	−1,856	†−33	−840	−1,517	−401	185	27	38	−3,377	−3,346	†−396
321x Domestic.................................	−2,675	−1,780	†60	....	....	....	....	....	....	....	....	†−304
322x Foreign.................................	−47	−76	†−93	....	....	....	....	....	....	....	....	†−93
323 Monetary gold and SDRs.................	—	—	†—	—	—	—	—	—	—	—	—	†—
33 Net incurrence of liabilities.................	−11,945	−3,203	†−2,430	−2,687	−1,255	323	−1,469	−1,324	−1,103	−16,101	−5,782	†−3,210
331 Domestic.................................	−11,945	−3,203	†−2,430	−2,687	−1,255	323	−1,469	−1,324	−1,103	−16,101	−5,782	†−3,210
332 Foreign.................................	—	—	†—	—	—	—	—	—	—	—	—	†—
NFB Net cash inflow from fin. activities.................	−9,223	−1,347	†−2,397	−1,847	262	725	−1,654	−1,351	−1,141	−12,724	−2,436	†−2,814
NCB *Net change in the stock of cash.............*	....	....	....	....	....	....	....	....	....	....	....	....
Table 1 Revenue												
1 **Revenue.................................**	**117,172**	**81,727**	**†85,785**	**60,862**	**63,203**	**64,904**	**41,435**	**42,372**	**43,496**	**179,544**	**158,720**	**†165,098**
11 **Taxes..................................**	**46,795**	**43,200**	**†43,215**	**28,850**	**30,174**	**31,988**	**20,226**	**21,056**	**21,195**	**95,871**	**94,430**	**†96,399**
111 Taxes on income, profits, & capital gains......	16,850	13,072	†13,946	21,738	22,978	24,374	17,077	17,501	17,627	55,665	53,551	†55,947
1111 Individuals..............................	11,945	7,246	†8,975	17,685	18,446	20,294	14,595	14,918	15,244	44,225	40,610	†44,513
1112 Corporations and other enterprises.............	4,905	5,826	†4,971	....	....	4,081	....	....	2,382	....	....	†11,433
112 Taxes on payroll and workforce.............	—	—	†—	—	—	—	—	—	—	—	—	†—
113 Taxes on property.......................	3,629	2,908	†2,189	5,033	5,073	5,430	3,088	3,497	3,510	11,750	11,478	†11,130
114 Taxes on goods and services.............	25,271	26,196	†26,031	2,079	2,123	2,184	61	58	38	27,411	28,377	†28,252
1141 General taxes on goods and services..........	16,594	17,033	†16,857	—	—	—	—	—	—	16,594	17,033	†16,857
1142 Excises..............................	7,110	7,177	†6,924	—	—	—	—	—	—	7,110	7,177	†6,924
115 Taxes on int'l. trade and transactions........	1,045	1,024	†1,049	—	—	—	—	—	—	1,045	1,024	†1,049
116 Other taxes...........................	—	—	†—	—	—	—	—	—	21	—	—	†21
12 **Social contributions................................**	**48,603**	**32,391**	**†33,185**	**—**	**—**	**—**	**—**	**—**	**—**	**48,603**	**32,391**	**†33,185**
121 Social security contributions..................	48,603	32,391	†33,185	—	—	—	—	—	—	48,603	32,391	†33,185
122 Other social contributions...................	—	—	†—	—	—	—	—	—	—	—	—	†—
13 **Grants..**	**14,536**	**2,307**	**†2,350**	**19,307**	**20,513**	**19,475**	**7,286**	**7,487**	**7,262**	**1,204**	**1,725**	**†—**
131 From foreign governments...................	—	—	†—	726	1,231	—	478	494	—	1,204	1,725	†—
132 From international organizations..............	—	—	†—	—	—	—	—	—	—	—	—	†—
133 From other general government units...........	14,536	2,307	†2,350	18,581	19,282	19,475	6,808	6,993	7,262	—	—	†—
14 **Other revenue...............................**	**7,238**	**3,829**	**†7,035**	**12,705**	**12,516**	**13,441**	**13,923**	**13,829**	**15,039**	**33,866**	**30,174**	**†35,514**
Table 2 Expense by economic type												
2 **Expense..**	**107,684**	**79,991**	**†82,475**	**54,392**	**58,444**	**60,486**	**35,720**	**36,828**	**37,535**	**157,871**	**146,681**	**†151,409**
21 **Compensation of employees................**	**5,405**	**4,711**	**†6,050**	**21,794**	**23,415**	**24,379**	**15,495**	**15,944**	**17,040**	**42,694**	**44,070**	**†47,469**
211 Wages and salaries........................	4,567	3,388	†4,785	21,794	23,415	20,796	15,495	15,944	14,566	41,856	42,747	†40,148
212 Social contributions.......................	838	1,323	†1,265	—	—	3,583	—	—	2,474	838	1,323	†7,321
22 **Use of goods and services.....................**	**24,486**	**6,821**	**†7,350**	**6,999**	**7,652**	**7,916**	**8,539**	**8,906**	**9,056**	**40,024**	**23,379**	**†24,322**
23 **Consumption of fixed capital..............**	....	....	....	....	....	....	....	....	....	....	....	....
24 **Interest..**	**3,664**	**3,645**	**†3,901**	**2,341**	**2,253**	**2,065**	**2,093**	**2,000**	**1,889**	**8,098**	**7,898**	**†7,855**
25 **Subsidies.......................................**	**3,999**	**3,797**	**†4,200**	....	....	**8,458**	....	....	**2,409**	....	....	**†15,068**

In Millions of Francs / Year Ending December 31 / Cash Reporter

		Central Government			State Government			Local Government			General Government		
		2000	2001	2002	2000	2001	2002	2000	2001	2002	2000	2001	2002
26	Grants...................................	25,912	16,740	†17,441	....	....	9,642	....	....	4,374	....	....	†2,370
261	To foreign govenments.................	1,931	2,205	†492	....	....	—	....	....	—	....	....	†492
262	To international organizations........	—	—	†1,878	....	....	—	....	....	—	....	....	†1,878
263	To other general government units.......	23,981	14,535	†15,071	11,493	9,238	9,642	4,451	4,809	4,374	—	—	†—
2631	Current................................	21,459	12,049	†12,497	10,681	8,485	8,919	4,371	4,709	4,274	—	—	†—
2632	Capital................................	2,522	2,486	†2,574	812	753	724	80	100	100	—	—	†—
27	Social benefits........................	42,194	41,890	†39,397	....	....	—	....	....	—	....	....	†39,397
28	Other expense.........................	2,024	2,387	†4,136	....	....	8,026	....	....	2,767	....	....	†14,929
281	Property expense other than interest..........	—	—	†—	....	....	—	....	....	—	....	....	†—
282	Miscellaneous other expense...........	2,024	2,387	†4,136	....	....	8,026	....	....	2,767	....	....	†14,929
2821	Current................................	—	—	†2,684	....	....	6,864	....	....	2,573	....	....	†12,121
2822	Capital................................	2,024	2,387	†1,452	....	....	1,162	....	....	194	....	....	†2,808
Table 3 Transactions in assets and liabilities													
3	Change in net worth from transactns....	....	....	....	....	....	....	....	....	....	....	....	....
31	Net acquisition of nonfinancial assets...	265	389	†912	4,623	5,021	5,143	4,061	4,193	4,820	8,949	9,603	†10,876
311	Fixed assets...........................	111	244	†523	....	....	5,098	....	....	4,581	....	....	†10,202
3111	Buildings and structures...........	....	....		....	....		....	....		....	....	
3112	Machinery and equipment...........	....	....		....	....		....	....		....	....	
3113	Other fixed assets.................	....	....		....	....		....	....		....	....	
312	Inventories............................	−30	−81	†—	....	....	—	....	....	—	....	....	†—
313	Valuables..............................	—	—	†—	....	....	—	....	....	—	....	....	†—
314	Nonproduced assets....................	184	226	†390	....	....	45	....	....	239	....	....	†674
3141	Land..................................	....	....		....	....		....	....		....	....	
3142	Subsoil assets.......................	....	....		....	....		....	....		....	....	
3143	Other naturally occurring assets......	....	....		....	....		....	....		....	....	
3144	Intangible nonproduced assets.........	....	....		....	....		....	....		....	....	
32	Net acquisition of financial assets........	−2,722	−1,856	†−33	−840	−1,517	−401	185	27	38	−3,377	−3,346	†−396
321	Domestic...............................	−2,675	−1,780	†60	....	....	−401	....	....	38	....	....	†−304
3212	Currency and deposits...............	....	....		....	....		....	....		....	....	
3213	Securities other than shares........	....	....		....	....		....	....		....	....	
3214	Loans................................	....	....		....	....		....	....		....	....	
3215	Shares and other equity.............	....	....		....	....		....	....		....	....	
3216	Insurance technical reserves........	....	....		....	....		....	....		....	....	
3217	Financial derivatives................	....	....		....	....		....	....		....	....	
3218	Other accounts receivable...........	....	....		....	....		....	....		....	....	
322	Foreign................................	−47	−76	†−93	....	....	—	....	....	—	....	....	†−93
3222	Currency and deposits...............	....	....		....	....	—	....	....	—	....	....	
3223	Securities other than shares........	....	....		....	....	—	....	....	—	....	....	
3224	Loans................................	....	....		....	....	—	....	....	—	....	....	
3225	Shares and other equity.............	....	....		....	....	—	....	....	—	....	....	
3226	Insurance technical reserves........	....	....		....	....	—	....	....	—	....	....	
3227	Financial derivatives................	....	....		....	....		....	....		....	....	
3228	Other accounts receivable...........	....	....		....	....		....	....		....	....	
323	Monetary gold and SDRs..............	—	—	†—	—	—	—	—	—	—	—	—	†—
33	Net incurrence of liabilities...................	−11,945	−3,203	†−2,430	−2,687	−1,255	323	−1,469	−1,324	−1,103	−16,101	−5,782	†−3,210
331	Domestic...............................	−11,945	−3,203	†−2,430	−2,687	−1,255	323	−1,469	−1,324	−1,103	−16,101	−5,782	†−3,210
3312	Currency and deposits...............	....	....		....	....		....	....		....	....	
3313	Securities other than shares........	....	....		....	....		....	....		....	....	
3314	Loans................................	....	....		....	....		....	....		....	....	
3316	Insurance technical reserves........	....	....		....	....		....	....		....	....	
3317	Financial derivatives................	....	....		....	....		....	....		....	....	
3318	Other accounts payable..............	....	....		....	....		....	....		....	....	
332	Foreign................................	—	—	†—	—	—	—	—	—	—	—	—	†—
3322	Currency and deposits...............	—	—	†—	—	—	—	—	—	—	—	—	†—
3323	Securities other than shares........	—	—	†—	—	—	—	—	—	—	—	—	†—
3324	Loans................................	—	—	†—	—	—	—	—	—	—	—	—	†—
3326	Insurance technical reserves........	—	—	†—	—	—	—	—	—	—	—	—	†—
3327	Financial derivatives................	—	—	†—	—	—	—	—	—	—	—	—	†—
3328	Other accounts payable..............	....	....		....	....		....	....		....	....	

In Millions of Francs / Year Ending December 31 / Cash Reporter

	Central Government			State Government			Local Government			General Government		
	2000	2001	2002	2000	2001	2002	2000	2001	2002	2000	2001	2002
Table 4 Holding gains in assets and liabilities												
Table 5 Other changes in the volume of assets and liabilities												
Table 6 Balance sheet												
6 Net worth......	....	....	....	....	....	....	....	....	....	....	....	....
61 Nonfinancial assets......	....	....	....	....	....	....	....	....	....	....	....	....
611 Fixed assets......	....	....	....	....	....	....	....	....	....	....	....	....
6111 Buildings and structures......	....	....	....	....	....	....	....	....	....	....	....	....
6112 Machinery and equipment......	....	....	....	....	....	....	....	....	....	....	....	....
6113 Other fixed assets......	....	....	....	....	....	....	....	....	....	....	....	....
612 Inventories......	....	....	....	....	....	....	....	....	....	....	....	....
613 Valuables......	....	....	....	....	....	....	....	....	....	....	....	....
614 Nonproduced assets......	....	....	....	....	....	....	....	....	....	....	....	....
6141 Land......	....	....	....	....	....	....	....	....	....	....	....	....
6142 Subsoil assets......	....	....	....	....	....	....	....	....	....	....	....	....
6143 Other naturally occurring assets......	....	....	....	....	....	....	....	....	....	....	....	....
6144 Intangible nonproduced assets......	....	....	....	....	....	....	....	....	....	....	....	....
62 Financial assets......	....	....	....	....	....	....	....	....	....	....	....	....
621 Domestic......	....	....	....	....	....	....	....	....	....	....	....	....
6212 Currency and deposits......	....	....	....	....	....	....	....	....	....	....	....	....
6213 Securities other than shares......	....	....	....	....	....	....	....	....	....	....	....	....
6214 Loans......	....	....	....	....	....	....	....	....	....	....	....	....
6215 Shares and other equity......	....	....	....	....	....	....	....	....	....	....	....	....
6216 Insurance technical reserves......	....	....	....	....	....	....	....	....	....	....	....	....
6217 Financial derivatives......	....	....	....	....	....	....	....	....	....	....	....	....
6218 Other accounts receivable......	....	....	....	....	....	....	....	....	....	....	....	....
622 Foreign......	....	....	....	....	....	....	....	....	....	....	....	....
6222 Currency and deposits......	....	....	....	....	....	....	....	....	....	....	....	....
6223 Securities other than shares......	....	....	....	....	....	....	....	....	....	....	....	....
6224 Loans......	....	....	....	....	....	....	....	....	....	....	....	....
6225 Shares and other equity......	....	....	....	....	....	....	....	....	....	....	....	....
6226 Insurance technical reserves......	....	....	....	....	....	....	....	....	....	....	....	....
6227 Financial derivatives......	....	....	....	....	....	....	....	....	....	....	....	....
6228 Other accounts receivable......	....	....	....	....	....	....	....	....	....	....	....	....
623 Monetary gold and SDRs......	....	....	....	....	....	....	....	....	....	....	....	....
63 Liabilities......	108,108	106,813	122,923	64,261	69,161	73,408	38,000	38,000	38,500	210,369	213,974	234,831
631 Domestic......	108,108	106,813	122,923	64,261	69,161	73,408	38,000	38,000	38,500	210,369	213,974	234,831
6312 Currency and deposits......	....	....	....	....	....	....	....	....	....	....	....	....
6313 Securities other than shares......	....	....	....	....	....	....	....	....	....	....	....	....
6314 Loans......	....	....	....	....	....	....	....	....	....	....	....	....
6316 Insurance technical reserves......	....	....	....	....	....	....	....	....	....	....	....	....
6317 Financial derivatives......	....	....	....	....	....	....	....	....	....	....	....	....
6318 Other accounts payable......	....	....	....	....	....	....	....	....	....	....	....	....
632 Foreign......	—	—	—	—	—	—	—	—	—	—	—	—
6322 Currency and deposits......	—	—	—	—	—	—	—	—	—	—	—	—
6323 Securities other than shares......	—	—	—	—	—	—	—	—	—	—	—	—
6324 Loans......	—	—	—	—	—	—	—	—	—	—	—	—
6326 Insurance technical reserves......	—	—	—	—	—	—	—	—	—	—	—	—
6327 Financial derivatives......	—	—	—	—	—	—	—	—	—	—	—	—
6328 Other accounts payable......	....	....	....	....	....	....	....	....	....	....	....	....
Memorandum items:												
6M2 Net financial worth......	....	....	....	....	....	....	....	....	....	....	....	....
6M3 Debt at market value......	....	....	....	....	....	....	....	....	....	....	....	....
6M4 Debt at nominal value......	....	....	....	....	....	....	....	....	....	....	....	....
6M5 Arrears......	....	....	....	....	....	....	....	....	....	....	....	....
6M6 Obligations for social security benefits......	....	....	....	....	....	....	....	....	....	....	....	....
6M7 Contingent liabilities......	....	....	....	....	....	....	....	....	....	....	....	....
6M8 Uncapitalized military weapons, systems......	....	....	....	....	....	....	....	....	....	....	....	....
Table 7 Outlays by functions of govt.												
7 Total outlays......	108,024	80,498	†83,387	59,216	63,617	65,629	40,345	41,599	42,355	167,660	157,132	†162,285
701 General public services......	14,121	14,566	†14,932	6,957	7,360	7,324	6,367	6,627	6,671	....	....	†22,493
7017 Public debt transactions......	3,664	3,645	†3,901	2,341	2,253	2,065	2,093	2,000	1,889	8,098	7,898	†7,855
7018 General transfers between levels of govt......	....	....	†5,804	....	....	1,530	....	....	552			
702 Defense......	5,004	4,956	†4,782	285	258	245	249	238	231	....	....	†5,142
703 Public order and safety......	543	620	†710	4,830	5,007	5,209	1,833	1,897	1,966	....	....	†7,511

In Millions of Francs / Year Ending December 31 / Cash Reporter

	Central Government			State Government			Local Government			General Government		
	2000	2001	2002	2000	2001	2002	2000	2001	2002	2000	2001	2002
704 **Economic affairs**........................	11,137	11,749	†11,247	9,646	10,691	10,025	3,840	4,075	3,672	....	....	†18,465
7042 Agriculture, forestry, fishing, and hunting.....	3,929	4,114	†4,142	3,313	3,439	3,442	485	455	429	....	....	†5,086
7043 Fuel and energy.........................	192	216	†194	105	215	97	125	224	121	....	....	†404
7044 Mining, manufacturing, and construction.....	—	—	†410	—	—	498	—	—	101	....	....	†995
7045 Transport.............................	6,539	6,946	†6,424	5,776	6,034	5,989	2,898	3,006	3,021	....	....	†11,904
7046 Communication........................	477	473	†77	452	1,003	—	332	390	—	....	....	†77
705 **Environmental protection**......................	....	....	†218	....	....	644	....	....	2,492	....	....	†2,825
706 **Housing and community amenities**........	719	781	†486	1,273	1,320	719	3,320	3,320	1,040	....	....	†17,967
707 **Health**.................................	21,042	215	†230	9,834	11,021	11,814	7,393	7,737	8,141	....	....	†17,967
7072 Outpatient services......................	—	—	†—	....	....	215	....	....	183	....	....	†391
7073 Hospital services.......................	—	—	†10	....	....	11,049	....	....	7,677	....	....	†16,551
7074 Public health services...................	....	....	†220	....	....	551	....	....	280	....	....	†1,025
708 **Recreation, culture, and religion**..........	443	482	†506	1,236	1,297	1,335	2,107	2,191	2,280	....	....	†3,996
709 **Education**..............................	2,581	2,650	†3,267	14,640	15,569	16,470	9,282	9,663	9,755	....	....	†24,966
7091 Pre-primary and primary education.........	....	....	†47	....	....	6,535	....	....	9,154	....	....	†12,736
7092 Secondary education.....................	—	—	†524	....	....	5,910	....	....	585	....	....	†6,270
7094 Tertiary education......................	2,059	2,116	†2,696	....	....	4,025	....	....	15	....	....	†5,959
710 **Social protection**.........................	52,434	44,479	†47,010	10,515	11,094	11,844	5,954	5,851	6,108	....	....	†57,018
7 Statistical discrepancy: Total outlays............	—	—	†—	—	—	—	—	—	—	....	....	†—

Table 8 Transactions in financial assets and liabilities by sector

	2000	2001	2002	2000	2001	2002	2000	2001	2002	2000	2001	2002
82 **Net acquisition of financial assets**........	−2,722	−1,856	†−33	−840	−1,517	−402	185	27	38	−3,377	−3,346	†−396
821 Domestic.............................	−2,675	−1,780	†60	....	....	−402	....	....	38	....	....	†−304
8211 General government...................	−2,259	−2,455	....	12	22	....	....	....	....	....	....	....
8212 Central bank.........................	....	....	....	....	....	....	....	....	....	....	....	....
8213 Other depository corporations..................	....	....	....	....	....	....	....	....	....	....	....	....
8214 Financial corporations n.e.c.............	....	....	....	....	....	....	....	....	....	....	....	....
8215 Nonfinancial corporations...............	−288	−179	....	....	....	....	....	....	....	....	....	....
8216 Households & NPIs serving households......	....	....	....	....	....	....	....	....	....	....	....	....
822 Foreign.............................	−47	−76	†−93	....	....	—	....	....	—	....	....	†−93
8221 General government...................	....	....	....	....	....	—	....	....	—	....	....	....
8227 International organizations...............	....	....	....	....	....	—	....	....	—	....	....	....
8228 Financial corporations other than international organizations.................	....	....	....	....	....	—	....	....	—	....	....	....
8229 Other nonresidents.....................	....	....	....	....	....	—	....	....	—	....	....	....
823 Monetary gold and SDRs................	—	—	†—	—	—	—	—	—	—	—	—	†—
83 **Net incurrence of liabilities**..................	−11,945	−3,203	†−2,430	−2,687	−1,255	323	−1,469	−1,324	−1,103	−16,101	−5,782	†−3,210
831 Domestic.............................	−11,945	−3,203	†−2,430	−2,687	−1,255	323	−1,469	−1,324	−1,103	−16,101	−5,782	†−3,210
8311 General government...................	....	....	....	....	....	....	....	....	....	....	....	....
8312 Central bank.........................	....	....	....	....	....	....	....	....	....	....	....	....
8313 Other depository corporations..................	....	....	....	....	....	....	....	....	....	....	....	....
8314 Financial corporations n.e.c.............	....	....	....	....	....	....	....	....	....	....	....	....
8315 Nonfinancial corporations...............	....	....	....	....	....	....	....	....	....	....	....	....
8316 Households & NPIs serving households......	....	....	....	....	....	....	....	....	....	....	....	....
832 Foreign.............................	—	—	†—	—	—	—	—	—	—	—	—	†—
8321 General government...................	—	—	†—	—	—	—	—	—	—	—	—	†—
8327 International organizations...............	—	—	†—	—	—	—	—	—	—	—	—	†—
8328 Financial corporations other than international organizations.................	—	—	†—	—	—	—	—	—	—	—	—	†—
8329 Other nonresidents.....................	—	—	†—	—	—	—	—	—	—	—	—	†—

In Millions of Pounds / Year Ending December 31 / Cash Reporter

	Budgetary Central Government			Central Government			Local Government			General Government		
	1997	1998	1999	1997	1998	1999	1997	1998	1999	1997	1998	1999
Statement of government operations												
Statement of other economic flows												
Balance sheet												
Statement of sources and uses of cash												
1 Cash receipts from operating activities...........	....	....	....	179,995	180,411	196,096	....	....	....	....	....	....
11 Taxes..................	....	....	....	121,510	124,210	142,748	....	....	....	....	....	....
12 Social contributions................	....	....	....	512	595	531	....	....	....	....	....	....
13 Grants................	....	....	....	798	2	—	....	....	....	....	....	....
14 Other receipts..................	....	....	....	57,175	55,604	52,817	....	....	....	....	....	....
2 Cash payments for operating activities...........	....	....	....	....	....	....	....	....	....	....	....	....
21 Compensation of employees...............	....	....	....	....	....	....	....	....	....	....	....	....
22 Purchases of goods and services..................	....	....	....	....	....	....	....	....	....	....	....	....
24 Interest................	....	....	....	....	....	....	....	....	....	....	....	....
25 Subsidies..................	....	....	....	....	....	....	....	....	....	....	....	....
26 Grants..................	....	....	....	....	....	....	....	....	....	....	....	....
27 Social benefits..................	....	....	....	....	....	....	....	....	....	....	....	....
28 Other payments..................	....	....	....	....	....	....	....	....	....	....	....	....
CIO *Net cash inflow from oper. activities.....*	....	....		....	....		....	....	....	....	....	....
31.1 Purchases of nonfinancial assets..................	....	....	....	....	....		....	....	....	....	....	....
31.2 Sales of nonfinancial assets........................	....	....	....	5	28	31	....	....	....	....	....	....
31 Net cash outflow from investments in nonfinancial assets........................	....	....	....	....	....	....	....	....	....	....	....	....
CSD *Cash surplus/deficit........................*	....	....	....	*−1,723*	*−5,534*	*5,827*	....	....	....	....	....	....
32x Net acquisition of fin assets, excl. cash...........	—	—	—				....	....	....	....	....	....
321x Domestic........................	....	....	....	—	—	—	....	....	....	....	....	....
322x Foreign..........................	—	—	—				....	....	....	....	....	....
323 Monetary gold and SDRs........................	—	—	—				....	....	....	....	....	....
33 Net incurrence of liabilities........................	....	....	....	....	....	....	....	....	....	....	....	....
331 Domestic..................	....	....	....	....	....	....	....	....	....	....	....	....
332 Foreign........................	....	....	....	....	....	....	....	....	....	....	....	....
NFB Net cash inflow from fin. activities................	....	....	....	....	....	....	....	....	....	....	....	....
NCB *Net change in the stock of cash.............*	....	....	....	....	....	....	....	....	....	....	....	....
Table 1 Revenue												
1 **Revenue........................**	....	....	....	**179,995**	**180,411**	**196,096**	....	....	....	....	....	....
11 **Taxes........................**	....	....	....	**121,510**	**124,210**	**142,748**	....	....	....	....	....	....
111 Taxes on income, profits, & capital gains......	....	....	....	54,034	60,700	73,537	....	....	....	....	....	....
1111 Individuals..................	....	....	....	....	60,700	73,537	....	....	....	....	....	....
1112 Corporations and other enterprises...........	....	....	....	....			....	....	....	....	....	....
112 Taxes on payroll and workforce..................	....	....	....	5,063	5,403	6,045	....	....	....	....	....	....
113 Taxes on property..................	....	....	....	1,767	1,711	2,011	....	....	....	....	....	....
114 Taxes on goods and services........................	....	....	....	37,132	30,537	37,426	....	....	....	....	....	....
1141 General taxes on goods and services..........	....	....	....	—	—	—	....	....	....	....	....	....
1142 Excises..................	....	....	....	2,138	2,110	2,301	....	....	....	....	....	....
115 Taxes on int'l. trade and transactions..........	....	....	....	18,971	21,254	19,344	....	....	....	....	....	....
116 Other taxes..................	....	....	....	4,543	4,605	4,385	....	....	....	....	....	....
12 **Social contributions........................**	....	....	....	**512**	**595**	**531**	....	....	....	....	....	....
121 Social security contributions........................	....	....	....	—	—	—	....	....	....	....	....	....
122 Other social contributions........................	....	....	....	512	595	531	....	....	....	....	....	....
13 **Grants........................**	....	....	....	**798**	**2**	**—**	....	....	....	....	....	....
131 From foreign governments........................	....	....	....	....	....	—	....	....	....	....	....	....
132 From international organizations..................	....	....	....	....	....	—	....	....	....	....	....	....
133 From other general government units..........	....	....	....	....	....	—	....	....	....	....	....	....
14 **Other revenue........................**	....	....	....	57,175	55,604	52,817	....	....	....	....	....	....

	Budgetary Central Government			Central Government			Local Government			General Government		
	1997	1998	1999	1997	1998	1999	1997	1998	1999	1997	1998	1999
Table 2 Expense by economic type												
Table 3 Transactions in assets and liabilities												
Table 4 Holding gains in assets and liabilities												
Table 5 Other changes in the volume of assets and liabilities												
Table 6 Balance sheet												
Table 7 Outlays by functions of govt.												
7 **Total outlays**..................	....	....	....	181,723	185,973	190,300	....	....	....	....	....	....
701 **General public services**..........	....	....	....	22,577	24,179	24,559	....	....	....	....	....	....
7017 Public debt transactions..........	....	....	....	....	....	....	....	....	....	....	....	....
7018 General transfers between levels of govt......	....	....	....	....	....	....	....	....	....	....	....	....
702 **Defense**..........	....	....	....	42,842	46,064	44,984	....	....	....	....	....	....
703 **Public order and safety**..........	....	....	....	—	—	—	....	....	....	....	....	....
704 **Economic affairs**..........	....	....	....	83,709	74,950	83,810	....	....	....	....	....	....
7042 Agriculture, forestry, fishing, and hunting.....	....	....	....	17,616	16,811	14,278	....	....	....	....	....	....
7043 Fuel and energy..........	....	....	....	21,302	17,009	13,613	....	....	....	....	....	....
7044 Mining, manufacturing, and construction.....	....	....	....	2,794	6,368	8,000	....	....	....	....	....	....
7045 Transport..........	....	....	....	4,766	7,813	6,343	....	....	....	....	....	....
7046 Communication..........	....	....	....	....	....	....	....	....	....	....	....	....
705 **Environmental protection**..........	....	....	....	....	....	....	....	....	....	....	....	....
706 **Housing and community amenities**........	....	....	....	3,112	3,221	1,910	....	....	....	....	....	....
707 **Health**..........	....	....	....	4,980	5,125	4,459	....	....	....	....	....	....
7072 Outpatient services..........	....	....	....	—	—	—	....	....	....	....	....	....
7073 Hospital services..........	....	....	....	3,090	3,514	3,033	....	....	....	....	....	....
7074 Public health services..........	....	....	....	....	....	....	....	....	....	....	....	....
708 **Recreation, culture, and religion**..........	....	....	....	2,770	3,334	2,937	....	....	....	....	....	....
709 **Education**..........	....	....	....	16,761	18,969	17,533	....	....	....	....	....	....
7091 Pre-primary and primary education..........	....	....	....	....	....	....	....	....	....	....	....	....
7092 Secondary education..........	....	....	....	10,251	11,969	11,295	....	....	....	....	....	....
7094 Tertiary education..........	....	....	....	4,174	4,354	4,002	....	....	....	....	....	....
710 **Social protection**..........	....	....	....	4,972	10,131	10,108	....	....	....	....	....	....
7 Statistical discrepancy: Total outlays..........	....	....	....	—	—	—	....	....	....	....	....	....
Table 8 Transactions in financial assets and liabilities by sector												

In Millions of Somoni / Year Ending December 31 / Cash Reporter

	Budgetary Central Government			Central Government			Local Government			General Government		
	2002	2003	2004	2002	2003	2004	2002	2003	2004	2002	2003	2004
Statement of government operations												
Statement of other economic flows												
Balance sheet												
Statement of sources and uses of cash												
1 Cash receipts from operating activities......	....	561.27	761.54	....	640.89	870.16	....	183.46	234.21	....	824.35	1,104.37
11 Taxes......	....	461.96	605.69	....	461.96	605.69	....	149.08	174.79	....	611.04	780.48
12 Social contributions......	....	—	—	....	79.62	108.62	....	—	—	....	79.62	108.62
13 Grants......	....	14.61	40.60	....	14.61	40.60	....	—	—	....	14.61	40.60
14 Other receipts......	....	84.70	115.25	....	84.70	115.25	....	34.39	59.42	....	119.09	174.67
2 Cash payments for operating activities......	....	454.61	744.88	....	531.78	847.85	....	240.41	324.66	....	772.18	1,172.51
21 Compensation of employees......	....	58.43	78.11	....	59.13	79.11	....	98.38	127.63	....	157.50	206.74
22 Purchases of goods and services......	....	173.69	237.39	....	176.20	243.80	....	74.66	101.17	....	250.86	344.98
24 Interest......	....	59.05	44.31	....	59.05	44.31	....	—	—	....	59.05	44.31
25 Subsidies......	....	90.44	126.03	....	90.44	126.03	....	13.39	3.80	....	103.83	129.83
26 Grants......	....	—	—	....	—	—	....	....	....	....	—	—
27 Social benefits......	....	16.82	7.56	....	90.77	103.11	....	7.56	9.83	....	98.33	112.95
28 Other payments......	....	56.19	251.49	....	56.19	251.49	....	46.43	82.22	....	102.61	333.71
CIO *Net cash inflow from oper. activities.....*	....	....	....	....	*109.12*	*22.31*	....	....	....	....	*52.17*	*−68.14*
31.1 Purchases of nonfinancial assets......	....	326.83	430.18	....	326.83	430.18	....	224.50	319.37	....	551.32	749.56
31.2 Sales of nonfinancial assets......	....	—	—	....	....	....	....	....	....	....	—	—
31 Net cash outflow from investments in nonfinancial assets......	....	326.83	430.18	....	326.83	430.18	....	224.50	319.37	....	551.32	749.56
CSD *Cash surplus/deficit...............*	....	....	....	....	*−217.71*	*−407.87*	....	....	....	....	*−499.15*	*−817.69*
32x Net acquisition of fin assets, excl. cash......	....	....	....	....	....	....	....	....	....	....	....	....
321x Domestic......	....	....	....	....	....	....	....	....	....	....	....	....
322x Foreign......	....	....	....	....	....	....	....	....	....	....	....	....
323 Monetary gold and SDRs......	....	....	....	....	....	....	....	....	....	....	....	....
33 Net incurrence of liabilities......	....	....	....	....	....	....	....	....	....	....	....	....
331 Domestic......	....	....	....	....	....	....	....	....	....	....	....	....
332 Foreign......	....	....	....	....	....	....	....	....	....	....	....	....
NFB Net cash inflow from fin. activities......	....	....	....	....	....	....	....	....	....	....	....	....
NCB *Net change in the stock of cash............*	....	....	....	....	....	....	....	....	....	....	....	....

Table 1   Revenue

	Budgetary Central Government			Central Government			Local Government			General Government		
	2002	2003	2004	2002	2003	2004	2002	2003	2004	2002	2003	2004
1 **Revenue......**	....	**561.27**	**761.54**	....	**640.89**	**870.16**	....	**183.46**	**234.21**	....	**824.35**	**1,104.37**
11 **Taxes......**	....	**461.96**	**605.69**	....	**461.96**	**605.69**	....	**149.08**	**174.79**	....	**611.04**	**780.48**
111 Taxes on income, profits, & capital gains......	....	14.16	27.10	....	14.16	27.10	....	61.05	78.01	....	75.21	105.11
1111 Individuals......	....	3.73	4.96	....	3.73	4.96	....	47.27	63.67	....	51.00	68.63
1112 Corporations and other enterprises......	....	10.44	22.13	....	10.44	22.13	....	13.78	14.34	....	24.21	36.48
112 Taxes on payroll and workforce......	....	—	—	....	—	—	....	—	—	....	—	—
113 Taxes on property......	....	7.63	9.64	....	7.63	9.64	....	4.27	5.36	....	11.90	15.01
114 Taxes on goods and services......	....	367.69	470.67	....	367.69	470.67	....	83.76	91.41	....	451.44	562.08
1141 General taxes on goods and services......	....	302.87	393.73	....	302.87	393.73	....	45.16	61.94	....	348.04	455.67
1142 Excises......	....	48.09	57.31	....	48.09	57.31	....	.70	—	....	48.79	57.31
115 Taxes on int'l. trade and transactions......	....	72.49	96.57	....	72.49	96.57	....	—	—	....	72.49	96.57
116 Other taxes......	....	—	1.71	....	—	1.71	....	—	—	....	—	1.71
12 **Social contributions......**	....	—	—	....	**79.62**	**108.62**	....	—	—	....	**79.62**	**108.62**
121 Social security contributions......	....	—	—	....	79.62	108.62	....	—	—	....	79.62	108.62
122 Other social contributions......	....	—	—	....	—	—	....	—	—	....	—	—
13 **Grants......**	....	**14.61**	**40.60**	....	**14.61**	**40.60**	....	—	—	....	**14.61**	**40.60**
131 From foreign governments......	....	14.61	40.60	....	14.61	40.60	....	—	—	....	14.61	40.60
132 From international organizations......	....	—	—	....	—	—	....	—	—	....	—	—
133 From other general government units......	....	—	—	....	—	—	....	—	—	....	—	—
14 **Other revenue......**	....	**84.70**	**115.25**	....	**84.70**	**115.25**	....	**34.39**	**59.42**	....	**119.09**	**174.67**

Table 2   Expense by economic type

	Budgetary Central Government			Central Government			Local Government			General Government		
	2002	2003	2004	2002	2003	2004	2002	2003	2004	2002	2003	2004
2 **Expense......**	....	**454.61**	**744.88**	....	**531.78**	**847.85**	....	**240.41**	**324.66**	....	**772.18**	**1,172.51**
21 **Compensation of employees......**	....	**58.43**	**78.11**	....	**59.13**	**79.11**	....	**98.38**	**127.63**	....	**157.50**	**206.74**
211 Wages and salaries......	....	52.58	70.46	....	53.18	71.26	....	79.71	103.46	....	132.88	174.72
212 Social contributions......	....	5.85	7.65	....	5.95	7.85	....	18.67	24.17	....	24.62	32.02
22 **Use of goods and services......**	....	**173.69**	**237.39**	....	**176.20**	**243.80**	....	**74.66**	**101.17**	....	**250.86**	**344.98**
23 **Consumption of fixed capital......**	....	....	....	....	....	....	....	....	....	....	....	....
24 **Interest......**	....	**59.05**	**44.31**	....	**59.05**	**44.31**	....	—	—	....	**59.05**	**44.31**
25 **Subsidies......**	....	**90.44**	**126.03**	....	**90.44**	**126.03**	....	**13.39**	**3.80**	....	**103.83**	**129.83**

		Budgetary Central Government			Central Government			Local Government			General Government		
		2002	2003	2004	2002	2003	2004	2002	2003	2004	2002	2003	2004
26	**Grants**.....................................	....	—	—	....	—	—	....	—	—	....	—	—
261	To foreign govenments...................	....	—	—	....	—	—	....	—	—	....	—	—
262	To international organizations...........	....	—	—	....	—	—	....	—	—	....	—	—
263	To other general government units..............	....	—	—	....	—	—	....	—	—	....	—	—
2631	Current................................	....	—	—	....	—	—	....	—	—	....	—	—
2632	Capital.................................	....	—	—	....	—	—	....	—	—	....	—	—
27	**Social benefits**..........................	....	16.82	7.56	....	90.77	103.11	....	7.56	9.83	....	98.33	112.95
28	**Other expense**...........................	....	56.19	251.49	....	56.19	251.49	....	46.43	82.22	....	102.61	333.71
281	Property expense other than interest............	....	—	—	....	—	—	....	—	—	....	—	—
282	Miscellaneous other expense............	....	56.19	251.49	....	56.19	251.49	....	46.43	82.22	....	102.61	333.71
2821	Current................................	....	....	....	....	....	....	....	....	....	....	....	....
2822	Capital.................................	....	....	....	....	....	....	....	....	....	....	....	....

Table 3   Transactions in assets and liabilities

		Budgetary Central Government			Central Government			Local Government			General Government		
		2002	2003	2004	2002	2003	2004	2002	2003	2004	2002	2003	2004
3	**Change in net worth from transactns....**	....	....	....	....	....	....	....	....	....	....	....	....
31	**Net acquisition of nonfinancial assets...**	....	326.83	430.18	....	326.83	430.18	....	224.50	319.37	....	551.32	749.56
311	Fixed assets..............................	....	192.15	430.18	....	192.15	430.18	....	224.50	319.37	....	416.65	749.56
3111	Buildings and structures..............	....	108.38	125.78	....	108.38	125.78	....	183.00	319.37	....	291.38	445.15
3112	Machinery and equipment...........	....	72.27	120.51	....	72.27	120.51	....	41.50	—	....	113.77	120.51
3113	Other fixed assets....................	....	11.49	183.90	....	11.49	183.90	....	—	—	....	11.49	183.90
312	Inventories...............................	....	—	—	....	—	—	....	—	—	....	—	—
313	Valuables................................	....	—	—	....	—	—	....	—	—	....	—	—
314	Nonproduced assets...................	....	134.68	—	....	134.68	—	....	—	—	....	134.68	—
3141	Land...................................	....	....	—	....	....	—	....	....	—	....	....	—
3142	Subsoil assets.........................	....	....	—	....	....	—	....	....	—	....	....	—
3143	Other naturally occurring assets.........	....	....	—	....	....	—	....	....	—	....	....	—
3144	Intangible nonproduced assets.......	....	....	—	....	....	—	....	....	—	....	....	—
32	**Net acquisition of financial assets........**	....	....	....	....	....	....	....	....	....	....	....	....
321	Domestic.................................	....	....	....	....	....	....	....	....	....	....	....	....
3212	Currency and deposits...............	....	....	....	....	....	....	....	....	....	....	....	....
3213	Securities other than shares........	....	....	....	....	....	....	....	....	....	....	....	....
3214	Loans..................................	....	....	....	....	....	....	....	....	....	....	....	....
3215	Shares and other equity..............	....	....	....	....	....	....	....	....	....	....	....	....
3216	Insurance technical reserves.........	....	....	....	....	....	....	....	....	....	....	....	....
3217	Financial derivatives..................	....	....	....	....	....	....	....	....	....	....	....	....
3218	Other accounts receivable...........	....	....	....	....	....	....	....	....	....	....	....	....
322	Foreign..................................	....	....	....	....	....	....	....	....	....	....	....	....
3222	Currency and deposits...............	....	....	....	....	....	....	....	....	....	....	....	....
3223	Securities other than shares........	....	....	....	....	....	....	....	....	....	....	....	....
3224	Loans..................................	....	....	....	....	....	....	....	....	....	....	....	....
3225	Shares and other equity..............	....	....	....	....	....	....	....	....	....	....	....	....
3226	Insurance technical reserves.........	....	....	....	....	....	....	....	....	....	....	....	....
3227	Financial derivatives..................	....	....	....	....	....	....	....	....	....	....	....	....
3228	Other accounts receivable...........	....	....	....	....	....	....	....	....	....	....	....	....
323	Monetary gold and SDRs.............	....	....	....	....	....	....	....	....	....	....	....	....
33	**Net incurrence of liabilities...................**	....	....	....	....	....	....	....	....	....	....	....	....
331	Domestic.................................	....	....	....	....	....	....	....	....	....	....	....	....
3312	Currency and deposits...............	....	....	....	....	....	....	....	....	....	....	....	....
3313	Securities other than shares........	....	....	....	....	....	....	....	....	....	....	....	....
3314	Loans..................................	....	....	....	....	....	....	....	....	....	....	....	....
3316	Insurance technical reserves.........	....	....	....	....	....	....	....	....	....	....	....	....
3317	Financial derivatives..................	....	....	....	....	....	....	....	....	....	....	....	....
3318	Other accounts payable..............	....	....	....	....	....	....	....	....	....	....	....	....
332	Foreign..................................	....	....	....	....	....	....	....	....	....	....	....	....
3322	Currency and deposits...............	....	....	....	....	....	....	....	....	....	....	....	....
3323	Securities other than shares........	....	....	....	....	....	....	....	....	....	....	....	....
3324	Loans..................................	....	....	....	....	....	....	....	....	....	....	....	....
3326	Insurance technical reserves.........	....	....	....	....	....	....	....	....	....	....	....	....
3327	Financial derivatives..................	....	....	....	....	....	....	....	....	....	....	....	....
3328	Other accounts payable..............	....	....	....	....	....	....	....	....	....	....	....	....

	Budgetary Central Government			Central Government			Local Government			General Government		
	2002	2003	2004	2002	2003	2004	2002	2003	2004	2002	2003	2004
Table 4 Holding gains in assets and liabilities												
Table 5 Other changes in the volume of assets and liabilities												
Table 6 Balance sheet												
Table 7 Outlays by functions of govt.												
7 Total outlays................................	....	781.43	1,175.07	....	858.60	1,278.03	....	464.91	644.03	....	1,323.51	1,922.06
701 **General public services**........................	....	....	....	....	....	....	....	....	....	....	....	....
7017 Public debt transactions............................	....	59.05	44.31	....	59.05	44.31	....	—	—	....	59.05	44.31
7018 General transfers between levels of govt......	....	....	....	....	....	....	....	....	....	....	....	....
702 **Defense**...	....	....	....	....	....	....	....	....	....	....	....	....
703 **Public order and safety**........................	....	....	....	....	....	....	....	....	....	....	....	....
704 **Economic affairs**................................	....	....	....	....	....	....	....	....	....	....	....	....
7042 Agriculture, forestry, fishing, and hunting.....	....	....	....	....	....	....	....	....	....	....	....	....
7043 Fuel and energy..	....	....	....	....	....	....	....	....	....	....	....	....
7044 Mining, manufacturing, and construction.....	....	....	....	....	....	....	....	....	....	....	....	....
7045 Transport...	....	....	....	....	....	....	....	....	....	....	....	....
7046 Communication...	....	....	....	....	....	....	....	....	....	....	....	....
705 **Environmental protection**......................	....	....	....	....	....	....	....	....	....	....	....	....
706 **Housing and community amenities**........	....	....	....	....	....	....	....	....	....	....	....	....
707 **Health**...	....	....	....	....	....	....	....	....	....	....	....	....
7072 Outpatient services..................................	....	....	....	....	....	....	....	....	....	....	....	....
7073 Hospital services......................................	....	....	....	....	....	....	....	....	....	....	....	....
7074 Public health services...............................	....	....	....	....	....	....	....	....	....	....	....	....
708 **Recreation, culture, and religion**............	....	....	....	....	....	....	....	....	....	....	....	....
709 **Education**...	....	....	....	....	....	....	....	....	....	....	....	....
7091 Pre-primary and primary education............	....	....	....	....	....	....	....	....	....	....	....	....
7092 Secondary education................................	....	....	....	....	....	....	....	....	....	....	....	....
7094 Tertiary education....................................	....	....	....	....	....	....	....	....	....	....	....	....
710 **Social protection**...................................	....	....	....	....	....	....	....	....	....	....	....	....
7 Statistical discrepancy: Total outlays..............	....	....	....	....	....	....	....	....	....	....	....	....
Table 8 Transactions in financial assets and liabilities by sector												

Thailand 578

In Billions of Baht / Year Ending September 30 / Noncash Reporter

		Budgetary Central Government			Central Government			Local Government			General Government		
		2002	2003	2004p	2002	2003	2004p	2002	2003	2004p	2002	2003	2004p
Statement of government operations													
1	Revenue.........	....	1,045.6	1,168.7	....	1,159.2	1,275.1	....	183.9	225.3	....	1,250.0	1,381.1
2	Expense.........	....	921.1	1,084.5	....	938.4	1,114.5	....	70.6	109.8	....	915.9	1,105.0
GOB	*Gross operating balance......*	....	*124.5*	*84.2*	....	*221.1*	*161.1*	....	*113.3*	*115.5*	....	*334.5*	*276.5*
NOB	*Net operating balance......*	....	....	....	....	....	....	....	....	....	....	....	....
31	Net acquisition of nonfinancial assets.....	....	120.3	112.1	....	133.3	124.6	....	78.8	76.8	....	212.1	201.4
NLB	*Net lending/borrowing......*	....	*4.1*	*−27.9*	....	*87.5*	*36.1*	....	*34.5*	*38.7*	....	*122.0*	*74.8*
32	Net acquisition of financial assets.....	....	11.4	149.0	....	104.3	279.5	....	35.6	39.2	....	139.9	318.7
33	Net incurrence of liabilities.....	....	7.3	177.0	....	16.8	243.4	....	1.1	.5	....	17.9	243.9
NLB	Statistical discrepancy.....	....	—	—	....	—	—	....	—	—	....	—	—
Statement of other economic flows													
Balance sheet													
6	*Net worth......*	....	....	....	....	....	....	....	....	....	....	....	....
61	Nonfinancial assets.....	....	....	....	....	....	....	....	....	....	....	....	....
62	Financial assets.....	....	....	....	....	....	....	....	....	....	....	....	....
63	Liabilities.....	1,670.5	1,651.6	1,639.6	1,734.9	1,708.6	1,696.6	....	....	....	....	....	....
Statement of sources and uses of cash													
1	Cash receipts from operating activities.....	871.7	1,045.6	1,168.7	937.6	....	....	165.0	183.9	225.3	1,015.2	....	....
11	Taxes.....	763.8	897.6	1,023.6	777.2	....	....	69.9	83.0	97.7	847.0	....	....
12	Social contributions.....	—	—	—	30.2	....	....	—	—	—	30.2	....	....
13	Grants.....	3.1	2.5	2.2	3.1	....	....	87.5	93.1	119.3	3.1	....	....
14	Other receipts.....	104.8	145.5	142.9	127.2	....	....	7.7	7.8	8.2	134.8	....	....
2	Cash payments for operating activities.....	1,155.0	921.1	1,084.5	1,165.0	....	....	64.1	70.6	109.8	1,141.6	....	....
21	Compensation of employees.....	306.8	328.1	354.1	308.5	....	....	19.3	21.3	34.6	327.8	....	....
22	Purchases of goods and services.....	186.4	211.0	214.6	223.7	....	....	35.3	38.7	63.8	259.0	....	....
24	Interest.....	69.0	65.1	84.4	71.6	....	....	—	—	—	71.6	....	....
25	Subsidies.....	35.4	29.6	27.4	43.8	....	....	—	—	—	43.8	....	....
26	Grants.....	171.3	177.9	208.5	91.3	....	....	—	—	—	3.8	....	....
27	Social benefits.....	67.7	70.9	124.4	81.6	....	....	1.9	1.9	1.5	83.5	....	....
28	Other payments.....	318.4	38.5	71.0	344.4	....	....	7.6	8.7	9.9	352.1	....	....
CIO	*Net cash inflow from oper. activities.....*	*−283.3*	*124.5*	*84.2*	*−227.3*	....	....	*100.9*	*113.3*	*115.5*	*−126.4*	....	....
31.1	Purchases of nonfinancial assets.....	156.4	120.4	112.3	164.2	....	....	68.9	78.8	76.8	233.1	....	....
31.2	Sales of nonfinancial assets.....	.1	.1	.2	.1	....	....	—	—	—	.1	....	....
31	Net cash outflow from investments in nonfinancial assets.....	156.3	120.3	112.1	164.1	....	....	68.9	78.8	76.8	233.0	....	....
CSD	*Cash surplus/deficit.....*	*−439.6*	*4.1*	*−27.9*	*−391.4*	....	....	*32.1*	*34.5*	*38.7*	*−359.4*	....	....
32x	Net acquisition of fin assets, excl. cash.....	−16.6	−2.8	−43.0	36.5	....	....	—	—	—	36.5	....	....
321x	Domestic.....	−16.6	−2.8	−43.0	36.5	....	....	—	—	—	36.5	....	....
322x	Foreign.....	—	—	—	—	....	....	—	—	—	—	....	....
323	Monetary gold and SDRs.....	—	—	—	—	....	....	—	—	—	—	....	....
33	Net incurrence of liabilities.....	375.7	7.3	177.0	387.8	....	....	3.5	1.1	.5	391.3	....	....
331	Domestic.....	436.8	41.2	195.2	448.9	....	....	3.5	1.1	.5	452.4	....	....
332	Foreign.....	−61.1	−33.9	−18.2	−61.1	....	....	—	—	—	−61.1	....	....
NFB	Net cash inflow from fin. activities.....	392.4	10.0	220.0	351.3	....	....	3.5	1.1	.5	354.8	....	....
NCB	*Net change in the stock of cash.....*	*−47.3*	*14.2*	*192.1*	*−40.1*	....	....	*35.6*	*35.6*	*39.2*	*−4.5*	....	....
Table 1 Revenue													
1	**Revenue......**	**871.7**	**1,045.6**	**1,168.7**	**937.6**	**†1,159.2**	**1,275.1**	**165.0**	**183.9**	**225.3**	**1,015.2**	**†1,250.0**	**1,381.1**
11	**Taxes......**	**763.8**	**897.6**	**1,023.6**	**777.2**	**†914.8**	**1,032.9**	**69.9**	**83.0**	**97.7**	**847.0**	**†997.8**	**1,130.7**
111	Taxes on income, profits, & capital gains......	279.3	332.6	407.9	279.3	†332.6	407.9	—	—	—	279.3	†332.6	407.9
1111	Individuals.....	103.2	111.4	128.7	103.2	†111.4	128.7	—	—	—	103.2	†111.4	128.7
1112	Corporations and other enterprises.....	176.1	221.2	279.2	176.1	†221.2	279.2	—	—	—	176.1	†221.2	279.2
112	Taxes on payroll and workforce.....	—	—	—	—	†—	—	—	—	—	—	†—	—
113	Taxes on property.....	.3	.3	.4	.3	†.3	.4	18.9	22.4	28.6	19.2	†22.7	29.0
114	Taxes on goods and services.....	384.8	449.3	505.0	396.1	†463.9	510.8	51.0	60.5	69.1	447.0	†524.5	579.9
1141	General taxes on goods and services.....	169.7	196.0	229.1	169.7	†196.0	229.1	21.8	24.5	26.9	191.5	†220.4	255.9
1142	Excises.....	205.7	237.1	259.2	217.0	†251.7	265.1	17.6	20.1	25.1	234.5	†271.7	290.2
115	Taxes on int'l. trade and transactions.....	95.4	110.0	103.6	97.5	†112.7	107.1	—	—	—	97.5	†112.7	107.1
116	Other taxes.....	4.0	5.3	6.7	4.0	†5.3	6.7	—	—	—	4.0	†5.3	6.7
12	**Social contributions......**	**—**	**—**	**—**	**30.2**	**†46.0**	**62.0**	**—**	**—**	**—**	**30.2**	**†46.0**	**62.0**
121	Social security contributions.....	—	—	—	30.2	†42.1	57.8	—	—	—	30.2	†42.1	57.8
122	Other social contributions.....	—	—	—	—	†3.9	4.2	—	—	—	—	†3.9	4.2
13	**Grants......**	**3.1**	**2.5**	**2.2**	**3.1**	**†2.5**	**2.2**	**87.5**	**93.1**	**119.3**	**3.1**	**†2.5**	**2.2**
131	From foreign governments.....	3.1	2.4	2.2	3.1	†2.4	2.2	—	—	—	3.1	†2.4	2.2
132	From international organizations.....	—	.2	—	—	†.2	—	—	—	—	—	†.2	—
133	From other general government units.....	—	—	—	—	†—	—	87.5	93.1	119.3	—	†—	—
14	**Other revenue......**	**104.8**	**145.5**	**142.9**	**127.2**	**†195.8**	**178.0**	**7.7**	**7.8**	**8.2**	**134.8**	**†203.6**	**186.2**

Thailand 578

In Billions of Baht / Year Ending September 30 / Noncash Reporter

Table 2 Expense by economic type

	Budgetary Central Government			Central Government			Local Government			General Government		
	2002	2003	2004p	2002	2003	2004p	2002	2003	2004p	2002	2003	2004p
2 **Expense**	**1,155.0**	**921.1**	**1,084.5**	**1,165.0**	**†938.4**	**1,114.5**	**64.1**	**70.6**	**109.8**	**1,141.6**	**†915.9**	**1,105.0**
21 **Compensation of employees**	**306.8**	**328.1**	**354.1**	**308.5**	**†330.1**	**357.9**	**19.3**	**21.3**	**34.6**	**327.8**	**†351.4**	**392.6**
211 Wages and salaries	306.8	328.1	354.1	308.5	†330.1	356.4	19.3	21.3	34.6	327.8	†351.4	391.1
212 Social contributions	—	—	—	—	†—	1.5	—	—	—	—	†—	1.5
22 **Use of goods and services**	**186.4**	**211.0**	**214.6**	**223.7**	**†257.9**	**229.1**	**35.3**	**38.7**	**63.8**	**259.0**	**†296.5**	**292.9**
23 **Consumption of fixed capital**	....	....	....	....	....	....	....	....	....	....	....	....
24 **Interest**	**69.0**	**65.1**	**84.4**	**71.6**	**†67.6**	**85.1**	—	—	—	**71.6**	**†67.6**	**85.1**
25 **Subsidies**	**35.4**	**29.6**	**27.4**	**43.8**	**†46.5**	**67.7**	—	—	—	**43.8**	**†46.5**	**67.7**
26 **Grants**	**171.3**	**177.9**	**208.5**	**91.3**	**†94.7**	**120.9**	—	—	—	**3.8**	**†1.6**	**1.6**
261 To foreign governments	3.8	1.6	1.7	3.8	†1.6	1.7	—	—	—	3.8	†1.6	1.7
262 To international organizations	—	—	—	—	†—	—	—	—	—	—	†—	—
263 To other general government units	167.5	176.3	207.0	87.5	†93.1	119.3	—	—	—	—	†—	—
2631 Current	105.2	136.0	105.5	39.4	†63.9	57.0	—	—	—	—	†—	—
2632 Capital	62.3	40.3	101.5	48.1	†29.2	62.4	—	—	—	—	†—	—
27 **Social benefits**	**67.7**	**70.9**	**124.4**	**81.6**	**†86.2**	**178.3**	**1.9**	**1.9**	**1.5**	**83.5**	**†88.1**	**179.8**
28 **Other expense**	**318.4**	**38.5**	**71.0**	**344.4**	**†55.1**	**75.0**	**7.6**	**8.7**	**9.9**	**352.1**	**†63.8**	**85.0**
281 Property expense other than interest	—	—	.1	—	†—	.1	—	—	—	—	†—	.1
282 Miscellaneous other expense	318.4	38.5	71.0	344.4	†55.1	75.0	7.6	8.7	9.9	352.1	†63.8	84.9
2821 Current	25.6	27.7	42.5	25.6	†27.9	43.0	7.6	8.7	9.9	33.2	†36.6	52.9
2822 Capital	292.9	10.8	28.5	318.8	†27.2	32.0	—	—	—	318.8	†27.2	32.0

Table 3 Transactions in assets and liabilities

	Budgetary Central Government			Central Government			Local Government			General Government		
	2002	2003	2004p	2002	2003	2004p	2002	2003	2004p	2002	2003	2004p
3 **Change in net worth from transactns**	....	....	....	....	....	....	....	....	....	....	....	....
31 **Net acquisition of nonfinancial assets**	**156.3**	**120.3**	**112.1**	**164.1**	**†133.3**	**124.6**	**68.9**	**78.8**	**76.8**	**233.0**	**†212.1**	**201.4**
311 Fixed assets	156.2	120.3	111.8	164.1	†130.9	121.9	68.9	78.8	73.9	233.0	†209.7	195.8
3111 Buildings and structures	86.3	63.8	53.2	86.3	†65.7	55.0	40.6	52.7	50.0	126.8	†118.4	104.9
3112 Machinery and equipment	70.0	56.5	53.5	77.8	†65.2	61.8	28.3	26.0	24.0	106.1	†91.2	85.8
3113 Other fixed assets	—	—	5.1	—	†—	5.1	—	—	—	—	†—	5.1
312 Inventories	—	—	.4	—	†2.4	2.7	—	—	2.7	—	†2.4	5.4
313 Valuables	—	—	—	—	†—	—	—	—	—	—	†—	—
314 Nonproduced assets	—	—	—	—	†—	—	—	—	.2	—	†—	.2
3141 Land	—	—	—	—	†—	—	—	—	.2	—	†—	.2
3142 Subsoil assets	—	—	—	—	†—	—	—	—	—	—	†—	—
3143 Other naturally occurring assets	—	—	—	—	†—	—	—	—	—	—	†—	—
3144 Intangible nonproduced assets	—	—	—	—	†—	—	—	—	—	—	†—	—
32 **Net acquisition of financial assets**	**−63.9**	**11.4**	**149.0**	**−3.7**	**†104.3**	**279.5**	**35.6**	**35.6**	**39.2**	**31.9**	**†139.9**	**318.7**
321 Domestic	−63.9	11.4	149.0	−3.7	†104.3	279.5	35.6	35.6	39.2	31.9	†139.9	318.7
3212 Currency and deposits	−47.3	14.2	192.1	−40.1	†8.3	261.1	35.6	35.6	39.2	−4.5	†44.0	300.3
3213 Securities other than shares	—	—	—	28.6	†14.2	−40.9	—	—	—	28.6	†14.2	−40.9
3214 Loans	−12.3	−2.8	—	12.3	†49.6	58.6	—	—	—	12.3	†49.6	58.6
3215 Shares and other equity	−4.4	—	−43.0	−4.4	†28.2	−1.6	—	—	—	−4.4	†28.2	−1.6
3216 Insurance technical reserves	—	—	—	—	†—	—	—	—	—	—	†—	—
3217 Financial derivatives	—	—	—	—	†—	—	—	—	—	—	†—	—
3218 Other accounts receivable	....	....	....	....	....	....	....	....	....	....	....	....
322 Foreign	—	—	—	—	†—	—	—	—	—	—	†—	—
3222 Currency and deposits	—	—	—	—	†—	—	—	—	—	—	†—	—
3223 Securities other than shares	—	—	—	—	†—	—	—	—	—	—	†—	—
3224 Loans	—	—	—	—	†—	—	—	—	—	—	†—	—
3225 Shares and other equity	—	—	—	—	†—	—	—	—	—	—	†—	—
3226 Insurance technical reserves	—	—	—	—	†—	—	—	—	—	—	†—	—
3227 Financial derivatives	—	—	—	—	†—	—	—	—	—	—	†—	—
3228 Other accounts receivable	....	....	....	....	....	....	....	....	....	....	....	....
323 Monetary gold and SDRs	—	—	—	—	†—	—	—	—	—	—	†—	....
33 **Net incurrence of liabilities**	**375.7**	**7.3**	**177.0**	**387.8**	**†16.8**	**243.4**	**3.5**	**1.1**	**.5**	**391.3**	**†17.9**	**243.9**
331 Domestic	436.8	41.2	195.2	448.9	†50.7	261.7	3.5	1.1	.5	452.4	†51.8	262.2
3312 Currency and deposits	—	—	−2.8	—	†—	−2.8	—	—	—	—	†—	−2.8
3313 Securities other than shares	444.6	54.4	198.0	444.6	†54.4	198.0	—	—	—	444.6	†54.4	198.0
3314 Loans	−7.8	−13.2	—	4.3	†−11.1	43.3	3.5	1.1	.5	7.8	†−10.0	43.8
3316 Insurance technical reserves	—	—	—	—	†—	—	—	—	—	—	†—	—
3317 Financial derivatives	—	—	—	—	†—	—	—	—	—	—	†—	—
3318 Other accounts payable	....	....	....	....	....	....	....	....	....	....	....	....

In Billions of Baht / Year Ending September 30 / Noncash Reporter

		Budgetary Central Government			Central Government			Local Government			General Government		
		2002	2003	2004p	2002	2003	2004p	2002	2003	2004p	2002	2003	2004p
332	Foreign...............................	−61.1	−33.9	−18.2	−61.1	†−33.9	−18.2	—	—	—	−61.1	†−33.9	−18.2
3322	Currency and deposits.................	—	—	—	—	†—	—	—	—	—	—	†—	—
3323	Securities other than shares...........	—	—	—	—	†—	—	—	—	—	—	†—	—
3324	Loans....................................	−61.1	−33.9	−18.2	−61.1	†−33.9	−18.2	—	—	—	−61.1	†−33.9	−18.2
3326	Insurance technical reserves...........	—	—	—	—	†—	—	—	—	—	—	†—	—
3327	Financial derivatives....................	—	—	—	—	†—	—	—	—	—	—	†—	—
3328	Other accounts payable................	....	....	....	....	....	....	....	....	....	....	....	....

Table 4   Holding gains in assets and liabilities

Table 5   Other changes in the volume of assets and liabilities

Table 6   Balance sheet

		Budgetary Central Government			Central Government			Local Government			General Government		
6	**Net worth**....................	....	....	....	....	....	....	....	....	....	....	....	....
61	**Nonfinancial assets**.........	....	....	....	....	....	....	....	....	....	....	....	....
611	Fixed assets.......................	....	....	....	....	....	....	....	....	....	....	....	....
6111	Buildings and structures.........	....	....	....	....	....	....	....	....	....	....	....	....
6112	Machinery and equipment........	....	....	....	....	....	....	....	....	....	....	....	....
6113	Other fixed assets.................	....	....	....	....	....	....	....	....	....	....	....	....
612	Inventories........................	....	....	....	....	....	....	....	....	....	....	....	....
613	Valuables..........................	....	....	....	....	....	....	....	....	....	....	....	....
614	Nonproduced assets..............	....	....	....	....	....	....	....	....	....	....	....	....
6141	Land...............................	....	....	....	....	....	....	....	....	....	....	....	....
6142	Subsoil assets.....................	....	....	....	....	....	....	....	....	....	....	....	....
6143	Other naturally occurring assets..	....	....	....	....	....	....	....	....	....	....	....	....
6144	Intangible nonproduced assets...	....	....	....	....	....	....	....	....	....	....	....	....
62	**Financial assets**..............	....	....	....	....	....	....	....	....	....	....	....	....
621	Domestic...........................	....	....	....	....	....	....	....	....	....	....	....	....
6212	Currency and deposits............	....	....	....	....	....	....	....	....	....	....	....	....
6213	Securities other than shares......	....	....	....	....	....	....	....	....	....	....	....	....
6214	Loans..............................	....	....	....	....	....	....	....	....	....	....	....	....
6215	Shares and other equity..........	....	....	....	....	....	....	....	....	....	....	....	....
6216	Insurance technical reserves......	....	....	....	....	....	....	....	....	....	....	....	....
6217	Financial derivatives..............	....	....	....	....	....	....	....	....	....	....	....	....
6218	Other accounts receivable........	....	....	....	....	....	....	....	....	....	....	....	....
622	Foreign............................	....	....	....	....	....	....	....	....	....	....	....	....
6222	Currency and deposits............	....	....	....	....	....	....	....	....	....	....	....	....
6223	Securities other than shares......	....	....	....	....	....	....	....	....	....	....	....	....
6224	Loans..............................	....	....	....	....	....	....	....	....	....	....	....	....
6225	Shares and other equity..........	....	....	....	....	....	....	....	....	....	....	....	....
6226	Insurance technical reserves......	....	....	....	....	....	....	....	....	....	....	....	....
6227	Financial derivatives..............	....	....	....	....	....	....	....	....	....	....	....	....
6228	Other accounts receivable........	....	....	....	....	....	....	....	....	....	....	....	....
623	Monetary gold and SDRs..........	....	....	....	....	....	....	....	....	....	....	....	....
63	**Liabilities**....................	**1,670.5**	**1,651.6**	**1,639.6**	**1,734.9**	**1,708.6**	**1,696.6**	....	....	....	....	....	....
631	Domestic...........................	1,261.0	1,307.4	1,307.4	1,325.4	1,364.3	1,364.3	....	....	....	....	....	....
6312	Currency and deposits............	—	—	—	—	—	—	....	....	....	....	....	....
6313	Securities other than shares......	1,261.0	1,307.4	1,307.4	1,261.0	1,307.4	1,307.4	....	....	....	....	....	....
6314	Loans..............................	—	—	—	64.4	57.0	57.0	....	....	....	....	....	....
6316	Insurance technical reserves......	—	—	—	—	—	—	....	....	....	....	....	....
6317	Financial derivatives..............	—	—	—	—	—	—	....	....	....	....	....	....
6318	Other accounts payable...........	....	....	....	....	....	....	....	....	....	....	....	....
632	Foreign............................	409.6	344.3	332.3	409.6	344.3	332.3	....	....	....	....	....	....
6322	Currency and deposits............	—	—	—	—	—	—	....	....	....	....	....	....
6323	Securities other than shares......	—	—	—	—	—	—	....	....	....	....	....	....
6324	Loans..............................	409.6	344.3	332.3	409.6	344.3	332.3	....	....	....	....	....	....
6326	Insurance technical reserves......	—	—	—	—	—	—	....	....	....	....	....	....
6327	Financial derivatives..............	—	—	—	—	—	—	....	....	....	....	....	....
6328	Other accounts payable...........	....	....	....	....	....	....	....	....	....	....	....	....

In Billions of Baht / Year Ending September 30 / Noncash Reporter

	Budgetary Central Government			Central Government			Local Government			General Government		
	2002	2003	2004p	2002	2003	2004p	2002	2003	2004p	2002	2003	2004p
Memorandum items:												
6M2 Net financial worth..................................	....	....	....	....	....	....	....	....	....	....	....	....
6M3 Debt at market value..............................	....	....	....	....	....	....	....	....	....	....	....	....
6M4 Debt at nominal value.............................	....	....	....	....	....	....	....	....	....	....	....	....
6M5 Arrears...	....	....	....	....	....	....	....	....	....	....	....	....
6M6 Obligations for social security benefits...........	....	....	....	....	....	....	....	....	....	....	....	....
6M7 Contingent liabilities................................	....	....	....	....	....	....	....	....	....	....	....	....
6M8 Uncapitalized military weapons, systems........	....	....	....	....	....	....	....	....	....	....	....	....
Table 7 Outlays by functions of govt.												
7 **Total outlays....................................**	**1,311.4**	**1,041.5**	**1,196.8**	**1,329.2**	**†1,071.8**	**1,239.2**	**133.0**	**149.4**	**186.6**	**1,374.6**	**†1,128.0**	**1,306.5**
701 **General public services........................**	**484.5**	**222.9**	**279.8**	**409.4**	**†144.1**	**193.8**	....	....	....	....	....	....
7017 Public debt transactions..............................	69.0	65.1	84.4	71.6	†67.6	85.1	—	—	—	71.6	†67.6	85.1
7018 General transfers between levels of govt......	—	—	—		†		....	....	....	....	....	....
702 **Defense..**	**79.4**	**75.8**	**81.0**	**79.7**	**†76.1**	**81.2**	....	....	....	....	....	....
703 **Public order and safety.......................**	**57.8**	**62.8**	**67.8**	**57.9**	**†62.8**	**67.8**	....	....	....	....	....	....
704 **Economic affairs...............................**	**230.3**	**207.5**	**242.7**	**290.1**	**†257.9**	**301.2**	....	....	....	....	....	....
7042 Agriculture, forestry, fishing, and hunting......	84.1	71.5	69.1	107.6	†84.7	76.3	....	....	....	....	....	....
7043 Fuel and energy..	1.7	1.4	1.9	16.6	†32.8	30.0	....	....	....	....	....	....
7044 Mining, manufacturing, and construction.....	7.5	7.5	6.4	20.1	†8.4	6.8	....	....	....	....	....	....
7045 Transport...	73.5	54.3	64.1	77.2	†55.7	64.7	....	....	....	....	....	....
7046 Communication.......................................	2.4	.6	1.6	2.4	†.6	1.6	....	....	....	....	....	....
705 **Environmental protection....................**	**1.7**	**1.0**	**11.0**	**2.3**	**†1.6**	**11.2**	....	....	....	....	....	....
706 **Housing and community amenities........**	**54.3**	**22.2**	**9.5**	**54.5**	**†37.1**	**10.9**	....	....	....	....	....	....
707 **Health..**	**88.4**	**97.1**	**102.1**	**107.8**	**†119.0**	**118.0**	....	....	....	....	....	....
7072 Outpatient services..................................	.2	—	—	.2	†—	—	....	....	....	....	....	....
7073 Hospital services......................................	43.5	55.5	58.1	51.7	†65.2	68.5	....	....	....	....	....	....
7074 Public health services..............................	44.6	32.1	—	44.6	†32.1	—	....	....	....	....	....	....
708 **Recreation, culture, and religion...........**	**7.2**	**7.8**	**7.4**	**7.3**	**†8.0**	**7.5**	....	....	....	....	....	....
709 **Education....................................**	**226.5**	**235.3**	**263.0**	**230.0**	**†237.4**	**265.0**	....	....	....	....	....	....
7091 Pre-primary and primary education...............	....	—	186.4	....	†.5	186.4	....	....	....	....	....	....
7092 Secondary education................................	153.9	164.5	.3	155.0	†165.0	.3	....	....	....	....	....	....
7094 Tertiary education....................................	34.1	32.1	35.2	34.1	†32.1	35.2	....	....	....	....	....	....
710 **Social protection.............................**	**81.3**	**109.2**	**132.5**	**90.3**	**†127.7**	**182.7**	....	....	....	....	....	....
7 Statistical discrepancy: Total outlays...............	—	—	—	—	†—	—	....	....	....	....	....	....
Table 8 Transactions in financial assets and liabilities by sector												
82 **Net acquisition of financial assets........**	**−63.9**	**11.4**	**149.0**	**−3.7**	**†104.3**	**279.5**	**35.6**	**35.6**	**39.2**	**31.9**	**†139.9**	**318.7**
821 Domestic..	−63.9	11.4	149.0	−3.7	†104.3	279.5	35.6	35.6	39.2	31.9	†139.9	318.7
8211 General government..............................	−9.2	—	—	19.3	†9.4	—	—	—	—	19.3	†9.4	—
8212 Central bank.....................................	−22.3	21.3	197.0	−20.1	†21.3	197.6	—	—	—	−20.1	†21.3	197.6
8213 Other depository corporations..................	−15.8	−7.1	−4.9	−10.9	†−13.0	94.7	35.6	35.6	39.2	24.7	†22.7	133.9
8214 Financial corporations n.e.c....................	—	—	−43.0	—	†—	−43.0	—	—	—	—	†—	−43.0
8215 Nonfinancial corporations.......................	−16.6	−2.8	—	−16.6	†34.2	41.1	—	—	—	−16.6	†34.2	41.1
8216 Households & NPIs serving households......	—	—	—	24.5	†52.4	−10.9	—	—	—	24.5	†52.4	−10.9
822 Foreign...	—	—	—	—	†—	—	—	—	—	—	†—	—
8221 General government..............................	—	—	—	—	†—	—	—	—	—	—	†—	—
8227 International organizations......................	—	—	—	—	†—	—	—	—	—	—	†—	—
8228 Financial corporations other than international organizations............	—	—	—	—	†—	—	—	—	—	—	†—	—
8229 Other nonresidents...............................	—	—	—	—	†—	—	—	—	—	—	†—	—
823 Monetary gold and SDRs.........................	—	—	—	—	†—	—	—	—	—	—	†—	—
83 **Net incurrence of liabilities..................**	**375.7**	**7.3**	**177.0**	**387.8**	**†16.8**	**243.4**	**3.5**	**1.1**	**.5**	**391.3**	**†17.9**	**243.9**
831 Domestic..	436.8	41.2	195.2	448.9	†50.7	261.7	3.5	1.1	.5	452.4	†51.8	262.2
8311 General government..............................	—	—	−1.1	—	†—	−1.1	—	—	—	—	†—	−1.1
8312 Central bank.....................................	−28.9	5.9	7.9	−28.9	†5.9	7.9	—	—	—	−28.9	†5.9	7.9
8313 Other depository corporations..................	144.9	−19.6	−45.6	155.2	†−19.6	−7.6	—	—	—	155.2	†−19.6	−7.6
8314 Financial corporations n.e.c....................	—	58.8	90.8	—	†58.8	90.8	3.5	1.1	.5	3.5	†59.9	91.3
8315 Nonfinancial corporations.......................	—	—	85.0	—	†9.8	113.5	—	—	—	—	†9.8	113.5
8316 Households & NPIs serving households......	320.8	−3.8	58.2	322.7	†−4.1	58.2	—	—	—	322.7	†−4.1	58.2
832 Foreign...	−61.1	−33.9	−18.2	−61.1	†−33.9	−18.2	—	—	—	−61.1	†−33.9	−18.2
8321 General government..............................	−.9	−20.0	−9.4	−.9	†−20.0	−9.4	—	—	—	−.9	†−20.0	−9.4
8327 International organizations......................	−52.9	−5.1	−45.6	−52.9	†−5.1	−45.6	—	—	—	−52.9	†−5.1	−45.6
8328 Financial corporations other than international organizations..............	−7.4	−8.8	36.8	−7.4	†−8.8	36.8	—	—	—	−7.4	†−8.8	36.8
8329 Other nonresidents...............................	—	—	—	—	†—	—	—	—	—	—	†—	—

	Budgetary Central Government			Central Government			Local Government			General Government		
	2003	2004p	2005f	2003	2004p	2005f	2003	2004	2005	2003	2004	2005
Statement of government operations												
Statement of other economic flows												
Balance sheet												
6 *Net worth*...............	....	....	....	....	....	....	....	....	....	....	....	....
61 Nonfinancial assets...............	....	....	....	....	....	....	....	....	....	....	....	....
62 Financial assets...............	....	....	....	....	....	....	....	....	....	....	....	....
63 Liabilities...............	19,463	20,912	22,301	19,463	20,912	22,301	....	....	....	....	....	....
Statement of sources and uses of cash												
1 Cash receipts from operating activities...........	7,611	8,381	8,778	9,553	10,490	10,991	....	....	....	....	....	....
11 Taxes...............	6,631	7,254	7,672	6,631	7,254	7,672	....	....	....	....	....	....
12 Social contributions...............	—	—	—	1,781	1,938	2,047	....	....	....	....	....	....
13 Grants...............	77	73	81	77	73	81	....	....	....	....	....	....
14 Other receipts...............	904	1,055	1,025	1,065	1,226	1,191	....	....	....	....	....	....
2 Cash payments for operating activities...........	6,956	7,738	8,033	8,974	9,961	10,409	....	....	....	....	....	....
21 Compensation of employees...............	3,651	3,919	4,176	3,719	3,999	4,258	....	....	....	....	....	....
22 Purchases of goods and services...............	658	699	661	689	733	696	....	....	....	....	....	....
24 Interest...............	904	989	1,028	904	989	1,028	....	....	....	....	....	....
25 Subsidies...............	....	....	....	....	....	....	....	....	....	....	....	....
26 Grants...............	....	....	....	....	....	....	....	....	....	....	....	....
27 Social benefits...............	....	....	....	....	....	....	....	....	....	....	....	....
28 Other payments...............	....	....	....	....	....	....	....	....	....	....	....	....
CIO *Net cash inflow from oper. activities.....*	*656*	*643*	*745*	*579*	*529*	*582*	....	....	....	....	....	....
31.1 Purchases of nonfinancial assets...............	1,335	1,346	1,512	1,362	1,365	1,536	....	....	....	....	....	....
31.2 Sales of nonfinancial assets...............	19	9	10	19	9	10	....	....	....	....	....	....
31 Net cash outflow from investments in nonfinancial assets...............	1,316	1,337	1,502	1,343	1,356	1,526	....	....	....	....	....	....
CSD *Cash surplus/deficit...............*	*−661*	*−694*	*−757*	*−764*	*−827*	*−944*	....	....	....	....	....	....
32x Net acquisition of fin assets, excl. cash...........	100	−158	−186	210	−104	−133	....	....	....	....	....	....
321x Domestic...............	100	−158	−186	210	−104	−133	....	....	....	....	....	....
322x Foreign...............	—	—	—	—	—	—	....	....	....	....	....	....
323 Monetary gold and SDRs...............	—	—	—	—	—	—	....	....	....	....	....	....
33 Net incurrence of liabilities...............	1,030	545	855	1,030	545	855	....	....	....	....	....	....
331 Domestic...............	222	332	648	222	332	648	....	....	....	....	....	....
332 Foreign...............	808	213	207	808	213	207	....	....	....	....	....	....
NFB Net cash inflow from fin. activities...............	930	703	1,041	820	648	988	....	....	....	....	....	....
NCB *Net change in the stock of cash...............*	*269*	*9*	*284*	*56*	*−178*	*44*	....	....	....	....	....	....
Table 1 Revenue												
1 **Revenue**	**7,611**	**8,381**	**8,778**	**9,553**	**10,490**	**10,991**	....	....	....	....	....	....
11 **Taxes............**	**6,631**	**7,254**	**7,672**	**6,631**	**7,254**	**7,672**	....	....	....	....	....	....
111 Taxes on income, profits, & capital gains......	2,177	2,385	2,593	2,177	2,385	2,593	....	....	....	....	....	....
1111 Individuals...............	1,309	1,437	1,584	1,309	1,437	1,584	....	....	....	....	....	....
1112 Corporations and other enterprises............	868	948	1,009	868	948	1,009	....	....	....	....	....	....
112 Taxes on payroll and workforce...............	118	121	74	118	121	74	....	....	....	....	....	....
113 Taxes on property...............	136	149	173	136	149	173	....	....	....	....	....	....
114 Taxes on goods and services...............	3,360	3,691	3,893	3,360	3,691	3,893	....	....	....	....	....	....
1141 General taxes on goods and services.........	2,171	2,427	2,525	2,171	2,427	2,525	....	....	....	....	....	....
1142 Excises...............	954	1,021	1,101	954	1,021	1,101	....	....	....	....	....	....
115 Taxes on int'l. trade and transactions...............	726	752	775	726	752	775	....	....	....	....	....	....
116 Other taxes...............	114	156	163	114	156	163	....	....	....	....	....	....
12 **Social contributions............**	**—**	**—**	**—**	**1,781**	**1,938**	**2,047**	....	....	....	....	....	....
121 Social security contributions...............	—	—	—	1,781	1,938	2,047	....	....	....	....	....	....
122 Other social contributions...............	—	—	—	—	—	—	....	....	....	....	....	....
13 **Grants............**	**77**	**73**	**81**	**77**	**73**	**81**	....	....	....	....	....	....
131 From foreign governments...............	54	41	81	54	41	81	....	....	....	....	....	....
132 From international organizations...............	—	—	—	—	—	—	....	....	....	....	....	....
133 From other general government units...............	23	32	—	23	32	—	....	....	....	....	....	....
14 **Other revenue............**	**904**	**1,055**	**1,025**	**1,065**	**1,226**	**1,191**	....	....	....	....	....	....
Table 2 Expense by economic type												
2 **Expense............**	**6,956**	**7,738**	**8,033**	**8,974**	**9,961**	**10,409**	....	....	....	....	....	....
21 **Compensation of employees............**	**3,651**	**3,919**	**4,176**	**3,719**	**3,999**	**4,258**	....	....	....	....	....	....
211 Wages and salaries...............	3,651	3,919	4,176	3,719	3,999	4,258	....	....	....	....	....	....
212 Social contributions...............	—	—	—	—	—	—	....	....	....	....	....	....
22 **Use of goods and services............**	**658**	**699**	**661**	**689**	**733**	**696**	....	....	....	....	....	....
23 **Consumption of fixed capital............**	....	....	....	....	....	....	....	....	....	....	....	....
24 Interest...............	904	989	1,028	904	989	1,028	....	....	....	....	....	....
25 Subsidies...............	....	....	....	....	....	....	....	....	....	....	....	....

Tunisia   744

In Millions of Dinars / Year Ending December 31 / Cash Reporter

		Budgetary Central Government			Central Government			Local Government			General Government		
		2003	2004p	2005f	2003	2004p	2005f	2003	2004	2005	2003	2004	2005
26	**Grants**................................	....	....	....	....	....	....	....	....	....	....	....	....
261	To foreign govenments.............	....	....	....	....	....	....	....	....	....	....	....	....
262	To international organizations...........	....	....	....	....	....	....	....	....	....	....	....	....
263	To other general government units...........	....	....	....	....	....	....	....	....	....	....	....	....
2631	Current..............................	....	....	....	....	....	....	....	....	....	....	....	....
2632	Capital..............................	....	....	....	....	....	....	....	....	....	....	....	....
27	**Social benefits**.......................	....	....	....	....	....	....	....	....	....	....	....	....
28	**Other expense**........................	....	....	....	....	....	....	....	....	....	....	....	....
281	Property expense other than interest...........	....	....	....	....	....	....	....	....	....	....	....	....
282	Miscellaneous other expense................	....	....	....	....	....	....	....	....	....	....	....	....
2821	Current..............................	....	....	....	....	....	....	....	....	....	....	....	....
2822	Capital..............................	....	....	....	....	....	....	....	....	....	....	....	....
Table 3	**Transactions in assets and liabilities**												
3	**Change in net worth from transactns....**	....	....	....	....	....	....	....	....	....	....	....	....
31	**Net acquisition of nonfinancial assets...**	1,316	1,337	1,502	1,343	1,356	1,526	....	....	....	....	....	....
311	Fixed assets...........................	1,316	1,337	1,502	1,343	1,356	1,526	....	....	....	....	....	....
3111	Buildings and structures..............	....	....	....	....	....	....	....	....	....	....	....	....
3112	Machinery and equipment.......................	....	....	....	....	....	....	....	....	....	....	....	....
3113	Other fixed assets..................	....	....	....	....	....	....	....	....	....	....	....	....
312	Inventories..........................	—	—	—	—	—	—	....	....	....	....	....	....
313	Valuables............................	—	—	—	—	—	—	....	....	....	....	....	....
314	Nonproduced assets..................	—	—	—	—	—	—	....	....	....	....	....	....
3141	Land................................	—	—	—	—	—	—	....	....	....	....	....	....
3142	Subsoil assets.......................	—	—	—	—	—	—	....	....	....	....	....	....
3143	Other naturally occurring assets........	—	—	—	—	—	—	....	....	....	....	....	....
3144	Intangible nonproduced assets........	—	—	—	—	—	—	....	....	....	....	....	....
32	**Net acquisition of financial assets........**	369	−149	98	266	−282	−89	....	....	....	....	....	....
321	Domestic.............................	369	−149	98	266	−282	−89	....	....	....	....	....	....
3212	Currency and deposits...............	269	9	284	56	−178	44	....	....	....	....	....	....
3213	Securities other than shares..............	—	—	—	—	—	—	....	....	....	....	....	....
3214	Loans...............................	100	−158	−186	210	−104	−133	....	....	....	....	....	....
3215	Shares and other equity.............	—	—	—	—	—	—	....	....	....	....	....	....
3216	Insurance technical reserves.............	—	—	—	—	—	—	....	....	....	....	....	....
3217	Financial derivatives..................	—	—	—	—	—	—	....	....	....	....	....	....
3218	Other accounts receivable.................	....	....	....	....	....	....	....	....	....	....	....	....
322	Foreign..............................	—	—	—	—	—	—	....	....	....	....	....	....
3222	Currency and deposits...............	—	—	—	—	—	—	....	....	....	....	....	....
3223	Securities other than shares..............	—	—	—	—	—	—	....	....	....	....	....	....
3224	Loans...............................	—	—	—	—	—	—	....	....	....	....	....	....
3225	Shares and other equity.............	—	—	—	—	—	—	....	....	....	....	....	....
3226	Insurance technical reserves.............	—	—	—	—	—	—	....	....	....	....	....	....
3227	Financial derivatives..................	—	—	—	—	—	—	....	....	....	....	....	....
3228	Other accounts receivable.................	....	....	....	....	....	....	....	....	....	....	....	....
323	Monetary gold and SDRs..............	—	—	—	—	—	—	....	....	....	....	....	....
33	**Net incurrence of liabilities...................**	1,030	545	855	1,030	545	855	....	....	....	....	....	....
331	Domestic.............................	222	332	648	222	332	648	....	....	....	....	....	....
3312	Currency and deposits................	—	—	—	—	—	—	....	....	....	....	....	....
3313	Securities other than shares..............	222	332	648	222	332	648	....	....	....	....	....	....
3314	Loans...............................	—	—	—	—	—	—	....	....	....	....	....	....
3316	Insurance technical reserves.............	—	—	—	—	—	—	....	....	....	....	....	....
3317	Financial derivatives..................	—	—	—	—	—	—	....	....	....	....	....	....
3318	Other accounts payable.................	....	....	....	....	....	....	....	....	....	....	....	....
332	Foreign..............................	808	213	207	808	213	207	....	....	....	....	....	....
3322	Currency and deposits...............	—	—	—	—	—	—	....	....	....	....	....	....
3323	Securities other than shares..............	717	347	128	717	347	128	....	....	....	....	....	....
3324	Loans...............................	91	−134	80	91	−134	80	....	....	....	....	....	....
3326	Insurance technical reserves.............	—	—	—	—	—	—	....	....	....	....	....	....
3327	Financial derivatives..................	—	—	—	—	—	—	....	....	....	....	....	....
3328	Other accounts payable..............	....	....	....	....	....	....	....	....	....	....	....	....

Tunisia   744

In Millions of Dinars / Year Ending December 31 / Cash Reporter

	Budgetary Central Government			Central Government			Local Government			General Government		
	2003	2004p	2005f	2003	2004p	2005f	2003	2004	2005	2003	2004	2005
Table 4 Holding gains in assets and liabilities												
Table 5 Other changes in the volume of assets and liabilities												
Table 6 Balance sheet												
6 Net worth........................	....	....	....	....	....	....	....	....	....	....	....	....
61 Nonfinancial assets...................	....	....	....	....	....	....	....	....	....	....	....	....
611 Fixed assets................	....	....	....	....	....	....	....	....	....	....	....	....
6111 Buildings and structures............	....	....	....	....	....	....	....	....	....	....	....	....
6112 Machinery and equipment...........	....	....	....	....	....	....	....	....	....	....	....	....
6113 Other fixed assets................	....	....	....	....	....	....	....	....	....	....	....	....
612 Inventories..................	....	....	....	....	....	....	....	....	....	....	....	....
613 Valuables.....................	....	....	....	....	....	....	....	....	....	....	....	....
614 Nonproduced assets.............	....	....	....	....	....	....	....	....	....	....	....	....
6141 Land..................	....	....	....	....	....	....	....	....	....	....	....	....
6142 Subsoil assets................	....	....	....	....	....	....	....	....	....	....	....	....
6143 Other naturally occurring assets.........	....	....	....	....	....	....	....	....	....	....	....	....
6144 Intangible nonproduced assets........	....	....	....	....	....	....	....	....	....	....	....	....
62 Financial assets..................	....	....	....	....	....	....	....	....	....	....	....	....
621 Domestic...................	....	....	....	....	....	....	....	....	....	....	....	....
6212 Currency and deposits.............	....	....	....	....	....	....	....	....	....	....	....	....
6213 Securities other than shares........	....	....	....	....	....	....	....	....	....	....	....	....
6214 Loans...................	....	....	....	....	....	....	....	....	....	....	....	....
6215 Shares and other equity............	....	....	....	....	....	....	....	....	....	....	....	....
6216 Insurance technical reserves.........	....	....	....	....	....	....	....	....	....	....	....	....
6217 Financial derivatives................	....	....	....	....	....	....	....	....	....	....	....	....
6218 Other accounts receivable...........	....	....	....	....	....	....	....	....	....	....	....	....
622 Foreign..................	....	....	....	....	....	....	....	....	....	....	....	....
6222 Currency and deposits.............	....	....	....	....	....	....	....	....	....	....	....	....
6223 Securities other than shares........	....	....	....	....	....	....	....	....	....	....	....	....
6224 Loans...................	....	....	....	....	....	....	....	....	....	....	....	....
6225 Shares and other equity............	....	....	....	....	....	....	....	....	....	....	....	....
6226 Insurance technical reserves.........	....	....	....	....	....	....	....	....	....	....	....	....
6227 Financial derivatives................	....	....	....	....	....	....	....	....	....	....	....	....
6228 Other accounts receivable...........	....	....	....	....	....	....	....	....	....	....	....	....
623 Monetary gold and SDRs...........	....	....	....	....	....	....	....	....	....	....	....	....
63 **Liabilities**........................	**19,463**	**20,912**	**22,301**	**19,463**	**20,912**	**22,301**	....	....	....	....	....	....
631 Domestic....................	6,934	7,707	8,789	6,934	7,707	8,789	....	....	....	....	....	....
6312 Currency and deposits.............	....	....	....	....	....	....	....	....	....	....	....	....
6313 Securities other than shares........	....	....	....	....	....	....	....	....	....	....	....	....
6314 Loans...................	....	....	....	....	....	....	....	....	....	....	....	....
6316 Insurance technical reserves.........	....	....	....	....	....	....	....	....	....	....	....	....
6317 Financial derivatives................	....	....	....	....	....	....	....	....	....	....	....	....
6318 Other accounts payable............	....	....	....	....	....	....	....	....	....	....	....	....
632 Foreign..................	12,529	13,205	13,512	12,529	13,205	13,512	....	....	....	....	....	....
6322 Currency and deposits.............	....	....	....	....	....	....	....	....	....	....	....	....
6323 Securities other than shares........	....	....	....	....	....	....	....	....	....	....	....	....
6324 Loans...................	....	....	....	....	....	....	....	....	....	....	....	....
6326 Insurance technical reserves.........	....	....	....	....	....	....	....	....	....	....	....	....
6327 Financial derivatives................	....	....	....	....	....	....	....	....	....	....	....	....
6328 Other accounts payable............	....	....	....	....	....	....	....	....	....	....	....	....
Memorandum items:												
6M2 Net financial worth.....................	....	....	....									
6M3 Debt at market value..................	....	....	....									
6M4 Debt at nominal value...............	....	....	....									
6M5 Arrears................................	....	....	....									
6M6 Obligations for social security benefits...........	....	....	....									
6M7 Contingent liabilities.......................	....	....	....									
6M8 Uncapitalized military weapons, systems........	....	....	....									
Table 7 Outlays by functions of govt.												
7 **Total outlays**..................	**8,291**	**9,084**	**9,545**	**10,336**	**11,326**	**11,945**	....	....	....	....	....	....
701 **General public services**........................	**1,643**	**1,806**	**1,823**	**1,643**	**1,806**	**1,823**	....	....	....	....	....	....
7017 Public debt transactions....................	904	989	1,028	904	989	1,028	....	....	....	....	....	....
7018 General transfers between levels of govt......	....	....	....	....	....	....	....	....	....	....	....	....
702 **Defense**..........................	**525**	**554**	**555**	**525**	**554**	**555**	....	....	....	....	....	....
703 **Public order and safety**......................	**806**	**874**	**900**	**806**	**874**	**900**	....	....	....	....	....	....

458   2005, International Monetary Fund: *Government Finance Statistics Yearbook*

In Millions of Dinars / Year Ending December 31 / Cash Reporter

	Budgetary Central Government			Central Government			Local Government			General Government		
	2003	2004p	2005f	2003	2004p	2005f	2003	2004	2005	2003	2004	2005
704 **Economic affairs**................................	**1,705**	**1,883**	**2,132**	**1,705**	**1,883**	**2,132**	....	....	....	....	....	....
7042 Agriculture, forestry, fishing, and hunting.....	736	692	727	736	692	727	....	....	....	....	....	....
7043 Fuel and energy...............................	—	—	—	—	—	—	....	....	....	....	....	....
7044 Mining, manufacturing, and construction.....	134	341	321	134	341	321	....	....	....	....	....	....
7045 Transport.......................................	283	286	311	283	286	311	....	....	....	....	....	....
7046 Communication...............................	....	....	....	....	....	....	....	....	....	....	....	....
705 **Environmental protection**....................	....	....	....	....	....	....	....	....	....	....	....	....
706 **Housing and community amenities**........	**497**	**603**	**601**	**497**	**603**	**601**	....	....	....	....	....	....
707 **Health**..	**590**	**604**	**637**	**590**	**604**	**637**	....	....	....	....	....	....
7072 Outpatient services............................	....	....	....	....	....	....	....	....	....	....	....	....
7073 Hospital services...............................	....	....	....	....	....	....	....	....	....	....	....	....
7074 Public health services.........................	....	....	....	....	....	....	....	....	....	....	....	....
708 **Recreation, culture, and religion**...........	**287**	**336**	**366**	**287**	**336**	**366**	....	....	....	....	....	....
709 **Education**......................................	**2,087**	**2,260**	**2,371**	**2,087**	**2,260**	**2,371**	....	....	....	....	....	....
7091 Pre-primary and primary education.............	....	....	....	....	....	....	....	....	....	....	....	....
7092 Secondary education...........................	1,570	1,663	1,752	1,570	1,663	1,752	....	....	....	....	....	....
7094 Tertiary education..............................	517	598	618	517	598	618	....	....	....	....	....	....
710 **Social protection**.............................	**151**	**166**	**160**	**2,196**	**2,408**	**2,560**	....	....	....	....	....	....
7 Statistical discrepancy: Total outlays..............	—	—	—	—	—	—	....	....	....	....	....	....
Table 8 Transactions in financial assets and liabilities by sector												
82 **Net acquisition of financial assets**........	**369**	**−149**	**98**	**266**	**−282**	**−89**	....	....	....	....	....	....
821 Domestic...	369	−149	98	266	−282	−89	....	....	....	....	....	....
8211 General government...........................	....	....	....	....	....	....	....	....	....	....	....	....
8212 Central bank...................................	....	....	....	....	....	....	....	....	....	....	....	....
8213 Other depository corporations.................	....	....	....	....	....	....	....	....	....	....	....	....
8214 Financial corporations n.e.c...................	....	....	....	....	....	....	....	....	....	....	....	....
8215 Nonfinancial corporations.....................	....	....	....	....	....	....	....	....	....	....	....	....
8216 Households & NPIs serving households......	....	....	....	....	....	....	....	....	....	....	....	....
822 Foreign...	—	—	—	—	—	—	....	....	....	....	....	....
8221 General government...........................	—	—	—	—	—	—	....	....	....	....	....	....
8227 International organizations....................	—	—	—	—	—	—	....	....	....	....	....	....
8228 Financial corporations other than international organizations..............	—	—	—	—	—	—	....	....	....	....	....	....
8229 Other nonresidents............................	—	—	—	—	—	—	....	....	....	....	....	....
823 Monetary gold and SDRs.......................	—	—	—	—	—	—	....	....	....	....	....	....
83 **Net incurrence of liabilities**.................	**1,030**	**545**	**855**	**1,030**	**545**	**855**	....	....	....	....	....	....
831 Domestic...	222	332	648	222	332	648	....	....	....	....	....	....
8311 General government...........................	....	....	....	....	....	....	....	....	....	....	....	....
8312 Central bank...................................	....	....	....	....	....	....	....	....	....	....	....	....
8313 Other depository corporations.................	....	....	....	....	....	....	....	....	....	....	....	....
8314 Financial corporations n.e.c...................	....	....	....	....	....	....	....	....	....	....	....	....
8315 Nonfinancial corporations.....................	....	....	....	....	....	....	....	....	....	....	....	....
8316 Households & NPIs serving households......	....	....	....	....	....	....	....	....	....	....	....	....
832 Foreign...	808	213	207	808	213	207	....	....	....	....	....	....
8321 General government...........................	−21	−91	−77	−21	−91	−77	....	....	....	....	....	....
8327 International organizations....................	134	−22	168	134	−22	168	....	....	....	....	....	....
8328 Financial corporations other than international organizations..............	—	—	—	—	—	—	....	....	....	....	....	....
8329 Other nonresidents............................	695	326	115	695	326	115	....	....	....	....	....	....

Turkey 186

In Trillions of Liras / Year Ending December 31 / Cash Reporter

		Budgetary Central Government			Extrabudgetary Accounts			Central Government			General Government		
		1999	2000	2001	1999	2000	2001	1999	2000	2001	1999	2000	2001
Statement of government operations													
Statement of other economic flows													
Balance sheet													
Statement of sources and uses of cash													
1	Cash receipts from operating activities...........	19,537.7	34,613.6	51,324.7	240.7	364.1	587.1	....	....	....	....	....	....
11	Taxes..	16,471.4	27,528.9	43,126.5	—	—	—	....	....	....	....	....	....
12	Social contributions...............................	—	—	—	—	—	—	....	....	....	....	....	....
13	Grants..	7.5	—	—	—	—	—	....	....	....	....	....	....
14	Other receipts..	3,058.8	7,084.7	8,198.1	240.7	364.1	587.1	....	....	....	....	....	....
2	Cash payments for operating activities...........	26,210.9	43,910.6	80,025.4	1,641.8	2,583.8	4,021.9	....	....	....	....	....	....
21	Compensation of employees.....................	5,744.7	8,153.0	12,467.8	1,292.7	2,001.7	3,013.1	....	....	....	....	....	....
22	Purchases of goods and services..................	2,140.0	3,455.8	4,905.8	177.2	281.0	474.7	....	....	....	....	....	....
24	Interest..	10,720.8	20,535.9	44,189.7	—	—	—	....	....	....	....	....	....
25	Subsidies..	119.7	330.8	673.4	—	—	—	....	....	....	....	....	....
26	Grants..	5,523.6	7,586.9	12,874.7	27.7	43.1	57.5	....	....	....	....	....	....
27	Social benefits..	1,461.6	2,771.0	3,389.2	144.1	258.0	476.6	....	....	....	....	....	....
28	Other payments.......................................	500.4	1,077.2	1,524.8	—	—	—	....	....	....	....	....	....
CIO	*Net cash inflow from oper. activities.....*	....	....	....	....	....	....	....	....	....	....	....	....
31.1	Purchases of nonfinancial assets...................	650.0	1,015.2	1,520.6	964.6	1,624.6	2,835.2	....	....	....			
31.2	Sales of nonfinancial assets........................	26.6	446.9	2,516.2	.7	1.2	4.5	....	....	....			
31	Net cash outflow from investments in nonfinancial assets............................	623.4	568.3	−995.7	963.8	1,623.4	2,830.7						
CSD	*Cash surplus/deficit...........................*	....	....	....	....	....	....						
32x	Net acquisition of fin assets, excl. cash..........	414.3	554.4	992.5	—	—	—	....	....	....			
321x	Domestic..	414.3	554.4	992.5	—	—	—	....	....	....			
322x	Foreign..	—	—	—	—	—	—	....	....	....			
323	Monetary gold and SDRs.........................	—	—	—				....	....	....			
33	Net incurrence of liabilities......................	....	....	....	....	....	....	....	....	....			
331	Domestic..	....	....	....	....	....	....	....	....	....			
332	Foreign..	....	....	....	....	....	....	....	....	....			
NFB	Net cash inflow from fin. activities..............	....	....	....	....	....	....	....	....	....			
NCB	*Net change in the stock of cash..............*	....	....	....	....	....	....	....	....	....	....	....	....

Table 1   Revenue

		1999	2000	2001	1999	2000	2001	1999	2000	2001	1999	2000	2001
1	**Revenue**..	**19,537.7**	**34,613.6**	**51,324.7**	**240.7**	**364.1**	**587.1**	....	....	....	....	....	....
11	**Taxes**..	**16,471.4**	**27,528.9**	**43,126.5**	—	—	—	....	....	....	....	....	....
111	Taxes on income, profits, & capital gains......	7,443.1	10,308.8	18,217.6	—	—	—	....	....	....	....	....	....
1111	Individuals..	5,187.6	6,806.0	12,849.1	—	—	—	....	....	....	....	....	....
1112	Corporations and other enterprises............	1,810.9	2,831.8	4,178.8	—	—	—	....	....	....	....	....	....
112	Taxes on payroll and workforce..................	—	—	—	—	—	—	....	....	....	....	....	....
113	Taxes on property..................................	560.5	1,107.2	1,842.8	—	—	—	....	....	....	....	....	....
114	Taxes on goods and services.....................	7,473.1	14,340.4	20,641.4	—	—	—	....	....	....	....	....	....
1141	General taxes on goods and services..........	4,370.4	8,872.2	12,474.7	—	—	—	....	....	....	....	....	....
1142	Excises..	2,913.6	5,162.3	7,690.3	—	—	—	....	....	....	....	....	....
115	Taxes on int'l. trade and transactions...........	286.5	467.8	475.5	—	—	—	....	....	....	....	....	....
116	Other taxes..	708.1	1,304.7	1,949.2	—	—	—	....	....	....	....	....	....
12	**Social contributions**.............................	—	—	—	—	—	—	....	....	....	....	....	....
121	Social security contributions.....................	—	—	—	—	—	—	....	....	....	....	....	....
122	Other social contributions........................	—	—	—	—	—	—	....	....	....	....	....	....
13	**Grants**..	7.5	—	—	—	—	—	....	....	....	....	....	....
131	From foreign governments........................	7.5	—	—	—	—	—	....	....	....	....	....	....
132	From international organizations.................	—	—	—	—	—	—	....	....	....	....	....	....
133	From other general government units...........	—	—	—	—	—	—	....	....	....	....	....	....
14	**Other revenue**....................................	3,058.8	7,084.7	8,198.1	240.7	364.1	587.1	....	....	....	....	....	....

Table 2   Expense by economic type

		1999	2000	2001	1999	2000	2001	1999	2000	2001	1999	2000	2001
2	**Expense**...	**26,210.9**	**43,910.6**	**80,025.4**	**1,641.8**	**2,583.8**	**4,021.9**	....	....	....	....	....	....
21	**Compensation of employees**..................	**5,744.7**	**8,153.0**	**12,467.8**	**1,292.7**	**2,001.7**	**3,013.1**	....	....	....	....	....	....
211	Wages and salaries.................................	5,744.7	8,153.0	12,467.8	1,292.7	2,001.7	3,013.1	....	....	....	....	....	....
212	Social contributions...............................							....	....	....	....	....	....
22	**Use of goods and services**....................	**2,140.0**	**3,455.8**	**4,905.8**	**177.2**	**281.0**	**474.7**	....	....	....	....	....	....
23	**Consumption of fixed capital**.................	....	....	....	....	....	....	....	....	....	....	....	....
24	**Interest**..	**10,720.8**	**20,535.9**	**44,189.7**	—	—	—	....	....	....	....	....	....
25	**Subsidies**..	**119.7**	**330.8**	**673.4**	—	—	—	....	....	....	....	....	....

In Trillions of Liras / Year Ending December 31 / Cash Reporter

		Budgetary Central Government			Extrabudgetary Accounts			Central Government			General Government		
		1999	2000	2001	1999	2000	2001	1999	2000	2001	1999	2000	2001
26	**Grants**................................	**5,523.6**	**7,586.9**	**12,874.7**	**27.7**	**43.1**	**57.5**	....	....	....	....	....	....
261	To foreign govenments..................	125.7	218.7	399.1	.1	.1	.2	....	....	....	....	....	....
262	To international organizations..........	—	—	—	—	—	—	....	....	....	....	....	....
263	To other general government units...........	5,397.9	7,368.2	12,475.7	27.7	43.0	57.3	....	....	....	....	....	....
2631	Current..................................	5,397.9	7,368.2	12,475.7	27.7	43.0	57.3	....	....	....	....	....	....
2632	Capital..................................	—	—	—	—	—	—	....	....	....	....	....	....
27	**Social benefits**........................	**1,461.6**	**2,771.0**	**3,389.2**	**144.1**	**258.0**	**476.6**	....	....	....	....	....	....
28	**Other expense**..........................	**500.4**	**1,077.2**	**1,524.8**	**—**	**—**	**—**	....	....	....	....	....	....
281	Property expense other than interest...........	—	—	—	—	—	—	....	....	....	....	....	....
282	Miscellaneous other expense................	500.4	1,077.2	1,524.8	—	—	—	....	....	....	....	....	....
2821	Current..................................	—	—	—	—	—	—	....	....	....	....	....	....
2822	Capital..................................	500.4	1,077.2	1,524.8	—	—	—	....	....	....	....	....	....
Table 3	**Transactions in assets and liabilities**												
3	**Change in net worth from transactns....**	....	....	....	....	....	....	....	....	....	....	....	....
31	**Net acquisition of nonfinancial assets...**	**623.4**	**568.3**	**−995.7**	**963.8**	**1,623.4**	**2,830.7**	....	....	....	....	....	....
311	Fixed assets..............................	612.5	925.1	1,384.2	918.2	1,543.5	2,755.6	....	....	....	....	....	....
3111	Buildings and structures..............	....	....	....	....	....	....	....	....	....	....	....	....
3112	Machinery and equipment..............	....	....	....	....	....	....	....	....	....	....	....	....
3113	Other fixed assets....................	....	....	....	....	....	....	....	....	....	....	....	....
312	Inventories...............................	—	—	—	—	—	—	....	....	....	....	....	....
313	Valuables.................................	—	—	—	—	—	—	....	....	....	....	....	....
314	Nonproduced assets.......................	10.9	−356.8	−2,379.9	45.6	79.9	75.1	....	....	....	....	....	....
3141	Land.....................................	....	....	....	....	....	....	....	....	....	....	....	....
3142	Subsoil assets........................	....	....	....	....	....	....	....	....	....	....	....	....
3143	Other naturally occurring assets..........	....	....	....	....	....	....	....	....	....	....	....	....
3144	Intangible nonproduced assets................	....	....	....	....	....	....	....	....	....	....	....	....
32	**Net acquisition of financial assets........**	....	....	....	....	....	....	....	....	....	....	....	....
321	Domestic.................................	....	....	....	....	....	....	....	....	....	....	....	....
3212	Currency and deposits.................	....	....	....	....	....	....	....	....	....	....	....	....
3213	Securities other than shares..........	....	....	....	....	....	....	....	....	....	....	....	....
3214	Loans....................................	....	....	....	....	....	....	....	....	....	....	....	....
3215	Shares and other equity...............	....	....	....	....	....	....	....	....	....	....	....	....
3216	Insurance technical reserves..........	....	....	....	....	....	....	....	....	....	....	....	....
3217	Financial derivatives.................	....	....	....	....	....	....	....	....	....	....	....	....
3218	Other accounts receivable.............	....	....	....	....	....	....	....	....	....	....	....	....
322	Foreign..................................	....	....	....	....	....	....	....	....	....	....	....	....
3222	Currency and deposits.................	....	....	....	....	....	....	....	....	....	....	....	....
3223	Securities other than shares..........	....	....	....	....	....	....	....	....	....	....	....	....
3224	Loans....................................	....	....	....	....	....	....	....	....	....	....	....	....
3225	Shares and other equity...............	....	....	....	....	....	....	....	....	....	....	....	....
3226	Insurance technical reserves..........	....	....	....	....	....	....	....	....	....	....	....	....
3227	Financial derivatives.................	....	....	....	....	....	....	....	....	....	....	....	....
3228	Other accounts receivable.............	....	....	....	....	....	....	....	....	....	....	....	....
323	Monetary gold and SDRs...................	....	....	....	....	....	....	....	....	....	....	....	....
33	**Net incurrence of liabilities...................**	....	....	....	....	....	....	....	....	....	....	....	....
331	Domestic.................................	....	....	....	....	....	....	....	....	....	....	....	....
3312	Currency and deposits.................	....	....	....	....	....	....	....	....	....	....	....	....
3313	Securities other than shares..........	....	....	....	....	....	....	....	....	....	....	....	....
3314	Loans....................................	....	....	....	....	....	....	....	....	....	....	....	....
3316	Insurance technical reserves..........	....	....	....	....	....	....	....	....	....	....	....	....
3317	Financial derivatives.................	....	....	....	....	....	....	....	....	....	....	....	....
3318	Other accounts payable................	....	....	....	....	....	....	....	....	....	....	....	....
332	Foreign..................................	....	....	....	....	....	....	....	....	....	....	....	....
3322	Currency and deposits.................	....	....	....	....	....	....	....	....	....	....	....	....
3323	Securities other than shares..........	....	....	....	....	....	....	....	....	....	....	....	....
3324	Loans....................................	....	....	....	....	....	....	....	....	....	....	....	....
3326	Insurance technical reserves..........	....	....	....	....	....	....	....	....	....	....	....	....
3327	Financial derivatives.................	....	....	....	....	....	....	....	....	....	....	....	....
3328	Other accounts payable................	....	....	....	....	....	....	....	....	....	....	....	....

In Trillions of Liras / Year Ending December 31 / Cash Reporter

	Budgetary Central Government			Extrabudgetary Accounts			Central Government			General Government		
	1999	2000	2001	1999	2000	2001	1999	2000	2001	1999	2000	2001
Table 4 Holding gains in assets and liabilities												
Table 5 Other changes in the volume of assets and liabilities												
Table 6 Balance sheet												
Table 7 Outlays by functions of govt.												
7 Total outlays................	26,860.9	44,925.8	81,545.9	2,606.4	4,208.4	6,857.1	....	....	....	....	....	....
701 General public services................	14,948.7	27,506.9	56,229.4	—	—	—	....	....	....	....	....	....
7017 Public debt transactions................	10,720.8	20,535.9	44,189.7	—	—	—	....	....	....	....	....	....
7018 General transfers between levels of govt......	....	....	....	—	—	—	....	....	....	....	....	....
702 Defense................	2,402.5	3,768.3	5,456.9	—	—	—	....	....	....	....	....	....
703 Public order and safety................	1,352.2	2,013.1	3,063.7	—	—	—	....	....	....	....	....	....
704 Economic affairs................	1,434.7	2,066.5	2,569.0	1,307.3	2,192.3	3,870.4	....	....	....	....	....	....
7042 Agriculture, forestry, fishing, and hunting.....	900.3	1,269.1	1,825.1	82.0	162.5	219.7	....	....	....	....	....	....
7043 Fuel and energy................	27.2	119.4	85.3	310.9	501.5	636.9	....	....	....	....	....	....
7044 Mining, manufacturing, and construction.....	101.7	166.3	219.9	—	—	—	....	....	....	....	....	....
7045 Transport................	50.0	75.1	97.6	592.1	967.3	2,125.9	....	....	....	....	....	....
7046 Communication................	....	....	....	....	....	....	....	....	....	....	....	....
705 Environmental protection................	....	....	....	....	....	....	....	....	....	....	....	....
706 Housing and community amenities........	77.3	741.6	706.7	342.6	579.2	845.2	....	....	....	....	....	....
707 Health................	1,086.0	1,580.1	2,598.5	55.7	86.4	136.8	....	....	....	....	....	....
7072 Outpatient services................	223.9	302.7	470.0	—	—	—	....	....	....	....	....	....
7073 Hospital services................	481.0	689.9	1,108.4	30.3	44.8	67.6	....	....	....	....	....	....
7074 Public health services................	....	....	....	....	....	....	....	....	....	....	....	....
708 Recreation, culture, and religion...........	268.0	374.3	557.9	62.7	78.8	122.8	....	....	....	....	....	....
709 Education................	2,531.0	3,539.0	5,233.7	791.9	1,194.7	1,773.0	....	....	....	....	....	....
7091 Pre-primary and primary education.............	....	....	....	....	....	....	....	....	....	....	....	....
7092 Secondary education................	2,195.9	3,015.2	4,468.8	—	—	—	....	....	....	....	....	....
7094 Tertiary education................	.4	.5	1.1	789.4	1,191.2	1,768.3	....	....	....	....	....	....
710 Social protection................	2,760.5	3,336.0	5,130.2	46.1	77.0	108.9	....	....	....	....	....	....
7 Statistical discrepancy: Total outlays.............	—	—	—	—	—	—	....	....	....	....	....	....
Table 8 Transactions in financial assets and liabilities by sector												
82 Net acquisition of financial assets........	....	....	....	....	....	....	....	....	....	....	....	....
821 Domestic................	....	....	....	....	....	....	....	....	....	....	....	....
8211 General government................	265.4	269.8	638.0	....	....	....	....	....	....	....	....	....
8212 Central bank................	....	....	....	....	....	....	....	....	....	....	....	....
8213 Other depository corporations................	....	....	....	....	....	....	....	....	....	....	....	....
8214 Financial corporations n.e.c................	....	....	....	....	....	....	....	....	....	....	....	....
8215 Nonfinancial corporations................	133.2	195.2	436.4	....	....	....	....	....	....	....	....	....
8216 Households & NPIs serving households......	....	....	....	....	....	....	....	....	....	....	....	....
822 Foreign................	....	....	....	....	....	....	....	....	....	....	....	....
8221 General government................	....	....	....	....	....	....	....	....	....	....	....	....
8227 International organizations................	....	....	....	....	....	....	....	....	....	....	....	....
8228 Financial corporations other than international organizations.............	....	....	....	....	....	....	....	....	....	....	....	....
8229 Other nonresidents................	....	....	....	....	....	....	....	....	....	....	....	....
823 Monetary gold and SDRs................	....	....	....	....	....	....	....	....	....	....	....	....
83 Net incurrence of liabilities................	....	....	....	....	....	....	....	....	....	....	....	....
831 Domestic................	....	....	....	....	....	....	....	....	....	....	....	....
8311 General government................	....	....	....	....	....	....	....	....	....	....	....	....
8312 Central bank................	....	....	....	....	....	....	....	....	....	....	....	....
8313 Other depository corporations................	....	....	....	....	....	....	....	....	....	....	....	....
8314 Financial corporations n.e.c................	....	....	....	....	....	....	....	....	....	....	....	....
8315 Nonfinancial corporations................	....	....	....	....	....	....	....	....	....	....	....	....
8316 Households & NPIs serving households......	....	....	....	....	....	....	....	....	....	....	....	....
832 Foreign................	....	....	....	....	....	....	....	....	....	....	....	....
8321 General government................	....	....	....	....	....	....	....	....	....	....	....	....
8327 International organizations................	....	....	....	....	....	....	....	....	....	....	....	....
8328 Financial corporations other than international organizations.............	....	....	....	....	....	....	....	....	....	....	....	....
8329 Other nonresidents................	....	....	....	....	....	....	....	....	....	....	....	....

Uganda 746

In Billions of Shillings / Year Ending June 30 / Cash Reporter

	Budgetary Central Government			Central Government			Local Government			General Government		
	2001	2002	2003	2001	2002	2003	2001	2002	2003	2001	2002	2003
Statement of government operations												
Statement of other economic flows												
Balance sheet												
Statement of sources and uses of cash												
1 Cash receipts from operating activities...........	2,531.9	2,539.9	2,695.1	....	....	....	565.6	659.3	773.5	....	....	....
11 Taxes..	1,074.9	1,212.0	1,401.3	....	....	....	35.6	38.2	43.3	....	....	....
12 Social contributions...........................				....	....	....	—	—	—	....	....	....
13 Grants...	1,448.7	1,286.5	1,269.1	....	....	....	506.8	598.0	703.0	....	....	....
14 Other receipts.................................	8.3	41.4	24.7	....	....	....	23.2	23.1	27.2	....	....	....
2 Cash payments for operating activities...........	2,219.7	2,473.8	2,687.7	....	....	....	468.7	533.5	639.1	....	....	....
21 Compensation of employees....................	225.9	253.5	284.8	....	....	....	240.7	293.2	344.2	....	....	....
22 Purchases of goods and services...............	743.4	878.0	971.6	....	....	....	145.8	161.3	201.4	....	....	....
24 Interest......................................	116.2	146.1	174.1	....	....	....	—	—	—	....	....	....
25 Subsidies.....................................	24.4	9.1	27.6	....	....	....	—	—	—	....	....	....
26 Grants.......................................	1,087.2	1,142.8	1,170.8	....	....	....	82.3	78.9	93.2	....	....	....
27 Social benefits...............................	22.4	44.2	58.8	....	....	....	—	—	—	....	....	....
28 Other payments..............................	—	—	—	....	....	....	—	.1	.3	....	....	....
CIO *Net cash inflow from oper. activities.....*	*312.3*	*66.1*	*7.3*	....	....	....	*96.9*	*125.8*	*134.4*	....	....	....
31.1 Purchases of nonfinancial assets..................	409.9	447.0	451.2	....	....	....	87.6	124.9	118.6	....	....	....
31.2 Sales of nonfinancial assets......................	—	—	—	....	....	....	—	—	—	....	....	....
31 Net cash outflow from investments in nonfinancial assets......................	409.9	447.0	451.2	....	....	....	87.6	124.9	118.6	....	....	....
CSD *Cash surplus/deficit................................*	*−97.7*	*−380.8*	*−443.9*	....	....	....	*9.3*	*.9*	*15.8*	....	....	....
32x Net acquisition of fin assets, excl. cash...........	170.9	307.9	60.2	....	....	....	7.2	1.5	−1.5	....	....	....
321x Domestic..	170.9	307.9	60.2	....	....	....	7.2	1.5	−1.5	....	....	....
322x Foreign...	—	—	—	....	....	....	—	—	—	....	....	....
323 Monetary gold and SDRs.........................	—	—	—	....	....	....	—	—	—	....	....	....
33 Net incurrence of liabilities......................	252.0	627.4	550.3	....	....	....	−.7	−2.3	7.7	....	....	....
331 Domestic......................................	−15.5	158.1	59.0	....	....	....	−.7	−2.3	4.7	....	....	....
332 Foreign..	267.5	469.2	491.2	....	....	....	—	—	3.1	....	....	....
NFB Net cash inflow from fin. activities................	81.2	319.5	490.1	....	....	....	−7.8	−3.8	9.3	....	....	....
NCB *Net change in the stock of cash...........*	*−16.5*	*−61.3*	*46.2*	....	....	....	*1.5*	*−2.9*	*25.1*	....	....	....
Table 1 Revenue												
1 **Revenue..**	**2,531.9**	**2,539.9**	**2,695.1**	....	....	....	**565.7**	**659.3**	**773.5**	....	....	....
11 **Taxes...**	**1,074.9**	**1,212.0**	**1,401.3**	....	....	....	**35.6**	**38.2**	**43.3**	....	....	....
111 Taxes on income, profits, & capital gains......	199.9	259.3	318.7	....	....	....	20.5	17.8	22.2	....	....	....
1111 Individuals..................................	6.3	6.6	19.1	....	....	....	20.5	17.8	22.2	....	....	....
1112 Corporations and other enterprises...........	193.7	252.7	299.6	....	....	....	—	—	—	....	....	....
112 Taxes on payroll and workforce..................	—	—	—	....	....	....	—	—	—	....	....	....
113 Taxes on property.............................				....	....	....	7.9	14.1	12.7	....	....	....
114 Taxes on goods and services.....................	492.8	567.0	647.5	....	....	....	3.7	4.5	6.0	....	....	....
1141 General taxes on goods and services..........	339.2	392.9	458.9	....	....	....	—	—	—	....	....	....
1142 Excises....................................	125.6	139.3	148.1	....	....	....	—	—	—	....	....	....
115 Taxes on int'l. trade and transactions..........	382.2	385.7	429.8	....	....	....	—	—	—	....	....	....
116 Other taxes...................................	—	—	5.3	....	....	....	3.5	1.8	2.4	....	....	....
12 **Social contributions.............................**	**—**	**—**	**—**	....	....	....	**—**	**—**	**—**	....	....	....
121 Social security contributions........................	—	—	—	....	....	....	—	—	—	....	....	....
122 Other social contributions........................	—	—	—	....	....	....	—	—	—	....	....	....
13 **Grants..**	**1,448.7**	**1,286.5**	**1,269.1**	....	....	....	**506.8**	**598.0**	**703.0**	....	....	....
131 From foreign governments.........................	....	....	....	....	....	....	—	—	—	....	....	....
132 From international organizations.................	....	....	....	....	....	....	43.9	57.6	58.5	....	....	....
133 From other general government units...........	628.7	531.7	516.6	....	....	....	463.0	540.4	644.6	....	....	....
14 **Other revenue...............................**	**8.3**	**41.4**	**24.7**	....	....	....	**23.2**	**23.1**	**27.2**	....	....	....
Table 2 Expense by economic type												
2 **Expense..**	**2,219.7**	**2,473.8**	**2,687.7**	....	....	....	**468.7**	**533.5**	**639.1**	....	....	....
21 **Compensation of employees..................**	**225.9**	**253.5**	**284.8**	....	....	....	**240.7**	**293.2**	**344.2**	....	....	....
211 Wages and salaries.............................	225.9	253.5	284.8	....	....	....	240.7	293.2	344.2	....	....	....
212 Social contributions...........................	—	—	—	....	....	....	—	—	—	....	....	....
22 **Use of goods and services.....................**	**743.4**	**878.0**	**971.6**	....	....	....	**145.8**	**161.3**	**201.4**	....	....	....
23 **Consumption of fixed capital................**	....	....	....	....	....	....	....	....	....	....	....	....
24 **Interest..**	**116.2**	**146.1**	**174.1**	....	....	....	**—**	**—**	**—**	....	....	....
25 **Subsidies...**	**24.4**	**9.1**	**27.6**	....	....	....	**—**	**—**	**—**	....	....	....

In Billions of Shillings / Year Ending June 30 / Cash Reporter

		Budgetary Central Government			Central Government			Local Government			General Government		
		2001	2002	2003	2001	2002	2003	2001	2002	2003	2001	2002	2003
26	Grants..................................	**1,087.2**	**1,142.8**	**1,170.8**	....	....	....	**82.3**	**78.9**	**93.2**	....	....	....
261	To foreign govenments................	—	—	—	....	....	....	—	—	—	....	....	....
262	To international organizations.........	—	—	—	....	....	....	—	—	—	....	....	....
263	To other general government units........	1,087.2	1,142.8	1,170.8	....	....	....	82.3	78.9	93.2	....	....	....
2631	Current............................	....	....	....	....	....	....	....	....	....	....	....	....
2632	Capital............................	....	....	....	....	....	....	....	....	....	....	....	....
27	**Social benefits.....................**	**22.4**	**44.2**	**58.8**	....	....	....	—	—	—	....	....	....
28	**Other expense.......................**	—	—	—	....	....	....	—	.1	.3	....	....	....
281	Property expense other than interest...........	—	—	—	....	....	....	—	—	—	....	....	....
282	Miscellaneous other expense...............	—	—	—	....	....	....	—	.1	.3	....	....	....
2821	Current............................	—	—	—	....	....	....	—	.1	.3	....	....	....
2822	Capital............................	—	—	—	....	....	....	—	—	—	....	....	....

Table 3 Transactions in assets and liabilities

		Budgetary Central Government			Central Government			Local Government			General Government		
		2001	2002	2003	2001	2002	2003	2001	2002	2003	2001	2002	2003
3	**Change in net worth from transactns....**	....	....	....	....	....	....	....	....	....	....	....	....
31	**Net acquisition of nonfinancial assets...**	**409.9**	**447.0**	**451.2**	....	....	....	**87.6**	**124.9**	**118.6**	....	....	....
311	Fixed assets..........................	409.9	447.0	451.2	....	....	....	87.6	124.9	118.6	....	....	....
3111	Buildings and structures.............	....	....	....	....	....	....	....	....	....	....	....	....
3112	Machinery and equipment.............	....	....	....	....	....	....	....	....	....	....	....	....
3113	Other fixed assets...................	....	....	....	....	....	....	....	....	....	....	....	....
312	Inventories...........................	—	—	—	....	....	....	—	—	—	....	....	....
313	Valuables............................	—	—	—	....	....	....	—	—	—	....	....	....
314	Nonproduced assets....................	—	—	—	....	....	....	—	—	—	....	....	....
3141	Land................................	—	—	—	....	....	....	—	—	—	....	....	....
3142	Subsoil assets.......................	—	—	—	....	....	....	—	—	—	....	....	....
3143	Other naturally occurring assets........	—	—	—	....	....	....	—	—	—	....	....	....
3144	Intangible nonproduced assets........	—	—	—	....	....	....	—	—	—	....	....	....
32	**Net acquisition of financial assets........**	**154.4**	**246.5**	**106.4**	....	....	....	**8.6**	**−1.4**	**23.6**	....	....	....
321	Domestic............................	154.4	246.5	106.4	....	....	....	8.6	−1.4	23.6	....	....	....
3212	Currency and deposits................	−16.5	−61.3	46.2	....	....	....	1.5	−2.9	25.1	....	....	....
3213	Securities other than shares..........	....	....	....	....	....	....	....	....	....	....	....	....
3214	Loans..............................	....	....	....	....	....	....	....	....	....	....	....	....
3215	Shares and other equity.............	....	....	....	....	....	....	....	....	....	....	....	....
3216	Insurance technical reserves..........	....	....	....	....	....	....	....	....	....	....	....	....
3217	Financial derivatives.................	....	....	....	....	....	....	....	....	....	....	....	....
3218	Other accounts receivable............	....	....	....	....	....	....	....	....	....	....	....	....
322	Foreign.............................	—	—	—	....	....	....	—	—	—	....	....	....
3222	Currency and deposits................	—	—	—	....	....	....	—	—	—	....	....	....
3223	Securities other than shares..........	—	—	—	....	....	....	—	—	—	....	....	....
3224	Loans..............................	—	—	—	....	....	....	—	—	—	....	....	....
3225	Shares and other equity.............	—	—	—	....	....	....	—	—	—	....	....	....
3226	Insurance technical reserves..........	—	—	—	....	....	....	—	—	—	....	....	....
3227	Financial derivatives.................	—	—	—	....	....	....	—	—	—	....	....	....
3228	Other accounts receivable............	—	—	—	....	....	....	—	—	—	....	....	....
323	Monetary gold and SDRs..............	—	—	—	....	....	....	—	—	—	....	....	....
33	**Net incurrence of liabilities...................**	**252.0**	**627.4**	**550.3**	....	....	....	**−.7**	**−2.3**	**7.7**	....	....	....
331	Domestic............................	−15.5	158.1	59.0	....	....	....	−.7	−2.3	4.7	....	....	....
3312	Currency and deposits................	....	....	....	....	....	....	....	....	....	....	....	....
3313	Securities other than shares..........	....	....	....	....	....	....	....	....	....	....	....	....
3314	Loans..............................	....	....	....	....	....	....	....	....	....	....	....	....
3316	Insurance technical reserves..........	....	....	....	....	....	....	....	....	....	....	....	....
3317	Financial derivatives.................	....	....	....	....	....	....	....	....	....	....	....	....
3318	Other accounts payable..............	....	....	....	....	....	....	....	....	....	....	....	....
332	Foreign.............................	267.5	469.2	491.2	....	....	....	—	—	3.1	....	....	....
3322	Currency and deposits................	....	....	....	....	....	....	—	—	....	....	....	....
3323	Securities other than shares..........	....	....	....	....	....	....	—	—	....	....	....	....
3324	Loans..............................	....	....	....	....	....	....	—	—	....	....	....	....
3326	Insurance technical reserves..........	....	....	....	....	....	....	—	—	....	....	....	....
3327	Financial derivatives.................	....	....	....	....	....	....	—	—	....	....	....	....
3328	Other accounts payable..............	....	....	....	....	....	....	....	....	....	....	....	....

Uganda 746

	Budgetary Central Government			Central Government			Local Government			General Government		
	2001	2002	2003	2001	2002	2003	2001	2002	2003	2001	2002	2003
Table 4 Holding gains in assets and liabilities												
Table 5 Other changes in the volume of assets and liabilities												
Table 6 Balance sheet												
Table 7 Outlays by functions of govt.												
7　　**Total outlays**..................................	2,629.6	2,920.7	3,139.0	....	....	....	556.3	658.4	757.7	....	....	....
701　　**General public services**.........................	432.3	562.9	583.0	....	....	....	153.2	148.9	197.4	....	....	....
7017　　Public debt transactions..................	116.2	146.1	174.1	....	....	....	—	—	—			
7018　　General transfers between levels of govt......	....	....	....	....	....	....	....	....	....			
702　　**Defense**..	208.4	234.9	278.9	....	....	....	—	—	—	....	....	....
703　　**Public order and safety**........................	104.8	136.5	150.0	....	....	....	9.9	7.8	7.9	....	....	....
704　　**Economic affairs**.................................	909.1	827.1	935.9	....	....	....	66.7	76.6	71.1	....	....	....
7042　　Agriculture, forestry, fishing, and hunting.....	105.6	121.8	130.9	....	....	....	....	....	....			
7043　　Fuel and energy..................................	36.9	50.8	41.5	....	....	....	....	....	....			
7044　　Mining, manufacturing, and construction.....	....	....	....	....	....	....	....	....	....			
7045　　Transport..	395.9	278.8	339.7	....	....	....	....	....	....			
7046　　Communication...................................	....	....	....	....	....	....	....	....	....			
705　　**Environmental protection**.....................	—	64.7	65.2	....	....	....	3.4	.4	1.7	....	....	....
706　　**Housing and community amenities**........	184.1	140.7	145.3	....	....	....	22.9	27.0	22.5	....	....	....
707　　**Health**...	314.7	390.6	399.4	....	....	....	66.6	95.7	101.7	....	....	....
7072　　Outpatient services.............................	—	....	....	....	....	....	....	....	....			
7073　　Hospital services.................................	22.0	43.3	44.2	....	....	....	....	....	....			
7074　　Public health services..........................	35.9	77.2	74.3	....	....	....	....	....	....			
708　　**Recreation, culture, and religion**............	—	—	—	....	....	....	4.4	4.1	7.1	....	....	....
709　　**Education**...	436.8	544.3	561.4	....	....	....	248.4	302.2	341.7	....	....	....
7091　　Pre-primary and primary education...............	347.3	430.4	424.6	....	....	....	....	....	....			
7092　　Secondary education............................	41.1	55.7	64.3	....	....	....	....	....	....			
7094　　Tertiary education...............................	48.5	58.2	72.5	....	....	....	....	....	....			
710　　**Social protection**...............................	39.3	19.0	19.8	....	....	....	19.3	5.5	7.0	....	....	....
7　　Statistical discrepancy: Total outlays..............	—	—	—	....	....	....	−38.4	−9.8	−.5	....	....	....
Table 8 Transactions in financial assets and liabilities by sector												
82　　**Net acquisition of financial assets**........	154.4	246.5	106.4	....	....	....	8.6	−1.4	23.6	....	....	....
821　　Domestic...	154.4	246.5	106.4	....	....	....	8.6	−1.4	23.6	....	....	....
8211　　General government................................	....	....	....	....	....	....	....	....	....	....	....	....
8212　　Central bank.......................................	....	....	....	....	....	....	....	....	....	....	....	....
8213　　Other depository corporations....................	....	....	....	....	....	....	....	....	....	....	....	....
8214　　Financial corporations n.e.c.....................	....	....	....	....	....	....	....	....	....	....	....	....
8215　　Nonfinancial corporations........................	....	....	....	....	....	....	....	....	....	....	....	....
8216　　Households & NPIs serving households.......	....	....	....	....	....	....	....	....	....	....	....	....
822　　Foreign...	—	—	—	....	....	....	....	....	....	....	....	....
8221　　General government................................	—	—	—	....	....	....	....	....	....	....	....	....
8227　　International organizations.......................	—	—	—	....	....	....	....	....	....	....	....	....
8228　　Financial corporations other than international organizations..............	—	—	—	....	....	....	—	—	—	....	....	....
8229　　Other nonresidents...............................	—	—	—	....	....	....	—	—	—	....	....	....
823　　Monetary gold and SDRs..........................	—	—	—	....	....	....	—	—	—	....	....	....
83　　**Net incurrence of liabilities**...................	252.0	627.4	550.3	....	....	....	−.7	−2.3	7.7	....	....	....
831　　Domestic...	−15.5	158.1	59.0	....	....	....	−.7	−2.3	4.7	....	....	....
8311　　General government................................	....	....	....	....	....	....	....	....	....	....	....	....
8312　　Central bank.......................................	....	....	....	....	....	....	....	....	....	....	....	....
8313　　Other depository corporations....................	....	....	....	....	....	....	....	....	....	....	....	....
8314　　Financial corporations n.e.c.....................	....	....	....	....	....	....	....	....	....	....	....	....
8315　　Nonfinancial corporations........................	....	....	....	....	....	....	....	....	....	....	....	....
8316　　Households & NPIs serving households......	....	....	....	....	....	....	....	....	....	....	....	....
832　　Foreign...	267.5	469.2	491.2	....	....	....	—	—	3.1	....	....	....
8321　　General government................................	....	....	....	....	....	....	—	—	....	....	....	....
8327　　International organizations.......................	....	....	....	....	....	....	—	—	....	....	....	....
8328　　Financial corporations other than international organizations..............	....	....	....	....	....	....	—	—	....	....	....	....
8329　　Other nonresidents...............................	....	....	....	....	....	....	—	—	....	....	....	....

	Budgetary Central Government			Central Government			Local Government			General Government		
	2002	2003p	2004p	2002	2003p	2004p	2002	2003p	2004p	2002	2003p	2004p
Statement of government operations												
Statement of other economic flows												
Balance sheet												
6 *Net worth*............	....	....	....	....	....	....	....	....	....	....	....	....
61 Nonfinancial assets............	....	....	....	....	....	....	....	....	....	....	....	....
62 Financial assets............	479	363	429	....	....	....	....	....	....	....	....	....
63 Liabilities............	75,729	77,533	85,401	....	....	....	....	....	....	....	....	....
Statement of sources and uses of cash												
1 Cash receipts from operating activities..........	44,983	54,270	69,487	69,248	82,482	108,007	27,626	33,275	37,914	85,113	101,660	127,509
11 Taxes............	29,578	36,504	45,816	29,578	36,504	45,816	16,191	18,235	17,798	45,769	54,740	63,614
12 Social contributions............	1,511	1,844	2,595	25,073	29,905	40,912	—	—	—	25,073	29,905	40,912
13 Grants............	3,235	2,581	2,011	3,238	2,586	2,021	8,818	11,729	16,819	296	217	428
14 Other receipts............	10,659	13,340	19,065	11,358	13,487	19,258	2,617	3,311	3,297	13,976	16,798	22,555
2 Cash payments for operating activities............	41,257	51,616	73,844	65,473	79,438	113,833	25,556	29,867	35,526	79,269	95,207	130,946
21 Compensation of employees............	10,755	13,426	17,161	11,183	13,927	17,883	9,900	12,249	15,628	21,083	26,176	33,511
22 Purchases of goods and services............	8,158	11,148	12,032	8,772	11,908	12,954	5,996	7,013	7,672	14,768	18,921	20,627
24 Interest............	2,750	2,520	3,054	2,750	2,520	3,054	70	23	93	2,821	2,543	3,147
25 Subsidies............	2,792	3,622	5,015	3,038	4,115	5,735	1,721	2,196	2,477	4,759	6,312	8,213
26 Grants............	11,549	13,985	23,039	8,926	12,010	17,037	2,943	2,369	1,593	108	281	218
27 Social benefits............	3,343	3,579	4,706	28,870	31,619	48,324	4,357	4,872	5,265	33,226	36,491	53,589
28 Other payments............	1,909	3,336	8,837	1,934	3,338	8,845	570	1,144	2,796	2,504	4,482	11,641
CIO *Net cash inflow from oper. activities.....*	*3,726*	*2,653*	*–4,357*	*3,774*	*3,044*	*–5,826*	*2,070*	*3,409*	*2,389*	*5,845*	*6,453*	*–3,437*
31.1 Purchases of nonfinancial assets............	3,212	4,141	5,628	3,532	4,356	6,041	2,226	3,904	4,831	5,757	8,260	10,872
31.2 Sales of nonfinancial assets............	484	807	851	484	807	851	621	1,031	1,690	1,106	1,838	2,540
31 Net cash outflow from investments in nonfinancial assets............	2,728	3,334	4,777	3,047	3,549	5,190	1,604	2,873	3,141	4,652	6,422	8,331
CSD *Cash surplus/deficit............*	*999*	*–680*	*–9,134*	*727*	*–505*	*–11,016*	*466*	*536*	*–752*	*1,193*	*31*	*–11,768*
32x Net acquisition of fin assets, excl. cash..........	–121	363	1,083	–123	360	1,080	–50	—	40	–173	714	1,119
321x Domestic............	–121	363	1,083	–123	360	1,080	–50	—	40	–173	714	1,119
322x Foreign............	—	—	—	—	—	—	—	—	—	—	—	—
323 Monetary gold and SDRs............	—	—	—	—	—	—	—	—	—	—	—	—
33 Net incurrence of liabilities............	–1	1,953	10,641	–1	1,953	10,641	32	738	1,377	31	3,045	12,017
331 Domestic............	933	1,371	9,972	933	1,371	9,972	32	–62	314	965	1,663	10,285
332 Foreign............	–934	582	669	–934	582	669	—	800	1,063	–934	1,382	1,732
NFB Net cash inflow from fin. activities............	119	1,590	9,558	122	1,593	9,561	82	738	1,337	204	2,331	10,898
NCB *Net change in the stock of cash............*	*1,118*	*910*	*425*	*849*	*1,088*	*–1,455*	*548*	*1,274*	*585*	*1,397*	*2,362*	*–870*

Table 1 Revenue

	2002	2003p	2004p	2002	2003p	2004p	2002	2003p	2004p	2002	2003p	2004p
1 **Revenue............**	**44,983**	**54,270**	**69,487**	**69,248**	**82,482**	**108,007**	**27,626**	**33,275**	**37,914**	**85,113**	**101,660**	**127,509**
11 **Taxes............**	**29,578**	**36,504**	**45,816**	**29,578**	**36,504**	**45,816**	**16,191**	**18,235**	**17,798**	**45,769**	**54,740**	**63,614**
111 Taxes on income, profits, & capital gains......	8,162	13,087	16,660	8,162	13,087	16,660	12,833	14,672	13,879	20,995	27,759	30,539
1111 Individuals............	—	—	635	—	—	635	11,108	13,909	13,042	11,108	13,909	13,677
1112 Corporations and other enterprises............	8,162	13,087	16,025	8,162	13,087	16,025	1,600	655	722	9,761	13,742	16,748
112 Taxes on payroll and workforce............	51	10	15	51	10	15	146	143	150	197	153	165
113 Taxes on property............	—	—	—	—	—	—	1,479	1,545	1,544	1,479	1,545	1,544
114 Taxes on goods and services............	18,368	18,876	23,220	18,368	18,876	23,220	1,731	1,872	2,223	20,099	20,748	25,444
1141 General taxes on goods and services............	13,471	12,598	14,808	13,471	12,598	14,808	7	8	7	13,478	12,606	14,815
1142 Excises............	3,887	5,141	6,661	3,887	5,141	6,661	211	105	44	4,098	5,246	6,704
115 Taxes on int'l. trade and transactions............	2,881	4,463	5,892	2,881	4,463	5,892	—	—	—	2,881	4,463	5,892
116 Other taxes............	117	68	29	117	68	29	2	3	—	118	71	29
12 **Social contributions............**	**1,511**	**1,844**	**2,595**	**25,073**	**29,905**	**40,912**	**—**	**—**	**—**	**25,073**	**29,905**	**40,912**
121 Social security contributions............	—	—	—	23,562	28,061	38,317	—	—	—	23,562	28,061	38,317
122 Other social contributions............	1,511	1,844	2,595	1,511	1,844	2,595	—	—	—	1,511	1,844	2,595
13 **Grants............**	**3,235**	**2,581**	**2,011**	**3,238**	**2,586**	**2,021**	**8,818**	**11,729**	**16,819**	**296**	**217**	**428**
131 From foreign governments............	—	—	—	1	4	5	—	—	—	1	4	5
132 From international organizations............	292	213	418	294	214	423	—	—	—	294	214	423
133 From other general government units............	2,943	2,369	1,593	2,943	2,369	1,593	8,818	11,729	16,819	—	—	—
14 **Other revenue............**	**10,659**	**13,340**	**19,065**	**11,358**	**13,487**	**19,258**	**2,617**	**3,311**	**3,297**	**13,976**	**16,798**	**22,555**

Table 2 Expense by economic type

	2002	2003p	2004p	2002	2003p	2004p	2002	2003p	2004p	2002	2003p	2004p
2 **Expense............**	**41,257**	**51,616**	**73,844**	**65,473**	**79,438**	**113,833**	**25,556**	**29,867**	**35,526**	**79,269**	**95,207**	**130,946**
21 **Compensation of employees............**	**10,755**	**13,426**	**17,161**	**11,183**	**13,927**	**17,883**	**9,900**	**12,249**	**15,628**	**21,083**	**26,176**	**33,511**
211 Wages and salaries............	8,890	11,169	14,188	9,209	11,541	14,714	7,304	9,048	11,422	16,513	20,589	26,136
212 Social contributions............	1,865	2,257	2,973	1,974	2,387	3,168	2,596	3,201	4,206	4,570	5,587	7,374
22 **Use of goods and services............**	**8,158**	**11,148**	**12,032**	**8,772**	**11,908**	**12,954**	**5,996**	**7,013**	**7,672**	**14,768**	**18,921**	**20,627**
23 **Consumption of fixed capital............**	....	....	....	....	....	....	....	....	....	....	....	....
24 **Interest............**	**2,750**	**2,520**	**3,054**	**2,750**	**2,520**	**3,054**	**70**	**23**	**93**	**2,821**	**2,543**	**3,147**
25 **Subsidies............**	**2,792**	**3,622**	**5,015**	**3,038**	**4,115**	**5,735**	**1,721**	**2,196**	**2,477**	**4,759**	**6,312**	**8,213**

In Millions of Hryvnias / Year Ending December 31 / Cash Reporter

		Budgetary Central Government			Central Government			Local Government			General Government		
		2002	2003p	2004p	2002	2003p	2004p	2002	2003p	2004p	2002	2003p	2004p
26	Grants................................	11,549	13,985	23,039	8,926	12,010	17,037	2,943	2,369	1,593	108	281	218
261	To foreign govenments...............	108	281	218	108	281	218	—	—	—	108	281	218
262	To international organizations.........	—	—	—	—	—	—	—	—	—	—	—	—
263	To other general government units...	11,441	13,704	22,821	8,818	11,729	16,819	2,943	2,369	1,593	—	—	—
2631	Current............................	11,271	13,265	20,961	8,648	11,290	14,959	2,942	2,369	1,593	—	—	—
2632	Capital............................	170	439	1,861	170	439	1,861	—	—	—	—	—	—
27	Social benefits......................	3,343	3,579	4,706	28,870	31,619	48,324	4,357	4,872	5,265	33,226	36,491	53,589
28	Other expense......................	1,909	3,336	8,837	1,934	3,338	8,845	570	1,144	2,796	2,504	4,482	11,641
281	Property expense other than interest...........	—	—	—	—	—	—	—	—	—	—	—	—
282	Miscellaneous other expense.....................	1,909	3,336	8,837	1,934	3,338	8,845	570	1,144	2,796	2,504	4,482	11,641
2821	Current............................	1,008	1,036	1,337	1,033	1,039	1,346	31	38	59	1,063	1,076	1,404
2822	Capital............................	902	2,300	7,500	902	2,300	7,500	539	1,106	2,737	1,440	3,406	10,237
Table 3	**Transactions in assets and liabilities**												
3	Change in net worth from transactns....	....	....	....	....	....	....	....	....	....	....	....	....
31	Net acquisition of nonfinancial assets...	2,728	3,334	4,777	3,047	3,549	5,190	1,604	2,873	3,141	4,652	6,422	8,331
311	Fixed assets.......................	2,867	3,440	4,744	3,186	3,655	5,157	1,740	3,179	3,749	4,926	6,834	8,906
3111	Buildings and structures..........	....	....	....	....	....	....	....	....	....	....	....	....
3112	Machinery and equipment.........	....	....	....	....	....	....	....	....	....	....	....	....
3113	Other fixed assets...............	....	....	....	....	....	....	....	....	....	....	....	....
312	Inventories........................	−154	−113	45	−154	−113	45	—	1	1	−154	−112	45
313	Valuables.........................	—	—	—	—	—	—	—	—	—	—	—	—
314	Nonproduced assets................	16	7	−11	16	7	−11	−135	−307	−609	−120	−300	−620
3141	Land............................	16	7	−11	16	7	−11	−135	−307	−609	−120	−300	−620
3142	Subsoil assets....................	—	—	—	—	—	—	—	—	—	—	—	—
3143	Other naturally occurring assets...	—	—	—	—	—	—	—	—	—	—	—	—
3144	Intangible nonproduced assets..........	—	—	—	—	—	—	—	—	—	—	—	—
32	Net acquisition of financial assets........	997	1,273	1,507	726	1,448	−375	498	1,274	625	1,224	3,075	249
321	Domestic..........................	580	1,453	1,439	308	1,628	−443	489	1,274	259	796	3,255	−186
3212	Currency and deposits..............	700	1,090	356	431	1,268	−1,523	538	1,274	219	970	2,542	−1,305
3213	Securities other than shares.........	—	—	—	—	—	—	—	—	—	—	—	—
3214	Loans...........................	−121	363	1,083	−123	360	1,080	−50	—	40	−173	714	1,119
3215	Shares and other equity............	—	—	—	—	—	—	—	—	—	—	—	—
3216	Insurance technical reserves.........	—	—	—	—	—	—	—	—	—	—	—	—
3217	Financial derivatives...............	—	—	—	—	—	—	—	—	—	—	—	—
3218	Other accounts receivable..........	....	....	....	....	....	....	....	....	....	....	....	....
322	Foreign...........................	418	−180	68	418	−180	68	10	—	366	427	−180	434
3222	Currency and deposits..............	418	−180	68	418	−180	68	10	—	366	427	−180	434
3223	Securities other than shares.........	—	—	—	—	—	—	—	—	—	—	—	—
3224	Loans...........................	—	—	—	—	—	—	—	—	—	—	—	—
3225	Shares and other equity............	—	—	—	—	—	—	—	—	—	—	—	—
3226	Insurance technical reserves.........	—	—	—	—	—	—	—	—	—	—	—	—
3227	Financial derivatives...............	—	—	—	—	—	—	—	—	—	—	—	—
3228	Other accounts receivable..........	....	....	....	....	....	....	....	....	....	....	....	....
323	Monetary gold and SDRs.............	—	—	—	—	—	—	—	—	—	—	—	—
33	Net incurrence of liabilities...................	−1	1,953	10,641	−1	1,953	10,641	32	738	1,377	31	3,045	12,017
331	Domestic..........................	933	1,371	9,972	933	1,371	9,972	32	−62	314	965	1,663	10,285
3312	Currency and deposits.............	603	2,174	9,502	603	2,174	9,502	—	—	325	603	2,528	9,825
3313	Securities other than shares..........	330	−803	471	330	−803	471	32	−62	−11	362	−865	460
3314	Loans...........................	—	—	—	—	—	—	—	—	—	—	—	—
3316	Insurance technical reserves.........	—	—	—	—	—	—	—	—	—	—	—	—
3317	Financial derivatives...............	—	—	—	—	—	—	—	—	—	—	—	—
3318	Other accounts payable..........	....	....	....	....	....	....	....	....	....	....	....	....
332	Foreign...........................	−934	582	669	−934	582	669	—	800	1,063	−934	1,382	1,732
3322	Currency and deposits.............	—	—	—	—	—	—	—	—	—	—	—	—
3323	Securities other than shares..........	−934	582	669	−934	582	669	—	800	1,063	−934	1,382	1,732
3324	Loans...........................	—	—	—	—	—	—	—	—	—	—	—	—
3326	Insurance technical reserves.........	—	—	—	—	—	—	—	—	—	—	—	—
3327	Financial derivatives...............	—	—	—	—	—	—	—	—	—	—	—	—
3328	Other accounts payable............	....	....	....	....	....	....	....	....	....	....	....	....

In Millions of Hryvnias / Year Ending December 31 / Cash Reporter

	Budgetary Central Government			Central Government			Local Government			General Government		
	2002	2003p	2004p	2002	2003p	2004p	2002	2003p	2004p	2002	2003p	2004p
Table 4 Holding gains in assets and liabilities												
Table 5 Other changes in the volume of assets and liabilities												
Table 6 Balance sheet												
6 Net worth....................	....	....	....	....	....	....	....	....	....	....	....	....
61 Nonfinancial assets....................	....	....	....	....	....	....	....	....	....	....	....	....
611 Fixed assets....................	....	....	....	....	....	....	....	....	....	....	....	....
6111 Buildings and structures....................	....	....	....	....	....	....	....	....	....	....	....	....
6112 Machinery and equipment....................	....	....	....	....	....	....	....	....	....	....	....	....
6113 Other fixed assets....................	....	....	....	....	....	....	....	....	....	....	....	....
612 Inventories....................	....	....	....	....	....	....	....	....	....	....	....	....
613 Valuables....................	....	....	....	....	....	....	....	....	....	....	....	....
614 Nonproduced assets....................	....	....	....	....	....	....	....	....	....	....	....	....
6141 Land....................	....	....	....	....	....	....	....	....	....	....	....	....
6142 Subsoil assets....................	....	....	....	....	....	....	....	....	....	....	....	....
6143 Other naturally occurring assets....................	....	....	....	....	....	....	....	....	....	....	....	....
6144 Intangible nonproduced assets....................	....	....	....	....	....	....	....	....	....	....	....	....
62 **Financial assets**....................	**479**	**363**	**429**	....	....	....	....	....	....	....	....	....
621 Domestic....................	—	—	—	....	....	....	....	....	....	....	....	....
6212 Currency and deposits....................	—	—	—	....	....	....	....	....	....	....	....	....
6213 Securities other than shares....................	—	—	—	....	....	....	....	....	....	....	....	....
6214 Loans....................	—	—	—	....	....	....	....	....	....	....	....	....
6215 Shares and other equity....................	—	—	—	....	....	....	....	....	....	....	....	....
6216 Insurance technical reserves....................	—	—	—	....	....	....	....	....	....	....	....	....
6217 Financial derivatives....................	—	—	—	....	....	....	....	....	....	....	....	....
6218 Other accounts receivable....................	....	....	....	....	....	....	....	....	....	....	....	....
622 Foreign....................	479	363	429	....	....	....	....	....	....	....	....	....
6222 Currency and deposits....................	—	—	—	....	....	....	....	....	....	....	....	....
6223 Securities other than shares....................	479	363	429	....	....	....	....	....	....	....	....	....
6224 Loans....................	—	—	—	....	....	....	....	....	....	....	....	....
6225 Shares and other equity....................	—	—	—	....	....	....	....	....	....	....	....	....
6226 Insurance technical reserves....................	—	—	—	....	....	....	....	....	....	....	....	....
6227 Financial derivatives....................	—	—	—	....	....	....	....	....	....	....	....	....
6228 Other accounts receivable....................	....	....	....	....	....	....	....	....	....	....	....	....
623 Monetary gold and SDRs....................	—	—	—	....	....	....	....	....	....	....	....	....
63 **Liabilities**....................	**75,729**	**77,533**	**85,401**	....	....	....	....	....	....	....	....	....
631 Domestic....................	21,387	20,525	20,954	....	....	....	....	....	....	....	....	....
6312 Currency and deposits....................	—	—	—	....	....	....	....	....	....	....	....	....
6313 Securities other than shares....................	10,924	10,063	11,234	....	....	....	....	....	....	....	....	....
6314 Loans....................	10,463	10,462	9,721	....	....	....	....	....	....	....	....	....
6316 Insurance technical reserves....................	—	—	—	....	....	....	....	....	....	....	....	....
6317 Financial derivatives....................	—	—	—	....	....	....	....	....	....	....	....	....
6318 Other accounts payable....................	....	....	....	....	....	....	....	....	....	....	....	....
632 Foreign....................	54,342	57,009	64,447	....	....	....	....	....	....	....	....	....
6322 Currency and deposits....................	—	—	—	....	....	....	....	....	....	....	....	....
6323 Securities other than shares....................	13,391	16,736	19,616	....	....	....	....	....	....	....	....	....
6324 Loans....................	40,951	40,273	44,831	....	....	....	....	....	....	....	....	....
6326 Insurance technical reserves....................	—	—	—	....	....	....	....	....	....	....	....	....
6327 Financial derivatives....................	—	—	—	....	....	....	....	....	....	....	....	....
6328 Other accounts payable....................	....	....	....	....	....	....	....	....	....	....	....	....
Memorandum items:												
6M2 Net financial worth....................	−75,250	−77,170	−84,972	....	....	....	....	....	....	....	....	....
6M3 Debt at market value....................	....	....	....	....	....	....	....	....	....	....	....	....
6M4 Debt at nominal value....................	....	....	....	....	....	....	....	....	....	....	....	....
6M5 Arrears....................	....	....	....	....	....	....	....	....	....	....	....	....
6M6 Obligations for social security benefits....................	....	....	....	....	....	....	....	....	....	....	....	....
6M7 Contingent liabilities....................	11,260	11,400	17,719	....	....	....	....	....	....	....	....	....
6M8 Uncapitalized military weapons, systems........	....	....	....	....	....	....	....	....	....	....	....	....
Table 7 Outlays by functions of govt.												
7 **Total outlays**....................	**44,469**	**55,757**	**79,472**	**69,005**	**83,794**	**119,874**	**27,781**	**33,771**	**40,357**	**85,026**	**103,467**	**141,818**
701 **General public services**....................	**15,647**	**19,576**	**26,277**	**15,647**	**19,576**	**26,277**	**4,643**	**4,535**	**4,252**	**8,529**	**10,013**	**12,116**
7017 Public debt transactions....................	2,750	2,520	3,054	2,750	2,520	3,054	70	23	93	2,821	2,543	3,147
7018 General transfers between levels of govt......	8,818	11,729	16,819	8,818	11,729	16,819	2,943	2,369	1,593	—	—	—
702 **Defense**....................	**2,997**	**3,562**	**5,111**	**2,997**	**3,562**	**5,111**	—	—	—	**2,997**	**3,562**	**5,111**
703 **Public order and safety**....................	**4,660**	**5,685**	**7,708**	**4,660**	**5,685**	**7,708**	364	139	148	**5,024**	**5,823**	**7,855**

In Millions of Hryvnias / Year Ending December 31 / Cash Reporter

		Budgetary Central Government			Central Government			Local Government			General Government		
		2002	2003p	2004p	2002	2003p	2004p	2002	2003p	2004p	2002	2003p	2004p
704	**Economic affairs**	**6,572**	**10,235**	**15,347**	**6,913**	**10,827**	**16,274**	**2,167**	**3,541**	**5,246**	**9,080**	**14,368**	**21,520**
7042	Agriculture, forestry, fishing, and hunting	1,408	2,729	2,985	....	....	2,985	6,728	27	33	....	....	3,018
7043	Fuel and energy	2,404	3,540	4,726	....	....	4,726	28,994	43	94	....	....	4,820
7044	Mining, manufacturing, and construction	278	328	376	....	....	376	4,468	7	595	....	....	970
7045	Transport	1,098	1,926	5,408	....	....	5,408	1,074	1,217	1,777	....	....	7,185
7046	Communication	21	33	36	....	....	36	11,537	11	20	....	....	57
705	**Environmental protection**	**233**	**361**	**534**	**233**	**361**	**534**	**167**	**233**	**355**	**400**	**594**	**889**
706	**Housing and community amenities**	**593**	**479**	**639**	**594**	**479**	**639**	**1,282**	**1,634**	**2,370**	**1,876**	**2,113**	**3,008**
707	**Health**	**2,060**	**2,944**	**4,106**	**2,474**	**3,474**	**4,706**	**5,875**	**7,254**	**8,607**	**8,350**	**10,728**	**13,313**
7072	Outpatient services	60	77	205	62	80	208	689	872	1,097	752	952	1,304
7073	Hospital services	1,234	1,546	1,818	1,641	2,066	2,406	4,825	5,936	7,041	6,466	8,002	9,446
7074	Public health services	344	523	623	344	523	623	65	72	80	409	595	702
708	**Recreation, culture, and religion**	**434**	**659**	**1,029**	**482**	**716**	**1,096**	**1,000**	**1,418**	**1,705**	**1,483**	**2,135**	**2,802**
709	**Education**	**5,314**	**5,998**	**7,493**	**5,318**	**6,001**	**7,496**	**6,845**	**8,678**	**10,503**	**12,163**	**14,679**	**17,999**
7091	Pre-primary and primary education	9	9	15	....	....	15	1,309	1,631	1,968	....	....	1,982
7092	Secondary education	62	36	51	....	....	51	4,492	5,718	6,913	....	....	6,964
7094	Tertiary education	3,900	4,307	5,424	....	....	5,424	262	314	392	....	....	5,816
710	**Social protection**	**5,958**	**6,258**	**11,228**	**29,685**	**33,113**	**50,034**	**5,439**	**6,339**	**7,171**	**35,125**	**39,452**	**57,205**
7	Statistical discrepancy: Total outlays	—	—	—	—	—	—	—	—	—	—	—	—

Table 8   Transactions in financial assets and liabilities by sector

		2002	2003p	2004p	2002	2003p	2004p	2002	2003p	2004p	2002	2003p	2004p
82	**Net acquisition of financial assets**	**997**	**1,273**	**1,507**	**726**	**1,448**	**−375**	**498**	**1,274**	**625**	**1,224**	**3,075**	**249**
821	Domestic	580	1,453	1,439	308	1,628	−443	489	1,274	259	796	3,255	−186
8211	General government	15	−354	—	15	−354	—	—	−9	1	15	−9	—
8212	Central bank	700	1,090	356	431	1,268	−1,523	538	1,274	219	970	2,542	−1,305
8213	Other depository corporations	—	—	—	—	—	—	—	—	—	—	—	—
8214	Financial corporations n.e.c.	—	—	—	—	—	—	—	—	—	—	—	—
8215	Nonfinancial corporations	−187	616	1,222	−189	613	1,219	−50	−21	−7	−239	593	1,212
8216	Households & NPIs serving households	51	101	−139	51	101	−139	—	29	46	51	130	−93
822	Foreign	418	−180	68	418	−180	68	10	—	366	427	−180	434
8221	General government	—	−180	—	—	−180	—	—	—	—	—	−180	—
8227	International organizations	—	—	—	—	—	—	—	—	—	—	—	—
8228	Financial corporations other than international organizations	—	—	—	—	—	—	—	—	—	—	—	—
8229	Other nonresidents	418	—	68	418	—	68	10	—	366	427	—	434
823	Monetary gold and SDRs	—	—	—	—	—	—	—	—	—	—	—	—
83	**Net incurrence of liabilities**	**−1**	**1,953**	**10,641**	**−1**	**1,953**	**10,641**	**32**	**738**	**1,377**	**31**	**3,045**	**12,017**
831	Domestic	933	1,371	9,972	933	1,371	9,972	32	−62	314	965	1,663	10,285
8311	General government	603	1,371	9,502	603	1,371	9,502	—	−62	325	603	1,663	9,825
8312	Central bank	—	—	−708	—	—	−708	—	—	—	—	—	−708
8313	Other depository corporations	—	—	—	—	—	—	—	—	—	—	—	—
8314	Financial corporations n.e.c.	330	—	1,179	330	—	1,179	44	—	−11	374	—	1,167
8315	Nonfinancial corporations	—	—	—	—	—	—	−12	—	—	−12	—	—
8316	Households & NPIs serving households	—	—	—	—	—	—	—	—	—	—	—	—
832	Foreign	−934	582	669	−934	582	669	—	800	1,063	−934	1,382	1,732
8321	General government	−700	−1,267	−1,112	−700	−1,267	−1,112	—	800	—	−700	−468	−1,112
8327	International organizations	−799	−442	−894	−799	−442	−894	—	—	1,063	−799	−442	170
8328	Financial corporations other than international organizations	−32	—	—	−32	—	—				−32	—	—
8329	Other nonresidents	597	2,292	2,675	597	2,292	2,675	—	—	—	597	2,292	2,675

United Arab Emirates   466

In Millions of Dirhams / Year Ending December 31 / Cash Reporter

		Central Government			State Government			Local Government			General Government		
		1997	1998	1999p	1997	1998	1999	1997	1998	1999	1997	1998	1999
Statement of government operations													
Statement of other economic flows													
Balance sheet													
Statement of sources and uses of cash													
1	Cash receipts from operating activities...........	18,996	19,212	20,217	....	....	....	....	....	....	....	....	....
11	Taxes........................	2,872	2,990	3,481	....	....	....	....	....	....	....	....	....
12	Social contributions......................	103	122	92	....	....	....	....	....	....	....	....	....
13	Grants.................................	—	—	—	....	....	....	....	....	....	....	....	....
14	Other receipts.................................	16,021	16,100	16,644	....	....	....	....	....	....	....	....	....
2	Cash payments for operating activities...........	17,521	18,200	19,228	....	....	....	....	....	....	....	....	....
21	Compensation of employees...................	6,458	6,695	6,922	....	....	....	....	....	....	....	....	....
22	Purchases of goods and services..................	8,786	8,851	8,787	....	....	....	....	....	....	....	....	....
24	Interest.............................	—	—	—	....	....	....	....	....	....	....	....	....
25	Subsidies...........................	....	....	....	....	....	....	....	....	....	....	....	....
26	Grants.............................	....	....	....	....	....	....	....	....	....	....	....	....
27	Social benefits.........................	....	....	....	....	....	....	....	....	....	....	....	....
28	Other payments........................	—	—	—	....	....	....	....	....	....	....	....	....
CIO	*Net cash inflow from oper. activities.....*	*1,475*	*1,012*	*989*	....	....	....	....	....	....	....	....	....
31.1	Purchases of nonfinancial assets...................	529	970	822	....	....	....	....	....	....	....	....	....
31.2	Sales of nonfinancial assets.....................	16	44	17	....	....	....	....	....	....	....	....	....
31	Net cash outflow from investments in nonfinancial assets...........	513	926	805	....	....	....	....	....	....	....	....	....
CSD	*Cash surplus/deficit.................*	*962*	*86*	*184*	....	....	....	....	....	....	....	....	....
32x	Net acquisition of fin assets, excl. cash...........	65	618	127	....	....	....	....	....	....	....	....	....
321x	Domestic.................................	46	613	127	....	....	....	....	....	....	....	....	....
322x	Foreign.................................	19	5	—	....	....	....	....	....	....	....	....	....
323	Monetary gold and SDRs.................	—	—	—	....	....	....	....	....	....	....	....	....
33	Net incurrence of liabilities................	....	....	....	....	....	....	....	....	....	....	....	....
331	Domestic.................................	....	....	....	....	....	....	....	....	....	....	....	....
332	Foreign.................................	....	....	....	....	....	....	....	....	....	....	....	....
NFB	Net cash inflow from fin. activities...........	....	....	....	....	....	....	....	....	....	....	....	....
NCB	*Net change in the stock of cash............*	....	....	....	....	....	....	....	....	....	....	....	....
Table 1 Revenue													
1	**Revenue**	**18,996**	**19,212**	**20,217**	....	....	....	....	....	....	....	....	....
11	**Taxes........................**	**2,872**	**2,990**	**3,481**	....	....	....	....	....	....	....	....	....
111	Taxes on income, profits, & capital gains......	—	—	—	....	....	....	....	....	....	....	....	....
1111	Individuals..............................	—	—	—	....	....	....	....	....	....	....	....	....
1112	Corporations and other enterprises............	—	—	—	....	....	....	....	....	....	....	....	....
112	Taxes on payroll and workforce..................	—	—	—	....	....	....	....	....	....	....	....	....
113	Taxes on property.............................	—	—	—	....	....	....	....	....	....	....	....	....
114	Taxes on goods and services..................	2,872	2,990	3,481	....	....	....	....	....	....	....	....	....
1141	General taxes on goods and services..........	....	....	....	....	....	....	....	....	....	....	....	....
1142	Excises..................................	....	....	....	....	....	....	....	....	....	....	....	....
115	Taxes on int'l. trade and transactions...........	—	—	—	....	....	....	....	....	....	....	....	....
116	Other taxes.................................	—	—	—	....	....	....	....	....	....	....	....	....
12	**Social contributions..............................**	**103**	**122**	**92**	....	....	....	....	....	....	....	....	....
121	Social security contributions......................	103	122	92	....	....	....	....	....	....	....	....	....
122	Other social contributions...........................	—	—	—	....	....	....	....	....	....	....	....	....
13	**Grants................................**	**—**	**—**	**—**	....	....	....	....	....	....	....	....	....
131	From foreign governments.........................	—	—	—	....	....	....	....	....	....	....	....	....
132	From international organizations..................	—	—	—	....	....	....	....	....	....	....	....	....
133	From other general government units...........	—	—	—	....	....	....	....	....	....	....	....	....
14	**Other revenue..........................**	**16,021**	**16,100**	**16,644**	....	....	....	....	....	....	....	....	....
Table 2 Expense by economic type													
2	**Expense..........................**	**17,521**	**18,200**	**19,228**	....	....	....	....	....	....	....	....	....
21	**Compensation of employees.................**	**6,458**	**6,695**	**6,922**	....	....	....	....	....	....	....	....	....
211	Wages and salaries.........................	6,458	6,695	6,922	....	....	....	....	....	....	....	....	....
212	Social contributions..........................	....	....	....	....	....	....	....	....	....	....	....	....
22	**Use of goods and services....................**	**8,786**	**8,851**	**8,787**	....	....	....	....	....	....	....	....	....
23	**Consumption of fixed capital.................**	....	....	....	....	....	....	....	....	....	....	....	....
24	**Interest...................................**	**—**	**—**	**—**	....	....	....	....	....	....	....	....	....
25	**Subsidies..........................**	....	....	....	....	....	....	....	....	....	....	....	....

2005, International Monetary Fund: *Government Finance Statistics Yearbook*

In Millions of Dirhams / Year Ending December 31 / Cash Reporter

		Central Government			State Government			Local Government			General Government		
		1997	1998	1999p	1997	1998	1999	1997	1998	1999	1997	1998	1999
26	**Grants**................................	....	....	....	....	....	....	....	....	....	....	....	....
261	To foreign govenments................	....	....	....	....	....	....	....	....	....	....	....	....
262	To international organizations..........	....	....	....	....	....	....	....	....	....	....	....	....
263	To other general government units........	....	....	....	....	....	....	....	....	....	....	....	....
2631	Current............................	....	....	....	....	....	....	....	....	....	....	....	....
2632	Capital............................	—	—	—	....	....	....	....	....	....	....	....	....
27	**Social benefits**.......................	....	....	....	....	....	....	....	....	....	....	....	....
28	**Other expense**.......................	—	—	—	....	....	....	....	....	....	....	....	....
281	Property expense other than interest........	—	—	—	....	....	....	....	....	....	....	....	....
282	Miscellaneous other expense.............	—	—	—	....	....	....	....	....	....	....	....	....
2821	Current............................	—	—	—	....	....	....	....	....	....	....	....	....
2822	Capital............................	—	—	—	....	....	....	....	....	....	....	....	....

Table 3   Transactions in assets and liabilities

		Central Government			State Government			Local Government			General Government		
3	**Change in net worth from transactns....**	....	....	....	....	....	....	....	....	....	....	....	....
31	**Net acquisition of nonfinancial assets...**	513	926	805	....	....	....	....	....	....	....	....	....
311	Fixed assets..........................	....	....	....	....	....	....	....	....	....	....	....	....
3111	Buildings and structures..............	....	....	....	....	....	....	....	....	....	....	....	....
3112	Machinery and equipment.............	....	....	....	....	....	....	....	....	....	....	....	....
3113	Other fixed assets....................	....	....	....	....	....	....	....	....	....	....	....	....
312	Inventories..........................	....	....	....	....	....	....	....	....	....	....	....	....
313	Valuables...........................	....	....	....	....	....	....	....	....	....	....	....	....
314	Nonproduced assets....................	....	....	....	....	....	....	....	....	....	....	....	....
3141	Land..............................	....	....	....	....	....	....	....	....	....	....	....	....
3142	Subsoil assets.......................	....	....	....	....	....	....	....	....	....	....	....	....
3143	Other naturally occurring assets........	....	....	....	....	....	....	....	....	....	....	....	....
3144	Intangible nonproduced assets..........	....	....	....	....	....	....	....	....	....	....	....	....
32	**Net acquisition of financial assets........**	....	....	....	....	....	....	....	....	....	....	....	....
321	Domestic............................	....	....	....	....	....	....	....	....	....	....	....	....
3212	Currency and deposits.................	....	....	....	....	....	....	....	....	....	....	....	....
3213	Securities other than shares...........	....	....	....	....	....	....	....	....	....	....	....	....
3214	Loans..............................	....	....	....	....	....	....	....	....	....	....	....	....
3215	Shares and other equity...............	....	....	....	....	....	....	....	....	....	....	....	....
3216	Insurance technical reserves...........	....	....	....	....	....	....	....	....	....	....	....	....
3217	Financial derivatives..................	....	....	....	....	....	....	....	....	....	....	....	....
3218	Other accounts receivable..............	....	....	....	....	....	....	....	....	....	....	....	....
322	Foreign.............................	....	....	....	....	....	....	....	....	....	....	....	....
3222	Currency and deposits.................	....	....	....	....	....	....	....	....	....	....	....	....
3223	Securities other than shares...........	....	....	....	....	....	....	....	....	....	....	....	....
3224	Loans..............................	....	....	....	....	....	....	....	....	....	....	....	....
3225	Shares and other equity...............	....	....	....	....	....	....	....	....	....	....	....	....
3226	Insurance technical reserves...........	....	....	....	....	....	....	....	....	....	....	....	....
3227	Financial derivatives..................	....	....	....	....	....	....	....	....	....	....	....	....
3228	Other accounts receivable..............	....	....	....	....	....	....	....	....	....	....	....	....
323	Monetary gold and SDRs................	....	....	....	....	....	....	....	....	....	....	....	....
33	**Net incurrence of liabilities...................**	....	....	....	....	....	....	....	....	....	....	....	....
331	Domestic............................	....	....	....	....	....	....	....	....	....	....	....	....
3312	Currency and deposits.................	....	....	....	....	....	....	....	....	....	....	....	....
3313	Securities other than shares...........	....	....	....	....	....	....	....	....	....	....	....	....
3314	Loans..............................	....	....	....	....	....	....	....	....	....	....	....	....
3316	Insurance technical reserves...........	....	....	....	....	....	....	....	....	....	....	....	....
3317	Financial derivatives..................	....	....	....	....	....	....	....	....	....	....	....	....
3318	Other accounts payable................	....	....	....	....	....	....	....	....	....	....	....	....
332	Foreign.............................	....	....	....	....	....	....	....	....	....	....	....	....
3322	Currency and deposits.................	....	....	....	....	....	....	....	....	....	....	....	....
3323	Securities other than shares...........	....	....	....	....	....	....	....	....	....	....	....	....
3324	Loans..............................	....	....	....	....	....	....	....	....	....	....	....	....
3326	Insurance technical reserves...........	....	....	....	....	....	....	....	....	....	....	....	....
3327	Financial derivatives..................	....	....	....	....	....	....	....	....	....	....	....	....
3328	Other accounts payable................	....	....	....	....	....	....	....	....	....	....	....	....

In Millions of Dirhams / Year Ending December 31 / Cash Reporter

	Central Government			State Government			Local Government			General Government		
	1997	1998	1999p	1997	1998	1999	1997	1998	1999	1997	1998	1999
Table 4 Holding gains in assets and liabilities												
Table 5 Other changes in the volume of assets and liabilities												
Table 6 Balance sheet												
Table 7 Outlays by functions of govt.												
7 **Total outlays**.............................	18,050	19,170	20,050	....	....	....	....	....	....	....	....	....
701 **General public services**....................	2,945	3,336	4,167	....	....	....	....	....	....	....	....	....
7017 Public debt transactions....................	—	—	—	....	....	....	....	....	....	....	....	....
7018 General transfers between levels of govt......	....	....	....	....	....	....	....	....	....	....	....	....
702 **Defense**...	6,027	6,027	6,027	....	....	....	....	....	....	....	....	....
703 **Public order and safety**......................	2,602	2,685	2,763	....	....	....	....	....	....	....	....	....
704 **Economic affairs**..............................	643	1,091	910	....	....	....	....	....	....	....	....	....
7042 Agriculture, forestry, fishing, and hunting.....	127	145	135	....	....	....	....	....	....	....	....	....
7043 Fuel and energy.................................	268	694	548	....	....	....	....	....	....	....	....	....
7044 Mining, manufacturing, and construction.....	16	16	15	....	....	....	....	....	....	....	....	....
7045 Transport...	43	47	25	....	....	....	....	....	....	....	....	....
7046 Communication..................................	....	....	....	....	....	....	....	....	....	....	....	....
705 **Environmental protection**................	—	—	—	....	....	....	....	....	....	....	....	....
706 **Housing and community amenities**........	128	234	329	....	....	....	....	....	....	....	....	....
707 **Health**...	1,391	1,450	1,448	....	....	....	....	....	....	....	....	....
7072 Outpatient services.............................	....	....	....	....	....	....	....	....	....	....	....	....
7073 Hospital services................................	....	....	....	....	....	....	....	....	....	....	....	....
7074 Public health services..........................	....	....	....	....	....	....	....	....	....	....	....	....
708 **Recreation, culture, and religion**...........	273	297	290	....	....	....	....	....	....	....	....	....
709 **Education**..	3,379	3,396	3,474	....	....	....	....	....	....	....	....	....
7091 Pre-primary and primary education..............	....	....	....	....	....	....	....	....	....	....	....	....
7092 Secondary education...........................	....	....	....	....	....	....	....	....	....	....	....	....
7094 Tertiary education...............................	....	....	....	....	....	....	....	....	....	....	....	....
710 **Social protection**.............................	662	654	642	....	....	....	....	....	....	....	....	....
7 Statistical discrepancy: Total outlays..............	—	—	—	....	....	....	....	....	....	....	....	....
Table 8 Transactions in financial assets and liabilities by sector												

In Millions of Pounds / Year Ending December 31 / Noncash Reporter

		Budgetary Central Government			Central Government			Local Government			General Government		
		2002	2003	2004	2002	2003	2004	2002	2003	2004	2002	2003	2004
	Statement of government operations												
1	Revenue...	....	....	....	381,501	401,413	428,815	124,740	138,092	147,016	418,842	441,372	472,921
2	Expense..	....	....	....	397,681	436,933	462,595	120,688	131,536	140,254	430,970	470,336	499,939
GOB	*Gross operating balance*................	....	....	....	*-10,749*	*-29,960*	*-28,096*	*8,677*	*11,399*	*11,866*	*-2,072*	*-18,561*	*-16,230*
NOB	*Net operating balance*...................	....	....	....	*-16,180*	*-35,520*	*-33,780*	*4,052*	*6,556*	*6,762*	*-12,128*	*-28,964*	*-27,018*
31	Net acquisition of nonfinancial assets.........	....	....	....	1,724	2,918	3,590	2,735	3,966	5,246	4,459	6,884	8,836
NLB	*Net lending/borrowing*...................	....	....	....	*-17,904*	*-38,438*	*-37,370*	*1,317*	*2,590*	*1,516*	*-16,587*	*-35,848*	*-35,854*
32	Net acquisition of financial assets...........	....	....	....	-5,164	-1,672	4,320	789	1,480	3,128	-4,375	-192	7,448
33	Net incurrence of liabilities.................	....	....	....	13,369	37,023	41,793	-1,461	-2,093	3,181	11,908	34,930	44,974
NLB	Statistical discrepancy......................	....	....	....	-629	-257	-103	933	983	-1,569	304	726	-1,672
	Statement of other economic flows												
	Balance sheet												
6	*Net worth*..................................	....	....	....	....	....	....	....	....	....	....	....	....
61	Nonfinancial assets.........................	....	....	....	....	....	....	....	....	....	....	....	....
62	Financial assets.............................	....	....	....	....	....	....	....	....	....	165,119	166,405	173,839
63	Liabilities...................................	....	....	....	....	....	....	....	....	....	522,529	548,613	602,100
	Statement of sources and uses of cash												
	Table 1 Revenue												
1	**Revenue**....................................	....	....	....	381,501	401,413	428,815	124,740	138,092	147,016	418,842	441,372	472,921
11	**Taxes**......................................	....	....	....	287,703	296,480	318,413	15,828	17,828	19,350	303,531	314,308	337,763
111	Taxes on income, profits, & capital gains......	....	....	....	142,456	143,602	156,442	—	—	—	142,456	143,602	156,442
1111	Individuals................................	....	....	....	109,047	111,051	119,959	—	—	—	109,047	111,051	119,959
1112	Corporations and other enterprises...........	....	....	....	33,409	32,551	36,483	—	—	—	33,409	32,551	36,483
112	Taxes on payroll and workforce.............	....	....	....									
113	Taxes on property..........................	....	....	....	19,208	19,531	20,317	173	188	204	19,381	19,719	20,521
114	Taxes on goods and services.................	....	....	....	121,480	128,708	136,748	15,655	17,640	19,146	137,135	146,348	155,894
1141	General taxes on goods and services.........	....	....	....	68,566	74,925	79,958	—	—	—	68,566	74,925	79,958
1142	Excises....................................	....	....	....	37,497	38,421	39,709	—	—	—	37,497	38,421	39,709
115	Taxes on int'l. trade and transactions...........	....	....	....	—	—	—	—	—	—			
116	Other taxes................................	....	....	....	4,559	4,639	4,906	—	—	—	4,559	4,639	4,906
12	**Social contributions**......................	....	....	....	76,421	86,946	92,971	2,703	2,804	2,919	79,124	89,750	95,890
121	Social security contributions.................	....	....	....	70,139	82,158	88,693	637	659	701	70,776	82,817	89,394
122	Other social contributions...................	....	....	....	6,282	4,788	4,278	2,066	2,145	2,218	8,348	6,933	6,496
13	**Grants**.....................................	....	....	....	3,112	3,570	3,604	83,371	92,505	99,935	3,261	3,881	4,135
131	From foreign governments...................	....	....	....	—	—	—	—	—	—	—	—	—
132	From international organizations.............	....	....	....	3,112	3,570	3,604	149	311	531	3,261	3,881	4,135
133	From other general government units.........	....	....	....	—	—	—	83,222	92,194	99,404	—	—	—
14	**Other revenue**.............................	....	....	....	14,265	14,417	13,827	22,838	24,955	24,812	32,926	33,433	35,133
	Table 2 Expense by economic type												
2	**Expense**....................................	....	....	....	397,681	436,933	462,595	120,688	131,536	140,254	430,970	470,336	499,939
21	**Compensation of employees**................	....	....	....	55,737	59,129	61,410	52,008	55,505	59,699	107,745	114,634	121,109
211	Wages and salaries.........................	....	....	....	45,342	47,937	49,865	42,707	45,772	49,481	88,049	93,709	99,346
212	Social contributions........................	....	....	....	10,395	11,192	11,545	9,301	9,733	10,218	19,696	20,925	21,763
22	**Use of goods and services**.................	....	....	....	71,329	80,447	87,018	41,847	47,404	50,701	113,176	127,851	137,719
23	**Consumption of fixed capital**..............	....	....	....	5,431	5,560	5,684	4,625	4,843	5,104	10,056	10,403	10,788
24	**Interest**...................................	....	....	....	21,440	22,431	23,316	4,023	4,602	3,799	21,541	22,667	23,700
25	**Subsidies**..................................	....	....	....	4,218	4,951	4,537	1,055	1,281	2,195	5,273	6,232	6,732
26	**Grants**.....................................	....	....	....	85,795	94,909	102,580	—	—	—	2,573	2,715	3,176
261	To foreign govenments.....................	....	....	....	—	—	—						
262	To international organizations...............	....	....	....	2,573	2,715	3,176	—	—	—	2,573	2,715	3,176
263	To other general government units..............	....	....	....	83,222	92,194	99,404	—	—	—			
2631	Current...................................	....	....	....	77,259	85,153	91,683	—	—	—	—	—	—
2632	Capital....................................	....	....	....	5,963	7,041	7,721	—	—	—	—	—	—
27	**Social benefits**............................	....	....	....	123,029	131,138	139,245	15,863	16,415	17,196	138,892	147,553	156,441
28	**Other expense**.............................	....	....	....	30,702	38,368	38,805	1,267	1,486	1,560	31,714	38,281	40,274
281	Property expense other than interest...........	....	....	....	—	—	—	—	—	—	—	—	—
282	Miscellaneous other expense.................	....	....	....	30,702	38,368	38,805	1,267	1,486	1,560	31,714	38,281	40,274
2821	Current...................................	....	....	....	24,195	28,756	30,783	423	319	359	24,618	29,075	31,142
2822	Capital....................................	....	....	....	6,507	9,612	8,022	844	1,167	1,201	7,096	9,206	9,132

In Millions of Pounds / Year Ending December 31 / Noncash Reporter

	Budgetary Central Government			Central Government			Local Government			General Government		
	2002	2003	2004	2002	2003	2004	2002	2003	2004	2002	2003	2004
Table 3 Transactions in assets and liabilities												
3 Change in net worth from transactns....	....	....	....	−16,809	−35,777	−33,883	4,985	7,539	5,193	−11,824	−28,238	−28,690
31 Net acquisition of nonfinancial assets...	....	....	....	1,724	2,918	3,590	2,735	3,966	5,246	4,459	6,884	8,836
311 Fixed assets...........	....	....	....	2,029	3,044	3,764	3,495	4,766	6,103	5,524	7,810	9,867
3111 Buildings and structures...........	....	....	....	....	....	....	....	....	....	....	....	....
3112 Machinery and equipment...........	....	....	....	....	....	....	....	....	....	....	....	....
3113 Other fixed assets...........	....	....	....	....	....	....	....	....	....	....	....	....
312 Inventories...........	....	....	....	—	15	20	—	—	—	—	15	20
313 Valuables...........	....	....	....	22	16	20	—	—	—	22	16	20
314 Nonproduced assets...........	....	....	....	−327	−157	−214	−760	−800	−857	−1,087	−957	−1,071
3141 Land...........	....	....	....	....	....	....	....	....	....	....	....	....
3142 Subsoil assets...........	....	....	....	....	....	....	....	....	....	....	....	....
3143 Other naturally occurring assets...........	....	....	....	....	....	....	....	....	....	....	....	....
3144 Intangible nonproduced assets...........	....	....	....	....	....	....	....	....	....	....	....	....
32 Net acquisition of financial assets........	....	....	....	−5,164	−1,672	4,320	789	1,480	3,128	−4,375	−192	7,448
321 Domestic...........	....	....	....	−5,419	497	4,009	789	1,480	3,128	−4,630	1,977	7,137
3212 Currency and deposits...........	....	....	....	−4,433	482	−2,488	1,598	1,448	3,844	−2,835	1,930	1,356
3213 Securities other than shares...........	....	....	....	−7	−1,128	751	93	−153	−457	86	−1,281	294
3214 Loans...........	....	....	....	−231	−2,231	2,735	123	168	−95	−108	−2,063	2,640
3215 Shares and other equity...........	....	....	....	32	76	−4	−218	45	−117	−186	121	−121
3216 Insurance technical reserves...........	....	....	....	—	—	—	27	8	35	27	8	35
3217 Financial derivatives...........	....	....	....	−238	−136	−173	—	—	—	−238	−136	−173
3218 Other accounts receivable...........	....	....	....	−542	3,434	3,188	−834	−36	−82	−1,376	3,398	3,106
322 Foreign...........	....	....	....	495	−2,167	348	—	—	—	495	−2,167	348
3222 Currency and deposits...........	....	....	....	−299	−916	−1,407	—	—	—	−299	−916	−1,407
3223 Securities other than shares...........	....	....	....	704	−1,377	1,657	—	—	—	704	−1,377	1,657
3224 Loans...........	....	....	....	—	—	—	—	—	—	—	—	—
3225 Shares and other equity...........	....	....	....	90	126	98	—	—	—	90	126	98
3226 Insurance technical reserves...........	....	....	....	—	—	—	—	—	—	—	—	—
3227 Financial derivatives...........	....	....	....	—	—	—	—	—	—	—	—	—
3228 Other accounts receivable...........	....	....	....	—	—	—	—	—	—	—	—	—
323 Monetary gold and SDRs...........	....	....	....	−240	−2	−37	—	—	—	−240	−2	−37
33 Net incurrence of liabilities...........	....	....	....	13,369	37,023	41,793	−1,461	−2,093	3,181	11,908	34,930	44,974
331 Domestic...........	....	....	....	13,418	37,068	41,839	−1,487	−2,297	2,548	11,931	34,771	44,387
3312 Currency and deposits...........	....	....	....	2,126	3,482	2,589	—	—	—	2,126	3,482	2,589
3313 Securities other than shares...........	....	....	....	11,885	32,811	35,311	47	18	−225	11,932	32,829	35,086
3314 Loans...........	....	....	....	899	−63	5,876	−883	−2,719	2,088	16	−2,782	7,964
3316 Insurance technical reserves...........	....	....	....	—	—	—	—	—	—	—	—	—
3317 Financial derivatives...........	....	....	....	—	—	—	—	—	—	—	—	—
3318 Other accounts payable...........	....	....	....	−1,492	838	−1,937	−651	404	685	−2,143	1,242	−1,252
332 Foreign...........	....	....	....	−49	−45	−46	26	204	633	−23	159	587
3322 Currency and deposits...........	....	....	....	—	—	—	—	—	—	—	—	—
3323 Securities other than shares...........	....	....	....	—	—	—	—	—	—	—	—	—
3324 Loans...........	....	....	....	−49	−45	−46	26	204	633	−23	159	587
3326 Insurance technical reserves...........	....	....	....	—	—	—	—	—	—	—	—	—
3327 Financial derivatives...........	....	....	....	—	—	—	—	—	—	—	—	—
3328 Other accounts payable...........	....	....	....	—	—	—	—	—	—	—	—	—
Table 4 Holding gains in assets and liabilities												
Table 5 Other changes in the volume of assets and liabilities												
Table 6 Balance sheet												
6 Net worth...........	....	....	....	....	....	....	....	....	....	....	....	....
61 Nonfinancial assets...........	....	....	....	....	....	....	....	....	....	....	....	....
611 Fixed assets...........	....	....	....	....	....	....	....	....	....	....	....	....
6111 Buildings and structures...........	....	....	....	....	....	....	....	....	....	....	....	....
6112 Machinery and equipment...........	....	....	....	....	....	....	....	....	....	....	....	....
6113 Other fixed assets...........	....	....	....	....	....	....	....	....	....	....	....	....
612 Inventories...........	....	....	....	....	....	....	....	....	....	....	....	....
613 Valuables...........	....	....	....	....	....	....	....	....	....	....	....	....
614 Nonproduced assets...........	....	....	....	....	....	....	....	....	....	....	....	....
6141 Land...........	....	....	....	....	....	....	....	....	....	....	....	....
6142 Subsoil assets...........	....	....	....	....	....	....	....	....	....	....	....	....
6143 Other naturally occurring assets...........	....	....	....	....	....	....	....	....	....	....	....	....
6144 Intangible nonproduced assets...........	....	....	....	....	....	....	....	....	....	....	....	....

In Millions of Pounds / Year Ending December 31 / Noncash Reporter

		Budgetary Central Government			Central Government			Local Government			General Government		
		2002	2003	2004	2002	2003	2004	2002	2003	2004	2002	2003	2004
62	**Financial assets**................	....	....	....	....	....	....	....	....	....	**165,119**	**166,405**	**173,839**
621	Domestic....................	....	....	....	....	....	....	....	....	....	136,887	140,445	148,430
6212	Currency and deposits............	....	....	....	....	....	....	....	....	....	21,258	24,348	27,157
6213	Securities other than shares........	....	....	....	....	....	....	....	....	....	5,865	4,585	4,909
6214	Loans..........................	....	....	....	....	....	....	....	....	....	68,920	67,205	69,302
6215	Shares and other equity..........	....	....	....	....	....	....	....	....	....	1,891	2,106	2,071
6216	Insurance technical reserves........	....	....	....	....	....	....	....	....	....	942	762	797
6217	Financial derivatives.............	....	....	....	....	....	....	....	....	....	209	−10	182
6218	Other accounts receivable.........	....	....	....	....	....	....	....	....	....	37,802	41,449	44,012
622	Foreign.......................	....	....	....	....	....	....	....	....	....	25,867	23,401	22,949
6222	Currency and deposits............	....	....	....	....	....	....	....	....	....	5,882	4,889	3,304
6223	Securities other than shares........	....	....	....	....	....	....	....	....	....	17,969	16,370	17,405
6224	Loans..........................	....	....	....	....	....	....	....	....	....			
6225	Shares and other equity..........	....	....	....	....	....	....	....	....	....	2,016	2,142	2,240
6226	Insurance technical reserves........	....	....	....	....	....	....	....	....	....	—	—	—
6227	Financial derivatives.............	....	....	....	....	....	....	....	....	....	—	—	—
6228	Other accounts receivable.........	....	....	....	....	....	....	....	....	....	—	—	—
623	Monetary gold and SDRs...........	....	....	....	....	....	....	....	....	....	2,365	2,559	2,460
63	**Liabilities**................	....	....	....	....	....	....	....	....	....	**522,529**	**548,613**	**602,100**
631	Domestic....................	....	....	....	....	....	....	....	....	....	521,316	547,287	600,227
6312	Currency and deposits............	....	....	....	....	....	....	....	....	....	77,672	79,610	82,209
6313	Securities other than shares........	....	....	....	....	....	....	....	....	....	330,187	353,572	393,555
6314	Loans..........................	....	....	....	....	....	....	....	....	....	73,784	72,196	80,281
6316	Insurance technical reserves........	....	....	....	....	....	....	....	....	....			
6317	Financial derivatives.............	....	....	....	....	....	....	....	....	....	—	—	—
6318	Other accounts payable...........	....	....	....	....	....	....	....	....	....	39,673	41,909	44,182
632	Foreign.......................	....	....	....	....	....	....	....	....	....	1,213	1,326	1,873
6322	Currency and deposits............	....	....	....	....	....	....	....	....	....	—	—	—
6323	Securities other than shares........	....	....	....	....	....	....	....	....	....	—	—	—
6324	Loans..........................	....	....	....	....	....	....	....	....	....	1,213	1,326	1,873
6326	Insurance technical reserves........	....	....	....	....	....	....	....	....	....	—	—	—
6327	Financial derivatives.............	....	....	....	....	....	....	....	....	....	—	—	—
6328	Other accounts payable...........	....	....	....	....	....	....	....	....	....			
Memorandum items:													
6M2	Net financial worth...............	....	....	....	....	....	....	....	....	....	−357,410	−382,208	−428,261
6M3	Debt at market value.............	....	....	....	....	....	....	....	....	....	....	....	....
6M4	Debt at nominal value............	....	....	....	....	....	....	....	....	....	....	....	....
6M5	Arrears........................	....	....	....	....	....	....	....	....	....	....	....	....
6M6	Obligations for social security benefits...........	....	....	....	....	....	....	....	....	....	....	....	....
6M7	Contingent liabilities.............	....	....	....	....	....	....	....	....	....	....	....	....
6M8	Uncapitalized military weapons, systems........	....	....	....	....	....	....	....	....	....	....	....	....

Table 7   Outlays by functions of govt.

		Budgetary Central Government			Central Government			Local Government			General Government		
		2002	2003	2004	2002	2003	2004	2002	2003	2004	2002	2003	2004
7	**Total outlays**................	....	....	....	399,405	439,851	466,185	123,423	135,502	145,500	435,429	477,220	508,775
701	**General public services**............	....	....	....	....	....	....	....	....	....	43,859	49,757	53,356
7017	Public debt transactions............	....	....	....	21,440	22,431	23,316	4,023	4,602	3,799	21,541	22,667	23,700
7018	General transfers between levels of govt......	....	....	....	....	....	....	....	....	....			
702	**Defense**................	....	....	....	....	....	....	....	....	....	28,127	31,305	32,400
703	**Public order and safety**............	....	....	....	....	....	....	....	....	....	25,566	27,661	29,814
704	**Economic affairs**................	....	....	....	....	....	....	....	....	....	28,121	31,813	33,256
7042	Agriculture, forestry, fishing, and hunting.....	....	....	....	....	....	....	....	....	....	....	....	....
7043	Fuel and energy.................	....	....	....	....	....	....	....	....	....	....	....	....
7044	Mining, manufacturing, and construction.....	....	....	....	....	....	....	....	....	....	....	....	....
7045	Transport......................	....	....	....	....	....	....	....	....	....	....	....	....
7046	Communication.................	....	....	....	....	....	....	....	....	....	....	....	....
705	**Environmental protection**............	....	....	....	....	....	....	....	....	....	6,800	7,247	7,271
706	**Housing and community amenities**........	....	....	....	....	....	....	....	....	....	6,831	7,416	8,132
707	**Health**................	....	....	....	....	....	....	....	....	....	68,726	76,610	84,217
7072	Outpatient services...............	....	....	....	....	....	....	....	....	....	....	....	....
7073	Hospital services.................	....	....	....	....	....	....	....	....	....	....	....	....
7074	Public health services.............	....	....	....	....	....	....	....	....	....	....	....	....
708	**Recreation, culture, and religion**............	....	....	....	....	....	....	....	....	....	5,522	5,637	5,148

In Millions of Pounds / Year Ending December 31 / Noncash Reporter

	Budgetary Central Government			Central Government			Local Government			General Government		
	2002	2003	2004	2002	2003	2004	2002	2003	2004	2002	2003	2004
709 **Education**........................	....	....	....	....	....	....	....	....	....	56,016	61,923	65,370
7091 Pre-primary and primary education...............	....	....	....	....	....	....	....	....	....	....	....	....
7092 Secondary education........................	....	....	....	....	....	....	....	....	....	....	....	....
7094 Tertiary education........................	....	....	....	....	....	....	....	....	....	....	....	....
710 **Social protection**........................	....	....	....	....	....	....	....	....	....	165,861	177,851	189,811
7 Statistical discrepancy: Total outlays...............	....	....	....	....	....	....	....	....	....	—	—	—

Table 8 Transactions in financial assets and liabilities by sector

	Budgetary Central Government			Central Government			Local Government			General Government		
	2002	2003	2004	2002	2003	2004	2002	2003	2004	2002	2003	2004
82 **Net acquisition of financial assets**.........	....	....	....	−5,164	−1,672	4,320	789	1,480	3,128	−4,375	−192	7,448
821 Domestic........................	....	....	....	−5,419	497	4,009	789	1,480	3,128	−4,630	1,977	7,137
8211 General government........................	....	....	....	....	....	....	....	....	....	....	....	....
8212 Central bank........................	....	....	....	....	....	....	....	....	....	....	....	....
8213 Other depository corporations.................	....	....	....	....	....	....	....	....	....	....	....	....
8214 Financial corporations n.e.c.................	....	....	....	....	....	....	....	....	....	....	....	....
8215 Nonfinancial corporations.................	....	....	....	....	....	....	....	....	....	....	....	....
8216 Households & NPIs serving households......	....	....	....	....	....	....	....	....	....	....	....	....
822 Foreign........................	....	....	....	495	−2,167	348	—	—	—	495	−2,167	348
8221 General government........................	....	....	....	....	....	....	—	—	—	....	....	....
8227 International organizations.................	....	....	....	....	....	....	—	—	—	....	....	....
8228 Financial corporations other than international organizations.............	....	....	....	....	....	....	—	—	—	....	....	....
8229 Other nonresidents........................	....	....	....	−240	−2	−37	—	—	—	−240	−2	−37
823 Monetary gold and SDRs........................	....	....	....	−240	−2	−37				−240	−2	−37
83 **Net incurrence of liabilities**.................	....	....	....	13,369	37,023	41,793	−1,461	−2,093	3,181	11,908	34,930	44,974
831 Domestic........................	....	....	....	13,418	37,068	41,839	−1,487	−2,297	2,548	11,931	34,771	44,387
8311 General government........................	....	....	....	....	....	....	....	....	....	....	....	....
8312 Central bank........................	....	....	....	....	....	....	....	....	....	....	....	....
8313 Other depository corporations.................	....	....	....	....	....	....	....	....	....	....	....	....
8314 Financial corporations n.e.c.................	....	....	....	....	....	....	....	....	....	....	....	....
8315 Nonfinancial corporations.................	....	....	....	....	....	....	....	....	....	....	....	....
8316 Households & NPIs serving households......	....	....	....	....	....	....	....	....	....	....	....	....
832 Foreign........................	....	....	....	−49	−45	−46	26	204	633	−23	159	587
8321 General government........................	....	....	....	....	....	....	....	....	....	....	....	....
8327 International organizations.................	....	....	....	....	....	....	....	....	....	....	....	....
8328 Financial corporations other than international organizations.............	....	....	....	....	....	....	....	....	....	....	....	....
8329 Other nonresidents........................	....	....	....	....	....	....	....	....	....	....	....	....

In Billions of Dollars / Year Ending December 31 / Noncash Reporter

	Central Government			State Government			Local Government			General Government		
	2003	2004	2005f	2003	2004	2005	2003	2004	2005	2003	2004	2005
Statement of government operations												
1 Revenue...............	1,898.7	2,011.2	2,277.9	....	....	....	....	....	....	3,474.3	3,706.6	....
2 Expense...............	2,313.1	2,450.3	2,601.6	....	....	....	....	....	....	3,859.4	4,097.6	....
GOB *Gross operating balance........*	*−386.4*	*−410.1*	*−225.9*	....	....	....	....	....	....	*−241.4*	*−239.9*	....
NOB *Net operating balance........*	*−414.4*	*−439.1*	*−323.7*	....	....	....	....	....	....	*−385.1*	*−391.0*	....
31 Net acquisition of nonfinancial assets........	10.4	10.0	8.6	....	....	....	....	....	....	147.3	149.2	....
NLB *Net lending/borrowing........*	*−424.8*	*−449.1*	*−332.3*	....	....	....	....	....	....	*−532.4*	*−540.2*	....
32 Net acquisition of financial assets........	5.7	−34.7	....	....	....	....	....	....	....	....	....	....
33 Net incurrence of liabilities........	399.4	369.7	....	....	....	....	....	....	....	....	....	....
NLB Statistical discrepancy........	31.1	44.7	....	....	....	....	....	....	....	....	....	....
Statement of other economic flows												
Balance sheet												
6 *Net worth........*	....	....	....	....	....	....	....	....	....	....	....	....
61 Nonfinancial assets........	....	....	....	....	....	....	....	....	....	....	....	....
62 Financial assets........	....	....	....	....	....	....	....	....	....	....	....	....
63 Liabilities........	4,092.7	4,462.4	....	....	....	....	....	....	....	5,981.7		
Statement of sources and uses of cash												
Table 1 Revenue												
1 **Revenue........**	**1,898.7**	**2,011.2**	**2,277.9**	....	....	....	....	....	....	**3,474.3**	**3,706.6**	....
11 **Taxes........**	**1,081.1**	**1,147.0**	**1,370.3**	....	....	....	....	....	....	**2,059.8**	**2,200.1**	....
111 Taxes on income, profits, & capital gains......	969.5	1,028.4	1,247.3	....	....	....	....	....	....	1,208.4	1,293.9	....
1111 Individuals........	782.8	811.0	949.9	....	....	....	....	....	....	986.5	1,035.0	....
1112 Corporations and other enterprises........	186.7	217.4	297.5	....	....	....	....	....	....	221.9	258.9	....
112 Taxes on payroll and workforce........	—	—	—	....	....	....	....	....	....	—	—	....
113 Taxes on property........	22.0	24.6	24.8	....	....	....	....	....	....	337.1	359.0	....
114 Taxes on goods and services........	68.3	70.7	72.4	....	....	....	....	....	....	492.9	524.0	....
1141 General taxes on goods and services........	—	—	....	....	....	....	....	....	....	236.4	252.9	....
1142 Excises........	48.3	49.0	....	....	....	....	....	....	....	120.4	124.6	....
115 Taxes on int'l. trade and transactions........	21.4	23.3	25.8	....	....	....	....	....	....	21.4	23.3	....
116 Other taxes........	—	—	—	....	....	....	....	....	....	—	—	....
12 **Social contributions........**	**759.1**	**802.5**	**856.9**	....	....	....	....	....	....	**776.6**	**822.2**	....
121 Social security contributions........	754.2	797.2	....	....	....	....	....	....	....	771.7	816.8	....
122 Other social contributions........	4.9	5.4	....	....	....	....	....	....	....	4.9	5.4	....
13 **Grants........**	**—**	**—**	**—**	....	....	....	....	....	....	**—**	**—**	....
131 From foreign governments........	—	—	—	....	....	....	....	....	....	—	—	
132 From international organizations........	—	—	—	....	....	....	....	....	....	—	—	
133 From other general government units........	—	—	—	....	....	....	....	....	....	—	—	
14 **Other revenue........**	**58.5**	**61.7**	**50.7**	....	....	....	....	....	....	**638.0**	**684.3**	....
Table 2 Expense by economic type												
2 **Expense........**	**2,313.1**	**2,450.3**	**2,601.6**	....	....	....	....	....	....	**3,859.4**	**4,097.6**	....
21 **Compensation of employees........**	**295.5**	**317.6**	....	....	....	....	....	....	....	**1,123.9**	**1,180.5**	....
211 Wages and salaries........	....	....	....	....	....	....	....	....	....	....	....	....
212 Social contributions........	....	....	....	....	....	....	....	....	....	....	....	....
22 **Use of goods and services........**	**332.6**	**379.8**	....	....	....	....	....	....	....	**866.2**	**950.6**	....
23 **Consumption of fixed capital........**	**28.0**	**29.0**	**97.9**	....	....	....	....	....	....	**143.7**	**151.1**	....
24 **Interest........**	**214.3**	**220.7**	**251.2**	....	....	....	....	....	....	**299.4**	**308.5**	....
25 **Subsidies........**	**46.5**	**43.0**	**52.1**	....	....	....	....	....	....	**46.6**	**43.5**	....
26 **Grants........**	**410.1**	**420.7**	**458.0**	....	....	....	....	....	....	**25.5**	**26.1**	....
261 To foreign governments........	25.5	26.1	29.0	....	....	....	....	....	....	25.5	26.1	....
262 To international organizations........	—	—	—	....	....	....	....	....	....	—	—	....
263 To other general government units........	384.6	394.6	429.0	....	....	....	....	....	....	—	—	....
2631 Current........	339.1	348.3	358.7	....	....	....	....	....	....	—	—	....
2632 Capital........	45.5	46.3	70.3	....	....	....	....	....	....	—	—	....
27 **Social benefits........**	**965.0**	**1,017.1**	**1,081.9**	....	....	....	....	....	....	**1,316.3**	**1,397.6**	....
28 **Other expense........**	**21.0**	**22.3**	....	....	....	....	....	....	....	**37.7**	**39.7**	....
281 Property expense other than interest........	....	....	....	....	....	....	....	....	....	....	....	....
282 Miscellaneous other expense........	....	....	....	....	....	....	....	....	....	....	....	....
2821 Current........	....	....	....	....	....	....	....	....	....	....	....	....
2822 Capital........	....	....	....	....	....	....	....	....	....	....	....	....

In Billions of Dollars / Year Ending December 31 / Noncash Reporter

	Central Government			State Government			Local Government			General Government		
	2003	2004	2005f	2003	2004	2005	2003	2004	2005	2003	2004	2005
Table 3 Transactions in assets and liabilities												
3 Change in net worth from transactns....	−414.4	−439.1	−323.7	....	....	....	....	....	....	−385.1	−391.0	....
31 Net acquisition of nonfinancial assets...	10.4	10.0	8.6	....	....	....	....	....	....	147.3	149.2	....
311 Fixed assets............................	9.5	9.9	9.0	....	....	....	....	....	....	135.1	137.4	....
3111 Buildings and structures..........	....	....	....	....	....	....	....	....	....	....	....	....
3112 Machinery and equipment.........	....	....	....	....	....	....	....	....	....	....	....	....
3113 Other fixed assets.................	....	....	....	....	....	....	....	....	....	....	....	....
312 Inventories...........................	1.1	.1	—	....	....	....	....	....	....	1.1	.1	....
313 Valuables.............................	—	—	—	....	....	....	....	....	....	—	—	....
314 Nonproduced assets.................	−.2	—	−.4	....	....	....	....	....	....	11.1	11.7	....
3141 Land.............................	....	....	....	....	....	....	....	....	....	....	....	....
3142 Subsoil assets.....................	....	—	....	....	....	....	....	....	....	....	....	....
3143 Other naturally occurring assets..	....	—	....	....	....	....	....	....	....	....	....	....
3144 Intangible nonproduced assets..	....	—	....	....	....	....	....	....	....	....	....	....
32 **Net acquisition of financial assets........**	**5.7**	**−34.7**	....	....	....	....	....	....	....	....	....	....
321 Domestic.............................	5.7	−34.7	....	....	....	....	....	....	....	....	....	....
3212 Currency and deposits...........	....	....	....	....	....	....	....	....	....	....	....	....
3213 Securities other than shares......	....	....	....	....	....	....	....	....	....	....	....	....
3214 Loans.............................	....	....	....	....	....	....	....	....	....	....	....	....
3215 Shares and other equity..........	....	....	....	....	....	....	....	....	....	....	....	....
3216 Insurance technical reserves......	....	....	....	....	....	....	....	....	....	....	....	....
3217 Financial derivatives.............	....	....	....	....	....	....	....	....	....	....	....	....
3218 Other accounts receivable........	....	....	....	....	....	....	....	....	....	....	....	....
322 Foreign..............................	—	—	—	....	....	....	....	....	....	....	....	....
3222 Currency and deposits...........	—	—	—	....	....	....	....	....	....	....	....	....
3223 Securities other than shares......	—	—	—	....	....	....	....	....	....	....	....	....
3224 Loans.............................	—	—	—	....	....	....	....	....	....	....	....	....
3225 Shares and other equity..........	—	—	—	....	....	....	....	....	....	....	....	....
3226 Insurance technical reserves......	—	—	—	....	....	....	....	....	....	....	....	....
3227 Financial derivatives.............	—	—	—	....	....	....	....	....	....	....	....	....
3228 Other accounts receivable........	—	—	—	....	....	....	....	....	....	....	....	....
323 Monetary gold and SDRs............	—	—	—	....	....	....	....	....	....	....	....	....
33 **Net incurrence of liabilities...................**	**399.4**	**369.7**	....	....	....	....	....	....	....	....	....	....
331 Domestic.............................	108.3	13.0	....	....	....	....	....	....	....	....	....	....
3312 Currency and deposits...........	5.3	−6.7	....	....	....	....	....	....	....	....	....	....
3313 Securities other than shares......	77.2	23.2	....	....	....	....	....	....	....	....	....	....
3314 Loans.............................	25.8	−3.5	....	....	....	....	....	....	....	....	....	....
3316 Insurance technical reserves......	—	—	....	....	....	....	....	....	....	....	....	....
3317 Financial derivatives.............	—	—	....	....	....	....	....	....	....	....	....	....
3318 Other accounts payable..........	—	—	....	....	....	....	....	....	....	....	....	....
332 Foreign..............................	291.1	356.7	....	....	....	....	....	....	....	....	....	....
3322 Currency and deposits...........	—	—	....	....	....	....	....	....	....	....	....	....
3323 Securities other than shares......	291.5	357.7	....	....	....	....	....	....	....	....	....	....
3324 Loans.............................	−.4	−1.0	....	....	....	....	....	....	....	....	....	....
3326 Insurance technical reserves......	....	....	....	....	....	....	....	....	....	....	....	....
3327 Financial derivatives.............	—	—	....	....	....	....	....	....	....	....	....	....
3328 Other accounts payable..........	—	—	....	....	....	....	....	....	....	....	....	....
Table 4 Holding gains in assets and liabilities												
Table 5 Other changes in the volume of assets and liabilities												
Table 6 Balance sheet												
6 **Net worth.........................**	....	....	....	....	....	....	....	....	....	....	....	....
61 **Nonfinancial assets..............**	....	....	....	....	....	....	....	....	....	....	....	....
611 Fixed assets.........................	....	....	....	....	....	....	....	....	....	....	....	....
6111 Buildings and structures..........	....	....	....	....	....	....	....	....	....	....	....	....
6112 Machinery and equipment.........	....	....	....	....	....	....	....	....	....	....	....	....
6113 Other fixed assets.................	....	....	....	....	....	....	....	....	....	....	....	....
612 Inventories...........................	....	....	....	....	....	....	....	....	....	....	....	....
613 Valuables.............................	....	....	....	....	....	....	....	....	....	....	....	....
614 Nonproduced assets.................	....	....	....	....	....	....	....	....	....	....	....	....
6141 Land.............................	....	....	....	....	....	....	....	....	....	....	....	....
6142 Subsoil assets.....................	....	....	....	....	....	....	....	....	....	....	....	....
6143 Other naturally occurring assets..	....	....	....	....	....	....	....	....	....	....	....	....
6144 Intangible nonproduced assets..	....	....	....	....	....	....	....	....	....	....	....	....

United States 111

In Billions of Dollars / Year Ending December 31 / Noncash Reporter

	Central Government 2003	2004	2005f	State Government 2003	2004	2005	Local Government 2003	2004	2005	General Government 2003	2004	2005
62 **Financial assets**....................	....	....	....	....	....	....	....	....	....	....	....	....
621 Domestic.................................	....	....	....	....	....	....	....	....	....	....	....	....
6212 Currency and deposits.............	....	....	....	....	....	....	....	....	....	....	....	....
6213 Securities other than shares.......	....	....	....	....	....	....	....	....	....	....	....	....
6214 Loans......................................	....	....	....	....	....	....	....	....	....	....	....	....
6215 Shares and other equity..............	....	....	....	....	....	....	....	....	....	....	....	....
6216 Insurance technical reserves........	....	....	....	....	....	....	....	....	....	....	....	....
6217 Financial derivatives.................	....	....	....	....	....	....	....	....	....	....	....	....
6218 Other accounts receivable...........	....	....	....	....	....	....	....	....	....	....	....	....
622 Foreign..................................	....	....	....	....	....	....	....	....	....	....	....	....
6222 Currency and deposits.............	....	....	....	....	....	....	....	....	....	....	....	....
6223 Securities other than shares.......	....	....	....	....	....	....	....	....	....	....	....	....
6224 Loans......................................	....	....	....	....	....	....	....	....	....	....	....	....
6225 Shares and other equity..............	....	....	....	....	....	....	....	....	....	....	....	....
6226 Insurance technical reserves........	....	....	....	....	....	....	....	....	....	....	....	....
6227 Financial derivatives.................	....	....	....	....	....	....	....	....	....	....	....	....
6228 Other accounts receivable...........	....	....	....	....	....	....	....	....	....	....	....	....
623 Monetary gold and SDRs............	....	....	....	....	....	....	....	....	....	....	....	....
63 **Liabilities**.............................	**4,092.7**	**4,462.4**	....	....	....	....	....	....	....	**5,981.7**	....	....
631 Domestic.................................	2,562.8	2,575.8	....	....	....	....	....	....	....	4,451.8	....	....
6312 Currency and deposits.............	....	....	....	....	....	....	....	....	....	....	....	....
6313 Securities other than shares.......	....	....	....	....	....	....	....	....	....	....	....	....
6314 Loans......................................	....	....	....	....	....	....	....	....	....	....	....	....
6316 Insurance technical reserves........	....	....	....	....	....	....	....	....	....	....	....	....
6317 Financial derivatives.................	....	....	....	....	....	....	....	....	....	....	....	....
6318 Other accounts payable.............	....	....	....	....	....	....	....	....	....	....	....	....
632 Foreign..................................	1,529.9	1,886.6	....	....	....	....	....	....	....	1,529.9	....	....
6322 Currency and deposits.............	....	....	....	....	....	....	....	....	....	....	....	....
6323 Securities other than shares.......	....	....	....	....	....	....	....	....	....	....	....	....
6324 Loans......................................	....	....	....	....	....	....	....	....	....	....	....	....
6326 Insurance technical reserves........	....	....	....	....	....	....	....	....	....	....	....	....
6327 Financial derivatives.................	....	....	....	....	....	....	....	....	....	....	....	....
6328 Other accounts payable.............	....	....	....	....	....	....	....	....	....	....	....	....
Memorandum items:												
6M2 Net financial worth...................	....	....	....	....	....	....	....	....	....	....	....	....
6M3 Debt at market value.................	....	....	....	....	....	....	....	....	....	....	....	....
6M4 Debt at nominal value................	....	....	....	....	....	....	....	....	....	....	....	....
6M5 Arrears....................................	....	....	....	....	....	....	....	....	....	....	....	....
6M6 Obligations for social security benefits........	....	....	....	....	....	....	....	....	....	....	....	....
6M7 Contingent liabilities..................	....	....	....	....	....	....	....	....	....	....	....	....
6M8 Uncapitalized military weapons, systems.......	....	....	....	....	....	....	....	....	....	....	....	....
Table 7 Outlays by functions of govt.												
7 Total outlays.............................	**2,323.5**	**2,460.3**	**2,610.2**	....	....	....	....	....	....	**4,006.7**	**4,246.7**	....
701 General public services.............	**285.9**	**290.5**	....	....	....	....	....	....	....	**523.3**	**548.4**	....
7017 Public debt transactions.............	214.3	220.7	251.2	....	....	....	....	....	....	299.4	308.5	....
7018 General transfers between levels of govt......	....	....	....	....	....	....	....	....	....	....	....	....
702 Defense.................................	**443.3**	**496.4**	....	....	....	....	....	....	....	**439.6**	**492.8**	....
703 Public order and safety.............	**33.1**	**37.0**	....	....	....	....	....	....	....	**231.4**	**246.9**	....
704 Economic affairs......................	**161.0**	**160.6**	....	....	....	....	....	....	....	**411.6**	**426.8**	....
7042 Agriculture, forestry, fishing, and hunting....	....	....	....	....	....	....	....	....	....	....	....	....
7043 Fuel and energy.........................	....	....	....	....	....	....	....	....	....	....	....	....
7044 Mining, manufacturing, and construction.....	....	....	....	....	....	....	....	....	....	....	....	....
7045 Transport.................................	....	....	....	....	....	....	....	....	....	....	....	....
7046 Communication..........................	....	....	....	....	....	....	....	....	....	....	....	....
705 Environmental protection....................	....	....	....	....	....	....	....	....	....	....	....	....
706 Housing and community amenities........	**46.9**	**47.1**	....	....	....	....	....	....	....	**80.3**	**83.0**	....
707 Health..................................	**547.8**	**594.3**	....	....	....	....	....	....	....	**802.2**	**871.1**	....
7072 Outpatient services.....................	....	....	....	....	....	....	....	....	....	....	....	....
7073 Hospital services........................	....	....	....	....	....	....	....	....	....	....	....	....
7074 Public health services..................	....	....	....	....	....	....	....	....	....	....	....	....
708 Recreation, culture, and religion............	**4.1**	**4.3**	....	....	....	....	....	....	....	**36.4**	**37.7**	....

In Billions of Dollars / Year Ending December 31 / Noncash Reporter

		Central Government			State Government			Local Government			General Government		
		2003	2004	2005f	2003	2004	2005	2003	2004	2005	2003	2004	2005
709	**Education**..............	**60.9**	**67.7**	....	....	....	....	....	....	....	**684.4**	**711.9**	....
7091	Pre-primary and primary education..............	....	....	....	....	....	....	....	....	....	....	....	....
7092	Secondary education..............	....	....	....	....	....	....	....	....	....	....	....	....
7094	Tertiary education..............	....	....	....	....	....	....	....	....	....	....	....	....
710	**Social protection**..............	**740.5**	**762.4**	....	....	....	....	....	....	....	**797.5**	**828.0**	....
7	Statistical discrepancy: Total outlays..............	—	—	....	....	....	....	....	....	....	—	—	....
Table 8 Transactions in financial assets and liabilities by sector													
82	**Net acquisition of financial assets**........	**5.7**	**−34.7**	....	....	....	....	....	....	....	....	....	....
821	Domestic..............	5.7	−34.7	....	....	....	....	....	....	....	....	....	....
8211	General government..............	....	....	....	....	....	....	....	....	....	....	....	....
8212	Central bank..............	....	....	....	....	....	....	....	....	....	....	....	....
8213	Other depository corporations..............	....	....	....	....	....	....	....	....	....	....	....	....
8214	Financial corporations n.e.c.............	....	....	....	....	....	....	....	....	....	....	....	....
8215	Nonfinancial corporations..............	....	....	....	....	....	....	....	....	....	....	....	....
8216	Households & NPIs serving households......	....	....	....	....	....	....	....	....	....	....	....	....
822	Foreign..............	—	—	....	....	....	....	....	....	....	....	....	....
8221	General government..............	—	—	....	....	....	....	....	....	....	....	....	....
8227	International organizations..............	—	—	....	....	....	....	....	....	....	....	....	....
8228	Financial corporations other than international organizations..............	—	—	....	....	....	....	....	....	....	....	....	....
8229	Other nonresidents..............	—	—	....	....	....	....	....	....	....	....	....	....
823	Monetary gold and SDRs..............	—	—	....	....	....	....	....	....	....	....	....	....
83	**Net incurrence of liabilities**..................	**399.4**	**369.7**	....	....	....	....	....	....	....	....	....	....
831	Domestic..............	108.3	13.0	....	....	....	....	....	....	....	....	....	....
8311	General government..............	....	....	....	....	....	....	....	....	....	....	....	....
8312	Central bank..............	....	....	....	....	....	....	....	....	....	....	....	....
8313	Other depository corporations..............	....	....	....	....	....	....	....	....	....	....	....	....
8314	Financial corporations n.e.c.............	....	....	....	....	....	....	....	....	....	....	....	....
8315	Nonfinancial corporations..............	....	....	....	....	....	....	....	....	....	....	....	....
8316	Households & NPIs serving households......	....	....	....	....	....	....	....	....	....	....	....	....
832	Foreign..............	291.1	356.7	....	....	....	....	....	....	....	....	....	....
8321	General government..............	173.9	297.9	....	....	....	....	....	....	....	....	....	....
8327	International organizations..............	−1.6	9.1	....	....	....	....	....	....	....	....	....	....
8328	Financial corporations other than international organizations..............	—	—	....	....	....	....	....	....	....	....	....	....
8329	Other nonresidents..............	118.8	49.7	....	....	....	....	....	....	....	....	....	....

In Millions of Pesos / Year Ending December 31 / Cash Reporter

		Budgetary Central Government			Central Government			Local Government			General Government		
		2002	2003	2004p	2002	2003	2004p	2002	2003	2004p	2002	2003	2004p
Statement of government operations													
Statement of other economic flows													
Balance sheet													
Statement of sources and uses of cash													
1	Cash receipts from operating activities...........	52,788	64,521	76,519	71,656	84,501	100,589	....	....	....	....	....	....
11	Taxes..	45,634	58,465	70,109	45,634	58,465	70,109	....	....	....	....	....	....
12	Social contributions.................................	—	—	—	16,158	16,351	18,846	....	....	....	....	....	....
13	Grants..	—	—	—				....	....	....	....	....	....
14	Other receipts.......................................	7,154	6,056	6,411	9,863	9,686	11,634	....	....	....	....	....	....
2	Cash payments for operating activities...........	61,757	74,863	81,346	80,670	94,845	104,466	....	....	....	....	....	....
21	Compensation of employees.........................	16,466	18,038	20,498	17,930	19,822	22,771	....	....	....	....	....	....
22	Purchases of goods and services...................	7,005	9,198	10,907	9,583	12,271	14,812	....	....	....	....	....	....
24	Interest..	10,592	17,803	18,646	10,592	17,803	18,646	....	....	....	....	....	....
25	Subsidies..	8,008	8,622	9,358	8,159	8,880	9,542	....	....	....	....	....	....
26	Grants..	19,686	21,202	21,937	—	—	—	....	....	....	....	....	....
27	Social benefits......................................	—	—	—	34,406	36,069	38,694	....	....	....	....	....	....
28	Other payments.....................................	—	—	—	—	—	—	....	....	....	....	....	....
CIO	*Net cash inflow from oper. activities.....*	*–8,969*	*–10,343*	*–4,827*	*–9,014*	*–10,344*	*–3,877*	....	....	....	....	....	....
31.1	Purchases of nonfinancial assets...................	3,281	3,625	5,260	3,701	4,074	5,646	....	....	....			
31.2	Sales of nonfinancial assets........................	—	—	—	—	—	—	....	....	....			
31	Net cash outflow from investments in nonfinancial assets..............................	3,281	3,625	5,260	3,701	4,074	5,646	....	....	....			
CSD	*Cash surplus/deficit...............................*	*–12,250*	*–13,967*	*–10,087*	*–12,715*	*–14,418*	*–9,523*	*133*	*–231*	*69*	*–12,582*	*–14,649*	*–9,454*
32x	Net acquisition of fin assets, excl. cash...........	9,736	–7,970	4,366	9,736	–7,970	4,366	—	—	—	9,736	–7,970	4,366
321x	Domestic..	9,736	–8,260	4,276	9,736	–8,260	4,276	—	—	—	9,736	–8,260	4,276
322x	Foreign..	—	290	91	—	290	91	—	—	—	—	290	91
323	Monetary gold and SDRs...........................	—	—	—	—	—	—	—	—	—	—	—	—
33	Net incurrence of liabilities.........................	57,391	5,468	4,921	57,450	5,477	4,854	–328	352	180	57,122	5,829	5,034
331	Domestic..	–5,042	–17,406	–1,781	–4,983	–17,397	–1,848	–474	54	82	–5,457	–17,343	–1,766
332	Foreign..	62,433	22,873	6,702	62,433	22,873	6,702	146	298	98	62,579	23,172	6,800
NFB	Net cash inflow from fin. activities.................	47,655	13,437	555	47,713	13,447	487	–328	352	180	47,385	13,799	668
NCB	*Net change in the stock of cash.............*	*35,181*	*–1,036*	*–8,543*	*35,141*	*–890*	*–8,603*	*–195*	*121*	*249*	*34,946*	*–769*	*–8,354*
Table 1 Revenue													
1	**Revenue..**	**52,788**	**64,521**	**76,519**	**71,656**	**84,501**	**100,589**	....	....	....	....	....	....
11	**Taxes...**	**45,634**	**58,465**	**70,109**	**45,634**	**58,465**	**70,109**	....	....	....	....	....	....
111	Taxes on income, profits, & capital gains......	5,186	5,408	9,651	5,186	5,408	9,651	....	....	....	....	....	....
1111	Individuals..	—	—	—	—	—	—	....	....	....	....	....	....
1112	Corporations and other enterprises...........	5,186	5,408	9,651	5,186	5,408	9,651	....	....	....	....	....	....
112	Taxes on payroll and workforce..................	4,909	6,610	4,947	4,909	6,610	4,947	....	....	....	....	....	....
113	Taxes on property.................................	4,774	6,681	6,748	4,774	6,681	6,748	....	....	....	....	....	....
114	Taxes on goods and services......................	30,741	38,892	48,959	30,741	38,892	48,959	....	....	....	....	....	....
1141	General taxes on goods and services..........	22,603	29,315	37,424	22,603	29,315	37,424	....	....	....	....	....	....
1142	Excises...	7,169	8,042	9,735	7,169	8,042	9,735	....	....	....	....	....	....
115	Taxes on int'l. trade and transactions...........	3,008	4,148	5,422	3,008	4,148	5,422	....	....	....	....	....	....
116	Other taxes..	–2,983	–3,274	–5,617	–2,983	–3,274	–5,617	....	....	....	....	....	....
12	**Social contributions........................**	**—**	**—**	**—**	**16,158**	**16,351**	**18,846**	....	....	....	....	....	....
121	Social security contributions.....................	—	—	—	16,158	16,351	18,846	....	....	....	....	....	....
122	Other social contributions........................	—	—	—	—	—	—	....	....	....	....	....	....
13	**Grants...**	**—**	**—**	**—**	**—**	**—**	**—**	....	....	....	....	....	....
131	From foreign governments........................	—	—	—	—	—	—	....	....	....	....	....	....
132	From international organizations..................	—	—	—	—	—	—	....	....	....	....	....	....
133	From other general government units...........	—	—	—	—	—	—	....	....	....	....	....	....
14	**Other revenue................................**	**7,154**	**6,056**	**6,411**	**9,863**	**9,686**	**11,634**	....	....	....	....	....	....
Table 2 Expense by economic type													
2	**Expense.......................................**	**61,757**	**74,863**	**81,346**	**80,670**	**94,845**	**104,466**	....	....	....	....	....	....
21	**Compensation of employees................**	**16,466**	**18,038**	**20,498**	**17,930**	**19,822**	**22,771**	....	....	....	....	....	....
211	Wages and salaries................................	12,590	13,428	15,334	14,053	15,212	17,608	....	....	....	....	....	....
212	Social contributions...............................	3,876	4,610	5,164	3,876	4,610	5,164	....	....	....	....	....	....
22	**Use of goods and services...................**	**7,005**	**9,198**	**10,907**	**9,583**	**12,271**	**14,812**	....	....	....	....	....	....
23	**Consumption of fixed capital...............**	....	....	....	....	....	....	....	....	....	....	....	....
24	**Interest..**	**10,592**	**17,803**	**18,646**	**10,592**	**17,803**	**18,646**	....	....	....	....	....	....
25	**Subsidies......................................**	**8,008**	**8,622**	**9,358**	**8,159**	**8,880**	**9,542**	....	....	....	....	....	....

	Budgetary Central Government			Central Government			Local Government			General Government		
	2002	2003	2004p	2002	2003	2004p	2002	2003	2004p	2002	2003	2004p
26 Grants.............	19,686	21,202	21,937	—	—	—	....	....	....	....	....	....
261 To foreign govenments.............	—	—	—	—	—	—	....	....	....	....	....	....
262 To international organizations.............	—	—	—	—	—	—	....	....	....	....	....	....
263 To other general government units.............	19,686	21,202	21,937	—	—	—	....	....	....	....	....	....
2631 Current.............	19,686	21,202	21,937	—	—	—	....	....	....	....	....	....
2632 Capital.............	—	—	—	—	—	—	....	....	....	....	....	....
27 Social benefits.............	—	—	—	34,406	36,069	38,694	....	....	....	....	....	....
28 Other expense.............	—	—	—	—	—	—	....	....	....	....	....	....
281 Property expense other than interest.............	—	—	—	—	—	—	....	....	....	....	....	....
282 Miscellaneous other expense.............	—	—	—	—	—	—	....	....	....	....	....	....
2821 Current.............	—	—	—	—	—	—	....	....	....	....	....	....
2822 Capital.............	—	—	—	—	—	—	....	....	....	....	....	....

Table 3   Transactions in assets and liabilities

	Budgetary Central Government			Central Government			Local Government			General Government		
	2002	2003	2004p	2002	2003	2004p	2002	2003	2004p	2002	2003	2004p
3 Change in net worth from transactns....	....	....	....	....	....	....	....	....	....	....	....	....
31 Net acquisition of nonfinancial assets...	3,281	3,625	5,260	3,701	4,074	5,646	....	....	....	....	....	....
311 Fixed assets.............	3,281	3,625	5,260	3,701	4,074	5,646	....	....	....	....	....	....
3111 Buildings and structures.............	....	....	....	....	....	....	....	....	....	....	....	....
3112 Machinery and equipment.............	....	....	....	....	....	....	....	....	....	....	....	....
3113 Other fixed assets.............	....	....	....	....	....	....	....	....	....	....	....	....
312 Inventories.............	—	—	—	—	—	—	....	....	....	....	....	....
313 Valuables.............	—	—	—	—	—	—	....	....	....	....	....	....
314 Nonproduced assets.............	—	—	—	—	—	—	....	....	....	....	....	....
3141 Land.............	—	—	—	—	—	—	....	....	....	....	....	....
3142 Subsoil assets.............	—	—	—	—	—	—	....	....	....	....	....	....
3143 Other naturally occurring assets.............	—	—	—	—	—	—	....	....	....	....	....	....
3144 Intangible nonproduced assets.............	—	—	—	—	—	—	....	....	....	....	....	....
32 Net acquisition of financial assets...	44,917	−9,005	−4,177	44,877	−8,860	−4,237	−195	121	249	44,682	−8,739	−3,988
321 Domestic.............	7,448	−1,181	1,758	7,408	−1,036	1,697	−195	121	249	7,213	−915	1,947
3212 Currency and deposits.............	−2,288	7,079	−2,518	−2,328	7,225	−2,578	−195	121	249	−2,523	7,346	−2,329
3213 Securities other than shares.............	—	−20	−60	—	−20	−60	—	—	—	—	−20	−60
3214 Loans.............	8,532	−8,430	4,335	8,532	−8,430	4,335	—	—	—	8,532	−8,430	4,335
3215 Shares and other equity.............	1,205	190	—	1,205	190	—	—	—	—	1,205	190	—
3216 Insurance technical reserves.............	—	—	—	—	—	—	—	—	—	—	—	—
3217 Financial derivatives.............	—	—	—	—	—	—	—	—	—	—	—	—
3218 Other accounts receivable.............	....	....	....	....	....	....	....	....	....	....	....	....
322 Foreign.............	37,469	−7,824	−5,934	37,469	−7,824	−5,934	—	—	—	37,469	−7,824	−5,934
3222 Currency and deposits.............	37,469	−8,115	−6,025	37,469	−8,115	−6,025	—	—	—	37,469	−8,115	−6,025
3223 Securities other than shares.............	—	290	91	—	290	91	—	—	—	—	290	91
3224 Loans.............	—	—	—	—	—	—	—	—	—	—	—	—
3225 Shares and other equity.............	—	—	—	—	—	—	—	—	—	—	—	—
3226 Insurance technical reserves.............	—	—	—	—	—	—	—	—	—	—	—	—
3227 Financial derivatives.............	—	—	—	—	—	—	—	—	—	—	—	—
3228 Other accounts receivable.............	—	—	—	—	—	—	—	—	—	—	—	—
323 Monetary gold and SDRs.............	—	—	—	—	—	—	—	—	—	—	—	—
33 Net incurrence of liabilities.............	57,391	5,468	4,921	57,450	5,477	4,854	−328	352	180	57,122	5,829	5,034
331 Domestic.............	−5,042	−17,406	−1,781	−4,983	−17,397	−1,848	−474	54	82	−5,457	−17,343	−1,766
3312 Currency and deposits.............												
3313 Securities other than shares.............	−871	1,970	−1,943	−871	1,970	−1,943	—	—	—	−871	1,970	−1,943
3314 Loans.............	−4,171	−19,376	163	−4,113	−19,366	95	−474	54	82	−4,587	−19,313	177
3316 Insurance technical reserves.............	—	—	—	—	—	—	—	—	—	—	—	—
3317 Financial derivatives.............	—	—	—	—	—	—	—	—	—	—	—	—
3318 Other accounts payable.............	....	....	....	....	....	....	....	....	....	....	....	....
332 Foreign.............	62,433	22,873	6,702	62,433	22,873	6,702	146	298	98	62,579	23,172	6,800
3322 Currency and deposits.............												
3323 Securities other than shares.............	1,184	14,778	9,646	1,184	14,778	9,646	—	—	—	1,184	14,778	9,646
3324 Loans.............	61,249	8,095	−2,944	61,249	8,095	−2,944	146	298	98	61,396	8,393	−2,845
3326 Insurance technical reserves.............	—	—	—	—	—	—	—	—	—	—	—	—
3327 Financial derivatives.............	—	—	—	—	—	—	—	—	—	—	—	—
3328 Other accounts payable.............	....	....	....	....	....	....	....	....	....	....	....	....

Uruguay 298

In Millions of Pesos / Year Ending December 31 / Cash Reporter

	Budgetary Central Government			Central Government			Local Government			General Government		
	2002	2003	2004p	2002	2003	2004p	2002	2003	2004p	2002	2003	2004p
Table 4 Holding gains in assets and liabilities												
Table 5 Other changes in the volume of assets and liabilities												
Table 6 Balance sheet												
6 Net worth	….	….	….	….	….	….	….	….	….	….	….	….
61 Nonfinancial assets	….	….	….	….	….	….	….	….	….	….	….	….
611 Fixed assets	….	….	….	….	….	….	….	….	….	….	….	….
6111 Buildings and structures	….	….	….	….	….	….	….	….	….	….	….	….
6112 Machinery and equipment	….	….	….	….	….	….	….	….	….	….	….	….
6113 Other fixed assets	….	….	….	….	….	….	….	….	….	….	….	….
612 Inventories	….	….	….	….	….	….	….	….	….	….	….	….
613 Valuables	….	….	….	….	….	….	….	….	….	….	….	….
614 Nonproduced assets	….	….	….	….	….	….	….	….	….	….	….	….
6141 Land	….	….	….	….	….	….	….	….	….	….	….	….
6142 Subsoil assets	….	….	….	….	….	….	….	….	….	….	….	….
6143 Other naturally occurring assets	….	….	….	….	….	….	….	….	….	….	….	….
6144 Intangible nonproduced assets	….	….	….	….	….	….	….	….	….	….	….	….
62 Financial assets	65,370	66,236	56,050	66,373	66,727	57,272	459	566	752	66,831	67,293	58,024
621 Domestic	51,701	59,325	55,620	52,704	59,816	56,842	459	566	752	53,163	60,382	57,594
6212 Currency and deposits	25,967	33,814	29,350	26,971	34,305	30,572	459	566	752	27,429	34,871	31,324
6213 Securities other than shares	947	562	72	947	562	72	—	—	—	947	562	72
6214 Loans	24,786	24,760	26,008	24,786	24,760	26,008	—	—	—	24,786	24,760	26,008
6215 Shares and other equity	—	190	190	—	190	190	—	—	—	—	190	190
6216 Insurance technical reserves	—	—	—	—	—	—	—	—	—	—	—	—
6217 Financial derivatives	—	—	—	—	—	—	—	—	—	—	—	—
6218 Other accounts receivable	….	….	….	….	….	….				….	….	….
622 Foreign	13,669	6,911	430	13,669	6,911	430	—	—	—	13,669	6,911	430
6222 Currency and deposits	13,669	6,690	148	13,669	6,690	148	—	—	—	13,669	6,690	148
6223 Securities other than shares	—	221	282	—	221	282	—	—	—	—	221	282
6224 Loans	—	—	—	—	—	—	—	—	—	—	—	—
6225 Shares and other equity	—	—	—	—	—	—	—	—	—	—	—	—
6226 Insurance technical reserves	—	—	—	—	—	—	—	—	—	—	—	—
6227 Financial derivatives	—	—	—	—	—	—	—	—	—	—	—	—
6228 Other accounts receivable	….	….	….	….	….	….				….	….	….
623 Monetary gold and SDRs	—	….	….	—	….	….				—	….	….
63 Liabilities	275,488	358,762	335,628	275,546	358,829	335,628	5,784	6,840	6,623	281,330	365,669	342,252
631 Domestic	80,566	118,170	107,589	80,624	118,238	107,589	2,090	2,523	2,624	82,714	120,760	110,212
6312 Currency and deposits												
6313 Securities other than shares	73,831	82,642	76,281	73,831	82,642	76,281	—	—	—	73,831	82,642	76,281
6314 Loans	6,735	35,527	31,308	6,793	35,595	31,308	2,090	2,523	2,624	8,883	38,118	33,931
6316 Insurance technical reserves	—	—	—	—	—	—	—	—	—	—	—	—
6317 Financial derivatives	—	—	—	—	—	—	—	—	—	—	—	—
6318 Other accounts payable	….	….	….	….	….	….				….	….	….
632 Foreign	194,922	240,592	228,040	194,922	240,592	228,040	3,694	4,317	4,000	198,616	244,909	232,040
6322 Currency and deposits	—	—	—	—	—	—			—	—	—	—
6323 Securities other than shares	80,422	103,891	105,069	80,422	103,891	105,069	—	—	—	80,422	103,891	105,069
6324 Loans	114,500	136,701	122,971	114,500	136,701	122,971	3,694	4,317	4,000	118,194	141,018	126,971
6326 Insurance technical reserves	—	—	—	—	—	—	—	—	—	—	—	—
6327 Financial derivatives	—	—	—	—	—	—	—	—	—	—	—	—
6328 Other accounts payable	….	….	….	….	….	….				….	….	….
Memorandum items:												
6M2 Net financial worth	−210,118	−292,526	−279,578	−209,174	−292,102	−278,356	−5,325	−6,274	−5,872	−214,499	−298,376	−284,227
6M3 Debt at market value	….	….	….	….	….	….	….	….	….	….	….	….
6M4 Debt at nominal value	….	….	….	….	….	….	….	….	….	….	….	….
6M5 Arrears	….	….	….	….	….	….	….	….	….	….	….	….
6M6 Obligations for social security benefits	….	….	….	….	….	….	….	….	….	….	….	….
6M7 Contingent liabilities	….	….	….	….	….	….	….	….	….	….	….	….
6M8 Uncapitalized military weapons, systems	….	….	….	….	….	….	….	….	….	….	….	….
Table 7 Outlays by functions of govt.												
7 Total outlays	65,038	78,488	86,606	84,371	98,919	110,111	….	….	….	….	….	….
701 General public services	….	….	….	….	….	….	….	….	….	….	….	….
7017 Public debt transactions	10,592	17,803	18,646	10,592	17,803	18,646	….	….	….	….	….	….
7018 General transfers between levels of govt.	….	….	….	….	….	….	….	….	….	….	….	….
702 Defense	….	….	….	….	….	….	….	….	….	….	….	….
703 Public order and safety	….	….	….	….	….	….	….	….	….	….	….	….

In Millions of Pesos / Year Ending December 31 / Cash Reporter

	Budgetary Central Government			Central Government			Local Government			General Government		
	2002	2003	2004p	2002	2003	2004p	2002	2003	2004p	2002	2003	2004p
704 **Economic affairs**...............	....	....	....	....	....	....	....	....	....	....	....	....
7042 Agriculture, forestry, fishing, and hunting.....	....	....	....	....	....	....	....	....	....	....	....	....
7043 Fuel and energy.....	....	....	....	....	....	....	....	....	....	....	....	....
7044 Mining, manufacturing, and construction.....	....	....	....	....	....	....	....	....	....	....	....	....
7045 Transport.....	....	....	....	....	....	....	....	....	....	....	....	....
7046 Communication.....	....	....	....	....	....	....	....	....	....	....	....	....
705 **Environmental protection**.....	....	....	....	....	....	....	....	....	....	....	....	....
706 **Housing and community amenities**.......	....	....	....	....	....	....	....	....	....	....	....	....
707 **Health**.....	....	....	....	....	....	....	....	....	....	....	....	....
7072 Outpatient services.....	....	....	....	....	....	....	....	....	....	....	....	....
7073 Hospital services.....	....	....	....	....	....	....	....	....	....	....	....	....
7074 Public health services.....	....	....	....	....	....	....	....	....	....	....	....	....
708 **Recreation, culture, and religion**.....	....	....	....	....	....	....	....	....	....	....	....	....
709 **Education**.....	....	....	....	....	....	....	....	....	....	....	....	....
7091 Pre-primary and primary education.....	....	....	....	....	....	....	....	....	....	....	....	....
7092 Secondary education.....	....	....	....	....	....	....	....	....	....	....	....	....
7094 Tertiary education.....	....	....	....	....	....	....	....	....	....	....	....	....
710 **Social protection**.....	....	....	....	....	....	....	....	....	....	....	....	....
7 Statistical discrepancy: Total outlays.....	....	....	....	....	....	....	....	....	....	....	....	....

Table 8   Transactions in financial assets and liabilities by sector

	Budgetary Central Government			Central Government			Local Government			General Government		
	2002	2003	2004p	2002	2003	2004p	2002	2003	2004p	2002	2003	2004p
82 **Net acquisition of financial assets**.....	44,917	−9,005	−4,177	44,877	−8,860	−4,237	−195	121	249	44,682	−8,739	−3,988
821 Domestic.....	7,448	−1,181	1,758	7,408	−1,036	1,697	−195	121	249	7,213	−915	1,947
8211 General government.....	—	—	—	—	—	—	—	—	—	—	—	—
8212 Central bank.....	−5,085	−5,881	4,407	−5,142	−5,820	4,362	—	—	—	−5,142	−5,820	4,362
8213 Other depository corporations.....	12,533	4,700	−8,040	12,550	4,785	−8,055	−195	121	249	12,355	4,906	−7,806
8214 Financial corporations n.e.c.....	—	—	4,840	—	—	4,840	—	—	—	—	—	4,840
8215 Nonfinancial corporations.....	—	—	582	—	—	582	—	—	—	—	—	582
8216 Households & NPIs serving households.....	—	—	−32	—	—	−32	—	—	—	—	—	−32
822 Foreign.....	37,469	−7,824	−5,934	37,469	−7,824	−5,934	—	—	—	37,469	−7,824	−5,934
8221 General government.....	—	—	—	—	—	—	—	—	—	—	—	—
8227 International organizations.....	—	—	—	—	—	—	—	—	—	—	—	—
8228 Financial corporations other than international organizations.....	37,469	−8,115	−6,025	37,469	−8,115	−6,025	—	—	—	37,469	−8,115	−6,025
8229 Other nonresidents.....	—	290	91	—	290	91	—	—	—	—	290	91
823 Monetary gold and SDRs.....	—	—	—	—	—	—	—	—	—	—	—	—
83 **Net incurrence of liabilities**.....	57,391	5,468	4,921	57,450	5,477	4,854	−328	352	180	57,122	5,829	5,034
831 Domestic.....	−5,042	−17,406	−1,781	−4,983	−17,397	−1,848	−474	54	82	−5,457	−17,343	−1,766
8311 General government.....	—	—	—	—	—	—	—	—	—	—	—	—
8312 Central bank.....	23,675	−7,173	102	23,675	−7,173	102	—	—	—	23,675	−7,173	102
8313 Other depository corporations.....	−916	−7,329	−1,645	−857	−7,319	−1,712	−474	12	82	−1,331	−7,307	−1,630
8314 Financial corporations n.e.c.....	2,698	−4,593	2,141	2,698	−4,593	2,141	—	—	—	2,698	−4,593	2,141
8315 Nonfinancial corporations.....	−100	−227	789	−100	−227	789	—	—	—	−100	−227	789
8316 Households & NPIs serving households.....	−30,399	1,915	−3,168	−30,399	1,915	−3,168	—	42	—	−30,399	1,957	−3,168
832 Foreign.....	62,433	22,873	6,702	62,433	22,873	6,702	146	298	98	62,579	23,172	6,800
8321 General government.....	—	—	—	—	—	—	—	—	—	—	—	—
8327 International organizations.....	61,301	8,603	−2,874	61,301	8,603	−2,874	145	298	98	61,446	8,901	−2,775
8328 Financial corporations other than international organizations.....	−31	−43	−42	−31	−43	−42	—	—	—	−31	−43	−42
8329 Other nonresidents.....	1,163	14,313	9,618	1,163	14,313	9,618	1	—	—	1,164	14,313	9,618

Vanuatu 846

In Millions of Vatu / Year Ending December 31 / Cash Reporter

	Budgetary Central Government			Central Government			Local Government			General Government		
	1997	1998	1999	1997	1998	1999	1997	1998	1999	1997	1998	1999
Statement of government operations												
Statement of other economic flows												
Balance sheet												
6 *Net worth*...........	....	....	....	....	....	....	....	....	....	....	....	....
61 Nonfinancial assets...........	....	....	....	....	....	....	....	....	....	....	....	....
62 Financial assets...........	....	....	....	....	....	....	....	....	....	....	....	....
63 Liabilities...........	7,381	9,500	9,445	7,381	9,500	9,445	....	....	....	....	....	....
Statement of sources and uses of cash												
1 Cash receipts from operating activities...........	6,205	6,675	6,721	6,858	7,046	7,246	....	....	....	....	....	....
11 Taxes...........	5,718	5,932	5,924	5,718	5,932	5,924	....	....	....	....	....	....
12 Social contributions...........	—	—	—	—	—	—	....	....	....	....	....	....
13 Grants...........	—	—	—	653	371	525	....	....	....	....	....	....
14 Other receipts...........	487	743	797	487	743	797	....	....	....	....	....	....
2 Cash payments for operating activities...........	6,424	6,401	6,509	6,424	6,401	6,885	....	....	....	....	....	....
21 Compensation of employees...........	2,938	3,645	3,741	2,938	3,645	3,807	....	....	....	....	....	....
22 Purchases of goods and services...........	2,560	1,900	1,909	2,560	1,900	2,219	....	....	....	....	....	....
24 Interest...........	146	161	247	146	161	247	....	....	....	....	....	....
25 Subsidies...........	....	....	....	....	....	....	....	....	....	....	....	....
26 Grants...........	....	....	....	....	....	....	....	....	....	....	....	....
27 Social benefits...........	....	....	....	....	....	....	....	....	....	....	....	....
28 Other payments...........	—	—	—	—	—	—	....	....	....	....	....	....
CIO *Net cash inflow from oper. activities*...........	....	....	....	*434*	*645*	*361*	....	....	....	....	....	....
31.1 Purchases of nonfinancial assets...........	—	366	289	599	2,818	646	....	....	....	....	....	....
31.2 Sales of nonfinancial assets...........	1	7	31	1	7	31	....	....	....	....	....	....
31 Net cash outflow from investments in nonfinancial assets...........	−1	359	258	598	2,811	615	....	....	....	....	....	....
CSD *Cash surplus/deficit*...........	....	....	....	*−164*	*−2,166*	*−254*	....	....	....	....	....	....
32x Net acquisition of fin assets, excl. cash...........	....	891	−2	—	891	121	....	....	....	....	....	....
321x Domestic...........	....	....	....	—	....	....	....	....	....	....	....	....
322x Foreign...........	....	....	....	—	....	....	....	....	....	....	....	....
323 Monetary gold and SDRs...........	—	—	—	—	—	—	....	....	....	....	....	....
33 Net incurrence of liabilities...........	....	....	....	143	3,231	578	....	....	....	....	....	....
331 Domestic...........	....	....	....	300	1,858	−65	....	....	....	....	....	....
332 Foreign...........	....	....	....	−157	1,373	643	....	....	....	....	....	....
NFB Net cash inflow from fin. activities...........	....	....	....	143	2,340	457	....	....	....	....	....	....
NCB *Net change in the stock of cash*...........	....	....	....	*−21*	*174*	*203*	....	....	....	....	....	....
Table 1 Revenue												
1 **Revenue**...........	**6,205**	**6,675**	**6,721**	**6,858**	**7,046**	**7,246**	....	....	....	....	....	....
11 **Taxes**...........	**5,718**	**5,932**	**5,924**	**5,718**	**5,932**	**5,924**	....	....	....	....	....	....
111 Taxes on income, profits, & capital gains...........	—	—	—	—	—	—	....	....	....	....	....	....
1111 Individuals...........	—	—	—	—	—	—	....	....	....	....	....	....
1112 Corporations and other enterprises...........	—	—	—	—	—	—	....	....	....	....	....	....
112 Taxes on payroll and workforce...........	—	—	—	—	—	—	....	....	....	....	....	....
113 Taxes on property...........	187	163	119	187	163	119	....	....	....	....	....	....
114 Taxes on goods and services...........	2,230	2,669	3,369	2,230	2,669	3,369	....	....	....	....	....	....
1141 General taxes on goods and services...........	501	1,313	2,431	501	1,313	2,431	....	....	....	....	....	....
1142 Excises...........	30	31	36	30	31	36	....	....	....	....	....	....
115 Taxes on int'l. trade and transactions...........	3,301	3,100	2,436	3,301	3,100	2,436	....	....	....	....	....	....
116 Other taxes...........	—	—	—	—	—	—	....	....	....	....	....	....
12 **Social contributions**...........	—	—	—	—	—	—	....	....	....	....	....	....
121 Social security contributions...........	—	—	—	—	—	—	....	....	....	....	....	....
122 Other social contributions...........	—	—	—	—	—	—	....	....	....	....	....	....
13 **Grants**...........	—	—	—	653	371	525	....	....	....	....	....	....
131 From foreign governments...........	—	—	—	....	....	....	....	....	....	....	....	....
132 From international organizations...........	—	—	—	....	....	....	....	....	....	....	....	....
133 From other general government units...........	—	—	—	....	....	....	....	....	....	....	....	....
14 **Other revenue**...........	**487**	**743**	**797**	**487**	**743**	**797**	....	....	....	....	....	....
Table 2 Expense by economic type												
2 **Expense**...........	**6,424**	**6,401**	**6,509**	**6,424**	**6,401**	**6,885**	....	....	....	....	....	....
21 **Compensation of employees**...........	**2,938**	**3,645**	**3,741**	**2,938**	**3,645**	**3,807**	....	....	....	....	....	....
211 Wages and salaries...........	2,938	3,645	3,741	2,938	3,645	3,807	....	....	....	....	....	....
212 Social contributions...........	....	....	....	....	....	....	....	....	....	....	....	....
22 **Use of goods and services**...........	**2,560**	**1,900**	**1,909**	**2,560**	**1,900**	**2,219**	....	....	....	....	....	....
23 **Consumption of fixed capital**...........	....	....	....	....	....	....	....	....	....	....	....	....
24 **Interest**...........	**146**	**161**	**247**	**146**	**161**	**247**	....	....	....	....	....	....
25 **Subsidies**...........	....	....	....	....	....	....	....	....	....	....	....	....

Vanuatu 846

In Millions of Vatu / Year Ending December 31 / Cash Reporter

		Budgetary Central Government			Central Government			Local Government			General Government		
		1997	1998	1999	1997	1998	1999	1997	1998	1999	1997	1998	1999
26	**Grants**....................	....	....	....	....	....	....	....	....	....	....	....	....
261	To foreign govenments.............	....	....	....	....	....	....	....	....	....	....		....
262	To international organizations........	....	....	....	....	....	....	....	....	....	....	....	....
263	To other general government units.......	....	....	....	....	....	....	....	....	....	....	....	....
2631	Current...................	....	....	....	....	....	....	....	....	....	....	....	....
2632	Capital....................	—	—	—	—	—	—	....	....	....	....	....	....
27	**Social benefits**..............	....	....	....	....	....	....	....	....	....	...	....	....
28	**Other expense**................	—	—	—	—	—	—	....	....	....	....	....	....
281	Property expense other than interest...........	—	—	—	—	—	—	....	....	....	....	....	....
282	Miscellaneous other expense.........	—	—	—	—	—	—	....	....	....	....	....	....
2821	Current..................	—	—	—	—	—	—	....	....	....	....	....	....
2822	Capital..................	—	—	—	—	—	—	....	....	....	....	....	....
Table 3	**Transactions in assets and liabilities**												
3	**Change in net worth from transactns....**	....	....	....	....	....	....	....	....	....	....	....	....
31	**Net acquisition of nonfinancial assets...**	−1	359	258	598	2,811	615	....	....	....	....	....	....
311	Fixed assets..................	....	....	....	....	....	....	....	....	....	....	....	....
3111	Buildings and structures.........	....	....	....	....	....	....	....	....	....	....	....	....
3112	Machinery and equipment.........	....	....	....	....	....	....	....	....	....	....	....	....
3113	Other fixed assets............	....	....	....	....	....	....	....	....	....	....	....	....
312	Inventories..................	....	....	....	....	....	....	....	....	....	....	....	....
313	Valuables..................	....	....	....	....	....	....	....	....	....	....	....	....
314	Nonproduced assets............	....	....	....	....	....	....	....	....	....	....	....	....
3141	Land....................	....	....	....	....	....	....	....	....	....	....	....	....
3142	Subsoil assets..............	....	....	....	....	....	....	....	....	....	....	....	....
3143	Other naturally occurring assets........	....	....	....	....	....	....	....	....	....	....	....	....
3144	Intangible nonproduced assets......	....	....	....	....	....	....	....	....	....	....	....	....
32	**Net acquisition of financial assets........**	....	....	....	−21	1,065	324	....	....	....	....	....	....
321	Domestic..................	....	....	....	−21			....	....	....	....	....	....
3212	Currency and deposits..........	....	....	....	−21	174	203	....	....	....	....	....	....
3213	Securities other than shares........	....	....	....	—	....	....	....	....	....	....	....	....
3214	Loans...................	....	....	....	—	....	....	....	....	....	....	....	....
3215	Shares and other equity..........	....	....	....	—	....	....	....	....	....	....	....	....
3216	Insurance technical reserves........	....	....	....	—	....	....	....	....	....	....	....	....
3217	Financial derivatives...........	....	....	....	—	....	....	....	....	....	....	....	....
3218	Other accounts receivable.........	....	....	....	....	....	....	....	....	....	....	....	....
322	Foreign...................	....	....	....	....	....	....	....	....	....	....	....	....
3222	Currency and deposits..........	....	....	....	—	—	—	....	....	....	....	....	....
3223	Securities other than shares........	....	....	....	—	....	....	....	....	....	....	....	....
3224	Loans...................	....	....	....	—	....	....	....	....	....	....	....	....
3225	Shares and other equity..........	....	....	....	—	....	....	....	....	....	....	....	....
3226	Insurance technical reserves........	....	....	....	—	....	....	....	....	....	....	....	....
3227	Financial derivatives...........	....	....	....	—	....	....	....	....	....	....	....	....
3228	Other accounts receivable.........	....	....	....	....	....	....	....	....	....	....	....	....
323	Monetary gold and SDRs...........	....	....	....	....	....	....	....	....	....	....	....	....
33	**Net incurrence of liabilities...................**	....	....	....	143	3,231	578	....	....	....	....	....	....
331	Domestic..................	....	....	....	300	1,858	−65	....	....	....	....	....	....
3312	Currency and deposits..........	....	....	....	—	—	—	....	....	....	....	....	....
3313	Securities other than shares........	....	....	....	300	1,858	−65	....	....	....	....	....	....
3314	Loans...................	....	....	....	—	—	—	....	....	....	....	....	....
3316	Insurance technical reserves........	....	....	....	—	—	—	....	....	....	....	....	....
3317	Financial derivatives...........	....	....	....	—	—	—	....	....	....	....	....	....
3318	Other accounts payable...........	....	....	....	....	....	....	....	....	....	....	....	....
332	Foreign...................	....	....	....	−157	1,373	643	....	....	....	....	....	....
3322	Currency and deposits..........	....	....	....	—	—	—	....	....	....	....	....	....
3323	Securities other than shares........	....	....	....	−157	1,373	643	....	....	....	....	....	....
3324	Loans...................	....	....	....	—	—	—	....	....	....	....	....	....
3326	Insurance technical reserves........	....	....	....	—	—	—	....	....	....	....	....	....
3327	Financial derivatives...........	....	....	....	—	—	—	....	....	....	....	....	....
3328	Other accounts payable...........	....	....	....	....	....	....	....	....	....	....	....	....

In Millions of Vatu / Year Ending December 31 / Cash Reporter

	Budgetary Central Government			Central Government			Local Government			General Government		
	1997	1998	1999	1997	1998	1999	1997	1998	1999	1997	1998	1999
Table 4 Holding gains in assets and liabilities												
Table 5 Other changes in the volume of assets and liabilities												
Table 6 Balance sheet												
6 **Net worth**....................	....	....	....	....	....	....	....	....	....	....	....	....
61 **Nonfinancial assets**........................	....	....	....	....	....	....	....	....	....	....	....	....
611 Fixed assets..........................	....	....	....	....	....	....	....	....	....	....	....	....
6111 Buildings and structures....................	....	....	....	....	....	....	....	....	....	....	....	....
6112 Machinery and equipment......................	....	....	....	....	....	....	....	....	....	....	....	....
6113 Other fixed assets............................	....	....	....	....	....	....	....	....	....	....	....	....
612 Inventories.............................	....	....	....	....	....	....	....	....	....	....	....	....
613 Valuables..............................	....	....	....	....	....	....	....	....	....	....	....	....
614 Nonproduced assets........................	....	....	....	....	....	....	....	....	....	....	....	....
6141 Land.................................	....	....	....	....	....	....	....	....	....	....	....	....
6142 Subsoil assets........................	....	....	....	....	....	....	....	....	....	....	....	....
6143 Other naturally occurring assets............	....	....	....	....	....	....	....	....	....	....	....	....
6144 Intangible nonproduced assets............	....	....	....	....	....	....	....	....	....	....	....	....
62 **Financial assets**........................	....	....	....	....	....	....	....	....	....	....	....	....
621 Domestic..............................	....	....	....	....	....	....	....	....	....	....	....	....
6212 Currency and deposits.....................	....	....	....	....	....	....	....	....	....	....	....	....
6213 Securities other than shares................	....	....	....	....	....	....	....	....	....	....	....	....
6214 Loans.................................	....	....	....	....	....	....	....	....	....	....	....	....
6215 Shares and other equity....................	....	....	....	....	....	....	....	....	....	....	....	....
6216 Insurance technical reserves................	....	....	....	....	....	....	....	....	....	....	....	....
6217 Financial derivatives......................	....	....	....	....	....	....	....	....	....	....	....	....
6218 Other accounts receivable..................	....	....	....	....	....	....	....	....	....	....	....	....
622 Foreign...............................	....	....	....	....	....	....	....	....	....	....	....	....
6222 Currency and deposits.....................	....	....	....	....	....	....	....	....	....	....	....	....
6223 Securities other than shares................	....	....	....	....	....	....	....	....	....	....	....	....
6224 Loans.................................	....	....	....	....	....	....	....	....	....	....	....	....
6225 Shares and other equity....................	....	....	....	....	....	....	....	....	....	....	....	....
6226 Insurance technical reserves................	....	....	....	....	....	....	....	....	....	....	....	....
6227 Financial derivatives......................	....	....	....	....	....	....	....	....	....	....	....	....
6228 Other accounts receivable..................	....	....	....	....	....	....	....	....	....	....	....	....
623 Monetary gold and SDRs....................	....	....	....	....	....	....	....	....	....	....	....	....
63 **Liabilities**.............................	**7,381**	**9,500**	**9,445**	**7,381**	**9,500**	**9,445**	....	....	....	....	....	....
631 Domestic..............................	2,457	2,761	2,706	2,457	2,761	2,706	....	....	....	....	....	....
6312 Currency and deposits.....................	....	....	....	....	....	....	....	....	....	....	....	....
6313 Securities other than shares................	....	....	....	....	....	....	....	....	....	....	....	....
6314 Loans.................................	....	....	....	....	....	....	....	....	....	....	....	....
6316 Insurance technical reserves................	....	....	....	....	....	....	....	....	....	....	....	....
6317 Financial derivatives......................	....	....	....	....	....	....	....	....	....	....	....	....
6318 Other accounts payable....................	....	....	....	....	....	....	....	....	....	....	....	....
632 Foreign...............................	4,924	6,739	6,739	4,924	6,739	6,739	....	....	....	....	....	....
6322 Currency and deposits.....................	....	....	....	....	....	....	....	....	....	....	....	....
6323 Securities other than shares................	....	....	....	....	....	....	....	....	....	....	....	....
6324 Loans.................................	....	....	....	....	....	....	....	....	....	....	....	....
6326 Insurance technical reserves................	....	....	....	....	....	....	....	....	....	....	....	....
6327 Financial derivatives......................	....	....	....	....	....	....	....	....	....	....	....	....
6328 Other accounts payable....................	....	....	....	....	....	....	....	....	....	....	....	....
Memorandum items:												
6M2 Net financial worth..........................	....	....	....	....	....	....	....	....	....	....	....	....
6M3 Debt at market value........................	....	....	....	....	....	....	....	....	....	....	....	....
6M4 Debt at nominal value.......................	....	....	....	....	....	....	....	....	....	....	....	....
6M5 Arrears....................................	....	....	....	....	....	....	....	....	....	....	....	....
6M6 Obligations for social security benefits...........	....	....	....	....	....	....	....	....	....	....	....	....
6M7 Contingent liabilities.......................	....	....	....	....	....	....	....	....	....	....	....	....
6M8 Uncapitalized military weapons, systems........	....	....	....	....	....	....	....	....	....	....	....	....
Table 7 Outlays by functions of govt.												
7 **Total outlays**........................	**6,424**	**6,767**	**6,798**	**7,023**	**9,219**	**7,531**	....	....	....	....	....	....
701 **General public services**........................	**1,773**	....	....	**2,372**	....	....	....	....	....	....	....	....
7017 Public debt transactions............................	146	161	247	146	161	247	....	....	....	....	....	....
7018 General transfers between levels of govt......	....	....	....	....	....	....	....	....	....	....	....	....
702 **Defense**................................	—	....	....	—	....	....	....	....	....	....	....	....
703 **Public order and safety**........................	**587**	....	....	**587**	....	....	....	....	....	....	....	....

In Millions of Vatu / Year Ending December 31 / Cash Reporter

	Budgetary Central Government			Central Government			Local Government			General Government		
	1997	1998	1999	1997	1998	1999	1997	1998	1999	1997	1998	1999
704 **Economic affairs**.....................	**1,846**	....	....	**1,846**	....	....	....	....	....	....	....	....
7042 Agriculture, forestry, fishing, and hunting.....	232	....	....	232	....	....	....	....	....	....	....	....
7043 Fuel and energy......................	—	....	....	—	....	....	....	....	....	....	....	....
7044 Mining, manufacturing, and construction.....	653	....	....	653	....	....	....	....	....	....	....	....
7045 Transport................................	346	....	....	346	....	....	....	....	....	....	....	....
7046 Communication.....................	....	....	....	....	....	....	....	....	....	....	....	....
705 **Environmental protection**.....................	....	....	....	....	....	....	....	....	....	....	....	....
706 **Housing and community amenities**........	**259**	....	....	**259**	....	....	....	....	....	....	....	....
707 **Health**...................................	**655**	....	....	**655**	....	....	....	....	....	....	....	....
7072 Outpatient services..................	....	....	....	....	....	....	....	....	....	....	....	....
7073 Hospital services.....................	....	....	....	....	....	....	....	....	....	....	....	....
7074 Public health services...............	....	....	....	....	....	....	....	....	....	....	....	....
708 **Recreation, culture, and religion**...........	**35**	....	....	**35**	....	....	....	....	....	....	....	....
709 **Education**..................................	**1,269**	....	....	**1,269**	....	....	....	....	....	....	....	....
7091 Pre-primary and primary education.......	....	....	....	....	....	....	....	....	....	....	....	....
7092 Secondary education................	....	....	....	....	....	....	....	....	....	....	....	....
7094 Tertiary education...................	....	....	....	....	....	....	....	....	....	....	....	....
710 **Social protection**....................	—	....	....	—	....	....	....	....	....	....	....	....
7 Statistical discrepancy: Total outlays............	—	....	....	—	....	....	....	....	....	....	....	....

Table 8 Transactions in financial assets and liabilities by sector

	Budgetary Central Government			Central Government			Local Government			General Government		
82 **Net acquisition of financial assets**........	....	....	....	**−21**	**1,065**	**324**	....	....	....	....	....	....
821 Domestic.............................	....	....	....	−21	....	....	....	....	....	....	....	....
8211 General government..................	....	....	....	....	....	....	....	....	....	....	....	....
8212 Central bank........................	....	....	....	....	....	....	....	....	....	....	....	....
8213 Other depository corporations..................	....	....	....	....	....	....	....	....	....	....	....	....
8214 Financial corporations n.e.c...........	....	....	....	....	....	....	....	....	....	....	....	....
8215 Nonfinancial corporations............	....	....	....	....	....	....	....	....	....	....	....	....
8216 Households & NPIs serving households......	....	....	....	....	....	....	....	....	....	....	....	....
822 Foreign..............................	....	....	....	—	....	....	....	....	....	....	....	....
8221 General government.................	....	....	....	—	....	....	....	....	....	....	....	....
8227 International organizations............	....	....	....	—	....	....	....	....	....	....	....	....
8228 Financial corporations other than international organizations.............	....	....	....	—	....	....	....	....	....	....	....	....
8229 Other nonresidents................	....	....	....	—	....	....	....	....	....	....	....	....
823 Monetary gold and SDRs................	....	....	....	—	—	—	....	....	....	....	....	....
83 **Net incurrence of liabilities**....................	....	....	....	**143**	**3,231**	**578**	....	....	....	....	....	....
831 Domestic.............................	....	....	....	300	1,858	−65	....	....	....	....	....	....
8311 General government..................	....	....	....	....	....	....	....	....	....	....	....	....
8312 Central bank........................	....	....	....	....	....	....	....	....	....	....	....	....
8313 Other depository corporations..................	....	....	....	....	....	....	....	....	....	....	....	....
8314 Financial corporations n.e.c...........	....	....	....	....	....	....	....	....	....	....	....	....
8315 Nonfinancial corporations............	....	....	....	....	....	....	....	....	....	....	....	....
8316 Households & NPIs serving households......	....	....	....	....	....	....	....	....	....	....	....	....
832 Foreign..............................	....	....	....	−157	1,373	643	....	....	....	....	....	....
8321 General government.................	....	....	....	−263	−1	−37	....	....	....	....	....	....
8327 International organizations............	....	....	....	106	1,374	680	....	....	....	....	....	....
8328 Financial corporations other than international organizations.............	....	....	....	—	—	—	....	....	....	....	....	....
8329 Other nonresidents................	....	....	....	—	—	—	....	....	....	....	....	....

In billions of Bolivares / Year Ending December 31 / Cash Reporter

		Central Government			State Government			Local Government			General Government		
		2001	2002	2003p	2001	2002	2003	2001	2002	2003	2001	2002	2003
Statement of government operations													
Statement of other economic flows													
Balance sheet													
Statement of sources and uses of cash													
1	Cash receipts from operating activities...........	19,326.5	24,632.8	32,252.9	....	....	....	....	....	....	....	....	....
11	Taxes..	10,492.3	11,809.0	15,482.0	....	....	....	....	....	....	....	....	....
12	Social contributions..................................	673.5	650.4	796.8	....	....	....	....	....	....	....	....	....
13	Grants..	—	—	—	....	....	....	....	....	....	....	....	....
14	Other receipts................................	8,160.7	12,173.4	15,974.1	....	....	....	....	....	....	....	....	....
2	Cash payments for operating activities...........	21,420.4	25,150.0	33,765.3	....	....	....	....	....	....	....	....	....
21	Compensation of employees.......................	4,470.1	4,995.8	6,518.3	....	....	....	....	....	....	....	....	....
22	Purchases of goods and services.................	1,439.8	2,013.7	2,550.3	....	....	....	....	....	....	....	....	....
24	Interest..	2,581.0	4,954.0	6,300.8	....	....	....	....	....	....	....	....	....
25	Subsidies.......................................	.3	.5	.2	....	....	....	....	....	....	....	....	....
26	Grants..	10,793.5	11,044.7	15,507.6	....	....	....	....	....	....	....	....	....
27	Social benefits................................	1,857.9	1,656.6	2,361.7	....	....	....	....	....	....	....	....	....
28	Other payments...............................	277.8	484.7	526.5	....	....	....	....	....	....	....	....	....
CIO	*Net cash inflow from oper. activities.....*	*–2,093.9*	*–517.2*	*–1,512.4*	....	....	....	....	....	....	....	....	....
31.1	Purchases of nonfinancial assets...................	1,463.4	2,967.4	4,020.7	....	....	....	....	....	....	....	....	....
31.2	Sales of nonfinancial assets........................	—	—	—	....	....	....	....	....	....	....	....	....
31	Net cash outflow from investments in nonfinancial assets........................	1,463.3	2,967.4	4,020.7	....	....	....	....	....	....	....	....	....
CSD	*Cash surplus/deficit...............................*	*–3,557.3*	*–3,484.6*	*–5,533.1*	....	....	....	....	....	....	....	....	....
32x	Net acquisition of fin assets, excl. cash..........	383.8	793.6	315.3	....	....	....	....	....	....	....	....	....
321x	Domestic.......................................	336.1	748.6	231.9	....	....	....	....	....	....	....	....	....
322x	Foreign..	47.7	44.9	83.4	....	....	....	....	....	....	....	....	....
323	Monetary gold and SDRs.......................	—	—	—	....	....	....	....	....	....	....	....	....
33	Net incurrence of liabilities......................	3,541.3	2,722.9	8,617.5	....	....	....	....	....	....	....	....	....
331	Domestic.......................................	3,373.8	3,412.3	8,395.7	....	....	....	....	....	....	....	....	....
332	Foreign..	167.5	–689.4	221.8	....	....	....	....	....	....	....	....	....
NFB	Net cash inflow from fin. activities................	3,157.5	1,929.3	8,302.2	....	....	....	....	....	....	....	....	....
NCB	*Net change in the stock of cash...........*	*–399.7*	*–1,555.3*	*2,769.1*	....	....	....	....	....	....	....	....	....
Table 1 Revenue													
1	**Revenue..**	**19,326.5**	**24,632.8**	**32,252.9**	....	....	....	....	....	....	....	....	....
11	**Taxes...**	**10,492.3**	**11,809.0**	**15,482.0**	....	....	....	....	....	....	....	....	....
111	Taxes on income, profits, & capital gains......	3,792.0	2,964.4	4,325.4	....	....	....	....	....	....	....	....	....
1111	Individuals..................................	198.7	330.3	333.2	....	....	....	....	....	....	....	....	....
1112	Corporations and other enterprises............	3,593.0	2,634.1	3,992.3	....	....	....	....	....	....	....	....	....
112	Taxes on payroll and workforce..................	—	—	—	....	....	....	....	....	....	....	....	....
113	Taxes on property................................	372.0	1,832.3	2,327.4	....	....	....	....	....	....	....	....	....
114	Taxes on goods and services.....................	4,861.2	5,533.0	7,570.7	....	....	....	....	....	....	....	....	....
1141	General taxes on goods and services..........	3,729.0	4,515.6	6,476.0	....	....	....	....	....	....	....	....	....
1142	Excises.......................................	895.9	902.2	994.6	....	....	....	....	....	....	....	....	....
115	Taxes on int'l. trade and transactions...........	1,355.4	1,351.5	1,137.2	....	....	....	....	....	....	....	....	....
116	Other taxes....................................	111.5	127.9	121.2	....	....	....	....	....	....	....	....	....
12	**Social contributions...............................**	**673.5**	**650.4**	**796.8**	....	....	....	....	....	....	....	....	....
121	Social security contributions........................	673.5	650.4	796.8	....	....	....	....	....	....	....	....	....
122	Other social contributions.........................	—	—	—	....	....	....	....	....	....	....	....	....
13	**Grants..**	**—**	**—**	**—**	....	....	....	....	....	....	....	....	....
131	From foreign governments.........................	—	—	—	....	....	....	....	....	....	....	....	....
132	From international organizations..................	—	—	—	....	....	....	....	....	....	....	....	....
133	From other general government units...........	—	—	—	....	....	....	....	....	....	....	....	....
14	**Other revenue...............................**	**8,160.7**	**12,173.4**	**15,974.1**	....	....	....	....	....	....	....	....	....
Table 2 Expense by economic type													
2	**Expense..**	**21,420.4**	**25,150.0**	**33,765.3**	....	....	....	....	....	....	....	....	....
21	**Compensation of employees..................**	**4,470.1**	**4,995.8**	**6,518.3**	....	....	....	....	....	....	....	....	....
211	Wages and salaries...............................	4,365.9	4,952.9	6,210.0	....	....	....	....	....	....	....	....	....
212	Social contributions..............................	104.2	42.9	308.3	....	....	....	....	....	....	....	....	....
22	**Use of goods and services.....................**	**1,439.8**	**2,013.7**	**2,550.3**	....	....	....	....	....	....	....	....	....
23	**Consumption of fixed capital...............**	....	....	....	....	....	....	....	....	....	....	....	....
24	**Interest..**	**2,581.0**	**4,954.0**	**6,300.8**	....	....	....	....	....	....	....	....	....
25	**Subsidies..**	**.3**	**.5**	**.2**	....	....	....	....	....	....	....	....	....

		Central Government			State Government			Local Government			General Government		
		2001	2002	2003p	2001	2002	2003	2001	2002	2003	2001	2002	2003
26	**Grants**................................	**10,793.5**	**11,044.7**	**15,507.6**	....	....	....	....	....	....	....	....	....
261	To foreign govenments.........................	5.7	4.6	8.3	....	....	....	....	....	....	....	....	....
262	To international organizations..................	—	—	—	....	....	....	....	....	....	....	....	....
263	To other general government units...........	10,787.8	11,040.1	15,499.3	....	....	....	....	....	....	....	....	....
2631	Current...	7,707.8	7,694.9	10,969.2	....	....	....	....	....	....	....	....	....
2632	Capital..	3,080.0	3,345.2	4,530.1	....	....	....	....	....	....	....	....	....
27	**Social benefits**...........................	**1,857.9**	**1,656.6**	**2,361.7**	....	....	....	....	....	....	....	....	....
28	**Other expense**............................	**277.8**	**484.7**	**526.5**	....	....	....	....	....	....	....	....	....
281	Property expense other than interest............	—	—	—	....	....	....	....	....	....	....	....	....
282	Miscellaneous other expense..................	277.8	484.7	526.5	....	....	....	....	....	....	....	....	....
2821	Current...	—	—	—	....	....	....	....	....	....	....	....	....
2822	Capital..	277.8	484.7	526.5	....	....	....	....	....	....	....	....	....

Table 3   Transactions in assets and liabilities

		Central Government			State Government			Local Government			General Government		
3	**Change in net worth from transactns....**	....	....	....	....	....	....	....	....	....	....	....	....
31	**Net acquisition of nonfinancial assets...**	**1,463.3**	**2,967.4**	**4,020.7**	....	....	....	....	....	....	....	....	....
311	Fixed assets.......................................	1,462.9	2,965.6	4,019.7	....	....	....	....	....	....	....	....	....
3111	Buildings and structures.......................	....	....	....	....	....	....	....	....	....	....	....	....
3112	Machinery and equipment.....................	....	....	....	....	....	....	....	....	....	....	....	....
3113	Other fixed assets..............................	....	....	....	....	....	....	....	....	....	....	....	....
312	Inventories..	.4	1.8	1.1	....	....	....	....	....	....	....	....	....
313	Valuables..	—	—	—	....	....	....	....	....	....	....	....	....
314	Nonproduced assets.............................	—	—	—	....	....	....	....	....	....	....	....	....
3141	Land...	—	—	—	....	....	....	....	....	....	....	....	....
3142	Subsoil assets....................................	—	—	—	....	....	....	....	....	....	....	....	....
3143	Other naturally occurring assets................	—	—	—	....	....	....	....	....	....	....	....	....
3144	Intangible nonproduced assets..................	—	—	—	....	....	....	....	....	....	....	....	....
32	**Net acquisition of financial assets.........**	**−15.9**	**−761.7**	**3,084.4**	....	....	....	....	....	....	....	....	....
321	Domestic...	69.6	829.4	4,222.2	....	....	....	....	....	....	....	....	....
3212	Currency and deposits..........................	−266.5	80.7	3,990.3	....	....	....	....	....	....	....	....	....
3213	Securities other than shares...................	....			....	....	....	....	....	....	....	....	....
3214	Loans...	....	748.6	231.9	....	....	....	....	....	....	....	....	....
3215	Shares and other equity........................	....			....	....	....	....	....	....	....	....	....
3216	Insurance technical reserves...................	—	—	—	....	....	....	....	....	....	....	....	....
3217	Financial derivatives............................	—	—	—	....	....	....	....	....	....	....	....	....
3218	Other accounts receivable......................	....	....	....	....	....	....	....	....	....	....	....	....
322	Foreign...	−85.5	−1,591.1	−1,137.8	....	....	....	....	....	....	....	....	....
3222	Currency and deposits..........................	−133.2	−1,636.0	−1,221.3	....	....	....	....	....	....	....	....	....
3223	Securities other than shares...................	....	44.9	—	....	....	....	....	....	....	....	....	....
3224	Loans...	....	—	83.4	....	....	....	....	....	....	....	....	....
3225	Shares and other equity........................	....	—	—	....	....	....	....	....	....	....	....	....
3226	Insurance technical reserves...................	—	—	—	....	....	....	....	....	....	....	....	....
3227	Financial derivatives............................	—	—	—	....	....	....	....	....	....	....	....	....
3228	Other accounts receivable......................	....	....	....	....	....	....	....	....	....	....	....	....
323	Monetary gold and SDRs.........................	—	—	—	....	....	....	....	....	....	....	....	....
33	**Net incurrence of liabilities...................**	**3,541.3**	**2,722.9**	**8,617.5**	....	....	....	....	....	....	....	....	....
331	Domestic...	3,373.8	3,412.3	8,395.7	....	....	....	....	....	....	....	....	....
3312	Currency and deposits..........................	—	—	22.9	....	....	....	....	....	....	....	....	....
3313	Securities other than shares...................	3,374.5	3,337.6	8,412.3	....	....	....	....	....	....	....	....	....
3314	Loans...	−.6	74.7	−39.6	....	....	....	....	....	....	....	....	....
3316	Insurance technical reserves...................	—	—	—	....	....	....	....	....	....	....	....	....
3317	Financial derivatives............................	—	—	—	....	....	....	....	....	....	....	....	....
3318	Other accounts payable.........................	....	....	....	....	....	....	....	....	....	....	....	....
332	Foreign...	167.5	−689.4	221.8	....	....	....	....	....	....	....	....	....
3322	Currency and deposits..........................	—	—	—	....	....	....	....	....	....	....	....	....
3323	Securities other than shares...................	—	281.7	—	....	....	....	....	....	....	....	....	....
3324	Loans...	167.5	−971.1	221.8	....	....	....	....	....	....	....	....	....
3326	Insurance technical reserves...................	—	—	—	....	....	....	....	....	....	....	....	....
3327	Financial derivatives............................	—	—	—	....	....	....	....	....	....	....	....	....
3328	Other accounts payable.........................	....	....	....	....	....	....	....	....	....	....	....	....

In billions of Bolivares / Year Ending December 31 / Cash Reporter

	Central Government			State Government			Local Government			General Government		
	2001	2002	2003p	2001	2002	2003	2001	2002	2003	2001	2002	2003
Table 4 Holding gains in assets and liabilities												
Table 5 Other changes in the volume of assets and liabilities												
Table 6 Balance sheet												
Table 7 Outlays by functions of govt.												
7 Total outlays	22,883.8	28,117.4	37,786.0	....	....	....	....	....	....	....	....	....
701 **General public services**	8,826.8	12,732.7	18,008.4	....	....	....	....	....	....	....	....	....
7017 Public debt transactions	2,581.0	4,954.0	6,300.8	....	....	....	....	....	....	....	....	....
7018 General transfers between levels of govt.	....	....	....	....	....	....	....	....	....	....	....	....
702 **Defense**	1,373.3	1,396.4	1,665.8	....	....	....	....	....	....	....	....	....
703 **Public order and safety**	742.6	855.7	1,120.6	....	....	....	....	....	....	....	....	....
704 **Economic affairs**	1,940.8	1,549.1	1,892.3	....	....	....	....	....	....	....	....	....
7042 Agriculture, forestry, fishing, and hunting	88.8	194.8	308.1	....	....	....	....	....	....	....	....	....
7043 Fuel and energy	154.8	180.0	121.7	....	....	....	....	....	....	....	....	....
7044 Mining, manufacturing, and construction	706.8	216.7	953.7	....	....	....	....	....	....	....	....	....
7045 Transport	610.8	804.9	....	....	....	....	....	....	....	....	....	....
7046 Communication	....	....	....	....	....	....	....	....	....	....	....	....
705 **Environmental protection**	—	—	—	....	....	....	....	....	....	....	....	....
706 **Housing and community amenities**	1,328.0	1,555.3	1,307.8	....	....	....	....	....	....	....	....	....
707 **Health**	1,482.9	1,782.7	2,852.9	....	....	....	....	....	....	....	....	....
7072 Outpatient services	29.9	....	....	....	....	....	....	....	....	....	....	....
7073 Hospital services	966.3	....	....	....	....	....	....	....	....	....	....	....
7074 Public health services	....	....	....	....	....	....	....	....	....	....	....	....
708 **Recreation, culture, and religion**	183.6	185.5	583.4	....	....	....	....	....	....	....	....	....
709 **Education**	4,716.2	5,649.0	6,993.6	....	....	....	....	....	....	....	....	....
7091 Pre-primary and primary education	....	....	....	....	....	....	....	....	....	....	....	....
7092 Secondary education	....	....	....	....	....	....	....	....	....	....	....	....
7094 Tertiary education	....	....	....	....	....	....	....	....	....	....	....	....
710 **Social protection**	2,289.6	2,411.0	3,361.3	....	....	....	....	....	....	....	....	....
7 Statistical discrepancy: Total outlays	—	—	—	....	....	....	....	....	....	....	....	....
Table 8 Transactions in financial assets and liabilities by sector												
82 **Net acquisition of financial assets**	−15.9	−761.7	3,084.4	....	....	....	....	....	....	....	....	....
821 Domestic	69.6	829.4	4,222.2	....	....	....	....	....	....	....	....	....
8211 General government	....	—	....	....	....	....	....	....	....	....	....	....
8212 Central bank	....	85.5	3,937.0	....	....	....	....	....	....	....	....	....
8213 Other depository corporations	....	—	53.3	....	....	....	....	....	....	....	....	....
8214 Financial corporations n.e.c.	....	161.2	169.7	....	....	....	....	....	....	....	....	....
8215 Nonfinancial corporations	237.7	582.7	62.2	....	....	....	....	....	....	....	....	....
8216 Households & NPIs serving households	....	—	—	....	....	....	....	....	....	....	....	....
822 Foreign	−85.5	−1,591.1	−1,137.8	....	....	....	....	....	....	....	....	....
8221 General government	....	—	—	....	....	....	....	....	....	....	....	....
8227 International organizations	....	—	—	....	....	....	....	....	....	....	....	....
8228 Financial corporations other than international organizations	....	−1,636.0	−1,221.3	....	....	....	....	....	....	....	....	....
8229 Other nonresidents	....	44.9	83.4	....	....	....	....	....	....	....	....	....
823 Monetary gold and SDRs	—	—	—	....	....	....	....	....	....	....	....	....
83 **Net incurrence of liabilities**	3,541.3	2,722.9	8,617.5	....	....	....	....	....	....	....	....	....
831 Domestic	3,373.8	3,412.3	8,395.7	....	....	....	....	....	....	....	....	....
8311 General government	....	—	—	....	....	....	....	....	....	....	....	....
8312 Central bank	....	—	—	....	....	....	....	....	....	....	....	....
8313 Other depository corporations	....	3,337.6	8,435.2	....	....	....	....	....	....	....	....	....
8314 Financial corporations n.e.c.	....	74.7	−39.6	....	....	....	....	....	....	....	....	....
8315 Nonfinancial corporations	....	—	—	....	....	....	....	....	....	....	....	....
8316 Households & NPIs serving households	....	—	—	....	....	....	....	....	....	....	....	....
832 Foreign	167.5	−689.4	221.8	....	....	....	....	....	....	....	....	....
8321 General government	−12.1	668.7	822.9	....	....	....	....	....	....	....	....	....
8327 International organizations	−224.9	−331.4	192.1	....	....	....	....	....	....	....	....	....
8328 Financial corporations other than international organizations	—	—	—	....	....	....	....	....	....	....	....	....
8329 Other nonresidents	404.5	−1,026.7	−793.2	....	....	....	....	....	....	....	....	....

In Billions of Dong / Year Ending December 31 / Cash Reporter

	Budgetary Central Government			Central Government			Local Government			General Government		
	2002	2003	2004	2002	2003	2004	2002	2003	2004	2002	2003p	2004f
Statement of government operations												
Statement of other economic flows												
Balance sheet												
Statement of sources and uses of cash												
1 Cash receipts from operating activities...........	....	....	....	....	....	....	....	....	....	120,596	147,791	179,292
11 Taxes................................	....	....	....	....	....	....	....	....	....	106,322	127,080	153,472
12 Social contributions...................	....	....	....	....	....	....	....	....	....	—	—	—
13 Grants............................	....	....	....	....	....	....	....	....	....	2,250	2,969	2,314
14 Other receipts......................	....	....	....	....	....	....	....	....	....	12,024	17,742	23,506
2 Cash payments for operating activities...........	....	....	....	....	....	....	....	....	....	....	....	....
21 Compensation of employees................	....	....	....	....	....	....	....	....	....	....	....	....
22 Purchases of goods and services...............	....	....	....	....	....	....	....	....	....	....	....	....
24 Interest............................	....	....	....	....	....	....	....	....	....	5,330	6,395	6,450
25 Subsidies...........................	....	....	....	....	....	....	....	....	....			
26 Grants.............................	....	....	....	....	....	....	....	....	....			
27 Social benefits.......................	....	....	....	....	....	....	....	....	....			
28 Other payments......................	....	....	....	....	....	....	....	....	....			
CIO *Net cash inflow from oper. activities.....*	....	....	....	....	....	....	....	....	....	....	....	....
31.1 Purchases of nonfinancial assets.............	....	....	....	....	....	....	....	....	....	....	....	....
31.2 Sales of nonfinancial assets.................	....	....	....						....	1,120	9,265	1,105
31 Net cash outflow from investments in nonfinancial assets.................	....	....	....	....	....				....	....	....	....
CSD *Cash surplus/deficit........................*	....	....	....	....	....				....	−13,774	−21,485	−28,415
32x Net acquisition of fin assets, excl. cash........	....	....	....	....	....	....	....	....	....	—	—	—
321x Domestic..........................	....	....	....	....	....	....	....	....	....	—	—	—
322x Foreign...........................	....	....	....	....	....	....	....	....	....	—	—	—
323 Monetary gold and SDRs................	....	....	....	....	....	....	....	....	....	—	—	—
33 Net incurrence of liabilities.................	....	....	....	....	....	....	....	....	....	10,018	11,904	12,025
331 Domestic..........................	....	....	....	....	....	....	....	....	....	4,711	7,327	9,250
332 Foreign...........................	....	....	....	....	....	....	....	....	....	5,307	4,577	2,775
NFB Net cash inflow from fin. activities.................	....	....	....	....	....	....	....	....	....	10,018	11,904	12,025
NCB *Net change in the stock of cash.............*	....	....	....	....	....	....	....	....	....	−3,756	−9,581	−16,390
Table 1 Revenue												
1 **Revenue...........................**	....	....	....	....	....	....	....	....	....	**120,596**	**147,791**	**179,292**
11 **Taxes................................**	....	....	....	....	....	....	....	....	....	**106,322**	**127,080**	**153,472**
111 Taxes on income, profits, & capital gains......	....	....	....	....	....	....	....	....	....	39,164	50,361	58,811
1111 Individuals.........................	....	....	....	....	....	....	....	....	....	2,338	2,951	3,521
1112 Corporations and other enterprises...........	....	....	....	....	....	....	....	....	....	36,826	47,410	55,290
112 Taxes on payroll and workforce............	....	....	....	....	....	....	....	....	....	—	—	—
113 Taxes on property......................	....	....	....	....	....	....	....	....	....	1,995	2,584	3,688
114 Taxes on goods and services..............	....	....	....	....	....	....	....	....	....	42,910	52,628	69,391
1141 General taxes on goods and services..........	....	....	....	....	....	....	....	....	....	25,916	33,130	41,394
1142 Excises............................	....	....	....	....	....	....	....	....	....	7,272	8,850	14,212
115 Taxes on int'l. trade and transactions...........	....	....	....	....	....	....	....	....	....	22,083	21,507	21,582
116 Other taxes.........................	....	....	....	....	....	....	....	....	....	170	—	—
12 **Social contributions.............................**	....	....	....	....	....	....	....	....	....	—	—	—
121 Social security contributions.........................	....	....	....	....	....	....	....	....	....	—	—	—
122 Other social contributions........................	....	....	....	....	....	....	....	....	....	—	—	—
13 **Grants..............................**	....	....	....	....	....	....	....	....	....	**2,250**	**2,969**	**2,314**
131 From foreign governments................	....	....	....	....	....	....	....	....	....	....	....	....
132 From international organizations.............	....	....	....	....	....	....	....	....	....	....	....	....
133 From other general government units........	....	....	....	....	....	....	....	....	....	....	....	....
14 **Other revenue.........................**	....	....	....	....	....	....	....	....	....	**12,024**	**17,742**	**23,506**
Table 2 Expense by economic type												
2 **Expense............................**	....	....	....	....	....	....	....	....	....	....	....	....
21 **Compensation of employees.................**	....	....	....	....	....	....	....	....	....	....	....	....
211 Wages and salaries.....................	....	....	....	....	....	....	....	....	....	....	....	....
212 Social contributions....................	....	....	....	....	....	....	....	....	....	....	....	....
22 **Use of goods and services...................**	....	....	....	....	....	....	....	....	....	....	....	....
23 **Consumption of fixed capital................**	....	....	....	....	....	....	....	....	....	....	....	....
24 **Interest............................**	....	....	....	....	....	....	....	....	....	**5,330**	**6,395**	**6,450**
25 **Subsidies...........................**	....	....	....	....	....	....	....	....	....	....	....	....

In Billions of Dong / Year Ending December 31 / Cash Reporter

		Budgetary Central Government			Central Government			Local Government			General Government		
		2002	2003	2004	2002	2003	2004	2002	2003	2004	2002	2003p	2004f
26	**Grants**..................................	....	....	....	....	....	....	....	....	....	....	....	....
261	To foreign govenments..........................	....	....	....	....	....	....	....	....	....	....	....	....
262	To international organizations..................	....	....	....	....	....	....	....	....	....	....	....	....
263	To other general government units.............	....	....	....	....	....	....	....	....	....	....	....	....
2631	Current...	....	....	....	....	....	....	....	....	....	....	....	....
2632	Capital...	....	....	....	....	....	....	....	....	....	....	....	....
27	**Social benefits**...........................	....	....	....	....	....	....	....	....	....	....	....	....
28	**Other expense**............................	....	....	....	....	....	....	....	....	....	....	....	....
281	Property expense other than interest...........	....	....	....	....	....	....	....	....	....	....	....	....
282	Miscellaneous other expense..................	....	....	....	....	....	....	....	....	....	....	....	....
2821	Current...	....	....	....	....	....	....	....	....	....	....	....	....
2822	Capital...	....	....	....	....	....	....	....	....	....	....	....	....

Table 3   Transactions in assets and liabilities

		Budgetary Central Government			Central Government			Local Government			General Government		
		2002	2003	2004	2002	2003	2004	2002	2003	2004	2002	2003p	2004f
3	**Change in net worth from transactns....**	....	....	....	....	....	....	....	....	....	....	....	....
31	**Net acquisition of nonfinancial assets...**	....	....	....	....	....	....	....	....	....	....	....	....
311	Fixed assets....................................	....	....	....	....	....	....	....	....	....	....	....	....
3111	Buildings and structures....................	....	....	....	....	....	....	....	....	....	....	....	....
3112	Machinery and equipment....................	....	....	....	....	....	....	....	....	....	....	....	....
3113	Other fixed assets..........................	....	....	....	....	....	....	....	....	....	....	....	....
312	Inventories.....................................	....	....	....	....	....	....	....	....	....	....	....	....
313	Valuables.......................................	....	....	....	....	....	....	....	....	....	....	....	....
314	Nonproduced assets............................	....	....	....	....	....	....	....	....	....	....	....	....
3141	Land...	....	....	....	....	....	....	....	....	....	....	....	....
3142	Subsoil assets................................	....	....	....	....	....	....	....	....	....	....	....	....
3143	Other naturally occurring assets.............	....	....	....	....	....	....	....	....	....	....	....	....
3144	Intangible nonproduced assets...............	....	....	....	....	....	....	....	....	....	....	....	....
32	**Net acquisition of financial assets.........**	....	....	....	....	....	....	....	....	....	−3,756	−9,581	−16,390
321	Domestic.......................................	....	....	....	....	....	....	....	....	....	−3,756	−9,581	−16,390
3212	Currency and deposits......................	....	....	....	....	....	....	....	....	....	−3,756	−9,581	−16,390
3213	Securities other than shares...............	....	....	....	....	....	....	....	....	....	—	—	—
3214	Loans..	....	....	....	....	....	....	....	....	....	—	—	—
3215	Shares and other equity.....................	....	....	....	....	....	....	....	....	....	—	—	—
3216	Insurance technical reserves................	....	....	....	....	....	....	....	....	....	—	—	—
3217	Financial derivatives........................	....	....	....	....	....	....	....	....	....	—	—	—
3218	Other accounts receivable...................	....	....	....	....	....	....	....	....	....	....	....	....
322	Foreign..	....	....	....	....	....	....	....	....	....	—	—	—
3222	Currency and deposits......................	....	....	....	....	....	....	....	....	....	—	—	—
3223	Securities other than shares...............	....	....	....	....	....	....	....	....	....	—	—	—
3224	Loans..	....	....	....	....	....	....	....	....	....	—	—	—
3225	Shares and other equity.....................	....	....	....	....	....	....	....	....	....	—	—	—
3226	Insurance technical reserves................	....	....	....	....	....	....	....	....	....	—	—	—
3227	Financial derivatives........................	....	....	....	....	....	....	....	....	....	—	—	—
3228	Other accounts receivable..................	....	....	....	....	....	....	....	....	....	....	....	....
323	Monetary gold and SDRs......................	....	....	....	....	....	....	....	....	....	—	—	—
33	**Net incurrence of liabilities...................**	....	....	....	....	....	....	....	....	....	10,018	11,904	12,025
331	Domestic.......................................	....	....	....	....	....	....	....	....	....	4,711	7,327	9,250
3312	Currency and deposits......................	....	....	....	....	....	....	....	....	....	—	—	—
3313	Securities other than shares...............	....	....	....	....	....	....	....	....	....	4,711	7,327	9,250
3314	Loans..	....	....	....	....	....	....	....	....	....	—	—	—
3316	Insurance technical reserves................	....	....	....	....	....	....	....	....	....	—	—	—
3317	Financial derivatives........................	....	....	....	....	....	....	....	....	....	—	—	—
3318	Other accounts payable.....................	....	....	....	....	....	....	....	....	....	....	....	....
332	Foreign..	....	....	....	....	....	....	....	....	....	5,307	4,577	2,775
3322	Currency and deposits......................	....	....	....	....	....	....	....	....	....	—	—	—
3323	Securities other than shares...............	....	....	....	....	....	....	....	....	....	—	—	—
3324	Loans..	....	....	....	....	....	....	....	....	....	5,307	4,577	2,775
3326	Insurance technical reserves................	....	....	....	....	....	....	....	....	....	—	—	—
3327	Financial derivatives........................	....	....	....	....	....	....	....	....	....	—	—	—
3328	Other accounts payable.....................	....	....	....	....	....	....	....	....	....	....	....	....

	Budgetary Central Government			Central Government			Local Government			General Government		
	2002	2003	2004	2002	2003	2004	2002	2003	2004	2002	2003p	2004f
Table 4 Holding gains in assets and liabilities												
Table 5 Other changes in the volume of assets and liabilities												
Table 6 Balance sheet												
Table 7 Outlays by functions of govt.												
7 Total outlays...................	....	....	....	....	....	....	....	....	....	135,490	178,541	208,812
701 **General public services................**	....	....	....	....	....	....	....	....	....	....	....	....
7017 Public debt transactions................	....	....	....	....	....	....	....	....	....	5,330	6,395	6,450
7018 General transfers between levels of govt......	....	....	....	....	....	....	....	....	....	....	....	....
702 **Defense................**	....	....	....	....	....	....	....	....	....	....	....	....
703 **Public order and safety................**	....	....	....	....	....	....	....	....	....	....	....	....
704 **Economic affairs................**	....	....	....	....	....	....	....	....	....	....	....	....
7042 Agriculture, forestry, fishing, and hunting......	....	....	....	....	....	....	....	....	....	....	....	....
7043 Fuel and energy................	....	....	....	....	....	....	....	....	....	....	....	....
7044 Mining, manufacturing, and construction......	....	....	....	....	....	....	....	....	....	....	....	....
7045 Transport................	....	....	....	....	....	....	....	....	....	....	....	....
7046 Communication................	....	....	....	....	....	....	....	....	....	....	....	....
705 **Environmental protection................**	....	....	....	....	....	....	....	....	....	....	....	....
706 **Housing and community amenities........**	....	....	....	....	....	....	....	....	....	....	....	....
707 **Health................**	....	....	....	....	....	....	....	....	....	....	....	....
7072 Outpatient services................	....	....	....	....	....	....	....	....	....	....	....	....
7073 Hospital services................	....	....	....	....	....	....	....	....	....	....	....	....
7074 Public health services................	....	....	....	....	....	....	....	....	....	....	....	....
708 **Recreation, culture, and religion............**	....	....	....	....	....	....	....	....	....	....	....	....
709 **Education................**	....	....	....	....	....	....	....	....	....	....	....	....
7091 Pre-primary and primary education................	....	....	....	....	....	....	....	....	....	....	....	....
7092 Secondary education................	....	....	....	....	....	....	....	....	....	....	....	....
7094 Tertiary education................	....	....	....	....	....	....	....	....	....	....	....	....
710 **Social protection................**	....	....	....	....	....	....	....	....	....	13,221	16,451	19,034
7 Statistical discrepancy: Total outlays...............	....	....	....	....	....	....	....	....	....	....	....	....
Table 8 Transactions in financial assets and liabilities by sector												
82 **Net acquisition of financial assets.........**	....	....	....	....	....	....	....	....	....	−3,756	−9,581	−16,390
821 Domestic................	....	....	....	....	....	....	....	....	....	−3,756	−9,581	−16,390
8211 General government................	....	....	....	....	....	....	....	....	....	—	—	—
8212 Central bank................	....	....	....	....	....	....	....	....	....	−3,756	−9,581	−16,390
8213 Other depository corporations................	....	....	....	....	....	....	....	....	....	—	—	—
8214 Financial corporations n.e.c................	....	....	....	....	....	....	....	....	....	—	—	—
8215 Nonfinancial corporations................	....	....	....	....	....	....	....	....	....	—	—	—
8216 Households & NPIs serving households......	....	....	....	....	....	....	....	....	....	—	—	—
822 Foreign................	....	....	....	....	....	....	....	....	....	—	—	—
8221 General government................	....	....	....	....	....	....	....	....	....	—	—	—
8227 International organizations................	....	....	....	....	....	....	....	....	....	—	—	—
8228 Financial corporations other than international organizations.............	....	....	....	....	....	....	....	....	....	—	—	—
8229 Other nonresidents................	....	....	....	....	....	....	....	....	....	—	—	—
823 Monetary gold and SDRs................	....	....	....	....	....	....	....	....	....	—	—	—
83 **Net incurrence of liabilities...................**	....	....	....	....	....	....	....	....	....	10,018	11,904	12,025
831 Domestic................	....	....	....	....	....	....	....	....	....	4,711	7,327	9,250
8311 General government................	....	....	....	....	....	....	....	....	....	....	....	....
8312 Central bank................	....	....	....	....	....	....	....	....	....	....	....	....
8313 Other depository corporations................	....	....	....	....	....	....	....	....	....	....	....	....
8314 Financial corporations n.e.c................	....	....	....	....	....	....	....	....	....	....	....	....
8315 Nonfinancial corporations................	....	....	....	....	....	....	....	....	....	....	....	....
8316 Households & NPIs serving households......	....	....	....	....	....	....	....	....	....	....	....	....
832 Foreign................	....	....	....	....	....	....	....	....	....	5,307	4,577	2,775
8321 General government................	....	....	....	....	....	....	....	....	....	....	....	....
8327 International organizations................	....	....	....	....	....	....	....	....	....	....	....	....
8328 Financial corporations other than international organizations.............	....	....	....	....	....	....	....	....	....	....	....	....
8329 Other nonresidents................	....	....	....	....	....	....	....	....	....	....	....	....

Yemen, Republic of 474

In Millions of Rials / Year Ending December 31 / Cash Reporter

	Budgetary Central Government			Extrabudgetary Accounts			Central Government			General Government		
	1997	1998	1999f	1997	1998	1999	1997	1998	1999	1997	1998	1999
Statement of government operations												
Statement of other economic flows												
Balance sheet												
Statement of sources and uses of cash												
1 Cash receipts from operating activities............	288,738	304,903	282,268	....	....	....	....	....	....	....	....	....
11 Taxes...	96,699	111,693	109,548	....	....	....	....	....	....	....	....	....
12 Social contributions................................	—	—	—	....	....	....	....	....	....	....	....	....
13 Grants..	1,938	5,480	4,219	....	....	....	....	....	....	....	....	....
14 Other receipts..	190,101	187,730	168,501	....	....	....	....	....	....	....	....	....
2 Cash payments for operating activities...........	239,858	254,406	257,575	....	....	....	....	....	....	....	....	....
21 Compensation of employees.......................	84,375	102,663	125,828	....	....	....	....	....	....	....	....	....
22 Purchases of goods and services.................	34,106	38,780	43,266	....	....	....	....	....	....	....	....	....
24 Interest...	20,707	29,000	27,339	....	....	....	....	....	....	....	....	....
25 Subsidies..	74,801	53,626	23,088	....	....	....	....	....	....	....	....	....
26 Grants..	3,451	4,790	5,100	....	....	....	....	....	....	....	....	....
27 Social benefits.......................................	20,675	21,011	27,003	....	....	....	....	....	....	....	....	....
28 Other payments......................................	—	—	—	....	....	....	....	....	....	....	....	....
CIO *Net cash inflow from oper. activities.....*	*48,880*	*50,497*	*24,693*	....	....	....	....	....	....	....	....	....
31.1 Purchases of nonfinancial assets...................	46,052	55,536	53,127	....	....	....	....	....	....	....	....	....
31.2 Sales of nonfinancial assets........................	547	1,368	1,369	....	....	....	....	....	....	....	....	....
31 Net cash outflow from investments in nonfinancial assets.............................	45,505	54,168	51,758	....	....	....	....	....	....	....	....	....
CSD *Cash surplus/deficit...........................*	*3,375*	*–3,671*	*–27,065*	....	....	....	....	....	....	....	....	....
32x Net acquisition of fin assets, excl. cash........	12,460	15,445	13,213	....	....	....	....	....	....	....	....	....
321x Domestic...	12,000	14,888	12,782	....	....	....	....	....	....	....	....	....
322x Foreign...	460	557	431	....	....	....	....	....	....	....	....	....
323 Monetary gold and SDRs...........................	—	—	—	....	....	....	....	....	....	....	....	....
33 Net incurrence of liabilities......................	....	....	....	....	....	....	....	....	....	....	....	....
331 Domestic...	....	....	....	....	....	....	....	....	....	....	....	....
332 Foreign...	....	....	....	....	....	....	....	....	....	....	....	....
NFB Net cash inflow from fin. activities...............	....	....	....	....	....	....	....	....	....	....	....	....
NCB *Net change in the stock of cash............*	....	....	....	....	....	....	....	....	....	....	....	....
Table 1 Revenue												
1 **Revenue**...	**288,738**	**304,903**	**282,268**	....	....	....	....	....	....	....	....	....
11 **Taxes**..	**96,699**	**111,693**	**109,548**	....	....	....	....	....	....	....	....	....
111 Taxes on income, profits, & capital gains......	45,595	54,441	50,246	....	....	....	....	....	....	....	....	....
1111 Individuals...	11,018	11,069	15,940	....	....	....	....	....	....	....	....	....
1112 Corporations and other enterprises.............	34,576	43,372	34,305	....	....	....	....	....	....	....	....	....
112 Taxes on payroll and workforce..................	—	—	—	....	....	....	....	....	....	....	....	....
113 Taxes on property....................................	1,690	513	513	....	....	....	....	....	....	....	....	....
114 Taxes on goods and services......................	19,740	21,416	25,768	....	....	....	....	....	....	....	....	....
1141 General taxes on goods and services...........	—	—	—	....	....	....	....	....	....	....	....	....
1142 Excises...	19,005	20,595	24,861	....	....	....	....	....	....	....	....	....
115 Taxes on int'l. trade and transactions...........	25,785	31,015	28,701	....	....	....	....	....	....	....	....	....
116 Other taxes...	3,889	4,308	4,320	....	....	....	....	....	....	....	....	....
12 **Social contributions**...............................	**—**	**—**	**—**	....	....	....	....	....	....	....	....	....
121 Social security contributions........................	—	—	—	....	....	....	....	....	....	....	....	....
122 Other social contributions..........................	—	—	—	....	....	....	....	....	....	....	....	....
13 **Grants**..	**1,938**	**5,480**	**4,219**	....	....	....	....	....	....	....	....	....
131 From foreign governments.........................	1,938	5,480	4,219	....	....	....	....	....	....	....	....	....
132 From international organizations..................	—	—	—	....	....	....	....	....	....	....	....	....
133 From other general government units...........	—	—	—	....	....	....	....	....	....	....	....	....
14 **Other revenue**..	**190,101**	**187,730**	**168,501**	....	....	....	....	....	....	....	....	....
Table 2 Expense by economic type												
2 **Expense**...	**239,858**	**254,406**	**257,575**	....	....	....	....	....	....	....	....	....
21 **Compensation of employees**..................	**84,375**	**102,663**	**125,828**	....	....	....	....	....	....	....	....	....
211 Wages and salaries..................................	82,150	100,198	122,103	....	....	....	....	....	....	....	....	....
212 Social contributions..................................	2,225	2,465	3,725	....	....	....	....	....	....	....	....	....
22 **Use of goods and services**.....................	**34,106**	**38,780**	**43,266**	....	....	....	....	....	....	....	....	....
23 **Consumption of fixed capital**.................	....	....	....	....	....	....	....	....	....	....	....	....
24 **Interest**..	**20,707**	**29,000**	**27,339**	....	....	....	....	....	....	....	....	....
25 **Subsidies**..	**74,801**	**53,626**	**23,088**	....	....	....	....	....	....	....	....	....

		Budgetary Central Government			Extrabudgetary Accounts			Central Government			General Government		
		1997	1998	1999f	1997	1998	1999	1997	1998	1999	1997	1998	1999
26	**Grants**..................................	**3,451**	**4,790**	**5,100**	....	....	....	....	....	....	....	....	....
261	To foreign govenments..................	3,451	4,790	5,100	....	....	....	....	....	....	....	....	....
262	To international organizations.................	—	—	—	....	....	....	....	....	....	....	....	....
263	To other general government units...........	—	—	—	....	....	....	....	....	....	....	....	....
2631	Current..	—	—	—	....	....	....	....	....	....	....	....	....
2632	Capital...	—	—	—	....	....	....	....	....	....	....	....	....
27	**Social benefits**...........................	**20,675**	**21,011**	**27,003**	....	....	....	....	....	....	....	....	....
28	**Other expense**.............................	—	—	—	....	....	....	....	....	....	....	....	....
281	Property expense other than interest............	—	—	—	....	....	....	....	....	....	....	....	....
282	Miscellaneous other expense..................	—	—	—	....	....	....	....	....	....	....	....	....
2821	Current.......................................	—	—	—	....	....	....	....	....	....	....	....	....
2822	Capital..	—	—	—	....	....	....	....	....	....	....	....	....

Table 3   Transactions in assets and liabilities

3	**Change in net worth from transactns....**	....	....	....	....	....	....	....	....	....	....	....	....
31	**Net acquisition of nonfinancial assets...**	**45,505**	**54,168**	**51,758**	....	....	....	....	....	....	....	....	....
311	Fixed assets..................................	45,687	53,325	51,131	....	....	....	....	....	....	....	....	....
3111	Buildings and structures....................	....	....	....	....	....	....	....	....	....	....	....	....
3112	Machinery and equipment.....................	....	....	....	....	....	....	....	....	....	....	....	....
3113	Other fixed assets...........................	....	....	....	....	....	....	....	....	....	....	....	....
312	Inventories..................................	−17	−11	−11	....	....	....	....	....	....	....	....	....
313	Valuables....................................	—	—	—	....	....	....	....	....	....	....	....	....
314	Nonproduced assets...........................	−165	854	638	....	....	....	....	....	....	....	....	....
3141	Land...	....	....	....	....	....	....	....	....	....	....	....	....
3142	Subsoil assets...............................	....	....	....	....	....	....	....	....	....	....	....	....
3143	Other naturally occurring assets.............	....	....	....	....	....	....	....	....	....	....	....	....
3144	Intangible nonproduced assets................	....	....	....	....	....	....	....	....	....	....	....	....
32	**Net acquisition of financial assets.........**	....	....	....	....	....	....	....	....	....	....	....	....
321	Domestic.....................................	....	....	....	....	....	....	....	....	....	....	....	....
3212	Currency and deposits........................	....	....	....	....	....	....	....	....	....	....	....	....
3213	Securities other than shares.................	....	....	....	....	....	....	....	....	....	....	....	....
3214	Loans..	....	....	....	....	....	....	....	....	....	....	....	....
3215	Shares and other equity......................	....	....	....	....	....	....	....	....	....	....	....	....
3216	Insurance technical reserves.................	....	....	....	....	....	....	....	....	....	....	....	....
3217	Financial derivatives........................	....	....	....	....	....	....	....	....	....	....	....	....
3218	Other accounts receivable....................	....	....	....	....	....	....	....	....	....	....	....	....
322	Foreign......................................	....	....	....	....	....	....	....	....	....	....	....	....
3222	Currency and deposits........................	....	....	....	....	....	....	....	....	....	....	....	....
3223	Securities other than shares.................	....	....	....	....	....	....	....	....	....	....	....	....
3224	Loans..	....	....	....	....	....	....	....	....	....	....	....	....
3225	Shares and other equity......................	....	....	....	....	....	....	....	....	....	....	....	....
3226	Insurance technical reserves.................	....	....	....	....	....	....	....	....	....	....	....	....
3227	Financial derivatives........................	....	....	....	....	....	....	....	....	....	....	....	....
3228	Other accounts receivable....................	....	....	....	....	....	....	....	....	....	....	....	....
323	Monetary gold and SDRs.......................	....	....	....	....	....	....	....	....	....	....	....	....
33	**Net incurrence of liabilities...................**	....	....	....	....	....	....	....	....	....	....	....	....
331	Domestic.....................................	....	....	....	....	....	....	....	....	....	....	....	....
3312	Currency and deposits........................	....	....	....	....	....	....	....	....	....	....	....	....
3313	Securities other than shares.................	....	....	....	....	....	....	....	....	....	....	....	....
3314	Loans..	....	....	....	....	....	....	....	....	....	....	....	....
3316	Insurance technical reserves.................	....	....	....	....	....	....	....	....	....	....	....	....
3317	Financial derivatives........................	....	....	....	....	....	....	....	....	....	....	....	....
3318	Other accounts payable.......................	....	....	....	....	....	....	....	....	....	....	....	....
332	Foreign......................................	....	....	....	....	....	....	....	....	....	....	....	....
3322	Currency and deposits........................	....	....	....	....	....	....	....	....	....	....	....	....
3323	Securities other than shares.................	....	....	....	....	....	....	....	....	....	....	....	....
3324	Loans..	....	....	....	....	....	....	....	....	....	....	....	....
3326	Insurance technical reserves.................	....	....	....	....	....	....	....	....	....	....	....	....
3327	Financial derivatives........................	....	....	....	....	....	....	....	....	....	....	....	....
3328	Other accounts payable.......................	....	....	....	....	....	....	....	....	....	....	....	....

	Budgetary Central Government			Extrabudgetary Accounts			Central Government			General Government		
	1997	1998	1999f	1997	1998	1999	1997	1998	1999	1997	1998	1999
Table 4 Holding gains in assets and liabilities												
Table 5 Other changes in the volume of assets and liabilities												
Table 6 Balance sheet												
Table 7 Outlays by functions of govt.												
7 **Total outlays**............................	285,910	309,942	310,702	....	....	....	....	....	....	....	....	....
701 **General public services**.........................	66,120	79,742	95,665	....	....	....	....	....	....	....	....	....
7017 Public debt transactions...............................	20,707	29,000	27,339	....	....	....	....	....	....	....	....	....
7018 General transfers between levels of govt......	....	....	....	....	....	....	....	....	....	....	....	....
702 **Defense**..	55,104	53,824	58,311	....	....	....	....	....	....	....	....	....
703 **Public order and safety**.........................	18,578	22,418	25,830	....	....	....	....	....	....	....	....	....
704 **Economic affairs**................................	86,093	63,496	35,642	....	....	....	....	....	....	....	....	....
7042 Agriculture, forestry, fishing, and hunting.....	76,984	54,337	24,288	....	....	....	....	....	....	....	....	....
7043 Fuel and energy..	563	749	917	....	....	....	....	....	....	....	....	....
7044 Mining, manufacturing, and construction......	354	204	205	....	....	....	....	....	....	....	....	....
7045 Transport...	7,628	7,654	9,632	....	....	....	....	....	....	....	....	....
7046 Communication..	....	....	....	....	....	....	....	....	....	....	....	....
705 **Environmental protection**......................	....	....	....	....	....	....	....	....	....	....	....	....
706 **Housing and community amenities**........	4,090	4,359	5,076	....	....	....	....	....	....	....	....	....
707 **Health**..	9,485	12,067	13,672	....	....	....	....	....	....	....	....	....
7072 Outpatient services....................................	....	....	....	....	....	....	....	....	....	....	....	....
7073 Hospital services..	....	....	....	....	....	....	....	....	....	....	....	....
7074 Public health services.................................	....	....	....	....	....	....	....	....	....	....	....	....
708 **Recreation, culture, and religion**...........	5,142	7,005	8,757	....	....	....	....	....	....	....	....	....
709 **Education**...	45,535	56,462	67,749	....	....	....	....	....	....	....	....	....
7091 Pre-primary and primary education..............	....	....	....	....	....	....	....	....	....	....	....	....
7092 Secondary education...................................	34,570	47,039	57,428	....	....	....	....	....	....	....	....	....
7094 Tertiary education......................................	6,143	9,423	6,221	....	....	....	....	....	....	....	....	....
710 **Social protection**.................................	—	—	—	....	....	....	....	....	....	....	....	....
7 Statistical discrepancy: Total outlays.............	–4,237	10,569	—	....	....	....	....	....	....	....	....	....
Table 8 Transactions in financial assets and liabilities by sector												

	Budgetary Central Government			Central Government			Local Government			General Government		
	1997	1998p	1999f	1997	1998	1999	1997	1998	1999	1997	1998	1999
Statement of government operations												
Statement of other economic flows												
Balance sheet												
6 *Net worth*................	....	....	....	....	....	....	....	....	....	....	....	....
61 Nonfinancial assets...........	....	....	....	....	....	....	....	....	....	....	....	....
62 Financial assets.............	....	....	....	....	....	....	....	....	....	....	....	....
63 Liabilities.................	8,489.1	10,621.2	....	....	....	....	....	....	....	....	....	....
Statement of sources and uses of cash												
1 Cash receipts from operating activities..........	950.0	1,530.1	1,844.4	....	....	....	....	....	....	....	....	....
11 Taxes...................	907.9	1,066.4	1,378.3	....	....	....	....	....	....	....	....	....
12 Social contributions...........	—	—	—	....	....	....	....	....	....	....	....	....
13 Grants..................	4.7	432.7	414.2	....	....	....	....	....	....	....	....	....
14 Other receipts.............	37.4	31.0	51.9	....	....	....	....	....	....	....	....	....
2 Cash payments for operating activities...........	....	1,291.8	1,303.5	....	....	....	....	....	....	....	....	....
21 Compensation of employees.........	....	448.7	405.8	....	....	....	....	....	....	....	....	....
22 Purchases of goods and services........	....	414.8	369.2	....	....	....	....	....	....	....	....	....
24 Interest.................	....	206.0	259.3	....	....	....	....	....	....	....	....	....
25 Subsidies...............	....	—	—	....	....	....	....	....	....	....	....	....
26 Grants..................	....	243.9	261.5	....	....	....	....	....	....	....	....	....
27 Social benefits.............	....	—	—	....	....	....	....	....	....	....	....	....
28 Other payments..............	....	2.6	7.7	....	....	....	....	....	....	....	....	....
CIO *Net cash inflow from oper. activities.....*	....	**238.3**	**540.9**	....	....	....	....	....	....	....	....	....
31.1 Purchases of nonfinancial assets..............	....	425.3	570.7	....	....	....	....	....	....	....	....	....
31.2 Sales of nonfinancial assets.............	11.7	.2	.2	....	....	....	....	....	....	....	....	....
31 Net cash outflow from investments in nonfinancial assets..................	....	425.1	570.5	....	....	....	....	....	....	....	....	....
CSD *Cash surplus/deficit...............*	**−351.9**	**−186.8**	**−29.7**	....	....	....	....	....	....	....	....	....
32x Net acquisition of fin assets, excl. cash..........	136.6	143.6	245.7	....	....	....	....	....	....	....	....	....
321x Domestic.................	136.4	139.6	204.9	....	....	....	....	....	....	....	....	....
322x Foreign..................	.2	4.0	40.8	....	....	....	....	....	....	....	....	....
323 Monetary gold and SDRs..........	—	—	—	....	....	....	....	....	....	....	....	....
33 Net incurrence of liabilities.............	....	....	....	....	....	....	....	....	....	....	....	....
331 Domestic.................	....	....	....	....	....	....	....	....	....	....	....	....
332 Foreign.................	772.4	280.2	....	....	....	....	....	....	....	....	....	....
NFB Net cash inflow from fin. activities.............	....	....	....	....	....	....	....	....	....	....	....	....
NCB *Net change in the stock of cash.............*	....	....	....	....	....	....	....	....	....	....	....	....
Table 1 Revenue												
1 **Revenue................**	**950.0**	**1,530.1**	**1,844.4**	....	....	....	....	....	....	....	....	....
11 **Taxes.................**	**907.9**	**1,066.4**	**1,378.3**	....	....	....	....	....	....	....	....	....
111 Taxes on income, profits, & capital gains......	305.1	395.8	477.7	....	....	....	....	....	....	....	....	....
1111 Individuals.............	98.7	260.5	312.8	....	....	....	....	....	....	....	....	....
1112 Corporations and other enterprises...........	89.8	105.5	128.0	....	....	....	....	....	....	....	....	....
112 Taxes on payroll and workforce............	—	—	—	....	....	....	....	....	....	....	....	....
113 Taxes on property............	.6	2.1	2.3	....	....	....	....	....	....	....	....	....
114 Taxes on goods and services...........	478.5	484.6	662.3	....	....	....	....	....	....	....	....	....
1141 General taxes on goods and services..........	269.4	299.5	435.0	....	....	....	....	....	....	....	....	....
1142 Excises..............	206.5	181.5	222.5	....	....	....	....	....	....	....	....	....
115 Taxes on int'l. trade and transactions..........	123.7	183.9	236.0	....	....	....	....	....	....	....	....	....
116 Other taxes..............	—	—	—	....	....	....	....	....	....	....	....	....
12 **Social contributions................**	**—**	**—**	**—**	....	....	....	....	....	....	....	....	....
121 Social security contributions..............	—	—	—	....	....	....	....	....	....	....	....	....
122 Other social contributions............	—	—	—	....	....	....	....	....	....	....	....	....
13 **Grants................**	**4.7**	**432.7**	**414.2**	....	....	....	....	....	....	....	....	....
131 From foreign governments..............	4.7	432.7	414.2	....	....	....	....	....	....	....	....	....
132 From international organizations............	—	—	—	....	....	....	....	....	....	....	....	....
133 From other general government units..........	—	—	—	....	....	....	....	....	....	....	....	....
14 **Other revenue.................**	**37.4**	**31.0**	**51.9**	....	....	....	....	....	....	....	....	....
Table 2 Expense by economic type												
2 **Expense.................**	....	**1,291.8**	**1,303.5**	....	....	....	....	....	....	....	....	....
21 **Compensation of employees..................**	....	**448.7**	**405.8**	....	....	....	....	....	....	....	....	....
211 Wages and salaries............	....	447.1	404.1	....	....	....	....	....	....	....	....	....
212 Social contributions.............	....	1.6	1.7	....	....	....	....	....	....	....	....	....
22 **Use of goods and services...............**	....	**414.8**	**369.2**	....	....	....	....	....	....	....	....	....
23 **Consumption of fixed capital................**	....	....	....	....	....	....	....	....	....	....	....	....
24 **Interest.................**	....	**206.0**	**259.3**	....	....	....	....	....	....	....	....	....
25 **Subsidies................**	....	**—**	**—**	....	....	....	....	....	....	....	....	....

In Billions of Kwacha / Year Ending December 31 / Cash Reporter

	Budgetary Central Government			Central Government			Local Government			General Government		
	1997	1998p	1999f	1997	1998	1999	1997	1998	1999	1997	1998	1999
26 Grants..................................	....	243.9	261.5	....	....	....	....	....	....	....	....	....
261 To foreign govenments.............	....	—	.4	....	....	....	....	....	....	....	....	....
262 To international organizations..............	....	—	—	....	....	....	....	....	....	....	....	....
263 To other general government units.............	....	243.9	261.1	....	....	....	....	....	....	....	....	....
2631 Current..............	....	243.9	261.0	....	....	....	....	....	....	....	....	....
2632 Capital..............	....	—	.1	....	....	....	....	....	....	....	....	....
27 Social benefits....................	....	—	—	....	....	....	....	....	....	....	....	....
28 Other expense......................	....	2.6	7.7	....	....	....	....	....	....	....	....	....
281 Property expense other than interest.............	....	—	—	....	....	....	....	....	....	....	....	....
282 Miscellaneous other expense.....................	....	2.6	7.7	....	....	....	....	....	....	....	....	....
2821 Current......................	....	—	—	....	....	....	....	....	....	....	....	....
2822 Capital......................	....	2.6	7.7	....	....	....	....	....	....	....	....	....
Table 3 Transactions in assets and liabilities												
3 Change in net worth from transactns....	....	....	....	....	....	....	....	....	....	....	....	....
31 Net acquisition of nonfinancial assets...	....	425.1	570.5	....	....	....	....	....	....	....	....	....
311 Fixed assets...................	....	425.1	570.5	....	....	....	....	....	....	....	....	....
3111 Buildings and structures..............	....	....	....	....	....	....	....	....	....	....	....	....
3112 Machinery and equipment..............	....	....	....	....	....	....	....	....	....	....	....	....
3113 Other fixed assets.............	....	....	....	....	....	....	....	....	....	....	....	....
312 Inventories..............	....	—	—	....	....	....	....	....	....	....	....	....
313 Valuables..............	....	—	—	....	....	....	....	....	....	....	....	....
314 Nonproduced assets..............	....	—	—	....	....	....	....	....	....	....	....	....
3141 Land..............	....	—	—	....	....	....	....	....	....	....	....	....
3142 Subsoil assets..............	....	—	—	....	....	....	....	....	....	....	....	....
3143 Other naturally occurring assets.............	....	—	—	....	....	....	....	....	....	....	....	....
3144 Intangible nonproduced assets.................	....	—	—	....	....	....	....	....	....	....	....	....
32 Net acquisition of financial assets........	....	....	....	....	....	....	....	....	....	....	....	....
321 Domestic.............	....	....	....	....	....	....	....	....	....	....	....	....
3212 Currency and deposits.................	....	....	....	....	....	....	....	....	....	....	....	....
3213 Securities other than shares..............	....	....	....	....	....	....	....	....	....	....	....	....
3214 Loans.................	....	....	....	....	....	....	....	....	....	....	....	....
3215 Shares and other equity.................	....	....	....	....	....	....	....	....	....	....	....	....
3216 Insurance technical reserves.................	....	....	....	....	....	....	....	....	....	....	....	....
3217 Financial derivatives.................	....	....	....	....	....	....	....	....	....	....	....	....
3218 Other accounts receivable.............	....	....	....	....	....	....	....	....	....	....	....	....
322 Foreign.............	.2	4.0	....	....	....	....	....	....	....	....	....	....
3222 Currency and deposits.............	—	....	....	....	....	....	....	....	....	....	....	....
3223 Securities other than shares.............	....	....	....	....	....	....	....	....	....	....	....	....
3224 Loans.............	....	....	....	....	....	....	....	....	....	....	....	....
3225 Shares and other equity.............	....	....	....	....	....	....	....	....	....	....	....	....
3226 Insurance technical reserves.............	....	....	....	....	....	....	....	....	....	....	....	....
3227 Financial derivatives.............	....	....	....	....	....	....	....	....	....	....	....	....
3228 Other accounts receivable.............	....	....	....	....	....	....	....	....	....	....	....	....
323 Monetary gold and SDRs.............	—	—	....	....	....	....	....	....	....	....	....	....
33 Net incurrence of liabilities....................	....	....	....	....	....	....	....	....	....	....	....	....
331 Domestic.............	....	....	....	....	....	....	....	....	....	....	....	....
3312 Currency and deposits.............	....	....	....	....	....	....	....	....	....	....	....	....
3313 Securities other than shares.............	....	....	....	....	....	....	....	....	....	....	....	....
3314 Loans.............	....	....	....	....	....	....	....	....	....	....	....	....
3316 Insurance technical reserves.............	....	....	....	....	....	....	....	....	....	....	....	....
3317 Financial derivatives.............	....	....	....	....	....	....	....	....	....	....	....	....
3318 Other accounts payable.............	....	....	....	....	....	....	....	....	....	....	....	....
332 Foreign.............	772.4	280.2	....	....	....	....	....	....	....	....	....	....
3322 Currency and deposits.............	—	—	....	....	....	....	....	....	....	....	....	....
3323 Securities other than shares.............	—	—	....	....	....	....	....	....	....	....	....	....
3324 Loans.............	772.4	280.2	....	....	....	....	....	....	....	....	....	....
3326 Insurance technical reserves.............	—	—	....	....	....	....	....	....	....	....	....	....
3327 Financial derivatives.............	—	—	....	....	....	....	....	....	....	....	....	....
3328 Other accounts payable.............	....	....	....	....	....	....	....	....	....	....	....	....

Zambia   754

In Billions of Kwacha / Year Ending December 31 / Cash Reporter

	Budgetary Central Government			Central Government			Local Government			General Government		
	1997	1998p	1999f	1997	1998	1999	1997	1998	1999	1997	1998	1999
Table 4 Holding gains in assets and liabilities												
Table 5 Other changes in the volume of assets and liabilities												
Table 6 Balance sheet												
6 **Net worth**..........	....	....	....	....	....	....	....	....	....	....	....	....
61 **Nonfinancial assets**..........	....	....	....	....	....	....	....	....	....	....	....	....
611 Fixed assets..........	....	....	....	....	....	....	....	....	....	....	....	....
6111 Buildings and structures..........	....	....	....	....	....	....	....	....	....	....	....	....
6112 Machinery and equipment..........	....	....	....	....	....	....	....	....	....	....	....	....
6113 Other fixed assets..........	....	....	....	....	....	....	....	....	....	....	....	....
612 Inventories..........	....	....	....	....	....	....	....	....	....	....	....	....
613 Valuables..........	....	....	....	....	....	....	....	....	....	....	....	....
614 Nonproduced assets..........	....	....	....	....	....	....	....	....	....	....	....	....
6141 Land..........	....	....	....	....	....	....	....	....	....	....	....	....
6142 Subsoil assets..........	....	....	....	....	....	....	....	....	....	....	....	....
6143 Other naturally occurring assets..........	....	....	....	....	....	....	....	....	....	....	....	....
6144 Intangible nonproduced assets..........	....	....	....	....	....	....	....	....	....	....	....	....
62 **Financial assets**..........	....	....	....	....	....	....	....	....	....	....	....	....
621 Domestic..........	....	....	....	....	....	....	....	....	....	....	....	....
6212 Currency and deposits..........	....	....	....	....	....	....	....	....	....	....	....	....
6213 Securities other than shares..........	....	....	....	....	....	....	....	....	....	....	....	....
6214 Loans..........	....	....	....	....	....	....	....	....	....	....	....	....
6215 Shares and other equity..........	....	....	....	....	....	....	....	....	....	....	....	....
6216 Insurance technical reserves..........	....	....	....	....	....	....	....	....	....	....	....	....
6217 Financial derivatives..........	....	....	....	....	....	....	....	....	....	....	....	....
6218 Other accounts receivable..........	....	....	....	....	....	....	....	....	....	....	....	....
622 Foreign..........	....	....	....	....	....	....	....	....	....	....	....	....
6222 Currency and deposits..........	....	....	....	....	....	....	....	....	....	....	....	....
6223 Securities other than shares..........	....	....	....	....	....	....	....	....	....	....	....	....
6224 Loans..........	....	....	....	....	....	....	....	....	....	....	....	....
6225 Shares and other equity..........	....	....	....	....	....	....	....	....	....	....	....	....
6226 Insurance technical reserves..........	....	....	....	....	....	....	....	....	....	....	....	....
6227 Financial derivatives..........	....	....	....	....	....	....	....	....	....	....	....	....
6228 Other accounts receivable..........	....	....	....	....	....	....	....	....	....	....	....	....
623 Monetary gold and SDRs..........	....	....	....	....	....	....	....	....	....	....	....	....
63 **Liabilities**..........	**8,489.1**	**10,621.2**	....	....	....	....	....	....	....	....	....	....
631 Domestic..........	303.2	212.8	....	....	....	....	....	....	....	....	....	....
6312 Currency and deposits..........	....	....	....	....	....	....	....	....	....	....	....	....
6313 Securities other than shares..........	....	....	....	....	....	....	....	....	....	....	....	....
6314 Loans..........	....	....	....	....	....	....	....	....	....	....	....	....
6316 Insurance technical reserves..........	....	....	....	....	....	....	....	....	....	....	....	....
6317 Financial derivatives..........	....	....	....	....	....	....	....	....	....	....	....	....
6318 Other accounts payable..........	....	....	....	....	....	....	....	....	....	....	....	....
632 Foreign..........	8,185.9	10,408.4	....	....	....	....	....	....	....	....	....	....
6322 Currency and deposits..........	....	....	....	....	....	....	....	....	....	....	....	....
6323 Securities other than shares..........	....	....	....	....	....	....	....	....	....	....	....	....
6324 Loans..........	....	....	....	....	....	....	....	....	....	....	....	....
6326 Insurance technical reserves..........	....	....	....	....	....	....	....	....	....	....	....	....
6327 Financial derivatives..........	....	....	....	....	....	....	....	....	....	....	....	....
6328 Other accounts payable..........	....	....	....	....	....	....	....	....	....	....	....	....
Memorandum items:												
6M2 Net financial worth..........	....	....	....	....	....	....	....	....	....	....	....	....
6M3 Debt at market value..........	....	....	....	....	....	....	....	....	....	....	....	....
6M4 Debt at nominal value..........	....	....	....	....	....	....	....	....	....	....	....	....
6M5 Arrears..........	....	....	....	....	....	....	....	....	....	....	....	....
6M6 Obligations for social security benefits..........	....	....	....	....	....	....	....	....	....	....	....	....
6M7 Contingent liabilities..........	....	....	....	....	....	....	....	....	....	....	....	....
6M8 Uncapitalized military weapons, systems..........	....	....	....	....	....	....	....	....	....	....	....	....
Table 7 Outlays by functions of govt.												
7 **Total outlays**..........	**1,313.6**	**1,717.1**	**1,874.3**	....	....	....	....	....	....	....	....	....
701 **General public services**..........	**721.4**	**784.9**	**758.9**	....	....	....	....	....	....	....	....	....
7017 Public debt transactions..........	....	206.0	259.3	....	....	....	....	....	....	....	....	....
7018 General transfers between levels of govt.......	....	....	....	....	....	....	....	....	....	....	....	....
702 **Defense**..........	**90.8**	**113.8**	**73.7**	....	....	....	....	....	....	....	....	....
703 **Public order and safety**..........	**46.6**	**77.5**	**61.4**	....	....	....	....	....	....	....	....	....

2005, International Monetary Fund: *Government Finance Statistics Yearbook*

In Billions of Kwacha / Year Ending December 31 / Cash Reporter

		Budgetary Central Government			Central Government			Local Government			General Government		
		1997	1998p	1999f	1997	1998	1999	1997	1998	1999	1997	1998	1999
704	**Economic affairs**................................	**108.7**	**250.7**	**383.4**	....	....	....	....	....	....	....	....	....
7042	Agriculture, forestry, fishing, and hunting.....	54.3	75.4	88.0	....	....	....	....	....	....	....	....	....
7043	Fuel and energy............................	.6	5.3	4.8	....	....	....	....	....	....	....	....	....
7044	Mining, manufacturing, and construction.....	7.6	12.3	19.4	....	....	....	....	....	....	....	....	....
7045	Transport....................................	33.8	140.4	256.0	....	....	....	....	....	....	....	....	....
7046	Communication..........................	....	....	....	....	....	....	....	....	....	....	....	....
705	**Environmental protection**.................	....	....	....	....	....	....	....	....	....	....	....	....
706	**Housing and community amenities**........	**4.4**	**40.6**	**43.3**	....	....	....	....	....	....	....	....	....
707	**Health**.......................................	**102.6**	**197.0**	**248.0**	....	....	....	....	....	....	....	....	....
7072	Outpatient services.......................	23.3	62.5	75.7	....	....	....	....	....	....	....	....	....
7073	Hospital services..........................	28.2	24.4	26.6	....	....	....	....	....	....	....	....	....
7074	Public health services.....................	....	....	....	....	....	....	....	....	....	....	....	....
708	**Recreation, culture, and religion**...........	**7.5**	**11.9**	**10.5**	....	....	....	....	....	....	....	....	....
709	**Education**....................................	**221.4**	**243.5**	**270.8**	....	....	....	....	....	....	....	....	....
7091	Pre-primary and primary education.............	....	....	....	....	....	....	....	....	....	....	....	....
7092	Secondary education......................	72.8	104.4	126.7	....	....	....	....	....	....	....	....	....
7094	Tertiary education.........................	27.7	55.3	42.1	....	....	....	....	....	....	....	....	....
710	**Social protection**...........................	**10.2**	**21.3**	**24.3**	....	....	....	....	....	....	....	....	....
7	Statistical discrepancy: Total outlays...............	—	−24.1	—	....	....	....	....	....	....	....	....	....
Table 8 Transactions in financial assets and liabilities by sector													
82	**Net acquisition of financial assets**........	....	....	....	....	....	....	....	....	....	....	....	....
821	Domestic..................................	....	....	....	....	....	....	....	....	....	....	....	....
8211	General government.........................	—	76.4	110.5	....	....	....	....	....	....	....	....	....
8212	Central bank...............................	....	....	....	....	....	....	....	....	....	....	....	....
8213	Other depository corporations...................	....	....	....	....	....	....	....	....	....	....	....	....
8214	Financial corporations n.e.c..................	....	....	....	....	....	....	....	....	....	....	....	....
8215	Nonfinancial corporations...................	7.2	13.8	8.4	....	....	....	....	....	....	....	....	....
8216	Households & NPIs serving households......	....	....	....	....	....	....	....	....	....	....	....	....
822	Foreign....................................	.2	4.0	....	....	....	....	....	....	....	....	....	....
8221	General government.........................	....	....	....	....	....	....	....	....	....	....	....	....
8227	International organizations.....................	....	....	....	....	....	....	....	....	....	....	....	....
8228	Financial corporations other than international organizations..............	....	....	....	....	....	....	....	....	....	....	....	....
8229	Other nonresidents.....................	....	....	....	....	....	....	....	....	....	....	....	....
823	Monetary gold and SDRs.................	—	—	—	....	....	....	....	....	....	....	....	....
83	**Net incurrence of liabilities**..................	....	....	....	....	....	....	....	....	....	....	....	....
831	Domestic..................................	....	....	....	....	....	....	....	....	....	....	....	....
8311	General government.........................	....	....	....	....	....	....	....	....	....	....	....	....
8312	Central bank...............................	....	....	....	....	....	....	....	....	....	....	....	....
8313	Other depository corporations...................	....	....	....	....	....	....	....	....	....	....	....	....
8314	Financial corporations n.e.c..................	....	....	....	....	....	....	....	....	....	....	....	....
8315	Nonfinancial corporations...................	....	....	....	....	....	....	....	....	....	....	....	....
8316	Households & NPIs serving households......	....	....	....	....	....	....	....	....	....	....	....	....
832	Foreign....................................	772.4	280.2	....	....	....	....	....	....	....	....	....	....
8321	General government.........................	....	....	....	....	....	....	....	....	....	....	....	....
8327	International organizations.....................	....	....	....	....	....	....	....	....	....	....	....	....
8328	Financial corporations other than international organizations..............	....	....	....	....	....	....	....	....	....	....	....	....
8329	Other nonresidents.....................	....	....	....	....	....	....	....	....	....	....	....	....

Institutional Tables

Afghanistan, Islamic Rep. of   512

Units of General Government

Central Government

Subsector 1.   Budgetary central government
  1.1   Audit office
  1.2   Central statistics office
  1.3   General attorney
  1.4   Ministries
  1.5   National security agency
  1.6   Office of the Father of the Nation
  1.7   President's office
  1.8   Science academy
  1.9   Supreme court

Subsector 2.   Extrabudgetary units/entities
  2.1   Administrative reform and civil service
  2.2   Geodesy and Cartography
  2.3   Narcotics Eradication
  2.4   National Olympic Committee
  2.5   Other self-financing government agencies

Subsector 3.   Social security funds
  3.1   Pension Fund

State Governments

Subsector 4.   State governments
  4.1   34 provinces (Badakhshan, Badghis, Baghlan, Balkh, Bamyan, Dikondy, Farah, Faryab, Ghazni, Ghor, Heart, Helmand, Jawzjan, Kabul, Kandahar, Kapisa, Khost, Kunar, Kunduz, Laghman, Logar, Nangarhar, Nimroz, Nooristan, Paktika, Paktiya, Pangsher, Parwan, Samangan, Sar-e-Pul, Takhar, Uruzgan, Wardak, and Zabul)

Local Governments

Subsector 5.   Local governments
  5.1   Not applicable

Data Coverage

Data in central government tables cover operations of subsector 1.

Not included are the transactions in kind, including foreign grants, if the cash transactions are not processed through the official accounts of the government of the Islamic Republic of Afghanistan.

Accounting Practices

1. Liquidation or complementary period:
   Not reported.
2. Valuation of assets and liabilities:
   Not reported.

GFSM 2001 Implementation Plan

Not reported.

This institutional table is based on information reported in 2005.

Albania   914

Units of General Government

Central Government

Subsector 1.   Budgetary central government
  1.1   Budgetary institutions, council of ministers, ministries, nonministerial departments, parliament, and president.

Subsector 2.   Extrabudgetary units/entities
  2.1   National Health Institute

Subsector 3.   Social security funds
  3.1   Social Security Institute

State Governments

Subsector 4.   State governments
  4.1   Not applicable

Local Governments

Subsector 5.   Local governments
  5.1   36 districts and 43 municipalities

Data Coverage

Data in central government tables cover operations of subsectors 1–3.

Data in local government tables cover operations of subsector 5.

Accounting Practices

1. Liquidation or complementary period:
   Not reported.
2. Valuation of assets and liabilities:
   Not reported.

GFSM 2001 Implementation Plan

Not reported.

This institutional table is based on information reported in or prior to 1996.

Algeria   612

Units of General Government

Central Government

Subsector 1.   Budgetary central government
  1.1   Constitutional council, council of state, court of accounts, government departments and ministries, national assembly, and presidency
  1.2   7 commissions and councils, including Amazirité High Commission, Arab Language Academy, Higher Council for Education, Higher Council for Youth, and National Institute for Global Strategic Studies

Subsector 2.   Extrabudgetary units/entities
  2.1   Administrative bodies and hospitals
  2.2   Algerian Development Bank

Subsector 3.   Social security funds
  3.1   4 social security funds

State Governments

Subsector 4.   State governments
  4.1   Not applicable

Local Governments

Subsector 5.   Local governments
  5.1   1,552 communes
  5.2   48 wilayate

Data Coverage

Data in budgetary central government tables cover operations of subsector 1.

† Central government debt takes into account debt assumptions in 1996 (171 billion dinars) and in 1999 (346 billion dinars) that were not accounted as transactions (financing).

Accounting Practices

1. Liquidation or complementary period:
   Not reported.
2. Valuation of assets and liabilities:
   Not reported.

GFSM 2001 Implementation Plan

Not reported.

This institutional table is based on information reported in 2000.

Argentina 213

Units of General Government

Central Government

Subsector 1. Budgetary central government
  1.1 Judiciary, legislature, 12 ministries, presidency, and secretariats of the National Executive and Public Ministry

Subsector 2. Extrabudgetary units/entities
  2.1 57 government agencies, such as the Argentine Mining and Geological Service; National Agrofood Health and Quality Service; National Drug, Food, and Medical Technology Administration; National Fisheries Research and Development Institute; National Institute of Agricultural Technology; National Institute of Industrial Technology; and National Transportation Regulation Commission

Subsector 3. Social security funds
  3.1 National Social Security Administration

State Governments

Subsector 4. State governments
  4.1 23 provinces and Ciudad Autónoma de Buenos Aires

Local Governments

Subsector 5. Local governments
  5.1 1,617 municipalities

Data Coverage

Data in central government tables cover operations of subsectors 1–3.

Prior to 1993, data on corporate taxes were included in line 1113, other unallocated taxes on income, of Table 1, Revenue.

Data in state government tables cover operations of subsector 4.

Data in local government tables cover operations of subsector 5.

† Data through 2001 are on a cash basis. Starting in 2002, data are on an accrual basis. Also, through 2001 the subsectors of central government are presented on a net basis (i.e., after consolidation). Starting in 2002, the subsectors of central government are presented on a gross basis (i.e., before consolidation).

Accounting Practices

1. Liquidation or complementary period:
   Not reported.
2. Valuation of assets and liabilities:
   Not reported.

GFSM 2001 Implementation Plan

Not reported.

This institutional table is based on information reported in 2005.

Armenia 911

Units of General Government

Central Government

Subsector 1. Budgetary central government
  1.1 Agencies and departments, judiciary, ministries, parliament, president, state committees

Subsector 2. Extrabudgetary units/entities
  2.1 Various government nonprofit institutions, including schools, hospitals, and universitities

Subsector 3. Social security funds
  3.1 Social security fund

State Governments

Subsector 4. State governments
  4.1 Not applicable

Local Governments

Subsector 5. Local governments
  5.1 900+ communities (marzes)

Data Coverage

Data in central government tables cover operations of subsectors 1–3.

Data in local government tables cover operations of subsector 5.

Accounting Practices

1. Liquidation or complementary period:
   Complementary period is one month.
2. Valuation of assets and liabilities:
   Fixed assets are valued at historical cost, financial assets at market prices, and loans and bonds at face value.

GFSM 2001 Implementation Plan

It is planned to bring budgetary central government revenues, expense, and transactions in nonfinancial assets in line with the GFSM 2001.

This institutional table is based on information reported in 2004.

Australia 193

Units of General Government

Central Government

Subsector 1. Budgetary central government
  1.1 Agencies, departments, governor general's office, judiciary, and parliament

Subsector 2. Extrabudgetary units/entities
  2.1 Government agencies
  2.2 6 government commissions
  2.3 3 government corporations
  2.4 Health Insurance Commission
  2.5 2 national universities

Subsector 3. Social security funds
  3.1 Not applicable

State Governments

Subsector 4. State governments
  4.1 8 state governments

Local Governments

Subsector 5. Local governments
  5.1 900 (approximately) cities, district councils, municipalities, shires, and towns

Data Coverage

Data in central government tables cover operations of subsectors 1 and 2.

Data in state government tables cover operations of subsector 4 and are based on information from all state governments. Data in local government tables cover operations of subsector 5 and are based on information from all local governments.

Subsector 2 comprises some entities with individual budgets financed wholly or largely by transfers from the central government budget.

† From 1996 onward, all local government data are compiled on a year ending June 30.

Accounting Practices

1. Liquidation or complementary period:
   None.
2. Valuation of assets and liabilities:
   Not reported.

GFSM 2001 Implementation Plan

From 1999 onward, the Australian Bureau of Statistics has implemented the recording of GFS on an accrual basis, and detailed data are no longer available on a cash basis. The 1999 data provided for publication in the *GFS Yearbook* are aggregates from the Cash Flow Statement, which is prepared as part of the accrual reporting system.

This institutional table is based on information reported in 1999.

Austria   122

Units of General Government

Central Government

Subsector 1.   Budgetary central government
1.1   Agencies, audit commissioner's office, judiciary, ministries, national assembly, ombudsman, presidency

Subsector 2.   Extrabudgetary units/entities
2.1   Austrian Academy of Science
2.2   1 Austrian advertising association
2.3   14 Austrian associations of students
2.4   13 federal chambers of commerce, labor, and professionals
2.5   38 federal funds
2.6   13 outsourced companies classified to sector government

Subsector 3.   Social security funds
3.1   244 social insurance institutions; hospitals of social insurance

State Governments

Subsector 4.   State governments
4.1   8 states
4.2   71 state chambers of commerce, labor, and professionals
4.3   73 state funds

Local Governments

Subsector 5.   Local governments
5.1   2,358 municipalities (without Vienna)
5.2   475 municipal associations (education and music services)
5.3   10 municipal funds
5.4   Vienna as municipality

Data Coverage

Data in central government tables cover operations of subsectors 1–3.

Data in state government tables cover operations of subsector 4.

Data in local government tables cover operations of subsector 5.

† From 1998 onwards, in line with the presentation adopted within the European Union, data on domestic financial assets and liabilities include foreign financial assets and liabilities.

† Until 1996, the Motorway and Toll Road Financing Company (ASFINAG) was part of the central government, and its data were included in data on extrabudgetary funds.

† Until 1996, the hospital managing companies were part of state government, and their data were included in data on state government.

† From 1995 onwards, data are compiled in accordance with the *1995 ESA*.

Accounting Practices

1. Liquidation or complementary period:
   Complementary period is 3 weeks for subsector 1 and 4 weeks for all other subsectors.
2. Valuation of assets and liabilities:
   Financial assets and liabilities at market prices.

GFSM 2001 Implementation Plan

The implementation of *GFSM 2001* is made in accordance with the implementation of the *1995 ESA*.

This institutional table is based on information reported in 2004.

Azerbaijan   912

Units of General Government

Central Government

Subsector 1.   Budgetary central government
1.1   Cabinet of ministers, judiciary, 17 ministries, parliament, presidency, and 20 state committees

Subsector 2.   Extrabudgetary units/entities
2.1   Ecology Fund
2.2   President's Fund
2.3   Roads Fund
2.4   Unified Foreign Exchange Fund

Subsector 3.   Social security funds
3.1   State Fund for Assistance to Employment
3.2   State Social Protection Fund

State Governments

Subsector 4.   State governments
4.1   Not applicable

Local Governments

Subsector 5.   Local governments
5.1   65 regions (rayon) including 9 cities and the Autonomous Republic of Nakhichevan

Data Coverage

Data in central government tables cover operations of subsectors 1 and 3 and components 2.1 and 2.3.

Data in local government tables cover operations of subsector 5.

Accounting Practices

1. Liquidation or complementary period:
   Not reported.
2. Valuation of assets and liabilities:
   Not reported.

GFSM 2001 Implementation Plan

Not reported.

This institutional table is based on information reported in 1998.

Bahamas, The 313

Units of General Government

Central Government

Subsector 1. Budgetary central government
  1.1 Audit, cabinet, governorate, house of assembly, judiciary, law courts, ministries, senate, and service commissions

Subsector 2. Extrabudgetary units/entities
  2.1 Not applicable

Subsector 3. Social security funds
  3.1 National Insurance Board

State Governments

Subsector 4. State governments
  4.1 Not applicable

Local Governments

Subsector 5. Local governments
  5.1 Not applicable

Data Coverage

Data in central government tables cover operations of subsector 1.

Accounting Practices

1. Liquidation or complementary period:
   Complementary period is 30 days.
2. Valuation of assets and liabilities:
   Loans and bonds are valued at remaining amounts of face values.

GFSM 2001 Implementation Plan

Not reported.
This institutional table is based on information reported in 2005.

Bahrain, Kingdom of 419

Units of General Government

Central Government

Subsector 1. Budgetary central government
  1.1 Cabinet, ministries, prime minister's office, and ruler's court

Subsector 2. Extrabudgetary units/entities
  2.1 Extrabudgetary funds

Subsector 3. Social security funds
  3.1 General Organization for Social Insurance

State Governments

Subsector 4. State governments
  4.1 Not applicable

Local Governments

Subsector 5. Local governments
  5.1 Hamad Town municipal council
  5.2 Hidd municipal council
  5.3 Isa Town municipal council
  5.4 Jidafs municipal council
  5.5 Manama municipal council
  5.6 Middle Zone municipal council
  5.7 Moharraq municipal council
  5.8 North Zone municipal council
  5.9 Riffa municipal council
  5.10 Sitra municipal council
  5.11 Western Zone municipal council

Data Coverage

Data in central government tables cover operations of subsectors 1–3.
† Prior to 1996 in Table 7, data on public order and safety were included in the line on general public services.

Accounting Practices

1. Liquidation or complementary period:
   Not reported.
2. Valuation of assets and liabilities:
   Not reported.

GFSM 2001 Implementation Plan

Not reported.
This institutional table is based on information reported in 2000.

Bangladesh 513

Units of General Government

Central Government

Subsector 1. Budgetary central government
  1.1 Divisions, ministries, parliament, planning division, presidency, prime minister's office, public service commission, rural development and cooperatives division, and supreme court

Subsector 2. Extrabudgetary units/entities
  2.1 Not applicable

Subsector 3. Social security funds
  3.1 Not applicable

State Governments

Subsector 4. State governments
  4.1 Not applicable

Local Governments

Subsector 5. Local governments
  5.1 City corporations, district councils, and municipalities

Data Coverage

Data in central government tables cover operations of subsector 1.

Accounting Practices

1. Liquidation or complementary period:
   Data for one month after the end of the fiscal year are included in the previous year's data.
2. Valuation of assets and liabilities:
   Fixed loans and bonds are valued at face value.

GFSM 2001 Implementation Plan

Not reported.
This institutional table is based on information reported in 2004.

Barbados 316

Units of General Government

Central Government

Subsector 1. Budgetary central government
  1.1 Attorney general, cabinet office, 14 ministries, prime minister's office

Subsector 2. Extrabudgetary units/entities
2.1 Barbados Cadet Corps
2.2 Barbados Defense Force
2.3 Barbados Defense Force—Sports Program
2.4 Barbados Investment and Development Corporation
2.5 Barbados Tourism Authority
2.6 Child Care Board
2.7 National Assistance Board
2.8 National Conservation Commission
2.9 Sanitation Service
2.10 University of the West Indies

Subsector 3. Social security funds
3.1 National Insurance Fund
3.2 Severance Fund
3.3 Unemployment Fund

State Governments

Subsector 4. State governments
4.1 Not applicable

Local Governments

Subsector 5. Local governments
5.1 Not applicable

Data Coverage

Data in central and general government tables cover operations of subsectors 1–3.

Accounting Practices

1. Liquidation or complementary period:
    Complementary period is four months.
2. Valuation of assets and liabilities:
    Not reported.

GFSM 2001 Implementation Plan

Not reported.

This institutional table is based on information reported in 2004.

Belarus   913

Units of General Government

Central Government

Subsector 1. Budgetary central government
1.1 Council of ministers, funds (Construction Science Development Fund, funds of free economic zones, innovation funds, ministries' centralized funds, Precautionary Measures Fund, and Stabilization Fund of the Ministry of Communication and Information Technology), law courts, ministries, national assembly, office of public prosecutor, other committees and agencies, presidency, and state committees

Subsector 2. Extrabudgetary units/entities
2.1 Not applicable

Subsector 3. Social security funds
3.1 Social Protection Fund of the Ministry of Labor and Social Protection of Population

State Governments

Subsector 4. State governments
4.1 Not applicable

Local Governments

Subsector 5. Local governments
5.1 7 regional governments, including 6 oblasts and 1 city (Minsk)

Data Coverage

Data in central government tables cover operations of subsectors 1 and 3.

Data in local government tables cover operations of subsector 5.

† On August 20, 1994, the rubel was redenominated with the removal of one zero from the currency.

† Starting in 1998, the operations of funds previously classified as extrabudgetary are included in the budgetary central government data.

† On January 1, 2000, the rubel was redenominated with the removal of three zeros from the currency.

† Starting in 2003 for central government subsectors, data are presented on a gross basis (i.e., before consolidation).

Accounting Practices

1. Liquidation or complementary period:
    One month after the end of the fiscal year.
2. Valuation of assets and liabilities:
    Financial assets and liabilities are valued at face value.

GFSM 2001 Implementation Plan

Starting in 2006, data on a cash basis will be compiled using the new classifications of revenue and outlays by functions of government. These classifications are broadly consistent with the recommendations of the *GFSM 2001* analytical framework..

This institutional table is based on information reported in 2005.

Belgium   124

Units of General Government

Central Government

Subsector 1. Budgetary central government
1.1 Judiciary, ministries, monarchy, and parliament
1.2 Councils of the communities and regions

Subsector 2. Extrabudgetary units/entities
2.1 Approximately 80 government agencies and extrabudgetary funds

Subsector 3. Social security funds
3.1 National Pension Fund for Employees
3.2 National Retirement and Old Age Pension Fund
3.3 Special Family Allowance Funds
3.4 Work Accidents Fund
3.5 13 other social security funds

State Governments

Subsector 4. State governments
4.1 9 provinces

Local Governments

Subsector 5. Local governments
5.1 Metropolitan Brussels
5.2 589 communes

Data Coverage

Some entities of component 2.1 have individual budgets but are included in budgets of ministries.

Data in budgetary central government tables cover operations of components 1.1, 1.2, and 2.1, for the most part. Some financial transactions of component 2.1 are reflected in the extrabudgetary central government tables.

Data in state government tables cover operations of subsector 4.

Data in local government tables cover operations of subsector 5.

Accounting Practices

1. Liquidation or complementary period:
   Not reported.
2. Valuation of assets and liabilities:
   Not reported.

GFSM 2001 Implementation Plan

Data in accordance with *ESA95* methodology were reported for publication in the *GFS Yearbook*.

This institutional table is based on information reported in 2005.

Bhutan 514

Units of General Government

Central Government

Subsector 1. Budgetary central government
  1.1 Bhutan Olympic Committee; Cabinet Secretariat; Center for Bhutan Studies; Council for Ecclesiastical Affairs; Department of Planning; Dzongkha Development Authority; His Majesty's Secretariat; judiciary; 10 ministries; National Assembly Secretariat; National Commission for Cultural Affairs; National Environment Commission; Office of Legal Affairs; Royal Advisory Council; Royal Audit Authority; Royal Civil Service Commission; and Royal Institute of Management
  1.2 20 district administrations
      201 subdistrict administrations
Subsector 2. Extrabudgetary units/entities
  2.1 Not applicable
Subsector 3. Social security funds
  3.1 Not applicable

State Governments

Subsector 4. State governments
  4.1 Not applicable

Local Governments

Subsector 5. Local governments
  5.1 Not applicable

Data Coverage

Data in central budgetary government tables cover operations of subsector 1.

Fiscal year begins on July 1.

Accounting Practices

1. Liquidation or complementary period:
   None.
2. Valuation of assets and liabilities:
   Not reported.

GFSM 2001 Implementation Plan

Not reported.

This institutional table is based on information reported in 2005.

Bolivia 218

Units of General Government

Central Government

Subsector 1. Budgetary central government
  1.1 Comptroller general's office, judiciary, legislative,

ministries (16), national electoral court, national supreme council of defense, and treasury
Subsector 2. Extrabudgetary units/entities
  2.1 75 government agencies
Subsector 3. Social security funds
  3.1 Military Social Security
  3.2 National Health Scheme
  3.3 Oil Health Scheme
  3.4 State Banking Health Scheme
  3.5 National Highway Service Health Scheme

State Governments

Subsector 4. State governments
  4.1 9 departmental prefectures

Local Governments

Subsector 5. Local governments
  5.1 9 municipalities of departmental capitals and numerous other municipalities

Data Coverage

Data for central government cover operations carried out through the General Fund for subsectors 1–3.

† From 2002 onwards, data are reported on an accrual basis. Data prior to 2002 are reported on a cash basis. Also, starting in 2002, data for the central government subsectors are presented on a gross basis (i.e., before consolidation). Data prior to 2002 for these subsectors are presented on a net basis (i.e., after consolidation).

† From 1996 onwards, the structure of expense changed. The central government transferred health and education functions to other levels of government, which resulted in a significant reduction of wages and salaries paid by the central government and an increase of central government transfers to other levels of government.

Accounting Practices

1. Liquidation or complementary period:
   None.
2. Valuation of assets and liabilities:
   At market prices.

GFSM 2001 Implementation Plan

Not reported.

This institutional table is based on information reported in 2005.

Bosnia and Herzegovina 963

Units of General Government

Central Government

Subsector 1. Budgetary central government
  1.1 Bosnia and Herzegovina institutions (state-level)
  1.2 Federation of Bosnia and Herzegovina (including 10 cantons) (entity-level)
  1.3 Republika Srpska (entity-level)
  1.4 Brčko District
Subsector 2. Extrabudgetary units/entities
  2.1 Extrabudgetary units of the State, the Federation of Bosnia and Herzegovina, the Republika Srpska, and the Brčko District
Subsector 3. Social security funds
  3.1 Social security funds of the Federation of Bosnia and

Herzegovina and the Republika Srpska, covering retirement, health, unemployment, and child protection benefits

State Governments

Subsector 4.   State governments
   4.1   Not applicable

Local Governments

Subsector 5.   Local governments
   5.1   141 municipalities

Data Coverage

Data for central government cover operations of subsectors 1 and 3. The data do not include foreign expenditures directly financed from abroad.

Accounting Practices

1.   Liquidation or complementary period:
     Two months after the end of the fiscal year.
2.   Valuation of assets and liabilities:
     Fixed assets are valued at historical cost, financial assets at market prices, and loans and bonds at face value.

GFSM 2001 Implementation Plan

The main steps and target dates of the implementation plan are divided into two development phases:

Development phase 1 (mid-2004 to mid-2005) comprises the compilation of central government sector quarterly data.

Development phase 2 (from mid-2005) will encompass the extension of the coverage of GFS to include municipalities and the production of the full range of GFS statements and tables, including the sources and uses of cash statement, outlays by function, and balance sheets. Estimates of consumption of fixed capital will be added at a later stage.

This institutional table is based on information reported in 2005.

Brazil   223

Units of General Government

Central Government

Subsector 1.   Budgetary central government
   1.1   Congress, judiciary, ministries, and presidency
Subsector 2.   Extrabudgetary units/entities
   2.1   Federal universities and federal university foundations
   2.2   Government agencies, boards, and commissions; 17 foundations; 48 funds; 11 institutes; 42 services; and 2 superintendencies
   2.3   National and regional development agencies
   2.4   National Highway Department
   2.5   Technical schools
Subsector 3.   Social security funds
   3.1   Social security institutes and funds

State Governments

Subsector 4.   State governments
   4.1   27 state governments and the federal district

Local Governments

Subsector 5.   Local governments
   5.1   5,508 municipal governments

Data Coverage

Data in central government tables cover operations of subsectors 1–3.

Data in state government tables cover operations of subsector 4.
Data in local government tables cover operations of subsector 5.

Accounting Practices

1.   Liquidation or complementary period:
     Not reported.
2.   Valuation of assets and liabilities:
     Not reported.

GFSM 2001 Implementation Plan

Not reported.

This institutional table is based on information reported in 2001.

Bulgaria   918

Units of General Government

Central Government

Subsector 1.   Budgetary central government
   1.1   Committees, government agencies, judiciary, ministries, national assembly, and president's office
Subsector 2.   Extrabudgetary units/entities
   2.1   Agriculture Fund, Privatization Fund, National Fund
Subsector 3.   Social security funds
   3.1   National Social Security Institute, in charge of pension and many social benefit funds (Pension Fund, General Illness and Maternity Fund, Industrial Injuries and Professional Illness Funds, and others), National Health Insurance Fund, Employees' Receivables Guarantee Fund, Teachers' Pension Fund

State Governments

Subsector 4.   State governments
   4.1   Not applicable

Local Governments

Subsector 5.   Local governments
   5.1   264 municipalities

Data Coverage

Data in central government tables cover operations of subsectors 1–3.

Data in local government tables cover operations of subsector 5.

† Starting in 2000, the subsectors of central government are presented on a gross basis (i.e., before consolidation). Until 1999, the data were presented on a net basis (i.e., after consolidation).

Accounting Practices

1.   Liquidation or complementary period:
     None.
2.   Valuation of assets and liabilities:
     Only valuation of foreign currency is reported.

GFSM 2001 Implementation Plan

Not reported.

This institutional table is based on information reported in 2005.

Burundi   618

Units of General Government

Central Government

Subsector 1.   Budgetary central government
   1.1   Budgetary agencies, executive committee, ministries,

national assembly, presidency, provinces, and specialized schools

Subsector 2. Extrabudgetary units/entities
2.1 Burundi National Commission for UNESCO, Prince Louis Rwagasose Clinic, radio station, university, and various government centers and institutions

Subsector 3. Social security funds
3.1 Civil Servants Mutual Insurance
3.2 National Social Security Institute of Burundi

State Governments

Subsector 4. State governments
4.1 Not applicable

Local Governments

Subsector 5. Local governments
5.1 114 communal administrations

Data Coverage

Data in central government tables cover operations of subsectors 1 and 3.

Data in local government tables cover operations of subsector 5.

Accounting Practices

1. Liquidation or complementary period:
    Not reported.
2. Valuation of assets and liabilities:
    Not reported.

GFSM 2001 Implementation Plan

Not reported.

This institutional table is based on information reported in 1998.

Cambodia 522

Units of General Government

Central Government

Subsector 1. Budgetary central government
1.1 Judiciary, ministries (30), monarchy, national assembly, and prime minister's office

Subsector 2. Extrabudgetary units/entities
2.1 Not applicable

Subsector 3. Social security funds
3.1 Not applicable

State Governments

Subsector 4. State governments
4.1 Not applicable

Local Governments

Subsector 5. Local governments
5.1 1,609 communes
5.2 185 districts
5.3 24 provinces
5.4 About 14,000 villages

Data Coverage

Data in central government tables cover operations of subsector 1, including foreign-financed expenditures conducted outside the Treasury.

Accounting Practices

1. Liquidation or complementary period:
    Not reported.

2. Valuation of assets and liabilities:
    Not applicable: no balance sheet data are reported.

GFSM 2001 Implementation Plan

Cambodia will gradually implement, over several years, the recommendations of the *GFSM 2001*. In the short to medium run, the Ministry of Economy and Finance will focus on improving current compilation procedures and on adopting the *GFSM 2001* analytical framework and classifications. Over the medium term, it is intended to expand the coverage to include local government units and to compile government financial balance sheet statements, including debt statistics. Accrual recording will be introduced gradually in line with the reform of public accounting systems.

This institutional table is based on information reported in 2005.

Cameroon 622

Units of General Government

Central Government

Subsector 1. Budgetary central government
1.1 Economic and social council, ministries, national assembly, and presidency

Subsector 2. Extrabudgetary units/entities
2.1 Agricultural institutions; Committee for Human Rights; cooperatives; government centers, councils, and offices; noncommercial projects; and schools and universities
2.2 Autonomous Amortization Fund
2.3 Maritime Fishing Development Fund
2.4 National Employment Fund
2.5 National Hydrocarbons Company of Cameroon

Subsector 3. Social security funds
3.1 National Social Security Fund

State Governments

Subsector 4. State governments
4.1 Not applicable

Local Governments

Subsector 5. Local governments
5.1 38 associations of communes
5.2 Center for Municipal Administrative Training
5.3 192 communes
5.4 Special Fund for Intercommunal Development and Assistance
5.5 Stock-raising funds

Data Coverage

Data in central government tables cover operations of subsectors 1–3.

Accounting Practices

1. Liquidation or complementary period:
    Not reported.
2. Valuation of assets and liabilities:
    Not reported.

GFSM 2001 Implementation Plan

Not reported.

This institutional table is based on information reported in or prior to 1996.

Canada 156

Units of General Government

Central Government

Subsector 1.   Budgetary central government
- 1.1   Departments, governor general's office, judiciary, ministries, parliament, and prime minister's office

Subsector 2.   Extrabudgetary units/entities
- 2.1   Agricultural Commodities Stabilization Account
- 2.2   Atlantic Pilotage Authority
- 2.3   Blue Water Bridge Authority
- 2.4   Canada Council
- 2.5   Canada Deposit Insurance Corporation
- 2.6   Canada Development Investment Corporation
- 2.7   Canada Foundation for Innovation
- 2.8   Canada Health Infoway Inc.
- 2.9   Canada Hibernia Holding Corporation
- 2.10 Canada Lands—Old Port of Montreal
- 2.11 Canada Millennium Scholarship Foundation
- 2.12 Canadian Air Transport Security Authority
- 2.13 Canadian Broadcasting Corporation
- 2.14 Canadian Commercial Bank and Northland Bank Holdback Account
- 2.15 Canadian Commercial Corporation
- 2.16 Canadian Dairy Commission
- 2.17 Canadian Film Development Corporation
- 2.18 Canadian Forces
- 2.19 Canadian Forces Death Benefit Account
- 2.20 Canadian Foundation for Climate and Atmospheric Sciences
- 2.21 Canadian Health Services Research Foundation
- 2.22 Canadian Institute for Health Information
- 2.23 Canadian Museum of Civilization
- 2.24 Canadian Museum of Nature
- 2.25 Canadian Policy Research Network Inc.
- 2.26 Canadian Race Relations Foundation
- 2.27 Canadian Television Fund—Licence Fee Program
- 2.28 Canadian Tourism Commission
- 2.29 Cape Breton Growth Fund Corporation
- 2.30 Crop Reinsurance Fund
- 2.31 Defense Construction (1951) Ltd.
- 2.32 Employment Insurance Account
- 2.33 Endowments for Health Research
- 2.34 Enterprise Cape Breton Corporation
- 2.35 Environmental Damages Fund
- 2.36 Environmental Studies Research Fund
- 2.37 Fines for the Transportation of Dangerous Goods
- 2.38 Flight Recorder Software Systems Account
- 2.39 Foundation for Sustainable Development Technology
- 2.40 Genome Canada
- 2.41 Great Lakes Pilotage Authority
- 2.42 Green Municipal Funds—Green Municipal Enabling Fund & Green Municipal Investment Fund
- 2.43 Health Insurance Supplementary Fund
- 2.44 International Development Research Center
- 2.45 Investors' Indemnity Account
- 2.46 Jacques Cartier and Champlain Bridges Inc.
- 2.47 Laurentian Pilotage Authority
- 2.48 Mackenzie King Trust Account
- 2.49 National Arts Center Corporation
- 2.50 National Battlefields Commission Trust Fund
- 2.51 National Capital Commission
- 2.52 National Gallery of Canada
- 2.53 National Museum of Science and Technology
- 2.54 New Parks and Historic Sites Accounts
- 2.55 Nonautonomus Superannuation and Retirement Funds for Public Service Employees
- 2.56 Nuclear Liability Reinsurance Account
- 2.57 Pacific Pilotage Authority
- 2.58 Pierre Elliot Trudeau Foundation
- 2.59 Public Service Death Benefit Account
- 2.60 Queen's Fellowship Fund
- 2.61 Queen's Quay West Land Corp.
- 2.62 Royal Canadian Mounted Police
- 2.63 Seized Property Proceeds Account
- 2.64 Ship-Source Oil Pollution Fund
- 2.65 Standards Council
- 2.66 Supplementary Fines Fish Account
- 2.67 Western Grain Stabilization Account

Subsector 3.   Social security funds
- 3.1   Canada Pension Plan
- 3.2   Quebec Pension Plan

State Governments

Subsector 4.   State governments
- 4.1   10 provincial and 3 territorial governments, related agencies, boards, and commissions
- 4.2   Health and social services institutions, colleges, and universities
- 4.3   Nonautonomous superannuation and retirement funds for public service employees

Local Governments

Subsector 5.   Local governments
- 5.1   Municipal governments; agency boards, commissions, and local school boards

Data Coverage

Data in the central government tables cover the operations of subsectors 1–3.

Data in the state government tables cover the operations of subsector 4.

Data in the local government tables cover the operations of subsector 5 and are based on information from a sample of local governments.

Accounting Practices

1.   Liquidation or complementary period:
     None for revenue; 30 days for expenditure.
2.   Valuation of assets and liabilities:
     Not reported.

GFSM 2001 Implementation Plan

Not reported.

This institutional table is based on information reported in 2003.

Chile 228

Units of General Government

Central Government

Subsector 1.   Budgetary central government
- 1.1   Comptroller general's office, judiciary, legislature, ministries, presidency, and approximately 100 government institutions

Subsector 2.   Extrabudgetary units/entities
- 2.1   Oil Price Stabilization Fund, Law No 13.196 (Reserved

Law), Funds in Administration by Central Bank, and Accrued Interest on Recognition Bonds

Subsector 3.   Social security funds
3.1   Directorate of Social Security for Chilean Police
3.2   National Fund for Welfare Pensions
3.3   Social Security Fund for Those Employed in National Defense
3.4   Social Security Standardization Institute

State Governments

Subsector 4.   State governments
4.1   Not applicable

Local Governments

Subsector 5.   Local governments
5.1   341 municipalities

Data Coverage

Data in central government tables cover operations of subsectors 1–3. Data for subsector 3 are included in budgetary central government.

Data in local government tables cover operations of subsector 5.

The data for budgetary central government and extrabudgetary units are reported after consolidation.

Accounting Practices

1.   Liquidation or complementary period:
     None.
2.   Valuation of assets and liabilities:
     Not reported.

GFSM 2001 Implementation Plan

Classify adjusted cash data in *GFSM 2001* format and collect data for extrabudgetary operations in 2004.

Compile balance sheet for financial assets and liabilities in 2005. Collect data on accrual basis and compile balance sheet in 2006. This institutional table is based on information reported in 2005.

China People's Republic: Mainland   924

Units of General Government

Central Government

Subsector 1.   Budgetary central government
1.1   Departments and institutions under the CPC Central Committee; General Office of the National People's Congress; General Office of the National People's Political Consultative Conference; State Council (administrations and bureaus [10] under the ministries and commissions, general office, institutions [14], ministries and commissions [28], organizations [20], and working organs [4]); State-Owned Assets Supervision and Administration Commission; State-owned enterprises subject to the central government; the Supreme People's Court; and the Supreme People's Procuratorate

Subsector 2.   Extrabudgetary units/entities
2.1   Extrabudgetary operations of central government ministries and local governments
2.2   Government units with individual budgets

Subsector 3.   Social security funds
3.1   Insurance for Work-Related Injuries Plan
3.2   Maternity Insurance Plan
3.3   Medical Insurance Plan
3.4   National Social Security Fund

3.5   Old Age Insurance Plan
3.6   Unemployment Insurance Plan

State Governments

Subsector 4.   State governments
4.1   Not applicable

Local Governments

Subsector 5.   Local governments
5.1   656 cities; 2,487 counties; 44,067 townships; and 678,589 villages
5.2   31 provinces (excluding Taiwan, Hong Kong, and Macao and including Beijing, Shanghai, Chongqing, and Tianjin)
5.3   333 subprovincial administrative regions

Data Coverage

Data in central government tables cover operations of subsector 1, part of subsector 2, and unit 3.6.

Data in local government tables cover operations of subsector 5, part of subsector 2, and units 3.1–3.5.

† Data from 1994 onward include tax revenue.

† Data from 1999 onward include social security.

† Data from 2002 onward include extrabudgetary fund transactions.

Accounting Practices

1.   Liquidation or complementary period:
     None.
2.   Valuation of assets and liabilities:
     Not reported.

GFSM 2001 Implementation Plan

Not reported.

This institutional table is based on information reported in 2005.

China, People's Republic: Hong Kong   532

Units of General Government

1.   Government bureaus and departments, judiciary, and legislature
2.   Funds under the Public Finance Ordinance
3.   Other funds established by the government for specific purposes, with their funding mainly from the government, and the government responsible for their use
4.   The Hong Kong Housing Authority

Data Coverage

Because of the special administrative arrangements that are applied to Hong Kong SAR, there are no data in central, state, or local government tables. Data in general government tables cover operations of units 1–4.

Accounting Practices

1.   Liquidation or complementary period:
     Not applicable.
2.   Valuation of assets and liabilities:
     Reported fixed assets, which belong to the Hong Kong Housing Authority, are stated at cost less accumulated depreciation (except capital works/projects in progress, which are stated at cost). Inventories are stated at the lower of cost and net realizable value. Investments are mainly valued at fair value. Pension liabilities were assessed by an independent qualified actuary using the Projected Unit Credit Method. Contract gratuities and

leave are accrued, while other employee benefits such as housing, medical, and education are recognized when they are paid. For the government, no accrual is made for accounts receivable and accounts payable (except for the employee benefits indicated).

GFSM 2001 Implementation Plan

Starting from the fiscal year 2002–03, the government of Hong Kong SAR has prepared a set of consolidated accounts on an accrual basis, in addition to the cash-based accounts. This set of accrual-based accounts reflects the first phase of the implementation of the accrual accounts for the government. The set has yet to include reporting of fixed assets and the corresponding depreciation, which will only start with the accounts for the financial year 2004–05. Reported fixed assets and depreciation relate to those owned by the Hong Kong Housing Authority only. The GFS data are prepared based on this set of accrual-based consolidated accounts, but are adjusted, where necessary, to conform with the scope, definition, and guidelines laid down in the *GFSM 2001*.

This institutional table is based on information reported in 2005.

China, People's Republic: Macao   546

Units of General Government

Central Government

Subsector 1.   Budgetary central government
 1.1   Courts, executive council, legislative assembly, 5 general secretariats, ministries, office of the chief executive, and several nonautonomous services

Subsector 2.   Extrabudgetary units/entities
 2.1   33 autonomous services and funds

Subsector 3.   Social security funds
 3.1   Social Security Fund

State Governments

Subsector 4.   State governments
 4.1   Not applicable

Local Governments

Subsector 5.   Local governments
 5.1   Not applicable

Data Coverage

Data in central government tables cover operations of subsectors 1–3.

Accounting Practices

1.   Liquidation or complementary period:
     None.
2.   Valuation of assets and liabilities:
     Not reported.

GFSM 2001 Implementation Plan

Not reported.

This institutional table is based on information reported in 2005.

Colombia   233

Units of General Government

Central Government

Subsector 1.   Budgetary central government
 1.1   Administrative Department of Security, congress, general

comptroller, general prosecutor, judiciary, ministries, national administrative departments (3), national police, national registry, presidency, special administrative units, and superintendences (3)

Subsector 2.   Extrabudgetary units/entities
 2.1   Public agencies (130)
 2.2   Public funds (21)
 2.3   Public universities

Subsector 3.   Social security funds
 3.1   Fund of Health Warranties and Solidarities
 3.2   Fund of Social Solidarity
 3.3   Institute of Social Insurances
 3.4   Military Force Retirement Fund
 3.5   National Fund of Social Assistance of Teachers
 3.6   National Police Retirement Fund
 3.7   National Social Security Fund
 3.8   National Social Security Fund of Banking Superintendence
 3.9   National Social Security Fund of Communications
 3.10 Public Retirement Fund
 3.11 Retirement Fund of National Railroad
 3.12 Retirement Fund of Petroleum Company
 3.13 Retirement Fund of Telephone Company
 3.14 Social Security Fund of Congress
 3.15 Other funds

State Governments

Subsector 4.   State governments
 4.1   32 state governments
 4.2   805 state government agencies
 4.3   32 social security funds of state governments

Local Governments

Subsector 5.   Local governments
 5.1   60 agencies of the municipality of Bogotá
 5.2   1,099 municipalities (including the municipality of Bogotá)
 5.3   162 municipal agencies
 5.4   33 social security funds of municipalities (including some social security funds of public universities)

Data Coverage

Data in central government tables cover operations of subsectors 1–3.

Data in state government tables cover operations of subsector 4.

Data in local government tables cover operations of subsector 5.

The data for 2001, 2002, and 2003 are based on a sample of 258 entities (153 from the central government, 46 from the state governments, and 59 from the local governments). Data for 2004 are based on a sample of 242 entities (123 from the central government, 56 from the state governments, and 63 from the local governments).

† Starting in 1998, data for subsectors of central government are presented on gross basis (i.e., before consolidation). From 2001 onwards, data are reported on an accrual basis.

Accounting Practices

1.   Liquidation or complementary period:
     None.
2.   Valuation of assets and liabilities:
     For nonfinancial assets, the valuation is based on the historical costs, and for financial assets and liabilities, the valuation is based on current market prices.

GFSM 2001 Implementation Plan

The authorities of the accounting entity use a chart of accounts based on the classifications and definitions of *GFSM 2001*.

This institutional table is based on information reported in 2005.

Congo, Democratic Republic of   636

Units of General Government

Central Government

Subsector 1.   Budgetary central government
  1.1   Auxiliary units, departments, national legislative council, and presidency

Subsector 2.   Extrabudgetary units/entities
  2.1   Not reported

Subsector 3.   Social security funds
  3.1   National Social Security Institute

State Governments

Subsector 4.   State governments
  4.1   Not applicable

Local Governments

Subsector 5.   Local governments
  5.1   9 regions, 27 subregions, and 15 towns

Data Coverage

Data in central government tables cover operations of subsector 1 and include foreign-financed operations not recorded in the budget.

† Data prior to 1994 include social security operations.

Accounting Practices

1.   Liquidation or complementary period:
     None.
2.   Valuation of assets and liabilities:
     Not reported.

GFSM 2001 Implementation Plan

Not reported.

This institutional table is based on information reported in 2001.

Congo, Republic of   634

Units of General Government

Central Government

Subsector 1.   Budgetary central government
  1.1   Congolese Information Agency
  1.2   Congolese radio and Congolese television
  1.3   Judiciary, legislature, 35 ministries, and presidency
  1.4   La Nouvelle République (daily newspaper)

Subsector 2.   Extrabudgetary units/entities
  2.1   Agence Nationale de l'Aviation Civile (National Civil Aviation Agency); Bureau Congolais des Droits d'Auteurs; Bureau de Contrôle des Batiments et Travaux Publics (construction and public works); Bureau d'Etudes en Batiments et Travaux Publics (construction and public works); Caisse Congolaise d'Ammortissement (Congolese Amortization Fund); Caisse de Stabilisation des Prix des Produits Agricoles et Forestiers (Agricultural and Forest Products Price Stabilization Fund); Centre Congolais du Commerce Extérieur (Congolese Foreign Trade Center); Centre de Formalités des Entreprises; Centre Hospitalier Universitaire de Brazzaville (University Hospital Center of Brazzaville); Centre National de Gestion (National Management Center); Centre National de Transfusion Sanguine; Chambre de Commerce; Commissariat National aux Comptes (National Commission for Accounts);

Direction Générale de la Marine Marchande; Fonds Routier; Laboratoire National de Santé Publique (National Public Health Laboratory); Office Congolais d'Informatique (daily processing); Office National de l'Emploi et de la main d'Œuvre (National Office of Employment); Palais du Parlement; Pompes funèbres de Brazzaville (funeral services); Service National de Reboisement (National Reforestation Service); Stade Massamba Débat de Brazzaville (Massamba Débat Stadium); Université Marien N'Gouabi de Brazzaville (University of Brazzaville)

Subsector 3.   Social security funds
  3.1   National Social Security Fund
  3.2   Civil Service Pension Fund

State Governments

Subsector 4.   State governments
  4.1   Not applicable

Local Governments

Subsector 5.   Local governments
  5.1   Brazzaville and 5 other municipalities
  5.2   11 departments

Data Coverage

Data in central government tables cover operations of subsectors 1–3. Data on local governments do not cover the Pool region.

Accounting Practices

1.   Liquidation or complementary period:
     One month after the end of the fiscal year
     for expenditures.
2.   Valuation of assets and liabilities:
     Not reported.

GFSM 2001 Implementation Plan

Not reported.

This institutional table is based on information reported in 2005.

Costa Rica   238

Units of General Government

Central Government

Subsector 1.   Budgetary central government
  1.1   Comptroller general's office, Defense Office for the Inhabitants, electoral court, judiciary, legislative assembly, 18 ministries, presidency, public debt service, special pension regimes, and specific works

Subsector 2.   Extrabudgetary units/entities
  2.1   58 assigned entities and 31 public service agencies

Subsector 3.   Social security funds
  3.1   Costa Rican Social Security Agency

State Governments

Subsector 4.   State governments
  4.1   Not applicable

Local Governments

Subsector 5.   Local governments
  5.1   81 municipalities

Data Coverage

Data in central government tables cover operations of subsectors 1–3.

Data in local government tables cover operations of subsector 5.

† From 1991 onward, tax revenue data are not adjusted to deduct payments made with tax credit certificates.

Accounting Practices

1. Liquidation or complementary period:
   None.
2. Valuation of assets and liabilities:
   Not reported.

GFSM 2001 Implementation Plan

A commission comprised of staff from the accounting and compilation offices has been created to prepare a migration plan and to implement the *GFSM 2001*.

This institutional table is based on information reported in 2004.

Côte d'Ivoire   662

Units of General Government

Central Government

Subsector 1.   Budgetary central government
  1.1   Constitutional council, economic and social council, ministries, national assembly, presidency, prime minister services, supreme court, and various agencies

Subsector 2.   Extrabudgetary units/entities
  2.1   General Pension fund for Civil Servants
  2.2   Autonomous agencies

Subsector 3.   Social security funds
  3.1   National Social Security Fund

State Governments

Subsector 4.   State governments
  4.1   Not applicable

Local Governments

Subsector 5.   Local governments
  5.1   225 municipalities

Data Coverage

Data in central government tables cover subsectors 1–3.

Accounting Practices

1. Liquidation or complementary period:
   Not reported.
2. Valuation of assets and liabilities:
   Not reported.

GFSM 2001 Implementation Plan

Not reported.

This institutional table is based on information reported in 2002.

Croatia   960

Units of General Government

Central Government

Subsector 1.   Budgetary central government
  1.1   Agencies, funds, institutes, judiciary, ministries, parliament, and presidency

Subsector 2.   Extrabudgetary units/entities
  2.1   Croatian Motorways Ltd.
  2.2   Croatian Privatization Fund
  2.3   Croatian Roads Ltd.
  2.4   Croatian Waters
  2.5   Development and Employment Fund
  2.6   Environment Protection Fund
  2.7   Regional Development
  2.8   State Agency for Deposit Insurance and Bank Rehabilitation

Subsector 3.   Social security funds
  3.1   Croatian Employment Service
  3.2   Croatian Health Insurance Institute
  3.3   Croatian Institute for Pension Insurance

State Governments

Subsector 4.   State governments
  4.1   Not applicable

Local Governments

Subsector 5.   Local governments
  5.1   20 counties, City of Zagreb, 123 towns, and 426 municipalities

Data Coverage

Data in central government tables cover subsectors 1–3. Units 2.5 and 2.7 existed as extrabudgetary units only in 2002. In later years, they have been part of budgetary central government. Unit 2.6 started operating in 2004.

Data in local government tables cover the operations of 20 counties, City of Zagreb, and 32 towns, representing between 70 and 80 percent of the total operations in this subsector.

† Starting in 2002, data for subsectors of central government are presented on gross basis (i.e., before consolidation).

Accounting Practices

1. Liquidation or complementary period:
   Not applicable.
2. Valuation of assets and liabilities:
   Not reported.

GFSM 2001 Implementation Plan

Reporting in the *GFSM 2001* format started in 2004. There is an intention to compile data for local governments with complete coverage in the near future.

This institutional table is based on information reported in 2005.

Cyprus   423

Units of General Government

Central Government

Subsector 1.   Budgetary central government
  1.1   Agencies, council of ministries, house of representatives, judiciary, ministries, and presidency

Subsector 2.   Extrabudgetary units/entities
  2.1   Grain Commission
  2.2   National Defense Fund
  2.3   Public Loans funds
  2.4   Sinking funds
  2.5   Special Relief Fund

Subsector 3.   Social security funds
  3.1   Central Holiday Fund
  3.2   Redundancy Fund
  3.3   Social Insurance Fund
  3.4   Social security schemes
  3.5   Unemployment Benefits Fund

State Governments

Subsector 4.   State governments
   4.1   Not applicable

Local Governments

Subsector 5.   Local governments
   5.1   Municipalities
   5.2   Other local governments, including improvement boards

Data Coverage

Data in central government tables cover operations of subsectors 1–3.

Accounting Practices

1.   Liquidation or complementary period:
     Not reported.
2.   Valuation of assets and liabilities:
     Not reported.

GFSM 2001 Implementation Plan

Not reported.

This institutional table is based on information reported in 1999.

Czech Republic   935

Units of General Government

Central Government

Subsector 1.   Budgetary central government
   1.1   State budget (41 chapters)
   1.2   National Fund

Subsector 2.   Extrabudgetary units/entities
   2.1   Czech Land Fund
   2.2   National Property Fund
   2.3   State Environmental Fund
   2.4   State Fund for Agricultural Intervention
   2.5   State Fund for Culture
   2.6   State Fund for Czech Cinematography
   2.7   State Fund for Soil Fertilization
   2.8   State Fund of Transportation Infrastructure
   2.9   State Housing Development Fund

Subsector 3.   Social security funds
   3.1   Public health insurance organizations (9 units)

State Governments

Subsector 4.   State governments
   4.1   Not applicable

Local Governments

Subsector 5.   Local governments
   5.1   Municipalities (ca 6,300 units)
   5.2   Regions (14 units)

Data Coverage

Data in central government tables cover operations of subsectors 1–3.

Data in local government tables cover operations of subsector 5.

Accounting Practices

1.   Liquidation or complementary period:
     None.
2.   Valuation of assets and liabilities:
     Loans and bonds are valued at face value.

GFSM 2001 Implementation Plan

On an experimental basis, the compilation of accrual fiscal data for some segments of general government has started gradually, and bridge tables between financial statements of various government units and *GFSM 2001* have been created. The new general government coverage has been introduced in line with *GFSM 2001* and *ESA95*.

This institutional table is based on information reported in 2005.

Denmark   128

Units of General Government

Central Government

Subsector 1.   Budgetary central government
   1.1   Judiciary, legislature, ministries, and monarchy

Subsector 2.   Extrabudgetary units/entities
   2.1   Government agencies
   2.2   State church

Subsector 3.   Social security funds
   3.1   Social security funds

State Governments

Subsector 4.   State governments
   4.1   Not applicable

Local Governments

Subsector 5.   Local governments
   5.1   City of Copenhagen
   5.2   14 counties
   5.3   County agencies
   5.4   275 municipalities
   5.5   Municipal agencies

Data Coverage

Data for budgetary central government also cover extrabudgetary units and entities.

Data in central government tables cover operations of subsectors 1–3.

Data in local government tables cover operations of subsector 5.

In line with the presentation adopted within the European Union, data on domestic financial assets and liabilities include foreign financial assets and liabilities.

† Starting with 1991, data are compiled in accordance with the *ESA 1995.*

Accounting Practices

1.   Liquidation or complementary period:
     Not reported.
2.   Valuation of assets and liabilities:
     Not reported.

GFSM 2001 Implementation Plan

Not reported.

This institutional table is based on information reported in 2000.

Dominican Republic   243

Units of General Government

Central Government

Subsector 1.   Budgetary central government
   1.1   Central electoral board, chamber of accounts,

congress, general procurement office, judiciary, presidency, and 17 secretariats

Subsector 2.   Extrabudgetary units/entities
  2.1   Autonomous University of Santo Domingo, Civil Protection Office, commissions (2), councils (3), Dominican Center for Exports Promotion, Dominican Red Cross, Museum of Natural History, National Aquarium, National Botanical Garden, National Office of Industrial Property, National Zoo, public institutes (10), superintendencies (6), and other entities (3)

Subsector 3.   Social security funds
  3.1   Dominican Social Security Institute
  3.2   Institute of Assistance and Housing
  3.3   Social Security Institute of Military
  3.4   Social Security Institute of Police

State Governments

Subsector 4.   State governments
  4.1   Not applicable

Local Governments

Subsector 5.   Local governments
  5.1   Dominican Municipal League
  5.2   148 municipalities

Data Coverage

Data in central government tables cover operations of subsectors 1–3.

Data in local government tables cover operations of subsector 5.

† Through 2002, the subsectors of central government are presented on a net basis (i.e., after consolidation).

Accounting Practices

1.   Liquidation or complementary period:
     Not reported.
2.   Valuation of assets and liabilities:
     Not reported.

GFSM 2001 Implementation Plan

Not reported.

This institutional table is based on information reported in 2005.

Egypt   469

Units of General Government

Central Government

Subsector 1.   Budgetary central government
  1.1   Cabinet, 14 central agencies and authorities, 27 local authorities, ministries, office of the attorney general, parliament, presidency, and 90 public service authorities

Subsector 2.   Extrabudgetary units/entities
  2.1   General Authority for Supply of Commodities (GASC)
  2.2   National Investment Bank

Subsector 3.   Social security funds
  3.1   Social Development Fund

State Governments

Subsector 4.   State governments
  4.1   Not applicable

Local Governments

Subsector 5.   Local governments
  5.1   Not applicable

Data Coverage

Data in central government tables cover operations of subsectors 1–3.

† Prior to 1996, data in the central government tables include the operations of the Public Authority for Insurance and Pensions (pensions for government employees) and the Public Authority for Social Insurance (pensions for public enterprise employees), which were incorrectly included as social security funds, and exclude the operations of GASC.

Accounting Practices

1.   Liquidation or complementary period:
     None.
2.   Valuation of assets and liabilities:
     Not reported.

GFSM 2001 Implementation Plan

Not reported.

This institutional table is based on information reported in 2003.

El Salvador   253

Units of General Government

Central Government

Subsector 1.   Budgetary central government
  1.1   Civil service court, court of accounts, electoral supreme court, general prosecutor's office, judiciary, judiciary national council, legislative assembly, ministries (12), presidency, procurator for the defense of human rights office, procurator general's office, and public treasury.

Subsector 2.   Extrabudgetary units/entities
  2.1   9 funds, 30 national hospitals, 9 public institutes, 1 public university, 3 superintendences, and 22 other public units

Subsector 3.   Social security funds
  3.1   Institute of Social Security for Defense
  3.2   National Institute of Civil Servant pensions
  3.3   Salvadoran Social Security Institute

State Governments

Subsector 4.   State governments
  4.1   Not applicable

Local Governments

Subsector 5.   Local governments
  5.1   262 local governments, of which 134 with detailed financial information

Data Coverage

Data in central government tables cover operations of subsectors 1–3.

Data in local government tables cover operations of subsector 5.

† Starting in 2002, data are on an accrual basis. Data through 2001 are on a cash basis.

† Through 2000, millions of colones and, starting in 2001, millions of dollars.

Accounting Practices

1.   Liquidation or complementary period:
     Liquidation: calendar year
2.   Valuation of assets and liabilities:
     Fixed assets at historical cost, financial assets at market prices, and loans and bonds at face value.

GFSM 2001 Implementation Plan

The Ministry of Finance (MoF) has developed an action plan to fully implement the *GFSM 2001* analytical framework for compiling fiscal data. During the next two years, the MoF will update the accounting legislation according to the *GFSM 2001* and international accounting standards. Also, additional changes in the current legislation will allow the MoF to collect data on a timely basis and with a more complete coverage, especially for local government data.

This institutional table is based on information reported in 2005.

Estonia   939

Units of General Government

Central Government

Subsector 1.   Budgetary central government
1.1   Chancellor of justice, counties, ministries, parliament, president's office, state audit office, state chancery, and supreme court

Subsector 2.   Extrabudgetary units/entities
2.1   Center of Environmental Investments Foundation
2.2   Enterprise Estonia Foundation
2.3   Estonian Disabled People Foundation
2.4   Estonian Migration Foundation
2.5   Estonian Movie Foundation
2.6   Estonian Science Foundation
2.7   Estonian Sea Education Center Foundation
2.8   Jõgevamaa County Entrepreneurship Foundation
2.9   Jõulumäe Recreation Center Foundation
2.10 Kääriku-Tehvandi Olympic Center Foundation
2.11 Medical Insurance Fund
2.12 Old Town Theater Foundation
2.13 Raplamaa County Entrepreneurship Foundation
2.14 Tartu Business Counseling Foundation
2.15 Tartumaa Recreation Center Foundation
2.16 Tiger Leap Foundation (IT development)
2.17 Viljandimaa County Entrepreneurship Foundation
2.18 Võrumaa County Entrepreneurship Foundation

Subsector 3.   Social security funds
3.1   Social Insurance Fund

State Governments

Subsector 4.   State governments
4.1   Not applicable

Local Governments

Subsector 5.   Local governments
5.1   245 local governments

Data Coverage

Data in central government tables cover operations of subsectors 1–3.

Data in local government tables cover operations of subsector 5.

Through 1993 and from 1996 onward, fiscal years ended December 31 for all local government units; fiscal years 1994 and 1995 ended March 31 for local government.

From 1992 onward, data on local governments include data on local government communes.

Accounting Practices

1.   Liquidation or complementary period:
     Not reported.

2.   Valuation of assets and liabilities:
     Not reported.

GFSM 2001 Implementation Plan

Not reported.

This institutional table is based on information reported in 2002.

Ethiopia   644

Units of General Government

Central Government

Subsector 1.   Budgetary central government
1.1   Authorities (16), commissions (11), federal supreme court, house of the people's representative and other executive bodies, institutes (6), ministries (18), office of the president, other entities (29), and universities (6)

Subsector 2.   Extrabudgetary units/entities
2.1   Fuel Administration Fund
2.2   Industrial Development Fund and Privatization
2.3   National Disaster Prevention and Preparedness Fund Administration
2.4   Road Fund Administration Office

Subsector 3.   Social security funds
3.1   Not reported.

State Governments

Subsector 4.   State governments
4.1   9 regional governments and 2 administrative councils

Local Governments

Subsector 5.   Local governments
5.1   550 woredas (districts)

Data Coverage

Data in central government tables cover operations of subsector 1.

Data are provided for subsectors 2 and 3 from 2002 only.

No data are provided for subsector 5.

Accounting Practices

1.   Liquidation or complementary period:
     None.

2.   Valuation of assets and liabilities:
     Not reported.

GFSM 2001 Implementation Plan

Not reported.

This institutional table is based on information reported in 2005.

Fiji   819

Units of General Government

Central Government

Subsector 1.   Budgetary central government
1.1   Departments, judiciary, ministries, parliament, president's office, prime minister's office

Subsector 2.   Extrabudgetary units/entities
2.1   Air Transport Licensing Board
2.2   Board of Fire Commissioners

2.3   Central Board of Health
2.4   Central Liquor Board
2.5   Central Traffic Authority
2.6   Coconut Board
2.7   Consumer Council of Fiji
2.8   Drainage Board
2.9   Fiji Arts Council
2.10 Fiji Dental Council
2.11 Fiji Marine Board
2.12 Fiji Meat Industry Board
2.13 Fiji Medical Council
2.14 Fiji Mining Board
2.15 Fiji Museum
2.16 Fiji National Training Council
2.17 Fiji Optometrists Board
2.18 Fiji Sports Council
2.19 Fiji Trade and Investment Board
2.20 Fiji Visitors' Bureau
2.21 Fijian Affairs Board
2.22 Fijian Development Fund Board
2.23 Film Control Board
2.24 Forestry Board
2.25 Hotels and Licensing Board
2.26 Labor and Advisory Board
2.27 Land Conservation Board
2.28 National Trust of Fiji
2.29 Native Land Trust Board
2.30 Pharmacy and Poisons Board
2.31 Prices and Incomes Board
2.32 PWD Water and Sewerage Section
2.33 Sugar Cane Growers' Fund Authority
2.34 Surveyors and Registration Board
2.35 Transport Control Board
2.36 Valuers Registration Board

Subsector 3.   Social security funds
3.1   Not applicable

State governments

Subsector 4.   State governments
4.1   Not applicable

Local Governments

Subsector 5.   Local governments
5.1   14 provincial councils, 2 city councils, 9 town councils, and 5 local authorities in rural areas

Data Coverage

Data in central government tables cover operations of subsector 1.

† Prior to 1993 in Table 7, data on public order and safety were included in the line on general public services.

Accounting Practices

1.   Liquidation or complementary period:
     Not reported.
2.   Valuation of assets and liabilities:
     Not reported.

GFSM 2001 Implementation Plan

Not reported.

This institutional table is based on information reported in 1997.

Units of General Government

Central Government

Subsector 1.   Budgetary central government
1.1   Central government agencies, central government regional and public authorities, institutions and other bodies, judiciary, ministries, parliament, and presidency

Subsector 2.   Extrabudgetary units/entities
2.1   Central Government Pension Fund
2.2   Fire Protection Fund
2.3   Fund for Compensation of Oil Damages
2.4   Fund for Development of Farm Economy
2.5   Fund for Security of Supply
2.6   Government Guarantee Fund
2.7   Housing Fund
2.8   Intervention Fund for Agriculture
2.9   Nuclear Waste Fund
2.10 State Guarantee Fund
2.11 State Television and Radio Fund

Subsector 3.   Social security funds
3.1   Burial and redundancy assistance funds
3.2   Education Fund
3.3   Employment pension funds
3.4   Sickness funds
3.5   Social Insurance Institution
3.6   Unemployment benefit funds (about 65)
3.7   Unemployment Insurance Fund

State Governments

Subsector 4.   State governments
4.1   Not applicable

Local Governments

Subsector 5.   Local governments
5.1   444 municipalities
5.2   237 joint municipal boards established by municipalities

Data Coverage

Data for budgetary central government also cover extrabudgetary units and entities.

Data in central government tables cover operations of subsectors 1–3.

Data in local government tables cover operations of subsector 5.

† Break symbols in Table 7 for health and social protection indicate that, from 1991 onward, data for social protection include partial data for health.

† Break symbols in Table 3 indicate that beginning in 1991 a separation between long- and short-term bonds cannot be made for domestic financing or financing abroad.

Accounting Practices

1.   Liquidation or complementary period:
     Not reported.
2.   Valuation of assets and liabilities:
     Not reported.

GFSM 2001 Implementation Plan

Starting in 2001, data are reported on an accrual basis, in accordance with the requirements of the European Commission Council Regulation No. 2223/96.

This institutional table is based on information reported in 2005.

France   132

Units of General Government

Central Government

Subsector 1.
  1.1 Budget agencies, judiciary, ministries, parliament, presidency, and prime minister

Subsector 2. Extrabudgetary units/entities
  2.1 About 800 government agencies involved in agriculture, cultural activities, health and social welfare, housing, and other economic and general services, and universities

Subsector 3. Social security funds
  3.1 One main general social security scheme (Illness, Old Age, Family Benefits, Worker's Compensation) and numerous other schemes, assorted organizations dependent on social insurance, and government hospitals
  3.2 Unemployment compensation schemes

State Governments

Subsector 4. State governments
  4.1 Not applicable

Local Governments

Subsector 5. Local governments
  5.1 36,000 (approximately) communes
  5.2 96 departments
  5.3 Local government agencies (including primary and secondary schools)
  5.4 22 regions

Data Coverage

Data in central government tables cover operations of subsectors 1–3. Data for budgetary central government also cover extrabudgetary central government units and entities.

Data in local government tables cover operations of subsector 5 and are based on information from all local governments.

Accounting Practices
  1. Liquidation or complementary period:
      One month after the end of the fiscal year for expenditures.
  2. Valuation of assets and liabilities:
      Assets and liabilities are valued at market prices.

GFSM 2001 Implementation Plan

Not reported.

This institutional table is based on information reported in 2005.

Georgia   915

Units of General Government

Central Government

Subsector 1. Budgetary central government
  1.1 Constitutional court, control chamber, judicial agencies, ministries, parliament, presidential office, office of prime minister, presidential offices in regions, state departments, and several scientific academies and inspectorates

Subsector 2. Extrabudgetary units/entities
  2.1 Road Fund

Subsector 3. Social security funds
  3.1 United Fund of Social Protection and Health Care

State Governments

Subsector 4. State governments
  4.1 Not applicable

Local Governments

Subsector 5. Local governments
  5.1 2 autonomous republics
  5.2 59 administrative districts, towns, and cities

Data Coverage

Data on the central government cover operations of subsectors 1–3.

Data on local government cover operations of component 5.2 and part of component 5.1, which covers only the budget of the Adjaria Autonomous Republic and does not cover the budget of the Abkhazia Autonomous Republic.

† As of 2003, data are consolidated and are more closely classified in accordance with *GFSM 2001*.

Accounting Practices

  1. Liquidation or complementary period:
      Transaction data cover only the accounting period. "Late transactions" are not included in the accounting period. Data corrections are made within 3 months after accounting period. Fiscal year matches the calendar year.
  2. Valuation of assets and liabilities:
      Liabilities are valued at nominal value.

GFSM 2001 Implementation Plan

The plan is to more closely align national classifications with *GFSM 2001* classifications in 2004 and implement them in 2005. There are no plans to move to accrual accounting.

This institutional table is based on information reported in 2004.

Germany   134

Units of General Government

Central Government

Subsector 1. Budgetary central government
  1.1 Chancellorship, judiciary, legislature (Bundesrat–Federal Council of Länder; and Bundestag–federal parliament), ministries, presidency, and special funds

Subsector 2. Extrabudgetary units/entities
  2.1 Credit Repayment Fund
  2.2 Equalization of Burdens Fund
  2.3 European Recovery Program Special Fund
  2.4 Federal Railroad Fund
  2.5 German Unity Fund
  2.6 Indemnity and Equilization Fund to Ensure Hard Coal Usage
  2.7 Redemption Fund for Inherited Liabilities
  2.8 Special Fund for Disabled Persons
  2.9 Special Fund for Flood Damages

Subsector 3. Social security funds
  3.1 Accident Insurance
  3.2 Federal Institute of Labor
  3.3 Health Insurance
  3.4 Miners' Pension Fund
  3.5 Old Age Assistance to Farmers
  3.6 Old Age Care Insurance
  3.7 Pension Fund for Manual and Nonmanual Workers
  3.8 Supplementary Public Pension Insurance (until 1994)

State Governments

Subsector 4.   State governments
   4.1 16 Länder

Local Governments

Subsector 5.   Local governments
   5.1 Municipal special-purpose associations and nonprofit organizations
   5.2 15,000 (approximately) municipalities and municipal associations

Data Coverage

Data in central government tables cover operations of subsectors 1–3.

Data in state government tables cover operations of subsector 4.

Data in local government tables cover operations of subsector 5.

Data for subsectors 4 and 5 cover all Länder, city states, and local governments.

† From 1995 onward, the data are in line with the European system of national accounts (*1995 ESA*).

† From 1992 onward, data refer to government operations within the territory of unified Germany; through 1991, data cover government operations within the territory of the former Federal Republic of Germany.

† From 1990 onward, central government extrabudgetary operations include the operations of the German Unity Fund.

Accounting Practices

1. Liquidation or complementary period:
From 1995 onward, time adjustments are made for taxes, social contributions, interest, and construction. Balance of payments data are used to obtain information about debt cancellation and debt assumption.
2. Valuation of assets and liabilities:
Not reported.

GFSM 2001 Implementation Plan

From 1995 onward, data in accordance with *1995 ESA* methodology were reported for publication in the *GFS Yearbook*. Data for 1970 through 1990 are available for the former Federal Republic of Germany, and from 1991, for united Germany. Cash data for compilation of *GFSM 2001* Statement II are not available.

This institutional table is based on information reported in 2005.

Ghana   652

Units of General Government

Central Government

Subsector 1.   Budgetary central government
   1.1 Boards, councils, ministries and related agencies and departments, and regional organizations

Subsector 2.   Extrabudgetary units/entities
   2.1 Ghana Broadcasting Corporation
   2.2 Ghana Export Promotion Council
   2.3 Grains and Legumes Development Board
   2.4 National Trust Fund
   2.5 Other "subvented" organizations
   2.6 Public universities

Subsector 3.   Social security funds
   3.1 Not applicable

State Governments

Subsector 4.   State governments
   4.1 Not applicable

Local Governments

Subsector 5.   Local governments
   5.1 138 district councils; 273 municipal councils, urban councils, area councils, and local councils; and numerous town and village committees

Data Coverage

Data in central government tables cover operations of subsector 1.

Accounting Practices

1. Liquidation or complementary period:
Not reported.
2. Valuation of assets and liabilities:
Not reported.

GFSM 2001 Implementation Plan

Not reported.

This institutional table is based on information reported in 2005.

Greece   174

Units of General Government

Central Government

Subsector 1.   Budgetary central government
   1.1 Judiciary, ministries, parliament, prefectures, and presidency

Subsector 2.   Extrabudgetary units/entities
   2.1 Air Defense Fund
   2.2 Apostoliki Diakonia of the Church of Greece
   2.3 Autonomous Workers' Housing Organization
   2.4 Center of Visual Teaching Aids
   2.5 Central funds for agriculture, livestock, and forests
   2.6 Chambers of commerce, trade, arts, etc. (61)
   2.7 Civil Aviation Authority
   2.8 Cultural service agencies (21)
   2.9 Field Police Account
  2.10 National Defense Fund
  2.11 National Defense Fund
  2.12 National Legacy Fund
  2.13 National Navy Fund
  2.14 Public works institutions (151 miscellaneous)
  2.15 Social welfare and charity agencies (600 approximately)
  2.16 Special Farmers' Resettlement Fund
  2.17 Special Resettlement Fund
  2.18 State universities, colleges, and other educational institutions

Subsector 3.   Social security funds
   3.1 Farmers' Social Insurance Organization
   3.2 Other social insurance organizations

State Governments

Subsector 4.   State governments
   4.1 Not applicable

Local Governments

Subsector 5.   Local governments
   5.1 277 municipalities and 5,757 communities

Data Coverage

Data in central government tables cover operations of subsectors 1–3.

† Starting in 1998, data are on an accrual basis. Prior to 1998, data were on a cash basis.

Accounting Practices

1. Liquidation or complementary period:
   Not reported.
2. Valuation of assets and liabilities:
   Not reported.

GFSM 2001 Implementation Plan

Not reported.

This institutional table is based on information reported in 1997.

Guatemala 258

Units of General Government

Central Government

Subsector 1.   Budgetary central government
   1.1   Accountant general's office, judiciary, legislature, ministries, and presidency

Subsector 2.   Extrabudgetary units/entities
   2.1   San Carlos University of Guatemala and approximately 20 government agencies and institutes

Subsector 3.   Social security funds
   3.1   Guatemalan Social Security Institute

State Governments

Subsector 4.   State governments
   4.1   Not applicable

Local Governments

Subsector 5.   Local governments
   5.1   330 municipalities and other local authorities

Data Coverage

Data in central government tables cover operations of subsectors 1 and 2 (part). Data on own revenues for expenditure of subsector 2 are not included.

Data in local government tables cover operations of subsector 5.

† From 1996 onward, data are not comparable because of reclassifications in line with GFS methodology.

Accounting Practices

1. Liquidation or complementary period:
   Not reported.
2. Valuation of assets and liabilities:
   Not reported.

GFSM 2001 Implementation Plan

Not reported.

This institutional table is based on information reported in 1997.

Guinea 656

Units of General Government

Central Government

Subsector 1.   Budgetary central government
   1.1   Judiciary, Military Committee for National Advancement, ministries, presidency, and 13 secretariats of state

Subsector 2.   Extrabudgetary units/entities
   2.1   Not applicable

Subsector 3.   Social security funds
   3.1   Social security fund

State Governments

Subsector 4.   State governments
   4.1   Not applicable

Local Governments

Subsector 5.   Local governments
   5.1   Districts
   5.2   34 regions, including Conakry (divided into 3 communes)

Data Coverage

Data in budgetary central government tables cover operations of subsector 1, including French pensions.

Accounting Practices

1. Liquidation or complementary period:
   Not reported.
2. Valuation of assets and liabilities:
   Not reported.

GFSM 2001 Implementation Plan

Not reported.

This institutional table is based on information reported reported in or prior to 1996.

Hungary 944

Units of General Government

Central Government

Subsector 1.   Budgetary central government
   1.1   Constitutional court, law courts, ministries, office of ombudsman, office of public prosecutors, parliament, presidency of the republic, prime minister's office, state audit office
   1.2   Central Statistical Office, Economic Competition Office, Historical Documents Office, and Hungarian Academy of Science

Subsector 2.   Extrabudgetary units/entities
   2.1   CASA Co.
   2.2   Central Nuclear Financial Fund
   2.3   Labor Market Fund
   2.4   National Road Construction Co.
   2.5   Participation Management Co.
   2.6   State Debt Management Co.
   2.7   State Privatization and Property Management Co.
   2.8   State Treasury Co.
   2.9   Various nonprofit institutions, public foundations, and public nonprofit corporations

Subsector 3.   Social security funds
   3.1   Health Care Fund
   3.2   Pension Fund

State Governments

Subsector 4.   State governments
   4.1   Not applicable

Local Governments

Subsector 5.   Local governments
   5.1   3,200 municipalities and 20 county governments
   5.2   1,845 local minority governments

Data Coverage

Data in central government tables cover operations of subsectors 1–3. Certain data—financing, stocks of financial assets and liabilities, and consumption of fixed capital—cannot be broken down into GFS budgetary and extrabudgetary subsectors.

Data in local government tables cover operations of subsector 5 and are based on information from all local governments.

Accounting Practices

1. Liquidation or complementary period:
   None.
2. Valuation of assets and liabilities:
   Market value for financial accounts, as in the national accounts. Nonfinancial assets are recorded using acquisition cost less tax depreciation. Debt at nominal value—memorandum item in Table 6—is calculated according to EU Excessive Deficit Procedure. National accounts data on nonfinancial assets and consumption of fixed capital (CFC) are available within 2–3 years. CFC is only available for SNA/ESA sectors (central government, social security, local government) and cannot be classified according to COFOG, in Table 7, or in Tables 2 and 3 and Statement I.

GFSM 2001 Implementation Plan

Not reported.

This institutional table is based on information reported in 2004.

Iceland   176

Units of General Government

Central Government

Subsector 1.   Budgetary central government
   1.1   Departments, government agencies, judiciary, legislature, ministries, presidency, public colleges and universities, and public health service units

Subsector 2.   Extrabudgetary units/entities
   2.1   Not applicable

Subsector 3.   Social security funds
   3.1   Health Insurance Scheme
   3.2   Insurance for occupational injuries
   3.3   Pension and disability schemes
   3.4   Unemployment Insurance Scheme

State Governments

Subsector 4.   State governments
   4.1   Not applicable

Local Governments

Subsector 5.   Local governments
   5.1   165 municipalities, including public nursery and primary schools, and old persons' residential institutions
   5.2   Municipal Equalization Fund

Data Coverage

Data in central government tables cover operations of subsectors 1 and 3.

Data in local government tables cover operations of subsector 5.

† In August 1996, some education functions (mainly teachers' salaries) were transferred from central government to local governments. In 1996, these expenditures were financed by way

of an increased transfer from central government to local governments, and from 1997 onward, by way of higher individual income tax at local government level (central government individual income tax was lowered accordingly).

Accounting Practices

1. Liquidation or complementary period:
   Not reported.
2. Valuation of assets and liabilities:
   Not reported.

GFSM 2001 Implementation Plan

Not reported.

This institutional table is based on information reported in 2000.

India   534

Units of General Government

Central Government

Subsector 1.   Budgetary central government
   1.1   Judiciary, ministries, parliament, presidency, and prime minister's office

Subsector 2.   Extrabudgetary units/entities
   2.1   Not applicable

Subsector 3.   Social security funds
   3.1   Not applicable

State Governments

Subsector 4.   State governments
   4.1   25 states (with separate legislatures)
   4.2   1 union territory (with separate legislatures)

Local Governments

Subsector 5.   Local governments
   5.1   Committees
   5.2   Development boards
   5.3   Municipal boards
   5.4   Other local units
   5.5   Port trusts

Data Coverage

Data in central government tables cover operations of subsector 1.

Data in state government tables cover operations of subsector 4 and are based on information from all state governments and the union territory.

In Table 7, Outlays by Functions of Government, data for line 703 are included in 702, data for line 7043 are included in line 7044, and data for lines 708 and 710 are included in line 706.

Accounting Practices

1. Liquidation or complementary period:
   Not reported.
2. Valuation of assets and liabilities:
   Loans and bonds at face value.

GFSM 2001 Implementation Plan

Not reported.

This institutional table is based on information reported in or prior to 1996.

Indonesia 536

Units of General Government

Central Government

Subsector 1. Budgetary central government
 1.1 Judiciary, ministries, nonministerial agencies, People's Consultative Assembly, presidency, Supreme Advisory Council, and supreme auditor's office

Subsector 2. Extrabudgetary units/entities
 2.1 Investment Fund
 2.2 Reforestation Fund

Subsector 3. Social security funds
 3.1 3 social security schemes

State Governments

Subsector 4. State governments
 4.1 27 provinces (including the capital and 2 special districts)

Local Governments

Subsector 5. Local governments
 5.1 277 municipalities and local governments

Data Coverage

Data in central government tables cover operations of subsectors 1–3. Extrabudgetary operations comprise operations of subsector 2 and operations carried out through foreign loan accounts and prefinancing accounts.

Data in provincial government tables cover operations of subsector 4 and are based on information from all provinces.

† Prior to 2000, natural resources oil and gas revenue were classified as corporate income tax.

† Prior to 1999, tax on income, profits, and capital gains could not be broken into its components, and almost all of the income tax was classified as taxes paid by individuals.

† Prior to 1994, certain revenue components of Other Revenue were not separately identified and were instead included under Miscellaneous and Unidentified Revenue.

† Also prior to 1994, certain expenditure items of Social Protection; Housing and Community Amenities; and Agriculture, Forestry, Fishing, and Hunting were not separately identified and were instead included under General Public Services.

Accounting Practices

1. Liquidation or complementary period:
 Not reported.
2. Valuation of assets and liabilities:
 Not reported.

GFSM 2001 Implementation Plan

Not reported.

This institutional table is based on information reported in 2002.

Iran, Islamic Republic of 429

Units of General Government

Central Government

Subsector 1. Budgetary central government
 1.1 Judiciary, legislature, ministries, Organization for Protection of Consumers and Producers, presidency, and universities

Subsector 2. Extrabudgetary units/entities
 2.1 4 pension funds
 2.2 5 procurement and distribution centers
 2.3 Special purpose funds

Subsector 3. Social security funds
 3.2 Social insurance organization

State Governments

Subsector 4. State governments
 4.1 Not applicable

Local Governments

Subsector 5. Local governments
 5.1 700 municipalities

Data Coverage

Data in central government tables cover operations of components 1.1, 2.3, and 3.2, and are not consolidated.

Accounting Practices

1. Liquidation or complementary period:
 Not reported.
2. Valuation of assets and liabilities:
 Not reported.

GFSM 2001 Implementation Plan

Not reported.

This institutional table is based on information reported in 2005.

Israel 436

Units of General Government

Central Government

Subsector 1. Budgetary central government
 1.1 Legislature, ministries, presidency, prime minister's office, and state comptroller's office

Subsector 2. Extrabudgetary units/entities
 2.1 4 binational research funds
 2.2 Various nonprofit institutions controlled and mainly financed by the government, such as sick funds; universities, education, research, culture, religion, and welfare institutions; environmental organizations; etc.
 2.3 Compensation Fund

Subsector 3. Social security funds
 3.1 National insurance institute

State Governments

Subsector 4. State governments
 4.1 Not applicable

Local Governments

Subsector 5. Local governments
 5.1 Approximately 260 units of local government (local councils, municipalities, regional councils)
 5.2 Approximately 180 religious councils

Data Coverage

Data in central government tables cover operations of subsectors 1–3.

Data in local government tables cover operations of subsector 5.

Accounting Practices

1. Liquidation or complementary period:
 Not reported.
2. Valuation of assets and liabilities:
 Not reported.

GFSM 2001 Implementation Plan

Not reported.

This institutional table is based on information reported in 2004.

Italy 136

Units of General Government

Central Government

Subsector 1. Budgetary central government
- 1.1 8 constitutional bodies, including the court of auditors, judiciary, parliament, and presidency
- 1.2 19 ministries

Subsector 2. Extrabudgetary units/entities, 159, comprising:
- 2.1 Associations (5)
- 2.2 Cultural services providers (58)
- 2.3 Economic services providers (13)
- 2.4 Experimental research bodies (47)
- 2.5 Independent administrative bodies (6)
- 2.6 Regulatory bodies (6)
- 2.7 Research bodies (24)

Subsector 3. Social security funds
- 3.1 26 social security institutions and funds

State Governments

Subsector 4. State governments
- 4.1 Not applicable

Local Governments

Subsector 5. Local governments, 9,494 bodies, including:
- 5.1 Local agencies other than health (883)
- 5.2 Local health units and hospitals (321)
- 5.3 Municipalities (8,101)
- 5.4 Provinces (100)
- 5.5 Regions (20) and autonomous provinces (2)
- 5.6 Universities (65)

Data Coverage

Data in central government tables cover operations of subsectors 1–3.

Data in local government tables cover operations of subsector 5.

Accounting Practices

1. Liquidation or complementary period:
   Not applicable.
2. Valuation of assets and liabilities:
   Not reported.

GFSM 2001 Implementation Plan

Not reported.

This institutional table is based on information reported in 2004.

Jamaica 343

Units of General Government

Central Government

Subsector 1. Budgetary central government
- 1.1 Audit department, governor general's office, houses of parliament, 15 ministries, parliamentary ombudsman's office, prime minister's office, and service commissions

Subsector 2. Extrabudgetary units/entities
- 2.1 Capital Development Fund
- 2.2 Human Employment and Resources Training (HEART) Trust
- 2.3 National Housing Trust
- 2.4 Students' Loan Council
- 2.5 Statutory bodies and agencies

Subsector 3. Social security funds
- 3.1 National Insurance Fund

State Governments

Subsector 4. State governments
- 4.1 Not applicable

Local Governments

Subsector 5. Local governments
- 5.1 Kingston and St. Andrew Corp.
- 5.2 Municipal Services Commission
- 5.3 Parish Council Services Commission
- 5.4 13 parish councils

Data Coverage

Data in central government tables cover operations of subsectors 1–3.

Data from 2003 onward are not strictly comparable with those through 2002, owing to changes in classifications.

Accounting Practices

1. Liquidation or complementary period:
   Not reported.
2. Valuation of assets and liabilities:
   Not reported.

GFSM 2001 Implementation Plan

Not reported.

This institutional table is based on information reported in or prior to 1994.

Japan 158

Units of General Government

Central Government

Subsector 1. Budgetary central government
- 1.1 Agencies, board of audit, cabinet, courts, emperor, legislature [diet], ministries, prime minister's office

Subsector 2. Extrabudgetary units/entities
- 2.1 National Public Service Employees' Mutual Aid Association
- 2.2 Private School Teachers' and Employees' Mutual Aid Association

Subsector 3. Social security funds
- 3.1 Social security funds

State Governments

Subsector 4. State governments
- 4.1 Not applicable

Local Governments

Subsector 5. Local governments
- 5.1 655 cities and 2,586 towns and villages
- 5.2 Cooperative services of local governments
- 5.3 47 prefectures
- 5.4 Special wards of Tokyo

Data Coverage

Data in central government tables cover operations of subsectors 1–3. Subsector 1 includes the operations of central government social security funds.

Data in local government tables cover operations, other than social security funds, of subsector 5.

Data in general government tables cover operations of subsectors 1–3 and 5, derived from the national accounts' general government account.

† Break symbols indicate that, prior to 1991, data include budgetary central government only. From 1991 onward, data (other than data on debt) are presented on a consolidated central government basis.

† From 1991 onward, data for financing abroad and foreign debt are included, respectively, in domestic financing and domestic debt.

Accounting Practices

1. Liquidation or complementary period:
   Not reported.
2. Valuation of assets and liabilities:
   Not reported.

GFSM 2001 Implementation Plan

Not reported.

This institutional table is based on information reported in or prior to 1996.

Jordan   439

Units of General Government

Central Government

Subsector 1.   Budgetary central government
  1.1   Audit bureau, civil service commission, council of ministers, ministries, parliament, prime minister's office, and Royal Hashemite Court
  1.2   Chief justice for religious affairs
  1.3   Jordan Valley Authority
  1.4   Royal Jordanian Geographic Center
Subsector 2.   Extrabudgetary units/entities
  2.1   9 government agencies
Subsector 3.   Social security funds
  3.1   Health Security Fund

State Governments

Subsector 4.   State governments
  4.1   Not applicable

Local Governments

Subsector 5.   Local governments
  5.1   Greater Amman Municipality
  5.2   172 municipalities
  5.3   350 village councils

Data Coverage

Data in central government tables cover operations of components 1.1–1.3.

Through 2001, in Tables 3 and 8, lines for adjustments to liabilities include amortization data that could not be classified in component items.

Accounting Practices

1. Liquidation or complementary period:
   None.
2. Valuation of assets and liabilities:
   Not reported.

GFSM 2001 Implementation Plan

Not reported.

This institutional table is based on information reported in 2005.

Kazakhstan   916

Units of General Government

Central Government

Subsector 1.   Budgetary central government
  1.1   Administration of the president, agencies, chancellery of the prime minister, ministries, and other central state bodies
  1.2   State institutions funded from the republican budget
Subsector 2.   Extrabudgetary units/entities
  2.1   National Fund of the Republic of Kazakhstan
Subsector 3.   Social security funds
  3.1   Not reported

State Governments

Subsector 4.   State governments
  4.1   Not applicable

Local Governments

Subsector 5.   Local governments
  5.1   16 local administrative bodies, including 2 cities (Almaty and Astana) and 14 oblast bodies

Data Coverage

Data in central government tables cover operations of subsectors 1 and 2.

Data in local government tables cover operations of subsector 5.

† From 1999 onwards, the social security and extrabudgetary funds, except the National Fund of the Republic of Kazakhstan, have been incorporated into the central government budget.

Accounting Practices

1. Liquidation or complementary period:
   The financial year ends on December 31. A complementary period exists ("counting period") to allow for investment projects that were not provided with funding before the financial year expires, as well as for official transfers remitted to the budget. The "counting period" ends on March 15 of the following year.
2. Valuation of assets and liabilities:
   Fixed assets are valued at purchase cost, financial assets at market price, and bonds and loans at face value.

GFSM 2001 Implementation Plan

According to the Budget Code Act, since January 1, 2005, operations of a current financial year, connected to the remittance of revenue to the budget, begin on January 1 and end on December 31 of a current calendar year. The act also provides for changes in the budget structure, following the *GFSM 2001* presentation; at the same time, cash methods are preserved.

This institutional table is based on information reported in 2005.

Kenya   664

Units of General Government

Central Government

Subsector 1.   Budgetary central government
  1.1   Consolidated Fund Services

1.2 Department of Defense
1.3 Directorate of Personnel Management
1.4 Electoral Commission
1.5 Judicial Department
1.6 Ministries (all)
1.7 National Assembly
1.8 Office of Attorney General
1.9 Office of the Controller and Auditor General
1.10 Office of the Vice President
1.11 Public Service Commission
1.12 State House

Subsector 2.   Extrabudgetary units/entities
2.1 Local Authorities Transfer Fund
2.2 Petroleum Development Fund
2.3 Roads Maintenance Levy Fund
2.4 Rural Electrification Program

Subsector 3.   Social security funds
3.1 National Hospital Insurance Fund
3.2 National Social Security Fund

State Governments
Subsector 4.   State governments
4.1 Not applicable

Local Governments
Subsector 5.   Local governments
5.1 66 county councils
5.2 43 municipal councils
5.3 62 town councils

Data Coverage
Data in central government tables cover operations of subsector 1.

† From 1997 onward, data are not comparable because of reclassifications in line with GFS methodology.

Accounting Practices
1.   Liquidation or complementary period:
     Not reported.
2.   Valuation of assets and liabilities:
     The assets are valued at historical cost, and a comprehensive list of assets is yet to be compiled.

GFSM 2001 Implementation Plan
The cash data have been compiled according to the *GFSM 2001* format. The coverage will be gradually improved to cover the general government, that is, to incorporate extrabudgetary units, social security funds, and local governments.

This institutional table is based on information reported in 2004.

Korea, Republic of   542

Units of General Government
Central Government
Subsector 1.   Budgetary central government
1.1 Boards, committees, and councils; judiciary; ministries; national assembly; 11 offices; and presidency
Subsector 2.   Extrabudgetary units/entities
2.1 Various units
Subsector 3.   Social security funds
3.1 Not applicable

State Governments
Subsector 4.   State governments
4.1 1 special city (Seoul)

4.2 5 direct jurisdiction cities (Busan, Daegu, Daejon, Gwangju, and Incheon)
4.3 9 provinces

Local Governments
Subsector 5.   Local governments
5.1 67 cities
5.2 137 counties

Data Coverage
Data in central government tables cover operations of subsector 1 and operations of extrabudgetary special accounts and funds controlled by this subsector.

Accounting Practices
1.   Liquidation or complementary period:
     None for subsector 1; 2 months for subsectors 4 and 5.
2.   Valuation of assets and liabilities:
     Loans and bonds at face value.

GFSM 2001 Implementation Plan
Not reported.

This institutional table is based on information reported in or prior to 1996.

Kuwait   443

Units of General Government
Central Government
Subsector 1.   Budgetary central government
1.1 Departments, head of state, and ministries
Subsector 2.   Extrabudgetary units/entities
2.1 Kuwait Fire Department
2.2 Kuwait Institute for Scientific Research (KISR)
2.3 Kuwait University
2.4 8 public authorities (including the Public Authority for Assessment of Damages Resulting from Iraqi Invasion (PAAD) and the Environment Public Authority)
2.5 Municipality of Kuwait
2.6 National Assembly of Kuwait
2.7 Zakat House (religious provident endowment fund)

Subsector 3.   Social security funds
3.1 Public Institution for Social Security

State Governments
Subsector 4.   State governments
4.1 Not applicable

Local Governments
Subsector 5.   Local governments
5.1 Not applicable

Data Coverage
Data in central government tables cover operations of subsectors 1–3.

† From 1997 onward, data include the operations of the Environment Public Authority.

Accounting Practices
1.   Liquidation or complementary period:
     Not reported.
2.   Valuation of assets and liabilities:
     Not reported.

GFSM 2001 Implementation Plan

Not reported.

This institutional table is based on information reported in 2000.

Kyrgyz Republic   917

Units of General Government

Central Government
Subsector 1. Budgetary central government
  1.1 Agencies, commissions, judicial and legislative authorities, ministries, and presidency
Subsector 2. Extrabudgetary units/entities
  2.1 Funds, government agencies, and institutions
Subsector 3. Social security funds
  3.1 Social Fund

State Governments
Subsector 4. State governments
  4.1 Not applicable

Local Governments
Subsector 5. Local governments
  5.1 Local governments

Data Coverage

Data in central government tables cover operations of subsector 1.
Data in local government tables cover operations of subsector 5.

Accounting Practices

1. Liquidation or complementary period:
    Not reported.
2. Valuation of assets and liabilities:
    Not reported.

GFSM 2001 Implementation Plan

Not reported.

This institutional table is based on information reported in 1999.

Latvia   941

Units of General Government

Central Government
Subsector 1. Budgetary central government
  1.1 Budgetary institutions, ministries, parliament, president's office, and prime minister's office
Subsector 2. Extrabudgetary units/entities
  2.1 Not applicable
Subsector 3. Social security funds
  3.1 Government Special Social Insurance Budget

State Governments
Subsector 4. State governments
  4.1 Not applicable

Local Governments
Subsector 5. Local governments
  5.1 Municipal Privatization Fund and other special funds
  5.2 Amalgamated municipalities (26), regional governments/districts (26), rural municipalities (444), towns (63)

Data Coverage

Data in central government tables cover operations of subsectors 1–3.

Data in local government tables cover operations of subsector 5.

† From 2004 onwards, all extrabudgetary funds are included in the budgetary central government.

† From 2002 onwards, revenue and expense data for budgetary central government, extrabudgetary accounts, and social security funds are presented on a gross basis. Before 2002, these data are presented net of transfers among these central government units.

† In 1997, there were shifts of education and health functions within the components of central government, and between local government and central government.

† From 1996 onwards, data in the local government tables cover the operations of subsector 5; prior to 1996, data cover the operations of component 5.2 only.

† Prior to 1996, social security operations were included in the budgetary accounts. Also, prior to 1996, data exclude the operations of extrabudgetary funds (subsector 2).

Accounting Practices

1. Liquidation or complementary period:
    Not applicable.
2. Valuation of assets and liabilities:
    Not applicable.

GFSM 2001 Implementation Plan

Reclassify existing cash-based data to the *GFSM 2001* framework, which has been completed. No further migration plans to the *GFSM 2001* methodology exist at this stage.

This institutional table is based on information reported in 2005.

Lebanon   446

Units of General Government

Central Government
Subsector 1. Budgetary central government
  1.1 Budget agencies, constitutional council, ministries, parliament, presidency, and presidency of the council of ministers
Subsector 2. Extrabudgetary units/entities
  2.1 Autonomous Fuel Fund
  2.2 Bureau for Tobacco
  2.3 Council for Development and Reconstruction
  2.4 University of Lebanon
Subsector 3. Social security funds
  3.1 General social security scheme

State Governments
Subsector 4. State governments
  4.1 Not applicable

Local Governments
Subsector 5. Local governments
  5.1 Municipalities

Data Coverage

Data in central government tables cover operations of subsector 1.

† Prior to 1999, excise taxes levied on imported products are included with other import duties.

Accounting Practices

1. Liquidation or complementary period:
    1 month.
2. Valuation of assets and liabilities:
    Not reported.

GFSM 2001 Implementation Plan

Lebanon has started reclassifying its government finance statistics according the *GFSM 2001*. Budgetary expenditure data are reported on a modified cash basis, corresponding to the issuance of payment orders.

This institutional table is based on information reported in 2003.

Lesotho   666

Units of General Government

Central Government

Subsector 1.   Budgetary central government
  1.1   Auditor general's office, ministries, monarchy, and public service commission

Subsector 2.   Extrabudgetary units/entities
  2.1   Lesotho Highlands Water Revenue Fund (LHWRF)

Subsector 3.   Social security funds
  3.1   Not applicable

State Governments

Subsector 4.   State governments
  4.1   Not applicable

Local Governments

Subsector 5.   Local governments
  5.1   Not applicable

Data Coverage

Data cover the operations of subsectors 1 and 2.

Accounting Practices

1.   Liquidation or complementary period:
   Not reported.
2.   Valuation of assets and liabilities:
   Not reported.

GFSM 2001 Implementation Plan

Not reported.

This institutional table is based on information reported in or prior to 1996.

Lithuania   946

Units of General Government

Central Government

Subsector 1.   Budgetary central government
  1.1   Budgetary institutions, law courts, ministries, national museums, national parks, office of the government, office of the president, parliament, public universities, regional offices, research institutes, and state control

Subsector 2.   Extrabudgetary units/entities
  2.1   1990 Blockade Fund
  2.2   Fund for Decommission of Ignalina Nuclear Power Station
  2.3   Guarantee Fund
  2.4   Privatization Fund
  2.5   Reserve (Stabilization) Fund
  2.6   Savings Restitution Account

Subsector 3.   Social security funds
  3.1   Compulsory Health Insurance Fund
  3.2   State Social Security Fund

State Governments

Subsector 4.   State governments
  4.1   Not applicable

Local Governments

Subsector 5.   Local governments
  5.1   60 local governments and nonprofit institutions (including pre-primary, primary, and secondary schools, nursing homes, etc.), which are controlled and mainly financed by local governments

Data Coverage

Data in central government tables cover operations of subsectors 1–3.

† Starting in 2001, revenue includes grants received from the European Union. Also accruals of value-added taxes and excises are derived from time-adjusted cash data. Accruals of interest are calculated for budgetary central government. Adjustments for the Bank of Lithuania profit transferred to the state budget are made to correspond to the period when profit was earned. Consumption of fixed capital is taken into account starting in 2001; consumption of fixed capital data of budgetary central government and local governments are provided by Statistics Lithuania.

† Starting in 2000, data for social security funds are on an accrual basis. Data prior to 2000 are on a cash basis.

† Prior to 1999, expenditure of the privatization funds was not allocated among functional expenditures of government.

† In 1997 health functions shifted within the components of central government and between local government and central government. At the same time, the income tax revenue sharing formula among budgetary central government, the Compulsory Health Insurance Fund, and local governments was changed.

Prior to 1996, data in local government tables cover operations of subsector 5 and the Municipal Privatization Fund; from 1996 onward, data cover operations of subsector 5 only.

Accounting Practices

1.   Liquidation or complementary period:
   None, except for unused appropriations for financing special programs and construction, which have to be refunded within 10 days after year end.
2.   Valuation of assets and liabilities:
   Loans and bonds are valued at face value. Accrued interest is not added to the principal of the underlying instrument but is classified under accounts payable.

GFSM 2001 Implementation Plan

The budget classification system consistent with *GFSM 2001* was introduced starting with the 2004 budget (central and local government). An action plan has been drawn up for implementing accrual accounting, to be fully introduced by 2006.

This institutional table is based on information reported in 2004.

Luxembourg   137

Units of General Government

Central Government

Subsector 1.   Budgetary central government
  1.1   Judiciary, legislature, ministries, and monarchy
  1.2   34 special funds

Subsector 2. Extrabudgetary units/entities
2.1 National Solidarity Fund
2.2 Regional Development Fund for the Kirchberg Plateau
2.3 Various nonmarket public establishments with financial autonomy

Subsector 3. Social security funds
3.1 19 social protection institutions

State Governments
Subsector 4. State governments
4.1 Not applicable

Local Governments
Subsector 5. Local governments
5.1 118 municipalities and communal administrations
5.2 Various intercommunal associations

Data Coverage

Data in central government tables cover operations of subsectors 1–3. Data for subsector 2 are included in subsector 1.

Data in local government tables cover operations of subsector 5 and are based on information from all local governments.

Accounting Practices

1. Liquidation or complementary period:
   One month after the end of the fiscal year for expenditures.
2. Valuation of assets and liabilities:
   Financial assets at market prices; loans and bonds at market value.

GFSM 2001 Implementation Plan

Data are consistent with public sector accounts and are on an accrual basis in accordance with *ESA95*.

This institutional table is based on information reported in 2005.

Madagascar   674

Units of General Government

Central Government
Subsector 1. Budgetary central government
1.1 Agencies, judiciary, military development committee, ministries, national assembly, presidency, prime minister's cabinet, and Supreme Revolutionary Council

Subsector 2. Extrabudgetary units/entities
2.1 Approximately 60 government agencies (including 12 chambers of commerce)
2.2 Veterans' office

Subsector 3. Social security funds
3.1 National Social Security Fund

State Governments
Subsector 4. State governments
4.1 Not applicable

Local Governments
Subsector 5. Local governments
5.1 11,333 cantons and rural communes
5.2 110 prefectures (including 9 urban municipalities)
5.3 6 provinces
5.4 28 social welfare offices
5.5 1,252 subprefectures (including 37 urban municipalities)

Data Coverage

Data in budgetary central government tables cover budgetary and extrabudgetary operations of subsector 1.

† Prior to 1996 in Table 7, data on public order and safety were included in the line on defense.

Accounting Practices

1. Liquidation or complementary period:
   Not reported.
2. Valuation of assets and liabilities:
   Not reported.

GFSM 2001 Implementation Plan

Not reported.

This institutional table is based on information reported in 1996.

Malaysia   548

Units of General Government

Central Government
Subsector 1. Budgetary central government
1.1 Judiciary, 25 ministries with related departments and regulatory agencies, monarchy, and parliament

Subsector 2. Extrabudgetary units/entities
2.1 59 statutory bodies

Subsector 3. Social security funds
3.1 Social security organization

State Governments
Subsector 4. State governments
4.1 13 state governments

Local Governments
Subsector 5. Local governments
5.1 4 city councils, 21 municipal councils, and 118 district councils

Data Coverage

Data in central government tables cover operations of subsectors 1–3.

Data in state government tables cover operations of subsector 4 and are based on information from all state governments.

Data in local government tables cover operations of subsector 5 and are based on information from all local governments.

Accounting Practices

1. Liquidation or complementary period:
   Not reported.
2. Valuation of assets and liabilities:
   Not reported.

GFSM 2001 Implementation Plan

Not reported.

This institutional table is based on information reported in 1996.

Maldives   556

Units of General Government

Central Government
Subsector 1. Budgetary central government
1.1 Attorney general's office, ministries, and office of the president (including Anti-corruption Board, audit office, Citizen's Majilis Chamber, high court, and presidency)

Subsector 2. Extrabudgetary units/entities
  2.1 Not applicable
Subsector 3. Social security funds
  3.1 Not applicable

State Governments

Subsector 4. State governments
  4.1 Not applicable

Local Governments

Subsector 5. Local governments
  5.1 Not applicable

Data Coverage

Data in central government tables cover operations of subsector 1.

Accounting Practices

1. Liquidation or complementary period:
    None.
2. Valuation of assets and liabilities:
    Not reported.

GFSM 2001 Implementation Plan

Not reported.

This institutional table is based on information reported in 2001.

Malta   181

Units of General Government

Central Government

Subsector 1. Budgetary central government
  1.1 House of representatives, judiciary, 13 ministries, national audit office, ombudsman's office, president's office, and prime minister's office
Subsector 2. Extrabudgetary units/entities
  2.1 62 government agencies, boards, and commissions
Subsector 3. Social security funds
  3.1 Not applicable

State Governments

Subsector 4. State governments
  4.1 Not applicable

Local Governments

Subsector 5. Local governments
  5.1 Not applicable

Data Coverage

Data in central government tables cover operations of subsectors 1 and 2. Data on own revenues for expenditures of subsector 2 are not included.

† From 1996 onward, data are not comparable because of reclassifications in line with *GFSM 1986* methodology.

Accounting Practices

1. Liquidation or complementary period:
    Not reported.
2. Valuation of assets and liabilities:
    Not reported.

GFSM 2001 Implementation Plan

Not reported.

This institutional table is based on information reported in 1998.

Mauritius   684

Units of General Government

Central Government

Subsector 1. Budgetary central government
  1.1 Departments, judiciary, ministries, national assembly, and president's office
Subsector 2. Extrabudgetary units/entities
  2.1 91 government agencies
Subsector 3. Social security funds
  3.1 Social security fund

State Governments

Subsector 4. State governments
  4.1 Rodrigues Regional Assembly

Local Governments

Subsector 5. Local governments
  5.1 4 district councils
  5.2 5 municipal councils

Data Coverage

Data in central government tables cover operations of subsectors 1–3.

Data in state government tables cover operations of subsector 4.

Data in local government tables cover operations of subsector 5.

† A break symbol in 2002 indicates a change in the consolidation methodology. Prior to 2002, data for the subsectors of central government were presented net of transactions among them. Starting in 2002, data for the subsectors of central government are presented on a gross basis, and transactions among them are eliminated separately. In addition, consolidation for 2002 is more complete than for the earlier years.

† Break symbols in 1992, 1993, 1994, 1999, and 2001 indicate that coverage of subsector 2 was expanded.

† Break symbol in 1992 indicates that coverage of subsector 3 was expanded.

Accounting Practices

1. Liquidation or complementary period:
    None.
2. Valuation of assets and liabilities:
    Debt liabilities are valued at nominal value.

GFSM 2001 Implementation Plan

Not reported.

This institutional table is based on information reported in 2005.

Mexico   273

Units of General Government

Central Government

Subsector 1. Budgetary central government
  1.1 Administrative agencies
  1.2 Congress, electoral authorities, judiciary, presidency, secretariats, and tribunals
  1.3 Government agencies
Subsector 2. Extrabudgetary units/entities
  2.1 Not applicable
Subsector 3. Social security funds
  3.1 Social Security Institute for the Mexican Armed Forces

3.2 Institute of Security and Social Services for Government Workers
3.3 Mexican Social Security Institute

State Governments

Subsector 4. State governments
4.1 Federal district
4.2 31 state governments

Local Governments

Subsector 5. Local governments
5.1 2,430 municipal governments

Note: Component 1.3 comprises approximately 52 agencies. Among these are the Council for Mineral Resources, Foundation for Mining Promotion, Mexican Petroleum Institute, National Agricultural Training Institute, national unit for seed production, and retirees of the National Printing Office.

Data Coverage

Data in central government tables cover operations of components 1.2, 1.3, 3.2, and 3.3. Under a tax revenue sharing agreement, the central government collects the taxes that are shared and immediately transfers them to other levels of government. The central government payment of the taxes shared is recorded as a negative tax revenue in Table 1.

The adjustment to the cash surplus/deficit in the Statement of Sources and Uses of Cash is the net result of unclassified receipts and expenditures included in suspense accounts.

Data in state government tables cover operations of subsector 4.

Data in local government tables cover operations of subsector 5.

Accounting Practices

1. Liquidation or complementary period:
   Not reported.
2. Valuation of assets and liabilities:
   Not reported.

GFSM 2001 Implementation Plan

Not reported.

This institutional table is based on information reported in 2002.

Moldova 921

Units of General Government

Central Government

Subsector 1. Budgetary central government
1.1 Apparatus of the parliament, apparatus of the president, chamber of accounts, constitutional court, courts (43), economic court of appeal, human rights center, information and security service, ministries (15), national committee for stocks and shares, other central administrative authorities (14), other institutions and agencies (16), public administration academy, public prosecuter's office, state chancellery, superior council of magistracy, supreme court of justice, and other institutions (48)

Subsector 2. Extrabudgetary units/entities
2.1 Central government institutions and organizations (697)
2.2 Extrabudgetary funds (14)

Subsector 3. Social security funds
3.1 Compulsory medical insurance funds
3.2 State Social Insurance Budget

State Governments

Subsector 4. State governments
4.1 Not applicable

Local Governments

Subsector 5. Local governments
5.1 Autonomous territorial unit (1)
5.2 City halls of municipalities, towns, and villages (901)
5.3 Extrabudgetary funds (35)
5.4 Local government budgetary organizations (8,499)
5.5 Municipalities (2)
5.6 Rayons (32)

Data Coverage

Data in central government tables cover operations of subsectors 1–3.

Data in local government tables cover operations of subsector 5.

† Prior to 2002, data exclude operations of subsector 2. Also, data are classified more closely according to the *GFSM 2001* methodology and are thus not strictly comparable with those before.

Accounting Practices

1. Liquidation or complementary period:
   None. The budget year is closed on December 31.
2. Valuation of assets and liabilities:
   The accounting for assets is carried out on initial cost basis, that is, at the price of purchase, including the tax added to cost, and the assets which were reassessed as of January 1, 1996, on a replacement cost basis.

GFSM 2001 Implementation Plan

1. Review current budget classification and fit it to the requirements of *GFSM 2001* (2005–06);

2. Review current accounting system and current charts of accounts (now there are 4 charts of accounts, for each level of budget) and create one chart of accounts for all budget operations (2005–06);

3. Review current reporting system for budget execution and fit it to the new budget classification (2005–06);

4. Review and develop new normative and legislative documentation (2007);

5. Introduce, adjust, and test the new budget classification into the informational system of the public finance administration (2008);

6. Explain and make public for all budget executors the new budget classification, new account system, chart of accounts, and reporting system (2008); and

7. Implement the new budget classification, the new chart of accounts, and the reporting system (beginning January 1, 2009).

This institutional table is based on information reported in 2005.

Mongolia 948

Units of General Government

Central Government

Subsector 1. Budgetary central government
1.1 Cabinet office, constitutional council, general prosecutor's office, ministries, parliament, president's office, and supreme court
1.2 Culture and Art Fund
1.3 Employment and Promotion Fund
1.4 Environment Fund
1.5 Government agencies (except self-financed)

1.6 Road Department
1.7 State Property Committee (before 2002 and from 2004 onward)

Subsector 2. Extrabudgetary units/entities
2.1 State Property Committee (2002 and 2003)
2.2 10 agencies (Fuel and Energy Authority, State Center of Standardization and Metrology, State Citizens' Registration and Information Center, and the following departments: Construction, Foreign Citizens and Citizenship Issues, Intellectual Rights, Oil and Gas, Postal and Telecommunications, Service of Diplomatic Missions, and Transportation)
2.3 13 funds (Assistance of Disabled Citizens, Departments Development, Environment Protection, Grains, Herd Protection, KR–1, KR–2, three Ministry of Food and Agriculture funds [USA1; USA2; Ukraine], Road, Travel, and Wild Goats)

Subsector 3. Social security funds
3.1 Health Insurance Fund
3.2 Industrial Accidents and Occupational Disease Insurance Fund
3.3 Pension Insurance Fund
3.4 Social Benefits Insurance Fund
3.5 Unemployment Insurance Fund

State Governments

Subsector 4. State governments
4.1 Not applicable

Local Governments

Subsector 5. Local governments
5.1 City and 9 districts of Ulaanbaatar
5.2 331 districts (soums)
5.3 21 provinces (aimags)

Data Coverage

Data in central government tables cover operations of subsectors 1–3.

Data in local government tables cover operations of subsector 5.

† Data in 2003 for extrabudgetary units, central government, and general government are on a noncash basis. Data prior to 2003 are on a cash basis.

† Starting in 2002, data for central government subsectors are presented on a gross basis (i.e., before consolidation). Data through 2001 for these subsectors are presented on a net basis (i.e., after consolidation).

† From 1997 onward, the data cover the expenditures of the Reserve Funds.

† Before 1993, Table 7 data on public order and safety were included in the line·on general public services.

Accounting Practices

1. Liquidation or complementary period:
   None.
2. Valuation of assets and liabilities:
   Fixed assets are valued at market value; loans and bonds at face value.

GFSM 2001 Implementation Plan

Classify cash data in *GFSM 2001* format for reporting to the IMF's Statistics Department in 2003 and 2004. A new budget accounting system introduced in 2004 will allow implementation of modified accrual accounting.

This institutional table is based on information reported in 2004.

Morocco 686

Units of General Government

Central Government

Subsector 1. Budgetary central government
1.1 Annexed budgets*
1.2 Chamber of representatives, ministries, monarchy, and prime minister's office
1.3 Treasury special accounts

Subsector 2. Extrabudgetary units/entities
2.1 16 government agencies
2.2 Moroccan Pension Fund

Subsector 3. Social security funds
3.1 National Social Security Fund
3.2 Pension Fund (Régime Collectif d'Allocation de Retraites)

State Governments

Subsector 4. State governments
4.1 Not applicable

Local Governments

Subsector 5. Local governments
5.1 26 prefectures
5.2 45 provinces
5.3 16 regions
5.4 1,298 rural communes
5.5 249 urban municipalities
5.6 17 *wilayas*

Data Coverage

Data in central government tables cover operations of subsectors 1 and 3 and component 2.2.

Data in local government tables cover operations of subsector 5.

† Prior to 1995, the data exclude operations of component 2.2.

† Year ending December 31 through 1995; year ending June 30 thereafter.

* 4 annexed budgets reduced to 2 starting in 1998/99.

Accounting Practices

1. Liquidation or complementary period:
   Not reported.
2. Valuation of assets and liabilities:
   Not reported.

GFSM 2001 Implementation Plan

Not reported.

This institutional table is based on information reported in 2001.

Myanmar 518

Units of General Government

Central Government

Subsector 1. Budgetary central government
1.1 Attorney general, auditor general, cabinet, chief justice, departments, general election commission, ministries, state administrative organizations, and state law and order restoration council

Subsector 2. Extrabudgetary units/entities
2.1 Not applicable

Subsector 3. Social security funds
3.1 Social security board

State Governments
Subsector 4. State governments
  4.1 Not applicable

Local Governments
Subsector 5. Local governments
  5.1 9 cantonment development committees
  5.2 272 city and township development committees

Data Coverage

Data in central government tables cover operations of subsectors 1 and 3.

† Prior to 1992, data in central government tables include operations of component 5.2.

Accounting Practices

1. Liquidation or complementary period:
    Not reported.
2. Valuation of assets and liabilities:
    Not reported.

GFSM 2001 Implementation Plan

Not reported.

This institutional table is based on information reported in 2001.

Namibia   728

Units of General Government

Central Government
Subsector 1. Budgetary central government
  1.1 Auditor general's office, ministries, national planning office, parliament, president's office, and prime minister's office
Subsector 2. Extrabudgetary units/entities
  2.1 Guardian's Fund, Intelligence and Security Agency, Labor Promotion Fund, Namibia Press Agency (NAMPA), National Monuments Council, New Era Publications Corporation, Sea Fisheries Research Fund, University of Namibia, and Workmen's Compensation Fund
Subsector 3. Social security funds
  3.1 Not applicable

State Governments
Subsector 4. State governments
  4.1 Not applicable

Local Governments
Subsector 5. Local governments
  5.1 48 local authority councils comprising 15 municipalities, 12 towns, and 21 villages 5.2 13 regional councils

Data Coverage

Data in central government tables cover operations of subsector 1.

Accounting Practices

1. Liquidation or complementary period:
    None.
2. Valuation of assets and liabilities:
    Not reported.

GFSM 2001 Implementation Plan

There are no plans to implement the *GFSM 2001* soon.

This institutional table is based on information reported in 2004.

Nepal   558

Units of General Government

Central Government
Subsector 1. Budgetary central government
  1.1 Cabinet, departments, judiciary, legislature, ministries, monarchy, and prime minister's office
Subsector 2. Extrabudgetary units/entities
  2.1 Not applicable
Subsector 3. Social security funds
  3.1 Not applicable

State Governments
Subsector 4. State governments
  4.1 Not applicable

Local Governments
Subsector 5. Local governments
  5.1 75 districts, 58 municipalities, and 3,912 village development committees

Data Coverage

Data in central government tables cover operations of subsector 1.

Data include foreign transactions in kind.

Data for foreign grants and borrowing have been adjusted to eliminate receivable items.

From 1991 onward, data on public order and safety were included in the line on general public services in Table 7.

Accounting Practices

1. Liquidation or complementary period:
    Not reported.
2. Valuation of assets and liabilities:
    Not reported.

GFSM 2001 Implementation Plan

Not reported.

This institutional table is based on information reported in 1999.

Netherlands   138

Units of General Government

Central Government
Subsector 1. Budgetary central government
  1.1 Council of state, judiciary, legislature (states general), ministries, and monarchy
  1.2 Six funds, comprising Agricultural Equalization Fund (Part A), Government Road Fund, Investment Account Fund, Mobility Fund, Municipalities Fund, and Provinces Fund
Subsector 2. Extrabudgetary units/entities
  2.1 Government agencies, comprising the Delft Hydraulics Laboratory, Food Board, Foundation for Land Administration, Health Board, institutes for research and development, National Aerospace Laboratory, Netherlands Emigration Agency, Netherlands Organization for Applied Scientific Research, and public nonprofit institutions serving enterprises, universities, and various foundations
Subsector 3. Social security funds
  3.1 17 social security funds and 130 social security agencies

State Governments
Subsector 4. State governments
  4.1 Not applicable

Local Governments

Subsector 5.   Local governments
- 5.1   487 intermunicipal corporations and the Union of Netherlands Municipalities
- 5.2   633 municipalities and 584 municipal agencies
- 5.3   85 polder boards
- 5.4   12 provinces

Data Coverage

Data in central government tables cover operations of subsectors 1–3. Data on budgetary central government also cover the operations of the extrabudgetary units.

Data in local government tables cover operations of subsector 5 and are based on information from all units in 5.1 and 5.3–5.4, and on a stratified sample of units in 5.2.

In line with the presentation adopted within the European Union, data on domestic financial assets and liabilities include foreign financial assets and liabilities.

† From 1999 onward, data are reported on an accrual basis. Data prior to 1999 are on a cash basis.

Accounting Practices

1. Liquidation or complementary period:
    None for subsectors 1–3; 3 months for subsector 5.
2. Valuation of assets and liabilities:
    Not reported.

GFSM 2001 Implementation Plan

Not reported.

This institutional table is based on information reported in or prior to 1996.

New Zealand   196

Units of General Government

Central Government

Subsector 1.   Budgetary central government
- 1.1   Executive council, governor general's office, house of representatives, judiciary, and parliamentary departments and offices
- 1.2   New Zealand Superannuation Fund

Subsector 2.   Extrabudgetary units/entities
- 2.1   Accident Compensation Corporation
- 2.2   Accounting Standards Review Board
- 2.3   Agricultural and Marketing Research and Development Trust
- 2.4   Alcohol Advisory Council of New Zealand
- 2.5   Animal Control Products Limited
- 2.6   Arts Council of New Zealand Toi Aotearoa (Creative NZ)
- 2.7   Asia 2000 Foundation of New Zealand
- 2.8   Broadcasting Commission
- 2.9   Broadcasting Standards Authority
- 2.10 Building Industry Authority
- 2.11 Career Services
- 2.12 Casino Control Authority
- 2.13 Children's Commissioner
- 2.14 Civil Aviation Authority of New Zealand
- 2.15 Commerce Commission
- 2.16 Crown research institutes (9)
- 2.17 District health boards (21)
- 2.18 Earthquake Commission
- 2.19 Electoral Commission
- 2.20 Electricity Governance Board
- 2.21 Energy Efficiency and Conservation Authority
- 2.22 Environmental Risk Management Authority (ERMA)
- 2.23 Fish and Game Councils (12)
- 2.24 Foundation for Research, Science and Technology
- 2.25 Government Superannuation Fund Authority
- 2.26 The Guardians of New Zealand Superannuation
- 2.27 Health and Disability Services Commissioner
- 2.28 Health Research Council of New Zealand
- 2.29 Health Sponsorship Council
- 2.30 Housing New Zealand Corporation
- 2.31 Human Rights Commission
- 2.32 Land Transport Safety Authority of New Zealand
- 2.33 Law Commission
- 2.34 Leadership Development Centre Trust
- 2.35 Learning Media Limited
- 2.36 Legal Services Agency
- 2.37 Maritime Safety Authority of New Zealand
- 2.38 Mental Health Commission
- 2.39 Museum of New Zealand Te Papa
- 2.40 New Zealand Antarctic Institute (Antarctic New Zealand)
- 2.41 New Zealand Artificial Limb Board
- 2.42 New Zealand Blood Service
- 2.43 New Zealand Film Commission
- 2.44 New Zealand Fire Service Commission
- 2.45 New Zealand Fish and Game Council
- 2.46 New Zealand Game Bird Habitat Trust Board
- 2.47 New Zealand Government Property Corporation
- 2.48 New Zealand Lotteries Commission
- 2.49 New Zealand Lottery Grants Board
- 2.50 New Zealand Qualifications Authority
- 2.51 New Zealand Sports Drug Agency
- 2.52 New Zealand Symphony Orchestra
- 2.53 New Zealand Teachers Council
- 2.54 New Zealand Tourism Board
- 2.55 New Zealand Trade and Enterprise
- 2.56 New Zealand Venture Investment Fund
- 2.57 Ngai Tahu Ancillary Claims Trust
- 2.58 Office of Film and Literature Classification
- 2.59 Pacific Island Business Development Trust
- 2.60 Pharmaceutical Management Agency
- 2.61 Police Complaints Authority
- 2.62 Privacy Commissioner
- 2.63 Public Trust
- 2.64 Quotable Value New Zealand
- 2.65 Radio New Zealand Limited
- 2.66 Residual Health Management Unit
- 2.67 Reserve boards (26)
- 2.68 Road Safety Trust
- 2.69 Retirement Commissioner
- 2.70 Schools—TAMU
- 2.71 Securities Commission
- 2.72 Social Workers Registration Board
- 2.73 Sport and Recreation New Zealand
- 2.74 Standards New Zealand (Standards Council)
- 2.75 Takeovers Panel
- 2.76 Te Reo Whakapuaki Irirangi (Te Mangai Paho)
- 2.77 Te Taura Whiri I Te rao maori (Maori Language Commission)
- 2.78 Telarc Limited (Testing Laboratory, Registration Council) (Int. Accreditation NZ)
- 2.79 Television New Zealand Limited
- 2.80 Tertiary Education Commission
- 2.81 Tertiary education institutions (35)

2.82 Transfund New Zealand
2.83 Transit New Zealand
2.84 Transportation Accident Investigation Commission
Subsector 3.   Social security funds
  3.1 Government Superannuation Fund

State Governments
Subsector 4.   State governments
  4.1 Not applicable

Local Governments
Subsector 5.   Local governments
  5.1 86 local government units

Data Coverage

Data in central government tables cover operations of subsectors 1–3.

Data in local government tables cover operations of subsector 5.

† Prior to 2001, data in all tables are compiled in accordance with the methodology of the *GFSM 1986*.

† Prior to 1991, data on public order and safety were included in the line on general public services.

From 1990 onward, fiscal years end June 30.

Accounting Practices

1. Liquidation or complementary period:
    None.
2. Valuation of assets and liabilities:
    Fixed assets at market prices; financial assets at market prices; loans and bonds at face value.

GFSM 2001 Implementation Plan

The data provided in the attached tables have been classified to the *GFSM 2001* classification system. This output is still in development. This release incorporates an expanded range of data, including:

- central government—amended data supply to match *GFSM 2001* reporting requirements,
- local government—expanded data collection to meet reporting requirements (with some exceptions), and
- general government—development of consolidation transactions.

Work continues to develop (expected to be completed in 2006):

- increased time series,
- coverage review (central government), and
- review transaction classifications.

This institutional table is based on information reported in 2005.

Nicaragua   278

Units of General Government

Central Government
Subsector 1.   Budgetary central government
  1.1 Decentralized entities (7), electoral council, general controller office, judiciary, ministries (12), national assembly, and presidency
Subsector 2.   Extrabudgetary units/entities
  2.1 General Procurement of Human Rights
  2.2 Pension Superintendence
  2.3 Public Prosecutor Office
  2.4 Public universities (8)

Subsector 3.   Social security funds
  3.1 Nicaraguan Social Security Institute

State Governments
Subsector 4.   State governments
  4.1 Regional government of North Atlantic
  4.2 Regional government of South Atlantic

Local Governments
Subsector 5.   Local governments
  5.1 152 municipalities

Data Coverage

Data in central government tables cover operations of subsectors 1–3. Extrabudgetary funds are not reported separately, although they are covered in the budget through transfers. However, public universities are partially covered, since they do not report data on own revenues and their spending. The authorities reported that the volume of these transactions can be considered marginal.

Accounting Practices

1. Liquidation or complementary period:
    Not reported.
2. Valuation of assets and liabilities:
    Not reported.

GFSM 2001 Implementation Plan

Not reported.

This institutional table is based on information reported in 2005.

Norway   142

Units of General Government

Central Government
Subsector 1.   Budgetary central government
  1.1 Auditor general's office, cabinet, legislature, ministries, monarchy, and supreme court
Subsector 2.   Extrabudgetary units/entities
  2.1 Extrabudgetary funds (includes advance and deposit accounts, special accounts of the central government, and other guarantee funds)
  2.2 Government funds
  2.3 Government Petroleum Fund
  2.4 Government Petroleum Insurance Fund
  2.5 Norwegian Research Council and Norwegian Trade Council
  2.6 Price regulation funds
  2.7 Public hospitals
  2.8 Public universities and public colleges
Subsector 3.   Social security funds
  3.1 Child Allowance Scheme
  3.2 National Insurance Scheme
  3.3 National Insurance Fund
  3.4 Public Service Pension Fund
  3.5 Seamen's Pension Insurance Fund
  3.6 War Pension Scheme for the Military

State Governments
Subsector 4.   State governments
  4.1 Not applicable

Local Governments
Subsector 5.   Local governments
  5.1 18 counties and 434 municipalities

Data Coverage

Data in central government tables cover operations of subsectors 1–3.

Data in local government tables cover operations of subsector 5.

In line with the presentation adopted within the European Union, data on domestic financial assets and liabilities include foreign financial assets and liabilities.

Accounting Practices

1. Liquidation or complementary period:
    Subsector 1 applies modified cash-based accounting principles.
    Subsector 2 applies a variety of accounting principles, but the far most used is accrual accounting.
    Subsector 5 applies modified cash-based accounting principles.
2. Valuation of assets and liabilities:
    Nominal values. However, an exception is the Government Petroleum Fund, for which the lowest value of average buying price and market value is used.

GFSM 2001 Implementation Plan

Not reported.

This institutional table is based on information reported in 2005.

Oman   449

Units of General Government

Central Government

Subsector 1.   Budgetary central government
  1.1   Agencies, Cabinet Secretariat Office of the Personal Representative to His Majesty the Sultan, magistrate court, ministries, ruler's court, Secretariat of the Supreme Committee for Town Planning, and Sultan Qaboos University

Subsector 2.   Extrabudgetary units/entities
  2.1   State General Reserve Fund

Subsector 3.   Social security funds
  3.1   Not applicable

State Governments

Subsector 4.   State governments
  4.1   Not applicable

Local Governments

Subsector 5.   Local governments
  5.1   Not applicable

Data Coverage

Data in budgetary central government tables cover operations of subsector 1.

Accounting Practices

1. Liquidation or complementary period:
    Not reported.
2. Valuation of assets and liabilities:
    Not reported.

GFSM 2001 Implementation Plan

Not reported.

This institutional table is based on information reported in 2002.

Pakistan   564

Units of General Government

Central Government

Subsector 1.   Budgetary central government
  1.1   Cabinet secretariat, judiciary, legislature, 26 ministries, presidency, and prime minister's secretariat

Subsector 2.   Extrabudgetary units/entities
  2.1   Not applicable

Subsector 3.   Social security funds
  3.1   Not applicable

State Governments

Subsector 4.   State governments
  4.1   Baluchistan
  4.2   Northwest Frontier Province
  4.3   Punjab
  4.4   Sind

Local Governments

Subsector 5.   Local governments
  5.1   District councils, local councils, and municipalities

Data Coverage

Data in central government tables cover operations of subsector 1.

Accounting Practices

1. Liquidation or complementary period:
    Not reported.
2. Valuation of assets and liabilities:
    Liabilities are valued at face value.

GFSM 2001 Implementation Plan

Not reported.

This institutional table is based on information reported in 2004.

Panama   283

Units of General Government

Central Government

Subsector 1.   Budgetary central government
  1.1   Comptroller general's office, electoral court, judiciary, legislative assembly, 3 ministries, and presidency

Subsector 2.   Extrabudgetary units/entities
  2.1   Government institutions and 4 universities

Subsector 3.   Social security funds
  3.1   Social security fund

State Governments

Subsector 4.   State governments
  4.1   Not applicable

Local Governments

Subsector 5.   Local governments
  5.1   75 municipalities, including the indigenous territories of Emberá, Kuna Yala, and Ngobe Buglé

Data Coverage

Data in central government tables cover operations of subsectors 1–3.

Data in local government tables cover operations of subsector 5.

Accounting Practices

1. Liquidation or complementary period:
   Not reported.
2. Valuation of assets and liabilities:
   Not reported.

GFSM 2001 Implementation Plan

A *GFSM 2001* implementation plan and an assessment of the institutional coverage of the public sector of Panama is under preparation. A public accounting system is to be applied, and collection of detailed financial information is to be requested from all general government units.

This institutional table is based on information reported in 2003.

Papua New Guinea 853

Units of General Government

Central Government

Subsector 1. Budgetary central government
  1.1 Auditor general's office, 41 departments, governor general's office, judiciary, and national parliament
Subsector 2. Extrabudgetary units/entities
  2.1 Defense Force Retirement Benefits Fund
  2.2 Papua New Guinea Retirement Benefits Fund
  2.3 Public Officers' Superannuation Fund
  2.4 17 statutory bodies
  2.5 4 universities
Subsector 3. Social security funds
  3.1 Not applicable

State Governments

Subsector 4. State governments
  4.1 20 provincial governments and national capital district

Local Governments

Subsector 5. Local governments
  5.1 150 (approximately) local government councils and community governments

Data Coverage

Data in budgetary central government tables cover the operations of subsector 1.

† From 1994 onward, data are compiled using a different database and classification system.

Accounting Practices

1. Liquidation or complementary period:
   Not reported.
2. Valuation of assets and liabilities:
   Not reported.

GFSM 2001 Implementation Plan

Not reported.

This institutional table is based on information reported in 2000.

Paraguay 288

Units of General Government

Central Government

Subsector 1. Budgetary central government
  1.1 Comptroller general's office, council of state, electoral court, judiciary, ministries, national congress, national

council of the magistrate, office of ombudsman, office of public prosecutor, and presidency
  1.2 Retirement and Pension Fund of Government Employees
Subsector 2. Extrabudgetary units/entities
  2.1 Government institutions (13) including Municipal Development Institute, National Animal Health Service, National Commission of Communications, National Commission of Stock Market, National Council of Housing, National Directorate of Welfare, National Environmental Restoration Service, National Fund of Culture and Arts, National Institute for Indigenous People, National Institute of Technology and Normalization, and Rural Welfare Institute
  2.2 Universities (4)
Subsector 3. Social security funds
  3.1 Social security funds (5) comprise Pension Fund of Banking Employees, Retirement and Pension Fund for Employees of the National Electricity Administration, Social Security Fund of Railway Employees and Workers, and Social Security Institute

State Governments

Subsector 4. State governments
  4.1 Regional governments (17)

Local Governments

Subsector 5. Local governments
  5.1 Capital and municipalities (224)

Data Coverage

Data in budgetary central government tables cover operations of subsector 1.

From 1990 to 1993, data in local government tables cover operations of Asunción (capital) only.

Accounting Practices

1. Liquidation or complementary period:
   Not reported.
2. Valuation of assets and liabilities:
   Not reported.

GFSM 2001 Implementation Plan

Not reported.

This institutional table is based on information reported in 2004.

Peru 293

Units of General Government

Central Government

Subsector 1. Budgetary central government
  1.1 Comptroller general's office, congress, constitutional tribunal, judiciary, ministries (15), national council of the magistrate, national electoral court, national office of electoral processes, national registry of identification and civil status, office of ombudsman, office of the prime minister, and office of the public prosecutor
  1.2 Entities of enterprise treatment (9)
  1.3 Other decentralized agencies (7)
  1.4 Public institutions (58)
  1.5 Public welfare agencies (101)
  1.6 Universities (31)
Subsector 2. Extrabudgetary units/entities
  2.1 National Fund for Housing (in liquidation)
  2.2 Mortgage Fund for Housing Promotion

Subsector 3.   Social security funds
3.1   Consolidated Pensions Reserves Fund (Fondo Consolidado de Reservas Previsionales)
3.2   Public Pension Fund (Oficina de Normalización Previsional)
3.3   Social Security of Health

State Governments
Subsector 4.   State governments
4.1   25 regional governments

Local Governments
Subsector 5.   Local governments
5.1   7 decentralized agencies
5.2   1,836 district councils
5.3   194 provincial councils

Data Coverage

Data in central government tables cover operations of subsectors 1–3.

Data in state government tables cover operations of subsector 4.

Data in local government tables cover operations of subsector 5.

Component 1.5 includes the National Superintendency of Customs, National Superintendency of Tax Administration, Supervisory Agency for Investment in Energy, and others.

Data in the provincial and local government subsector (subsector 5) are based on information from a sample of provincial and district councils.

Revenue data include adjustments, because some tax refunds are not classified by tax categories.

† Starting in 1995, data for subsectors of central government are presented on a gross basis (i.e., before consolidation).

Accounting Practices

1.   Liquidation or complementary period: None.
2.   Valuation of assets and liabilities: Not reported.

GFSM 2001 Implementation Plan

Not reported.

This institutional table is based on information reported in 2004.

Philippines   566

Units of General Government

Central Government
Subsector 1.   Budgetary central government
1.1   2 autonomous regions, Commission on Human Rights, congress, 3 constitutional offices, departments, executive offices, Joint Legislative Executive Debt Council, judiciary, ombudsman's office, presidency, and vice presidency
Subsector 2.   Extrabudgetary units/entities
2.1   Central Bank Board of Liquidators
2.2   Government service insurance system
2.3   Lung Center of the Philippines
2.4   Medical care plan
2.5   National Kidney Institute
2.6   National Post-harvest Institute for Research and Extension
2.7   Philippine Children's Medical Center
2.8   Philippine Heart Center
2.9   Philippine High School for the Arts
2.10 Philippine Rice Research Institute

2.11 Philippine Tourism Authority
Subsector 3.   Social security funds
3.1   Social security system

State Governments
Subsector 4.   State governments
4.1   Not applicable

Local Governments
Subsector 5.   Local governments
5.1   41,924 barangays (municipal subunits)
5.2   64 cities
5.3   1,541 municipalities
5.4   76 provinces
5.5   13 regions

Data Coverage

Data in budgetary central government tables cover operations of subsector 1.

† Through 2001, the net operations of "nonbudget accounts" are incorrectly classified as domestic financing. Starting in 2002, the "nonbudget accounts" transactions are appropriately classified to revenues, expenses, and financing.

† Starting in 1998, the budgetary central government stock of liabilities (outstanding debt data) has been consolidated with the Bond Sinking Fund, and other subsectors of general government's debt have been appropriately consolidated.

† Starting in 1994, data exclude interest paid for restructuring of the Central Bank of the Philippines.

† Through 1992, data available in local government tables cover operations of subsector 5 and are based on information from all local governments. For the most recent available year, data on local governments are provisional.

Accounting Practices

1.   Liquidation or complementary period: None.
2.   Valuation of assets and liabilities: Fixed assets at historical cost; loans and bonds at face value.

GFSM 2001 Implementation Plan

It is envisaged to approve a migration plan to the *GFSM 2001* by the end of 2005.

This institutional table is based on information reported in 2005.

Poland   964

Units of General Government

Central Government
Subsector 1.   Budgetary central government
1.1   Chancellery of the president, chancellery of the prime minister, constitutional tribunal, governmental center strategic studies, sejm (lower house of parliament), ministries, ombudsman's office, senate (upper house of parliament), supreme administrate court, supreme chamber of control (audit), supreme court, and other institutions
1.2   Energy Regulatory Authority
1.3   Insurance and Pension Funds Supervisory Commission
1.4   Office for Competition and Consumer Protection
1.5   Office of Public Procurement
1.6   Other various agencies
1.7   Polish Committee for Standardization

1.8 Polish Patent Office
1.9 State Mining Authority

Subsector 2. Extrabudgetary units/entities
2.1 Agencies (6 units)
2.2 Agency of Agricultural Property of the State Treasury
2.3 Agency of Material Stocks
2.4 Agency of Military Property
2.5 Agency of Restructurization and Modernization of Agriculture
2.6 Alimony Fund
2.7 Arts Promotion Fund
2.8 Auxiliary units, budget establishments, special units, universities
2.9 Central Fund for Management of Geodetic and Cartographic Resources
2.10 Fund for Guaranteed Employee Benefits
2.11 Fund for Protection of Agricultural Land
2.12 Military Agency for Housing
2.13 National Fund for Environmental Protection and Water Management
2.14 Non-social security special-purpose funds (8 units)
2.15 Polish Agency for Enterprise Development
2.16 State Fund for Rehabilitation of the Disabled
2.17 State Veterans' Fund

Subsector 3. Social security funds
3.1 Administrative Fund of the Board for the Social Insurance of Farmers
3.2 Contribution' Fund and Motivation Fund
3.3 Demographic Reserve Fund and Labor Fund
3.4 Fund for Prevention and Rehabilitation
3.5 National Health Fund (until 2002, health funds were included in local governments)
3.6 Pension and Disability Fund (for farmers)
3.7 Reserve Fund and Social Insurance Fund
3.8 Social security special-purpose funds (9 units)
3.9 Social Insurance Institution

State Governments
Subsector 4. State governments
4.1 Not applicable

Local Governments
Subsector 5. Local governments
5.1 Auxiliary units, budget establishments, special-purpose funds, and special units
5.2 2,489 communes
5.3 373 counties
5.4 16 districts

Data Coverage

Data in central government tables cover operations of subsectors 1–3. Data in subsector 3 include data on fully funded open pension funds, which is not in accordance with the methodological guidelines of GFSM 2001.

Data in local government tables cover operations of subsector 5.

† From 2001 onward, data are compiled partially on an accrual basis and are classified in accordance with GFSM 2001.

Accounting Practices
1. Liquidation or complementary period:
   25 days.
2. Valuation of assets and liabilities:
   Nominal value for domestic debt; end-of-year exchange rates for foreign debt.

GFSM 2001 Implementation Plan

An interinstitutional working group has been established with the main objective to discuss and resolve technical and

methodological issues regarding the implementation of the ESA 1995. The implementation of the GFSM 2001 will follow upon this work.

This institutional table is based on information reported in 2004.

Portugal   182

Units of General Government

Central Government
Subsector 1. Budgetary central government
1.1 Account court, cabinets for Azores and Madeira, constitutional court, independent scientific commission, ministries (17), ombudsman service, parliament, presidency, and presidency of the council of ministers
1.2 Health Service for Government Employees (Assistência na Doença aos Servidores do Estado); universities

Subsector 2. Extrabudgetary units/entities
2.1 Government agencies (includes 6 agencies in agriculture, 13 in cultural activities, 2 in defense, 9 in economy, 173 in education (including universities), 3 in environment, 4 in finance, 3 in foreign affairs, 115 in health, 7 in internal affairs, 8 in justice, 33 in labor and solidarity, 3 in miscellaneous activities, 7 in planning, 2 in public administration reform, 6 in science and technology, and 8 in social equipment)
2.2 Government funds (includes 1 in agriculture, 1 in cultural activities, 1 in education, 4 in finance, 1 in foreign affairs, and 1 science and technology)

Subsector 3. Social security funds
3.1 Pension Fund for Government Employees (Caixa Geral de Aposentações e Montepio dos Servidores do Estado)
3.2 Social Security Financial Management Institute (Instituto de Gestão Financeira da Segurança Social)

State Governments
Subsector 4. State governments
4.1 Not applicable

Local Governments
Subsector 5. Local governments
5.1 2 autonomous regional governments (Azores and Madeira)
5.2 18 districts
5.3 308 municipal councils
5.4 4,220 parochial authorities

Data Coverage

Data for budgetary central government also cover extrabudgetary central government units and entities.

Data in central government tables cover operations of subsectors 1–3.

Data in local government tables cover operations of subsector 5.

From 1993 onwards, data on current and capital transfers to other levels of government exclude budgetary central government transfers abroad (Table 2).

Also beginning in 1993, some of the special funds (fundos privativos) are included in the budgetary central government (subsector 1) rather than in unit 2.2.

Accounting Practices
1. Liquidation or complementary period:
   Not reported.

2. Valuation of assets and liabilities:
Not reported.

GFSM 2001 Implementation Plan

Not reported.

This institutional table is based on information reported in 2005.

Romania 968

Units of General Government

Central Government

Subsector 1.   Budgetary central government
1.1   Central government agencies, judiciary, ministries, parliament, and presidency

Subsector 2.   Extrabudgetary units/entities
2.1   Agency for Recovery State Assets (formerly Agency for Bank Asset Recovery and the Authority for Privatization and Management of State Ownership)
2.2   Self-financing institutions subordinated to ministries

Subsector 3.   Social security funds
3.1   State Social Security Budget
3.2   Unemployment Fund
3.3   Health Social Insurance Fund

State Governments

Subsector 4.   State governments
4.1   Not applicable

Local Governments

Subsector 5.   Local governments
5.1   Bucharest, 2,686 communes, 41 counties, 96 municipalities, and 265 towns
5.2   Self-financing institutions subordinated to local authorities

Data Coverage

Data in central government tables cover operations of subsectors 1–3, except for transactions of the Agency for Recovery State Assets.

Data in local government tables cover operations of subsector 5.

† From 2002 onward, data are reported on an accrual basis. Accrual data are derived from cash data using various methods: tax revenue data are adjusted using time-adjusted cash method; expense data are adjusted using due-for-payments data; and interest payments are calculated on an accrual basis. Furthermore, cash data for budgetary central government, extrabudgetary accounts, and social security funds are not comparable, owing to the change in consolidation method. Beginning in 2002, the Special Fund for Development of the Energy System, Special Fund for Public Roads, Special Fund "Romanian Agriculture Development," and Special Fund "Romania" were included in the state budget, while the Special Fund for Insured Protection was eliminated from general government accounts.

† From 2000 onward, data for social security funds include the health social insurance fund.

† From 1997 onward, substantial amounts of central government securities were issued in exchange for nonperforming bank claims. These transactions, which should be classified both as net acquisition of financial assets from financial institutions and as net incurrence of liabilities to depository corporations (through the net issuance of long-term bonds), are not included in reported data.

† Prior to 1992, operations of the Unemployment Fund were included under extrabudgetary accounts.

Accounting Practices

1. Liquidation or complementary period:
Not reported.
2. Valuation of assets and liabilities:
Not reported.

GFSM 2001 Implementation Plan

Implement accrual accounting, including new budgetary classifications, in 2006.

This institutional table is based on information reported in 2005.

Russian Federation 922

Units of General Government

Central Government

Subsector 1.   Budgetary central government
1.1   Chief prosecutor's office, commissions, constitutional court, federal agencies, federal assembly, high arbitrage court, ministries, president's office, state committees, and supreme court
1.2   Extrabudgetary resources of the federal budgetary institutions
1.3   Research units and universities

Subsector 2.   Extrabudgetary units/entities
2.1   Fund for Scientific Research, Design, and Construction (NIOKR)
2.2   Russian Fund for Technological Development

Subsector 3.   Social security funds
3.1   Funds for social support of the population—federal and territorial
3.2   Mandatory medical insurance funds—federal and territorial
3.3   Pension Fund of the Russian Federation
3.4   Russian Federation Social Insurance Fund

State Governments

Subsector 4.   State governments
4.1   Not applicable

Local Governments

Subsector 5.   Local governments
5.1   89 regional governments ("subjects"), including 1 autonomous oblast, 10 autonomous districts, 2 cities (Moscow and St. Petersburg), 6 krays, 49 oblasts, and 21 republics
5.2   Extrabudgetary resources of the subnational budgetary institutions

Data Coverage

Data in central government tables cover operations of subsectors 1–3.

Data in local government tables cover operations of subsector 5.

† Starting in 2002, data are on an accrual basis. Data through 2001 are on a cash basis.

† In 2002, federal budget data include the operations of the Ministry of Atomic Energy Fund, and the local government budgets data include the operations of the Territorial Road Funds and the Territorial Ecological Funds.

† In 2002, the opening balances of budgetary, central government, local governments, and general government

liabilities were different from the 2001 closing balances. The 2001 closing balances were replaced by 2002 opening balances for publication purposes.

† For 2001, central and local government extrabudgetary data include a wider coverage of off-budget transactions of budget institutions.

† Before 2000, local government debt guaranteed by the central government is included under central government debt.

† From 1999 onward, the budgetary data include transactions of budgetary organizations related to own revenue and its expenditure.

† For 1998, debt data exclude certain operations on the rescheduling of government debt in the form of securities, which should have been included under internal debt.

† From 1998 onward, the operations of three additional extrabudgetary funds—the Atomic Energy Ministry Fund, Earmarked Budgetary Fund to Assist Military Reform, and Federal Fund for Replenishment of Mineral and Raw Material Base—are included with budgetary data.

† From 1995 onward, the operations of six former extrabudgetary funds—the Federal Ecological Fund, Federal Roads Fund, Fund for Development of the Customs System, State Fund for Combating Criminal Activities, Tax Police Fund, and Tax Service Fund—are included with budgetary data.

Accounting Practices

1. Liquidation or complementary period:
   Three and one-half months in 1998; none from 1999 onward.
2. Valuation of assets and liabilities:
   Not reported.

GFSM 2001 Implementation Plan

On January 1, 2005, a single accounting instruction was introduced. It is based on the accrual concept and applies to budgets at all levels of the Russian Federation's budgetary system.

This institutional table is based on information reported in 2005.

St. Kitts and Nevis   361

Units of General Government

Central Government

Subsector 1.   Budgetary central government
  1.1 Audit; deputy governor general; governor general; ministries (Ministry of Education and Youth; Ministry of Finance, Technology, and Sustainable Development; Ministry of Foreign Affairs, International Trade, Industry, and Commerce; Ministry of Health; Ministry of Housing, Agriculture, Fisheries, and Consumer Affairs; Ministry of Legal Affairs; Ministry of National Security, Justice, Immigration, and Labor; Ministry of Public Works, Utilities, Transport, and Post; Ministry of Social and Community Development and Gender Affairs; Ministry of Tourism, Sports, and Culture); parliament; premier's ministry; and prime minister's office

Subsector 2.   Extrabudgetary units/entities
  2.1 National Handicraft and Cottage Industries Development Board
  2.2 Tourism Authority
  2.3 Trust funds

Subsector 3.   Social security funds
  3.1 Social security fund

State Governments

Subsector 4.   State governments
  4.1 Not applicable

Local Governments

Subsector 5.   Local governments
  5.1 Not applicable

Data Coverage

Data in central government tables cover operations of subsectors 1–3. Data for subsector 2 are included with the budgetary data.

Accounting Practices

1. Liquidation or complementary period:
   Not reported.
2. Valuation of assets and liabilities:
   Not reported.

GFSM 2001 Implementation Plan

Not reported.

This institutional table is based on information reported in 2005.

St. Vincent and The Grenadines   364

Units of General Government

General Government

  1. Government departments: Audit department, director of public prosecution's office, electoral office, governor general's office, judiciary, ministries, parliament, prime minister's office, and service commissions
  2. Social security funds
  3. Local governments

Data Coverage

Data in general government tables cover operations of components 1–3.

Accounting Practices

1. Liquidation or complementary period:
   Not reported.
2. Valuation of assets and liabilities:
   Not reported.

GFSM 2001 Implementation Plan

Not reported.

This institutional table is based on information reported in 2005.

San Marino   135

Units of General Government

Central Government

Subsector 1.   Budgetary central government:
  1.1 Department of Education, University, and Social Affairs
  1.2 Department of Finance and Budget Office, Economic Planning, and Relations with the Coin Minting and Stamp Printing Company, and Transportation
  1.3 Department of Foreign and Political Affairs
  1.4 Department of Health and Social Security
  1.5 Department of Industry, Craftsmanship, and Economic

Cooperation, Relations with the Public Works Company and Public Services Company
- 1.6 Department of Internal Affairs, Postal and Telecommunication Services, Civil Protection
- 1.7 Department of Justice, Relations with the Municipalities and Information
- 1.8 Department of Labor and Cooperation
- 1.9 Department of the Territory, Environment, and Agriculture
- 1.10 Department of Tourism, Commerce and Sport

Subsector 2. Extrabudgetary units/entities
- 2.1 Coin Minting and Stamp Printing Company
- 2.2 National Olympic Committee
- 2.3 Public Services Company
- 2.4 Public Works Company
- 2.5 State Dairy
- 2.6 University of San Marino

Subsector 3. Social security funds
- 3.1 Social Security Institute

State Governments

Subsector 4. State governments
- 4.1 Not applicable

Local Governments

Subsector 5. Local governments
- 5.1 Not applicable

Data Coverage

Data in central and general government tables cover operations of subsectors 1–3.

Accounting Practices

1. Liquidation or complementary period:
   Not reported.
2. Valuation of assets and liabilities:
   Fixed assets are valued at historical cost; financial assets and loans are valued at face value.

GFSM 2001 Implementation Plan

Not reported.

This institutional table is based on information reported in 2002.

Senegal   722

Units of General Government

Central Government

Subsector 1. Budgetary central government
- 1.1 Economic and Social Council, judiciary, ministries, national assembly, and presidency

Subsector 2. Extrabudgetary units/entities
- 2.1 Administrative government agencies

Subsector 3. Social security funds
- 3.1 Social security fund

State Governments

Subsector 4. State governments
- 4.1 Not applicable

Local Governments

Subsector 5. Local governments
- 5.1 Communes (municipalities) and rural districts

Data Coverage

Data in budgetary central government tables cover operations of subsector 1 (including operations financed by extrabudgetary foreign grants and loans for capital expenditures not recorded in the Treasury accounts).

Data in local government tables cover operations of subsector 5.

Accounting Practices

1. Liquidation or complementary period:
   None.
2. Valuation of assets and liabilities:
   Not reported.

GFSM 2001 Implementation Plan

Not reported.

This institutional table is based on information reported in 2001.

Serbia and Montenegro   965

Units of General Government

Central Government

Subsector 1. Budgetary central government
- 1.1 Budget agencies, judiciary, legislature, ministries, parliament, president's office, and prime minister's office

Subsector 2. Extrabudgetary units/entities
- 2.1 Not applicable

Subsector 3. Social security funds
- 3.1 Health Fund
- 3.2 Labor Market Fund
- 3.3 Pension Fund

State Governments

Subsector 4. State governments
- 4.1 Vojvodina

Local Governments

Subsector 5. Local governments
- 5.1 City of Belgrade
- 5.2 City of Kragujevac
- 5.3 City of Niš
- 5.4 City of Novi Sad
- 5.5 141 municipalities

Data Coverage

Data in central government tables cover operations of subsectors 1–3.

Data in state government tables cover operations of subsector 4.

Data in local government tables cover operations of subsector 5.

Accounting Practices

1. Liquidation or complementary period:
   Not reported.
2. Valuation of assets and liabilities:
   Not reported.

GFSM 2001 Implementation Plan

Not reported.

This institutional table is based on information reported in 2003.

Seychelles   718

Units of General Government

Central Government

Subsector 1.   Budgetary central government
  1.1   18 ministries, office of the president (comprising 8 departments), and 5 regulatory bodies

Subsector 2.   Extrabudgetary units
  2.1   Not applicable

Subsector 3.   Social security funds
  3.1   Social security institution

State Governments

Subsector 4.   State governments
  4.1   Not applicable

Local Governments

Subsector 5.   Local governments
  5.1   Not applicable

Data Coverage

Data in central government tables cover operations of subsectors 1 and 3.

Accounting Practices

1. Liquidation or complementary period:
    Not reported.
2. Valuation of assets and liabilities:
    Not reported.

GFSM 2001 Implementation Plan

Not reported.

This institutional table is based on information reported in 2004.

Sierra Leone   724

Units of General Government

Central Government

Subsector 1.   Budgetary central government
  1.1   24 departments headed by ministers and cabinet members, president, and vice president

Subsector 2.   Extrabudgetary units/entities
  2.1   Institute of Education
  2.2   Land and Other Development Division
  2.3   Milton Margai Cheircher Home
  2.4   National Agricultural Research Coordinating Council
  2.5   National Authorizing Office
  2.6   National Sports Council
  2.7   Planning, Evaluation, Monitoring, and Services Unit
  2.8   Public Archives
  2.9   Rokupr Rice Research Station
  2.10 Secretariat for Coordination of National Aid
  2.11 Sierra Leone Library Board
  2.12 Sierra Leone School for the Blind
  2.13 Sierra Leone School for the Deaf
  2.14 State-sponsored primary and secondary schools
  2.15 5 teacher-training colleges
  2.16 University of Sierra Leone

Subsector 3.   Social security funds
  3.1   Not applicable

State Governments

Subsector 4.   State governments
  4.1   Not applicable

Local Governments

Subsector 5.   Local governments
  5.1   Freetown City Council1
  5.2   49 chiefdom committees
  5.3   12 district councils
  5.4   1 rural area council
  5.5   4 rural district councils (Koya, Mountain, Waterloo, and York)
  5.6   5 town councils (Bo, Kenema, Koidu, Makeni, and Sherbro Urban District)

Data Coverage

Data in budgetary central government tables cover operations of subsector 1.

† From 1998 onward, fiscal years end December 31; through 1997, fiscal years end June 30.

† From 1991 onward, revenue data include loan repayments, and expense data include lending operations. Data on loan repayments and lending operations should be included in the net acquisition of financial assets aggregate but cannot be disaggregated from existing source data.

Accounting Practices

1. Liquidation or complementary period:
    Not reported.
2. Valuation of assets and liabilities:
    Not reported.

GFSM 2001 Implementation Plan

Not reported.

This institutional table is based on information reported in 2001.

Singapore   576

Units of General Government

Central Government

Subsector 1.   Budgetary central government
  1.1   Attorney general's chambers, audit department, cabinet, judiciary, ministries, parliament, presidency, presidential council, prime minister's office, and public service commission

Subsector 2.   Extrabudgetary units/entities
  2.1   5 community development authorities, boards, and councils
  2.2   7 economic affairs and services agencies, boards, and councils
  2.3   11 education agencies (including universities and polytechnics)

Subsector 3.   Social security funds
  3.1   Not applicable

State Governments

Subsector 4.   State governments
  4.1   Not applicable

Local Governments

Subsector 5.   Local governments
  5.1   Not applicable

Data Coverage

Data in central government tables cover operations of subsectors 1 and 2.

† Full consolidation for the subsectors of central government could not be effected prior to 1994.

Accounting Practices

1. Liquidation or complementary period:
   Not reported.
2. Valuation of assets and liabilities:
   Not reported.

GFSM 2001 Implementation Plan

Not reported.

This institutional table is based on information reported in 2005.

Slovak Republic   936

Units of General Government

Central Government

Subsector 1.   Budgetary central government
   1.1   Constitutional court, ministries, office of the attorney general, office of the government, office of the national council, office of the ombudsman, office of the president, regional offices, supreme audit office, and various agencies

Subsector 2.   Extrabudgetary units/entities
   2.1   National Property Fund
   2.2   Slovak Consolidation Agency
   2.3   Slovak Land Fund
   2.4   State Fund for Dwelling Development
   2.5   State Fund for Nuclear Energy Installation and Processing of Nuclear Fuel and Radioactive Waste

Subsector 3.   Social security funds
   3.1   Apollo Chemical Health Insurance Company
   3.2   General Health Insurance Institution
   3.3   National Labor Office (obligatory unemployment insurance)
   3.4   Sideria-Istota Health Insurance Company
   3.5   Social Insurance Company (obligatory pension and sickness insurance)
   3.6   Spolocna Health Insurance Company
   3.7   Vzajomna Health Insurance Company

State Governments

Subsector 4.   State governments
   4.1   Not applicable

Local Governments

Subsector 5.   Local governments
   5.1   8 regions and approximately 2,900 municipalities and budgetary and semibudgetary organizations established by municipalities

Data Coverage

Data in central government tables cover operations of subsectors 1–3.

Data in local government tables cover operations of subsector 5.

---

† Data through 2002 are on a cash basis. Starting in 2003, data are on an accrual basis.

Accounting Practices

1. Liquidation or complementary period:
   None.
2. Valuation of assets and liabilities:
   Face value for domestic debt; end-of-year exchange rates for foreign debt.

GFSM 2001 Implementation Plan

Starting in 2003, data are compiled on an accrual basis, in accordance with the EU Council Regulation No. 2223/96. Accrual data are prepared in accordance with the Slovak Republic Accounting Act 431/2001, Regulation of Chart of Accounts and Procedures for Accounting for Budgetary and Semibudgetary Organizations and Municipalities.

This institutional table is based on information reported in 2004.

Slovenia   961

Units of General Government

Central Government

Subsector 1.   Budgetary central government
   1.1   Administrative units (58), constitutional court, court of auditors, government offices, judiciary, ministries and related offices, nonministerial departments, ombudsman, parliament, and president of the Republic

Subsector 2.   Extrabudgetary central government units/entities
   2.1   Ad-futura Science and Education Foundation
   2.2   Agency for Energy
   2.3   Agency for Public Legal Records and Related Services
   2.4   Agency for Radioactive Waste
   2.5   Agency for Railways
   2.6   Agency for Regional Development
   2.7   Agency for Telecommunication
   2.8   Ecological Development Fund
   2.9   Employment Service of Slovenia
   2.10 Film Fund
   2.11 Fund for Employment of the Disabled
   2.12 Guarantee and Alimony Fund
   2.13 Krsko Nuclear Plant Decommissioning Fund
   2.14 Nonprofessional Cultural Activities Fund
   2.15 Regional Development Fund
   2.16 Slovene Enterprise Fund
   2.17 Slovenian Research Agency
   2.18 Slovenian Technology Agency
   2.19 Succession Fund
   2.20 Various other government institutions (316 units)

Subsector 3.   Social security funds
   3.1   Health Insurance Fund
   3.2   Pension and Disability Insurance Fund

State Governments

Subsector 4.   State governments
   4.1   Not applicable

Local Governments

Subsector 5.   Local governments
   5.1   193 municipalities
   5.2   Other local government institutions (987 units)

Data Coverage

Data in central government tables cover operations of subsector 1.

Data in local government tables cover operations of subsector 5 and are based on information from all local governments.

Accounting Practices

1. Liquidation or complementary period:
   Not reported.
3. Valuation of assets and liabilities:
   Not reported.

GFSM 2001 Implementation Plan

The Republic of Slovenia will gradually implement, over several years, the accrual accounting and *GFSM 2001* accrual reporting principles.

This institutional table is based on information reported in 2005.

South Africa   199

Units of General Government

Central Government
Subsector 1.   Budgetary central government
1.1   National budgetary accounts comprising 34 government departments, standing appropriations, and statutory payments
Subsector 2.   Extrabudgetary units
2.1   Extrabudgetary accounts of approximately 121 major councils, funds, museums, 22 sector education and training authorities (with effect from 2000), and other agencies for the development of specific activities
2.2   9 technikons (colleges providing advanced technical education)
2.3   17 universities
Subsector 3.   Social security funds
3.1   Compensation Fund
3.2   Mines and Workmen Compensation Fund
3.3   Road Accident Fund (since 1996)
3.4   Unemployment Insurance Fund

State Governments
Subsector 4.   State governments
4.1   9 provinces (Eastern Cape, Free State, Gauteng, KwaZulu/Natal, Limpopo [previously Northern Province], Mpumalanga, North West, Northern Cape, and Western Cape)

Local Governments
Subsector 5.   Local governments
5.1   47 district municipalities
5.2   231 local municipalities
5.3   6 metropolitan municipalities

Data Coverage

Data in central government tables cover operations of subsectors 1–3.

Data in state government tables cover operations of subsector 4 and are based on information from all provincial governments.

Data in local government tables cover operations of subsector 5 and are based on an annual stratified sample survey, supplemented by a survey of all local governments every four years.

For 2003 and 2004, cash data are used as a proxy for the accrual extrabudgetary and social security funds' data.

† Starting in 2002, data for extrabudgetary funds are on an accrual basis.

† In December 2000, local government elections for newly demarcated local governments were held. The demarcation process reduced the number of local governments to 284 units. Financial reporting on the new structures took effect from July 2001.

† Starting in 2000, data for social security funds are on an accrual basis.

† From 1997 onward, domestic debt data include part of Namibia's debt, guaranteed by South Africa before Namibia's independence and subsequently assumed by South Africa.

† From 1996 onward, local government data are based on the 1996 full census of the new local government structures that include those of the former self-governing territories and independent states. From 1996 onward, local government data are provided by Statistics South Africa. The data were revised based on a census conducted by Statistics South Africa for local government financial year 1997 and an annual survey for financial year 1998. Local governments include metropolitan, district, and local municipalities.

† From 1996 onward, data for the social security funds include the Road Accident Fund. The Multilateral Motor Vehicle Accident Fund, which was a public insurer, was transformed into a social security fund.

† From 1996 onward, data are classified according to the *GFSM 2001* classifications, and the subsectors of central government's data are presented on a gross basis (i.e., before consolidation). Prior to 1996, the subsectors of central government's data are presented on a net basis (i.e., after consolidation). As a result, the subsectors of central government, but not central government's data, are not comparable.

† Data for 1995 reflect further changes, which also were implemented according to the 1993 constitution, in the composition of government. Receipts from certain taxes formerly constituted a portion of the revenue of self-governing territories and independent states (and, in 1994, of the provincial administrations). In 1995, receipts from these taxes became part of budgetary central government revenue. Transfers from budgetary central government to the provincial governments were increased correspondingly to compensate for lost revenue and the devolution of further functions to provinces associated with implementation of the 1993 constitution.

† From 1994 onwards, data reflect changes that were implemented, according to the 1993 constitution, in the composition of government. Through 1993, the former Transkei, Bophuthatswana, Venda, Ciskei (TBVC-countries), and self-governing territories were treated as extrabudgetary institutions of the central government. In 1994, these self-governing territories and independent states were phased out; the number of provinces increased from four to nine; and operations of the self-governing territories and independent states were transferred either to national government or new provincial governments or were abolished. Domestic debt data include debt of the former independent states; this debt was assumed, on the basis of section 239 of the 1993 constitution, by the central government.

Accounting Practices

1. Liquidation or complementary period:
   Complementary period is seven days after month-end.

2. Valuation of assets and liabilities:
Liabilities, representing outstanding debt, are valued at face value.

GFSM 2001 Implementation Plan

The South African Reserve Bank converted cash GFS data into the *GFSM 2001* format in 2003. Starting in 2005, additional noncash data, as prescribed for the Financial Statements, are included. The release of the Public Finance Management Act, Act 1 of 1999 (as amended), lays the foundation for a number of reforms; the Minister of Finance established the Accounting Standards Board as a juristic person to establish generally recognized accounting practices. The Minister of Finance will, in due course, determine a date of implementation of Statements of Generally Recognized Accounting Practices. Full implementation is regarded as a medium- to long-term project.

This institutional table is based on information reported in 2005.

Spain   184

Units of General Government

Central Government
Subsector 1. Budgetary central government
   1.1 Judiciary, legislature, ministries, and monarchy
Subsector 2. Extrabudgetary units/entities
   2.1 Government agencies
Subsector 3. Social security funds
   3.1 Social security funds

State Governments
Subsector 4. State governments
   4.1 17 autonomous communities and several government agencies

that belong to these autonomous communities

Local Governments
Subsector 5. Local governments
   5.1 8,000 (approximately) municipalities and other local authorities

Data Coverage

Data for budgetary central government also cover extrabudgetary central government units and entities.

Data in central government tables cover operations of subsectors 1–3. Subsector 3 includes the National Mutual Pension Fund for local governments.

Data for state governments cover operations of subsector 4.

Data for local governments cover operations of subsector 5. These data are based on information from all municipalities with populations of more than 5,000 and on a sample of municipalities with populations of fewer than 5,000.

Domestic financing data (financial assets and liabilities) include foreign financing.

Accounting Practices

1. Liquidation or complementary period:
   None.
2. Valuation of assets and liabilities:
   Not reported.

GFSM 2001 Implementation Plan

Not reported.
This institutional table is based on information reported in 2004.

Sri Lanka   524

Units of General Government

Central Government
Subsector 1. Budgetary central government
   1.1 Judiciary, ministries, parliament, and presidency
Subsector 2. Extrabudgetary units/entities
   2.1 Rubber Control Fund
   2.2 Tea Board
   2.3 Tea Control Fund
   2.4 Tea Subsidy Fund
Subsector 3. Social security funds
   3.1 Not applicable

State Governments
Subsector 4. State governments
   4.1 8 provincial councils

Local Governments
Subsector 5. Local governments
   5.1 18 municipal councils
   5.2 37 urban councils
   5.3 256 village councils (pradesheeya sabhas)

Data Coverage

Data in budgetary central government tables cover operations of subsector 1.

Accounting Practices

1. Liquidation or complementary period:
   None.
2. Valuation of assets and liabilities:
   Fixed assets at historical cost; loans and bonds at face value.

GFSM 2001 Implementation Plan

A migration path for *GFSM 2001* is under consideration.
This institutional table is based on information reported in 2003.

Sudan   732

Units of General Government

Central Government
Subsector 1. Budgetary central government
   1.1 Council of ministers, ministries and department, national assembly, presidency, and various government agencies
   1.2 State Support Fund
Subsector 2. Extrabudgetary units/entities
   2.1 26 national universities
   2.2 6 social subsides programs
Subsector 3. Social security funds
   3.1 National Pension Fund
   3.2 Social Security Fund

State Governments
Subsector 4. State governments
   4.1 26 state governments

Local Governments
Subsector 5. Local governments
   5.1 615 localities
   5.2 118 provinces

Data Coverage

Data in budgetary central government tables cover operations of component 1.1.

Accounting Practices

1. Liquidation or complementary period:
   None.
2. Valuation of assets and liabilities:
   Not reported.

GFSM 2001 Implementation Plan

Not reported.

This institutional table is based on information reported in 2001.

Swaziland   734

Units of General Government

Central Government

Subsector 1. Budgetary central government
1.1 Judiciary, ministries and departments, monarchy, office of the prime minister and office of the deputy prime minister, and parliament

Subsector 2. Extrabudgetary units/entities
2.1 Swazi National Council (traditional or tribal government)

Subsector 3. Social security funds
3.1 Not applicable

State Governments

Subsector 4. State governments
4.1 Not applicable

Local Governments

Subsector 5. Local governments
5.1 2 city councils, 3 town boards, and 3 town councils

Data Coverage

Data in budgetary central government tables cover operations of subsector 1.

Data in local government tables cover operations of subsector 5.

Accounting Practices

1. Liquidation or complementary period:
   Not reported.
2. Valuation of assets and liabilities:
   Not reported.

GFSM 2001 Implementation Plan

Not reported.

This institutional table is based on information reported in 2001.

Sweden   144

Units of General Government

Central Government

Subsector 1. Budgetary central government
1.1 Agencies, judiciary, legislature, ministries, and monarchy
1.2 National Debt Office

Subsector 2. Extrabudgetary units/entities
2.1 Not applicable

Subsector 3. Social security funds
3.1 Regional agencies of the Public Health Insurance Society
3.2 Swedish National Social Insurance Board

State Governments

Subsector 4. State governments
4.1 Not applicable

Local Governments

Subsector 5. Local governments
5.1 23 county councils, 288 municipalities, and 2,545 parishes

Data Coverage

Data in central government tables cover operations of subsectors 1 and 3.

Data in local government tables cover operations of subsector 5 and are based on information from all county councils, all municipalities, and a sample of parishes.

In line with the presentation adopted within the European Union, data on domestic financial assets and liabilities include foreign financial assets and liabilities.

† From 1998 onward, the Unemployment Fund is included in the budgetary central government. Previously, this fund formed part of social security funds.

† From 1995 onward, fiscal years end December 31.

Accounting Practices

1. Liquidation or complementary period:
   Not reported.
2. Valuation of assets and liabilities:
   Not reported.

GFSM 2001 Implementation Plan

Not reported.

This institutional table is based on information reported in 1999.

Switzerland   146

Units of General Government

Central Government

Subsector 1. Budgetary central government
1.1 Departments, federal assembly, federal council, and judiciary

Subsector 2. Extrabudgetary units/entities
2.1 Federal Alcohol Administration
2.2 Railway Infrastructure Financing Fund
2.3 Swiss Federal Institute of Technology

Subsector 3. Social security funds
3.1 Health insurance
3.2 Social security schemes (allocations for loss of income for the military, disability insurance, old age and survivors' insurance, and unemployment insurance)

State Governments

Subsector 4. State governments
4.1 26 cantons

Local Governments

Subsector 5. Local governments
5.1 3,000 (approximately) communes

Data Coverage

Data in central government tables cover operations of subsectors 1–3 but exclude revenue of subsector 2.

Data in state government tables cover operations of subsector 4.

Data in local government tables cover operations of subsector 5. These data are based on information from approximately 80 percent of local governments and on sample-based estimates for the remainder.

† Beginning in 2002, the coverage of extrabudgetary units was broadened to include 2.2 and 2.3.

In Table 1, prior to 1991, data on excises levied on imported goods were included in taxes on international trade.

Accounting Practices

1. Liquidation or complementary period:
   Not reported.
2. Valuation of assets and liabilities:
   Not reported.

GFSM 2001 Implementation Plan

Not reported.

This institutional table is based on information reported in 2005.

Syrian Arab Republic   463

Units of General Government

Central Government

Subsector 1.   Budgetary central government
   1.1   Council of state, judiciary, legislature, ministries, offices and organizations, presidency, and prime minister's office

Subsector 2.   Extrabudgetary units/entities
   2.1   Governmental administrative agencies
   2.2   Public Debt Fund

Subsector 3.   Social security funds
   3.1   Not applicable

State Governments

Subsector 4.   State governments
   4.1   Not applicable

Local Governments

Subsector 5.   Local governments
   5.1   Administrative units of local government

Data Coverage

Data in central government tables cover operations of subsector 1 and component 2.2.

† After 1990, data on public order and safety are included in the line on general public services in Table 7.

Accounting Practices

1. Liquidation or complementary period:
   Not reported.
2. Valuation of assets and liabilities:
   Not reported.

GFSM 2001 Implementation Plan

Not reported.

This institutional table is based on information reported in or prior to 1996.

Tajikistan   923

Units of General Government

Central Government

Subsector 1.   Budgetary central government
   1.1   Budgetary institutions, committees, and government agencies
   1.2   Judiciary, ministries, office of the president, office of the prime minister, and parliament

Subsector 2.   Extrabudgetary units/entities
   2.1   Not applicable

Subsector 3.   Social security funds
   3.1   Social Protection Fund

State Governments

Subsector 4.   State governments
   4.1   Not applicable

Local Governments

Subsector 5.   Local governments
   5.1   1 autonomous province comprising 1 city and 7 districts
   5.2   1 city comprising 4 districts; also 2 provinces comprising 13 cities and 30 districts
   5.3   13 districts and towns

Data Coverage

Data in central government tables cover operations of subsectors 1 and 3.

Data in local government tables cover operations of subsector 5.

† The Road Fund, which was included in central government extrabudgetary accounts, was abolished in 2000.

† The Tajik ruble (TR) was introduced in May 1995. Starting in November 2000, the somoni (SM) replaced the TR at the rate of SM 1 = TR 1000.

Accounting Practices

1. Liquidation or complementary period:
   Not reported.
2. Valuation of assets and liabilities:
   Not reported.

GFSM 2001 Implementation Plan

Not reported.

This institutional table is based on information reported in 2001.

Thailand   578

Units of General Government

Central Government

Subsector 1.   Budgetary central government
   1.1   Administrative courts office, attorney general's office, botanical garden organization, Bureau of Royal Household, Civil Aviation Training Center, constitution court office, election board office, His Majesty's principal private secretary's office, house of representatives secretariat, Institute for Science and Technology, justice court office, King Prajadhipok's Institute, 20 ministries, National Buddhism Office, National Counter Corruption Commission Office, national human rights commission

office, national police office, National Research Council of Thailand, National Science Museum, ombudsman's office, Prevention and Suppression of Money Laundering Office, prime minister's office, Royal Development Project Board Office, Royal Institute, Thailand senate secretariat, Thailand sports authority, state audit office, Thailand tourism authority, and waste water management authority

Subsector 2. Extrabudgetary units/entities
2.1 Departmental agencies, comprising Boat Building Training Center, Committee for

the Coordination of the Investigation of the Lower Mekong Basin, Fisheries Development Center, Hoop Krapong Community Development Center, National Institution of Metrology, Plant Protection Service Center, public hospitals, public schools, Red Cross Society, Thai Health Promotion Foundation, Thailand Management and Productivity Development Center, 24 universities, Vegetable Seed Research Center, and War Veterans' Organization

2.2 Education Fund
2.3 Environment Fund
2.4 Farmers' Aid Fund
2.5 Fund for Distribution of Production and Employment to Rural Areas
2.6 Fund for Farmers Assistance
2.7 Oil Fund
2.8 Rubber Replanting Aid Fund
2.9 Rural Development Fund
2.10 Students' Lunch Fund
2.11 Urban Community Development Fund
2.12 Village and Urban Community Fund
2.13 81 extrabudgetary funds
2.14 Other special purpose funds of spending agencies

Subsector 3. Social security funds
3.1 Workman Compensation Fund
3.2 Social Security Fund

State Governments

Subsector 4. State governments
4.1 Not applicable

Local Governments

Subsector 5. Local governments
5.1 Bangkok Metropolitan Administration, 75 Changwad administrative organizations, 6,745 district administrative organizations, 1,129 municipalities, and Pattaya City

Data Coverage

Data in central government tables cover operations of subsector 1, components 2.2–2.13, and subsector 3. In 2001 and 2002, the coverage of data in the central government tables was expanded to extrabudgetary funds previously not included, such as components 2.3, 2.5, and 2.9–2.13.

Data in local government tables cover operations of subsector 5.

† Starting in 2003, central and general government data are a mixture of the cash and accrual basis of recording: budgetary central government and local government data are on a cash basis, while extrabudgetary central government and social security funds data are on an accrual basis.

Accounting Practices
1. Liquidation or complementary period:
    None.
2. Valuation of assets and liabilities:
    The outstanding stock of liabilities is at face value.

GFSM 2001 Implementation Plan

Thailand compiles existing cash data for general government based on the *GFSM 2001*. Implementation of an accrual accounting system for the budgetary central government started in the 2003/04 fiscal year, and the accrual data will be available in early 2006. Further plans for implementing the *GFSM 2001* are as follows. By end–2005, cash data are to be supplemented with some accrual data and noncash transactions. By end–2006, an incomplete financial balance sheet (not valued at market prices) will be compiled. By end–2007, accrual data will be compiled, including all government equity in public corporations and a consolidated financial balance sheet (not valued at market prices). By end–2008, a complete balance sheet, with nonfinancial assets not yet valued at market prices, will be compiled. The implementation date of valuing nonfinancial assets at market prices is not yet in the migration plan.

This institutional table is based on information reported in 2005.

Tunisia   744

Units of General Government

Central Government

Subsector 1. Budgetary central government
1.1 Judiciary, 24 ministries, national assembly, presidency, 19 secretariats of state, and secretariat general of the Tunisian government

Subsector 2. Extrabudgetary units/entities
2.1 Administrative government agencies
2.2 39 economic and social government agencies

Subsector 3. Social security funds
3.1 National Pension and Social Welfare Fund
3.2 National Social Security Fund

State Governments

Subsector 4. State governments
4.1 Not applicable

Local Governments

Subsector 5. Local governments
5.1 24 government councils and 264 municipalities

Data Coverage

Data in consolidated central government tables cover operations of subsectors 1 and 3. The domestic budget excludes foreign-financed spending and lending for policy purposes. Data for budgetary central government include those transactions.

† From 1994 onward, data for the Old Age, Disability, and Survivor Insurance Fund are included in the accounts of the National Social Security Fund. Until 1998, outstanding external debt as of December 31 is valued at average annual exchange rates. Thereafter, end-of-year exchange rates are used.

In Table 7, data for expenditures on fuel and energy are included in other economic affairs and services categories.

Accounting Practices
1. Liquidation or complementary period:
    20 days for subsectors 1–2 and 5. No complementary period for subsector 3.
2. Valuation of assets and liabilities:
    Not reported.

Not reported.

This institutional table is based on information reported in 2003.

Turkey 186

Units of General Government

Central Government

Subsector 1. Budgetary central government
  1.1 Grand National Assembly of Turkey, judiciary, ministries, and presidency

Subsector 2. Extrabudgetary units/entities
  2.1 Annex budget agencies—mainly universities
  2.2 Extrabudgetary funds
  2.3 Revolving funds
  2.4 State economic enterprises
  2.5 State economic enterprises under privatization

Subsector 3. Social security funds
  3.1 Social security institutions

State Governments

Subsector 4. State governments

Not applicable

Local Governments

Subsector 5. Local governments
  5.1 3,227 municipalities
  5.2 81 provinces

Data Coverage

Data in budgetary central government tables cover operations of subsector 1. Subsector 1 includes net revenue of revolving funds (component 2.3).

Data in extrabudgetary central government tables cover only operations of component 2.1.

† From 1997 onward, data on public order and safety, instead of being included in data on general public services, are reported separately in Table 7.

Accounting Practices

1. Liquidation or complementary period:
    Not reported.
2. Valuation of assets and liabilities:
    Not reported.

GFSM 2001 Implementation Plan

Not reported.

This institutional table is based on information reported in 2000.

Uganda 746

Units of General Government

Central Government

Subsector 1. Budgetary central government
  1.1 19 agencies and commissions, embassies and missions abroad, judiciary, 15 ministries, parliament, president's office, prime minister's office, and state house

Subsector 2. Extrabudgetary units/entities
  2.1 National agricultural research organization, referral hospitals, and universities

Subsector 3. Social security funds
  3.1 National social security fund

State Governments

Subsector 4. State governments
  4.1 Not applicable

Local Governments

Subsector 5. Local governments
  5.1 1 city council, 55 districts, 13 municipalities, and 60 town councils

Data Coverage

Data in central government tables cover operations of subsector 1.

Data in local government tables cover operations of subsector 5.

Accounting Practices

1. Liquidation or complementary period:
    None.
2. Valuation of assets and liabilities:
    Not reported.

GFSM 2001 Implementation Plan

Not reported.

This institutional table is based on information reported in 2003.

Ukraine 926

Units of General Government

Central Government

Subsector 1. Budgetary central government
  1.1 Committees, judiciary, ministries, parliament, president's office, research institutions, state funds for special purposes, and universities

Subsector 2. Extrabudgetary units/entities
  2.1 Not applicable

Subsector 3. Social security funds
  3.1 Accident Social Insurance Fund
  3.2 Pension Fund
  3.3 Temporary Disability Social Insurance Fund
  3.4 Unemployment Social Insurance Fund

State Governments

Subsector 4. State governments
  4.1 Not applicable

Local Governments

Subsector 5. Local governments
  5.1 24 oblast, 2 cities (Kyiv and Sevastopol), 1 republic (Crimea)
  5.2 175 municipalities, 488 districts

Data Coverage

Data of central government cover operations of subsectors 1 and 3.

Data of local government cover operations of subsector 5.

Data of foreign government debt cover direct government debt and guaranteed government debt.

† In 1999–2001, privatization receipts have been included as part of domestic financing and excluded from net lending minus repayments. In 1999, budgetary central government privatization receipts were 694 millions hryvnias, in 2000 they were 2,075.3 millions hryvnias, and in 2001 they were 2,208.0 million hryvnias. For local government in 1999–2001, the

amounts were 127.8 million hryvnias, 215.7 million hryvnias, and 355.7 million hryvnias, respectively.

† In 2000, budgetary central government data (Subsector 1) included operations of the Social Insurance Fund (Subsector 3). Starting in 2001, the Social Insurance Fund was liquidated, and at the same time the Accident Social Insurance Fund and the Temporary Disability Social Insurance Fund were established and data for these institutions reported under Subsector 3.

† In 1996–2000, budgetary central government data (Subsector 1) included operations of the Unemployment Social Insurance Fund (Subsector 3.3).

† In 1994–1996, budgetary central government data (Subsector 1) included operations of the Pension Fund (Subsector 3.1).

Accounting Practices

1. Liquidation or complementary period:
   None.
2. Valuation of assets and liabilities:
   Not reported.

GFSM 2001 Implementation Plan

The cash general government data have been compiled according to *GFSM 2001* format.

This institutional table is based on information reported in 2005.

United Arab Emirates   466

Units of General Government

Central Government

Subsector 1.   Budgetary central government
  1.1   Cabinet Affairs Office, Federal Audit Bureau, ministries, Ministry of State for Supreme Council Affairs, National Federal Council, presidency, prime minister's office, Protocol and Hospitality Office, and Supreme Council of Rulers

Subsector 2.   Extrabudgetary units/entities
  Not applicable

Subsector 3.   Social security funds
  Not applicable

State Governments

Subsector 4.   State governments
  4.1   Abu Dhabi: Ruler's court, executive and consultative councils, presidential court, ruler's representative east region, ruler's representative west region, Shari'a court, 11 departments, and 2 municipalities
  4.2   Ajman: Ruler's court, judiciary, 2 departments, and 1 municipality
  4.3   Dubai: Ruler's court, judiciary, 10 departments, and 1 municipality
  4.4   Fujairah: Ruler's court, 1 department, and 1 municipality
  4.5   Ras Al-Khaimah: Ruler's court, judiciary, 7 departments, and 1 municipality
  4.6   Sharjah: Ruler's court, judiciary, 9 departments, and 3 municipalities
  4.7   Umm Al-Quwain: Ruler's court, judiciary, 2 departments, and 1 municipality

Local Governments

Subsector 5.   Local governments
  5.1   Not applicable

Data Coverage

Data in central government tables cover operations of subsector 1.

Accounting Practices

1. Liquidation or complementary period:
   Not reported.
2. Valuation of assets and liabilities:
   Not reported.

GFSM 2001 Implementation Plan

Not reported.

This institutional table is based on information reported in or prior to 1996.

United Kingdom   112

Units of General Government

Central Government

Subsector 1.   Budgetary central government
  1.1   143 (approximately) agencies

Subsector 2.   Extrabudgetary units/entities
  2.1   Departments, judiciary, ministries, monarchy, national insurance funds, nondepartmental public bodies such as national museums, and parliament

Subsector 3.   Social security funds
  3.1   National Health Service (not including NHS hospitals that are public corporations)

State Governments

Subsector 4.   State governments
  4.1   Not applicable

Local Governments

Subsector 5.   Local governments
  5.1   540 (approximately) local councils and local government units

Data Coverage

Data in central government tables cover operations of subsectors 1–3 (including those of the National Insurance Fund).

Data in local government tables cover operations of subsector 5 and are based on information from all local governments.

Accounting Practices

1. Liquidation or complementary period:
   Not reported.
2. Valuation of assets and liabilities:
   Not reported.

GFSM 2001 Implementation Plan

Not reported.

This institutional table is based on information reported in 1999.

United States   111

Units of General Government

Central Government

Subsector 1.   Budgetary central government
  1.1   Congress; departments; judiciary; 3 major independent offices; presidency; and 90 smaller boards, councils, and offices
  1.2   3 employee retirement funds
  1.3   2 major transportation trust funds

Subsector 2. Extrabudgetary units/entities
2.1 Not applicable
Subsector 3. Social security funds
3.1 6 social security funds

State Governments

Subsector 4. State governments
4.1 50 state governments
4.2 4 state temporary disability insurance systems
4.3 44 state workers' compensation systems

Local Governments

Subsector 5. Local governments
5.1 There are approximately 87,525 units of local governments in the U.S., based on the 2002 Census of Governments, which was first released in 2004. The total includes 38,967 general purpose governments, 35,052 special district governments, and 13,506 public school systems (out of a total of 15,014) that are not dependent on their state or local government.

Notes: The three major independent offices in component 1.1 are the Environmental Protection Agency, General Services Administration, and National Aeronautics and Space Administration.

Component 1.2 comprises the Civil Service Retirement and Disability Fund, Foreign Service Retirement and Disability Fund, and Military Retirement Fund.

Component 1.3 comprises the Airport and Airway Trust Fund and Highway Trust Fund.

Subsector 3 comprises the Federal Disability Insurance Fund, Federal Hospital Insurance Fund, Federal Old-Age and Survivors Insurance Fund, Federal Supplementary Medical Insurance Fund, Railroad Retirement Fund, and Unemployment Insurance Fund.

Component 4.2 comprises the California Unemployment Compensation Disability Fund, New Jersey State Disability Benefits, New York Special Fund for Disability Benefits, and Rhode Island Temporary Disability Insurance.

Component 4.3 includes systems in Arizona, California, Colorado, Idaho, Kentucky, Maryland, Michigan, Minnesota, Montana, Nevada, North Dakota, Ohio, Oklahoma, Oregon, Pennsylvania, Utah, Washington, West Virginia, Wyoming, and smaller-scale workers' compensation systems in 25 other states.

Data Coverage

Data in central government tables cover operations of subsectors 1–3.

Data in the state and local government tables cover operations of subsectors 4 and 5, respectively.

† Starting in 2001, all data are on a calendar year and accrual basis. Data through 2000 are on a fiscal year (ending September 30) and cash basis.

Accounting Practices

1. Liquidation or complementary period:
    None.
2. Valuation of assets and liabilities:
    Data on government debt (liabilities) and assets are valued at book value (historic cost) for financial liabilities and assets. Fixed capital assets are valued at current prices net of depreciation.

GFSM 2001 Implementation Plan

Data from 2001 onwards reflect full movement to calendar-year estimates based on accrual accounting, which is consistent with the U.S. National Income and Product Accounts. Over the next three years, it is planned to research and expand the economic

and financial statistics that pertain to the balance-sheet components of the GFS system. To do so, possibilities for reporting such information based on the U.S. Federal Reserve Bank's "Flow of Funds" reports will be examined.

This institutional table is based on information reported in 2005.

Uruguay 298

Units of General Government

Central Government

Subsector 1. Budgetary central government
1.1 Legislature, ministries, and presidency
1.2 Court of accounts, electoral court, judiciary, and Tribunal for Administrative Disputes
1.3 National Administration for Public Education and University of the Republic
Subsector 2. Extrabudgetary units/entities
FLD ("Fondos de Libre Disponibilidad")
Subsector 3. Social security funds
3.1 Social insurance fund

State Governments

Subsector 4. State governments
4.1 Not applicable

Local Governments

Subsector 5. Local governments
5.1 19 departmental governments

Data Coverage

Data in central government tables cover operations of subsectors 1–3.

Data in local government tables cover operations of subsector 5. However, only financing data are available.

† In 1999 a new integrated financial information system (SIIF) began operating, which provides more complete and detailed data. Furthermore, new budget classifications were introduced.

Accounting Practices

1. Liquidation or complementary period:
    None.
2. Valuation of assets and liabilities:
    Not reported.

GFSM 2001 Implementation Plan

Not reported.

This institutional table is based on information reported in 2005.

Vanuatu 846

Units of General Government

Central Government

Subsector 1. Budgetary central government
1.1 Ministries, parliament, and presidency
Subsector 2. Extrabudgetary units/entities
2.1 Community Development Fund
2.2 European Union Stabex Fund
2.3 Forum Fisheries Agency
2.4 27 special funds
Subsector 3. Social security funds
3.1 Not applicable

State Governments

Subsector 4.   State governments
  4.1   Not applicable

Local Governments

Subsector 5.   Local governments
  5.1   Municipalities of Luganville and Port Vila
  5.2   6 provinces

Data Coverage

Data in central government tables cover operations of subsectors 1–3.

Data in local government tables cover operations of subsector 5.

Accounting Practices

1.   Liquidation or complementary period:
     Not reported.
2.   Valuation of assets and liabilities:
     Not reported.

GFSM 2001 Implementation Plan

Not reported.

This institutional table is based on information reported in 1998.

República Bolivariana de Venezuela   299

Units of General Government

Central Government

Subsector 1.   Budgetary central government
  1.1   Attorney general's office, comptroller general's office, national assembly, judiciary, ministries, national electoral council, presidency, supreme court, vice presidency

Subsector 2.   Extrabudgetary units/entities
  2.1   251 decentralized administrative entities.

Subsector 3.   Social Security Funds
  3.1   Armed Forces Social Security Institute
  3.2   Ministry of Education Personnel Social Security Institute
  3.3   Technical Staff of the Judiciary Police Social Security Institute
  3.4   Venezuelan Institute of Social Security

State Governments

Subsector 4.   State governments
  4.1   24 state governments

Local Governments

Subsector 5.   Local governments
  5.1   335 local governments

Data Coverage

Data in central government tables cover operations of subsector 1 and component 3.4.

† Data from 1998 onward are reported by the Ministry of Finance (Oficina de Estadísticas de Finanzas Públicas). Earlier data were reported by the Central Bank.

† For 1990–93, each revenue item has been reported on a cash basis, without including payments in documents. For all other years, the amounts paid in documents are included in item adjustment to cash basis with negative sign.

Accounting Practices

1.   Liquidation or complementary period:
     The fiscal year ends December 31 of each year. However, the budgetary execution for the budgetary central government includes the 12 months of the corresponding

year and 12 additional months from the following year. In that period no new expenditure commitments are allowed; only payments of prior commitments that were not canceled within the fiscal year are allowed.
2.   Valuation of assets and liabilities:
     Not reported.

GFSM 2001 Implementation Plan

The compiling office is preparing an implementation plan, which includes an evaluation of the resources needed.

This institutional table is based on information reported in 2004.

Vietnam   582

Units of General Government

Central Government

Subsector 1.   Budgetary central government
  1.1   Agencies, bureaus, institutes, ministries, national assembly, and office of the prime minister

Subsector 2.   Extrabudgetary units/entities
  2.1   Export Support Fund (formerly the Price Stabilization Fund)
  2.2   National Development Support Fund
  2.3   Reforestation Program lending Fund
  2.4   Restructuring Support Fund
  2.5   Sinking Fund

Subsector 3.   Social security funds
  3.1   General Security Fund
  3.2   Health Fund

State Governments

Subsector 4.   State governments

Not applicable

Local Governments

Subsector 5.   Local governments
  5.1   District government for 598 districts
  5.2   Commune governments for 10,500 communes, district towns, and wards
  5.3   Provincial governments for 61 provinces
  5.4   Various funds at the local government level

Data Coverage

Data in the general government tables cover the operations of subsectors 1 and 5 (5.1, 5.2, and 5.3).

Accounting Practices

1.   Liquidation or complementary period:
     Not reported.
2.   Valuation of assets and liabilities:
     Not reported.

GFSM 2001 Implementation Plan

Not reported.

This institutional table is based on information reported in 2001.

Yemen, Republic of   474

Units of General Government

Central Government

Subsector 1.   Budgetary central government
  1.1   Centers, council of consultancy, council of deputies

(parliament), judiciary, ministries, presidency, prime minister's office, and universities
1.2 1 municipal and 17 provincial administrations
Subsector 2.   Extrabudgetary units/entities
2.1 General Board for Agricultural Development
2.2 General Board for Agricultural Research
2.3 General Board for Al-Thawra Hospital
2.4 General Board for Development of Eastern Region
2.5 General Board for Development of Tihama
2.6 Martyrs' Bureau
2.7 Ministry of Interior Employee Fund
2.8 Promotion of Agricultural and Fisheries Production Fund
2.9 Roads and Bridges Maintenance Fund
2.10 Social Development Fund
2.11 Social Welfare Fund
2.12 Waqf Fund (religious endowments authority)
2.13 Youths and Sports Care Fund
Subsector 3.   Social security funds
3.1 General Authority for Social Security (Government and Public Enterprise Employees' Pension Fund)
3.2 Defense Employees' Pension Fund

State Governments

Subsector 4.   State governments
Not applicable

Local Governments

Subsector 5.   Local governments
Not applicable

Data Coverage

Data in budgetary central government tables cover operations of subsector 1.

† From 1997 onward, components 2.7–2.11, 2.13, and 3.2 were included in the coverage of subsector 1.

† From 1996 onward, data on expenditure for agriculture, forestry, fishing, and hunting affairs and services include subsidy schemes supporting the importers of agricultural products and the producers of petroleum products.

On May 22, 1990, the Yemen Arab Republic and the People's Democratic Republic of Yemen merged to become a single state—the Republic of Yemen.

Accounting Practices

1. Liquidation or complementary period:
    Not reported.
2. Valuation of assets and liabilities:
    Not reported.

GFSM 2001 Implementation Plan

Not reported.

This institutional table is based on information reported in 1998.

Zambia   754

Units of General Government

Central Government

Subsector 1.   Budgetary central government
1.1 Departments, House of Chiefs, judiciary, ministries, national assembly, and presidency
Subsector 2.   Extrabudgetary units/entities
2.1 Agencies, funds, and institutions
Subsector 3.   Social security funds
3.1 Workmen's Compensation Fund

State Governments

Subsector 4.   State governments
4.1 Not applicable

Local Governments

Subsector 5.   Local governments
5.1 55 districts councils

Data Coverage

Data in budgetary central government tables cover operations of subsector 1.

Subsector 2 comprises Bangwelu Water Transport, Copperbelt University, counterpart funds of budgetary organizations, Government Communication Flight, Government Stores Department, Hostel Board of Management, Industrial Plantations Division, Land Development Services Account, miscellaneous funds, Mweru Water Transport, Prices and Income Commission, special (revolving) funds, state-supported schools, University of Zambia, and Zambia National Tourist Bureau.

Data in local government tables cover operations of subsector 5.

Accounting Practices

1. Liquidation or complementary period:
    Not reported.
2. Valuation of assets and liabilities:
    Not reported.

GFSM 2001 Implementation Plan

Not reported.

This institutional table is based on information reported in 1997.

The Kenneth Gordon School

Macdonald Countries

China

L.L.Ref 900-M